W9-BCM-319

Networking Fundamentals

Second Edition

Richard M. Roberts

Publisher
The Goodheart-Willcox Company, Inc.
Tinley Park, Illinois
www.g-w.com

Manufactured in the United States of America.

Library of Congress Catalog Card Number 2010040071

ISBN 978-1-60525-356-5

2 3 4 5 6 7 8 9 – 12 – 16 15 14 13

The Goodheart-Willcox Company, Inc. Brand Disclaimer: Brand names, company names, and illustrations for products and services included in this text are provided for educational purposes only and do not represent or imply endorsement or recommendation by the author or the publisher.

The Goodheart-Willcox Company, Inc. Safety Notice: The reader is expressly advised to carefully read, understand, and apply all safety precautions and warnings described in this book or that might also be indicated in undertaking the activities and exercises described herein to minimize risk of personal injury or injury to others. Common sense and good judgment should also be exercised and applied to help avoid all potential hazards. The reader should always refer to the appropriate manufacturer's technical information, directions, and recommendations; then proceed with care to follow specific equipment operating instructions. The reader should understand these notices and cautions are not exhaustive.

The publisher makes no warranty or representation whatsoever, either expressed or implied, including but not limited to equipment, procedures, and applications described or referred to herein, their quality, performance, merchantability, or fitness for a particular purpose. The publisher assumes no responsibility for any changes, errors, or omissions in this book. The publisher specifically disclaims any liability whatsoever, including any direct, indirect, incidental, consequential, special, or exemplary damages resulting, in whole or in part, from the reader's use or reliance upon the information, instructions, procedures, warnings, cautions, applications, or other matter contained in this book. The publisher assumes no responsibility for the activities of the reader.

Library of Congress Cataloging-in-Publication Data

Roberts, Richard M.
Networking fundamentals / Richard M. Roberts. -- 2nd ed.
p. cm.
Includes index.
ISBN 978-1-60525-356-5
1. Computer networks. I. Title.

TK5105.5.R625 2011
004.6--dc22 2010040071

Introduction

The *Networking Fundamentals* textbook is beneficial to anyone wishing to pursue a career in information technology. It provides the skills and basic knowledge required before pursuing studies in specific networking fields, such as network administration, network design, and the support of specific network operating systems. This textbook and the accompanying ***Laboratory Manual*** and ***Study Guide*** meet all the required knowledge for the CompTIA Network+ Certification exam and provide the basic skills and knowledge needed to successfully enter the field of networking.

While many books on the market prepare students to pass the Network+ Certification exam, they do not take the time to explain in detail how the various network technologies work. You may be prepared for the exam, but lack the technical foundation to understand the networking technologies underlying everyday operations. In contrast, the ***Networking Fundamentals*** textbook contains detailed explanations about concepts, rather than just presentations of key points and specifications.

Many concepts may seem confusing or incomplete when first presented. As you progress through the textbook, you will learn other knowledge that will help you grasp previously presented concepts. This is why it is imperative that you constantly review previously learned subjects. Many of the concepts covered in early chapters will not become completely clear until later in the textbook. For example, throughout the textbook, references are made to protocols and the OSI model. These concepts are difficult to fully master until other concepts are presented and learned. Later in the textbook, an entire chapter is devoted to the OSI model and how it is directly related to protocols and equipment. Learning and reviewing the material presented should be a continuous process.

Be sure to visit the recommended Web sites and perform the ***Suggested Laboratory Activities***. A ***Laboratory Manual*** and a ***Study Guide*** have been designed to accompany this textbook. I strongly recommend that you complete all laboratory and study guide activities. The ***Laboratory Manual*** will provide you with a guided opportunity to perform many of the jobs required in a typical network setting. The ***Study Guide*** will provide you with a valuable means of review and practice essential for mastery of basic network knowledge and skills. By completing all activities and related class work, your opportunity for success on the Network+ Certification exam and in the workplace will be greatly enhanced.

I want to take this opportunity to wish you success in your future.

Sincerely,
Richard Roberts

The Author

For the past 45 years, Richard Roberts has been designing curriculum, teaching Electricity and Electronics as well as Computer Technology, and supervising technical teachers. Mr. Roberts is an accomplished programmer and computer technician. He has experience as the system administrator for Novell NetWare, Microsoft NT, and IBM Token Ring networking systems. He possesses a Bachelor's degree in Technical Education and a Master's degree in Administration/Supervision. He also has current CompTIA A+, Network+, and iNet+ certifications.

His computer experiences started as early as 1974, when he began programming and teaching the Motorola 6800, which eventually evolved into the Motorola 68000—the core processor of the Apple Macintosh computer system. Since then, Mr. Roberts has maintained his teaching status to both instructors and students as the technology has evolved, and he has remained at a state-of-the-art technical level through research, teaching, and applications. He is currently an adjunct instructor at South Florida Community College. He has authored the ***Computer Service and Repair*** textbook and its ancillaries and coauthored the ***Electricity and Electronics*** textbook as well as designed and programmed the accompanying interactive CD.

In addition to his current position, Mr. Roberts has taught at Erwin Technical Center and Tampa Bay Technical High School, and he has taught adults in the military service. His time is now divided between computer consulting and applications, teaching students and instructors, and writing textbooks and other ancillary instructional materials. Occasionally, he goes fishing, but not too often.

Using This Text

Each chapter begins with a number of learning objectives. These are the goals you should set to accomplish while working through the chapter. In addition to your objectives, each chapter begins with a list of new terms, which are important for you to learn as you move through the chapter. When these new terms are introduced in the text, they are printed in a ***bold italic*** typeface. At that point in the text, you will find these terms defined in the margin.

As you read this text, you will also notice some other words or phrases that stand out. File names that you encounter will appear like notepad.exe and student.txt. Any data you must enter, be it by typing at the command and Run prompts or button/tabs/menus that you will click with your mouse are set out like **dir C:** or **Start | All Programs | Accessories | System Tools**. Internet addresses within the text are in the traditional Web style and in blue, such as www.g-w.com. Internet addresses listed under ***Interesting Web Sites for More Information*** at the end of each chapter are in the traditional Web style, underlined, and in blue, such as www.g-w.com.

Be sure to read any Network+ Notes, Tech Tips, or Cautions that you encounter. Network+ Notes contain tips that will help you study for the CompTIA Network+ Certification exam. Tech Tips are useful tidbits that might come in handy in the field. Take heed when you see a Caution. Cautions alert you when an act may damage your computer or computer components or cause injury to yourself. Damaging a computer component or device through electrostatic discharge is the most common danger you will encounter with computers and networking. You may also encounter some dangerous voltages that can cause serious or fatal injury, especially when dealing with monitors. Most of those repairs should be left to special technicians.

Each chapter concludes with a summary of some of the key information you should take from the chapter, a large number of questions, a list of useful Web sites, and laboratory activities for you to try. Each chapter has two sets of questions. The first set of questions tests your general comprehension of the material in the chapter. The second set of questions mimics the style of the CompTIA Network+ Certification exam. The questions asked here are on topics that the exams commonly probe.

Hands-on experience is the only way to become proficient in networking, so be sure to attempt the activities at the end of each chapter. If you can complete the activities in this text and in the accompanying laboratory manual, you should have no problem passing the Network+ Certification exam. Each chapter concludes with a complete ***Laboratory Activity***. Be sure to work through each of these activities. ***Suggested Laboratory Activities*** are also included. These activities are loosely structured proceedings that you can attempt on your own or if you have free time in class.

Never forget, the world of networking changes rapidly. Consequently, network administration and the CompTIA Network+ Certification exam must change with it. Each chapter includes a list of Web sites where you can find the latest information on the topics covered. Be sure to check the CompTIA Web site (www.comptia.org) frequently for the latest information on what subjects are being added to the exam and what subjects are being dropped. Also, check the author's Web site (www.RMRoberts.com) for text updates, interesting links, and bonus laboratory material.

Acknowledgments

I would like to thank the following people who helped make this textbook possible by supplying information, details, photographs, artwork, and software.

Aimee Leclerc, American Power Conversion
Ana M. Bakas, PCTEL, Maxrad Product Group
Beverly Summers, Fluke Corporation
Ed Woodward, Hewlett Packard Company
Irene Bammer, Liza Meyers, Ortronics
Sheri Najafi, WildPackets Inc.
Tamara Borg, GFI Software, LTD
Vivian Lien, SOYO Group, Inc.

I would also like to thank the following companies for supplying information, details, photographs, artwork, and software.

3Com Corporation
American Power Conversion
Cisco Systems
Fluke Corporation
Gemplus
GFI Software, LTD
Hewlett-Packard Company
Ortronics
PCTEL, Maxrad Product Group
Precise Biometrics
Siecor Corporation, Hickory, NC
SOYO Group, Inc.
WildPackets, Inc.

CompTIA Authorized Quality Curriculum

The logo of the CompTIA Authorized Quality Curriculum (CAQC) program and the status of this or other training material as "Authorized" under the CompTIA Authorized Quality Curriculum program signifies that, in CompTIA's opinion, such training material covers the content of the CompTIA's related certification exam. CompTIA has not reviewed or approved the accuracy of the contents of this training material and specifically disclaims any warranties of merchantability or fitness for a particular purpose. CompTIA makes no guarantee concerning the success of persons using any such "Authorized" or other training material in order to prepare for any CompTIA certification exam.

The contents of this training material were created for the CompTIA Network+ exam covering CompTIA certification objectives that were current as of 2009.

How To Become CompTIA Certified

This training material can help you prepare for and pass a related CompTIA certification exam(s). In order to achieve CompTIA certification, you must register for and pass a CompTIA certification exam(s).

In order to become CompTIA certified, you must:

1. Select a certification exam provider. For more information please visit http://www.comptia.org/certifications/testprep/testingcenters.aspx.
2. Register for and schedule a time to take the CompTIA certification exam(s) at a convenient location.
3. Read and sign the Candidate Agreement, which will be presented at the time of the exam(s). The text of the Candidate Agreement can be found at http://www.comptia.org/certifications/policies/agreement.aspx.
4. Take and pass the CompTIA certification exam(s).

For more information about CompTIA's certifications, such as its industry acceptance, benefits, or program news, please visit www.comptia.org/certification.

CompTIA is a not-for-profit trade information technology (IT) trade association. CompTIA's certifications are designed by subject matter experts from across the IT industry. Each CompTIA certification is vendor-neutral, covers multiple technologies, and requires demonstration of skills and knowledge widely sought after by the IT industry.

To contact CompTIA with any questions or comments, please call (1) (630) 678 8300 or e-mail questions@comptia.org.

Chapter Listing

Table of Contents

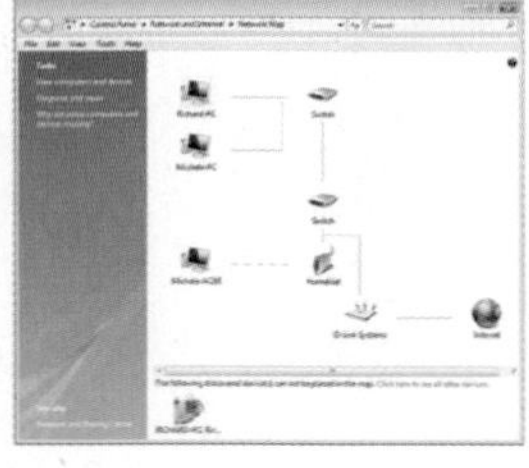

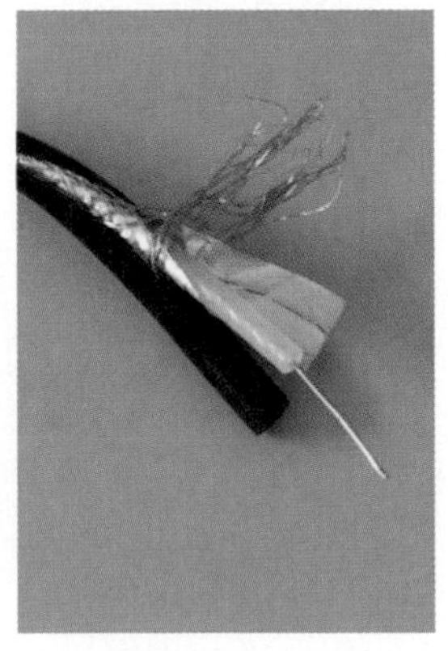

Chapter 10

TCP/IP Fundamentals. 403

Chapter 11

Subnetting. 451

Chapter 12

Multimedia Transmission. 487

Windows Features
Turn Windows features on or off
OK
Cancel

Chapter 14

Remote Access and Long-Distance Communications . . . 561

Chapter 15

Network Security 597

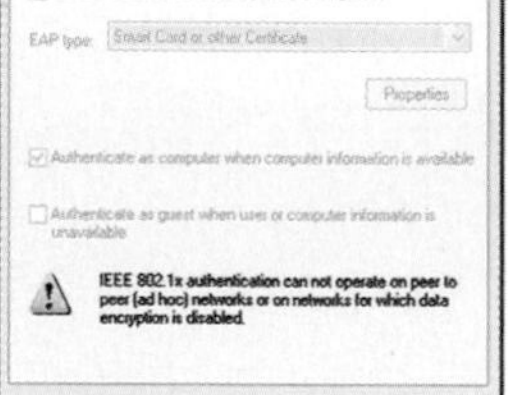

Chapter 18

Fundamentals of Troubleshooting the Network 719

Chapter 19 ■ ■ ■ ■ ■ ■ ■ ■
Designing and Installing a New Network 781

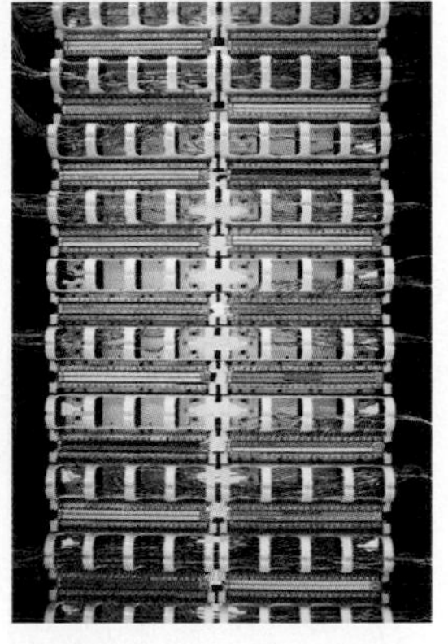

Chapter 20 ■ ■ ■ ■ ■ ■ ■ ■
Network+ Certification Exam Preparation 819

Domain	Percentage	Approximate Number of Questions
1.0 Network Technologies	20 %	20
2.0 Network Media and Topologies	20 %	20
3.0 Network Devices	17 %	17
4.0 Network Management	20 %	20
5.0 Network Tools	12 %	12
6.0 Network Security	11 %	11
Total	100 %	100

Chapter 21 ■ ■ ■ ■ ■ ■ ■ ■
Employment in the Field of Networking Technology 845

1 Introduction to Networking

After studying this chapter, you will be able to:

- ❑ Summarize the advantages and disadvantages of a network system.
- ❑ Classify a network as a LAN, MAN, or WAN.
- ❑ Identify the basic network topologies.
- ❑ Compare and contrast a peer-to-peer network with a client/server network.
- ❑ Summarize how data is packaged and transmitted.
- ❑ Recall the common networking protocols.
- ❑ Summarize the purpose of general network devices.
- ❑ Identify the major standards organizations.
- ❑ Recall the layers of the OSI model.
- ❑ Give examples of the function of each OSI layer.

Network+ Exam—Key Points

The following subject areas are frequently tested by the CompTIA Network+ Certification exam:

- Network topologies.
- Network protocols.
- Network models.
- Network connectivity.
- LAN, MAN, and WAN.
- Network standards.
- Network equipment.
- OSI model.

These subject areas are introduced in this chapter. Many of them appear in more detail later in the textbook. Begin studying them now as simple concepts, and you will be better prepared to comprehend the information presented in later chapters.

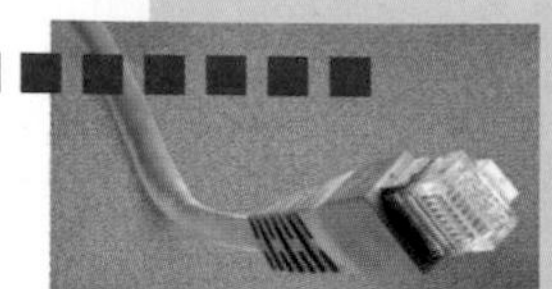

Key Words and Terms

The following words and terms will become important pieces of your networking vocabulary. Be sure you can define them.

active hub
access port
administrative server
American National Standards Institute (ANSI)
application layer
ATM (Asynchronous Transfer Mode)
attenuation
backbone
bridge
brouter
bus topology
cell
centralized administration
CERN
client/server network
concentrator
connectionless-oriented
connection-oriented
copper core cable
data link layer
database server
decentralized administration
dedicated server
driver
Electronic Industry Association (EIA)
FIR (Fast Infrared)
fiber-optic cable
file server
gateway
hierarchical star
hub
hybrid topology
Institute of Electrical and Electronic Engineers (IEEE)
International Organization for Standardization (ISO)
layer 1 device
layer 2 device
layer 3 device
Link-Layer Discovery Protocol (LLDP)
local area network (LAN)
logical identification
MAC (media access control) address
media
media converter
mesh topology
metropolitan area network (MAN)
multilayer switch
multistation access unit (MAU)
network
network administrator
network interface card (NIC)
network layer
network operating system (NOS)
network topology
node
Open Systems Interconnection (OSI) model
passive hub
peer-to-peer network
physical layer
presentation layer
print server
protocol
repeater
ring topology
router
server
session layer
standard
star topology
switch
TCP/IP (Transmission Control Protocol/Internet Protocol)
Telecommunications Industry Association (TIA)
terminating resistor
transport layer
tree
Underwriters Laboratories (UL)
wide area network (WAN)
wireless topology
World Wide Web Consortium (W3C)

This chapter presents a general overview of networking and introduces basic networking concepts. Each topic presented is expanded and explained in detail in later chapters. For full comprehension of the concepts presented throughout the textbook, it is essential that you complete the correlating labs in the lab manual and perform the suggested lab activities at the end of each chapter. The lab manual and suggested lab activities provide for a valuable learning experience.

Definition of a Network

A ***network*** is an interconnected collection of computers, computer-related equipment, and communications devices. This collection could include a PC, laptop computer, personal digital assistant, tablet PC, printer, cell phone, telephone, pager, fax machine, camera, satellite, satellite dish, or a bar code scanner, **Figure 1-1.** A network can be as simple as two computers in one room or as large as thousands of computers, computer equipment, and communications devices spread across the entire globe.

network
an interconnected collection of computers, computer-related equipment, and communications devices.

The purpose of a network is to share computer-related equipment and data. Examples of data are text files, spreadsheets, database information, images, video, music, and voice. Examples of computer-related equipment are printers, Internet access devices, and fax machines.

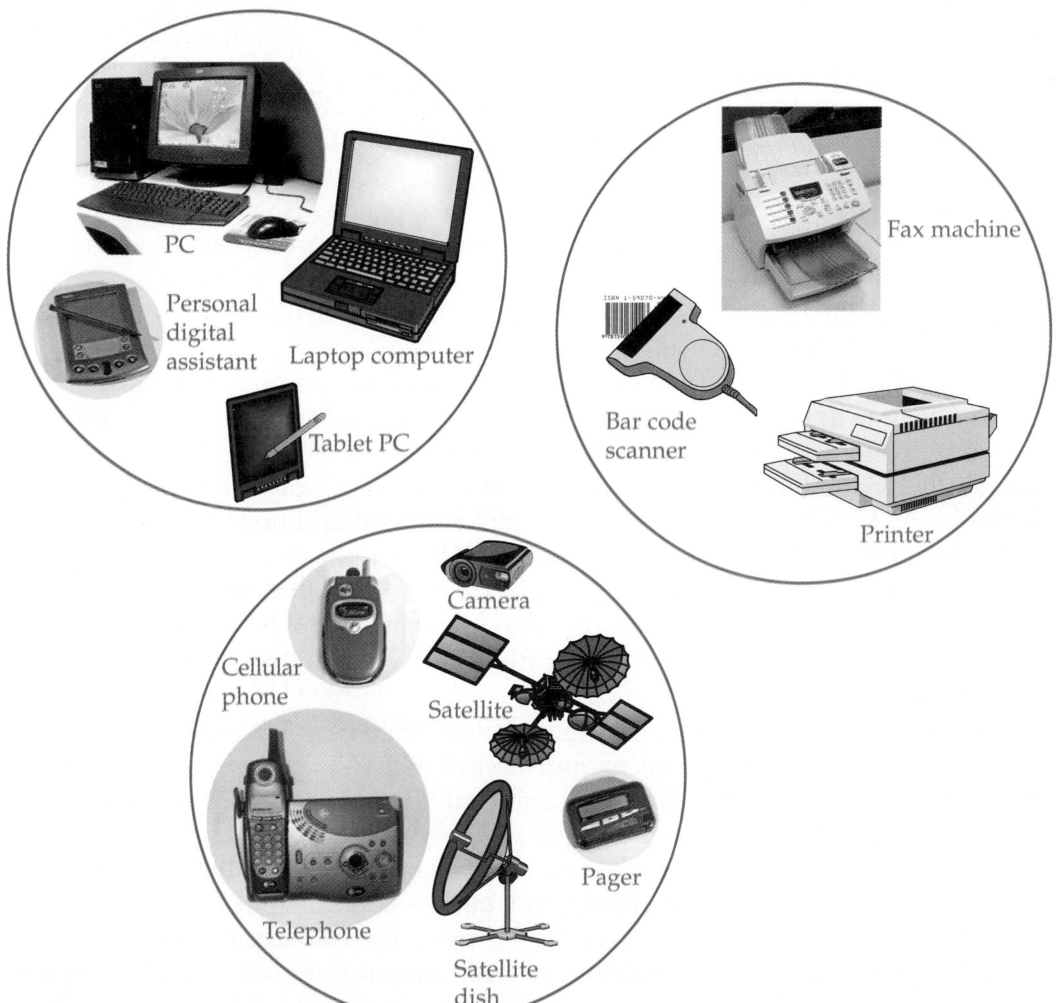

Figure 1-1.
Various devices that can be part of a network.

A network is not the best answer for every situation and should be justified. You must compare the need versus the cost. Next, we will look at the advantages and disadvantages of networking.

Advantages of Networking

Networks provide a means to share software, data, equipment, and communications quickly, easily, and inexpensively. They also provide a means to secure data. A corporate network saves time and money by providing quick access to files and resources throughout the corporation. By using a network system to its full potential, data and communication can be exchanged in the same day in a series of e-mails, phone conversations, and networking conferences. Network meetings can take place quickly and easily between individuals from all over the world, costing only a fraction of what it would cost if the participants had to travel. A small-office or a home-office network can easily share a single printer or data, eliminating the need to transport files via a USB flash drive or CD.

If it were not for networks, sharing data would not be quick, easy, or inexpensive. Think about what it would take to share data with another person without the use of a network. You could copy the file to be shared to a USB flash drive or CD-RW disc and then physically transport the file to the person. The transportation may involve a short walk or a drive, or it may involve shipping. A walk may not cost much, but a drive or mailing a package can be costly and may not be practical to meet deadlines.

A network can facilitate the delivery of the file to anyone anywhere on the network in a very short time at very little cost. Prior to the use of the Internet, editors and writers were required to exchange work via the US Postal Service. A manuscript would be mailed and delivered in two or three days. The manuscript would be read and edited and then returned within a few days via the public mail system. The writer would review the remarks, changes would be made, and the manuscript would be mailed once again. This process was slow and would typically take a week or more for each chapter. Today, material indicating corrections or clarifications can be exchanged via the network in the same day, saving time and shipping costs.

The ability to share network devices can also save a company a significant amount of time and money. A very expensive poster printer used in commercial advertising and art can be connected to the network. If a person located at another PC wished to print their artwork, they could simply send it there via the network. In fact, everyone in the art department could do the same. There would be no need to buy multiple printers. If the printer was not connected to the network, printing a graphic would be much more difficult and would consume a significant amount of time. The file would have to be copied to a USB flash drive or a CD-RW disc and physically transported to the PC to which the printer was attached.

Another advantage of networking is security. Security is a vital part of an organization's structure. It protects information such as customer lists, patient records, legal material, and ideas from being stolen or destroyed. Networks can keep data more secure than a traditional paper system. In an old hard-copy system, data can be photocopied and distributed by anyone having access to the original documents without the company's permission. Customer lists, patient files, financial records, and such can all be copied. The network can be structured to allow users to access only what they need to use for their individual job. Users can be set up as individuals or groups to access particular files, collections of files, and equipment. Allowing specific access is known as assigning user rights or permissions. Security will be covered in detail in Chapter 15—Network Security.

Disadvantages of Networking

Although networking has many advantages, it has its disadvantages as well. These disadvantages include needing additional personnel, losing access to files when the network is down, and vulnerability to hackers, viruses, and disgruntled workers.

Additional personnel are often needed to maintain and modify the network. This adds to the business's operational costs. The number of staff is directly related to the size of the network and the complexity of its design. A small, peer-to-peer network is cost-effective and requires few network administration skills for installation and maintenance. A large, client/server-type network can be very expensive and require users to have specialized training prior to its installation and operation. This type of network typically requires a network administrator and additional networking staff. The original cost of installing a network, as well as overcoming the complexity of its usage, can be a disadvantage. However, after long-term use and training, the costs can be justified.

One of the largest disadvantages of a network depends on how it is designed and configured. Often, when a network goes down, files may not be accessible. Unless a backup system is in place, files that are shared from the file server cannot be retrieved until the administrator repairs the network.

Security can be a double-edged sword. A network can provide an excellent means of security, yet fail to provide security because of the many variables involved. A network can be susceptible to hackers, viruses, and disgruntled workers.

Network Classifications—LAN, MAN, and WAN

Networks are classified into three major categories: local area network (LAN), metropolitan area network (MAN), and wide area network (WAN). These categories are based on the physical size of the network, management, and the use of a private or public communications system.

A public communications system can be accessed by anyone who has a telephone. A private system can only be accessed by designated personnel. For example, a telephone line between company offices can be either public or private. A public line is part of the general public telephone system. A private line between company offices is a privately-leased line accessible by only designated company employees. An example of a private line is a T1 line. You will learn about T1 lines in Chapter 14—Remote Access and Long-Distance Communications. Company networks in which security is a high priority often use private telephone lines rather than public lines.

A ***local area network (LAN)*** is a network that is usually confined to a single building and is managed by a single entity such as a company. An example of a LAN is a network system connecting computers in an office. A ***metropolitan area network (MAN)*** consists of two or more LANs connected with private or public communications lines within the same geographic area, such as a city or a university campus. A MAN is also managed by a single entity. The ***wide area network (WAN)*** consists of a large number of networks and PCs connected with private and public communications lines throughout many geographic areas, **Figure 1-2.** Both public and private telephone companies make communication over a WAN possible. A good

local area network (LAN)
a network that is usually confined to a single building and is managed by a single entity such as a company.

metropolitan area network (MAN)
a network that consists of two or more LANs connected with private or public communications lines within the same geographic area, such as a city or a university campus. It is managed by a single entity.

wide area network (WAN)
a network that consists of a large number of networks and PCs connected with private and public communications lines throughout many geographic areas.

Figure 1-2.
A wide area network connects networks and PCs together over a large geographic area.

example of a WAN is the Internet. The Internet consists of millions of networks spread across the entire globe. A WAN usually requires the services of a telephone company to connect LANs that are under different management.

network topology
the physical arrangement of computers, computer-related devices, communications devices, and cabling in a network.

node
any device attached to the network that is capable of processing and forwarding data.

Network Topologies

The physical arrangement of computers, computer-related devices, communications devices, and cabling in a network is referred to as ***network topology.*** The four major topologies are bus, ring, star, and mesh. Combining two or more of the four major topologies creates a hybrid topology, **Figure 1-3.**

The most distinctive identifier of network topology is the cable and node arrangement. A ***node*** is any device attached to the network that is capable of processing and forwarding data. Some of these devices could be a PC, hub, switch, router, server, and repeater, **Figure 1-4.** In a wireless network, cabling is not used

Figure 1-3.
A hybrid topology can be formed from two or more of the major network topologies.

Hybrid			
Bus	Star	Ring	Mesh

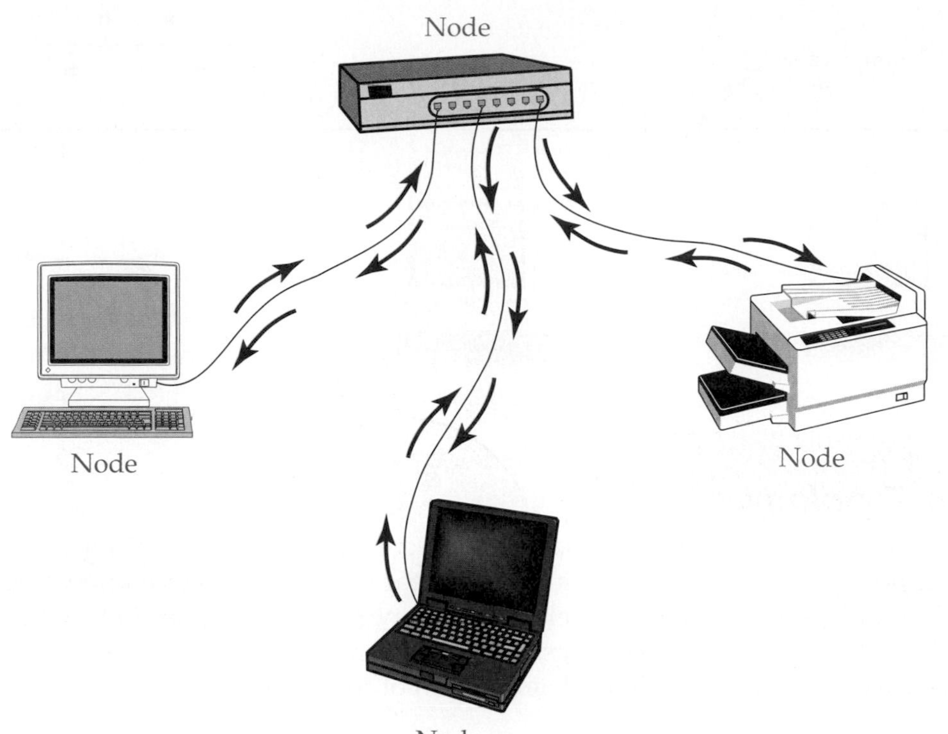

Figure 1-4.
A node denotes any device on the network that is capable of processing and forwarding data.

and nodes do not have to be arranged in a set pattern; however, each network device in a wireless network is capable of processing and forwarding data. Wireless technology is a popular form of linking networks. For these reasons, we will include wireless in our discussion of topologies.

As you read the following sections on each topology, note that each topology is a result of the type of media and network device used to form the network. The following sections briefly mention the type of media and network devices used in each topology. You will learn more about network media and devices later in this chapter and in the following chapters.

bus topology
a network topology that uses a single cable or conductor to connect all nodes on the network.

backbone
a common cable path that often employs high-speed network cable such as fiber-optic.

Bus Topology

A ***bus topology*** uses a single cable or conductor to connect all nodes on the network. Look at **Figure 1-5.** Each node is connected to a common cable. A bus topology uses the least amount of cable when compared to other topologies. The bus topology is often used as a backbone to link other topologies. A ***backbone*** serves as a common path and often employs high-speed network cable such as fiber-optic.

Tech Tip

The term *backbone* may change somewhat when applied to specific types of network topology. In the bus topology, it is the common connecting cable. In a star topology, it describes the cable that connects different portions of the network, or different LANs.

terminating resistor
an electrical device that absorbs transmitted signals, preventing the signals from deflecting and distorting.

A bus topology that uses coaxial cable requires a terminating resistor at each cable end. A ***terminating resistor*** absorbs the transmitted signals when they reach the end of the bus. Without the terminating resistor, the transmitted signals would deflect, causing the data to be distorted. Terminating resistors are covered in detail in Chapter 2—Network Media and Copper Core Cable.

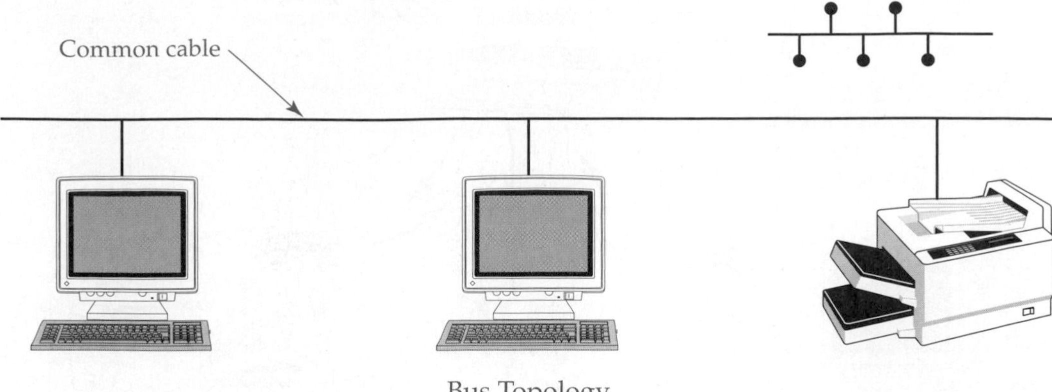

Figure 1-5.
In a bus topology, all nodes connect to a common cable.

star topology
a network topology in which cables running from each node connect to a single point, such as a hub.

Star Topology

Cables running from each node to connect to a single point distinguish the ***star topology*, Figure 1-6.** The center of the star is usually a device known as a hub. A *hub* provides a common electrical connection to all nodes in the star topology. Each network cable plugs into a hub connection called an ***access port.*** Hubs are discussed in detail in a later section of this chapter.

Ring Topology

The ***ring topology*** consists of a single cable that runs continuously from node to node, **Figure 1-7.** The cable begins and ends at the first node in the network. The ring must remain unbroken.

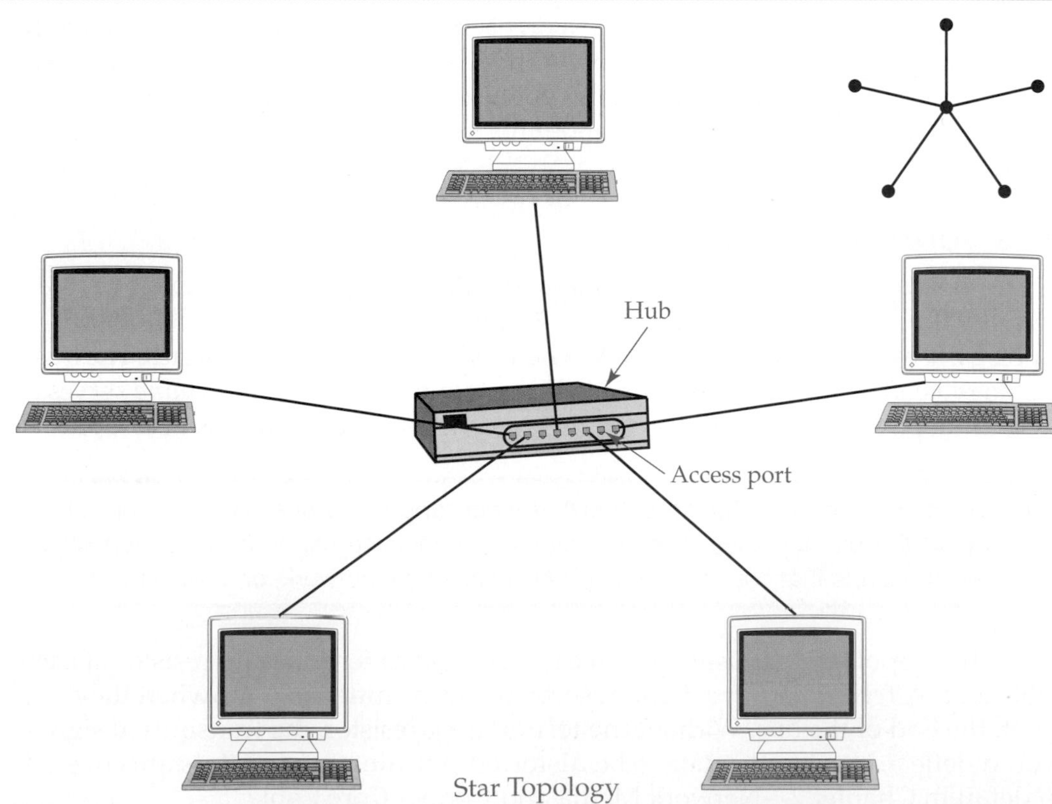

Figure 1-6.
In a star topology, all nodes connect to a central point.

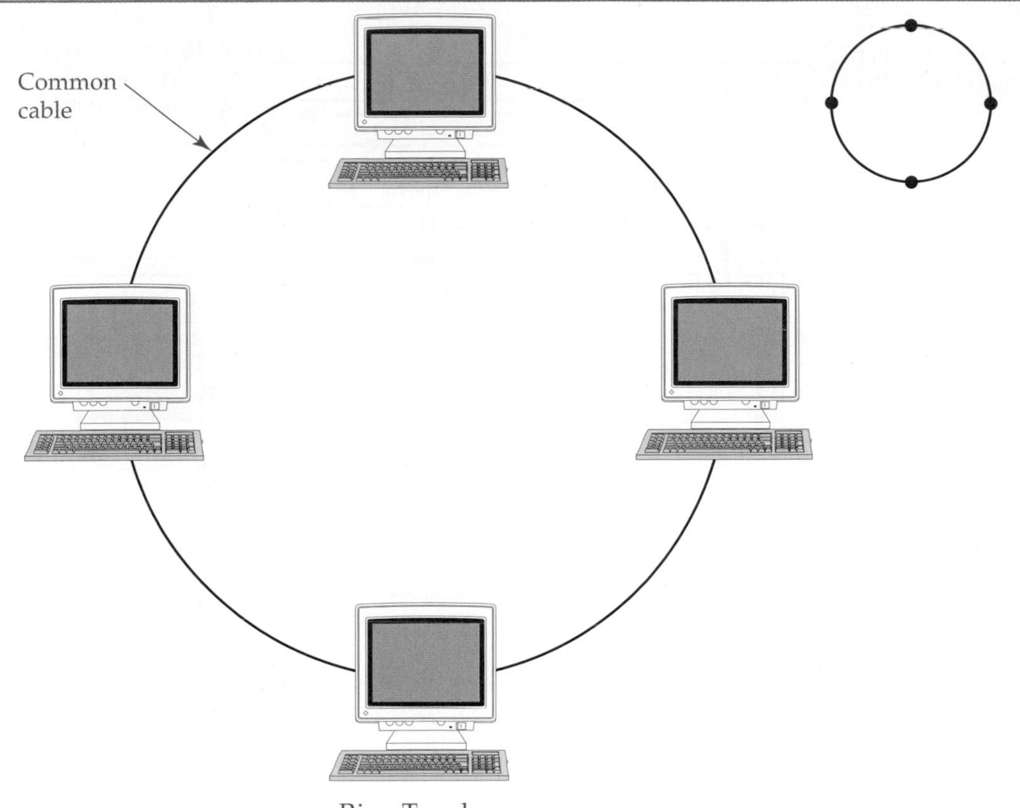

Figure 1-7. In a ring topology, all nodes connect to a cable, forming a circle or ring.

A ring topology may also resemble a star topology, but because of the equipment it uses, it is really connected as a ring. When laid out as a physical star, each node is wired directly to a central location called a ***multistation access unit (MAU).*** A MAU is similar to a hub, but does not function exactly like a hub. A MAU allows for the quick connection and disconnection of Token Ring cables while maintaining the logic of the ring topology. In other words, the MAU keeps the circle intact when one of the Token Ring cables is removed.

Switches at the access ports maintain the ring. See **Figure 1-8.** The unused ports act as closed switches, which maintain the logic of the ring topology. When a cable is plugged into the access port, the switch is opened. The pair of wires inside the cable run to and from the node and MAU. The integrity of the ring is maintained.

access port
a connection on a hub to which cables attach.

ring topology
a network topology that consists of a single cable that runs continuously from node to node.

Tech Tip

MAU is also referred to as a *MSAU (multi station access unit).*

Mesh Topology

In a ***mesh topology,*** each node on the network connects to every other node on the network. This is the most reliable network topology and the most expensive because of the additional cost of cabling and equipment. A mesh is only practical when the network is mission critical and cost is not a barrier. A network consisting of multiple servers may use a mesh topology to ensure the reliability of the servers. See **Figure 1-9.**

multistation access unit (MAU)
a network device that allows for the quick connection and disconnection of Token Ring cables while maintaining the logic of the ring topology.

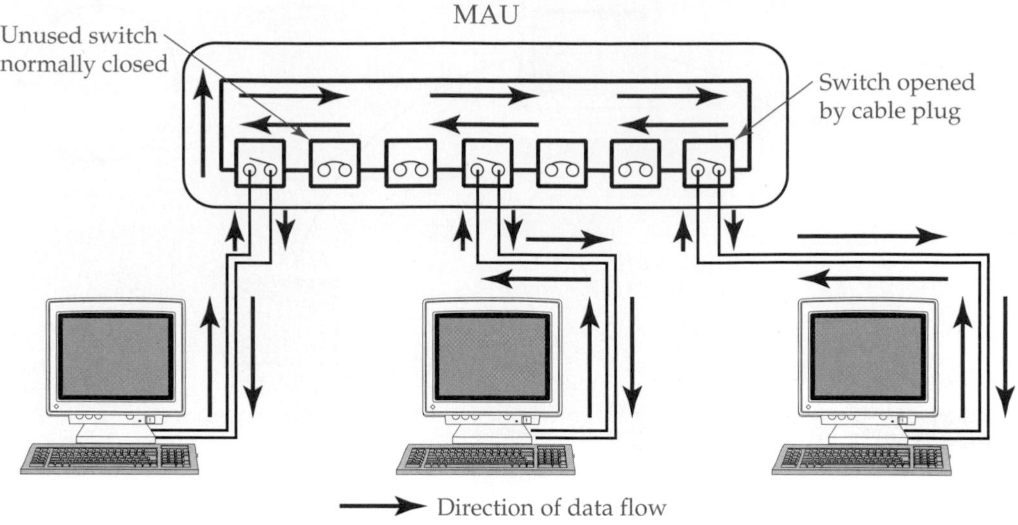

Figure 1-8.
A MAU maintains ring integrity while cables are connected to and disconnected from the network.

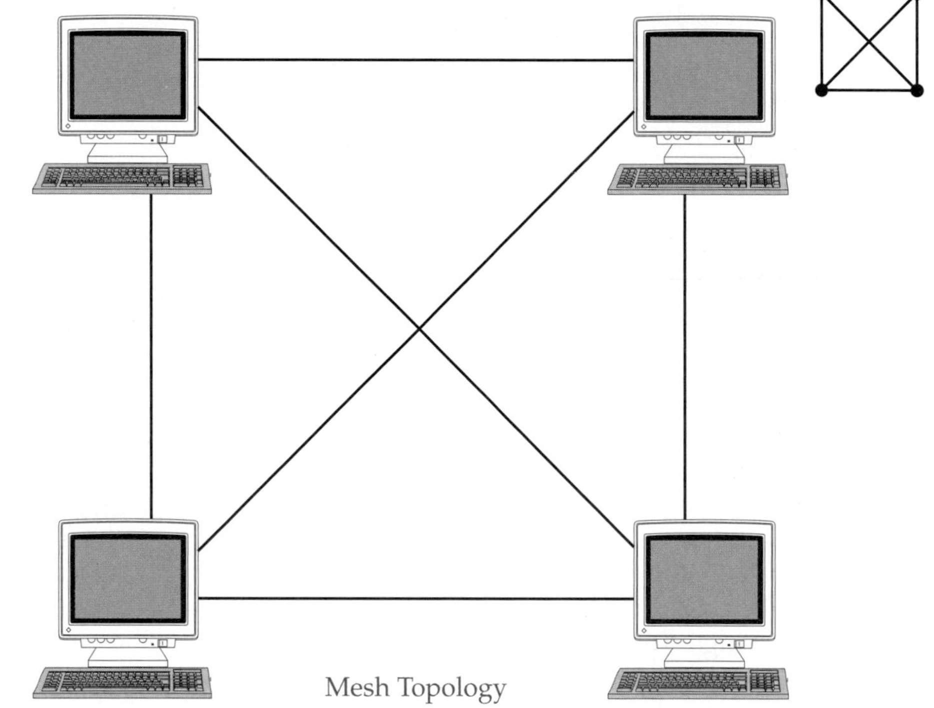

Figure 1-9.
In a mesh topology, each node is connected to each of the other nodes. The number of cable paths rapidly increases as more nodes are added to the mesh topology.

mesh topology
a network topology in which each node on the network connects to every other node on the network.

wireless topology
a network topology that does not use cabling.

Wireless Topology

As the name implies, a ***wireless topology*** does not use cabling. It uses either infrared light or radio transmission to communicate between nodes. Infrared light requires line-of-sight for nodes. This means that nothing that would block the light beam during communications should be placed between the nodes. Radio transmission can experience difficulties caused by building structure and interference generated by other electrical equipment such as radios, motors, welders, and microwave ovens.

Despite these disadvantages, a wireless topology does have many advantages. It is the only answer for communicating with vehicles. The transmission can originate

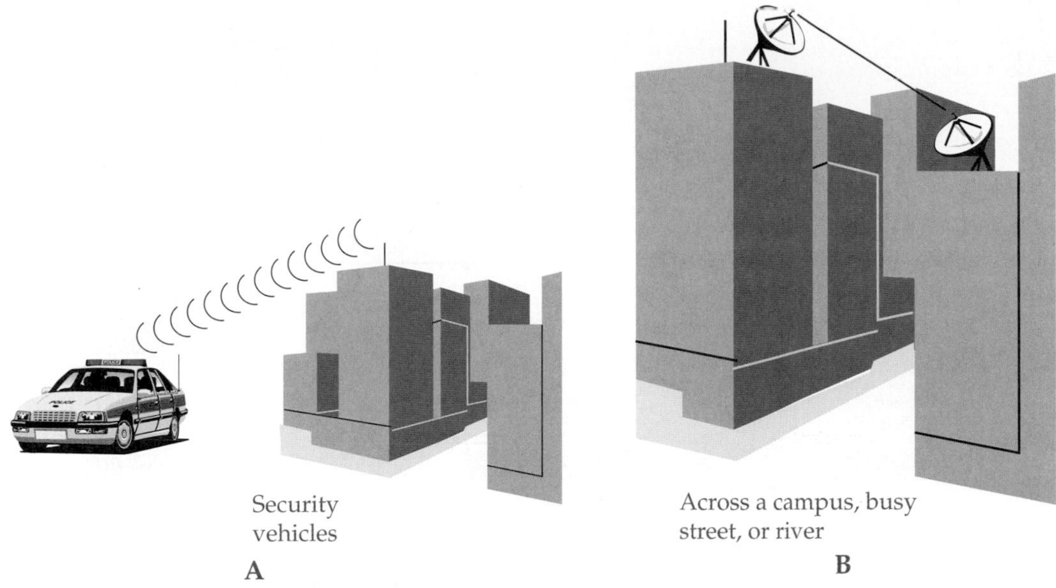

Figure 1-10.
A wireless topology allows nodes to connect to one another in areas where cabling would be impossible or difficult.
A—A security vehicle receives a transmission from an antenna located on top of a building.
B—Wireless technology connecting a network in one building with a network in another building.

from a building antenna or from a satellite, **Figure 1-10A.** Using cable to connect two buildings could be very expensive and time-consuming when compared to installing a wireless network. Two buildings separated by a metropolitan street or a river, or which need immediate connection, can be connected through wireless technology, **Figure 1-10B.** A wireless topology provides a quick way to reconfigure a computer arrangement, whereas moving cables to rearrange computers may not be as easy.

Wireless communications also use cell topology. A ***cell*** is an area that is served by a radio access tower. The towers are configured throughout an area and divide the area into zones known as *cells*. A similar technology is used for cellular telephone communications.

cell
an area or zone that is served by a radio access tower.

hybrid topology
a network topology that consists of a mixture of topology types connected together.

hierarchical star
a network topology created when two or more star topologies are merged using network devices such as hubs, switches, or routers.

tree
a network topology created from two or more star topologies connected together by a common backbone.

Hybrid Topology

As a network grows, it typically changes from a simple network topology, such as a bus or a star, into a hybrid topology. A ***hybrid topology*** is a mixture of topologies. Look at **Figure 1-11.** Notice the different sections of the network. Two star topologies, a bus topology, and a ring topology are connected together.

The design of a hybrid topology changes by the addition of backbones and additional stars or rings. Two subclassifications of the hybrid topology are the hierarchical star and the tree. A ***hierarchical star*** is created when two or more star topologies are merged using network devices such as hubs, switches, or routers, **Figure 1-12.** A ***tree*** is created when two or more star topologies are connected together by a common backbone, **Figure 1-13.**

Network+ Note

Point-to-point and point-to-multipoint was first identified as topologies for the CompTIA 2009 Network+ Certification exam. Point-to-point topology generally refers to two nodes connected directly to each other either by cable or by wireless means. A point-to-multipoint topology is when one node is connected directly to two or more nodes. For example, when one computer broadcasts wireless signals to multiple computers.

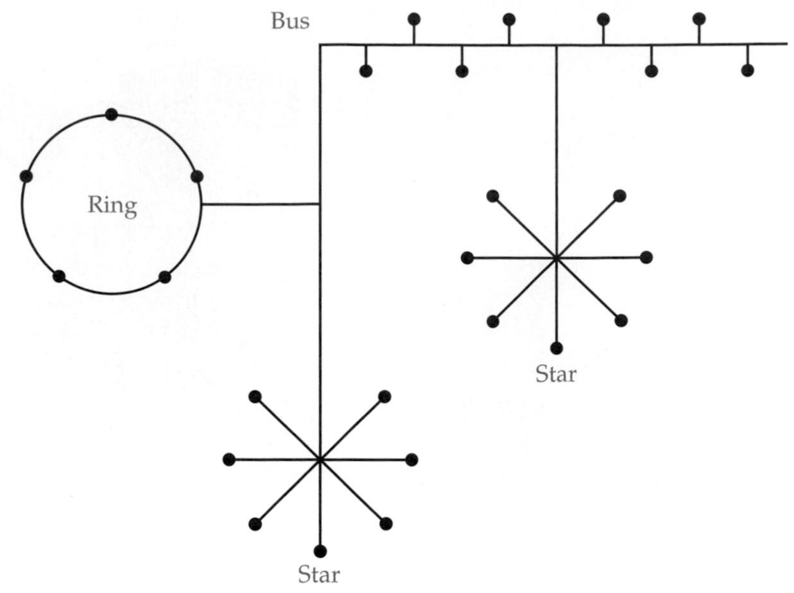

Figure 1-11. This hybrid topology consists of a ring topology, bus topology, and two star topologies.

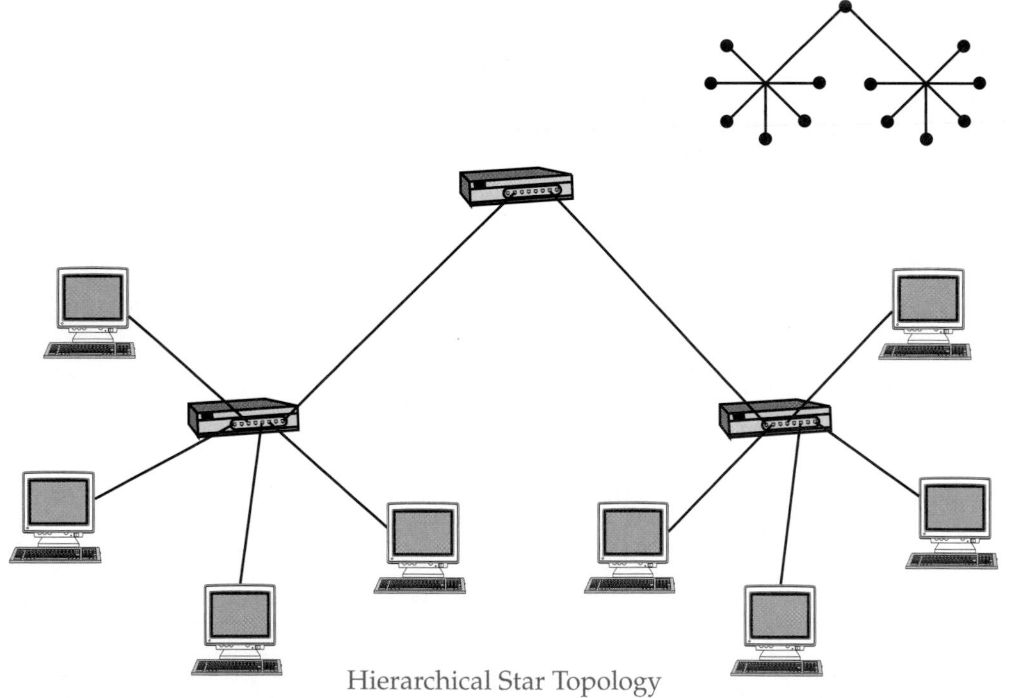

Figure 1-12. Example of a hierarchical star topology.

Basic Network Administration Models

The term *network administration model* refers to how a network is designed and administered. There are two basic network administration models: peer-to-peer and client/server. The client/server network uses centralized administration, and the peer-to-peer uses decentralized administration.

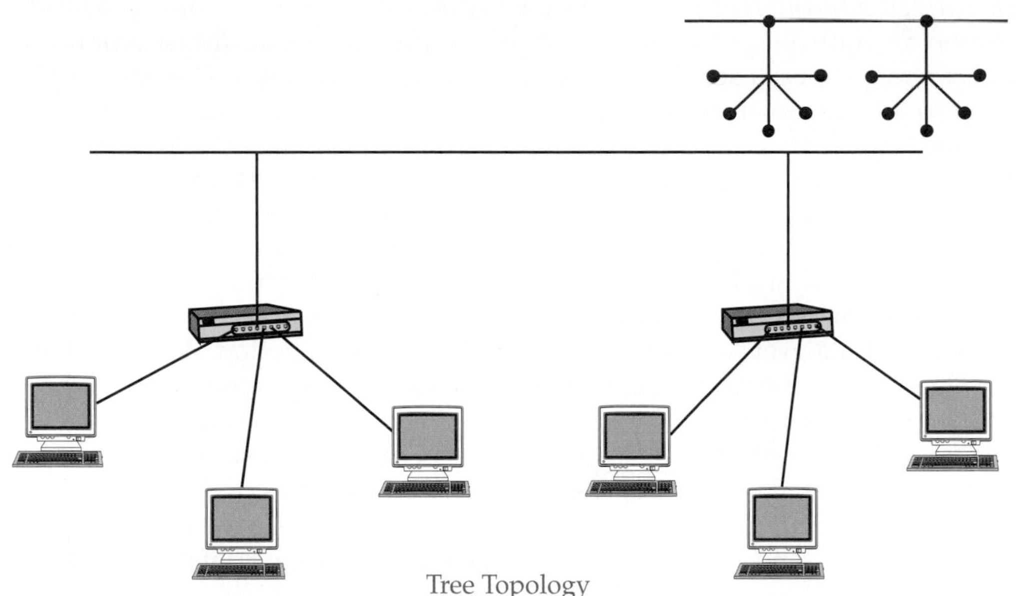

Figure 1-13.
Example of a tree topology.

Client/Server Network

client/server network
a network that consists of computers connected to one or more servers.

server
a computer that provides services to networked computers, or clients.

The ***client/server network*** consists of computers connected via a network to one or more servers, **Figure 1-14.** As its name implies, the ***server*** provides services to networked computers, or clients. Typical services are security, database applications, data storage, Internet access, Web page hosting, and e-mail.

A client/server network has an overall administrator who controls access to the network and to its shares. This person is called the ***network administrator.*** The methodology used to administer a client/server network is called

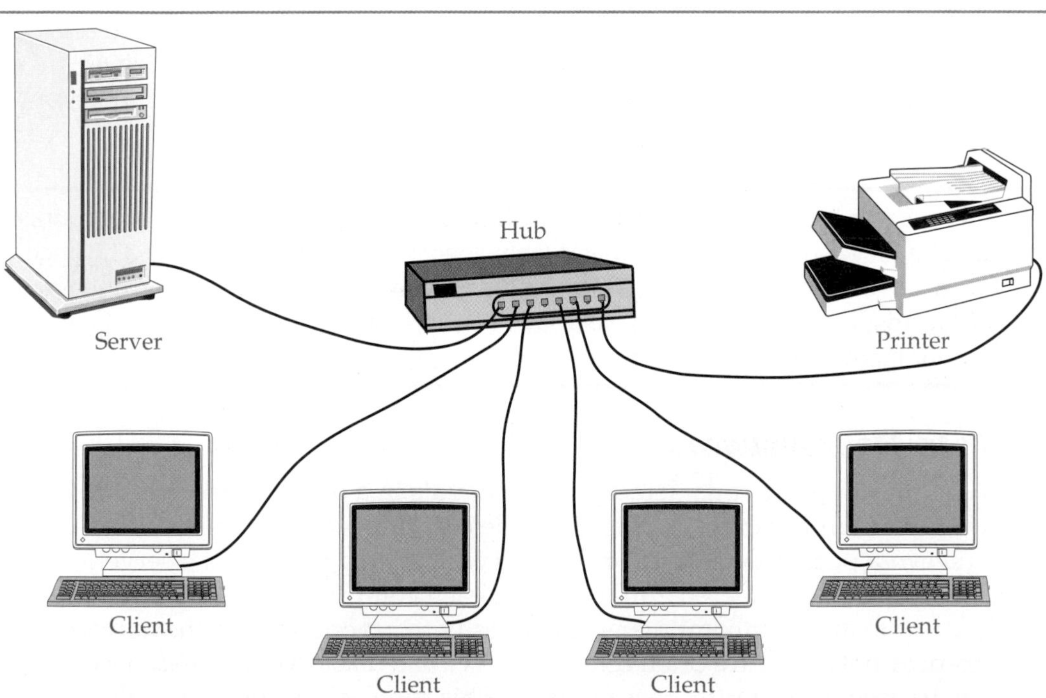

Figure 1-14.
A client/server model has a central computer called a *server,* which controls network security and user access to hardware, software, and programs.

network administrator an overall administrator who controls access to the network and to its shares.

centralized administration the methodology used to administer a client/server network.

dedicated server a server that provides a single function.

file server a server that stores data files that can be accessed by a client.

centralized administration. Centralized administration is the only practical solution for controlling a large number of computers. The administrator does not have to go to each server to perform administrative tasks. The administrator can view and access all resource and security information from a central location. Storing this information in a common database or directory makes this possible. An administrator accesses this database to perform administrative tasks such as adding a user or a share. Two examples of such databases are Microsoft's Active Directory Domain Services (AD DS) and Novell's eDirectory. AD DS is covered in Chapter 7—Microsoft Network Operating Systems.

A server may provide a multitude of services, such as access to files, the Internet, and mail services, or it may provide a single function. A server that provides a single function is referred to as a ***dedicated server.*** Some types of dedicated servers are file servers, print servers, database servers, Web page servers, and administrative servers. A ***file server*** is used to store data files that can be accessed by a client. A ***print server*** coordinates printing activities between clients and printers. An ***administrative server*** is used to administer network security and activities. A ***database server*** contains data files and software programs that query the data.

Tech Tip

Query is a term used to describe extracting data from a database system. Microsoft SQL Server is a typical database query software package.

print server a server that coordinates printing activities between clients and printers.

administrative server a server that administers network security and activities.

A server is similar to the standard PC in design, and, in fact, many small networks use a standard PC as a server. For large networks, the server is an enhanced PC. It may contain two or more CPUs and ten times or more the normal amount of RAM found in a typical PC. The additional RAM and CPUs allow information to be processed faster, which is useful when the server has many client requests to service at one time. A server is usually equipped with several hard drives. The server may also have one or more duplicate sets of hard drives used to back up the data saved on the first set of hard drives. Backup systems are key to network success. They are covered, along with server hardware, in greater depth in Chapter 9—Introduction to the Server.

Tech Tip

The term *server* can be used in two ways, which can be very confusing to a networking novice. The first and most obvious way is when identifying a physical server. The second is when a server is identified by a service such as a proxy server, Web server, or gateway. In other words, a single network server may be referred to by many different names and be used for more than one purpose.

database server a server that contains data files and software programs to query the data.

peer-to-peer network a network in which all computers are considered peers or equals.

Peer-to-Peer Network

All computers are considered peers or equals in a ***peer-to-peer network.*** As you can see in **Figure 1-15,** there is no designated server in this model. A computer in a peer-to-peer network can serve as both a client and a server. Each computer is considered equal because each computer's user has equal authority to share their computer's resources with other users on the network. Peer-to-peer networks are often referred to as *workgroups*. Many small networks are constructed as a peer-to-peer network. This type of network is usually inexpensive and easy to install.

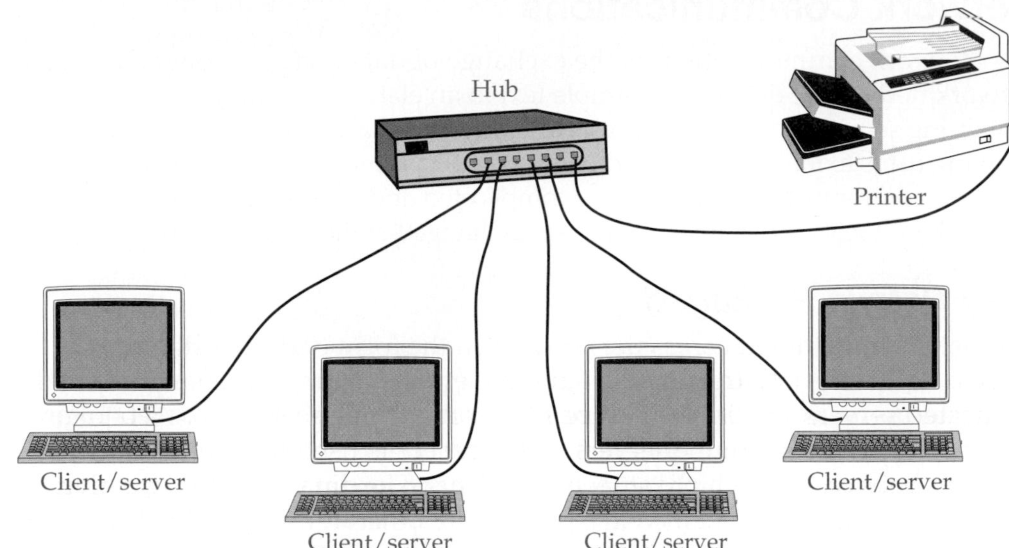

Figure 1-15.
In a simple peer-to-peer network, each computer has equal powers, or administration. Each computer controls the sharing of its data and hardware resources.

In a peer-to-peer network, a computer's user may determine and control which files, drives, and printers will be shared. The computer's user may also determine and control access to the share and designate a password to use the share. Because administration is spread across the entire network, the methodology used to administer a peer-to-peer network is called ***decentralized administration.*** Administration of this type of network can be very difficult. Without a common database, it is often hard to keep track of all the available users, resources, and access rights. This model is usually used on small networks of less than 25 computers.

decentralized administration
the methodology used to administer a peer-to-peer network.

Approximately 45% of all business networks are composed of less than 25 computers.

The advantages of a peer-to-peer network, however, is that it is inexpensive to install and simple to administer as long as it remains small. No special, costly networking software is required for operation as it is with the client/server model. A simple Microsoft peer-to-peer network can be assembled using only Windows 95 or later.

Network Operating Systems (NOS)

The ***network operating system (NOS)*** provides a communications system between the computers, printers, and other intelligent hardware that exist on the network. Some common network operating systems in use are Windows Server 2003, Windows Server 2008, UNIX, Linux, and to some limited extent Novell NetWare.

network operating system (NOS)
an operating system that provides communications between the computers, printers, and other intelligent hardware that exist on the network.

All networks provide communication between different operating systems, different brands of hardware, and various ages of equipment. The network operating system is also composed of software programs that provide for security, user identity, remote access, printer sharing, and other services. In reality, the network operating system *is* the network; everything else is hardware.

Network Communications

Network communications is the exchange of data and commands between network nodes. The data can be simple text to an elaborate multimedia presentation containing sound and full motion video. The network also communicates commands allowing users to log on, share hardware, and check conditions of the network system. Network communications can be very complicated and is based on network protocols. Network protocols determine how data is exchanged at the packet level.

How Data Is Packaged

Data is transmitted across the network in the form of digital signals, or pulses. Digital signals are rapidly changing levels of voltage often represented in binary terms as 1s and 0s. See **Figure 1-16.** For data to be sent across a network from node to node, a common scheme of packaging must be decided on.

Data is often divided into smaller segments. The data segments are given a sequence number and combined in a packet with other information, such as routing and error-checking code. The packet sequence number allows the receiving computer to reassemble the message in the order it was transmitted. An error-checking code ensures the data was not corrupted. Other information that may be coded into the packet is the packet's destination, the address of the node that originated the packet, and the time it was originated. The type of data and information contained in the packet varies depending on the protocol used. Protocols are discussed in an upcoming section of this chapter and are revisited throughout the textbook.

connection-oriented a type of network connection that requires a direct connection between the source and the destination.

connectionless-oriented a type of network connection that does not use a direct connection between the destination and the source.

Network Connectivity

Connections between two nodes can be classified as either connection-oriented or connectionless-oriented. ***Connection-oriented*** requires a direct connection between the source and the destination. For example, a telephone modem is used to make a direct connection between the Internet service provider and your computer. The telephone line usually provides a direct connection from one modem to another. Cable television is also an example of a connection-oriented communications system.

Connectionless-oriented means there is no direct connection between the destination and the source. For example, when a typical Internet connection is established between a PC in Florida and another in California using the Internet, many different paths are used between the destination and source. In fact, the

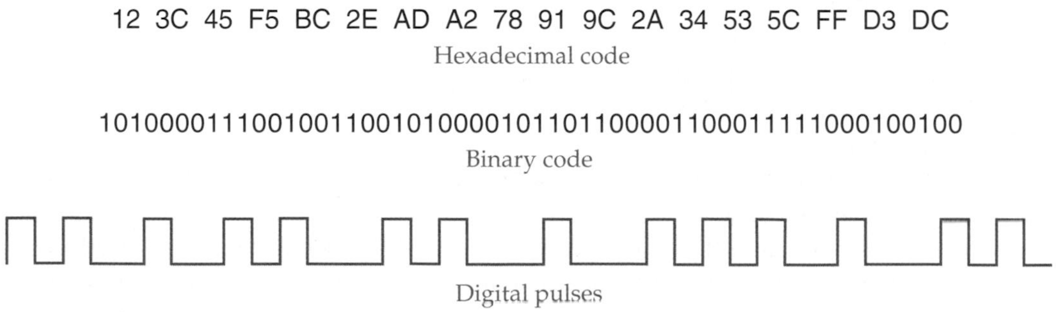

12 3C 45 F5 BC 2E AD A2 78 91 9C 2A 34 53 5C FF D3 DC

Hexadecimal code

101000011100100110010100001011011000011000111110001001 00

Binary code

Digital pulses

Figure 1-16. Data is transferred across a network as a series of digital signals, or pulses. These signals are sometimes expressed as binary numbers (1, 0) or as hexadecimal values (1B, F5, etc.). The way the data is presented is determined by the technology used.

path may change during the process of information exchange between the two PCs. Packets can be exchanged using several different routes. Each packet must be packaged with the source address when a connectionless-oriented transmission mode is used.

Protocols

For intelligent hardware to communicate across a network, they must use the same protocol. A ***protocol*** is a group of computer programs that handle packet formatting and control data transmission. A protocol can also be defined as a set of rules governing communication between devices on a network. Some of the things a protocol is responsible for include the following:

protocol
a group of computer programs that handle packet formatting and control data transmission.

- Determining how devices identify each other.
- Determining the method of data exchange.
- Determining the size of each packet.
- Determining the timing for packet transmission.
- Compressing data.
- Determining the signal to be used to end a session.
- Establishing the end of a session.
- Providing and establishing error checking.

The term *protocol* is often used as a label for a software program, a networking standard, or specification. Many times the exact definition depends on the context of the information it is applied to.

A protocol determines how to identify other computers that are running the same protocol. For example, a protocol establishes how the two computers will identify each other—by name, such as *Station1* and *Station25*, or by number, such as 192.168.000.010. A protocol also establishes the method for information exchange. Examples of data exchange methods are ASCII code or bitmap graphics.

Data may be transmitted between two computers by dividing the entire message into smaller packets, or it may be transmitted as a steady stream of data. The protocol determines the size of each packet and the timing of its release onto the network. If the packet is too large, the computer hardware may not be able to process it. The protocol divides data into packets of varying lengths. Some packets are as small as 52 bytes and others are several thousand bytes in length. Since only one or two computers may dominate the network usage time, breaking the message into packets and timing its release helps to balance network traffic when many computers are trying to communicate over the network at the same time.

A protocol may compress a packet's contents to allow for faster transmission rates. It also dictates when the communications session will end and what signal will denote this.

A protocol usually has some error-checking capabilities. Error checking ensures the information received is complete and is reassembled in the correct order. Some network systems, such as the Internet, are very complex. The packets may not be routed to their destination using the same route. Consequently, packets may arrive at different times and would be garbled when reassembled, if not for error checking.

You will study many different protocols and their characteristics throughout the textbook. For now, remember that the protocol is the set of communications rules between two or more devices.

TCP/IP

TCP/IP (Transmission Control Protocol/Internet Protocol) a protocol that was developed by the Defense Advanced Research Project Agency (DARPA) in the early 1970s and was designed to support communications over the Internet.

TCP/IP (Transmission Control Protocol/Internet Protocol) was developed by the Defense Advanced Research Project Agency (DARPA) in the early 1970s and was designed to support communications over the Internet. TCP/IP has become the default protocol used to communicate across the Internet and on local area networks.

The name *TCP/IP* consists of two separate protocols: TCP and IP. TCP/IP is an entire suite of protocols, each serving different functions. For example, TCP/IP network communications consist of mainly three protocols: IP, TCP, and UDP. IP routes information across a network by the use of IP addresses. TCP sends a packet to a destination and waits for a confirmation that the packet arrived intact. UDP sends packets without confirmation of their arrival.

Another protocol in the TCP/IP suite is the Network Time Protocol (NTP). NTP synchronizes time between network devices. All devices must have the same time reference to ensure security in the network. Time can be examined to determine if a packet has been tampered with. The File Transfer Protocol (FTP) is used to upload and download files to Web servers. Simple Mail Transfer Protocol (SMTP) is designed to send e-mail. To view a complete collection list of protocols in the TCP/IP suite, visit www.protocols.com.

There are two versions of the TCP/IP protocol: TCP/IPv4 and TCP/IPv6. The lower case *v* represents *version*. TCP/IPv4 was adopted as a standard in 1981 and is still in use to support Internet communications. TCP/IPv6 was first introduced as an official standard in 1995 but was slowly adopted and put into service by network operating software designers. TCP/IPv6 and TCP/IPv4 coexist today. For example, Windows Vista, Windows 7, and Windows Server 2008 operating systems use TCP/IPv4 as the primary Internet communications protocol but use TCP/IPv6 as the primary protocol to communicate on a local area network, **Figure 1-17.** The main reason TCP/IPv4 is still in use is to ensure downward compatibility with older network devices that do not recognize the IPv6 protocol.

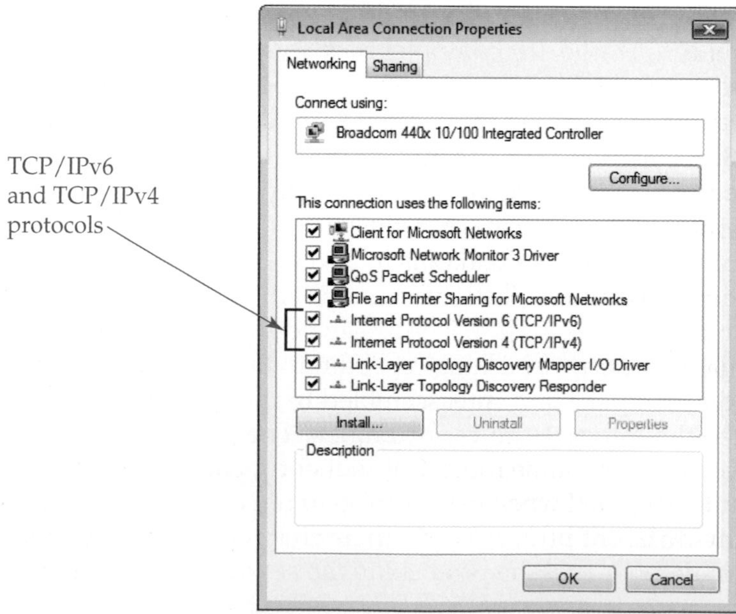

Figure 1-17. Windows Vista **Local Area Connection Properties** dialog box. Notice that both TCP/IPv4 and TCP/IPv6 are installed by default.

FIR

FIR (Fast Infrared) is used for transmitting data from laptop computers to desktop computers without the use of cables. Data is transmitted by infrared light. Because FIR is based on wireless technology, a different protocol specification than those developed for wired technology is required. Wireless technology features are discussed in more depth in Chapter 4—Wireless Technology. Then, the difference between communication based on wire and wireless devices will become more evident.

FIR (Fast Infrared) a protocol used for transmitting data from laptop computers to desktop computers without the use of cables.

ATM

ATM (Asynchronous Transfer Mode) is a protocol designed especially for transmitting data, voice, and video. Data is segmented into packets containing 53 bytes each, which are switched between any two nodes in the system at rates ranging from 1.5 Mbps to 622 Mbps. Voice and video data contain thousands more data packets than a typical Microsoft Word document. Transferring massive amounts of data between two points using existing technology such as copper wire systems requires a protocol designed to accomplish this. The ATM protocol is designed specifically to transfer large amounts of data in an uninterrupted stream required by audio and video communications across the Internet. Other existing protocols at the time would not meet this requirement.

ATM (Asynchronous Transfer Mode) a protocol designed especially for transmitting data, voice, and video.

There are many other protocols that are designed for specific communications requirements. Some protocols deal with security issues, others with the effective routing of data packets, and some with the remote access of network equipment. Protocol technologies are explored throughout this textbook.

LLDP

The ***Link-Layer Discovery Protocol (LLDP)*** standard was released by the Institute of Electrical and Electronic Engineers (IEEE) in 2005. LLDP allows network devices, such as computers, routers, and servers, to automatically exchange information. Microsoft first incorporated LLDP into Windows Vista and then later included it in Windows 7 and Windows Server 2008.

Link-Layer Discovery Protocol (LLDP) a protocol that identifies devices connected on the local area network and allows them to automatically exchange information.

Microsoft refers to their implementation of LLDP as two separate protocols: *Link-Layer Topology Discovery Mapper I/O Driver* and *Link-Layer Topology Discovery Responder.* The LLTD Mapper I/O Driver sends out packets containing information about the computer. The LLTD Responder responds to inquires. Together, the two versions of LLDP allow the computer to construct a map similar to the one in **Figure 1-18.** As you can see, all network devices capable of using LLDP can exchange information, thus creating a map of logical locations of each device. A dashed line represents a wireless connection. A solid line represents a wired connection. The paths are not to scale, but rather logically arranged to represent their location in the network.

Pay particular attention to the computer icon at the bottom of the map, which means the computer could not be placed in the map. Computers running an earlier version of an operating system, such as Windows XP, will not appear in the map. However, a software patch can be downloaded and installed on a Windows XP computer that will allow it to run LLDP and thus exchange information with other LLDP-enabled devices. Many legacy devices, such as some switches and routers, will not appear in the map because they are not capable of supporting LLDP, and there is no software patch available to update them.

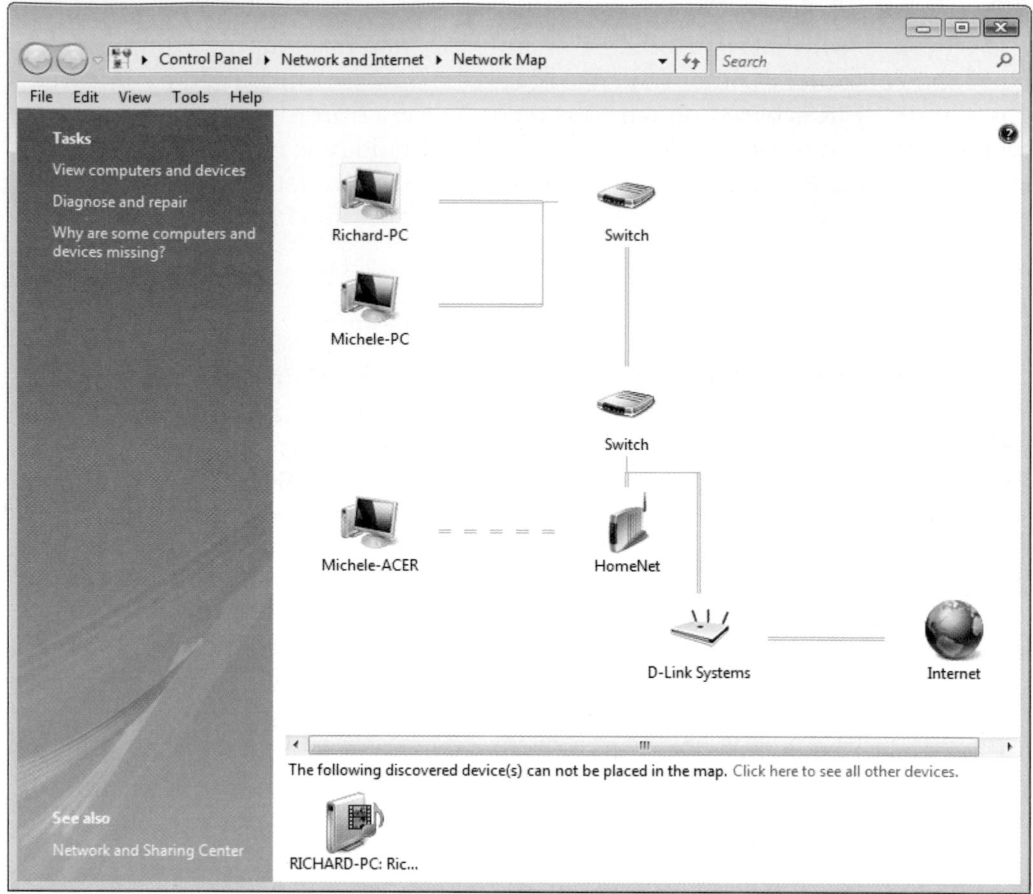

Figure 1-18. The Windows Vista Network Map utility uses the LLDP protocol to collect information about the location of nodes on the network.

Today, many devices support the LLDP standard. For example, many telephones, cameras, and other Bluetooth devices can communicate directly with local area networks and automatically identify themselves to the network using a form of LLDP.

There are several proprietary implementations of LLDP. For example, Cisco Systems created the Cisco Discovery Protocol (CDP). This protocol is used primarily to exchange information between routers and other Cisco networking devices. Nortel Networks created the Nortel Discovery Protocol (NDP) to allow telephones and telephone equipment to automatically exchange information across Ethernet networks. Enterasys Networks uses a form of LLDP called Enterasys Discovery Protocol (EDP) to configure routers and network security equipment. It was originally called Cabletron Discovery Protocol (CDP).

The most remarkable feature of LLDP is how it provides information about network equipment, which then allows operating systems such as Microsoft Vista and Windows 7 to configure a computer as a member of a local area network with little or no need for user input. You can take a Windows Vista or Windows 7 computer right out of the box and add it to an existing local area network. Once connected and booted, the computer will automatically discover the other network devices and automatically configure itself as part of the network. But don't worry. This feature will not replace network technicians. There are still plenty of things that can go wrong with a network. In many cases, a computer cannot automatically configure itself to join a network domain that is securely designed to prevent unauthorized attachment.

Usually if you see the words "Discovery Protocol," the protocol is most likely a variation of LLDP. Many early implementations of LLDP were referred to as *Neighbor Discovery Protocol* or *Neighborhood Discovery Protocol.*

NetBIOS and NetBEUI

NetBEUI and NetBIOS were common protocols that were an integral part of the Microsoft network operating system. NetBIOS was an early Microsoft network standard and protocol. One of its specifications was limiting network device names to 15 characters. Even today, Microsoft limits computer names to 15 characters.

NetBEUI was installed by default on Microsoft operating systems earlier than Windows XP. Be aware that you can still encounter the term *NetBIOS* when configuring network adapters in Windows Vista, Windows 7, and Windows Server 2008. You may also encounter references to NetBIOS and NetBEUI in other references and especially in practice questions and study guides found on the Internet.

Notice that in **Figure 1-19,** options are listed for the NetBIOS protocol in the **Windows Vista Advanced TCP/IP Settings** dialog box. Windows 7 and Windows Server 2008 have the same advanced TCP/IP settings for NetBIOS over TCP/IP.

As you can see, some protocols can be a part of networking for many years after they are considered obsolete. Microsoft has always preserved options, even ones considered obsolete, so that its operating system will be downward compatible with older Microsoft operating systems.

Network+ Note

Protocols and network technology rapidly changes. NetBIOS and NetBEUI are no longer a valid CompTIA topic but still have influence on today's network and computer technology.

NetBIOS settings

Figure 1-19.
The Windows Vista **Advanced TCP/IP Settings** dialog box includes settings for the NetBIOS protocol to ensure downward compatibility with older Windows operating systems.

To learn more about protocols, visit www.protocols.com. This Web site provides extensive information for hundreds of protocols. You should bookmark this Web site for future reference.

Network Media and Devices

A variety of media and devices are associated with networking. This section contains a brief description of each. Some of the network devices presented here may be difficult to distinguish because they are similar in function; however, their differences will become more apparent as protocols and the OSI model are further investigated. Also, each media type and network device is revisited in later chapters, and more detail regarding their use and operation is presented.

Media

media
the general term that identifies the material used to transport packets and data streams between nodes.

copper core cable
a type of cable that consists of a copper wire surrounded by plastic or synthetic insulation.

fiber-optic cable
a type of cable that has a glass or clear plastic core.

Media is the general term that identifies the material used to transport packets and data streams between nodes. There are several broad classifications of media. Each type of media has advantages and disadvantages. The most common media is ***copper core cable.*** Copper core cable consists of a copper wire surrounded by plastic or synthetic insulation. There are many different types of copper core cable used in networking. These types are discussed in depth in Chapter 2—Network Media and Copper Core Cable.

Another type of media, referred to as ***fiber-optic cable,*** uses a glass or clear plastic core rather than copper. The core is thin and flexible. Under normal circumstances, it will not break. Fiber-optic cable carries pulses of light that represent commands and data.

In wireless networks, radio waves carry digital signals between various pieces of equipment in the network. Radio waves are the media, and transmission is similar to cell phone technology. Wireless technology is commonly used where cables are impractical, such as to connect a computer installed in a police car to a main network system.

Infrared light is another form of media in which an infrared beam is used to transport a digital signal. Infrared transmission uses a transmitter/receiver unit at each end of the transmission path. A transmitter converts the digital signal into a series of infrared light flashes and sends them to a receiver unit. The receiver unit decodes the signal. Infrared light transmission is similar to the remote control used for televisions.

Media Converter

media converter
a device that changes one type of electrical signal into another or interfaces one cable type to another.

A ***media converter*** changes one type of electrical signal into another or interfaces one cable type to another. For example, a media converter can connect an Ethernet 100-Mbps copper core cable to an Ethernet 1-Gbps fiber-optic cable. The term *media converter* can also apply to other network equipment, such as a bridge or switch. This type of equipment often performs more than one function. Some media converters may even act as a repeater.

Network Interface Card

network interface card (NIC)
a network device that contains the electronic components needed to send and receive a digital signal.

A ***network interface card (NIC)*** contains the electronic components needed to send and receive a digital signal. A network card is known by many other names such as a *network host adapter*, *network expansion card*, and *network adapter card*. Look at **Figure 1-20** to see what a typical network interface card looks like.

Figure 1-20.
A typical Ethernet network card equipped with an RJ-45 connector. (Courtesy of Cisco Systems, Inc.)

The network interface card fits into one of the motherboard slots inside a PC. This provides a way for the PC to connect to the network media. The network interface card must be equipped with the suitable connector for the type of network media used. Network connectors are discussed in Chapter 2—Network Media and Copper Core Cable and Chapter 3—Fiber-Optic Cable.

A network interface card must first match the physical communication requirements of the network it is installed for, such as Ethernet, Token Ring, wireless, or high speed FDDI. Next, a driver must be installed so that the computer can communicate with the network interface card. A ***driver*** is a software program that allows a PC to communicate with and transfer data to and from computer hardware, such as the network interface card. The network interface card must also be configured with a protocol, such as TCP/IP or ATM, to support network communications. The network interface card may be configured for a combination of more than one protocol. The exact requirements will become apparent as you progress through this course. Remember that a protocol is a set of rules for communication between two nodes. In general, all network interface cards in the LAN must be configured with the same protocol to communicate with each other.

driver
a software program that allows a PC to communicate with and to transfer data to and from computer hardware, such as the network interface card.

After the network interface card driver and protocol are installed, the PC must be uniquely identified. There are two types of identification used on a typical network: a physical ID and a logical ID. The network card contains the physical ID, called a ***MAC (media access control) address.*** The MAC address is a six-byte, hexadecimal number, such as 00 C0 12 2B 14 C5. The first three bytes identify the network interface card's manufacturer, and the second three bytes uniquely identify the card. Together, these two sets of numbers give the network card its own unique, physical identification. The manufacturer stores the MAC address inside an electronic chip on the network interface card.

MAC (media access control) address
the physical ID of a network card, which is a six-byte, hexadecimal number such as 00 C0 12 2B 14 C5.

A ***logical identification*** is provided by the technician at the time of installation. It is usually a name that uniquely identifies the computer on the network. For example, the name *Station24* would be given to a computer that is the 24th to be added to a group of computers.

logical identification
a name provided by the technician at the time of installation that uniquely identifies the computer on the network.

attenuation
the loss of signal strength.

repeater
an electrical device that amplifies or reshapes a weak signal into its original strength and form.

hub
a central connection point where all network cables are concentrated. It is classified as either active or passive. Also called a *concentrator.*

concentrator
a central connection point where all network cables are concentrated. It is classified as either active or passive. Also called a *hub.*

passive hub
a hub that acts only as a central connection point for network cables.

active hub
a hub that can determine whether a packet should remain in an isolated section of the network or pass through to another section of the network. Also called an *intelligent hub* or *switch.*

Repeater

As digital signals travel across copper wire, the signals lose strength and become distorted. The loss of signal strength is called ***attenuation.*** To reshape and regenerate the strength of the digital signal, a ***repeater*** is used. The repeater amplifies or reshapes the weak signal into its original strength and form. See **Figure 1-21.** A repeater allows the network media to exceed its recommended maximum length.

Hub

A ***hub*** is a central connection point where all network cables are concentrated, **Figure 1-22.** A hub is often called a ***concentrator*** and is classified as either active or passive. A ***passive hub*** simply acts as a central connection point for network cables. Packets transmitted from one node are passed to all nodes connected to the passive hub and through the hub to other sections of the network.

An ***active hub,*** sometimes called an *intelligent hub* or *switch,* is an enhanced passive hub. It is designed with a power supply. The active hub not only acts as a central connection point for the network cabling, it also regenerates digital signals like a repeater. The active hub can also determine whether a packet should remain in the isolated section of the network or pass the packet through the hub to another section of the network.

Look at **Figure 1-23.** *Station3* attempts to communicate with *Station1.* The intelligent hub does not allow the packets to be transmitted through the hub to the other areas of the network. The hub directs the packets to only those computers that are attached to it. Active hubs are used to reduce excessive data transmission on a network. A network with an excessive number of collisions can be broken into segments by using active hubs. This can reduce the amount of packets transmitted over the entire network. However, this will only reduce the traffic if there are a significant number of transmissions to computers in the same area.

Gateway

Today, local area networks use the TCP/IP protocol like the Internet does, so the definition of gateway has changed. The accepted definition of ***gateway*** is a device that connects the local area network to the Internet.

In the early days of networking, the Internet used the TCP/IP protocol for communications, but local area networks used proprietary protocols such as NetBEUI and IPX/SPX. The local area network packets would need to be translated or

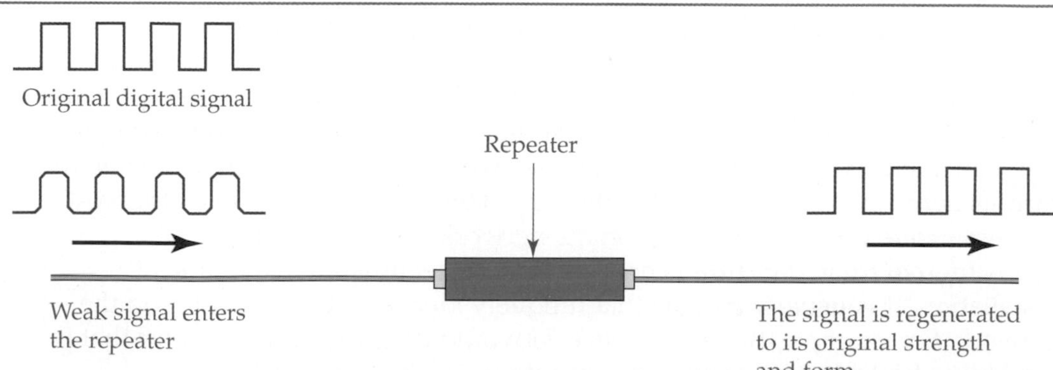

Figure 1-21.
Digital signals lose their strength as they travel along a wire. A repeater is used to regenerate a signal so that it is returned to its original strength and form.

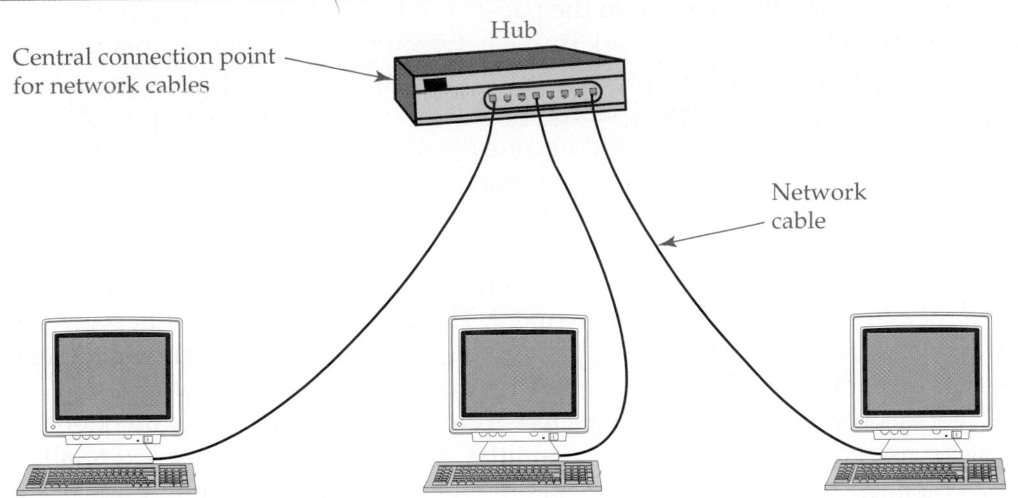

Figure 1-22.
A hub is commonly used to connect computers on a network.

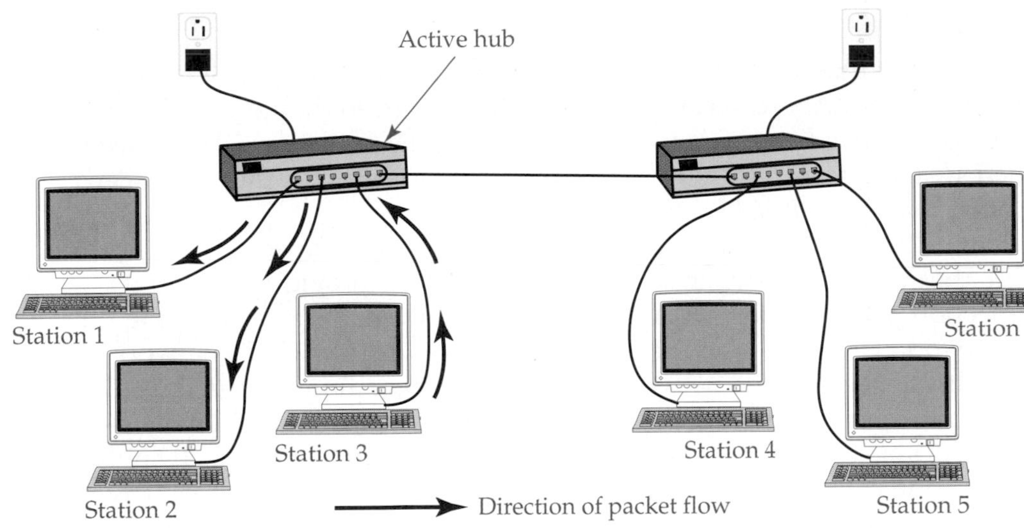

Figure 1-23.
In this example, *Station3* communicates with *Station1*. Rather than sending packets to other areas of the network, the active hub directs the packets to only those computers that are attached to it.

encapsulated before they could be carried across the Internet to their destination. The network device that connected the local area network to the Internet was referred to as the *gateway* and the definition referred to translating or connecting two different networks that operate using different protocols.

gateway
a network device that connects the local area network to the Internet.

Network+ Note

A server can be classified as a gateway if it provides gateway services to its clients.

Bridge

A ***bridge*** can be used to divide the network into smaller segments, reducing the chance of collisions. Networks, such as Ethernet, broadcast packets throughout the entire segment of the network. When two packets are sent across the network at the same time, a collision occurs, destroying each packet. As a network becomes larger and more and more packets are transmitted

bridge
a network device that can be used to divide the network into smaller segments, reducing the chance of collisions.

across the network, it is likely that the packets will collide and be destroyed. A bridge controls the flow of network traffic between two segments by reading the destination of a network packet. The bridge either allows a packet to pass through to the other segment or restricts the packet to the originating segment.

In **Figure 1-24,** a bridge is used to control network traffic. The network has been divided into two segments: one segment is for the business management department, and the other segment is for the engineering department. The engineering department is responsible for designing new products and for making drawings of the product's parts. The engineers often share the drawings with others in the engineering department. The business management segment contains executives and marketing personnel. By the nature of the arrangement, most of the packets broadcast in the engineering segment are between the engineers' computers. Most of the packets broadcast in the business management segment are between the executives' and the marketing personnel's computers. Only when the business management and engineering departments wish to communicate, packets pass through the bridge.

Switch

switch
a network device that filters network traffic or creates subnetworks from a larger network.

A ***switch*** filters network traffic or creates subnetworks from a larger network. Some LANs can easily have hundreds or even thousands of nodes. A switch can be used to divide the transmission paths to improve data delivery. When switches form logical networks from a large network, they are called *virtual networks* or *virtual LANs.* See **Figure 1-25.**

In the illustration, you can see that all the PCs are connected to one central point, the switch. The switch acts similar to a hub by providing a central connection point for the PCs. A switch also acts like a bridge by limiting traffic on the network. However, a bridge physically isolates segments of a network, while a switch isolates PCs into network segments, thus creating a virtual network. Virtual networks are configured by programming information into the switch, which permits the packets to only flow between designated nodes. By only allowing the packets to flow between the designated nodes, a virtual network within a network is created. The term *virtual,* when applied to networking, means "to simulate," rather than "a physical network."

Figure 1-24.
A bridge can be used to divide a network into segments. This reduces the amount of overall packet movement on the network media.

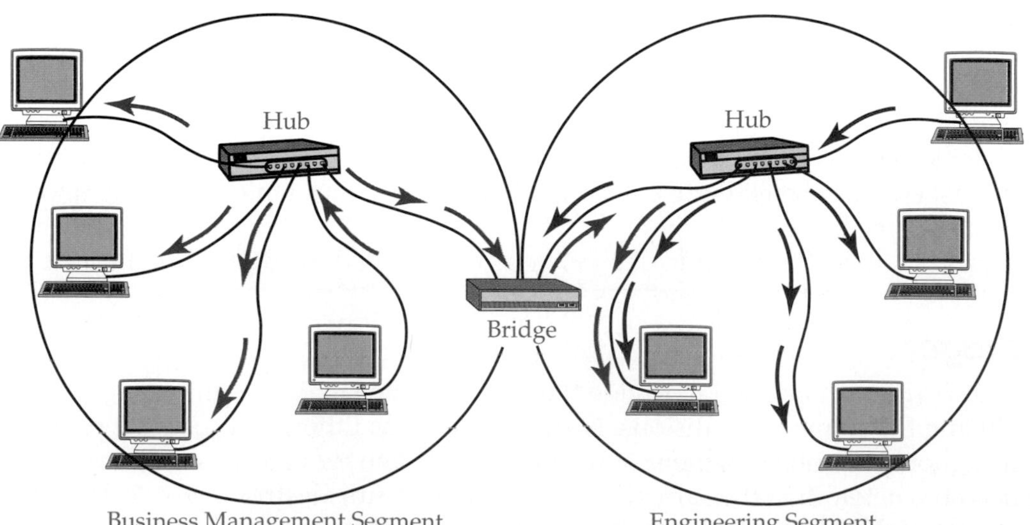

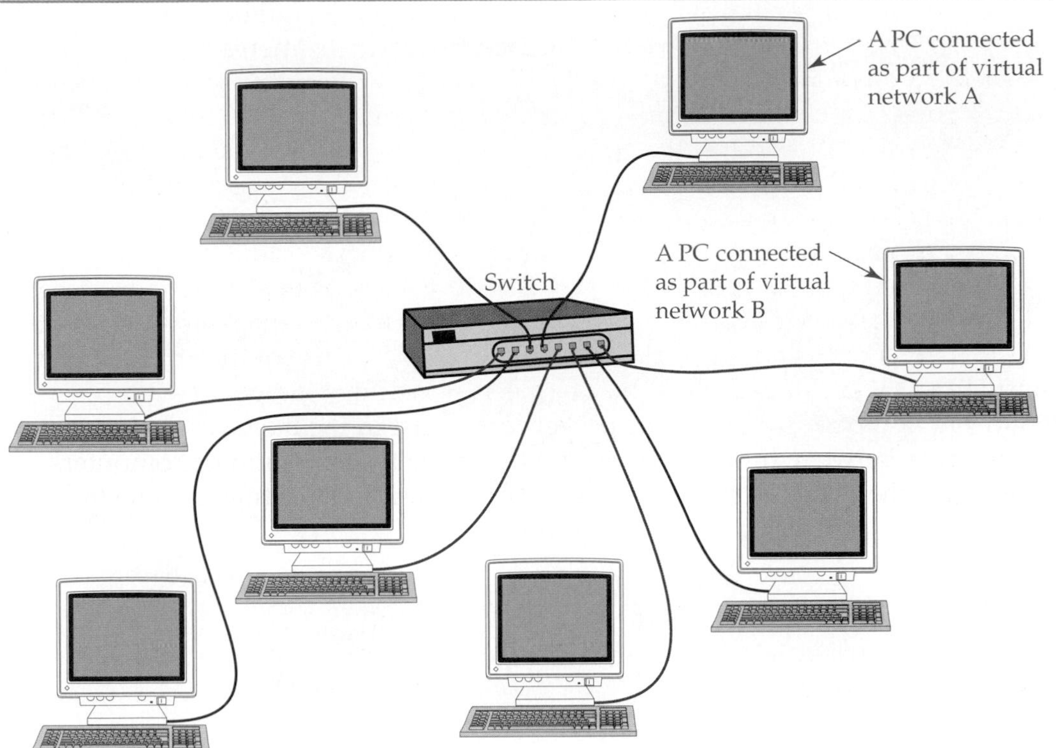

Figure 1-25. A switch is similar to a bridge in that it can isolate packets. It is similar to a hub in that it acts as a central connection point. However, a switch can do more than a bridge or a hub. It can be used to create virtual networks.

Multilayer Switch

A ***multilayer switch*** is an enhanced switch designed to perform more than basic switch functions. For example, the basic switch makes decisions about routing packets based on IP addresses. A multilayer switch can make decisions about routing a packet based on packet content. It can inspect the content of a packet to determine the type of material being downloaded. If a user is downloading a vast amount of multimedia packets containing video or music content, the switch can limit the amount of network bandwidth allocated to that user.

multilayer switch a switch that can make decisions about routing a packet based on packet content.

The basic switch functions at layer 2 of the OSI model, whereas a multilayer switch functions at higher layers of the OSI model.

Router

A ***router*** navigates packets across large networks, such as the Internet, using the most efficient route, **Figure 1-26.** A router maintains a table of information containing the location of other routers and their identification. Routers are typically installed between LANs, but may be installed inside a LAN if traffic conditions warrant their installation. Routers "route" data packets across WANs using the TCP/IP protocol addressing scheme. TCP/IP is the standard protocol used for WANs and LANs.

router a network device that navigates packets across large networks, such as the Internet, using the most efficient route.

Router communication is extremely technical. Cisco Systems has its own certification for router technology. Cisco network academies are located all over the United States.

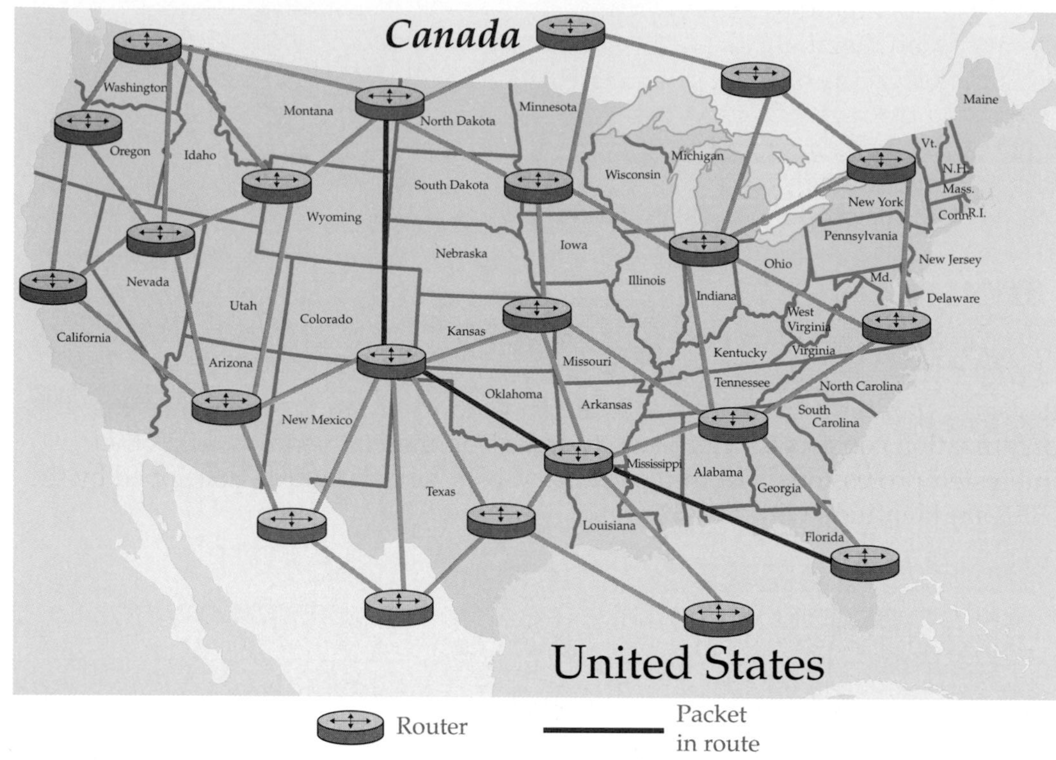

Figure 1-26.
Routers are used to transfer packets across small and large networks. The Internet uses thousands of routers to route packets across the United States and the world.

Brouter

brouter
a network device that combines router and bridge functions.

A ***brouter*** combines router and bridge functions. The brouter functions as a bridge by restricting or passing packets to other sections of a LAN based on the MAC address. It functions as a router by forwarding packets based on the IP address. The main difference between a router and a brouter is that a router typically provides many more functions than a brouter.

Standards and Organizations

standard
a set of recommendations or practices presented by an organization that defines specific aspects about a technology.

A ***standard*** is a set of recommendations or practices presented by an organization that defines specific aspects about a technology. For example, an organization may design the specifications for a type of connector that connects to a certain type of cable. Every company that manufactures connectors for this type of cable must know the physical and electrical specifications of the connector to make the connector compatible with the cable. The physical qualities may be length, width, height, and the amount of weight the connector can support. The electrical qualities may specify the amount of voltage and current the connector can handle.

Many times standards are adopted as law by local jurisdictions. For example, city, county, state, or country may adopt an organization's standards and make them the minimum standard to be followed by contractors or employees. In other words, a company might contract with a contractor to install a network for its business. Since the company wants the network to be installed properly, it will write into the contract "all work shall follow the IEEE standards for networking." Those standards will also serve as the minimum standards for installing the cabling and network devices. The contract will usually specify that all cable and network devices used for the installation must be UL approved. UL stands for Underwriters Laboratories, which is an organization that tests products for safety purposes.

A number of organizations are referred to throughout this textbook. Organization membership is made up of personnel who have an interest in the technology the organization represents. Some of the organizations that are referenced throughout this textbook are IEEE, ISO, UL, ANSI, EIA, and TIA. The following is just a brief explanation of a few of the many organizations that exist. It is recommended that you visit these organizations' Web sites to gain better insight into the scope, membership, and function of each.

IEEE

The ***Institute of Electrical and Electronic Engineers (IEEE)*** (pronounced "I triple E"), founded in 1884, is a professional organization that continually develops standards for the networking and communications industry. This organization consists of scientists, students, commercial vendors, and other interested professionals from the industry. Network standards developed by the IEEE are identified with an 802 prefix. See **Figure 1-27.**

Institute of Electrical and Electronic Engineers (IEEE) an organization that continually develops standards for the networking and communications industry.

IEEE Standard	Description
802.1	**High Layer LAN Protocols**
802.2	Logical Link Control (Inactive)
802.3	**Ethernet**
802.4	Token Bus (Disbanded)
802.5	Token Ring (Inactive)
802.6	Metropolitan Area Network (Disbanded)
802.7	Broadband (Disbanded)
802.8	Fiber Optic (Disbanded)
802.9	Integrated Services (Disbanded)
802.10	Security (Disbanded)
802.11	**Wireless Local Area Networking (WLAN)**
802.12	Demand Priority (Disbanded)
802.13	Not used
802.14	Cable Modem (Disbanded)
802.15	**Wireless Personal Area Network (WPAN), Bluetooth, and ZigBee**
802.16	**Wireless Metropolitan Area Network (WMAN), WiMAX, and Mobile Wireless**
802.17	**Resilient Packet Ring (RPR)**
802.18	**Radio Regulatory**
802.19	**Coexistence**
802.20	**Mobile Broadband Wireless Access (MBWA)**
802.21	**Media Independent Handover (MIH)**
802.22	**Wireless Regional Area Network (WRAN)**

Figure 1-27.
IEEE 802 standards. The standards in bold represent those that are still active.

The specifications outlined in the 802 standards are not laws but rather a set of recommended practices that ensure quality of work as well as the interoperability of equipment designed by different companies. The standards should only be thought of as a law if a contract to install a network requires the network to meet or exceed the IEEE standards. If a problem arises after the work is completed and the contractor did not follow the IEEE standards, the contractor can be held liable.

The 802 standards are referred to throughout your studies of networking, but be aware that the standards are constantly changing. The IEEE forms committees for each standard. Each committee is charged with creating, reviewing, and revising standards as needed. Over time, some of the standards become obsolete, which results in the disbanding of the committee or the committee becoming inactive.

In Figure 1-27, you will see that many of the standards that were once active are now disbanded or inactive. At times, the responsibility of a standard is absorbed by another entity, usually a communications organization or a newly-formed professional organization that is interested in a particular aspect of the industry. For example, the Cable modem industry has its own organization known as Data-Over-Cable Service Interface Specification (DOCSIS) that ensures interoperability between Cable television vendor hardware and software products. Soon after forming DOCSIS, the IEEE disbanded the IEEE 802.14 Cable Modem committee and discontinued writing specifications for Cable modem hardware and software.

Many different trade magazines provide articles about changes in IEEE standards. Most networking professionals have at least a few periodicals or newsletters to which they subscribe to keep up-to-date with changes in the networking industry.

ISO

International Organization for Standardization (ISO) an organization interested in the standardization of computer equipment.

The letters ***ISO*** are not an acronym, but have been adopted by the organization called the ***International Organization for Standardization.*** The term *iso* is of Greek origin and means *equal*. The ISO organization was founded in 1946 and comprises 46 different countries and other organizations such as the ANSI (American National Standards Institute) organization. The ISO, interested in the standardization of computer equipment, developed the OSI model for networking technologies. The OSI model is discussed in more detail later in this chapter and again throughout the textbook.

W3C

World Wide Web Consortium (W3C) an organization that provides recommendations for Web page language standards.

The ***World Wide Web Consortium (W3C)*** was established in 1994. The primary concern of the W3C is to provide recommendations for Web page language standards. The organization focuses on the development of programming language standards used for displaying information in the form of Web pages.

Some of the language standards developed and approved by W3C are Hypertext Markup Language (HTML), eXtensible Markup Language (XML), eXtensible Hypertext Markup Language (XHTML), and Cascading Style Sheets (CSS). The Internet uses these programming languages to present text, graphics, and sound. A protocol known as *Hypertext Transport Protocol (HTTP)* delivers Web pages to a user's computer.

The Internet has become a standard tool for business. An entire chapter in this textbook is devoted to Web servers. It includes an introduction to HTML and Web server communications.

CERN

CERN is an acronym for *Centre European pour la Recherche Nucléaire* (European Center for Nuclear Research). It is located in Geneva, Switzerland. One of the first Hypertext Transfer Protocol servers was placed online in Geneva and is still in operation. This organization is responsible for the original development of the World Wide Web.

UL

Underwriters Laboratories (UL) is a nonprofit organization that tests products and materials for safety standards. Typically, electrical materials and equipment must be UL approved before they can be used in many facilities or as part of a contract specification.

EIA

The ***Electronic Industry Association (EIA)*** began in 1948 as a trade association concerned with radio communications. It was originally formed as the Radio Manufacturers Association and was responsible for standards such as RS-232. The EIA sponsors many trade shows and conferences throughout the United States.

TIA

The ***Telecommunications Industry Association (TIA)*** was founded in 1924 by a small group of suppliers who wished to promote the independent telephone industry and to organize trade shows. It soon evolved into a standards maintenance organization. The main areas that TIA is concerned with are fiber optics, user equipment, network equipment, wireless communications, and satellite communications.

ANSI

In 1918, five engineering societies and three government organizations founded the ***American National Standards Institute (ANSI).*** ANSI is a private, nonprofit organization that does not develop standards, but rather prompts voluntary conformity and standardization. ANSI is the official representative of many international organizations such as the ISO. ANSI is also one of the founders of the ISO organization. ANSI facilitates meetings and brings together interested parties to resolve issues and create a general census among its members to be presented to other standards committees.

OSI Model

The ***Open Systems Interconnection (OSI) model*** describes how hardware and software should work together to form a network communications system. It serves as a guide for troubleshooting and designing networks.

The OSI model consists of seven layers, **Figure 1-28.** Each layer in the OSI model is assigned a specific function. This section provides a brief description

CERN
an organization responsible for the original development of the World Wide Web.

Underwriters Laboratories (UL)
a nonprofit organization that tests products and materials for safety standards.

Electronic Industry Association (EIA)
a trade association that is concerned with radio communications.

Telecommunications Industry Association (TIA)
a standards maintenance organization mainly concerned with fiber optics, user equipment, network equipment, wireless communications, and satellite communications.

American National Standards Institute (ANSI)
a private, nonprofit organization that does not develop standards, but rather prompts voluntary conformity and standardization.

Open Systems Interconnection (OSI) model
a model that describes how hardware and software should work together to form a network communications system.

Figure 1-28.
The seven layers of the OSI model.

Application
Presentation
Session
Transport
Network
Data link
Physical

of each layer. It is intended as an overview of how networking components work together to send and receive information. The OSI model is referenced throughout the textbook and is discussed in detail in Chapter 16—A Closer Look at the OSI Model.

Tech Tip

The OSI model is a joint effort of international members to standardize networking communications systems. Not all software companies follow the strict guidelines of the OSI model. Many systems were in place long before the OSI model was developed and adopted. Some models combine two or more layers into a single unit. It is important to remember that the OSI model simply serves as a guide for future development and illustrates the complexity of transmitting data between network devices.

physical layer
a layer of the OSI model that is concerned with how digital signals, the binary 1s and 0s, are carried electrically from one networked device to another.

Physical Layer

The ***physical layer*** is the lowest layer of the model. It consists of the cable and connectors used for constructing the network. This layer is only concerned with how digital signals, the binary 1s and 0s, are carried electrically from one networked device to another. When you think of the physical layer, think of cables, radio waves or light pulses, 1s and 0s, and digital signals.

data link layer
a layer of the OSI model that describes how raw data is packaged for transfer from one network interface card to another.

Data Link Layer

The ***data link layer*** describes how the raw data is packaged for transfer from one network interface card to another. The data link layer also contains information such as the address of the source and destination and the size of the packet, and it provides for error checking. When you think of the data link layer, think of packaging and placing the packet as a stream of digital pulses on the network media.

network layer
a layer of the OSI model that is responsible for routing packets from one network to another using the IP addressing format.

Network Layer

The ***network layer*** is responsible for routing packets from one network to another using the IP addressing format. Routing prevents or limits network congestion. It also can prioritize the transmission of packets. As packets are transmitted from one network to another, several different routes may be used. If there is too much traffic on one cable section, the packet may be transmitted along a different route to avoid congestion. When you think of the network layer, think of navigating between networks.

Transport Layer

The main responsibility of the ***transport layer*** is to ensure reliable data by sequencing packets and reassembling them into their correct order. Packets are transmitted over many miles and may use different routes. The packets may not arrive in the same sequence they were transmitted and may require reassembly into their correct order. Reassembly into the correct order is especially important in transmitting digital images. When you think of the transport layer, think of packet quality.

transport layer
a layer of the OSI model that ensures reliable data by sequencing packets and reassembling them into their correct order.

Session Layer

The ***session layer*** establishes a connection between two different computers and provides security based on computer and user name recognition. The two computers may not normally be compatible for data exchange, such as a PC and a Macintosh. The session layer and transport layers are sometimes combined. When you think of the session layer, think of a handshake at the introduction and at the end of the meeting.

session layer
a layer of the OSI model that establishes a connection between two different computers and provides security based on computer and user name recognition.

Presentation Layer

The ***presentation layer*** ensures character-code recognition. It is responsible for converting character codes into a code that is recognizable by a computer that uses a different character code. For example, Extended Binary Coded Decimal Interchange Code (EBCDIC) is widely used on mainframes, while most PCs use ASCII. EBCDIC uses numbers to represent characters similar to the way ASCII number codes represent character codes. When a PC communicates with a mainframe, the ASCII code must be converted to EBCDIC. When you think of the presentation layer, think of how the data must look for both parties to interpret or understand it.

presentation layer
a layer of the OSI model that is responsible for converting character codes into a code that is recognizable by a computer that uses a different character code.

Application Layer

The ***application layer*** should not be confused with general software applications. The application layer works with specific networking applications such as Web browser programs, file transfer programs, and e-mail. When you think of the application layer, think of establishing communication with the network.

application layer
a layer of the OSI model that works with specific networking applications such as Web browser programs, file transfer programs, and e-mail.

Network+ Note

The Network+ Certification exam by CompTIA requires extensive knowledge of the OSI model and how it relates to network devices, protocols, and network technologies. If the OSI model seems confusing to you, you are not alone. You cannot have a complete understanding of the OSI model until you have a basic understanding of all the networking technologies and how they relate to each other.

OSI Model and Network Devices

It is important to understand how the OSI model and network devices correlate. Look at **Figure 1-29.** In this figure you will see the generally accepted classifications of network devices, such as hubs, switches, and routers, as

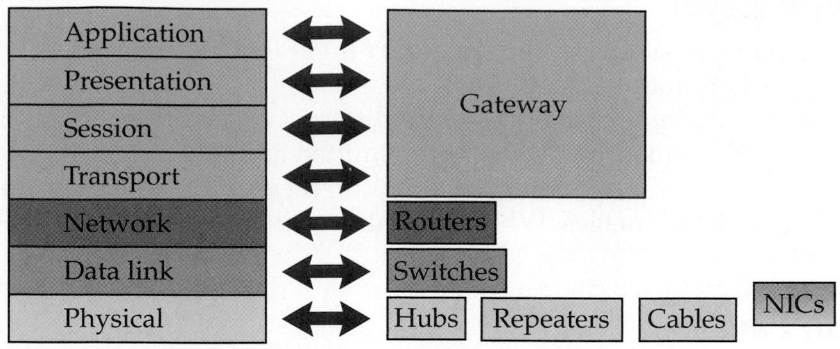

Figure 1-29.
A general correlation between network devices and the layers of the OSI model. This is only a general correlation. Some specific technologies may correlate a network device to a different OSI layer.

layer 1 device
a network device that makes no decision about where a packet is sent.

layer 2 device
a network device that makes decisions about where a packet is sent based on a MAC address or a logical name.

layer 3 device
a network device that makes decisions about where a packet is sent based on the Internet protocol.

compared to the OSI model. However, some alterations in the network device's technology may cause a network device to correlate to a different OSI layer.

Network devices are classified according to whether the device makes decisions about how a packet is sent. If the network device makes no decision about where a packet is sent, it is a ***layer 1 device.*** The device simply moves the packet along the network path such as through cabling, hubs, and repeaters. If decisions are made based on a MAC address or a logical name, it is a ***layer 2 device.*** If the network device makes a decision about where to move the data based on a protocol such as the Internet protocol, it is a ***layer 3 device.***

A network device is often reclassified when its normal function is altered. For example, a switch, normally classified as a layer 2 device, may be reclassified as a layer 3 device if more intelligent decision making is incorporated into it. The decision making of a layer 3 switch is based on some similar information that routers use. A hub, which is normally a layer 1 device, may be reclassified as a layer 2 device when it acts as an intelligent hub. Intelligent hubs make decisions based on MAC addresses and behave more like a switch.

Tech Tip

Some switches may be classified as a layer 2, layer 3, or layer 4 device. The generally accepted classification for a switch is layer 2. However, some companies advertise their switch as a layer 3 device if it has some router capabilities and as a layer 4 device if it is able to monitor a session.

As you progress through the text and learn more about protocols and network communications, the exact placement of certain network devices on the OSI model will become clear.

Summary

- Networks provide a way to share equipment and data.
- The three classifications of networks based on size, management, and use of private or public communications systems are LAN, MAN, and WAN.
- The four common network topologies are star, ring, bus, and mesh.
- The methodology used to administer a client/server network is centralized administration.
- The methodology used to administer a peer-to-peer network is decentralized administration.
- A network operating system provides a communications system between nodes.
- Data that is to be transmitted on a network is divided into segments.
- A typical packet contains a data segment, source and destination address, error checking, and sequence identification.
- A protocol is a set of rules that controls communication between two nodes.
- In general, two computers need to use the same protocol to communicate with each other.
- Link-Layer Discovery Protocol (LLDP) is designed to exchange information between network devices in the same local area network.
- A media converter is used to convert one type of electrical signal into another type of electrical signal.
- A repeater regenerates digital signals, allowing the network media to exceed its recommended length.
- A hub provides a central connection point for a network.
- A gateway device provides a connection between the local area network and the Internet.
- A bridge is used to segment a larger network to reduce the chance of collisions.
- A switch serves as a central connection point and can provide network segmentation.
- A router connects various networks together and provides a number of alternate routes for a data packet to travel.
- The OSI model serves as a guide for troubleshooting and designing networks.

Review Questions

Answer the following questions on a separate sheet of paper. Please do not write in this book.

1. List some things that might be shared on a network.
2. What are the advantages of using a network?
3. What are the three classifications of networks based on the size and complexity of the network system?
4. The Internet would be best described as a _____.
   A. LAN
   B. MAN
   C. WAN
   D. PAN
5. Rank by size, starting with the smallest: MAN, LAN, and WAN.
6. Six computers connected with a hub in your classroom would *most likely* be classified as a(n) _____ network.

7. Your instructor has a computer that is connected to a powerful computer in another building. This would *most likely* be a(n) _____ network.
8. What are the four major classifications of network topologies?
9. Define *node* and give two examples.
10. What does the term *client* mean in the context of a network?
11. Which type of administrative model uses centralized administration?
12. Name three types of dedicated servers.
13. How does a server differ from a typical PC?
14. Describe how data is transmitted across a network.
15. Data is divided into _____.
16. What does a packet contain?
17. What two versions of TCP/IP are used today?
18. Which Microsoft operating system first installed TCP/IPv4 and TCP/IPv6 by default?
19. Which protocol is designed to discover other devices on a local area network?
20. Which Microsoft operating system first introduced LLDP?
21. Link-Layer Discovery Protocol (LLDP) is designed to exchange information between _____ in the same local area network.
22. List the layers of the OSI model starting at the application layer.
23. Which layer of the OSI model is mainly concerned with network cables and connectors?
24. Convert the following acronyms into complete words.
    A. MAU
    B. LAN
    C. MAN
    D. WAN
    E. ATM
    F. LLDP
    G. TCP/IP
    H. IEEE
    I. FIR
    J. NIC

Sample Network+ Questions

Answer the following questions on a separate sheet of paper. Please do not write in this book.

1. Which of the following is *not* a typical LAN topology?
    A. Ring
    B. Star
    C. Bus
    D. Square
2. A protocol is best described as a _____.
    A. set of standards that serve as an installation guide for network media and devices
    B. set of rules and procedures that govern how two points on a network communicate
    C. special software utility that determines the amount of traffic on a network
    D. set of rules that assists personnel in using networks to communicate

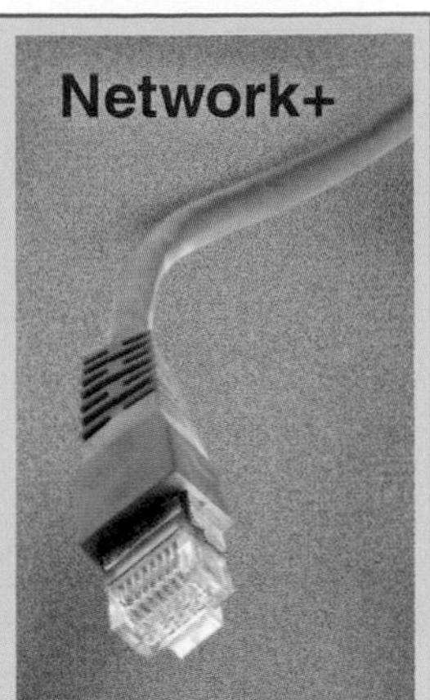

3. Network cabling is assigned to the ____ layer of the OSI model.
   A. presentation
   B. physical
   C. network
   D. materials
4. Which standard organization is responsible for the 802 standards?
   A. ISO
   B. EIA
   C. ANSI
   D. IEEE
5. Which of the following statements is true about a peer-to-peer network? (Select all that apply.)
   A. It is controlled or administered from one central computer.
   B. Each user controls his or her personal resources.
   C. It is the best method for controlling a large number of networked PCs.
   D. There is no central file server.
6. What protocol delivers Web page content from a Web server to a user's computer?
   A. XTML
   B. XML
   C. HTTP
   D. HTML
7. Which piece of equipment would *most likely* be used to provide communications between the local area network and the Internet?
   A. Hub
   B. Bridge
   C. Gateway
   D. Repeater
8. Which protocol is specifically designed to support audio and video communications?
   A. FTP
   B. ATM
   C. HTML
   D. IPX
9. Which item can be shared on a peer-to-peer network?
   A. Hard disk drive
   B. Floppy drive
   C. Printer
   D. Any of the above devices can be shared.
10. What is *attenuation*?
   A. The loss of network digital signal strength along a cable.
   B. Interference between two network cables.
   C. Network cable resistance measured in ohms.
   D. The term used to describe the procedure for calling attention to a particular node.

Discussion Questions

Answer the following questions on a separate sheet of paper. Please do not write in this book.

1. How many different ways could you deliver a message to a location, such as a business, ten miles away from your school location? What is the advantage and disadvantage of each method?

Interesting Web Sites for More Information

www.blackbox.com
www.howstuffworks.com
www.microsoft.com
www.novell.com

Chapter 1
Laboratory Activity

Identifying a Workstation's IP Configuration Settings

After completing this laboratory activity, you will be able to:

- Use the **ipconfig** command to determine the IP configuration settings of a workstation.
- Summarize the function of each IP configuration setting.

Introduction

This laboratory activity is extremely important because it provides you with the information necessary to reconfigure the network adapter properties assigned to your workstation. You will learn to quickly check the network configuration properties using the **ipconfig** command with and without the **/all** switch.

This lab activity does not require an in-depth understanding of the configuration properties or an in-depth understanding of the **ipconfig** command and associated switches. You will simply learn to use the command to quickly identify specific information.

On a separate sheet or paper, record your assigned user name, password, the number or name of your assigned workstation, and the server you are logged on to. You will most likely need to record the server name if there is more than one server for students to log on to. The default server specified in the logon box could be different than the server used for the Networking Fundamentals class, or there may not be any server specified at all. Your instructor will provide you with all required pertinent information, such as your user name and password, the workstation number or name and the server name.

To access the workstation IP configuration, you will issue an **ipconfig** command from the command prompt. The following image is a typical display provided by the **ipconfig** command issued from Windows Vista.

```
C:\Windows\system32\cmd.exe
Microsoft Windows [Version 6.0.6002]
Copyright (c) 2006 Microsoft Corporation.  All rights reserved.

C:\Users\Richard>ipconfig

Windows IP Configuration


Wireless LAN adapter Wireless Network Connection:

   Connection-specific DNS Suffix  . : hsd1.fl.comcast.net.
   Link-local IPv6 Address . . . . . : fe80::8c62:b6aa:704d:22b1%10
   IPv4 Address. . . . . . . . . . . : 192.168.1.104
   Subnet Mask . . . . . . . . . . . : 255.255.255.0
   Default Gateway . . . . . . . . . : 192.168.1.1

Tunnel adapter Local Area Connection* 6:

   Media State . . . . . . . . . . . : Media disconnected
   Connection-specific DNS Suffix  . : hsd1.fl.comcast.net.

Tunnel adapter Local Area Connection* 9:

   Connection-specific DNS Suffix  . :
   IPv6 Address. . . . . . . . . . . : 2001:0:4137:9e50:34a2:3f47:3f57:fe97
   Link-local IPv6 Address . . . . . : fe80::34a2:3f47:3f57:fe97%9
   Default Gateway . . . . . . . . . : ::

C:\Users\Richard>_
```

When the **ipconfig** command is issued, important information about the network connection is revealed. For this particular lab activity, you are interested in the IPv4 address, the subnet mask, and the default gateway. You can ignore the IPv6 address at this time. The IPv6 address will be covered in greater detail in a later lab activity. A TCP/IP network system uses the IPv4 assigned IP address to identify each device on the network. Every computer on the local area network must have a unique IP address. Each computer must also have a subnet mask to go with the assigned IPv4 address. The subnet mask is a set of four numbers separated by a period, such as 255.255.255.000. The subnet mask identifies the network portion of the address. There will be much more about subnet masks later in the course.

The default gateway is typically the device that is used to connect through to another network, such as the Internet. The gateway can be a device such as a router, a server, or another computer. Again, there will be much more about the function of a gateway later in the course.

When the **ipconfig** command is issued with the **/all** switch, much more detailed information is revealed about the connection configuration. Look at the following screen capture to see a sample of what is displayed after issuing the **ipconfig/all** command.

```
C:\Windows\system32\cmd.exe

C:\Users\Richard>ipconfig/all

Windows IP Configuration

   Host Name . . . . . . . . . . . . : AcerLapTop
   Primary Dns Suffix  . . . . . . . :
   Node Type . . . . . . . . . . . . : Hybrid
   IP Routing Enabled. . . . . . . . : No
   WINS Proxy Enabled. . . . . . . . : No
   DNS Suffix Search List. . . . . . : hsd1.fl.comcast.net.

Wireless LAN adapter Wireless Network Connection:

   Connection-specific DNS Suffix  . : hsd1.fl.comcast.net.
   Description . . . . . . . . . . . : Intel(R) PRO/Wireless 3945ABG Network Con
   Physical Address. . . . . . . . . : 00-19-D2-B3-5E-45
   DHCP Enabled. . . . . . . . . . . : Yes
   Autoconfiguration Enabled . . . . : Yes
   Link-local IPv6 Address . . . . . : fe80::8c62:b6aa:704d:22b1%10(Preferred)
   IPv4 Address. . . . . . . . . . . : 192.168.1.104(Preferred)
   Subnet Mask . . . . . . . . . . . : 255.255.255.0
   Lease Obtained. . . . . . . . . . : Monday, July 27, 2009 12:28:09 PM
   Lease Expires . . . . . . . . . . : Tuesday, August 11, 2009 11:06:48 AM
   Default Gateway . . . . . . . . . : 192.168.1.1
   DHCP Server . . . . . . . . . . . : 192.168.1.1
   DHCPv6 IAID . . . . . . . . . . . : 251664850
   DHCPv6 Client DUID. . . . . . . . : 00-01-00-01-0D-AD-1C-07-00-16-D4-4E-17-5C
   DNS Servers . . . . . . . . . . . : 68.87.74.166
                                       68.87.68.166
   NetBIOS over Tcpip. . . . . . . . : Enabled

Tunnel adapter Local Area Connection* 6:

   Media State . . . . . . . . . . . : Media disconnected
   Connection-specific DNS Suffix  . : hsd1.fl.comcast.net.
   Description . . . . . . . . . . . : isatap.hsd1.fl.comcast.net.
   Physical Address. . . . . . . . . : 00-00-00-00-00-00-00-E0
   DHCP Enabled. . . . . . . . . . . : No
   Autoconfiguration Enabled . . . . : Yes

Tunnel adapter Local Area Connection* 9:

   Connection-specific DNS Suffix  . :
   Description . . . . . . . . . . . : Teredo Tunneling Pseudo-Interface
   Physical Address. . . . . . . . . : 02-00-54-55-4E-01
   DHCP Enabled. . . . . . . . . . . : No
   Autoconfiguration Enabled . . . . : Yes
   IPv6 Address. . . . . . . . . . . : 2001:0:4137:9e50:34a2:3f47:3f57:fe97(Pref
   Link-local IPv6 Address . . . . . : fe80::34a2:3f47:3f57:fe97%9(Preferred)
   Default Gateway . . . . . . . . . : ::
   NetBIOS over Tcpip. . . . . . . . : Disabled

C:\Users\Richard>
```

Additional information is displayed, such as the physical address of the network adapter, IPv6 address of the DNS servers, if the adapter is DHCP enabled, the assigned address of the DHCP server, and if the adapter is configured to use NetBIOS over TCP/IP. Please note that the physical address is another name for the MAC address. The additional detailed information can be of great importance when troubleshooting a networking problem. For now, all this information is most likely overwhelming you. Be patient and you will learn all the details of the network adapter connection configuration. For now, just be familiar with how to issue the **ipconfig** and **ipconfig/all** commands.

IPv6 is automatically configured and first appeared by default in Windows Vista. IPv6 is intended to replace IPv4 in the near future. As of this writing, IPv6 is only used to communicate on the local area network, not on the Internet. IPv4 is used for both the local area network and the Internet. IPv4 requires a subnet mask; IPv6 does not.

IPv4 addresses can be assigned manually or automatically. The network device responsible for issuing unique IPv4 addresses automatically to workstations is called the *DHCP server*. Many times the same network device is responsible for more than one task such as acting as a gateway and as a DHCP server.

Equipment and Materials

- Assigned computer with Windows Vista or Windows 7 installed. The computer must be installed as part of a network or have a direct connection to the Internet for the lab activity to work correctly.
- The following information from your instructor, recorded on a separate sheet of paper:

  User name: ____________________

  Password: ____________________

  Workstation number or name: ____________________

  Server name: ____________________

  Note
  You will need administrator privileges to access and run **ipconfig**.

Procedure

1. ______ Report to your assigned workstation for this activity.
2. ______ Boot the computer and look for the logon screen. There may or may not be a logon screen for your computer, depending on how it is configured in a network system. You will use your assigned user name and password to log on to the network if required.
3. ______ In the **Search** box located on the **Start** menu, type **cmd** and wait for a moment. You will see "cmd" listed at the top of the **Search** list under **Programs**. If you pressed [Enter] after typing **cmd** in the **Search** box, the command prompt automatically appeared on the screen in its own dialog box.

   The command prompt can also be accessed in Windows Vista or Windows 7 by following the path **Start | All Programs | Accessories | Command Prompt**.

4. _____ At the command prompt, type and enter the **ipconfig** command. On a separate sheet of paper, record the follow information:

   IPv4 address: ______________________

   Subnet mask: ______________________

   Default gateway: ______________________

   IPv6 address: ______________________

5. _____ At the command prompt, type and enter **ipconfig/all**. On a separate sheet of paper, record the follow information:

   Physical address (MAC): ______________________

   DHCP enabled (Yes/No): ______________________

   DHCP server address: ______________________

   DNS server addresses (2): ______________________

   ____

6. _____ After recoding the information, answer the review questions.

7. _____ When you have finished the review questions, shut down your workstation and return all materials to their proper storage area.

Review Questions

Answer the following questions on a separate sheet of paper. Please do not write in this book.

1. What is the purpose of the IPv4 address?
2. What is the purpose of the IPv4 subnet mask?
3. What command is issued from the command prompt to reveal the assigned IP address?
4. What is another name for the physical address?
5. Does IPv6 require a subnet mask?
6. What is the purpose of the gateway?
7. Which operating system first used IPv6 by default?
8. What is the purpose of a DHCP server?
9. What is the path used to access the command prompt in Windows Vista and Windows 7?

2 Network Media—Copper Core Cable

After studying this chapter, you will be able to:

- ❑ Match the five forms of electronic signals to the media types on which they travel.
- ❑ Differentiate between analog and digital signals.
- ❑ Summarize the two methods of data transmission: Broadband and Baseband.
- ❑ Compare simplex, half-duplex, and full-duplex communication.
- ❑ Recall the meaning of electronic terms *resistance, impedance, reflected loss*, and *crosstalk*.
- ❑ Recall the characteristics of the 802.3 classifications.
- ❑ Identify the various types of wiring faults.

Network+ Exam—Key Points

To prepare for the Network+ Certification exam, you must be very familiar with IEEE 802.3 network media such as copper cable characteristics. The characteristics include the following:

- Cable type.
- Connectors.
- Topology.
- Data rates.
- Maximum and minimum cable lengths.

The Network+ Certification requirements are constantly changing. Always check the www.comptia.org Web site for the latest information!

Key Words and Terms

The following words and terms will become important pieces of your networking vocabulary. Be sure you can define them.

1000BaseCX
1000BaseT
100BaseT4
100BaseTX
10Base2
10Base5
10BaseT
10GBaseT
Alien Crosstalk (AXT)
amplifier
amplitude
analog signal
attenuation
Automatic Medium-Dependent Interface Crossover (Auto-MDIX)
AWG rating
bandwidth
Baseband
Broadband
coaxial cable
crossed pair
crosstalk
CSMA/CD (Carrier Sense Multiple Access with Collision Detection)
decibel (dB)
digital signal
Equal Level Far-End Crosstalk (ELFEXT)
Far-End Crosstalk (FEXT)
frequency
full-duplex
ground
half-duplex
impedance
interference
latency
magnetic induction
Near-End Crosstalk (NEXT)
network media
noise
open
plenum-rated
Power over Ethernet (PoE)
reflected loss
resistance
reversed pair
RG-58
RG-6
RG-8
rollover cable
short
simplex
split pair
terminating resistor
Time to Live (TTL)
twisted pair

Whether you are troubleshooting or designing a network, you must be familiar with the various types of network media. This chapter presents a general overview of network media and its electrical characteristics and covers in detail copper core cable. In the following chapters, fiber-optic and wireless network media are covered, respectively. To understand the characteristics and limitations of copper core cable, you will first be introduced to some electronics terminology. Later, the IEEE 802.3 and 802.5 standards are covered. You will see how these standards relate to network design and will understand the importance of knowing their specifications.

Network+ Note

In this chapter, 10Base2, 10Base5, and Token Ring have been presented as a historical reference to networking. You will see these particular technologies referenced on the Internet when you conduct networking related searches. You will most likely *not* see any questions related to these technologies on the CompTIA Network+ exam.

Network Media

Network media is a general term for all forms of pathways that support network communication. There are two general classifications of network media: cable-based and wireless, **Figure 2-1.** Cable-based network media comprises copper core cabling, such as coaxial and twisted pair, and glass/plastic core cabling, such as fiber-optic. Wireless network media comprises air, or the atmosphere.

network media
a general term for all forms of pathways that support network communication.

All network communication originates from electronic signals. Electronic signals can take many forms, such as electrical energy, light waves, radio waves, infrared light waves, and microwaves. For example, electronic signals are sent through coaxial and twisted pair cable as pulsating electrical energy; through fiber-optic cable as pulsating light waves; and through the atmosphere as pulsating radio waves, infrared light waves, or microwaves.

To understand the terminology related to network media and network communication, you must first learn some basics about electronic signals. In the following section, we will look at the characteristics of two general types of electronic signals: analog and digital.

Analog and Digital Signals

Electronic signals are classified into two general types: analog and digital. An ***analog signal*** is an electronic signal that varies in values, such as a light that varies in intensity. A ***digital signal*** is an electronic signal that has discrete values. Discrete values can be on and off, high and low, or 5 volts and 0 volts.

analog signal
an electronic signal that varies in values.

digital signal
an electronic signal that has discrete values.

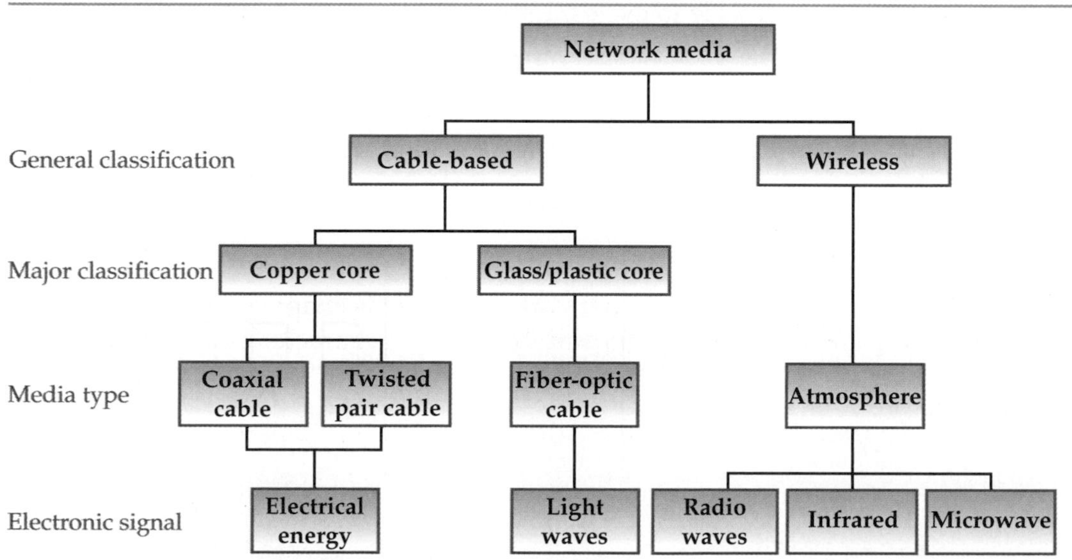

Figure 2-1. Network media classifications and media types. At the bottom of the hierarchy are the types of electronic signals that each media type carries.

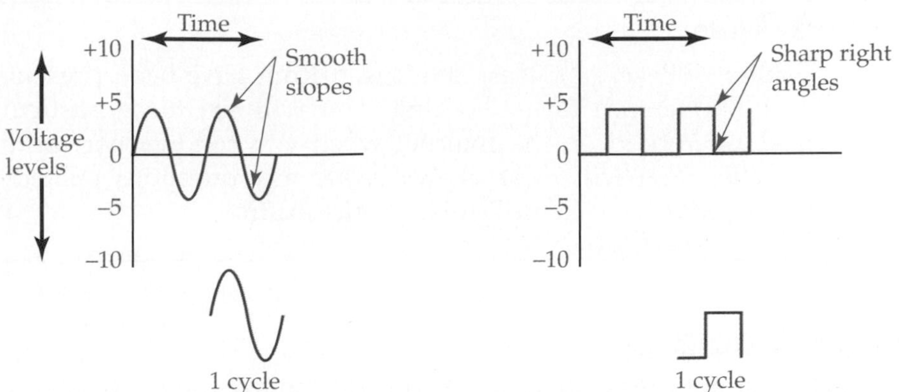

Figure 2-2.
Analog and digital signals plotted on a simple graph. Note that time affects the degree of the slope in an analog signal and the duration of the voltage level in a digital signal.

The major difference between analog and digital signals can be seen in the shape of the waveform. Look at **Figure 2-2.** The analog and digital signals of electrical energy are plotted on a simple graph that compares voltage levels to time. Note that the analog signal forms a series of slopes; whereas, the digital signal rises and falls sharply at right angles. In the analog signal, the degree of the slope is related to the varying degrees of voltage over time; whereas, the digital signal holds to discrete voltages (0 volts or +5 volts) over a length of time.

Each type of electronic signal has a cycle, or a pattern of fluctuations. Look again at Figure 2-2 and note the cycle for an analog and digital signal. In this example, a cycle for an analog signal begins at 0 volts, rises to +5 volts, falls to –5 volts, and rises to 0 volts. A cycle for a digital signal begins at 0 volts, rises sharply to +5 volts, and then falls sharply to 0 volts.

Frequency

frequency
the number of cycles of an electronic signal that occur in 1 second. It is measured in Hertz (Hz).

An electronic signal can be measured by its frequency. ***Frequency*** is the number of cycles of an electronic signal that occur in 1 second. It is measured in Hertz (Hz). Look at the analog and digital signal in **Figure 2-3** as plotted on a graph showing voltage and time. In each graph, the time interval is set to 1 second. The first graph shows an analog signal that achieves 5 cycles in 1 second. The analog signal, therefore, has a frequency of 5 Hz (5 cycles/1 second). The second graph shows a digital signal that achieves 5 cycles in 1 second. The digital signal also has a frequency of 5 Hz (5 cycles/1 second). If a cycle for an electronic signal is repeated 100 times in 1 second, the signal has a frequency of 100 Hz (100 cycles/1 second).

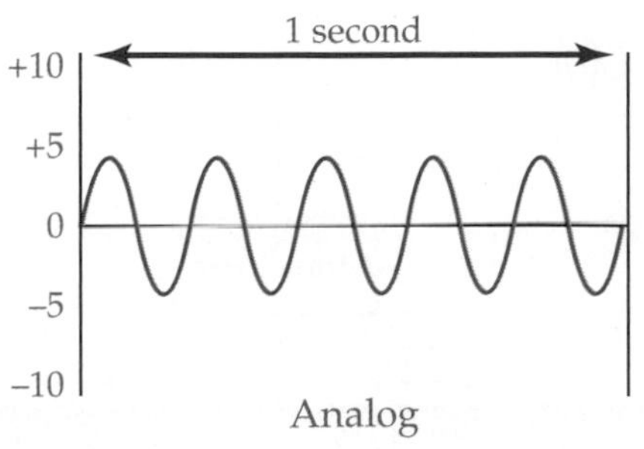

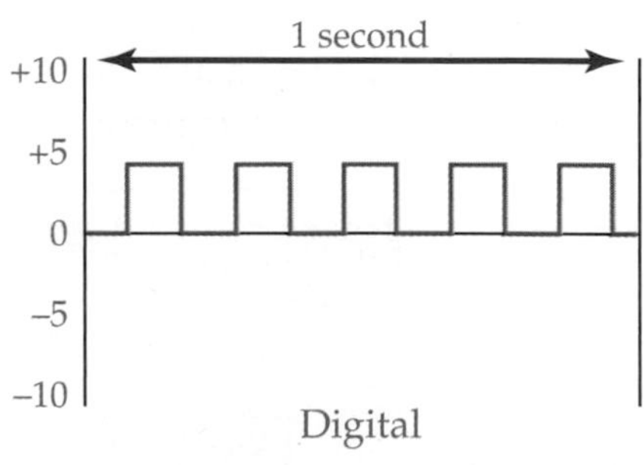

Figure 2-3.
The 5-Hz frequencies of an analog and a digital signal. On each graph an analog and digital cycle occurs 5 times in 1 second.

Attenuation

All electronic signals degenerate, or lose amplitude, over long distances. Losing signal strength is referred to as ***attenuation.*** As an electronic signal travels across the media, the amplitude of the signal is lessened, **Figure 2-4.** ***Amplitude*** is the maximum voltage, or height, of an electronic signal. The amplitude can be augmented to its original level with an amplifier. An ***amplifier*** is an electronic device designed to raise a signal's amplitude.

attenuation the loss of signal strength.

amplitude the maximum voltage, or height, of an electronic signal.

amplifier an electronic device designed to raise a signal's amplitude.

Interference

In addition to attenuation, most electronic signals pick up interference from sources such as motors, fluorescent lights, transformers, radio transmitters, and other conductors carrying electronic signals. ***Interference*** is an undesired electromagnetic signal imposed on a desired signal that distorts or corrupts the desired signal. Electromagnetic interference is generally referred to as ***noise.*** Interference that comes from neighboring conductors inside a wire's insulating jacket is called ***crosstalk.*** Crosstalk is covered later in detail.

interference an undesired electromagnetic signal imposed on a desired signal that distorts or corrupts the desired signal.

noise electromagnetic interference.

crosstalk interference that comes from neighboring conductors inside a wire's insulating jacket.

Noise and crosstalk are unwanted signals that need to be removed from the desired signal, especially before it is amplified. When an analog or digital signal is amplified, the unwanted signals caused by interference are also amplified. To get rid of the unwanted signals, the signal must be filtered. *Filtering* electronic signals is the removal of unwanted signals.

Amplifiers often incorporate filters. The filter removes the unwanted signals before amplification so when the signal is amplified, it is an exact duplicate of the original signal. Networks use repeaters to amplify and filter signals. A repeater is not actually an amplifier. However, in the networking environment, a repeater is often referred to as an amplifier because it counters attenuation by reshaping the signal to its original form.

While both analog and digital signals can be used to express data in network communication, the digital signal is preferred. It is very difficult and sometimes impossible to filter out all of the unwanted signals from an analog signal without changing the analog signal. Amplifying an analog signal not only amplifies the original signal, but also the unwanted signals, which results in a signal that no longer represents the original. However, when a digital signal is amplified, the unwanted signals are more easily filtered to restore the original look of the original signal.

Digital signals have a square or rectangular waveform and are produced at a fixed frequency. When digital signals are regenerated, they are regenerated by digital devices that also produce a square or rectangular waveform. A typical signal from a radio station is an analog signal composed of various amplitudes and a mixture of frequencies inside a set range of frequencies. Because the radio signal comprises various frequencies, the interference is sometimes impossible to separate or filter. This is a major drawback of using analog signals. Since interference can be easily removed from digital signals, the digital signal has become the norm for transmitting data over network cables.

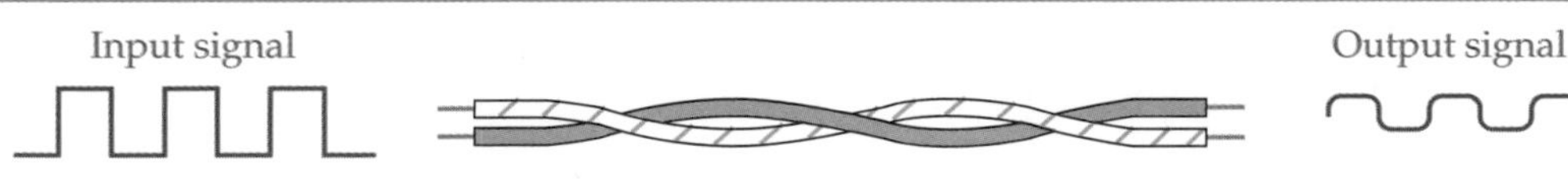

Figure 2-4. Attenuation is the loss of signal strength as the signal travels along a conductor.

Look at **Figure 2-5.** At the top is the original signal in digital and analog form. These signals represent the transmitted data. Below each signal (middle) is a representation of the same signal after attenuation and added interference. The bottom drawings are a representation of the distorted signals after amplification and filtering. Notice that the analog signal is distorted after amplification and is not an exact match of the original signal. The digital signal, however, looks exactly like the original signal after amplification. This is because the repeater is only capable of reproducing the original signal as 5-volt and 0-volt levels. Interference consists of many different levels of analog voltage (amplitude) and cannot be reproduced by the repeater because the repeater only generates two levels of signal strength.

Excessively strong interference, however, can be impossible to filter from a digital signal. Interference strength is directly related to the distance from the digital signal and the power of the source producing the interference. For example, a portable telephone may interfere with a digital signal at a close proximity of five to ten feet but not generate sufficient signal strength at thirty feet to interfere with the digital signal.

Latency

latency
the amount of time it takes a signal to travel from its source to its destination.

Latency is the amount of time it takes a signal to travel from its source to its destination. A general cause of latency is network equipment along the signal's path. Some networking equipment regenerate, or reshape, a digital signal after it is received. For example, a repeater is used to extend the maximum distance that a signal can normally travel by reshaping the signal. A digital signal may travel through several repeaters before reaching its destination, thus slowing the time it takes the signal to reach its destination.

Time to Live (TTL)
the maximum amount of time a packet is allowed to circulate through a network before it is destroyed.

There is normally a maximum amount of time a packet is allowed to circulate through a network before it is destroyed. If the overall latency is too great, the packet is dropped from the network. The maximum amount of time allowed is referred to as the ***Time to Live (TTL).*** If a signal exceeds the allocated TTL, it is removed from the network to prevent it from circulating forever. If signals could circulate forever, they would accumulate and eventually cause the entire system to shut down.

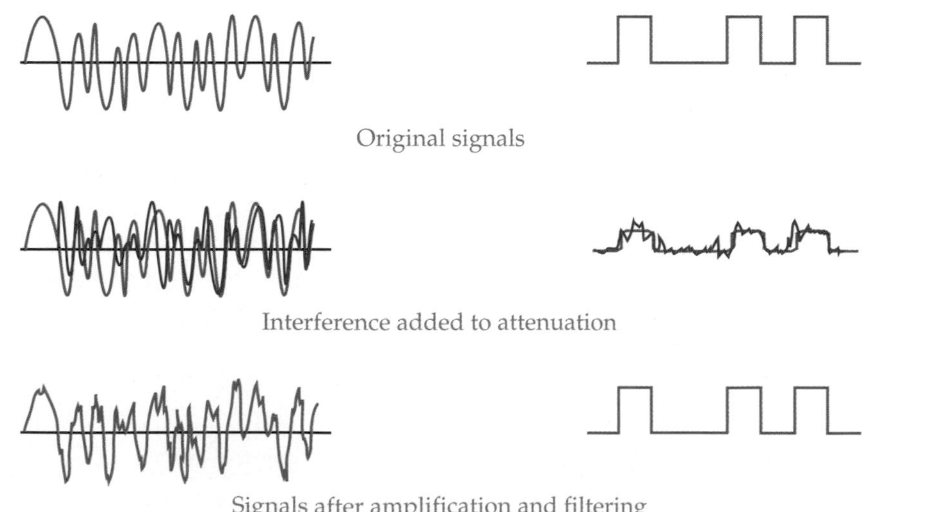

Figure 2-5.
The effects of filtering analog and digital signals. Top—Analog and digital signals in their original form. Middle—Analog and digital signals affected by interference and attenuation. Bottom—Analog and digital signals amplified and filtered. Note the fidelity of the digital signal in comparison to the analog signal after amplification and filtering.

Data Transmission

Data transmission terminology and concepts are often referenced in network standards and equipment specifications. A good understanding of data transmission terminology will help you master some of the most difficult concepts of networking. Much of the original network terminology has its roots in the field of electronics. Electronic terminology often requires an extensive background in electronics theory to fully grasp the concept being introduced. As networking has evolved over time, network technicians have coined their own terminology and have used electronics terms in some contexts that have slightly changed the original meaning of the term. Several of these terms and their influence on the data rate of data transmission are introduced in this section.

bandwidth
a measurement of the network media's ability to carry data.

Bandwidth

Bandwidth is a measurement of the network media's ability to carry data. The definition of bandwidth varies according to the context to which it is applied. For example, when referring to a network cable, bandwidth refers to the amount of digital signal the cable can carry based on a given time. Network cable bandwidth is measured in bits per second (bps).

The term *bandwidth,* when applied to network cabling, can be confused with the term *frequency*. Technically speaking, frequency is a measurement of the network media's ability to carry an electronic signal. For example, a network cable can have a frequency rating of 250 MHz but a permissible bandwidth of 1000 MHz. The frequency rating is the rating of the individual wires inside the cable assembly; the bandwidth is the entire cable assembly's (4 pairs of conductors) ability to carry digital signals. In general, the higher the bandwidth, the more data that can be carried. Please take note of the fact that bandwidth does not always match data rates because data rates can be influenced by data compression techniques.

When referring to an analog signal, the term *bandwidth* means a measurement of the maximum frequency of a device or the total range of analog frequencies. Bandwidth in analog transmission is measured in hertz (Hz). A range of frequencies would be all analog signal frequencies between two specific frequencies. An example would be television or radio analog signals transmitted and identified as channels. A typical television channel is assigned a 6-MHz bandwidth.

The bandwidth of analog transmission can support several different frequencies at once; whereas, the bandwidth of digital transmission usually supports only one frequency. In other words, when data is transmitted over a cable using a digital signal, the digital signal uses the entire bandwidth. When data is transmitted over a cable using analog signals, many different analog signals, or frequencies, representing data can be transmitted at once. See **Figure 2-6.**

Baseband

Baseband is a method of transmitting data in the form of a digital signal, using the entire bandwidth of a cable. Remember that the bandwidth of network media is its total capacity to transmit data and that a digital signal uses the entire bandwidth. The network media may be able to support more than one frequency, but in application, it is typically used to carry only one chosen frequency. For example, a copper core cable may be used to transmit several analog signals, or

Baseband
a method of transmitting data in the form of a digital signal, using the entire bandwidth of a cable.

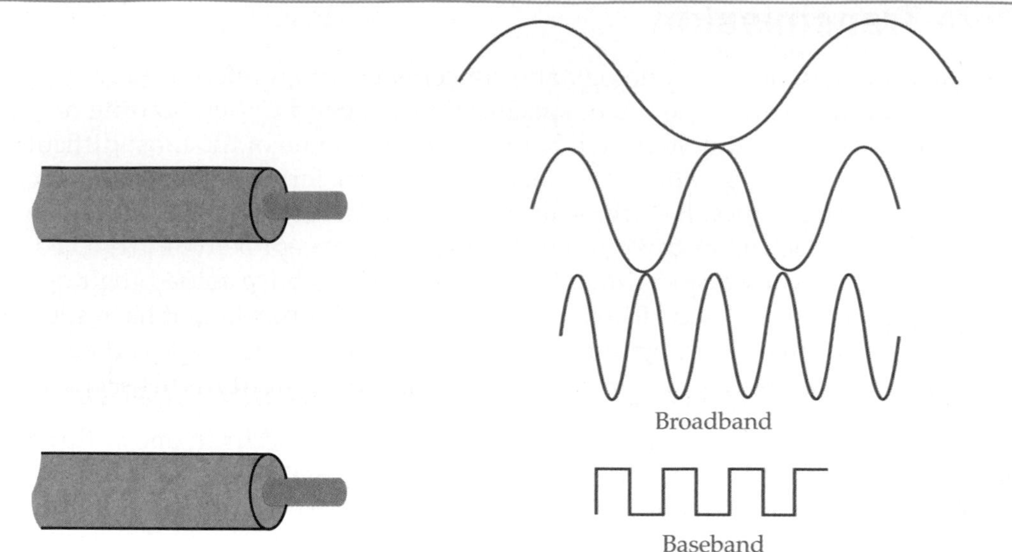

Figure 2-6.
Baseband transmission allows only one digital signal to be transmitted at a time. The digital signal uses the entire bandwidth of the network media. Broadband transmission allows multiple analog signals to be transmitted simultaneously, each of differing frequencies and amplitudes.

frequencies, at once, but when used as part of an Ethernet network, will transmit digital signals at only one frequency. This frequency will consume the entire bandwidth of the cable.

You cannot send two digital signals on the same wire because they have matching frequencies and voltage levels. **Figure 2-7** illustrates the effects of transmitting more than one digital signal on a wire. Each digital signal consists of a pattern of high and low voltage levels which represent data such as letters and numbers. When both signals are placed on one wire, the two signals combine to form a new digital pattern. The new digital pattern of the combined signals cannot be separated into two individual signals; thus, all data is distorted and cannot be read at its destination.

Broadband

Broadband
a method of transmitting data in the form of several analog signals at the same time.

Broadband is a method of transmitting data in the form of several analog signals at the same time. Certain electronic techniques can be incorporated into communications systems that allow network media to carry more than one frequency at a time. In general, a network conductor that carries a single series of digital signals is Baseband. A conductor that carries two or more analog signals is Broadband.

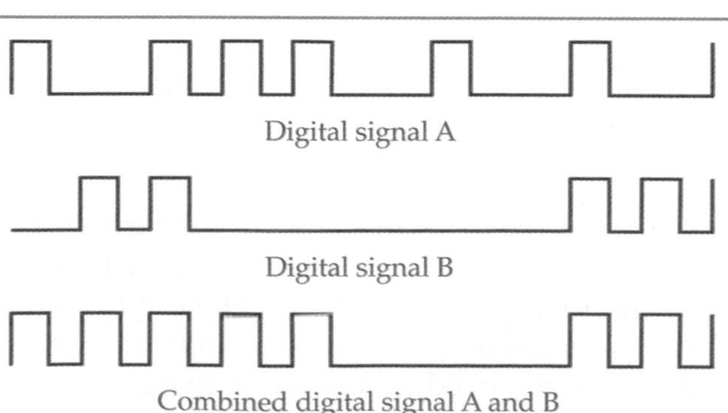

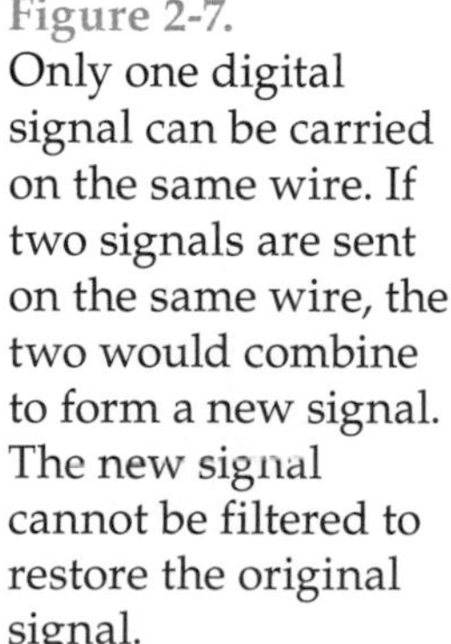

Figure 2-7.
Only one digital signal can be carried on the same wire. If two signals are sent on the same wire, the two would combine to form a new signal. The new signal cannot be filtered to restore the original signal.

Wireless media, such as radio, is an example of Broadband transmission. In this case, the atmosphere is capable of carrying many different radio frequencies at the same time. For example, television signals range from 7 MHz to 1002 MHz. Inside this range of frequencies are individual channels specified in smaller ranges. For example, Channel 8 has a frequency range of 180 MHz to 186 MHz. Channel 9 has a frequency range of 186 MHz to 192 MHz. Each of the channels has a bandwidth of 6 MHz inside the allocated television bandwidth of 7 MHz to 1002 MHz. Wireless networks use radio waves as the network medium and use the terms *bandwidth* and *channel* when describing each radio signal path.

Simplex, Full-Duplex, and Half-Duplex Communication

Communication between two electronic devices can occur in one of three modes: simplex, full-duplex, and half-duplex. See **Figure 2-8.**

Simplex means that communication occurs in one direction only. An example of simplex communication is the transmission that occurs between a television station and a television.

Full-duplex communication is the bi-directional communication that occurs between two devices simultaneously. An example of full-duplex communication is communication via telephone.

Half-duplex communication is also bi-directional communication; however, it can only occur in one direction at a time. Half-duplex communication is used with walkie-talkies. Also, most LANs use half-duplex communication. Ethernet is an excellent example. In an Ethernet network, only one computer or node can successfully transmit data over the network cable at a time. If two computers transmit data at the same time, a collision occurs and the data is destroyed.

simplex communication that occurs in one direction only. An example of simplex communication is the transmission that occurs between a television station and a television.

full-duplex communication that occurs bi-directionally and simultaneously between two devices. An example of full-duplex communication is communication via telephone.

half-duplex communication that is bi-directional but can only occur in one direction at a time.

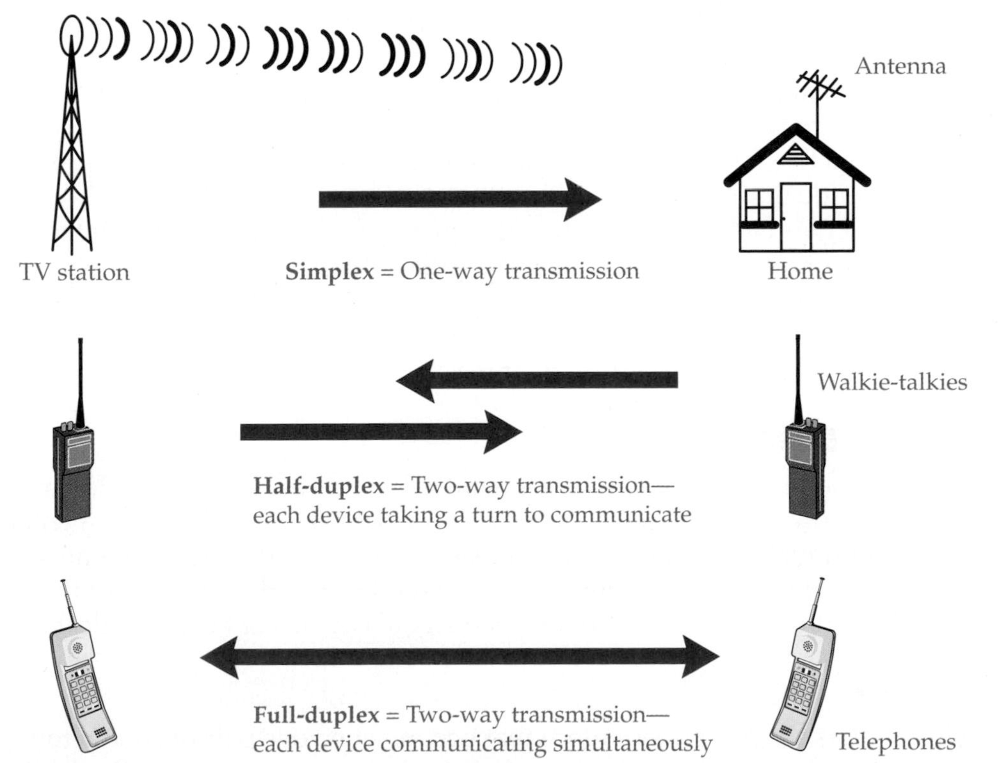

Figure 2-8. Examples of simplex, half-duplex, and full-duplex communication.

Electronic Terms

Networks that incorporate copper cable have limits to the type of cable, length, number of segments, and the number of nodes that can be connected. These limits are based on certain electrical characteristics. As you read about the copper cable types and the IEEE 802 classifications, you will learn what these limitations are. However, there are several basic electronics terms you must first master to fully understand these limitations. These terms are *resistance, impedance, reflected loss*, and *crosstalk*.

Direct Current and Alternating Current

The flow of electrical energy is described as either direct current (DC) or alternating current (AC). The term *current* describes the flow of electrons, which is the actual form of electrical energy. DC means that the current is in one steady direction. One of the most common sources of direct current is a battery. Battery electrical energy flows in a steady direction from the negative (–) terminal to the positive (+) terminal. AC does not flow in one direction. It alternates from a negative charge to a positive charge. The most common source of alternating current is the wall outlet.

Since the two forms of electrical energy flow differently, they produce different electrical characteristics. Because the two systems have different characteristics, different terminology is used to describe their characteristics. Two terms applied to these characteristics are *resistance* and *impedance*. These terms are inherited from the electronics industry and are applied to networking cable.

Resistance and Impedance

resistance
the opposition to direct current (DC) in a conductor.

impedance
the opposition to alternating current.

Resistance is the opposition to direct current (DC). Every conductor has a certain amount of resistance that affects current—the longer the conductor, the greater the resistance.

Resistance is a DC term and should not be confused with ***impedance,*** which refers to the opposition to AC. Impedance increases as frequency increases. In other words, the higher the frequency, the faster the speed of data transmission. However, the quality or integrity of the data will diminish because of impedance. This is why there are limitations to the speed at which data can be delivered across a conductor. The length of a conductor also influences impedance. As the length of a conductor increases, so does the total impedance.

Digital signals change current direction just as analog signals do. Digital signals consist of a series of square or rectangular waveforms which sharply change current direction after a set time period. For this reason, digital signals are affected by impedance the same way analog signals are affected by impedance. See **Figure 2-9** for a comparative summary of resistance and impedance.

Reflected Loss

reflected loss
the amount of signal reflected from the end of a cable.

In high-speed networks, data is transmitted in full-duplex mode. This means that data can flow in both directions at the same time. The original signal enters the cable and travels to the end. When it reaches the end, part of the signal is reflected. ***Reflected loss*** is the amount of signal reflected from the end of the cable. If it is of sufficient value, the reflected signal can disrupt communication.

Crosstalk

Crosstalk is a type of interference that occurs when one pair of conductors imposes a signal on another pair of parallel conductors, **Figure 2-10.** All energized

Electrical Term	Definition	Symbol	Comments
Resistance	Opposition to direct current.	Ω (ohm)	Current flow affected by cable length. Resistance is present in battery-powered circuits.
Impedance	Opposition to alternating current.	Z	Current flow is affected by frequency, cable length, induction, and capacitance. Impedance is present in AC-powered circuits.

Figure 2-9. Comparison of resistance and impedance.

conductors are surrounded by a magnetic field, Figure 2-10A. The magnetic field runs the length of the conductor. The strength of the magnetic field is determined by the amount of current traveling through the conductor. Frequency also affects the strength of the magnetic field. When another conductor is placed in close proximity to a current carrying conductor, the magnetic field encircles the other conductor and induces current, Figure 2-10B. This electronic phenomenon is referred to as ***magnetic induction,*** or ***mutual induction.*** When a conductor in a cable assembly carries digital pulses, the digital pulses create a magnetic field pattern similar to the digital pulses. The magnetic field induces in a neighboring conductor an electrical current resembling the digital pulse pattern of the original conductor, thus creating crosstalk.

magnetic induction an electrical phenomenon in which the magnetic field encircling a current-carrying conductor induces current in a conductor of close proximity. Also called *mutual induction.*

Analog telephone systems also suffer from crosstalk. In fact, the term *crosstalk* originated in telephone communications to describe the effect of hearing an additional telephone conversation from a neighboring telephone line while talking to someone else.

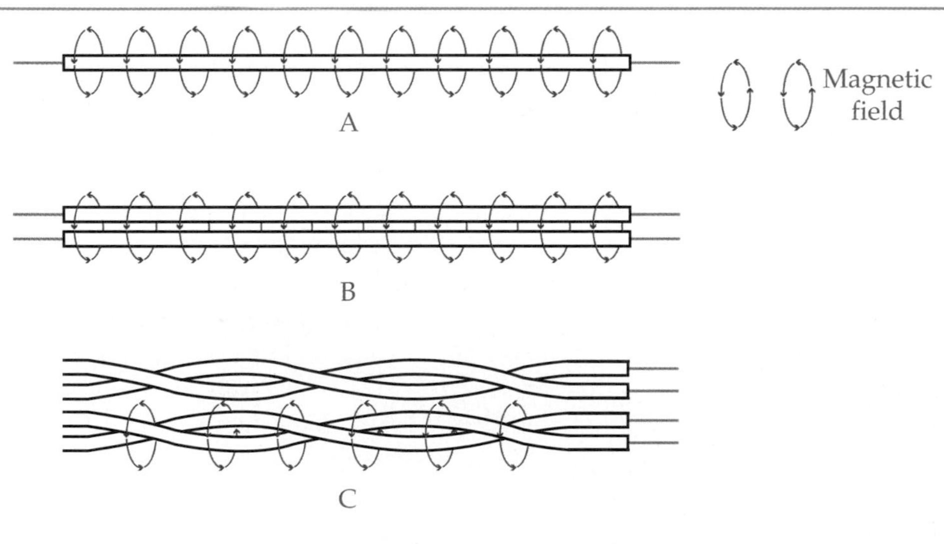

Figure 2-10. The occurrence of crosstalk. A—An energized conductor is surrounded by a magnetic field. B—Any conductor placed near the energized conductor and in the magnetic field will have electrical energy transferred to it. C—Twisting the pairs of conductors reduces the amount of electrical energy transferred between the pairs.

Network conductors, such as twisted pair, are designed to limit the effects of crosstalk by reducing the amount of contact between a pair of conductors, Figure 2-10C. This is why twisted pair must be used in place of the older style of telephone cable that has no twist. However, one place where crosstalk can be generated on twisted pair cable is at the ends near the connectors. When cables are made by hand, the technician may leave too much untwisted conductor near the connector, leaving the cable vulnerable to crosstalk.

Figure 2-11 shows a twisted pair cable properly connected to a connector and a twisted pair cable improperly connected to a connector. Note that the improperly connected twisted pair cable has too much wire exposed and that the pairs are not twisted. The improperly connected cable will produce crosstalk.

Twisted pair cable segments are limited to 100 meters (328 ft.) maximum in length. Longer segment lengths produce crosstalk, as well as a reduction in signal strength. Cable shielding of wire mesh or foil also reduces crosstalk. The shielding absorbs and contains the magnetic field generated by a conductor and protects the pairs from electromagnetic interference generated by an outside source.

Four types of measurement can be taken on twisted pair cable to measure the effects of crosstalk: Near-End Crosstalk (NEXT), Far-End Crosstalk (FEXT), Equal Level Far-End Crosstalk (ELFEXT), and Alien Crosstalk (AXT). The first three measurements are taken by a manufacturer to determine cable specifications so that the cable can be correctly labeled. They are only taken in the field to see if an existing Category 5 cable could be used as a Category 5e cable. AXT was introduced as part of the Category 6a standard.

Near-End Crosstalk (NEXT)
a measurement of the reflected loss at the near end, or input end, of a cable. Losses are typically expressed in decibels.

decibel (dB)
a unit of measurement that expresses the relationship of power between two electrical forces.

Near-End Crosstalk (NEXT)

Near-End Crosstalk (NEXT) is a measurement of the reflected loss at the near end, or input end, of a cable. Look at **Figure 2-12.**

Losses are typically expressed in decibels. A ***decibel (dB)*** is a unit of measurement that expresses the relationship of power between two electrical forces. This measurement is often used to show the output-to-input ratio of a signal. For twisted pair cable, it is used to compare the difference between the amount of power in the input signal and the amount of power generated by

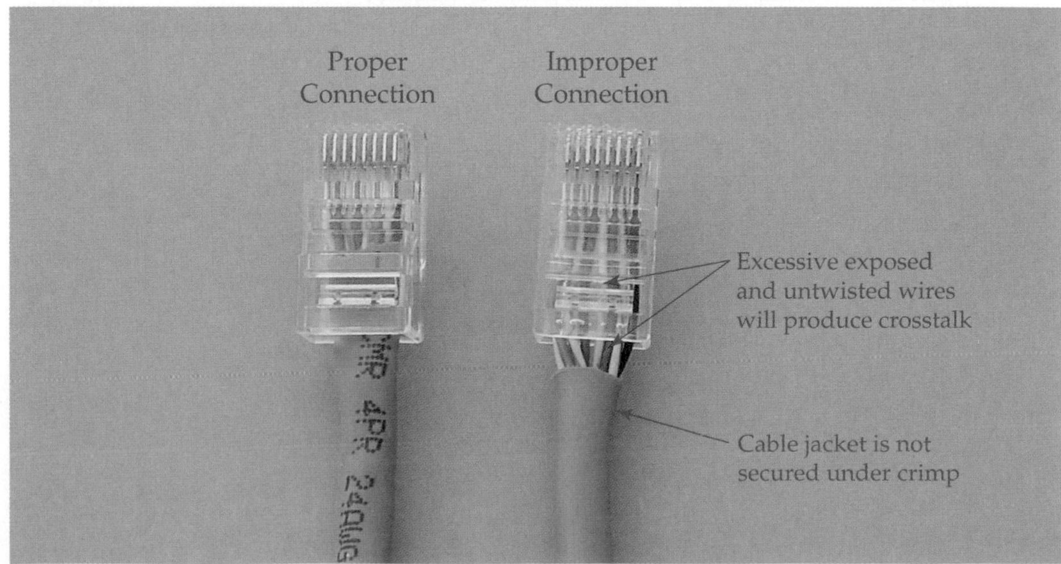

Figure 2-11. Example of a twisted pair cable properly connected to a connector and a twisted pair cable improperly connected to a connector. Note the exposed, untwisted pairs of wire in the improper connection.

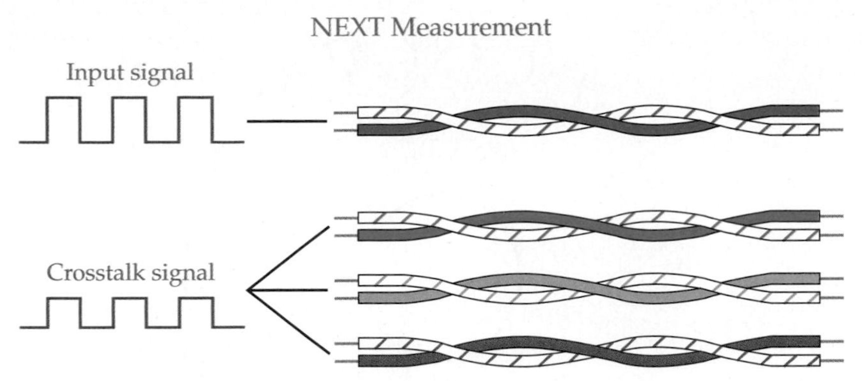

Figure 2-12.
Near-End Crosstalk (NEXT) is a measurement of crosstalk taken at the near end, or input end, of a cable.

crosstalk. For networking fundamentals, it is the relationship of the input signal compared to the crosstalk signal.

Far-End Crosstalk (FEXT)

As the name implies, ***Far-End Crosstalk (FEXT)*** is a measurement of reflective loss at the far end, or output end, of the cable, **Figure 2-13.** Far-end losses are also expressed in decibels.

Far-End Crosstalk (FEXT) a measurement of reflective loss at the far end, or output end, of a cable. Far-end losses are expressed in decibels.

Equal Level Far-End Crosstalk (ELFEXT)

Equal Level Far-End Crosstalk (ELFEXT) is a measurement calculated by subtracting the effects of attenuation from the FEXT. ELFEXT negates much of the attenuation by raising the attenuated signal by a value equal to the attenuation. This brings the attenuated signal back to the desired level. This is what the term *ELFEXT* implies by "equal level." It equalizes the loss with a gain.

Equal Level Far-End Crosstalk (ELFEXT) a measurement calculated by subtracting the effects of attenuation from the Far-End Crosstalk (FEXT) measurement.

Alien Crosstalk (AXT)

Alien Crosstalk (AXT) is a measurement of noise introduced outside the cable jacket, typically caused by other network cables in close proximity. This measurement was first introduced in February 2008 as part of the Category 6a standard because of the high-frequency capabilities of this cable. Cables that carry high-frequency signals are susceptible to AXT. At lower frequencies, AXT is not a problem.

Alien Crosstalk (AXT) a measurement of the noise introduced outside the cable jacket, typically caused by other network cables in close proximity.

Copper Core Cables

Copper core cables are commonly constructed of a center core of copper surrounded by an insulating jacket. All copper core cables have an AWG rating. The

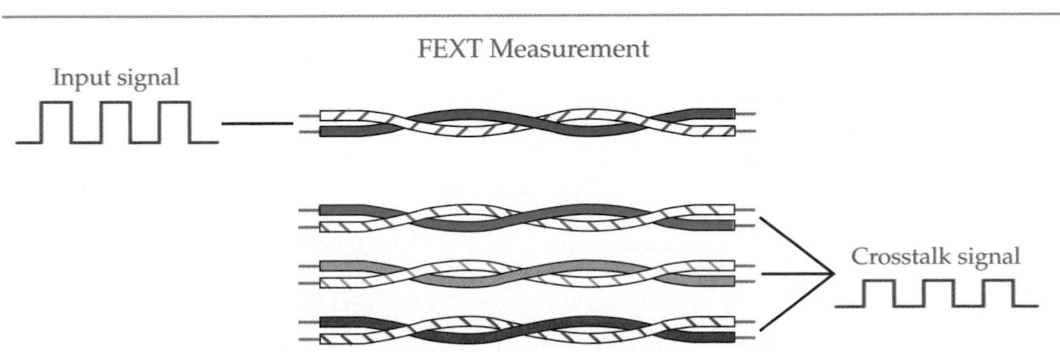

Figure 2-13.
Far-End Crosstalk (FEXT) is a measurement of crosstalk taken at the far end, or output end, of the cable.

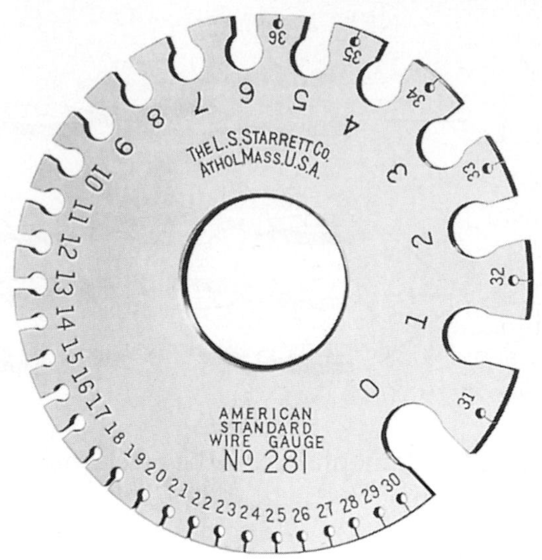

Figure 2-14. Note the AWG ratings on this wire gauge. The AWG rating of 0 indicates the largest wire size on the gauge; whereas, the AWG rating of 36 indicates the smallest wire size on the gauge.

AWG rating
a rating that describes the size of a conductor's diameter.

plenum-rated
a rating that means a cable has a special type of insulation that will not give off toxic gases should the cable be consumed by fire.

AWG rating describes the size of a conductor's diameter. The abbreviation AWG represents American Wire Gauge, which is the accepted standard for specifying the size of a conductor. The size of a conductor is expressed as a numeric value such as 22, 20, and 18. The smaller the number, the larger the diameter of the wire.

Figure 2-14 shows a wire gauge. A wire gauge is used to determine the AWG rating or the size of a conductor. Notice that the largest wire measurement on the gauge is marked by the AWG rating 0, and the smallest wire measurement on the gauge is marked by AWG rating 36.

Cables are often identified as plenum-rated. ***Plenum-rated*** means that the cable has a special type of insulation that will not give off toxic gases should the cable be consumed by fire. The term *plenum-rated* is derived from the plenum in a building. The plenum is the area above a drop ceiling and under a raised floor, **Figure 2-15.** Cables designed to pass through a building plenum must be plenum-rated.

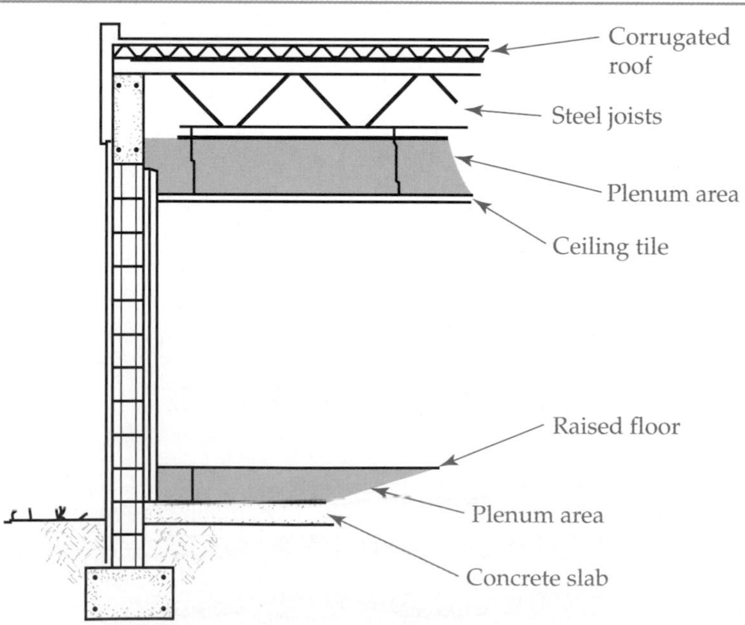

Figure 2-15. The plenum area of a building is located above a drop ceiling and under a raised floor.

Two types of copper core cable are used in networking: coaxial and twisted pair. Twisted pair was derived from the telephone industry. Twisted pair was not originally designed for high frequencies. Voice signals are relatively low frequency when compared with other forms of electrical signals, such as radio, and did not require cable designed for high frequencies. Also, the original networks ran at only 1 Mbps to 4 Mbps. Early versions of telephone communications cables worked fine for these applications.

Coaxial cable was designed to carry high-frequency signals and was first used in high-frequency radio communications to conduct a radio signal to and from an antenna. Coaxial cable was also used in early networks. It is used to some degree today because of its shielding effect. We will explore more about these two types of cables in the next section.

Coaxial Cable

Coaxial cable, or ***coax,*** consists of a copper core conductor surrounded by an insulator referred to as a *dielectric*. Look at **Figure 2-16.** The photo is of a typical RG-58 coaxial cable assembly. The dielectric is covered with two shields: a foil shield and a braided copper shield. The shields protect the core from electromagnetic interference (EMI). The shields prevent the cable from transmitting EMI to other cables. The entire cable assembly is covered by an insulating outer jacket, which protects the shielding. Coaxial cable is very difficult to work with and relatively expensive when compared with some other cable-based media.

coaxial cable
a type of cable that consists of a copper core conductor surrounded by an insulator referred to as a *dielectric*. Also called *coax*.

The core of a coaxial cable can be either solid or stranded. A solid core is stiffer and more difficult to work with than a stranded core. However, neither is as flexible as twisted pair and fiber-optic cable. Another interesting fact is a stranded core has the ability to carry more electrical energy (current) than a solid core of equal dimensions. Stranded core coaxial cable, therefore, can contribute to a better quality of signal than solid core coaxial cable.

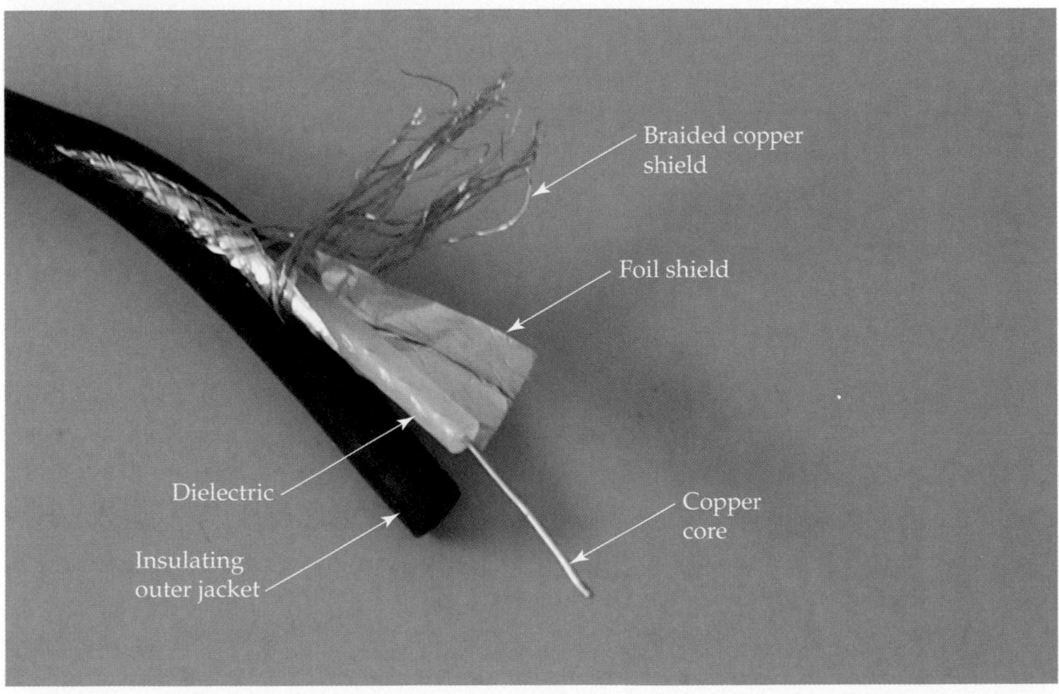

Figure 2-16.
Coaxial cable layers.

Many times, the most important factor in determining which cable type to use is cost. Solid copper core coaxial cable is less expensive than stranded copper core coaxial cable. This is true for all copper cable types manufactured. The exact type used typically varies according to installer preferences or the specifications of the installation.

Tech Tip

Do *not* assume all types of coaxial cable can be used to extend a network. The electrical characteristics of each type of coaxial cable vary greatly, and some coaxial cable types can only be used for specific applications.

Coaxial Connectors

Coaxial cable uses two main types of connectors: BNC and F-type. BNC makes a connection by pushing the connector onto the connection post and then twisting to the right, **Figure 2-17.** F-type connectors have threads and make a much better connection, **Figure 2-18.**

Coaxial Applications

You may encounter coaxial cable being used from an antenna or satellite dish to a network system or as a network backbone. A media converter or bridge device is used to convert the signal from coaxial cable to a twisted pair cable.

Video applications, such as Cable and satellite TV, typically use coaxial cable "RG" as the medium to carry their high-frequency signals rather than twisted pair cable. High-frequency signals are affected by twists in cables. When a video or audio signal is transmitted over a twisted conductor, the maximum length the signal can travel is drastically reduced. The twist in the cable causes an electronic characteristic known as *induction* which will distort the high-frequency signal. The distorted signal results in a distorted image or audio at the destination.

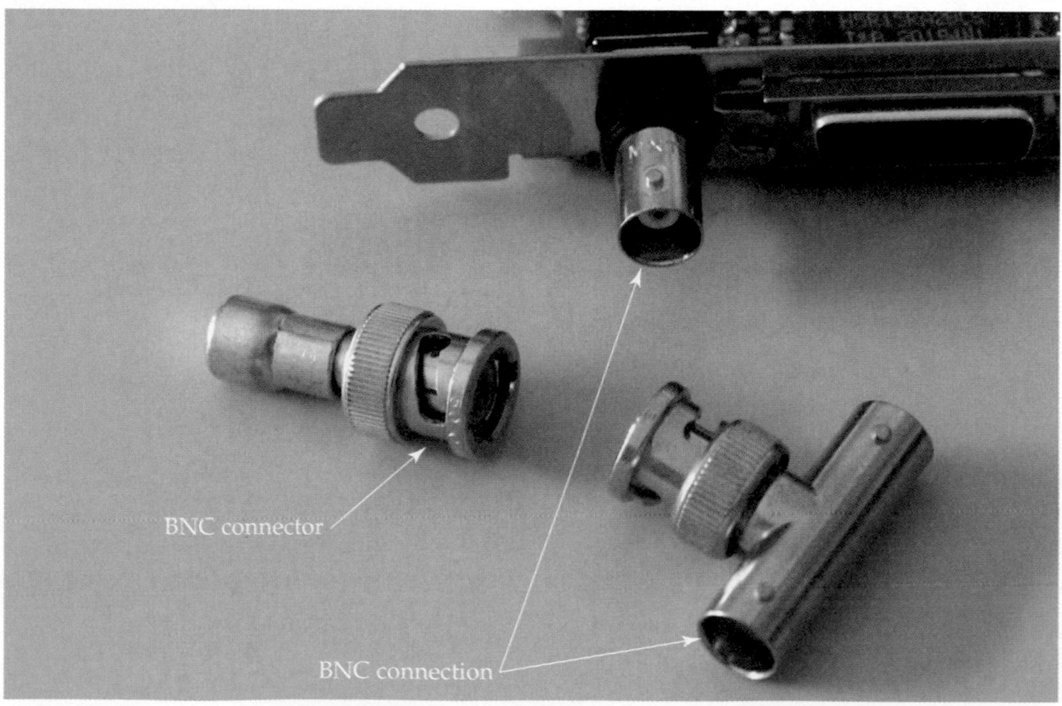

Figure 2-17.
A BNC connector is pushed onto the BNC connection and twisted until it "locks" in place.

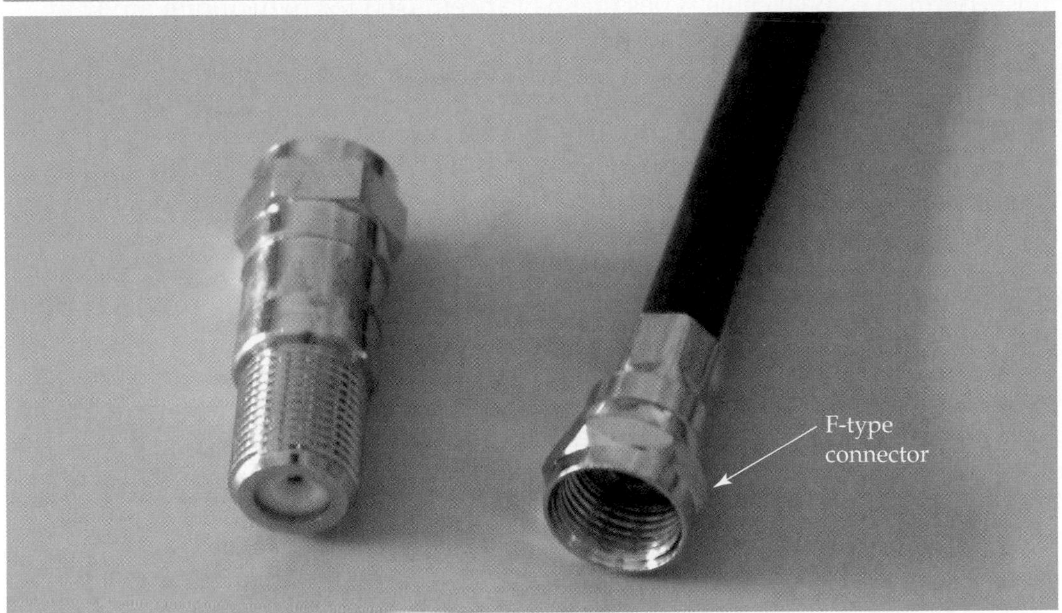

Figure 2-18.
An F-type connector is screwed onto an F-type connection.

Tech Tip

RG is an acronym for Radio Guide. Coaxial cables were first used in the emerging field of electronics to carry radio signals from the antenna to the receiver or from the transmitter to the antenna.

Areas that are prewired with coaxial cable may be used as a part of a twisted pair cabled network. D-Link, NETGEAR, and several other manufacturers have starter kits for using existing coax. The kit includes media bridges, or media converters, which have an F-type connection for the coaxial cable and an RJ-45 connection for twisted pair cable.

Coaxial Cable Classifications

There are several classifications of network coaxial cable. **Figure 2-19** lists some of the most common types of coaxial cable and their application. The three

Cable	Common Name	Impedance	Actual Size in Diameter	Description
RG-6	Broadband	75 Ω	0.332	Used for Cable TV.
RG-8	Thicknet	50 Ω	0.405	Used for Ethernet networks.
RG-11	Thick coax	75 Ω	0.475	Used for Cable TV trunk lines.
RG-58	Thinnet	50 Ω	0.195	Used for Ethernet networks.
RG-59	CATV	75 Ω	0.242	Used for Cable TV and sometimes used for ARCnet.
RG-62	Baseband	93 Ω	0.249	Used for ARCnet.

Figure 2-19.
Coaxial cable types and their applications.

most common coaxial cable types that have been used for networking are RG-6, RG-8 (thicknet), and RG-58 (thinnet).

RG-6
a type of coaxial cable that has become the standard for Cable television (CATV) systems and satellite systems

RG-6

RG-6 has become the standard for Cable television (CATV) systems and satellite systems, replacing other types of cable such as RG-59 for new installations. RG-6 in television applications typically use F-type connectors. RG-6 is often marked as RG-6/U and RG-6/UQ. The "U" represents "universal specification," which is an old military grade standard. The "Q" in RG-6/UQ represents "Quad" for quad shielding. Quad shielding has four layers of shielding rather than the typical two layers like that in RG-6/U.

Coaxial cable used for television is not acceptable for use as a network cable. Its characteristics work well for television transmission but will cause problems if used for computer networks.

Tech Tip

The EIA/TIA 570 residential communication standard recommends RG-6 for new residential installations.

RG-8
a thick, rigid coaxial cable used in a 10Base5 network. Also called *thicknet*.

RG-8

RG-8, or ***thicknet***, is a very rigid coaxial cable. It has a solid copper conductor in the center, which adds to its rigidity and to its overall thickness. RG-8 allows for longer segments than other copper core cables, but because of the difficulty in handling the cable and its wide diameter, it severely limits the number of cables that can be placed inside a conduit. Thicknet can be found in some network backbones because of its capability to carry a network signal as far as 500 meters.

Tech Tip

You may see references to 10base2 and 10base5 in outdated materials located on the Internet. 10base2 and 10base5 were early implementations of network media created from RG-58 and RG-8 cables, respectively.

RG-58
a thin, flexible coaxial cable used in a 10Base2 network. Also called *thinnet*.

RG-58

RG-58, or ***thinnet***, is smaller in diameter and easier to work with than thicknet coaxial cable but does not carry a signal as far. RG-58 is still permitted but not recommended for use in new network installations.

Network+ Note

The only RG type of cable listed in the CompTIA Network+ exam objectives are RG-6 and RG-58.

twisted pair
a type of cable that consists of four pairs of twisted conductors.

Twisted Pair

Twisted pair consists of four pairs of twisted conductors. Twisted pair cable has been available for many years and was first used by telephone companies to carry voice transmissions. Today, twisted pair is the most common choice of network cable. AWG wire sizes range from 18 to 26. The AWG wire size 24 is used most often.

There are seven categories of twisted pair cable: Category 1 through Category 7. The categories are based on the physical design, such as the number of pairs or twists per foot, and the capabilities of the cable, such as the maximum frequency rating and the data rate. The maximum frequency rating and data rate are only two of the measurements of a cable's capabilities. Other measurements to consider are crosstalk, NEXT, and impedance.

Twisted pair cable can also be labeled as UTP (unshielded twisted pair) and STP (shielded twisted pair). Shielding can be applied over the entire cable assembly or over individual pairs of conductors. When shielding is applied to individual pairs of conductors, the shielding protects against crosstalk and outside sources of interference. The problem with shielding individual pairs of conductors is it makes the cable much harder to work with when applying connectors. This type of cable is also more expensive than twisted pair cable that does not shield the individual pairs of conductors.

Two different classifications of cable can have the same maximum frequency rating, but as a standard, they will support two different data rates. An example of a cable having the same frequency rating is Category 5 and Category 5e. Both have a frequency rating of 100 MHz, but because Category 5e has a better reflected loss rating based on NEXT and FEXT, it can be used in networks with a higher data rate standard. What makes this section so confusing is that information about cable specifications can change between applications. The two main cable applications are voice (low-frequency analog) and data (high-frequency digital) signals. Also, different manufacturers sometimes post higher ratings for their cable than the minimum rating.

For a complete listing of twisted pair categories, see the chart in **Figure 2-20.** Note that Category 5e is not a separate category but rather an addendum to the Category 5 specification.

When referring to a category of twisted pair cable, it is common to use the term *Cat* for short. For example, it is common to use the term *Cat 5* instead of *Category 5*.

Category 1

Category 1 cable is limited to low-frequency applications, such as voice signals. It consists of two conductors. The two conductors are not twisted. While this design is sufficient for electrical signals representing voice transmission, it is inadequate for computer networks.

Category 2

Category 2 cable consists of four pairs and has a maximum frequency rating of 1 MHz. It was once used in networks that were limited to 4 Mbps.

Category 3

Category 3 cable has a maximum frequency rating of 16 MHz. It consists of four twisted pairs and three twists per foot. This cable is rarely encountered today in network applications but may be found in many existing telephone installations.

Figure 2-20.
Twisted pair categories and their characteristics. There are seven twisted pair categories. Category 5e is an addendum to Category 5, not a separate category.

Category	Type	Maximum Frequency Rating	Data Rate	Number of Pairs	Comments
Category 1	UTP	None	Less than 1 Mbps	2	Used for electrical signals representing voice transmission.
Category 2	UTP	1 MHz	4 Mbps	4	Used in earlier networks that were limited to 4 Mbps.
Category 3	UTP or STP	16 MHz	10 Mbps 16 Mbps	4	Can be found in existing networks rated at 10 Mbps and 16 Mbps and in some telephone installations.
Category 4	UTP or STP	20 MHz	16 Mbps	4	This cable type was only a slight improvement over Category 3.
Category 5	UTP or STP	100 MHz	100 Mbps 1000 Mbps (using 4 pairs)	4	Commonly used in 10BaseT and 100BaseTX network installations.
Category 5e	UTP or STP	100 MHz	100 Mbps 1000 Mbps (using 4 pairs)	4	This cable type is not a replacement for the Category 5 cable. It is an addendum to the cable classification.
Category 6	UTP or STP	250 MHz	1 Gbps	4	Has a plastic spine used to separate the conductors.
Category 6a	UTP or STP	500 MHz	10 Gbps	4	Introduced AXT.
Category 7	UTP or STP	600 MHz	10 Gbps	4	Each pair of twisted conductors is protected by foil shielding. Then, all four pairs are surrounded by foil or braided shielding.

Note: NS = No standard.

Category 4

Category 4 cable has a maximum frequency rating of 20 MHz. It consists of four twisted pairs. This cable has a data rate of 16 Mbps. It is only a slight improvement over Category 3 cable.

Category 5

Category 5 cable has a maximum frequency rating of 100 MHz. It is capable of data rates of 100 Mbps (using two pairs) and 1000 Mbps (using four pairs). It is found commonly in 10BaseT and 100BaseTX networks.

Category 5e cable has a maximum frequency rating of 100 MHz. Category 5e is not a replacement for Category 5 cable but rather an addendum to the cable classification. With the growing need for cable that could support higher data rates, Category 5 standards were revised to Category 5e. Category 5e can support data rates up to 1000 Mbps using all four pairs of conductors. The improvements to Category 5 are based on Near-End Crosstalk (NEXT) and Equal Level Far-End Crosstalk (ELFEXT).

At the time of the introduction of Category 5e, any existing Category 5 cable was eligible to be reclassified as Category 5e if it met the requirements of the new standard. This would allow the use of Category 5 cable for newer network installations. Existing Category 5 cable could be tested to see if it met the Category 5e standard. If it met the standard, then it could be used. If not, it would require replacement. Some of the factors that determine the results of the tests are the AWG of the conductors and the insulation.

Category 6

Category 6 has a maximum frequency rating of 250 MHz and a data rate of 1 Gbps. It is similar in construction to Category 5 and 5e but does not require special shielding. Category 6 is similar to Category 5 in that it has four pairs of conductors. The main physical difference is that Category 6 has more twist per pair of conductors, and the pairs are separated by a plastic spacer in the core of the cable. Look at **Figure 2-21,** which compares Category 5 to Category 6 cable.

Notice that Category 6 has more twist per pair than Category 5 cable. The tighter twist is especially apparent when comparing the blue and blue/white pairs. Category 6 also has a plastic center cable core, which provides more space between the conductor pairs. The tight pair twist and the plastic center core are physical features which allow the Category 6 cable to support higher frequencies as well as higher data rates than Category 5e.

Enhanced Category 6 cable known as *Category 6e* is not a true standard but rather a marketing term used to identify Category 6 cable that exceeds the Category 6 standard. Category 6a is a TIA recognized standard. The "a" in Category 6a stands for "augmented." The classification Category 6a is applied to any cable that was originally designed for the Category 6a standard but can actually meet the TIA Category 6a standard specifications, such as supporting frequencies as high as 500 MHz.

Category 6a is an excellent choice of network cable for noisy environments such as heavy industrial manufacturing. High-amperage industrial cables and equipment

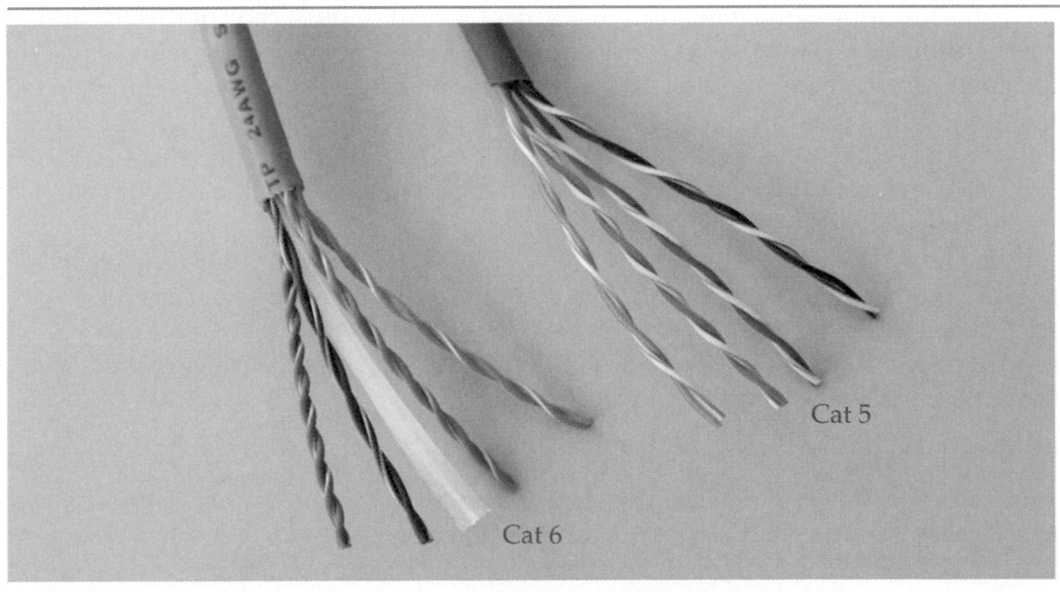

Figure 2-21. Category 5 and Category 6 cable.

such as welders generate a great deal of EMI. It has a maximum frequency rating of 500 MHz and a data rate of 10 Gbps. Do *not* confuse Category 6e with Category 6a.

Category 7

Category 7 cable has a maximum frequency rating of 600 MHz. It uses a different cable construction to achieve a high data rate. Category 7 is constructed of four pairs of twisted conductors with a protective foil or a conductive braid surrounding each pair. In addition to the individually covered pairs, there is an overall protective foil or conductive braid surrounding the complete assembly.

IEEE 802.3 Standard

In Chapter 1—Introduction to Networking, you learned that the Institute of Electrical and Electronic Engineers (IEEE) develops standards for the networking and communications industry. These standards begin with an 802 prefix, such as 802.1 for Internetworking and 802.2 for Logical Link Control. (See Figure 1-25.) In this section, you will learn specifically about the 802.3 standard, which describes Ethernet network specifications and specifies the use of copper cabling.

IEEE 802.3 Classifications

The IEEE 802.3 standard comprises various Ethernet classifications. These classifications differ by data rate, topology, and media type and are named with short descriptions, such as 10BaseT and 10Base2. The chart in **Figure 2-22** lists all of the IEEE 802.3 classifications along with the maximum and minimum segment lengths in meters, data rate, cable type, and the topology of each. The 802.3 classifications are divided into four categories: 10 Mbps, Fast Ethernet, Gigabit Ethernet, and 10 Gigabit Ethernet.

To help you decode the cryptic names of the classifications and to remember the specifications for each, look at **Figure 2-23.** In the first two examples, the *10* represents the data rate, which is 10 Mbps. In the third example, the 100 represents 100 Mbps. The *Base* in these examples stands for *Baseband,* which means that the digital signal is transmitted at one frequency, and this frequency consumes the entire bandwidth of the cable.

The last symbol in a cable classification is usually a number or a letter. A number indicates the approximate maximum segment length in hundreds of meters, and a letter indicates the media type. For example, in Figure 2-23A, the 2 represents the approximate maximum length of a segment in meters. A 10Base2 segment can therefore have a maximum length of approximately 200 meters (2 × 100). The actual maximum length, however, is 185 meters, but the *2* serves as an approximate. The 10Base5 classification specifies a maximum segment length of 500 meters (5 × 100). In this case, 500 meters is the actual maximum segment length.

In Figure 2-23B, the last character is a letter and represents the media type—twisted pair. Sometimes a classification will have two characters at the end, such as *VG* in 100BaseVG or *TX* in 100BaseTX. In the case of 100BaseVG, the *VG* represents *voice grade.* However, in 100BaseTX, the *T* represents *twisted pair* and the *X* represents *Fast Ethernet,* Figure 2-23C.

Tech Tip

The IEEE specification for 802.3 is over 1,000 pages long. You can download the complete specification from the IEEE Web site as an Adobe Acrobat file.

Category	Classification	Data Rate	Maximum Segment Length	Minimum Segment Length	Cable Type	Topology
10 Mbps	10Base2	10 Mbps	185 m	0.5 m	RG-58 (thinnet)	Bus
	10Base5	10 Mbps	500 m	2.5 m	RG-8 (thicknet)	Bus
	10BaseT	10 Mbps	100 m	0.6 m	Category 3, 4, and 5	Star
Fast Ethernet	100BaseT4	100 Mbps	100 m	0.6 m	Category 3, 4, and 5	Star
	100BaseTX	100 Mbps	100 m	0.6 m	Category 5	Star
Gigabit Ethernet	1000BaseCX	1000 Mbps	25 m	0.6 m	Category 5	Star
	1000BaseT	1000 Mbps	100 m	0 .6 m	Category 5e	Star
10 Gigabit Ethernet	10GBaseT	10 Gbps	55 m	0.6 m	Category 6	Star
	10GBaseT	10 Gbps	100 m	0.6 m	Category 6a	Star

Note: 1000BaseCX is obsolete and is no longer recognized.

Figure 2-22. IEEE 802.3 categories and classifications.

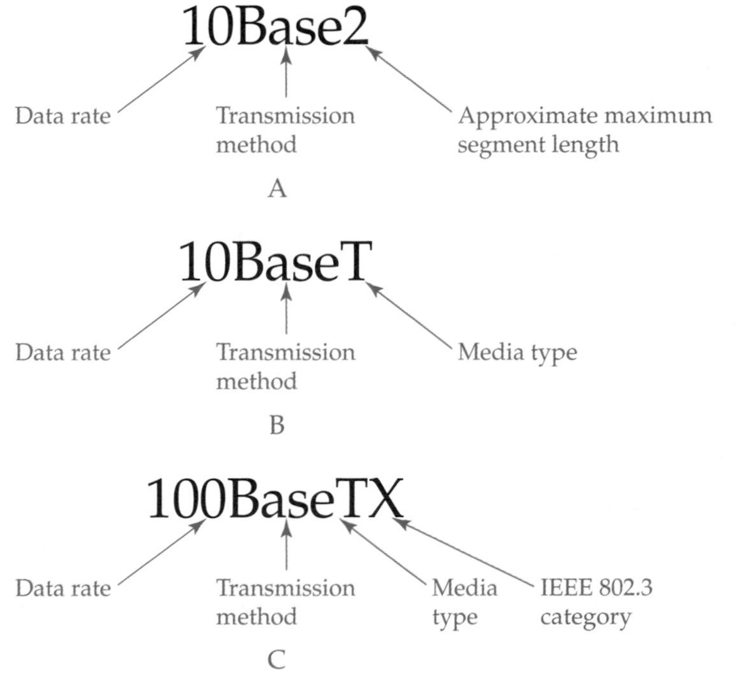

Figure 2-23. Each IEEE 802.3 classification has an identifying name that reveals the classification's data rate, transmission method, and either the approximate maximum segment length or media type. A—10Base2 means 10 Mbps, Baseband, with a maximum segment length of 200 meters. B—10BaseT means 10 Mbps, Baseband, using twisted pair cable. C—100BaseTX means 10 Mbps, Baseband, using twisted pair cable and the Fast Ethernet specification.

10 Mbps

Early networks were used primarily to transfer numeric or text data. A 10 Mbps transfer speed was more than adequate for most applications. The three classifications of 10 Mbps that were used are 10Base2, 10Base5, and 10BaseT.

10Base2

10Base2 an IEEE 802.3 classification that specifies the use of RG-58 (thinnet) cable and a data rate of 10 Mbps.

The ***10Base2*** classification specifies the use of RG-58 (thinnet) cable and a data rate of 10 Mbps. **Figure 2-24** illustrates the physical characteristics of a 10Base2 network. Note that a 10Base2 network is configured in a bus topology and that the maximum segment length is 185 meters. This means that the segment length cannot exceed 185 meters. If it does, the signal strength will deteriorate due to attenuation and impedance. Also, note that the minimum segment length between nodes is 0.5 meters.

terminating resistor an electrical device that absorbs transmitted signals when they reach the end of a network segment, preventing the signals from deflecting and distorting.

The ***terminating resistor*** absorbs the electrical signals when they reach the end of the segment. If a terminating resistor were not installed, the signal would reflect, causing the other signals transmitted across the cable to distort. Also, one end of the segment must be electrically grounded. Remember, a fluctuating digital signal traveling along a cable's core produces an electromagnetic wave, which can be absorbed by a neighboring conductor. In the case of a copper core cable, the cable's shielding absorbs the electromagnetic wave. Grounding one end of the cable helps to drain this interference so that the original signal is not affected.

Remember, if there is a break in the cabling or a problem with a BNC connector or a terminating resistor, no communication will take place. This is a major reason why coaxial cable is no longer used in networking.

10Base5

10Base5 an IEEE 802.3 classification that specifies the use of RG-8 (thicknet) and a data rate of 10 Mbps.

The ***10Base5*** classification was the first IEEE 802.3 classification developed for Ethernet. The 10Base5 classification specifies the use of RG-8 (thicknet) and a 10 Mbps data rate. The 10Base5 network, like 10Base2, uses a bus topology. However, the maximum segment length for a 10Base5 network is 500 meters. Each of the three segments that can connect to computers can connect to a maximum of 100. This allows a 10Base5 network to have a total of 300 computers.

A computer attaches to the thicknet coaxial cable through an AUI cable and AUI connectors. AUI is the acronym for Attachment Unit Interface. The AUI connector is a 15-pin D-shell connector that is used to attach a cable to a network interface card or network device. One end of the AUI connector connects to the network interface card and the other end connects to a transceiver unit, **Figure 2-25.** The transceiver unit

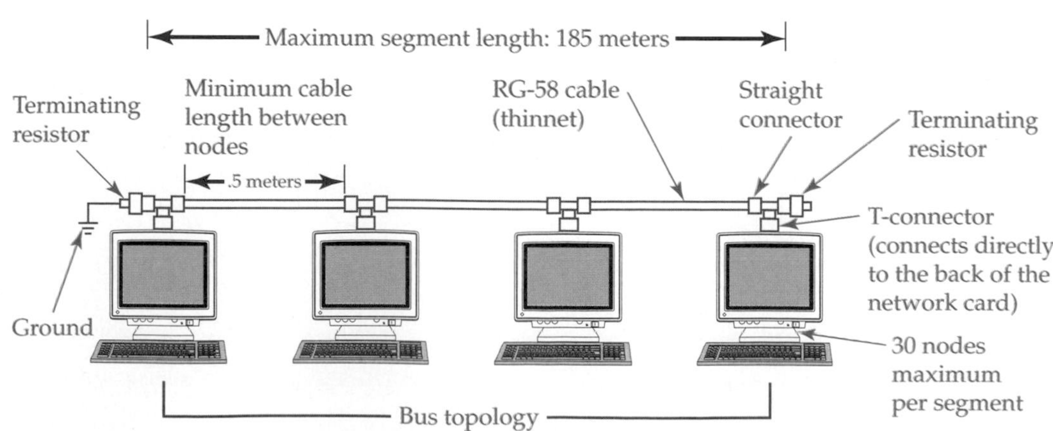

Figure 2-24. Physical characteristics of a 10Base2 network.

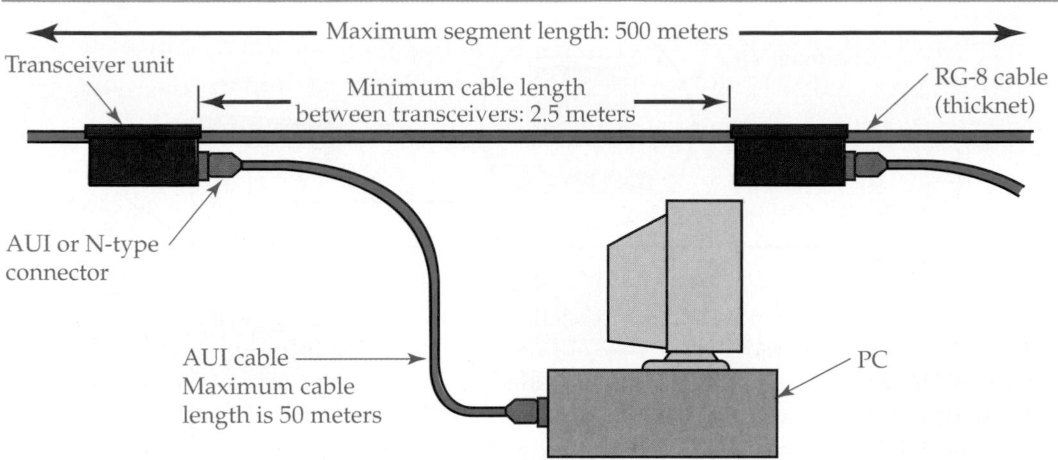

Figure 2-25. 10Base5 connections using a vampire tap, a transceiver unit, and an Attachment Unit Interface (AUI). Cable lengths and type are also indicated.

has a pair of spikes that pierce the cable's insulating jacket, shield, and insulator and makes a connection with the center core conductor. The transceiver unit is often called a *vampire tap.*

Tech Tip

10Base2, 10Base5, and related devices such as AUI are considered obsolete technologies. You will seldom encounter them.

10BaseT

The ***10BaseT*** classification specifies the use of Category 3, 4, and 5 UTP cable. It is arranged in a star topology and follows the 100-meter rule, **Figure 2-26.** This rule specifies that any cable on the network should not exceed 100 meters. The 100-meter length ensures that the signal strength will be sufficient when reaching the final destination. A repeater, however, may be used to extend the distance to an additional 100 meters. Most hubs encountered are active hubs, which means they also act as a repeater, regenerating electrical signals.

10BaseT
an IEEE 802.3 classification that specifies the use of Category 3, 4, and 5 UTP cable. It is arranged in a star topology, follows the 100-meter rule, and has a data rate of 10 Mbps.

A 10BaseT network can have two types of hub configurations: daisy chain and cascade. Study the hub configurations in **Figure 2-27.** Note that in the daisy-chain configuration, Figure 2-27A, an electronic signal from *Computer 1* must pass

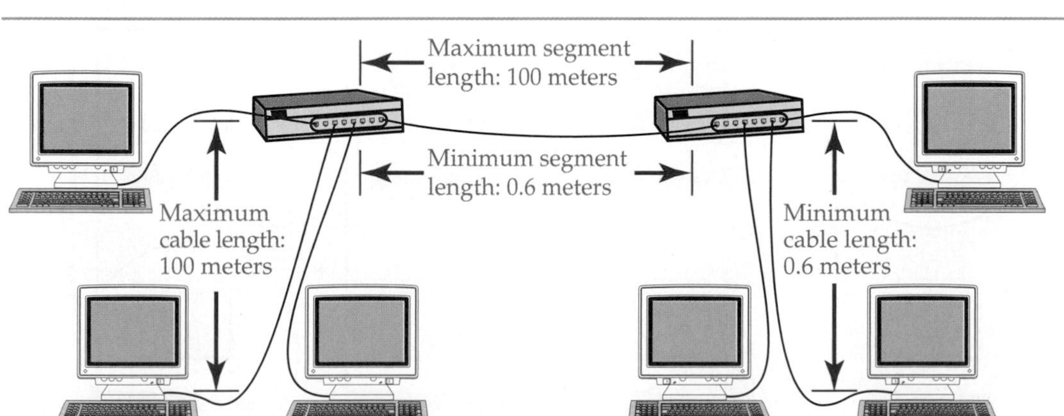

Figure 2-26. The 10BaseT network follows the 100-meter rule. This means that any cable used in a 10BaseT network should not exceed 100 meters in length.

Figure 2-27. Daisy-chain and cascade hub configurations. A—When hubs are arranged in a daisy-chain configuration, an electronic signal must pass through all hubs to arrive at a computer on the last hub in the chain. B—When hubs are arranged in a cascade configuration, an electronic signal never has to pass through more than three hubs to arrive at its destination.

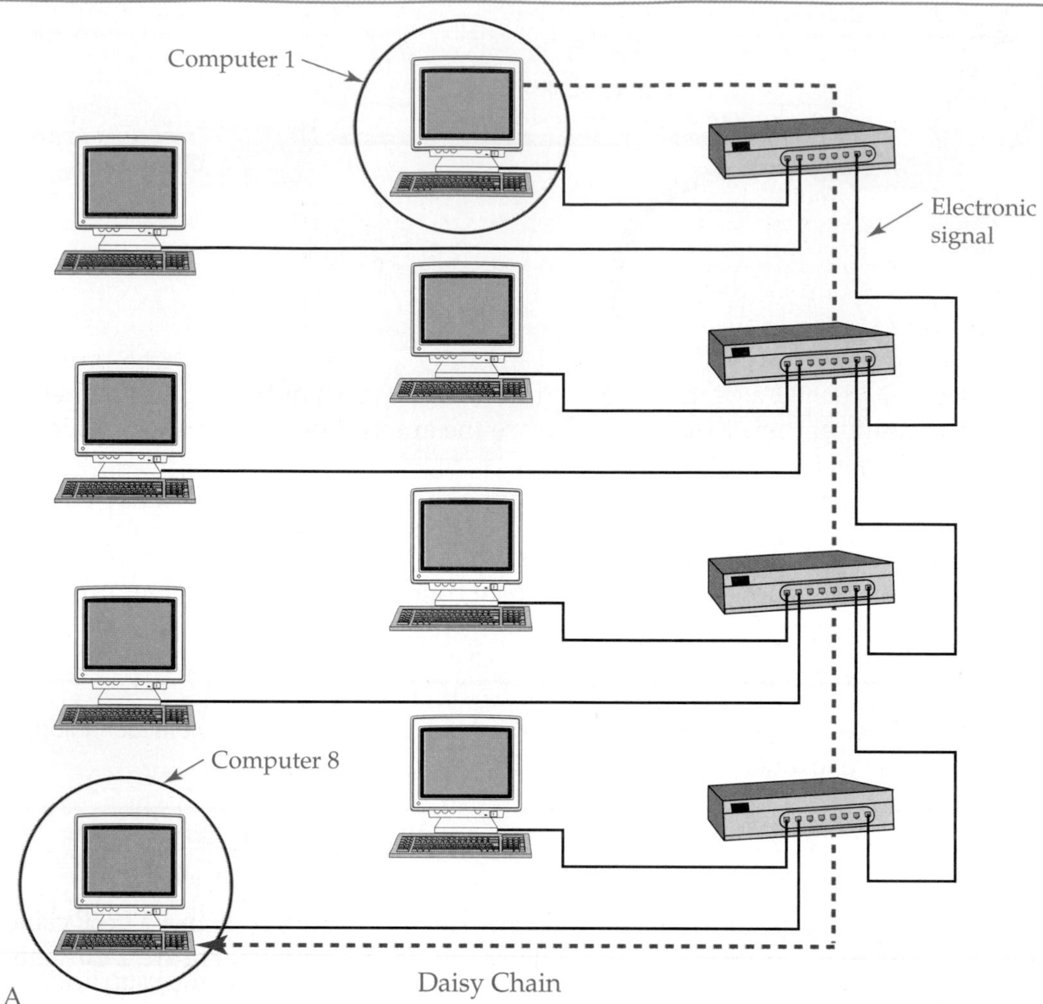

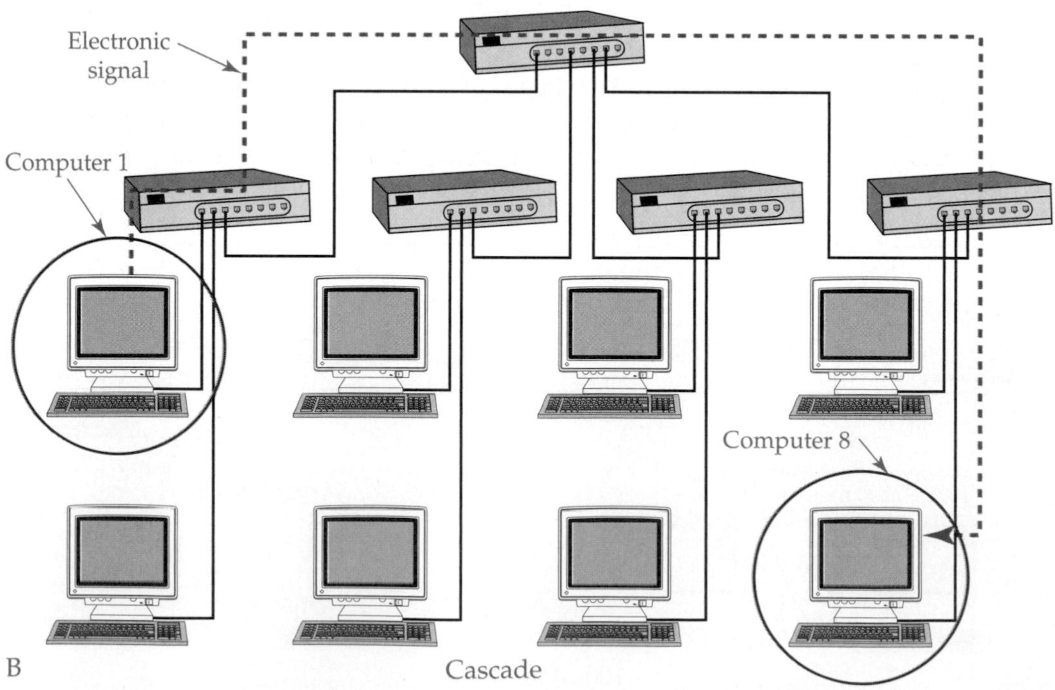

through four hubs before it reaches its destination, *Computer 8*. In the cascade configuration, Figure 2-27B, an electronic signal from *Computer 1* only has to pass through three hubs before it reaches its destination, *Computer 8*. This is a significant detail. Although both configurations have the same amount of hubs, an electronic signal does not have to pass through as many hubs in a cascade configuration as it does in a daisy-chain configuration.

If another hub were added to the daisy-chain configuration, an electronic signal from *Computer 1* would have to travel through five hubs before it reached a destination computer on the fifth hub, thus increasing the latency of the electronic signal. However, if another hub were added to the cascade configuration, an electronic signal from *Computer 1* would still only have to travel through three hubs before it reached a destination computer on the fifth hub. Adding another hub to the configuration would not increase the amount of hubs through which a signal has to travel.

As a general rule, no more than four hubs should be linked in a daisy-chain fashion. However, more than four hubs are allowed as long as an electronic signal does not need to travel through more than four hubs to arrive at its destination. If the signal passes through more than four hubs, the latency of the signal becomes excessive and causes the electronic signal to exceed its TTL setting. The electronic signal is then destroyed.

Fast Ethernet

Networks have rapidly grown in numbers and in applications. As networks and technology evolved, a demand for full motion video and audio was desired. Full motion video and audio requires a great deal of bandwidth because there is a much larger amount of data that needs to be transferred than with text-based data. In 1998, to accommodate the needs for greater bandwidth, the IEEE standards approved 100BaseT, also known as *Fast Ethernet*.

The Fast Ethernet classifications differ in the mode of communication and the number of twisted pairs that they use. Look at the chart in **Figure 2-28** for a summary of the two Fast Ethernet types that use copper cable: 100BaseT4 and 100BaseTX. Fast Ethernet works over most existing Category 5, 5e, and 6 cable.

100BaseT4

The ***100BaseT4*** classification specifies either half-duplex or full-duplex mode. In half-duplex mode, communication occurs on pairs 1 and 2, but in full-duplex mode, communication occurs on all four pairs. The 100BaseT4 classification specifies the use of all four pairs of Category 3, 4, or 5 cable.

100BaseT4
an IEEE 802.3 classification that specifies the use of all four pairs of Category 3, 4, or 5 cable and a data rate of 100 Mbps.

100BaseT4 was first introduced as a way to upgrade existing 10BaseT networks to 100 Mbps without the need to replace existing cables. Although the existing cable can be applied to the 100BaseT4 standard, existing network interface cards and other networking devices that are designed with a maximum throughput of only 10 Mbps need to be replaced to meet the 100 Mbps required

Fast Ethernet Classification	Communications Mode	Pairs Used
100BaseTX	Half-duplex	Pair 1 and 2
100BaseT4	Half-duplex Full-duplex	Pair 1 and 2 Pair 1, 2, 3, and 4

Figure 2-28. Communication modes used by the Fast Ethernet classifications.

by the 100BaseT4 standard. Remember, a network is only as fast as the slowest device or cable in the network.

100BaseTX

100BaseTX
an IEEE 802.3 classification that specifies the use of Category 5e cable on pairs 1 and 2 only. It is configured in a star topology and has a data rate of 100 Mbps.

The ***100BaseTX*** classification specifies the use of Category 5e cable and uses only pairs 1 and 2. Like 10BaseT, it is configured in a star topology, has the same cable limitations, and uses RJ-45 connectors; however, it has a data rate of 100 Mbps. 100BaseTX uses only the half-duplex mode. Remember that in half-duplex mode, transmission occurs in only one direction at a time. All half-duplex communication occurs on pairs 1 and 2.

Gigabit Ethernet

In 1999, 1000BaseT, also known as *Gigabit Ethernet*, was adopted. Higher speeds were accomplished by using cable that supported higher data rates and using all four of the cable pairs to allow for full-duplex transmission. It is important to note, however, that with Fast Ethernet and Gigabit Ethernet, not only must the cable be able to support the higher data rates, the network hardware, such as network cards and switches, must also be able to support the higher data rates.

Many network cards are manufactured as 10/100 and 10/100/1000, which means that they support 10 Mbps and 100 Mbps or 10 Mbps, 100 Mbps, and 1000 Mbps. The network cards and other network hardware automatically detect the data rate of the network and adjust accordingly.

1000BaseCX

1000BaseCX
an IEEE 802.3 classification that specifies a data rate of 1 Gbps, the use of Category 5 cable, a maximum segment length of 25 meters, and a minimum segment length of 0.6 meters.

The ***1000BaseCX*** classification specifies a data rate of 1 Gbps and uses Category 5 cable. It has a maximum segment length of 25 meters and a minimum segment length of 0.6 meters. It was intended for short runs, but has become obsolete due to the introduction of 1000BaseT.

1000BaseT

1000BaseT
an IEEE 802.3 classification that specifies a 1-Gbps data rate using all four pairs of Category 5e cable, a maximum segment length of 100 meters, and a minimum segment length of 0.6 meters. Also known as *Gigabit Ethernet*.

The ***1000BaseT*** classification, also known as *Gigabit Ethernet*, specifies a 1-Gbps data rate using all four pairs of Category 5e cable. It has a maximum segment length of 100 meters and a minimum segment length of 0.6 meters.

1000BaseT was originally introduced for network backbone installations, but now it is commonly used to connect workstations. 1000BaseT provides a less expensive alternative to fiber-optic cable when high-speed data rates are desired.

As you can see, the need to create faster network systems and the ability to use existing materials whenever possible has driven the creation of many different networking standards. At times, it can be confusing because many of the standards use the same category of cable, but in a different way. As new standards are created, older standards become obsolete, but can still be found in the field.

10 Gigabit Ethernet

10GBaseT
an IEEE 802.3 classification that specifies a data rate of 10 Gbps at a distance of 100 meters using unshielded Category 6a cable or a distance of 55 meters using Category 6 cable. Also known as *10 Gigabit Ethernet* or *10BbT*.

10 Gigabit Ethernet, also called ***10GBaseT,*** was adopted as a standard in 2006 by IEEE. It can provide 10 Gbps at a distance of 100 meters using unshielded Category 6a cable or a distance of 55 meters using Category 6 cable. 10GBaseT uses a special RJ-45 connector that looks very similar to the earlier version of RJ-45. The main difference is not so much physical as it is electrical. Because of the 10-Gbps data rate, the connector must meet an electrical standard of 650 MHz when tested. 10 Gigabit Ethernet is also referred to as *10GbT*.

IEEE 802.3 Media Access

Ethernet networks use a media access method called ***CSMA/CD (Carrier Sense Multiple Access with Collision Detection)*** to control and ensure data delivery. This is how CSMA/CD works. A workstation listens for data traffic on the network before transmitting data. When the network is silent, the workstation transmits data. If, however, another workstation submits data at the same time, the data collides on the network. When this happens, the two workstations wait a random period before retransmitting the data. The random period is less than a fraction of a second. A typical network can transmit thousands of data packets in one second. Collisions usually remain unnoticed on a properly-installed network. A poorly designed network may operate slowly due to too many collisions. As you see, one inherent problem with Ethernet communication is data collision on the network. When two data packets collide, they become corrupted and cannot be delivered.

CSMA/CD (Carrier Sense Multiple Access with Collision Detection) a media access method used in Ethernet networks.

The following will help you better understand CSMA/CD as a standard for network communication. The acronym CSMA/CD can be separated into three distinct pairs of letters/words that explain the operation requirements that must be met to match the CSMA/CD standard. Carrier Sense (CS) means that a network interface card can sense when data is transmitted on a network cable. Multiple Access (MA) means that the network cable provides multiple access at the same time to all network interface cards connected to the cable. Collision Detect (CD) means that the network interface card can detect when a collision has occurred and will automatically resend the damaged packet.

IEEE 802.3 Wiring and Connections

Wiring and connectors used for networking were first derived from the existing telephone communications industry. Even today, many of the cable standards apply to not only networking but also to other communications systems.

This section introduces the basics of twisted pair network cable, connectors, and standards. The two main cable termination standards in use for twisted pair cable are 568A and 568B as described by the TIA/EIA organization.

568A and 568B

When installing an RJ-45 connector, it is important that the conductors, which are color-coded, be inserted into the appropriate pin area. Two standard connections are recognized by industry: 568A and 568B. Long before standards existed, there were two common ways to make an RJ-45 connection. Since the industry was divided, both became standards but are denoted by the letters *A* and *B*. The only real difference in the connections is the color of the conductors inserted into the pin areas. Other than the color of the conductors, the electrical qualities are the same. Look at **Figure 2-29.** Compare the two standard connections, 568A and 568B, in Figure 2-29A. Notice that for the 10BaseT classification, Figure 2-29B, each connector uses only two pairs of conductors from the cable: the orange pair and the green pair. The other two pairs are not used for communication in a 10BaseT network.

UTP cables have two common classifications of assembly: straight-through and crossover. A straight-through cable is used to connect a computer with a hub, and a crossover cable is used to connect a computer with a computer. The straight-through cable is constructed with each numbered pin connecting to the matching numbered pin on the opposite end of the cable.

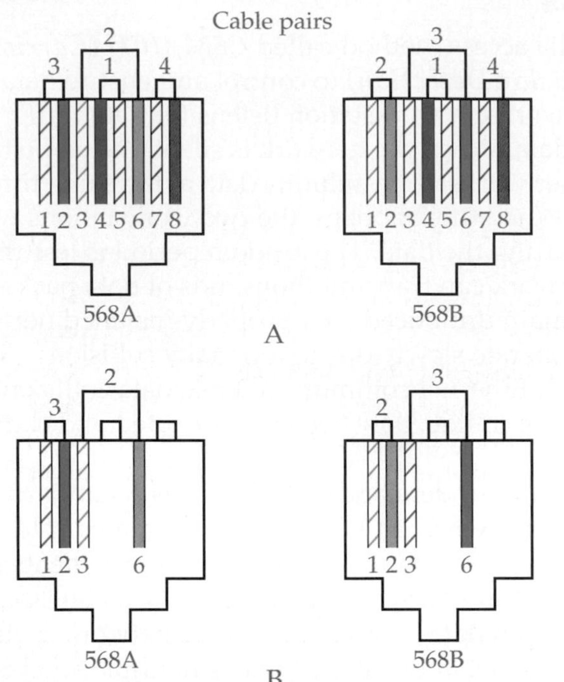

Figure 2-29. The 568A and 568B connection standards. A—The only difference between the two connection standards is the locations of pairs 2 and 3. B—The 10BaseT classification uses pairs 2 and 3. Either connection standard can be used.

Look at the wire map in **Figure 2-30.** Notice that pin 1 connects to pin 1, pin 2 connects to pin 2, and so on. When a two-workstation 10BaseT network is configured, a crossover cable must be used for the network cards to communicate. A crossover cable has two pairs (four individual conductors) that are cross-connected. Cross connecting the pairs allows a transmit signal from one computer to be sent to the receive pins of a network card on the other computer. This allows the computers to communicate without a hub. A crossover cable is not needed when a hub is used because the circuitry at each access port crosses the connection internally. Therefore in this situation, a straight-through cable is used.

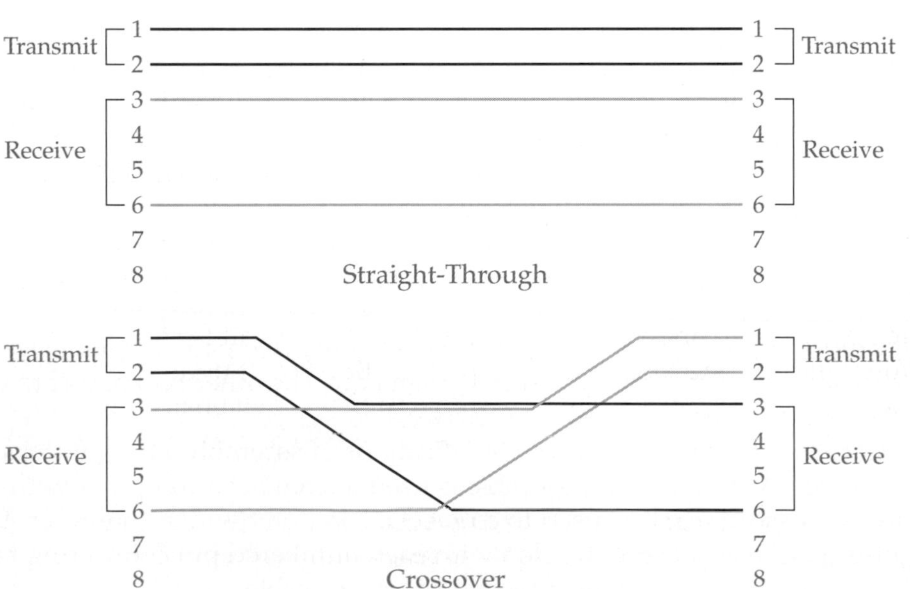

Figure 2-30. Wire map of a straight-through cable and a crossover cable.

A *wire map* is an illustration of the correct circuit path of conductors from one end of a cable run to the opposite end. Wire maps are used to illustrate proper cable connections for a technician who makes cable assemblies.

Look at the hub in **Figure 2-31.** Notice that each access port number on the hub has an *X* beside it. This indicates the access port's internal connection is crossed. Also, notice the uplink port. The uplink port serves a straight-through connection. It can be used to connect via a straight-through cable to an access port on another hub.

Some network devices, like switches and network adapters, are Auto-MDIX compliant. ***Automatic Medium-Dependent Interface Crossover (Auto-MDIX)*** is an electronic chip technology incorporated into Gigabit Ethernet devices to automatically reassign pin functions and eliminate the need for a crossover cable. It is a relatively new standard introduced by HP. To verify that the network device is Auto-MDIX compliant, look at the device specifications.

Automatic Medium-Dependent Interface Crossover (Auto-MDIX)
an electronic chip technology incorporated into Gigabit Ethernet devices to automatically reassign pin functions and eliminate the need for a crossover cable.

Installing an RJ-45 Connector

The RJ-45 connector contains eight connection points, or pins, inside its plastic housing, **Figure 2-32.** To install an RJ-45 connector on a UTP cable, the insulating jacket of the UTP cable is first stripped from the cable, exposing the conductor pairs, **Figure 2-33.** The pairs are untwisted so that each conductor can be inserted into one of the designated pin areas. When the RJ-45 connector is crimped, each conductor makes contact with one of the eight pins, **Figure 2-34.**

The RJ-45 is also known as the *8P8C connector.* The acronym 8P8C represents "8 pair 8 contacts."

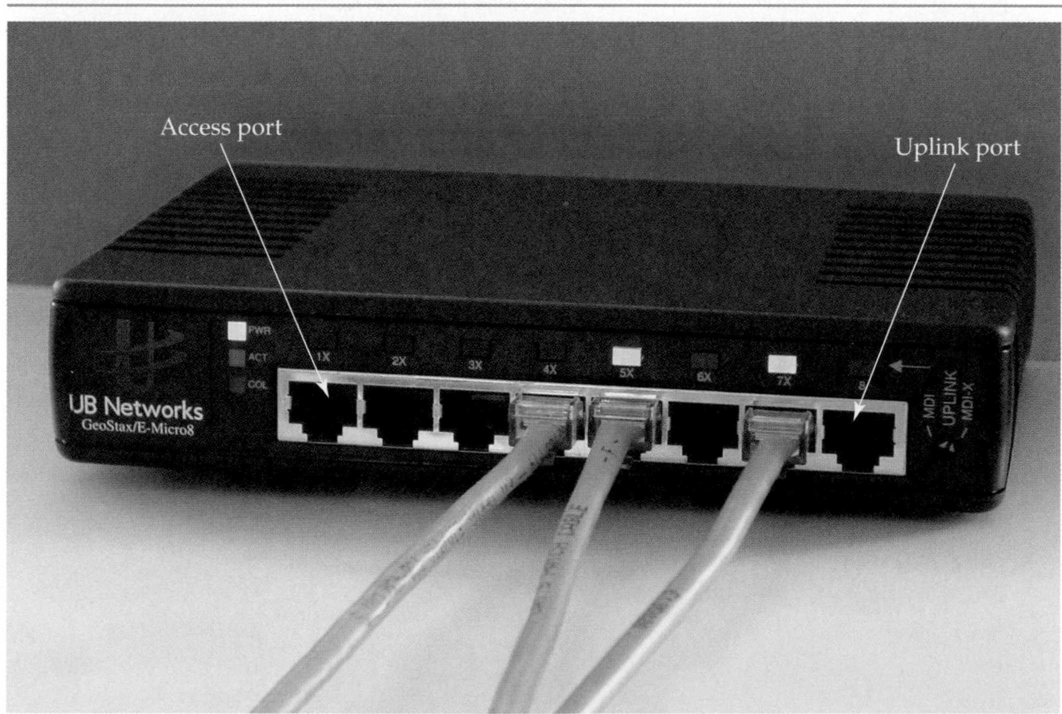

Figure 2-31.
A hub typically has many access ports and one uplink port. The circuitry inside the hub provides a crossed connection at each access port and allows for a straight-through connection at the uplink port.

Figure 2-32.
Close-up of an RJ-45 connector.

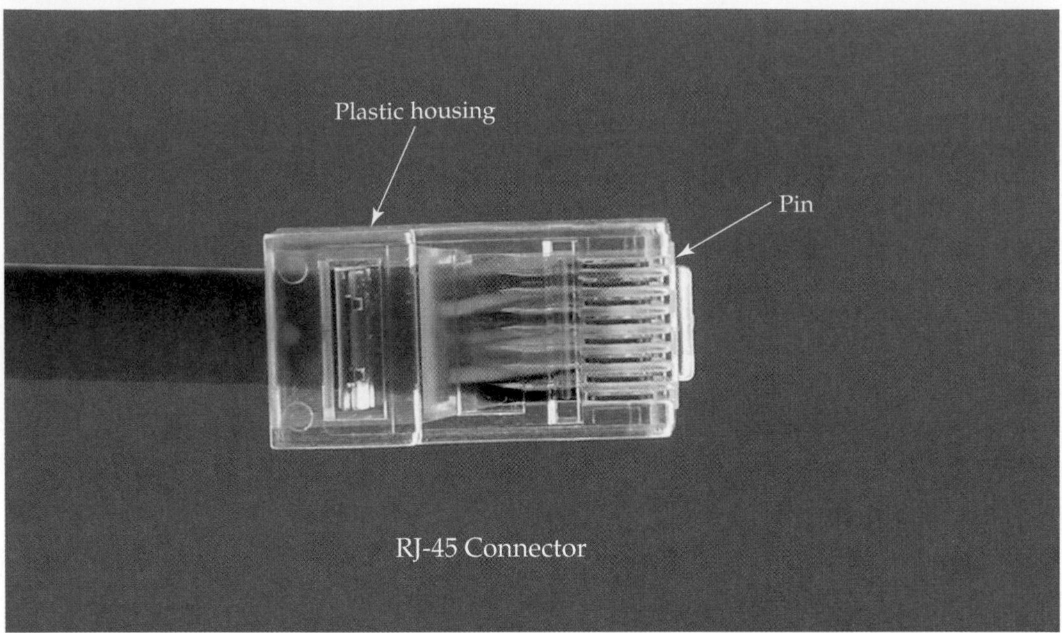

rollover cable
a special cable where the pin order is completely reversed on one end of the cable. Pin 1 connects to pin 8, pin 2 connects to pin 7, and so on.

Rollover Cable

A ***rollover cable*** is a special cable in which the pin order is completely reversed on one end of the cable. Pin 1 connects to pin 8, pin 2 connects to pin 7, and so on. The Cisco console cable is wired like a rollover cable in that the pin numbers are reversed. However, a Cisco console cable uses an RJ-45 connector on one end and a DB-9 serial connector on the other; whereas, a rollover cable uses an RJ-45 connector on each end.

Figure 2-33.
The insulating jacket on this UTP cable has been stripped to reveal the conductor pairs.

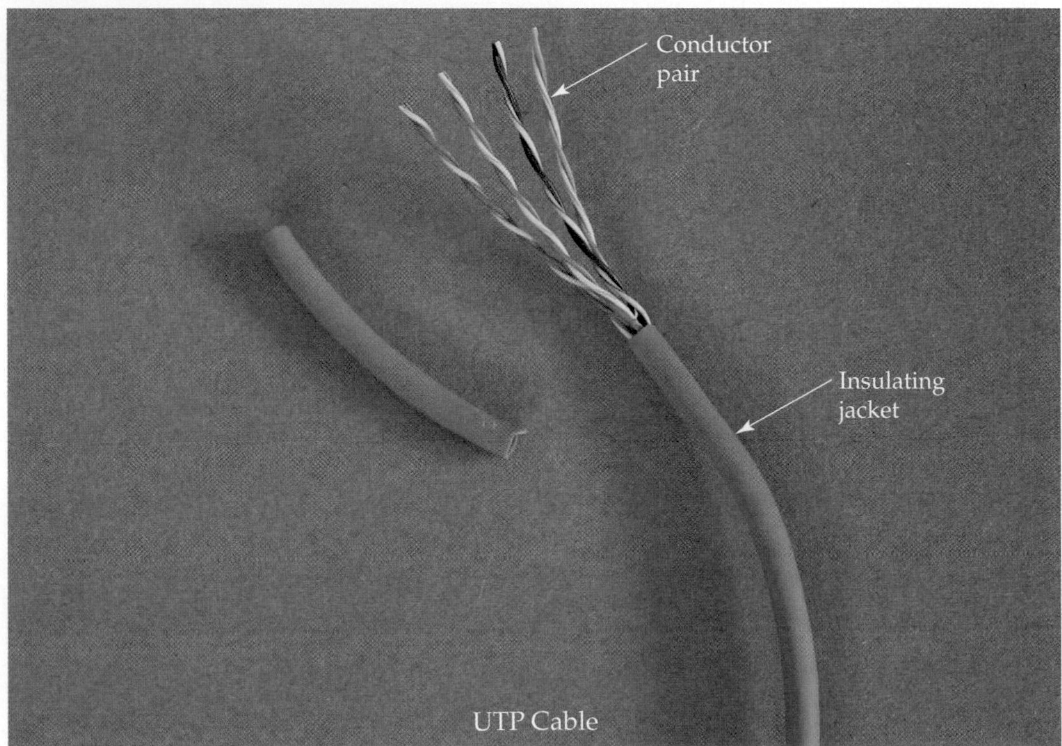

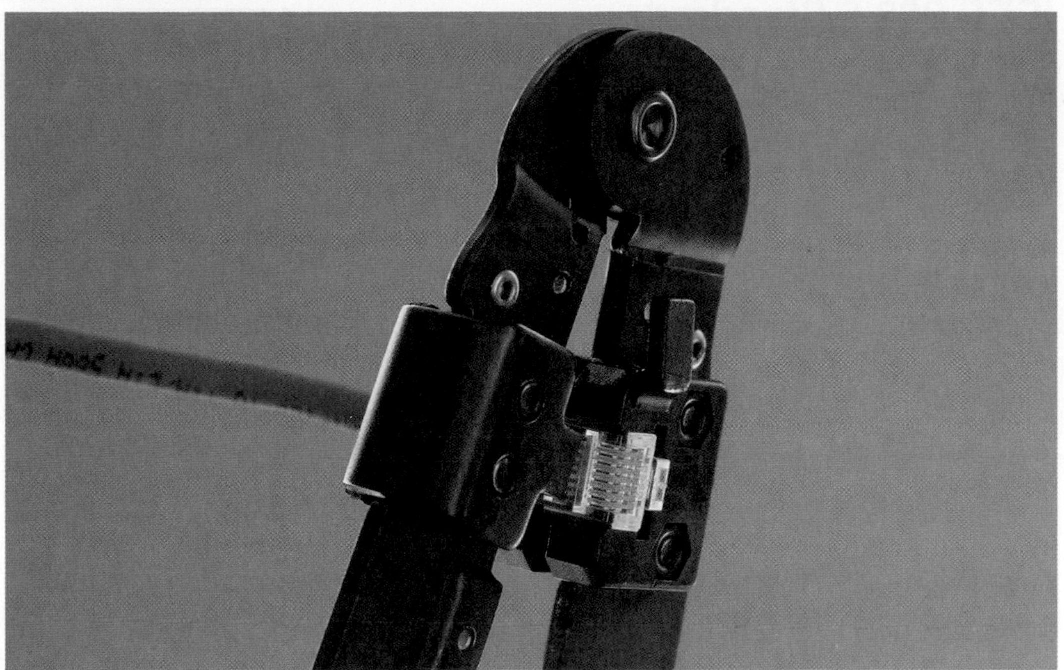

Figure 2-34.
An RJ-45 crimp tool is used to make the connection between the RJ-45 pins and the twisted pair conductors.

Bonding and Grounding

STP and coaxial cable requires equipment to be bonded and grounded before the shielding can be effective. All electrical systems have one centralized ground that is common for all electrical equipment. The centralized ground is typically located at the point in the building where the electrical company commercial power enters.

The ground path must be continuous from the equipment to which the cable is attached to the central ground in the electrical system. If the ground path is not continuous, the shielding will not effectively protect the network cables from electrical and radio interference. There will be more about grounding and bonding in Chapter 19—Designing and Installing a New Network.

Power over Ethernet (PoE)

The ***Power over Ethernet (PoE)*** IEEE standard 802.3af specifies the supply of small amounts of electrical power to network devices such as cameras, IP phones, Wireless Access Points, speakers, and phone or PDA chargers.

Power over Ethernet (PoE)
an IEEE standard that specifies the supply of small amounts of electrical power to network devices such as cameras, IP phones, Wireless Access Points, speakers, and phone or PDA chargers.

The amount of power delivered is approximately 13 watts at 48 volts. The cable used for PoE must be rated as Category 5 or better. Two pairs of cables are used for network communication and one pair is used to supply the electrical power.

A more electronically-sophisticated method of PoE is used for Gigabit networks in which all cable pairs are used to carry network communication. Electrical power is supplied via two of the existing cable pairs that provide communication.

A more technical explanation of how power is provided over a communications cable is beyond the purpose of this textbook. To learn more about the electronic aspect of PoE, visit www.poweroverethernet.com. For detailed electronic specifications, check the Texas Instruments Web site page focus.ti.com/docs/prod/folders/print/tps2370.html.

A common PoE application is building and area security when electrical power is not readily available. Using PoE is very cost-effective when compared with installing new electrical circuits to power devices such as cameras.

IEEE 802.5 Standard

The IEEE 802.5 standard describes the Token Ring network. The Token Ring network uses the token passing access method and is configured in a ring topology. Token Ring networks operate at 4 Mbps, 16 Mbps, and 100 Mbps. Token Ring can be used with proprietary cable such as IBM design or UTP and STP. The maximum number of nodes allowed for a Token Ring network varies according to the network distance, speed, cable media, and equipment used. Always check with the manufacturer for the latest specifications.

Tech Tip

Some Token Ring networks do not use UTP as the network media. They use a proprietary cable, but the electrical characteristics are similar.

While a Token Ring network can be wired as a physical ring, **Figure 2-35,** most Token Ring networks use a multiple access unit (MAU) for a center connection point, **Figure 2-36.** When a MAU is used, the network arrangement resembles a star topology. However, because of the circuitry in the MAU, the network is physically connected as a ring. Each port on the MAU is designed to maintain an electrical ring. Look closely at the illustration of the MAU in **Figure 2-37.**

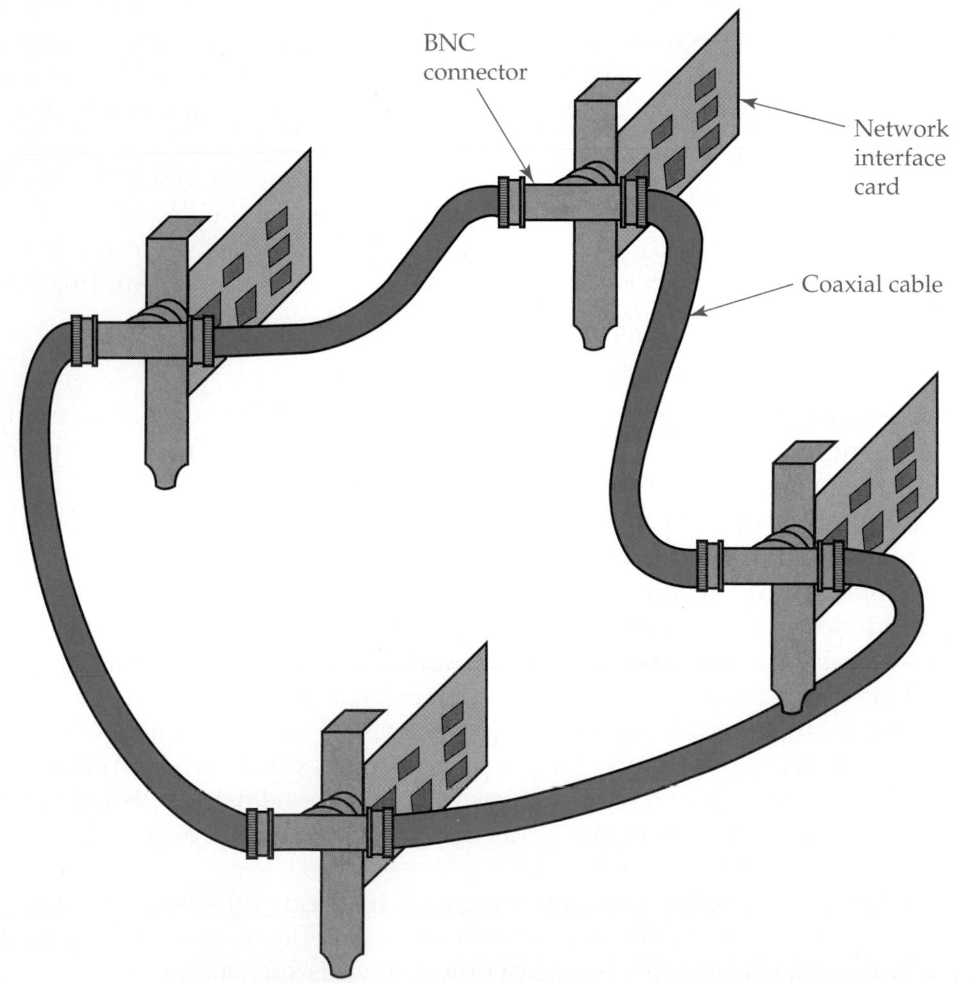

Figure 2-35.
Token Ring network using coaxial cable. When a Token Ring network uses coaxial cable, it resembles a physical ring.

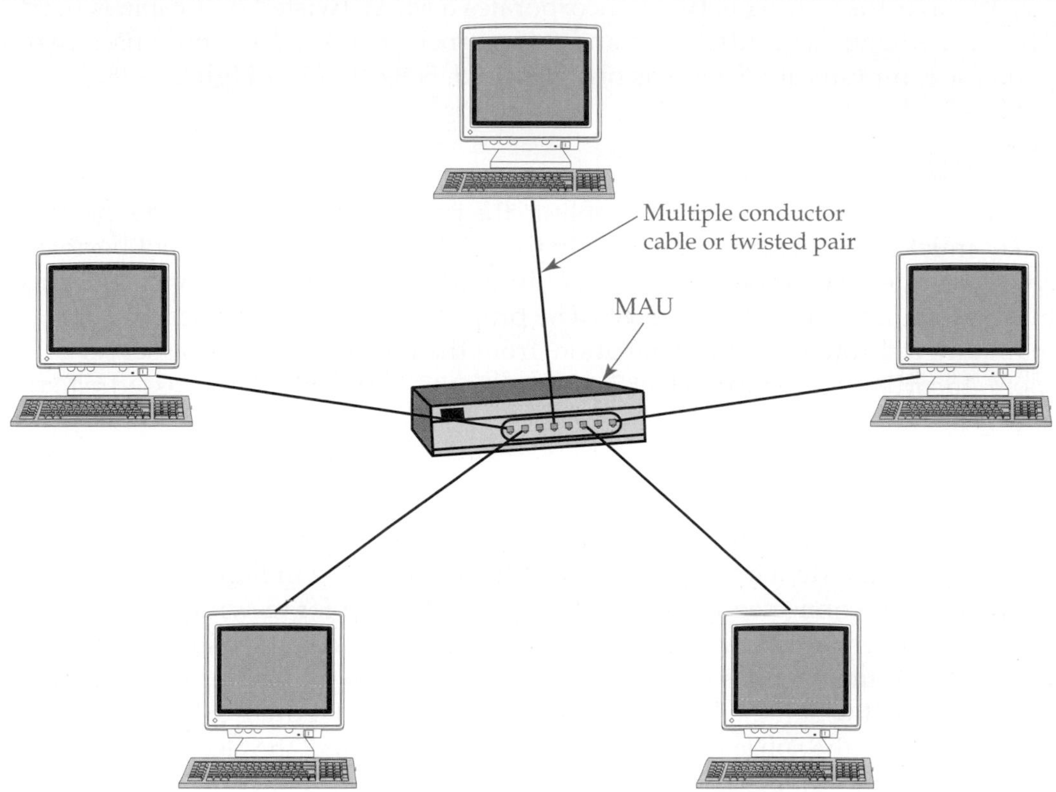

Figure 2-36.
Token Ring network using twisted pair cable. When a Token Ring network uses twisted pair cabling, it resembles a physical star.

Each port located at the MAU is normally closed to ensure the integrity of the ring. When a computer is added by plugging in the network cable, the port opens the normally-closed circuit allowing the added computer to join the ring.

A Token Ring network commonly uses several MAUs. When two or more MAUs exist in the ring, integrity is maintained in the same way as with added computers. MAUs, however, connect through special ports called *ring in* and *ring out*.

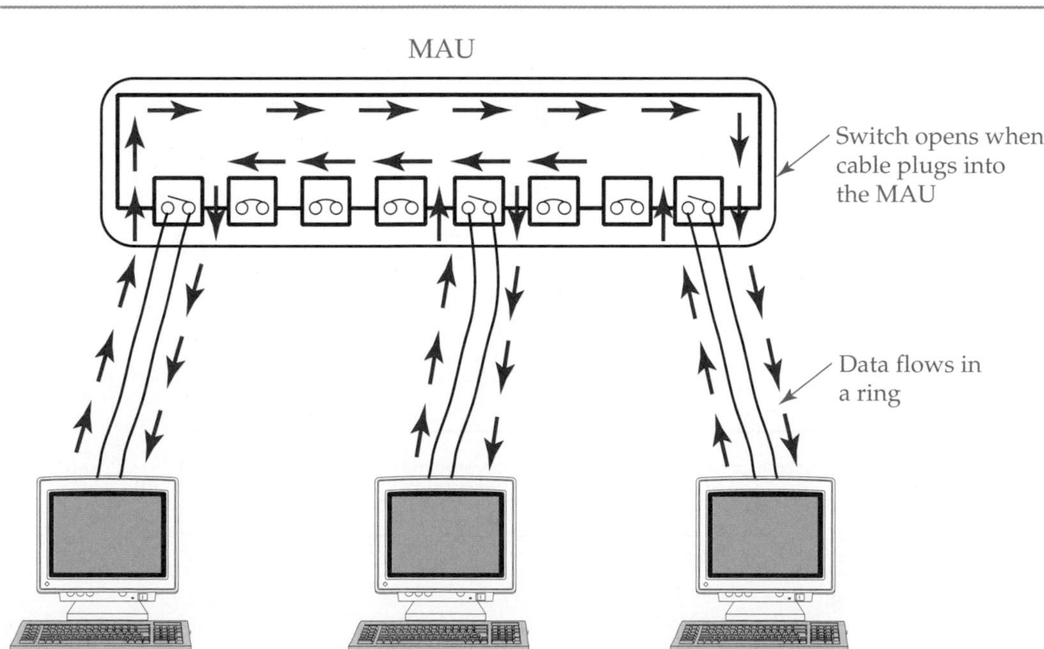

Figure 2-37.
Basic representation of the electronic circuitry inside a MAU. The MAU is designed to allow a continuous loop of data flow in the Token Ring topology. Look closely at the way the switches inside the unit are normally closed and then open when a cable plug is inserted.

When a Token Ring network incorporates a MAU, twisted pair cable is used. The twisted pair cable attaches to an RJ-45 connector. Token Ring only uses two pairs for communication and has one standard, 568A. Look at **Figure 2-38.**

Wiring Faults

When installing twisted pair cabling, the pairs of conductors inside the cable jacket must be connected correctly at both ends, or the network will not be able to communicate. The proper connection of individual conductors to pins is outlined in TIA standards: T568A and T568B. The proper connection sequence must be maintained throughout the installation, from the network card to the server room. Incorrect wiring can result in shorts, opens, reversed pairs, crossed pairs, and split pairs.

Short

short
a wiring fault that occurs in cabling when two conductors are improperly connected, resulting in a shorter circuit path.

A ***short*** occurs in cabling when two conductors are improperly connected, resulting in a shorter circuit path. Look at the lamp circuit in **Figure 2-39.** The lamp circuit is connected with the splice point left open for viewing. Most short circuits and open circuits occur at splice points and connection points. In Figure 2-39A, the circuit is correctly wired. When the switch is closed, electrical energy flows through the lamp, and the lamp lights. In Figure 2-39B, the wires are touching at the splice point. When the switch is closed, the electrical energy cannot reach the lamp because the electrical energy routes through the shortest path, the splice point. When a short occurs in a network cable, data takes a shorter route and does not reach its destination.

Open

open
a wiring fault that occurs when the length of a conductor has an open spot.

An ***open*** is just as the name implies. The circuit has an open spot along the length of the conductor. Look at **Figure 2-40.** In the illustration, you can see the open is at the splice point. When the switch is closed, no electrical energy can

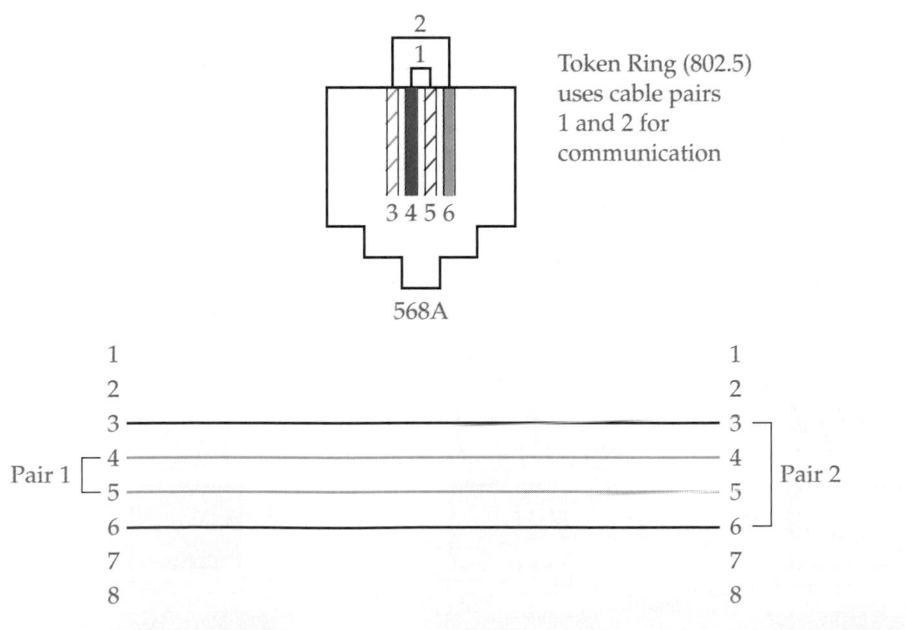

Figure 2-38.
The 802.5 standard specifies that only the 568A connection standard be used. Note that pairs 1 and 2 are used for communication.

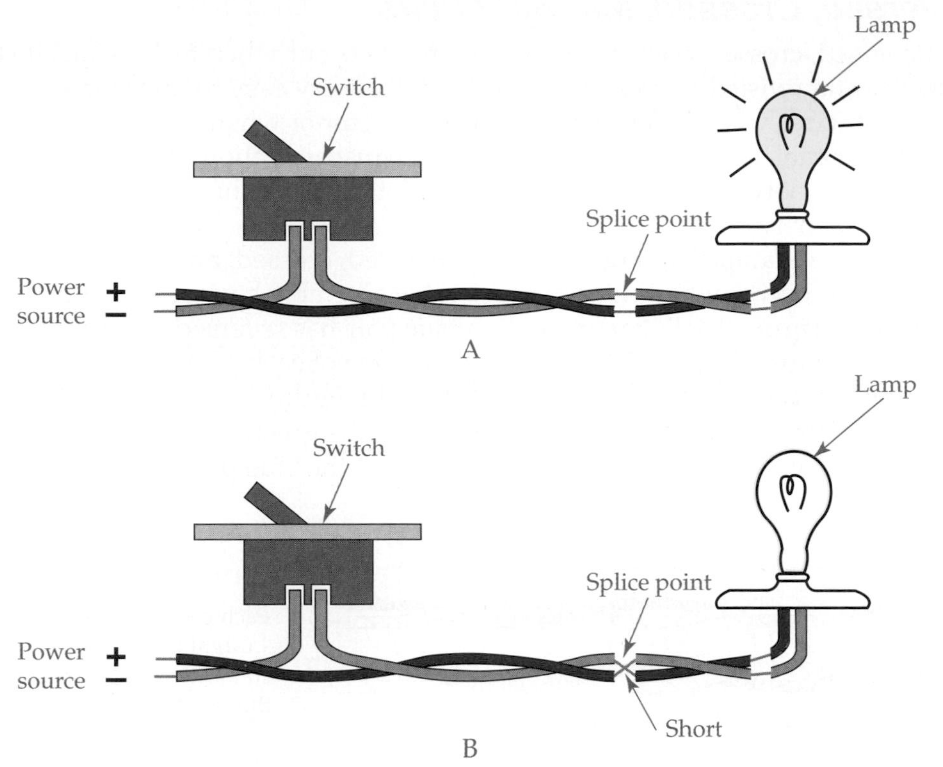

Figure 2-39.
A correctly-wired circuit and a shorted circuit. A—This circuit is correctly wired. When the switch is closed, the current flows through the complete circuit, lighting the lamp. B—In this circuit, the wires are shorted (touching). When the switch is closed, the current takes the shortest path, and the lamp does not light.

reach the lamp. The lamp will not light because the circuit is incomplete. When an open occurs in a network system, no data can travel past the point of the open.

Ground

A ***ground*** occurs when a conductor connects to the earth through a continuous path. Grounds typically occur where the conductor's insulating jacket is torn and the copper conductor makes contact with conduit or any other metal surface that is grounded. When a ground occurs in a network cable, all data is prevented from reaching its destination.

ground
a wiring fault that occurs when a conductor connects to the earth through a continuous path.

Tech Tip

Remember, a short occurs between two conductors, a ground occurs between a conductor and the earth. The connection to the earth is usually provided by a metallic enclosure, such as the metal pipe used to carry network cables, or exposed metal building parts, such as I beams or drop ceiling channels.

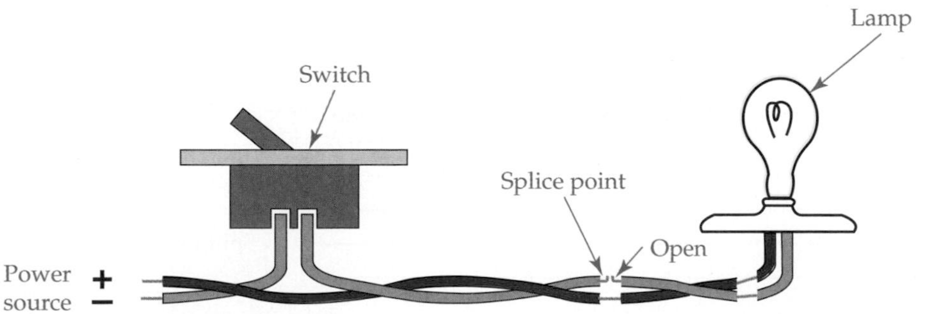

Figure 2-40.
In this circuit, there is a break in the wiring at the splice point. When the switch is closed, the lamp does light. This condition is called an *open*.

Reversed, Crossed, and Split Pairs

reversed pair a wiring fault that occurs when two pairs of a cable assembly have reversed two connections.

crossed pair a wiring fault that occurs when one of each of two cable pairs has become part of the other pair's connection.

Reversed, crossed, and split pairs commonly occur when technicians install connectors on twisted pair cables in the field. It is very easy to misconnect individual wires when installing an RJ-45 connector or when terminating a twisted pair cable in a punch down block. The misconnection may go unnoticed until after the network system is installed and a computer has a problem accessing the network.

Study the examples in **Figure 2-41** of reversed, crossed, and split pairs. A ***reversed pair*** occurs when two pairs of a cable assembly have reversed two connections, Figure 2-41B. For example, a blue pair has reversed pin connections with a green pair. A ***crossed pair*** occurs when one of each of the two cable pairs has become part of the other pair's connection. In Figure 2-41C, one conductor of the blue pair is connected as one conductor of the green pair. One conductor of the green pair is connected as one conductor of the blue pair. A ***split pair***

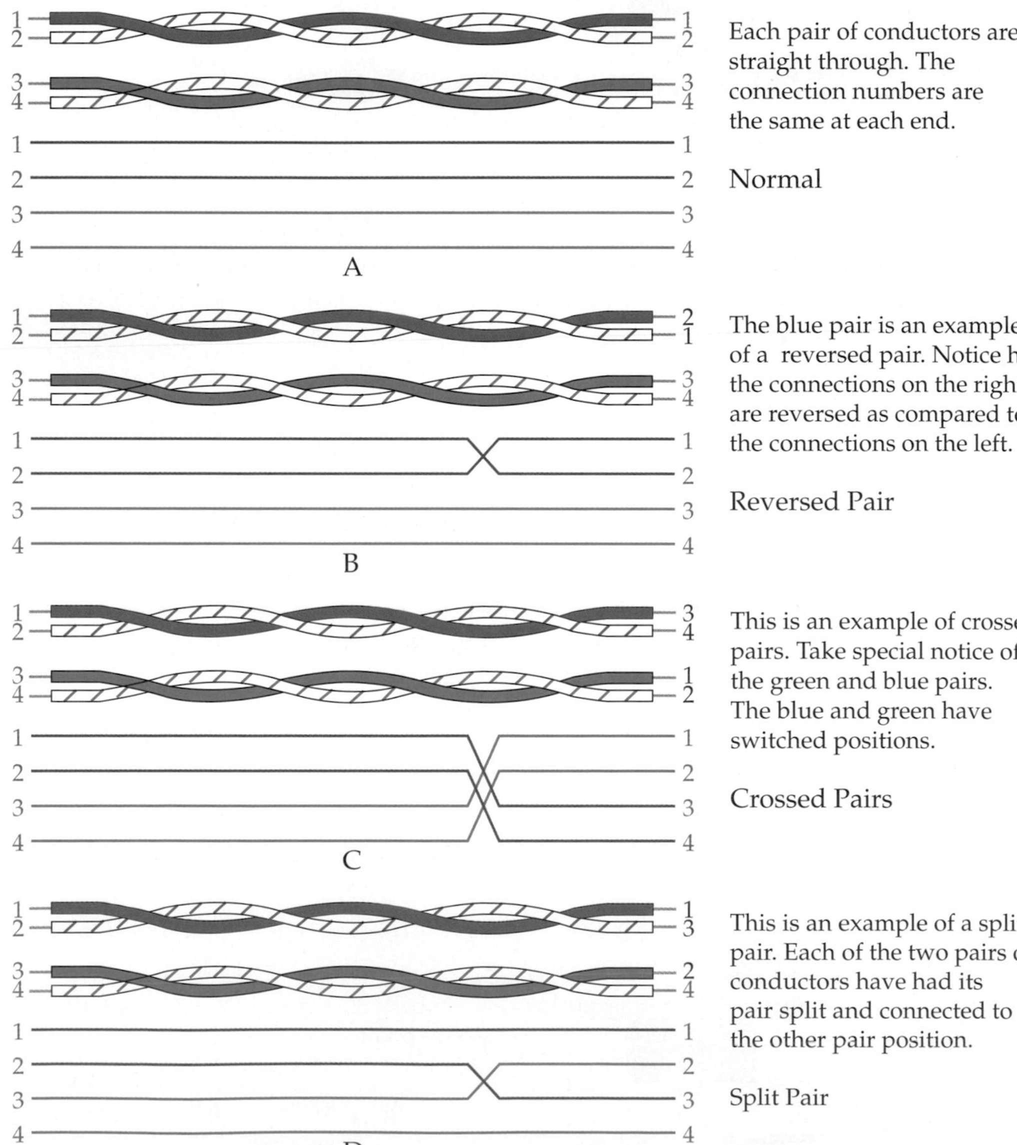

Figure 2-41. Common wiring errors: reversed pair, crossed pairs, and split pair. The red numbers indicate the errors. A—Normal connection is made. Each conductor is wired to a corresponding connection number. B—Reversed pair. Conductors within the pair reverse their connection at the opposite end of the cable. C—Crossed pairs. Two pairs have switched positions at the opposite end of the cable. D—Split pair. One conductor from each of two pairs have switched positions at the opposite end of the cable.

occurs when two pairs of conductors are reversed in connection with another pair. In Figure 2-41D, a complete pair of blue conductors has been reversed with connections intended for the green pair, and the green pair has taken the position intended for the blue pair.

split pair
a wiring fault that occurs when two pairs of conductors are reversed in connection with another pair.

Electronic cable testers are designed for testing a cable for the possibility of opens, crossed pairs, split pairs, and reversed pairs. You will use a cable tester often in the field when troubleshooting network communication problems. **Figure 2-42** shows a cable tester.

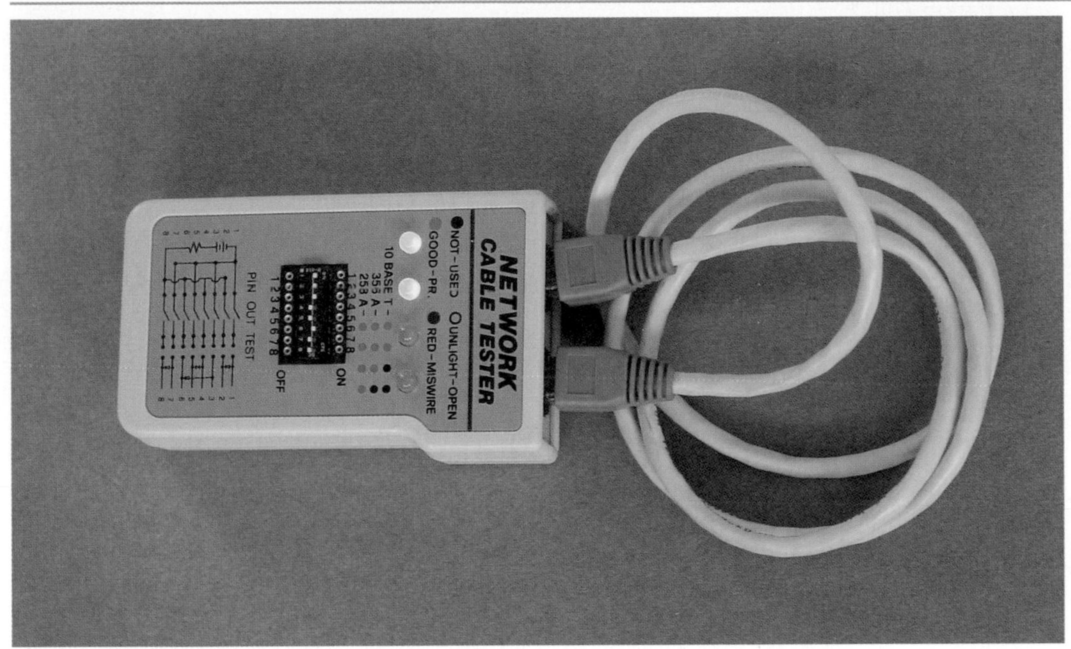

Figure 2-42.
An electronic cable tester is used to check for wiring faults such as crossed pairs, split pairs, and reversed pairs.

Summary

- The three major classifications of network media are copper cable, fiber-optic cable and wireless radio waves.
- Electronic signals are classified as analog and digital. Analog and digital signals differ by the shape of their waveforms.
- In the analog signal, time affects the degree of the slope. In the digital signal, time affects the duration of the voltage level.
- Both analog and digital waves have a frequency measurement. Frequency is the number of cycles that occur in 1 second and is measured in Hertz (Hz).
- Attenuation is the loss of signal strength.
- Interference is an unwanted signal that combines with and changes the waveform of the original signal.
- Latency is the amount of time it takes a signal to travel from its source to its destination.
- Bandwidth is a measurement of the ability of network media to carry data; whereas, frequency is a measurement of the ability of network media to carry an electronic signal.

- Baseband is a method of transmitting a single frequency, using the entire bandwidth of a cable.
- Broadband is a method of transmitting multiple frequencies or data across a cable at once.
- Communication can occur in one of three modes: simplex, half-duplex, and full-duplex. Simplex communication occurs in one direction only. Half-duplex communication occurs in both directions, but not at the same time. Full-duplex communication occurs in both directions at the same time.
- Electrical energy that travels in only one direction is referred to as *direct current (DC)*.
- Electrical energy that constantly reverses its direction of flow is referred to as *alternating current (AC)*.
- Electrical resistance is the opposition to the flow of electrical energy. Resistance is generally used to describe this effect in DC circuits.
- Impedance is also the opposition to the flow of electrical energy, but it expresses the amount of resistance encountered in an AC circuit.
- Reflected loss is the amount of signal reflected from the far end, or receiving end, of a cable.
- The electrical phenomenon of a current-carrying conductor inducing current in a cable of close proximity is called *crosstalk*.
- Near-End Crosstalk is a measurement of crosstalk at the near end, or sending end, of a cable.
- Alien Crosstalk is crosstalk generated from network cables in close proximity to each other.
- The decibel (dB) is an electrical measurement that is used to express the amount of power or energy gained or lost.
- Far-End Crosstalk is a measurement of crosstalk at the far end, or receiving end, of a cable.
- Equal Level Far-End Crosstalk is a measurement of the negated effects of cable attenuation caused by crosstalk.
- Copper conductor wire size is based on its diameter and is expressed as a size according to the American Wire Gauge AWG. The larger AWG the number, the smaller the wire size.
- Three common coaxial cable types that have been used for networking are RG-6, RG-8 (thicknet), and RG-58 (thinnet).
- Twisted pair cable is divided into seven categories. The categories are based on the physical design and capabilities of the cable such as the maximum frequency rating, the data rate that the cable is capable of, and number of twists per foot.
- The IEEE 802.3 standard describes the characteristics of various Ethernet technologies such as 10 Mbps, Fast Ethernet, Gigabit Ethernet, and 10 Gigabit Ethernet.
- An Auto-MDIX compliant device automatically reassigns the pin functions so that a crossover cable is not required for communication.
- Power over Ethernet (PoE) is a way of powering devices that consume small amounts of electrical energy, approximately 13 watts at 48 volts, over network cable.
- Wiring faults include shorts, opens, reversed pairs, crossed pairs, and split pairs.

Review Questions

Answer the following questions on a separate sheet of paper. Please do not write in this book.

1. _____ signals are sent through copper core cable as pulsating electrical energy.
2. Pulsating light waves are commonly sent through _____ cable.
3. Wireless technology commonly transmits _____ waves, _____ waves, and _____ through the atmosphere.
4. What are the two types of electrical signals?
5. Time affects the degree of the slope in a(n) _____ signal.
6. Time affects the duration of the voltage level in a(n) _____ signal.
7. How often an analog or digital cycle repeats in one second is called _____.
8. Frequency is measured in _____ and is represented by the abbreviation _____.
9. How many times does an analog cycle repeat in a 2.3-kHz electronic signal?
10. How many times does a digital cycle repeat in a 10-MHz electronic signal?
11. What is attenuation?
12. Noise and crosstalk are types of _____.
13. What is AXT?
14. What is latency?
15. A method of transmitting data in the form of a digital signal, using the entire bandwidth of a cable is called _____.
16. A method of transmitting data in the form of several analog signals at the same time is called _____.
17. List the three modes in which communication can occur.
18. What is the difference between half-duplex and full-duplex communication?
19. _____ is opposition to current flow in a DC circuit, and _____ is the opposition to current flow in an AC circuit.
20. The size of a conductor's diameter is described by what rating?
21. Which conductor is larger, one that has a 22 AWG rating or one that has a 24 AWG rating?
22. RG-58 is also referred to as _____.
23. What type of coaxial cable is recommended by the EIA/TIA 570 residential communication standard?
24. Which types of coaxial cable are referred to as *thicknet*?
25. What is the maximum frequency and data rate associated with Category 6a cable?
26. What Category 6 cable physical attributes provide improved data rates and higher frequencies when compared with Category 5 cable?
27. What is the difference between Category 6 and Category 6a?
28. List the following characteristics of a 10BaseT network: topology, cable type, connector type, maximum segment length, minimum cable length, and data rate.
29. What will happen to an electronic signal in a 10BaseT network if it passes through more than four hubs?
30. What does the acronym Auto-MDIX represent?
31. What is Auto-MDIX?
32. What is another acronym used to identify the RJ-45 connector?
33. What is the purpose of a rollover cable?
34. What does the acronym PoE represent?
35. What types of devices use PoE?
36. What is the maximum voltage delivered by PoE?
37. What is the term used for a circuit path that is shorter than its intended path?
38. What is the term used for an incomplete circuit path?

39. What is the term used to describe a wire that comes in contact with a metal enclosure that is touching the earth?
40. Name three possible cable problems that might result from improperly wiring twisted cable pairs.

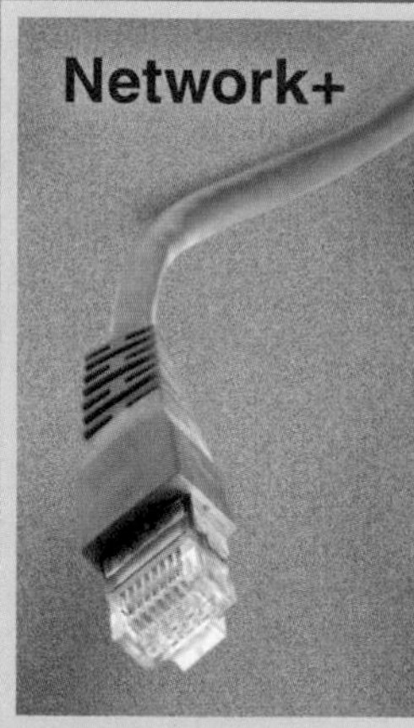

Sample Network+ Exam Questions

Answer the following questions on a separate sheet of paper. Please do not write in this book.

1. What type of cable is typically associated with a 10BaseT network?
   A. RG-58
   B. UTP
   C. Fiber-optic
   D. RG-8
2. Which of the following connectors is commonly associated with a 10BaseT network?
   A. BNC
   B. RJ-45
   C. AUI
   D. ST
3. What is the maximum segment length allowed for a Category 5 UTP cable?
   A. 100 meters
   B. 185 meters
   C. 200 meters
   D. 500 meters
4. The loss of signal strength from one end of a cable to the opposite end is expressed as _____.
   A. attenuation
   B. crosstalk
   C. NEXT
   D. resistance
5. What is the purpose of twisted pair shielding?
   A. To reduce the effects of environmental heat.
   B. To provide protection from EMI.
   C. To increase the rate of data flow.
   D. To identify which pair is used for transmitting data.
6. What is the difference in the 568B or 568A pinout sequence?
   A. The orange and green pairs are in reverse pin locations, and the blue and brown pairs remain in the same pin locations.
   B. The blue and brown pairs are in reverse pin locations, and the orange and green pairs remain in the same pin locations.
   C. The blue and red pairs are in opposite locations, and the gray and brown pairs remain in the same pin locations.
   D. All conductor pairs are in opposite locations.
7. Which electrical characteristic is used to measure signal loss in cable?
   A. Decibel
   B. Resistance
   C. Amperage
   D. Wattage

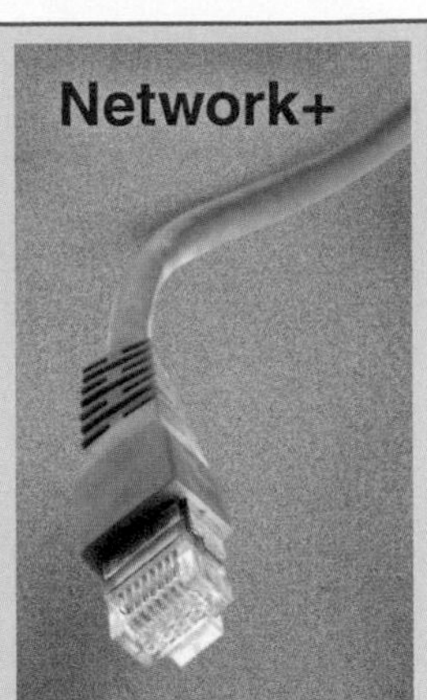

8. Which type of cable reverses the pin connections of the transmit and receive pairs?
   A. Rollover
   B. Crossover
   C. Pitchover
   D. 1000BaseT
9. What is the maximum data rate of a Category 5e cable if four cable pairs are used to transmit data?
   A. 10 Mbps
   B. 100 Mbps
   C. 1000 Mbps
   D. Only two cable pairs on a Category 5e cable can be used to transmit data.
10. A cable with a special type of insulation that will not give off toxic gases should the cable be consumed by fire is ____.
   A. AWG-rated
   B. fireproof-rated
   C. plenum-rated

Suggested Laboratory Activities

1. Make a straight-through patch cable.
2. Make a crossover cable.
3. Use a cable fault detector to verify a cable wire map.
4. Use a wire gauge to size different conductors.
5. Conduct an Internet search for network adapter PCI cards and see the variety available based on speed, cable type, and media such as copper core cable, fiber-optic cable, and wireless (radio signals).

Interesting Web Sites for More Information

www.belden.com
www.belden.com/03Products/03_CableBasics.cfm
www.blackbox.com
www.lanshack.com
www.techfest.com/index.htm

The IEEE Standards Association develops standards for the networking and communications industry. You will encounter many IEEE standards in your study of networking fundamentals. To learn more about the IEEE Standards Association, visit www.IEEE.org.

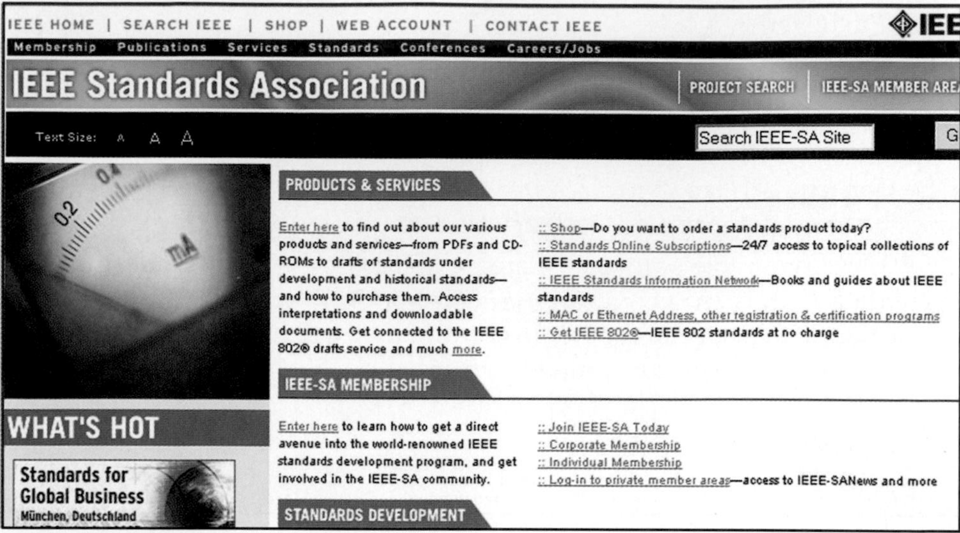

Chapter 2
Laboratory Activity

Making a Cat 6 Straight-Through Patch Cable

After completing this laboratory activity, you will be able to:

- Construct a Category 6 or Category 6e patch cable following the 568A or 568B standards.
- Explain the difference between the 568A and 568B wiring standard.
- Test a patch cable.

Introduction

In this laboratory activity, you will make a Category 6 or Category 6e straight-through patch cable. The following illustration shows the basic parts associated with a Category 6 connector: the boot, RJ-45 connector (8P8C), and load bar.

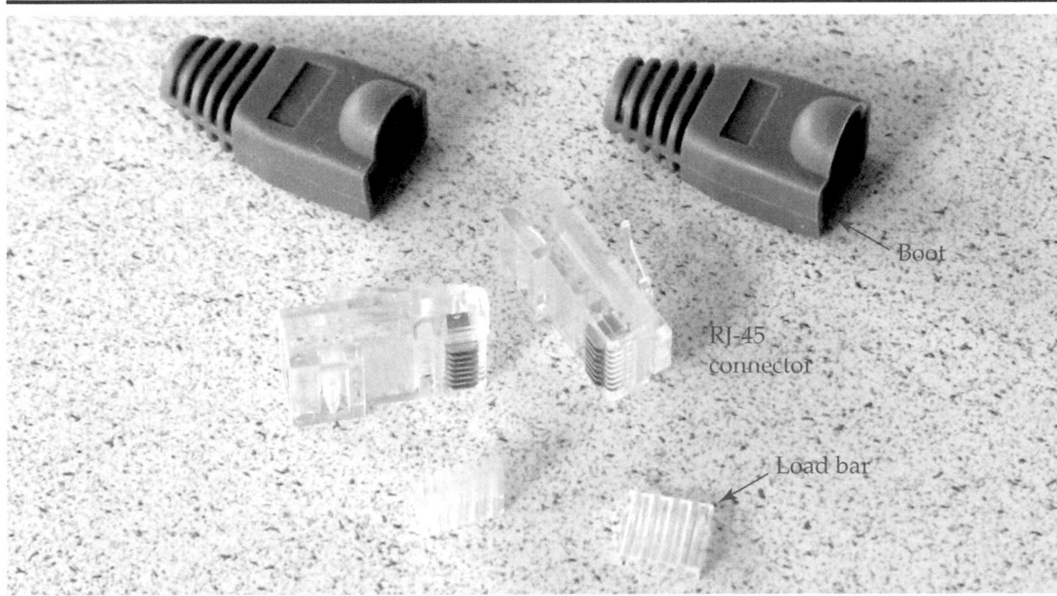

Note
Category 6 and Category 6e typically use the same type of RJ-45 connector. Category 6a connectors, however, are not the same as Category 6 or Cat6e connectors and are generally not compatible. Check with the cable connector manufacturer's Web site for more information about compatibility issues.

Not all Category 6 connector manufacturers use a load bar. A load bar helps arrange the conductors in their proper color sequence prior to insertion into the RJ-45 connector body. Category 6 cable uses a plastic spine to improve cable pair data-rate performance. The cable spine is a major design improvement over Category 5 and Category 5e cable. The plastic spine adds further separation distance between conductor pairs, thus allowing for high frequencies to be carried by each set of cable pairs. Notice the plastic spine located in the center of the cable in the following illustration.

You will use the following 568A and 568B color code illustration to assist you

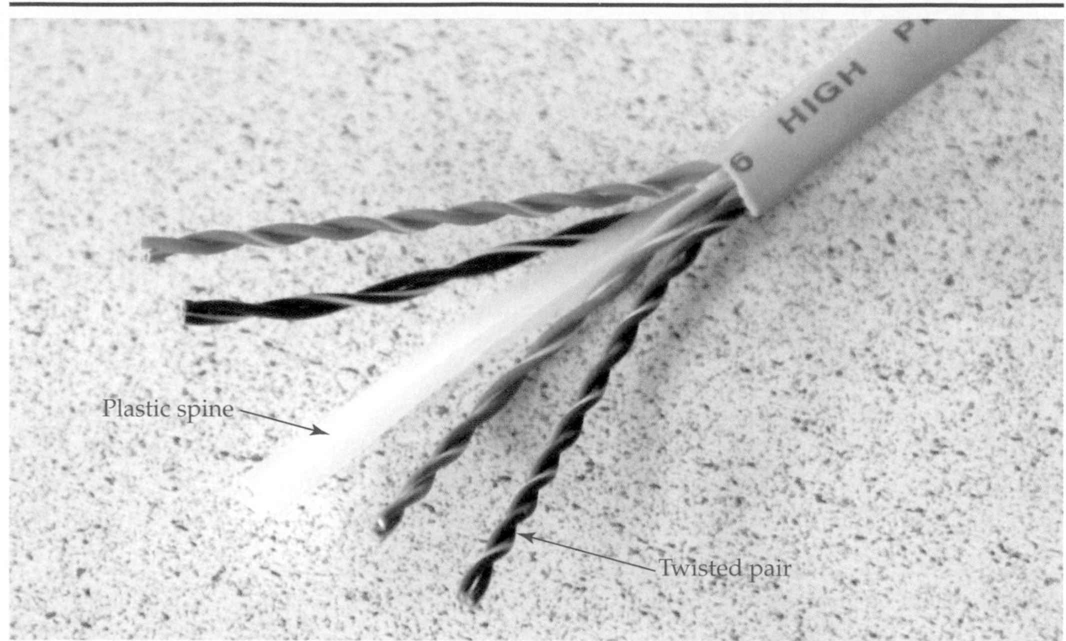

in the lab activity. Notice that the main difference between the 568A and 568B standard is the position of the orange and green pairs. The blue and brown pairs remain in the same locations. If you use the 568A color standard on one end and the 568B standard on the opposite end, you will create a crossover cable rather than a straight-through cable.

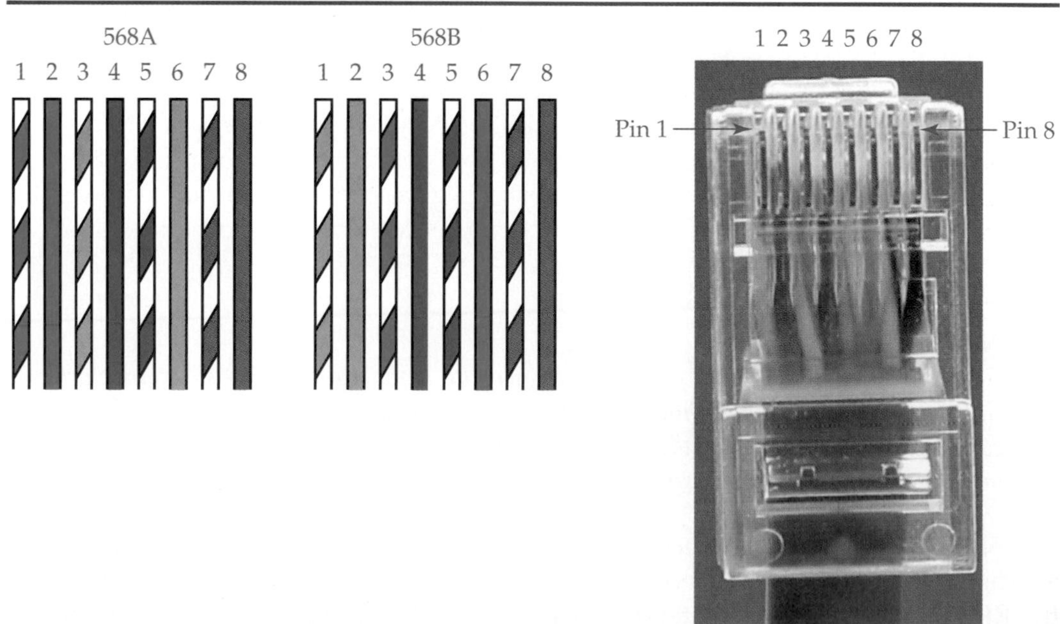

The two standards produce equal performance, and there is no real difference other than the color code. Most cable testers come with a copy of the 568A and 568B standard printed on the tester. Look at the following illustration of a cable tester.

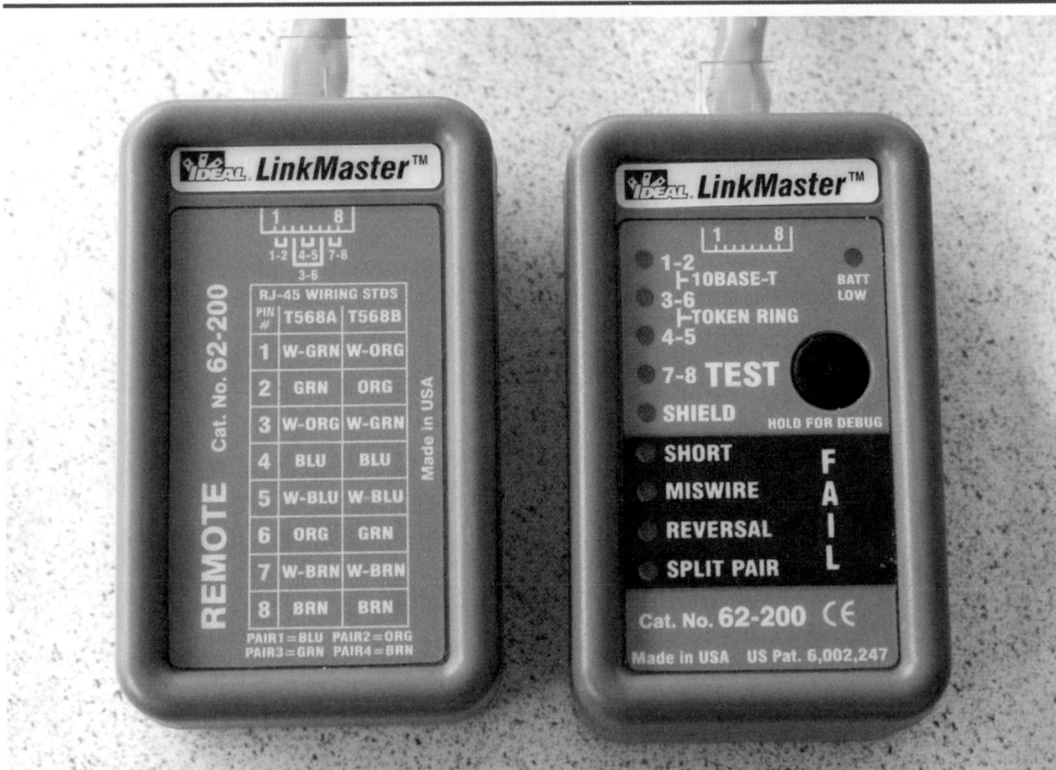

The cable tester you use in the lab activity will not necessarily match the one in the illustration, but it will be similar in design. You simply plug each end of the finished cable into the two cable tester modules and then press the "TEST" button. Faults will be indicated by a light.

Early 10BaseT and 100BaseTX cables only used two of the four pairs of conductors to transmit and receive. The two pairs corresponded with cable pins 1, 2, 3, and 6. High-speed cable, such as for 1000BaseT, still follow the 568A and 568B wire map but use all four pairs of conductors.

Stranded wire is preferred for patch cables because the cable needs to be flexible. Solid wire is flexible, but it tends to break at the connector if flexed excessively. Solid wire is typically used for horizontal runs. Horizontal runs are the network cable runs inside building walls. Because the horizontal run is installed inside building walls, the cable is not required to be as flexible as stranded wire.

Equipment and Materials

- Category 6 crimping tool.
- Cable cutter. (May be part of the cable crimping tool.)
- UTP cable jacket stripper. (May be part of the cable crimping tool.)
- Two Category 6 RJ-45 connectors, load bars, and boots.
- Length of Category 6 or Category 6e cable as indicated by your instructor.
- Cable tester.

- The following information provided by your instructor recorded on a separate sheet of paper:

  Cable length: ______________________________

  Cable color code (568A or 568B) to follow: ______________________

Procedure

1. _____ After gathering all required materials, report to your assigned workstation.
2. _____ Cut the cable to the desired length as indicated by your instructor. If you plan to use a cable boot to protect the finished connector, install the cable boot now. (You will need one boot for each end of the cable.)

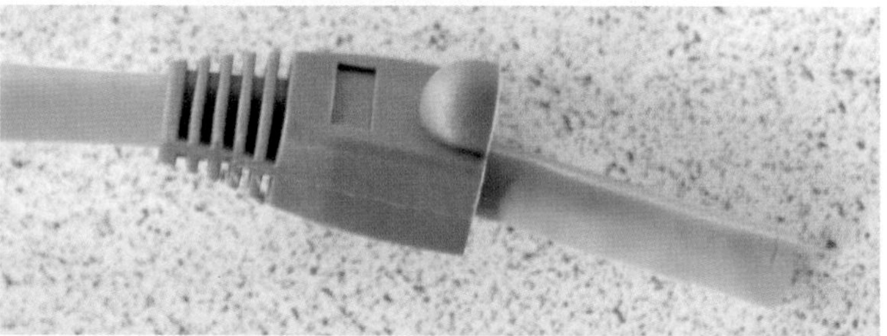

3. _____ Remove approximately 1 1/2″ to 2″ of cable insulating jacket.
4. _____ Separate the cable pairs. Bend the end of each pair to a 90° angle to help the conductor pair untwist easily.
5. _____ Bend the conductors out of the way and cut off the cable center spine as close as possible to the end of the insulating jacket.

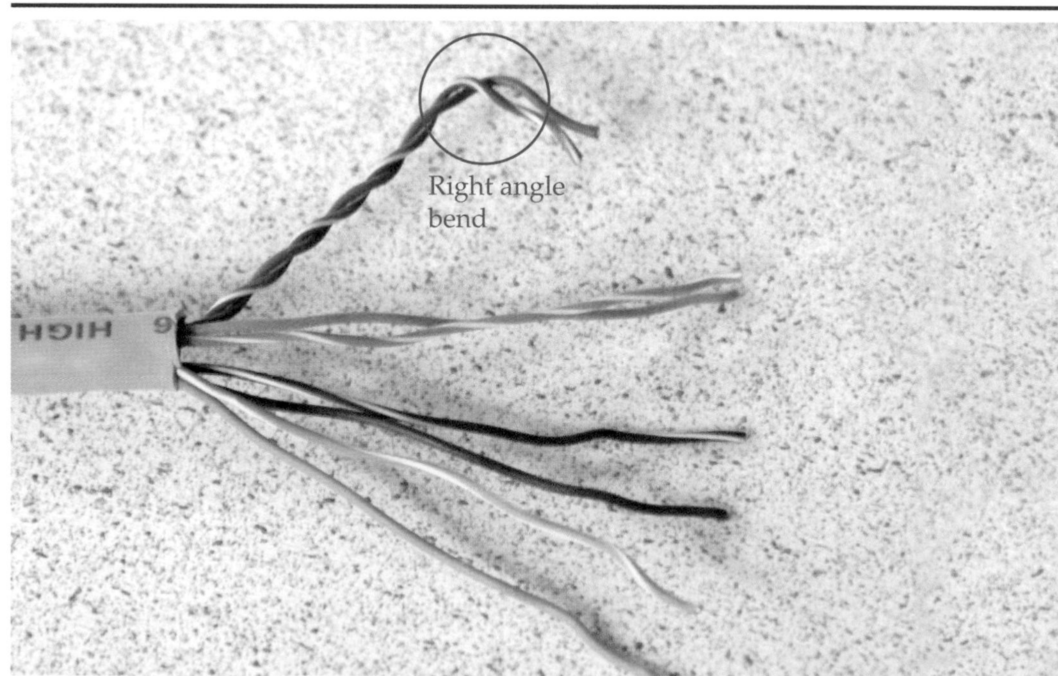

6. ______ Arrange individual conductors into the color order (568A or 568B) indicated by your instructor. Keep the conductors as straight as possible.

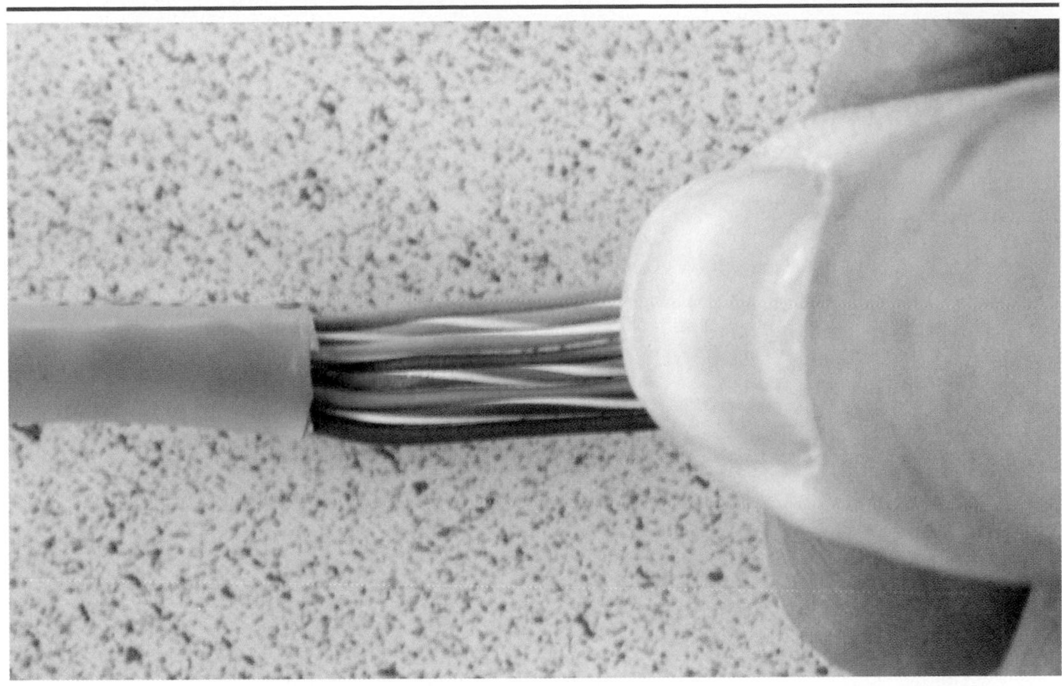

7. ______ If using a load bar, cut the conductors at slight angle. Cutting the conductors at an angle will make it easier to insert the conductors into the load bar. If using an RJ-45 without a load bar, cut the conductors at a right angle.

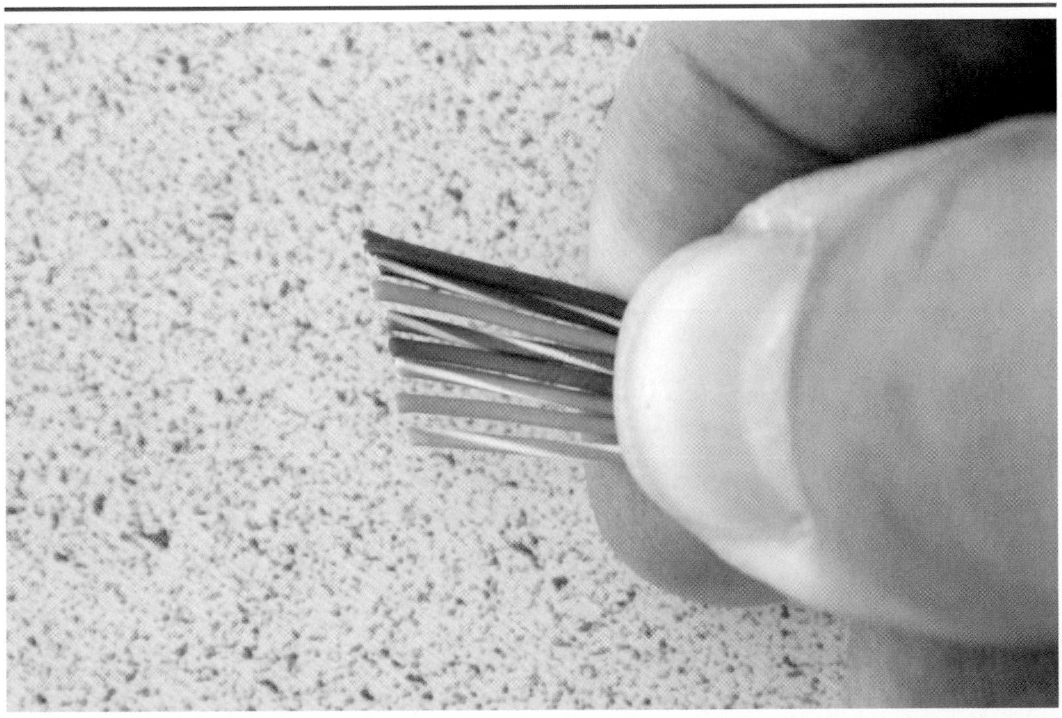

8. ______ If using a load bar, insert the conductors into the load bar and then slide the load bar down as close as possible to the cable jacket end.

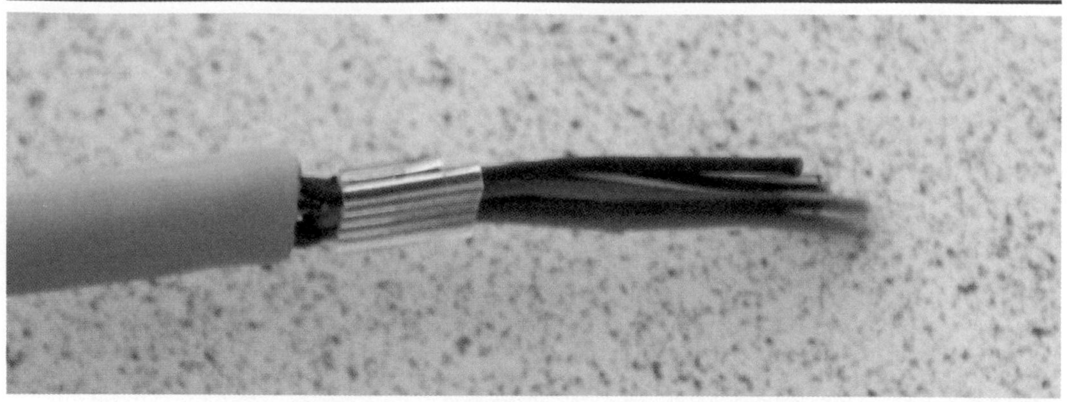

9. ______ Check the color code arrangement one more time.

10. ______ If using a load bar, cut the conductors off at approximately 1/4″ past the load bar.

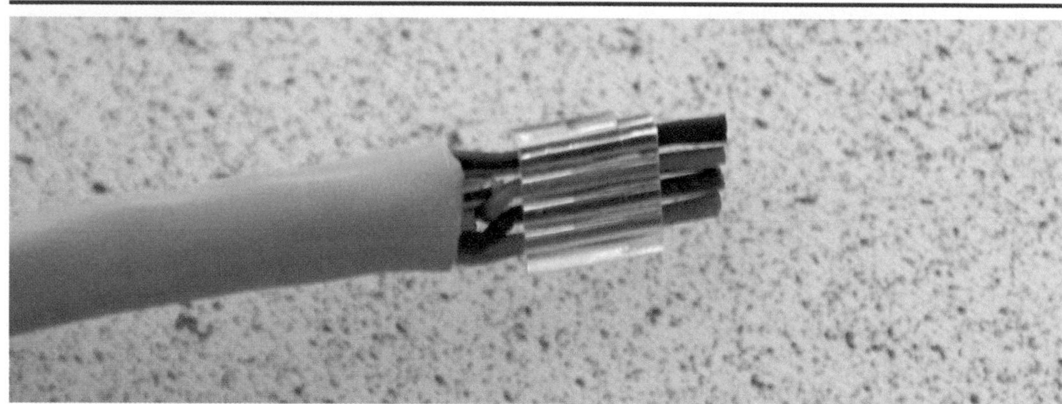

11. ______ Insert the conductors and load bar into the RJ-45 connector. Do *not* leave conductors exposed before the connector, as this may result in crosstalk.

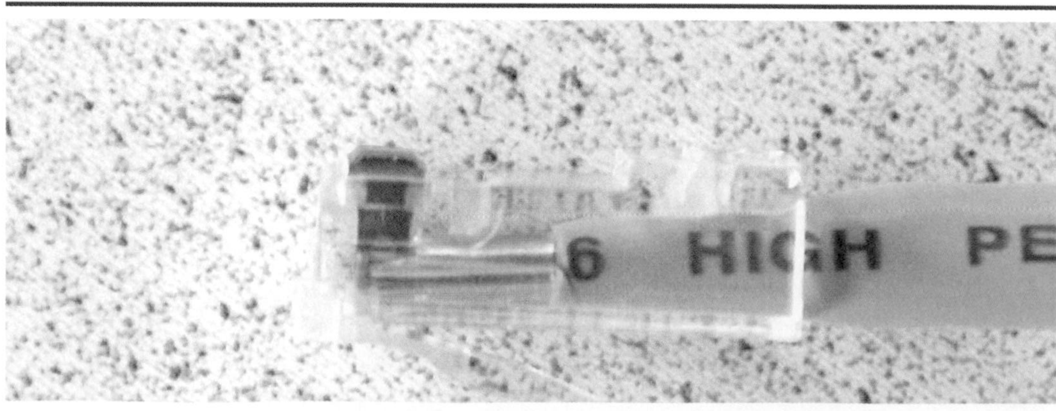

12. _____ Crimp the RJ-45 connector by squeezing the handles of the crimper firmly.

13. _____ Have your instructor inspect the connector before sliding the boot down.
14. _____ Repeat the installation operation for the other end of the cable.
15. _____ Use the cable tester to ensure the cable has been properly made. Demonstrate the results using the cable tester for your instructor. Simply plug both ends into the tester and then press the "Test" button. The LEDs will indicate the condition of the cable.
16. _____ Clean your workstation and return all tools and supplies to the proper storage area.

Review Questions

Answer the following questions on a separate sheet of paper. Please do not write in this book.

1. What physical feature improves the performance of Category 6 cable when compared with Category 5 cable?
2. What is the purpose of a load bar?
3. What is the difference between the 568A and 568B color code?
4. What will happen if you make one end of a patch cable according to the 568A standard and the opposite end according to the 568B standard?
5. What cable fault may occur if conductors are exposed before the connector?

6. How many pairs of conductors are used to communicate on a 10BaseT or 100BaseT network?
7. How many pairs of conductors are used to communicate on a 1000BaseT network?
8. Why is stranded core cable preferred for patch cables?
9. What is a horizontal run?
10. What type of copper conductor (solid or stranded) is typically used for horizontal runs?

3 Fiber-Optic Cable

After studying this chapter, you will be able to:

- ❑ Explain how fiber-optic cable is used to transmit data.
- ❑ Summarize the advantages of fiber-optic cable compared with copper core cable.
- ❑ Explain the properties of light.
- ❑ Compare multimode and single-mode fiber-optic cable.
- ❑ Recall the characteristics and specifications of the IEEE 802.3 fiber-optic standards.
- ❑ Recall the characteristics and specifications of the FDDI standard.
- ❑ Give examples of the problems associated with fiber-optic cable splices.
- ❑ Identify common fiber-optic cable test instruments and summarize how they are used.

Network+ Exam—Key Points

To prepare for the Network+ Certification exam, you must be able to do the following:

- ■ List the advantages of fiber-optic cable.
- ■ Identify the characteristics of fiber-optic cable.
- ■ Know the differences between single-mode and multimode fiber-optic cable.
- ■ Identify transmission-related issues.
- ■ Identify the main features of the FDDI and 802.3 fiber-optic standards, such as the type of cable and connectors used, speed, topology, and cable lengths.
- ■ Recognize SC, ST, FC, LC, and MTRJ connectors.

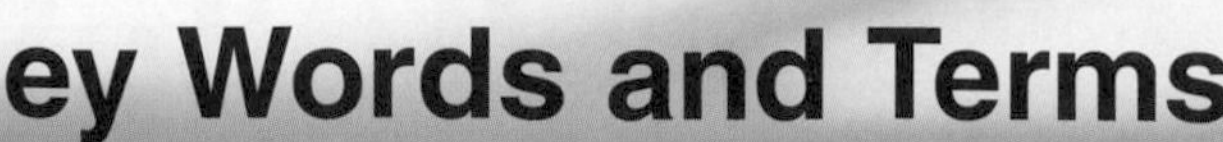

Key Words and Terms

The following words and terms will become important pieces of your networking vocabulary. Be sure you can define them.

dispersion
electromagnetic wave
extrinsic losses
Fiber Distributed Data Interface (FDDI)
Fresnel reflection loss
fusion splice
graded-index multimode fiber-optic cable
multimode fiber-optic cable
Optical Time Domain Reflectometer (OTDR)
scattering
single-mode fiber-optic cable
step-index multimode fiber-optic cable
wavelength

Fiber-optic cable supports transmission rates over 1 Gbps. It is primarily used for network backbones and long-distance runs. Soon it may be economical and common to install fiber-optic cable directly to the PC. Fiber-optic cable has many advantages over copper core cable and follows a different set of network standards such as FDDI and 802.3. This chapter explores the advantages of fiber-optic cable and its construction. It also covers the nature of light, transmission characteristics, the FDDI and 802.3 standards, and cable faults and testing.

Characteristics of Fiber-Optic Cable

Fiber-optic cable consists of a glass or plastic core that carries pulses of light. The pulses of light represent binary data. Look at **Figure 3-1.** A transmitter is located at the source and a receiver is located at the destination. The transmitter and receiver are connected by fiber-optic cable. The transmitter at the source converts the binary data represented by electrical, digital pulses into light pulses. A pulse of light represents a binary one and an absence of light represents a binary zero. The light pulses travel the fiber-optic cable to the receiver at the destination. The receiver converts the light pulses back into an electrical signal consisting of a series of digital pulses.

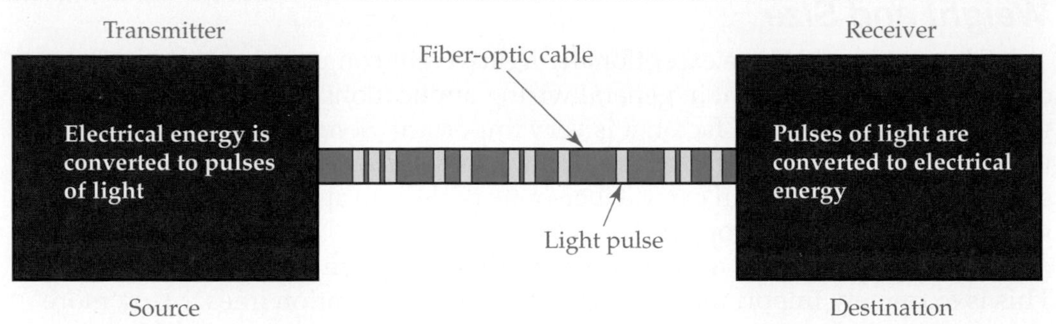

Figure 3-1. Electrical energy representing digital signals are transferred from the source to the destination. The transmitter converts electrical digital signals to light pulses representing digital data. The light pulses are converted to digital signals at the receiver.

It may seem like a lot of extra work to convert digital signals into light signals and then back to digital signals. One might question why it would not be more efficient to use copper core cable. There are several reasons fiber-optic cable might be chosen over copper core cable. These reasons are related to the following beneficial attributes of fiber-optic cable:

- Provides for data security.
- Immune to electromagnetic interference.
- Lightweight and small in diameter.
- Safety.
- Wide bandwidth.
- Corrosion- and water-resistant.
- Supports data transmission over longer distances than copper core cable.

Security

Information has become a profitable and, in some cases, a priceless commodity. In business, industry, and military applications, it is important to protect this information from unethical people who would seek to gain from using it. Fiber-optic cable is virtually impossible to tap into without being detected. Any cut made to the fiber-optic core disturbs the light signal and thus data transmission. Removing the protective material around the fiber-optic core causes signal loss. Fiber-optic cable is far more secure than copper core cable.

Immunity to Electromagnetic Interference

Fiber-optic cable conducts light waves instead of electrical energy, which makes it immune to electromagnetic interference generated by motors, radio signals, lighting, and other sources of electromagnetic energy. Conventional copper core cable must be shielded to prevent electromagnetic interference. Shielding cable causes cable to be large in diameter and heavy.

The military began research in fiber optics many years ago. Nuclear weapons create a powerful electromagnetic field, which destroys communication systems that consist of copper core cable. The destruction caused by an electromagnetic field could occur many miles from an actual nuclear explosion. Since fiber-optic cable is not affected by electromagnetic fields, military communications that use fiber-optic cable could remain intact.

Weight and Size

Fiber-optic cables are exceptionally lightweight compared with copper core cable. This is unimportant in general wiring applications, but for applications where weight is a critical factor, it is very important. Some of the applications in which weight is a critical factor are aircrafts and ships. The lighter the aircraft or ship, the more cargo it can carry. Fiber-optic cables are approximately 1/10th the weight of a comparable copper core cable.

Fiber-optic cable has a smaller overall diameter than copper core cable. This is extremely important when installing communication lines. Many more communication lines can be provided in the same conduit using fiber-optic cable rather than copper core cable. In a telephone communications system, over 1000 fiber-optic cables can easily fit in the same space as 100 copper core cables.

Safety

Fiber-optic cables are typically installed near explosive vapors and dust, such as in a petroleum factory or food processing plant. Using fiber-optic cable eliminates the possibility of an electrical spark causing an explosion due to a shorted or grounded circuit. In addition, light for illumination can be directly transmitted through fiber-optic cables in place of conventional lamps. When using electrical lamps for illumination in hazardous industries, the lamp fixtures must be the explosion-resistant type. Fiber-optic lamps are safer and less expensive.

Bandwidth

Fiber-optic cable has a greater bandwidth than copper core cable. Light can be transmitted at a much higher frequency through glass core than electronic digital signals through copper core cable. Copper wire suffers from data rate limitations caused by impedance. Fiber optic is not affected by impedance characteristics. Since a higher signal frequency can be used, more data can be transmitted through fiber-optic cable per second than copper core cable. Copper core cable has limitations and losses due to inductive reactance. Copper core cables lose their conduction capabilities at extremely high frequencies. Fiber-optic cable can handle high frequencies with little to no problem.

Corrosion and Water Resistance

The very nature of glass or plastic makes it resistant to most corrosives. Water does not affect the light conduction capabilities of a properly-installed fiber-optic system. The fiber-optic cables that have been installed under the world's oceans are expected to last for many, many years.

Greater Distances

Fiber-optic cable can support data transmission over greater distances than copper core cable. Copper core cable used for network systems is typically limited to 100 meters, but fiber-optic cable can be used for long-distance applications spanning 20 kilometers or more. Fiber-optic cable is typically used for network backbones of 2000 meters and 3000 meters in a single segment length. For certain applications such as FDDI, distances of 200 kilometers or approximately 124 miles can be supported.

The exact maximum distance for fiber-optic cable applications depends on many different factors such as the type of fiber-optic cable (multimode or single-mode), the official standard being applied (IEEE, ISO, or EIA/TIA), and manufacturer specifications.

The Nature of Light

Light is a form of energy closely related to electrical energy. While much is known about light, there are still many unanswered questions. One such question is what exactly is light energy? It has been debated whether it is a wave or a particle. For this reason, two main theories exist. The dominant theory, however, is that light is a wave. For the purpose of this textbook, the wave theory will be used to explain the nature of light.

Light is classified as electromagnetic energy and is identified in the electromagnetic wave spectrum chart along with radio waves, X-rays, and Gamma rays, **Figure 3-2.** An ***electromagnetic wave*** is a form of energy that behaves like a wave and can travel through a vacuum. It needs no other media for support. For example, sound is an energy that travels as a wave, but it must be carried by a gas (air), liquid (water), or solid (steel). Sound cannot travel through a vacuum like radio waves, X-rays, and light waves can. Hence, sound is not a form of electromagnetic energy.

electromagnetic wave
a form of energy that behaves like a wave and can travel through a vacuum.

In Chapter 2, Network Media—Copper Core Cable, electrical energy wave patterns were described using the term *frequency*. Remember, frequency is based on the number of complete cycles of an electrical wave that occur in one second. Light energy can also be described using the term *frequency*, but the preferred term is *wavelength*. ***Wavelength,*** in relation to light waves, is the distance of one complete cycle and is measured in meters. For example, visible light is composed of wavelengths between 390 nanometers and 770 nanometers. A nanometer is one billionth of a meter. The nanometer is used to measure the distance of the repeating light wave pattern or the distance of one complete light wave cycle.

wavelength
the total distance an electromagnetic or light wave travels during one full cycle.

The term *wavelength* originated from the field of physics. Many of the terms first introduced in physics have been directly adopted and used to describe the phenomena of fiber-optic cable. It is interesting to note that early on the term *wavelength* was used to describe the fluctuating patterns of radio waves and is still used in the design of antenna systems.

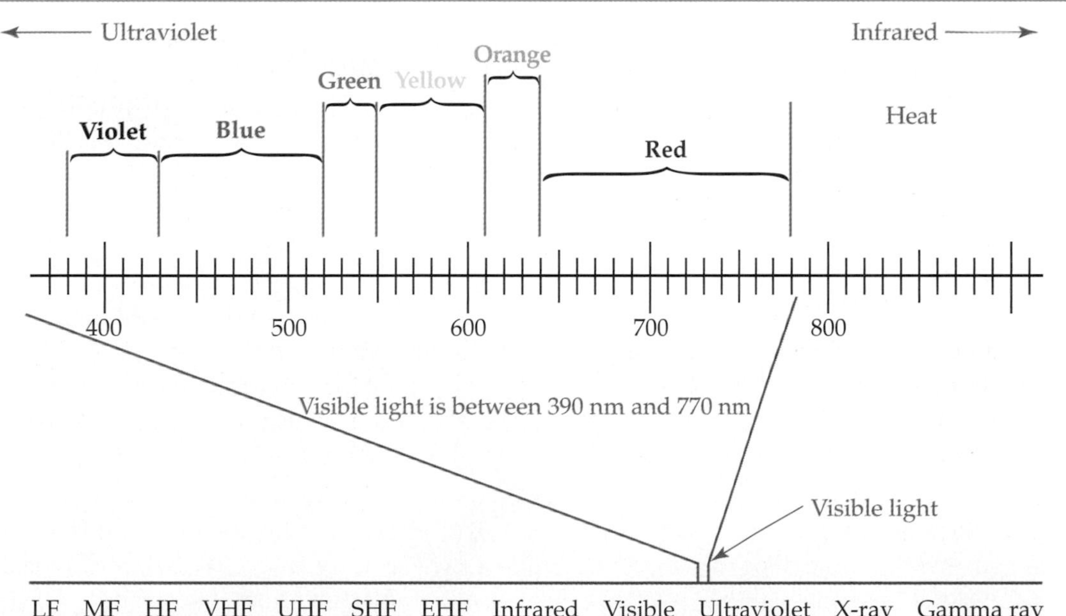

Figure 3-2. Visible light is only a small part of the total electromagnetic wave spectrum.

The three common wavelengths for fiber-optic communications are 850 nanometers, 1300 nanometers, and 1550 nanometers. Fiber-optic devices and cable, such as transmitters, receivers, and fiber-optic core diameters, are selected according to wavelength of the signal used. For example, a device such as a transmitter generates light at a specific wavelength. This requires that the receiver and fiber-optic core match the same wavelength to achieve the best performance.

Look again at Figure 3-2. Notice that the wavelength of visible light is between 390 nanometers and 770 nanometers. Below visible light are larger wavelengths, such as UHF and VHF television waves and radar waves. Above visible light are much shorter wavelengths, such as X-rays, Gamma rays, and cosmic rays. The actual spectrum of visible light is quite small compared with all other forms of electromagnetic wavelengths.

Most fiber-optic systems use infrared wavelengths between 850 nanometers to 1550 nanometers. At these wavelengths, there is less signal loss. A typical LED has a wavelength that is between 800 nanometers and 900 nanometers or 1250 nanometers and 1350 nanometers.

Fiber-Optic Cable Construction

Fiber-optic cable is composed of a glass or plastic core surrounded by a cladding. See **Figure 3-3.** The glass or plastic core is the medium for transferring light waves. The cladding surrounds the core and causes the transmitted light to remain in the core. Without the cladding on the core, the light would be lost through the sides of the core material. A buffer area surrounds the cladding and core. The buffer is wrapped

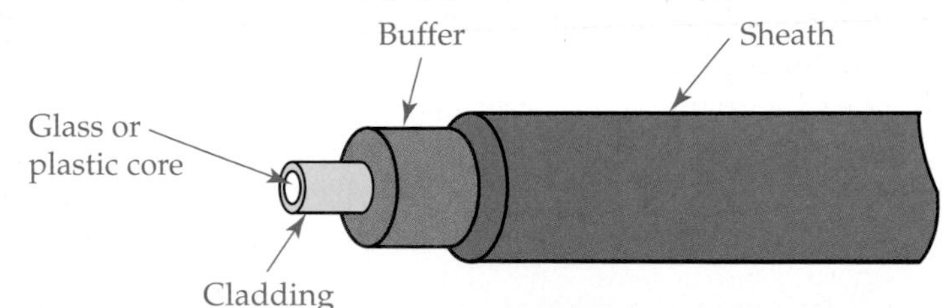

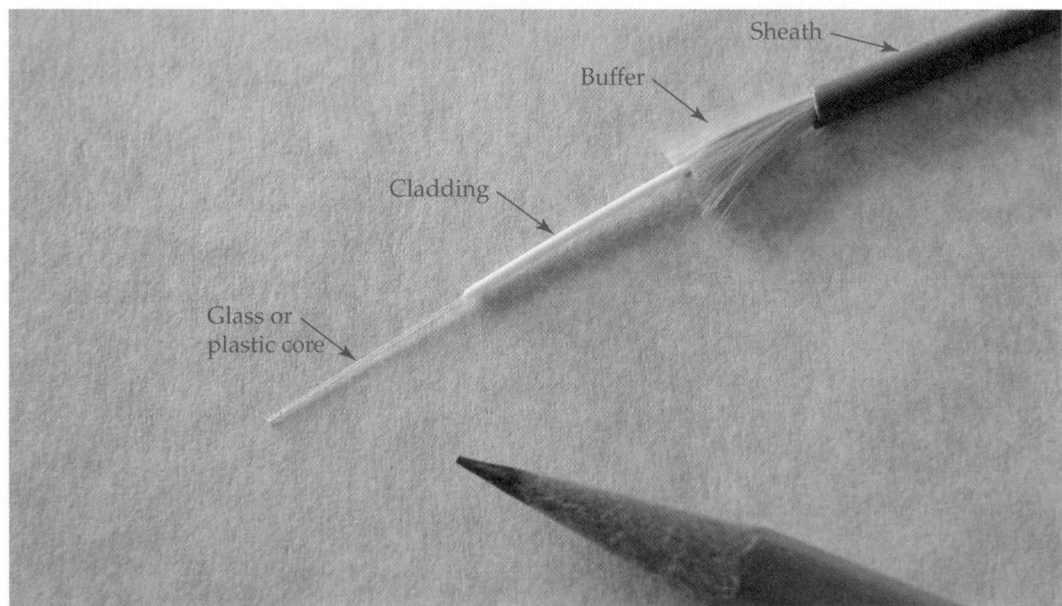

Figure 3-3. A typical fiber-optic cable is constructed of a glass or plastic core surrounded by cladding, a buffer, and a sheath. The buffer provides strength for pulling the cable and serves as a soft padding to protect the core and cladding. The sheath protects the cable from physical elements.

around the core and cladding to provide physical protection. In addition to the buffer area, waterproofing materials are sometimes inserted under the cable sheath. The sheath is similar to the insulating jacket on copper core conductors. Its composition depends on the environment in which the fiber-optic cable will be installed. Some sheaths are designed to be oil- or water-resistant. Others may be installed in saltwater or buried directly in the earth. Some may be installed in a building plenum area. The size of fiber-optic cable is expressed in micromils (μm).

Fiber-optic cable is generally classified as either loose tube or tight buffer. Loose tube is fiber-optic cable in which the core or cores are loosely fitted inside the sheath. The sheath is typically filled with gel to protect the core(s). The core or cores are free to move inside the jacket. Loose tube is typically used for long cable runs where pulling the cable into conduit could result in breaking the core(s). Tight buffer fiber-optic cable has a sheath that is tightly bound to the core(s). This produces a smaller overall diameter of the cable assembly. The selection of cable type is left to the designer or installer.

When fiber-optic cable is installed in a plenum area, the installation usually falls under the jurisdiction of the National Electrical Code (NEC). The NEC is referred to for building specifications or standards. The standards describe minimal requirements for installing cables and conduits. Many electrical contractors are responsible for installing all of a building's cables, including data cables. Electrical contractors and building codes refer to the NEC as a guide.

The NEC has strict regulations about the composition of the sheath of fiber-optic cables installed in a plenum area. Fumes produced by this covering in a fire may be dangerous to people in the building. In many buildings, the plenum area also contains the air-conditioning system. Fumes and vapors present in the plenum area could be harmful to personnel throughout the building.

Two broad classifications of fiber-optic cable commonly used are single-mode and multimode. To understand the characteristics of these fiber-optic cable classifications, you must first be familiar with the characteristics of fiber-optic transmission.

Fiber-Optic Cable Transmission Characteristics

Since fiber-optic cable carries light and not electrical energy, a new set of terms is needed to describe the characteristics of light carried over fiber-optic cable. While some of the terms might be familiar from the last chapter, some new terminology that is unique to light is introduced. The first characteristic presented is attenuation. Attenuation was discussed and related to copper core media in the previous chapter. The causes for the loss of an electrical signal over copper core cable, however, are different than for the loss of a light signal over fiber-optic cable. The major causes of attenuation in fiber-optic cable can be characterized as scattering, dispersion, extrinsic losses (bends, splices, and connectors), and Fresnel reflection loss.

Attenuation

In Chapter 2, Network Media—Copper Core Cable, you learned that the loss in transmission of signal power from one end of the cable to the other is called *attenuation*. Attenuation is expressed in decibels (dB), or decibels per kilometer (dB/km). The decibel is a relative measurement for signal strength. It is patterned after our sense of hearing.

Decibel measurement is nonlinear. It does not move in gradual increments, as does an analog speed gauge in an automobile. Look at the table in **Figure 3-4A** and compare the dB rating of 1, 3, 10, 20, and 50 to the power remaining and power loss values. Notice that a 50% power loss is represented by 3 dB. When the dB is doubled to 6, the power loss is only 75%, not the expected 100%. On close examination of the table, you will see that the relationship between power loss and dB is nonlinear. When decibel ratings are plotted as a chart, the result is a curve, not a straight line, **Figure 3-4B.**

The most common use of the decibel chart in fiber-optic cable specifications is to express the attenuation over a given distance. Each cable manufacturer has a slightly different decibel rating of loss for its fiber-optic core. The variation is caused by the amount of impurities left in the core after the refining and manufacturing process is complete. Engineers use these decibel ratings to calculate the expected attenuation of an installation. For example, the engineering staff of many communications carriers calculate the loss of light over a given distance when running fiber-optic cable in long-haul installations. A long-haul installation is the installation of fiber-optic cable between two end points that are many miles apart. It is not unusual for a long-haul installation to span more than 40 miles. Long-distance telephone carriers are a prime example.

Scattering

scattering
the loss of signal strength due to impurities in the core material.

Scattering is the loss of signal strength due to impurities in the core material. No core material can be made 100% pure. A microscopic amount of impurities will always remain. These impurities cause the light to scatter, **Figure 3-5.** The total amount of impurities along the length of the cable is cumulative—the longer the cable, the greater the signal loss.

Glass core is a better transmitter of light than plastic, but it is more expensive. To reduce attenuation, glass cores are used on very long runs of fiber-optic cable.

Dispersion

dispersion
the distortion of the light wave pattern as it reflects off the core cladding.

Dispersion is the distortion of the light wave pattern as it reflects off the core cladding. Dispersion is the main factor that limits the maximum length of a fiber-optic cable used as communications media.

Light beams transmitted through fiber-optic cable do not travel in a straight line. This causes the light to reflect off the cladding. Look at **Figure 3-6.** Due to dispersion, digital light pulses transmitted into one end of a fiber-optic cable reach the opposite end of the cable at different times. This factor causes the light pulse to be distorted in shape. The light pulse appears flattened and elongated. A receiver can quickly reshape the signal into a square. On a short run of fiber-optic cable there is no real problem with dispersion, but on a long run, not all of the light arrives at the end of the cable at the same time. The slight variation in time can be critical at high-frequency transmission rates.

extrinsic losses
signal losses caused by physical factors outside the normal core, such as splices, connectors, and bends in the fiber core.

Extrinsic Losses

Extrinsic losses are caused by physical factors outside the normal core. Physical factors can be splices, connectors, and bends in the fiber core. Splices in fiber-optic cable need special attention. Splices, couplings, and connectors are the main reasons for signal loss in normal runs of fiber-optic cable. Splices and connectors are covered in detail later in this chapter. Fiber-optic cables also have a minimum bend radius. Exceeding this radius causes attenuation.

Fresnel Reflection Loss

Fresnel reflection loss
a type of signal loss that commonly occurs at connection points in fiber-optic cabling and is due to refraction property differences in the core material, the connector materials used for sealing the connector, and air.

Fresnel reflection loss commonly occurs at connection points in fiber-optic cabling. It is typically due to the refraction property differences in the core

dB	Power Remaining in Percent	Power Loss in Percent	Fraction of Power
1	79	21	
2	63	37	
3	50	50	1/2 power
4	40	60	
5	32	68	
6	25	75	1/4
7	20	80	
8	16	84	
9	12	88	
10	10	90	1/10
11	8	92	
12	6.3	93.7	
13	5	95	
14	4	96	
15	3.2	96.8	
16	2.5	97.5	
17	2	98	
18	1.6	98.4	
19	1.3	98.7	
20	1	99	1/100
30	0.1	99.9	
40	0.01	99.99	
50	0.001	99.999	1/1000

A

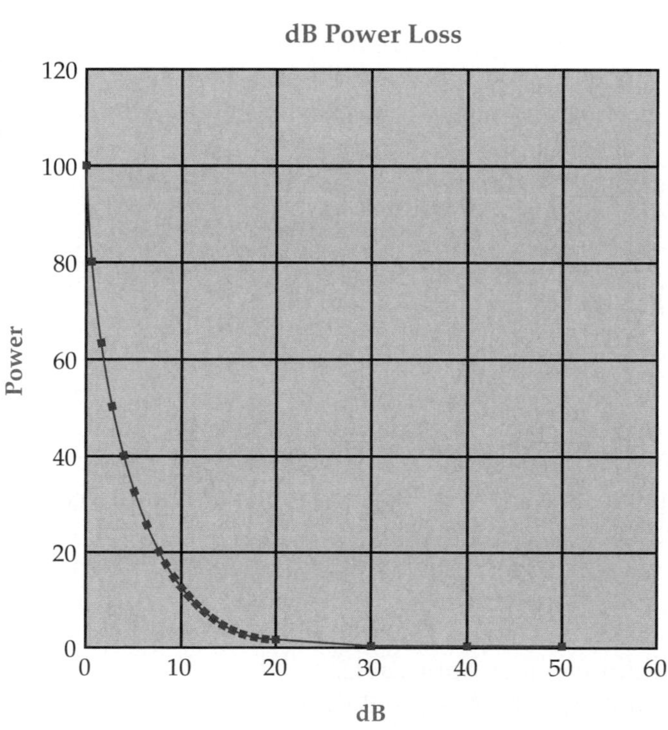

B

Figure 3-4. The common unit of measure for power loss or gain is the decibel (dB). Light, sound, and electrical energy are often expressed in decibels. The decibel is based on a complicated mathematical formula. A—Notice that a 3-dB loss equals 50% power loss, but an additional 3-dB loss results in a total loss of 75%. B—The chart plots the power in decibels against power loss. As you can plainly see, the relationship is not linear, but rather curved.

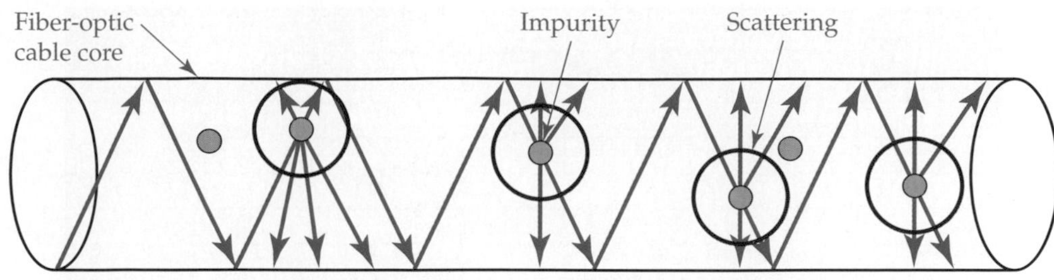

Figure 3-5. Impurities in the fiber-optic core cause the light signal to scatter and to decrease in strength.

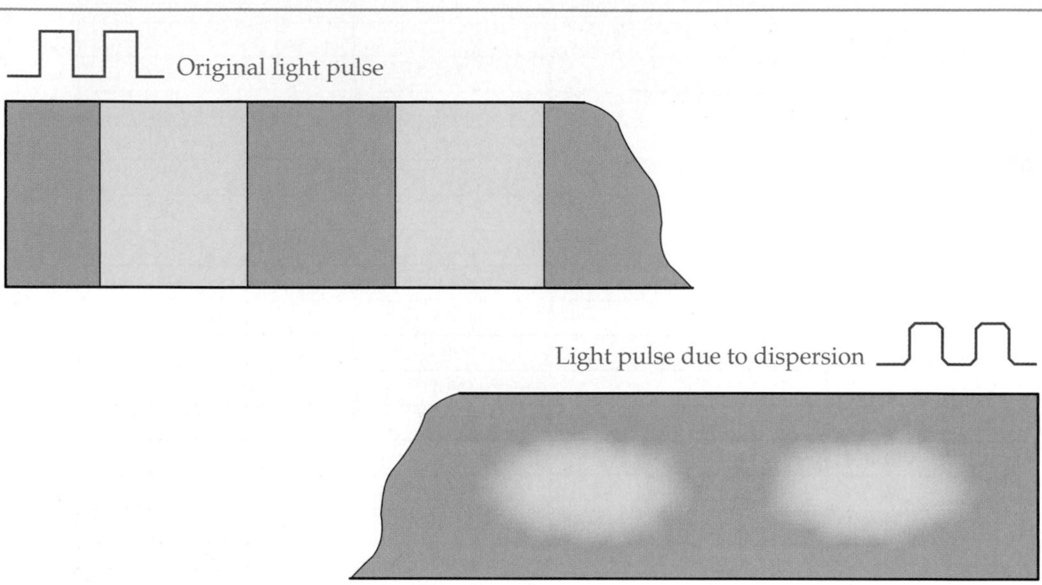

Figure 3-6. The original light pulse is a clean concentrated pulse of light. As the light pulse travels through the fiber-optic core, optical dispersion distorts the light pulse.

material, the connector materials used for sealing the connector, and air. Light waves traveling from one type of core material to another cause signal loss. All glass and plastic core materials, sealing materials, and air have different refraction indices, or properties. Using a sealing material minimizes this type of loss. The sealing material uses a refraction index closely matching the index of the glass or plastic core material. A mismatch of sealing agent to core material can cause an excessive amount of signal loss.

multimode fiber-optic cable a type of fiber-optic cable that has a large core diameter and is susceptible to attenuation due to dispersion.

single-mode fiber-optic cable a type of fiber-optic cable that has a small core diameter and limited dispersion. It can carry light farther than multimode fiber-optic cable.

Fiber-Optic Cable Specifications

The two broad classifications of fiber-optic cable based on the diameter of the core are multimode and single-mode. See **Figure 3-7.** In general, ***multimode fiber-optic cable*** has a larger core diameter than single-mode fiber-optic cable. A larger core diameter causes more light loss due to dispersion. ***Single-mode fiber-optic cable*** is much smaller in diameter than multimode cable. The diameter of single-mode fiber-optic cable is almost equal to the length of the light wave traveling through the cable. Because the core is designed to closely match the wavelength of the light wave, the light wave cannot readily disperse as it does in a large diameter core. The result is single-mode fiber-optic cable can carry light farther than multimode fiber-optic cable.

Look again at Figure 3-7. Note that the core dimensions are measured in micrometers (μm) or millionths of a meter. The size of a fiber-optic cable is expressed in two numerical values separated by a slash. For example, a fiber-optic cable

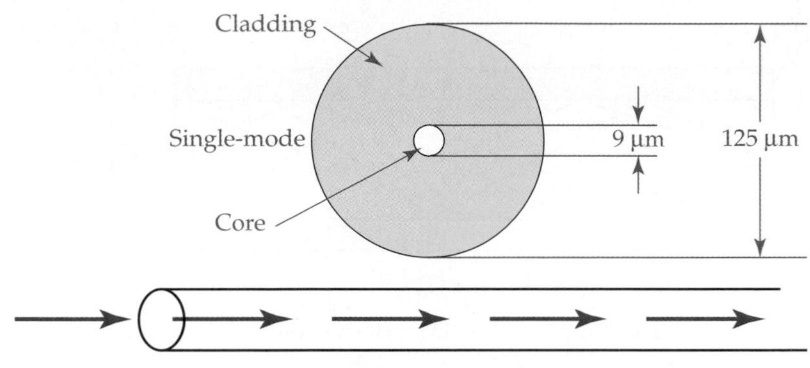

Single-mode fiber-optic cable has a small diameter and supports one light path.

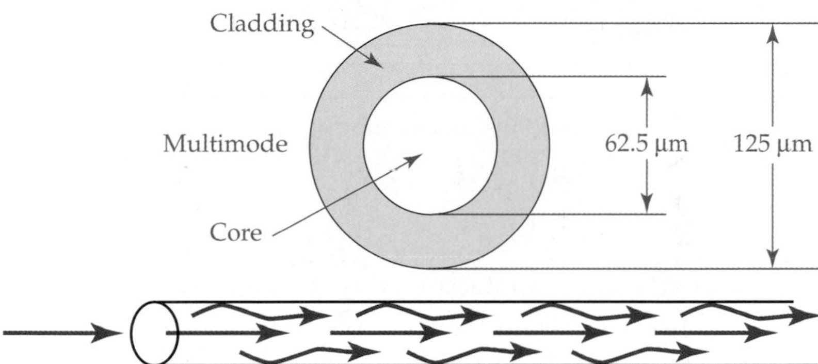

Multimode fiber-optic cable has a large diameter, causing multiple paths of light to be transmitted.

Figure 3-7. Fiber-optic cable is classified as either single-mode or multimode. Multimode fiber-optic cable has a larger core diameter than single-mode. A large-diameter core contributes to dispersion. Single-mode fiber-optic cable is much smaller in diameter and has a more restrictive light path, which results in less dispersion. Single-mode fiber-optic cable is used for long-distance applications.

identified as 65.5/125 indicates that the core diameter is equal to 65.5 micrometers, and the overall core and cladding diameter is 125 micrometers. Typical multimode core dimensions are 50/125, 62.5/125, and 100/140. However, 100/140 is an older technology and is not encountered very often. A typical single-mode core is 8.3/125.

Multimode cable is divided into two classifications: step-index and graded-index. These classifications are based on the design of the multimode cable core. ***Graded-index multimode fiber-optic cable*** is designed with a varying grade of core material. Look at **Figure 3-8.** Note that the core of the graded-index fiber-optic cable is designed with maximum light conduction at the center of the core. The ability of the core to conduct light is gradually reduced toward the cladding. This lessens the light's tendency to disperse. Less dispersion causes less signal distortion and attenuation. The ***step-index multimode fiber-optic cable*** does not counter dispersion.

graded-index multimode fiber-optic cable
a type of multimode fiber-optic cable that has a varying grade of core material. It is designed for maximum light conduction at the center of the core and gradually diminished light conduction toward the cladding.

step-index multimode fiber-optic cable
a general multimode fiber-optic cable that does not counter dispersion.

IEEE 802.3 Standards

IEEE is mainly concerned with the lower levels of the OSI model and develops standards that serve as guidelines for hardware applications. The original IEEE 802.3 Ethernet standard has evolved as the demand for higher data rates, greater distances, and new technologies are introduced. In **Figure 3-9,** you can readily see that single-mode fiber-optic cable supports much greater distances than multimode fiber-optic cable.

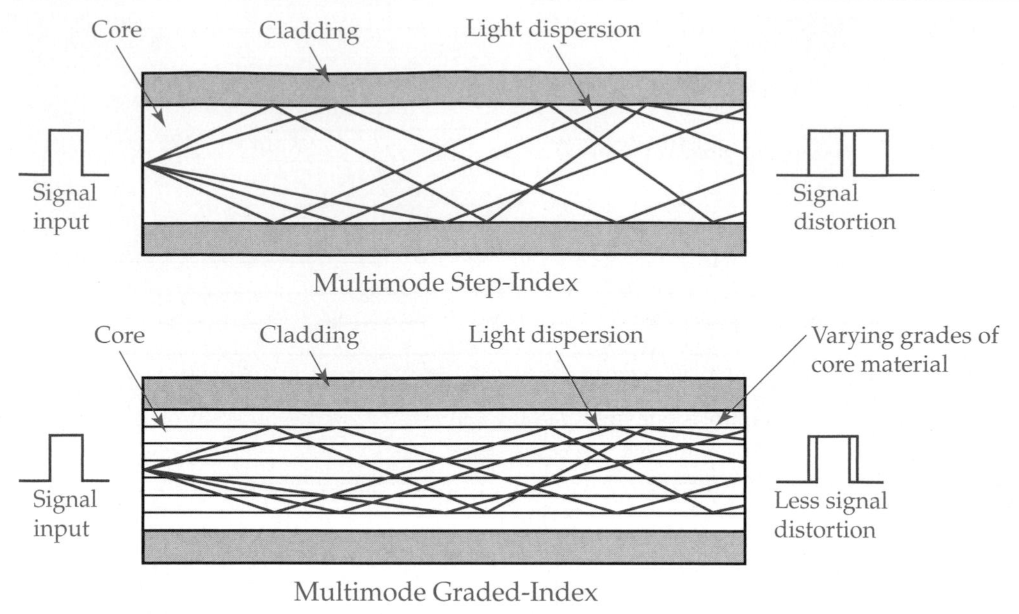

Figure 3-8. There are two types of multimode fiber-optic cable: graded-index and step-index. Graded-index multimode cable is designed with maximum light conduction in the center of the core. Conduction gradually diminishes toward the cladding, which reduces dispersion. Less light dispersion produces less digital signal distortion. No special design is applied to step-index.

At times, standards and manufacturers' tables conflict. Look at the ANSI/TIA/EIA 568-B 1 Standard table in **Figure 3-10.** You will see the recommended standard distances for network backbone distribution. This table is solely concerned with the maximum distance of backbone cabling without identifying specific IEEE cable standards. The chart simply categorizes backbone cable into one of three categories: UTP, multimode fiber-optic cable, and single-mode fiber-optic cable. The ANSI/TIA/EIA 568-B 1 standard makes no distinction for cable data rates. Data rates are specified in the IEEE standards.

Gigabit Ethernet

In the 1990s, the IEEE amended (modified) the 802.3 Ethernet standard to include Gigabit Ethernet. The amended standard is known as *IEEE 802.3z*. When an IEEE standard is modified, it is identified with a lowercase letter. Gigabit Ethernet describes the 1000BaseSX, 1000BaseLX, and 1000BaseCX classifications. Take note that 1000BaseCX is a copper core cable and not a fiber-optic cable. 1000BaseCX is limited to 25 meters and used to connect server room equipment. 1000BaseSX uses multimode fiber, and 1000BaseLX uses either single-mode or multimode fiber.

10 Gigabit Ethernet

In 2002, the IEEE amended the 802.3 Ethernet standard to include 10 Gigabit Ethernet. The amended standard is known as *IEEE 802.3ae*. The IEEE 802.ae standard only recognizes fiber-optic cables. It does not recognize copper core cables. The 802.3ae standard describes the 10GBaseSR (Short Range), 10GBaseLR (Long Range), and 10GBaseER (Extended Range) classifications. 10GBaseSR supports short distances using multimode fiber-optic cable, mainly 26 meters to 82 meters depending on the type of fiber-optic cable used. 10GBaseLR and 10GBaseER support 10 kilometers and 40 kilometers respectively. Long-distance communications use single-mode fiber-optic cable.

Standard	Single-mode (S) or Multimode (M)	Core Diameter in Microns	Wavelength in Nanometers (nm)	Cable Distance in Meters	Remarks
10BaseFL	M	62.5 50	850	2000	Early generic fiber-optic standard.
100BaseFX	M	62.5 50	1300	2000	Known as Fast Ethernet.
1000BaseSX	M	62.5 50	850	300	Known as Gigabit Ethernet.
1000BaseLX	M	62.5 50	1300	550	Known as Gigabit Ethernet.
1000BaseLX	S	9	1300	5 k	Known as Gigabit Ethernet.
10GBaseSR	M	62.5 50	850	66–300	Known as 10 Gigabit Ethernet. Distance dependent on bandwidth.
10GBaseLR	S	9	1310	10 k	Known as 10 Gigabit Ethernet.
10GBaseER	S	9	1310	40 k	Known as 10 Gigabit Ethernet.
10GBaseSW	M	50 62.5	850	300 33	Commonly used inside commercial buildings.
10GBaseLW	S	9	1310	10 k	Has a long wave-length and is used for relatively long distances.
10GBaseEW	S	9	1550	40 k	Used for "long-haul" connections.

Note: Companies may calculate greater distances based on manufacturer cable specifications and equipment requirements. Such engineering is common in long-haul communication systems such as long-distance telecommunications industries.

Figure 3-9. Fiber-optic cable classifications.

10GBaseW

10GBaseW is a collection of cable standards such as 10GBaseSW, 10GBaseLW, and 10GBaseEW. The *W* in the 10GBaseW standard represents *wide area network*. When the *W* is used in reference to a specific standard such as 10GBaseSW, the *W* represents *wavelength*. For example, 10GBaseSW represents *10 Gigabit Short Wavelength*.

10GBaseSW (Short Wavelength) can have two different core diameters: 50 micrometers and 62.5 micrometers. The 50 micrometers core diameter can support distances of up to 300 meters; while, the 62.5 micrometers core diameter can only support 33 meters. You can commonly find 10GBaseSW used in commercial building backbones and server rooms.

Figure 3-10.
The ANSI/TIA/EIA 568-B 1 standard for backbone distribution.

Media	Horizontal Cross Connect to Main Cross Connect in Meters	Horizontal Cross Connect to Intermediate Cross Connect in Meters	Main Cross Connect to Intermediate Cross Connect in Meters
UTP	800	300	500
62.5/125 and 50/125 Multimode Fiber-Optic Cable	2,000	300	1,700
Single-Mode Fiber-Optic Cable	3,000	300	2,700

Note: Single-mode fiber-optic cable can be installed to distances of 60 kilometers or greater based on engineering calculations and product manufacturers specifications.

10GBaseLW (Long Wavelength) is a single-mode fiber-optic cable capable of supporting distances of up to 10 kilometers. While this is a "long-haul" type of cable, it is being replaced by 10GBaseEW. 10GBbaseEW (Extended Wavelength) uses single-mode fiber-optic cable and is used for long-range applications. The wavelength for 10GBaseEW is 1550 nanometers; whereas, 10GBaseLW is 1350 nanometers and 10GBaseSW is 850 nanometers. 10GBaseEW is similarly used in SONET systems and supports cable length of up to 40,000 meters or approximately 25 miles.

All 10GBase fiber-optic long-distance cable are used in Synchronous Optical Network (SONET) applications. SONET technology was originally used for long-distance telephone communications, but today this technology is commonly used for long-distance network systems as well. There will be more about SONET in Chapter 14—Remote Access and Long-Distance Communications.

Network+ Note

Be sure to read any test items carefully for reference to ANSI/TIA/EIA or IEEE.

Fiber Distributed Data Interface (FDDI)
a standard developed by ANSI that employs fiber-optic cable that can reach distances as far as 40 kilometers in length and support data speeds of 100 Mbps or higher. It is used mainly as a backbone for large network systems such as a MAN or a WAN.

Fiber Distributed Data Interface (FDDI)

Fiber Distributed Data Interface (FDDI) is a standard developed by ANSI that employs fiber-optic cable over great distances. The distances can reach as far as 40 kilometers and support data speeds of 100 Mbps or higher. FDDI is used mainly as a backbone for large network systems such as a MAN or WAN.

FDDI is structured as a pair of rings, **Figure 3-11.** Two rings of fiber-optic cable connect to each node on the network system. One ring supports data flow in a clockwise rotation and the other ring supports data flow in a counterclockwise rotation.

Using FDDI guarantees continuous communication. If one ring fails, the other ring automatically takes over and provides the path for communication. One ring is considered the primary communication ring and the other the secondary communication ring. If a section fails in the primary ring, the

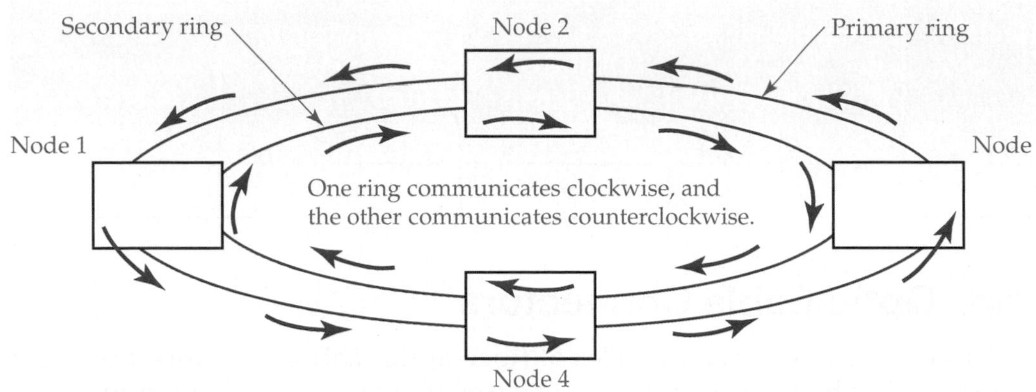

Figure 3-11. A typical FDDI system uses two fiber-optic paths to provide continuous data communication. If one ring fails, the other provides a path for communication.

secondary ring supports communication. If both the primary and secondary ring is cut or fails, the two rings join at the next node, forming a new ring and continuing communication, **Figure 3-12.**

FDDI uses a token passing method similar to IEEE 802.5. An enhanced version of FDDI called *FFDI Full Duplex Technology (FFDT)* supports speeds of 200 Mbps by allowing simultaneous communication in both directions. See **Figure 3-13** for a summary of FDDI data rates and cable lengths. FDDI can also use UTP cable.

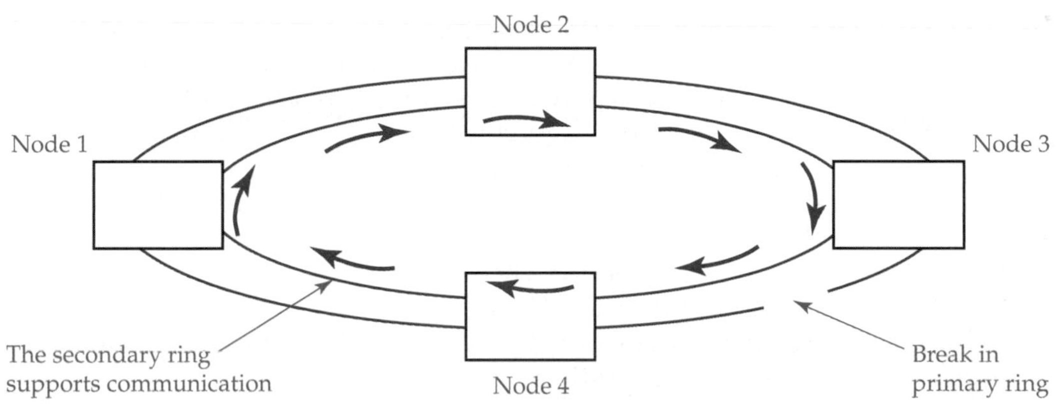

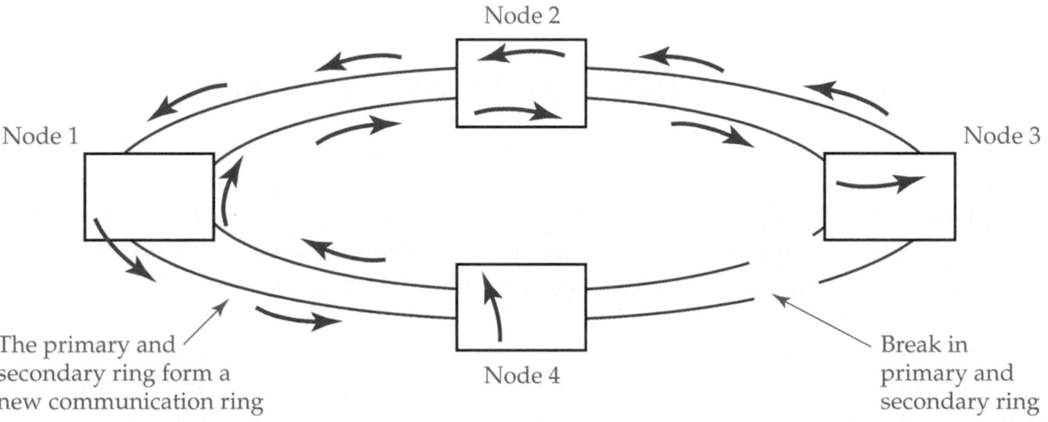

Figure 3-12. If the primary ring in an FDDI system fails, the secondary ring provides communication. When both rings break, the nodes closest to the break complete the circuit, allowing communication to continue.

Figure 3-13.
FDDI specifications.

Media	Single-Mode (S) or Multimode (M)	Core Diameter in Microns	Wavelength in Nanometers (nm)	Cable Distance in Meters
FDDI	M	62.5/125	1300	2 k
FDDI	S	9	1300	40 k

Fiber-Optic Cable Connectors

There are many different styles of fiber-optic cable connectors. Some are proprietary. It is best if you use connectors from the same manufacturer when installing a new fiber-optic network or extending an old one. The most common styles of fiber-optic cable connectors are SC, ST, FC, LC, and MTRJ.

Network+ Note

Although there are many different types of fiber-optic cable connectors, CompTIA lists only five in the Network+ Certification exam objectives: SC and ST, FC, LC, and MTRJ.

Look at the close-up of an ST and SC connector in **Figure 3-14A.** Note that the ST connector is round and uses a push and twist connection similar to the BNC. The SC connector is square and uses retaining clips to hold its position. When two SC or ST connectors are fabricated into a single unit, they are generally referred to as *duplex connectors.* A single connector is referred to as a *simplex connector.*

FC connectors are designed to provide a maximum physical connection, **Figure 3-14B.** The FC connector is designed with screw threads as part of the physical design. They are very similar in design to coaxial style screw on connectors.

The LC connector is a relatively new style developed by Lucent Technologies. The LC is classified as a small form factor connector. The term *form factor* refers to the physical attributes of a connector. The LC connector is approximately half the diameter of an SC or ST connector. The LC connector can be converted into a duplex connector by the addition of a clip designed to hold the two separate connectors together. See **Figure 3-14C.**

The MTRJ connector is unique in design because it incorporates two fiber-optic cores into one assembly without the use of a clip, **Figure 3-14D.** It is always considered a duplex connector. The MTRJ is also a small form factor connector.

Fiber-Optic Cable Installation and Troubleshooting

Fiber-optic cables are typically not made in the field but are prepared prior to installation in a controlled setting. Installing a fiber-optic connector on a fiber-optic cable requires a great deal of expertise. Typically, a technician who installs fiber-optic cable connectors must be certified. BICSI is an organization that provides certification. Another such organization is the Fiber Optic Association (FOA). Some companies, such as Ortronics, Corning Cable Systems, Nortel Networks, and Belden, oversee their own certification programs. Whether or not a technician requires certification is determined by the vendor or by installation specifications written for a new installation. Usually the purchasing company will prepare these.

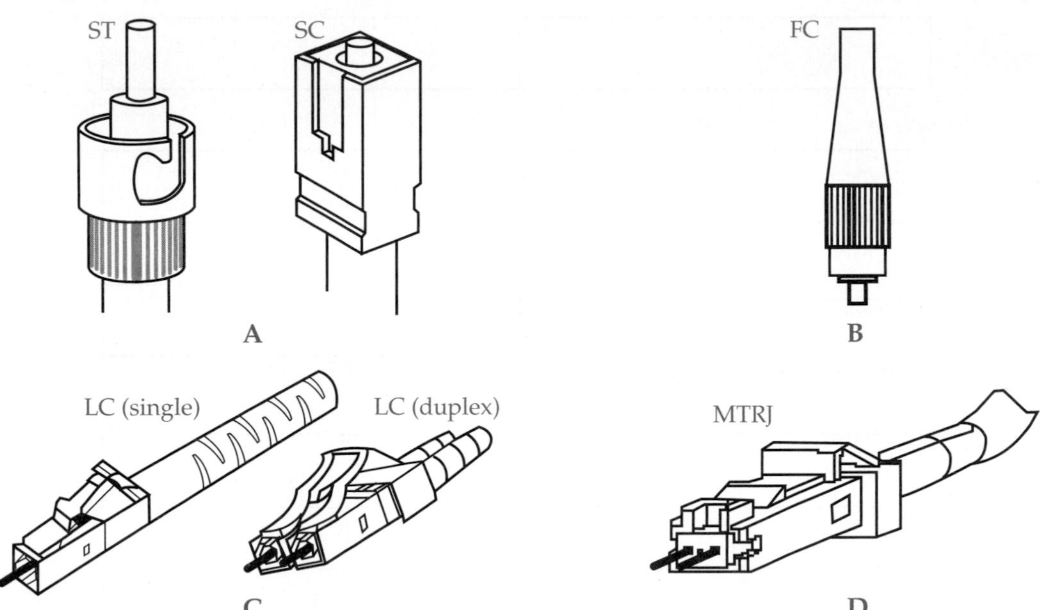

Figure 3-14. Fiber-optic cable connectors. A—ST and SC connectors. B—FC connector. C—LC connectors. D—MTRJ connector.

Installing Connectors

A supplier may provide the necessary cable for a small, fiber-optic network, such as a LAN. This includes taking measurements and preparing cable splices and connections prior to installation. When fiber-optic cabling is obtained in this way, the highest quality control standards are applied to cable preparation. However, this is not always possible. Cables may have to be installed in the field where factors such as dirt, dust, and chemicals can hamper the cable splicing, termination, and connector installation. Splices, couplings, and connections require special equipment and techniques. Fiber-optic cores must be in near-perfect alignment when splices are made. Misalignment or other improper splicing will cause attenuation. See **Figure 3-15.**

The fiber-optic cable is cleaved, not cut like copper core cable. To cleave the fiber-optic cable core, it must be scribed with a sharp, cleaving tool. The edge of the cleaving tool is made of diamond or ceramic material. Once the core has been scribed, pressure is applied to the scribed area until the core breaks. This produces a clean, clear surface at the end of the core. Traditional cutting tools used for copper core cable would badly scar the ends of the core. Marks or scratches on the ends of the core material cause attenuation due to reflection and refraction. The light scatters in many directions rather than transferring directly to the next cable or connector. Plastic core cables do not have to be cleaved. An extremely sharp cutter must be used to obtain a clean, clear cut.

Figure 3-16 shows a high-quality, fiber-optic cleaver and splicer. Note the eyepiece located at the top of the tool. Since the diameter of a fiber-optic core is small, a microscope with at least 30× magnification is needed to inspect the cut and splice. This tool is capable of cutting fiber-optic cable, polishing the ends, and fusing them together for a near-flawless splice.

Making a Fusion Splice

fusion splice joining two fiber-optic cores using heat to fuse the materials together.

A ***fusion splice*** is the joining of two fiber-optic cores using heat to fuse, or melt, the materials together. Another, more expensive fusion splicer is shown in

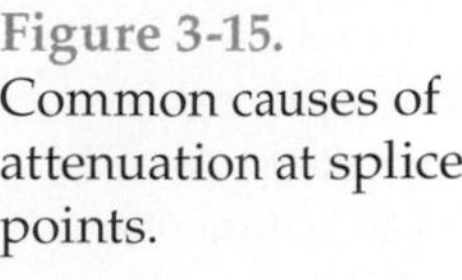

Figure 3-15.
Common causes of attenuation at splice points.

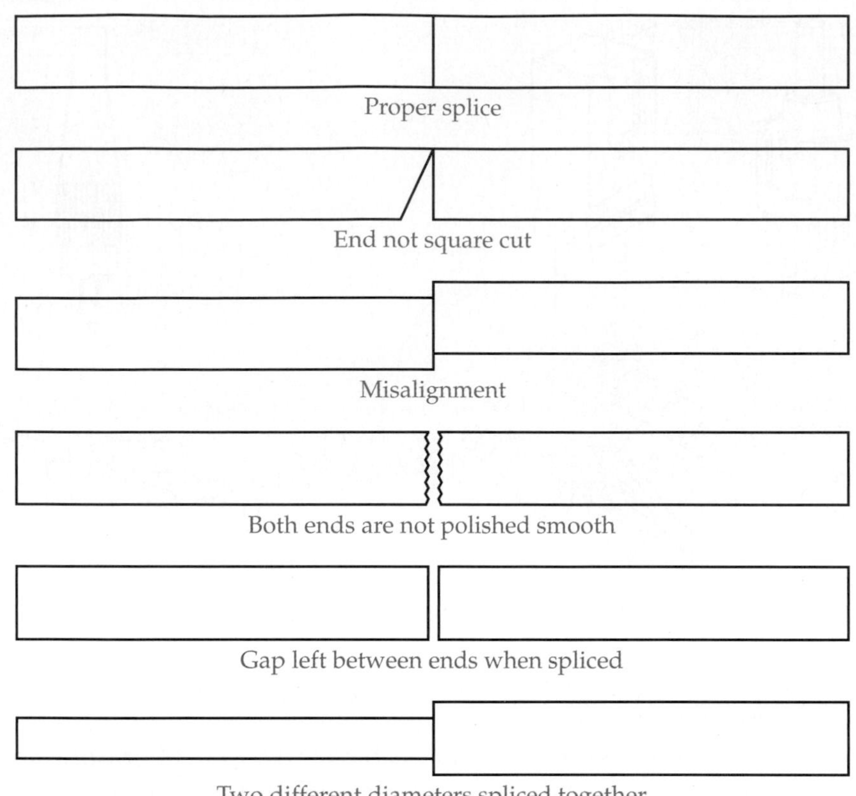

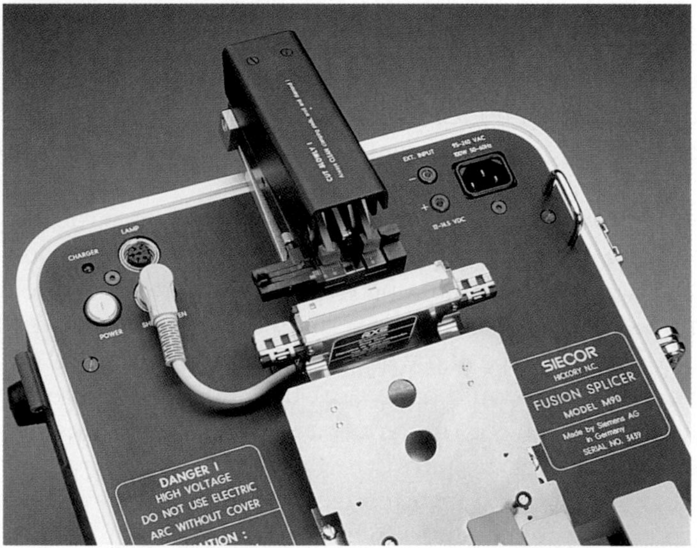

Figure 3-16.
Fiber-optic cable splicer with cleaver. (Siecor Corporation, Hickory, NC)

Figure 3-17. This fusion splicer performs all the functions of the splicer shown in Figure 3-16 and more. It is equipped with video cameras and a liquid crystal display for close, simultaneous inspection of the splice at two different angles.

Before making a fusion splice, the outer, protective sheath and buffer must be removed from the fiber-optic cable end. The splice area of the core must be very clean. Dust and debris can contaminate the splice, resulting in a poor data rate through the finished splice. The cladding must be carefully handled. Damage to the cladding will cause signal loss. Once the fiber-optic cable is prepared, the end

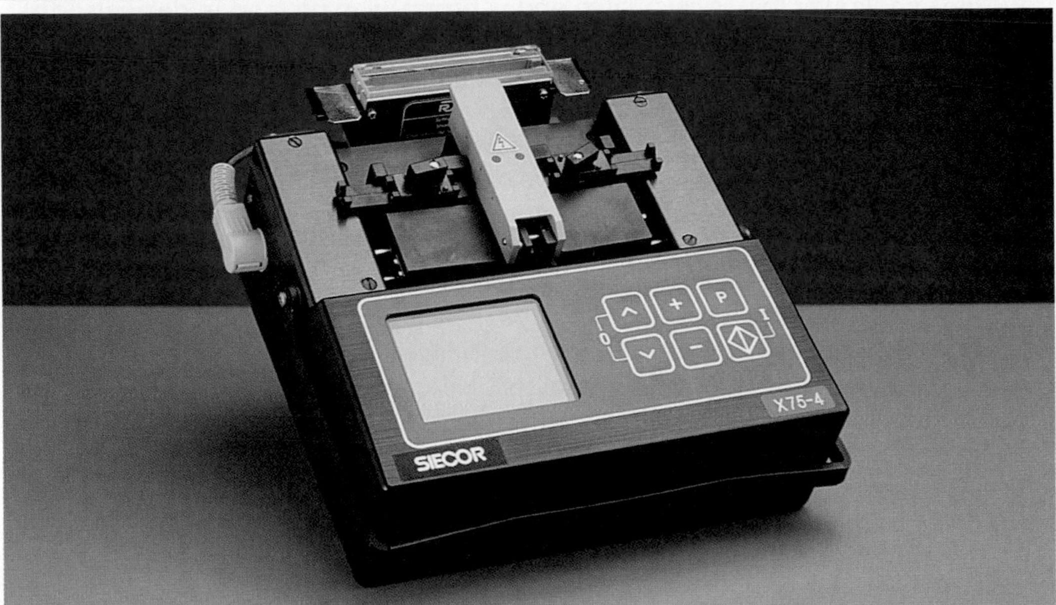

Figure 3-17. A multiprocessor-controlled fusion splicer. (Siecor Corporation, Hickory, NC)

of the fiber-optic core is cleaved. A cleaver simply nicks the core rather than cuts through it. The core can then be easily broken.

Next, the two ends of the fiber core must be perfectly aligned. Because of the small diameters of the core, a magnifier is used to aid in the alignment. Some of the more expensive fusion splicing units combine the cleaver magnifier and fuser into one package.

When the two ends are aligned, they are melted together by an electrical arc. The two ends become permanently welded together, or fused. After fusing the cores, the splice must be protected so it will not be damaged through handling or installation. The splice is covered using material such as heat shrink tubing, silicone gel, or mechanical crimps.

Mechanical splices are made in a similar way except for fusing the two cores. Mechanical splices do not use heat but rather a mechanical means of splicing the two cores. The two cores are aligned, and then the mechanical crimper clamps the two cores together. Between the two cores is a gel-like substance that maintains a consistent light path between the two ends by eliminating any air gap between the two cores. An air gap would cause the Fresnel effect, thus reducing the ability of the splice to carry light from one core to the other.

The main difference between the mechanical and the fusion splice is the cost of the equipment and the cost of each splice. The equipment for making a fusion splice is very expensive when compared with the equipment for making a mechanical splice. However, the cost of labor to make each splice is less expensive when using fusing equipment.

Using Fiber-Optic Cable Meters

Testing fiber-optic cable requires specialized instruments that employ the principles of light to obtain data. The most commonly used meter for testing short runs of fiber-optic cable consists of two items: a power meter and a light source. The light source is attached to one end of the fiber-optic cable, and the power meter is connected to the other end. The light source injects light into the fiber-optic cable, and the light meter measures the amount of light reaching the opposite end. Power loss is calculated and is typically expressed in decibels (dB) or microwatts (μW). The information gathered from the meter can be sent to and stored on a computer. For some new network installations, this test is more than adequate to assure a contractor that the fiber-optic cable installation is acceptable.

Optical Time Domain Reflectometer (OTDR) a meter for testing and troubleshooting long runs of fiber-optic cable. The OTDR conducts measurements based on the principle of attenuation.

Another type of meter is the ***Optical Time Domain Reflectometer (OTDR).*** The OTDR is a sophisticated and expensive meter for testing and troubleshooting long runs of fiber-optic cable. The OTDR accurately measures and records the effects of attenuation. It compares the amount of light injected into the fiber-optic cable core to the amount of light reflected to the meter. **Figure 3-18** shows the Fluke OFTM-5612 OTDR, which is used to inspect and analyze fiber-optic cable installations.

The OTDR can also accurately measure the total length of a cable run or locate breaks and faults in a cable and at its connections. The typical OTDR presents information in a graphical manner on a liquid crystal display (LCD). A slope is presented that represents the attenuation of the core. Major flaws in splices and such are presented as spikes, **Figure 3-19.** The distance to the fault and other pertinent information, such as signal loss in decibels (dB) or milliwatts (mW), is indicated along the bottom edge of the screen. **Figure 3-20** illustrates how faults and distance are represented on a graph.

Figure 3-21 shows an OTDR signal trace analysis indicating the attenuation of the cable and the location of a fault of 7.619 dB at approximately 53.481 kilometers from the meter. Using test equipment that can quickly identify the location of a fault can save many hours of testing by other means.

An OTDR is typically equipped with a port for connecting directly to a printer. Screen captures and a full report on the specifications of the fiber-optic cable can be printed. The OTDR is routinely used for the final inspection of a new fiber-optic cable installation. It not only provides information to prove the cable is flawless, but also provides a baseline of information for comparison at a later date when troubleshooting. The typical OTDR is an expensive piece of test equipment; however, it does not need to be purchased. To save money, contractors often rent

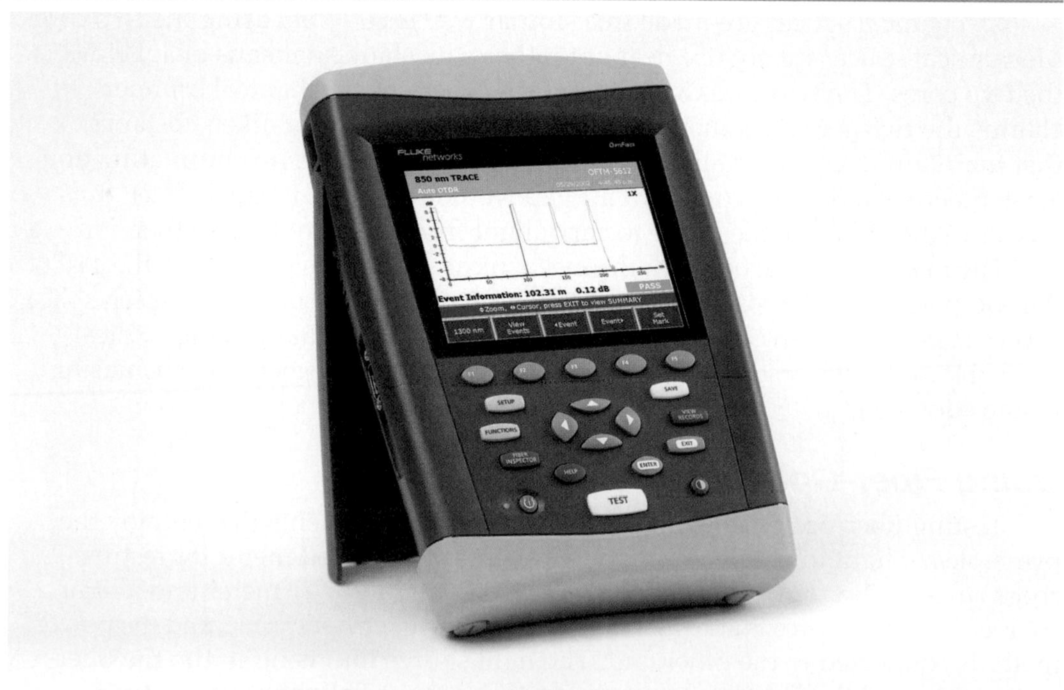

Figure 3-18. Fluke OFTM-5612 OTDR. (Reproduced with permission—Fluke Corp.)

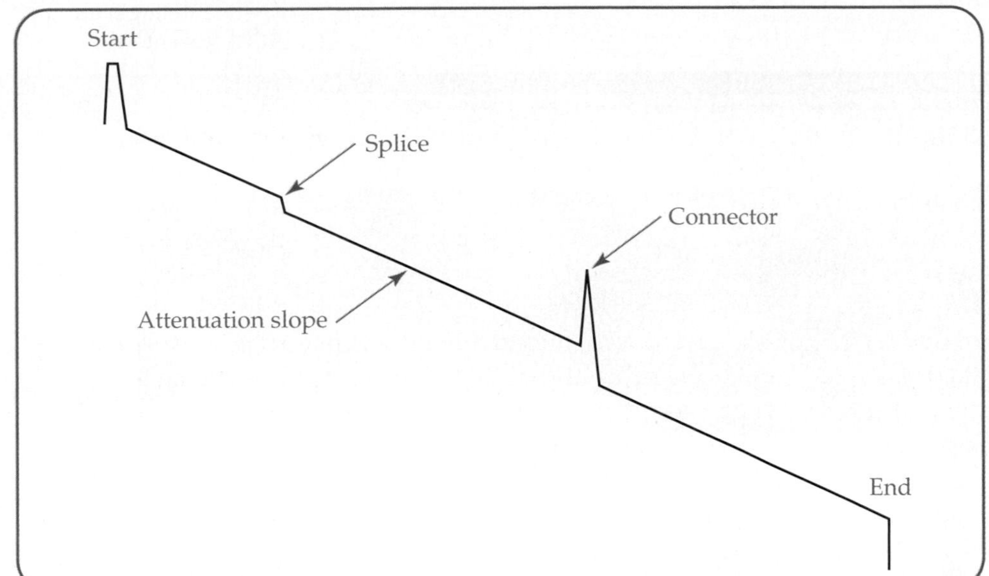

Figure 3-19. Attenuation and cable faults as indicated on an OTDR display. Note that faults are indicated by spikes.

an OTDR to test and certify a fiber-optic cable system they have installed. OTDR tests are not normally performed on short, fiber-optic cable runs associated with LANs. This type of installation is typically checked with a simple, handheld meter, not an OTDR. The OTDR is best suited for measuring cable runs spanning great distances like those found in network backbones.

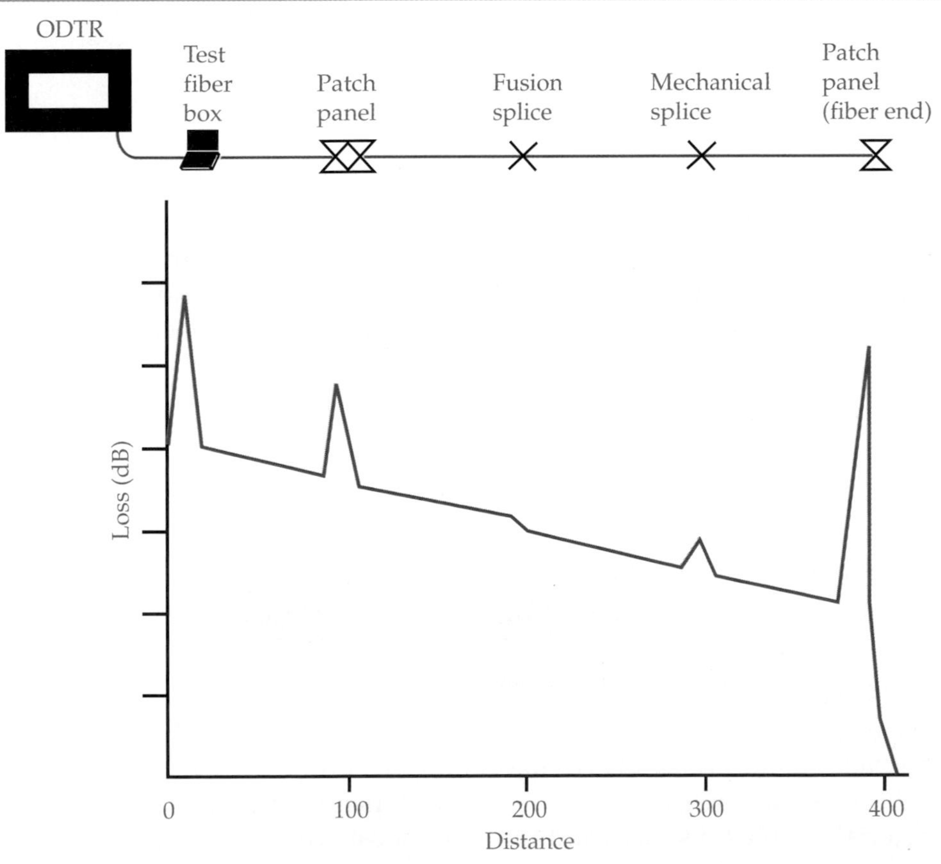

Figure 3-20. An OTDR can indicate loss in decibels and the exact distance from the OTDR to the fault.

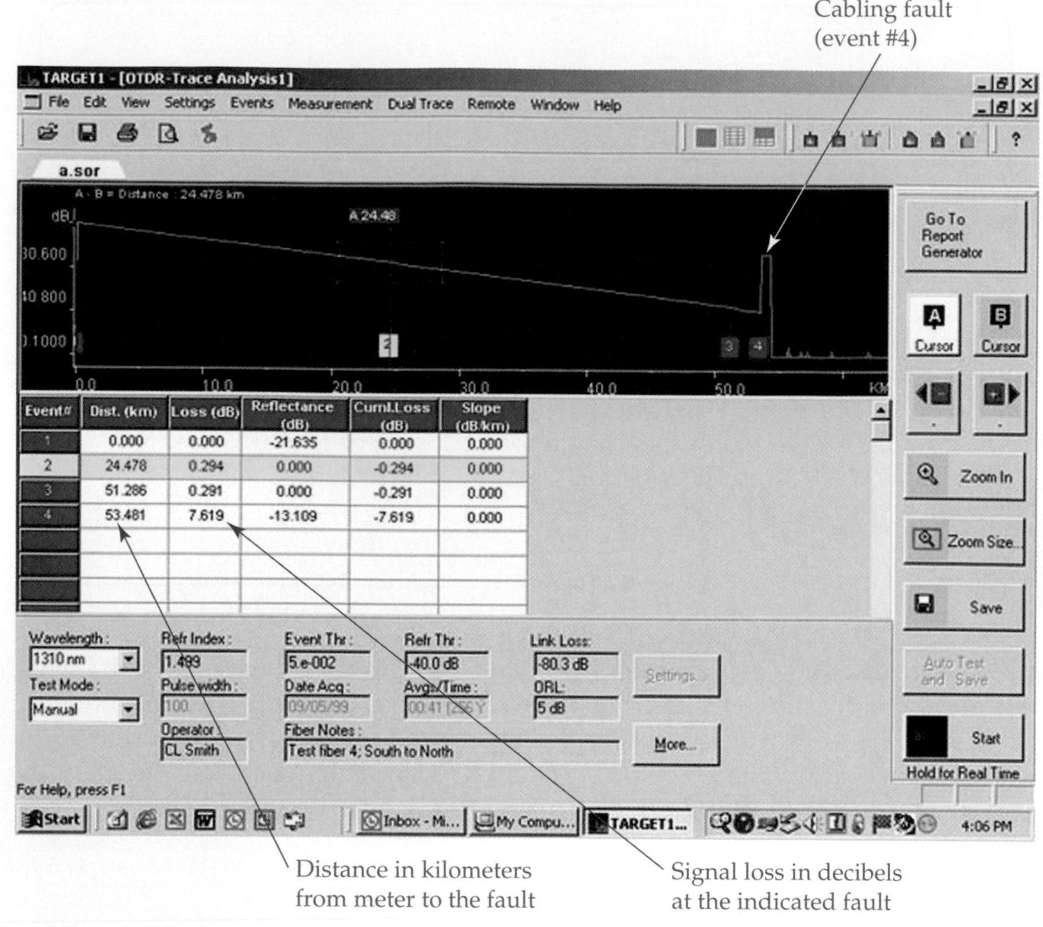

Figure 3-21.
A trace analysis is displayed on the LCD screen of an OTDR. Cable faults are indicated by the sharp spikes along the slope. Exact losses are also displayed in decibel units at the bottom of the display.

Summary

- Fiber-optic cable has the following advantages: provides for data security, immune to electromagnetic interference, lightweight and small in diameter, safe from fire and explosion, wide bandwidth, corrosion- and water-resistant, supports data transmission over longer distances than copper core cable.
- Light is described in wavelengths.
- A wavelength is the total distance the electromagnetic wave or light wave travels during one full cycle.
- Wavelengths are measured in nanometers (nanometer), or one billionth of a meter.
- Fiber-optic cable cores are composed of either glass or plastic.
- The glass or plastic core is surrounded by cladding, which restricts the light to the core area.
- Scattering is the loss of light due to impurities in the core material.
- Dispersion is the distortion of light waves caused by the light reflecting from the cladding material and arriving at different times at the far end of the cable.
- Extrinsic losses are caused by physical factors not normally found in the core material, such as at splices and connector locations.

- Two broad classifications of fiber-optic cable based on its ability to carry light are multimode and single-mode.
- Single-mode fiber-optic cable has a smaller core diameter than multimode fiber-optic cable and carries light farther and with less attenuation.
- Two classifications of multimode fiber-optic cable are graded-index and step-index.
- Graded-index multimode fiber-optic cable is designed with a varying grade of core material that allows for maximum light conduction at the center of the core. Step-index multimode fiber-optic cable does not have a special core design and is therefore greatly affected by dispersion.
- The 802.3z standard describes the 1000BaseSX, 1000BaseLX, and 1000BaseCX Gigabit Ethernet classifications.
- The 802.3ae 10 Gigabit Ethernet standard describes the 10GBaseSR, 10GBaseLR, 10GBaseEW, and 10GBaseER classifications.
- 10GBaseW is a collection of cable standards such as 10GBaseSW, 10GBaseLW, and 10GBaseEW.
- FDDI is used mainly as a backbone for large network systems such as a MAN or a WAN.
- FDDI is structured as a pair of rings.
- A splice that is joined by heat is called a *fusion splice.*
- A light source and fiber-optic light meter is used to test short runs of fiber-optic cable by comparing the amount of light injected in one end of the cable to the light power at the other end of the cable.
- The OTDR is used to measure the effects of scattering and cabling faults in long fiber-optic cable runs. It can also measure the distance to a cable fault or break.

Review Questions

Answer the following questions on a separate sheet of paper. Please do not write in this book.

1. What are seven advantages of fiber-optic cable?
2. Light is measured in _____.
3. What does the abbreviation *nm* represent?
4. What is the wavelength range of visible light?
5. What are the three common wavelengths associated with fiber-optic cable?
6. What is *dispersion*?
7. Name three physical factors that contribute to extrinsic losses.
8. What are the two classifications of fiber-optic cable based on the diameter of the core?
9. How does the diameter of the fiber-optic cable core affect the distance light can travel?
10. Fiber-optic cable core diameter is expressed in _____.
11. What are the two most common sizes of multimode fiber-optic cable?
12. How can the light distance-carrying capacity of a multimode cable be improved?
13. What do the following 10 Gigabit Ethernet acronyms represent: SW, LW, and EW?
14. How is FDDI structured?

15. Why does FDDI use two rings of cable?
16. What are the five most common types of fiber-optic cable connector?
17. What are some common causes of attenuation associated with fiber-optic cable splices?
18. Using heat to join two fiber-optic cores is called a(n) _____ splice.
19. What is required to test a short run of fiber-optic cable?
20. What device is commonly used to test long runs of fiber-optic cable?
21. What principle of fiber-optic cable loss does the OTDR use for measurements?

Sample Network+ Exam Questions

Answer the following questions on a separate sheet of paper. Please do not write in this book.

1. Which of the following network media is typically the most secure from eaves dropping devices or security taps?
   A. Fiber-optic cable
   B. Copper core cable
   C. Wireless
   D. Infrared
2. Identify the connector in the following exhibit.
   A. SC
   B. ST
   C. RJ-45
   D. BNC

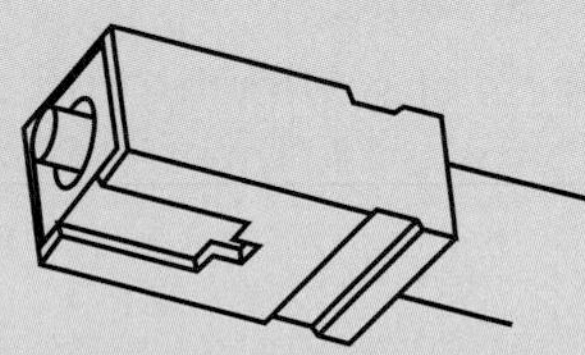

3. Identify the connector in the following exhibit.
   A. SC
   B. ST
   C. RJ-45
   D. BNC

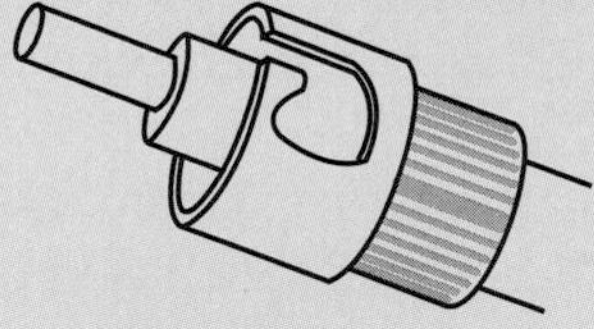

4. Where is fiber-optic cable typically found? (Select all that apply.)
   A. In network backbones.
   B. In network segments that are exposed to electromagnetic interference.
   C. Where security from wiretaps is of great concern.
   D. In network segments requiring slow data transmission rates.

5. Fiber-optic cable losses are expressed in which unit?
   A. Decibels
   B. Ohms
   C. Resistance
   D. Impedance
6. The loss of signal strength in the core of a fiber-optic cable caused by impurities in the core is referred to as _____.
   A. scattering
   B. dispersion
   C. diffusion
   D. reflection
7. Which cable standard supports the longest distances?
   A. 10GbaseER
   B. 10GBaseLX
   C. 1000BaseLX
   D. 100BaseCX
8. According to the ANSI/TIA/EIA standards for backbone distribution inside a premise, what is the maximum recommended distance for multimode fiber-optic cable?
   A. 100 meters
   B. 200 meters
   C. 500 meters
   D. 2000 meters
9. What type of networking media is used in FDDI?
   A. Fiber-optic multimode
   B. Fiber-optic single-mode
   C. UTP
   D. All the above materials can be used for FDDI.
10. Which is a correct description of the FDDI topology?
    A. Star
    B. Bus
    C. Single ring
    D. Dual ring

Suggested Laboratory Activities

1. Determine the core size of a fiber-optic cable using a micrometer.
2. Visit the Web sites of several network interface card vendors and see how much a fiber-optic network interface card would cost for your home computer.
3. Price 100 meters of multimode fiber-optic cable and compare it with the price of 100 meters of UTP cable.
4. Conduct an Internet search to locate the steps required to make a fiber-optic patch cable.
5. Visit the BICSI and Fiber Optic Association (FOA) Web site and see what it takes to become a certified fiber-optic technician.

Interesting Web Sites for More Information

www.cableu.net
www.fiber-optics.info
www.fiber-optics.info/fiber_optic_glossary
www.levitonvoicedata.com/learning/default.asp
www.lucent.com
www.occfiber.com
www.ortronics.com
www.siemon.com

Chapter 3 Laboratory Activity

Fiber-Optic Connector Identification

After completing this laboratory activity, you will be able to:

- Identify common fiber-optic connector types.
- Distinguish between common fiber-optic connectors by physical traits.

Introduction

This laboratory activity will familiarize you with various fiber-optic cable, connectors, and vendors. You will search the Internet for images of common, fiber-optic connectors. Once located, you will copy the images and paste them into a word processing document and then label the image with the appropriate acronym.

To copy a Web page image, right-click the image and then select **Copy** from the shortcut menu. To insert the image into a word processing document, right-click a blank area of the document page and click **Paste**. When you have finished copying the images specified in the laboratory activity, you will print two copies of the assignment, one for your reference and the other to turn in to your instructor.

Some fiber-optic cable manufacturers and distributors include the following: Ortronics, Siemon, Belden, Black Box, Agilent, Fluke, and 3Com. You may wish to visit their Web sites for information about various fiber-optic cables and connectors.

Equipment and Materials

- Computer with Internet access and word processing software, such as Microsoft WordPad. (WordPad is included in all Microsoft operating systems.)
- Printer access.

Procedure

1. ______ Report to your assigned workstation.
2. ______ Boot the computer and verify it is in working order.
3. ______ Open Internet Explorer.
4. ______ Conduct a search for fiber-optic connectors. Use the following phrases in your search:
   - Fiber-optic connectors.
   - Fiber optic connectors.
   - Fiber-optic cable connectors.
   - Fiber optic cable connectors.

5. ______ After locating images of fiber-optic connectors, copy each image from the Web page and paste it into a word processing document. Be sure to label each example. Use the following labels, one for each connector type: Biconic, ESCON, FC, FDDI, MTRJ, SC, SC Duplex, SMA, and ST.
6. ______ When you are finished, print out two copies of your document.
7. ______ Answer the review questions. You may use the Internet to research the answers.
8. ______ Return your workstation to its original condition.

Review Questions

Answer the following questions on a separate sheet of paper. Please do not write in this book.

1. What is the most obvious physical difference between an ST and an SC connector?
2. What is the main physical difference between an LC connector and an ST connector?
3. How many fiber-optic cores are typically associated with an FDDI connector?
4. How many fiber-optic cores are typically associated with an MTRJ connector?
5. How many fiber-optic cores are typically associated with an ST connector?
6. What does the acronym ESCON represent?
7. What does the acronym FDDI represent?
8. In general, what does the term *duplex* mean when referring to fiber-optic connectors?

4 Wireless Technology

After studying this chapter, you will be able to:

- ❑ Explain the principles of radio wave transmission.
- ❑ Identify the major antenna styles.
- ❑ Explain three transmission techniques used in radio wave-based transmission.
- ❑ Recall the characteristics of the U-NII classifications.
- ❑ Recall the key characteristics of the IEEE 802.11 wireless networking standards.
- ❑ Explain the CSMA/CA access method.
- ❑ Recall the key characteristics of the Bluetooth standard.
- ❑ Explain how cellular technology works.
- ❑ Compare the two types of microwave networks.
- ❑ Compare the two types of infrared transmission.
- ❑ Summarize the advantages and disadvantages of wireless networking.
- ❑ Recall the purpose of the SSID.
- ❑ Give examples of how security is provided in wireless networks.

Network+ Exam—Key Points

To prepare for the CompTIA Network+ exam, you must be able to specify the characteristics of the IEEE 802.11 standards. These characteristics include speed, cable lengths, and access method. You should also be able to define and identify an ad hoc wireless network and an infrastructure wireless network.

To better prepare yourself to answer questions on wireless technology, be sure to install and configure a wireless network card and view all of the configuration properties that are featured.

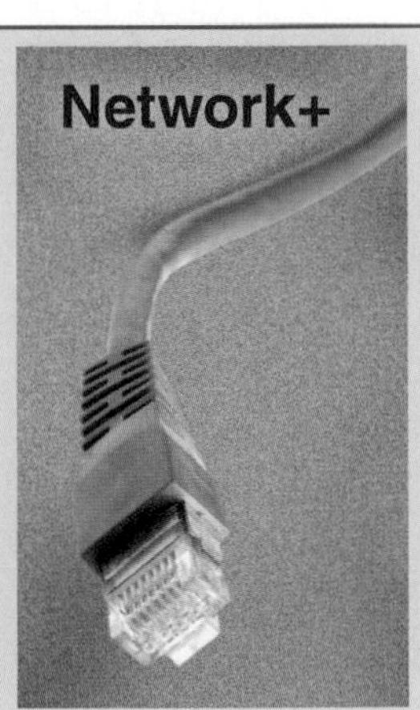

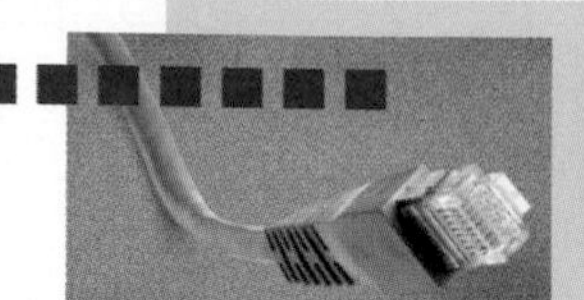

Key Words and Terms

The following words and terms will become important pieces of your networking vocabulary. Be sure you can define them.

- ad hoc mode
- Basic Service Set (BSS)
- carrier wave
- cellular technology
- channel
- demodulation
- direct sequencing
- directional
- Extended Service Set Identifier (ESSID)
- Extensible Authentication Protocol (EAP)
- frequency hopping
- geosynchronous orbit
- Independent Basic Service Set (IBSS)
- infrastructure mode
- ISM band
- modulation
- Multiple Input Multiple Output (MIMO)
- omni-directional
- orthogonal frequency-division multiplexing (OFDM)
- piconet
- propagation delay
- radio interference
- radio waves
- receiver
- spatial multiplexing
- spread spectrum
- transmitter
- unbounded media
- Wi-Fi
- Wi-Fi Protected Access (WPA)
- Wired Equivalent Privacy (WEP)
- Wireless Access Point (WAP)
- Wireless Application Protocol (WAP)
- Wireless Personal Area Networks (WPAN)
- working group

unbounded media an unrestricted path for network transmissions.

Wireless media is often referred to as ***unbounded media,*** which means the path for network transmissions is unrestricted. When copper core or fiber-optic cable is used, the transmitted network signals are bound to the medium. When the atmosphere is used, the transmission is spread throughout the atmosphere and is not limited to a single path.

Network signals transmitted through the atmosphere are electromagnetic waves. In Chapter 3—Fiber-Optic Cable, you learned that light waves are a part of the electromagnetic wave spectrum and are categorized as visible light. You learned specifically how light waves travel through fiber-optic cable to transmit data. In this chapter, you will learn about the three categories of electromagnetic waves that are used to transmit data across the atmosphere: radio waves, infrared, and microwaves. You will also learn about wireless transmission techniques and associated standards. To help you better understand wireless networking technologies, electromagnetic waves will be discussed in detail.

Electromagnetic Waves

The atmosphere is full of electromagnetic waves. Electromagnetic waves are categorized according to frequency ranges. For example, common radio waves used for communications start at 0.5 MHz for AM radio and span to 22 GHz for satellite communications. The frequency of an electromagnetic wave is based on the repeating pattern of its waveform just as it is with electrical energy. One complete waveform is called a *cycle,* **Figure 4-1,** and frequency is the number of times a cycle occurs in one second.

Electromagnetic waves are produced both intentionally and unintentionally as a by-product of electrical energy. Radio and television stations produce electromagnetic waves intentionally while many household appliances produce electromagnetic waves unintentionally. You should recall from Chapter 2, Network Media—Copper Core Cable that unintentional electromagnetic waves are referred to as *interference,* or more specifically, *noise.*

Radio and Microwave Transmission

Radio and microwave transmission works on the principle of producing a carrier wave as the means of communication between two wireless devices. A ***carrier wave*** is an electromagnetic wave of a set frequency that is used to carry data. It is identified by a frequency number. For example, radio and television stations are assigned specific frequencies on which they must transmit. A radio identification such as 104.5 FM represents a carrier wave of 104.5 MHz. The carrier wave is how individual stations are identified on a radio or television, **Figure 4-2.**

The carrier wave is mixed with the data signal. The mixing of the carrier wave and data signal is known as ***modulation.*** The technique of modulation is how AM radio, FM radio, and television operate. A simple radio broadcast

carrier wave an electromagnetic wave of a set frequency that is used to carry data.

modulation the process of mixing a data signal with a carrier wave.

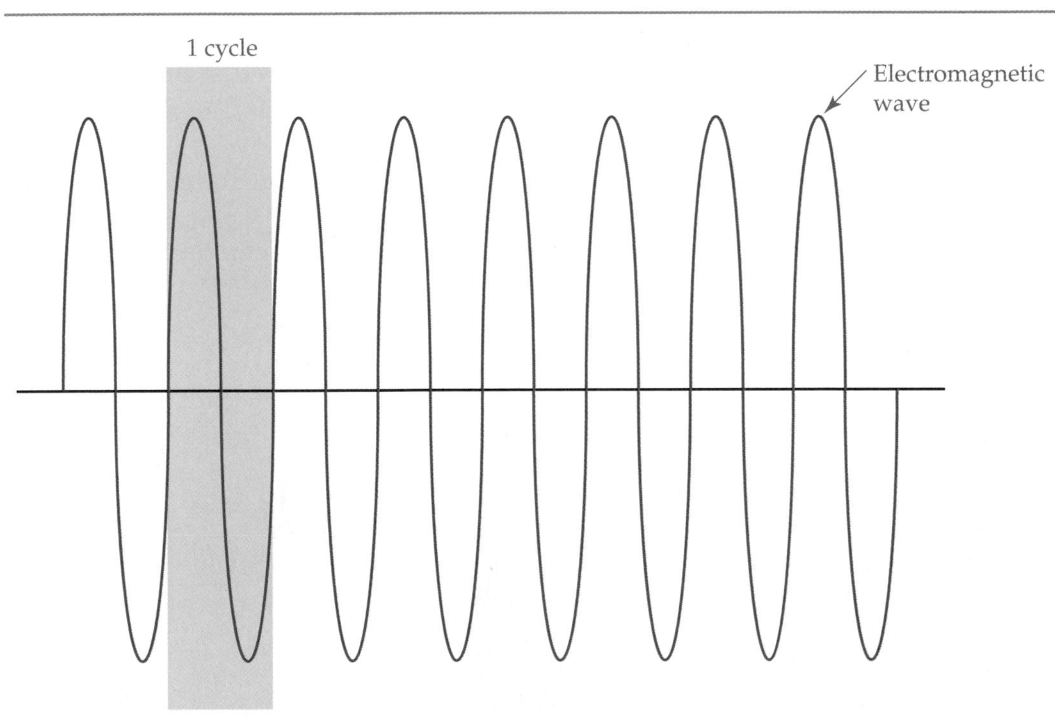

Figure 4-1. Electromagnetic frequency is based on the repeating pattern of a waveform. One complete waveform is called a *cycle.* The frequency is how many cycles occur in one second.

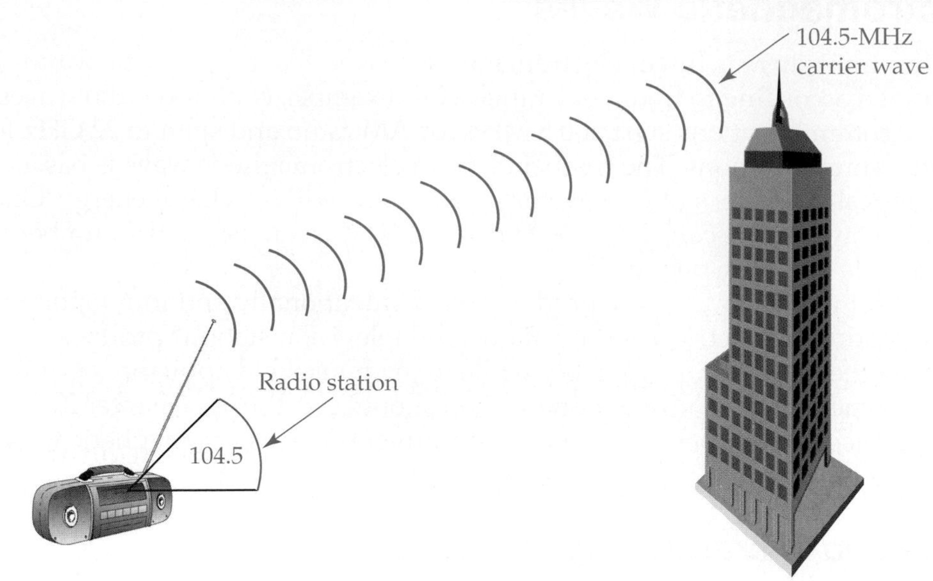

Figure 4-2.
A carrier wave is the means of communication between two wireless devices. In this example, a radio station assigned the 104.5-MHz frequency transmits data on a 104.5-MHz carrier wave. A radio with its dial set to 104.5 picks up the information broadcast from the radio station.

transmitter
an electronic device that generates a carrier wave and modulates the data signal into the carrier wave.

receiver
an electronic device that receives a modulated signal and demodulates it.

consists of a ***transmitter,*** which generates the carrier wave and modulates information into the carrier wave, and a ***receiver,*** which receives the modulated wave and demodulates it. The transceiver and receiver must both be at or very near the same carrier wave frequency for communication to occur.

Look at the example of a voice wave broadcast in **Figure 4-3.** In the example, a carrier wave of 104.5 MHz, is shown. The human voice produces sound at a much lower frequency, typically in a range from a 400 cycles per second to approximately 4,000 cycles per second. The human voice is converted into electrical energy using a microphone. The microphone produces a pattern of electrical energy in direct proportion to the human voice. The electrical energy is mixed with the carrier wave. The carrier wave has a much higher frequency than the electromagnetic wave produced by the human voice. The two are combined so that the human voice can be transmitted.

Figure 4-3.
Example of a voice wave broadcast.

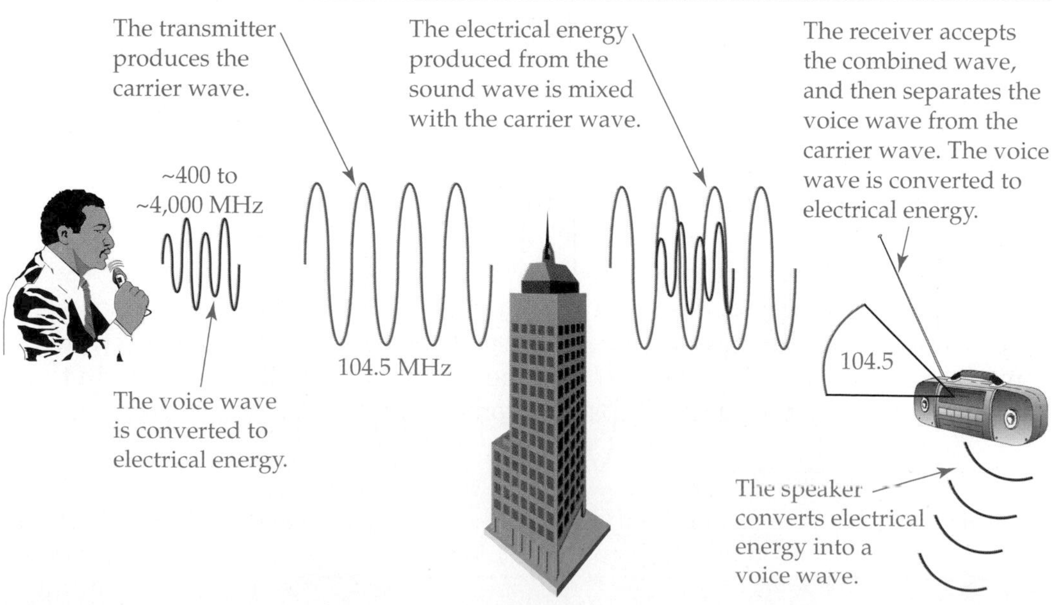

The combined wave is transmitted across the atmosphere. When the combined wave reaches the receiver and is accepted, the electromagnetic energy is converted into electrical energy. The receiver separates the voice wave from the carrier wave. This process is known as ***demodulation.*** After the combined wave is demodulated, the transceiver discards the carrier wave and then amplifies the voice wave and sends it to a speaker. The speaker converts the electrical energy into a voice wave. While this is a simple, nontechnical explanation, it is important to remember that the carrier wave and the voice wave are combined, or modulated, before they are transmitted and are separated, or demodulated, after they are received.

demodulation
the process of separating a data signal from a carrier wave.

channel
the bandwidth of a carrier wave.

The same principle is used to transmit digital data signals. A carrier wave establishes the transmitter/receiver relationship. The carrier wave is modulated with a wave pattern resembling the digital data signal. The two waves are combined before transmission and then separated at the receiver.

To modulate data, the carrier wave must be at a much higher frequency than the digital data. In the example of the voice wave and carrier wave frequency, the carrier wave is 104.5 MHz while the voice wave fluctuates between 400 Hz and 4,000 Hz. Based on an average voice frequency of 2,000 Hz, an approximate 500:1 ratio exists between the two frequencies. The carrier wave is only slightly distorted when combined with the voice wave. The same principle applies when a carrier wave is combined with a digital data signal. If the two signals do not have a high ratio, the digital data signal distorts the carrier wave to a point where the transmitter cannot recognize it.

A 104.5-MHz carrier wave is 200 kHz in width. Technically, a 104.5-MHz carrier wave has a bandwidth of 200 kHz. The bandwidth of a carrier wave is referred to as a ***channel.*** Technically, a channel is a small portion of the electromagnetic spectrum and is used to designate a set of frequencies for a particular electronic application. The FCC assigns channels and bandwidths for electromagnetic waves.

A channel is identified by the assigned frequency that represents the starting point of the band. For example, 104.5 is the identification of the channel even though the channel spans the next 200 kHz. Look at **Figure 4-4.** The 145 MHz is the designated channel for the carrier wave. This channel is a single position in the entire radio frequency spectrum represented by the 145-MHz designation. The carrier wave channel is 200 kHz wide starting at exactly 145 MHz and ending at 145.2 MHz. The carrier wave must stay within the 200-kHz band as specified by FCC regulation.

The exact center of the bandwidth area is 145.1 MHz. It is nearly impossible for the carrier wave to remain exactly at 145.1 MHz. The electronic components that are used to create the circuit that produce the exact frequency change directly with temperature. The components heat up because of the electrical energy passing through them and are also influenced by environmental temperatures. Electronic transmitters are enclosed and air-conditioned to keep the components at a predetermined temperature. The enclosure compensates for environmental changes in temperature and the heat effects of the electronic components. A change in component temperature causes a direct change in the carrier wave frequency produced by electronic components.

Infrared Transmission

Infrared uses a series of digital light pulses. The light is either on or off. A typical television remote control uses infrared technology rather than radio wave technology to transmit to the television receiver. There are two distinct disadvantages to infrared

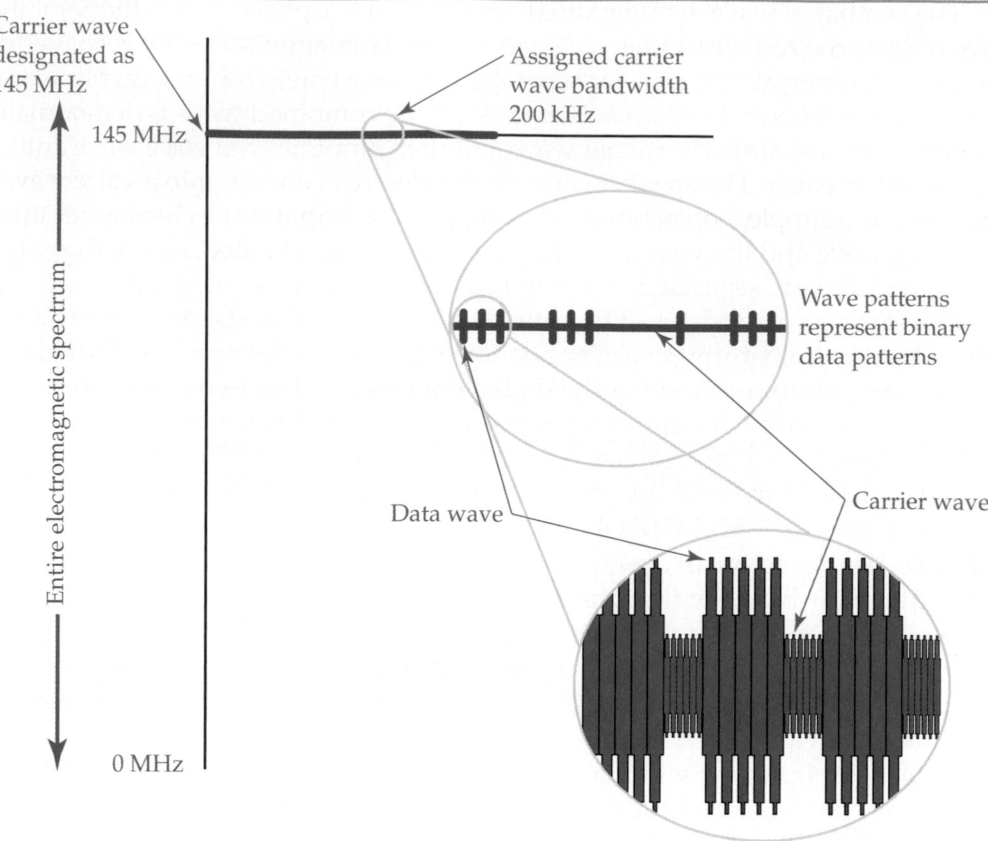

Figure 4-4. The carrier wave and the data wave are electronically combined or modulated. The modulated signal must remain inside the radio frequency range or channel assigned by the FCC.

technology. First, the two devices that are communicating must be in direct line of sight of each other. This means that the infrared receiver/transmitter of each device must be aimed, or at least positioned, in the general direction of the other.

The infrared beam is weak and must be transmitted through an optical lens to prevent dispersion. The other disadvantage is an infrared beam can travel a relatively limited distance when compared with wireless radio wave technologies. Some infrared communication links for networks use a laser to achieve greater distances.

Even with its disadvantages, infrared can be found in many of the same applications as Bluetooth. It is commonly used in some models of personal digital assistants, palm tops, and laptops. Typical data rates for infrared devices are 1 Mbps and 2 Mbps. Data rates can be much higher when lasers are used for the direct connection of two LANs.

Radio Interference

radio interference interference that matches the frequency of a carrier wave.

Radio interference is interference that matches the frequency of the carrier wave. The Federal Communications Commission (FCC) is responsible for dividing the entire electromagnetic spectrum to prevent electronic equipment from interfering with one another. However, this is not always possible. Think for a minute how many different devices use and produce electromagnetic waves—remote controls for remote control cars, remote control airplanes, garage door openers, television, AM radio, FM radio, satellites, pagers, cellular phones, electrical power lines, radar, motors, fluorescent lights, and such. The list is ever increasing. There are thousands of products that produce electromagnetic waves. The FCC regulates the electromagnetic spectrum and dictates the frequency that is to be used for each group of devices. Even with all these regulations, equipment fails and produces undesirable frequencies that can interfere with a regulated frequency. If you move the tuner of an AM radio across the various stations, you will hear an excellent example of interference.

AM radio is an old technology that was susceptible to radio interference. FM radio is an improvement over AM radio because it is less susceptible to radio interference.

Virtually any type of electrical equipment can produce radio interference even if it is not assigned to the radio frequency spectrum assigned to wireless LAN communications. For example, some other sources of radio interference that could corrupt data packets are fluorescent lighting, electric motors, electrical control systems, welding equipment, portable radios, and such. While not intended to produce radio interference in the assigned wireless spectrum, a defective piece of equipment can produce electrical radio harmonics. The harmonic signal is a multiple of an original signal. For example, a radio frequency of 12,000 can also produce signals of 24,000, 36,000, 48,000, and so on. This means that harmonic frequencies produced by other areas of the electromagnetic spectrum can cause interference with the wireless network.

Another major factor is proximity to the source of the signal. If radio interference is in close proximity to the wireless network system, it need not be at the same frequency. Close proximity and a powerful signal can disrupt the wireless communication. Radio signals can also reflect or bounce off surrounding materials, usually metallic surfaces, **Figure 4-5.** The reflected signal is an exact copy of the original signal. The reflected signal does not always disrupt the original signal. At times, it actually increases the strength of the original signal

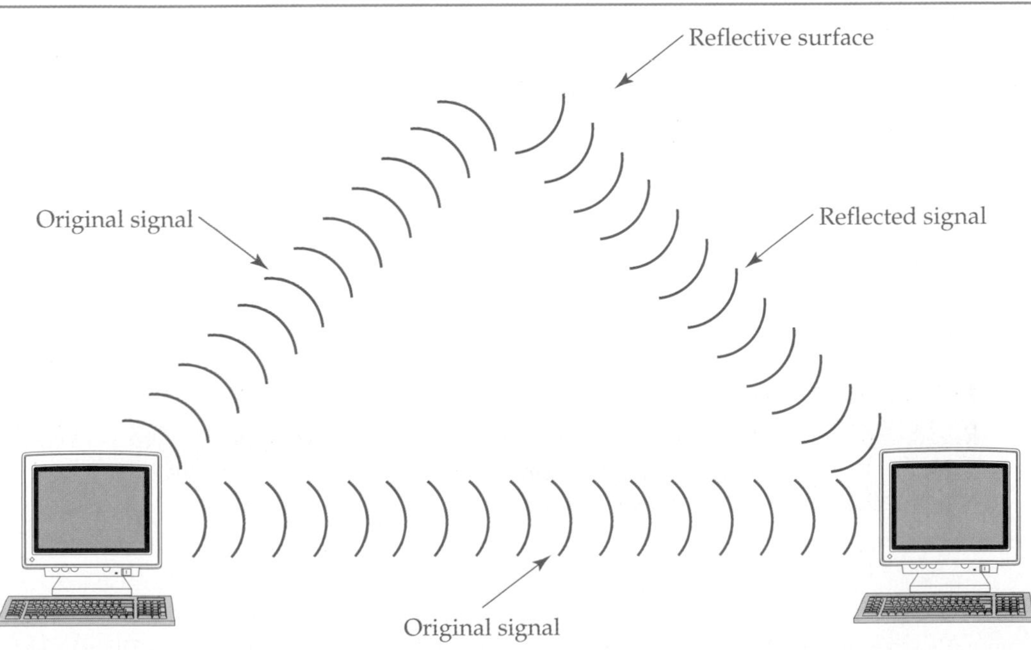

Figure 4-5.
A reflected radio signal can combine with the intended radio signal and either disrupt the intended signal or enhance it.

by combining with it. The problem occurs if there is too much delay between the original signal and the reflected signal. When there is too much delay, the two signals overlap causing the combined signal to be distorted. The difference in time it takes the two signals to travel from the source to the destination determines the level of distortion. The amount of time it takes to reach the destination depends on the angle and distance of the reflection.

There are many sources of radio interference that can affect communication on an IEEE 802.11 wireless LAN. Industrial, scientific, and medical devices occupy the frequency band allocated to the wireless network devices specified under the IEEE 802.11 standard. Wireless phones and microwave ovens are also included in the same frequency ranges. The band of radio frequencies associated with industrial, scientific, and medical devices is referred to as the ***ISM band***, **Figure 4-6.** The acronym ISM represents Industrial, Scientific, and Medical.

ISM band the band of radio frequencies associated with industrial, scientific, and medical devices.

omni-directional the ability of an antenna to transmit electromagnetic signals in all directions.

directional the ability of an antenna to transmit electromagnetic signals in a focused or aimed direction.

Antenna Styles

Two major classifications of antennae are associated with radio wave- and microwave-based wireless networks: omni-directional and directional. These classifications are based on an antenna's ability to transmit electromagnetic signals. ***Omni-directional*** is the transmission of electromagnetic signals in all directions. ***Directional*** is the transmission of electromagnetic signals in a focused or aimed direction. Antennae can be further broken down by their individual style of construction such as omni, dipole, flat panel, Yagi, and parabolic dish. **Figure 4-7** shows each antenna style and the electromagnetic wave pattern it produces. Note that the electromagnetic wave patterns are viewed from overhead.

Omni

The omni is a straight piece of wire. The wire is engineered to match the exact length or a fraction of the frequency's wavelength. For example, a frequency of 2.4 GHz produces a wavelength of approximately 2.19″. An antenna 2.19″ in length would match the wavelength exactly. Matching the antenna length to the wavelength of the radio frequency ensures the best possible reception and reduces the possibility of picking up interference.

The omni antenna is typically used for a wireless transmitter to broadcast in a 360° pattern. This type of antenna is used for the source of a wireless transmission. For example, a wireless Internet service provider would use an omni antenna to facilitate broadcasting in all directions to better serve customers throughout the area.

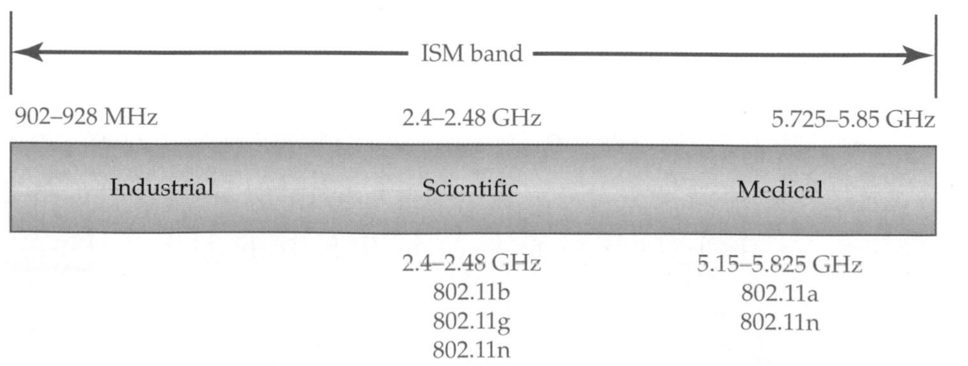

Figure 4-6. The Industrial, Scientific, and Medical (ISM) band is often a source of wireless network interference.

Dipole

The dipole is one of the most common radio antennae used. What makes it popular is it is relatively inexpensive to manufacture when compared with many other antenna styles. The dipole is commonly used as a client or receiver antenna rather than as a broadcast antenna. The dipole antenna is bidirectional, as seen in Figure 4-7. Rotating the antenna until the dipole aligns with the source of the radio wave transmission can enhance the received signal.

Yagi

The Yagi antenna is used for point-to-point links. It is a directional-type antenna. A Yagi antenna is typically designed from many radio antenna elements (tubes). Each element is progressively larger or smaller than the main element by approximately 5%. The way the Yagi antenna enhances the radiation of the electromagnetic wave is beyond the scope of this textbook. For now, just note and recognize the shape of the Yagi antenna and its electromagnetic wave pattern. Some Yagi antennae are constructed inside a metal tube to further enhance the reception and transmission of electromagnetic waves. See **Figure 4-8.**

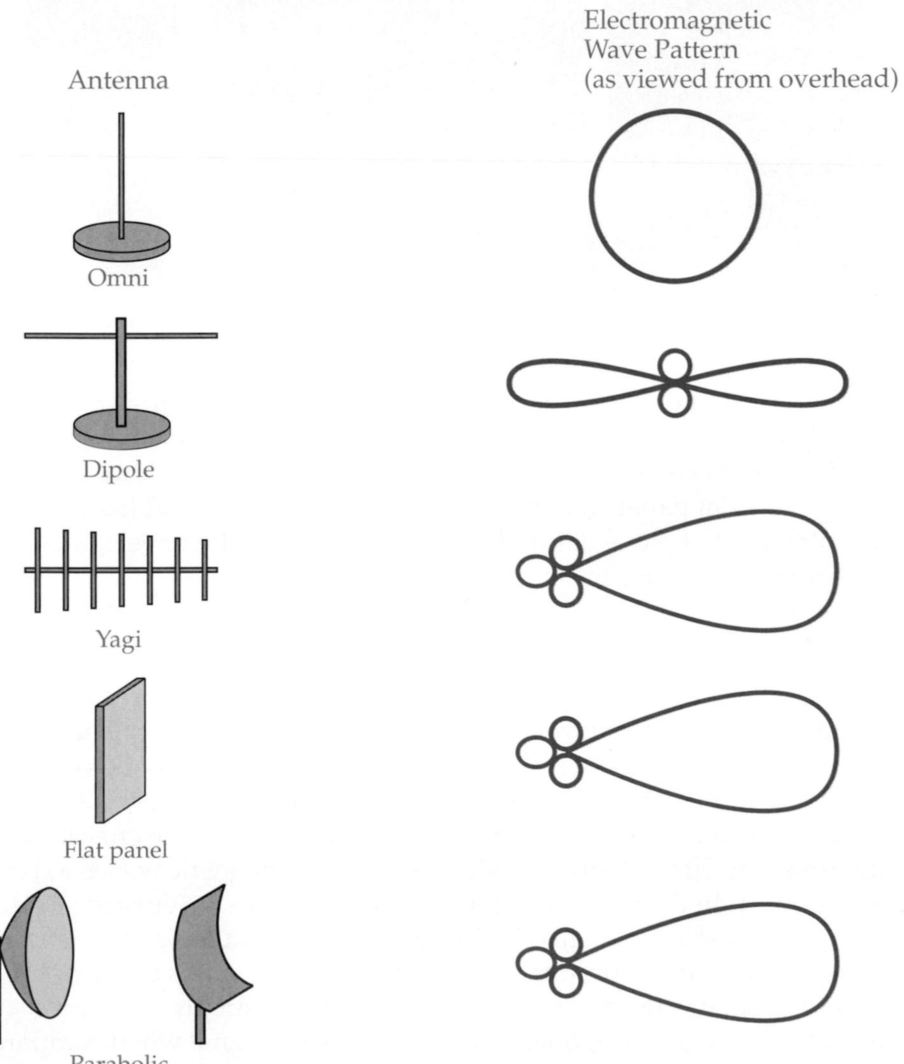

Figure 4-7. Basic antenna styles and the electromagnetic wave patterns they produce.

Figure 4-8. Yagi antenna constructed inside a metal tube. The metal tube enhances reception and transmission. (Photo reprinted with the permission of PCTEL, Maxrad Product Group.)

Flat Panel

The flat panel is a directional-type antenna used for point-to-point links. The main advantage of a flat panel is the aesthetics. The antenna blends in well with building architecture, and many times it is unnoticeable. However, the disadvantage of a flat panel antenna is the consideration of wind load. High wind areas can catch the flat panel design like a sail on a ship. Flat panels must be rigidly supported to reduce the effects of wind.

Parabolic

The parabolic antenna is used for point-to-point links. It a directional-type antenna typically constructed from a grid of rods or mesh wiring. The parabolic antenna enhances reception by reflecting incoming electromagnetic waves with its curved surface to a horn at its center. When the parabolic antenna transmits electromagnetic waves, the horn transmits the signal toward the curved surface of the antenna. The curved surface reflects the electromagnetic waves to produce a beamlike pattern in the same way light is reflected from the curved surface of a flashlight to produce a beam of light. The parabolic antenna is constructed as a simple, curved surface or in the shape of a dish. When it is constructed in the shape of a dish, it is usually called a *parabolic disk* or simply *dish antenna*. The parabolic antenna greatly amplifies a weak radio wave signal when compared with other antenna types.

Radio Wave Transmission Techniques and Networking

Radio waves are electromagnetic waves with a frequency range of 10 kHz to 3,000,000 MHz. They have the longest wavelength when compared with microwave and infrared. Radio waves are used in LANs. Radio wave-based networks adhere to the IEEE 802.11 and Bluetooth standards and operate at 2.4 GHz.

radio waves electromagnetic waves with a frequency range of 10 kHz to 3,000,000 MHz.

Radio Wave-Based Transmission Techniques

To communicate between radio-based wireless network devices, several transmission techniques are used: single-frequency, spread-spectrum, and orthogonal frequency-division multiplexing. You must become familiar with these techniques because most wireless network technologies are described using these terms. The techniques are based on the technology, the frequency band of operation, and the manufacturer's idea of the best way to achieve a high data rate. A high data rate not only relies on how fast the data can move between two points, but also on how much data has to be retransmitted because of interference.

Transmission techniques divide an allocated frequency band into many separate frequency ranges, or channels. After the frequency band is divided, a carrier wave is generated for each of the channels.

Spread Spectrum

Spread spectrum is a transmission technique that uses multiple channels to transmit data either simultaneously or sequentially. The term *spread spectrum* refers to transmission channels *spread* across the *spectrum* of the available bandwidth.

spread spectrum a transmission technique that uses multiple channels to transmit data either simultaneously or sequentially.

Spread spectrum transmission works in a similar manner that highways work. A highway system consists of several separate lanes to carry vehicles. You can think of spread spectrum as several radio wave paths designed to carry radio waves. In the highway system, trucks carry supplies to a store. Each truck uses a separate lane. If one of the lanes is blocked (interference), the other lanes can still carry the supplies to the store. This is the same method employed by spread spectrum. If one of the channels is blocked by radio interference, the other channels can still carry the radio wave data.

In the spread spectrum technique, data can be transmitted on multiple channels simultaneously or sequentially (one at a time). The spread spectrum technique that transmits data on multiple channels simultaneously is called ***frequency hopping.*** The spread spectrum technique that transmits data on multiple channels sequentially is called ***direct sequencing.***

frequency hopping a spread spectrum technique that transmits data on multiple channels simultaneously.

direct sequencing a spread spectrum technique that transmits data on multiple channels sequentially.

Spread spectrum is the chosen transmission method of most wireless technologies. Transmitting data on multiple channels decreases the likelihood of interference. Interference is typically limited to only one or two of the channels. The other channels in the frequency band are free to carry data undisturbed. Data that is lost can be easily retransmitted on a channel that is not affected by the interference.

Frequency hopping

Frequency hopping is also referred to as *frequency hopping spread spectrum (FHSS).* Frequency hopping is used with wireless devices that use the 2.4-GHz radio band. The 2.4-GHz frequency has a bandwidth of 83.5 MHz. Rather than use the entire range as a single channel to carry radio data, the frequency band is divided into 79 1-MHz channels. See **Figure 4-9.**

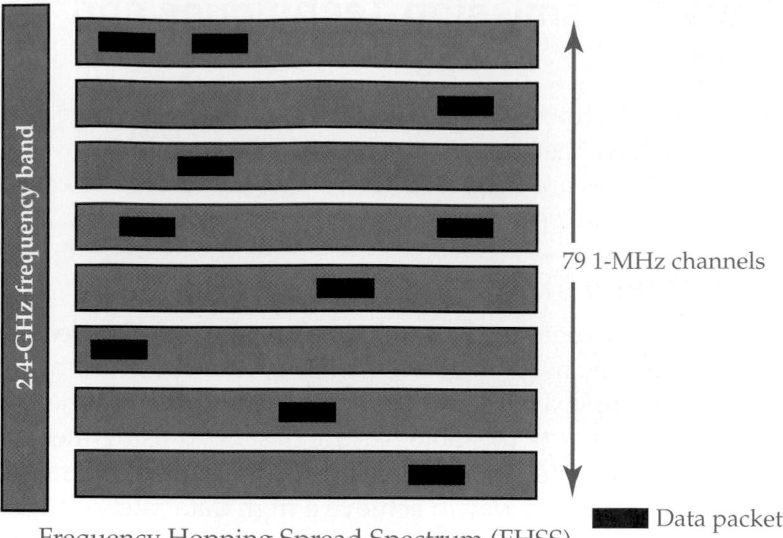

Figure 4-9. In frequency hopping, data is transmitted over 79 1-MHz channels. The data transmissions continuously use different channels in short increments of less than 0.4 seconds each.

Instead of transmitting the data packets over a single channel, the data packets hop from one channel to another in a set pattern determined by a software algorithm. None of the 79 channels are occupied for more than 0.4 seconds. Since the data packets switch from channel to channel, or rather frequency to frequency, this transmission technique is called *frequency hopping*.

Many people assume that because data packets hop to various channels, this transmission technique was designed as a security measure. This assumption is false. The reason that the frequency hopping technique is used is to avoid interference. If any interference matches the same frequency as the wireless networking devices, the data would be corrupted. If only one frequency was used and it encountered interference, then the network would be useless. By using the frequency hopping technique, interference can be tolerated. The interference would likely only affect one or two of the available frequencies in the entire 79 1-MHz channels. This allows more than an ample number of channels to ensure continuous transmission between wireless networking devices.

The frequency hopping technique is limited to a maximum of a 2-Mbps data rate. A much higher data rate can be accomplished using direct sequencing.

Direct sequencing

Direct sequencing divides the 2.4-GHz frequency band into eleven overlapping channels of 83 MHz each. Within the eleven channels are three channels with a 22-MHz bandwidth. The three channels do not overlap and can be used simultaneously. Using three channels at the same time results in higher data rates than frequency hopping. The data rates for direct sequencing are 11 Mbps and 33 Mbps. The 33 Mbps is a result of using all three 22-Mbps channels at the same time, **Figure 4-10.**

One disadvantage of direct sequencing is that a much larger portion of the transmitted data is affected by electromagnetic interference than with frequency hopping. The data rate of direct sequencing, therefore, is drastically affected by interference.

Direct sequencing is also referred to as *direct sequencing spread spectrum (DSSS)*. Most vendors use DSSS technology at 11 Mbps for wireless network systems.

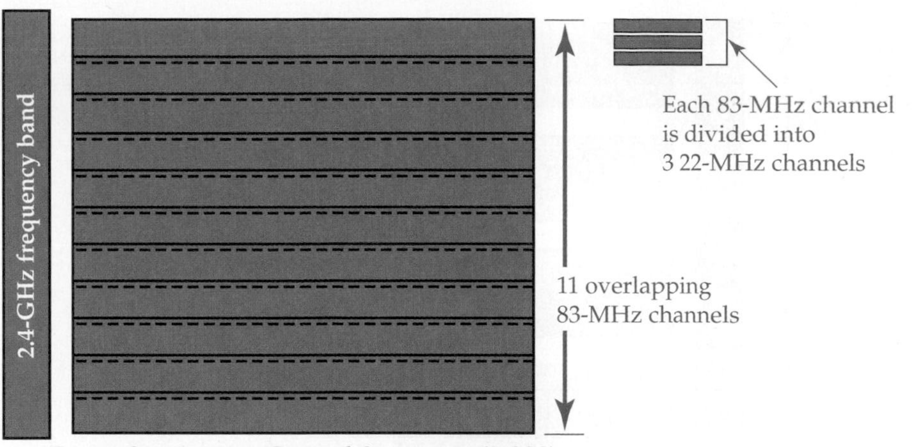

Figure 4-10. In direct sequencing, a 2.4-GHz frequency band is divided into eleven overlapping 83-MHz channels. Each 83-MHz channel is further divided into three 22-MHz channels.

Orthogonal Frequency-Division Multiplexing

The ***orthogonal frequency-division multiplexing (OFDM)*** transmission technique is used with wireless devices that use the 5-GHz radio band and can achieve a data rate as high as 54 Mbps. The OFDM transmission technique divides the allotted frequency into channels similar to frequency hopping and direct sequencing. *Orthogonal* means separate side by side over a range of values. In wireless application, the term *orthogonal* means there are multiple separate radio channels side by side within an assigned radio band. *Frequency division* means to divide the assigned frequency range into multiple, narrow sub-frequencies. *Multiplexing* is an electronics term, which means to combine content from different sources and transmit them collectively over a single, common carrier. By combining the three terms, OFDM means to communicate wireless data over several different channels within an assigned frequency range. However, in OFDM, each channel is broadcast separately and is referred to as *multiplexed*.

orthogonal frequency-division multiplexing (OFDM) a transmission technique that transmits data over different channels within an assigned frequency range. Each channel is broadcast separately and is referred to as *multiplexed*. It can achieve data rates as high as 54 Mbps.

OFDM is used in conjunction with the Unlicensed National Information Infrastructure (U-NII) frequency ranges. The FCC divided the 5-GHz radio frequency into three, 20-MHz channels and classified them as the Unlicensed National Information Infrastructure (U-NII). The three classifications are U-NII-1, U-NII-2, and U-NII-3. See **Figure 4-11.** Each of the three U-NII classifications has a frequency range of 100 MHz. Using the OFDM transmission technique, each 100-MHz frequency range is broken into four separate 20-MHz channels. Each of the 20-MHz channels is further divided into fifty-two, 300-kHz sub-channels. Forty-eight of the fifty-two sub-channels are used to transmit data, and the remaining four are used for error correction. It is the large number of channels that provide the high data rates. Additionally, communication is not affected as adversely by interference as it is with the other techniques mentioned. If one or two sub-channels are affected, the overall data rate is not affected.

The FCC U-NII classifications are based on the frequency range of the broadcast, the allowable maximum amount of power allotted to the broadcast, and the location of where the device may be used. There is no maximum distance measurement in feet or meters for the different classifications. The maximum distances are controlled by the maximum amount of output wattage that can be generated by the devices. The actual range varies considerably due to influences such as building structures and materials, the electromagnetic environment, and atmospheric conditions. Use the chart in **Figure 4-12** to get a relative idea of expected maximum distances.

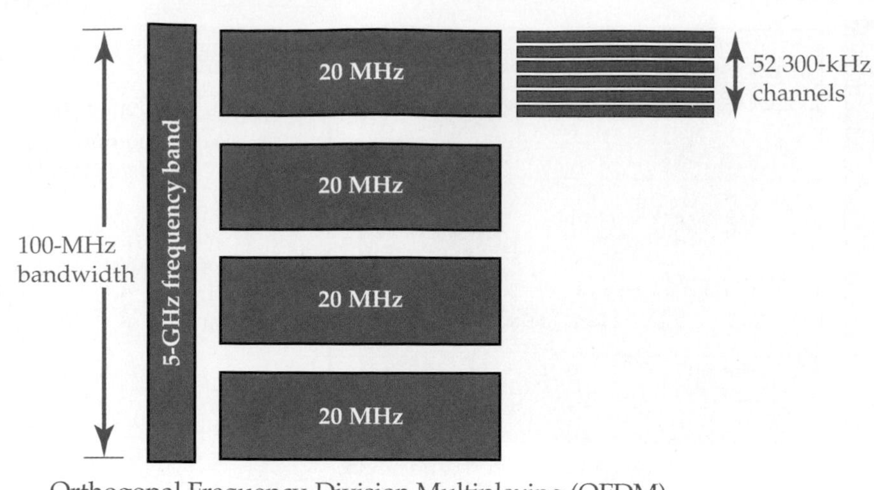

Figure 4-11. Orthogonal frequency-division multiplexing (OFDM) is used in conjunction with the U-NII frequency ranges to achieve a data rate as high as 54 Mbps. Each of the U-NII frequency ranges is 100 MHz wide. This bandwidth is divided into three 20-MHz channels, which are further divided into fifty-two 300-kHz channels.

Figure 4-12. U-NII classifications and their characteristics.

Classification	Frequency Range	Power	Comment
U-NII 1	5.15 GHz–5.25 GHz	50 mW	Indoors
U-NII 2	5.25 GHz–5.35 GHz	250 mW	Indoors/outdoors
U-NII 3	5.725 GHz–5.825 GHz	1 W	Outdoors

Distances vary by manufacturer and by location conditions such as placement of metal cabinets and building materials. The maximum power output of the device has a direct relationship to data throughput. Packet loss is generally caused by radio interference or excessive distance between two devices. When packet loss increases, the data rate decreases. The data rate is automatically adjusted to a lower rate when an excessive number of packets are lost. The data rate continues to be lowered until an acceptable packet loss is reached. The more powerful the signal, the less interference can disrupt the signal. This means that there will be fewer packets lost. Consequently, data rate is better when the signal is more powerful. The maximum transmission power rating for a wireless device is set by the FCC. Do *not* attempt to memorize distances because they are not standard.

Radio Wave-Based Networking

Wireless Access Point (WAP) a wireless network device that provides a connection between a wireless network and a cable-based network and controls the flow of all packets on the wireless network.

Radio wave-based networks are rapidly becoming the choice of many networking systems because of the fast and easy installation and the convenience of no wires. A simple wireless network, such as one designed for home or business use, consists of two or more computers with wireless network adapters. **Figure 4-13** shows a USB wireless network adapter.

Wireless Access Points

While not required, most wireless networks contain a Wireless Access Point (WAP) also referred to as an *access point (AP)*. A ***Wireless Access Point (WAP)*** provides a connection between a wireless network and a cable-based network.

Figure 4-13. USB wireless network adapter. (3Com Corporation)

Wireless Access Points typically provide access from wireless network devices to needed hardwired network devices, such as printers, modems, and routers.

A typical WAP comes equipped with two omni antennae, **Figure 4-14.** One antenna is used for transmitting, and the other is used for receiving. This allows for full-duplex communication, which makes the WAP more efficient than if a single antenna were used.

When a WAP is present in a wireless network, all communication must go through it. You can think of a WAP as a traffic director for packets. The WAP controls the flow of all packets on the wireless network. When multiple Wireless Access Points are used, the roaming device (laptop, palm top, personal digital assistant) automatically detects and connects to the WAP with the strongest signal, which is typically the closest WAP.

All Wireless Access Points in a wireless network use the same Service Set Identifier (SSID). The SSID is similar in nature to a workgroup name or domain name. It is a name that identifies Wireless Access Points within the same network.

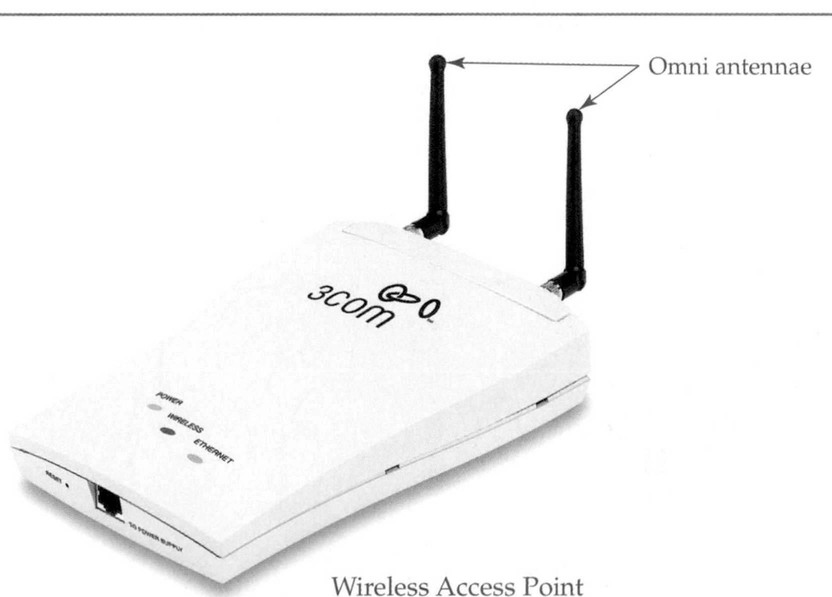

Figure 4-14. Wireless Access Point (WAP). Note that the WAP has two omni antennae. One antenna is used for receiving, and the other antenna is used for transmitting. (3Com Corporation)

Multiple Wireless Access Points within the same network should be configured with the same SSID to support network roaming. When separate network systems are within range of each other, the Wireless Access Points for each separate network should use a different SSID to distinguish themselves from each other. Most Wireless Access Points and wireless network adapters come with a default SSID. If they are installed with minimal or no configuration at all, all Wireless Access Points will have the same SSID. The SSID can be readily reconfigured.

Tech Tip

Service Set Identifier (SSID) names are case-sensitive.

Wireless network adapters and Wireless Access Points come with default settings to make configuration easy and, in some cases, automatic. However, easy or preconfigured settings make for weak security. Each device by the same manufacturer uses the same default SSID. The SSID should be changed to make the system more secure.

By default, most manufacturers do not enable encryption. The encryption process slows the overall data rate of the system. It takes time to encrypt and decrypt the packets. Encryption, however, should be enabled to make the network more secure.

infrastructure mode a wireless network that contains one or more Wireless Access Points.

ad hoc mode a wireless network that does not contain a Wireless Access Point.

Wireless Network Modes

A wireless network that contains one or more Wireless Access Points is arranged in ***infrastructure mode*,** **Figure 4-15.** When a WAP is not present in a wireless network, it is arranged in ***ad hoc mode*,** **Figure 4-16.** The reference to the term *ad hoc* means that the system is put together rapidly and is usually intended to be a temporary installation rather than a permanent installation. An ad hoc network can contain a maximum of 20 computers. Typically, an ad hoc network consists of a laptop and a desktop computer. An ad hoc network can be compared to a peer-to-peer network where all devices are equal.

Figure 4-15.
A wireless network in infrastructure mode.

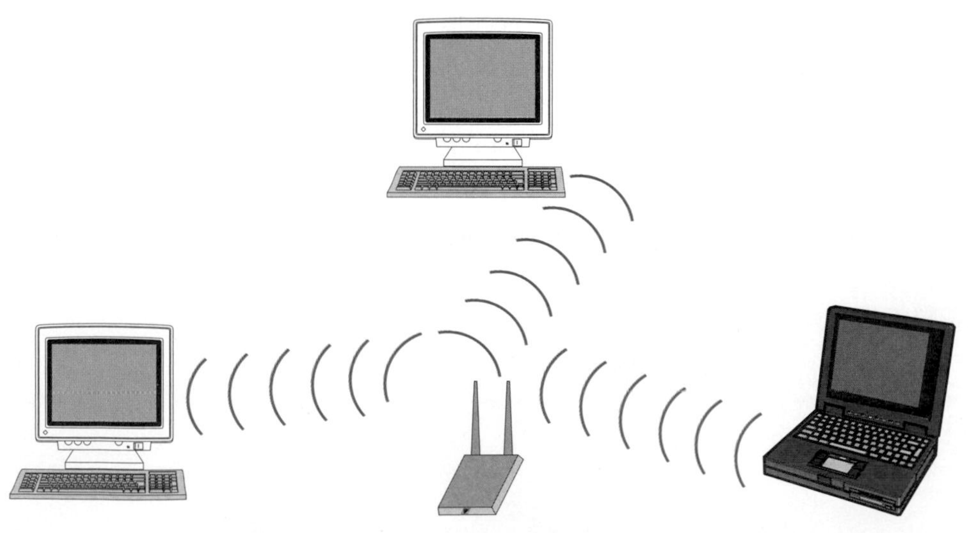

Infrastructure Mode

Figure 4-16.
A wireless network in ad hoc mode.

The IEEE 802.11 wireless network standard does not use the terms *ad hoc*, *SSID*, or *ESSID* when describing the technical aspects of a wireless network. These terms are encountered when reviewing product information provided by wireless manufacturers. The IEEE uses the terms *Basic Service Set (BSS)* and *Independent Basic Service Set (IBSS)*. A ***Basic Service Set (BSS)*** is a group of wireless devices connected as a network, which is described by manufacturers as an infrastructure network or an SSID. An ***Independent Basic Service Set (IBSS)*** is similar to an ad hoc network. The IBSS does not use an access point and usually is a direct connection between two wireless devices.

You will see the term *Enhanced Service Set Identifier (ESSID)* listed in the CompTIA Network+ 2009 objectives and acronyms list. The more commonly accepted translation of the acronym *ESSID* is *Extended Service Set Identifier.*

An ***Extended Service Set Identifier (ESSID)*** refers to two or more Wireless Access Points or wireless devices using the same SSID. In other words, the network has been "extended" by using the same SSID for more than one access point. When multiple access points use the same SSID, a portable wireless device can maintain a constant connection with the network as the user moves around the location.

Basic Service Set (BSS)
an IEEE term used to describe a group of wireless devices connected as an infrastructure network or an SSID.

Independent Basic Service Set (IBSS)
a network that does not use an access point and usually is a direct connection between two wireless devices.

Note

The exact meaning of networking terminology can be confusing because device manufacturers often present the terminology at a novice level rather than at a technical level. For example, some manufacturers use the term *enhanced* to indicate a feature that has been added by that particular manufacturer.

IEEE 802.11 Standard

Radio wave-based networks adhere to the 802.11 standard. The 802.11 standard consists of four classifications of wireless networks: 802.11a, 802.11b, 802.11g, and 802.11n. See **Figure 4-17** for a chart of the 802.11 standards and their characteristics.

Extended Service Set Identifier (ESSID)
two or more Wireless Access Points or wireless devices using the same SSID.

802.11a

The 802.11a standard operates at the 5-GHz frequency and has a maximum data rate of 54 Mbps. An 802.11a device may use lower data rates of 48 Mbps, 36 Mbps,

Figure 4-17.
IEEE 802.11 standards and their characteristics.

802.11 Standard	Radio Frequency	Frequency Range	Data Rate	Range (approximate)	Transmission Method
802.11a	5 GHz	5.15 GHz–5.825 GHz	6 Mbps 9 Mbps 12 Mbps 18 Mbps 24 Mbps 36 Mbps 54 Mbps	50 m	OFDM
802.11b	2.4 GHz	2.4 GHz–2.4835 GHz	1 Mbps 2 Mbps 5.5 Mbps 11 Mbps	100 m	DSSS
802.11g	2.4 GHz	2.4 GHz–2.4835 GHz	1 Mbps 2 Mbps 5.5 Mbps 11 Mbps	100 m	DSSS
	5 GHz	5.15 GHz-5.825 GHz	54 Mbps	50 m	OFDM
802.11n	2.4 GHz	2.4 GHz–2.4835 GHz	All previous data rates up to 300 Mbps and possibly as high as 600 Mbps	300 m	OFDM
	5 GHz	5.15 GHz-5.825 GHz			

24 Mbps, 18 Mbps, 12 Mbps, 9 Mbps, and 6 Mbps. At the 5-GHz frequency, 802.11a networking devices are not susceptible to interference from devices that cause interference at the 2.4-GHz frequency range. 802.11a devices are incompatible with 802.11b and 802.11g devices. Also, 802.11a devices use a higher frequency than 802.11b or 802.11g devices. The higher frequency cannot penetrate materials such as building walls like the lower frequency devices can. This results in 802.11a devices having a shorter range when compared with 802.11b, 802.11g, and 802.11n devices.

802.11b

Although the 802.11a and 802.11b standards were developed at the same time, 802.11b was the first to be adopted by industry. The maximum data rate for 802.11b is 11 Mbps. When the highest rate cannot be achieved because of distance or radio interference, a lower rate is automatically selected. The lower rates are 5.5 Mbps, 2 Mbps, and 1 Mbps. An 802.11b device can operate over any of 11 channels within the assigned bandwidth. When communicating between wireless devices, all devices should use the same channel. When using devices from the same manufacturer, the same channel is automatically selected by default. Two wireless networks, one constructed of 802.11b devices and the other constructed of 802.11a devices, can coexist without interfering with each other because they use different assigned frequencies. This allows for two different wireless networks to operate within the same area without interfering with the other.

Wi-Fi
a term coined by the Wi-Fi Alliance that refers to 802.11 wireless network products.

802.11 network devices are often referred to as ***Wi-Fi,*** which stands for "wireless fidelity." The use of the term *Wi-Fi* was due to manufacturers forming the Wireless Ethernet Compatibility Alliance (WECA) in an effort to standardize wireless network devices. Devices approved as compatible with the 802.11standards are given a "Wi-Fi compliant" seal, which means any device bearing the Wi-Fi seal is compatible with any other device bearing the seal, **Figure 4-18.** This process led to competing yet compatible standards by both organizations. As a result, users are able to mix and match components from various manufacturers. There are many proprietary devices and software products on the market that may not be fully compatible with other devices.

802.11g

The IEEE 802.11g standard followed the 802.11a and 802.11b standards. 802.11g operates in the 802.11b frequency range of 2.4 GHz. This makes it downward compatible with 802.11b devices. When communicating with 802.11b devices, the maximum data rate is reduced to 11 Mbps. The maximum throughput for the 802.11g standard is 54 Mbps, but the maximum distance is typically much shorter than an 802.11b device. An 802.11g device can use the lower data rates of 48 Mbps, 36 Mbps, 28 Mbps, 24 Mbps, 12 Mbps, 11 Mbps, 9 Mbps, 6 Mbps, 5.5 Mbps, 2 Mbps, and 1 Mbps. Since 802.11g is assigned to the same frequency range as 802.11b, it is susceptible to the same sources of radio interference.

802.11g and 802.11b devices are not compatible with 802.11a devices because they use different frequencies. It must be noted that while the standards are different, there are devices on the market that can communicate with any of the mentioned wireless standards. In other words, there are wireless devices that can communicate with 802.11a, 802.11b, and 802.11g devices.

802.11n

The 802.11n standard operates at 5 GHz and is backward compatible with the 2.4-GHz frequency range. In 2009, the Wi-Fi Alliance organization ratified (approved) a standard based on a draft version of 802.11n. However, manufacturers developed 802.11n wireless network devices before the 802.11n classification was ratified in an effort to offer superior wireless devices. Therefore, these devices may not exactly match the 802.11n ratified standard.

Note

There cannot be a definitive range for individual IEEE wireless standards, only approximations. Range is determined by radio wave power expressed in watts. There are many electronic factors that affect radio wave ranges.

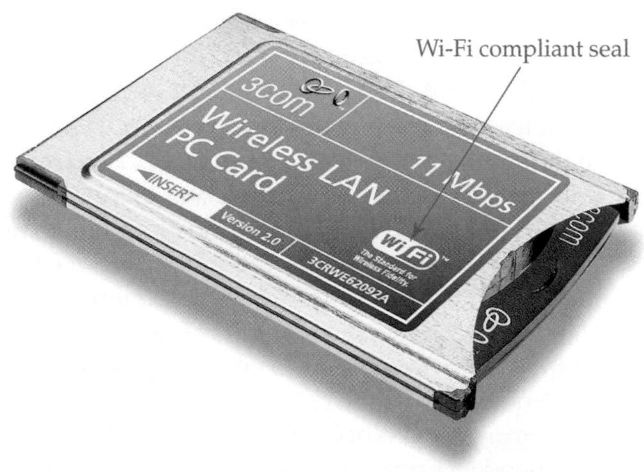

Figure 4-18. Wireless PCMCIA adapter card with the Wi-Fi compliant seal. (3Com Corporation)

Multiple Input Multiple Output (MIMO) a wireless networking technology that transmits two or more streams of data to increase data throughput and the range of the wireless network.

spatial multiplexing a wireless networking technology that transmits two or more streams of data in the same frequency channel.

An 802.11n device is compatible with 802.11a, 802.11b, and 802.11g, but may not support MIMO technology when paired with these devices. ***Multiple Input Multiple Output (MIMO)*** is a wireless networking technology that uses two or more streams of data transmission to increase data throughput and the range of the wireless network. Transmitting two or more streams of data in the same frequency channel is referred to as ***spatial multiplexing***.

802.11n incorporates the Multiple Input Multiple Output (MIMO) technology using 5-GHz and 2.4-GHz frequencies with an expected data rate of approximately 300 Mbps to 600 Mbps. The exact speed depends on the number of simultaneous data streams transmitted. Some 802.11n devices are advertised with data rates much higher than specified in the standard.

MIMO was designed as an integral part of the 802.11n standard. Some manufacturers have incorporated MIMO into the latest revisions of their 802.11g devices to take advantage of producing higher data rates.

Prior to MIMO, Wireless Access Points and devices sent a single stream of data between the transmitter and receiver. MIMO uses two or more antennae, thus creating two or more streams of data simultaneously. For example, an 802.11n wireless device that transmits data at 150 Mbps can apply MIMO and raise the data rate to 300 Mbps. The latest 802.11n standard is 144.4 Mbps or rounded up to 150 Mbps. By using MIMO, 802.11n devices can raise the expected data rate to nearly 300 Mbps when using a 20-MHz channel and 600 Mbps when using a 40-MHz channel inside the assigned 2.4-GHz frequency range. The 40-MHz channel can carry twice the data as the 20-MHz channel.

The WI-FI Alliance uses a similar method in its standard and achieves a maximum throughput of 450 Mbps as posted on their Web site at the time of this writing. Visit the Wi-Fi Alliance Web site (http://wi-fi.org).

802.11 Access Method

802.11 networks rely on Carrier Sense Multiple Access with Collision Avoidance (CSMA/CA) as a media access protocol. Do *not* confuse this with CSMA/CD, which is used by IEEE 802.3 networks. The Carrier Sense Multiple Access (CSMA) portion of the technology is the same for both the 802.11 and 802.3 networks. The difference is in the Collision Detection (CD) versus Collision Avoidance (CA). Collision Detection (CD) detects a collision on the network after it occurs, while Collision Avoidance (CA) attempts to avoid a collision.

To understand the CSMA/CA process, look at **Figure 4-19.** The laptop equipped with a wireless card first listens for network traffic. If the airwaves are clear, it signals the WAP with a request to send (RTS) message. The WAP returns either a clear to send (CTS) or busy signal to the laptop. The process is repeated until the laptop is cleared to send data. After the data has been sent to the WAP, the WAP sends an acknowledge (ACK) to the laptop. Collision avoidance technology solves the problem of broadcast storms, which are associated with collision detection technology. The collision detection technology is designed to accept network collisions, wait, and then resend the complete transmission.

The CSMA/CA access method was selected over CSMA/CD because of the nature of wireless media. In a typical Ethernet environment that uses cable, a collision can be detected anywhere on a segment by all nodes in that segment. The same is not true of a wireless network. Look at **Figure 4-20** and compare the two networking technologies. In the cable-based network, all nodes are connected to the same segment via a hub. All nodes can detect any broadcast that takes place. There is no need to broadcast an intention to communicate.

CSMA/CA Process

1. Request to send (RTS)
2. Busy or clear to send (CTS)
3. Sends data after clear to send (CTS)
4. Acknowledge (ACK)

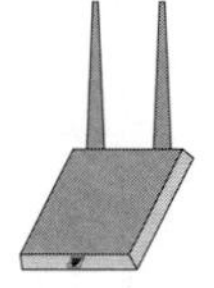

Figure 4-19. A laptop equipped with a wireless network adapter listens for network traffic. If all is clear, it sends a request to send (RTS) signal to the Wireless Access Point (WAP). The WAP returns a clear to send (CTS) or a busy signal to the laptop. This process is repeated until the laptop is cleared to send the data. After the data is sent to the WAP, the WAP sends an acknowledge (AWK) signal to the laptop.

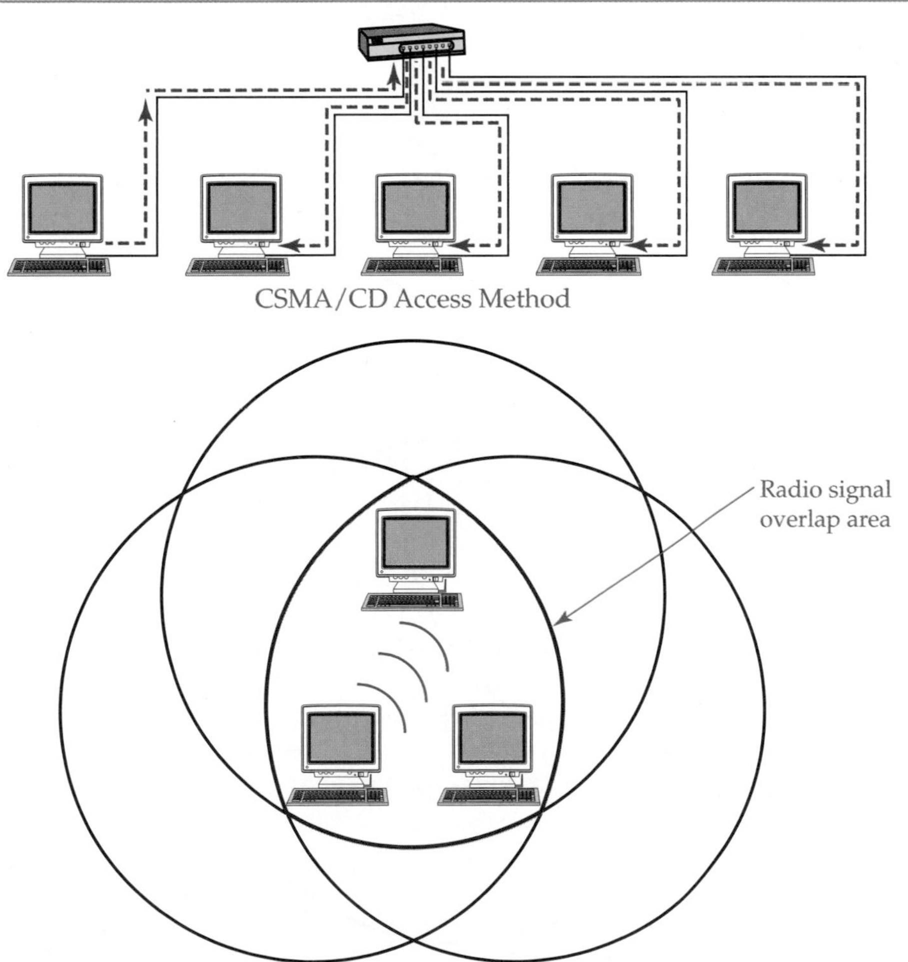

Figure 4-20. In an 802.3 network, which uses the CSMA/CD access method, all computers are wired to each other and each computer can hear traffic on the network. There is no need for a computer to send a signal notifying the other computers it is about to transmit data. In an 802.11 network, which uses the CSMA/CA access method, computers with wireless network interface cards communicate within an overlap area. A Wireless Access Point (WAP) controls all communication giving permission to the individual devices to communicate in an organized fashion.

For nodes to communicate with each other on a wireless network, all nodes must be inside the same broadcast area, called an *overlap area*. See **Figure 4-21.** This is not always possible, especially with mobile devices such as laptops, PDAs, cell phones, automobiles, and such. It is not unusual to have a mobile computer outside of the normal overlap area. There is also the possibility of mobile users moving in and out of the overlap area, further complicating communication. The best logical choice of media access for a wireless network is CSMA/CA.

Figure 4-21. Overlap area of an ad hoc and infrastructure wireless network. A—For computers in an ad hoc wireless network to communicate with each other, all computers must be in the same overlap area. B—In an infrastructure wireless network, the Wireless Access Point (WAP) must be in the common overlap area of the wireless network computers. The WAP controls all communication.

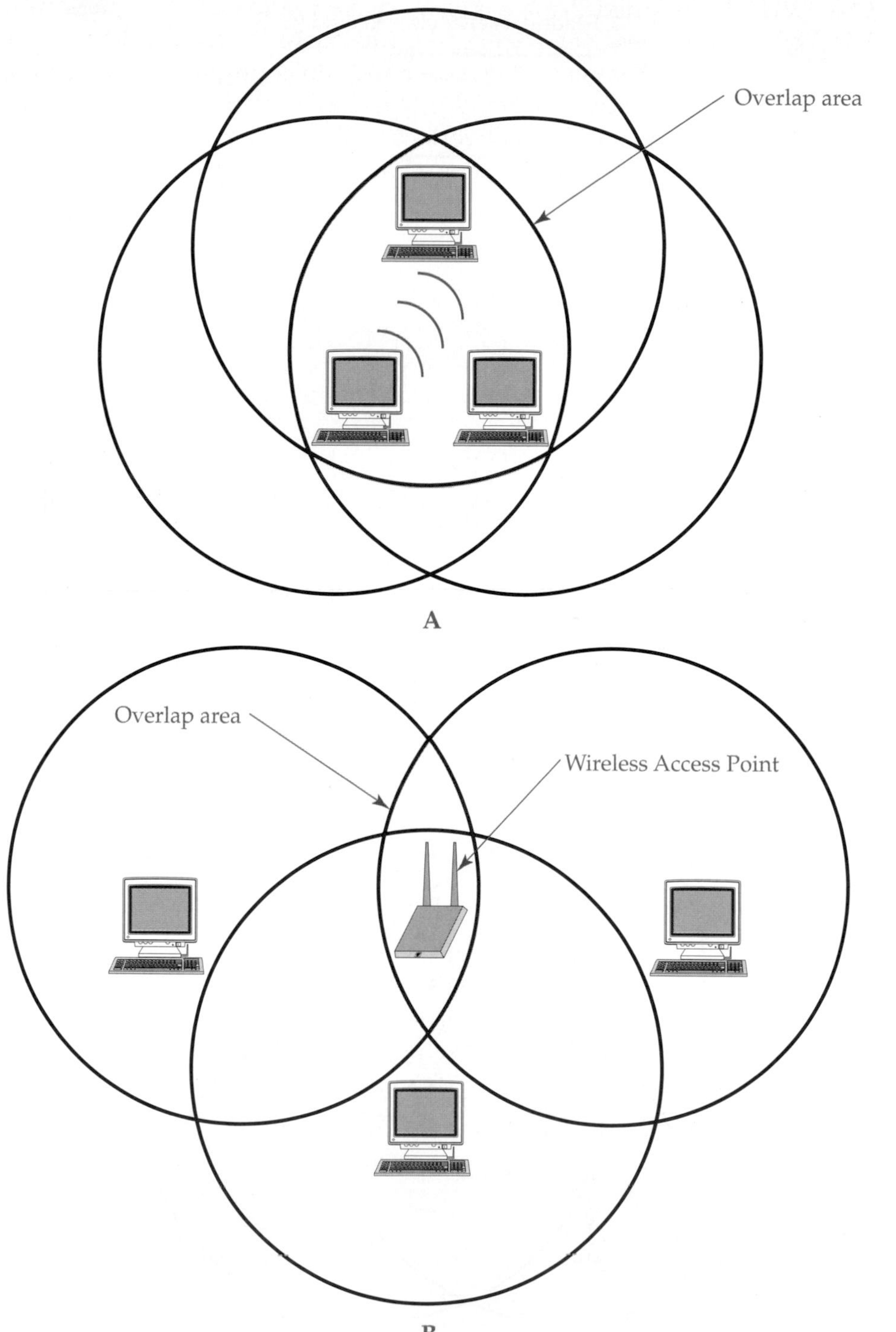

CSMA/CA is used because of the way wireless networks communicate as opposed to the way wired networks communicate. When communicating on a wired network, all devices in the same collision domain can hear each other when they are communicating. The idea is that each device waits for when the cable is clear of communication before it communicates on the cable. When a collection of wireless devices are connected as a network, not all devices will always be within the range of all other devices. This causes a problem because a wireless device may not be aware when other devices are communicating. This is why a wireless network system requires CSMA/CA to access the network media, the wireless network area.

CSMA/CA is designed to make the WAP in charge of all communication. The WAP permits wireless devices to communicate or denies wireless devices to communicate. The WAP is centrally located and can communicate with all the devices in the wireless network. The WAP hears all communication. A device sitting at the edge of the wireless network cannot hear the devices farthest from it, but the WAP can. If CSMA/CD was used as the access method, the devices would not take turns as permitted by the WAP and the result would be too many communication collisions on the network caused by two or more devices attempting to communicate at the same time.

Adding more Wireless Access Points can expand the geographic area covered by a wireless network, **Figure 4-22.** Connecting several WAPs with cable can also enlarge a wireless LAN. **Figure 4-23** shows several WAPs joined by copper core cable. This connection allows multiple WAPs to be spread over a large area

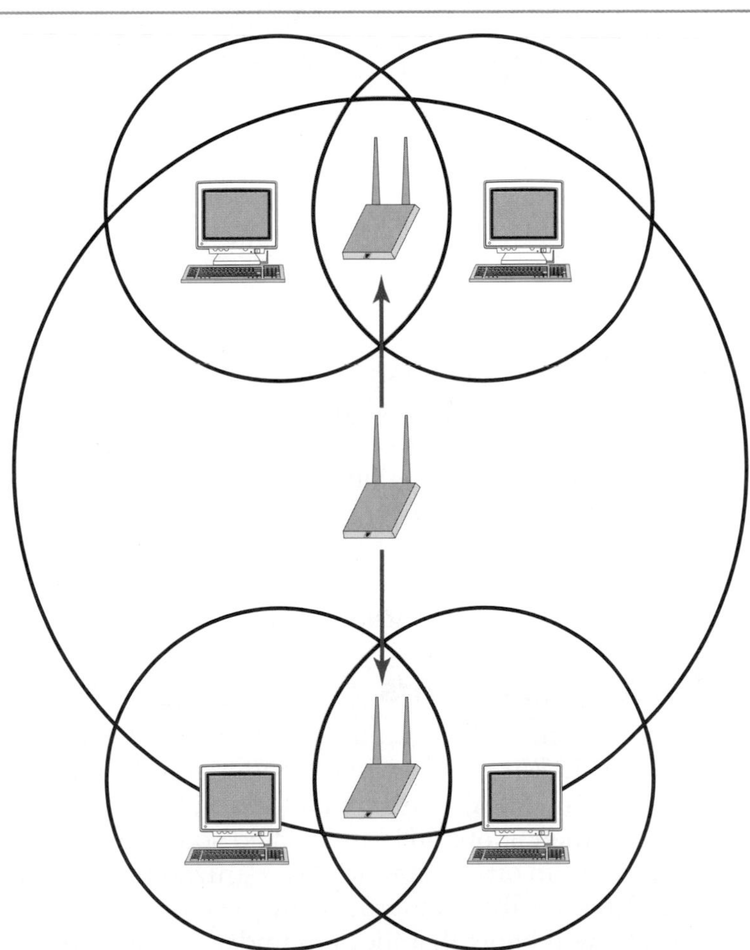

Figure 4-22.
The range of a wireless network can be extended by adding additional Wireless Access Points (WAPs).

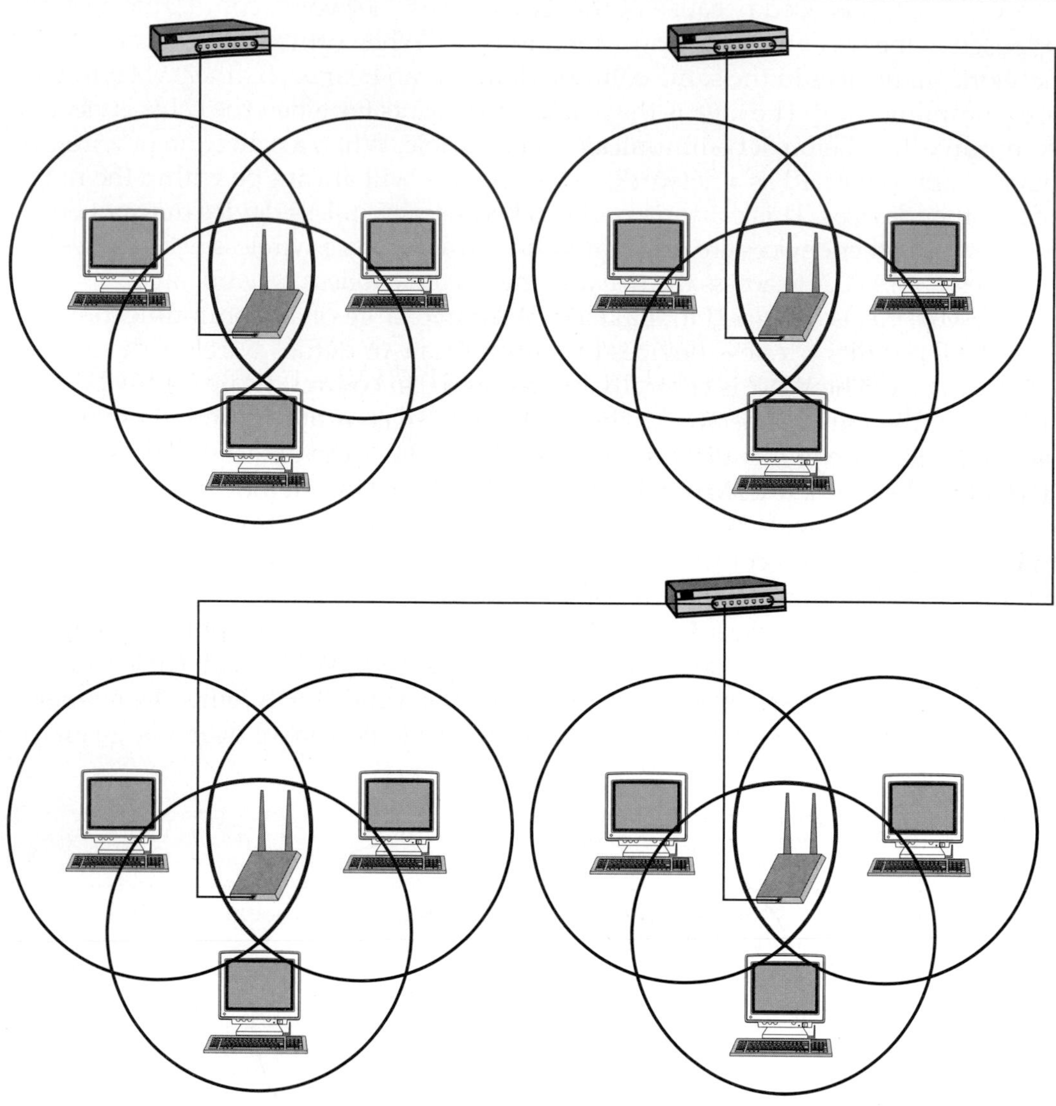

Figure 4-23. A wireless network can be greatly expanded by connecting multiple Wireless Access Points (WAPs) to a cable-based Ethernet network such as 10BaseT.

without the need for overlapping radio signals. This type of arrangement is ideal for mobile users. As the user travels through the network system with a mobile device such as a laptop, he or she can access the network system from anywhere. For example, a college campus spanning hundreds of acres could incorporate a mesh arrangement of WAPs throughout the campus area. A professor or student could use his or her laptop equipped with a wireless PCMCIA card to access the network system from anywhere on the campus such as classrooms, the library, cafeteria, a dorm room, or even from outside on the lawn areas.

New IEEE Wireless Standards

working group
a standard not fully developed and adopted as an official standard recognized by IEEE.

There are two other major IEEE standards that are directly related to wireless technology: 802.15 Wireless Personal Networks (WPAN) and 802.16 Broadband Wireless Access (BWA). While not adopted at this time, they are still worth mentioning since their adoption is anticipated soon. Standards not fully developed and adopted as an official standard recognized by IEEE are referred to as a ***working group.*** Titles for the standards being developed always use the term *working group* so people will know that they are under development.

Network+ Note

Questions concerning the IEEE standards can be tricky on the Network+ Certification exam because the standards are constantly changing. Before taking the certification exam, you should check the CompTIA Web site to see if any changes are reflected in the exam objectives.

802.15

The 802.15 Working Group for Wireless Personal Area Networks is better known as *Personal Area Networks (PAN)* or *Wireless Personal Area Networks (WPAN)*. A ***Wireless Personal Area Networks (WPAN)*** is typically a small Ethernet network consisting of personal wireless devices such as a cell phone, laptop, palmtop, wireless printer, Wireless Access Point, iPod, Xbox 360, and similar items. Many of the standards developed here coexist with standards already developed and adopted by 802.11 wireless LANs. One of the concerns of 802.15 is the compatibility of Bluetooth standards with other mobile communications devices such as telephones, portable computers, and personal digital assistants.

Wireless Personal Area Networks (WPAN) a small Ethernet network consisting of personal wireless devices such as a cell phone, laptop, palmtop, wireless printer, Wireless Access Point, iPod, Xbox 360, and similar items.

The 802.15 standard breaks down into additional separate specifications. These are listed and defined in the following table. A complete copy of the IEEE 802.15 standard is located at http://standards.ieee.org/getieee802/802.15.html.

802.15 Standard	Description
802.15.1	Low-speed PAN based on the Bluetooth standard.
802.15.2	Allows 802.11 and 802.15 devices to coexist in the 2.4-GHz band.
802.15.3	High-speed PAN with a data rate of 10 Mbps–55 Mbps at a range of 10 meters or less.
802.15.4	Low-speed PAN with a data rate of 2 kbps–200 kbps using DSSS for 2.4 and 915 MHz.

ZigBee is a standard developed by a consortium of electronic manufacturers for mainly residential applications of wireless devices as related to appliances and security and such. It is based on the 802.15.4 standard. What appears to be confusing is that the standard is represented by the name "ZigBee" rather than a number. The term *ZigBee* is used similar to the way the term *Wi-Fi* is used.

Keep in mind that the IEEE standards will constantly change and be amended as manufacturers try to improve the network wireless technologies.

802.16

The IEEE 802.16 Working Group on Broadband Wireless Access Standards is better known as *Broadband Wireless Access (BWA)* or *Wireless Metropolitan Area Networks (WMAN)*. This project is concerned with connecting LANs to each other using wireless technologies. The working group is hoping to design data rates as high as 70 Mbps over distances of 30 miles or more. The working group is also attempting to expand the radio frequencies assigned by the FCC and the radio frequencies dedicated to only wireless mesh-type networks, such as wireless MANs. At the present time, private companies can achieve high data rates over many miles, but there is no single standard that allows devices manufactured by different companies to communicate with the other.

USB Wireless

Wireless USB is a standard for devices that connect through the USB port of a PC. Wireless USB is most often used to support the transfer of data between the PC and devices such as cameras, printers, mobile phones, DVD players, televisions, external hard drives, and AV receivers. Wireless USB provides data speeds of up to 480 Mbps at a maximum range of 3 meters and up to 100 Mbps at a maximum range of 10 meters.

Bluetooth

Bluetooth is a short-range, wireless system that is designed for limited distances. Typical Bluetooth devices have an effective range of 30 meters or less. Look at the following table to see approximate values based on output wattage of the device.

Class	Power	Approximate Range
Class 1	100 mW	100 m
Class 2	2.5 mW	10 m
Class 3	1 mW	1 m

The abbreviation "mW" represents "milliwatt" or "1/1000 of a watt." As you can see, most Bluetooth devices have a very limited range.

The Bluetooth standard has evolved over the years in an effort to increase its data rates. Look at the maximum data rates for each Bluetooth standard listed in the following table.

Bluetooth Standard	Maximum Data Rate
1.0	1 Mbps
2.0	3 Mbps
3.0	24 Mbps

Tech Tip

As always when working with radio wave devices, expect that practical data rates will be much lower than the data rate printed for the standard, except in ideal conditions.

Bluetooth uses 79 channels that use the frequency hopping spread spectrum transmission technique, starting at 2.4 GHz. The Bluetooth standard was developed separately from the IEEE network standards. It was never intended as a networking standard designed to carry massive amounts of information. Bluetooth was designed for appliances such as telephones, laptops, palm tops, digital cameras, personal digital assistants, headsets, printers, keyboards, and mice.

piconet
a Bluetooth network. Also called a *Personal Area Network (PAN)*.

A Bluetooth network is referred to as a piconet or a Personal Area Network (PAN). A ***piconet*** is a very small network. Bluetooth became recognized by the IEEE organization and was incorporated into the IEEE 802.15 Working Group

Wireless Personal Area Networks in July, 2004. Bluetooth suffers from the same radio interference sources as other 802.11 devices, which are part of the ISM band. Bluetooth will not interfere with 802.11b devices when operated in the same area because they use different formats for configuring data. In other words, a wireless keyboard and mouse based on the Bluetooth standard will not interfere with the operation of an 802.11b wireless network.

For the very latest information about the Bluetooth standard, always check the Bluetooth organization Web site at www.Bluetooth.com and www.bluetooth.org.

Note

The name "Wireless Personal Area Network (WPAN)" is often used in place of "piconet."

Cellular Technology

Cellular technology is based on radio waves connecting to designated areas referred to as *cells*. Rather than communicate directly by radio wave from one cell to another, a remote device connects to a radio transmitter/receiver within its cell. The radio transmitter/receiver communicates to remote cells via microwave transmission or telephone lines. In the remote cell, the message is sent to a radio transceiver/receiver. The radio transceiver/receiver sends, via radio waves, the message to the remote device within its cell. See **Figure 4-24.**

cellular technology a technology based on radio waves connecting to designated areas referred to as *cells.*

Cellular technology is responsible for wireless telephone and telephone technology. The same technology connects mobile and stationary computer equipment. A text message can be transmitted to a pager by typing in a message using a desktop computer. The message is sent over an Internet connection to a mobile telephone switching office. From there, radio microwaves transmit the encoded message to the distant pager system. See **Figure 4-25.**

Cellular technology supports duplex communication using a device such as a personal digital assistant or a palmtop configured for wireless radio services.

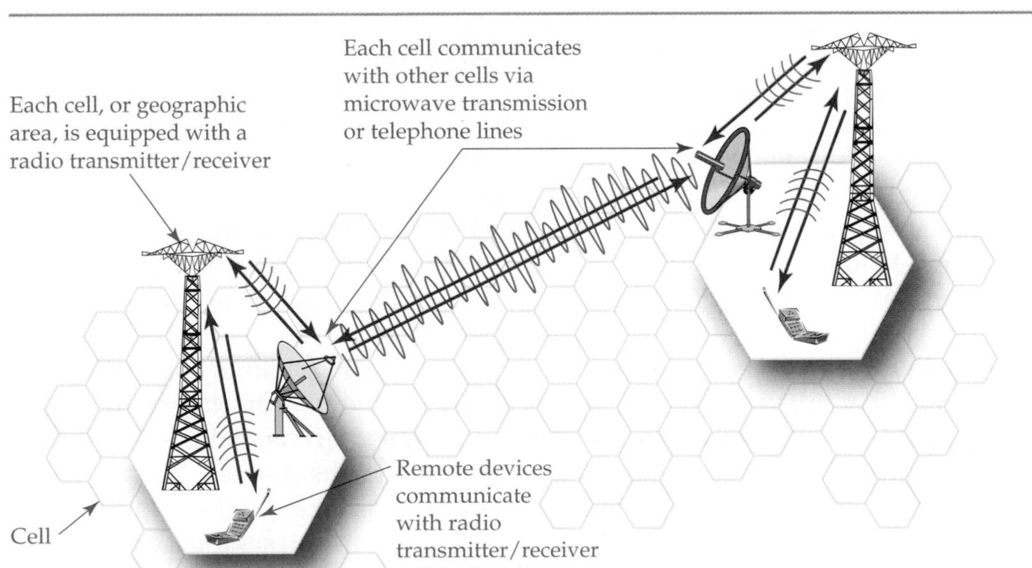

Figure 4-24. Cellular technology communications system.

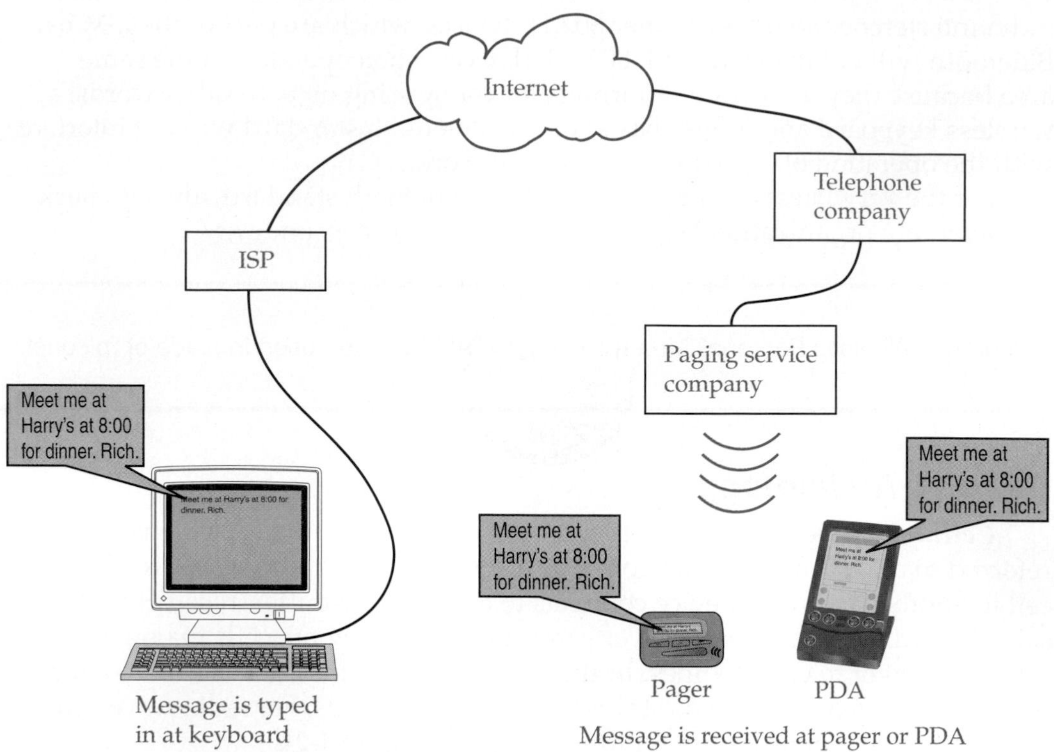

Figure 4-25.
An example of using cellular technology to send a message from a computer to a mobile network device such as a PDA.

Microwave Transmission and Networking

The term *microwave* is used to describe radio waves in the electromagnetic spectrum that have a wavelength from 1 millimeter (mm) to 30 centimeters (cm) and radio wave frequencies between 1 GHz and 300 GHz. The amount of data carried by a radio wave is directly proportional to its frequency. In short, the higher the frequency, the more data that can be transmitted in a given period of time. The portion of the electromagnetic spectrum identified as microwave is the preferred technology used for wireless networking. Its application is described in the IEEE 802.11 standards. Microwave radio wave transmission can be broadcast directly between wireless devices or routed through satellites orbiting the earth.

Satellites are often used as part of a WAN distribution. Satellites can offer the advantage of providing a wireless network connection to remote or mobile locations that cannot be achieved using conventional methods.

geosynchronous orbit
an orbit in which a satellite's rotational speed is synchronized with the earth's rotational speed, making the satellite appear to be in a stationary position.

propagation delay
the time it takes for data to be transmitted from the earth and satellite.

Look at **Figure 4-26.** The satellite in this illustration is positioned 22,300 miles (35,880 km) above the earth's surface and moves at a speed of approximately 68,000 mph. At this distance, it takes the satellite exactly 24 hours to make one revolution around the earth. This time is equal to the time of the earth's rotation. This equality causes the satellite to appear in a stationary position above the earth and is said to be in ***geosynchronous orbit.*** In other words, the satellite's speed is synchronized with the earth's rotational speed. If the satellite were in a lower orbit, it would need to move at a much higher orbital speed. This would result in the need to track the satellite as it moves across the sky. Tracking a satellite in stationary position is easy when compared with tracking a constantly moving satellite.

One significant disadvantage to satellite communications is propagation delay. ***Propagation delay*** is the time it takes for data to be transmitted from the earth

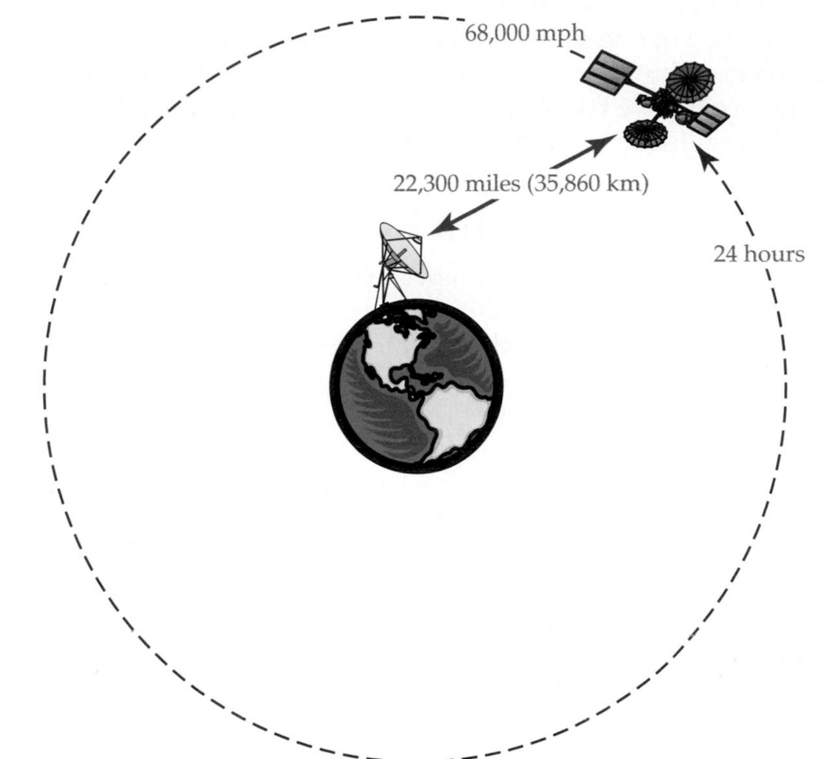

Figure 4-26.
A typical satellite in geosynchronous orbit is approximately 22,300 miles (35,860 km) above the earth's surface. At this distance, the satellite can maintain a fixed position above the earth.

and satellite. It is caused by the great distance between the satellite and earth and can be compared to latency. In the past, the Motorola Company attempted to send a large group of 66 satellites into orbit at approximately 460 miles (740 km) above the earth to eliminate much of the propagation delay. At this height, the propagation delay is significantly reduced and is relatively unnoticed by the users. Unfortunately, the project, called Iridium, proved too costly and was abandoned before it could be fully implemented.

The term *propagation delay* is used in satellite transmission in much the same way that the term *latency* is used for data delay in network systems.

While the propagation delay that normally occurs is generally short—only a fraction of a second—the effect of the delay depends on the type of data transmitted. For example, a delay of 250 milliseconds (ms) for a message consisting of several pages of text would go completely unnoticed by the end user. The same delay for data containing a telephone conversation would show slight pauses in the conversation. A series of frames containing millions of bits of picture or video data could show serious evidence of the delay. Picture or video data needs to be of relatively low resolution to limit the total amount of data transmitted. Transmitting high-resolution picture or video data would only be practical in half-duplex communication. Full-duplex communication for high-resolution picture or video data transmission is not yet practical. There are still very noticeable delays in high-resolution, two-way conference calls using satellite links in a network.

For one-way data transmission, buffering techniques similar to the buffering techniques used for downloading sound on a slow communications link, such as a 56 k modem, could be used to prevent jitter in the transmission of the video. But this can only be used in one direction. Two-way transmissions in real time could not take advantage of buffering to eliminate jitter. Delays of 250 milliseconds (ms) or less are tolerable for live telephone conversations and low-resolution graphics. Delays above 250 milliseconds (ms) are generally unacceptable.

Infrared Transmission and Networking

Infrared transmission is used in point-to-point communications, which are also known as *direct line of sight*. Direct line of sight means that both devices are in direct alignment with each other and that there are no objects between the two devices. The infrared light beam is positioned to aim directly at the receiving device. Each device must be oriented in a position that aims toward the other device. This is one of the main limitations to using infrared in networking applications.

Infrared is typically used for point-to-point communications between two devices such as a personal digital assistant and a desktop computer. Infrared point-to-point communications can also be used in place of radio wave communications where there might be excessive interference, such as in factory or manufacturing settings.

Advantages and Disadvantages of Wireless Technology

Wireless technology can be cost-effective as compared with cable-based network media when spanning long distances such as continents or oceans. Spanning across a city, a business district, or across a college campus can be difficult and expensive with copper-core cable or fiber-optic cable. The installation of landlines are not only expensive, they can cause major disruption while digging up streets and parking lots for installation. When installing a temporary network, wireless technology can be much more cost-effective than remodeling a building to accommodate wiring. Wireless technology is most appropriate for mobile devices such as palmtops, communicators, personal digital assistants, and laptops. Handheld scanners used to scan bar codes on product packages also use wireless technology to transmit data to a computer or cash register system.

Certain wireless technologies are also affected to various degrees by atmospheric conditions such as rain, lightning, fog, and sunspots. The greatest disadvantage or concern for wireless technology is security. Network signals are transmitted in the open air and are capable of being picked up by an unauthorized receiver. Of course, data transmission may be encrypted for security, but even the best security can sometimes be compromised.

Wireless Security

One major concern of wireless networks is security. Network infrastructures designed to use cable are inherently more secure than wireless networks. Cable can be installed so that it is physically secured. Cables can be installed inside walls, pipes, and locked server rooms. Because cables can be physically secured, cabled networks are considered more secure than wireless networks. Unauthorized persons cannot readily connect physically to a private, cabled network system. Wireless networks, on the other hand, transmit data through the air, making it possible for anyone with a standard wireless network card to intercept the radio waves.

Radio waves fill the building areas and areas outside the building. One of the most common building materials used today is glass, especially in commercial establishments. Windows do not limit radio wave transmissions. Anyone near a building that uses wireless devices can easily intercept the wireless network signals with a laptop equipped with a wireless network adapter. However, security features can be implemented that will secure the transmission.

This section covers common wireless security features and provides a brief overview of wireless security. A more in-depth exploration of security features, such as encryption methods, authentication, and security standards are covered in Chapter 15—Network Security.

802.1x Authentication

IEEE 802.1x is a draft standard for authentication methods for wireless networking. It is referred to as a *draft standard* because it is not complete. The 802.1x draft standard provides a means for a client and server to authenticate with each other. Authentication is typically achieved through the exchange of a user name and password based on the Extensible Authentication Protocol (EAP).

The ***Extensible Authentication Protocol (EAP)*** is used for both wired and wireless network systems. EAP ensures authorized access to the network system and network resources. The improved version of EAP is called PEAP, which represents Protected EAP.

Extensible Authentication Protocol (EAP) a protocol that ensures authorized access to the network system and network resources. It is used on both wired and wireless network systems.

Look at **Figure 4-27,** which shows the **WLAN properties**, **Authentication** page in Windows XP. Notice that the **Enable IEEE 802.1x authentication for this network** option has been selected and note the **EAP type** options, such as **Protected EAP (PEAP)** and **Smart Card or other Certificate**. The computer is authenticated, not the person using the computer. A person who has their password compromised could have their password used to access a wireless network. However, when configured to authenticate the computer, an intruder would have to use the computer to access the wireless network.

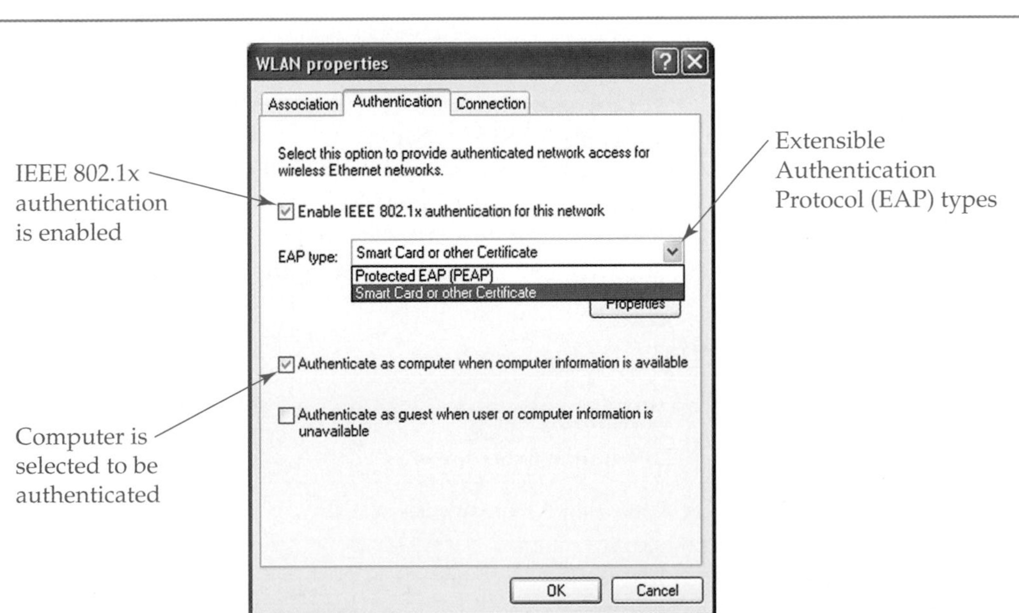

Figure 4-27. Windows XP **WLAN properties**, **Authentication** page.

802.1x Encryption

The second feature of the 802.1x standard is a way to hide the contents of network packets. Since the packets are broadcast through the open air, anyone could capture the packets and inspect the contents using a protocol analyzer or packet sniffer. A wireless network encryption key is used as part of the mathematical equation (algorithm) to encrypt data that is to be transmitted over a wireless network. There will be more about encryption keys in Chapter 15—Network Security.

The packets are encrypted using any one of a number of encryption software protocols. To make the encryption process unique to a particular network system, a key is used. You can think of a key as a string of alphanumeric characters that feed the random character generator used to encrypt the contents of each packet. The only way to crack the encryption would be to guess or steal the encryption key. The encryption key can be provided by a security service, manufactured into a hardware device, or created by the network administrator.

Look at **Figure 4-28,** which shows the **Association** page of the **WLAN properties** dialog box in Windows XP. Notice that the wireless network has been identified as *WLAN* and the data encryption protocol selected is WEP. The acronym *WEP* represents *Wired Equivalent Privacy*. You can see by its name that the ***Wired Equivalent Privacy (WEP)*** protocol is intended to make a wireless network as secure as a wired network.

Wired Equivalent Privacy (WEP) a data encryption protocol that makes a wireless network as secure as a wired network.

Wi-Fi Protected Access (WPA) a protocol that combines the authentication method with encryption.

Below the **Data encryption** option is an option labeled **Network key**. The administrator enters the network key into the text box and then enters the key once more in the option labeled **Confirm network key**. This procedure is repeated at other network clients and servers on the wireless network. Each computer must use the same key to be able to exchange encrypted data with each other.

WPA

The Wi-Fi Alliance introduced ***Wi-Fi Protected Access (WPA)*** as an improvement to overcome the weakness of WEP. You can think of WPA as an enhancement to WEP. WPA uses the most desirable features of the Temporal

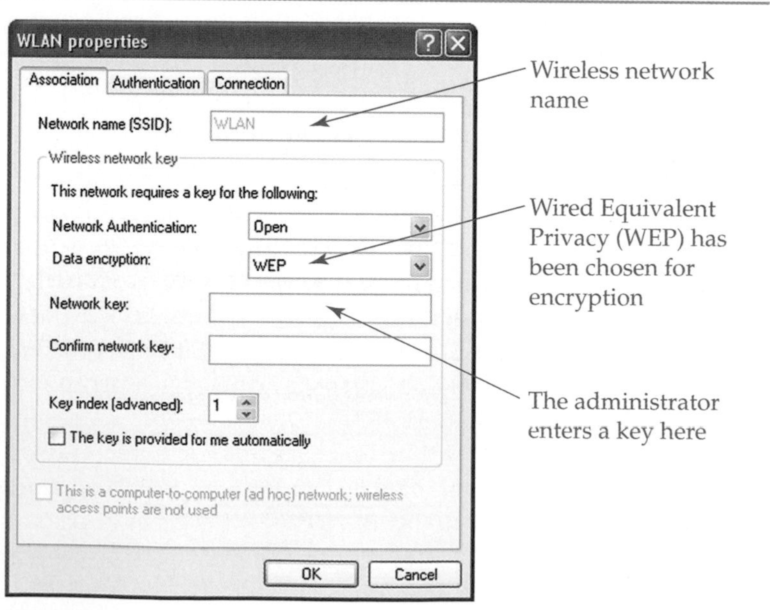

Figure 4-28. Windows XP **WLAN properties, Association** page.

Key Integrity Protocol (TKIP), which is part of the IEEE 802.11i standard. TKIP improves wireless security by constantly changing the security key rather than leaving it the same for all packets.

WPA was introduced in Windows XP Service Pack 1 and combined the authentication method with encryption. Both features are incorporated into one protocol. An additional improvement to encryption is that it is more difficult to crack than WEP encryption. This is because WPA automatically changes the encryption key with each packet exchanged on the network.

WPA-PSK

A variation of WPA is WPA-PSK. WPA-PSK represents *Wi-Fi Protected Access-Pre-Shared Key*. WPA-PSK was designed for small-office/home-office (SOHO) networks. It is designed to make it easy to configure encryption and authentication. WPA-PSK was incorporated into the Wireless Network Setup Wizard that came with Windows XP Service Pack 2. One of the improvements provided by WPA-PSK is the ability to automatically generate a new key after a specified length of time or after a number of packets are exchanged. Changing keys often improves security because the key can be guessed or cracked over time. The following is a sample of what an encryption key might look like:

- A1D4FFBB
- Opensezzime
- BigDogRunsHere

Keys are often referred to as a *passphrase* by some manufacturers. Also, some keys require all characters to be constructed from HEX characters, as in the first example. A key constructed from HEX characters typically is difficult to guess.

WPA-2

WPA-2 is an improved version of WPA. Both use the Extensible Authentication Protocol (EAP) for authentication and are based on the 802.11i standard. The main difference between WPA and WPA-2 is the fact that WPA-2 has a stronger encryption mechanism using the Advanced Encryption Standard (AES). WPA-2, is backward compatible with WPA devices. To learn more about WPA and WPA-2 visit www.wi-fi.org/knowledge_center/wpa2.

Be aware that both WPA and WPA-2 have a personal and an enterprise mode of operation. Check out the Microsoft article "4 steps to set up your home wireless network" located at www.microsoft.com/athome/moredone/wirelesssetup.mspx.

The Windows Vista operating system made advances in wireless security when compared with Windows XP. There are more options available to choose from. The exact number and type of options depends on the physical network adapter software drivers. Look at the screen capture showing the typical Windows Vista wireless network security properties, **Figure 4-29.**

In Figure 4-29A, you can see a wide variety of security options to choose from such as **No authentication (Open)**, **Shared**, **WPA2-Personal**, **WPA2-Enterprise**, **802.1x**, and **Intel-CCKM-Enterprise**. WPA-Enterprise and WPA2-Enterprise mode are designed for high security and uses a centralized security server for authentication. WPA-Personal and WPA2-Personal mode are designed for home- and small-office users that do not have an 802.1x server available.

The Cisco Centralized Key Management (CCKM) protocol was developed by Cisco systems as the name implies. CCKM is designed to allow a mobile user to move between access points without the need to reauthorize on a RADIUS server. A copy of the security certificate is stored on the access points so that the user

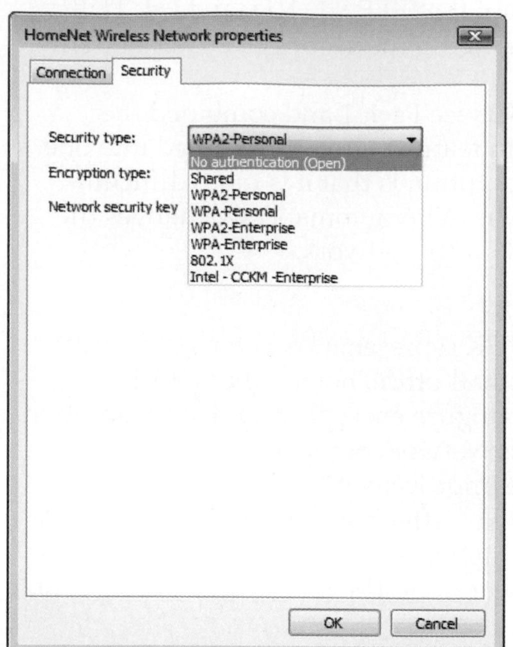

A

B

Figure 4-29. Windows Vista **Wireless Network Properties** dialog box. A—List of security types available. B—A network security key is entered.

will not need to be reauthorized by the 802.1x server each time he or she connects to another access point in the same network system.

In Figure 4-29B, you can see that the security type WPA2-Personal and AES encryption has been selected and that a network security key has been entered. The network security key is also known as a *passphrase*. All wireless devices must use the same network security key to communicate with each other. The wide variety of security types allows the user to maintain backward compatibility with older wireless equipment.

Wi-Fi Protected Access

Wireless Application Protocol (WAP) is an open standard developed by Unwired Planet, Motorola, Nokia, and Ericsson. WAP is used to ensure the safe exchange of data between a wireless network and a portable Wi-Fi device, such as a cell phone. WAP technology allows a cell phone to securely exchange data with the Internet and better protects wireless network systems from hackers, viruses, worms, and other problems. WAP uses a set of keys to identify a device and to encrypt the data during the exchange.

Network security and authentication is a very complex subject. There will be much more about encryption and authentication in Chapter 15—Network Security.

Wireless Application Protocol (WAP) a protocol that ensures the safe exchange of data between a wireless network and a portable Wi-Fi device, such as a cell phone. It uses a set of keys to identify a device and to encrypt the data exchanged.

Summary

- Radio wave and microwave transmissions work on the principle of producing a carrier wave as the means of communication between two network devices.
- Modulation is the mixing of two radio signals, typically a carrier wave with a data signal.
- Infrared is used in line of sight transmissions and is not susceptible to radio interference.
- The FCC regulates the use of the electromagnetic spectrum by assigning radio frequencies and maximum power ratings to devices.
- A common source of interference for wireless networks is industrial, scientific, and medical devices that use frequencies in the same range as wireless networks.
- Two main classifications of antennae based on the shape of the electromagnetic wave pattern it produces are directional and omni.
- Radio waves are electromagnetic waves that cover the 10 kHz to 3,000,000 MHz frequency range.
- Several transmission techniques are used to communicate between radio wave-based network devices: single-frequency, spread-spectrum, and orthogonal frequency-division multiplexing.
- Spread spectrum is the radio transmission technique that subdivides the allocated frequency range into smaller units called *channels*. The two types of spread spectrum transmission techniques are frequency hopping and direct sequencing.
- Frequency hopping avoids interference by changing channels while transmitting data.
- Another name for frequency hopping is *frequency hopping spread spectrum (FHSS)*.
- Direct sequencing consists of 11 overlapping channels of 83 MHz each in a 2.4-GHz spectrum. Within the 11 channels are three channels with a 22-MHz bandwidth. The three channels do not overlap and can be used simultaneously.
- Another name for direct sequencing is *direct sequencing spread spectrum (DSSS)*.
- Orthogonal frequency division multiplexing (OFDM) is similar to frequency hopping and direct sequencing and employs multiplexing.
- A Wireless Access Point (WAP) provides a connection between a wireless network and a cable-based network. It also serves as the center of communication in a wireless network.

- A wireless network that contains one or more Wireless Access Points is arranged in infrastructure mode.
- A wireless network that does not contain a Wireless Access Point (WAP) is arranged in ad hoc mode.
- The IEEE 802.11a standard describes wireless networks operating at 5 GHz with a maximum data rate of 54 Mbps.
- The IEEE 802.11b standard describes wireless networks operating at 2.4 GHz with a maximum data rate of 11 Mbps.
- The IEEE 802.11g standard describes wireless networks operating at either 2.4 GHz or 5 GHz with a maximum data rate of 54 Mbps.
- IEEE 802.11n standard operates at 5 GHZ and 2.4 GHz with a maximum data rate of 300 Mbps to 600 Mbps.
- Multiple Input Multiple Output (MIMO) uses two or more streams of data transmission to increase data throughput and the range of the wireless network. MIMO is described in the IEEE 802.11n standard.
- Spatial multiplexing is the transmission of two or more streams of data simultaneously.
- IEEE 802.15 standard describes the use of Wireless Personal Area Networks (WPANs).
- Wireless networks specified under the IEEE 802.11 standard use Carrier Sense Multiple Access with Collision Avoidance (CSMA/CA) as the media access method.
- Bluetooth is a standard developed by a group of manufacturers to allow their devices to interoperate. Bluetooth is recognized by the 802.11 standard and is used for short-range data transfer applications using the 2.4-GHz radio band.
- Infrared is commonly used for point-to-point transmission between two devices such as a personal digital assistant and a PC.
- Satellite communications experience propagation delay because of the great distance a signal must travel.
- Wireless technology can be cost-effective when compared with cable-based network media.
- A disadvantage of employing wireless technology is security.
- A Service Set Identifier (SSID) is similar in function to a workgroup name or domain name and must be assigned to a Wireless Access Point (WAP).
- Wireless networks are not secure when default settings are used for the configuration.
- Wireless encryption keys should be changed on a regular basis to maintain a high degree of security.

Review Questions

Answer the following questions on a separate sheet of paper. Please do not write in this book.

1. A(n) _____ is an electromagnetic wave of a set frequency that is used to carry data in radio wave- and microwave-based networks.
2. What is modulation?

3. A simple radio broadcast consists of a(n) _____, which generates a carrier wave and a(n) _____, which receives a carrier wave.
4. What is a channel?
5. What are the two major classifications of antennae?
6. Which of the following antenna types is not used in point-to-point links?
   A. Flat panel
   B. Omni
   C. Parabolic
   D. Yagi
7. Which antenna style was developed with aesthetics in mind?
8. What is spread spectrum?
9. The spread spectrum technique that transmits data on multiple channels simultaneously is called _____.
10. The spread spectrum technique that transmits data on multiple channels sequentially is called _____.
11. Why is frequency hopping used?
12. The _____ transmission technique uses the 5-GHz frequency and can achieve data rates as high as 54 Mbps.
13. List the frequency range and related power rating of each of the three U-NII classifications.
14. What is an SSID?
15. What frequency does the IEEE 802.11a standard specify, and what is the maximum achievable distance?
16. What frequency does IEEE 802.11b standard specify, and what is the maximum achievable distance?
17. What frequencies does IEEE 802.11g standard specify, and what are the related maximum achievable distances?
18. What is the maximum throughput based on the IEEE 802.11n standard?
19. Which media access method does the 802.11 wireless standard specify?
20. What is the difference between CSMA/CA and CSMA/CD?
21. What does the acronym MIMO represent?
22. What is MIMO wireless technology?
23. What is the maximum achievable distance of a Bluetooth device?
24. What is the data rate of the Bluetooth 2.0 standard?
25. What is the data rate of the Bluetooth 3.0 standard?
26. Which IEEE specification addresses WPAN?
27. _____ technology is based on radio waves connecting to designated areas referred to as *cells*.
28. What is a disadvantage of satellite communications?
29. What is a geosynchronous orbit?
30. What is generally the maximum amount of satellite transmission delay acceptable for telephone conversations?
31. What is an advantage of wireless networking?
32. What is the one major disadvantage of wireless technology?
33. What does the acronym WEP represent?
34. Write an example of an encryption key.
35. What does the acronym CCKM represent?

Sample Network+ Exam Questions

Answer the following questions on a separate sheet of paper. Please do not write in this book.

1. Which IEEE 802.11 standard specifies a data rate of 300 Mbps?
   A. 802.11a
   B. 802.11b
   C. 802.11g
   D. 802.11n
2. Which media access method is associated with wireless networks?
   A. ARCnet
   B. CSMA/CA
   C. CSMA/CD
   D. Token Ring
3. Which of the following items is used to connect a wireless network to an Ethernet network?
   A. Wireless Access Point
   B. Ad hoc converter
   C. Ethernet converter
   D. Ethernet sequencing device
4. What would *most likely* generate radio interference for an 802.11b network device?
   A. A cordless phone assigned to work at 2.4 GHz.
   B. Another computer using an 802.11g network adapter card.
   C. A wireless keyboard.
   D. An HP LaserJet printer.
5. Who is responsible for regulating the electromagnetic spectrum and dictating the frequency that is to be used for each group of devices?
   A. IEEE
   B. The telephone company in the local area.
   C. FCC
   D. WECA
6. Which item would *most likely* interfere with the operation of an 802.11b wireless network?
   A. Hub
   B. Cordless phone
   C. Incandescent lights
   D. Copier
7. What is the function of an SSID?
   A. To replace the network MAC address.
   B. To encrypt all wireless communication.
   C. To identify the wireless network by name.
   D. To increase the data throughput of a wireless network.
8. Which protocol is used to encrypt data inside packets on a wireless network?
   A. HTTP
   B. SNMP
   C. FTP
   D. WEP

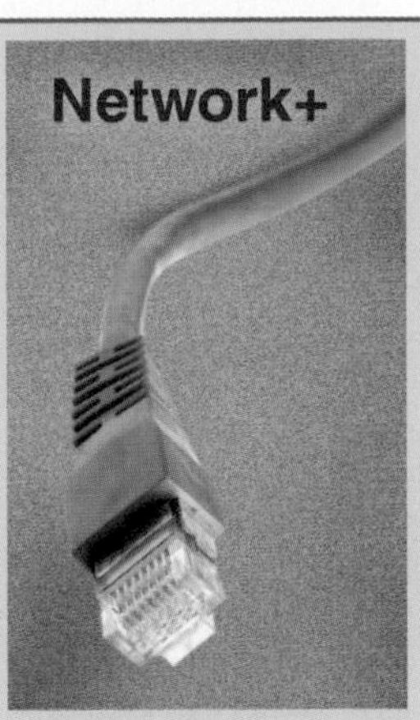

9. Which IEEE standard is used to describe how to achieve secure authentication to a wireless network?
   A. 802.3
   B. 802.1x
   C. 802.5b
   D. 802.4a
10. Which wireless transmission technique is used to transmit data according to the IEEE 802.11b standard?
    A. DSSS
    B. OFDM
    C. Both DSSS and OFDM
    D. Neither DSSS nor OFDM

Suggested Laboratory Activities

1. Set up an ad hoc network using a PC and a laptop.
2. Set up a two- or three-station wireless network using a Wireless Access Point (WAP).
3. Research a particular brand of wireless network device and list the expected transmission ranges and related speeds.
4. Transfer data between a laptop and a PC by using an infrared port.
5. Observe the effect of a variety of materials on a wireless network. For example, separate two computers on the wireless network with a wooden wall, sheet rock, metal door, or file cabinet. Note the effects on distance and data rate.
6. Observe the effect of a common electric drill being operated near the wireless network, and then observe the effects of a cell phone or walkie-talkie on the wireless network.

Interesting Web Sites for More Information

http://standards.ieee.org/getieee802/802.15.html
http://wi-fi.org
www.bluetooth.com/Bluetooth/Technology/Works/Compare
www.cwt.vt.edu
www.palowireless.com/ofdm/tutorials.asp
www.proxim.com
www.tech-faq.com

Wireless technology is ideal for college campuses. It can allow students to access the school network, Internet, and mail server from any location on campus, giving students more options on where and how they study.

Chapter 4
Laboratory Activity

Installing a USB Network Adapter and Configuring a Wireless Router

After completing this laboratory activity, you will be able to:

- Summarize the purpose of a Wireless Access Point (WAP).
- Recall typical wireless network configuration requirements.
- Summarize the purpose of an SSID.
- Summarize why wireless device default settings usually do not provide security.
- Carry out proper procedures to install an 802.11 USB network adapter.
- Carry out proper procedures to install an 802.11 wireless router/WAP.

Introduction

In this laboratory activity, you will install an 802.11 USB wireless network adapter and then install and configure a wireless router/WAP. Wireless devices fall into four categories as defined by the IEEE: 802.11a, 802.11b, 802.11g, and 802.11n.

IEEE Classification	Assigned Frequency	Maximum Data Rate	Comments
802.11a	5 GHz	54 Mbps	Not compatible with other wireless classifications. Obsolete at this time.
802.11b	2.4 GHz	11 Mbps	Compatible with 802.11g and 802.11n.
802.11g	2.4 GHz 5 GHz	11 Mbps in 802.11b mode 54 Mbps in 802.11g mode	Some manufacturers exceed the 54 Mbps as defined in the IEEE standard and can support over 100 Mbps.
802.11n	2.4 GHz 5 GHz	54 Mbps in 802.11a mode 11 Mbps in 802.11b mode 54 Mbps in 802.11g mode 300 Mbps in 802.11n mode	A maximum data rate as high as 600 Mbps has been reported.

Note

The chart reflects maximum theoretical data rates as defined by the IEEE standard. Some manufacturers specify data rates that exceed the data rates defined by IEEE. However, the actual throughput will be considerably lower than the advertised rate.

Maximum data rates can only be experienced under ideal conditions. For best data rates, devices need to be in close proximity and in direct line of sight with no partitions or other objects blocking the radio waves. Radio waves can penetrate through solid objects such as wood or concrete but not through metallic objects such as metal building walls, metallic file cabinets, or some types of window tint that is derived from metallic substances.

New wireless device technologies are typically designed to be backward compatible with other earlier wireless device technologies. As you can see in the table, 802.11n is backward compatible with all earlier wireless standards.

Microsoft Windows XP was the first operating system released by Microsoft that came with generic drivers and applications to support and configure wireless devices. Wireless device manufacturers almost always recommend using its installation CD/DVD to install device drivers and applications before installing the wireless device. Microsoft operating systems such as Windows Vista will typically recognize a new device, such as a USB adapter, and automatically configure the wireless device without the need of the manufacturer CD/DVD. When installing a wireless router, it is best to install the router software before connecting the wireless router.

Wireless routers typically provide both wireless connectivity and wired connection ports. Look at the wireless router in following illustration.

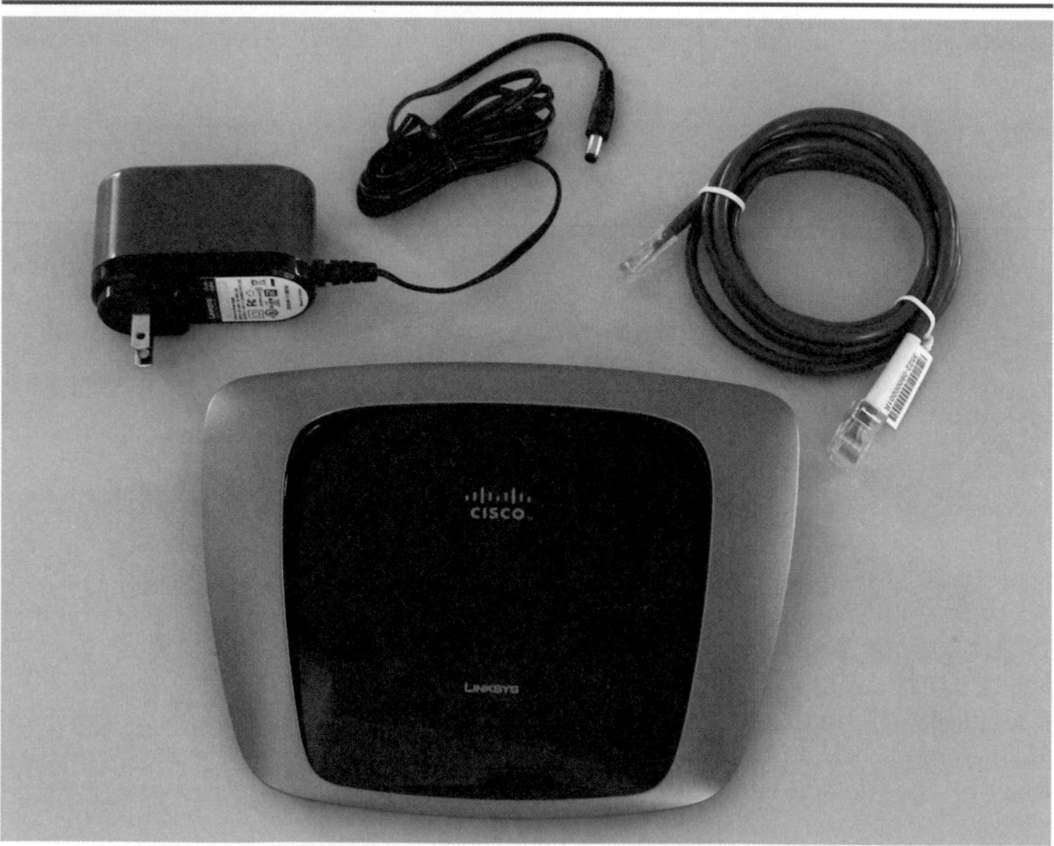

The router comes with an electrical power converter that changes the 120 volts AC to a much lower 12 volts DC. This particular router comes with one Ethernet cable to connect the router to the Internet modem or to a computer. The next illustration shows a close-up of typical router connections.

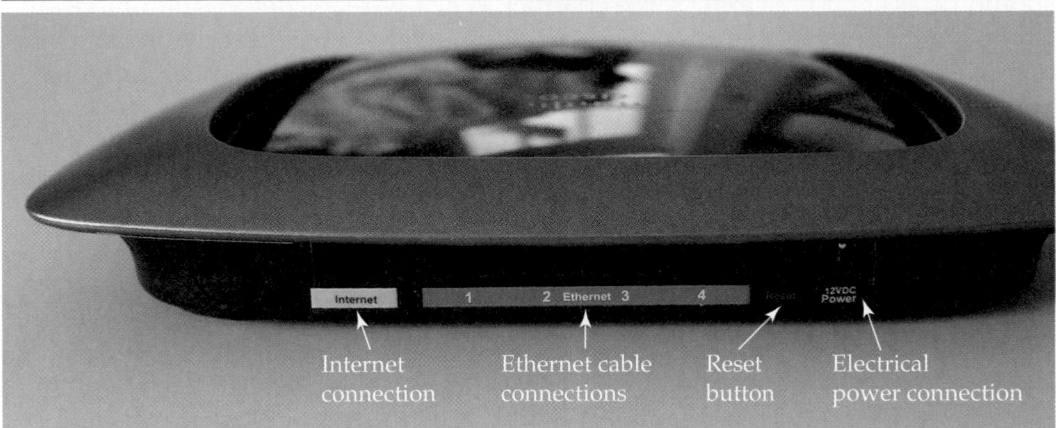

The Internet connection connects to the Cable or DSL modem, and the Ethernet cable connections connect to computers using network cable. The reset button is used to reset the router configuration to the default configuration set by the manufacturer. The electrical power connection connects to the electrical power converter.

Wireless routers are commonly encountered today and incorporate features such as Wireless Access Point (WAP) and Dynamic Host Configuration Protocol (DHCP). DHCP is a feature that automatically issues IP addresses to wireless client devices.

Wireless devices can be configured in two different configurations: Ad hoc and infrastructure mode. In ad hoc mode, wireless devices are free to communicate with each other and all devices are considered equal. Ad hoc mode does not use a router or WAP to control the connections between devices. In infrastructure mode, a WAP is used to control communication between devices. Wireless routers incorporate the WAP feature. Thus, the router controls communication between wireless devices and wired devices connected to the same router. Wireless devices such as routers and WAPs are also referred to at times as *bridges* because they bridge the connection between two dissimilar media types: wireless and cable.

The Service Set Identifier (SSID) is the name used to identify the wireless network. Manufacturers assign a default SSID to their wireless devices. For example, D-Link uses "WLAN" or "Default," Netgear uses "Wireless" or "NETGEAR," Linksys uses "Linksys," and 3Com uses "WLAN" or "3Com." You can usually locate the default SSID as well as the default user name and password to access the wireless router setup program by conducting a search on the Internet. Because it is so easy to locate the default SSID and user name and password, the default values are considered an extreme security risk. You can actually perform a Google search for the default user name and password for most router devices. During or after the initial configuration, you should change the SSID to a name other than the default name. Wireless devices from the same manufacturer will automatically connect to other wireless devices using the same SSID unless they are encrypted or have password authentication configured. The default SSID, user name, and password can be reset to the original manufacturer's values by pressing the reset button on the router for approximately 15 seconds or more.

The default wireless channel, or dedicated frequency, also varies according to manufacturer. In the United States, the FCC has assigned 11 wireless channels for use with wireless devices. Each wireless device in the wireless network should be assigned the exact same channel. When wireless devices automatically configure themselves, they assign a specific channel to themselves. You can manually assign the wireless channel if need be. For example, a specific channel may be experiencing radio interference resulting in very low data speeds or not connecting at all. You can sometimes overcome the effects of the radio interference by changing the assigned channel.

The wireless router configuration can be changed remotely from a wireless laptop or wireless workstation. The router or WAP is typically accessed by using a browser and entering the assigned IP address of the wireless router into the browser's address bar. Typical default assigned IP addresses are 192.168.0.1 and 192.168.1.1. Check the wireless router documentation for the assigned default IP address. During the connection process, you will be prompted for a user name and password. Again, the default user name and password assigned by the manufacturer should be changed to make the wireless network more secure.

Equipment and Materials

- 802.11(g or n) USB wireless network adapter with installation CD/DVD and manual.
- 802.11(g or n) Wireless Access Point or wireless router with installation CD/DVD and manual.
- Patch cable (Cat 5, Cat 5e, or Cat 6).
- Paper clip. (Used to press the reset button if needed.)
- Computer (desktop or laptop) running Windows Vista.
- On a separate sheet of paper, record the following information provided by your instructor:

User name: ____________________

Password: ____________________

IP address: ____________________

Subnet mask: ____________________

Default gateway: ____________________

Wireless channel: ____________________

Wireless router: ____________________

IP address: ____________________

Subnet mask: ____________________

Default gateway: ____________________

User name: ____________________

User password: ____________________

Wireless channel: ____________________

SSID: ____________________

Note

Both wireless devices should be the same IEEE standard, either 802.11g or 802.11n, and should (but not required) be the same brand to allow for easier set up and configuration.

Note
Most modern routers and USB wireless network adapters will automatically configure most of the values using the default settings. Review the manufacturer's installation procedures before attempting to install any devices or running the installation CD/DVD.

Part I—Installing a USB Wireless Network Adapter

Procedure

1. _____ Gather all required materials and report to your assigned workstation.
2. _____ Boot the computer and verify it is in working order.
3. _____ Review the manufacturer's installation manual for the USB wireless network adapter. You may have a "Quick Start" guide or need to open the CD/DVD that came with the device to view the installation manual. Typically, you install the software for the wireless device before installing the device. A typical installation consists of inserting the device's CD/DVD and having the disc automatically detected and its installation program started. A series of windows will appear prompting you for information while the device drivers are automatically installed. At the end of the software installation process, you will be prompted to insert the USB wireless network adapter.
4. _____ Insert the USB wireless network adapter. It should automatically be detected and configured by the operating system.
5. _____ After successfully installing the USB network adapter, an icon should appear in the taskbar representing the wireless network device.
6. _____ Verify that the USB wireless adapter card has been installed successfully by opening Device Manager. If you see a red *X* or a yellow exclamation mark (!) beside the device, there is a problem. Some older wireless device drivers are not compatible with Windows Vista or Windows 7. If there is a problem, check the manufacturer's Web site for troubleshooting information. Also, check the manufacturer's Web site for the very latest drivers.
7. _____ Call your instructor to inspect your USB wireless network adapter installation.

Part II—Configuring a Wireless Network Router

The screen captures used in this portion of the lab activity are based on a Cisco Linksys router and may not necessarily match your router configuration screens. However, they will be somewhat similar.

The wireless router CD/DVD will have a wizard program to assist you in the automatic configuration of the router. Because of the discovery-type protocols widely used today, the router cannot only discover information about your Internet provider, it can automatically configure your Internet connection in most cases. You will very seldom need to manually configure the wireless router, but you will still have the manual configuration option available to you.

Procedure

1. ______ Insert the router setup disc into the CD/DVD drive and wait for the installation program to open. A screen similar to the following will appear.

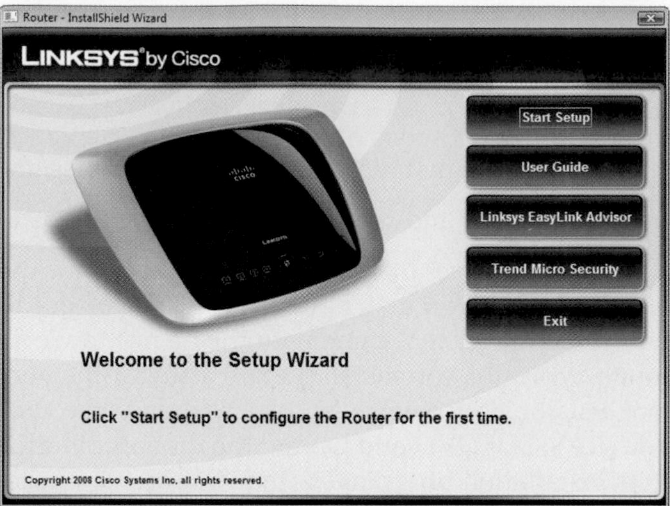

2. ______ Click the **Start Setup** button and then follow the instructions as presented in the setup wizard. The following is a series of some of the typical screens you will encounter while installing and configuring the router. These are not steps to perform but rather an overview of a typical wireless router configuration.

   The setup wizard will automatically check for an Internet connection and install and configure the router. You may be asked to respond to some simple questions as the router is configured.

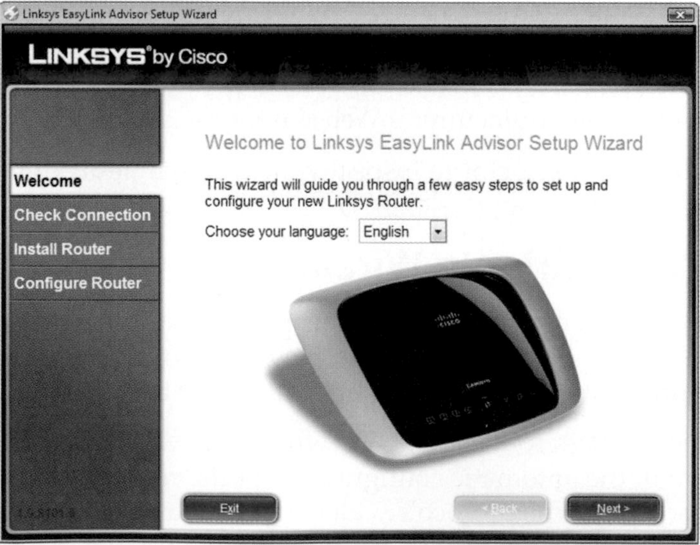

The installation wizard will even provide you with illustrations of how to connect your router to the Internet and to the computer.

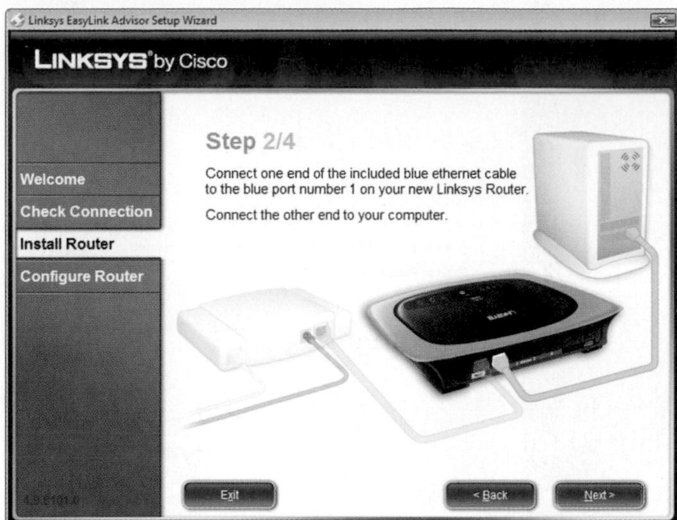

In the following screens, the setup wizard configures the router with minimal input from the user.

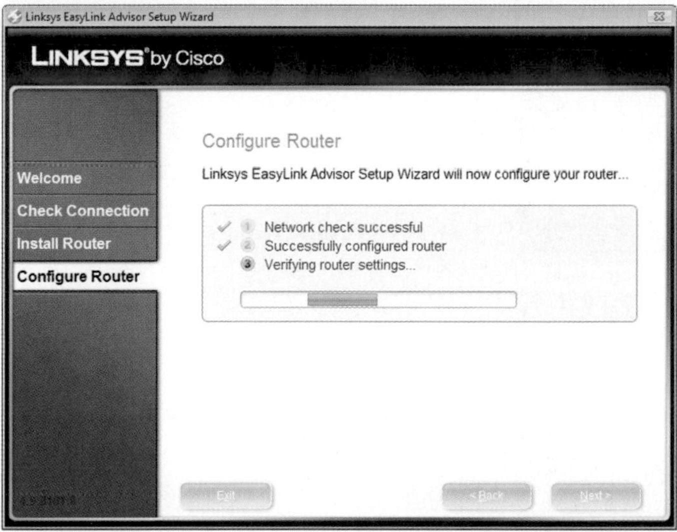

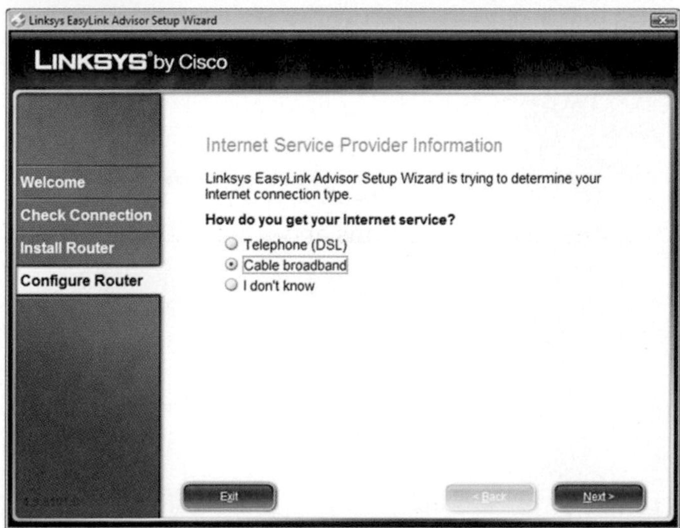

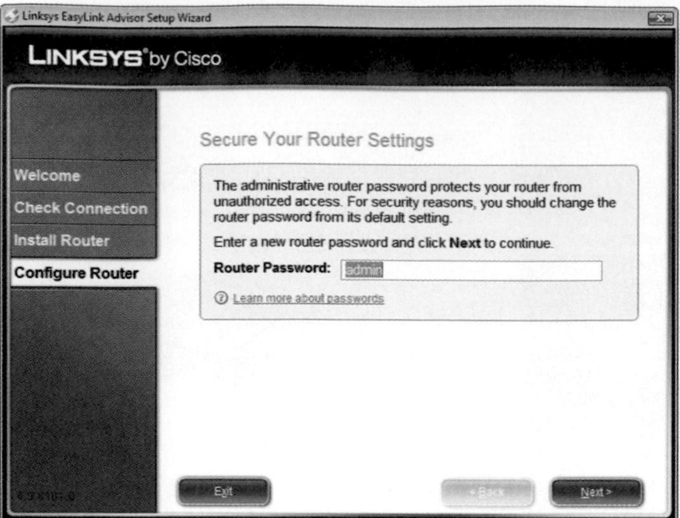

In the following two screens, notice the default SSID entry "linksys" has been replaced with the "HomeNet" SSID.

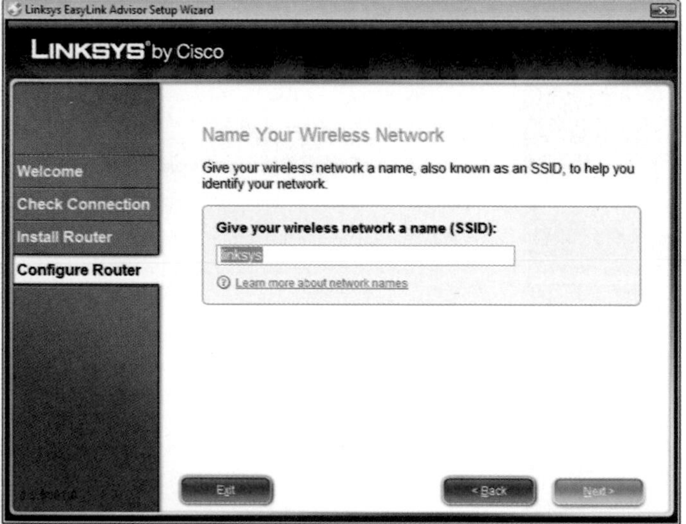

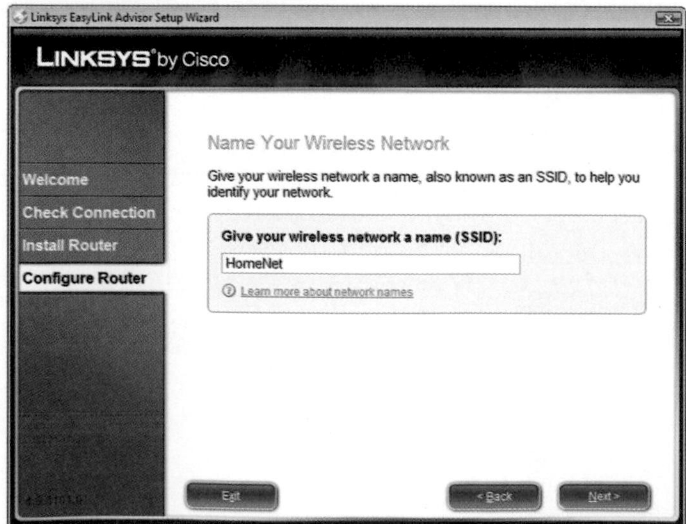

In the following screen, you are prompted to select the type of security you wish to configure.

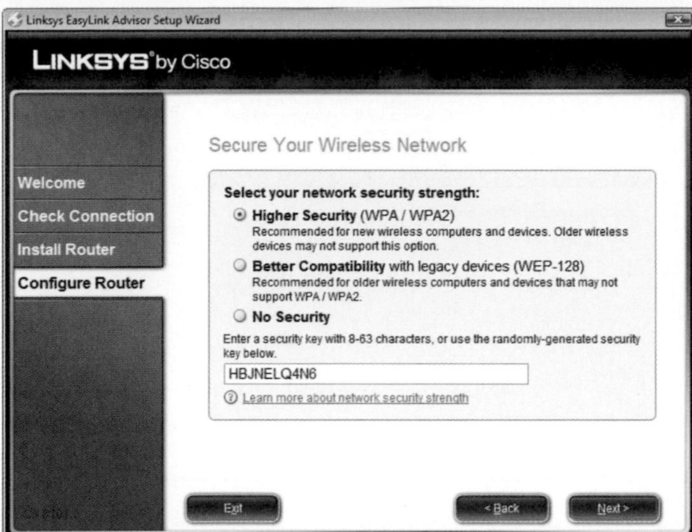

When the installation is finished, you should see a dialog box similar to the following.

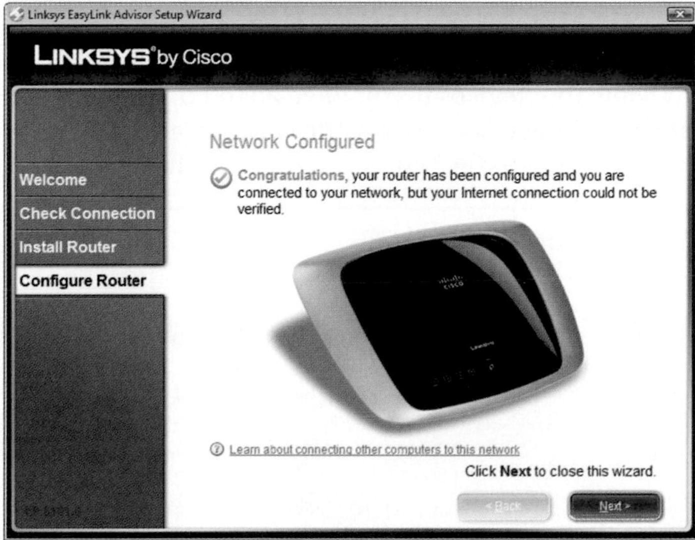

The Microsoft Vista operating system works in collaboration with the router when configuring the local area network. Security on the local area network is controlled by the Microsoft Vista operating system. As you can see in the following screen capture, you simply verify the network location, which is set to "Private" by default in the Network and Sharing Center. You may change the network location to "Public." The difference between public and private is that the Network Discovery feature is enabled in a private location and Network Discovery is disabled in public locations.

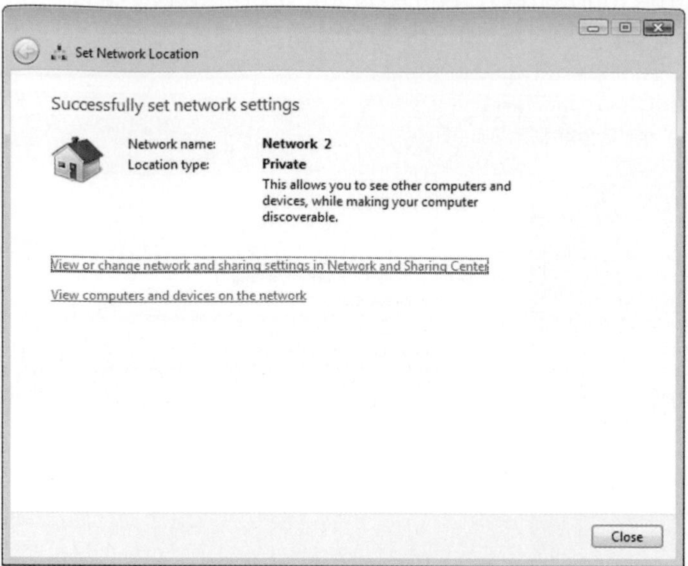

3. ______ After you have completed the configuration, open the network view to see all computers connected to the router. You can open the network view by selecting **Network** from the **Start** menu. You will have a view of all devices being served by the router, similar to that in the following screen capture. If you are performing the lab activity by yourself, you may have a view of only your computer. You can only view the devices if you have enabled the Network Discovery feature and have chosen the "Private" location. Network Discovery is disabled when the "Public" network setting is selected.

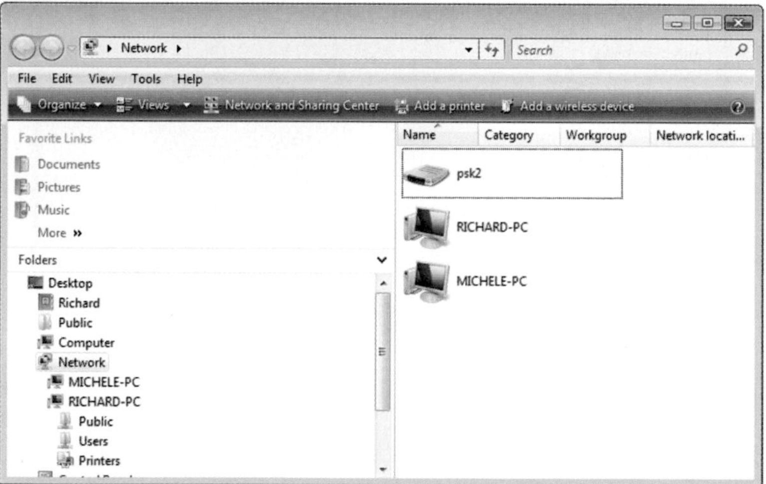

4. ______ To access the wireless router, you will need to type and enter the default IPv4 address of the router into the address bar of your Web browser. The default is typically 192.168.1.1, or very similar. Check the manufacturer's installation guide for the correct IPv4 address. You will be prompted for an administrator user name and a password. Again, check the manufacturer's information for the correct administrator user name and default password.

5. ______ After entering the administrator user name and password, you will see a user interface similar to the following. The user interface allows you to view and modify the router configuration. Take a few minutes to explore the various menu items and options, but do not change any settings at this time.

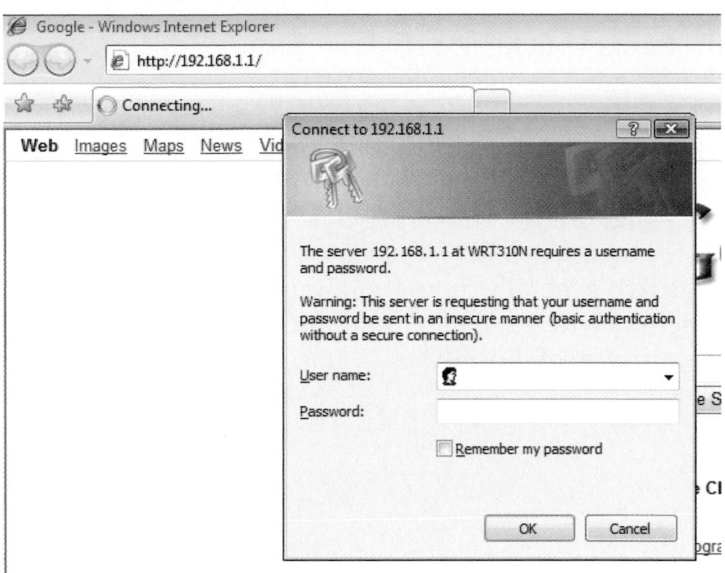

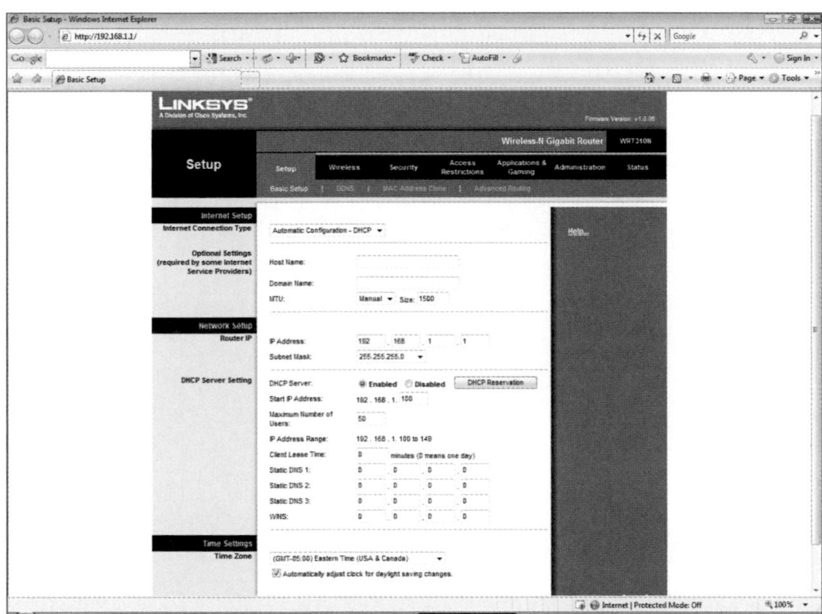

6. ______ Call your instructor to inspect this portion of your lab activity.

7. ______ Answer the review questions and then return all materials to their proper storage area.

Review Questions

Answer the following questions on a separate sheet of paper. Please do not write in this book.

1. What does the acronym WAP represent?
2. What is the maximum throughput for 802.11g?
3. What is the maximum throughput for 802.11b?
4. What is the maximum throughput for 802.11a?
5. What is the throughput for 802.11n?
6. What is the assigned frequency for 802.11b?
7. What is the assigned frequency for 802.11g?
8. What is the assigned frequency for 802.11a?
9. What is the assigned frequency for 802.11n?
10. With which standards are an 802.11g device backward compatible?
11. What does the acronym SSID represent?
12. What are the two general wireless configurations?
13. True *or* False? All wireless device manufacturers use the same SSID.
14. What is the purpose of the SSID?

5 Digital Encoding and Data Transmission

After studying this chapter, you will be able to:

- ❑ Give examples of digital signals.
- ❑ Identify the two modes of transmitting data between two points.
- ❑ Explain data integrity inspection using a parity check.
- ❑ Explain data integrity inspection using a Cyclic Redundancy Check (CRC).
- ❑ Explain the complete data packaging process.
- ❑ Compare connection-oriented transmission with connectionless data transmission.
- ❑ Compare packet switching with circuit switching.
- ❑ Identify the characteristics of the various data codes.
- ❑ Interpret the structure and contents of a UDP frame.
- ❑ Compare an Ethernet II frame with an IEEE 802.3 frame.
- ❑ Recall the function of each layer of the OSI model.

Network+ Exam—Key Points

Approximately 20% of the Network+ Certification exam is based on basic networking concepts such as those presented in this chapter. For example, when a protocol is described, it is often referred to as either connection-oriented or connectionless, whether it uses circuit switching or packet switching technology, and with which particular layer(s) of the OSI model it is associated.

The Network+ Certification exam tests the ability to understand these basic concepts. Review this chapter often as you progress through the course in preparation for the exam.

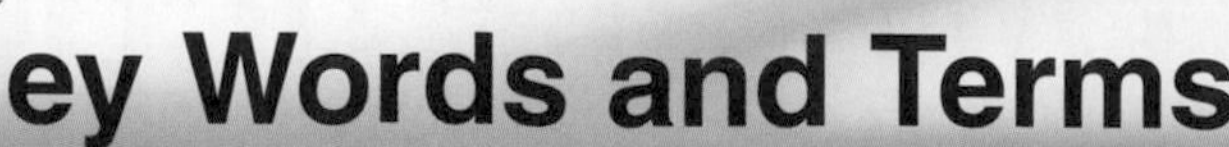

Key Words and Terms

The following words and terms will become important pieces of your networking vocabulary. Be sure you can define them.

American Standard Code for Information Interchange (ASCII)
asynchronous transmission
Binary Coded Decimal (BCD)
bipolar digital signal
broadcast frame
circuit switching
connectionless communication
connection-oriented communication
Cyclic Redundancy Check (CRC)
data encryption
digital encoding
encapsulation
Extended Binary Coded Decimal Interchange Code (EBCDIC)
frame
Hypertext Markup Language (HTML)
Manchester encoding
multicast frame
Non-Return to Zero (NRZ)
one's compliment
packet switching
parity check
port
segment
synchronous transmission
time period
Unicode
unipolar digital signal
virtual network

In this chapter, basic terminology about data packaging and transmission is presented. Learning this terminology will be beneficial when more specific aspects of networking are covered in later chapters. Also, a good understanding of the OSI model will help you when you further your networking education by studying security concepts, network infrastructure, and IEEE standards.

The chapter ends with a review of the OSI model and its relationship to digital encoding and data packaging. The OSI model is presented using some of the terminology you have learned thus far. The OSI model will be referenced throughout the textbook as you learn more network terminology and concepts. Presenting this material throughout the textbook will enable you to gain a solid understanding of the OSI model.

Digital Signals and Digital Encoding

Digital signals are used to transmit data and commands across network systems. In the Chapter 2, Network Media—Copper Core Cable, you learned that all network communication originates from electronic signals. Electronic signals take many forms, such as electrical energy, light waves, radio waves, infrared light waves, and microwaves. All of these forms of electronic signals originate from digital signals.

Digital encoding takes place when a network interface card converts data into a digital pattern acceptable to the network media. After the data is encoded into a digital pattern, it is placed on the network media. So that you can better understand digital encoding and digital patterns, the digital signal will be reviewed.

digital encoding
the conversion of data into a digital pattern acceptable to the network media.

As you have already learned, a digital signal is an electronic signal that has discrete values. Discrete values can be on and off, high and low, or 5 volts and 0 volts. The waveform of the digital signal is drawn at right angles, resembling a series of incomplete rectangles and squares, **Figure 5-1.** The height, or amplitude, of the digital signal represents the electrical voltage level. In Figure 5-1A, a positive voltage of 5 volts is illustrated. The digital signal fluctuates between a positive five-volt and zero-volt level. This pattern is similar to a light switch repeatedly turned on and off and is called a ***unipolar digital signal.***

unipolar digital signal
a digital signal that fluctuates between a positive five-volt and zero-volt level.

Some digital electronic circuit designs fluctuate between a positive voltage level and a negative voltage level. In Figure 5-1B, the digital signal fluctuates between a positive five-volt level and a negative five-volt level. This pattern is called a ***bipolar digital signal.***

bipolar digital signal
a digital signal that fluctuates between a positive five-volt level and a negative five-volt level.

The examples in Figure 5-1 are not meant to imply that all digital systems work at a standard five-volt level. Some systems work at lower voltage levels such as 3.3 volts.

Another important characteristic of the digital signal is the time period. The ***time period*** represents the rate of recurrence of an expected signal level change. The time period used to encode digital data should not be confused with the term *time period* used when talking about frequency or cycles. In the context of encoding a digital signal, the time period represents the time period of an expected digital wave shape. A digital signal may or may not change within a given time period, but a change is expected. In some digital encoding schemes, the time at which the digital signal changes voltage levels is important. The transition of the digital signal's voltage level may occur at the beginning of the time period or at the midpoint of the time period. See **Figure 5-2.**

time period
the rate of recurrence of an expected signal level change.

By changing the transitioning pattern and fluctuation pattern of a digital signal, many digital encoding schemes can be created. ***Non-Return to Zero (NRZ)*** is a special classification of digital encoding. Look at **Figure 5-3** and compare the two digital signal patterns. In the first digital signal pattern, the voltage level returns to zero after the digital pulse. In the second digital signal pattern, known as non-return to zero (NRZ), the signal fluctuates between the high (positive) voltage level and the low (negative) voltage level and never returns to zero for any measurable period of time.

Non-Return to Zero (NRZ)
a digital signal that fluctuates between a high (positive) voltage level and a low (negative) voltage level and never returns to zero for any measurable period of time.

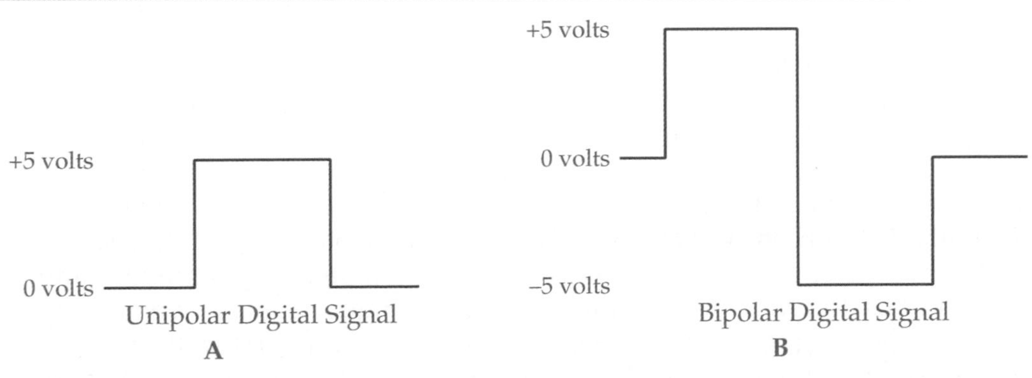

Figure 5-1.
A digital signal has discrete voltage levels. Its waveform resembles a series of incomplete squares and rectangles. A—A unipolar digital signal fluctuates between 0 volts and +5 volts. B—A bipolar digital signal fluctuates between +5 volts and –5 volts.

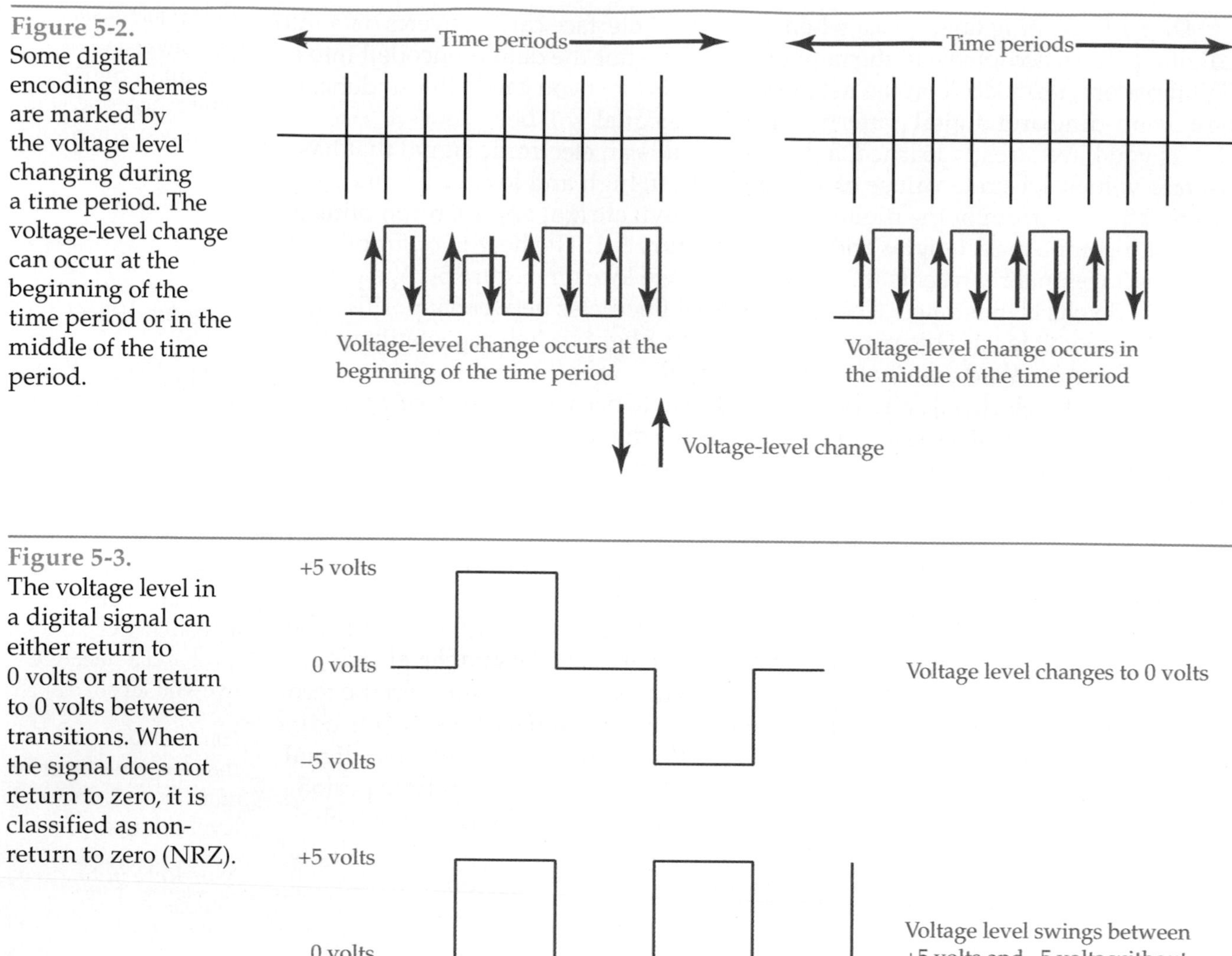

Figure 5-2. Some digital encoding schemes are marked by the voltage level changing during a time period. The voltage-level change can occur at the beginning of the time period or in the middle of the time period.

Figure 5-3. The voltage level in a digital signal can either return to 0 volts or not return to 0 volts between transitions. When the signal does not return to zero, it is classified as non-return to zero (NRZ).

Manchester encoding
an encoding scheme characterized by a digital pulse transitioning during the midpoint of the time period.

synchronous transmission
a type of transmission in which a digital signal is synchronized with a reference signal to ensure proper timing.

One of the most popular encoding schemes is called ***Manchester encoding.*** This encoding scheme is characterized by the digital pulse transitioning during the midpoint of the time period. Look at **Figure 5-4.** Note that a binary one is represented by a transition from five volts to zero volts in the midpoint of the time period. A binary zero is represented by a transition from zero to five volts in the midpoint of the time period.

Digital signal characteristics vary from one encoding scheme to another. The selection of the encoding scheme varies according to the electronic characteristics designed into the network hardware. Further study into the encoding schemes would require more detailed electronics study than this textbook provides. The main point to remember is digital encoding happens at the data link layer of OSI model.

Two modes of transmitting data between two points are synchronous and asynchronous. In ***synchronous transmission,*** the digital signal is synchronized with a reference signal to ensure proper timing. The timing of the digital signal is extremely important for decoding some variations of digital encoding patterns. In ***asynchronous transmission,*** no reference signal is present.

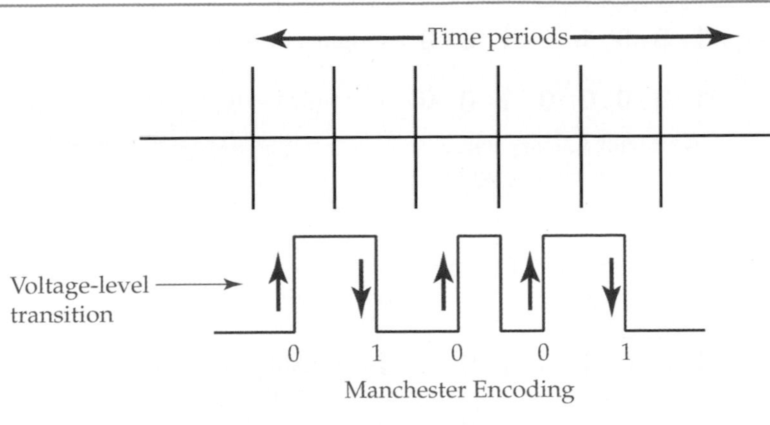

Figure 5-4.
The main characteristic of Manchester encoding is the direction of the voltage level during the midpoint of the time period, which is represented by a binary one or zero.

You may be wondering how a digital signal can be decoded without a reference signal. A reference signal is not needed if there is a way to determine when a byte or stream of data begins or ends. Some data transmission schemes use a series of ones and zeros to identify the beginning and end of a byte or stream of data. A long period of no digital signal can also be used to signify the beginning. Again, there are many different ways the beginning and end can be acknowledged. There is no one universal method. The methods with which data are encoded vary greatly between the computer bus system, network media, telephone signals, radio signals, and such.

asynchronous transmission
a type of transmission in which a digital signal is not synchronized with a reference signal.

Data Packaging and Transmission

To send data from one point to another across a network or the Internet, data is packaged with extra information to ensure its delivery and integrity. Often data is broken into smaller, deliverable pieces. Each piece is called a ***segment*** and contains information to aid in reassembly.

segment
raw data that is divided into smaller units.

Tech Tip

Be aware that many references refer to data segments as packets.

Sometimes, communication is established between a source and destination computer before data is sent. Other times, data is sent without establishing communication and without requiring a confirmation of delivery. Data routing can also differ among data transmissions. This section describes the components involved in data packaging, such as parity checks, segmentation, and encapsulation. It also covers communications and routing.

Parity Checks

Digital signals can become corrupted for different reasons. Some of the causes can be crosstalk, electromagnetic interference, loose connections, and faulty and improperly grounded equipment. A ***parity check*** is a method of verifying the integrity of transmitted data. Look at **Figure 5-5A.**

parity check
a method of verifying the integrity of transmitted data.

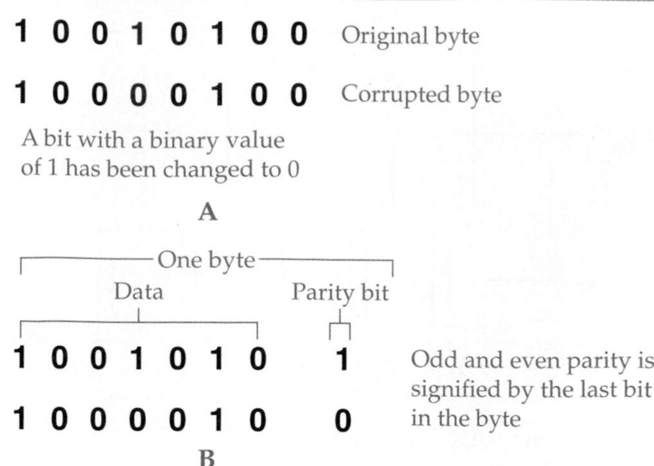

Figure 5-5. Parity check. A—To perform parity checks, the last bit position in an 8-bit data transmission can be used for the parity code. B—A value of 1 or 0 in the parity bit may indicate odd or even parity.

In the example, one bit in the entire byte has changed from a binary one to a zero. The meaning of the byte has therefore been altered. Originally, the byte might have represented the letter *A*, but now it represents the letter *R* or a command such as "end of transmission." One way to ensure that data sent from the source to the destination is intact is to include a parity code with the data. For example, rather than eight bits of a byte representing alphanumeric symbols, seven bits could represent alphanumeric symbols and the eighth bit could represent the parity code.

Look at **Figure 5-5B.** In the example, the total number of zeros in the data portion of the byte is used to validate data. An even number of zeros is represented by a parity code of a binary one. An odd number of zeros is represented by a parity code of a binary zero. When the destination receives the byte, it compares the parity code to the number of binary zeros to tell if the data has been corrupted. If the data is corrupted, the destination rejects the data and requests the data be resent.

Cyclic Redundancy Check (CRC)

Cyclic Redundancy Check (CRC) a sophisticated data integrity check that uses complicated mathematical algorithms to determine if one or more bits are corrupt.

A ***Cyclic Redundancy Check (CRC)*** is based on the same principle for error detection as the parity check. However, the CRC is a more sophisticated check. The main problem with the parity check is if an even number of bits is corrupt, the corruption goes undetected. The CRC uses complicated mathematical algorithms to determine if one or more bits are corrupt. A CRC can detect the corrupted bit and correct it without requiring the data be retransmitted. The only drawback is a CRC requires more data to be sent. The extra data is the parity code. This slows the data transmission rate. Still, the CRC is a popular method of verifying data. It is incorporated into many different network protocols when data integrity is critical.

Segmentation and Encapsulation

encapsulation the process of adding information to the segment that identifies such things as the source address, the destination address, the end of the segment, and the size of the segment.

Unless the amount of data transferred between two points is small, the data needs to be divided into smaller units, called *segments*. After the data is divided into segments, it is encapsulated. ***Encapsulation*** is the process of adding information to the segment that identifies such things as the source address, the destination address, the end of the segment, and the size of the segment.

Figure 5-6 shows the complete data packaging process, from raw data (text file, sound, or graphic) to digital signals. Raw data is first broken into segments. Segment size is determined by the networking technology, such as Ethernet or Token Ring,

Figure 5-6.
Data packaging process. Raw data is broken into segments (step 1). The segments are encapsulated into packets (step 2). The packets contain extra information such as source and destination addresses and error-checking codes. Since the data in this example will travel the Internet, the packets are encapsulated into a frame (step 3). The frame contains extra information needed to navigate the Internet. The frame is converted into binary code (step 4). The binary code is converted to digital signals and placed on the network media (step 5).

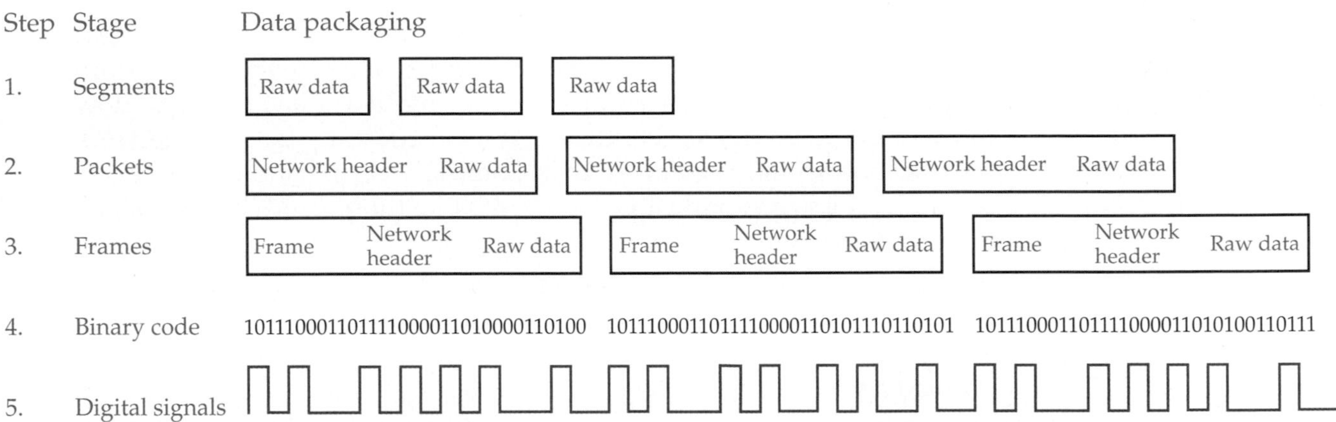

and the networking protocol, such as TCP/IP. The segmented data is then encapsulated into packets. Packets of data contain additional information needed to deliver the segments. This additional information is called the *network header*. The network header contains a source and destination address. Other additional information that can be added to the packet is error-checking codes. Error-checking codes ensure the packet is delivered without a distorted data signal.

Packets are limited to traversing only LANs. Since the data will be sent across the Internet, it is further encapsulated, or framed. A packet that is encapsulated with information needed to travel the Internet is called a ***frame***. The frame contains additional information such as an Internet address. An Internet address is different from a machine (MAC) address. The machine address is sufficient when delivering data on a LAN.

frame
a packet that is encapsulated with information needed to travel the Internet.

After the packet has been encapsulated, the frame is converted into binary code. The binary code is then converted to digital signals. The entire series of frames is placed on the network in the form of digital signals and is transmitted to the destination computer. The destination computer removes the information that is no longer needed, such as the destination address, and reconstructs the entire message by placing the packets into their proper sequence. Error checks are also performed to ensure the data has not been corrupted.

This explanation and Figure 5-6 is a generic example of how data is transmitted between two computers. Encapsulation varies depending on which technology and protocols are used. More information will be provided as each of the protocols are explored and explained.

The terms *segment, frame, data gram, protocol data unit (PDU),* and *packet* are often used interchangeably when discussing blocks of data. You can think of all of the terms as units of data transferred between two points. The ISO tends to use the term *PDU* when discussing data packaging. When discussing TCI/IP, the terms *packet* and *frame* are often used with packets described as fitting inside a frame. The term *PDU* is the most technically correct term, but it is awkward to use in conversation. Consequently, technicians tend to use the term *packet* to collectively represent all types of data units.

Many times it is acceptable to use any of the terms when discussing network data, but at other times, it is more important to be precise. Correct terminology is especially important when explaining protocols, OSI layers, and certain types of network equipment.

Network+ Note

Data packaging terminology can vary a great deal from one manufacturer to another. For example, one manufacturer may refer to the entire encapsulation process as *framing,* while another may break it down into different and distinct stages. When studying for the Network+ Certification exam, remember that CompTIA certifications are vendor-neutral and use generally accepted terms like those used in this textbook to describe various technologies.

If you are planning to take a certification exam for a specific networking technology, such as Microsoft or Novell, it is best to become familiar with the specific vendor's terminology. Many of the mentioned companies provide a vocabulary listing on their Web site.

Connection-Oriented and Connectionless Communication

connection-oriented communication a type of communication in which a connection is first established between the source and destination computers before data is transmitted.

connectionless communication a type of communication in which data is transmitted to the destination without first establishing a connection.

Communication between two computers can be classified as connection-oriented or connectionless. In ***connection-oriented communication,*** a connection is first established between the source and destination computers before data is transmitted. After the data is transferred, the connection is terminated. In ***connectionless communication,*** the data or commands are sent without an established connection. After the data is transferred, there is no need to terminate or release the connection. See **Figure 5-7.**

A protocol can be described as either connection-oriented or connectionless. IP is a connectionless protocol. It simply moves data from point A to point B. IP does not verify the delivery of the data. In contrast, TCP is a connection-oriented protocol. It verifies a connection before transmitting data and then terminates the connection when the data has been transferred. The best of both protocols is used when using TCP/IP in WAN communications. A connection is first established with the TCP protocol. Next, data is transferred with the IP protocol. After all data has been transferred, the connection is terminated with the TCP protocol.

Connectionless protocols are used to transfer audio or video data. Time is very important when conducting a conversation, and the fastest protocols for transferring data are connectionless. A connection-oriented protocol would slow the transfer of voice data since every frame of voice data would have to be verified. A connection-oriented protocol is used first to verify the destination of the call. A connectionless protocol is used to transfer the voice data. There is no need to verify that each packet of voice data has been received since it is assumed the connection will last through the entire conversation. If a packet is lost and does not reach the destination, a simple "What did you say?" will cause the sender to regenerate the lost data.

Commands can be sent between two computers with the UDP protocol. UDP is a connectionless protocol that requires minimal system resources. Think of a connectionless protocol as one that makes its best effort to send a command or data to a destination but has no way of guaranteeing its arrival. A connectionless

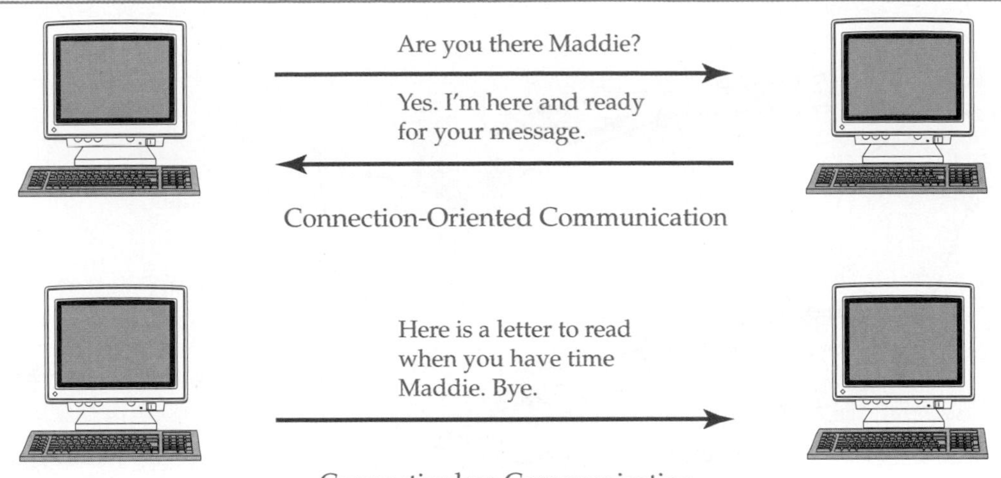

Figure 5-7. Connection-oriented communication establishes contact with the destination before sending data. Connectionless communication simply sends the data and does not bother to verify if the destination is there or if the message was received.

protocol typically depends on reliable equipment such as a dedicated line to ensure delivery.

Network+ Note

It is common to see a question on the Network+ Certification exam that identifies connection and connectionless protocols. Try to remember that IP is a connectionless protocol and TCP is a connection-oriented protocol.

Circuit Switching/Packet Switching

Two main categories describing the way data are routed between two points are packet switching and circuit switching. ***Circuit switching*** establishes a permanent connection between two points for the duration of the data transfer period. For example, a permanent connection is established when you connect to your Internet service provider using a Cable modem or a DSL modem. The permanent connection is equivalent to circuit switching. Other types of telephone lines that use circuit switching are ISDN, ATM, and T1. When you think of circuit switching, think of a permanent or dedicated line.

circuit switching a type of transmission which establishes a permanent connection between two points for the duration of the data transfer period.

Packet switching does not use a permanent connection. Packet switching breaks the data transmission into smaller parts called *packets*. Each packet has a source and destination address and a sequence number attached to it. You could say each small unit of data is encapsulated into a packet that contains source and destination addresses and a sequence number. The Internet uses packet switching to send data between two points on the Internet such as a home user and a Web server at a remote location. When a Web page is downloaded from the remote site to the home computer, the Web page is broken into smaller packets. The packets are sent out onto the Internet and may each take a different route to their destination, **Figure 5-8.**

packet switching a type of transmission which does not use a permanent connection between two points for the duration of the data transfer period. Packets may travel different routes to the same destination.

When packets travel across the maze of communications lines, many different factors can delay the packets, such as heavy traffic conditions in the different communications lines. The amount of traffic in each of the many communications lines constantly changes. Also, a communications line could be rendered unusable during transmission due to a lightning strike, maintenance,

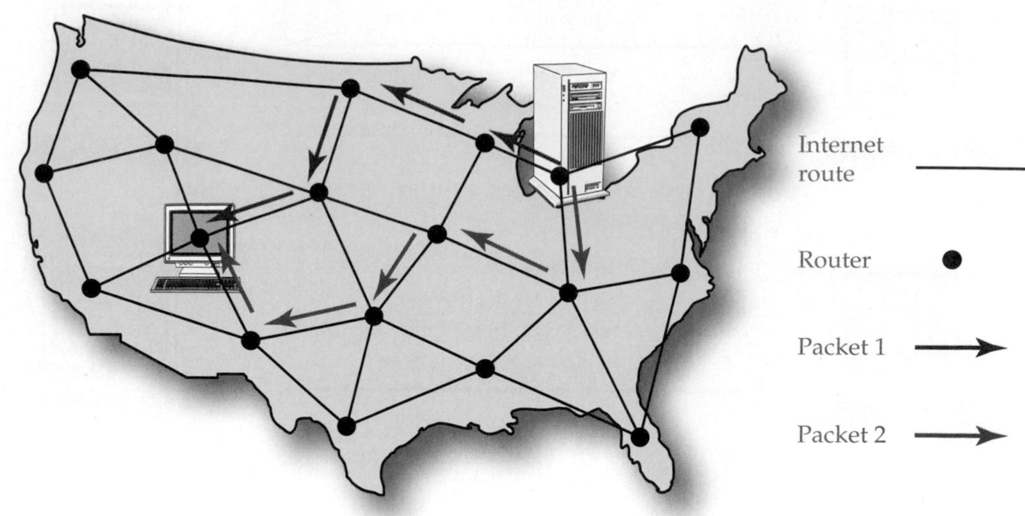

Figure 5-8. The Internet is an excellent example of how data transfer is based on packet switching. The total amount of data is divided into packets that may take different routes to their destination.

or equipment failure. The arrival time of the transmitted packets could be out of sequence due to the unforeseen circumstances. Sequence numbers included with the packets help to reconstruct the data. The sequence number also identifies missing packets that may have been destroyed en route to the destination. Some examples of packet switching technologies besides the Internet are FDDI, Frame Relay, and Ethernet.

Data Codes

There are many different coding standards, or data codes, for representing the written word. There are also many standards used for representing images, audio sound, and multimedia. Some you may be familiar with include JPEG, BMP, GIF, TIFF, and MPEG. Data codes must be converted for data exchange to take place. In the OSI model, this is addressed at the presentation layer. For example, a typical computer using ASCII and an IBM mainframe computer using EBCDIC cannot understand or decipher an exchange of information. The two encoding schemes must be converted so that the systems can understand the data when it is received. The most commonly encountered data codes are ASCII, BCD, EBCDIC, and UNICODE. Each of these data codes will be briefly introduced. Remember that in the OSI model, the presentation layer is responsible for putting the data into a format that is agreed on by the source and the destination.

ASCII

American Standard Code for Information Interchange (ASCII) a character code that uses eight bits to represent alphanumeric characters.

The ***American Standard Code for Information Interchange (ASCII)*** was an early attempt to standardize data codes. Look at the table of the ASCII character set in **Figure 5-9.** Note that 32 codes are command codes and 96 codes represent characters found on a standard keyboard. There are an additional 128 symbols not shown in Figure 5-9 that are operating system dependent. "Operating system dependent" means that the additional symbols are not standard but rather can only be interpreted by a specific software program. If the data file is opened by the wrong software application, the symbols are incorrectly interpreted and the result is unintelligible. The additional symbols represent such items as fractions, foreign

Standard ASCII Characters			(Continued)		(Continued)	
0	NUL	Null	43	+	86	V
1	SOH	Start of header	44	,	87	W
2	STX	Start of text	45	-	88	X
3	ETX	End of text	46	.	89	Y
4	EOT	End of transmission	47	/	90	Z
5	ENQ	Enquiry	48	0	91	[
6	ACK	Acknowledgment	49	1	92	\
7	BEL	Bell	50	2	93	]
8	BS	Backspace	51	3	94	^
9	HT	Horizontal tab	52	4	95	_
10	LF	Line feed	53	5	96	`
11	VT	Vertical tab	54	6	97	a
12	FF	Form feed	55	7	98	b
13	CR	Carriage return	56	8	99	c
14	SO	Shift out	57	9	100	d
15	SI	Shift in	58	:	101	e
16	DLE	Data link escape	59	;	102	f
17	DC1	Device control 1	60	<	103	g
18	DC2	Device control 2	61	=	104	h
19	DC3	Device control 3	62	>	105	i
20	DC4	Device control 4	63	?	106	j
21	NAK	Negative acknowledgment	64	@	107	k
22	SYN	Synchronous idle	65	A	108	l
23	ETB	End of transmit block	66	B	109	m
24	CAN	Cancel	67	C	110	n
25	EM	End of medium	68	D	111	o
26	SUB	Substitute	69	E	112	p
27	ESC	Escape	70	F	113	q
28	FS	File separator	71	G	114	r
29	GS	Group separator	72	H	115	s
30	RS	Record separator	73	I	116	t
31	US	Unit separator	74	J	117	u
32	SP	Space	75	K	118	v
33	!		76	L	119	w
34	"		77	M	120	x
35	#		78	N	121	y
36	$		79	O	122	z
37	%		80	P	123	{
38	&		81	Q	124	|
39	'		82	R	125	}
40	(		83	S	126	~
41	)		84	T	127	DEL
42	*		85	U		

Figure 5-9. ASCII character set.

letters, special symbols, lines, and more. The upper 128 characters are not standard. Also note that an ASCII symbol does not indicate font attributes such as size, shape, color, or spacing. ASCII characters interpreted by a software application such as Microsoft Word or Word Perfect can represent these additional attributes.

ASCII files are sometimes referred to as *plain text files*. They contain no special alphanumeric enhancements such as bold, italic, or underline. The ASCII file format is the most easily exchanged file format used by word processing programs. ASCII uses eight bits to represent individual characters. The bit pattern represents the digital pulses used to encode data as alphanumeric characters.

In the early days of computing, there were many problems because of a lack of standard encoding patterns. Many times an encoding pattern was proprietary. The hardware and software had to be purchased from the same vendor and may have been incompatible with other software programs or hardware devices. Today, some problems are encountered when exchanging text files. Two different versions of the same word processing software may not be compatible. Incompatibility may cause the file not to open when prompted. A good way to ensure a text file can be exchanged between two different systems is by saving the file as an ASCII file or as a plain text file. **Figure 5-10** shows some of the options for saving the text file Chap 5 Encoding and Transmitting Data.doc. Note that the **Text Only (*.txt)** option is selected.

Binary Coded Decimal (BCD) a binary number format in which each number is represented as a four-digit binary code.

BCD

Binary Coded Decimal (BCD) is a binary number format in which each number is represented as a four-digit binary code. For example, the three groups of four binary digits 0010 0011 1001 represent the decimal numbers 2, 3, and 9. The BCD is used only for numerical applications.

Extended Binary Coded Decimal Interchange Code (EBCDIC) an IBM character code similar to ASCII.

EBCDIC

Extended Binary Coded Decimal Interchange Code (EBCDIC) is an IBM character code similar to ASCII. EBCDIC is pronounced as "ebb si dik." It is widely used on IBM mainframe computers. See **Figure 5-11.**

Unicode a character code that uses 16 bits to represent individual characters.

Unicode

Unicode is similar in principal to ASCII but uses 16 bits to represent individual characters. By using 16 bits for each character, over 65,000 possible characters can be represented. This may seem like an extreme number of possibilities when thinking in terms of the English alphabet, but languages, such as Chinese, that rely on symbols require many more possibilities than the typical 8-bit ASCII code pattern will produce. There are also many characters that are unique to the various languages around the world, such as Russian, Hebrew, Tibetan, Mongolian, and Cherokee, which require extra bits. Unicode is also used in bar codes for scanning merchandise and in Braille for the blind.

Look at the various groups of Unicode listed in **Figure 5-12.** The Unicode groups Thai and Lao represent the Thai language symbols and the Laotian language symbols respectively. The references to CJK represent a joint collection of symbols used by China, Japan, and Korea. The Unicode collection represents over 96,000 symbols. To learn more about Unicode visit the Unicode Web site at www.unicode.org.

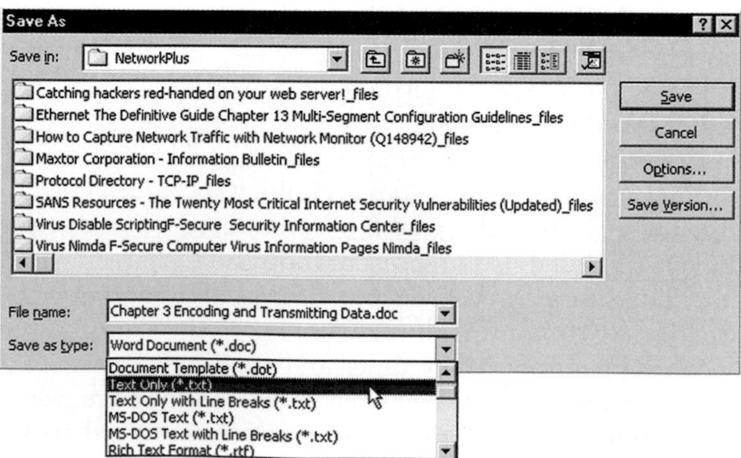

Figure 5-10. Options in a word processing program for saving a text file.

HTML

Hypertext Markup Language (HTML) is an authoring language used to create documents that can be downloaded from the Internet and viewed by a Web browser. Part of the HTML language is a standard set of color codes. The color codes are inserted into the coding of a Web page. When a Web browser interprets the page, the color code is translated into the color the code represents. **Figure 5-13** shows a partial listing of color codes. Note the color codes are expressed in hexadecimal form, such as FFFFFF, FFFFCC, FFFF99, FFFF66, FFFF33, and FFFF00. Web browsers, such as

Hypertext Markup Language (HTML) an authoring language used to create documents that can be downloaded from the Internet and viewed by a Web browser.

EBCDIC Characters

Dec	Hex	Code	Dec	Hex	Code	Dec	Hex	Code	Dec	Hex	Code
0	00	NUL	32	20		64	40	space	96	60	-
1	01	SOH	33	21		65	41		97	61	/
2	02	STX	34	22		66	42		98	62	
3	03	ETX	35	23		67	43		99	63	
4	04		36	24		68	44		100	64	
5	05	HT	37	25	LF	69	45		101	65	
6	06		38	26	ETB	70	46		102	66	
7	07	DEL	39	27	ESC	71	47		103	67	
8	08		40	28		72	48		104	68	
9	09		41	29		73	49		105	69	
10	0A		42	2A		74	4A	[	106	6A	|
11	0B	VT	43	2B		75	4B	.	107	6B	,
12	0C	FF	44	2C		76	4C	<	108	6C	%
13	0D	CR	45	2D	ENQ	77	4D	(	109	6D	_
14	0E	SO	46	2E	ACK	78	4E	+	110	6E	>
15	0F	SI	47	2F	BEL	79	4F	| !	111	6F	?
16	10	DLE	48	30		80	50	&	112	70	
17	11		49	31		81	51		113	71	
18	12		50	32	SYN	82	52		114	72	
19	13		51	33		83	53		115	73	
20	14		52	34		84	54		116	74	
21	15		53	35		85	55		117	75	
22	16	BS	54	36		86	56		118	76	
23	17		55	37	EOT	87	57		119	77	
24	18	CAN	56	38		88	58		120	78	
25	19	EM	57	39		89	59		121	79	'
26	1A		58	3A		90	5A	!]	122	7A	:
27	1B		59	3B		91	5B	$	123	7B	#
28	1C	IFS	60	3C		92	5C	*	124	7C	@
29	1D	IGS	61	3D	NAK	93	5D	)	125	7D	'
30	1E	IRS	62	3E		94	5E	;	126	7E	=
31	1F	IUS	63	3F	SUB	95	5F	^	127	7F	"

(Continued)

Figure 5-11. EBCDIC character set.

Figure 5-11.
(Continued.)

EBCDIC Characters

Dec	Hex	Code	Dec	Hex	Code	Dec	Hex	Code	Dec	Hex	Code
128	80		160	A0		192	C0	{	224	E0	\
129	81	a	161	A1	~	193	C1	A	225	E1	
130	82	b	162	A2	s	194	C2	B	226	E2	S
131	83	c	163	A3	t	195	C3	C	227	E3	T
132	84	d	164	A4	u	196	C4	D	228	E4	U
133	85	e	165	A5	v	197	C5	E	229	E5	V
134	86	f	166	A6	w	198	C6	F	230	E6	W
135	87	g	167	A7	x	199	C7	G	231	E7	X
136	88	h	168	A8	y	200	C8	H	232	E8	Y
137	89	i	169	A9	z	201	C9	I	233	E9	Z
138	8A		170	AA		202	CA		234	EA	
139	8B		171	AB		203	CB		235	EB	
140	8C		172	AC		204	CC		236	EC	
141	8D		173	AD		205	CD		237	ED	
142	8E		174	AE		206	CE		238	EE	
143	8F		175	AF		207	CF		239	EF	
144	90		176	B0		208	D0	}	240	F0	0
145	91	j	177	B1		209	D1	J	241	F1	1
146	92	k	178	B2		210	D2	K	242	F2	2
147	93	l	179	B3		211	D3	L	243	F3	3
148	94	m	180	B4		212	D4	M	244	F4	4
149	95	n	181	B5		213	D5	N	245	F5	5
150	96	o	182	B6		214	D6	O	246	F6	6
151	97	p	183	B7		215	D7	P	247	F7	7
152	98	q	184	B8		216	D8	Q	248	F8	8
153	99	r	185	B9		217	D9	R	249	F9	9
154	9A		186	BA		218	DA		250	FA	
155	9B		187	BB		219	DB		251	FB	
156	9C		188	BC		220	DC		252	FC	
157	9D		189	BD		221	DD		253	FD	
158	9E		190	BE		222	DE		254	FE	
159	9F		191	BF		223	DF		255	FF	

Internet Explorer or Firefox, interpret the color code and create the exact shade of color indicated.

Protocol Frame Structures

In Chapter 1—Introduction to Networking, you learned that a protocol is a set of rules that determines how two nodes will communicate. One part of a protocol determines how data and commands are structured into packages such as packets and frames. Many pieces of information have to be built into

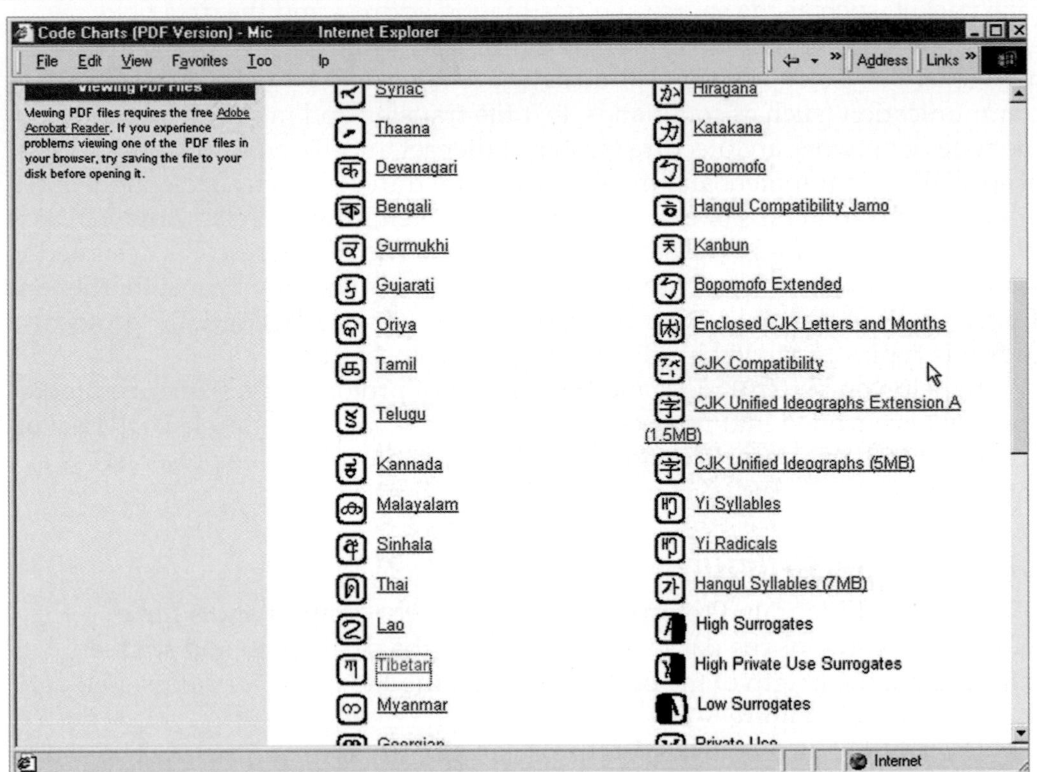

Figure 5-12. Various Unicode groups. Only languages are shown here, but Unicode also has charts for Braille patterns, mathematical symbols, and drawing symbols, such as arrows and boxes.

Color code	Color
#FFFFFF	
#FFFFCC	
#FFFF99	
#FFFF66	
#FFFF33	
#FFFF00	
#FFCCFF	
#FFCCCC	
#FFCC99	
#FFCC66	
#FFCC33	
#FFCC00	
#FF99FF	
#FF99CC	
#FF9999	
#FF9966	

Color code	Color
#FFCC33	
#FFCC00	
#FF99FF	
#FF99CC	
#FF9999	
#FF9966	
#FF9933	
#FF9900	
#FF66FF	
#FF66CC	
#FF6699	
#FF6666	
#FF6633	
#FF6600	
#FF33FF	
#FF33CC	

Figure 5-13. HTML color codes are written in hexadecimal format and represent various colors.

each packet, such as the source and destination address and the data field size. Many different protocol data structures are used to communicate across networks. The exact protocol data structure is determined by the purpose of the communication (such as commands, text file transfer, and multimedia transfer), the type of network architecture (such as Ethernet and Token Ring), and the use of specialized equipment and media during the transfer (such as telephone lines, modems, and routers). For example, Ethernet Token Ring, Wireless, and FDDI use different frame formats to match the technology. The PPP protocol is designed to establish telephone modem connections. Network protocols such as Ethernet and Token Ring can transport other protocols. For example, a TCP or UDP protocol packet is typically carried inside an Ethernet protocol frame.

To help you better understand the concept of protocol data structures and how data is encoded into packets, we will first look at how a simple UDP packet is constructed. Afterwards, a more complicated protocol will be presented as a comparison.

UDP Frame Structure

The User Datagram Protocol (UDP) is relatively compact and simple in design. It contains the data to be transferred, the destination and source information, the length of the packet, and a method to check for errors. Look at the illustration in **Figure 5-14.**

port
a logical connection that matches a service with a computer.

The first 16 bits (two bytes) of the packet identify the source port. The source port is the port from which the UDP originated. A ***port*** is a logical connection that matches a service with a computer. A computer uses many different port numbers when communicating. For example, the common port number for the HTTP service is port 80. There will be a much more detailed explanation about ports later in the textbook when discussing the TCP/IP protocol.

one's compliment
a digital-based mathematical calculation used to check for errors or corruption.

The second 16 bits contain the destination port number, which identifies the port to which the UDP is being delivered. The third 16 bits indicate the length of the entire UDP packet so that the destination can be sure the entire message or data package was delivered. Next, a 16-bit checksum block of information is included. The checksum is similar to the CRC discussed earlier. It uses a digital-based mathematical calculation called ***one's compliment*** to check for errors or corruption. The last block of information contains the actual data.

Figure 5-14.
UDP frame.

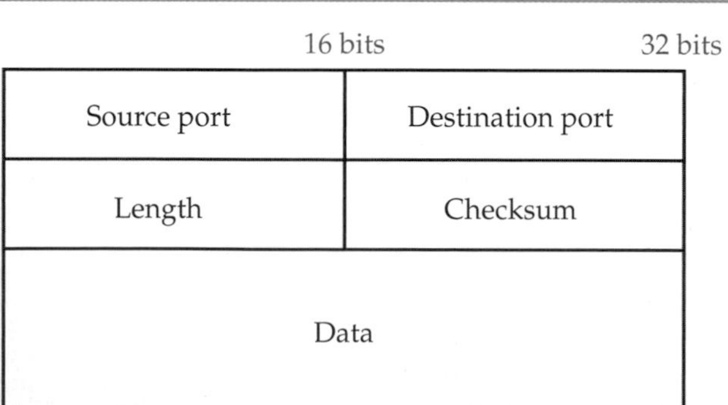

Source port	Destination port	Length	Checksum	Data

Ethernet Frame Structure

Four types of Ethernet frames exist in networking technology: Ethernet II (DIX), IEEE 802.2, IEEE 802.3, and Ethernet SNAP. The Xerox Corporation developed the original Ethernet standard in the early 1970s. In 1982, companies such as Digital Equipment, Intel, and Xerox joined to develop another release of Ethernet known as DIX (Digital, Intel, Xerox). The DIX Ethernet frame format became better known as Ethernet II.

The Institute of Electrical and Electronic Engineers (IEEE) developed and released their first standard for Ethernet in 1985. The standard is called *IEEE 802.3: Carrier Sense Multiple Access with Collision Detection (CSMA/CD) Access Method and Physical Layer Specifications.* It is interesting to note that *IEEE 802.3 CSMA/CD* is the technically correct terminology for the type of media access described, and the terms *Ethernet* and *802.3* have become generally accepted to mean the same as CSMA/CD.

The Ethernet II frame type was developed before the release of the IEEE 802.3 CSMA/CD standard. Consequently, they are two different frame types. While the two frame types Ethernet II and 802.3 are generally compatible, there is no guarantee of full compatibility. Network interface cards are usually set to automatically detect the frame type broadcast, but the network interface card can be configured to accept a specific frame type to improve network performance.

Ethernet SNAP is a modification of the original 802.3 and Ethernet II frame types. We will now look at two common frame types you will most likely encounter. A study of frame differences will help you better understand the compatibility issues that exist between different systems. Look at **Figure 5-15.**

You will notice that the two frame types, Ethernet II and 802.3, are similar in construction. In fact, both frame types can coexist within the same network.

Ethernet II Frame

Preamble	Destination address	Source address	Type	Data	Frame check sequence
64 bits	48 bits	48 bits	16 bits	368-12000 bits (1500 bytes)	32 bits

IEEE 802.3 Frame

Preamble	SFD	Destination address	Source address	Length	Data	Frame check sequence
56 bits	8 bits	48 bits	48 bits	16 bits	368-12000 bits (1500 bytes)	32 bits

Preamble: Identifies and synchronizes the start of frame.
Start Frame Delimiter (SFD): Indicates the start of frame with a one-byte binary pattern in an 802.3 frame.
Destination address: Where the data is being sent.
Source address: Where the data is coming from.
Type: Which upper layer provides guaranteed delivery.
Length: The length of the data field.
Data: The data being transmitted.
Frame Check Sequence: Ensures data integrity.

Figure 5-15.
Ethernet II and 802.3 frame comparison.

However, there is no guarantee that the two frames can be used to exchange information compatibly. This is due to the slight variation in frame construction. This variation exists in the length of the preamble fields.

The preamble is used to identify and synchronize the start of the frame. It consists of a series of alternating ones and zeros and ends with a series of steady ones. The start frame delimiter (SFD) in the 802.3 frame follows directly behind the preamble. Prior to Ethernet frame version IEEE 802.3, the SFD and preamble were combined. In the IEEE 802.3 frame, the SFD indicates the actual start of the frame information by using a one-byte field consisting of the following binary pattern: 10101011.

The preamble is followed by the destination address. In the Ethernet II and 802.3 frame types, there is a slight variation of the initial bits in the destination field. The variations in the binary pattern are used to indicate if the intended destination is multicast (a group of computers) or unicast (only one computer). The remaining destination field identifies the MAC address of the computer or device.

It is important to note that a frame containing only the MAC address can only be used for a LAN. To transmit the Ethernet frame to a distant network or across a WAN, additional destination information needs to encapsulate the frame. The Ethernet frame must contain both the source and destination IP addresses. The Internet is a WAN connected via routers. Routers are configured to recognize IP addresses, not MAC addresses. The router selects the proper route for the packet based on the IP address contained in the Ethernet frame. This is in contrast to NetBEUI, which does not use IP addresses to locate the destination. NetBEUI uses the name assigned to the destination and the MAC address. Since NetBEUI does not use IP addresses to identify the destination and source, a router cannot route NetBEUI transmissions.

broadcast frame
a frame intended for every computer on the network.

multicast frame
a frame intended for a preselected number of computers, such as a specific workgroup.

Another point of interest is that when the destination address is filled with all ones, it becomes a broadcast frame. A ***broadcast frame*** is intended for every computer on the network; whereas, a ***multicast frame*** is intended for a preselected number of computers, such as a specific workgroup. Ethernet is also described as broadcasting to every network interface card on the network with each frame it sends. This type of broadcasting is different than that described in the broadcast frame. When described as broadcasting, Ethernet frames are broadcast to every network interface card, but only a network card that matches the MAC address indicated in the destination field receives the frames. If the destination field does not match the MAC address of the network interface card, the frame will not pass through to the computer. The exception is when a broadcast frame is used.

Another difference between the two frame types is the type and length fields. The original Ethernet II frame was designed not to perform error checking at the data link layer. Since the original Ethernet II was not intended to perform data error correction at this level, the type field was used to indicate where error correction would occur. In other words, it identifies the upper layer of the OSI model that is responsible for checking damaged frames.

In the 802.3 frame, the length field exists in place of the type field. The length field indicates the total length of the frame (not including the preamble). This information is used to perform error checking at the data link layer rather than pass the responsibility to upper level layers of the OSI model. This is a fine example of how variations of network technology can occur because of developments in technology.

The data field contains the data, such as text, graphics, or sound, which is to be delivered to the destination. The two frames have identical data field maximum and minimum lengths.

The Frame Check Sequence (FCS) field is used to determine a successful delivery of the frame. The data link layer does not perform the check. Rather, an upper-level layer in the OSI model uses the FCS to verify the frame's integrity.

As you can see, the two Ethernet frames are very similar, but there are sufficient differences in the way the frames are constructed. The standard used today is Ethernet II, but most network adapters incorporate features to automatically detect the frame type. Many network adapter features are set to auto detect by default. These features can also be selected manually, usually through the **Network Connection Properties** dialog box under the **Advanced** tab.

Data Encoding, Transmission, and the OSI Model

The OSI model is used as a reference to determine how data can most effectively be transferred between networks. It is specifically designed for communication across WANs and MANs. LANs did not need a complex model when they were first developed. They were, in fact, proprietary in nature since communication was limited to nodes only on the local network. The network operating system could handle all that was required for identification, packet size, media access, security, and such. However, as the Internet grew, it became apparent that many different operating systems, networking devices, and media were going to be used to support communications. Some sort of standard or model was needed to help programmers and manufacturers design systems and computer programs to support the vast array of network technologies.

The OSI model is sometimes referred to as the *protocol stack* because it is, in essence, a stack of protocols. Various protocols are associated and designed to work at different levels of the OSI model. Some protocols are designed to work with specific types of media, some are designed for security, and others are designed to encapsulate various types of data such as text, audio, or video. The exact protocol needed is determined by the type of media and networking devices used, the nature of communication, and the type of data sent.

For example, you may use the Internet to access information on a distant server. As the signal travels between your computer and the remote server, it may pass through a maze of telephone exchanges, fiber-optic cables, wireless satellite connections, microwave stations, and such. It may also pass through multiplexers, switches, and routers. As the data passes through various network media and devices, the data is packaged to match the technology it encounters. This is all done at remarkably high speeds.

When negotiating a connection, the protocol used for making the initial connection may be different from the protocol used to transfer the data. For example, the Point-to-Point Protocol (PPP) may be used to initially attach to an Internet service provider through a dial-up telephone modem. After the connection is established, IP and UDP are used to make a connection at the distant site. After the connection is established, IP and TCP may be used to transfer the data. As you see, no one protocol is used.

As data moves through the layers of the OSI model, each layer is responsible for a specific aspect of communication. In other words, each layer has a different set of responsibilities. The following sections present an overview of how communication takes place at each layer of the OSI model. **Figure 5-16** provides a summary of each layer's function.

Figure 5-16.
OSI layers and functions.

Layer	Function
Application	Interfaces to the network system.
Presentation	Packages data into a universally agreed on form, such as ASCII, BCD, BMP, JPG, and WAV.
Session	Establishes and coordinates communication between two points.
Transport	Ensures accurate delivery.
Network	Encapsulates packets for routing.
Data link	Converts frames or packets into electronic signals and places them on the network media.
Physical	The network media.

Application Layer

The application layer is where the user interfaces with network operating system. The application layer is at the top of the OSI model and is the start and the final destination of all data communication. When a user generates a request, such as to connect to a Web page, the request is packaged, sent down the protocol stack to the physical layer, and sent across network media to the destination computer. At the destination computer, the request enters the physical layer and is sent up the protocol stack to the application layer. The data is finalized in the appropriate form, such as displaying the Web page. The application layer is associated with applications such as Web browsers and e-mail. The application layer also starts the file transfer mechanism associated with specific operating systems.

Presentation Layer

Data at the source computer leaves the application layer and enters the presentation layer where the raw data is packaged into a universally agreed on form. The data byte order must be agreed on and presented in the same manner. For example, originally most computer system CPUs were one of two types: Intel or Motorola. Mainframe computers were constructed from both. The two different CPUs wrote data in opposite order. The order of data written into the packets must be agreed on and presented in the same fashion; otherwise, the data will not be interpreted correctly. If all the hardware and software in the network were exactly the same, there would be no need for a presentation layer. Data encryption also takes place at the presentation layer. ***Data encryption*** is the encoding of data based on a mathematical formula, which converts the original data symbol into another symbol.

data encryption
the encoding of data based on a mathematical formula, which converts the original data symbol into another symbol.

Session Layer

The session layer establishes a dialog between the source and destination computers. It is easier to visualize the session layer as a negotiation rather than as a layer. The session layer negotiates decisions about how data flow is controlled and how a session ends. It decides on whether the destination computer needs to confirm that the data has been received or if the data will be sent without requiring a confirmation of its arrival. For example, video may need to be sent in one continuous flow to preserve the quality of the audio, such as in a telephone conversation. Confirming the arrival of each packet would not be possible. Sending an illustration or digital image, may require that each packet not only be confirmed but also that it be assembled in correct order so that the image is not distorted.

Transport Layer

The transport layer is responsible for the flow of data to and from the destination computer. The source and destination computers decide on an appropriate amount of data that can be sent at one time. They also identify if the data needs to be transmitted in sequential order or if a simple one-packet transmission is enough. For example, a large block of data may need to be segmented. Each segment would need a unique number assigned to it to ensure that it is assembled in the correct order. A simple authentication, which consists of a user name and password to access the destination computer, may only require one frame. Thus, one frame would not need to be assigned a sequence number.

The transport layer is also responsible for overseeing that the complete data package reaches the destination computer. When a large block of data is divided into many segments, it is most likely that a form of response will be needed. A response, such as a UDP packet, is sent from the destination to the source computer confirming that the packets were received and that the next group of packets may be sent or that all of the data has been received.

Network Layer

The network layer provides a means of routing data packets across a WAN or MAN. For example, sending a data packet across a LAN only requires the destination computer's address. This means the name of the computer or the MAC address can be used to identify the destination. When sending a data packet across a WAN or MAN, the packet must be encapsulated with an additional address. The MAC address and computer name is not a practical solution. A more precise address is required to negotiate a route across the Internet, specifically an IP address. Each packet of data must be repackaged according to a protocol standard such as TCP/IP. The protocol used depends on the need for verification of the delivered package. You should recall that the IP protocol does not require verification and is a connectionless protocol. TCP requires verification and is called a *connection-oriented protocol*.

It is at the network layer that data packets are turned into frames. The frame terminology comes from the fact that the network layer surrounds the data packet with a frame that can navigate across routers. Routers use IP addresses to transfer frames to their destination.

The network layer is also responsible for virtual networks. A ***virtual network*** is a logical network within a LAN. Virtual networks are created to help eliminate collisions, thus increasing the bandwidth capabilities of the LAN. A virtual network is typically created in a LAN to reduce the number of collisions.

virtual network a logical network within a LAN.

TCP/IP was designed to communicate over the Internet connecting millions of computers to each other. Originally, LANs used proprietary protocols to communicate. Today TCP/IP is the default protocol used to communicate over LANs and the Internet. TCP/IP is covered in detail in Chapter 10—TCP/IP Fundamentals.

Look at **Figure 5-17.** Two virtual networks have been created with a router. The physical network consists of six computers; however, the router creates two separate virtual networks. The router constructs a database of all connected devices by IP address. After all devices have been identified, the router can be programmed to limit packet broadcasts to only the devices identified or grouped together by IP addresses. In the example, two computers are grouped as virtual network A and four computers are grouped as virtual network B. Since broadcasts are limited to the designated virtual networks A and B, communication is limited to these networks. The two networks are not aware of each other. The router can also be programmed to allow communication beyond the virtual network.

This same type of virtual network can be created using a switch. A layer 2 switch creates networks based on MAC addresses. Remember, a layer 2 device operates at the data link layer.

Network switches have become more complex as networking science has evolved. Switches are classified as layer 2 and layer 3. Some switch manufacturers claim layer 4 because of the enhanced features added to the switch.

While the intent of the OSI model is to make data packaging appear as a precise sequence of operations, data packaging flows more freely. For example, if data is sent to a destination on a LAN and does not require an IP address, the network layer is not really needed. The data is passed through to the data link layer. The data link layer will have enough information to deliver the data package to the final destination on the LAN.

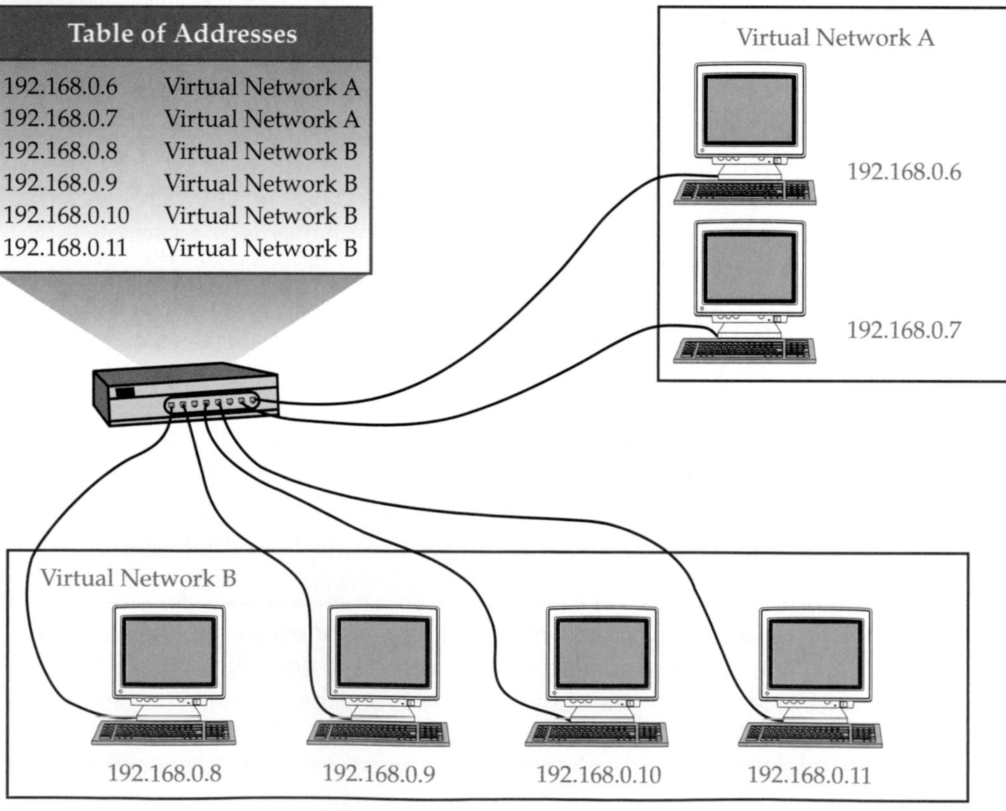

Figure 5-17. A switch or router can be used to divide a physical network into two or more virtual networks. The router or switch maintains a table of addresses, which it uses as a reference.

Data Link Layer

The data link layer converts the data package into electrical pulses and places the pulses on the network media. The data link layer is subdivided into the logical link control (LLC) sublayer and the MAC sublayer. At the MAC sublayer, the data code is converted into electrical pulses.

The MAC sublayer is not only concerned with how the data is encoded, but also with the type of topology and cable used. For example, it decides if the data frame needs to be converted for an 802.11 (wireless) network or an 802.3 10GBaseT network.

The LLC sublayer is only interested in getting the data to the destination on the LAN. The LLC sublayer uses the MAC address to address the packet.

If data is to be sent across a WAN, the data link layer sends the data to the appropriate router. The router forwards the package based on the IP address inside the package. The router does not need the MAC address to deliver the data package.

The data link layer, like the transport layer, is responsible for error checking. However, at this level, the error checks are based on the binary-coded digital patterns. Checks such as parity are made to detect missing binary information. CRC checks are also performed at the data link layer.

Network+ Note

For the Network+ Certification exam, remember that parity and CRC checks are performed at the data link layer. Checks at the transport layer ensure the entire data block was received intact. The transport layer also checks packet sequencing to ensure all data packets are reassembled in the proper order.

Physical Layer

The physical layer is concerned with the media, hardware, and topology of a network. The media may be infrared signals, copper wire, glass or plastic fiber, or electromagnetic radio waves. The choice of topology is typically a star, ring, mesh, or hybrid. The hardware is the connectors used for the media and unintelligible devices, such as hubs and repeaters.

An unintelligent device makes no decision about where the data will go. It simply passes electrical pulses though the device. An example of an unintelligent device is a repeater or a hub. In Chapter 1—Introduction to Networking, you learned that hubs could be either active or passive. A passive hub is an unintelligent device.

Network+ Note

For this textbook and for the Network+ Certification exam, a hub is considered unintelligent. It simply provides a connection for the physical media and passes signals without making any choices.

Summary

- Digital encoding is the conversion of data into a digital pattern acceptable to the network media.
- A digital signal that fluctuates between a positive voltage level and zero-volt level is called a *unipolar digital signal.*
- A digital signal that fluctuates between a positive voltage level and a negative voltage level is called a *bipolar digital signal.*
- Manchester encoding is a common digital-encoding scheme used on LANs. It is characterized by the digital pulse transitioning during the midpoint of the timing period.
- A digital signal that fluctuates between a positive voltage level and a negative voltage level and never returns to zero for any measurable period of time is known as *non-return to zero (NRZ).*
- A synchronous signal is synchronized with a reference signal to ensure proper timing.
- An asynchronous signal is not synchronized with a reference signal and typically uses a binary pattern to determine the stop and start of the signal.
- A parity check is used to check the integrity of data.
- A Cyclic Redundancy Check (CRC) is an enhanced parity check that not only identifies when an error occurs but also corrects the error.
- Data encapsulation is the process of surrounding the raw data with other information needed for delivery.
- The terms *segment*, *frame*, *datagram*, and *protocol data unit (PDU)* are used to describe blocks of data.
- The term *protocol data unit (PDU)* is the most technically correct term used to describe data packaging.
- A connection-oriented protocol establishes a connection with the destination, transfers the data, and then releases the connection after all communication has ended.
- A connectionless protocol simply sends data to the destination.
- A circuit-switching network establishes a physical connection between two points.
- A packet-switching network establishes a logical connection and may use many different, physical paths to send data from the source to the destination.
- ASCII, EBCDIC, and UNICODE are coding standards, or data codes, that represent the written word.
- Binary Coded Decimal (BCD) is a coding standard that uses a four-digit binary code to represent a number.
- Various protocols are designed to package data in particular ways.
- The OSI model is composed of seven layers, which explain the process of encapsulating data for communication between two points on a network system.

Review Questions

Answer the following questions on a separate sheet of paper. Please do not write in this book.

1. When does digital encoding take place?
2. Describe the Manchester digital encoding scheme and how it is related to binary signals.
3. The type of transmission in which the digital signal is synchronized with a reference signal to ensure proper timing is called _____ transmission.
4. The type of transmission in which no reference signal is present is called _____ transmission.
5. What is a parity check?
6. What is a Cyclic Redundancy Check (CRC)?
7. Describe the complete data packaging process, from raw data (text file, sound, or graphic) to digital signals.
8. A(n) _____ protocol first establishes a connection with the destination computer before transmitting data.
9. A(n) _____ protocol sends data to a destination computer without first establishing a connection.
10. What is the difference between packet switching and circuit switching?
11. Name three encoding standards used to represent written language as binary numbers.
12. What does the acronym ASCII represent?
13. Which standard was designed to represent plain text files?
14. What code is used to represent strictly numerical data?
15. What code format does IBM mainframe computers use?
16. What code can be used to represent over 65,000 different characters?
17. Draw and label a UDP frame.
18. Compare and contrast an Ethernet II frame with an IEEE 802.3 frame.
19. What layer of the OSI model is responsible for the conversion of different coding formats?
20. What layer of the OSI model routes data packages based on the IP address?
21. What layer of the OSI model is concerned with the media, hardware, and topology of the network?
22. What OSI layer is responsible for converting data into digital signals?
23. What OSI layer converts data into a form acceptable to both the source and destination?
24. What OSI layer is concerned with encrypting data?
25. What OSI layer is concerned with establishing and ending the connection to the destination?
26. What OSI layer negotiates the connection between the destination and source?
27. What OSI layer decides if TCP or UDP is to be used as the protocol for transmitting the data?

Sample Network+ Exam Questions

Answer the following questions on a separate sheet of paper. Please do not write in this book.

1. Data integrity of certain protocols is verified by using a technique known as _____.
   A. Cyclic Redundancy Check (CRC)
   B. Data Parity Reference (DPR)
   C. Kerberos Security Check (KSC)
   D. Parity Data Unit (PDU)
2. Which is true concerning a connectionless-oriented protocol? (Select all that apply.)
   A. When establishing a connection between the destination and source, the destination must send a "clear to send" signal to the source before data can be transmitted.
   B. When ending a session, the source must send a termination signal to the destination.
   C. There is no verification from the destination that the data arrived intact.
   D. A connectionless protocol typically relies on the integrity of the network equipment and assumes the packet arrived at the destination.
3. A connection established via modem over a telephone line with an ISP is an example of which of the following technologies?
   A. Packet switching
   B. Circuit switching
   C. Modular switching
   D. Enterprise switching
4. Which layer in the OSI model is responsible for converting data into electrical pulses?
   A. Physical
   B. Data link
   C. Application
   D. Presentation
5. The IEEE 802.3 standard is associated with which media access method?
   A. Carrier Sense Multiple Access with Collision Detection (CSMA/CD)
   B. Carrier Sense Multiple Access with Collision Avoidance (CSMA/CA)
   C. Asynchronous Transmission Mode (ATM)
   D. Wireless Ethernet Protocol (WEP)
6. What is the purpose of a port number?
   A. Identifies the network interface manufacturer.
   B. Identifies a computer operating system service.
   C. Identifies the data rate used by the protocol.
   D. Identifies what type of protocol is used for the transmission.
7. Which OSI layer is responsible for negotiating decisions about how data flow is controlled and how a session ends?
   A. Network
   B. Application
   C. Session
   D. Transport

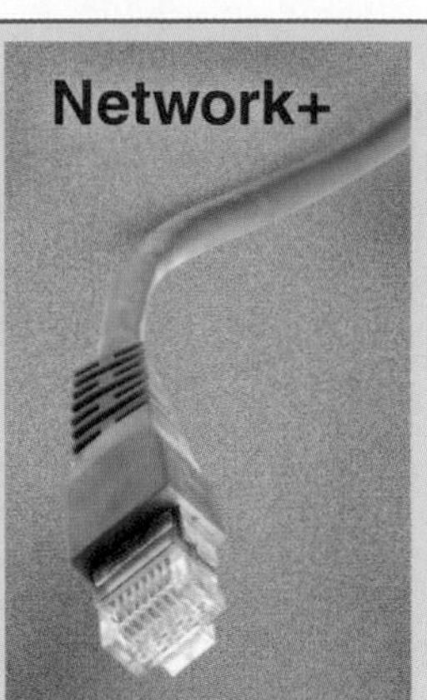

8. Which protocol is used to establish a connection with an ISP when using a dial-up telephone modem?
   A. TCP
   B. IP
   C. UDP
   D. PPP
9. Which items are responsible for identifying a destination computer? (Select all that apply.)
   A. IP number
   B. MAC address
   C. Port number
   D. Sequence number
10. What is the purpose of a multicast Ethernet frame?
    A. To broadcast a message to a specifically identified set of workstations.
    B. To broadcast a message to all workstations in the LAN.
    C. To broadcast a single frame to all servers in the WAN.
    D. There is no such thing as a multicast Ethernet frame.

Suggested Laboratory Activities

1. Using the Internet, research various Ethernet frame formats. List the contents of each section of the frame that surrounds the data. See if you can determine where the contents of the frame that is responsible for asynchronous data transmission are located. (Not all frame types will contain an asynchronous marker.)
2. Download a free or limited-time protocol analyzer from the Internet. Use the protocol analyzer to capture frames transmitted from your PC and analyze the contents. Determine where the MAC address, IP address, and data contents are located. See if you can decode the contents of the data frame and addresses.
3. On a Windows 7 computer, locate the properties for the network adapter and view the options available under the **Advanced** tab. To access this, right-click **Computer** and select **Manage** from the shortcut menu. The Computer Management utility will open. Select **Device Manager | Network adapters**. Then, right-click the network adapter that is listed and select **Properties** from the shortcut menu. The **Network Connection Properties** dialog box will display. Select the **Advanced** tab. Not all network adapters have the same advanced options, but some options that may exist are **Flow Control**, **Link Speed**, **Duplex**, and more.

Interesting Web Sites for More Information

www.protocols.com
www.unicode.org

Wireshark is a protocol analyzer that can be downloaded for free from the Wireshark Web site (www.wireshark.org). Using a protocol analyzer to study network activity is a good way to gain a better understanding of network protocols.

Chapter 5
Laboratory Activity

Introduction to Wireshark

After completing this lab activity, you will be able to:
- Identify the common features of a network protocol analyzer.
- Recall the purpose of WinPcap program.
- Differentiate between promiscuous and non-promiscuous mode as related to a network protocol analyzer.
- Use Wireshark to perform a simple capture.

Introduction

In this laboratory activity, you will download, install, and configure the network protocol analyzer program Wireshark previously known as *Ethereal* (pronounced "ether real").

Note
The name "Ethereal" was changed to "Wireshark" in 2006 because of a legal issue when its creator Gerald Combs changed employment.

There are many commercial network protocol analyzers available that cost a thousand dollars or more. Wireshark is a free, open source product developed under the GNU General Public License. While originally developed for Linux operating systems, it runs on all the latest versions of Windows. Many Linux operating systems incorporate a version of Ethereal or Wireshark as part of the administrative tools. Ethereal was originally written by Gerald Combs in 1998. Since that time, many programmers in the open source community have contributed to the development of Ethereal and now Wireshark.

You can still download a copy of the last version of Ethereal at www.ethereal.com or the very latest version called Wireshark at www.wireshark.org.

A network protocol analyzer captures network frames or packets and then displays details about the contents. Look at the following screen capture to see a sample Wireshark capture.

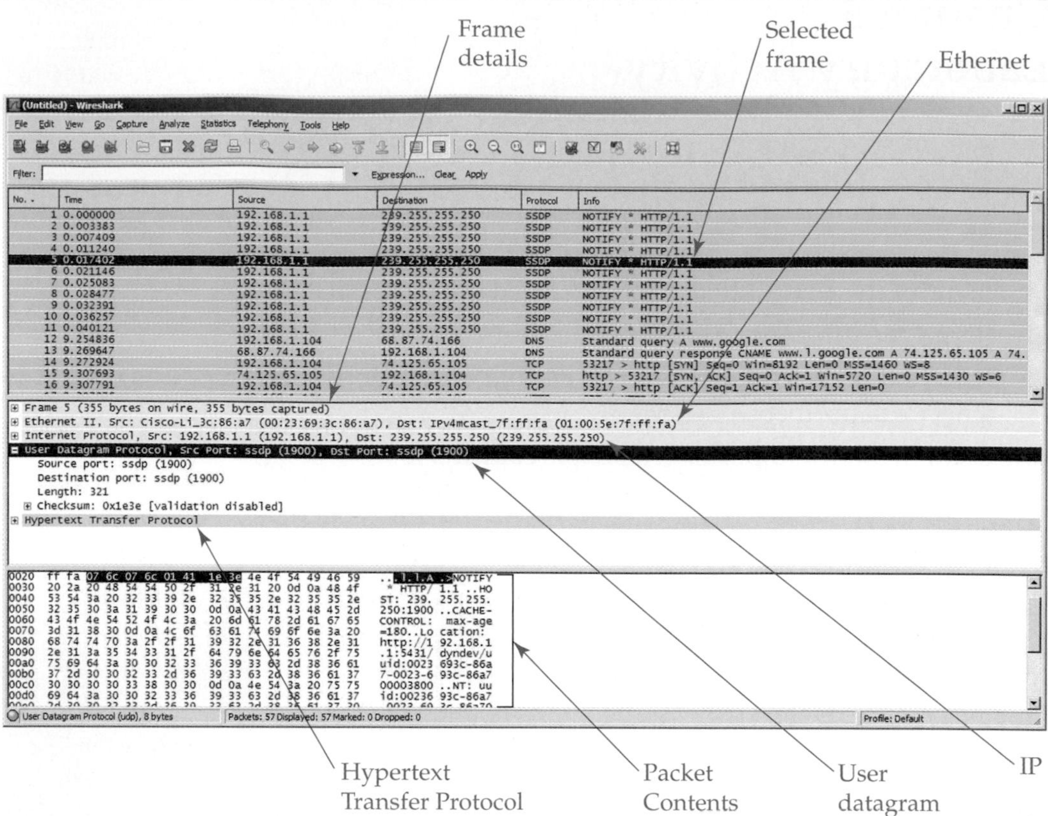

A frame is a collection of data transferred across a network as a single unit captured by the Wireshark protocol analyzer. The frame encapsulates protocol packets such as Ethernet, IP, UDP, and HTTP. All protocols that are part of the single transfer of data are collectively known as a *frame*.

There is a tremendous amount of information displayed in a Wireshark capture. Looking from left to right at the top half of the display, you will first see a number assigned to each frame starting with 1. The next column displays the exact amount of time from the start of Wireshark until the frame was captured. The next two columns display the source and destination IP address in IPv4 or IPv6 format, depending on which format is being used by the network operating system. In the fifth column, the protocol is identified such as ARP, DNS, DHCP, etc. Wireshark can identify approximately 700 different protocols—more protocols than you will ever normally need to monitor. The last column on the right provides a brief bit of information about each frame captured. Some examples of this information are a request to log on, DHCP information, and a response to another frame.

You can use Wireshark to study the protocols presented in your training course. You can either make your own captures or download sample captures of protocols that are available at the Wireshark Web link: http://wiki.wireshark.org/SampleCaptures.

You can also use Wireshark to conduct experiments such as watching the sequence of packets and protocols during the initial startup of a computer on a network. You can see how the booting computer sends out a series of frames to identify itself to other computers and devices on the local area network. You can also see it request an IP address from the DHCP server.

Conducting a protocol analysis will help you better understand how network systems operate. At first, Wireshark as any other protocol analyzer will be very intimidating, but the more you use it, the more comfortable you will be. Later, you will be able to use a protocol analyzer to inspect the network system and detect intruders, virus activities, and malfunctioning equipment.

Be sure to read the *Wireshark User's Guide* available at the Wireshark Web site (www.wireshark.org/docs/wsug_html_chunked). Look over the summary of features such as filtering, which allows you to capture only packets related to a particular protocol, a particular computer, or a group of computers identified by IP address.

A protocol analyzer is an extremely useful tool when it comes to network security. It will allow you to study how security protocols function and can be used to identify the source of an attack on a network system. If you are to become a true networking professional, you need to master how to use a protocol analyzer.

Note
Ethereal required that the WinPcap program be installed on a Windows operating system before installing the Ethereal program. WinPcap is a software program that must be installed to allow live packet captures on a Microsoft operating system. Wireshark will automatically detect any existing WinPcap version that might be already installed on the computer and will offer to install the latest version during the installation process.

Equipment and Materials

- Windows XP, Windows Vista, or Windows 7 computer.
- The location of where to store the Wireshark captures as indicated by your instructor and recorded on a separate sheet of paper.
- Captures: ______________________________

Note
This lab activity is based on Wireshark version 1.2.1 and may be different but similar to the version you will be using.

Procedure

1. _____ Report to your assigned workstation.
2. _____ Boot the computer and verify it is in working order.
3. _____ Connect to the Internet and locate the Wireshark home page or the Wireshark download page (www.wireshark.org/download.html).

Note
Wireshark may already be installed on the workstation by a previous student. If Wireshark is installed, go to step 6.

4. _____ Read the instructions for installing Wireshark. Select the correct version of Wireshark matching your operating system (32-bit or 64-bit). Download Wireshark and install it on the workstation following the instructions for your particular operating system. The installation program is very intuitive and makes it very easy to install Wireshark. Be sure to select the **Install desktop shortcut** option during the installation process.

5. _____ After Wireshark is installed, look for the desktop icon similar to the following. If you cannot locate the icon, call your instructor for assistance.

6. _____ Start Wireshark by double-clicking the **Wireshark** icon. You can also start Wireshark by selecting it from the **Start | All Programs**. After Wireshark is started, you should see a page similar to the one in the following screen capture.

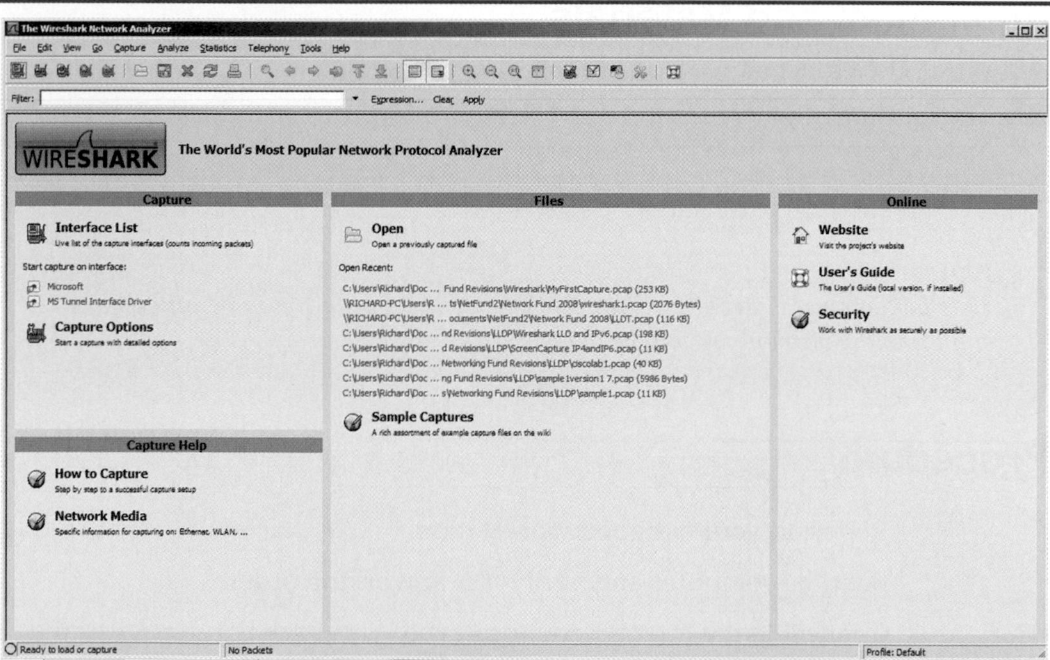

Take a few minutes to study the interface. Notice the **User's Guide** link in the right column. The *Wireshark User's Guide* provides a great deal of information on all topics related to Wireshark. Also, notice the **Sample Captures** link in the center column. The **Sample Captures** link will take you to a list of over 50 of the most common protocols encountered today. You will be making your own sample captures during this course.

7. ______ Wireshark must know which network interface to use before beginning a capture. Look at the following screen capture.

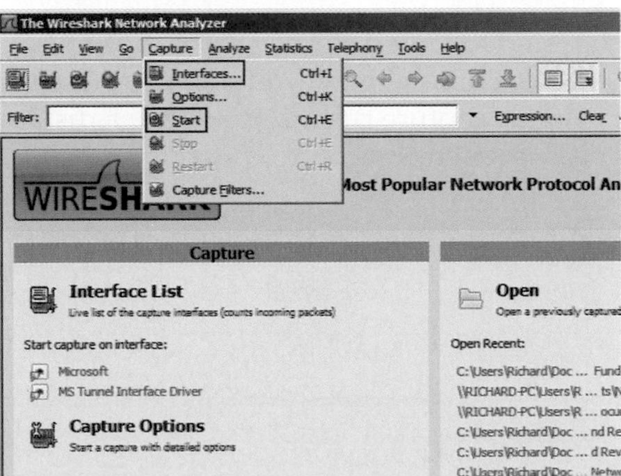

You must first select the network interface you will use for the capture. Some computers, especially laptops, have more than one network interface. They can have one or two network adapter cards that use an RJ-45 cable connector and may also have a wireless network card installed. A telephone modem also counts as a network interface. If you have more than one network interface, you will need to select the one you will be using. Look at the following screen captures to see a listing of interfaces on two different computers.

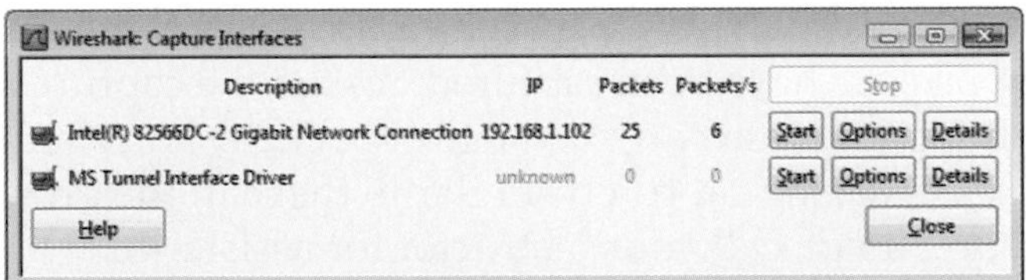

The first capture was taken from a Windows Vista laptop and the second from a Windows Vista desktop. The top capture used Wireshark version 1.0, and the second used Wireshark version 1.2.1. The version you are using may be even later, so there can be some differences between the screens in the captures and that on your computer.

Notice that the laptop (top screen capture) is using an IPv6 address and the desktop (bottom screen capture) is using an IPv4 address. You can use Control Panel to access the local area network adapter status and properties to help you identify the correct network adapter to use. Select the interface you will be using for this exercise. If you are not sure which one to use, ask your instructor.

8. ______ After choosing the interface, begin the capture series by selecting **Start** from the **Capture** menu. You may also use the shortcut keys [Ctrl] [E]. As the capture runs, you will see a display similar to the one in the following screen capture.

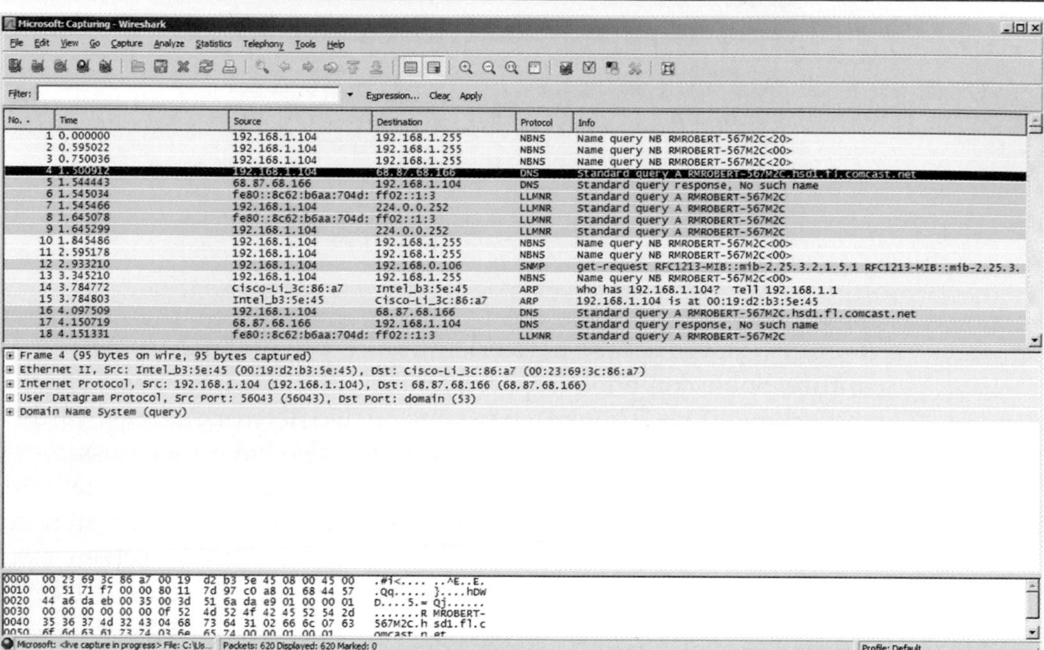

Wireshark will continue to capture frames until you stop the capture process. To stop the capture process, select **Stop** from the **Capture** menu or simply press [Ctrl] [E] once more. The keyboard combination [Ctrl] [E] not only starts a capture session, it also stops it.

After several packets have been captured, stop the capture process. If no packets have been captured, restart the capture and then access the Internet to start an exchange of packets. You should see a series of packets being captured similar to those in the previous screen capture. If not, call your instructor for assistance.

9. ______ Look closely at the capture. The columns are labeled left to right as follows: No., Time, Source, Destination, Protocol, and Info. You can rearrange the information in each column by simply clicking the top of the column in the area indicated in the following screen capture.

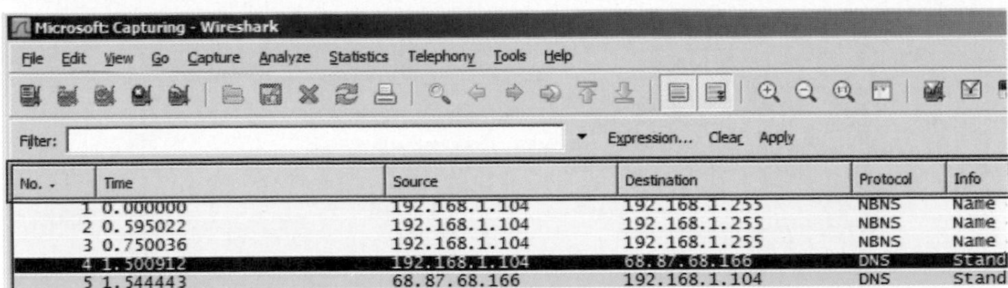

The frame numbers will change from ascending to descending order with a mouse click. You can also quickly sort other columns the same way. Click at the top of each column now to see how it affects the column contents.

10. _____ Select the **File** menu to see a list of menu items similar to those in the following screen capture.

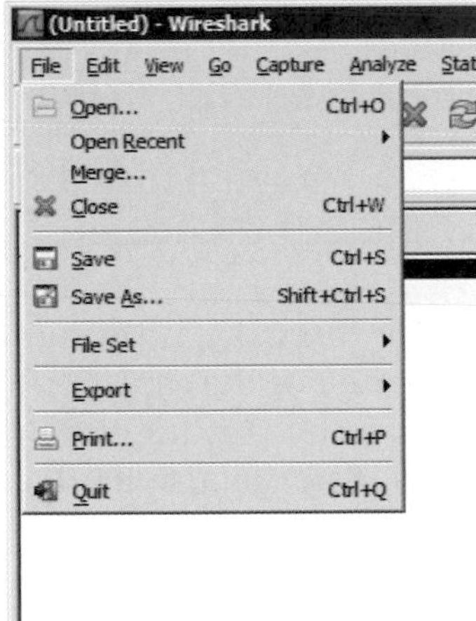

The **Close** menu option will close the display of captured packets. You will be prompted to save the capture or to continue without saving the capture.

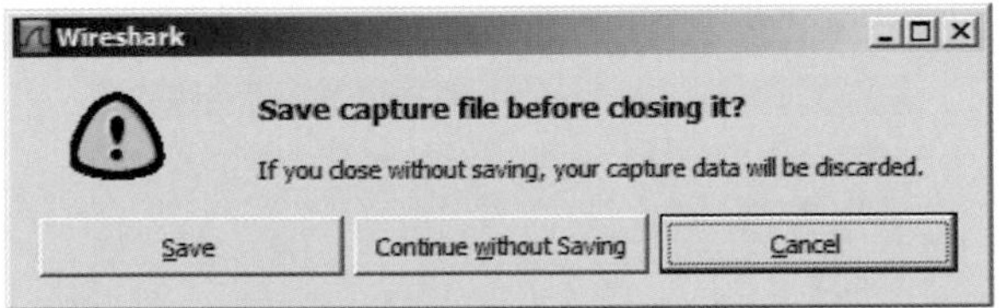

When you select the **Save** option, you will be prompted to select a location to which to save the contents of your capture. Look at the following screen capture of typical **Save file as** dialog box options.

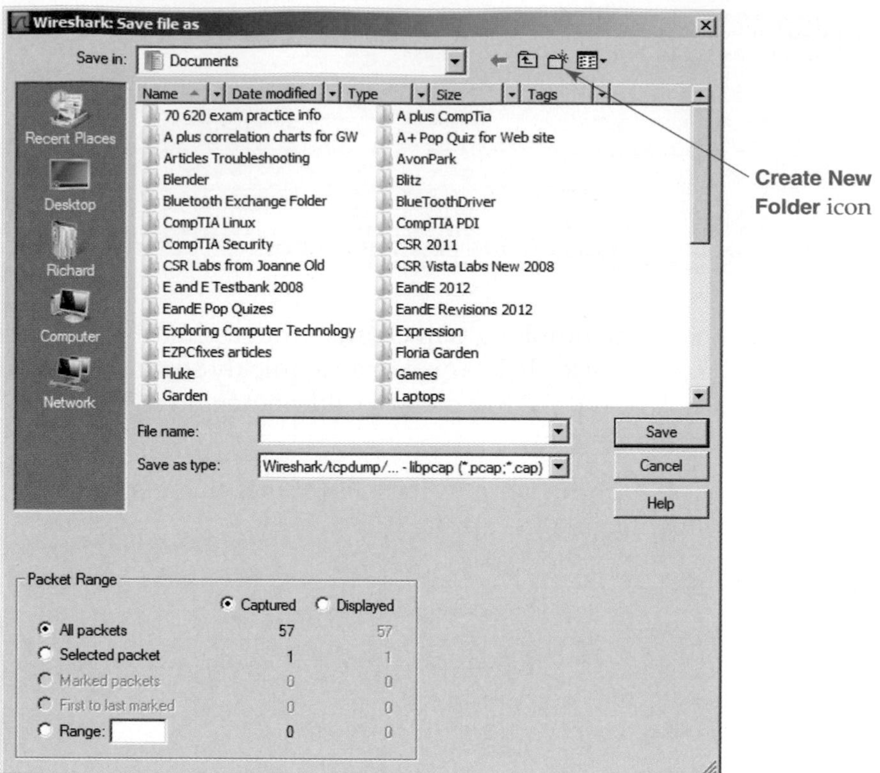

The operating system directory is presented. You will need to select a location and a file name for the capture. You can create a new folder to store your capture in by clicking the **Create New Folder** icon at the top of the dialog box. You can also navigate to a location other than Documents if you wish.

Also, notice that you are presented with options to save **All packets**, **Selected packet**, or a **Range** of packets.

Save your first capture to the location indicated by your instructor, and then call your instructor to inspect your lab.

11. ______ Select the **Capture** menu and then the **Options** menu item or use the keyboard combination [Ctrl] [K].

The **Wireshark Capture Options** dialog will display and will look similar to that in the following screen capture.

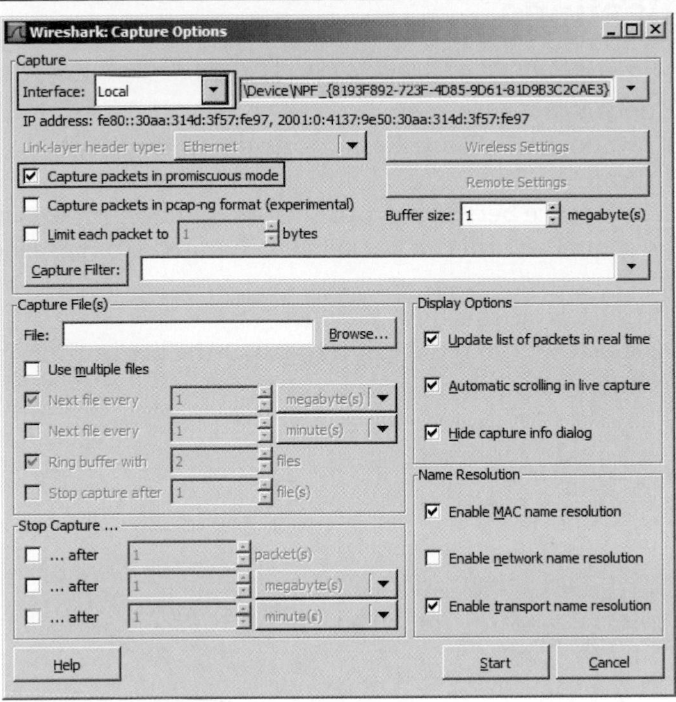

Here you can modify the default Wireshark capture options to meet your need. The first option to look at is **Interface**, which indicates the default network adapter to use for the capture.

Another option is **Capture packets in promiscuous mode**. Promiscuous mode enables all network traffic to be captured instead of only traffic to and from the chosen network interface. Pay particular attention to the section labeled **Name Resolution** located in the lower, right corner of the dialog box. In this section, you can configure Wireshark to automatically resolve (present) names in the frame capture based on such items as the MAC address, network name, or transport name. For example, MAC name resolution converts the MAC address's first six numbers to the adapter manufacturer name, such as "Intel." Network resolution converts an IP address to its Fully Qualified Domain Name such as mailserver.mynetwork.com. Transport name resolution converts the port number to the equivalent protocol, such as port 110 to POP3.

Another feature is the **Capture Filter** option. As you will see, networks generate a great deal of traffic displayed as frames. In fact, thousands of frames can be generated in a very short time. The **Capture Filter** option allows you to limit the scope of the capture to a particular area of the total network data being collected. For example, you can filter by IP address, MAC address, protocol, port number, and several other options.

To learn all the possible options, refer to the *Wireshark User's Guide*. Also, check out the following Wireshark link: http://wiki.wireshark.org/CaptureSetup.

12. ______ Answer the review questions and then close the Wireshark protocol analyzer.

Review Questions

Answer the following questions on a separate sheet of paper. Please do not write in this book.

1. How much does Wireshark cost?
2. How many protocols can Wireshark capture and identify?
3. What is WinPcap?
4. What is the difference between promiscuous and non-promiscuous mode?
5. How can the sequence order of packets be changed from ascending to descending?
6. How can you sort protocols by type?
7. What does the box with the plus sign mean at the beginning of an information line?

6 Network Operating Systems and Network Communications

After studying this chapter, you will be able to:

- Give examples of the common operating system features.
- Explain Ethernet, Token Ring, Token Bus, ARCnet, and AppleTalk communications.
- Explain how major operating systems use the TCP/IP protocol suite along with their own proprietary protocols.
- Recall the function of NetBIOS, NBNS, LLDP, LLTD, CDP, LLDP-MED, LLMNR, and ARP.

Network+ Exam—Key Points

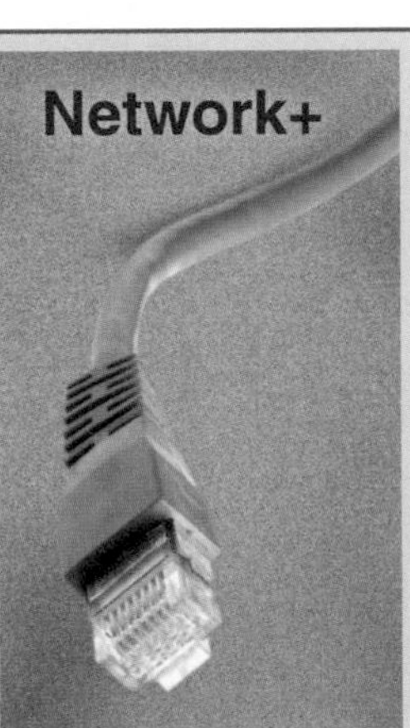

The CompTIA Network+ Certification exam emphasizes basic knowledge of the most common protocols encountered in networking. You should not expect to see reference to any of the older network technologies or proprietary protocols such as Token Ring, AppleTalk, and Token Bus. The majority of protocols presented on the CompTIA Network+ Certification exam are from the TCP/IP suite.

Key Words and Terms

The following words and terms will become important pieces of your networking vocabulary. Be sure you can define them.

access method
active monitor
Address Resolution Protocol (ARP)
AppleTalk
beaconing
broadcast storm
Cisco Discovery Protocol (CDP)
collision domain
command prompt
command syntax
datagram
de facto standard
dumb terminal
graphical user interface (GUI)
Link-Layer Discovery Protocol (LLDP)
Link-Layer Discovery Protocol–Media Endpoint Discovery (LLDP-MED)
Link-Layer Topology Discovery (LLTD)
Link-Local Multicast Name Resolution (LLMNR)
LocalTalk
loopback test
monitor contention
NetBIOS Name Server (NBNS)
ring polling
ring purge
segmenting
session
standby monitor
station address
token
Universal Naming Convention (UNC)
virtual circuit

As you have previously learned, digital data can be encoded in many different ways. It is the job of protocols to create a common language between different network hardware and network operating systems. In this chapter, the relationship between networking technologies, protocols, and network operating systems is explained. You will learn about the features that are common to all major network operating systems and will further explore network protocols and network access methods that make network communications possible. This chapter lays the foundation for the next two chapters, which cover two major network operating systems: Windows and UNIX/Linux.

The Evolution of Network Protocols

In the very early days of networking, the Internet had very limited access and was used almost exclusively by the Department of Defense (DoD) and certain universities. The TCP/IP suite of protocols was developed many years before computers were common in homes and businesses and Internet access was available to the public.

The very first network systems for business were designed by private companies such as Novell, IBM, Microsoft, and Apple. These early proprietary network systems developed protocols to work on their particular network system. These protocols were not designed to work on the Internet because no one knew at the time that the Internet would be used by the general public and the private business sector. Early business computer networks in different physical locations were joined together by telephone lines using telephone modems. There were no fiber-optic lines, wireless network communications, or high-speed cable.

Each network operating system developed its own network device naming system and protocols for logging on to the network, sharing files, and locating network devices and users. None of these original network systems used IP addresses to identify network devices.

Soon it became apparent that different proprietary networks needed to communicate with each other. Businesses such as banks demanded that different network systems exchange data, so new protocols were introduced by the various companies. Data exchange between the proprietary networks was very complicated and many different approaches were taken. An Internet backbone was developed as a way to connect different networks, but the proprietary networks needed to adopt the TCP/IP suite and make their systems compatible with Internet devices and Internet protocols.

Although all major operating systems now use TCP/IP, you may see many of the old proprietary protocols in use. The main reason so many old proprietary protocols still exist is to maintain backward compatibility with older devices that are using older operating systems—not just computers, but also network routers, gateways, and network storage devices.

Today, almost all protocols are developed to be used on the Internet. The very latest sets of new protocols are designed for IPv6, which will eventually replace IPv4. IPv6 has not yet been fully implemented. The implementation of IPv6 has been slow, and as a result, many companies have become impatient and developed their own solutions for communicating with IPv6.

At this time, there are three different generations of protocols being used: early proprietary, TCP/IP designed for IPv4, and TCP/IP designed for IPv6. There are also proprietary protocols designed for IPv6. Never before has there been such a diverse collection of protocols used for networking. So at this time, you are faced with learning some of the old proprietary protocols, the TCP/IP suite of protocols based on IPv4, and the TCP/IP suite of protocols based on IPv6.

Common Network Operating System Traits

Network operating systems share some common features. See **Figure 6-1.** For example, they provide a means of sharing computer resources. Resource sharing, such as sharing files and hardware, is the main purpose of a network system. All network operating systems provide a way to store and manage files in an organized manner. They also provide a means of backing up and encrypting data.

Network operating systems provide security through user authentication. Authentication is accomplished by entering a user name and password into a logon dialog box on a networked computer. Files, folders, and other resources are secured by setting permissions. Permissions are levels of security assigned to a resource. Permissions work by allowing only designated users to use the resource. Each user can also be assigned different access rights to the resource.

Figure 6-1.
Common features of network operating systems.

Common Features of a Network Operating System	Examples
Internet communications	TCP/IP protocol
Resource sharing	Printer, scanner, storage devices, files
Security	Logon/authentication and resource, file and directory permissions
Services	Web, e-mail, FTP
Storage and file management	File management utilities, backup utilities, encryption
Troubleshooting utilities	Network and server diagnostics
User interface	GUI and command line

You will learn more about permissions and access rights in Chapter 7—Microsoft Network Operating Systems.

All network operating systems provide a means of communicating over the Internet by using the TCP/IP protocol. The TCP/IP protocol can also be used to communicate within a LAN.

Network operating systems provide troubleshooting utilities and services such as e-mail. Each network operating system is also very portable. The term *portability* is a programming term that means the operating system can be ported (installed and run) on all major hardware systems.

Networks provide a user interface, both graphical and text-based. The network operating system is the software that interfaces the user with the network hardware. It determines the type of interface, such as a command-line or graphical user interface (GUI), to be used between the user and hardware. A ***graphical user interface (GUI)*** is a pictorial representation of commands and computer hardware that allows a user to access resources and programs with a click of a mouse button. In **Figure 6-2** a user has right-clicked the **Computer** icon to expose a hidden menu (shortcut menu). The menu contains commands, which the user can click to invoke. This is easier than typing commands at a command line.

graphical user interface (GUI)
a pictorial representation of commands and computer hardware that allow a user to access resources and programs with a click of a mouse button.

In a command-line environment, commands are typed and entered at a ***command prompt.*** A command prompt differs among operating systems and user settings. Compare the command prompts in **Figure 6-3** and **Figure 6-4.** The command prompt in Figure 6-3 is from Windows Server 2008. It consists of a directory path (C:\Users\Administrator) and a greater than symbol (>). The command prompt in Figure 6-4 is from the Novell SUSE operating system and consists of the user name, server name, colon, tilde (~) symbol, and the greater than sign. In UNIX/Linux operating systems, the tilde (~) symbol represents the user's home directory. When it appears in the command prompt, it means the current working directory is the user's home directory.

command prompt
a text-based interface where commands are typed and entered.

The user can change the command prompt format. Each operating system has a set of command prompt codes from which to choose. For example, a code to display the date and time can be added to the command prompt.

Commands are typed to the right of the command prompt. Many commands consist of several components. You will learn about these components in Chapter 8—UNIX/Linux Operating Systems. The command and its components have to be typed correctly and in the correct arrangement or an error will occur. The correct manner and arrangement in which a command is to be typed is referred to as the ***command syntax.***

command syntax
the correct manner and arrangement in which a command is to be typed.

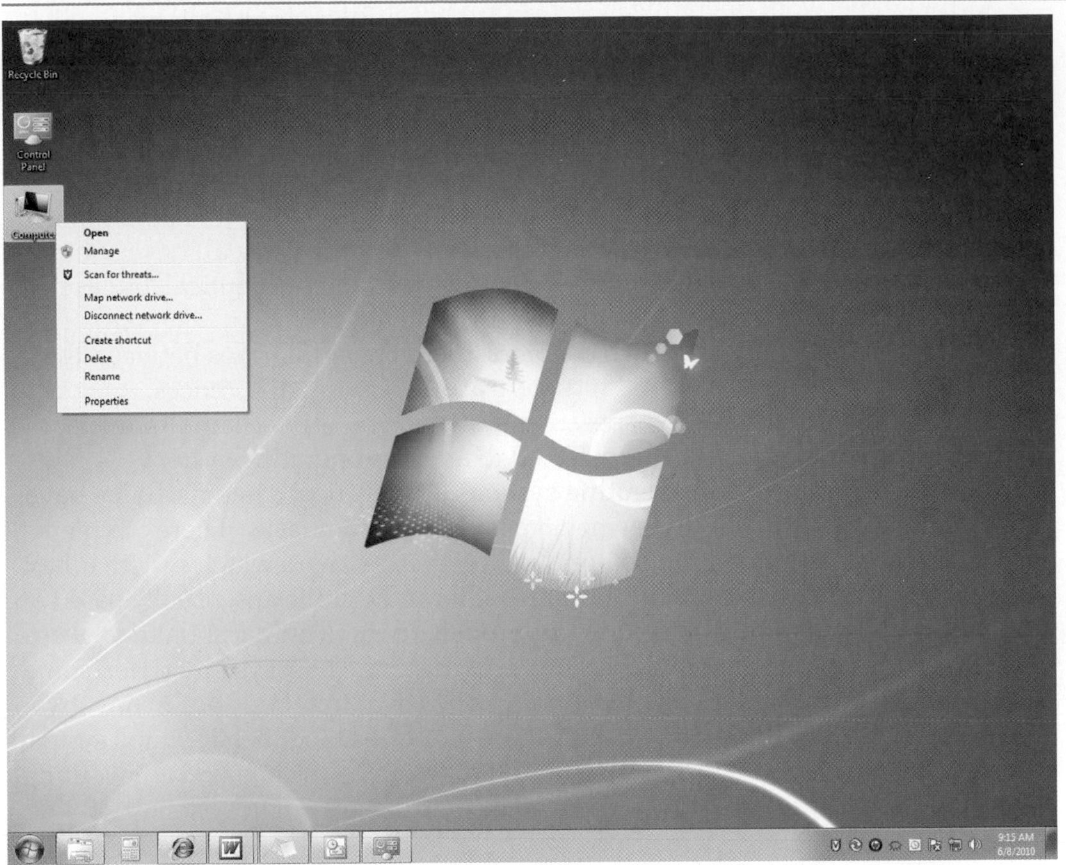

Figure 6-2. Windows 7 GUI. Right-clicking the mouse reveals a shortcut menu. The shortcut menu contains a list of commands.

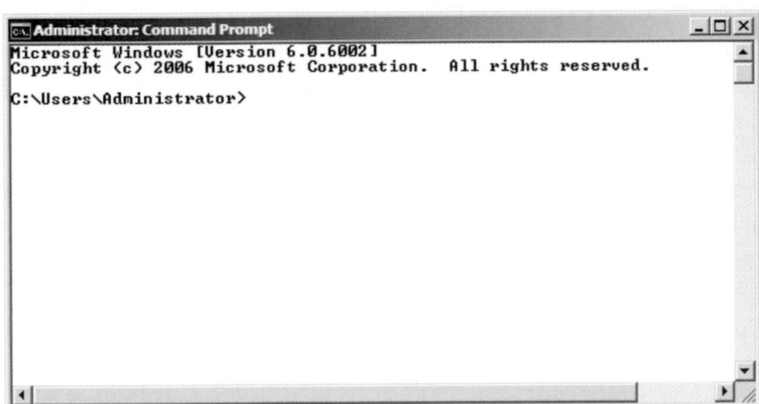

Figure 6-3. Command prompt in Windows Server 2008. A command prompt used in network operating systems is similar to the familiar DOS prompt. A command prompt appears on the screen and text commands are entered to the right of the prompt.

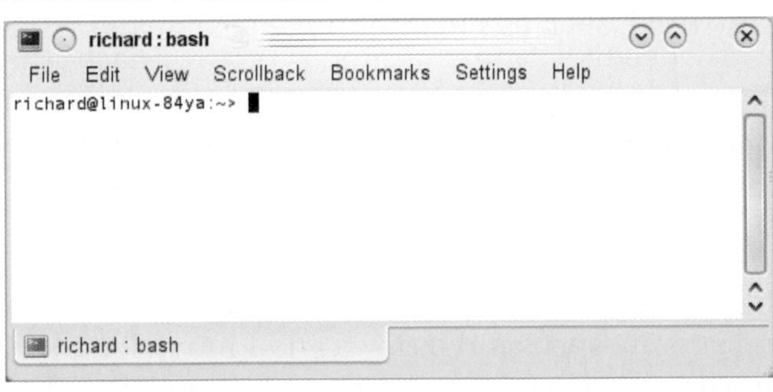

Figure 6-4. Command prompt in the Novell SUSE Linux operating system.

Although network operating systems provide similar services to users, such as file sharing, file management, a user interface, and authentication, there are many variations in these services. Network operating systems differ mainly in terminology and procedures, or methods, to accomplish networking tasks. The most confusion among users is due to network service vendors using a different term to name the same device, service, or function in their network operating system. Network operating systems can be compared to automobiles. All automobiles are designed to travel from point to point. They all have starters, engines, tires, and other components, some of which may be identical, but each automobile brand chooses to maintain a specific identity.

As you will see in the next two chapters, there are similarities between the major network operating systems, and there are also many differences. As you become familiar with one of the operating systems, you will be simultaneously gaining knowledge that can be transferred to another operating system.

All the various network operating systems are excellent systems. Some have better characteristics than others when it comes to certain tasks. There are many opinions among network administrators and technicians about which system is best. There are also strong biases among administrators and technicians, usually based on their own personal training or experiences. Students of networking should not waste valuable time in any negative discussions regarding the best system. Often some network systems are better suited to some purposes than others, but in any given situation, given many different variables, there may be another better-suited system. The best approach may be to know that the best system is the one you are working on at the time because it may be your job to move from system to system.

Network Operating Systems and Hardware Protocols

As you have learned in previous chapters, networking technologies such as Ethernet, Token Ring, and wireless are tied to certain standards that define the hardware, topology, access method, and other specifications of that technology. Each technology uses a different frame type or way of packaging data and other information for accessing the network media. This type of access takes place at the data link layer of the OSI model.

The data link layer is responsible for accessing the network media and either placing the data on the network media or receiving the data and passing it up the OSI layers, **Figure 6-5.** Token Ring and Ethernet are actually protocols that operate at the lower level of the OSI model. The method of gaining access to the network media is called an ***access method.*** Examples of access methods are CSMA/CD, CSMA/CA, and token passing. The access method is designed into the network interface card electronics. This is the reason network interface cards are designed to match the network technology used, such as Ethernet, Token Ring, and wireless.

access method
a method of gaining access to the network media.

Tech Tip

The name of the network technology is often used interchangeably with the name of the access method. For example, the term *Ethernet* may be used in place of the term *CSMA/CD.*

The operating system software interfaces with the access method. The network operating system, such as Windows and Linux, operates above the data link layer and can run on any of the networking technologies. The access method

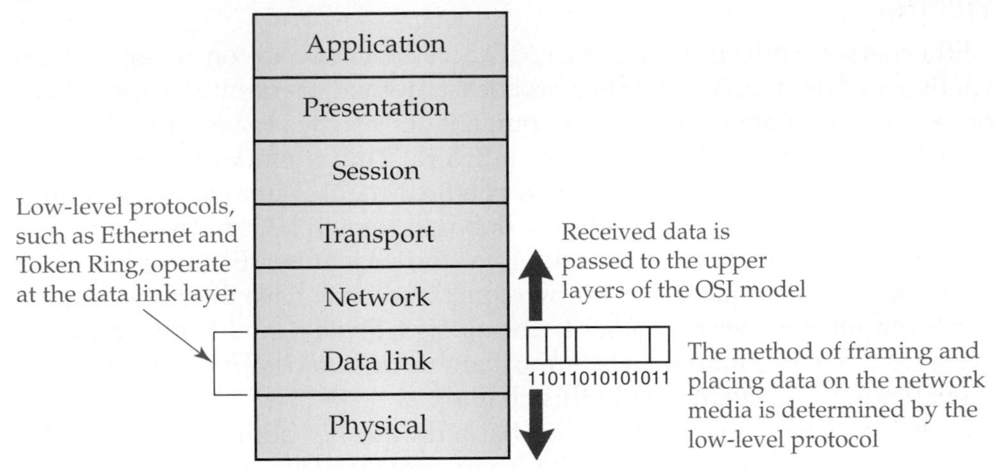

Figure 6-5.
The data link layer is responsible for framing the data unit, acknowledging the reception of data, error detection, recovery, and data frame flow control.

and the network operating system combine to create the characteristics of the various network operating systems.

Originally, layer 2 of the OSI model was called the *data link layer,* but later it was subdivided into two distinct sublayers called the *logical link control (LLC) sublayer* and the *media access control (MAC) sublayer,* **Figure 6-6.** The LLC sublayer serves an interface between the data link layer and network operating system. It is responsible for communicating with the upper layers of the OSI regardless of the network operating system. The LLC sublayer is described in the IEEE 802.2 standard.

The MAC sublayer is responsible for formatting the data into frames and placing the frames on the physical media. Examples of frame formats are Ethernet, Token Ring, and ATM. You can think of the MAC sublayer as the layer where raw data is converted into binary ones and zeros and packaged into frame formats according to the network architecture or network technology.

Before going on to discuss the high-level protocols associated with the various network operating systems, we will first take a closer look at some of the low-level protocols and the access methods they use.

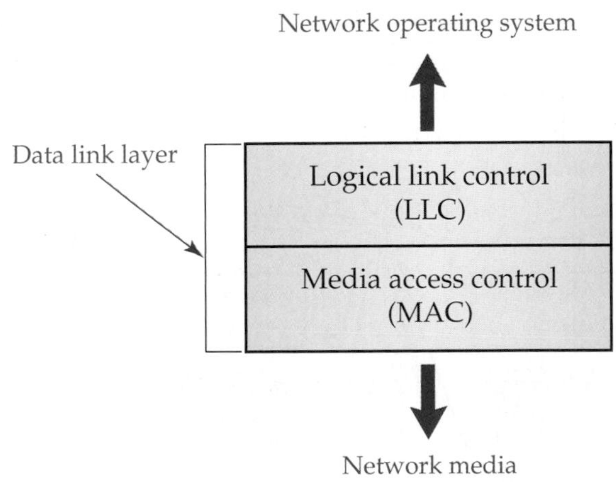

Figure 6-6.
The data link layer is divided into two distinct sublayers: logical link control (LLC) and media access control (MAC). The LLC sublayer is responsible for interfacing with the network operating system. The MAC sublayer is responsible for formatting the data into frames and placing the data on the network media.

Ethernet

Ethernet networks use the CSMA/CD access method to control and ensure the delivery of data. CSMA/CD is a broadcast method of communication. When a computer sends data to another computer, it does so by broadcasting the information to all the computers on the network. This is similar to one person yelling in a room full of people "Bob do you hear me?" Everyone in the room hears Bob's name being called, but only Bob will reply if he is in the room.

An Ethernet system communicates in a similar manner. Each computer on the network has a unique name; no two computers may have the same name. Typical computer names are *Station1, Accounting3, Smith_J,* and *Engineering_Bob.* However, a computer name can be almost anything you desire. Computer names are covered in more detail later in this chapter.

Each computer in the network also has a unique hex address, called a *MAC address*, programmed into the computer's network interface card. The MAC address is six bytes long. An example of a MAC address is C0 0B 08 1A 2D 2F. No other computer on the network has the same number. Using the hex numbering system to communicate is difficult for humans. Therefore, a database is used to match the MAC address of the network interface card to the unique name given to the computer.

A typical session on an Ethernet network would go something like this. Bob wants to send some data to Sue. Bob sends the data to Sue at a computer named *Station4*. When Bob sends a message to Sue, he is actually sending the message to all computers on the network. All computers on an Ethernet system hear the call from Bob to Sue, but only Sue's computer accepts the message, **Figure 6-7.**

Let's take a closer look at how this happens. First, review the Ethernet 802.3 frame in **Figure 6-8.** Note the frame sections and the size in bytes of each. After the preamble and the start frame delimiter (SFD), the six bytes that represent the address of the destination computer are transmitted on the network. When the six bytes match Sue's computer, the data packet is accepted. When the data packet is accepted, the next six bytes, which identify the source computer (Bob's computer), are decoded and stored for a return message. Next, the data portion of the packet is decoded and checked for errors. If no errors are detected, a return message is transmitted to Bob's PC. If a return message is not transmitted to

Figure 6-7.
A typical session on an Ethernet network. Note that all computers receive Bob's message, but only Sue's computer accepts the message.

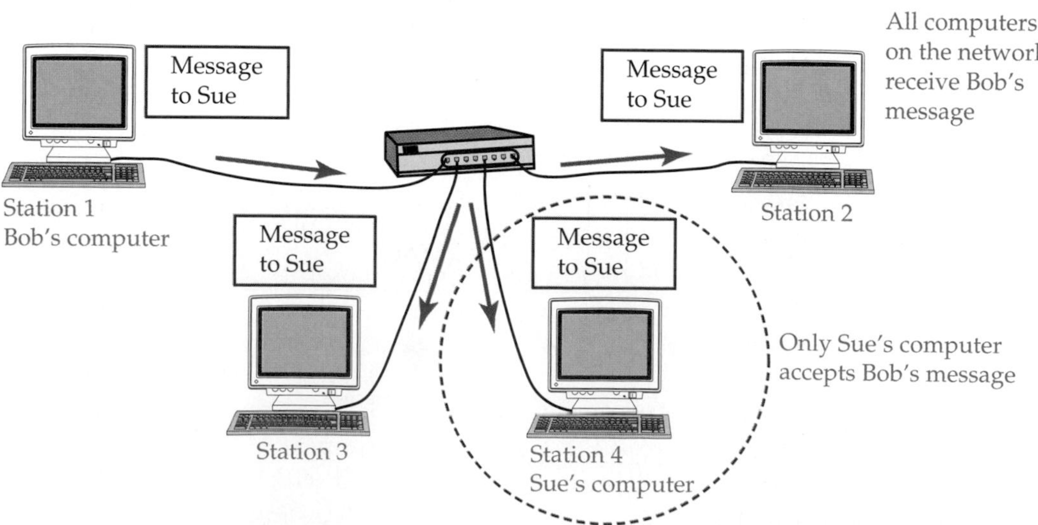

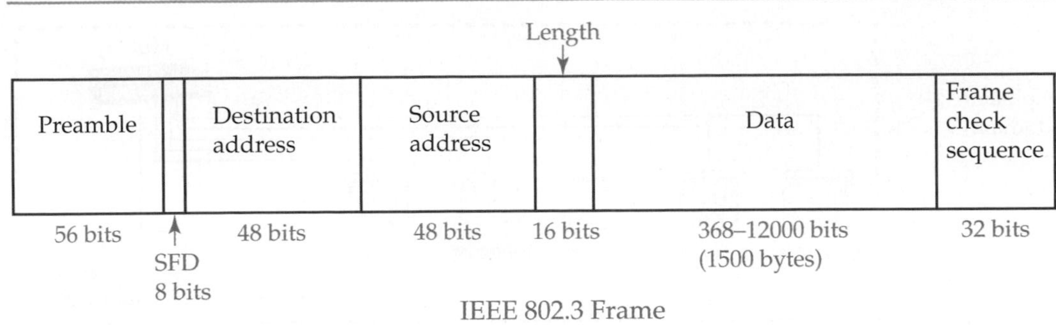

Figure 6-8.
Ethernet 802.3 frame.

Bob's PC, the data packet will be retransmitted. The data will be retransmitted several more times until a message is received from Sue's PC.

Collisions

Ethernet is an excellent networking system until collisions become excessive. As collisions increase, so does the likelihood of more collisions. Each time a collision occurs, each computer involved in generating the collision ceases broadcasting for a random period of time. After that time, each computer rebroadcasts the packet. This increases the likelihood of another collision. Each collision increases the possibility of additional collisions. If the number of collisions reaches a point that the network is flooded with a continuous number of collisions and rebroadcasts, a ***broadcast storm*** has occurred. When a broadcast storm occurs, there are so many collisions and rebroadcasts that no significant amount of packets can be exchanged. The only solution to a broadcast storm is to eliminate a significant number of network computers that are causing the problem or to shut down the entire network and then reboot it. Shutting down the network automatically disconnects the computers that have caused the broadcast storm.

broadcast storm
a condition in which a network is flooded with a continuous number of collisions and rebroadcasts.

Collision Domains

The section of a network where collisions occur is referred to as a ***collision domain.*** A collision domain consists of computers that can directly communicate with each other using broadcasts. The collision domain can be isolated by equipment that controls or limits the broadcasts. Equipment such as switches and routers control broadcasts by limiting the extent or physical boundary of a collision domain. Equipment such as hubs and repeaters do *not* limit broadcasts, and thus do *not* limit the physical size of the collision domain. Repeaters and hubs simply pass the packets and frames. Switches and routers sort packets and frames depending on the destination address. This helps to isolate the network into sections called *segments.* The act of dividing a network into smaller sections to avoid collisions is called ***segmenting.*** Collision domains can be resized by strategically installing network devices such as switches and routers in a network topology. Look at **Figure 6-9.**

collision domain
a section of a network where collisions occur.

segmenting
the act of dividing a network into smaller sections to avoid collisions.

In the illustration, a LAN is segmented by replacing the hubs with switches. The switches isolate communication to a particular segment of the network, reducing the amount of collisions. The network is further segmented into three distinct departments: Engineering, Sales, and Management. By limiting broadcasts to a particular department, the total number of broadcasts across the entire network is reduced. Each of these departments can still communicate with the entire network, but when communication is desired with a member of the department, the packets are limited to that particular segment of the network.

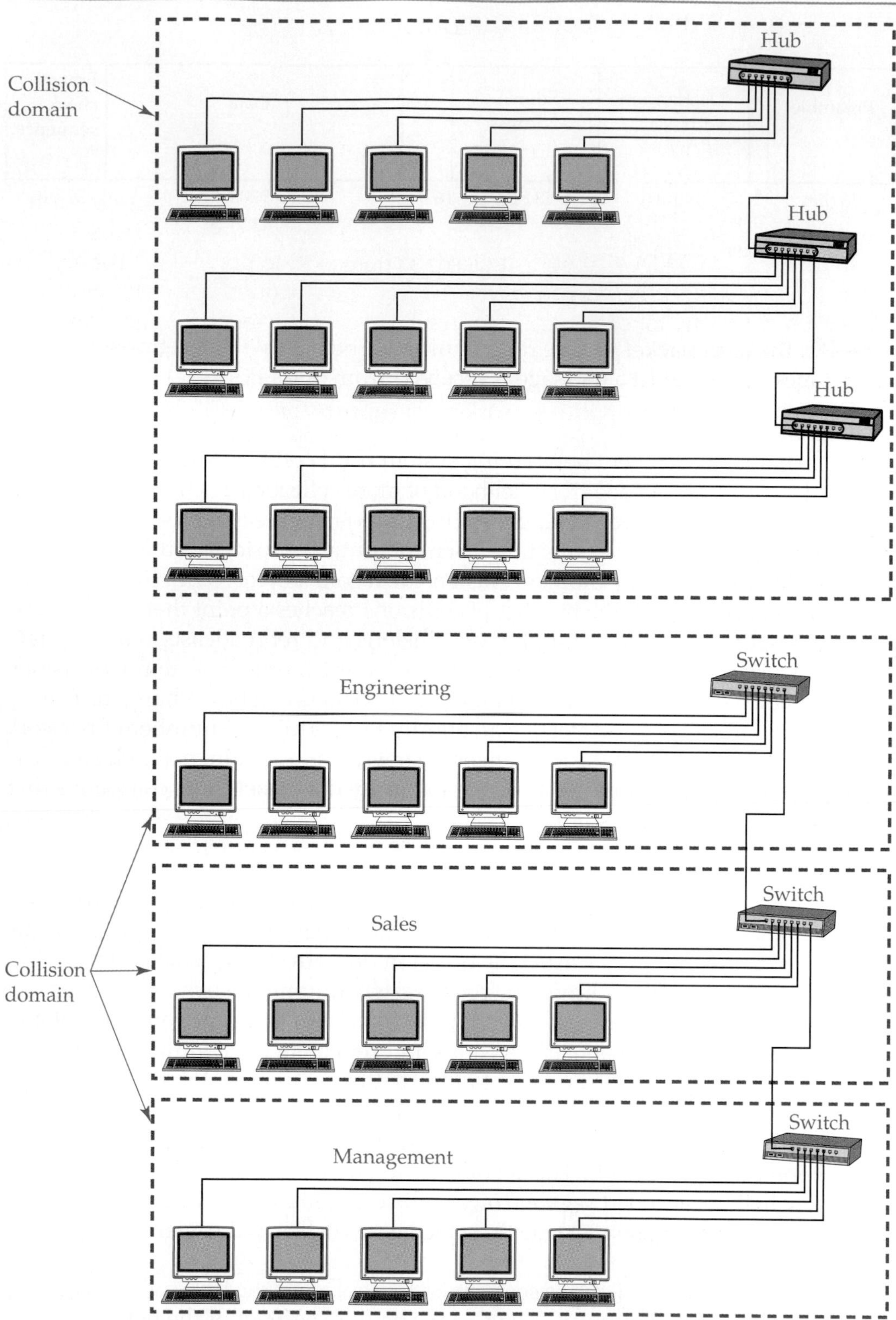

Figure 6-9. Replacing hubs with switches on an Ethernet network can reduce collisions. Switches limit broadcasts to specific areas of the network by creating virtual networks. In the illustration, the hubs are replaced with switches to create network segments, isolating some of the communication by departments, or workgroups.

As more computers are added to a network segment, the likelihood of collision becomes greater. When the number of computers grows to the point of unacceptable collisions, the network segment again needs to be segmented to reduce the number of collisions. It is important to note, however, that as more equipment is added to reduce the number of collisions, latency increases. Each piece of equipment that must analyze or repackage a packet increases the latency of the digital signal.

Token Ring

A Token Ring network uses the token passing access method. Before a computer can transmit information on the network, it must seize a token to take control of the network. A ***token*** is a short binary code that is passed around to the computers on a ring topology and, in some cases, a bus topology. See **Figure 6-10.**

token
a short binary code that is passed around to the computers on a ring topology and, in some cases, a bus topology.

In contrast to CSMA/CD, token passing is designed to prevent collisions. Transmission on the Token Ring network is organized around the computer that has possession of the token. A computer must possess the token before it can transmit data across the network.

A token is generated by the network software and is circulated throughout the network. Computers on the network must capture, or accept, the token before they are allowed to communicate. If a network interface card does not accept the token, it regenerates the token and passes it along to the next computer. By using this method, only one computer at a time can control the flow of data.

When a network interface card captures the token, it generates a new type of frame. The new frame contains source and destination addresses and data. See **Figure 6-11.** Although at first it may appear that the token passing method is time-consuming, you must remember that this process only takes a few milliseconds, in contrast to an Ethernet system that may generate many delays due to collisions.

Active Monitor

When a Token Ring network is first activated, a specific computer is selected as the active monitor. An ***active monitor*** is a computer that is responsible for

active monitor
a computer that is responsible for monitoring the necessary administrative functions associated with Token Ring technology.

Token Format

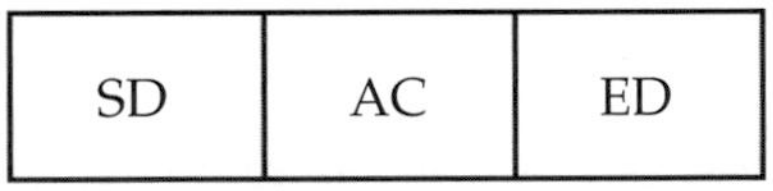

SD	AC	ED

SD = Starting delimeter 1 byte
AC = Access control 1 byte
ED = Ending delimeter 1 byte

Figure 6-10.
The token format consists only of three bytes. A workstation must first capture the token to send a Token Ring frame containing data.

Token Ring Frame Format

SD	AC	FC	D-MAC	S-MAC	Data	FC	ED	FS

SD = Starting delimeter 1 byte
AC = Access control 1 byte
FC = Frame control 1 byte
D-MAC = Destination MAC 6 bytes
S-MAC = Source MAC 6 bytes
Data Varies
FC = Frame check sequence 4 bytes
ED = Ending delimeter 1 byte
FS = Frame status 1 byte

Figure 6-11.
The Token Ring frame format is long when compared with the token. The Token Ring frame contains data and information such as the destination and source MAC addresses.

monitoring the necessary administrative functions associated with Token Ring technology. The functions of the active monitor include the following:

- Monitor the presence of the token on the ring.
- Identify added or deleted computers.
- Remove continuously circulating tokens.
- Insert a 24-bit delay between transmissions.
- Synchronize timing of all computers.

monitor contention the process of selecting an active monitor. Also called *monitor election.*

standby monitor a computer on a Token Ring network that can become an active monitor if the current active monitor fails or logs off the network.

The active monitor is selected through a process called ***monitor contention*** or ***monitor election.*** Active monitor selection is based on the MAC address of each network interface card on the ring. The network interface card with the highest MAC address number wins the election. Any computer can become an active monitor, and all other computers are considered a ***standby monitor.*** If the active monitor fails or logs off the network, one of the standby monitors becomes the new active monitor.

Let's take a closer look at Token Ring communications. As the name implies, the active monitor keeps track of the activities on the Token Ring network. It conducts periodic checks to ensure a token is circulating the ring. If a token is not detected in 10 milliseconds (default), a new token is generated and placed on the ring.

ring polling a process conducted by an active monitor to identify if a computer has logged on or off of the ring. Also called *polling the ring.*

ring purge the process of removing a defective token and replacing it with a new token.

The active monitor conducts a ring poll to identify any new computer logged on to the ring and detects any computers that have logged off the ring. This process is generally referred to as ***ring polling*** or ***polling the ring.*** The ring polling occurs every seven seconds. Remember that in Token Ring communications, each computer communicates with the computer immediately upstream and downstream of its location. A computer receives the token and data from its upstream neighbor and then regenerates the token and passes it to the computer immediately downstream of its location.

The active monitor is responsible for removing circulating tokens. If a token becomes corrupt, the token may circulate the ring forever, thus stopping all communication on the ring. The active monitor performs a ***ring purge,*** which means it removes the defective token and replaces it with a new one.

The active monitor enforces a 24-bit delay between tokens. The 24-bit delay is necessary to ensure that the complete frame (token) is deliverable. The 24-bit space is necessary because it is the exact length of an empty token. The delay is created by holding a frame until sufficient time (equaling 24-bits) lapses.

Lastly, the active monitor is responsible for synchronizing the timing of all computers on the ring. Timing is a critical part of Token Ring operation. Ethernet is random and chaotic, while Token Ring relies on a set timing pattern and orderly procedure for delivering data and monitoring functions. Therefore, all computers must be synchronized with each other so they measure time lapse equally and expect the appearance of a token at a specific time. Remember that any computer on the ring may need to assume the responsibilities of the active monitor and keep the timing sequence going.

Tech Tip

While synchronized timing is not required for Ethernet communications, it is used in Ethernet systems for security purposes. Security is covered in detail in Chapter 15—Network Security.

Beaconing

Beaconing is a recovery process used when a hardware failure occurs on the ring. The beaconing process is used to remove a defective computer from the ring. When a computer does not receive a token from its upstream neighbor within a set period of time, it begins the beaconing process. First, it generates a beacon frame and sends it to its downstream neighbor. The downstream computer regenerates the beacon frame and sends it to its downstream neighbor. This process continues around the ring. When any computer receives eight beacon frames, it temporarily takes itself off the ring and performs a self-test, which is known as a *loopback test*. The ***loopback test*** is simply a signal that tests the network interface card to ensure it is functioning properly. If the loopback test fails, the computer remains offline. If the loopback test indicates no problem with the network interface card, the computer reattaches itself to the ring. This process continues until the defective computer is identified or the network administrator intervenes.

beaconing
a recovery process used when a hardware failure occurs on the ring.

loopback test
a signal that tests the network interface card to ensure it is functioning properly.

It may seem like a lot of activity happens on the Token Ring network and that the various methods to ensure frame delivery slow down the transmission rate. Rest assured that data transfer occurs at a blazing speed (unless downloading graphics or sound). The activities previously described typically go unnoticed.

When transferring data, it is not done as one continuous steady stream but as parts of a total sequence of transmissions. When the token is captured, it can be held up to approximately 10 milliseconds (1/100 second). After that, it must be released. If the total transmission is not complete, the computer needs to recapture the token and continue doing so until complete. By incorporating a maximum time the token can be captured and released, the Token Ring system provides an opportunity for other computers to capture the token. Token passing is a well-organized access method that allows each computer to take its turn. If no other computer needs to send data or a command, the token returns to the computer that last sent the token. In less than a second, thousands of bits of data can be transmitted and received. It usually appears to the user that they have had complete control of the ring, when in reality, two, three, or hundreds of users have been communicating over the same network using the same token.

Token Bus

A Token Bus network is defined in the IEEE 802.4 standard and operates similar to a Token Ring network. The difference is in how the token is passed from computer to computer. In a typical Token Ring network, the token is passed to the next computer on the ring. Since the Token Bus topology uses a bus rather than a ring, a variation of token passing must be used. A list of computers is created in a database. Each computer is identified by a MAC address and computer name. A sequential list of addresses is generated which becomes the sequence for the token to follow. The token can also have a priority code set to allow a specific workstation to have the token before any of the other workstations.

ARCnet

ARCnet was originally designed for LANs, but has evolved into an industrial control field bus technology. ARCnet is a popular industrial control technology because of several features:

- The protocol design is simple and compact.
- The protocol uses very short packet lengths, which is critical in industrial manufacturing timing systems.

The ARCnet technology is based on token passing for accessing the media. Token passing ensures equal access to all nodes on the network. This is critical to the design of an industrial manufacturing type application where sharing and timing of machine control is critical. Any one computer on the network cannot be forced to wait too long to transmit data to another computer on the network. CSMA/CD does provide access to all nodes, but it is does not provide equal access.

The access method of ARCnet is similar to the access method of Token Ring. ARCnet, however, uses a deterministic method of cable access by passing the token to the next, highest assigned node number, not necessarily the closest node like Token Ring.

ARCnet allows a maximum number of 255 nodes per network. Each node on the network must be uniquely identified by numbers ranging from *1* to *255*. Zero is reserved for broadcast messages. Each node uses a network interface module (NIM) not a network interface card (NIC), and it is assigned a MAC ID for identification rather than having one burned in at the factory. Assigning a MAC ID is unique to ARCnet networks.

Tech Tip

Many times specific networking technologies use variations on acceptable terminology when identifying a particular type of equipment or technology. One such term associated with ARCnet is *network interface module (NIM)*. The term NIM is the equivalent to network interface card (NIC) when talking about the circuit board used to connect the network device to the network medium. ARCnet technology was among the first network systems ever used. Since the ARCnet standards use the acronym NIM not NIC, you should also use the preferred term NIM.

AppleTalk

AppleTalk
a suite of protocols developed to support the Macintosh computers when configured as a network. Uses CSMA/CA as its access method.

AppleTalk is a suite of protocols developed to support the Macintosh computers when configured as a network. AppleTalk uses CSMA/CA as its access method. You should recall that wireless LANs also use CSMA/CA. CSMA/CA is similar to the access method used in Ethernet networks. However, CSMA/CA attempts to avoid collisions, rather than detect collisions. In the CSMA/CA access method, a computer not only listens to the media (carrier sense) to detect communications, it also sends a short packet to the destination computer to see if it is ready to receive the data. The destination computer could be offline or busy with some other task. If the destination computer is free to receive the data, it will reply. This short packet also serves as an announcement to other computers on the cable that data transmission is about to take place.

Today, Macintosh computers use the OS X operating system which is a Linux design that runs on Intel-based CPUs just like Microsoft Windows. The OS X operating system uses the TCP/IP suite of protocols.

Network Operating Systems and Networking Protocols

There are numerous high-level network protocols in use today. Part of the reason is no one single protocol can adequately satisfy all possible network functions because network technology is constantly evolving. For example, originally network protocols were designed to exchange text documents. Before long, additional protocols were needed to support the exchange of media such as audio and video.

There is also the desire to maintain compatibility with older network devices that were not designed to handle the capabilities of the latest protocols. For example, the transition from IPv4 addresses to IPv6 addresses resulted in numerous new protocols that either replaced protocols designed exclusively for IPv4 or replaced protocols used to translate address information between IPv4 and IPv6 systems.

Also, as you've previously learned, when networking was in its infancy there were many different network operating systems. Each operating system was developed with its own way of communicating with network hardware. There were no standards, no OSI model, and no one set of protocols. Network companies were in direct competition with other companies and many kept secret the way they programmed their software and protocols. As time went by, it became apparent that people purchasing network operating systems and hardware wanted to be able to communicate with other network systems and use the Internet.

Network operating systems had to provide software programs and protocols that would enable the exchange of data between different network operating systems. The exchange of data between different network operating systems was not easy to establish. One of the reasons for the difficulty was many network operating systems used different ways to identify the nodes on a LAN.

The common denominator for communicating between different network operating systems finally became apparent. Each of the various network operating systems would use the same method to identify individual nodes while maintaining compatibility with its own set of protocols. For example, while Novell NetWare, Mac OS, and Microsoft Windows have different protocols, they all are capable of being encapsulated at the lower levels of the OSI model in protocols defined by the IEEE, such as Ethernet and Token Ring, **Figure 6-12.** The result was that numerous protocols were added to the various suites of vendor-specific protocols.

As you can see, network technology is never stagnant. It is constantly evolving, which results in new additional protocols or the replacement of existing protocols. As a student of networking technology you will constantly experience new protocols. For example, if you connect a protocol analyzer to view the traffic on a network, you will see a wide variety of old and new protocols being transmitted across the network. So when you study protocols, you not only need to learn about the very latest protocols but also the legacy protocols.

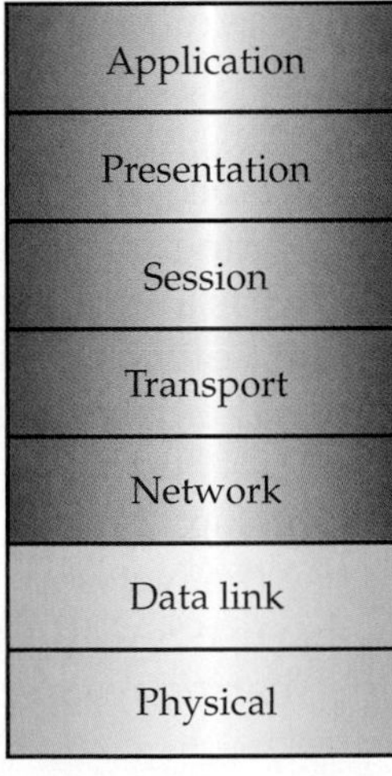

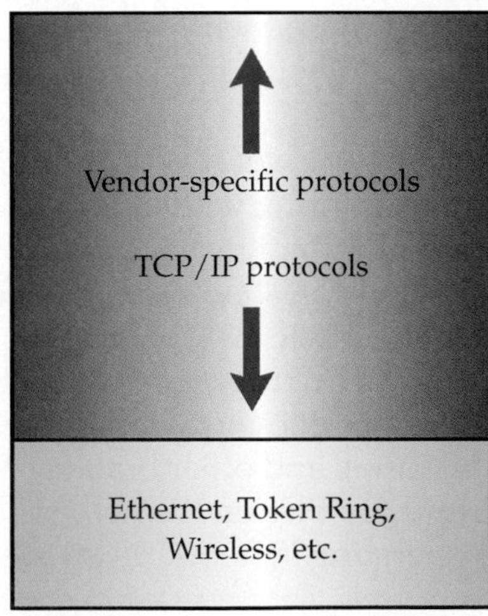

Figure 6-12. Different protocols such as those from Novell, Apple Computer, and Microsoft are capable of being encapsulated at the lower levels of the OSI model in the protocols defined by the IEEE.

This section presents TCP/IP as well as legacy protocols NetBIOS, NetBEUI, IPX/SPX, and AppleTalk. It emphasizes how modern network operating systems use the TCP/IP suite of protocols, while using their own set of proprietary protocols to maintain backward compatibility with legacy systems and for file sharing and printer access. Network discovery protocols, LLDP, LLTD, CDP, LLDP-MED, LLMNR, and ARP, are also covered. Discovery protocols are used to detect devices on the network.

TCP/IP

TCP/IP is not a single protocol but rather an entire suite of protocols designed specifically to support communication between computers and network devices connected via the Internet. TCP/IP is native to UNIX. UNIX was the original operating system designed to communicate via the Internet. Other network operating systems were not originally designed to communicate via the Internet, but rather were designed to communicate over a LAN. In these operating systems, two or more LANs could be connected to form a MAN or WAN. These operating systems used their own address formats and naming conventions to identify nodes on the network. The following table compares the various address formats that were used.

Network OS	Original Network Address Format
NetWare	2b.0000.0e23.12ab
Mac	2.12
Linux/UNIX	192.168.0.1
Windows	STATION1

Early Windows operating systems used 15-character NetBIOS names to identify network devices. They resolved the NetBIOS name to a corresponding MAC address.

Today, all major network operating systems can communicate across the Internet and adhere to the naming rules of TCP/IP. Modern networks are all based on the TCP/IP protocol suite and use the IPv4 and IPv6 address format for network and node identification.

Even though modern network operating systems use the TCP/IP suite of protocols, some still use their own set of proprietary protocols to maintain backward compatibility with legacy systems and for file sharing and printer access. Look at **Figure 6-13.**

Microsoft uses the Server Message Block (SMB) protocol for sharing files and NetBIOS for communicating with older Windows operating systems. Network adapters automatically configure NetBIOS over TCP/IP as a service for IPv4. Look at **Figure 6-14** which shows the **Advanced TCP/IP Settings** dialog box from a Windows Vista computer. As you can see, NetBIOS has a default setting which enables NetBIOS to be carried over TCP/IP if a static IPv4 address is used or when the DHCP server does not provide a NetBIOS setting.

Novell SUSE Linux and other brands of Linux use the Network File Sharing (NFS) protocol to share files on the network. They also use SAMBA to share files with Windows operating systems. SAMBA supports sharing resources using the SMB protocol.

OSI Model	TCP/IP	Microsoft	Novell SUSE Linux	Apple Mac OS X
Application	HTTP FTP POP3	SMB	NFS	AFP
Presentation				NFS
Session	DNS SNMP SSL	NetBIOS	SAMBA	SMB
Transport	TCP UDP			
Network	IPv4 IPv6			
Data link	LLC			
Physical	Ethernet 802.3			

Figure 6-13.
All major operating systems use the TCP/IP protocol as well as their own proprietary protocols to maintain backward compatibly with legacy operating systems and for file sharing and printer access.

Mac OS X uses the Apple File Protocol (AFP), Network File Sharing (NFS), and Server Message Block (SMB) for file sharing. AFP is native to all versions of MAC OS. NFS allows MAC OS X to share files with Linux-based computers, and the SMB protocol allows MAC OS X to share files with Windows computers.

There are many more protocols in use today than what is presented in Figure 6-13. For example, all the major network operating systems and desktop systems support the TCP/IP suite of protocols, such as FTP, HTTP, POP3, and DNS.

As we progress through the textbook, many new protocols will be introduced as they relate to network functions such as security, multimedia, and the Internet. While this was only a brief introduction to TCP/IP, Chapter 10—TCP/IP Fundamentals covers TCP/IP in detail.

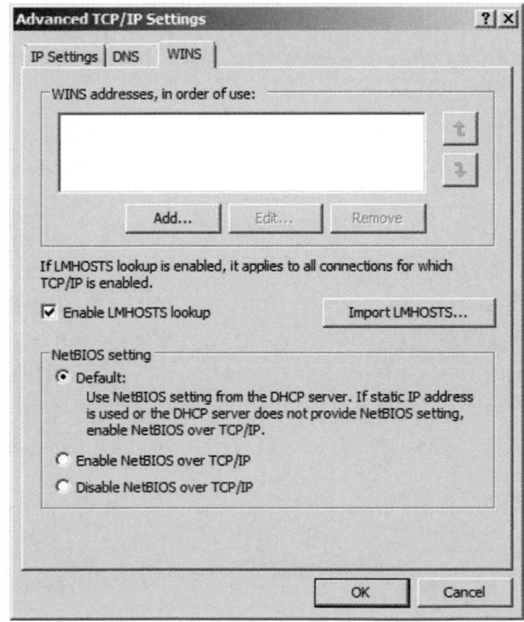

Figure 6-14.
Network adapters still automatically configure NetBIOS over TCP/IP as a service for IPv4.

NetBIOS

IBM originally developed the Network Basic Input/Output System (NetBIOS) to network IBM PCs. In a typical computer, the BIOS software supports communication between the computer software and hardware. The computer BIOS allows hardware and software programs created by different manufacturers to communicate. NetBIOS functions in a similar fashion to support communication between different computer systems through the use of a network interface card.

dumb terminal a type of computer that consists of only a display and keyboard. The keyboard contains the electronic components needed to support communication between the mainframe and the terminal. A dumb terminal does not contain a CPU.

de facto standard a standard developed because of its widely accepted use by industry.

datagram a short message block that can be sent to a particular computer, sent to a group of computers, or broadcast to all computers connected to the media.

Before NetBIOS was developed, the traditional method of networking was connecting a dumb terminal to a mainframe via cabling. A ***dumb terminal*** consists of only a display and keyboard. The keyboard contains the electronic components needed to support communication between the mainframe and the terminal. No separate microprocessor acts as the brain in the terminal. Consequently, the term *dumb* was used to infer that it contained no CPU. See **Figure 6-15.** In these systems, the mainframe contained the CPUs used to process data and the terminals did not. The mainframe also contained the storage media for retaining data on large magnetic spools of tape. The spools of tape stored data in much the same way as a hard disk drive stores data.

NetBIOS became the de facto standard for LAN communications. ***De facto standard*** means that the software became a standard because of its widely accepted use by industry, not because of the actions or ratification of any standards committee. NetBIOS was also the first protocol designed for communication between PCs rather than through a mainframe. For the first time, a network could be created without needing a mainframe. This made the network inexpensive when compared with the mainframe model.

Datagrams and Sessions

The NetBIOS protocol uses two common network communication methods: datagram and session. A ***datagram*** is a short message block that can be sent to a particular computer, sent to a group of computers, or broadcast to all computers connected to the media, **Figure 6-16.** When the datagram is broadcast to a group of specific computers, it is referred to as *multicast*. The multicast communication method sends the datagram to a specified group of computers on the network rather than to all the computers on the network. Broadcasts and multicasts are referred to as *connectionless communications*. They do not guarantee data delivery.

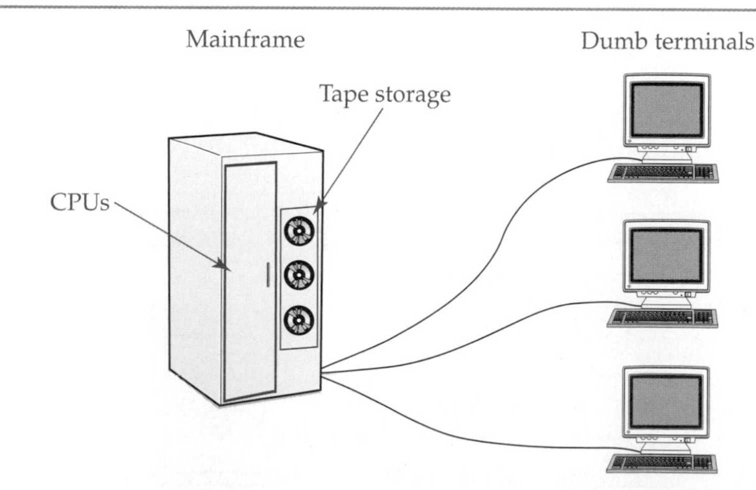

Figure 6-15.
Dumb terminals are wired directly to a mainframe computer. They communicate directly with the mainframe and cannot process data on their own because they do not contain a CPU. The CPU(s) are located in the mainframe.

NetBIOS Datagram

D-MAC	S-MAC	Data

D-MAC = Destination MAC 46 bytes
S-MAC = Source MAC 46 bytes
Data 32 bytes

Figure 6-16.
NetBIOS datagram.

When communicating on small network systems, broadcast messages do not interfere with network operation. When a large network is established, the broadcast method of communication is undesirable. Too many broadcast messages fill the network with communication traffic and create a broadcast storm. In this condition, so many broadcast messages occur they collide with one another and never reach their destination. On very large networks, session-type communication is much more effective. Network systems use both methods of communication while limiting the amount of direct broadcasts by users.

When communication is limited between two particular computers, it is referred to as a ***session.*** When computers establish a session, they create a connection-oriented communication known as a ***virtual circuit.*** A virtual circuit behaves like a direct connection between two or more devices. During a session, communication remains established until one of the participants terminates the session. Communication between two computers in an established session guarantees data delivery. It uses some form of error checking to ensure the delivery of each data packet.

session
communication that is limited between two particular computers.

virtual circuit
a connection-oriented communication.

NetBIOS Names, Group Names, and Addresses

NetBIOS can identify a computer by its MAC address, its logical name, or by the group to which it belongs. The MAC address is electronically encoded into the network interface card and cannot be changed. Each MAC address is specifically unique for proper computer identification on a network. Each computer also receives a unique name. When a network interface card is installed in a computer, a default name is automatically assigned. The default name is typically a randomly generated series of alphanumeric characters with no special meaning. The default name can be changed to one with more meaning, such as *Station1*, *PC3*, *Accounting*, or *Billy*. The user name must be unique like the MAC address. If two computers use the same name for identification, communication will not operate properly. The computer can also be assigned a group name to identify it as part of a special group of computers. Similar to the computer name, the group name is assigned a default group name. In the Windows networking environment, the default group name is *Workgroup*. The exception is Windows XP Home Edition in which the workgroup name is *MSHOME*.

Note

Do not be confused by the Windows 7 "HomeGroup." The Windows 7 HomeGroup is the default group used for sharing resources on a home network. The default workgroup name in Windows 7 is still *Workgroup*.

In older systems, the identification of each computer was originally stored in a text file located on each computer on the network. The text file contained the computer name and the associated MAC address. Any computer on a NetBIOS

Universal Naming Convention (UNC) a standard naming convention used by NetBIOS.

NetBIOS Name Server (NBNS) resolves NetBIOS computer names to IPv4 addresses.

network could read the text file of any of the other computers on the network. This system worked for earlier and smaller networks, but as networking evolved in size and capability, protocols were developed that allowed for an automated method of communicating identification information across the LAN. We will discuss these protocols in later chapters.

NetBIOS Names and UNC

NetBIOS computer names are used to identify computers and servers. NetBIOS names can contain a maximum of 15 characters. NetBIOS uses a standard naming convention called the ***Universal Naming Convention (UNC)*** to identify shared resources on the network. A typical UNC is \\server_name\share_name. The *server_name* is the name of the computer or server that contains a shared resource, and the *share_name* is the name assigned to the shared resource. The UNC can also include a path to a subdirectory beneath the shared resource such as \\server_name\My Documents\Projects\. In this example, My Documents is the shared resource and Projects is a subdirectory beneath the shared resource. Think of descending a hierarchical structure. The file server contains all shares, so it is the highest level of the hierarchical structure. Next is the share, and last, is the path.

NetBIOS Name Server

NetBIOS Name Server (NBNS) resolves NetBIOS computer names to IPv4 addresses. This is a very old protocol and was used by early Microsoft network systems in conjunction with the Windows Internet Naming Service (WINS). WINS is covered in detail in Chapter 10—TCP/IP Fundamentals.

Note

The acronym NBNS is translated as "NetBIOS Name Server" when found in Microsoft references and translated as "NetBIOS Name Service" when found in many other sources. The name used depends mainly on the context of the information. For example, when discussing WINS, Microsoft uses the term *Server*, and when talking about port number 137 and protocols, it uses the term *Service*.

NetBEUI

The NetBIOS Extended User Interface (NetBEUI) protocol was designed as an enhanced version of NetBIOS. It was also designed by IBM to support its LAN Manager network operating system. Later, Microsoft adopted NetBEUI into its networking products. NetBEUI is constantly referenced by technical documentation and can still be used to support LAN systems.

NetBEUI and NetBIOS are often referred to as the same protocol, but they are technically not the same. However, they do share similarities. NetBIOS and NetBEUI are broadcast-type network protocols, and a typical router will not pass broadcast-type protocols. To communicate with a PC in a large network such as the Internet, another protocol must be used such as IP.

Tech Tip

A protocol that can transmit packets across a router is referred to as a *routable protocol*. The most common routable protocol is TCP/IP.

Network+ Note

For the Network+ Certification exam, remember that NetBEUI is *not* a routable protocol.

Figure 6-17 shows the relationship of NetBEUI to the OSI model. The Server Message Block (SMB) protocol is an upper-layer protocol that initiates client requests to a server. The request is passed down to the NetBEUI protocol. NetBEUI passes the request to the data link layer. At the data link layer, the request is sent to the network media. As you can see, SMB and NetBEUI combine to cover five layers of the OSI model.

Note

Windows 98 was the first version of a Microsoft Windows to allow a LAN to be configured for TCP/IP only. Microsoft stopped support for NetBEUI with the introduction of Windows XP.

IPX/SPX

Novell NetWare was first introduced in the early 1980s. Early versions of Novell NetWare used the IPX/SPX protocol suite exclusively. Novell NetWare 5 offered TCP/IP as an alternative to IPX/SPX. A key point to remember is proprietary networks developed their local network communications system independent of Internet communications. Later, the proprietary networks modified their local network system to be compatible with the TCP/IP protocol suite to enable communication over the Internet. Today, the TCP/IP protocol suite is selected by default on network operating systems for communicating on a LAN and WAN.

Proprietary networks also incorporate methods to exchange data between each other. For example, Windows XP supports communication with IPX/SPX networks by implementing an IPX/SPX, NetBIOS-compatible protocol known as NWLink.

An IPX/SPX address consists of a network number, node address, and socket number. See **Figure 6-18.** The IPX/SPX address is written in hexadecimal form. The network number identifies the network segment. It is 32 bits, or 4 bytes, long.

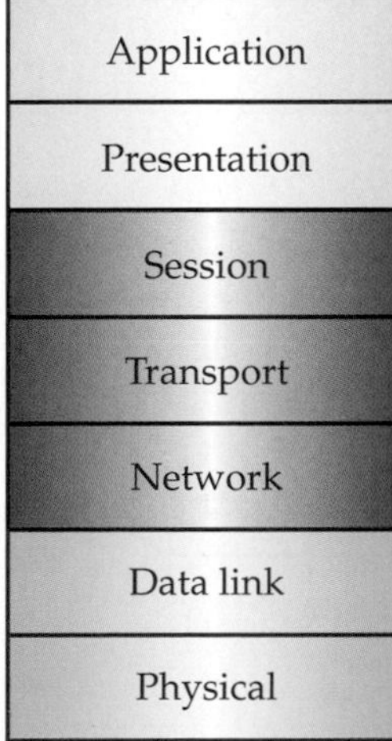

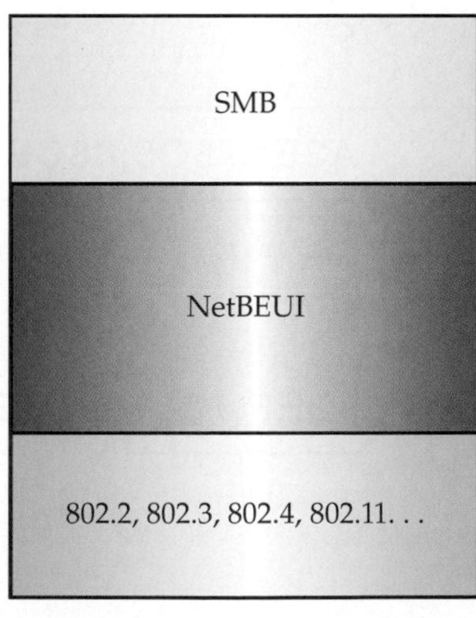

Figure 6-17.
The Server Message Block (SMB) and NetBEUI protocols span five layers of the OSI model. They were developed long before the OSI model was ever designed as a suggested standard.

A3EF78C5:88CEF538BA07:0451

Network number	Node address	Socket number
4 bytes	6 bytes	2 bytes

Figure 6-18. An IPX/SPX address consists of a network number, node address, and a socket number.

The node address is the physical address, or MAC address, of the workstation. This address is 48 bits, or 6 bytes, long. The socket number identifies a process. This number is 16 bits, or 2 bytes long.

station address an IPX/SPX-based address that consists of only a network number and node address.

An IPX/SPX address can also be written as a station address. A ***station address*** consists of only a network number and node address. Leading zeros in the network number are often truncated. **Figure 6-19** shows the two ways a station address can be written.

AppleTalk

AppleTalk was originally developed in the 1980s to support Macintosh computers connected as a network. AppleTalk consists of its own set of protocols such as EtherTalk, LocalTalk, TokenTalk, FDDITalk, AppleTalk Address Resolution Protocol (AARP), and more. The original version of AppleTalk simply operated as a local network and was limited to 254 nodes. ***LocalTalk*** was the commonly used term to describe the implementation of a LAN that supported Macintosh computers. Technically, LocalTalk refers to the network media, and AppleTalk refers to a suite of protocols.

LocalTalk the network media in an AppleTalk network.

Soon it was realized that larger network capabilities were needed. In 1989, AppleTalk Phase 2 was introduced. The original Apple Computer network became referred to as *AppleTalk Phase 1*. AppleTalk Phase 2 could support up to 16 million nodes.

The ability to increase the number of nodes was due to changing the node address to a more complex system. The new system consists of three parts: a network number, a node number, and a socket number. The network number is a 16-bit (2-byte) value that identifies the specific network. The node number is a unique, 8-bit (1-byte) value. The socket number is an 8-bit (1-byte) value.

AppleTalk Phase 2 introduced a feature called *AppleTalk Zones*. AppleTalk Zones are similar to the concept of workgroups and domains found in Microsoft network operating systems. An AppleTalk Zone allows for the logical grouping of computers. AppleTalk Zones also allow AppleTalk to support LANs consisting of

Figure 6-19. An IPX/SPX station address consists only of a network number and a node address. It can be written in two ways: a colon separating the network number and node address or a colon separating each four bytes of hexadecimal numbers.

more than 255 clients on 65,534 networks. Through the use of AppleTalk Zones, the new node addressing technique, and new Apple protocols that support packet routing between networks, the network size increased from 254 nodes to over 16 million nodes. This was a significant advancement for Apple Computer.

AppleTalk is a proprietary protocol that can only be interpreted directly by other AppleTalk computers. To support communication with Microsoft Windows computers and other computers that support TCP/IP communications, AppleTalk over IP was developed. This protocol was modified to support the naming requirements found in the TCP/IP suite of protocols.

Microsoft XP does not support direct communication with AppleTalk computers. To communicate with an AppleTalk computer, a Microsoft server must have the Services for Macintosh gateway installed. When a server is configured as a gateway for communication, Microsoft XP clients can access shared files on the AppleTalk network. For a Microsoft XP client to access a Macintosh printer, the AppleTalk protocol must be installed on the Microsoft XP client. Microsoft stopped direct support for AppleTalk with Windows XP in 2001. You can use a third-party vender for support.

In 2009, the Macintosh OS X Leopard operating system was introduced. This operating system can communicate directly with Windows Vista and Windows 7 using TCP/IP for sharing computer and network resources. Mac OS X will not run software applications designed for Windows operating systems. To accomplish the task of running a Windows software application on a Mac OS X computer, Apple provides a feature known as "Boot Camp," which is a dual-boot system. This system allows you to run either Mac OS X or Windows, but not both at the same time. If you want to run both operating systems at the same time, Apple recommends installing VMware or Parallels, which are third-party software applications. Once VMware or Parallels is installed on the Macintosh computer, you can run Windows at the same time as Mac OS. VMware and Parallels provide a virtual hosting system that allows Windows to run on the Macintosh computer.

Discovery Protocols

The development of IPv6 introduced a new array of protocols that dynamically discover network devices located in the network. These new protocols, LLDP, LLTD, CDP, LLDP-MED, and LLMNR, are covered in this section as well as the legacy protocol ARP. When there is a full implementation of IPv6, legacy discovery protocols such as ARP will no longer be a required for name resolution. However, until then, they are still part of network systems.

LLDP

The ***Link-Layer Discovery Protocol (LLDP)*** was developed as an IEEE specification found in section 802.1ab and referred to as "Station and Media Access Control Connectivity Discovery." The more common name used is *Link-Layer Discovery Protocol*. It is designed to identify devices connected on the local area network. As its name indicates, LLDP works at the data link layer of the OSI model. Since it works at the data link layer, it is designed to work in isolation on a small section of a network bound by a router or gateway.

Link-Layer Discovery Protocol (LLDP) a protocol that identifies devices connected on the local area network and allows them to automaticaly exchange information.

LLDP is the basis of many proprietary protocols introduced by router manufacturers such Cisco Systems, Juniper, and 3COM as well as telephone device manufacturers that rely on Ethernet network systems to support the Voice over Internet Protocol (VoIP). Many new protocol designs are based on LLDP, resulting in enhanced versions of LLDP. When LLDP is enhanced by a private company, the enhanced version changes the acronym but generally retains the terms *link* and *layer*. The enhanced versions are proprietary while the original LLDP is an open source protocol developed by IEEE and can be used by anyone.

LLTD

Link-Layer Topology Discovery (LLTD) Microsoft's version of the Link-Layer Discovery Protocol (LLDP).

Link-Layer Topology Discovery (LLTD) protocol is the core protocol behind the Microsoft Network and Sharing Center Map function in Windows Vista, Windows 7, and Windows Server 2008. When you open the Microsoft Network and Sharing Center and then select the **View Full Map** option, a series of inquiry packets are sent out to devices on the local network. The devices reply with information such as their MAC address, device name, and function. A map of the local area network is then constructed and presented to the user.

Microsoft implements two versions of the LLTD protocol: Link-Layer Topology Discovery Mapper I/O Driver and Link-Layer Topology Discovery Responder. **Figure 6-20** shows the two protocols listed in the **Wireless Network Connection Properties** dialog box.

Link-Layer Topology Discovery Mapper I/O Driver broadcasts information about the host computer to neighboring devices in the LAN. Link-Layer Topology Discovery Responder, as its name implies, responds to broadcasts sent by the Link-Layer Topology Discovery Mapper I/O Driver. Together, the two protocols produce a map of local devices similar to the one in **Figure 6-21.** Both wired and wireless devices are displayed. Devices that are not running LLTD and not configured for IPv6 can still be identified, but cannot be shown as a logical connection in the network map.

Windows XP operating systems can be discovered after downloading and installing a special "hot fix" called "Link-Layer Topology Discovery (LLTD) Responder." To learn more about this "hot fix" conduct a search using the key terms "Microsoft KB922120."

CDP

Cisco Discovery Protocol (CDP) a variation of the Link-Layer Discovery Protocol (LLDP) designed to support equipment such as Cisco routers, switches, and telephones.

Cisco Discovery Protocol (CDP) is a variation of LLDP designed to support equipment such as Cisco routers, switches, and telephones. It is an enhanced

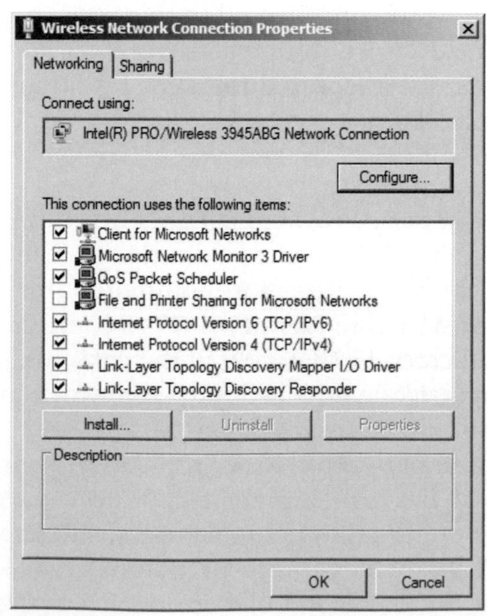

Figure 6-20. The two versions of the LLTD protocol, Link-Layer Topology Discovery Mapper I/O Driver and Link-Layer Topology Discovery Responder, are listed in the **Network Connection Properties** dialog box.

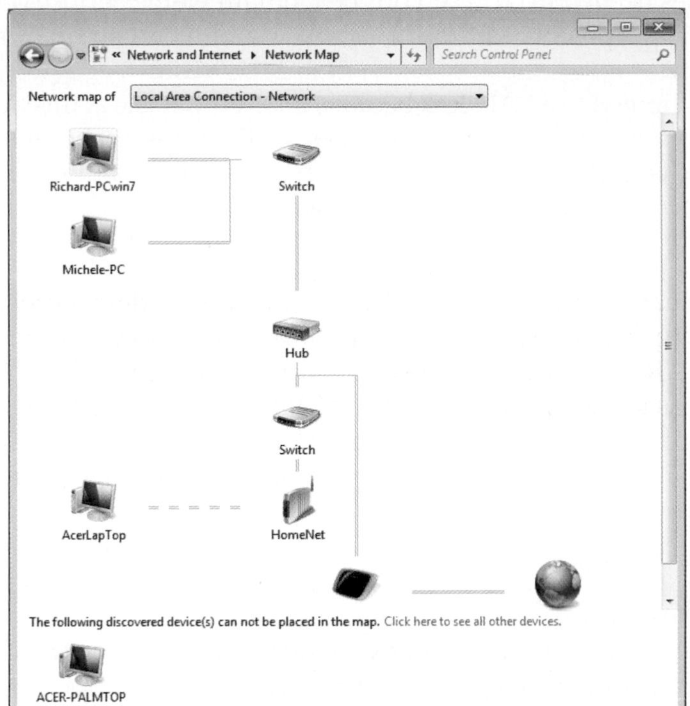

Figure 6-21
The Link-Layer Topology Discovery Responder and the Link-Layer Topology Discovery Mapper I/O Driver work together to produce a map of the devices on the local network.

version of LLDP, which can be routed and is not restricted to a single section of a network bounded by a gateway or router.

LLDP-MED

Link-Layer Discovery Protocol–Media Endpoint Discovery (LLDP-MED) is an enhanced version of LLDP used for routers, switches, Voice over Internet Protocol (VoIP) devices, and Power over Ethernet (PoE) devices. There are many different proprietary versions of LLDP-MED available. VoIP systems do not perform well when competing with other network activity such as workstations downloading or transferring large volumes of data. One way to provide better support for VoIP devices is to incorporate advanced switches into the local area network. Advanced switches will not only automatically locate and configure VoIP devices, they will provide better bandwidth by creating logical networks for the devices. The logical network, called a *Virtual LAN (VLAN)*, provides a dedicated bandwidth to VoIP devices, and does not share the bandwidth with workstations.

Link-Layer Discovery Protocol–Media Endpoint Discovery (LLDP-MED) an enhanced version of the Link-Layer Discovery Protocol (LLDP) used for routers, switches, Voice over Internet Protocol (VoIP) devices, and Power over Ethernet (PoE) devices.

LLMNR

Link-Local Multicast Name Resolution (LLMNR) protocol serves the same function as a DNS server when a DNS server cannot be reached. LLMNR resolves names of devices connected collectively on a local network.

Link-Local Multicast Name Resolution (LLMNR) a protocol that serves the same function as a DNS server when a DNS server cannot be reached. It resolves names of devices connected collectively on a local network.

Modern network operating systems are using a more sophisticated naming solution for devices rather than simple NetBIOS names. As a result, new protocols are needed to resolve names on a local area network when a DNS server cannot be reached. Early Microsoft network systems used Windows Internet Name Service (WINS) to resolve devices based on NetBIOS names. With the introduction of advanced networking technologies such as Lightweight Directory Name Service (LDNS) a better method to resolve names was needed. The method to resolve names needed to be based on the Domain Name Service (DNS). LLMNR serves the same purpose as a DNS server, but is not meant to replace the function of a DNS server.

LLMNR is limited to a LAN link because it is not routable at this time. LLMNR cannot be used for resolving Internet names to IP addresses, because resolving Internet names is under the jurisdiction of the Internet Assigned Numbers Authority (IANA) and is handled by DNS servers.

ARP

Address Resolution Protocol (ARP) a service that resolves IP addresses to MAC addresses.

Address Resolution Protocol (ARP) is one of the oldest protocols associated with networking. When a computer or network device is first booted, it sends out a series of ARP broadcasts with the purpose of resolving the assigned IPv4 network address to the physical address (MAC address). You can think of ARP as a protocol that can merge layer two (data link-layer) information with layer three (network layer) information. There will be more about ARP in Chapter 10—TCP/IP Fundamentals.

Summary

- Some common features that a network operating system provides are shared resources, file storage, file management, security, troubleshooting utilities, services, and a user interface.
- The data link layer is responsible for placing data on the network media or receiving data and passing it up the OSI layers.
- The data link layer is defined by the IEEE 802.2 standard.
- Ethernet uses CSMA/CD to access the network media.
- CSMA/CD broadcasts a message to all computers in a collision domain. Only the intended computer accepts the message.
- A collision domain is an area where collisions occur in an Ethernet network.
- Segmenting an Ethernet network can reduce collisions.
- A broadcast storm occurs when there is continuous activity on an Ethernet network.
- Macintosh computers used the AppleTalk protocol for communication and the CSMA/CA access method until the release of the OS X operating system.
- The CSMA/CA access method attempts to avoid collisions through detecting communications on the network media.
- Token Ring uses the token passing access method. Only one computer may control the token at any one moment.
- Token Bus uses a token passing access method similar to Token Ring. However, the token is passed according to a list of sequential addresses rather than to the proximate computer.
- Token Bus is defined by the IEEE 802.4 standard.
- ARCnet uses token passing for media access.
- ARCnet assigns the MAC address for each network interface module (NIM).
- NetBIOS was originally developed by IBM to network IBM PCs.
- NetBIOS uses two common network communication methods: datagram and session.

- A datagram is a short message block that can be sent to a particular computer, sent to a group of computers, or broadcast to all computers connected to the media.
- A datagram that is broadcast to a group of specific computers is referred to as *multicast*.
- A session is communication that is limited between two particular computers.
- NetBEUI is an enhanced version of NetBIOS.
- NetBEUI is *not* a routable protocol.
- NetBIOS Name Server (NBNS) is designed to resolve NetBIOS computer names to IPv4 addresses.
- AppleTalk Phase 1 could only support LANs.
- AppleTalk Phase 2 could support communications between LANs.
- Starting with Windows XP, the default network protocol for Windows operating systems is TCP/IP.
- The Link-Layer Discovery Protocol (LLDP) identifies devices connected on a local area network.
- The Microsoft Link-Layer Topology Discovery Mapper I/O Driver and Link-Layer Topology Discovery Responder protocols are both based on LLDP.
- Cisco Discovery Protocol (CDP) is based on LLDP.
- Link-Layer Discovery Protocol–Media Endpoint Discovery (LLDP-MED) is an enhanced version of LLDP used for switches, Voice over Internet Protocol (VoIP) devices, and Power over Ethernet (PoE) devices.
- Link-Local Multicast Name Resolution (LLMNR) serves the same function as a DNS server when a DNS server cannot be reached.

Review Questions

Answer the following questions on a separate sheet of paper. Please do not write in this book.

1. List some common features of network operating systems.
2. What is the purpose of the data link layer?
3. The data link layer is subdivided into what two layers?
4. The Ethernet protocol uses the _____ access method.
5. Describe a typical session on an Ethernet network.
6. When too many packets on a network collide, a(n) _____ storm has occurred.
7. On which type of network do broadcast storms typically occur?
8. Which access method does AppleTalk use?
9. Which access method does Token Ring use?
10. What is monitor contention?
11. What does the term *ring purge* mean?
12. Which computer on a Token Ring network starts the beaconing process?
13. Which IEEE standard describes Token Bus?
14. How does token passing in a Token Bus system differ from token passing in a Token Ring system?
15. Describe ARCnet's access method.
16. What acronym used in ARCnet technology means the same as network interface card?

17. What does the term *de facto standard* mean?
18. Define the term *broadcast*.
19. Define the term *multicast*.
20. Define the term *session*.
21. Which form of communication guarantees delivery of a packet—a session or a datagram?
22. Which form of communication relies on a broadcast-type of transmission—a session or a datagram?
23. Which form of communication is best for large networks—a session or a broadcast?
24. Define the term *virtual circuit*.
25. _____ and _____ are *not* routable protocols.
26. What is the purpose of NetBIOS Name Service?
27. What is the purpose of LLDP?
28. What two Microsoft protocols are based on LLDP and can be viewed in the **Network Connection Properties** dialog box?
29. Why would a network device such as a computer running Windows XP not appear in Network Map?
30. What is the name of the Cisco version of LLDP?
31. Which link layer protocol design is similar to DNS?
32. What is the purpose of ARP?

Sample Network+ Exam Questions

Answer the following questions on a separate sheet of paper. Please do not write in this book.

1. Which of the following is the UNC format for a shared directory called MyFiles on a server called *Server1*?
   A. //Server1/MyFiles
   B. //MyFiles /Server1
   C. \\Server1\MyFiles
   D. \Server1\MyFiles
2. Which protocol is designed to match IP addresses to the device physical address?
   A. IP
   B. ARP
   C. DNS
   D. TCP
3. How can you reduce network collisions?
   A. Assign static IP addresses to all devices.
   B. Replace network switches with hubs.
   C. Segment the network using switches.
   D. Add additional network servers.
4. Which protocol serves the same purpose as DNS but is limited in scope to a local network?
   A. FTP
   B. ARP
   C. HTML
   D. LLMNR

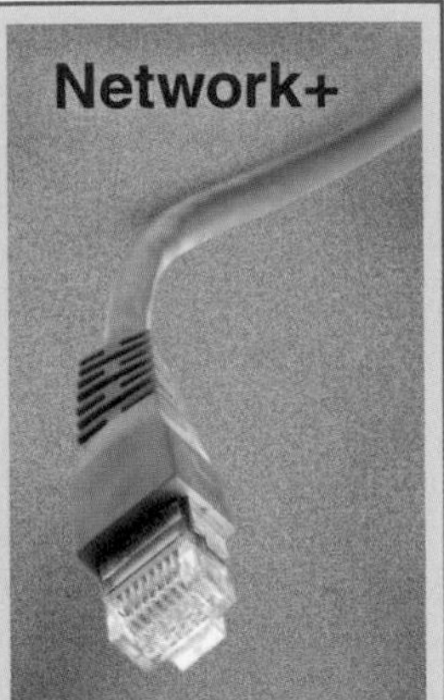

5. Broadcasting data to a few select workstations is referred to as _____.
   A. beaconing
   B. multicasting
   C. conferencing
   D. multiplexing
6. The IEEE 802.3 standard is associated with which access method?
   A. Carrier Sense Multiple Access with Collision Detection (CSMA/CD)
   B. Carrier Sense Multiple Access with Collision Avoidance (CSMA/CA)
   C. Asynchronous Transmission Mode (ATM)
   D. Wireless Ethernet Protocol (WEP)
7. Which two items are commonly used to segment a network and reduce collisions? (Select two.)
   A. Switch
   B. Hub
   C. Router
   D. Repeater
8. Which item is commonly used to provide dedicated bandwidth to VoIP devices?
   A. VLAN
   B Duplex NIC
   C. Protocol analyzer
   D. Proxy server
9. Which network operating system can communicate over Ethernet?
   A. Microsoft Windows
   B. OS X
   C. UNIX
   D. All of the above.
10. Which answer is a correct example of a MAC address?
   A. AB C3 D4 23 54 F2
   B. 192.168.000.123
   C. A12.34E.676.FF2
   D. 1926867721

Suggested Laboratory Activities

1. Install an Ethernet, peer-to-peer network.
2. Create a peer-to-peer network using Windows 7, OS X, and Linux.
3. Use a protocol analyzer to view how name resolution is performed on a peer-to-peer network.
4. On a Windows Vista, Windows 7, or Windows Server 2008 computer, open the Network and Sharing Center and then select the **View Full Map** option.

Interesting Web Sites for More Information

www.javvin.com/protocolsuite.html
www.protocols.com
www.wildpackets.com

Javvin Network Management & Security is an excellent Web site to visit when studying networking protocols. This site contains many valuable resources such as network-related dictionaries and in-depth information on various networking protocols. (www.javvin.com)

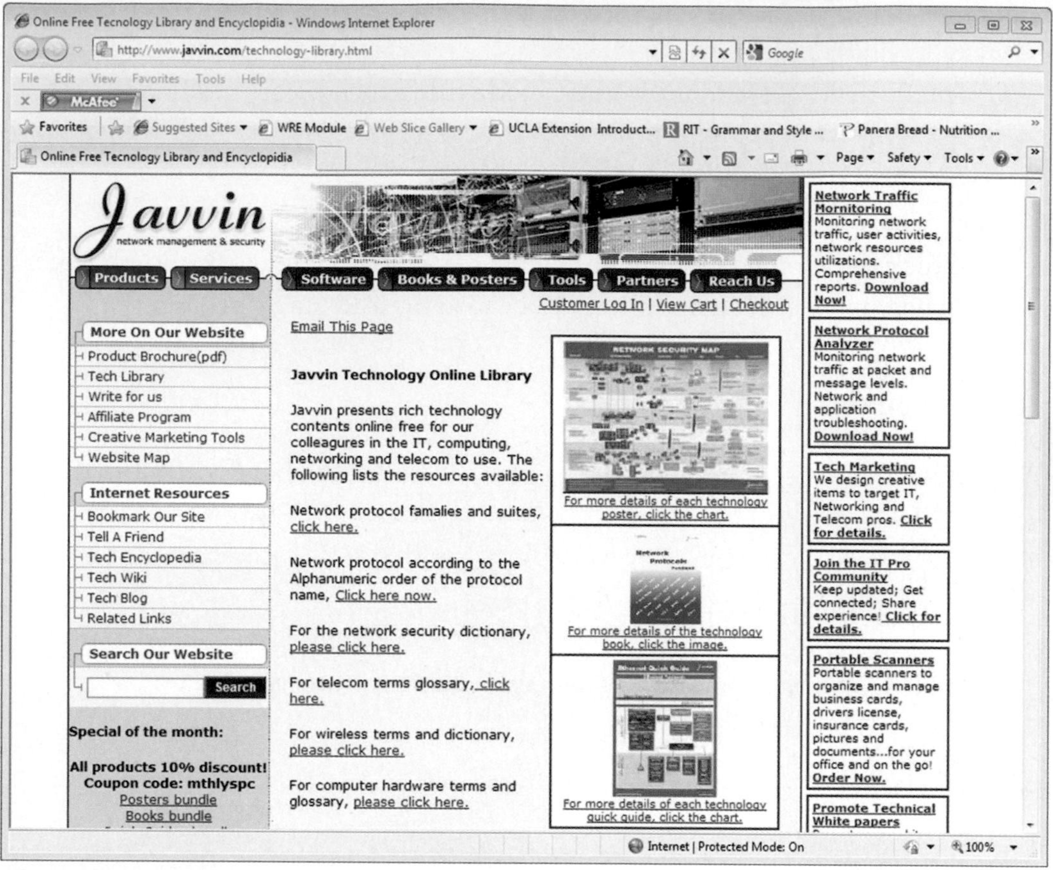

Chapter 6
Laboratory Activity

Using the ARP Command

After completing this laboratory activity, you will be able to:

- Recall the function of the Address Resolution Protocol (ARP).
- Use the **arp** command to identify contents of the ARP cache.
- Use the **arp** command to refresh and modify the contents of the ARP cache.
- Give examples of several utilities that cause the ARP cache to refresh.

Introduction

This laboratory activity will familiarize you with ARP as a protocol and as a command. ARP is used to resolve an assigned IP address to a MAC address on a local area network. The ARP cache is used in conjunction with the TCP/IP protocol to resolve IP addresses to MAC addresses. TCP/IP communications is only based on IP addresses, not MAC addresses or local computer names.

Look at the following illustration. It lists the typical sequence of ARP activity during the address resolution process. Notice the sequence of events that take place during an ARP request. Note that the ARP cache is updated at the computer sending the ARP request and at the computer receiving the ARP request.

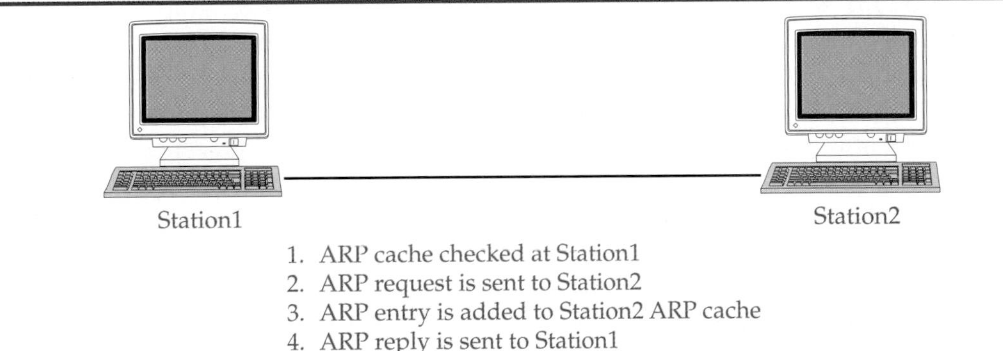

The ARP cache is used to speed the process of resolving IP to MAC addresses. The ARP cache in the Windows operating system typically lasts for approximately 2 minutes unless it is requested again during the 2 minutes. If the ARP request is sent again during the 2-minute period, then the ARP cache will stay intact for 10 minutes. After 10 minutes, it must be refreshed by a complete series of ARP request steps.

Note

Exact time may vary according to the operating system and version being used.

Several switches can be used with the **arp** command. The most common switch is **-a**, which reveals the contents of the ARP cache. Another common switch is **/?** or **/help** which reveals all switches associated with the **arp** command.

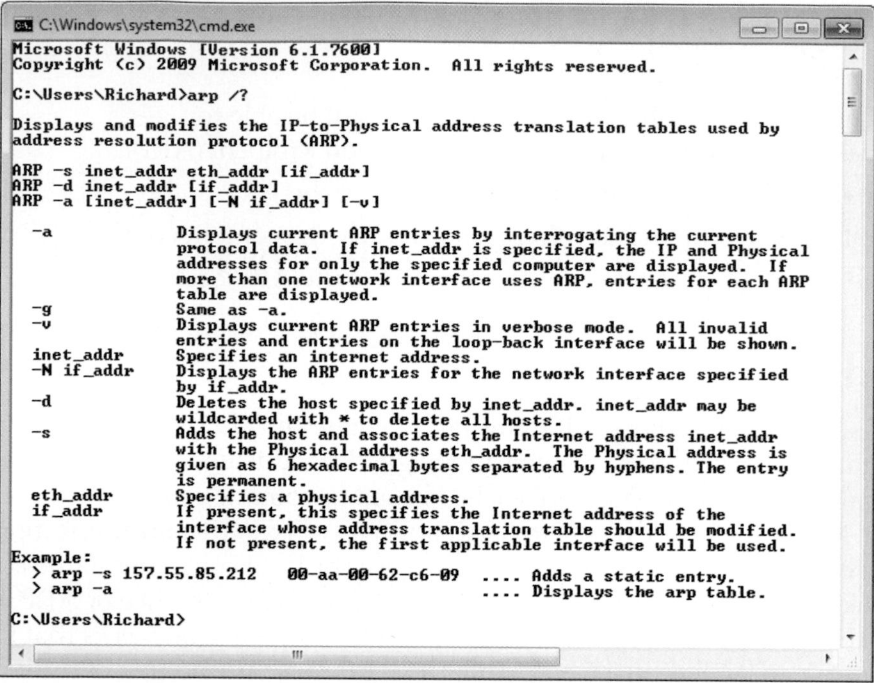

```
C:\Windows\system32\cmd.exe
Microsoft Windows [Version 6.1.7600]
Copyright (c) 2009 Microsoft Corporation.  All rights reserved.

C:\Users\Richard>arp /?

Displays and modifies the IP-to-Physical address translation tables used by
address resolution protocol (ARP).

ARP -s inet_addr eth_addr [if_addr]
ARP -d inet_addr [if_addr]
ARP -a [inet_addr] [-N if_addr] [-v]

  -a            Displays current ARP entries by interrogating the current
                protocol data.  If inet_addr is specified, the IP and Physical
                addresses for only the specified computer are displayed.  If
                more than one network interface uses ARP, entries for each ARP
                table are displayed.
  -g            Same as -a.
  -v            Displays current ARP entries in verbose mode.  All invalid
                entries and entries on the loop-back interface will be shown.
  inet_addr     Specifies an internet address.
  -N if_addr    Displays the ARP entries for the network interface specified
                by if_addr.
  -d            Deletes the host specified by inet_addr. inet_addr may be
                wildcarded with * to delete all hosts.
  -s            Adds the host and associates the Internet address inet_addr
                with the Physical address eth_addr.  The Physical address is
                given as 6 hexadecimal bytes separated by hyphens. The entry
                is permanent.
  eth_addr      Specifies a physical address.
  if_addr       If present, this specifies the Internet address of the
                interface whose address translation table should be modified.
                If not present, the first applicable interface will be used.
Example:
  > arp -s 157.55.85.212   00-aa-00-62-c6-09  .... Adds a static entry.
  > arp -a                                    .... Displays the arp table.

C:\Users\Richard>
```

To add entries to the ARP cache, a function that requires generating an ARP request needs to be performed. Such requests are generated by the **ping** command or by using the utilities that rely on the ARP request, such as viewing the network through Windows Explorer or looking at the **View Full Map** option in the Network and Sharing Center. Since the ARP cache can be refreshed by these various utilities, it is obvious that the utilities use ARP to identify local computers and equipment on the LAN.

Note

IPv6 does not use the ARP protocol to identify a workstation. The IPv6 protocol directly assigns an interface identifier to the network adapter. The interface identifier serves the same purpose as the MAC address. In the distant future, ARP will no longer be required to match an IP address to a MAC address. However, ARP will still exist for many years because Microsoft has always maintained backward compatibility with legacy operating systems.

When using Windows Vista or Windows 7, you must use an elevated permission to use all the various **arp** command switches. In the **Start** menu, simply right-click **Command Prompt** and select **Run as Administrator** from the shortcut menu.

Equipment and Materials

- Two networked computers running Windows XP, Windows Vista, or Windows 7.

Note
You can perform this lab with a lab partner.

Procedure

1. _____ Gather the required materials and report to your assigned workstations.
2. _____ Boot the computers and verify they are in working order.
3. _____ Identify the assigned IP address and MAC address for each computer in the lab activity. Use the **ipconfig/all** command as appropriate for the operating system. On a separate sheet of paper, record the following information. You will need this information to verify the ARP request.

   Station1 name: ______________________________

   MAC address: ______________________________

   IPv4 address: ______________________________

   Station2 name: ______________________________

   MAC address: ______________________________

   IPv4 address: ______________________________
4. _____ Open the Command Prompt and type and enter the **arp -a** command. The ARP cache should be empty and reveal no data. If not, wait approximately two minutes and then reissue the **arp -a** command. The ARP cache should clear after two minutes of no activity.

Note
If the computers are connected to a peer-to-peer network and if there is a gateway or router connected to it for Internet access, there will be a lot of background activity and the ARP cache will not clear. To clear the ARP cache, use the **-d** *switch.*

5. _____ Issue the **ping** command from Station1 to Station2 by typing and entering **ping Station2**. You need only send the command from one station, not both.
6. _____ Use the **arp -a** command at each of the two computers to see if the ARP cache has been updated. It should contain the IP address and MAC address of the other computer. If not, call your instructor for assistance.
7. _____ Wait two minutes to see if the ARP cache clears. Issue the **arp -a** command again to see if the cache is empty.

8. ______ After the ARP cache is empty, try using Network Neighborhood, My Network Places, or Computers Near Me to refresh the ARP cache. After using the appropriate utility, check the ARP cache at each computer using the **arp -a** command. The ARP cache should contain the IP address and MAC address of the opposite computer.

9. ______ Use the appropriate switch to view all the ARP command switches. On a separate piece of paper, list and record their function.

10. ______ Practice using the **arp** command until you feel comfortable using it and know the expected results.

11. ______ Answer the review questions and then return the computers to their pre-lab activity condition.

Review Questions

Answer the following questions on a separate sheet of paper. Please do not write in this book.

1. What is the purpose of ARP?
2. How long does the initial ARP cache hold the resolved MAC and IP address?
3. What is the maximum amount of time the ARP cache remains before it requires to be refreshed?
4. Name several utilities that cause the ARP cache to refresh?
5. Which ARP switch produces the same result as **arp -a**?

7

Microsoft Network Operating Systems

After studying this chapter, you will be able to:

- ❑ Differentiate between a Microsoft peer-to-peer network and a Microsoft client/server network.
- ❑ Differentiate between FAT16, FAT32, and NTFS.
- ❑ Differentiate between a domain, workgroup, and HomeGroup.
- ❑ Interpret the Active Directory structure.
- ❑ Use the Computer Management utility or the MMC Computer Management snap-in to set up local user and group accounts.
- ❑ Use the Active Directory Users and Computers utility to set up domain user and group accounts.

Network+ Exam—Key Points

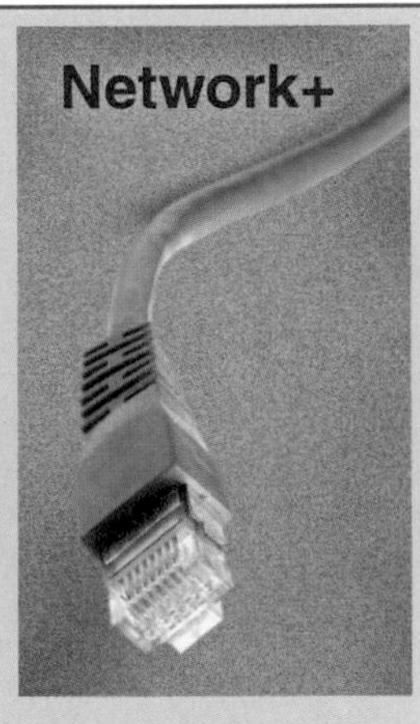

A question about Lightweight Directory Access Protocol (LDAP) is most likely to be on the Network+ Certification exam. Remember that LDAP is independent of the operating system. Basic principles discussed here may appear on the exam such as general questions about user accounts, user logon, and resource sharing.

The CompTIA Network+ Certification is not a certification for Windows Server or any other network operating system. It measures general knowledge, not specific systems. You will not need to know specifics about the Windows Server operating systems. Microsoft has its own collection of certifications for network administrators and network engineers.

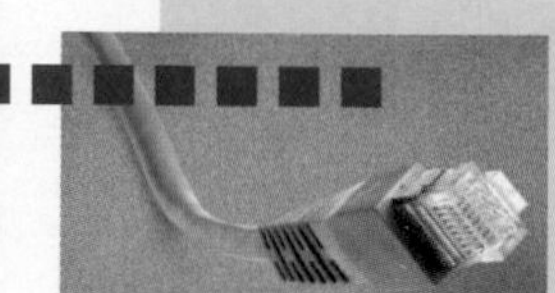

Key Words and Terms

The following words and terms will become important pieces of your networking vocabulary. Be sure you can define them.

Active Directory (AD)
auditing
basic disk
complex trust relationship
contiguous namespace
disjointed namespace
disk quota
distinguished name
domain
dynamic disk
EFI partition
extended partition
external trust
forest
forest trust
free space
global security policy
globally unique identifier (GUID)
group account
interactive logon
local security policy
Logical Disk Manager (LDM) partition
logical drive
logon right
Microsoft Reserved (MSR) partition
multimaster replication
namespace
network share
network authentication
Network File System (NFS)
New Technology File System (NTFS)
NTFS permissions
object
one-way trust relationship
organizational unit
partition
permission
physical drive
primary partition
realm trust
security policy
server cluster
Server Message Block (SMB)
share permissions
share-level security
simple volume
snap-in
spanned volume
striped volume
tree
trust relationship
two-way trust relationship
user-level security
volume
volume set
workgroup

This chapter and the next introduce the dominant Microsoft and UNIX/Linux network operating systems. As you cover the content of these chapters, you will see the similarities and differences among network operating systems. The material presented in these chapters is limited to an introductory level. Knowledge of these network operating systems fills volumes of textbooks. In fact, a typical resource book for any of these operating systems typically contains over a 1000 pages.

Network+ Note

The Network+ Certification exam only requires introductory-level knowledge of the Microsoft network operating system. After finishing this course on networking fundamentals, you may wish to expand your knowledge in this area.

A Brief History of Microsoft Network Operating Systems

Microsoft began developing network operating systems in 1993 when it introduced Windows for Workgroups and Windows NT 3.1. Windows for Workgroups was designed as a peer-to-peer technology, while Windows NT 3.1 was designed as a client/server technology. Both network operating systems became popular because of the GUI.

Windows for Workgroups was one of the first peer-to-peer network models developed. At the time, most networks were the client/server type requiring expensive server software and hardware or a system to access mainframes through dumb terminals. The peer-to-peer model allows a collection of computers to communicate in similar fashion as the client/server model, and also allows the computers to function as stand-alone computers.

Computers in a Windows for Workgroups peer-to-peer network are grouped as workgroups. A ***workgroup*** is a group of computers that share resources such as files and hardware, **Figure 7-1.** This type of network structure is limited in scope and is not used for large networks. In the peer-to-peer workgroup model, each computer contains its own database of users. Each user must have a separate account on each computer to use the computer's shared resources. As a peer-to-peer network grows in size, it becomes impractical to manage.

workgroup
a group of computers that share resources such as files and hardware.

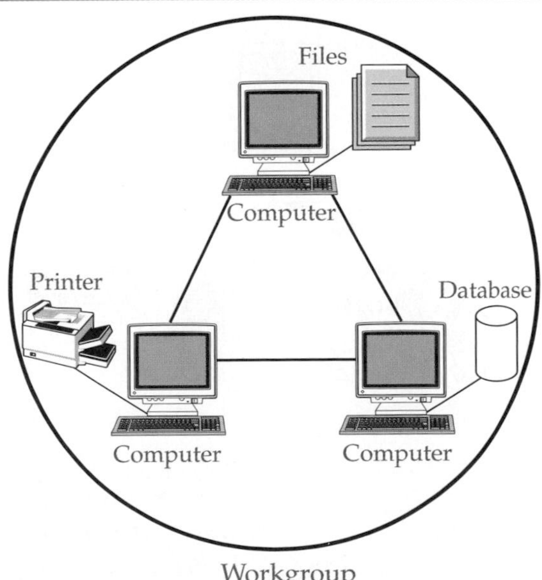

Figure 7-1.
A workgroup is a group of computers that share resources. Some examples of resources are files, directories, databases, and printers.

Windows NT 3.1 based its network administration on the client/server model. A client/server model stores user and resource information in one location called a *security database*. In a client/server network, the security database is stored on a server. The user logs on to the server and is then cleared to access the network resources.

domain
a logical grouping of users and equipment as defined by the network administrator.

Computers in a Windows client/server network are grouped together in a domain. A ***domain*** is a logical grouping of users and equipment as defined by the network administrator, **Figure 7-2.** Domain members share a common security database. It is much easier to manage a large number of users when the network is configured as a client/server.

Tech Tip

Workgroups can also be implemented on a client/server network. However, the ability of a Microsoft client/server model to organize users into groups makes workgroups obsolete.

It is interesting to note that the first release of Windows NT was called Windows NT 3.1. Typically, the first release number of software is labeled as 1.0. Major releases follow in whole numbers such as 2.0, 3.0, and 4.0. Revisions increment in tenths, such as 2.1 and 2.2, and minor revisions generally increment in one hundredths, such as 2.11 and 2.22. The first version of Windows NT, however, was labeled 3.1 to match the version of DOS that was available at the time.

In 1996, Microsoft introduced Windows NT Workstation 4.0 and Windows NT Server 4.0. The workstation version could function as a stand-alone computer or support up to ten computers in a peer-to-peer environment.

Two of the major differences between Windows NT 3.1 and Windows NT 4.0 are the interface and Plug-and-Play capabilities. Windows NT 4.0 was designed to look like Windows 95. The operating system was capable of recognizing and installing Plug-and-Play devices, a feature that NT 3.1 lacked.

In February of 2000, Microsoft introduced Windows 2000 Professional to replace Windows NT Workstation 4.0 and Windows 2000 Server to replace

Figure 7-2.
A domain consists of a collection of users and equipment under one administration.

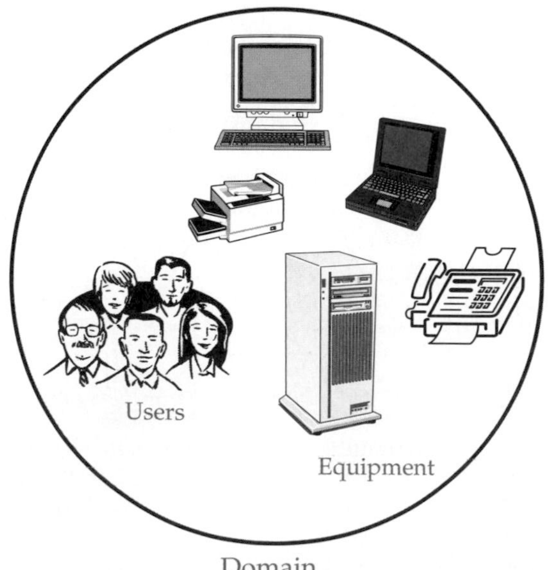

Domain

Windows NT Server 4.0. In addition, Microsoft introduced Windows 2000 Advanced Server, which was designed to replace Windows NT 5.0 Server Enterprise Edition and Windows 2000 Datacenter Server.

In 2003, Microsoft released Windows Server 2003. Windows Server 2003 comes in four versions: Standard Edition, Enterprise Edition, Datacenter Edition, and Web Edition. The names reflect the design and administrative tool collection of each. For example, the Standard Edition functions as a network server for controlling a simple network. The Enterprise Edition is designed especially for a large-scale network. The Datacenter Edition is designed to serve as a storage server for a central database. The Web Edition is designed to serve as a Web server with limited capabilities.

Each edition supports IPv6, Remote Desktop, Active Directory, IIS6, .NET Application Services, and the Encrypting File System (EFS). Each has a similar interface. The major differences are the technical features such as how much RAM and how many processors each can support and whether it supports hot-add memory and cluster services.

While network systems such as Windows NT are excellent systems and could be used for years to come, they become obsolete because of the lack of technical support provided by Microsoft. Microsoft supports its product line by constantly releasing patches and service packs that keep the system up-to-date with new hardware and security features. Once the company stops releasing new hardware and security features for a particular operating system, the operating system becomes obsolete. For example, as new hardware products are developed such as the USB port, there is a need for a software patch for existing operating systems that were released before the first USB port was introduced. If a patch that enables the operating system to recognize and use the USB port is not released, the operating system soon becomes obsolete. Normally users do not settle on using older hardware such as a parallel or serial port when newer, faster hardware is available.

Windows Server 2008

As of this writing, Windows Server 2008 is Microsoft's latest server operating system. There are many variations of Windows Server 2008. The variations range from a modest version known as Server Core, which does not use a GUI, to Server Enterprise, which is a GUI-based system designed to support thousands of workstations and devices worldwide. In this section, you will learn about the various Windows Server 2008 editions and their available features.

Windows Server 2008 Editions

There are seven different editions of Windows Server 2008: Foundation, Standard, Enterprise, Datacenter, Web Server, HPC Server, and Itanium-Based Systems. See the table in **Figure 7-3** for a brief description of each.

Foundation

Windows Foundation Server 2008 is an entry-level server operating system. While providing support for common server functions, it does not support many of Microsoft's enhanced features found in the Standard edition, such as Hyper-V™ technology. Also, the Foundation edition supports a limited maximum number of clients for remote access and remote desktop access. The Foundation edition only supports 10 Internet access connections, whereas the

Figure 7-3.
Windows Server 2008 editions.

Windows Server 2008 Edition	Description
Foundation	Entry-level Windows Server 2008 operating system.
Standard	As the name implies, the standard version of Microsoft Server 2008.
Enterprise	Designed for large networks and provides unlimited virtualization licenses.
Datacenter	Designed specifically for use as a datacenter using software applications such as SQL.
Web Server	Designed to support Web hosting on the Internet.
HPC	High Performance Computing (HPC) can be scaled to support thousands of processor cores, ensuring "high performance."
Itanium-Based Systems	Designed specifically for the Itanium processor.

Standard edition supports up to 50 connections and the Enterprise edition supports an unlimited number of connections. The Foundation edition is easily upgradable to the Standard edition.

Standard

This is one of the most commonly encountered Windows Server 2008 editions. Windows Server 2008 Standard satisfies the requirements for most network systems. It provides support for DNS, DHCP, file sharing, network security, firewall protection, Web server service, and more.

Enterprise

As the name implies, Windows Server 2008 Enterprise is designed for large scale network systems. The Enterprise edition can provide any and all services provided by the Windows Server 2008 editions. One of the big advantages of the Enterprise edition is that it allows for an unlimited number of remote connections.

Datacenter

Windows Server 2008 Datacenter provides all the same services as the Enterprise edition. The main difference is the Datacenter can utilize up to 64 processors while Enterprise can only utilize 8. The Standard edition can only utilize 4 processors. The Datacenter is intended for large volumes of critical data storage. There is no limit to the number of users that can connect to the Datacenter edition. The Datacenter also supports CPU and RAM hot swapping, which means you do not have to shut down the server to change a CPU or RAM.

Web Server

All of the Windows Server 2008 editions include Internet Information Service (IIS), which is a software package that supports Web hosting and Web hosting applications. The Windows Web Server edition provides only Web server hosting features and DNS. The Web Server edition does not provide other server features such as file server, Active Directory, and other features commonly associated with the Standard edition. The Web Server edition costs less than the Standard edition, which makes it cost-effective.

HPC Server

Windows HPC Server 2008 is designed for "high-performance" processing through thousands of processor cores. This type of processing is closest in design to a supercomputer, which is capable of processing thousands of programming instructions in a single second.

Itanium-Based Systems

Window Server 2008 for Itanium-Based Systems is based on the Itanium processor developed by Intel. The Intel Itanium processor can process more instructions per second than any existing x64 (64-bit) processors. While the Itanium processor will outperform current x64 processors, it is not directly backward compatible with x64 or x32 server software applications. There are software emulators available to provide backward compatibility, but at a loss of performance. As a result, you should only use software designed especially for the Itanium processor to achieve best performance. The Itanium supports CPU and RAM hot swapping.

Windows Server 2008 Features

Figure 7-4 lists some of the major features in Windows Server 2008. Note that most features are not available in all of the editions. This section details some of the features listed in Figure 7-4.

BranchCache™

BranchCache™ is new for Windows Server 2008 and Windows 7. The BranchCache feature is designed to improve network performance by storing information downloaded from the Internet or from a Web server onto a local area network client. In a peer-to-peer network such as a home office, one of the Windows 7 computers stores the downloaded content and has it available for other clients in the network.

In a client/server network, a copy of the downloaded content is stored on the server and made available to network clients. BranchCache greatly improves LAN performance by providing an alternate location of the requested information to reduce network traffic.

DirectAccess

DirectAccess is a new feature in Windows Server 2008. Prior to DirectAccess, users typically connected to a remote server using a Virtual Private Network (VPN). A VPN connection requires manual user authentication each time the connection is made. DirectAccess only requires user authentication the first time the connection is established. After that, connections are made automatically. Another important feature of DirectAccess is if a network remote connection is temporarily lost, the computer will automatically reconnect when the network remote connection is re-established. For example, mobile users use wireless connections while out of the office. A wireless connection can easily be disrupted by radio interference or loss of signal strength. When the wireless connection returns, the DirectAccess feature resumes the remote connection to the office.

Figure 7-4.
Windows Server 2008 editions and features comparison chart.

Feature	Enterprise	Datacenter	Standard	Web Server	Itanium-Based Systems	Foundation	HPC Server
64-bit RAM	2 TB	2TB	32 GB	32 GB	NA	8 GB	128 GB
AD Rights Management Services	Yes	Yes	Yes	No	No	Yes	No
Branchcache™ Content Server	Yes	Yes	Yes	Yes	Yes	Yes	
DirectAccess	Yes	Yes	Yes	No	No	No	No
Failover Cluster	Yes	Yes	No	No	Yes	No	No
Hot Swap CPU	No	Yes	No	No	Yes	No	No
Hot Swap Memory	No	Yes	No	No	Yes	No	No
Hyper-V™	Yes	Yes	Yes	No	No	No	Yes
Internet Information Services 7.5	Yes	Yes	Yes	Yes	Yes	Yes	Yes
Network Access Protection	Yes	Yes	Yes	No	No	Yes	No
Remote Access using VPN	Unlimited	Unlimited	250	NA	NA	50	250
Remote Access using RADIUS	Unlimited	Unlimited	50	NA	2	10	NA
Remote Desktop Services	Yes	Yes	Yes	No	No	Yes	Yes
Server Core	Yes	Yes	Yes	Yes	No	No	No

Network Access Protection (NAP) is incorporated into the DirectAccess feature. NAP automatically checks if the system is healthy. Being "healthy" means the computer has the latest critical updates and anti-malware definitions installed.

server cluster
a group of servers connected both physically and logically to ensure constant service to clients.

Failover Cluster

Failover Cluster is a group of individual servers connected both physically and logically to ensure constant service to clients. Microsoft refers to its server cluster as "Failover Cluster" while other venders generally use the term ***server cluster.*** An example of the function of a server cluster is when two or more servers provide file sharing, printer services, and mail service. When one server fails, the other server automatically begins servicing clients connected to the failed server. Failover clustering is a way to provide near perfect service, even during routine server maintenance or server failure. Failover Cluster is only available in Enterprise, Datacenter, and Itanium-Based Systems editions.

Load balancing is typically included with Failover Cluster. The client load is distributed evenly through all servers participating in the load-balancing service. Load-balancing software constantly checks the performance of each server and makes decisions based on client/server demand. When the demand is too high on one server, some of the client connections can be automatically switched to a different server that provides the same service. Load balancing is a key factor for server farms.

Hyper-V™

Hyper-V™ is the Microsoft version of server virtualization software. The computer running Hyper-V is referred to as the "host." When Hyper-V is installed, the host can run other server operating systems. Virtualization is a very economical way to run two or more servers simultaneously using only one computer. The host shares physical resources such as the CPU, RAM, and hard disk drive storage with the other installed operating systems.

Virtualization allows a network administrator to phase in a new server system such as Windows Server 2008 and run an earlier version such as Windows Server 2003 at the same time. After a test period, the administrator can migrate the entire network system to the new server operating system while both servers are running. There is no service interruption or network downtime during the migration. Network clients can continue to use network resources such as shared files during the migration. Hyper-V also allows the network administrator to host operating systems other than Microsoft, such as Linux. Many organizations prefer to use a Linux server as a Web server. Again, a separate computer is not required to host the Linux Web server.

Another advantage is redundancy of servers which provide services while a network server is taken off-line. For example if a company is using two physical servers, one as a system file server and the other as a Web server, client service could be denied if one of the two servers were to fail. However, with each of the two servers running Hyper-V and each server hosting a file server and a Web server, if one of the two physical servers fail, the other could still provide services to network clients.

Internet Information Service

Internet Information Services (IIS) is the Microsoft version of Web service hosting software. Once installed, a server with IIS can host Web page applications and Web services. Microsoft has a proprietary Web site development suite called Microsoft Expression Studio. The suite consists of Web page and Web site design tools as well as programming tools for constructing database Web pages. The suite is quite elaborate.

Network Access Protection

Network Access Protection (NAP) is a new feature in Windows Server 2008 R2. NAP inspects the "health" of the computer before it completes a connection to the domain, which means it checks if the latest software patches and updates and the latest anti-malware definitions are installed. If not, the user is denied access to the domain. This feature helps prevent the spread of malware through the network. It is especially useful for preventing infection through wireless connections, such as when using a laptop in a public environment.

Remote Access

Remote access to the server is typically performed in one of two ways. One way is by using a server that is running RADIUS. RADIUS is a security feature that requires clients connecting from remote locations to the network server to authenticate with a user name and password. In addition, the RADIUS server keeps track of user activity.

The other way is through a Virtual Private Network (VPN) connection, which does not require a server to be running RADIUS but does require a password. There will be much more about VPN connections and RADIUS in Chapter 15—Network Security.

To learn more about Windows Server 2008, visit the Windows Server 2008 Web page at www.microsoft.com/windowsserver2008/en/us/editions.aspx. You can also conduct an Internet search using the key terms "Microsoft Server 2008" or "Microsoft TechNet Server 2008."

Server Core

Server Core is a minimal server configuration that provides specialized or limited services. For example, Server Core can be configured to function as only a DHCP, DNS, or Web server. Server Core is available in all of the Windows Server 2008 editions except for Foundation, HPC, and Itanium-Based Systems.

The most drastic difference between Server Core and a full server version is Server Core does not use a GUI interface. Server Core only provides a command prompt interface for configuring the server and viewing server information. By providing a limited number of services or a single service without the enhancements of a typical server, Server Core is less vulnerable to network attacks. For example, Server Core does not use Windows Explorer, thus any malicious attack based on Windows Explorer will not affect it.

Small Business Server 2008

Small Business Server (SBS) is designed especially for the small-office environment, usually consisting of 50 to 75 computers. SBS comes in two editions: Standard and Premium. It is designed to automatically set up in a typical installation configuration and provide features such as e-mail, collaboration and messaging software, security features, automatic updating, and Web site support. The main difference between the Standard and Premium edition is Premium includes database server support using SQL. The database provides services for accounting.

Common Windows Server Administrative Components

This section provides an overview of the common administrative components and basic terminology of all Microsoft network operating systems. A basic understanding of Microsoft network operating systems will serve as a foundation when studying the specific Microsoft network operating systems.

Domain, Workgroup, and HomeGroup Membership

Students new to networking find it difficult to tell the difference between the terms *domain*, *workgroup*, and *HomeGroup*. The main differences are found by comparing security, administration features, and general limitations. See **Figure 7-5** for a brief comparison.

Note that HomeGroup membership is optional, whereas membership to a workgroup or domain is not. A computer must be a member of either workgroup or domain. By default, Microsoft operating systems are configured as a member of a workgroup unless otherwise specified.

HomeGroup was first introduced in Windows 7 and was designed to provide an easy way for users to share resources on a home network. It is configured automatically in addition to workgroup membership during the operating system installation process. HomeGroup membership is designed to share common folders such as Pictures, Music, Documents, and Videos, which are referred to as *Libraries*. Some hardware devices such as printers and media players can also be shared.

Note

HomeGroup is only available in Windows 7.

In a workgroup, all computers are equal or peers. Each computer has a set of user accounts. You must have a user account configured on a specific computer to access the computer. Each workstation controls access to its own resources. In a domain, there are one or more servers. The server designated as the domain controller controls access to the network and to the network's resources. A single user account can allow a user to log on to any computer in the entire domain. A

Figure 7-5. Workgroup, domain, and HomeGroup comparison.

Workgroup	Domain	HomeGroup
A computer must be a member of either workgroup or domain.	A computer must be a member of either workgroup or domain.	Membership is optional.
Peer-to-peer configuration.	Client/server configuration.	Peer-to-peer configuration.
Each computer has a set of user accounts.	User accounts are stored in a single location called a *security database*.	Each computer has a set of user accounts.
Passwords are optional.	Passwords are required.	Passwords are required.
All workgroup computers must be on the same LAN or subnet.	Domain membership is not limited to a subnet or local area network.	Must be a Windows 7 computer with the network location set to Home.
A workgroup typically contains 10–20 computers.	A domain can contain thousands of computers.	Same as the workgroup limit.

domain provides for centralized network control, typically by one person called the *administrator.*

Domain membership and HomeGroup membership require a password; workgroup membership does not. All computers in a workgroup must be on the same local area network or subnet. Domain membership is not limited to a subnet or local area network. A domain can span across the globe and comprise individual networks and computers. A domain can contain thousands of computers, whereas a workgroup typically contains 10 to 20 computers.

User Account

logon right
the ability to log on to the network.

permission
the ability to access a network share.

Each person who needs to access a Microsoft server and its resources must have a user account. The basic requirement for a user account is a user name and password. A user account can be assigned properties such as rights and restrictions. Rights include logon rights and permissions. A ***logon right*** is the ability to log on to the network. This ability may be restricted by disabling a user's account or by limiting the time the user is allowed to access the network. A ***permission*** is the ability to access a network share. Permissions may be limited. For example, a user can be given permission to read a file on the server, but not given permission to write to the file. A user can also be given permission to store personal files on the server's hard drive, yet restricted to using a limited amount of hard drive space.

When a computer running a Windows server operating system boots, a dialog box appears prompting the user to press [Ctrl] [Alt] [Del] to begin. After the user presses [Ctrl] [Alt] [Del], a logon dialog box displays, prompting the user for a user name and password. After the user name and password are authenticated, the user's default desktop appears.

One of the most common errors made by users is to incorrectly type their user name or password or to forget their password. The following is a typical Windows Server 2003 message that is displayed when a user incorrectly enters his or her name or password:

> The system could not log you on. Make sure your user name and domain are correct, and then type your password again. Letters in passwords must be typed using correct case. Make sure that CAPS LOCK is not accidentally on.

Network+

Network+ Note

Logon failures are a common question topic on the Network+ Certification exam. Practice logon procedures and create logon failures to observe error messages firsthand.

Group Account

group account
a collection of users that typically share a common job-oriented goal or similar function.

To simplify user and resource administration, a network administrator can create a group account and then add users to that account. A ***group account*** is a collection of users that typically share a common job-oriented goal or similar function. Think of a group as a container or a collection of users who share the same responsibilities, duties, or interest. The group account may also consist of equipment. A group account can be assigned rights and restrictions like a user. Assigning rights and restrictions to the group level rather than to the user level makes administration simpler. For example, if users of a group need to access a new folder, the administrator can simply change the rights of the group account rather than change each user account.

Some groups are created by default when a network operating system is installed. The following is a list of some typical default groups found in Windows Server:

- Administrators.
- Account Operators.
- Backup Operators.
- Guests.
- Server Operators.
- Remote Desktop Users.
- Event Log Readers.
- Network Configuration Operators.
- Performance Operators.
- Pre-Windows 2000 Compatibility Access.
- Print Operators.
- Replicator.
- Users.

The system administrator may create additional groups to better match the network environment. For example, typical groups that may be created for a school setting would be *Teachers, Students, Science, English, Math, Counseling*, and *Administration*. Once the groups are set up with permissions and restrictions, users can be assigned to the groups. Users may be assigned to more than one group. For example, a teacher may be assigned to the *Teacher* group, the *Math* group, and the default *Backup Operators* group.

Security Policy

A ***security policy*** is a blanket policy that secures resources on the network. This policy is set before users are added to the network. Users added to the network are automatically affected by these policies unless specific properties are assigned to the users that override the policy's settings. Two types of security policies exist: local security policies and global security policies. A ***local security policy*** affects local users. A ***global security policy*** affects users throughout the domain.

Security policies can define password requirements such as whether a user should be allowed to reuse an old password when a password change is required, **Figure 7-6.** Security policies can also be set that affect auditing. ***Auditing*** is a service that tracks the events, use, and access of network resources and writes these actions to a log. In **Figure 7-7,** a file server error is displayed in the Server Manager utility. Error logs for server versions of Windows are very similar to the error logs generated in desktop versions of Windows.

security policy
a blanket policy that secures resources on the network.

local security policy
a security policy that affects local users.

global security policy
a security policy that affects domain users.

auditing
a service that tracks the events, use, and access of network resources and writes these actions to a log.

Network Share

A ***network share,*** or ***shared resource,*** is a resource on the network that is shared among assigned users. Examples of resources include files, directories, hard drives, CD drives, and printers.

network share
a resource on the network that is shared among assigned users.

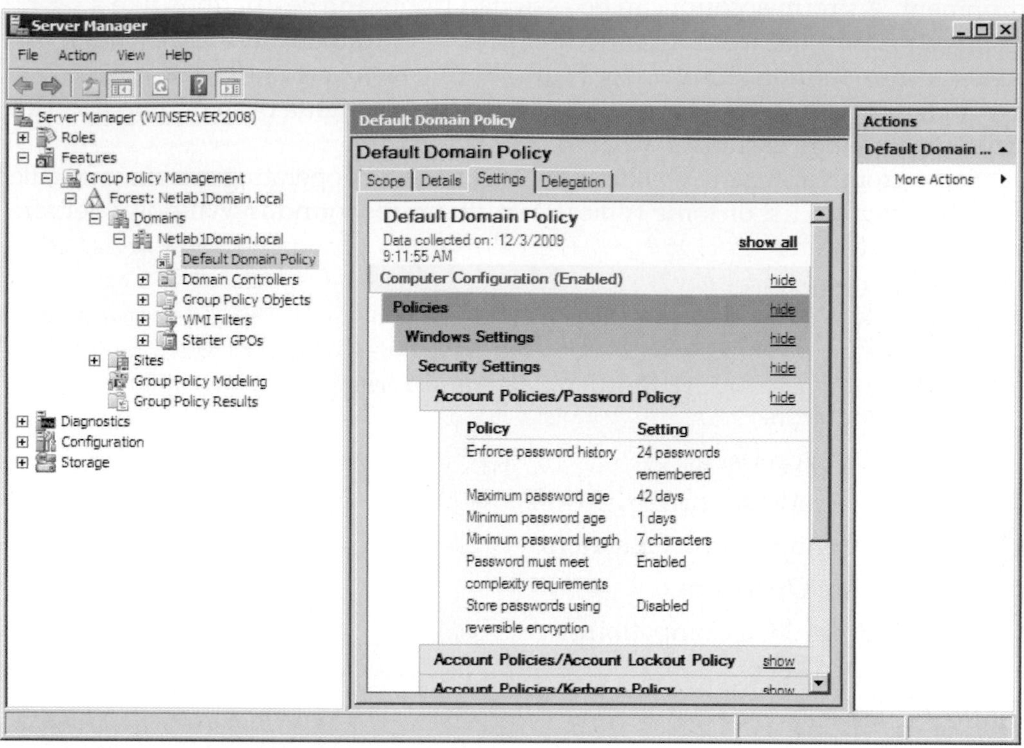

Figure 7-6. Policies are created and modified using the Server Manager.

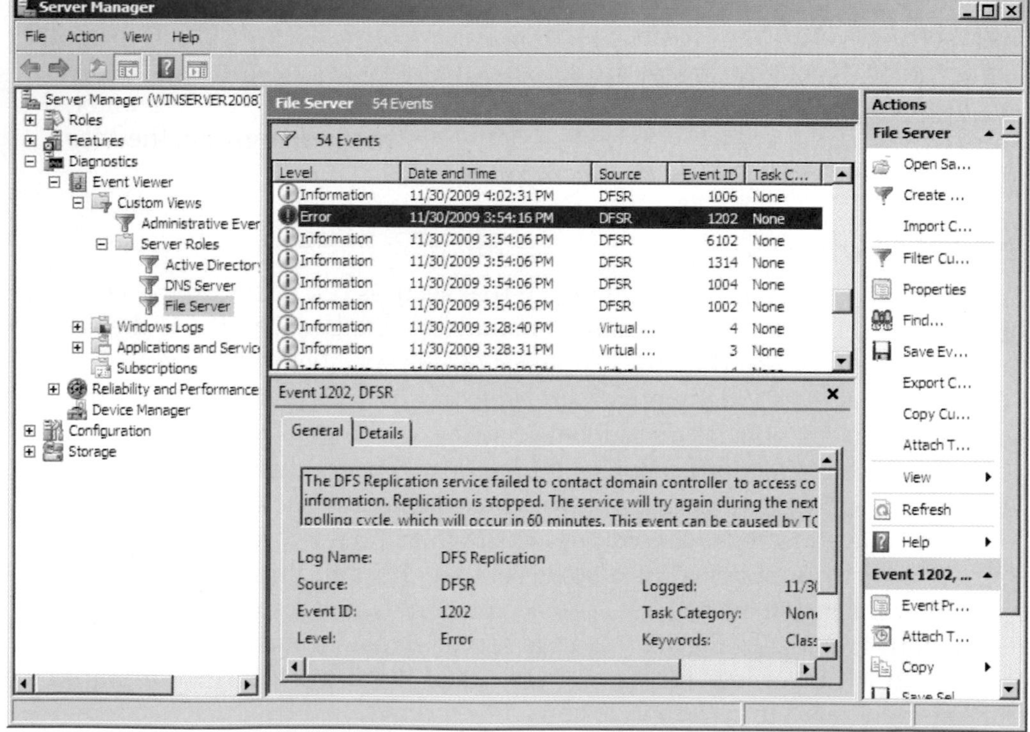

Figure 7-7. Server Manager provides a set of Event Viewer logs that contain information and error messages.

A network share as viewed from a computer workstation looks similar as that in **Figure 7-8.** Earlier systems used an open hand icon to indicate a shared object. An open hand beneath an object is still used by Windows 7 and Windows Server 2008 to indicate a shared object as a local share for access by local users, not a network share. A network share is indicated by a cable connected to the shared object. Originally, a public folder share was typically named *Public* in a Windows Server environment. Today, Windows Vista and Windows 7 use the term *Public* to indicate shared resources on a local computer.

Two administrative shares automatically created in the Windows Server 2008 environment are "netlogon" and "sysvol." They can only be accessed by the system administrator or a user with equal to system administrator privileges. The share labeled "Test Folder1" in Figure 7-8 was created for demonstration purposes. This shared folder can be accessed by anyone with the proper permissions.

Permissions granted to shares delegate who can use the share and in what way. Permissions to a share can be granted at the user or group level. Examples of permissions are Full Control, Modify, Read, and Write.

Tech Tip

The permissions available for selection will vary according to partition file type (NTFS, FAT, etc.), the type of user account (local or domain), and the operating system version or edition.

Figure 7-9 shows the permissions assigned to the group *Everyone* for the shared folder, Public ON Adv Server. The group *Everyone* is assigned the Full Control permission over the contents of the folder. When a user is assigned to the group *Everyone*, the user will be able to have full control over the shared folder, Public ON Adv Server.

File Sharing Protocols

Microsoft Windows Server uses the ***Server Message Block (SMB)*** protocol to support file sharing from a Windows operating system. SMB is also referred

Server Message Block (SMB) a protocol that supports file sharing from a Windows operating system.

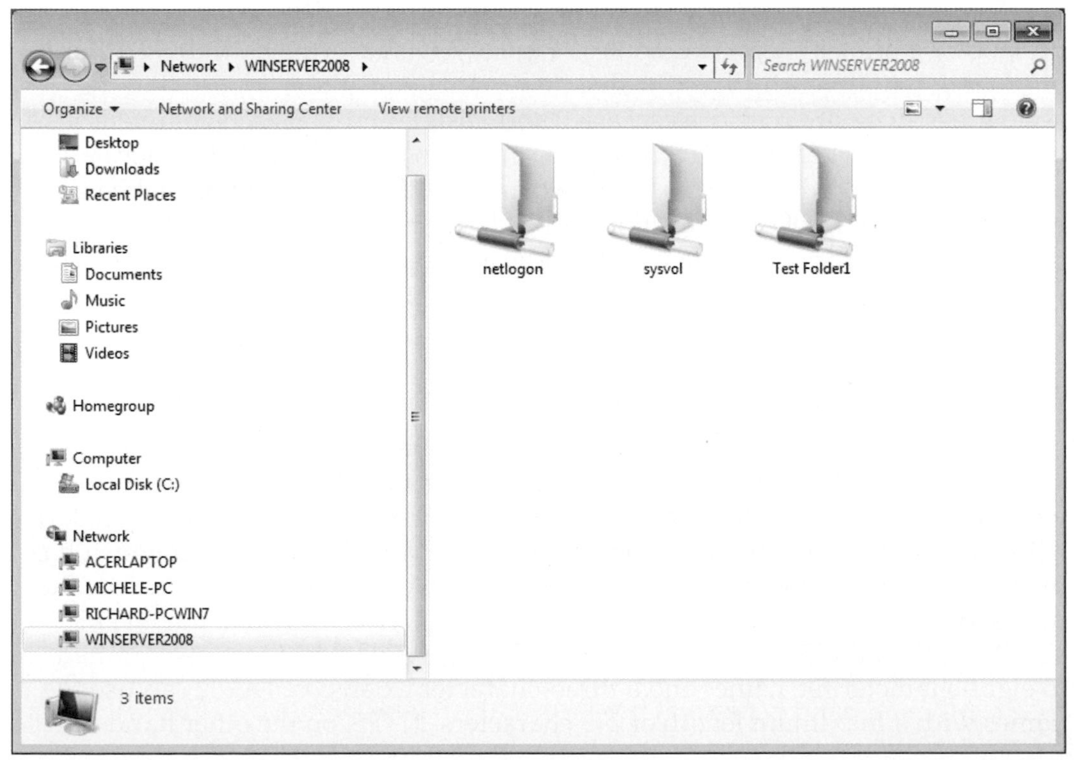

Figure 7-8. Shares are indicated by the object's icon with a cable connection. This indicates that the share is network accessible.

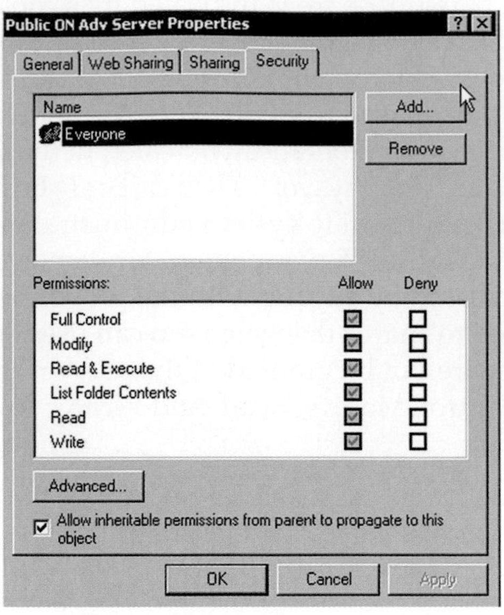

Figure 7-9. Permissions granted to the group *Everyone* for the Public On Adv Server folder.

to as *Common Internet File System (CIFS)*, which is technically incorrect. CIFS was an attempt by Microsoft to standardize a universal file sharing protocol for the Internet to be used by all operating systems. Today, CIFS is considered a dialect of SMB. SMB is not limited to file sharing. SMB is also used to support network printing, network browsing, and locating other SMB servers on the network.

Network File System (NFS) a protocol that supports file sharing from a UNIX and Linux operating system.

The other major file sharing protocol is ***Network File System (NFS)***, which is used by UNIX and Linux operating systems. There will be more about NFS in Chapter 8—UNIX/Linux Operating Systems.

Disk Management

The disk management tool that comes with Windows Server as well as desktop operating systems is graphical. **Figure 7-10** shows the hard drive volumes of a Windows Server displayed with a disk management tool. Notice that the system has two hard disk drives, Disk 0 and Disk 1, and that each volume is formatted with FAT32 or NTFS. There are also two areas labeled "Unallocated" and "Free space," which means these two areas of the disk have not yet been formatted. The size of each partition and its location in the directory structure is displayed. Note the color code used to indicate the primary partition, extended partition, and logical drives. Disk management tools and disk terminology are discussed in more detail later in this chapter.

New Technology File System

New Technology File System (NTFS) the native file format for Windows NT and Windows Server operating systems.

The ***New Technology File System (NTFS)*** is the native file format for Windows NT and Windows Server operating systems. NTFS was introduced with Windows NT 3.1. The original file system, known as File Allocation Table (FAT) or FAT16 has several limitations. It is limited to a 2-GB partition which has made it obsolete by today's standards. This is a severe limitation for a server that needs to provide a large amount of storage space. FAT32 overcame the FAT16 size limitation. FAT32 can create a partition size of 32 GB. FAT16 is also limited to eight-character file names and a three-character extension. FAT32 can use file names with a maximum length of 255 characters. NTFS, on the other hand, can

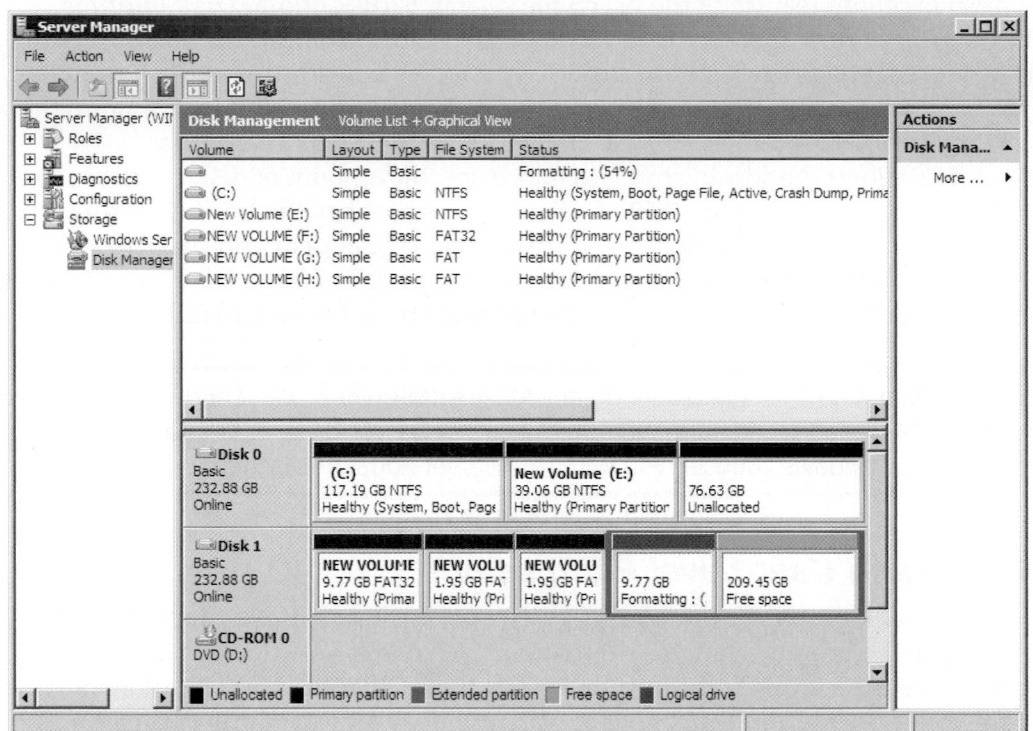

Figure 7-10.
The Disk Management tool provides a graphical display of disks, volumes, partitions, the type of file system, and more.

create partition sizes as large as 16 EB. NTFS file names can be as long as 255 characters and have multiple extensions. See **Figure 7-11** for a comparison of FAT16, FAT32, and NTFS.

Note that for FAT32 and NTFS the file extension is optional. Commonly used extensions have three characters to maintain backward compatibility, but this is less of an issue today. Some Microsoft Office documents are saved with four-letter extensions, such as docx. The main difference between the original DOS file extension and those used today is for the original DOS file you can only use the period symbol once to identify the file extension. Today, file names can contain more than one period, such as in MyFile.one.two.three.four.doc. The period is an accepted special symbol which can be used in the file path and file name.

When Windows 2000 was released, the NTFS file system was further improved and was introduced by Microsoft as dynamic disk. Since the release of dynamic disk, it has been renamed NTFS5.0. The original NT file system was renamed NTFS4.0 so the two could be easily distinguished. NTFS4.0 and NTFS5.0 are covered in detail later in this chapter.

File System	Partition Size (Maximum)	File Name (Maximum characters)	File Extension (Maximum characters)
FAT16	2 GB	8	3
FAT32	32 GB	255	*
NTFS	16 EB	255	*

*For FAT32 and NTFS the file extension is optional.

Figure 7-11.
File system comparison chart.

disk quota
the amount of disk space assigned to specific users.

An excellent feature of the NTFS file system is disk quota. ***Disk quota*** is the amount of disk space assigned to specific users. A common problem with networks that have shared hard disk drive space is users filling disk space with graphics and audio files. Graphics and audio files take a tremendous amount of storage space when compared with database files and document files.

NTFS allows the administrator to allot a specific amount of disk space to a user and a warning level, **Figure 7-12.** As the user approaches the limit (warning level) of his or her assigned disk space, a warning message appears on the screen. The message is displayed before the user runs out of space. This is so the user may purge some of his or her files or request additional space from the system administrator.

Tech Tip

Be aware that many resources refer to any Microsoft Server product and network system as simply Microsoft NT even though the Microsoft Server product is a later technology belonging to Windows 2000 Server, Windows Server 2003, and Windows Server 2008.

share-level security
a type of security that provides password protection and minimal share permissions to network shares. Share-level security applies only to shares that are accessed over the network.

share permissions
permissions assigned to a network share. Common share permissions are Full Control, Modify, Read, and Write.

Share- and User-Level Permissions

Not only does NTFS offer larger disk capacity, it also offers many security features that were not available directly for FAT16 and FAT32. NTFS can be set up to share directories and control access to files. FAT16 and FAT32 allow only for share-level security. ***Share-level security*** provides password protection for a share and minimal share permissions. Share-level permissions are commonly called ***share permissions.*** See **Figure 7-13.** Share-level security applies only to shares that are accessed over the network. It does not secure shares that are accessed locally. For example, a user who accesses a shared directory over the network may be asked to provide a password or may be limited to only Read access. If the same user accesses the shared directory locally (at the computer that hosts the share), no security would be enforced. The user would be able to make changes to the file.

An object which is to be shared such as a folder can be directly configured by simply right-clicking the desired folder and selecting **Share** from the shortcut menu. This applies to all Microsoft operating systems, both desktop versions and server versions. Once accessed, you are provided with two buttons: **Share Permissions** and **NTFS Permissions**. The **Share Permissions** option is

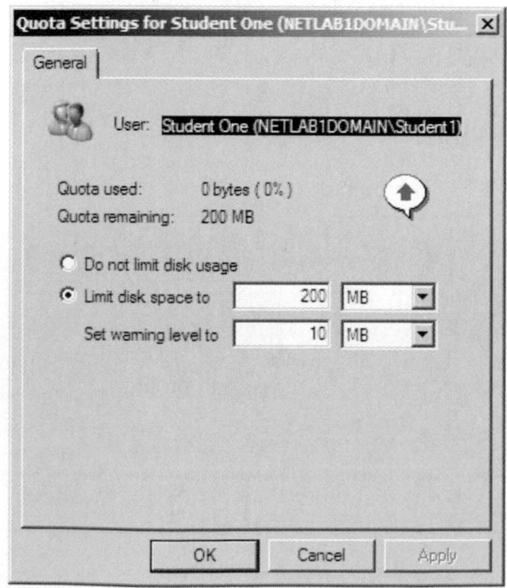

Figure 7-12.
Disk storage space can be controlled using the **Quota Settings** option.

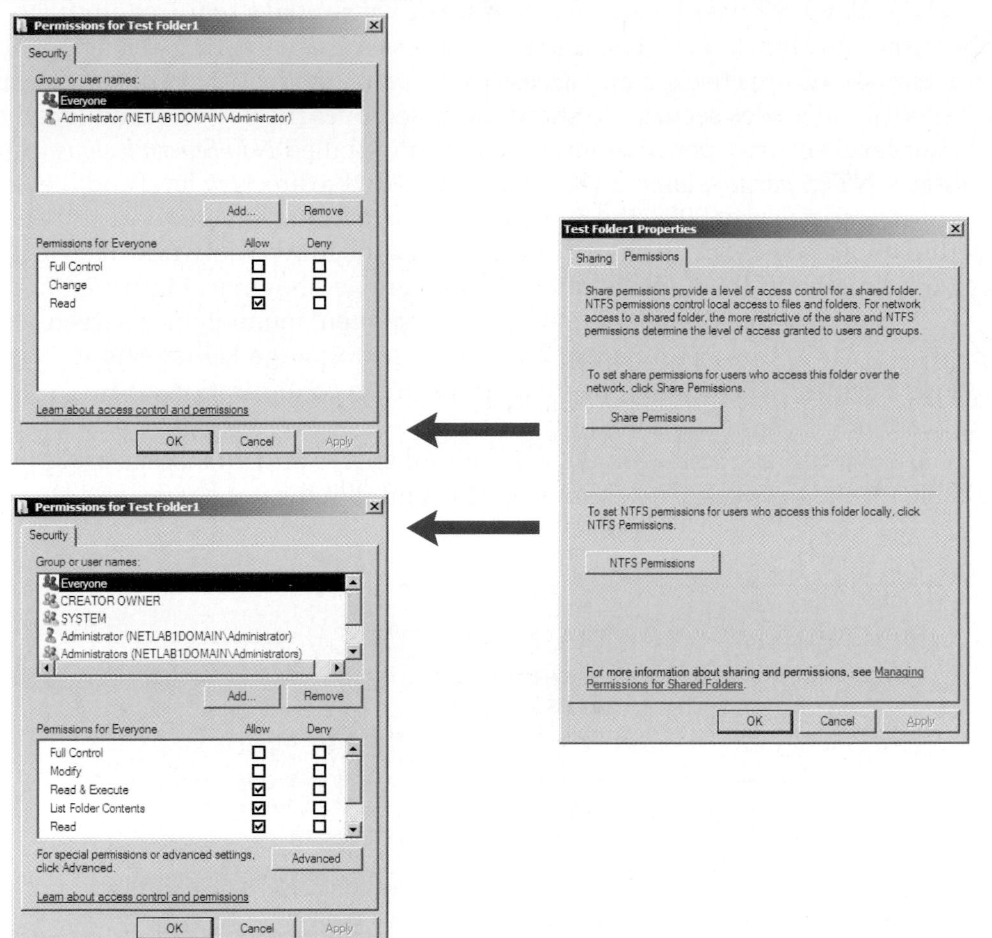

Figure 7-13.
A folder's **Properties** dialog box allows you to set up share permissions or NTFS permissions.

provided for configuring folders based on FAT file system permissions. The **NTFS Permissions** option is used to configure folder access based on NTFS permissions. You may use either system to configure permissions for an object. When both share permissions and NTFS permissions are applied to the same share, there can be a conflict. When a conflict with permissions occurs, the most restrictive permission is always applied to the object. The following are a list of NTFS and share permissions for the Windows operating systems:

NTFS Permissions

- Full Control.
- Modify.
- Read & Execute.
- List Folder Contents.
- Read.
- Write.
- Special Permissions.

Share Permissions

- Full Control.
- Change.
- Read.

user-level security a type of security that requires a user to authenticate through a security database to access a share.

NTFS permissions permissions assigned to directories and files. These permissions are effective locally and over the network.

NTFS allows for user-level security. ***User-level security*** requires a user to authenticate through a security database to access a share. During authentication, user permissions are checked and access to the share is given accordingly. User-level security provides security to shares accessed over the network and locally.

User-level security permissions are commonly called *NTFS permissions* or just *permissions*. ***NTFS permissions*** can be applied to both the directory level and file level.

In Microsoft Server 2008, the Share and Storage Management tool has been added to allow you to set up shares and permissions for the network. This tool is accessed directly off the **Administrative Tools** menu as shown in **Figure 7-14.**

After selecting the **Share and Storage Management** menu item, a screen appears similar to the one in **Figure 7-15. Share and Storage Management** provides a centralized location for share and storage configuration and modification.

Share and Storage Management displays all shares and all storage areas available for the network. The dollar sign ($) symbol indicates shares and storage

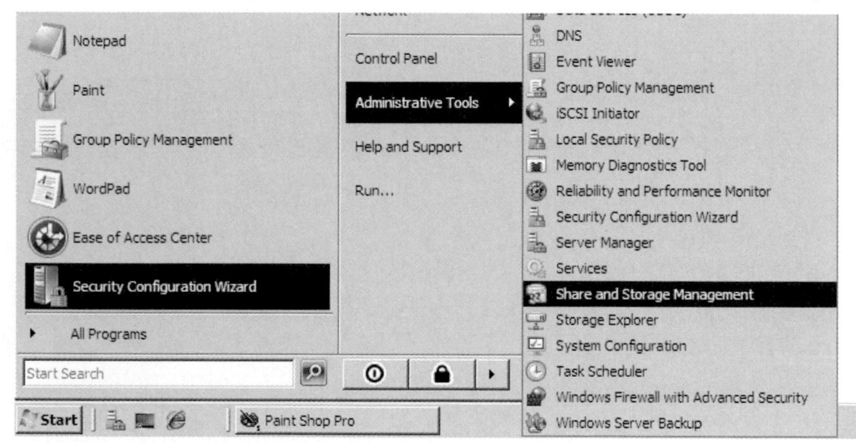

Figure 7-14. Shares and disk storage can be managed through Share and Storage Management.

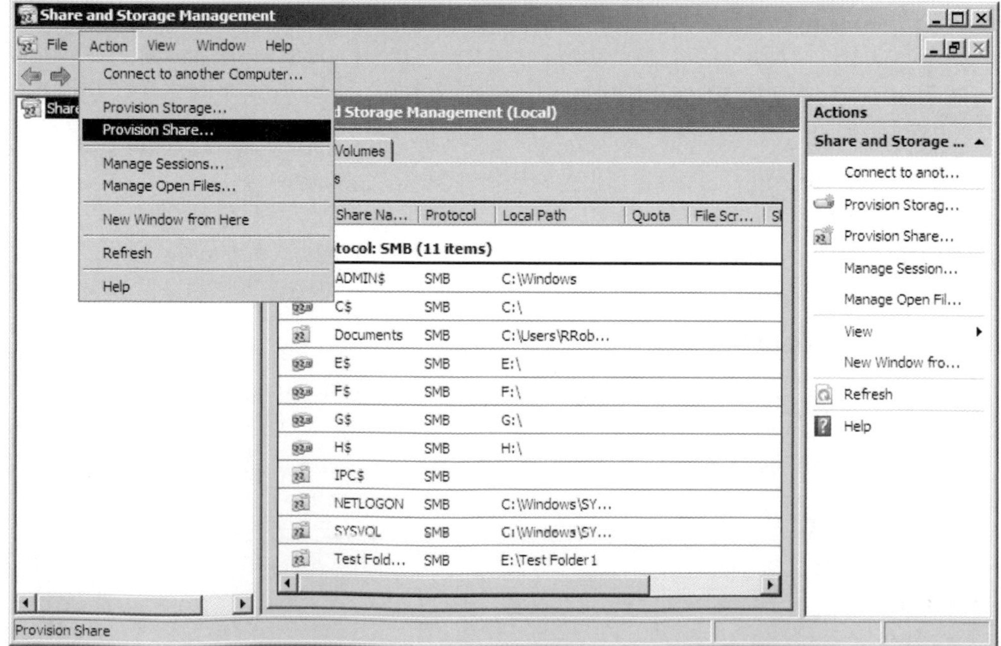

Figure 7-15. Share and Storage Management displays all shares and all storage areas available for the network.

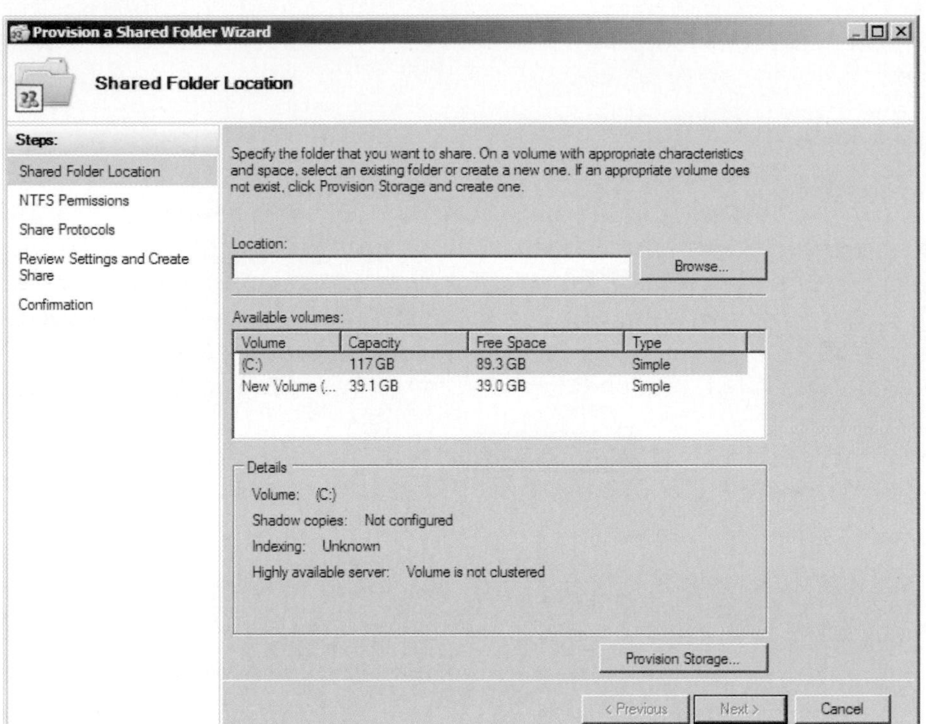

Figure 7-16.
The server provides a wizard to assist with creating a share.

controlled solely by the system administrator. You can create a new share by selecting the **Provision Share** located in the **Action** menu, Figure 7-15. Once **Provision Share** is selected, a wizard will open with a dialog box similar to the one in **Figure 7-16.**

The Provision a Shared Folder Wizard will guide the administrator through a series of dialog boxes that will automatically configure a new folder share or modify an existing share. You will be able to select features such as who can access the folder and what permissions to assign to the folder. You can also limit the number of users who can access the folder at one time. The wizard provides a foolproof method of creating a shared folder so that no aspect of a proper share creation is left out. The wizard can create shares not only on the server but also anywhere in the entire network domain.

Although both share permissions and NTFS permissions can be applied to a share, it is best to set only the NTFS permissions and to leave the share permissions set to their default. Working with both types of permissions is unnecessary and only complicates administration.

Administrative Tools

Administrative tools are designed to make network administration easy and convenient. Some of the tasks administrative tools allow the administrator to view logs, manage the domain, manage users and groups, configure the server, set security policies, and add and manage services. Windows Server provides a wide variety of administrative tools located directly off the **Start** menu, **Figure 7-17.** Some of the most commonly used administrative tools are Active Directory User and Computers, Computer Management, Event Viewer, and Share and Storage Management.

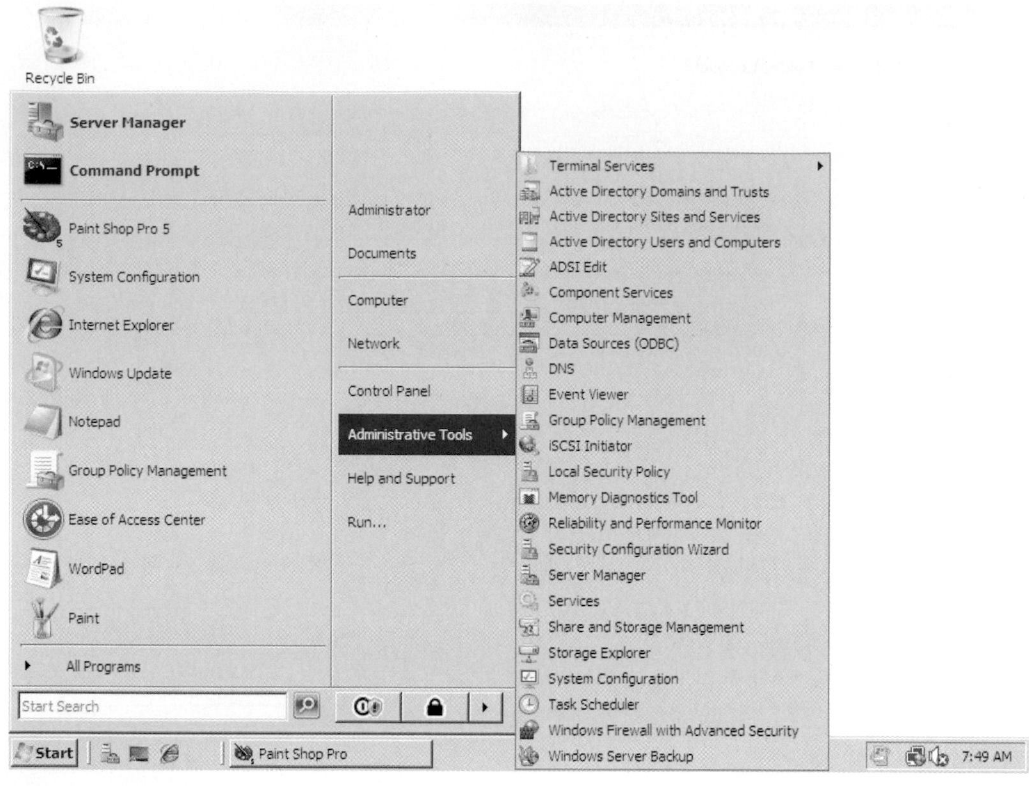

Figure 7-17.
Windows Server 2008 provides a wide variety of Administrative Tools located directly off the **Start** menu.

Note

The Active Directory tools will only appear as a menu item after the server is configured for Active Directory.

The Microsoft Management Console (MMC) is accessed by selecting **Computer Management** or running **MMC** in the **Start Search** box located at the bottom of the **Start** menu. MMC is an early version of an administrative tool that can be used to complete some of the most common administrative tasks in a centralized location. The MMC is covered in detail later in this chapter. You will find that the features of many of these administrative tools are very similar to administrative tools found in a typical Windows desktop operating system such as Windows Vista or Windows 7.

You have just received a very brief overview of some of the capabilities of the Microsoft network operating systems. The following sections explore Windows Server in more detail.

Active Directory (AD)
the Windows Server standard used to manage large and small network systems. It uses a hierarchical directory structure that is designed as a database containing information about objects belonging to the entire network.

object
any physical or logical unit that is defined as part of the network.

Active Directory Domain Services

Microsoft introduced Active Directory with the introduction of Windows Server 2000. Active Directory features vastly improved the way network systems shared information. Today, ***Active Directory (AD)*** is the Windows Server standard used to manage large and small network systems. It uses a hierarchical directory structure that is designed as a database containing information about objects belonging to the entire network. In the Active Directory environment, an ***object*** is any physical or logical unit that is defined as part of the network. Some examples of objects are users, groups, printers, volumes, directories, and services. Active Directory stores information about each object in its database. For example, for a user object, Active Directory stores information such as user name, password, permissions, and restrictions.

Starting with Windows Server 2008, Active Directory is referred to as *Active Directory Domain Services (AD DS)*.

AD is not installed by default when installing the server operating system. It is configured as a server role after the server operating system is installed.

Active Directory uses Lightweight Directory Access Protocol (LDAP) as well as Hypertext Transfer Protocol (HTTP) to transmit directory information between domain controllers. Both LDAP and HTTP are Internet standard protocols. LDAP allows the exchange of directory information between different computer platforms. For example, a server running Windows Server can freely exchange directory information with a Novell NetWare or UNIX/Linux server as long as both use LDAP. HTTP is the protocol used on the Internet that determines how Web pages are displayed. HTTP is used to display directory information across the network in a form of a Web page. Later in the textbook, you will see the striking similarity of the Active Directory structure and the Novell SUSE Linux directory structure. This is because both are based on LDAP technology.

Do not confuse HTTP with HTML. HTML is a hypertext markup language, which is an authoring language used to create documents that appear as Web pages. It is not a protocol.

Active Directory Structure

The Active Directory is a hierarchical structure that consists of a forest, trees, domains, and organizational units (OUs), **Figure 7-18.** The definition and an introduction to each are presented briefly in this section. An in-depth knowledge

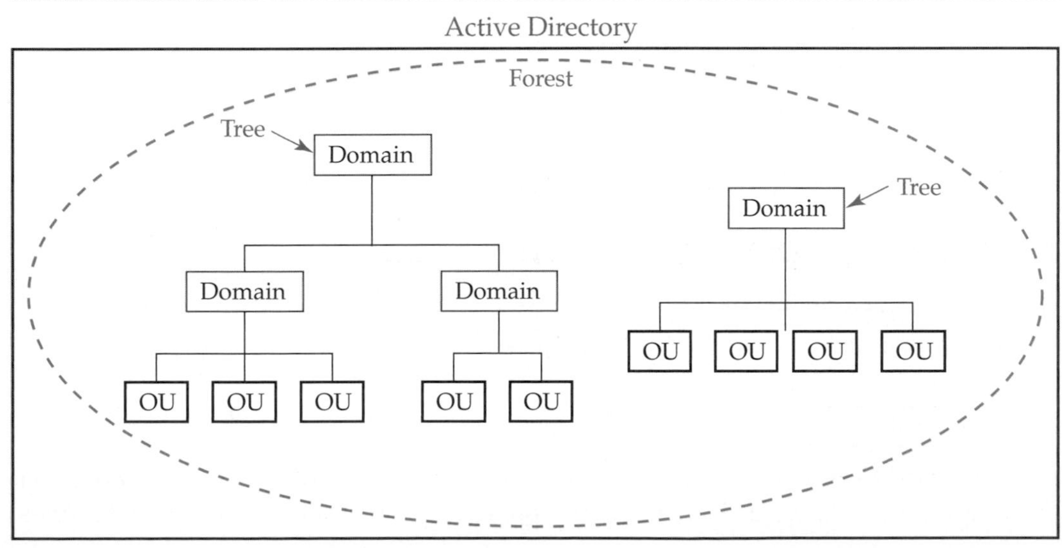

Figure 7-18. An Active Directory hierarchical structure consists of a forest, trees, domains, and organizational units.

of the Active Directory structure requires in-depth study and more information than can be presented here.

The hierarchical structure is designed like the Internet structure. Look at the **Figure 7-19.** Objects inside a hierarchical structure can be traced to a root, or root domain. Each object in the hierarchical structure is a part of the object above it.

Domains

As you've previously learned, a domain is a logical grouping of users and equipment as defined by the network administrator. Users and equipment, such as computers, are assigned to a domain for administrative purposes and security. A small company may use a single domain name for the entire business. A large company may divide the company into several distinct domains. For example, a company spanning the United States may divide the company into regions, such as San Francisco, New York, and Orlando. See **Figure 7-20.** The example consists of three distant locations connected via the Internet or a private line. Although each region is represented as a separate domain, it is set up to allow the free flow of data and communications between them. The flow of data and communications can also be restricted.

Tech Tip

The term *domain* as it is used here should not be confused with the term *domain* used in Internet terminology. The term *domain* when used in Internet terminology describes a collection of computers sharing an Internet name or address. A better understanding of the differences will become evident after reading Chapter 10—TCP/IP Fundamentals.

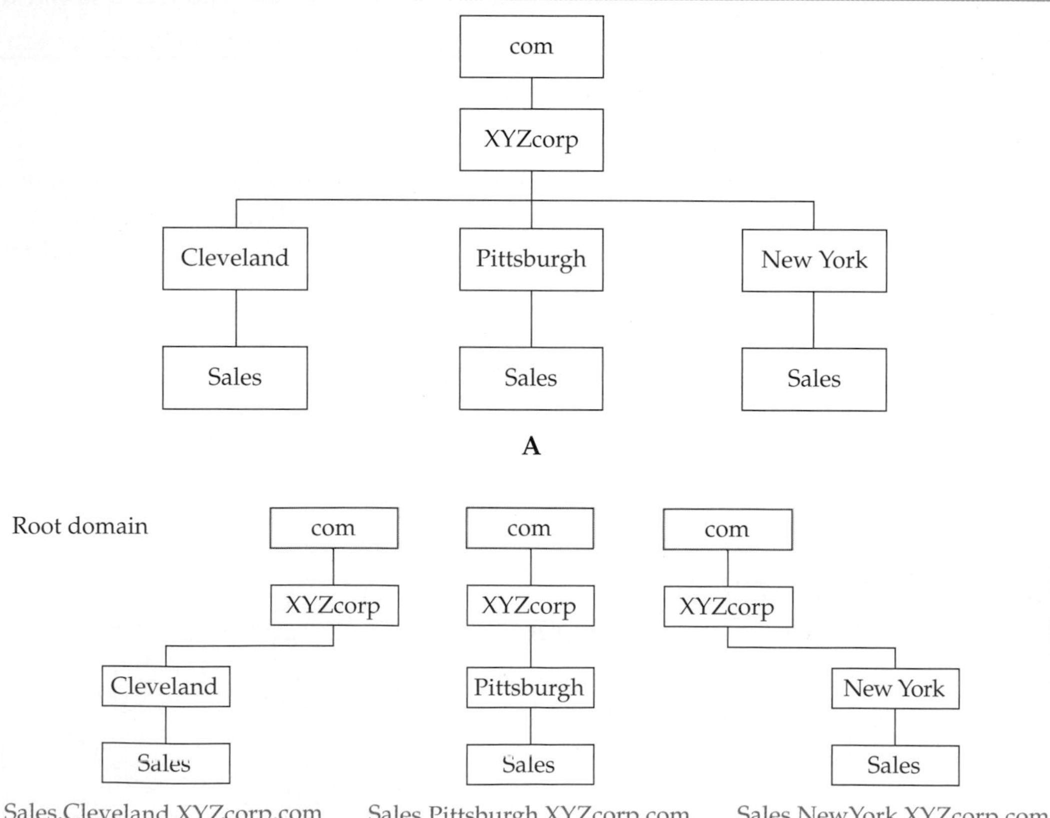

Figure 7-19. Internet domain structure. A—In an Internet domain structure, objects can be traced back to a root domain. The root domain in this example is com. B—The domain structure in this example has been broken into sections to illustrate how each object in the hierarchy belongs to the object above it.

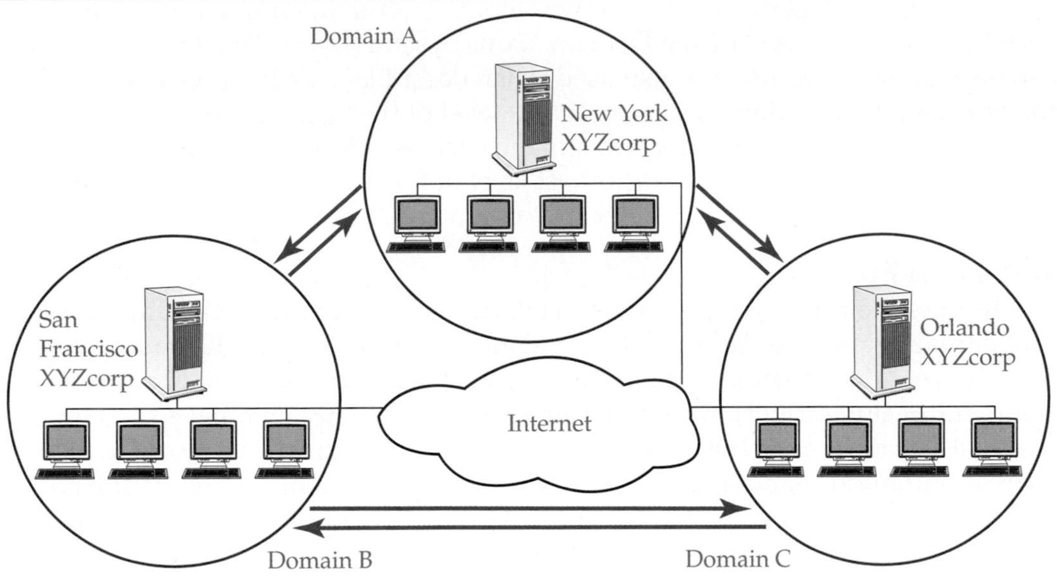

Figure 7-20.
The XYZcorp company has assigned each of its locations to a separate domain. The domains have been configured to allow the free flow of data between them.

Another scenario is the company illustrated in **Figure 7-21.** The company spans several distant locations yet is configured into a single domain. Typically, multiple domains are used to better organize a large company into logical working units such as research, sales, accounting, executive administration, and human resources. There is no one set method to arrange a domain structure. The size and arrangement of a domain structure design is left to the network engineer or administrator.

The members of the domain need not be physically located together. They are joined by using the same root domain name and having an account established in the domain.

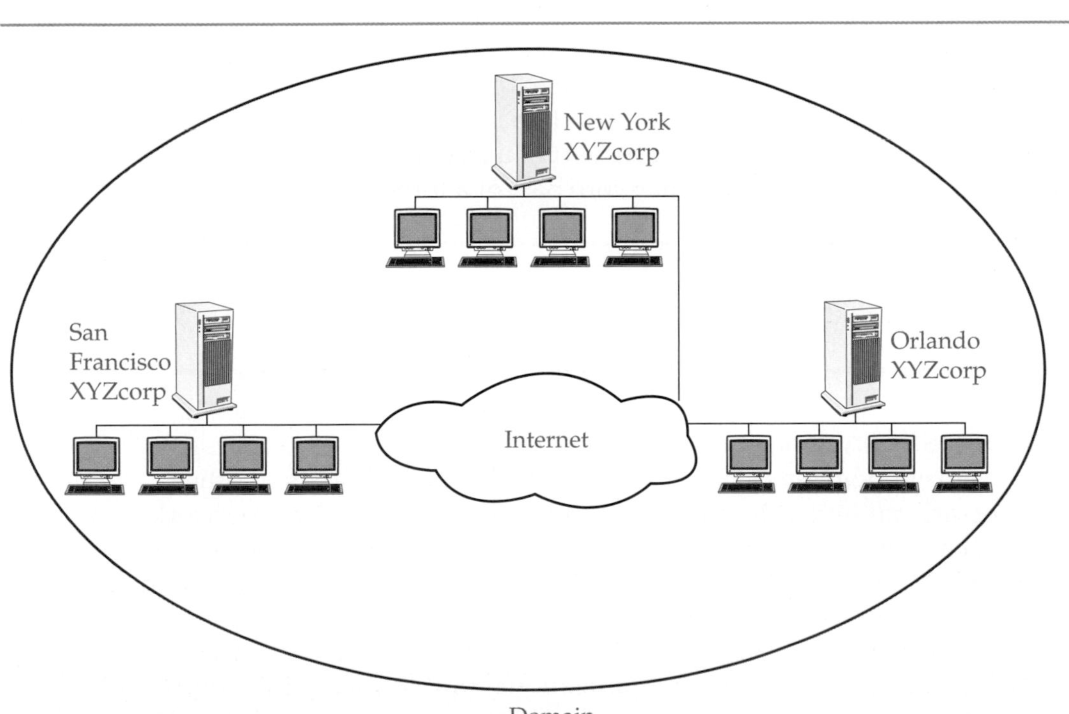

Figure 7-21.
A company may span several distant locations yet be configured as a single domain.

Typically, each domain in the Active Directory structure must conform to the naming convention used by the Domain Name System (DNS). The term *root domain* can be confusing because it is also used when describing the Internet structure. In the Internet, the root domain is the highest level of the organizational structure and is composed of a single dot and a name such as .edu and .com. In Active Directory, the root domain is the highest level of the organizational structure but consists of a name followed by a dot and a name such as XYZ.com.

tree
a collection of domains that share a common root domain name and Active Directory database.

forest
a collection of domain trees that share a common Active Directory database.

namespace
the label that identifies a unique location in a structure such as the Internet.

contiguous namespace
a namespace in which the location must use the root domain name as part of its URL or as its complete name.

disjointed namespace
a domain name that is a part of the Active Directory, but does not follow the contiguous namespace requirement.

Trees and Forests

In the simplest of terms, a ***tree*** is a collection of domains that share a common root domain name and Active Directory database. A ***forest*** is a collection of domain trees that share a common Active Directory database. The definitions are very similar, but the most important trait that distinguishes whether a domain is part of a tree or forest is the domain name. For a domain to belong to a tree it must share a contiguous namespace. A forest is a collection of domain trees that have a disjointed namespace. To better understand these definitions lets look at the terms *namespace, contiguous namespace,* and *disjointed namespace.*

A ***namespace*** is the label that identifies a unique location in a structure such as the Internet. The uniform resource locator (URL) standard uses a namespace to identify locations on the Internet. For an object or location to conform to a ***contiguous namespace*** standard, the location must use the root domain name as part of its URL or as its complete name. For example, the root domain name in an Active Directory structure is G-W.com. For a domain in the Active Directory to have a contiguous namespace with G-W.com, the G-W.com must be part of its domain name, for example, Chicago.G-W.com. Any domain name that is a part of the Active Directory, but does not follow the contiguous namespace requirement is considered a ***disjointed namespace.*** A disjointed namespace occurs commonly when two networks are merged or an existing network is upgraded using Windows 2000 Active Directory. When two organizations or companies merge, it is unlikely that they will have a contiguous namespace. Look at **Figure 7-22.**

In the illustration, you can see three domains with a contiguous namespace: Chicago.XYZcorp.com, Dallas. XYZcorp.com, and NewYork.XYZcorp.com. These three are in contrast to the other domain name, Chicago.DEFcorp.com, which has a different root domain name. The root domain name is the determining factor that distinguishes whether a domain is part of a tree or forest. Chicago.DEF.com is a disjointed namespace and is therefore part of a forest.

Tech Tip

Forest and tree definitions came after the original NT domain structure. Because of the radical changes, an existing NT domain may not meet the criteria to belong to a tree.

organizational unit
a container that holds objects or other organizational units and is used to organize a network into manageable units.

Organizational Unit

An ***organizational unit*** is a container that holds objects or other organizational units. Organizational units serve to organize a network into manageable units and often model a company's business structure. Look at **Figure 7-23.** A tree with a root domain name of XYZcorp.com has a domain named Chicago. This domain has an organizational unit for each department in the Chicago office. The Chicago.XYZcorp.com domain has an *Accounting, Administration,* and *Warehouse* organizational unit. Each organizational unit contains objects that belong to each department. An object in Active Directory

Figure 7-22.
Example of a contiguous namespace and a disjointed namespace. Domains that share a contiguous namespace have a common root domain name. A disjointed namespace does not share a common root domain with the other domains in the Active Directory. A disjointed namespace in an Active Directory indicates that the domains within it are a part of a forest.

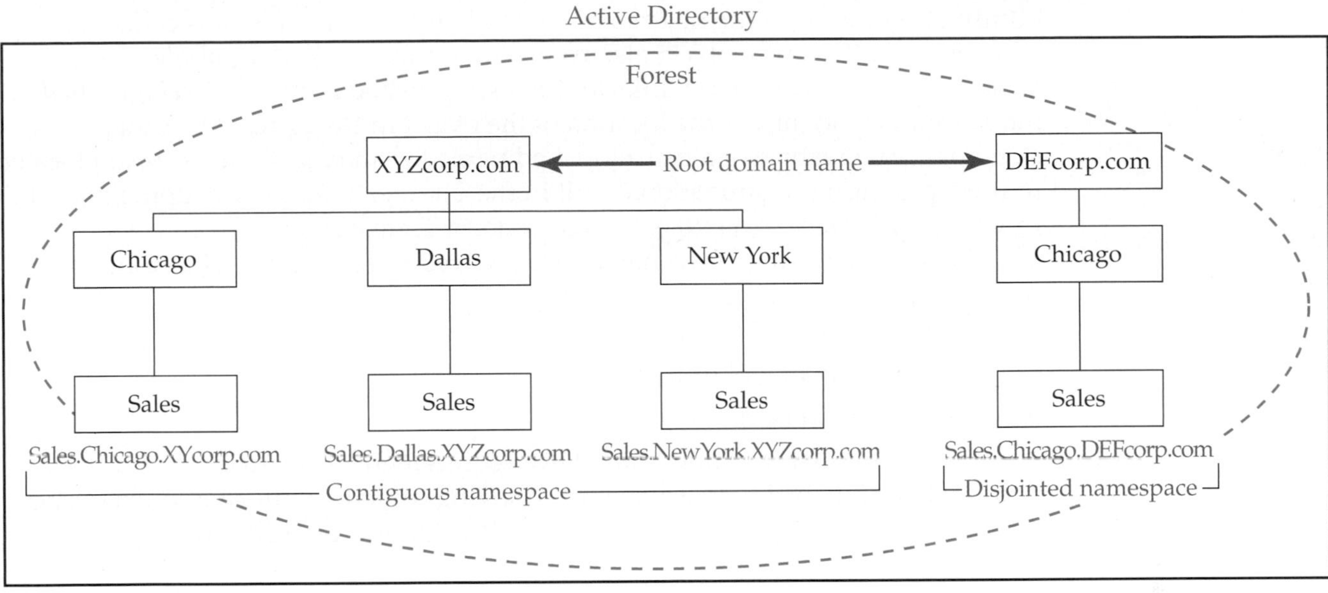

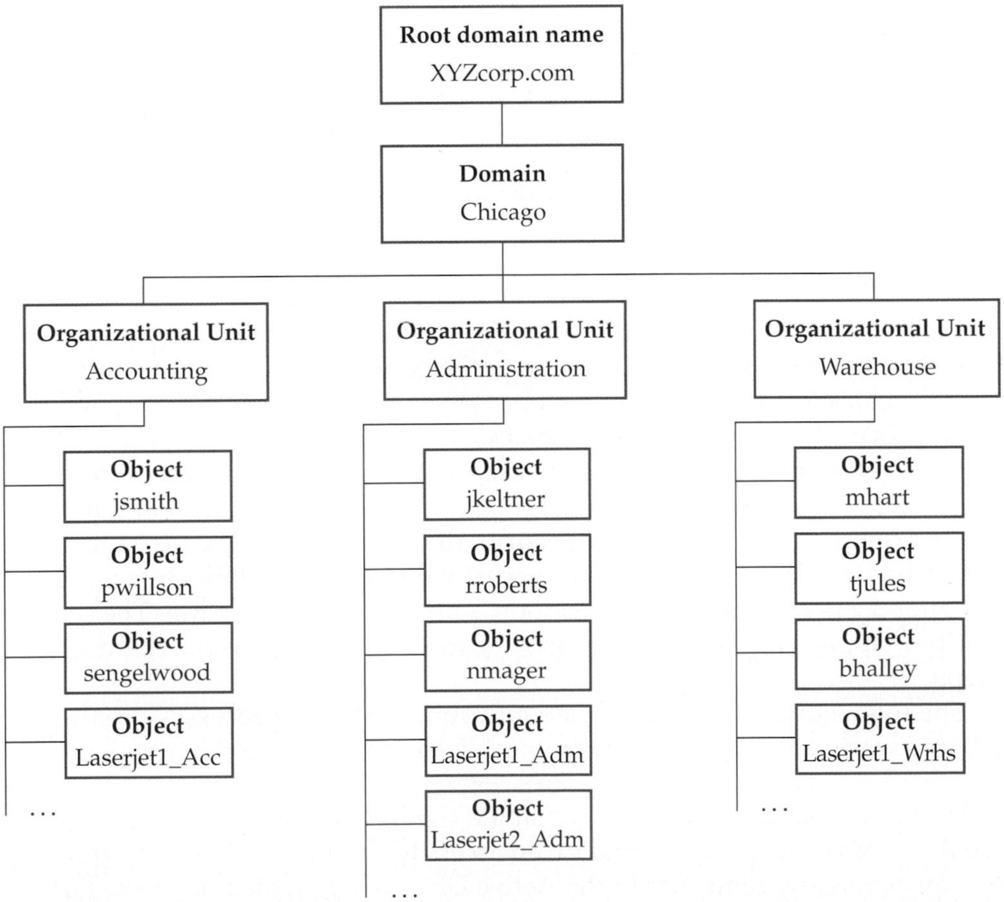

Root domain name
XYZcorp.com

Domain
Chicago

Organizational Unit
Accounting

Object jsmith
Object pwillson
Object sengelwood
Object Laserjet1_Acc
...

Organizational Unit
Administration

Object jkeltner
Object rroberts
Object nmager
Object Laserjet1_Adm
Object Laserjet2_Adm
...

Organizational Unit
Warehouse

Object mhart
Object tjules
Object bhalley
Object Laserjet1_Wrhs
...

Figure 7-23.
Organizational units are used to organize a network into manageable units. An organizational unit can contain organizational units and objects. Examples of objects are users, groups, computers, and printers.

can be any component that is part of the network, such as users, groups, computers, and printers.

Common Name

When an administrator creates a new object in the directory, the administrator assigns the object a name to identify it. This name is called a *common name (CN)*. The object also receives a number called a *globally unique identifier (GUID)*. The GUID links to the distinguished name. A ***distinguished name*** uniquely identifies the location of the object in the Active Directory structure. An example of a distinguished name for an object named *jsmith* located in the Accounting organizational unit in the Chicago.XYZcorp.com domain would be CN=*jsmith*, OU=*Accounting*, DC=Chicago.XYZcorp.com.

distinguished name a naming system that uniquely identifies the location of the object in the Active Directory structure.

The letters in front of the names are referred to as *attributes*. The following list defines each attribute:

- DC=Domain component.
- OU=Organizational unit.
- CN=Common name.

The distinguished name is an LDAP requirement. The attributes are used to decode distinguished names when transferring directory information between two dissimilar network operating system directories. You will see a similar naming structure in Novell SUSE.

Network+ Note

Be careful when answering a question that contains the term *domain*. Look at the context in which the term *domain* is used. The term *domain* in a Windows NT network content refers to the network, not to the Internet domain. In a Windows 2000/2003/2008 network, the term *domain* means the network name and Internet domain name.

Authentication

In a Windows 2000/2003/2008 network, authentication occurs during two types of processes: when a user logs on to the network and when the user requests access to a resource. The first process is called *interactive logon*, and the second process is called *network authentication*.

During the ***interactive logon,*** the user is verified and given access to the Active Directory. When the user accesses a resource, the ***network authentication*** process occurs. In this process, the security descriptor of the resource the user wishes to access is checked. The security descriptor contains information regarding users and groups, permissions, auditing, and ownership. The security descriptor applies to objects in the Active Directory, such as resources, users, and groups.

interactive logon an authentication process in which the user is verified and given access to the Active Directory.

network authentication an authentication process that occurs when a user accesses a resource.

The interactive logon and the network authentication processes use the Kerberos version 5 authentication protocol. Kerberos is covered in detail in Chapter 15—Network Security.

Windows 2000/2003/2008 uses a single sign-on method. This means that once the user is authenticated and given access to the Active Directory, the user can access any computer in the Active Directory to which he or she has permission. The user does not have to log on again. Authentication occurs behind the scenes and is handled through the network authentication process.

AD Replication

Active Directory allows the use of more than one domain controller within a domain. The Active Directory database is replicated on all domain controllers within the domain so that each has the current status of all objects in the network. For example, if an administrator disables a user account, the information is instantly transmitted to all domain controllers in the domain.

Windows NT servers use a primary domain controller (PDC) and a backup domain controller (BDC). Microsoft servers today configured with Active Directory no longer use the earlier design of a PDC and BDC. Servers in a Microsoft Windows 2000/2003/2008 network can perform one of three roles: domain controller (DC), member server, and stand-alone server. The Windows 2000/2003/2008 environment uses a process called ***multimaster replication.*** In this model, all DCs are equal. Each DC stores a copy of the Active Directory database, **Figure 7-24.** Changes to the database can be made at any DC in the domain. When changes to the database are made, the changes are replicated to the other DCs.

multimaster replication
a type of security database replication in which all domain controllers store a copy of the Active Directory database. Changes to the database can be made at any DC in the domain. When changes to the database are made, the changes are replicated to the other domain controllers.

Windows Server 2008 introduced the Read Only Domain Controller (RODC) as an optional configuration. RODC is designed to be used in locations that are hard to secure or locations such as branch offices that do not have IT support administrators assigned on site. The intention of RODC is to prevent personnel from "tinkering" with the server, which could result in disabling the system or creating a security problem. The RODC has a read only Active Directory structure, and the DNS portion of the server cannot be modified. As an option, a person at the RODC location can be given very limited administrative privileges,

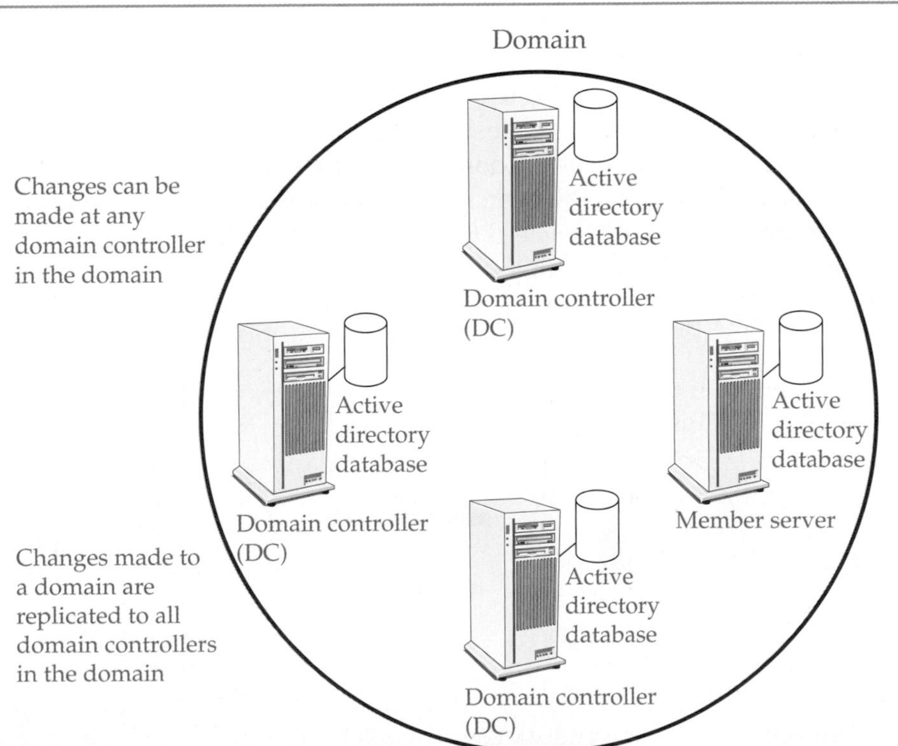

Figure 7-24. A Windows 2000/2003/2008 Active Directory can have multiple domain controllers. An administrator may make changes to the Active Directory at any of the domain controllers. Changes are replicated to every domain controller in the domain.

trust relationship
a relationship between domains, which allows users from one domain to access resources on another domain in which they do not have a user account. The user can then access resources on another domain without having to log on to that domain. The user, however, must have permissions to access the resources.

two-way trust relationship
a trust relationship in which both domains are designated as a trusted domain and a trusting domain. A two-way trust relationship allows both domains in the trust relationship to share its resources with the other.

one-way trust relationship
a trust relationship in which one domain is the trusted domain and the other is the trusting domain. The trusting domain allows the trusted

such as capabilities to install hardware drivers. User accounts at the RODC site cannot access other domain controllers at other locations. Also, users are not authenticated at the RODC. User authentication is performed through a regular domain controller at another site.

Windows Server 2008 uses a Primary Domain Controller Emulator to ensure backward compatibility with Windows NT, 2000, and 2003. The Primary Domain Controller Emulator provides the same function as the earlier PDC. When there are multiple servers in a domain providing similar services such as user logon service, there is still only one PDC emulator which is the ultimate authority for user account security. For example, when a user password is updated on one of the servers, it is automatically sent to the designated master PDC Emulator server. The master PDC Emulator is responsible for distributing up-to-date and accurate information to the other servers.

Trusts Relationships

To allow the free flow of data and communications between domains, a trust relationship between the domains must be established. A ***trust relationship*** is a relationship between domains that allows users from one domain to access resources on another domain in which they do not have a user account. The user can then access resources on another domain without having to log on to that domain. The user, however, must have permissions to access the resources.

A trust relationship can be set up to allow domains to have a two-way trust relationship or a one-way trust relationship. In a ***two-way trust relationship*** both domains are designated as a *trusted domain* and a *trusting domain*. A two-way trust relationship allows both domains in the trust relationship to share its resources with the other. A two-way trust relationship is sometimes referred to as a *full-trust relationship*. **Figure 7-25** shows an example of a two-way trust relationship. *Domain A* trusts *Domain B* and allows *Domain B* to access its resources. *Domain B* trusts *Domain A* and allows *Domain A* to access its resources.

In a ***one-way trust relationship***, one domain is the trusted domain and the other is the trusting domain. The trusting domain allows the trusted domain to access its resources. Look at **Figure 7-26.** A one-way trust relationship has been established. *Domain B* has been designated the trusting domain and *Domain A* has been designated the trusted domain. In other words, *Domain B* trusts *Domain A* to access its resources. However, since a one-way trust has been established, *Domain A* does not trust *Domain B* to access its resources.

Two-way trust relationships can be implemented to develop a complex trust relationship. A ***complex trust relationship*** is a trust relationship in which more

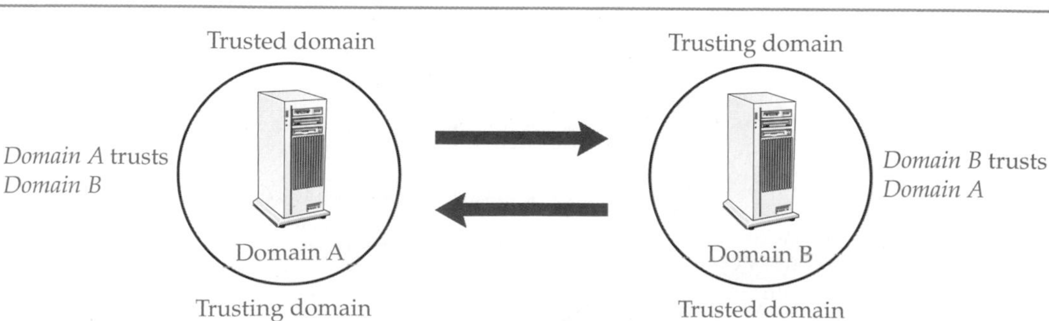

Figure 7-25.
This is an example of a two-way trust relationship established between two domains. Each domain can access resources on the other domain.

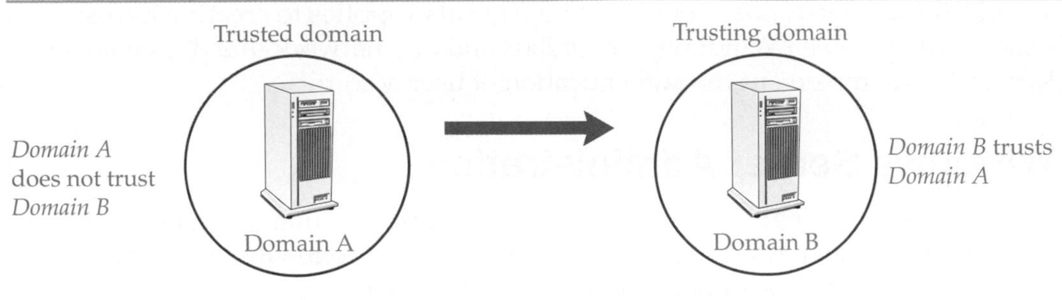

Figure 7-26.
In a one-way trust relationship, a domain may access resources on another domain even though there is no user account established on the other domain. The trust honors the logon authentication of the domain the user is in.

than two domains have a full-trust relationship. Look at **Figure 7-27.** Notice that a two-way trust relationship is established between all three domains. Trust relationships can also be formed between forests in addition to domains.

Forest Trusts

When you create a new domain in the same forest, you automatically create a two-way trust. A ***forest trust*** is a two-way trust and is designed to share resources between the two forests. In a forest trust, users can be authenticated in either forest.

External Trusts

An ***external trust*** is created when Windows Server 2008 configures a trust relationship with an older Windows Server operating system or with another Windows Server 2008 computer or when the other domain is located in an entirely separate forest. The two forests are not joined in an external trust relationship.

Realm Trusts

A ***realm trust*** is formed when you create a trust relationship between a Windows Server 2008 domain and a non-Windows domain. For example, when you wish to establish a trust relationship between Windows Server 2008 and

domain to access its resources, but the trusted domain does not allow the trusting domain to access it resources.

complex trust relationship
a trust relationship in which more than two domains have a full-trust relationship.

forest trust
a two-way trust that is designed to share resources between the two forests. In a forest trust, users can be authenticated in either forest.

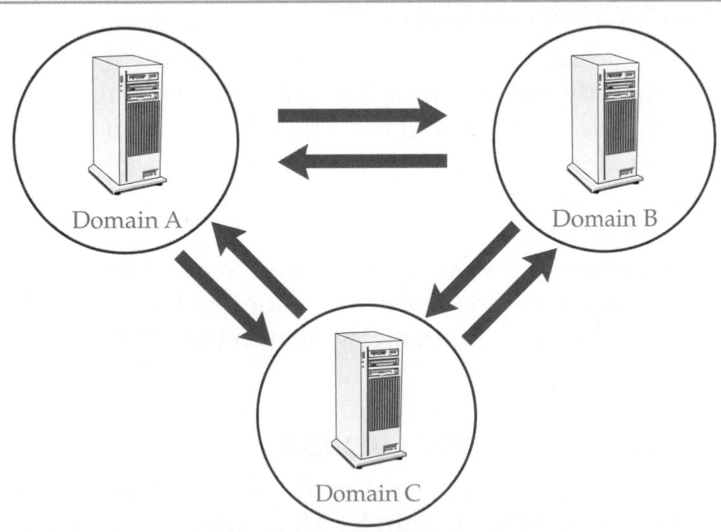

Figure 7-27.
An example of a complex trust relationship. You can think of a complex trust relationship as two-way trusts established between all domains in the configuration.

external trust
a trust relationship between Windows Server 2008 and an older server operating system or with another Windows Server 2008 computer or when the other domain is located in an entirely separate forest. The two forests are not joined in a trust relationship.

realm trust
a trust relationship between a Windows Server 2008 domain and a non-Windows domain.

a UNIX/Linux network system. A realm trust also applies to creating a trust relationship between Windows Server 2008 and any network that does not use Kerberos 5 to implement the authentication of user accounts.

Windows Server Administration

Windows server administration includes utilities for managing objects in the Active Directory and setting security policies. The following is a table of the utilities covered in this section and a description of each:

Utility	Description
Computer Management	Allows an administrator to add local users to a Windows server.
Active Directory Users and Computers	Allows an administrator to manage users, groups, computers, and OUs in the Active Directory.
Local Security Policy	Allows an administrator to set global security policies for a single computer.
Domain Security Policy	Allows an administrator to set global security policies for the entire domain.
Disk Management	Allows an administrator to manage a server's hard disk drives.

These utilities can be accessed individually or through the Microsoft Management Console (MMC). The MMC was first introduced with Windows 2000.

Note

Beginning with Windows Server 2008, the Domain Security Policy utility was modified and renamed *Group Policy Management Console.*

Microsoft Management Console

Windows 2000 and later uses the Microsoft Management Console (MMC) as an interface to commonly used utilities. The MMC can be used on any Microsoft system including Windows 95, 98, and NT. The MMC is not a utility itself, but rather a container that holds commonly used utilities. It is set up as a customized Windows interface. It is empty by default and allows the user to select utilities from one convenient location.

snap-in
a tool or utility that is added to the Microsoft Management Console (MMC).

A utility that is added to the MMC is referred to as a ***snap-in.*** **Figure 7-28** shows some of the many snap-ins that can be added to the MMC. When the snap-ins are selected, they are automatically sent to the MMC. **Figure 7-29** shows a customized MMC.

Managing Local Users and Groups

Local users and groups are managed on the server by using the Computer Management utility or the MMC Computer Management snap-in. To add a new user, right-click the **Users** folder in the left-hand pane of the Computer Management window or the MMC. Select **New User** from the shortcut menu. The **New User** dialog box displays, **Figure 7-30.** Complete the requested information.

You cannot create a local user account on a domain controller or view local user accounts on a server that has been promoted to domain controller status.

You may select a password option from the options beneath the **Confirm Password** text box or leave it set to the default. The default is set to the **User Must Change Password at Next Logon** option. This option means that the user needs to change his or her password when he or she logs on to the system the first time. When the user completes the logon, he or she will be prompted to change the password. The administrator will not know the user's password after the user changes it. As you can see, security starts with the user password and can be very strict.

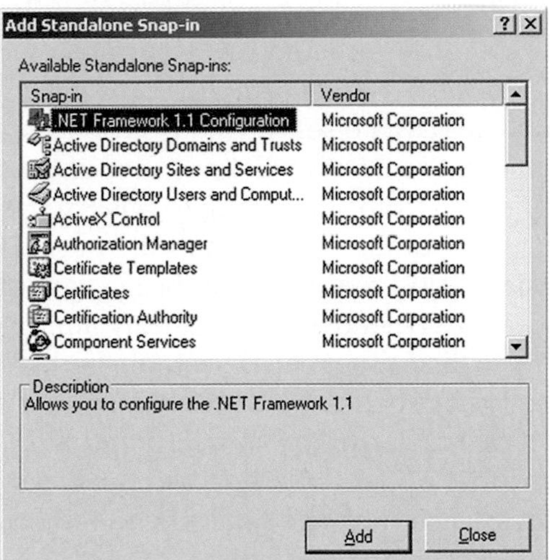

Figure 7-28. List of snap-ins that can be added to the Microsoft Management Console (MMC) in Windows Server 2003.

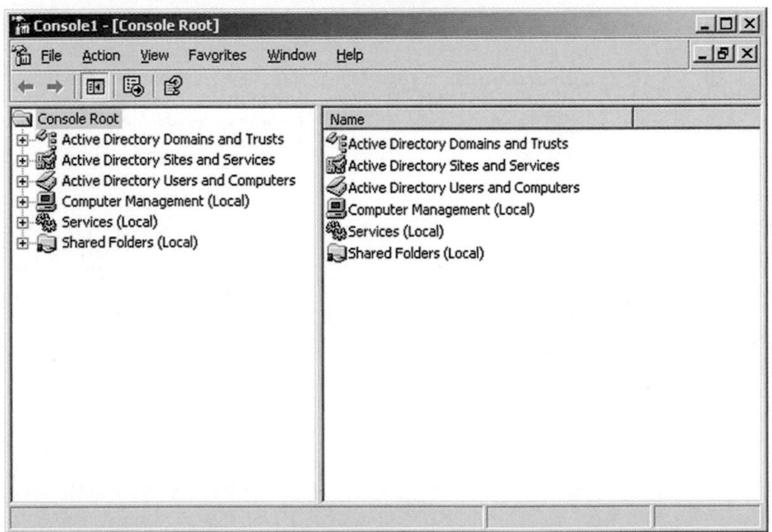

Figure 7-29. Example of a customized MMC.

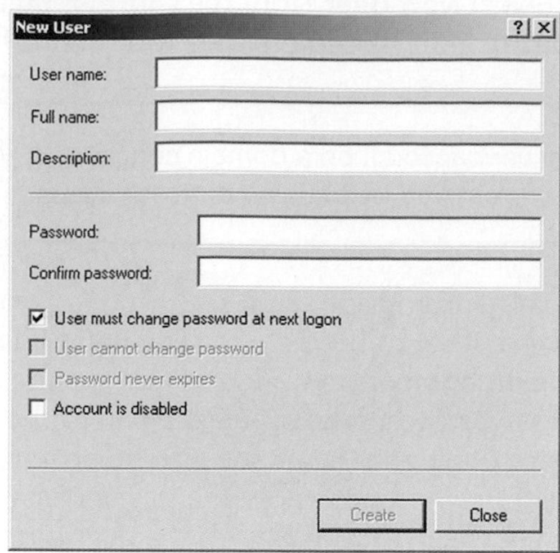

Figure 7-30. The Windows 2000 **New User** dialog box for adding local users.

Adding more restrictions to passwords can further enhance security. This can be accomplished in the Local Security Policy utility. Various policies can be set to increase password security, such as keeping a history of the user's password to prevent reuse, specifying a minimum and maximum password length, and forcing the user to select a password that meets complexity requirements.

Account lockout policies can be set that cause the user account to be locked if the user incorrectly enters the password a number of times, **Figure 7-31.** This prevents unauthorized persons from attempting to guess a user's password. Lockout times can be set to last a few minutes to an indefinite period of time. A lockout time that is set for an indefinite period requires that the system administrator unlock the account. This explanation is a brief overview of how a user account can be set up and some of the security policies that can be established.

You can add groups by right-clicking the **Groups** folder and selecting **New Group** from the shortcut menu. When the **New Group** dialog box displays, enter a group name and a description. To add members to the group, click **Add**. The **Select Users** dialog box displays. Click **Advanced** and then **Find Now**. You can select

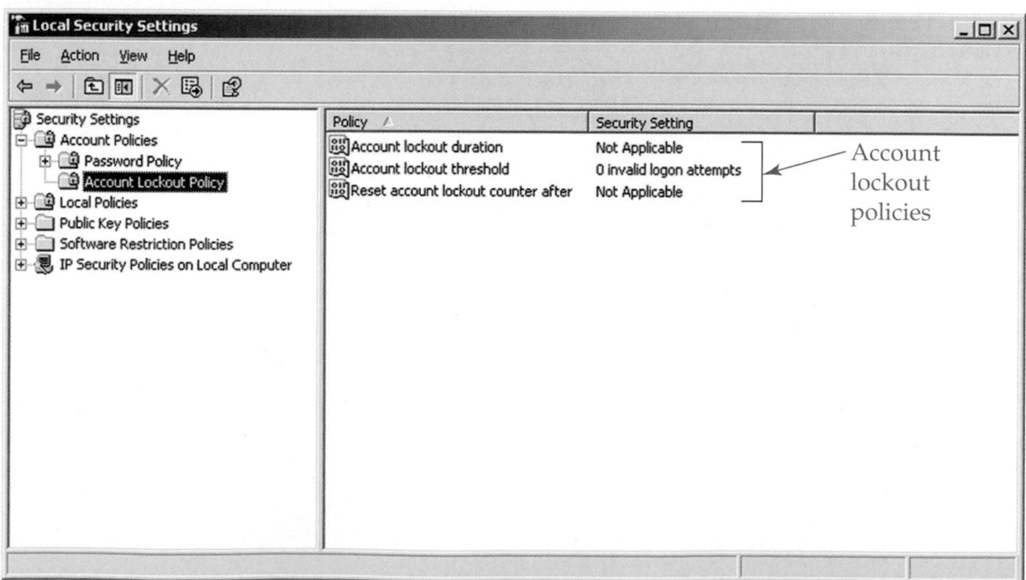

Figure 7-31. Account lockout policy settings.

multiple users by holding down the [Ctrl] key as you click each user's name. After you have selected the desired users, click **OK**. Click **OK** again to close the **Select Users** dialog box. In the **New Group** dialog box, click **Create** and then click **Close**.

Tech Tip

Network security has become such an issue in networking and e-commerce that it has created the demand for highly-trained specialists. If you wish to become a certified network administrator you must learn everything there is about a particular network operating system's security.

Managing Domain Users and Groups

Domain users and groups are accounts that are members of a domain. Domain user and group accounts can only be created at a server that is a domain controller. The Active Directory Users and Computers utility is used to add user accounts and group accounts to the domain.

To add a user to the domain, open the Active Directory Users and Computers utility. Right-click the container you wish to add the user to and select **New | User** from the shortcut menu. The **New Object—User** dialog box displays, **Figure 7-32.** Enter the user's first, middle, and last name in the appropriate text boxes, Figure 7-32A. The **Full name** text box automatically fills in as you enter this information. Enter a

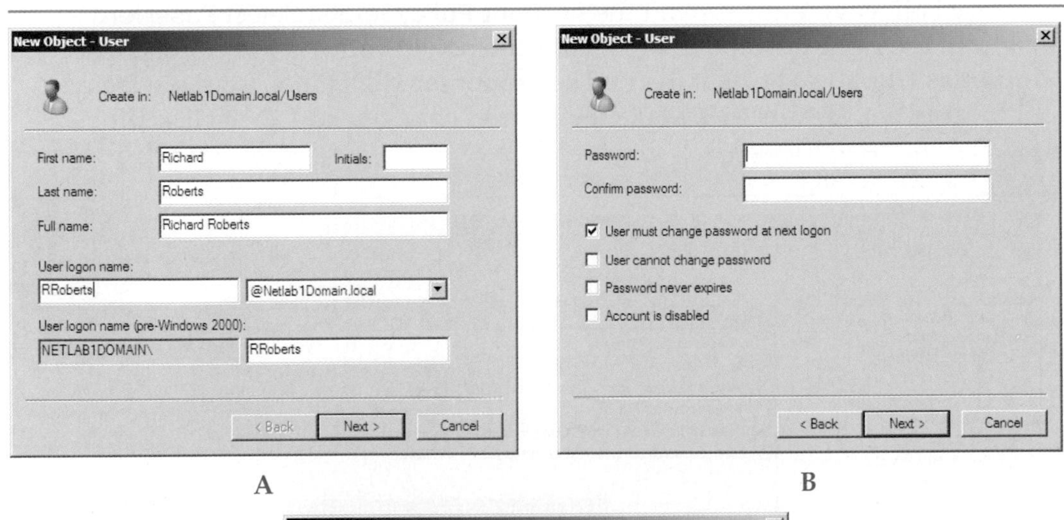

Figure 7-32. The **New Object—User** dialog box in the Active Directory Users and Computers utility. A—The user's full name is automatically entered when the first and last name and middle initial are entered. B—Enter and confirm the user account password and select password options. C—Review the new user account settings and click **Finish** if the settings are correct.

logon name and then click **Next**. Enter a password in the **Password** and **Confirm Password** text boxes, Figure 7-32B. Change the password options to reflect the security policies set for the network. Click **Next** and review the account settings, Figure 7-32C. Click **Finish** if the settings are correct. Otherwise, click **Back** to review and change the settings in the previous screens.

To add a group to the domain, open the Active Directory Users and Computers utility. Right-click the container you wish to add the group to and select **New | Group** from the shortcut menu. The **New Object—Group** dialog box will display. Enter the name of the group in the **Group name** text box. The **Group name (pre-Windows 2000)** text box will be completed automatically with this name. Leave the **Group scope** and **Group type** options at their default settings. To learn more about these options, see **Help and Support** located in the server's **Start** menu.

Password restrictions and account policies for a domain can be further enhanced through the Domain Security Policy utility. This utility provides the same policies as the Local Security Policy utility.

Note

Microsoft modified and renamed the Domain Security Policy utility to *Group Policy Management Console* beginning with Windows Server 2008.

To modify the password and account lockout policy settings for the domain, open the Domain Security Policy utility. In the left-hand pane of the Domain Security Policy window, expand the **Account Policy** folder. Select **Password Policy**. In the right-hand pane, right-click the policy you wish to modify. Select **Properties** from the shortcut menu. The **Properties** dialog box for the selected policy displays, **Figure 7-33.** Make the desired changes, and then click **OK**.

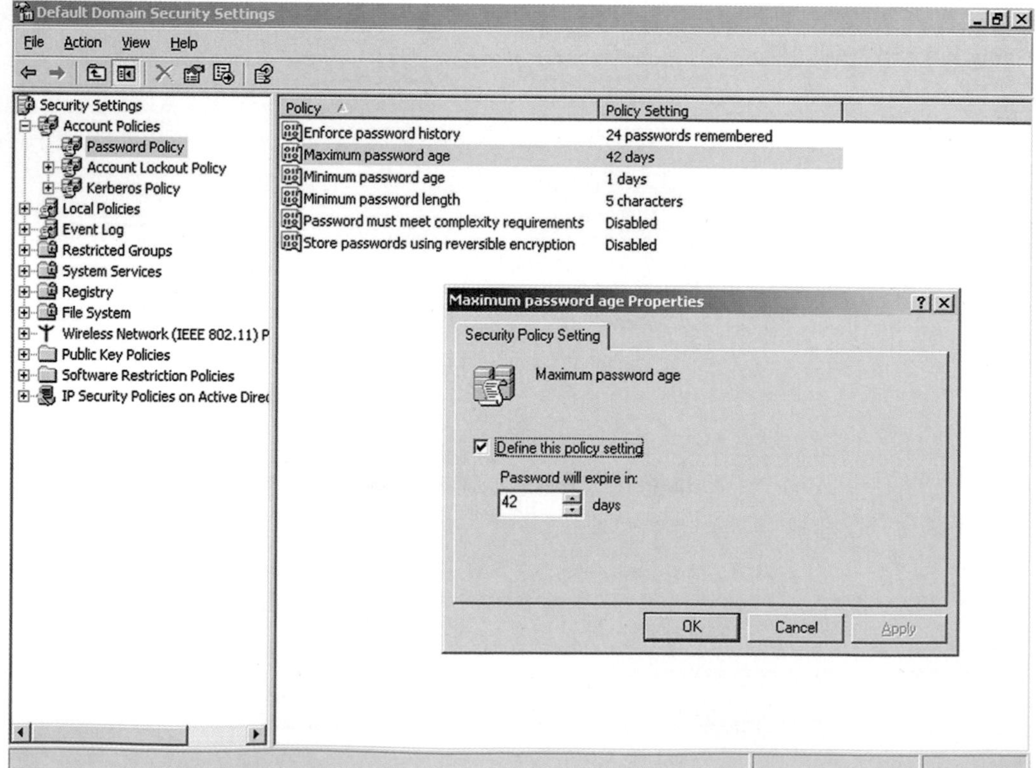

Figure 7-33. Password policies are modified by right-clicking the password policy, selecting **Properties** from the shortcut menu, and entering the changes.

Windows Disk Management

The Disk Management utility is used to create partitions and volumes, format volumes, and to add fault tolerance. Windows Server is installed on an NTFS partition. It also supports older file systems such as FAT16 and FAT32; however, these file systems are no longer options for installing a modern Windows server operating system.

physical drive
the hard disk drive that is inside the computer.

Windows 2000 Server and Windows Server 2003 can be installed on a FAT16, FAT32, and NTFS partition. An NTFS partition offers the highest level of security.

Disk Management Terminology

Some terminology you should be familiar with when working with the Disk Management utility is *physical drive, free space, partition, primary partition, extended partition, logical drive, volume,* and *volume set.* The ***physical drive*** is the hard disk drive that is inside the computer. The computer BIOS assigns a number to each physical drive in the computer. This number is displayed in Disk Management as *Disk 0, Disk 1,* and so on. See **Figure 7-34.** Displaying the disk number aids the administrator in properly identifying the hard disk drive before making changes to it.

Free space is the space on a hard disk drive that has not been partitioned. A ***partition*** is an area of the hard disk drive that is to be allocated to an operating system. When a hard disk drive is partitioned, it is assigned a drive letter and becomes a ***logical drive.*** This term makes sense when you think that a hard disk drive can be divided into multiple partitions and assigned a separate drive letter.

A hard disk drive may contain up to four primary partitions, **Figure 7-35.** A ***primary partition*** is a partition that stores a bootable copy of an operating

free space
the space on a hard disk drive that has not been partitioned.

partition
an area of the hard disk drive that is to be allocated to an operating system.

logical drive
a partition on a hard disk drive that is assigned a drive letter.

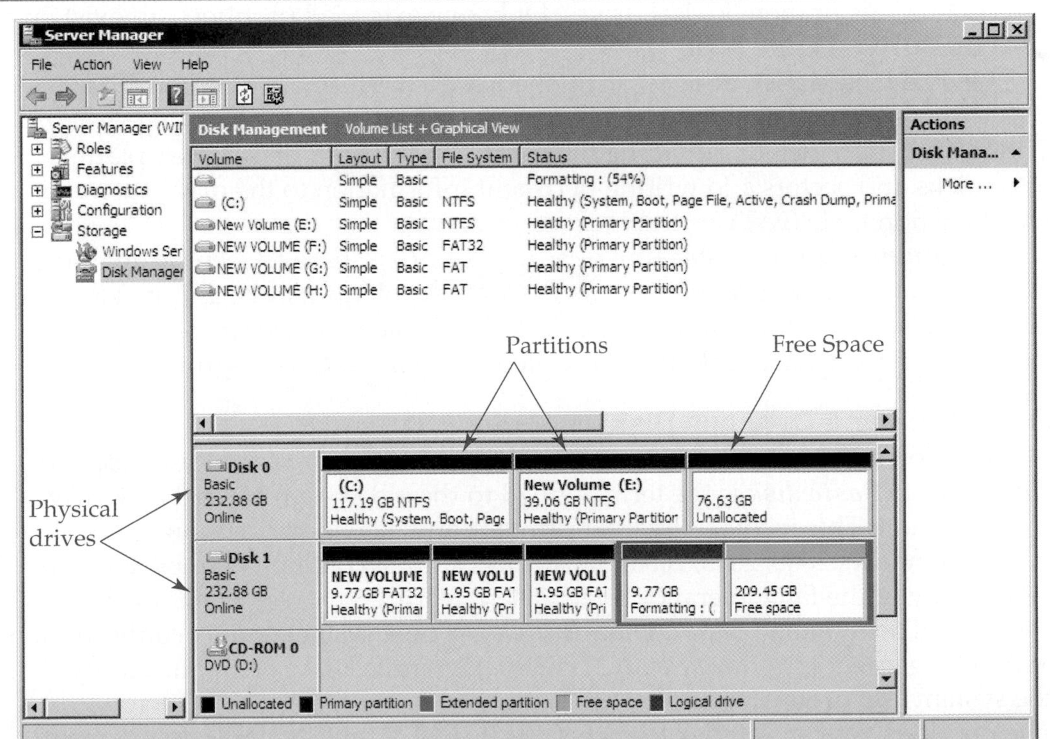

Figure 7-34. The Disk Management utility. Notice that colors are used to identify unallocated space, primary partition, extended partition, free space, and the logical drive.

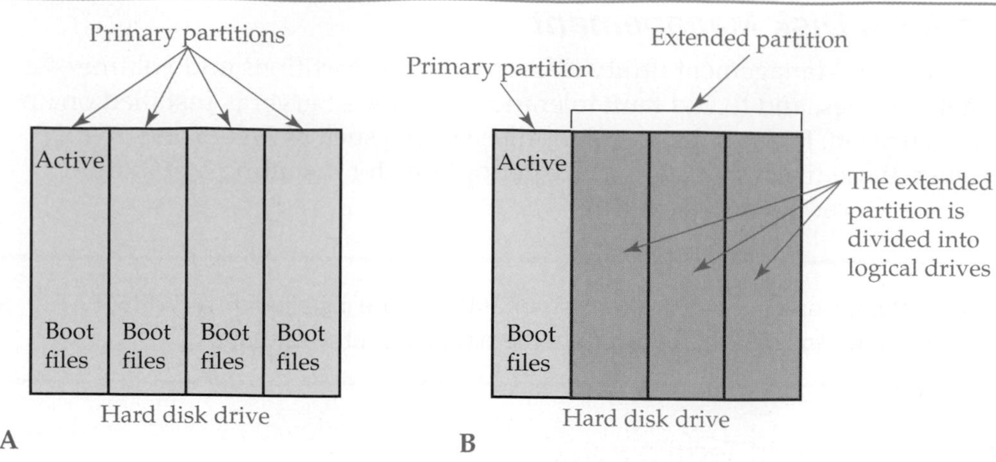

Figure 7-35. Hard disk drive partition configurations. A—A hard disk drive may contain up to four primary partitions. A primary partition contains an operating system's boot files. Only one primary partition on a hard disk drive may be marked active. B—A hard disk drive may contain only one extended partition. An extended partition is not assigned a drive letter. It is instead divided into logical drives, which are assigned drive letters.

primary partition
a partition that stores a bootable copy of an operating system. Four primary partitions, or bootable partitions, may exist on a single hard disk drive, but only one primary partition can be active at a time.

extended partition
a partition that can contain one or more logical drives. Only one extended partition can exist on a hard disk drive.

volume
an accessible unit of hard disk drive space as seen through the Windows interface, such as in Windows Explorer. A volume may be assigned a single drive letter yet contain multiple partitions.

system. Although four primary partitions, or bootable partitions, may exist on a single hard disk drive, only one primary partition can be active at a time, Figure 7-35A.

An administrator may want to store an operating system's boot files and system files on the primary partition and create an extended partition with logical drives on which to store data. An ***extended partition*** is a partition that can contain one or more logical drives. Only one extended partition can exist on a hard disk drive, Figure 7-35B.

Once the hard disk drive is partitioned, it can be formatted. When a hard disk drive is formatted, it is physically prepared to receive an operating system. This preparation includes dividing the surface of the hard disk drive's platters into tracks and sectors and writing pertinent information to the drive such as a file allocation table (FAT).

A ***volume*** is an accessible unit of hard disk drive space as seen through the Windows interface, such as in Windows Explorer. A volume may be assigned a single drive letter yet contain multiple partitions. A volume that consists of partitions from two or more hard disk drives is called a ***volume set.*** See **Figure 7-36.**

Basic Disk and Dynamic Disk

Windows 2000 introduced two new disk management terms: *basic disk* and *dynamic disk*. ***Basic disk*** is the term applied to the old system of hard disk drive configuration. This includes creating primary and extended partitions.

In Windows 2000/2003/2008, a basic disk cannot contain volumes, volume sets, or any of the fault tolerance levels. These features are reserved for drives configured as dynamic disk. ***Dynamic disk*** is a new system of disk configuration and management introduced with NTFS5.0. Dynamic Disks are managed by the system as a group. Dynamic Disk is a requirement for Active Directory. The previous versions of disk formats (FAT16, FAT32, and NTFS 4) do not meet

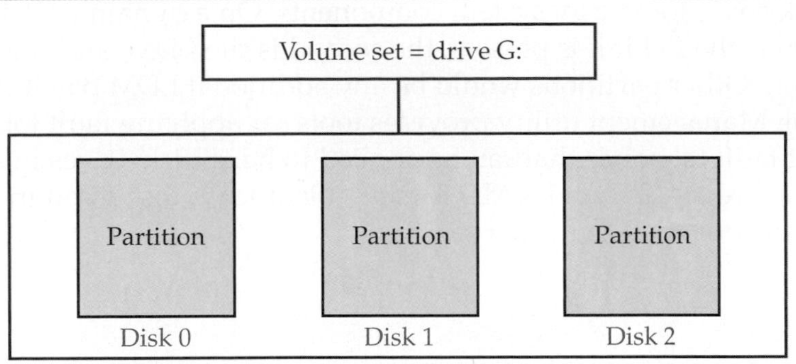

Figure 7-36. A volume set is assigned a single drive letter and consists of partitions from multiple hard disk drives.

the requirements of Active Directory. Dynamic disk allows the creation of five different volume types. These types include the following:

- Simple.
- Spanned.
- Mirrored.
- RAID-5.
- Striped.

A ***simple volume*** exists on a single drive. A simple volume is similar to a volume in Windows NT. It is an accessible unit of hard disk drive space as seen through the Windows interface, such as in Windows Explorer. A ***spanned volume*** is similar to a Windows NT volume set in that it is a single volume that combines two or more physical drives. Mirrored and RAID-5 volumes incorporate fault tolerance. Fault tolerance is discussed in detail in Chapter 9—Introduction to the Server. A ***striped volume*** increases the read/write access speed by spreading data across multiple hard disk drives. The disadvantage to this is if one of the hard disk drives in the striped set fails, the data will no longer be accessible from any of the hard disk drives in the striped volume. A striped volume, therefore, does not provide fault tolerance.

Globally Unique Identifier

Starting with the introduction of 64-bit processors, such as the Intel® Itanium®, and 64-bit operating systems, such as Windows XP Professional and Windows Enterprise Server 2003, a new partitioning style was developed. The new partitioning style is called ***globally unique identifier (GUID)***. It uses a partition table called GUID partition table (GPT).

The GPT partition table is required for a 64-bit operating system to boot. The GPT can support up to 18 Exabytes and 128 partitions per disk. You can have both MBR and GPT disks on the same computer. The GPT disk contains three new partitions in addition to any volumes created on the disk: EFI, Logical Disk Manager (LDM), and Microsoft Reserved (MSR). The EFI partition was developed as a replacement for BIOS functions. The ***EFI partition*** contains all programs required to boot the computer in the same way the BIOS boots the computer. The EFI is not a required partition. It can be created on a basic disk or on a GPT disk. At the time of this writing, EFI is an unproven technology and is only available for 64-bit operating systems.

The ***Logical Disk Manager (LDM) partition*** contains information about dynamic volumes and is created during the conversion from NTFS4.0 to dynamic disk. There can be more than one LDM partition in a system. The ***Microsoft Reserved (MSR) partition*** is a required partition on every GPT disk. The MSR

volume set
a volume that consists of partitions from two or more hard disk drives.

basic disk
the term applied to the old system of hard disk drive configuration, which includes creating primary and extended partitions.

dynamic disk
a new system of disk configuration and management introduced with NTFS5.0. Dynamic disks are managed by the system as a group and allow for the creation of five different volume types: simple, spanned, mirrored, RAID-5, and striped.

simple volume
a dynamic disk volume that exists on a single drive.

spanned volume
a single dynamic disk volume that spans many drives.

striped volume
a dynamic disk volume that increases the read/write access speed by spreading data across multiple hard disk drives.

reserves disk space for use by system components. On a dynamic GPT disk, the first partition is the EFI if it is present, the second is the LDM, and the third is the MSR partition. Other partitions would be any additional LDM partitions.

The Disk Management utility provides tools for applying fault tolerance. The two levels of fault tolerance that can be applied to hard disk drives in a Windows Server system are RAID 1 and RAID 5. Fault tolerance is discussed in detail in Chapter 9—Introduction to the Server.

globally unique identifier (GUID) a new partitioning style that uses a partition table called GUID partition table (GPT).

EFI partition a partition on a GPT disk that contains all programs required to boot the computer in the same way the BIOS boots the computer.

Logical Disk Manager (LDM) partition a partition on a GPT disk that contains information about dynamic volumes and is created during the conversion from NTFS4.0 to NTFS.0. There can be more than one LDM partition in a system.

Microsoft Reserved (MSR) partition a partition on a disk that reserves disk space for use by system components.

POSIX

Windows Server supports the POSIX standard as defined by the IEEE. The acronym POSIX represents Portable Operating System Interface. The term *portable* is a programming term, which means that the program can be installed and run on various computer hardware systems. The C programming language by nature is very portable. A program written in C language can be run on most hardware systems despite the hardware system's manufacturer.

The POSIX standard covers areas such as file name structure, file access, and file sharing. The POSIX standard was originally designed to ensure compatibility between applications and the UNIX operating system. POSIX had originally stood for Portable Operating System Interface for UNIX. The term has come to mean portability with all operating systems, not just UNIX.

Microsoft Windows Services for UNIX introduced with Windows Server 2003 far exceed the original POSIX standards. Windows XP and Windows Server 2003 can run some Linux programs, such as scripts designed for the C Shell and Korn Shell. Linux shells are covered in Chapter 8—UNIX/Linux Network Operating Systems.

Network Interoperability

Interoperability was once a major problem between different proprietary network operating systems. For example, it was often difficult and complex to configure communication between a Microsoft network and a Novell NetWare network because they both used different communications standards and protocols. Today, the default protocol for network systems is TCP/IP. Part of the TCP/IP suite of protocols is HTTP which is the protocol used to communicate across the Internet. The HTTP protocol is used to establish communication between two network systems using different operating systems such as Linux and Microsoft or Mac OS X.

Originally for networks of different operating systems to communicate, a gateway service was typically required. A gateway service provides translation between the different operating systems. The term *gateway* is also used to represent the network device that connects the local area network to the Internet.

Because all the major networking systems were redesigned for Internet communications and since the introduction of IPv6, networks of different design operating systems are now much easier to integrate.

Summary

- Computers in a Microsoft peer-to-peer network are grouped as workgroups.
- A workgroup is a group of computers that share resources.
- Computers in a Microsoft client/server network are grouped together in a domain.

- A domain is a logical grouping of users and equipment as defined by the network administrator.
- Windows native file sharing protocol is Server Message Block (SMB).
- The New Technology File System (NTFS) is the native file format for Windows NT and Windows Server operating systems.
- The NTFS file system is an improvement over FAT16 and FAT32.
- NTFS can create partition sizes as large as 16 EB. NTFS file names can be as long as 255 characters and have multiple extensions.
- FAT16 is limited to a 2-GB partition and to an eight-character file name with a three-character extension.
- FAT32 is limited to a 32-GB partition.
- Dynamic disk is an improved version of NTFS and is referred to as *NTFS5.0.*
- Network shares have assigned permissions, such as Full Control, Modify, Read, and Write.
- Administrative shares are indicated by a dollar sign ($) symbol.
- Active Directory uses LDAP and HTTP to transfer information between domain controllers.
- The Active Directory structure consists of trees, forests, organizational units, and objects.
- A tree is a collection of domains that have a contiguous namespace and share a common Active Directory database.
- A forest is a collection of domains that have a disjointed namespace and share a common Active Directory database.
- An organizational unit is a container that holds objects or other organizational units and serves to organize a network into manageable units.
- The two processes that handle authentication in a Windows network are interactive logon and network authentication.
- Windows Server networks use the Kerberos protocol for authentication.
- A Windows 2000/2003/2008 server can support one of three roles: domain controller (DC), member server, and stand-alone server.
- Windows Server 2000/2003/2008 supports multimaster replication.
- A trust relationship between Windows domains allows the free flow of data and communication between domains. Forests can also form trust relationships with other forests.
- The Microsoft Management Console (MMC) is a utility used to organize commonly used utilities.
- The Active Directory Users and Computers utility is used to add user and group accounts to a Windows domain.
- A POSIX compliant operating system can run on numerous hardware platforms.
- A gateway service provides communication between dissimilar network systems.
- A gateway is also the device used to provide a connection between the local area network and the Internet.

Review Questions

Answer the following questions on a separate sheet of paper. Please do not write in this book.

1. A(n) _____ is a group of computers that share resources such as files and hardware.
2. In a(n) _____ network, each computer contains its own database of users.
3. A(n) _____ network stores user and resource information in one location.
4. A(n) _____ is a logical grouping of users and equipment as defined by the network administrator.
5. What is the purpose of a server cluster?
6. What is the purpose of load balancing?
7. What protocol is native to Windows file sharing?
8. What other protocol is often identified as SMB?
9. What protocol is commonly associated with sharing on a UNIX/Linux system?
10. The _____ file system is limited to a 32-GB partition.
11. The _____ file system is limited to a 2-GB partition.
12. The _____ file system can create partition sizes as large as 16 EB.
13. The _____ file system can be set up to share directories and control access to files.
14. The _____ and _____ file systems allow only for share-level security.
15. What two Internet protocols are used by Active Directory to exchange directory information with other servers?
16. The Active Directory is a hierarchical structure that consists of _____, _____ _____, and _____.
17. What namespace feature determines if a domain is part of a tree or forest?
18. What is the difference between a disjointed and a contiguous namespace?
19. What two processes handle authentication in a Windows Server 2000/2003/2008 network?
20. What does the $ symbol indicate when located beside a share?
21. What is the Microsoft Management Console (MMC)?
22. What utility would an administrator use to add users and groups to an Active Directory?
23. Define *basic disk* and *dynamic disk*.
24. What is a gateway service?

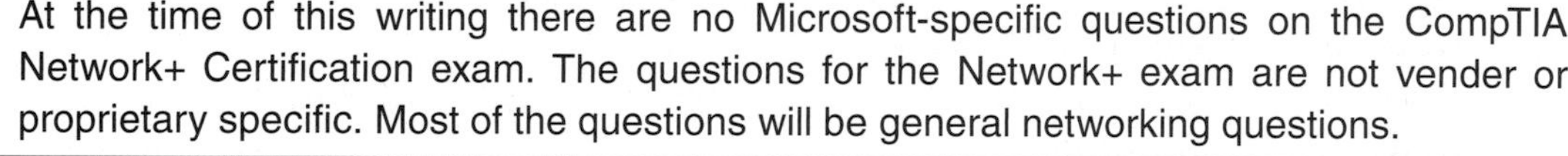

Note At the time of this writing there are no Microsoft-specific questions on the CompTIA Network+ Certification exam. The questions for the Network+ exam are not vender or proprietary specific. Most of the questions will be general networking questions.

Sample Network+ Exam Questions

Answer the following questions on a separate sheet of paper. Please do not write in this book.

1. What will happen on Windows Server if a user presses the [Ctrl] [Alt] [Del] keys simultaneously after the server boots?
   A. The system will reboot.
   B. The **Windows Security** dialog box will display.
   C. The **Logon** dialog box will appear.
   D. Nothing will happen. Only the system administrator can invoke [Ctrl] [Alt] [Del].
2. Which device is used to translate protocols when two different networks are connected together?
   A. Switch
   B. Router
   C. Hub
   D. Gateway
3. Which file system supports the largest disk partition?
   A. FAT16
   B. FAT32
   C. NTFS
   D. OS/2
4. What can RAID do for a network server?
   A. Provide a secure network connection.
   B. Provide data storage redundancy.
   C. Provide protection from malware.
   D. Provide a secure method of user authentication.
5. Which of the following is *not* a classification associated with LDAP?
   A. Forest
   B. Tree
   C. Branch
   D. Domain
6. Which of the following is an authentication protocol?
   A. FTP
   B. HTML
   C. Kerberos
   D. ARP
7. A client can log on to a network and see a network folder. She can read the contents of all documents located inside the network folder but cannot make changes to the documents. What is *most likely* the reason she cannot make changes to the documents in the folder?
   A. The client is configured with the wrong protocol.
   B. The folder is located on a different subnet.
   C. The client does not have the correct permission to change the contents of the folder.
   D. The client is using the wrong software application when attempting to make changes to the shared documents.

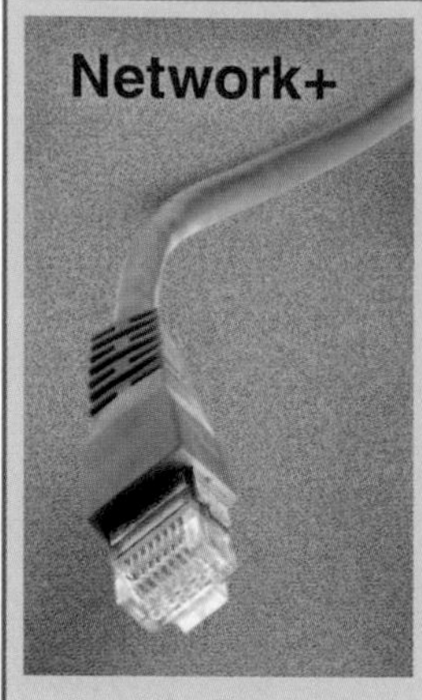

8. Which device is used to store user accounts in a client/server network?
   A. Each workstation stores user security account information and permissions.
   B. The server stores user account security information and permissions.
   C. Both the user workstation and the server store user security information and permissions.
   D. Security account information and permissions are stored at Microsoft headquarters, not on the actual network system.
9. Which three are typical characteristics of a peer-to-peer network? (Select three.)
   A. A centralized server to control user accounts.
   B. Each computer requires individual user accounts.
   C. There is no limit to number of workstations.
   D. Total clients are limited to 20.
   E. Each computer must be configured with LDAP.
   F. LDAP is not required.
10. What is the minimal requirement for a client/server network user account?
    A. User logon name and no password
    B. User logon name and password
    C. User logon name and a password shared folder
    D. No user logon name, just a password

Suggested Laboratory Activities

1. Log on to a Windows Server 2008 computer and set up a new user account.
2. Log on to a Windows Server 2008 computer and experiment with a user's password restrictions such as history, length, and lockout policy.
3. Set up a new group on a network and assign users to the group.
4. Make a list of suggested groups you might find in a typical high school network and list the types of objects they might typically share. Do not underestimate this assignment. It can be very involved if done correctly.
5. Using the knowledgebase on the Microsoft Support Web site, research common logon errors in Windows Server 2008. Note the reasons for their generation and their associated error messages.
6. Obtain information from the Microsoft Web site on how to install Windows Server 2008. Use this information to install the server's operating system.

Interesting Web Sites for More Information

www.microsoft.com
http://technet.microsoft.com/en-us/library/cc731574.aspx
http://technet.microsoft.com/en-us/library/cc770406.aspx

Chapter 7
Laboratory Activity

Adding Users to Windows Server 2008

After completing this laboratory activity, you will be able to:

- Recall the purpose of a user account.
- Recall the basic requirements of a user account.
- Identify the various password options available.
- Use Active Directory Users and Computers to create a new user account.

Introduction

In this laboratory activity, you will add a new user to a Windows 2008 Server domain. One of the most common jobs a network technician performs is adding new users and giving users new passwords when the user forgets his or her password. Adding new users to a network system is also known as *creating a user account*. A user cannot access system resources on a network without a user account. At minimum, the user account requires a user name and a password.

There are two types of user and group accounts that can be created: domain and local. A local account is created for accessing the local computer or server. A local account is typically used on a peer-to-peer network. The domain user account is created on a server that is a domain controller. With the proper permission, this domain account is good for the entire domain. Once the domain user account is created, a user can log on to the network from any workstation. (The user must have permissions to log on from any workstation.) A local account only allows a user to log on to the computer the user is at, not the entire network.

A domain user account serves two main purposes: authentication and authorization. Authorization is the process of verifying a user's rights to access specific network services, such as printers and shares. Authentication is the process of verifying a user's identity. The user name and password is used for this purpose. This is why it is so important to keep the password secret. Anyone who knows the user password can authenticate as the real user. Active Directory requires user passwords to be more than simple passwords. If you attempt to use a simple password, you will generate an error message similar to that in the following screen capture.

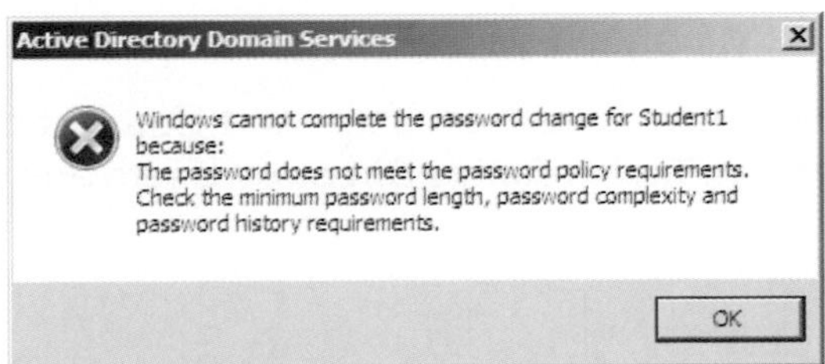

As you can see, the password failed to meet one or more of the following requirements: length, history, and complexity. The requirements are a minimum password length of six characters; a history of 24 passwords; and a complex password, which includes uppercase and lowercase letters, numbers, and at least one special character. You can learn more about user accounts by accessing **Help and Support** located off the **Start** menu. The following list includes a few basic rules for setting up user accounts:

- Passwords can contain a maximum of 127 characters.
- User names must be unique.
- User names should not contain the characters / \ [ ] ; : | = , + * ? < > because they have special meaning to the computer system and can cause an unexpected problem. You are free to use any remaining special characters, such as ! $ # % and &.

Companies generally have a naming convention in place for user names. Typically, they use a last name followed by the initial of the first name. The last name is placed first so that the user will be listed alphabetically in the Active Directory Users and Computers window. It makes it easy to locate a user when all names are listed alphabetically by last name.

For this laboratory activity, the naming scheme you will use for entering user names and group names will be a combination of your name and the name of the object you are creating followed by a decimal number: 1, 2, or 3. For example, a student named Karen will create the following users: KarenUser1, KarenUser2, and so on. This naming scheme will make it easy for your instructor to check your project.

Read the entire laboratory activity before you begin. The laboratory activity contains many examples. Familiarizing yourself with the examples and reading the laboratory activity will give you a clear understanding of what is to be accomplished. After reading the entire laboratory activity, you may begin.

Equipment and Materials

- A computer with Windows Server 2008.

Note

On a separate sheet of paper, record any additional instructor notes that will be needed to complete the laboratory activity.

Procedure

1. _____ Report to your assigned workstation.
2. _____ Boot the server and verify it is in working order.
3. _____ Access the Active Directory Users and Computers utility (**Start | Administrative Tools | Active Directory Users and Computers**).

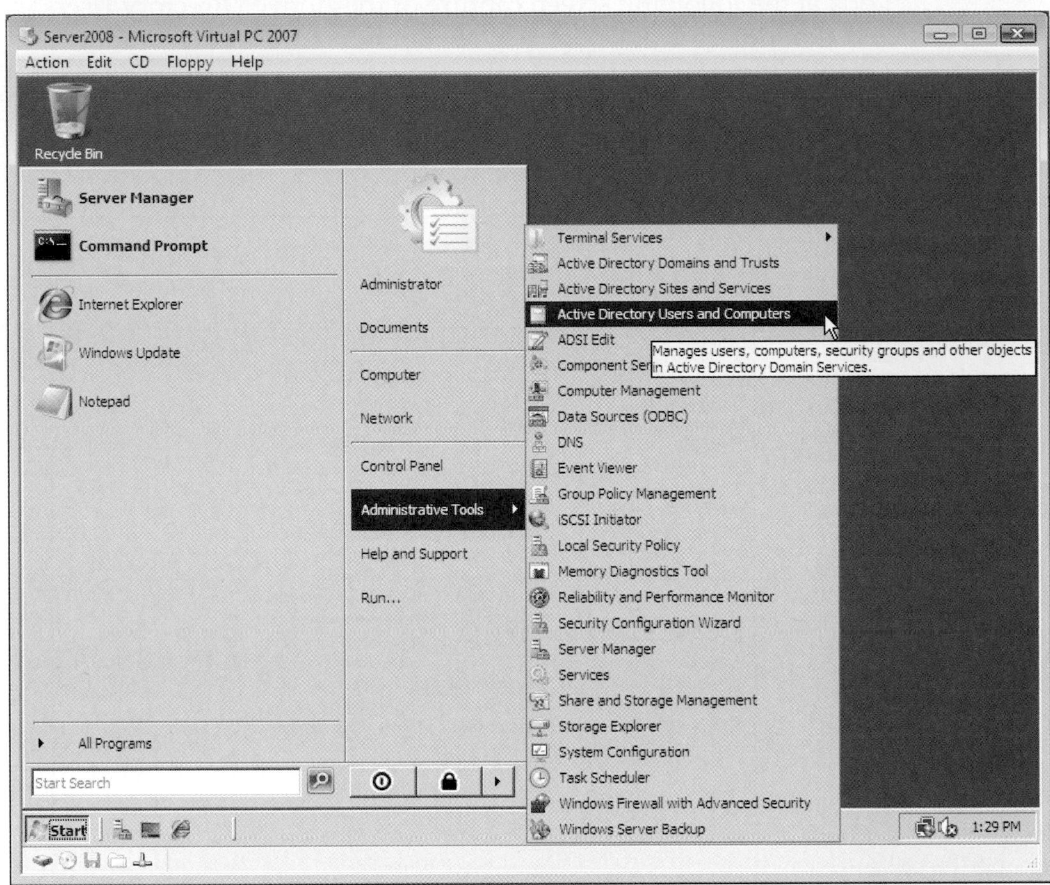

Note

If Active Directory is not installed, there will be no option for **Active Directory Users and Computers**. *Select* **Computer Management** *instead. Creating a new user in the Computer Management utility is similar to creating a new user in Active Directory Users and Computers.*

Look at the following screen capture of the Active Directory Users and Computers utility. Notice how the right pane of the window lists users and groups currently in the domain. The left pane is displayed in a typical, Windows directory format. At the top of the directory is the name of the Active Directory that contains all the listed users, groups, domain controllers, and more.

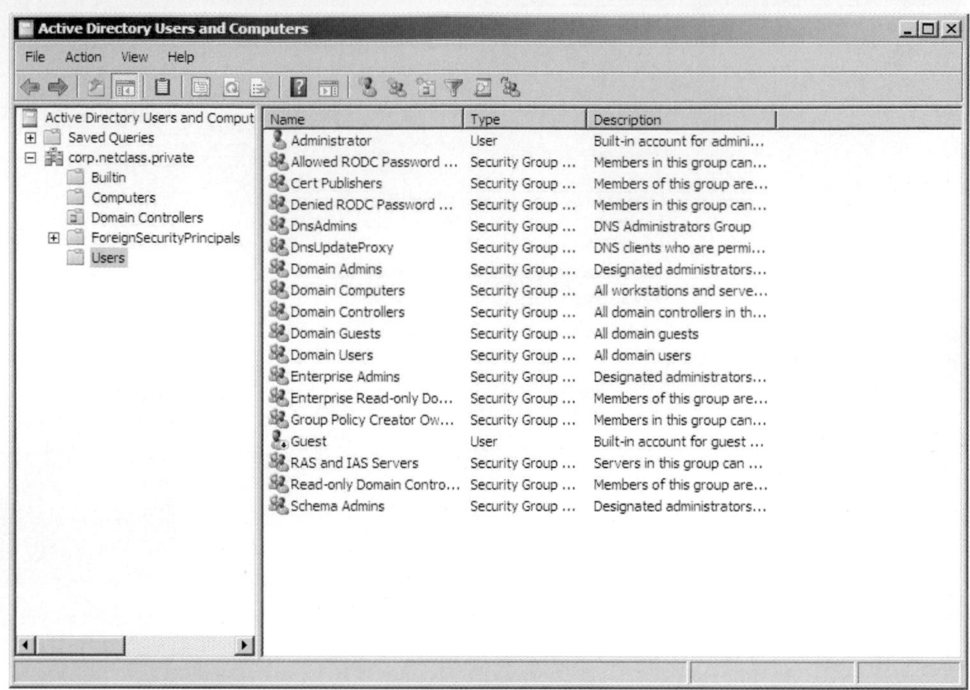

4. ______ From the **Action** menu, select **New | User**. Take note that you can also select **Computer**, **Contact**, **Group**, or **Printer**.

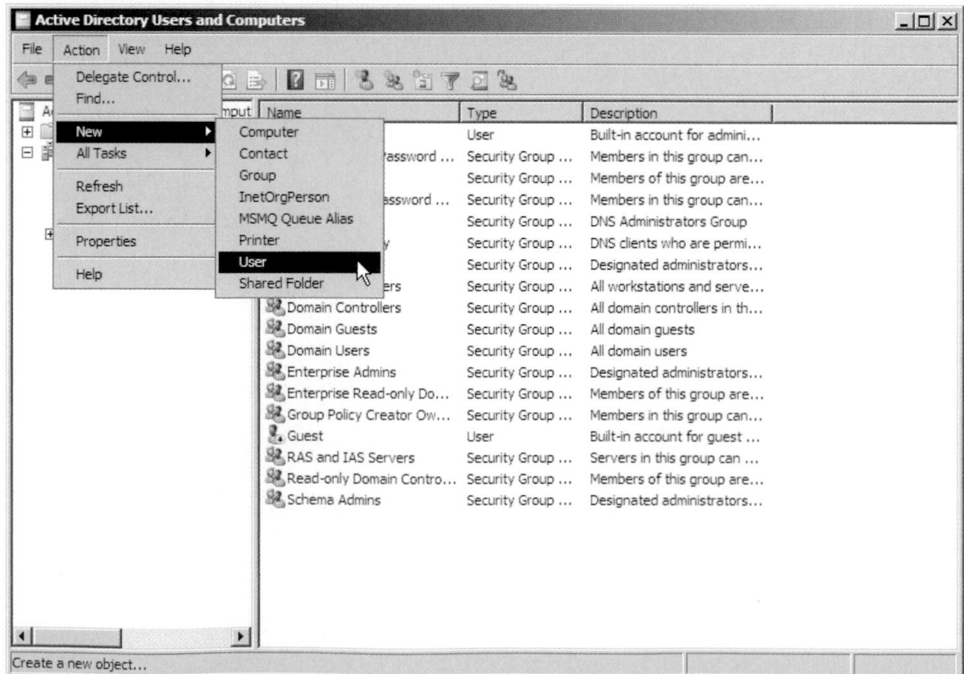

5. _____ The **New Object—User** dialog box will display. You will be required to fill in a series of dialog boxes. The first dialog box should look similar to that in the following screen capture. Fill in the required information and then click **Next**. Remember to create a new user based on your name, such as BillUser1.

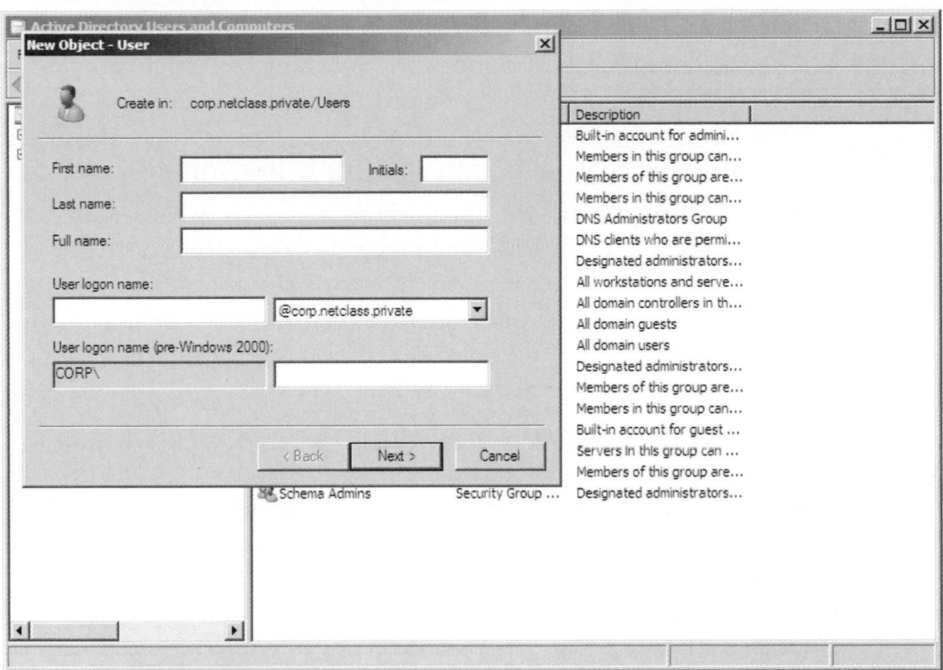

6. _____ In the next dialog box, enter a user password. For this laboratory activity, you will use the *PwD123#* for the password, unless otherwise instructed by your teacher. This password meets the complexity required by Active Directory.

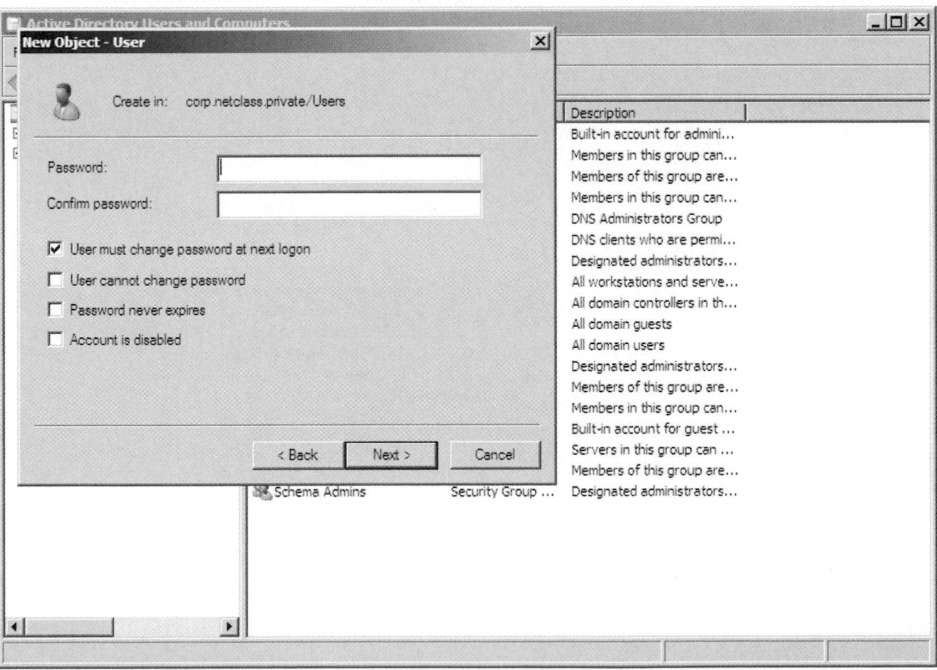

Take special note of the password options available. The first option, **User must change password at next logon**, means the administrator will assign a password. Then, the first time the user logs on to the system, the user will be prompted to change the password. This option allows users to choose their own password so that only they know what it is, not the administrator. Companies typically use the same password for all first time users.

The second option, **User cannot change password**, means the network administrator will assign a password to the user, and the user must use the assigned password each time he or she logs on to the system. The user cannot change the password, only the Administrator can.

The next option, **Password never expires**, means as stated that the assigned password will never expire. Typically, a network administrator sets an expiration date for passwords, forcing the user to change the password periodically to enhance security. This is a common practice. You will learn to set the expiration date and other features in a later laboratory activity.

The last option, **Account is disabled**, is used to disable a user account. This option is used when personnel go on vacation or take an extended leave. You would not delete the user account because the user would lose all permissions and privileges. The associated permissions and privileges would not be regained by creating a new user account using the previous user name and password. Permissions and privileges would have to be reassigned. It is much easier, therefore, to disable and re-enable an account.

7. _____ After entering the password information, click **Next**. A summary of the user information you entered will display. You can either accept the information by clicking **Finish**, or modify the information by clicking **Back** until you reach the appropriate dialog box to which you want to make changes.

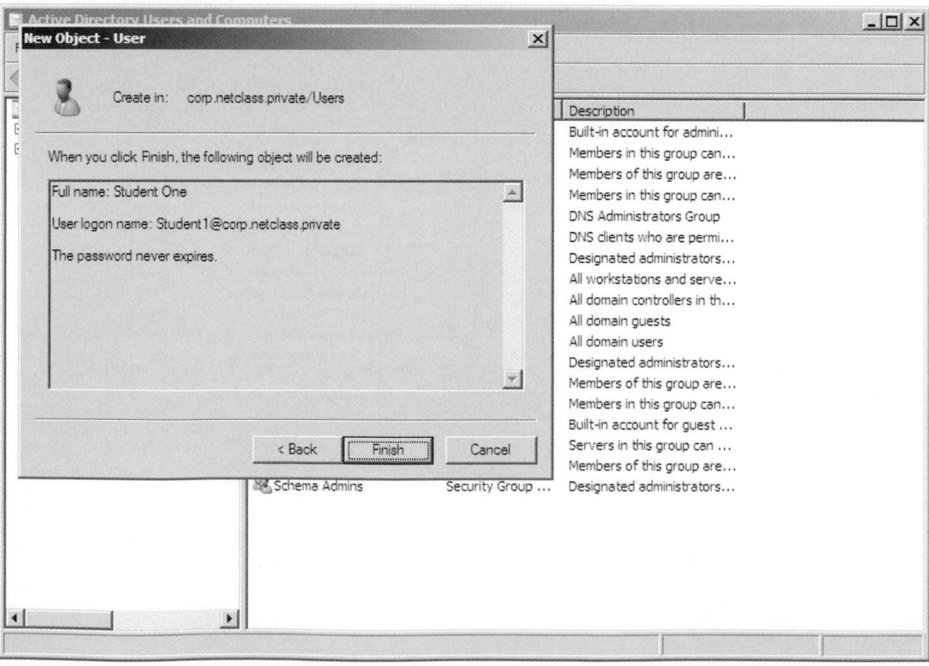

8. ______ After clicking **Finish**, the new user you just created will be automatically added to the list of users. Check the **Users** folder in the Active Directory Users and Computers utility for this user. If you have successfully created a new account, repeat the steps five through seven until you have created two more users. Remember to create user names based on your name, such as BillUser2 and BillUser3. If you do not see the user account you have just created, call your instructor.
9. ______ Answer the review questions.
10. ______ If required by your instructor, return the server to its original condition.

Review Questions

Answer the following questions on a separate sheet of paper. Please do not write in this book.

1. What are the minimum requirements for a user account? List two items.
2. What are the two main types of user accounts?
3. What are the two main reasons for a user account?
4. What options are available for the user password?
5. What must a password contain to meet the complexity requirement?

The Microsoft Web site includes many resources, such as training videos and product documentation, to help you learn about Windows Server 2008.

8 UNIX/Linux Operating Systems

After studying this chapter, you will be able to:

- Explain the structure of the UNIX/Linux operating system.
- Summarize the advantages and disadvantages of using the Linux operating system.
- Differentiate between copyleft and copyright.
- Explain the Linux boot process.
- Recall the common shell programs associated with UNIX/Linux.
- Use the **set** command to determine the default shell program.
- Use common UNIX/Linux commands.
- Recall the characteristics of the UNIX/Linux file system.
- Compare the UNIX/Linux file structure with the DOS file structure.
- Interpret the user, group, and other permissions assigned to directories and files.
- Summarize how UNIX/Linux can establish communications with Windows operating systems.

Network+ Exam—Key Points

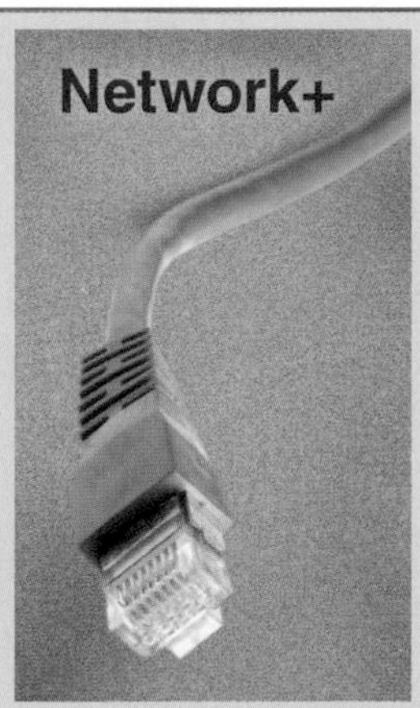

Starting with the CompTIA Network+ 2009 objectives, system interoperability is no longer a certification objective. You will most likely see nothing about UNIX or Linux on the examination. If UNIX/Linux is reinstated for the certification exam, it will most likely cover only the basics of UNIX/Linux.

Currently, the only reference to UNIX/Linux in the Network+ 2009 objectives are the **ifconfig**, **mtr**, **dig**, and **traceroute** commands listed in Domain 5.0.

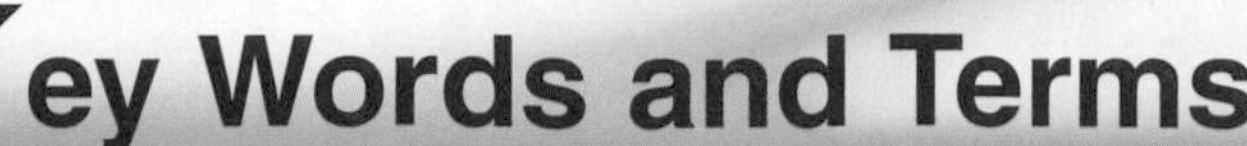

Key Words and Terms

The following words and terms will become important pieces of your networking vocabulary. Be sure you can define them.

boot loader
Common UNIX Printing System (CUPS)
daemon
device file
inode
journal file
journaling file system
kernel
module
mount point
session
shell
tar ball
windows manager
X client
X server
X Windows

UNIX is the fountainhead of modern network operating systems. After its inception, it served as a model of how network operating systems should operate. There have been many variations of UNIX. None of the variations produced a large-scale change in the networking industry until Linux was released. Linux has become a robust network and desktop operating system. Many software companies, such as IBM, Novell, and Apple Computer, have adopted the open-source technology of Linux into their networking operating systems.

While Microsoft Windows dominates the desktop computer world in the United States, Linux is the preferred desktop for most C and C++ programmers and computer science majors. Linux allows programmers complete control over the operating system and the kernel. In fact, a programmer can write a new kernel if they have sufficient skills. This is why Linux is popular with serious programmers.

This chapter presents a basic foundation of UNIX/Linux operating systems. The UNIX and Linux information in this chapter is combined because talking about one operating system is like talking about the other.

UNIX

UNIX was developed at the AT&T Bell Laboratories in the 1960s. It was the first major operating system for networking. Scientific communities, academic communities, and governmental agencies readily accepted UNIX. The original version of UNIX has spawned countless variations, such as Berkeley Software Distribution (BSD), Sun Solaris, HP, and IBM.

Many networking concepts originated from the early versions of UNIX. While UNIX was still in its early development, the TCP/IP protocol was developed to support communication between universities, government sites, and scientific research companies. UNIX adopted TCP/IP as its native communications protocol.

What makes UNIX and Linux unique when compared with Windows operating systems is the source code used for the components is readily available to anyone. Windows is a proprietary operating system; however, Microsoft has made some aspects of its Windows code available in a similar manner as open source. The availability of the source code has made the UNIX/Linux system a favorite among programmers and programming enthusiasts. If a program needs to be modified or to have a new procedure developed, the administrator can simply write the code for the change. The most common programming language used for writing UNIX/Linux code is the C programming language. If you cannot program, you can usually find the code you need through an Internet search. There are many organizations devoted to developing and sharing program code.

kernel
the core of an operating system.

module
a small program, such as a hardware driver or a kernel enhancement, used to expand the kernel and to allow for flexibility.

UNIX/Linux consists of the system kernel surrounded by modules, **Figure 8-1.** A ***kernel*** is the core of an operating system. A ***module*** is a small program, such as a hardware driver or a kernel enhancement. Modules are used to expand the kernel and to allow for flexibility. An administrator can load and unload modules as needed or configure the kernel to load them automatically during the system boot.

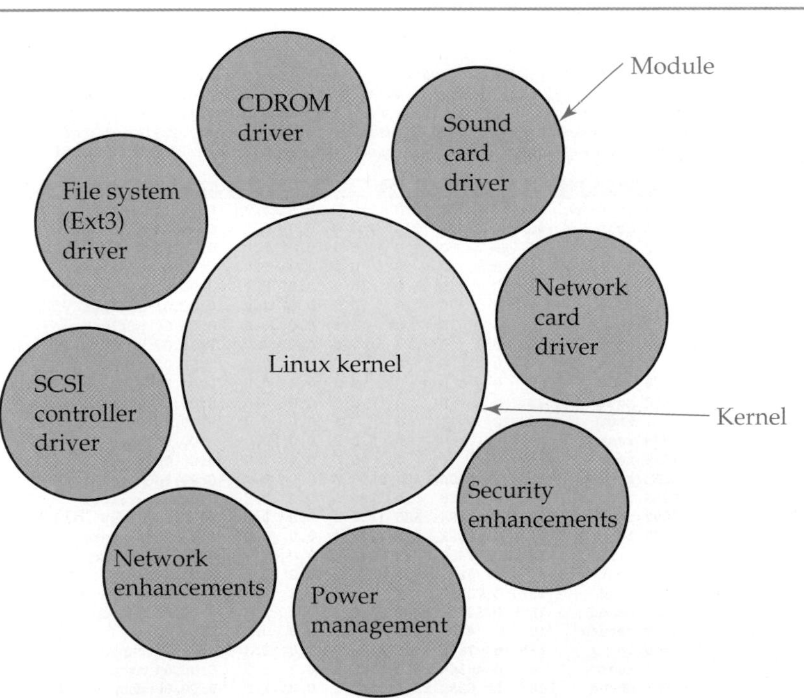

Figure 8-1.
The UNIX/Linux kernel is surrounded by modules. A module is typically a hardware driver, file system driver, or other kernel enhancement.

daemon
a program that runs in the background and waits for a client to request its services.

The UNIX/Linux system also consists of daemons. A ***daemon*** is a program that runs in the background and waits for a client to request its services. It is much like a service in Windows operating systems. An example of a daemon is the Simple Mail Transfer Protocol (SMTP). SMTP waits for e-mail to arrive. When e-mail does arrive, SMTP either transfers the e-mail to another server or delivers the e-mail to the recipient's mailbox. All of this is handled in the background without the user's knowledge until a message pops up on the screen notifying the user that they have mail. **Figure 8-2** shows a list of currently running programs and daemons on a Linux computer. Note that the file names of all daemons end in the letter *d*.

The kernel combined with modules and daemons defines the total operating system and its capabilities, **Figure 8-3.** An administrator can customize the operating system and load only the modules and services desired. By building a custom operating system, overall performance is improved. The operating system is more efficient than when loading an operating system with all of its possible components. The administrator can also unload modules and services no longer needed. The ability to load or unload separate modules to support the kernel results in efficient use of system resources, such as RAM. As each module is loaded, valuable RAM is used. There are also more demands on the CPU. Processor time is required for each running module.

Linux

In 1991, the University of Helsinki student, Linus Torvalds, developed the Linux (pronounced Lih-nucks) kernel and freely distributed the source code rather than retaining proprietary rights. What makes this operating system unique is that the code is a collaboration through the years of countless numbers of developers, programmers, students, and engineers. Linux is distributed for free or for a relatively small cost. It is licensed under the GNU (pronounced guh-noo) General Public License (GPL), which allows users to freely modify, copy, and distribute the Linux software system. We will discuss more about this subject later.

Figure 8-2.
In this example, a utility called **top** has been run to reveal currently running programs and daemons. Files on a UNIX/Linux system that are daemons, typically end with the letter *d*. Some of the daemons listed in this example have been pointed out. Can you identify other daemons in this example?

```
top - 00:41:43 up 23:47,  2 users,  load average: 0.00, 0.00, 0.00
Tasks:  40 total,   1 running,  39 sleeping,   0 stopped,   0 zombie
Cpu(s):  0.3% us,  0.3% sy,  0.0% ni, 99.3% id,  0.0% wa,  0.0% hi,  0.0% si
Mem:    256716k total,  249688k used,    7028k free,  109332k buffers
Swap:   514072k total,      12k used,  514060k free,   20968k cached

  PID USER      PR  NI  VIRT  RES  SHR S %CPU %MEM    TIME+  COMMAND
 6493 jkeltner  16   0  1752  892 1536 R  0.3  0.3   0:00.16 top
    1 root      16   0   588  244  444 S  0.0  0.1   0:06.34 init
    2 root      34  19     0    0    0 S  0.0  0.0   0:00.00 ksoftirqd/0
    3 root       5 -10     0    0    0 S  0.0  0.0   0:00.48 events/0
    4 root       5 -10     0    0    0 S  0.0  0.0   0:00.00 kblockd/0
    5 root       6 -10     0    0    0 S  0.0  0.0   0:00.01 khelper
    6 root      20   0     0    0    0 S  0.0  0.0   0:00.00 pdflush
    7 root      15   0     0    0    0 S  0.0  0.0   0:00.83 pdflush
    9 root      15 -10     0    0    0 S  0.0  0.0   0:00.00 aio/0
    8 root      15   0     0    0    0 S  0.0  0.0   0:00.31 kswapd0
  162 root      23   0     0    0    0 S  0.0  0.0   0:00.00 kseriod
  331 root       5 -10     0    0    0 S  0.0  0.0   0:00.00 reiserfs/0
  774 root       6 -10     0    0    0 S  0.0  0.0   0:00.00 kcopyd
 1516 root      15   0     0    0    0 S  0.0  0.0   0:00.00 khubd
 2182 root      15   0  1404  420 1196 S  0.0  0.2   0:00.00 hwscand
 2249 root      16   0  1428  624 1256 S  0.0  0.2   0:00.04 syslogd
 2298 root      15   0  1496  588 1208 S  0.0  0.2   0:00.00 klogd
 2367 root      25   0  1392  476 1232 S  0.0  0.2   0:00.00 resmgrd
 2373 bin       18   0  1400  472 1244 S  0.0  0.2   0:00.00 portmap
 2696 root      16   0  5260 1936 4832 S  0.0  0.8   0:00.89 sshd
 2851 ldap      18   0 72968 5100  26m S  0.0  2.0   0:00.00 slapd
 2927 named     18   0 32448 4348 5528 S  0.0  1.7   0:00.00 named
 3187 daemon    16   0  4352 1388 4092 S  0.0  0.5   0:00.02 slpd
 3359 lp        15   0  7656 3372 4604 S  0.0  1.3   0:01.25 cupsd
 3393 root      16   0 46364 2576 3892 S  0.0  1.0   0:00.04 nscd
 3457 dhcpd     16   0  6352 3276 4340 S  0.0  1.3   0:00.00 dhcpd
```

Daemons

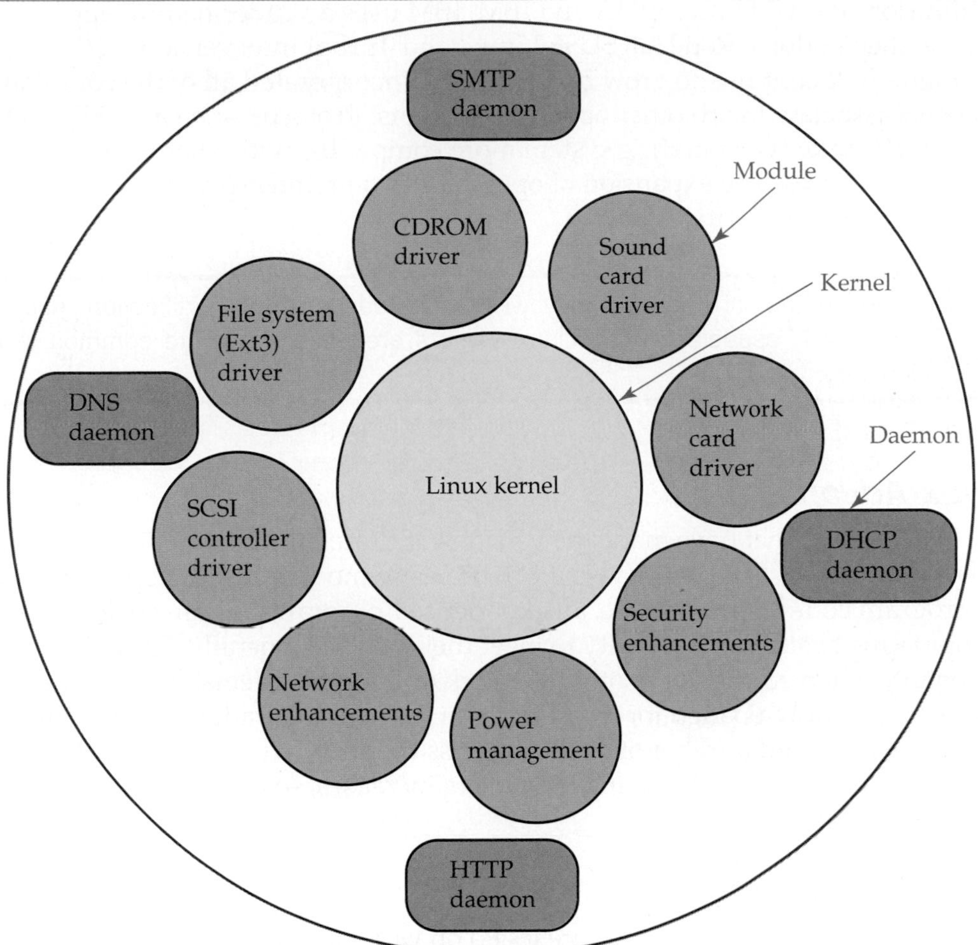

Figure 8-3. The kernel, modules, and daemons make up the UNIX/Linux operating system.

While Linux has been presented as an open source operating system, this can be misleading. The kernel and many other Linux components are free to download, but many versions are a mix of open source and proprietary programs and components. For example, Xandros Linux includes a proprietary file management system, proprietary applications, and proprietary utilities. It also contains several third-party applications such as Netscape Communicator and Adobe Acrobat Reader.

Since Linux was designed to emulate UNIX, most of its features are the same as UNIX. You can think of Linux as another version in the evolution of UNIX. There are many variations of Linux available such as Red Hat, Caldera, Mandrake, SUSE, Turbo, and Corel. You will see many similarities between the different versions of Linux. These similarities are due to all of the Linux operating systems using the most common, available programs to enhance the kernel, such as Gimp, KDE, GNOME, Mozilla, XFree86, Apache Web Server, Evolution, and Samba.

Linux has evolved rapidly and has been incorporated into other operating systems. Linux was once difficult to install, mainly because of the lack of hardware driver support by manufacturers. Since Novell and IBM have endorsed Linux, hardware manufacturers have increased their driver support.

There are also various Linux certifications available. They range from vendor-specific, such as Red Hat certification, to vender-neutral, such as Linux certification offered by CompTIA and IBM. IBM uses a vender-neutral approach because they endorse Red Hat, SUSE Linux, and TurboLinux versions.

Linux will continue to grow because it has incorporated all of the common protocols associated with other operating systems. Protocols such as SMB, LDAP, and SNMP make the operating system more compatible with Microsoft Windows operating systems. The expansion of operating system interoperability has helped to develop the popularity of Linux.

Tech Tip

After completing this course, you may wish to pursue a Linux certification, such as CompTIA's Linux+, especially since Linux servers are becoming more common in the network industry.

Linux Advantages

The features that have made the versions of Linux popular are its flexibility and price. Linux is flexible because it can be easily modified or customized. Since the program code is open source, an experienced programmer can customize the operating system and security to meet their needs. Generally, Linux is priced reasonably when compared to other network operating systems. In fact, an entire system can be downloaded for free. Prices for network operating systems that allow only a limited number of users to access the server typically start at several thousands of dollars. As the number of users increases, so does the cost of the network operating system.

Linux Disadvantages

Commercial versions of Linux are tested on various systems and have somewhat of a guarantee they will not harm your computer. Downloaded versions of Linux and associated files are not guaranteed. If the software destroys, causes loss of data, or crashes the system, the user has no recourse, no one to blame, or cost recovery source.

Many Linux companies do not have a highly-structured support system. Commercial versions of Linux, however, do provide support, either for free or for a low cost. Commercial versions Linux also have the broadest range of hardware compatibility when compared to the free download versions. Remember the old saying, "You get what you pay for." If the operating system is free, the support is typically less than desirable.

Also, since Linux is an open source operating system, the code is not secret. It can be hacked or cracked more easily than some other operating systems.

Another concern is independent-vendor support. There are not as many venders that provide driver support for UNIX/Linux in the same way as they do for Microsoft products. Also, not all versions of UNIX/Linux services or programs are interchangeable and compatible. You must be very careful when adding a free service or utility. It may not be compatible with the version of Linux you are running. Other operating systems may have problems too, but not to the extent as the Linux operating system. It is best to stick with a well-established Linux operating system such as Red Hat or SUSE.

Copyright and Copyleft

One of the most interesting and often misunderstood aspects of Linux is the copyright. Linux is copyrighted under the GNU General Public License

(GPL), often referred to as *copyleft*. See **Figure 8-4.** Many people are under the impression that you cannot sell Linux software. This is not true. The intent of the GNU GPL is to make the Linux kernel source code freely available. This allows anyone to modify the code to suit his or her needs. In short, the GNU GPL allows anyone the right to copy, modify, and distribute software without the permission of the original copyright holder, as long as they pass the same rights on to the next user. In other words, all users who receive a copy of the source code may freely modify the programs and freely distribute the programs.

Therefore, this may lead to the question of how do companies have the right to sell Linux? Commercial companies extend all the rights associated with the GNU GPL. The commercial companies distribute the source code and allow copies to be made and distributed under the same guidelines as stated above. What the companies are charging for is a neat package with manuals and support via the Internet and telephone for the consumer. The consumer actually pays for the enhancements while not being charged for the software. In fact, you can go to the commercial sites and download an image of the software to use on a computer. The fact that you can download and install the software from the commercial site and access the source code is what keeps the commercial sites in compliance with the GNU general public license. For more information on the GNU GPL visit www.gnu.org/copyleft/gpl.html.

The Free Software Foundation (FSF), a nonprofit organization founded in 1983, develops many different software packages that complement Linux systems. The FSF promotes the free distribution of software and source code similar to the GNU GPL. See **Figure 8-5.** The FSF develops utilities and programs that interface with GNU/Linux operating systems. For more information on the FSF visit www.gnu.org/fsf/fsf.html.

You should note that not all versions of Linux are under the free distribution plan. Many commercial versions are independent of the GNU GPL license and are very expensive.

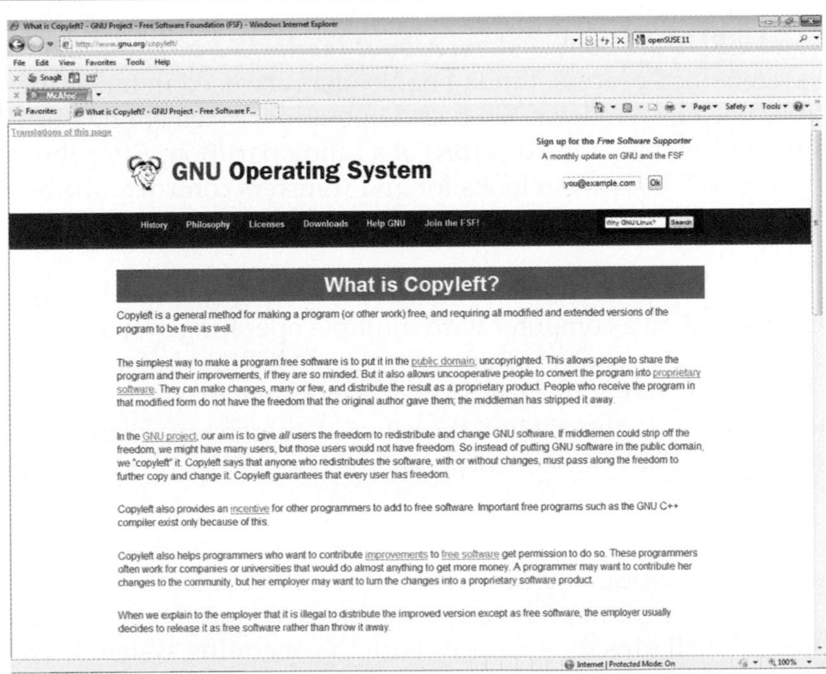

Figure 8-4. An explanation of *copyleft* can be viewed on the www.gnu.org/copyleft Web page.

Figure 8-5.
The www.fsf.org Web page provides information about the Free Software Foundation (FSF) and its purpose.

UNIX/Linux Basics

This section introduces the basics of the UNIX/Linux operating system. It is not comprehensive in its coverage. It would take a full textbook to cover the basics in detail. The intention of this section is to introduce you to some UNIX/Linux terminology and to the basic differences and likenesses between UNIX/Linux and other operating systems.

LILO and GRUB

The acronym LILO represents Linux Loader. GRUB represents Grand Unified Boot loader. LILO has been around for many years, but GRUB is relatively new.

boot loader
a program that starts the operating system load process.

LILO and GRUB are boot loaders. A ***boot loader*** is a program that starts the operating system load process. Linux boot loaders are used in much the same way as ntldr is used in Windows NT–based operating systems. LILO or GRUB installs in the master boot record (MBR) of a Linux partition. After the Power On Self-Test (POST), the system looks for and transfers control to the boot loader. The boot loader loads the kernel. When the kernel loads, the kernel loads the operating system.

LILO or GRUB can be used to load other operating systems. When LILO or GRUB is configured on a computer with multiple operating systems, the LILO or GRUB boot loader takes control after the system POST and before the operating system is selected. It allows the user to choose between two or more operating systems and then boots directly into the selected operating system. Modern Linux systems like Linux SUSE incorporate the boot loader into the YaST utility.

shell
a user interface that interprets and carries out commands from the user.

Shells

A ***shell*** is a user interface that interprets and carries out commands from the user similar to the way the command interpreter (cmd.exe) interprets and carries out commands. The shell directly interfaces with the operating system kernel. There are numerous shells available. Some are freeware and others are proprietary. Some of the more common shells are the Bourne Again Shell, Korn Shell, and Turbo C Shell. See **Figure 8-6** for a list of common UNIX/Linux shells.

The Bourne Again Shell is the default shell for Red Hat Linux. **Figure 8-7** shows the **set** command issued at the Bourne Again Shell. The UNIX/Linux **set** command is similar to the DOS **set** command. Entered without options, the **set** command displays a list of a user's shell variables, including the name of the current shell. In the example, you can see that the user's shell is set to bash, which is the Bourne Again Shell.

A user can change to a different shell by typing the desired shell name at the prompt. For example, to activate and use the Turbo C Shell, you would simply type **tcsh** at the prompt. In **Figure 8-8,** the user has issued the **tcsh** command and then entered **set** at the shell prompt. Since each shell has its own set of variables, the SHELL variable now reads /bin/tcsh. A user can also run another session of the current shell by entering the shell name. For example, to run another session of the bash shell, the user would enter **bash** at the prompt.

Note that each time a user enters the name of a new shell or the name of the current shell being used, a new session is invoked. One of the greatest advantages

Shell	Full Name
bash	Bourne Again Shell
bs	Bourne Shell
csh	C Shell
ksh	Korn Shell
tcsh	Turbo C Shell

Figure 8-6. Common UNIX/Linux shells.

```
jkeltner@linux:/> set
ACLOCAL_PATH=/opt/gnome/share/aclocal
BASH=/bin/bash
BASH_VERSINFO=([0]="2" [1]="05b" [2]="0" [3]="1" [4]="release" [5]="i586-suse-linux")
BASH_VERSION='2.05b.0(1)-release'
COLORTERM=1
COLUMNS=142
CPU=i686
CVS_RSH=ssh
DEFAULT_WM=kde
DIRSTACK=()
EUID=1000
GNOME2_PATH=/usr/local:/opt/gnome:/usr
GNOMEDIR=/opt/gnome
GNOME_PATH=:/opt/gnome:/usr
GROUPS=()
GTK_PATH=/usr/local/lib/gtk-2.0:/opt/gnome/lib/gtk-2.0:/usr/lib/gtk-2.0
G_BROKEN_FILENAMES=1
HISTCONTROL=ignoreboth
HISTFILE=/home/jkeltner/.bash_history
HISTFILESIZE=1000
HISTSIZE=1000
HOME=/home/jkeltner
HOST=linux
SHELL=/bin/bash
SHELLOPTS=braceexpand:emacs:hashall:histexpand:history:interactive-comments:monitor
SHLVL=1
SSH_CLIENT='::ffff:192.168.10.40 3032 22'
SSH_CONNECTION='::ffff:192.168.10.40 3032 ::ffff:192.168.10.20 22'
SSH_TTY=/dev/pts/0
TERM=xterm
TEXINPUTS=:/home/jkeltner/.TeX:/usr/share/doc/.TeX:/usr/doc/.TeX
UID=1000
USER=jkeltner
```

SHELL variable

Figure 8-7. The **set** command lists the current shell's variables. Note the value of the SHELL variable, /bin/bash. This means that the shell is currently set to use the bash shell.

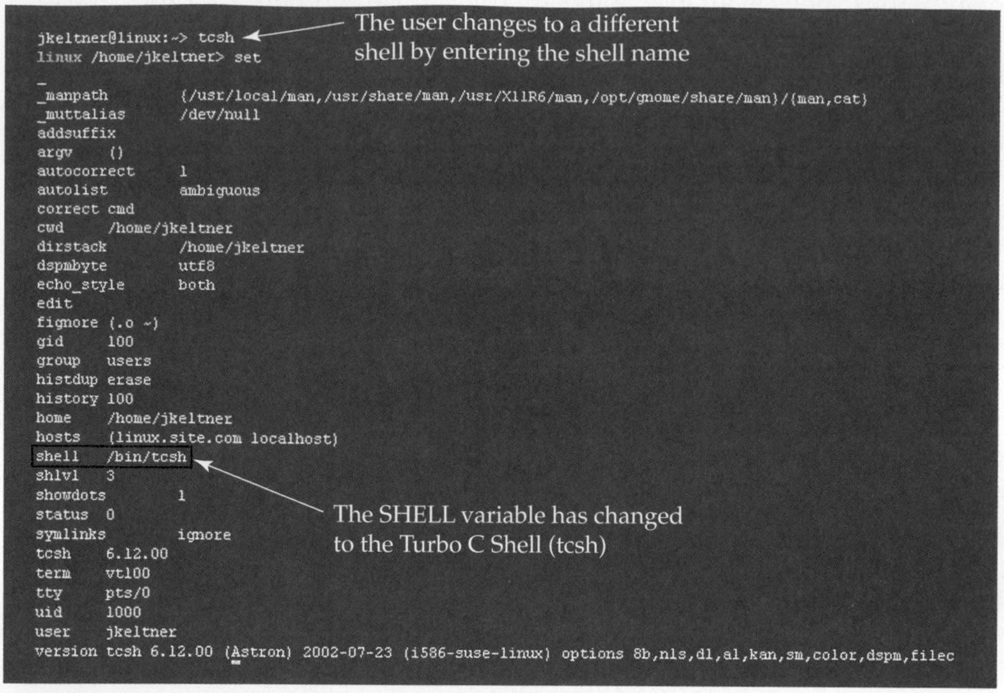
jkeltner@linux:~> tcsh
linux /home/jkeltner> set
_
_manpath {/usr/local/man,/usr/share/man,/usr/X11R6/man,/opt/gnome/share/man}/{man,cat}
_muttalias /dev/null
addsuffix
argv ()
autocorrect 1
autolist ambiguous
correct cmd
cwd /home/jkeltner
dirstack /home/jkeltner
dspmbyte utf8
echo_style both
edit
fignore (.o ~)
gid 100
group users
histdup erase
history 100
home /home/jkeltner
hosts (linux.site.com localhost)
shell /bin/tcsh
shlvl 3
showdots 1
status 0
symlinks ignore
tcsh 6.12.00
term vt100
tty pts/0
uid 1000
user jkeltner
version tcsh 6.12.00 (Astron) 2002-07-23 (i586-suse-linux) options 8b,nls,dl,al,kan,sm,color,dspm,filec
The user changes to a different shell by entering the shell name
The SHELL variable has changed to the Turbo C Shell (tcsh)

Figure 8-8.
The user has entered **tsch** at the shell prompt to change to the Turbo C Shell. The SHELL variable, as indicated by the **set** command, now reads /bin/tsch.

session
a logical connection with the Linux computer.

of the UNIX/Linux operating system is the ability to run multiple sessions on a single computer. A ***session*** is a logical connection with the Linux computer. Each session provides its own set of variables as shown in Figure 8-7 and Figure 8-8. A session allows for remote users to log on to a Linux computer and use the computer at the same time as the user sitting at the computer. It also allows a user to run a lengthy batch process in one session and perform other tasks in another session concurrently.

The user can end a session by entering the **exit** command. This will return a user to a previous session. If there is not a previous session, the **exit** command will log the user off the system.

Commands

Linux commands are similar among the various versions of Linux, but they do not match perfectly. This lack of standardization can be frustrating. You can usually type the command followed by **--help** (two dashes before the word *help*) at the shell prompt to obtain help about a particular command. You can also access the manual pages for a particular command by typing **man** followed by the command. However, even these commands are not universal.

The command syntax is similar to that of DOS commands. The command may stand alone or be followed by options, an argument, or both. The following shows the complete syntax of a Linux command:

command <options> <argument>

An *option* alters the output of a command. Some options must be preceded with a dash (-) or with two dashes (--). Some options do not need a dash at all. In any case, a space must exist between the command and the option. Options, like commands and file names, are case-sensitive.

An *argument* is what the command is to act on. It can be a file name, a directory name, wild card characters, such as the asterisk (*) or question mark (?); or other piece of information designated as an argument for a particular command.

Figure 8-9 shows an example of using a command without options and an argument. The **ls** command is used to list the contents of the current directory. Now look at **Figure 8-10.** In this example, entering **ls** with the **l** option displays the directory listing in a long form. The long form lists details about each file and directory, such as permissions and file size. The **ls** command can also be used with an argument. The argument can be a path name to list the contents of a directory other than the working directory. The argument can also be a file name or part of a file name with wild card characters. Look at **Figure 8-11.** In this example, the **ls** command is used with an argument that contains a wildcard character. This

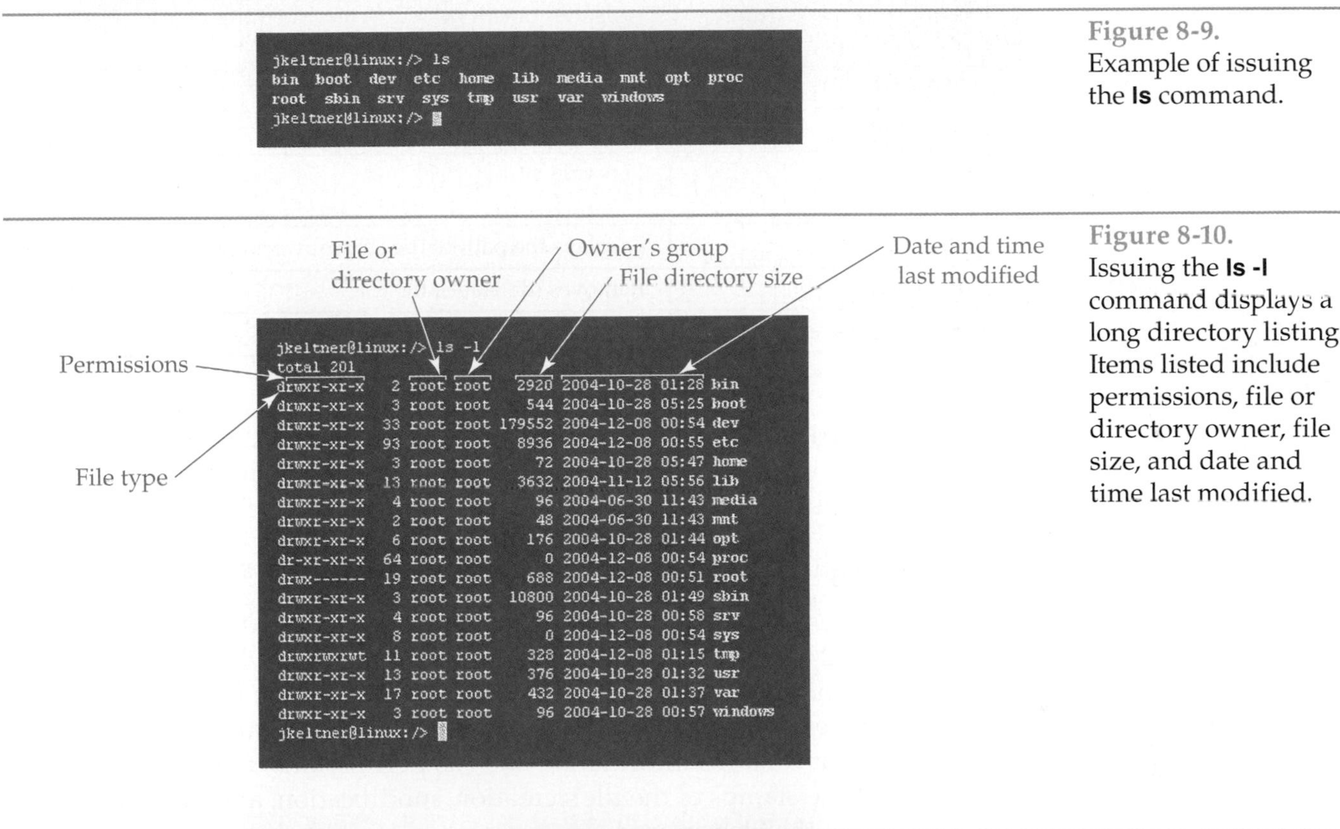

Figure 8-9.
Example of issuing the **ls** command.

Figure 8-10.
Issuing the **ls -l** command displays a long directory listing. Items listed include permissions, file or directory owner, file size, and date and time last modified.

```
jkeltner@linux:/> ls -ld s*
drwxr-xr-x  3 root root 10800 2004-10-28 01:49 sbin
drwxr-xr-x  4 root root    96 2004-10-28 00:58 srv
drwxr-xr-x  8 root root     0 2004-12-08 00:54 sys
jkeltner@linux:/>
```

Figure 8-11.
The **ls** command has been listed here with an argument. The argument in this example includes a wildcard character, the asterisk (*). Together with the letter *S*, it tells the **ls** command to list only those files and directories that begin with the letter *S*. The **-l** option tells the **ls** command to output the result of the argument in a long listing format.

Figure 8-12.
Common UNIX/Linux commands.

Linux command	Description
cd	Changes the directory to the user's home directory.
cd ..	Changes to the parent directory of the current working directory.
cd *<directory>*	Changes the directory to the specified directory.
cp *<filename> <directory>*	Copies a file to a specified directory.
ls	Lists the contents of the current working directory.
ls *<directory>*	Lists the contents of the specified directory.
ls l **ls l** *<directory>*	Lists the contents of a directory, including file and subdirectory details.
mkdir *<new directory>*	Makes (creates) a directory.
mv *<filename> <directory>*	Moves a file to a new directory.
mv *<filename>* *<new filename>*	Renames a file.
pwd	Displays the path of the current working directory.
rm *<filename>*	Removes (deletes) a file.
rmdir *<directory>*	Removes (deletes) a directory.

argument tells the **ls** command to list only files and directories that begin with the letter *S*. The **-l** option tells the **ls** command to list the results in long form. See **Figure 8-12** for a list of other common Linux commands and their function.

File Systems

inode
a table entry that contains information such as permissions; file size; name of the owner; the time stamps of the file's creation, modification, and last access; and a pointer to where the file is stored.

journaling file system
a type of file system that ensures file integrity whenever an unexpected system shutdown occurs, such as a power outage. The journaling file system maintains a log of all file activity.

journal file
a log of file activity.

Several choices of Linux file systems are available: Ext2, Ext3, Ext4, ReiserFS, JFS1, and JFS. Ext2 is the original Linux file system. It supports long file names (255 characters) and stores information in blocks much like the DOS and Windows file systems. Information about each file is stored in an inode. An ***inode*** is a table entry that contains information such as permissions; file size; name of the owner; the time stamps of the file's creation, modification, and last access; and a pointer to where the file is stored.

The Ext3 file system is basically the Ext2 file system with the journaling feature added. In fact, each of the Linux file systems, except for Ext2, is a journaling file system. A ***journaling file system*** ensures file integrity whenever an unexpected system shutdown occurs, such as a power outage. The journaling file system maintains a log of all file activity. This log is called the ***journal file.*** Three time stamps that contain information about the creation of the file, the last date the file was modified, and the last date the file was accessed are added to the journal file. The journaling file system uses the journal file to restore a file to its most usable state. This can be accomplished even if the file is corrupted or incomplete. A journaling file system also allows for faster boot time and consumes less memory than other file systems. For more information on journaling file systems, visit www.linux-mag.com/2002-10/jfs_01.html.

The Ext4 file system is a continuation of Ext2 and Ext3 and provides the largest storage capacity to date. Ext4 is backward compatible with Ext3 and Ext2.

The Journaled File System (JFS) was originally developed by IBM for the OS/2 Warp operating system. JFS is similar to Ext3 in that information is stored in blocks and metadata is stored in inodes. However, JFS is a 64-bit file system, which allows for a larger file system and larger file sizes.

File Structure

The UNIX/Linux file structure looks similar to the DOS file structure. However, the most noticeable difference between the UNIX/Linux file structure and the DOS file structure is the lack of drive letters. This means that your system does not have a storage limit based on the number of drive letters.

The root (/) directory is the top of the directory structure, **Figure 8-13.** All files and directories are under the root directory. The root directory can be subdivided into additional directories and files like it can with the DOS file structure. Unlike DOS, UNIX/Linux has the ability to append file structures from devices such as floppy disk, hard disk, CD-ROM, DVD, and ZIP drives and to append the file structures from remote computers. This ability makes the file structures appear to be part of the root file structure. To append a file structure to the root, the file structure or device that holds the file structure must be mounted.

Do *not* confuse the root of the directory (/) with the /root directory. The /root directory belongs to the root user, also known as the *superuser*. It is the superuser's home directory.

Mounting a device makes it appear as part of the directory structure. **Figure 8-14** shows the contents of the /etc/fstab file. This file indicates the drives and partitions that are to be mounted during the system boot. The first entry represents the device file associated with the device. In UNIX/Linux, each device

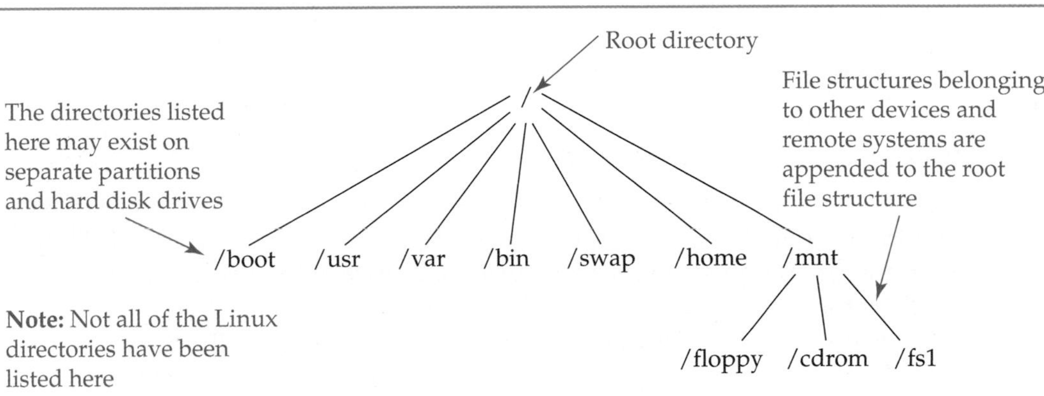

Figure 8-13. The root directory is the top of the directory structure. File structures belonging to other devices, such as hard disk drives, CD-ROMs, and remote systems, are appended to the root directory when they are mounted.

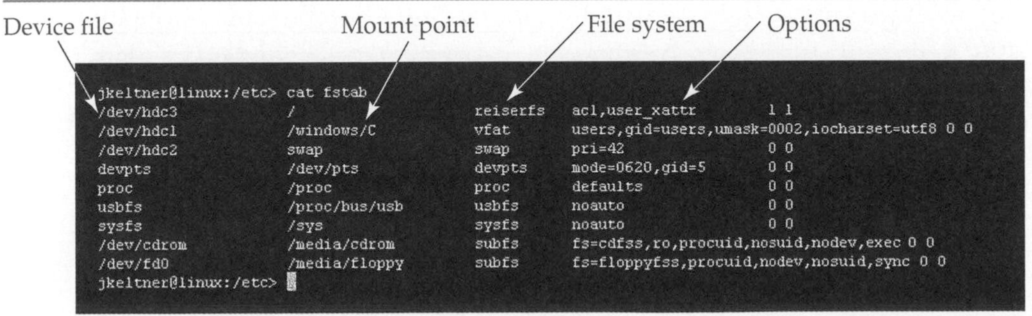

Figure 8-14. Contents of the /etc/fstab file.

device file
serves as a means of communication between the driver and the device.

on the local system has an associated device file in the /dev directory. The ***device file*** serves as a means of communication between the driver and the device. Devices are referred to by the device file name. For example, a primary drive designated as the master drive is called hda. The device file for this drive is /dev/hda. **Figure 8-15** shows the storage device naming scheme and related device files. Partitions are indicated by numbers, starting with the number one for the first partition. For example, the first partition on /dev/hda would be indicated as hda1.

mount point
the location in the directory structure where a device is mounted or inserted.

Look again at Figure 8-14. The second entry in the /etc/fstab file is the mount point. The ***mount point*** is the location in the directory structure where a device is mounted or inserted. For example, a mount point of /mnt/cdrom mounts the file structure of the /dev/hdc device in the /mnt/cdrom directory.

The third entry indicates the type of file system on the device. Note that various file systems can exist on the devices and still be a part of the complete file structure.

The fourth entry lists the options that should be used by the mount command to configure the device. For example, the **ro** option indicates that the device is to be mounted as read only. The **users** option indicates that all users should be allowed to mount and unmount the device. Finally, the fifth and sixth entries set administrative parameters. These will not be discussed because the details about these parameters are beyond the scope of this chapter.

Typical PC devices, such as the keyboard, mouse, and most common file systems are mounted during the system boot process. Before you can save a file to a device such as hard disk drive, CD, or floppy disk, the device must be mounted. Before removing a CD disc or floppy disk, the device should be unmounted. This will ensure that the file can be read by other systems. If the device is not unmounted, the file may be unreadable.

Tech Tip

Some Linux operating systems perform the unmount function automatically.

Common Files and Directories

There are many directories commonly associated with UNIX/Linux systems. This is not to say that all UNIX/Linux file system structures are identical. They do vary among operating systems and versions. **Figure 8-16** lists the most universal directories associated with UNIX/Linux systems.

While it is not necessary for the common user to navigate the directory structure, it is required for the system administrator who commonly modifies software packages designed for Linux. Typically, a common user has access to only part of the directory structure and can only modify his or her directories and files.

Figure 8-15.
Storage device naming scheme.

Hard Drives	Type	Description
hda	IDE	Master or single hard drive on primary controller
hdb	IDE	Slave hard drive on primary controller
hdc	IDE	Master or single hard drive on secondary controller
hdd	IDE	Slave hard drive on secondary controller
sda	SCSI	First SCSI drive in chain
sdb	SCSI	Second SCSI drive in chain, and so on

Directory	Description
/dev	Contains system device files.
/bin	Contains system commands.
/etc	Contains system configuration files.
/tmp	Used as a temporary storage area for files created by utilities and executables. It is emptied when the system is rebooted.
/var	Contains variable data associated with administrative, logging, and temporary files.
/home	Contains user directories and files. The startup files are located here by user.

Figure 8-16. Common UNIX/Linux directories.

UNIX/Linux file and directory names are case-sensitive. This means that two files can be spelled the same but be recognized by the operating system as two separate files. For example, Myfile and myfile are two separate files. Also, be aware that UNIX/Linux files typically do not use file extensions. For example, when looking for an executable file, you will not see the familiar .exe extension appended to the file name. An executable file is identifiable by the file's permissions accessed through one of the utilities that display the file name, directory, and permissions or by using the **ls -l** command.

File and Directory Security

Like other network operating systems, the UNIX/Linux operating system has the ability to assign permissions to files and directories. Look at the long directory listing in **Figure 8-17.** Note the first entry for each file and directory. This entry lists the file or directory type followed by permissions. There are ten spaces available for this information. The file or directory type occupies the first space. Some of the characters that may fill this space are *d*, *l*, or a dash (-) The following list shows the meaning of each:

d = directory

l = link

- = normal file

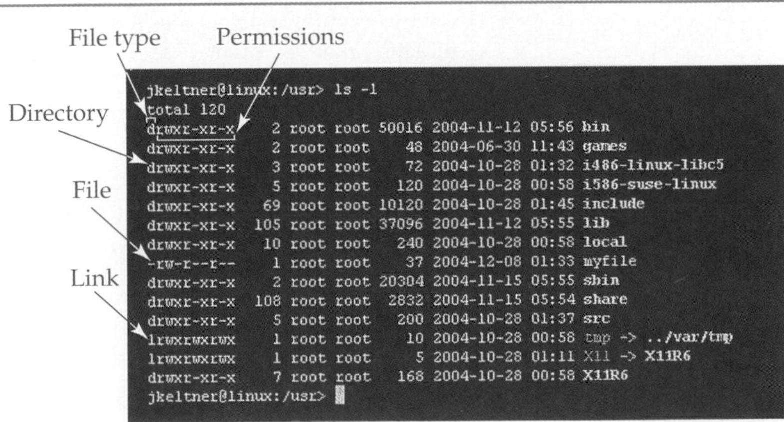

Figure 8-17. Note the permissions for the files and directories in this long directory listing.

The file and directory permissions occupy the other nine spaces. The permissions represent the file and directory permissions assigned to user, group, and other. The user is typically the owner of the file or directory. The group is typically the user's default group. Other is anyone else who is not the file's owner or a member of the group.

Note the letters *r*, *w*, and *x* as well as the dash (-) symbol. A dash within any of the file and directory permissions spaces indicates that no permission for that entry has been set. The permissions associated with the letters are as follows:

r = read

w= write

x = execute

These permissions vary in meaning depending on whether they are set for a file or for a directory. See **Figure 8-18.**

Each of the nine permission spaces is a placeholder for the read, write, and execute permissions for user, group, and other. If any of these values are not set, then a dash displays in its place. To better understand how to interpret permissions, look at **Figure 8-19.** Note that user, group, and other is each assigned three placeholders. Each of these placeholders can be filled with the read, write, or execute permission. In the example, the user and group have permission to read and write to the file. All other users are only able to read the file.

The administrator or user with equal administrative powers can set file and directory permissions. They can even change the owner of the file or of the default group. The owner of a file or a directory can also change permissions or the owner and group.

Figure 8-18.
File and directory permissions and their meaning.

File Permissions	Description
read	Open a file and view its contents.
write	Change a file's contents.
execute	Run a file. This attribute is assigned to executable files.
Directory Permissions	**Description**
read	Display the contents of a directory.
write	Create, modify, or delete files in the directory that you own.
execute	Change to that directory.

Figure 8-19.
In this example, the user and default group are granted the read and write permissions to a file. All other users can only read the file name.

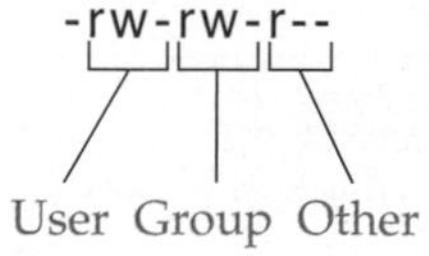

-rw-rw-r--

User Group Other

Network Authentication

Procedures for logging on and off UNIX/Linux systems are similar to other network operating systems. Logging on to the system can take place through a command-line prompt or a GUI-based prompt, depending on how Linux is configured. In either case, the user must supply a user name followed by a password. The user name and password is compared to that in the /etc/passwd file. The /etc/passwd file stores user account information. After the user is authenticated, the user may use the services for which he or she is authorized.

The highest level of administration is the superuser, which has the default user account name of *root*. The initial password for *root* is set during the installation of the operating system. The system administrator uses the root account to make changes in the system configuration. Changes in the system configuration or file structure can render the entire system inaccessible. When the administrator is using the system for normal tasks, the administrator logs on under a common user name and password similar to any typical user. Mistakes made by a common user can be fixed, and typically, the common user cannot access critical areas of the system.

File and Print Sharing

File sharing is made possible through the Network File System (NFS) protocol. NFS was originally developed by Sun Microsystems and later released to the public as an open standard. NFS allows a UNIX/Linux system to share its files with users from remote locations. The system that shares its files is called the *NFS server.* It runs the NFS service. The NFS service consists of several daemons. These daemons handle services such as authentication and client mount requests. NFS also relies on support from the kernel.

The system that accesses files on the NFS server is called the *client*. It relies on support from the kernel and from several NFS client daemons.

An administrator makes an NFS server's files available to remote users by listing in the /etc/exports file the directories to be shared, associated permissions, and the systems that are allowed to access each directory. The administrator then runs the **exportfs** command to export the directories. To view the exported directories, a user at the client computer must mount the directory. Mounting the directory makes the directory appear as if it were part of the client's file structure.

The line printer daemon (lpd) handles remote and local printing services. It listens for incoming print jobs and sends the jobs to the printer. Security is set through the /etc/host.equiv or /etc/host.lpd file. Remote access can be denied through the /ect/printcap file. Denying remote access allows only local users to send print jobs. The **lpr** command is used to send print jobs to the line printer daemon (lpd). For example, to print a file named chapter9 located in the /home/rroberts directory, the user would enter lpr /home/rroberts/chapter9 at the command prompt.

The ***Common UNIX Printing System (CUPS)*** daemon has been designed to support network printing using the Internet Printing Protocol (IPP). CUPS is used in many Linux operating systems as well as Mac OS X. Since CUPS is based on IPP, it is designed to locate and configure printers located on the LAN and WAN through the use of a browser. Linux systems typically provide the user with a choice of using the traditional lpd printing system or CUPS.

Common UNIX Printing System (CUPS)
a printer daemon designed to support network printing using the Internet Printing Protocol (IPP).

Remote Access Features

UNIX/Linux is designed to share resources but not in the same way that other networking systems share resources. For example, when you create and set up a share on a Windows network, the share is run on the client's computer. In UNIX/Linux, when a share is set up on the UNIX/Linux computer and is then accessed by the client, the program runs on the UNIX/Linux computer. This means that the client only needs minimal resources, but the resources of the UNIX/Linux computer must be increased as the number of clients increases.

Any operating system can access a UNIX/Linux system by using remote access protocols and services. There are several remote access protocols and services that you have probably heard of. They are FTP, TFTP, Telnet, and Apache. These various protocols and services provide remote access to clients anywhere in the world. Linux also provides the SFTP service as a way to secure the remote connection. The SFTP protocol differs from FTP and TFTP in that it encrypts the user password and data.

FTP

The File Transfer Protocol (FTP) is designed to transfer files between a server and a client. Using FTP, you cannot run a program or manipulate a file on the server. FTP transfers files rather than runs or manipulates them. In other words, using FTP, you can only download or upload files. If you need to edit a file on the server while using FTP, you can download the file, modify it, and then upload it to the server.

FTP can require a user name and password, or it can permit anonymous access. Most often, however, anonymous access requires some form of authentication, such as the client's e-mail address.

TFTP

Like FTP, the Trivial File Transfer Protocol (TFTP) is designed to transfer or copy files to and from a remote system. The main difference between FTP and TFTP is the protocol it uses to transfer the information. FTP uses the Transmission Control Protocol (TCP) to transfer data, while TFTP uses the User Datagram Protocol (UDP) to transfer data. TFTP does not require a user name or password and does not guarantee data delivery. It is a connectionless protocol.

Telnet

Telnet is designed to remotely access any computer running as a Telnet server. The Telnet service allows a user to log on using a user name and password. After the connection is made, the client communicates with the Telnet server using text-based commands. The Telnet session allows a user to manipulate a file on the remote computer. However, the amount of manipulation is limited to the set of Telnet commands. Telnet is often referred to as a *terminal emulation program* because it emulates a terminal connected to a mainframe. Telnet is commonly used to remotely control WAN servers and routers. See **Figure 8-20** for a comparison of FTP, TFTP, and Telnet.

Apache

Apache is Web server software developed in the public domain to run on UNIX/Linux. Many Web servers use the Apache Web server software. It is popular because not only is it a robust and stable system, it is free. The Apache Web server software was designed as a free distribution by a group of approximately 20 developers. Apache derives its name from the fact that it consists of a series of software patches for the original NCSA Web server software. Hence, the name Apache, which is a play on the words *"a patchy."* Apache is the default Web server package in most commercial Linux operating systems.

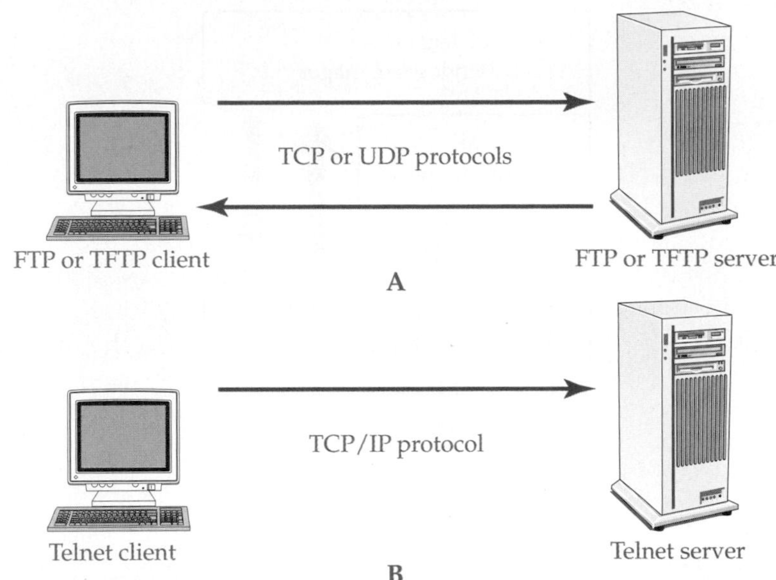

Figure 8-20. FTP, TFTP, and Telnet comparison. A—FTP and TFTP allow a client to transfer files to and from an FTP or TFTP server. FTP uses the TCP protocol and TFTP uses the UDP protocol. B—Telnet allows a client to manipulate files while they reside on the server.

X Windows System

The ***X Windows*** system provides a GUI for UNIX and Linux systems. Other operating systems integrate the GUI into the operating system. The operating system cannot be separated from the GUI to function as a single unit. The X Windows system is separate from the operating system. A user can operate a UNIX/Linux computer without ever installing the GUI.

X Windows provides a GUI for UNIX and Linux systems.

The X Windows system consists of the X server and the X client. ***X server*** is a program that communicates with the computer hardware, such as the keyboard, mouse, and monitor. The ***X client*** is an application, such as a word processing program. The X client can also be a windows manager. A ***windows manager*** controls the display. In other words, it provides the GUI such as the icons, boxes, and buttons. **Figure 8-21** shows the relationship between the hardware, X server, and X client applications and windows manager.

X server a program that communicates with the computer hardware, such as the keyboard, mouse, and monitor.

Tech Tip

X Windows is also referred to as *X*, *X11*, or *XFree86*.

The X Windows system has a client/server architecture. The X server and the X client can run on the same computer, **Figure 8-22,** or on separate computers, **Figure 8-23.** However, in contrast to a typical client/server architecture in which the client receives resources from the server, the X Windows system works in the opposite manner. The X client provides the processing power and display and the X server communicates with the hardware. The X server component serves as an interface between the system hardware and X clients. It allows the windows manager and X clients to operate independently of the hardware.

X client an application, such as a word processing program. The X client can also be a windows manager.

windows manager an application that controls the display such as by providing GUI icons, boxes, and buttons.

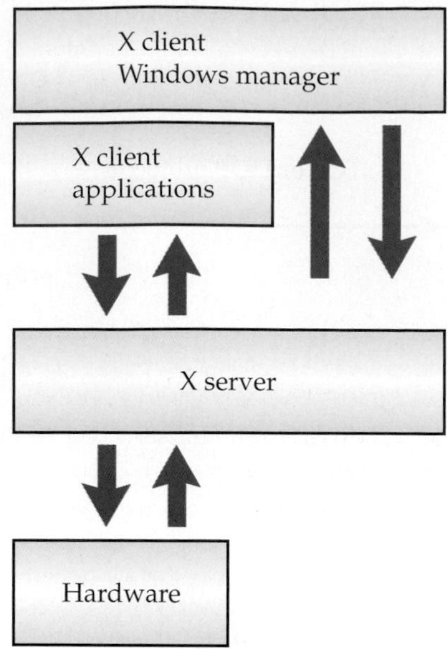

Figure 8-21.
Relationship between hardware, X server, and X client applications and windows manager.

Figure 8-22.
The X server and X client are typically installed on the same computer.

Figure 8-23.
The client/server architecture of the X Windows system allows the X server and X client to be installed on different computers on the network. Unlike the typical client/server design, the X client acts as the server in that it provides the processing power. The X client also sends display information to the X server.

Tech Tip

When the X client and the X server are installed on separate computers, the computer that runs the X clients is typically the more powerful of the two computers.

When X server is installed, it is configured for the system hardware. Typical configuration settings include mouse, keyboard, and video card type and monitor settings, such as the refresh rate and resolution.

An incorrect configuration of the monitor identification or frequency can permanently damage your monitor.

The X Windows system is an open source program for which many X clients or applications have been written. The various applications differ in appearance. To provide a common look among the various X clients, a desktop environment is often installed. A desktop environment is a software package that includes many applications (X clients) and a windows manager. The desktop environment provides a common look among X clients.

The term *X client* can refer to an application, windows manager, or the computer running the X client software. The term *X server* can refer to the X server program or to the computer running the X server program.

Two of the most commonly used desktop environments are K Desktop Environment (KDE) and GNU Network Object Model Environment (GNOME). **Figure 8-24** shows the KDE GUI. Notice that it is similar to the Windows GUI in that it contains a desktop area, icons, and a menu.

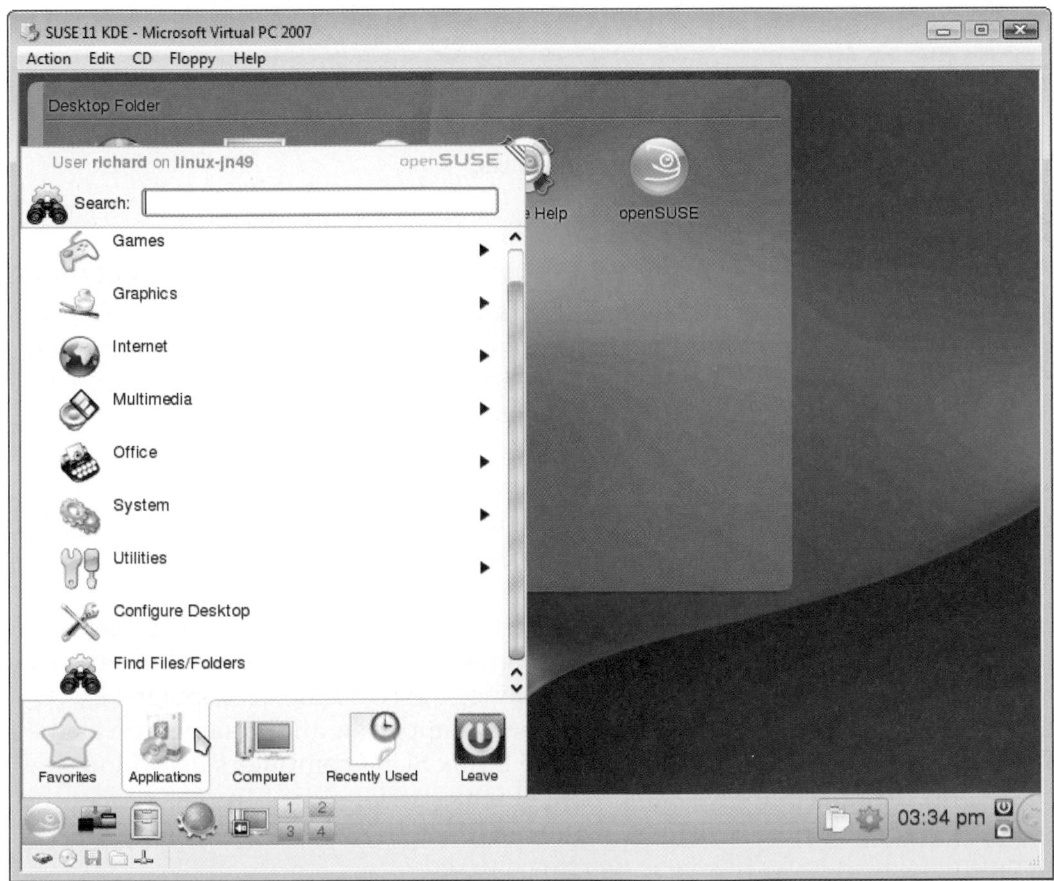

Figure 8-24.
The K Desktop Environment (KDE) with a view of the Applications Launcher.

Desktop environments offer a large assortment of software packages included as part of the installation or available for download. Many popular software packages are designed for both KDE and GNOME desktop environments. Software packages that are not included in the installation can be downloaded from the Internet, typically in a file format called a *tar ball*.

tar ball
a compressed file containing one or more software programs.

A ***tar ball*** is a compressed file containing one or more software programs. Once downloaded, it must be decompressed. Additional configuration may be required before the programs are installed. You should always read the documentation that is included in the tar ball. You will typically find a readme file, which contains an overview of the package, and an install file, which includes instructions for installing the software.

The X Windows system is started by entering **startx** at the command prompt. Most Linux systems can be configured to load and run the X Windows system automatically. When loaded automatically, a logon dialog box prompts for a user name and password. Many of the tasks an administrator performs at the command line, such as adding users or configuring services, can be performed in the GUI.

Interoperability

Interoperability is supported between Microsoft and UNIX/Linux systems using protocols such as Service Message Block (SMB and SMB2) and Network File System (NFS). SMB is the Microsoft Windows protocol designed for sharing system resources. SMB is used with IPv4, and SMB2 is designed for use with IPv6 communications. SMB2 requires fewer packet exchanges than SMB. This reduces network latency when accessing resources. SMB2 was first introduced in Windows Vista. The SMB protocol has been the traditional way to support file access and sharing between UNIX/Linux and Microsoft systems. NFS is the default file sharing protocol for UNIX/Linux systems.

There are also many third-party software applications and many open source software applications designed to support file access and sharing between UNIX/Linux systems and Microsoft systems.

Samba

Samba is a free, open source software package included in most UNIX/Linux systems. Samba is designed to share files on a UNIX/Linux computer with Windows computers using the SMB protocol. It is configured on a UNIX/Linux computer. **Figure 8-25** shows the option for **Samba Server** in the YaST Control Center. This option will allow you to configure the Linux computer as a Samba server.

The Linux computer and the Windows computer should be in the same workgroup, and both computers should have a user account with a matching user name and matching password. You will also need to configure the shared resource with the proper sharing permissions for the user account

After Samba is configured, a Windows computer can access the shared directory structure of a UNIX/Linux computer provided the Windows user has the proper permissions. **Figure 8-26** shows the devices available on the network as viewed from a Windows 7 computer. Notice the two Linux computers: LINUX-84YA and LINUX-GVFS. The Linux computers appear with the same icon as the Windows computers. You can see that the Linux SUSE computers use "Linux" as part of the default computer name. Some Linux versions use "Tux" as part of the default computer name. The term *Tux* refers to the traditional Linux mascot—the penguin—which looks like he is wearing a tuxedo.

Figure 8-25.
Samba Server option in the YaST Control Center.

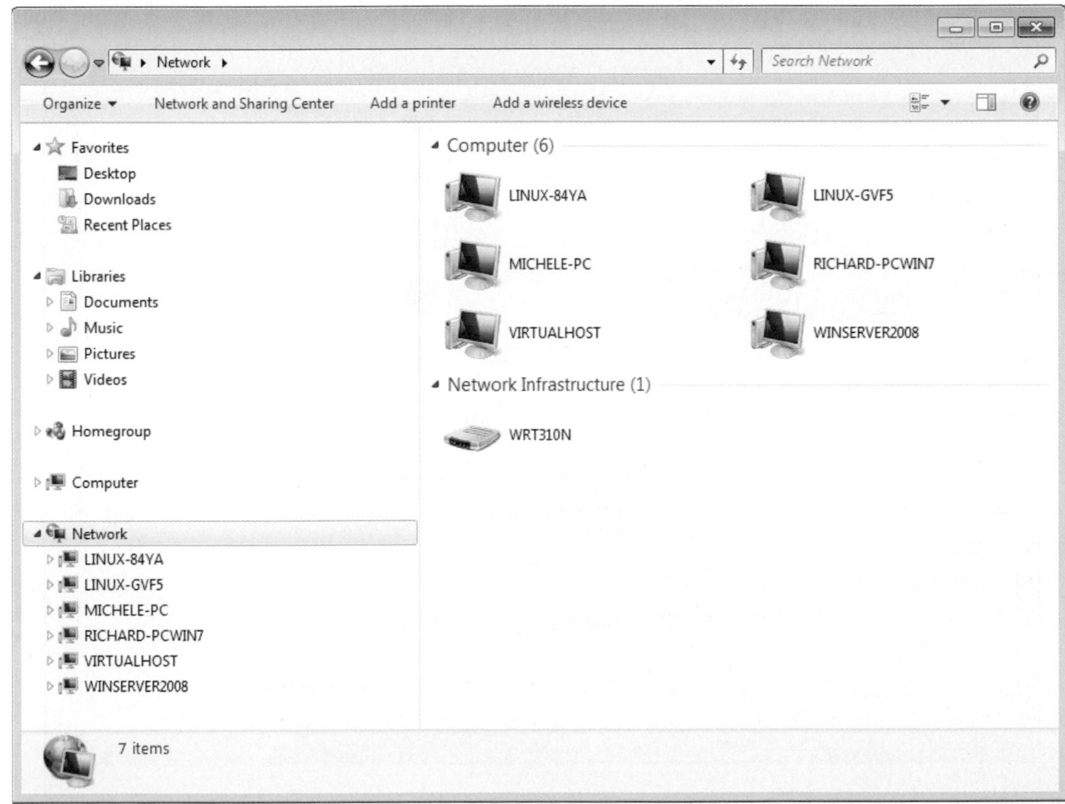

Figure 8-26.
When Samba is installed on a UNIX/Linux system, UNIX/Linux resources can be viewed through Network Neighborhood, My Network Places, or Network on a Windows workstation.

UNIX/Linux computers can be configured to require a user name and password when a Windows computer attaches to the UNIX/Linux shared folder. Shares can also be accessed anonymously, but this is not recommended because of obvious security problems.

Tech Tip

Firewall settings are the most common reason for failure to access shares between a Windows system and a Linux system.

Sharing resources from a Windows 7 and Windows Server 2008 computer with a SUSE Linux computer is very easy. Simply use the **Windows Domain Membership** option in the YaST Control Center on the SUSE Linux computer to join SUSE Linux users to the Windows workgroup or domain, **Figure 8-27.**

Shared resources from the Windows computer can be viewed from the SUSE Linux computer using the smb-Dolphin application. See **Figure 8-28.**

The most commonly encountered problem you may have is Windows Firewall blocking access from the Linux computer. You need to configure Windows Firewall to allow the Linux computer to access the Windows computer.

NFS

NFS is the default protocol used by UNIX/Linux systems to access and share files between UNIX/Linux computers. NFS can also be used to share files with Microsoft computers. Originally, Microsoft used a "gateway service" to translate

Figure 8-27. **Windows Domain Membership** option in the YaST Control Center.

Figure 8-28. Windows 7 shares viewed from a SUSE Linux computer using the smb-Dolphin utility.

the NFS protocol for interoperability between UNIX/Linux systems and Microsoft Windows systems. Microsoft also used Client for NFS as a way to support file sharing and access using the NFS protocol. The NFS translation occurs on the Microsoft gateway service server, thus supporting all Microsoft Windows clients. The other option for earlier Microsoft systems was to install Client for NFS on each Microsoft workstation. When Client for NFS is installed, a server running the gateway service is not required.

Windows Server 2008 supports NFS through the Services for Network File System server role. Once this server role is installed, you can use Server Manager to configure an NFS share. Through Server Manager, the Provision a Shared Folder Wizard can be used to configure a shared folder for NFS. To start this wizard, click the **Provision Share** option located in the right-hand pane, **Figure 8-29.** The Provision a Shared Folder Wizard is shown in **Figure 8-30.** After configuring NFS permissions on Windows Server 2008, UNIX/Linux computers will be able to access shared resources on the Windows Server.

There are options in Server Manager to configure NTFS share permissions for an NFS share. This provides access control for local users accessing the NFS share. NFS permissions used in UNIX/Linux systems are somewhat similar to NTFS permissions but are not an exact match. By clicking the **NTFS Permissions** button in the **Properties** dialog box for the NFS shared folder, you can configure the share permissions to react as NTFS permissions rather than as NFS permissions, **Figure 8-31.**

Figure 8-29.
To start the Provision a Shared Folder Wizard, click the **Provision Share** option.

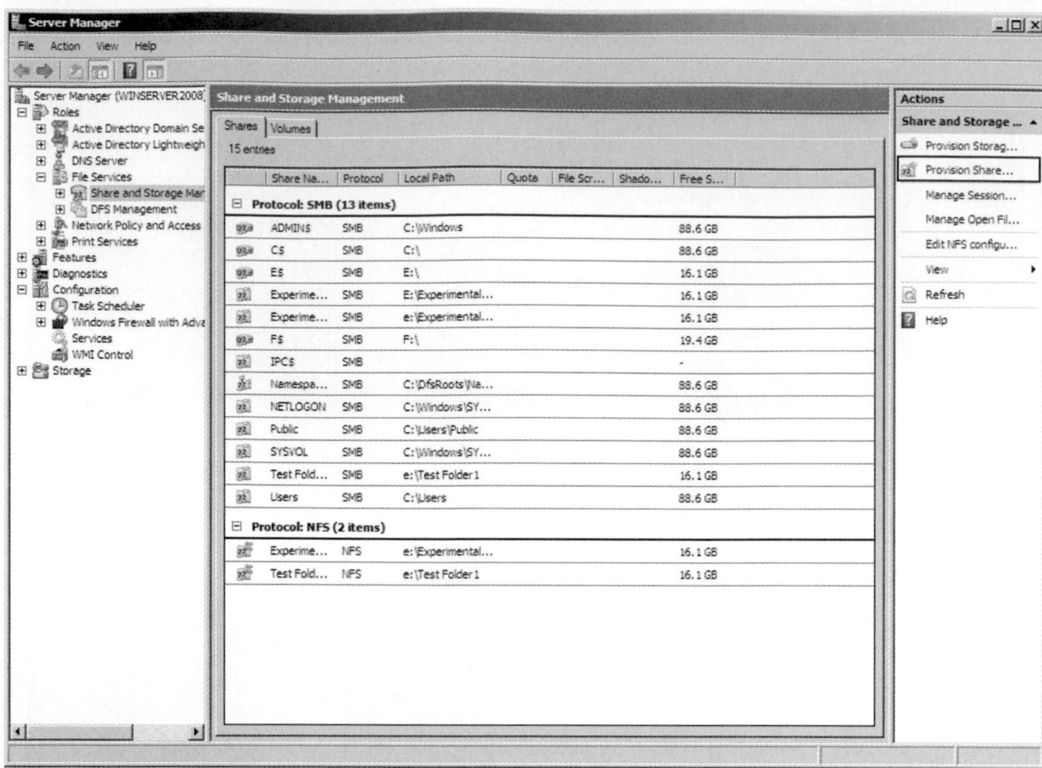

Figure 8-30.
Selecting NFS permissions when provisioning a share in Windows Server 2008.

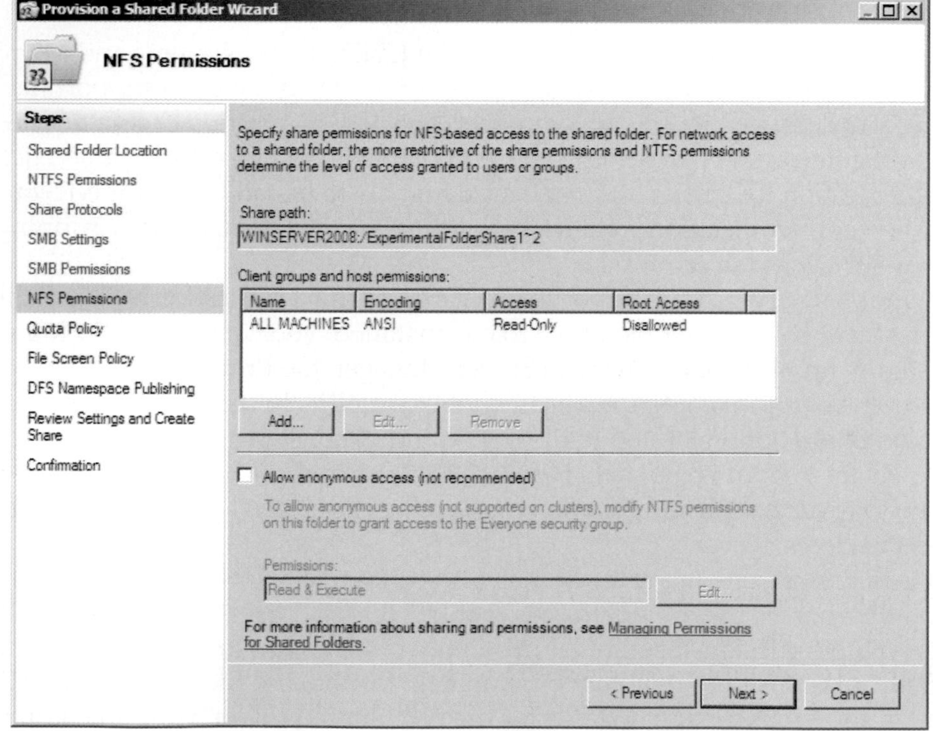

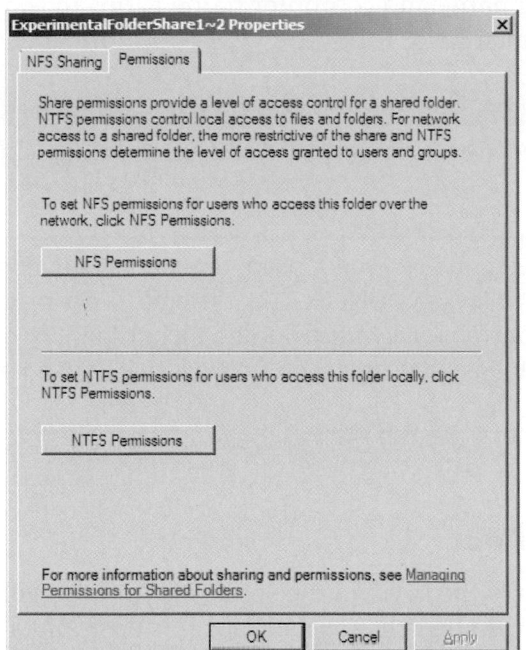

Figure 8-31. **Properties** dialog box for an NFS shared folder. Notice that NTFS permissions can be set for an NFS shared folder, thus providing access control to local users.

Network+ Note

When taking the Network+ Certification exam and you see a question referring to NFS, you can generally bet the right answer involves UNIX.

Troubleshooting Interoperability

A successful ping between computers of different operating systems confirms that the computers are correctly connected physically by network media and layer 2 and layer 3 devices such as hubs, bridges, switches, wireless access points, network adapter cards, and routers. If you can successfully ping computers of different operating systems but cannot view them or their shares, check the following:

- If the firewall is configured to block packets from the other operating systems. To check this, temporarily disable the firewall and attempt to view the computers and shares.
- That the computers are assigned to the same workgroup/domain. Correct if necessary.
- The IP assignment, subnet mask, and DNS server assignment to see if the network adapter is improperly configured.
- The Samba or NFS configuration.
- If the user attempting to access the share has a local user account with the proper permissions to access the share when configured as a peer-to-peer network.
- If the user and the user's computer is a member of the domain when configured as a client/server network.

- For user account name and computer name typos in share permissions and as domain members. Typos are very common when setting up a new system.

Always check the operating system FAQ for known issues involving interoperability. Check the Microsoft and the appropriate UNIX/Linux system support Web sites.

Note

At the time of this writing, the Network+ exam does not cover competencies associated with system interoperability and UNIX/Linux systems. This may change in the future because system interoperability is crucial for the technician. For example, many Internet service providers, Web host providers, and network backup and storage sites use UNIX and Linux servers.

Mac OS X Server

Mac OS X Server is the latest in the series of Apple server network operating systems. It is included in this chapter because it is basically a Linux system designed from open source software. The Mac OS X Server operating system contains all the features found in a typical Linux system, such as Samba, Apache, X Windows, CUPS, and LDAP.

The Mac OS X Server can be configured as a primary domain controller to control user authentication. When configured as a primary domain controller, Windows workstations can log directly on to the network using the Mac OS X Server for authentication. You can connect workstations running Mac OS X, Microsoft Windows, or Linux. A Mac OS X Server can also be integrated into a network that is managed by Microsoft or Novell servers.

Summary

- Linux uses a General Public License (GPL), known as a copyleft, to allow Linux users to copy, modify, and distribute Linux software.
- UNIX/Linux consists of a system kernel surrounded by modules.
- A *daemon* is a program that runs in the background and waits for a client to request its services.
- The Linux kernel is further enhanced by many software packages, such as GNOME, KDE, Apache, and Samba, which have become the de facto standard for distribution with Linux.
- Linux is a variation of the UNIX operating system.
- The term *Linux* refers to the operating system kernel.
- LILO and GRUB are boot loader programs that start the Linux operating system load process and can be used to load other operating systems.
- A *shell* is a user interface that interprets and carries out commands.
- UNIX/Linux file and directory names are case-sensitive.
- Several choices of Linux file systems are available such as Ext2, Ext3, Ext4, ReiserFS, JFS1, and JFS.
- ReiserFS, JFS, JFS1, Ext3 and Ext4 are journaling file systems.

- A journaling file system ensures file integrity by maintaining a log of all file activity whenever an unexpected system shutdown occurs.
- The UNIX/Linux file structure looks similar to the Microsoft file structure; however, UNIX/Linux does not use drive letters.
- The top of the UNIX/Linux directory structure is called the *root directory* and is indicated by the forward slash (/) symbol.
- All file structures from storage devices, such as CD-ROM drives and shared resources from remote systems, are appended to the root through the mounting process.
- Hardware such as the DVD device must be mounted before it can be used.
- The read, write, and execute permission can be set for a file or directory's owner, default group, and other users.
- The highest level of administration is the superuser and has the default user account name of *root*.
- The Network File System (NFS) was developed by Sun Microsystems for exchanging files on a network.
- NFS works in conjunction with TCP/IP to transfer files across a network system.
- Local and remote printing services are handled by the line printer daemon (lpd).
- Various protocols and services, such as FTP, TFTP, Telnet, and Apache provide remote access to clients anywhere in the world.
- Apache is the default Web server software package used with UNIX/Linux.
- The two main desktop environments used with Linux are GNOME and KDE.
- Samba is a free software package that allows UNIX/Linux systems to share files and printers with Windows-based clients.
- Originally Microsoft used gateway services to support interoperability between UNIX/Linux systems.
- Windows Server 2008 provides support for NFS through the Services for Network File System server role.
- Mac OS X Server is designed from open source software and contains all the features found in a typical Linux system, such as Samba, Apache, X Windows, CUPS, and LDAP.

Review Questions

Answer the following questions on a separate sheet of paper. Please do not write in this book.

1. What is the native network protocol used for UNIX?
2. Why are UNIX and Linux referred to as a programmer's operating system?
3. What is a daemon?
4. What is the purpose of LILO and GRUB?
5. What is the function of a shell?
6. List four common shells used with UNIX/Linux.
7. What is Ext2?
8. What is Ext3?
9. What is ReiserFS?
10. What is JFS?
11. What is a journaling file system?

12. Using the DOS file system as a comparison, describe the UNIX/Linux file system.
13. All files and all directories on a UNIX/Linux system are located under the _____ directory.
14. What does mounting a device do?
15. What is a mount point?
16. What is the /bin directory used for?
17. What are the three Linux file and directory permissions and how are they indicated?
18. What is the difference between FTP and TFTP?
19. What is Telnet used for?
20. What is X Windows?
21. What are the two most common desktop environments associated with X Windows?
22. What is the purpose of the Samba program?
23. What does the acronym NFS represent?
24. What is the purpose of NFS?

Sample Network+ Exam Questions

Answer the following questions on a separate sheet of paper. Please do not write in this book.

1. What program is *most* commonly used on UNIX/Linux systems to provide Web services?
   A. Samba
   B. TFTP
   C. Telnet
   D. Apache
2. In a Linux system, how is the second partition on the first hard disk drive identified?
   A. /dev/hda1
   B. /dev/hda2
   C. /hda/dev2
   D. /dev0/part2
3. What program is used to allow Windows workstations to access files on a Linux server?
   A. Samba
   B. Network File System
   C. TCP/IP
   D. Microsoft Client
4. Which file system is *not* typically associated with a Linux system?
   A. Ext2
   B. Ext3
   C. ReiserFS
   D. NTFS

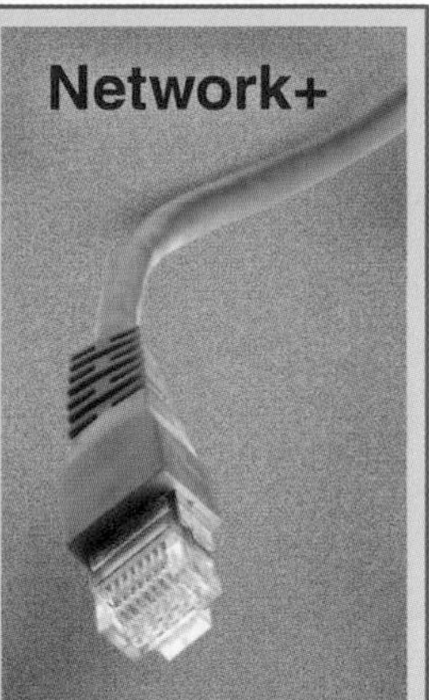

5. What protocol is used for communication between a UNIX and a Microsoft domain?
   A. SMB
   B. NetBEUI
   C. RIP
   D. DHCP
6. Which of the following server operating systems is based on UNIX design and open source software?
   A. Mac OS X
   B. Microsoft Enterprise Server 2003
   C. Microsoft NT 4.0
   D. Novell Netware 5.0
7. What is the default name of the server administrator in UNIX?
   A. Admin
   B. Administrator
   C. Root
   D. Man
8. Which of the following protocols is used by Windows to support communication with a UNIX system?
   A. IPX/SPX
   B. SMB
   C. NetBEUI
   D. AppleShare
9. Where is the C partition located in a Linux directory structure?
   A. Directly under the root.
   B. Between the B and D partition.
   C. Users have their own C partition created when their user account is created.
   D. There is never a C partition in the Linux directory structure.
10. What is required to run a graphical user interface on a Linux server?
   A. Samba
   B. Apache
   C. X Windows
   D. Inode

Suggested Laboratory Activities

1. Download and install a version of Linux. After the Linux system is installed, explore the basic file structure.
2. Visit the CompTIA Web site and look up the requirements for the Linux+ Certification.
3. Add a user to the Linux system.
4. Create a file and set up permissions such as read, write, and execute.
5. Create a group and set group permissions.
6. Create a user with limited permissions.
7. Set up a Linux system to communicate with a Windows 7 system.
8. Set up a printer share on a Windows 7 system to support a UNIX client.

Interesting Web Sites for More Information

www.debian.org
www.fsf.org
www.gnu.org
www.gnu.org/copyleft/gpl.html
www.gnu.org/fsf/fsf.html
www.kde.org
www.Linux.org/index.html
www.redhat.com
www.RMRoberts.com/FTP_files/OpenSUSE11Documentation
www.samba.org
www.opensuse.org/en

Chapter 8
Laboratory Activity

Installing openSUSE 11 Linux

After completing this laboratory activity, you will be able to:

- Carry out a default installation of openSUSE Linux.
- Recall the three default partitions created during the openSUSE installation process.
- Summarize the purpose of various installation options.
- Summarize the role of YaST when used as part of the installation process.
- Use the YaST installation program to modify the default configuration settings.

Introduction

In this laboratory activity, you will install openSUSE Linux, an open source version of the Novell SUSE Linux operating system. You can download a copy from the openSUSE organization located at http://software.opensuse.org/112/en. If this Web address is no longer valid, conduct an Internet search using the key words "openSUSE Linux download."

The two main problems typically encountered during a Linux installation are hardware compatibility and understanding terminology unique to UNIX/Linux operating systems. While the terminology problem still exists, hardware compatibility issues have become less of a problem. However, there is no need to fully understand Linux terminology to complete a successful installation process. This does not mean you do not need to understand the terminology, but rather how easy it has become to install Linux.

YaST is the default installer program for openSUSE 11. The YaST program automatically conducts a series of hardware probes to determine the best default configuration to use. In general, if you accept the defaults, you should not encounter any difficulties with the installation.

You can start the installation process in similar fashion to performing a Windows operating system installation. Place the openSUSE installation DVD into the DVD drive. The disk will be autodetected and the installation program started. You can also place the installation DVD into the drive and then reboot the computer. If the installation does not start from the DVD after the reboot, you may need to configure the boot device sequence so that the DVD drive is listed as the first boot device. You will need to configure the boot options in the BIOS setup.

After the installation DVD boots, you will be presented with several menu options such as those in the following table.

Menu Option	Description
Boot from Hard Disk	Boot directly from the hard disk drive. Only applicable after the operating system has been installed.
Installation	Normal installation of openSUSE Linux on the hard disk drive.
Repair Installed System	Boots to the graphic repair system.
Rescue System	Starts as a minimal, command-line only Linux operating system.
Firmware Test	Determines if the system BIOS or firmware is compatible.
Memory Test	Performs RAM memory tests to detect memory problems.
Boot Options	Allows for additional modified options entered as command syntax. For advanced users only.

Normally, you would select the **Installation** option to begin the installation process. The installation process typically starts the GRUB boot loader and then performs a quick system check to verify that the minimum required hardware exists. Next, the Linux kernel is loaded into RAM. After the kernel loads, the YaST program is loaded into RAM and continues the installation process using a graphical user interface. YaST is also the main system configuration tool used by SUSE Linux.

Note

YaST is an acronym for Yet Another Setup Program. As you will see in the study of UNIX/Linux, programmers have a strange sense of humor and reflect it in their choice of program names and acronyms.

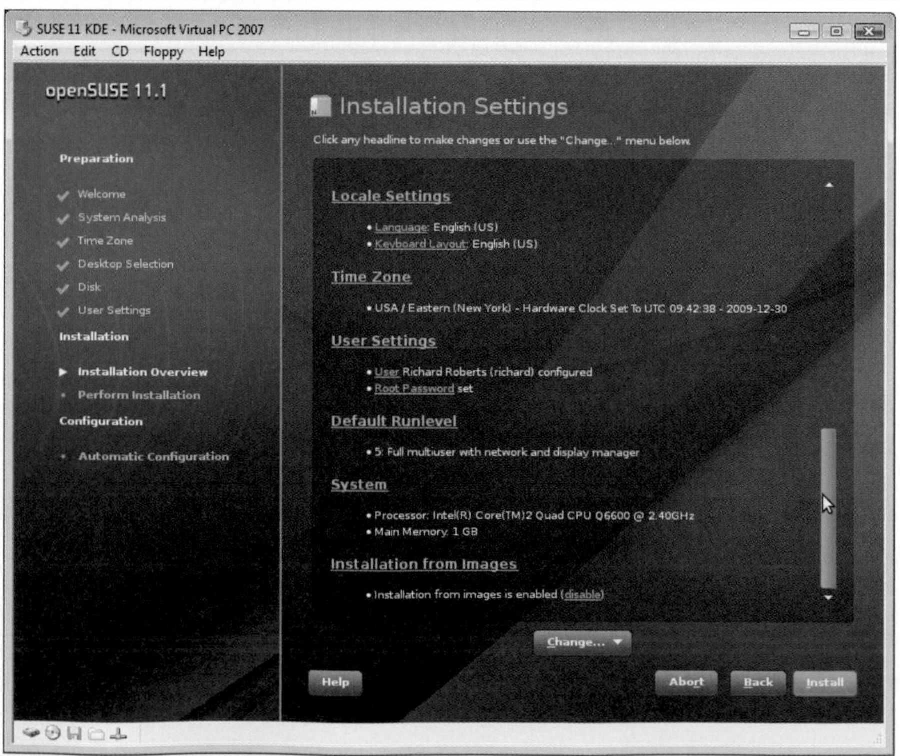

YaST performs the installation in two stages: the base installation stage and the system configuration stage. Base installation includes language selection, major hardware component detection, and hardware profile creation. It also installs the required files and drivers.

The second part of the installation is the system configuration. It includes setting up the root password and network settings, the online update, removing temporary installation files, and the final device configuration. The exact configuration will vary according to the version being installed. As the installation process moves through the various stages, you can interact with each stage to accept or modify the default recommendations. You can abort the installation at any time by clicking the **Abort** button at the bottom of the screen. You can access help at any time during the installation by clicking the **Help** button.

One problem that is commonly encountered in the classroom lab environment is the use of hard drives that contain previously-installed operating systems. This laboratory is intended for a clean installation. All previously-installed operating systems and all partitions should be removed prior to the openSUSE installation unless told otherwise by your instructor. The existence of an operating system on the hard drive could cause Linux to install as a dual-boot system.

During the openSUSE installation, the hard drive will be automatically partitioned into three partitions and formatted. The three partitions are /swap, /home, and / (root). The /swap partition is used in similar fashion as the Windows swap partition. The /swap partition supplements the available RAM. The /home partition is used for user home directories. The Linux operating system is installed in the root partition symbolized by the forward (/) symbol. This partition is also called the *system partition* and is where all the required operating system files are installed. It is not used for user storage.

Novell has chosen ext3 as the default file system for formatting the partitions. Other possible files systems are ReiserFS, ext, ext2, ext3, ext4 and JFS. Again, the default file system is dictated by the Linux operating system version.

During the installation process, you will create a password for the "superuser." *Superuser* is another name for *root user.* The password should consist of a combination of uppercase and lowercase letters as well as numbers and special keyboard symbols. You can even use spaces in a password. If the password does not meet the complexity recommendations, you will generate a warning message. The complexity of the password is not mandatory, just strongly recommended.

To find out more information about openSUSE Linux, go to the Novell Web page located at http://en.opensuse.org/Welcome_to_openSUSE.org. openSUSE documentation is also available at www.novell.com/documentation/opensuse110. To learn more about other Linux versions, look at the Linux organization Web site located at www.linux.org. You can access a selection of open source PDF booklets for openSUSE Linux at my Web site at www.RMRoberts.com/FTP_files/OpenSUSE11Documentation.

Note

When performing this lab, do not make changes to the recommended default configuration unless told to do so by your instructor.

Equipment and Materials

- openSuSE 11.1 or later set of DVD discs.
- Computer meeting the following requirements:
  - 512 MB RAM.
  - 5 GB or more available hard disk space.
  - CPU: Intel Pentium 1 to 4 or Xeon; AMD Duron, Athlon, Athlon XP, Athlon MP, Athlon 64, or Sempron.
- On a separate sheet of paper, record the following information, provided by your instructor.

  Root password: ______________________________

  User name: ______________________________

  User password: ______________________________

  Additional user names: ______________________________

Procedure

1. _____ Gather all required materials and report to your assigned workstation.
2. _____ Boot the computer and then place the first installation DVD in the DVD boot device.

Note
You may need to access the BIOS setup program to reconfigure the computer to boot from the DVD device first rather than from the hard disk drive.

3. _____ With the openSUSE installation DVD in the DVD drive, reboot the system to start the installation. In a few seconds, you will be presented with several options similar to those in following screen capture. The exact appearance and options will vary according to the version of Linux you are installing.

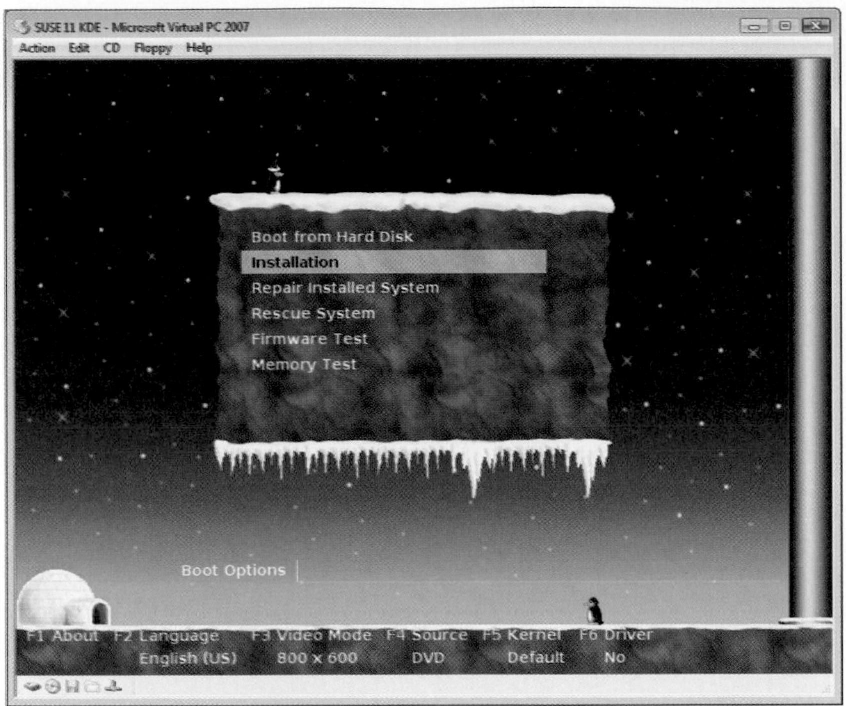

4. _____ Select **Installation**. A progress bar located under the word *openSUSE* will indicate the progress of loading the required minimal installation programs.

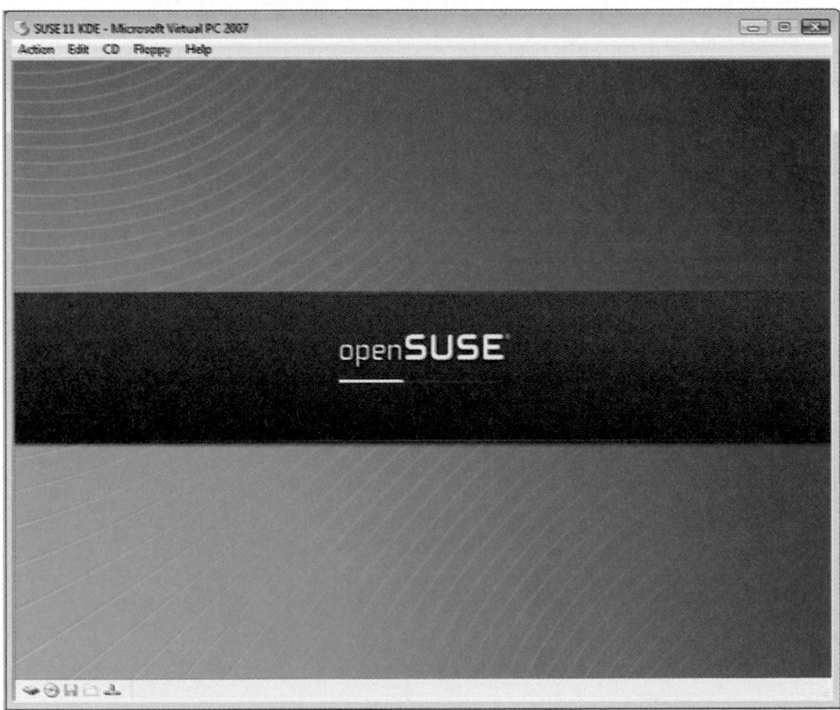

After about a few minutes to 20 minutes, a minimal SUSE Linux operating system will load and take control of the installation operation.

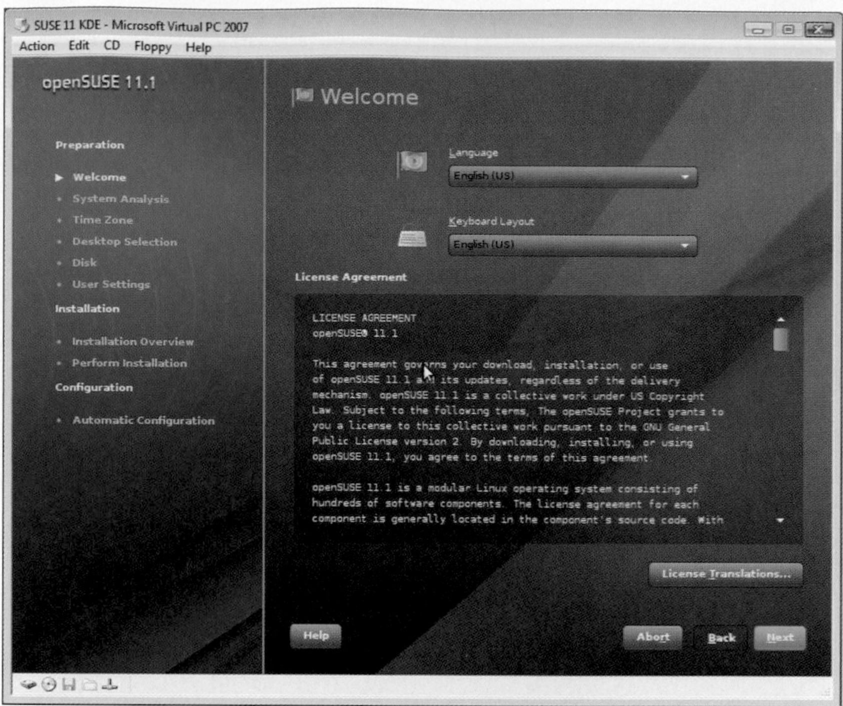

You are prompted to select the language and keyboard layout for the installation. You are also presented with the license agreement. Notice the list of preparation activities located in the left pane. It allows you to track the progress of the installation process. Completed steps are identified with a check mark.

5. ______ Click **Next** to continue. The installation program will probe the system to identify hardware and determine if any partitions are already created and if an operating system is already installed. This will take a few minutes.

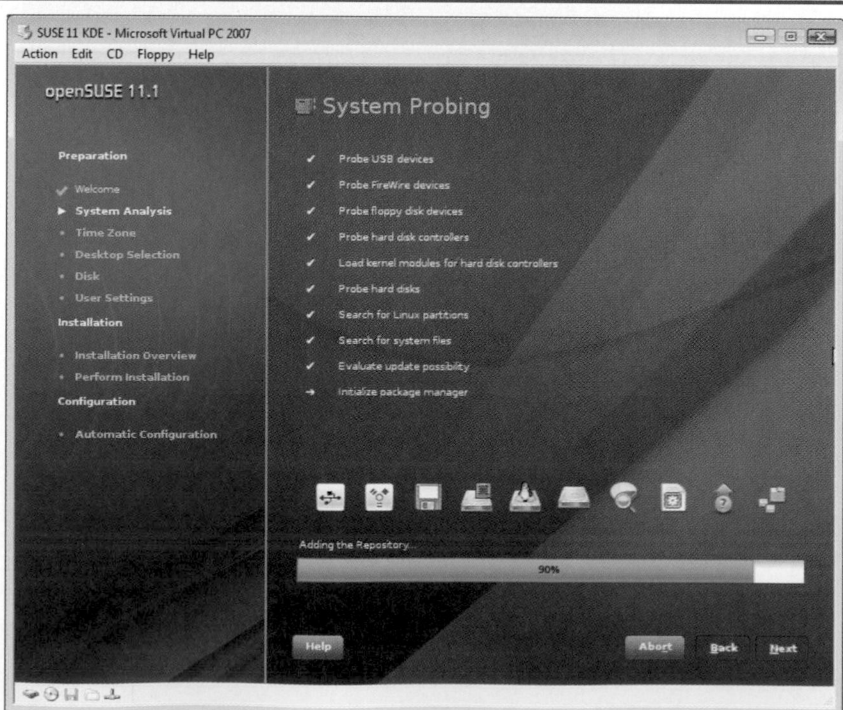

Note

You have the option to abort the installation at any time by clicking the **Abort** *button or by pressing the key combination [Ctrl] [Alt] [Del].*

6. ______ You are now prompted to select an installation mode. The three choices are **New Installation**, **Update**, and **Repair Installed System**. Select **New Installation** and then click **Next** to continue.

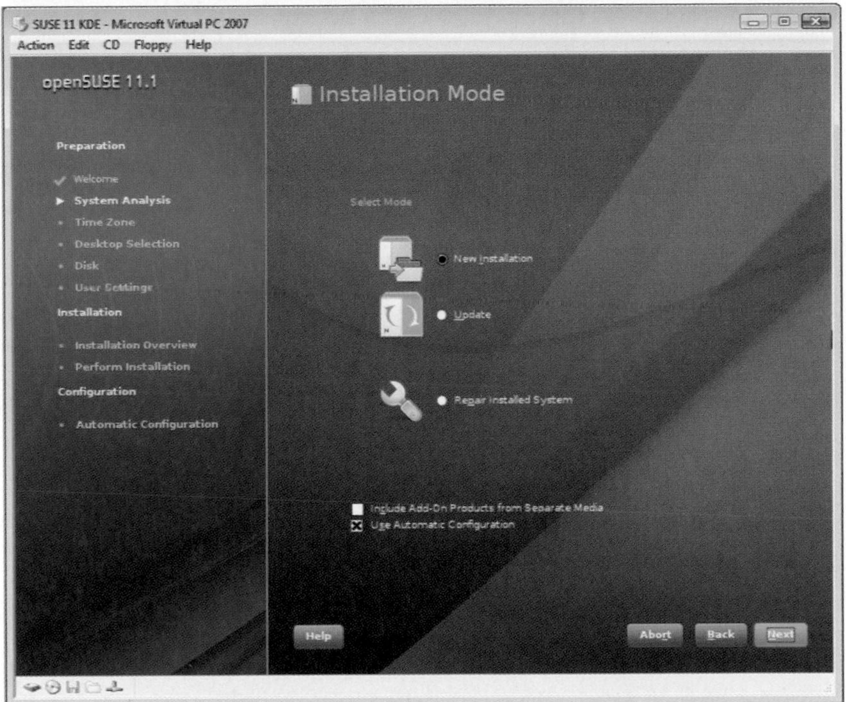

7. ______ You are prompted to set the clock and select the time zone. You can adjust the time by clicking the **Change** button or clicking **Next** to continue.

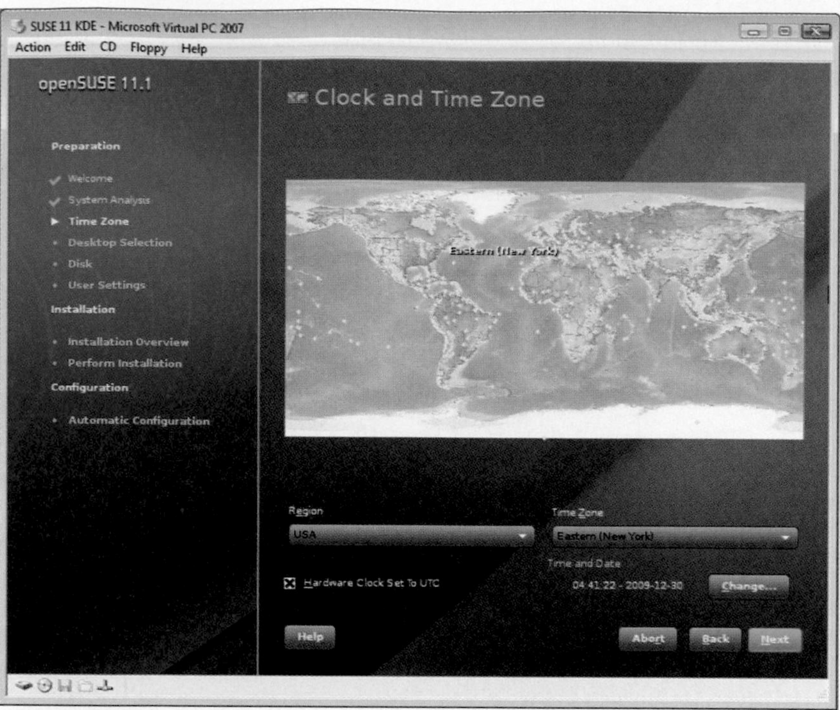

8. _____ You will be prompted to choose between Gnome or KDE for the user interface. Select **KDE 4.1** so that your system will match the screen captures in the upcoming lab activities.

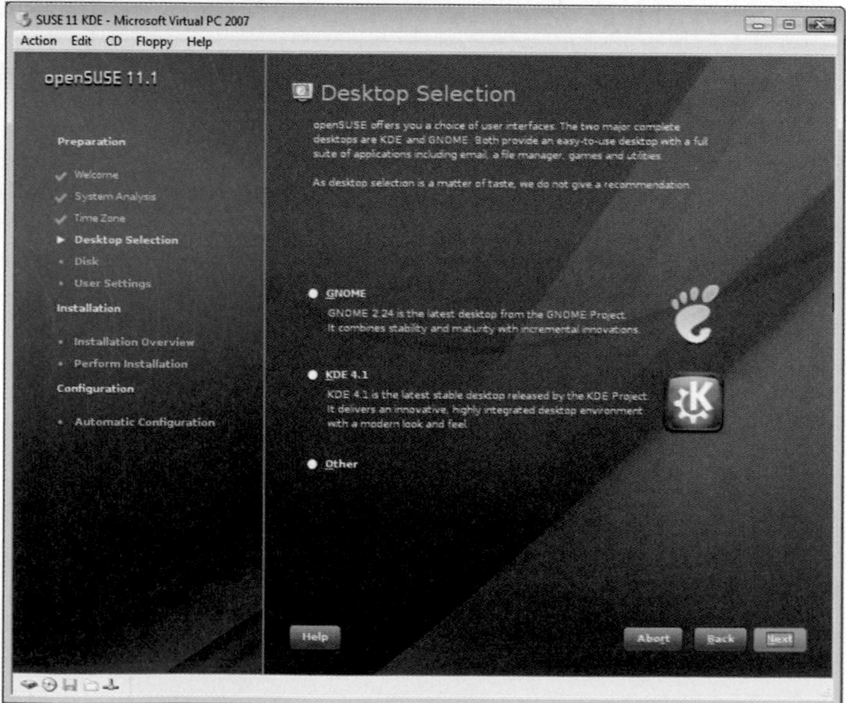

Note

You will not always be presented with two choices. Some versions of Linux only offer one user interface, especially if the Linux version is a beta release.

9. _____ Click **Next**. You are now prompted to choose a partition style. The **Partition Based** option will create a set of three typical Linux partitions using ext3. The **LVM Based** option represents the Logical Volume Manager (LVM). LVM is used to manage large disk volumes, such as a disk farm. It also has a feature to adjust the size of Microsoft partitions and volumes.

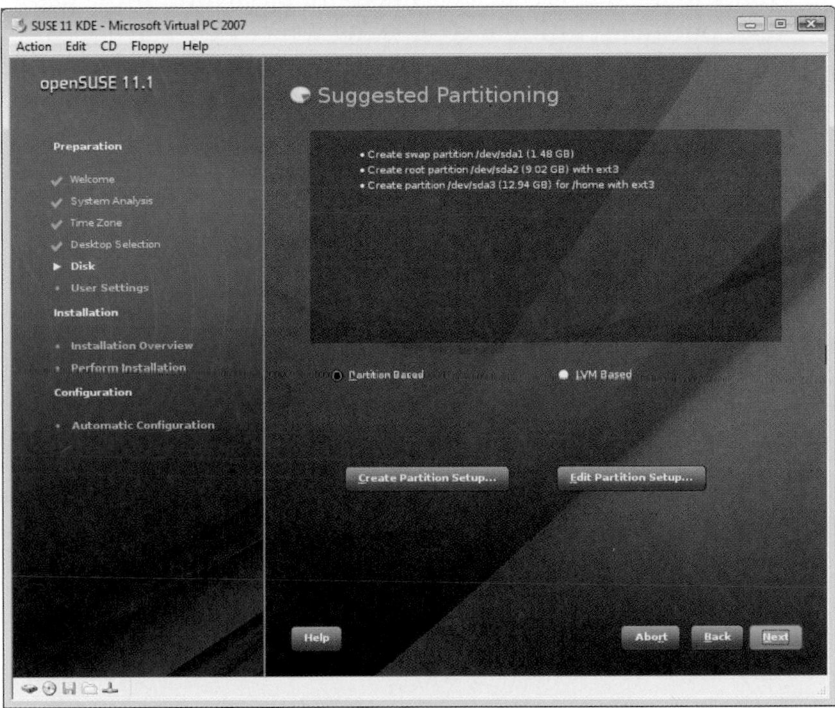

10. _____ Select the **Partition Based** option. You will be prompted to create the default user account and password.

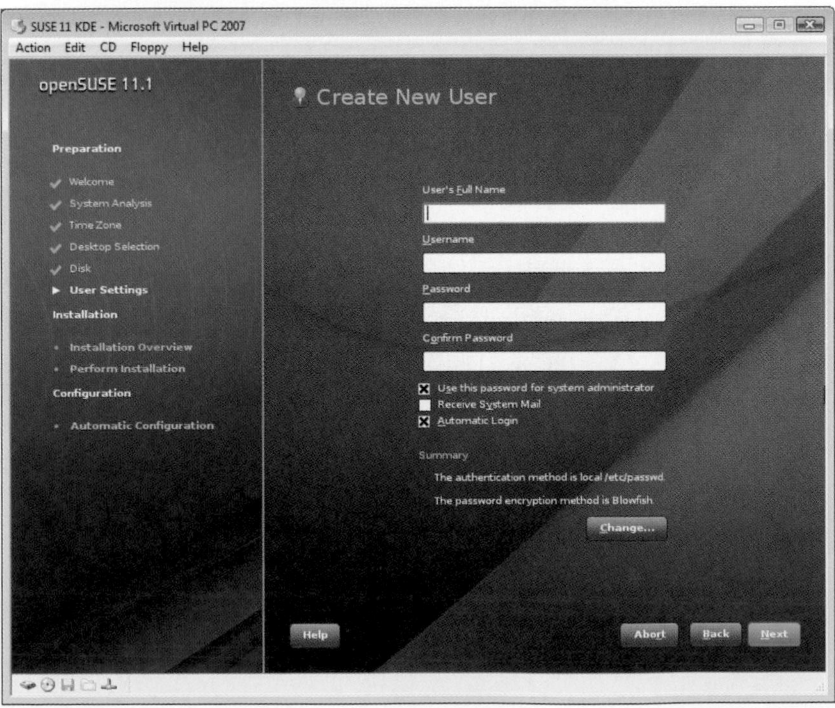

You must supply the user's full name. The user account name will be automatically created based on the user name. For example, the full user name "Richard M. Roberts" will automatically generate the user account name "richard." Notice that the automatically-generated user name is in all lowercase letters. You may change the user name to match an established naming scheme.

You will need to create a user account password. If the password does not meet sufficient complexity, a message will appear informing you that the password can be easily guessed. Click **Yes** to accept your password choice and to close this message box.

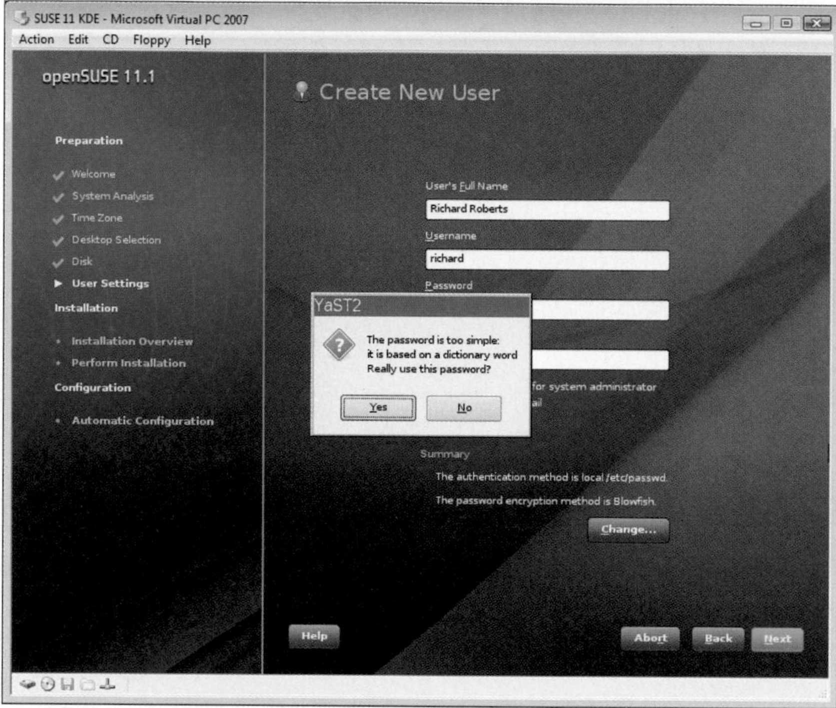

Notice the "Summary" information provided about the location of the password and the type of encryption used.

11. ______ Click **Next**. You will be presented with a list of installation settings. You can review the settings if you like before moving on. At this point in the installation, you can still make changes to the configuration selections. If the configuration selections are to your liking, click **Install**.

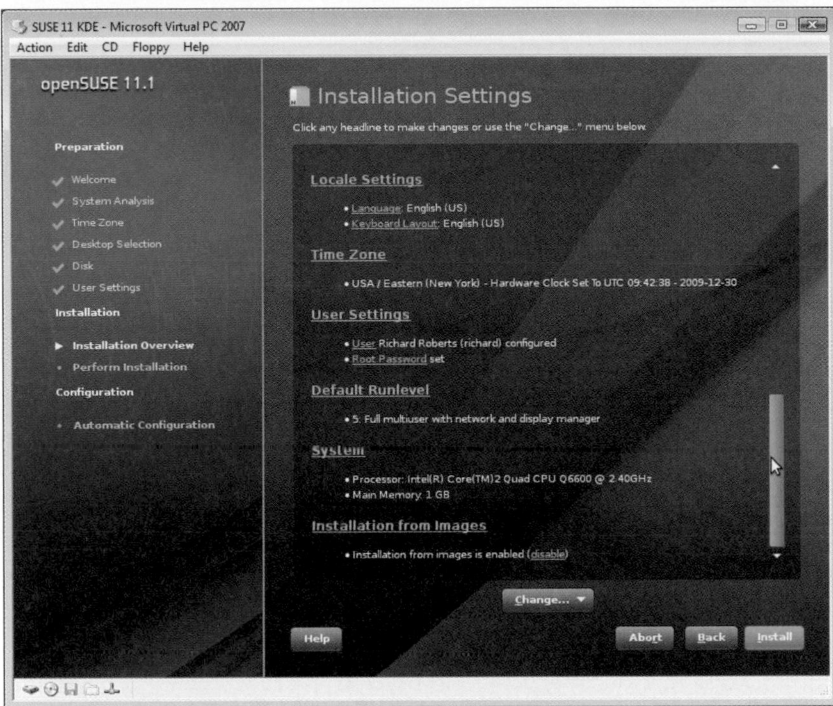

After accepting the settings in the last step, you will be prompted once more to confirm the selection.

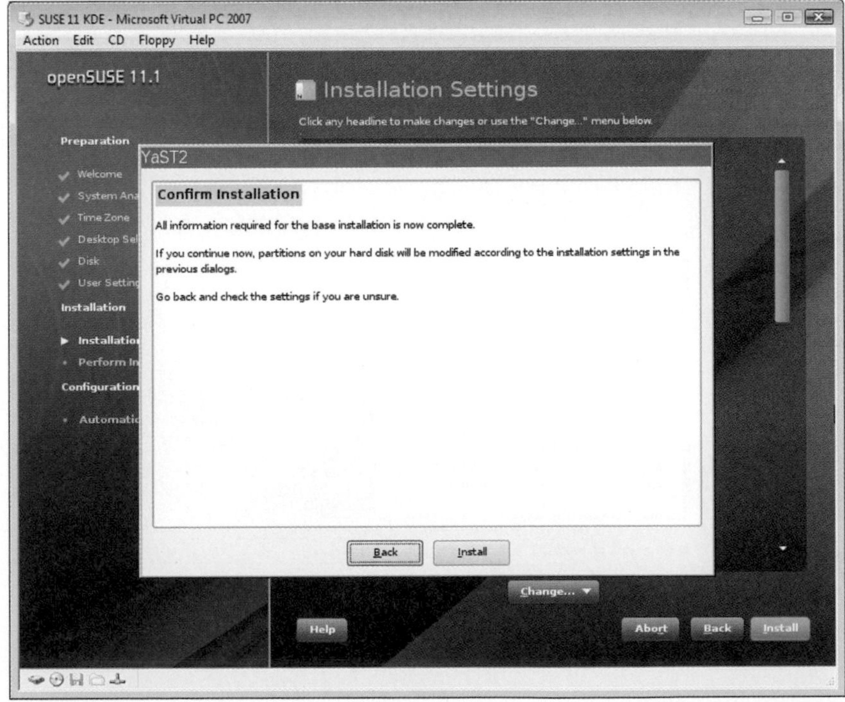

12. _____ Click **Install** to confirm the installation settings. A screen similar to the following will appear, showing the installation progress. It can take a long time (30 minutes or more) to complete the configuration.

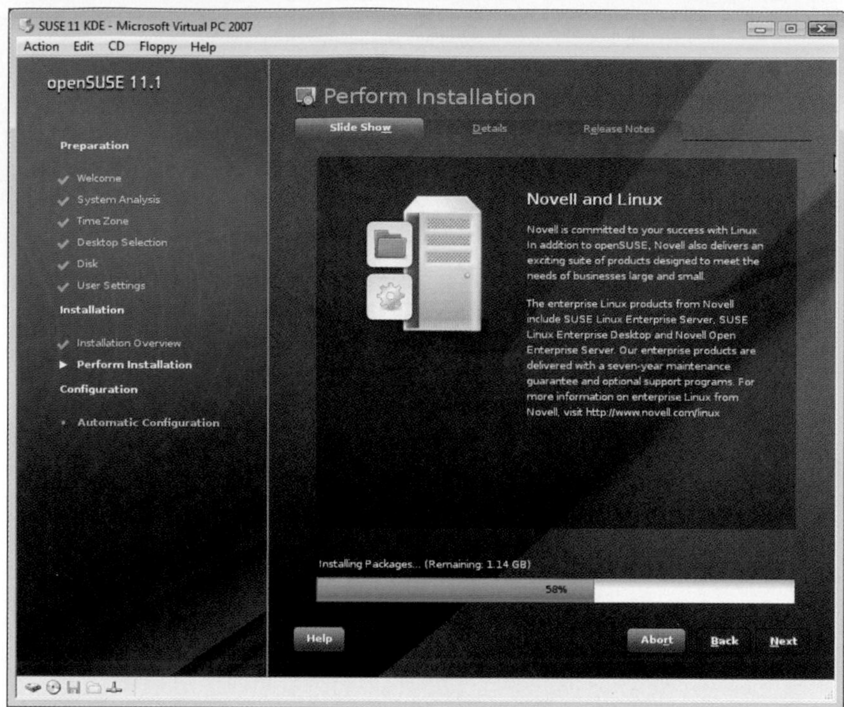

When the installation is complete, the desktop will load and a message box will appear similar to that in the following screen capture.

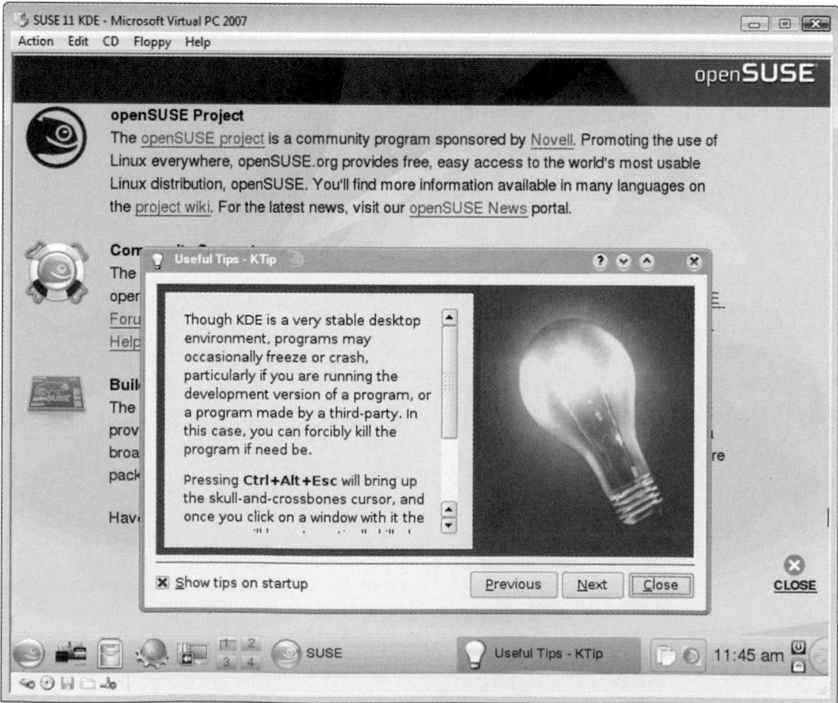

Typically, a **Useful Tips** message box will be displayed. Again, this type of screen display will vary according to the version of Linux you are installing. There may not be a message box at all. You can deselect the **Show tips at startup** option if you wish.

13. _____ Close the message box to see the **openSUSE** screen with links to information about openSUSE.

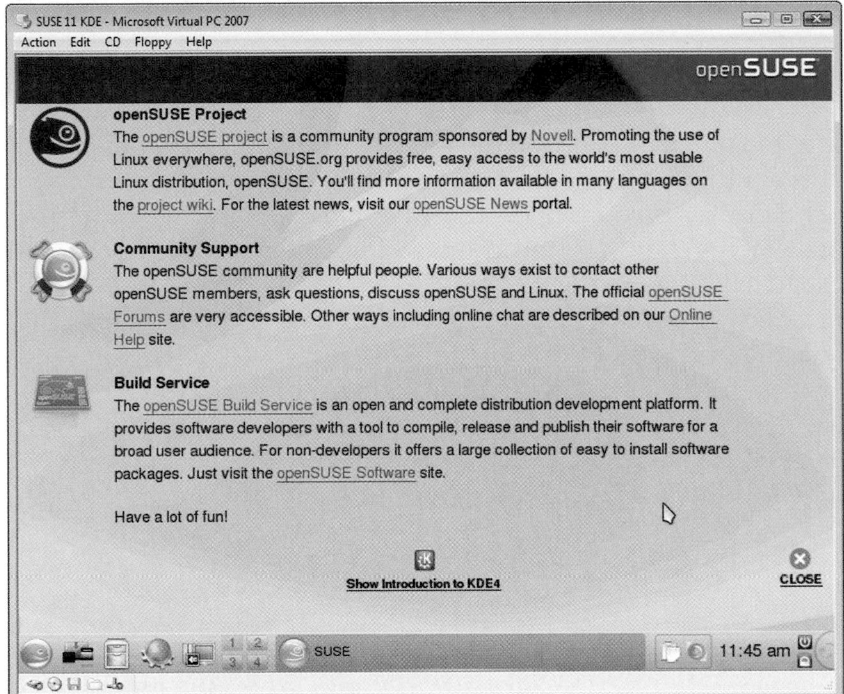

14. _____ Close the **openSUSE** screen. You will see a typical SUSE Linux desktop similar to the following.

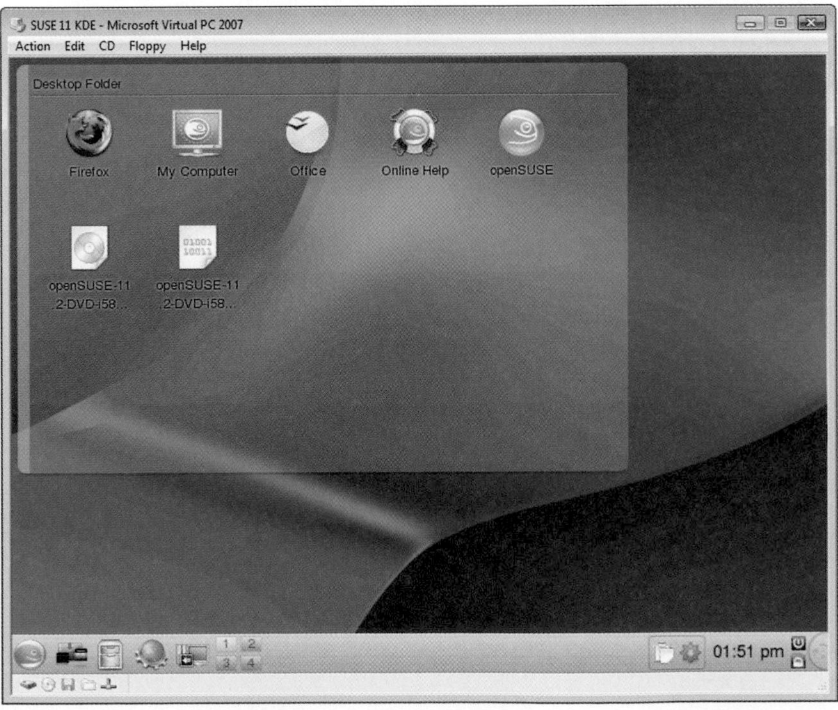

The exact appearance of the desktop will vary according to the version of Linux as well as which desktop package you selected. The desktop shown in the screen capture is based on openSUSE 11.1 KDE.

15. ______ Call your instructor to inspect your lab activity.
16. ______ Go on to answer the review questions. Return all materials to their proper storage area.

Review Questions

Answer the following questions on a separate sheet of paper. Please do not write in this book.

1. What is the name assigned to the Linux administrator by default?
2. What is another name for the root user?
3. What other user is equal to the root?
4. What elements should be incorporated into a secure Linux password?
5. Can spaces be used in the password?
6. What is the purpose of the /swap partition?
7. What is the purpose of the boot partition?
8. What are the two common Linux desktop user interfaces for openSUSE Linux?
9. What three partitions are created by default?
10. Which partition is used for user home directories?

9 Introduction to the Server

After studying this chapter, you will be able to:

- ❑ Recall the various roles of servers in a network environment.
- ❑ Give examples of uses for a thin server.
- ❑ Give examples of uses for a thin client server.
- ❑ Differentiate between a server and a PC.
- ❑ Identify the ID and LUN numbers of a Small Computer Systems Interface (SCSI) device.
- ❑ Identify the four types of system resources.
- ❑ Compare RAID systems.
- ❑ Recall the characteristics and purpose of network attached storage (NAS) technology.
- ❑ Recall the characteristics and purpose of storage area network (SAN) technology.
- ❑ Give examples of common Fibre Channel technology applications.
- ❑ Identify the Fibre Channel topologies.
- ❑ Interpret an iSCSI IQN address.

Network+ Exam—Key Points

The Network+ Certification exam specifically references fault tolerance and network storage. Pay particular attention to the characteristics of RAID 0, RAID 1, RAID 5, and RAID 6 and to network storage, such as storage area network (SAN) and network attached storage (NAS).

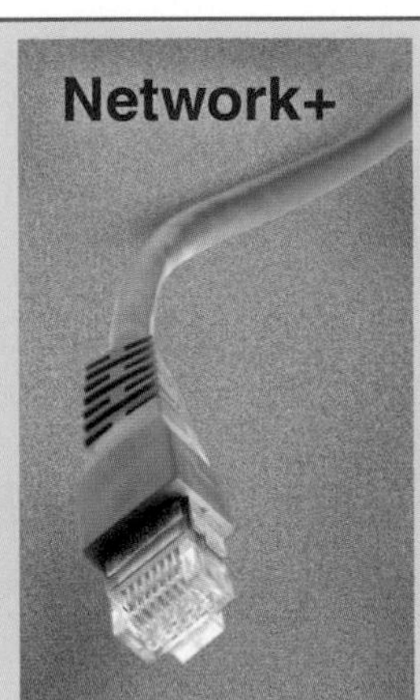

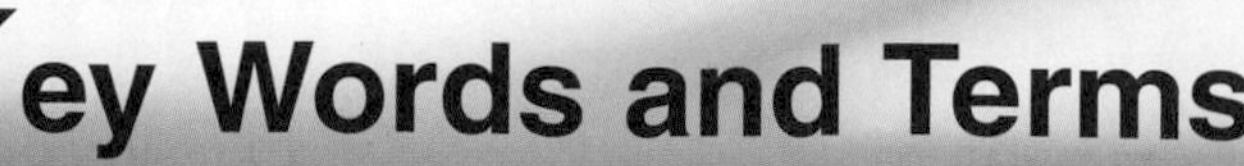

Key Words and Terms

The following words and terms will become important pieces of your networking vocabulary. Be sure you can define them.

ACPI Component Architecture (ACPICA)
Automatic Configuration and Power Interface (ACPI)
backplane
blade server
Direct Memory Access (DMA) channel
disk mirroring
disk striping
duplexing
error correction
fabric switch
fault tolerance
Fibre Channel
firmware
hot swapping
hot-swap technology
Input/Output (I/O) port
Internet Small Computer Systems Interface (iSCSI)
interrupt request (IRQ)
logical unit number (LUN)
memory address assignment
Network Address Authority (NAA)
network attached storage (NAS)
parallel processing
power-on self-test (POST)
Redundant Array of Independent Disks (RAID)
serial attached SCSI (SAS)
Small Computer Systems Interface (SCSI)
storage area network (SAN)
thin client
thin client server
thin server

A complete understanding of server hardware can take a great deal of study. This chapter provides an overview of the server and identifies different server types and their roles. You will be introduced to some of the hardware that makes the server unique from the ordinary PC, and you will learn about RAID and other storage systems.

Server Types and Services

Servers provide a variety of services. Some of the services a server can provide are authentication and security, Web, mail, and print. A server can be called by many names. For example, it can be called an *authentication and security database server, Web server, mail server,* and *print server,* **Figure 9-1.** A network may have a single server that provides a variety of services, or it may have a group of servers, each providing a specific service.

A small network usually has one server set up to handle many different services. A large network usually has several servers, each providing a different service or set of services. For example, a large corporation may use one server to handle e-mail requests and Web hosting, another server to serve as a domain

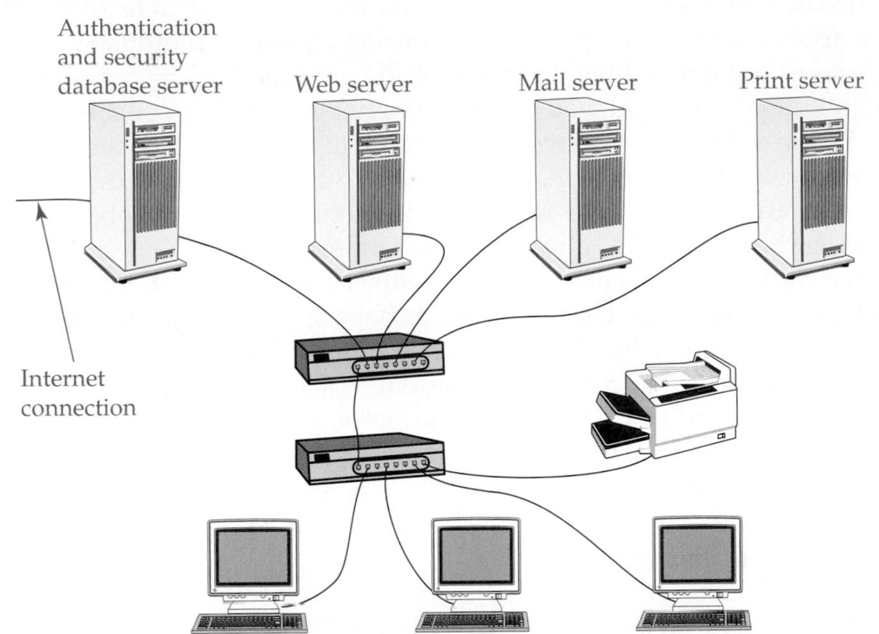

Figure 9-1. Servers provide a variety of services, such as authentication and security, Web, mail, and print.

controller to provide security for the entire network, and another server to provide application software, a database for its clients, and support for print operations.

The more services a server provides and the more clients it services creates a higher demand on the server. A single server with a limited amount of services may be fine for a relatively small number of users, typically less than 25. A commercial enterprise spanning across the country or world may require hundreds of servers. The network administrator or network designer decides the number and capacity of individual servers needed by taking into account the number of users and the system's predicted network traffic.

Each network system is uniquely designed, even though each network has many similarities. Some network equipment providers have software programs that help you design a network. You simply enter information, such as the number of clients, offices, cities, and countries and the type of software and services to be provided. After all the information is collected, the software program provides an estimate of the size and number of servers required. We will discuss this topic later in Chapter 19—Designing and Installing a New Network.

Thin Servers

A ***thin server*** is a server that has only the hardware and software needed to support and run a specific function, such as Web services, print services, and file services. It is more economical to use a thin server as a print server than to tie up a more expensive server simply to handle printing on a network. IBM markets a thin server, which consists of a sealed box that contains only the essential hardware and software required for supporting the server's dedicated function.

thin server
a server that has only the hardware and software needed to support and run a specific function, such as Web services, print services, and file services.

Thin Client Servers

A ***thin client server*** is a server that provides applications and processing power to a thin client. Thin client servers run terminal server software and may have more RAM and hard disk drive storage than needed. A ***thin client*** is a computer that typically has a minimal amount of processing power and memory.

thin client server
a server that provides applications and processing power to a thin client.

thin client
a computer that relies on the thin client server's processing power and memory.

It relies on the server's processor and memory for processing data and running software applications. Thin clients are becoming common in industry for such applications as hotel bookings, airline ticketing, and medical record access.

When budgets are tight, you can install what is normally considered an obsolete PC on a thin client network. The obsolete PC is obsolete because of its processing speed, lack of storage, and inability to run new software. The thin client server can provide all the services that are required by the obsolete PC, thus making the obsolete PC a useful workstation.

Do not confuse a thin client with a dumb terminal. A dumb terminal sends user input to a mainframe. Dumb terminals have absolutely no computing power, operating system, hard disk drive, BIOS, and RAM. A thin client may not need a hard disk drive or an operating system; however, it is still a full-fledged computer because it has a CPU and processing power.

Windows 2000 Server, Windows Server 2003, and Windows Server 2008 come with Terminal Services software. Once Terminal Services is set up on the server, you have the option to generate a disk that will assist you in automatically setting up thin client workstations.

Server Classification by Number of CPUs

Servers vary a great deal by size and power. The number of processors they contain usually classifies them. For example, Sun Microsystems has three classifications of servers: entry-level, midrange, and high-end. Sun Microsystems defines these classifications by the number of processors they contain. A Sun Microsystems entry-level server has up to 8 processors. A midrange server has up to 30 processors, and a high-end server has up to 106 processors. Other vendor's definitions vary somewhat, but this gives you a general idea. In this chapter, we focus on the HP ProLiant DL740 server. The HP ProLiant DL740 is one of the most powerful entry-level servers manufactured.

Major Server Components

It is assumed you have some PC hardware background from completing a course on PC service and repair or have a CompTIA A+ Certification. If not, it is strongly advised that you take a course in PC repair or, at the very least, complete a home study program. A good background in PC hardware proves to be beneficial to anyone working with network servers. As a matter of fact, IBM and other companies require the CompTIA A+ Certification as part of its progression toward certification as a server technician.

When handling electronic components, it is standard practice to use electrostatic discharge (ESD) safety practices. Electronic components based on complimentary metal oxide semiconductor (CMOS) technology can be easily damaged by static electricity. The human body and clothing can build up a tremendous static electricity charge. When touching a static-sensitive electronic component, the static electricity can discharge and cause the component to be destroyed. To avoid damaging electronic components, use an antistatic wrist strap, which is designed to drain static charges safely.

Caution

Do *not* use an antistatic wrist strap when servicing any component with live voltage present.

Do *not* open a CRT (monitor) while wearing an antistatic wrist strap, even if the CRT is unplugged. CRT screens can hold a high voltage charge for long periods of time after they have been disconnected from electrical power.

Caution

The major components of a server are similar to a typical PC. In fact, you can use a typical PC as a server for a small network. A network server can be as simple as a typical PC or as complex as a piece of equipment designed exclusively for networks. Some server models with multiple CPUs, large amounts of RAM, and vast amounts of storage space can be thought of as a "small" mainframe rather than as a PC. There are many server designs available. As part of your study of network servers, it is highly advisable to check the IBM, Sun Microsystems, HP, and Dell Web sites to see the available designs. This section looks at the following components: case, hot-swap components, power supply, motherboard, BIOS, and CPU.

Case

Server case styles vary greatly. Some are similar to desktop models. Some are designed to be mounted into a rack like the server in **Figure 9-2.**

Large enterprise servers are actually a group of individual servers mounted in a rack system or cabinet, **Figure 9-3.** The group of servers acts as one unit that has multiple CPUs and a large amount of system resources, such as hard disk drive storage and RAM.

A ***blade server*** derives its name from its size and shape. It is extremely thin compared to other servers and fits into a rack, **Figure 9-4.** Blade servers are especially designed to allow a large number of servers to be mounted in a small space. Blade servers are not to be confused with thin servers. A blade server can contain more than one processor and be quite powerful. They are often selected for applications where there is a requirement for many servers to perform the same or similar function. For example, they may be used in a large Web service facility or a file server farm.

blade server
a powerful server that is extremely thin. It is designed to be mounted in a small space with other blade servers.

Hot-Swap Components

Servers are generally designed to provide continuous service with minimal interruptions and data loss. The main feature that most servers use to provide this continuous service is hot-swap technology. ***Hot-swap technology*** allows a component to be removed or installed while the system is running. There is no need to power down the system while replacing or adding major components. Some common hot-swap components are hard disk drives, memory modules (RAM), CPUs, and power supplies.

hot-swap technology
a technology that allows a component to be removed or installed while the system is running.

Never assume a component is hot-swappable. Always check the system manual before removing any component while the system is powered on.

Figure 9-2.
The ProLiant DL740 can be mounted into a rack. (Hewlett-Packard Company)

Figure 9-3.
This cabinet can store many servers, allowing them to act as a single unit. (Hewlett-Packard Company)

A

B

Figure 9-4.
A blade server is thin, yet powerful. It is designed to allow many blade servers to be installed in a small area. A—A single blade server. B—Many blade servers installed in a single rack. (Hewlett-Packard Company)

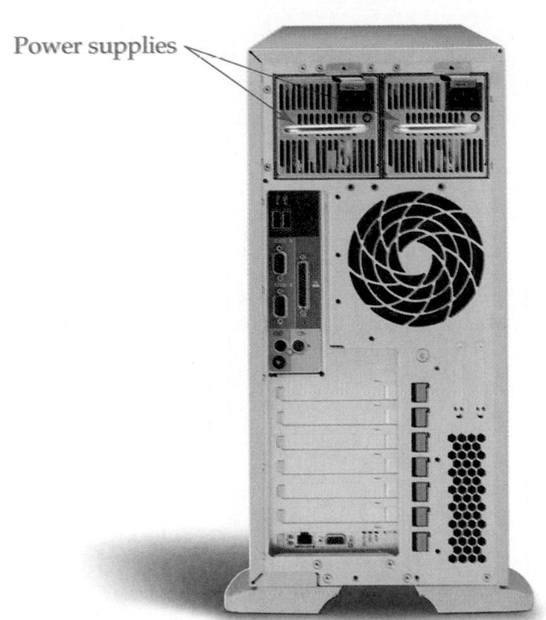

Figure 9-5.
Back view of the ProLiant ML350. This system comes with two power supplies that evenly distribute power throughout the system. When one power supply fails, the other carries the full load. (Hewlett-Packard Company)

Power Supply

The power supply converts standard 120-volt or 240-volt AC power into lower DC voltage levels that can be used by the motherboard and other devices inside the computer case. A typical power supply provides an assortment of output plugs. The plug style matches the intended piece of equipment. For example, a standard ATA drive uses a Molex plug, which supplies 5 volts DC and 12 volts DC to the ATA drive. An ATX-style motherboard plug supplies 3.3 volts, 5 volts, and 12 volts as well as a ground connection to the motherboard. It is also designed to plug into the motherboard correctly. Older style connections could be incorrectly plugged into the motherboard if you did not pay attention to the color-coding.

Entry-level servers are typically equipped with two power supplies, **Figure 9-5.** The two power supplies balance the load. If one power supply fails, the other power supply carries the full load. Some servers are designed with "hot-swappable" power supplies, which permit the defective power supply to be changed while the server is running.

To prevent the loss of data, most server manufacturers recommend disconnecting the server from the network while replacing hot-swappable power supplies.

Motherboard

Servers generally use a backplane. A ***backplane*** is a simple motherboard designed with minimal components. It typically serves as the interface of all the major components. It is designed to allow major components to be added or removed without powering down the system. Removing components without shutting down the system is call ***hot swapping.***

Figure 9-6 shows the general backplane layout of the HP ProLiant DL740 server with and without the added modules. An I/O board attaches to the backplane. It contains six PCI hot-swappable slots. The processor boards each contain 4 CPUs, for a total of 8 CPUs. Each memory module in the system is hot-swappable and contains 8 DIMMS. The HP ProLiant DL740 can contain up to 40 GB of RAM. The multiple CPUs and vast amount of RAM are required to provide the many different services to

backplane
a simple motherboard designed with minimal components. It typically serves as the interface of all the major components.

hot swapping
the process of removing components without shutting down the system.

Figure 9-6.
The backplane layout of the ProLiant DL740.

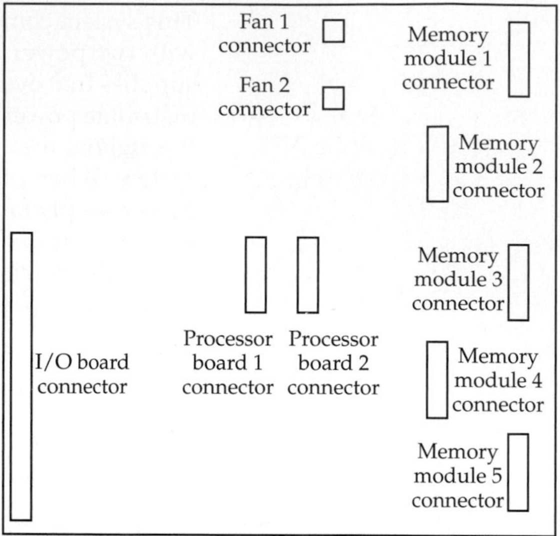

Backplane

Backplane with modules and I/O board

numerous network clients with minimal delay. The CPUs need not be the latest, high-speed processors available because there are numerous processors in the server.

BIOS

The BIOS contains a small software program that starts the server boot operation when power is applied to the server. The combination BIOS chip and the software program are usually referred to as ***firmware.*** The BIOS is responsible for the ***power-on self-test (POST),*** which is performed at startup. The POST does a quick, initial check of the major components, such as memory, disk drives, keyboard, mouse, and monitor, to be sure that a minimum working system is available. After a general check is made of the major hardware components, the BIOS turns control over to the operating system software. The operating system completes the boot process by loading more advanced hardware drivers than the BIOS did. It also performs a more sophisticated check of hardware and software systems. If all the software and hardware components appear to be in working order, the final screen, which serves as a user interface, appears.

firmware
the combination of BIOS chip and the software program within the chip.

power-on self-test (POST)
a BIOS routine that performs a series of hardware checks to determine if the computer is in minimal working order.

parallel processing
processing a program through more than one CPU simultaneously.

Central Processing Unit (CPU)

One major difference between a server and a typical PC is that many servers have multiple CPUs installed rather than just one. When multiple CPUs are installed, the server can perform ***parallel processing.*** This means that a program can be processed through more than one CPU simultaneously. Another advantage of multiple CPUs is several clients may be serviced at the same time rather than waiting their turn to access a single CPU. Supercomputers and enterprise servers may contain over 1,000 CPUs.

A small office server can get by with one processor, especially if demand on the server is low. A large enterprise system requires multiple processors to meet the demands of the server's clients. Some processor modules are hot-swappable. When a single CPU fails, it can easily be removed and replaced while the server is running and providing services to clients.

Small Computer Systems Interface (SCSI)

Small Computer Systems Interface (SCSI), pronounced *skuzzy,* is a computer bus technology that allows you to connect multiple devices to a single controller. The benefits of SCSI technology can be readily observed in the chart in **Figure 9-7.** SCSI technology not only allows multiple devices to connect to a single controller, it also supports high-data transfer rates. This is quite a performance improvement when compared to the traditional IDE or ATA attachment. SCSI is ideal for servers that must hold large amounts of data that is accessed by numerous clients.

Small Computer Systems Interface (SCSI)
a computer bus technology that allows you to connect multiple devices to a single controller.

Most SCSI drives are hot-swap devices. Often, SCSI drives are arranged in the server with hot-swap bays open to the outside of the case to provide easy access. This allows you to connect or disconnect a drive without opening the server case. See **Figure 9-8.**

SCSI technology has evolved over the years. With this evolution, new names have emerged to describe the improved technology. The term *Wide* is used to indicate 16-bit data transfers in place of 8-bit data transfers. To reflect the increase in frequency, the term *Fast* was used and then the term *Ultra*. Combination of the words, such as *Ultra/Wide*, are also used to express the newer technologies. Ultra/Wide means the SCSI device is faster and supports 16-bit transfers. A close

Common Name	Class	Devices	Bus Width in bits	Speed	MBps
SCSI-1	SCSI-1	8	8	5 MHz	4-5 MBps
Wide SCSI	SCSI-2	16	8	5 MHz	10 MBps
Fast SCSI	SCSI-2	8	8	10 MHz	10 MBps
Fast/Wide SCSI	SCSI-2	16	16	10 MHz	20 MBps
Ultra SCSI	SCSI-3	8	8	20 MHz	20 MBps
Ultra/Wide	SCSI-3	8	16	20 MHz	20 MBps
Ultra2	SCSI-3	8	8	40 MHz	40 MBps
Ultra2/Wide SCSI	SCSI-3	16	16	40 MHz	80 MBps
Ultra3 SCSI	SCSI-3	16	16	40 MHz	160 MBps
Ultra Wide 320	SCSI-3	16	16	80 MHz	320 MBps
Ultra Wide 640	SCSI-3	16	16	160 MHz	640 MBps

Figure 9-7.
SCSI technology specifications.

Figure 9-8.
Hot-swap drives are typically accessible from the front of the server for easy access. (Hewlett-Packard Company)

study of the table in Figure 9-7 will help you understand the evolution of the SCSI technology. To learn more about SCSI technology, visit the Adaptec Web page at www.adaptec.com. There you will find in-depth knowledge about SCSI systems and other technologies.

A SCSI hardware system consists of a host adapter or controller card, a flat ribbon cable to connect SCSI devices, and SCSI devices such as disk drives, CD-ROMs, and tape drives. SCSI cables come in a variety to match the many different classifications of SCSI. The cables come as DB-25, 50-pin, 68-pin, and 80-pin styles.

Look at **Figure 9-9** to see the way a typical SCSI host adapter, cable, and devices might appear. The host adapter and devices can connect to any part of the chain. The chain of SCSI devices must be terminated. Termination is typically completed at the last device with a termination block.

SCSI ID numbers

Each device, including the host adapter card, must have a unique ID number. The numbers start at zero and end at seven for an eight-device SCSI chain and end at fifteen for a sixteen-device SCSI chain. The host adapter typically is assigned the highest number.

SCSI ID numbers are assigned through pins and jumpers on the SCSI drive. The pins are arranged in pairs. When a jumper is applied across the pins, an

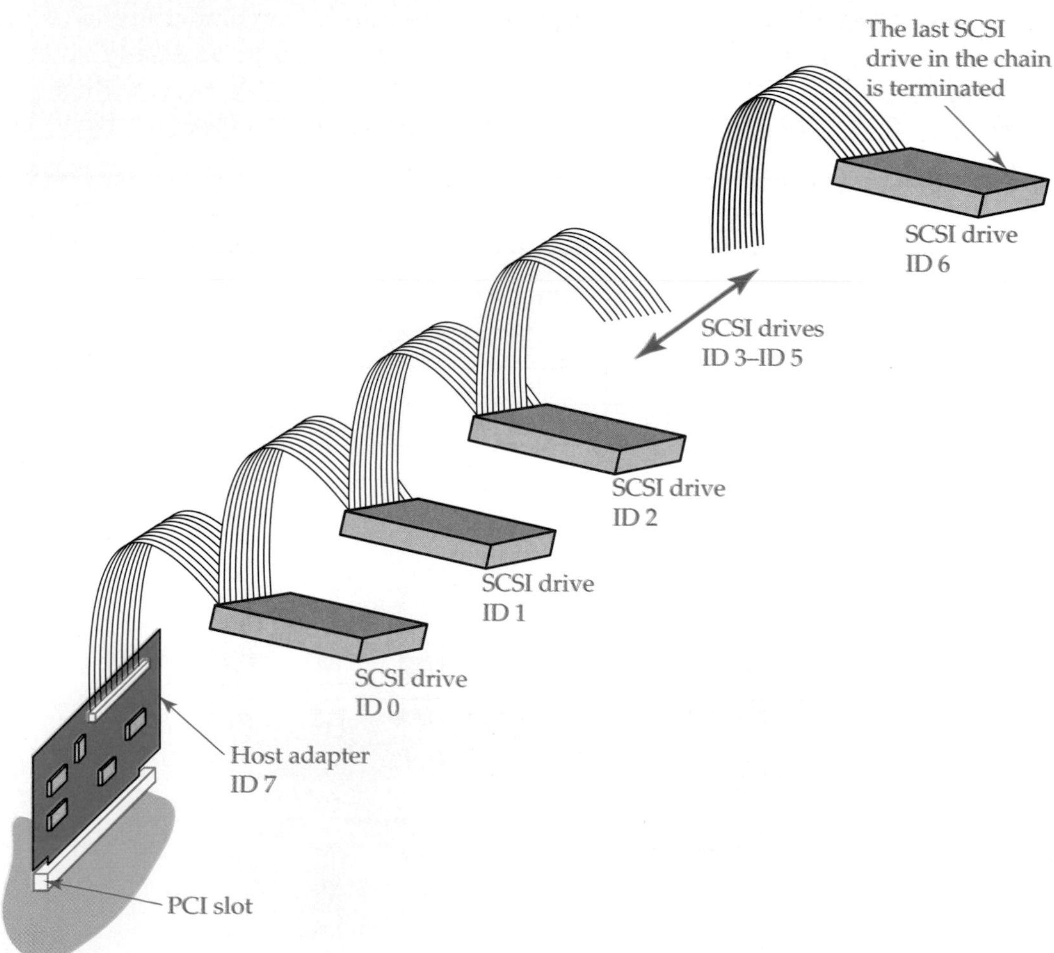

Figure 9-9. Typical SCSI drive arrangement.

electrical connection is made. The pairs of pins represent the binary number system. The jumpers are applied in a binary pattern that represents the SCSI ID number. **Figure 9-10** illustrates each of the binary patterns and the related SCSI ID number.

Logical unit number (LUN)

SCSI devices are not limited to internal devices. The SCSI chain can extend outside the case by adding an extender card to the SCSI chain. The extender card allows more devices to be attached to existing SCSI systems. The extender card is an integrated circuit card connected to the SCSI chain as a SCSI device. See **Figure 9-11.**

When additional devices are attached, they are identified separately from the original chain of devices. Each additional device connected to the SCSI extender is identified with a ***logical unit number (LUN).*** SCSI bus extenders are also referred to as *SCSI expanders, repeaters,* and *regenerators.*

logical unit number (LUN)
a numbering scheme to identify SCSI devices attached to an extender card.

External SCSI device chains are commonly used in RAID systems. RAID systems are covered later in this chapter.

Serial Attached SCSI

Serial attached SCSI (SAS) is the next generation of SCSI. It uses a serial port similar to the SATA serial drive port, **Figure 9-12.** This eliminates the need of the wide SCSI cable and produces faster data transfer rates. First generation SAS devices can achieve data rates as high as 3 Gbps. Second generation SAS devices can achieve rates of 6 Gbps. Note that these speeds are expressed in bits per second (bps), not bytes per second (Bps). This is because SAS transfers data in a serial fashion. The SAS design allows 128 devices to be attached directly.

Serial attached SCSI (SAS)
SCSI technology that transfers data in serial fashion.

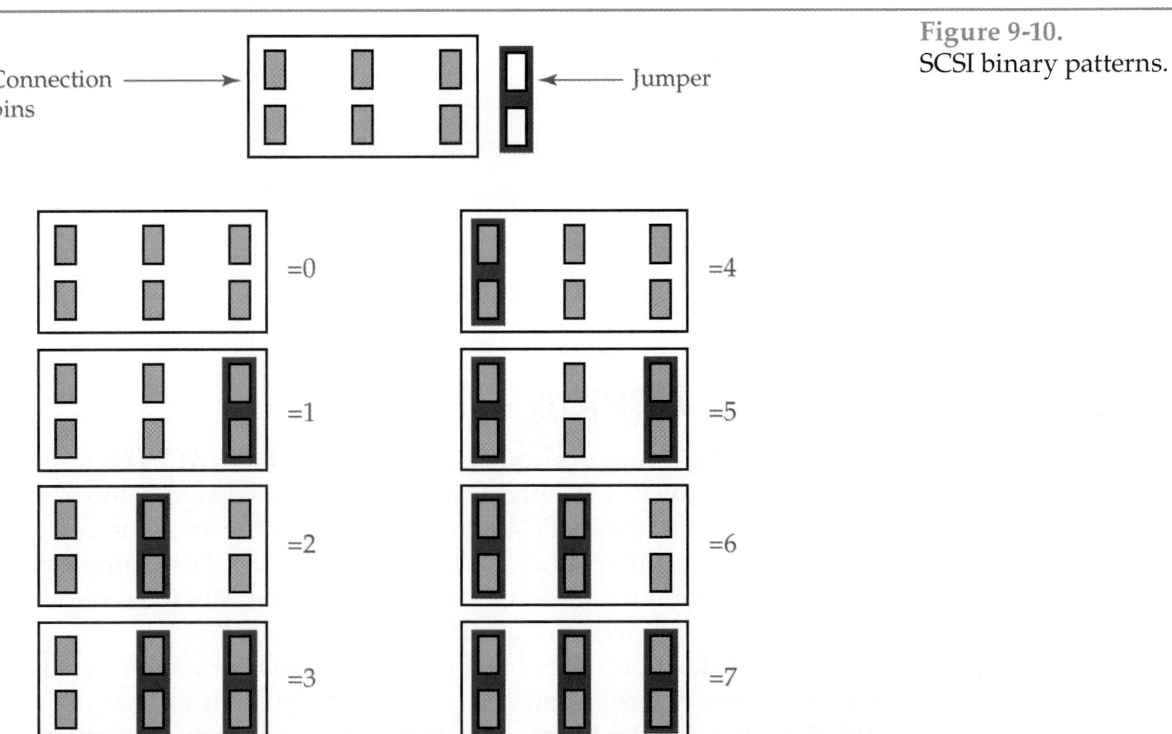

Figure 9-10.
SCSI binary patterns.

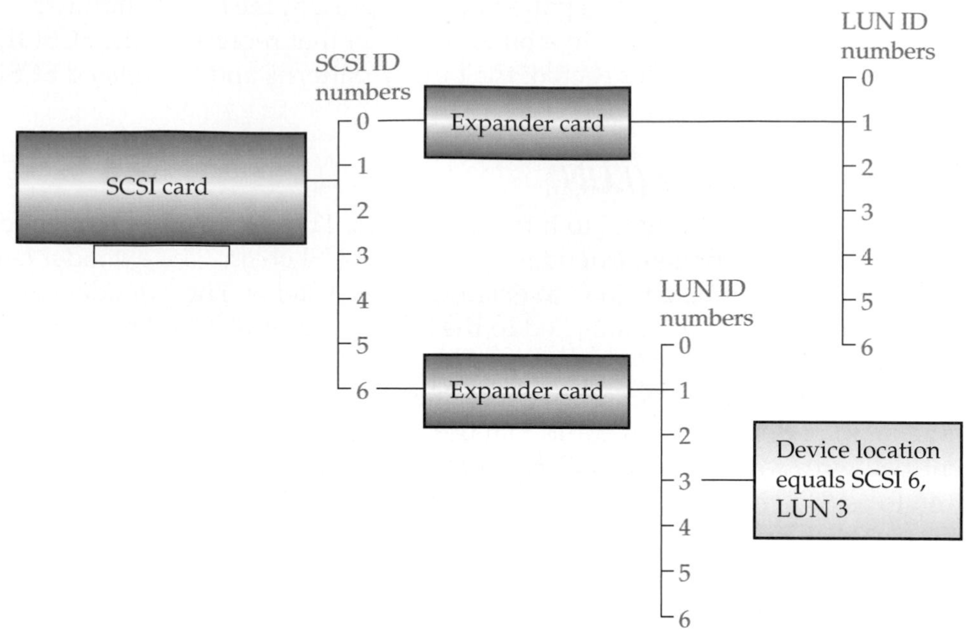

Figure 9-11. The SCSI limit of seven devices can be expanded by using expander cards. Each expander card allows an additional seven devices to be connected to the SCSI system. LUN numbers are assigned to the additional SCSI devices so they can be identified by the system software and BIOS.

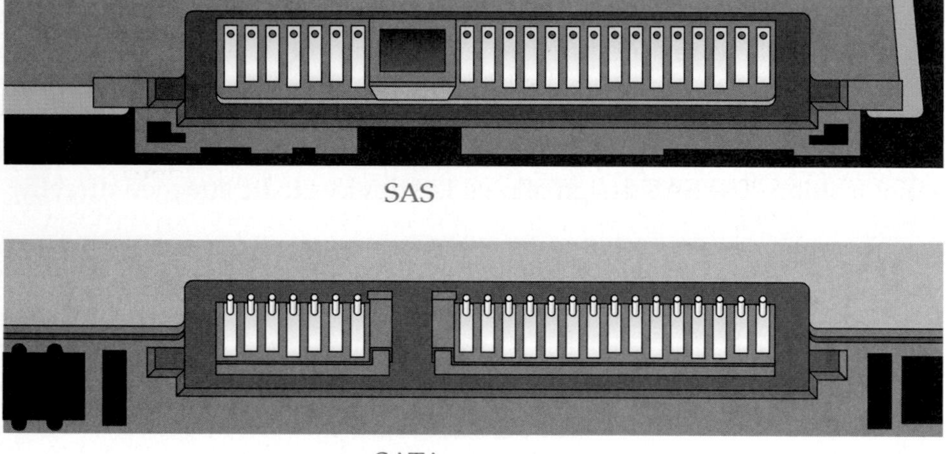

Figure 9-12. SAS and SATA disk drive connectors. Notice the two connector types are similar.

Through the use of edge expander devices, a maximum of 16,000 SAS devices can be connected.

ACPI and ACPICA

Automatic Configuration and Power Interface (ACPI) a standard for controlling the power options for computer hardware devices.

Automatic Configuration and Power Interface (ACPI) is a standard for controlling the power options for computer hardware devices. The first implementation of the ACPI standard gave users the ability to select how they wanted their computer to behave to conserve power. For example, the user could configure the computer or individual computer devices to go into a state of hibernation after a period of inactivity.

Figure 9-13 shows the power options available for a wireless network adapter. These options allow the computer to turn off the adapter to save power and allow the adapter to wake the computer when network activity occurs.

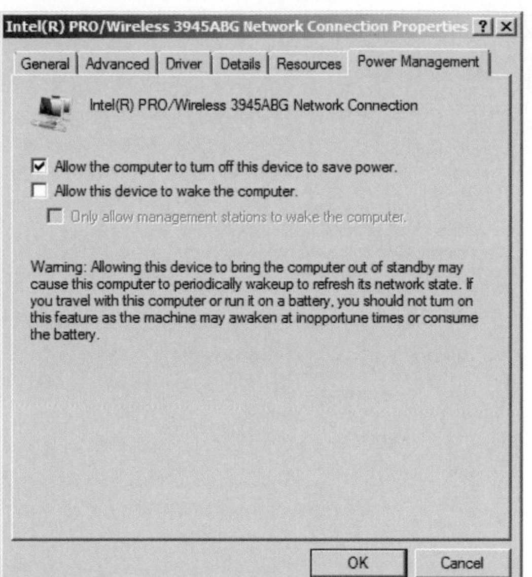

Figure 9-13. Power options for a wireless network adapter.

ACPI Component Architecture (ACPICA) is an extension to the original ACPI standard. The goal of ACPICA is to create a non-proprietary software package for configuring hardware. An ACPICA-compliant device is operating system independent. ACPICA is written in the C language and is an open standard allowing any computer software or hardware manufacturer to share power-saving features rather than developing proprietary power-saving features. ACPICA is compatible with both 32-bit and 64-bit systems.

ACPI Component Architecture (ACPICA)
an extension to the original ACPI standard that provides a non-proprietary software package for hardware configuration.

Some of the companies that participate with the goals of ACPICA are Microsoft, HP, Intel, and several Linux organizations. To learn more about ACPICA, check out the ACPICA Web site (www.acpica.org).

System Resources

System resources refer to resources such as interrupt requests, Direct Memory Access channels, Input/Output ports, and memory. System resources are assigned to components installed in the computer system such as hard disk drives, keyboards, and mice. In a Windows-based server, you can view system resource assignments in Device Manager.

Not all devices have all four types of resources assigned to them. For example, some devices do not require a DMA channel assignment. System resources typically cannot be shared between two devices. Sharing the same system resource causes a system resource conflict, referred to simply as a *conflict*. Conflicts must be resolved before the system can operate properly. An exception to this rule is motherboard chips used to bridge different bus systems. A motherboard chip can share an IRQ with a hardware device.

Interrupt Request (IRQ)

An ***interrupt request (IRQ)*** is a circuit that communicates with the CPU. Hardware devices send an electrical signal to the CPU using an assigned IRQ circuit. There are 16 IRQ assignments numbered from 0 to 15, **Figure 9-14.** Many of the assignments cannot be changed, but some can. When Plug and Play devices are used, the IRQ is automatically assigned. Typically, each hardware device must use a separate

interrupt request (IRQ)
a circuit that communicates with the CPU.

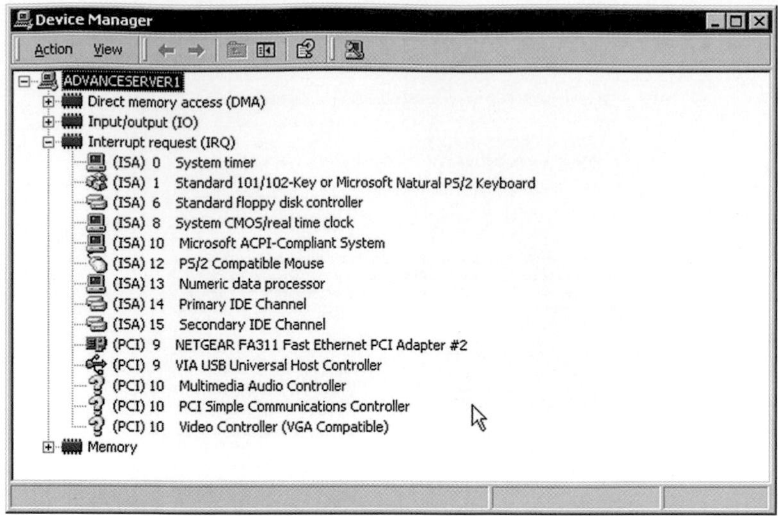

Figure 9-14.
IRQ assignments.

IRQ to communicate with the CPU. If two hardware devices are assigned the same IRQ, an IRQ conflict occurs. Once the first device contacts the CPU using the IRQ assignment, the other device cannot communicate with the CPU. An IRQ conflict can lead to problems such as an inoperable device, a system crash, and a system lockup. An IRQ can typically be assigned manually by first entering the BIOS setup program and disabling Plug and Play detection. Changes to the IRQ can then be made through Device Manager. After the problem device has been assigned the proper IRQ, the Plug and Play detection can be activated without a problem.

You may notice IRQ numbers higher than 16 in Device Manager. These numbers are virtual IRQ settings, rather than hardware-based IRQs. They work the same as the hardware-based interrupts, but they are not limited by physical properties. Virtual IRQ assignments are configured automatically by the operating system.

Tech Tip

Yellow question marks next to devices in Device Manager indicate there is a problem with the device or assignment.

Direct Memory Access (DMA) Channel

Direct Memory Access (DMA) channel
a circuit that allows devices to communicate and transfer data to and from RAM without the need of CPU intervention.

A ***Direct Memory Access (DMA) channel*** is a circuit that allows devices to communicate and transfer data to and from RAM without the need of CPU intervention. Computer systems were first designed with the CPU handling all communication. Every bit of data had to travel through the CPU. DMA technology was introduced to save valuable processor time.

DMA works in conjunction with the chipsets on the motherboard, BIOS software, and the CPU. Large blocks of data that need to be transferred between hardware devices and memory are transferred through a DMA channel that is assigned to the device. **Figure 9-15** shows the DMA controller identified by Device Manager.

One of the devices controlled by the DMA memory access controller is the computer ATA drive. **Figure 9-16** shows the **Advanced Settings** tab for the IDE channel. The IDE channel has been assigned to a DMA channel to take advantage of fast data transfer.

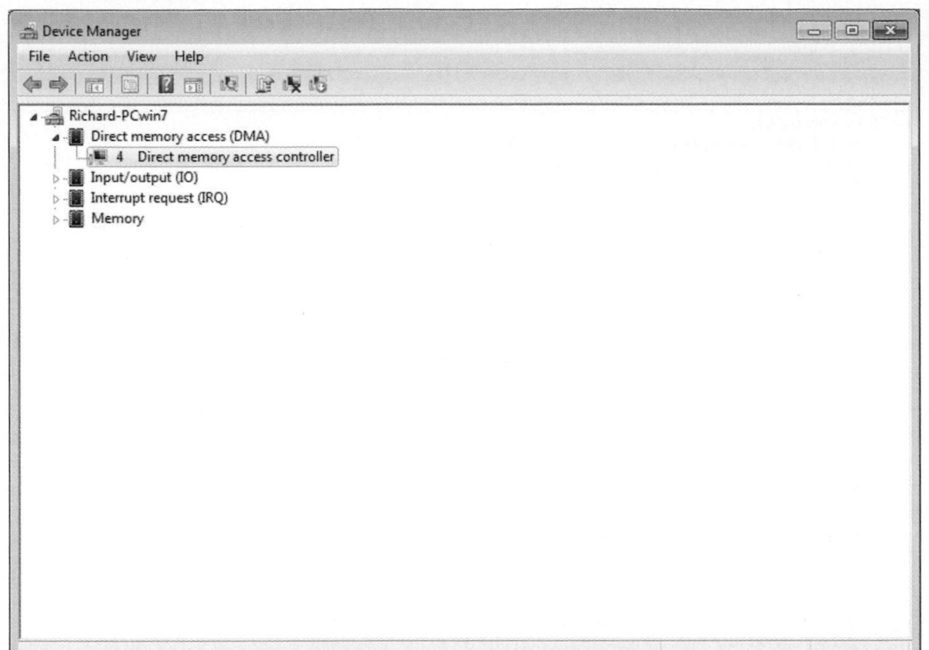

Figure 9-15.
DMA assignment.

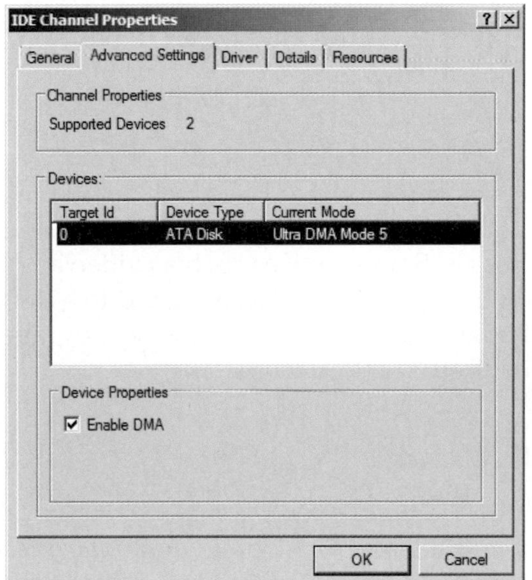

Figure 9-16.
IDE Channel Properties dialog box **Advanced Settings** tab. The IDE channel is assigned to a DMA channel by enabling DMA.

Input/Output (I/O) Port

The ***Input/Output (I/O) port*** is a small amount of memory assigned to a device that temporarily holds small amounts of data. It is used to transfer data between two locations. The data remains in the I/O port assignment until it can be moved.

Input/Output (I/O) port
a small amount of memory assigned to a device that temporarily holds small amounts of data. It is used to transfer data between two locations.

The system has many hardware devices and software programs that depend on transferring data between hardware and memory locations. When a device or software program wants to transfer data, it may need to wait until the CPU is finished with its current process. In fact, it may need to wait until several processes are completed before the CPU can handle the data. The I/O port stores

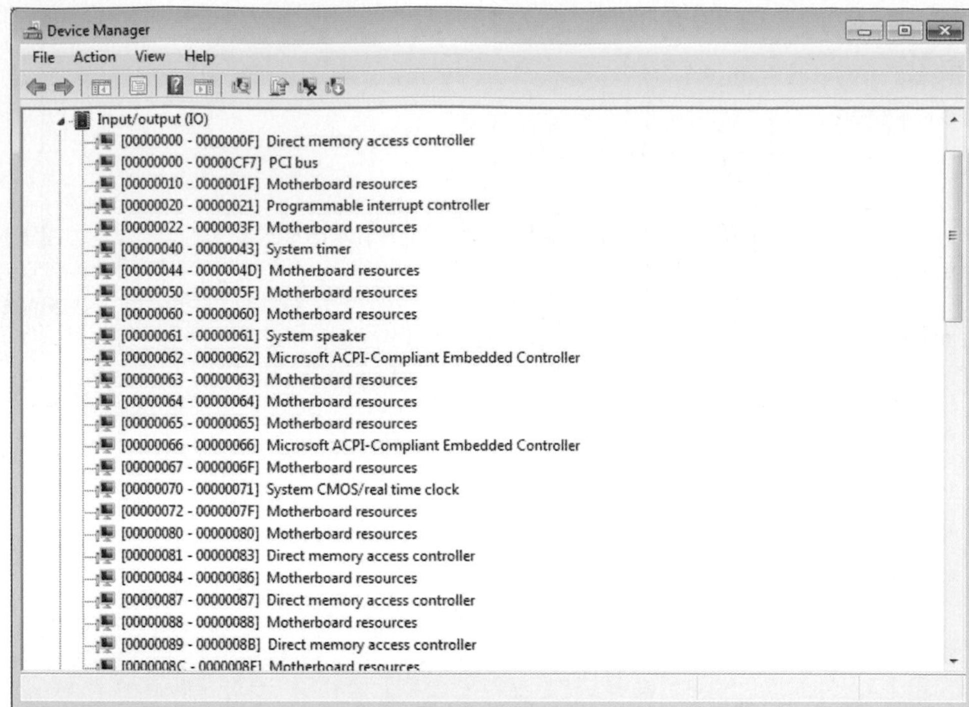

Figure 9-17. I/O port assignments.

this data until the CPU is free. **Figure 9-17** shows the I/O port assignments associated with a system's hardware devices.

Memory Address Assignment

memory address assignment a large block of memory assigned to a device. It is used to transfer data between two locations.

A ***memory address assignment*** is a large block of memory assigned to a device and is used to transfer data between two locations. A device is assigned a range of memory addresses. Some devices such as video and sound cards require a great deal of memory. The blocks of RAM assigned to a device cannot be used by any other device. **Figure 9-18** shows the memory assignments associated with a system's hardware devices.

RAID Systems

Redundant Array of Independent Disks (RAID) a system of disks arranged for speed or fault tolerance, or both.

Redundant Array of Independent Disks (RAID) is a system of disks arranged for speed or fault tolerance, or both. ***Fault tolerance*** as applied to RAID systems means the ability to recover from a hard disk or hard disk controller failure without the loss of stored data. Fault tolerance as applied to a network infrastructure means the ability to continue operation during a system hardware or software error. To achieve a high-data transfer rate, a technique known as *disk striping* is used. ***Disk striping*** involves dividing the data into separate sections and writing the data across several hard disk drives at the same time. This reduces the total amount of time it takes to store large amounts of data.

Tech Tip

Another accepted representation of the RAID acronym is Redundant Array of Inexpensive Disks.

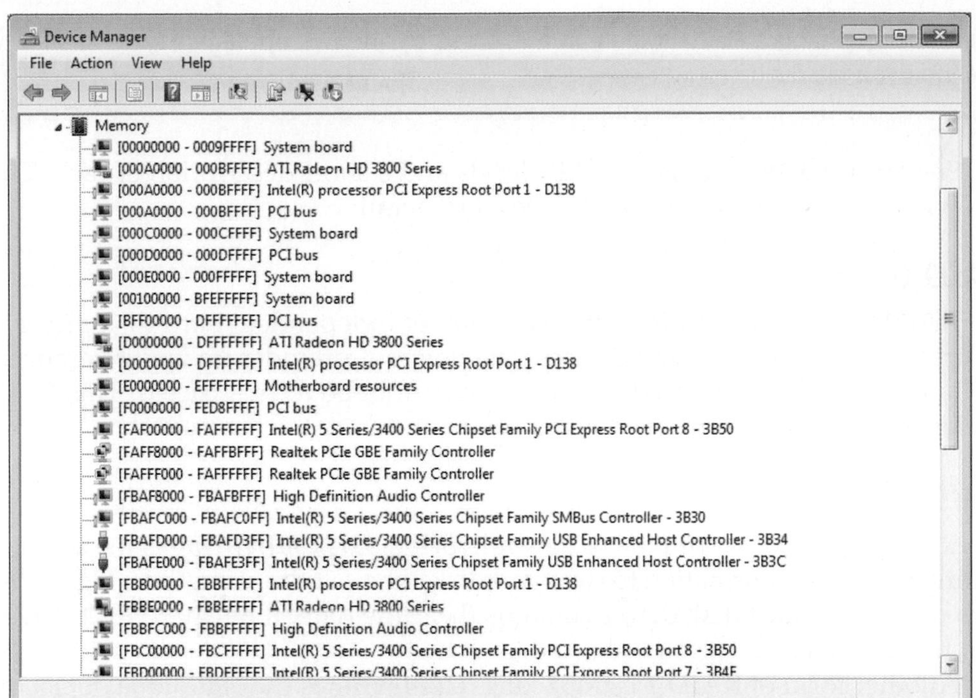

Figure 9-18. Memory assignments.

Another RAID technique is ***error correction,*** which can use traditional error-checking code (ECC) or parity. ECC is obsolete as a method for RAID because most hard disk drive systems use ECC as a standard way to protect data. Incorporating ECC into a RAID system would be redundant.

Parity is a technique that allows data to be recovered if one of the hard disk drives fails in a multiple disk drive system. A minimum of three hard disk drives must be used for this technique. If three hard disk drives are used, one hard disk drive is used to store parity and the other two are used to store data. Data is spread evenly between the two data storage drives, and the parity code for the sum of the two data storage drives is stored on the parity drive.

Parity is also a binary code that represents the total data pattern shared between the data storage drives. If any data storage drive fails, the system can use the parity bit to rebuild the missing data.

RAID systems are referred to as *RAID levels.* There are many RAID levels, each incorporating a different technique to increase speed or to provide data redundancy, or both.

Things to consider when selecting a RAID level are cost, reliability, and speed. There is no single, best RAID level. The appropriate level depends on the value of the data being protected and the amount of budget available. If a bank were protecting financial data, cost would most likely be of little concern. A RAID 0/5 with a tape backup would be quite appropriate. If you were protecting a personal computer, you would not likely need a RAID system.

Repairing a failed RAID system means the drive must be physically replaced and then the data reconstructed. In a Microsoft Windows operating system, the Disk Management utility is used to reconstruct data. If using proprietary SCSI drives, data is reconstructed by the data array manufacturer software package.

fault tolerance
as applied to RAID systems, it is the ability to recover from a hard disk or hard disk controller failure without the loss of stored data. As applied to a network infrastructure, it is the ability to continue operation during a system hardware or software error.

disk striping
a storage technique that divides the data into sections and writes the data across several hard disk drives at the same time.

error correction
a RAID technique that uses traditional error-checking code (ECC) or parity.

When implementing a RAID system in a Microsoft Windows operating system, all drives must be dynamic disk.

See **Figure 9-19** for a list of RAID levels and a short description of each. The following section looks at each RAID level in detail.

RAID 0

RAID 0 uses disk striping across a group of independent hard disk drives, **Figure 9-20.** This technique increases data flow but provides no fault tolerance. If one hard disk drive fails, all data is lost and cannot be reconstructed. This RAID level is most useful when speed is important, not fault tolerance.

RAID 1

disk mirroring the act of writing the same information to two hard disk drives at the same time.

duplexing the technique of placing each mirrored hard drive on a separate hard disk drive controller.

RAID 1 uses the technique of disk mirroring. ***Disk mirroring*** is the act of writing the same information to two hard disk drives at the same time, **Figure 9-21.** Each of the two hard disk drives contains the same data. If one hard disk drive fails, a copy exists on the other hard disk drive.

Another form of RAID 1 is duplexing. ***Duplexing*** is the technique of placing each mirrored hard drive on a separate hard disk drive controller. Duplexing adds another level of fault tolerance. If one hard disk drive controller fails, the other is still operable. Mirroring contains the risk of the hard disk drive controller failing and causing both hard disk drives to fail. RAID 1 provides data protection at the cost of speed when compared to RAID 0. When there is a small demand for disk read/writes, RAID 1 is an appropriate technique.

Figure 9-19.
RAID levels.

RAID Level	Description
RAID 0	Striping.
RAID 1	Mirroring or duplexing.
RAID 2	Error checking code (ECC).
RAID 3	Byte-level striping with parity.
RAID 4	Block-level striping with parity.
RAID 5	Block-level striping with distributed parity.
RAID 6	Dual parity.
RAID 0/1 or 10	Disk mirroring with striping.
RAID 0/5 or 50	Block striping with parity and striping.

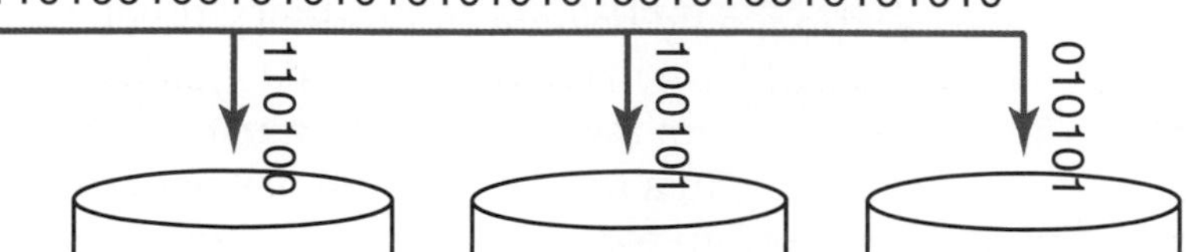

Figure 9-20.
RAID 0 divides data and writes it to multiple drives. It provides excellent data transfer rates but no data loss protection.

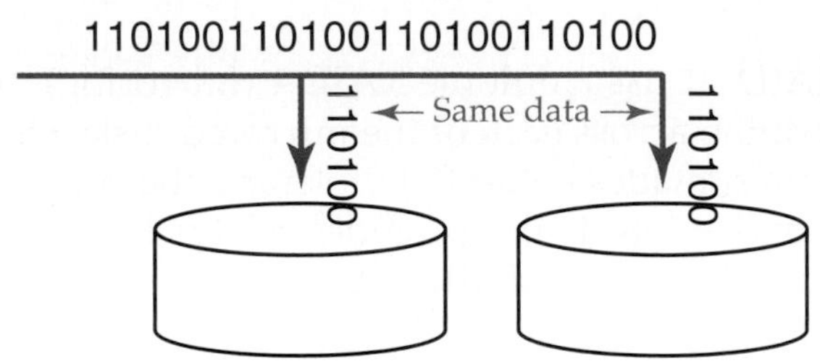

Figure 9-21.
RAID 1, or disk mirroring, provides a copy of data on two disk drives.

RAID 2

RAID 2 uses common ECC error-correction code to provide fault tolerance. All drives provide some sort of ECC, so this form of RAID is basically obsolete.

RAID 3

RAID 3 stripes data across multiple drives and stores parity on a separate drive. Data striping is performed at the byte level. See **Figure 9-22.**

RAID 4

RAID 4 stripes data across several drives and stores parity on a separate drive. The main difference between RAID 3 and RAID 4 is RAID 4 stores data in blocks. The size of the block can vary.

RAID 5

RAID 5 is also called *block striping with distributed parity*. RAID 5 distributes parity across all drives rather than writing parity to one drive. It provides fault tolerance and some increase in read-write data transfer. See **Figure 9-23.**

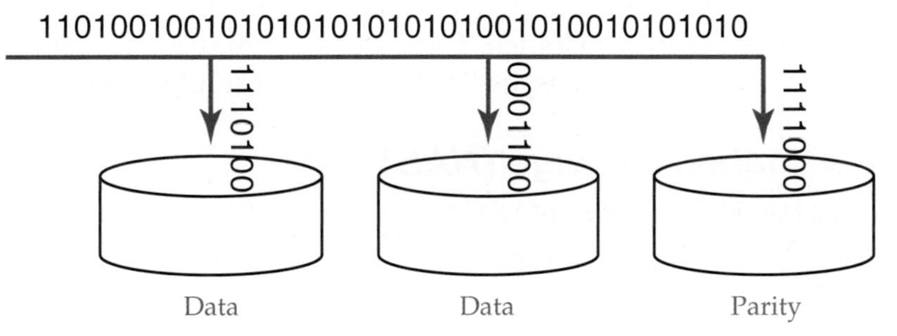

Figure 9-22.
RAID 3 writes across multiple drives with parity stored on a separate drive.

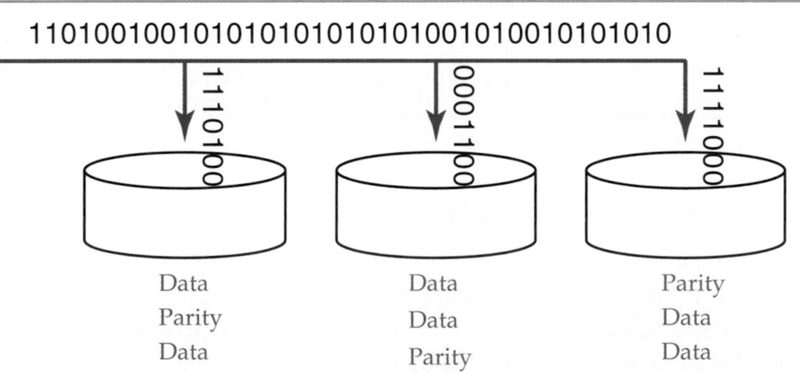

Figure 9-23.
RAID 5 provides both disk striping and parity. Parity and data is distributed across all drives.

RAID 0/1

RAID 0/1, or RAID 10, uses multiple RAID 1 (mirroring) disk systems. It also incorporates disk striping across each of the mirrored disk sets. When compared to RAID 1, this system provides better fault tolerance because data is duplicated on multiple mirrored disk sets. It also provides relatively fast data-transfer speeds by striping data across the mirrored disk sets.

RAID 0/5

RAID 0/5, or RAID 50, uses several RAID 5 (block striping with parity) sets and combines them with RAID 0 (disk striping). It provides increased fault tolerance when compared to a RAID 5 system.

RAID 6

RAID 6 is similar to RAID 5 in that it distributes parity across all drives, except RAID 6 uses a second set of parity. This technique is referred to as *dual parity*. The additional parity set allows for protection from simultaneous two-disk failure. Since two simultaneous disk failures are rarely encountered, RAID 6 is not commonly used.

Network+ Note

Pay particular attention to RAID 0, 1, and 5. These systems are the most commonly used and are the ones most likely to be covered on the Network+ Certification exam.

External Storage Systems

Data is often stored separately from a server. There are network devices that serve specifically as storage containers for network data. These devices are typically called *network attached storage (NAS)*. There are also facilities external to the local area network that provide data storage. These devices are typically called *storage area network (SAN)*. This section discusses both types of storage systems.

Network-Attached Storage (NAS)

Network attached storage (NAS) is a device or collection of devices that provide storage for network data. Network attached storage units are typically composed of disk arrays or tape arrays. The file systems used on the disk array and file array do not typically match the file system used by network clients or servers. The file systems are proprietary and are made to facilitate access speed and data integrity.

network attached storage (NAS)
a device or collection of devices that provide storage for network data.

This is how data on a NAS device is accessed. A client requesting data makes a request to the file server. The file server in turn makes a request to the NAS device. The NAS device retrieves the data and sends it to the file server. The file server, in turn, sends the data to the client. See **Figure 9-24.**

storage area network (SAN)
a separate, high-speed network that provides a storage facility for one or more networks.

Storage Area Network (SAN)

A ***storage area network (SAN)*** is a separate, high-speed network that provides a storage facility for one or more networks. Typically, a SAN uses a high-speed access media such as Fibre Channel. See **Figure 9-25.** Fibre Channel is discussed in the next section of the chapter.

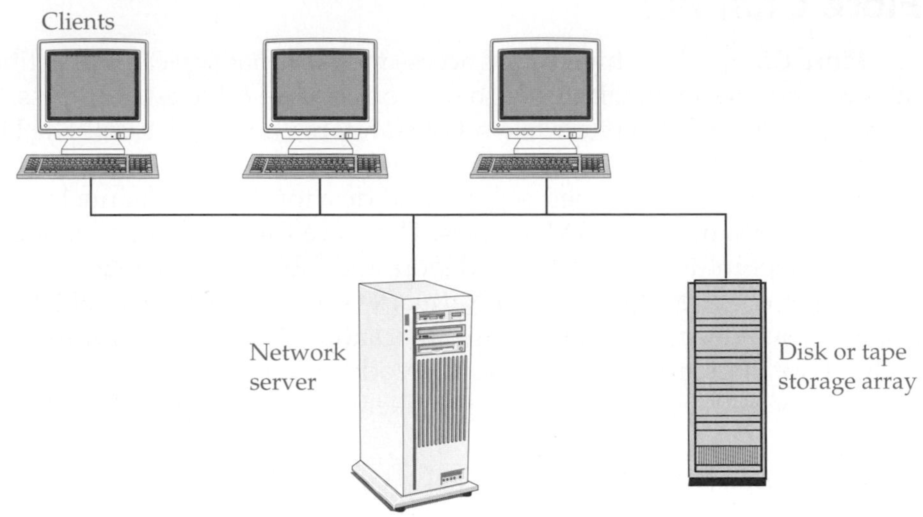

Figure 9-24. In a network attached storage (NAS) design, clients make requests for data through the network file server. The file server then makes a request to the NAS device. The NAS device retrieves the data and sends it to the file server. The file server forwards the data to the client.

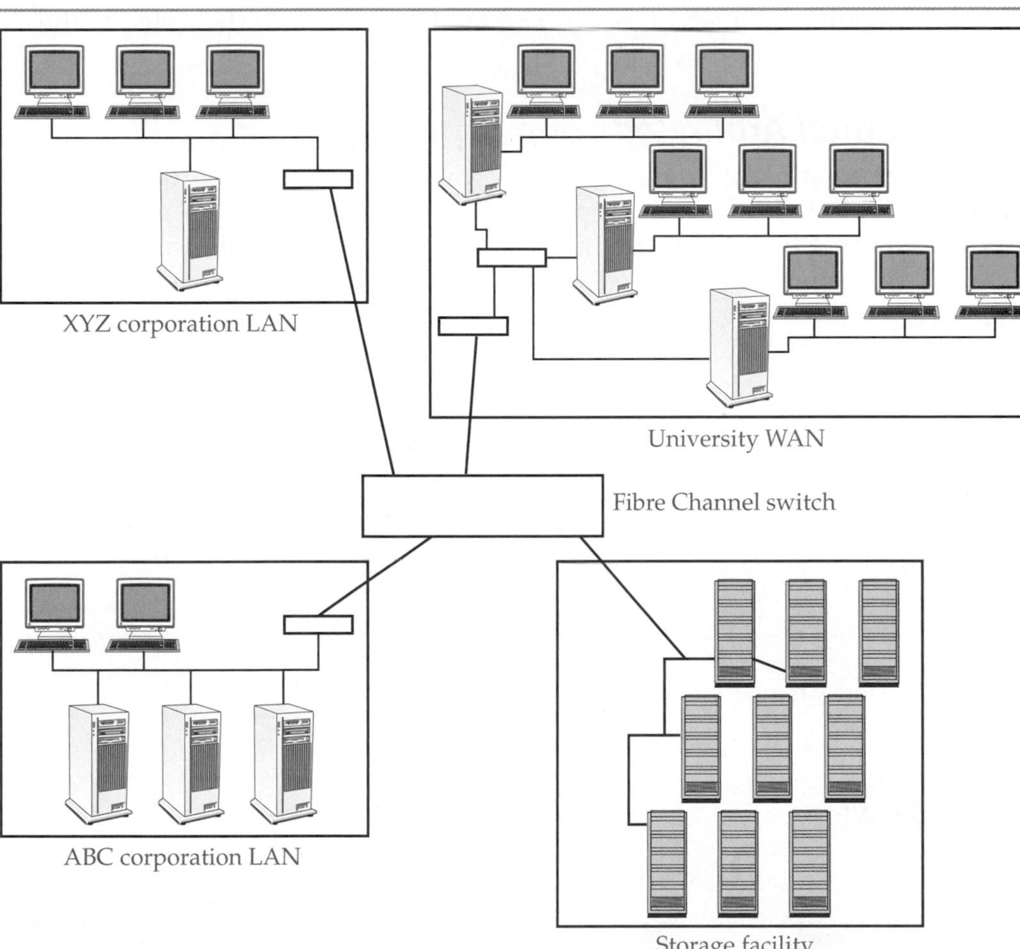

Figure 9-25. The storage area network (SAN) is a separate, high-speed network that provides a storage facility for other networks.

Exact definitions of storage area network vary according to different manufacturers. Often the differences are blurred.

Fibre Channel
a high-speed access method that typically uses fiber-optic cable as network media.

Network Address Authority (NAA)
a naming standard that consists of the "naa." prefix followed by a string of hexadecimal characters. It was developed by the International Committee for Information Technology Standards (ICITS).

Fibre Channel

Fibre Channel is a high-speed access method that typically uses fiber-optic cable as network media. It may also use copper core cable and wireless. The term *Fibre Channel* also refers to a set of standards and a protocol. The Fibre Channel standard provides a relatively high-data transmission rate between supercomputers, mainframes, servers, and desktops. Fibre Channel is often used for storage area network (SAN) access. There are three common Fibre Channel topologies: point-to-point, arbitrated loop, and fabric, **Figure 9-26.**

A fiber channel device uses a ***Network Address Authority (NAA)***, which is a naming standard developed by the International Committee for Information Technology Standards (ICITS). The NAA address consists of the "naa." prefix followed by a string of hexadecimal characters. For example, naa.02034D12B12124.

Fibre Channel Point-to-Point Topology

A Fibre Channel point-to-point topology is simply a straight connection or channel between two points, such as a mainframe and a server. The channel is isolated from other channels or media, and total bandwidth is dedicated to the channel between the two devices.

Fibre Channel Arbitrated Loop Topology

The Fibre Channel arbitrated loop is a common Fibre Channel topology. It looks similar to the Token Ring topology. The arbitrated loop differs from Token Ring in that two devices in the loop set up a direct communication link, or channel, for the duration of the data transfer. In Token Ring network, a token is passed around the ring while one device on the ring controls communication. Token Ring has a maximum control time of approximately 8 milliseconds in contrast to the arbitrated loop standard, which allows two devices to communicate until all the data requested has been transferred.

The arbitrated loop is limited to 127 connections. It is used to move large volumes of data between two devices such as a disk storage array and a server. It is not used for sporadic communication between multiple nodes as it is on a Token Ring network.

Figure 9-26.
Three major topologies associated with Fibre Channel systems are point-to-point, arbitrated loop, and fabric switched.

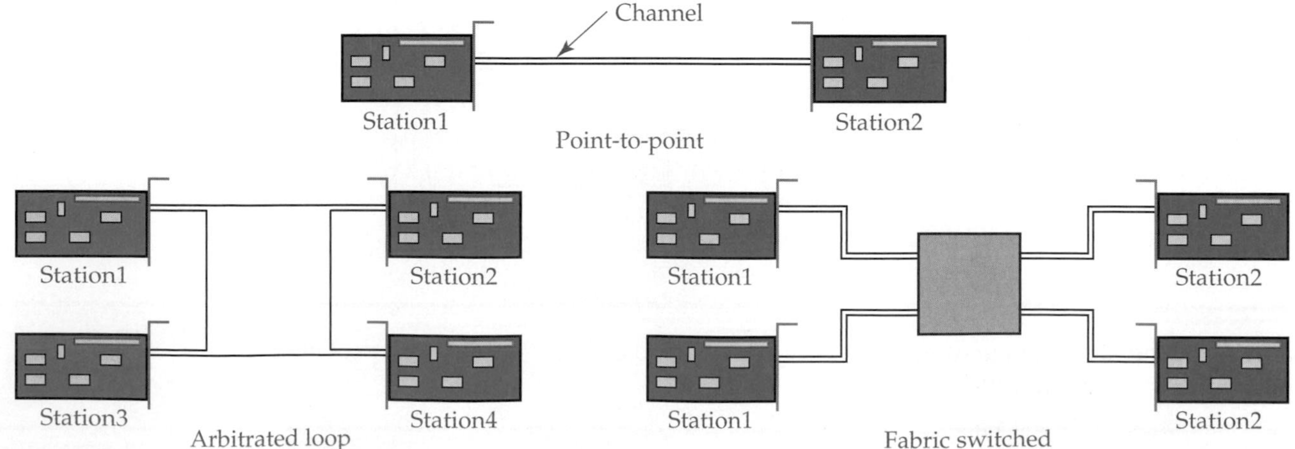

Fibre Channel Fabric Switched Topology

The fabric switched topology uses a device known as a *fabric switch*. A ***fabric switch*** is a switch designed especially for Fibre Channel networking. The fabric switch provides a direct or switched connection between two points. When two points wish to communicate, a private link, or channel, is set up between the two devices. This method is best used when numerous nodes wish to access the same disk storage array. For example, a university consisting of many buildings can connect each building's server to a common disk storage array using the fabric switched topology. This way, departments in each building can have access to research documents stored in the disk storage array. They can also access servers in other buildings through a high-speed connection.

fabric switch
a switch designed especially for Fibre Channel networking and that provides a direct or switched connection between two points.

Internet Small Computer Systems Interface

Internet Small Computer Systems Interface (iSCSI) is a network storage standard developed by the Internet Engineering Task Force (IETF). It is used to access a wide variety of storage devices such as tapes, disks, and storage arrays. The iSCSI (pronounced eye-scuzzy) standard is referred to as *IP-based storage* because it is designed to work on a LAN, MAN, or WAN using IPv4 and IPv6 network addresses to identify the storage device. iSCSI operates by sending SCSI commands over Ethernet using NFS or SMB/CIFS protocols. The two advantages of iSCSI are the following:

- Storage devices can be located at great distances from the client. This overcomes the limitations of systems such as Fibre Channel.
- It is less expensive than Fibre Channel SANs.

Internet Small Computer Systems Interface (iSCSI)
an IP-based storage technology that uses IPv4 and IPv6 network addresses to identify storage devices on a LAN, MAN, or WAN.

Windows 7 and Windows Server 2008 have a GUI interface called *iSCSI Initiator* for configuring iSCSI. It can be accessed from the **Administrative Tools** menu, **Figure 9-27.**

The iSCSI initiator is the workstation or server making the requests to the storage device. It is called the *target* and can be located either on the local area network or at some distant location across the Internet.

The iSCSI properties can be configured automatically through the Network Discovery feature or manually. Look at **Figure 9-28** to see how the Network Discovery feature can automatically locate an iSCSI device on the local area network. In this example, the iSCSI storage device is located on a Windows Server 2008 computer using IP address 192.168.1.103.

iSCSI devices can be located across the Internet by using an iSCSI qualified name (IQN) or an Enterprise Unique Name (EUI). The name can be automatically generated based on information provided by the Network Discovery feature. **Figure 9-29** shows an example of an IQN address. The IQN address in the example is iqn.1991-05.com.microsoft:richar7.netlab1domain.local. The IQN name format is *<type>–<date>–<authority>–<string defined by naming authority>*:
where

Type = iqn
Date = month and year domain was acquired
Authority = domain name
String defined by naming authority = String of characters identifying the iSCSI object

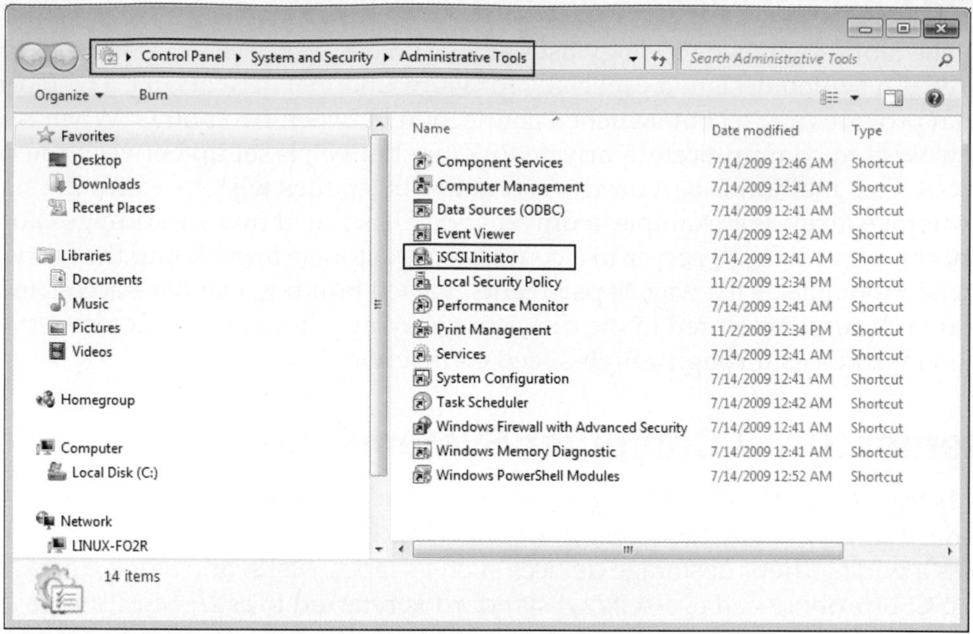

Figure 9-27.
The iSCSI Initiator, located under the **Administrative Tools** menu, is a GUI used for configuring an iSCSI system.

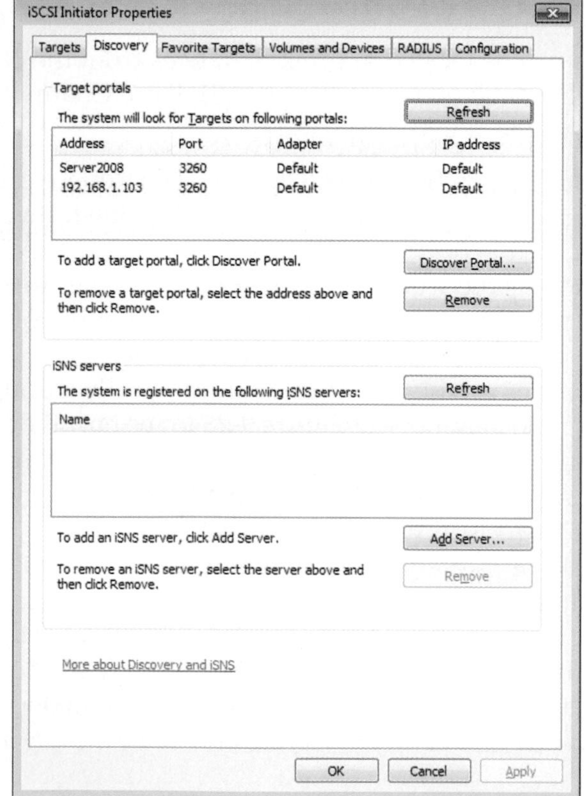

Figure 9-28.
Discovery tab of the **iSCSI Initiator Properties** dialog box.

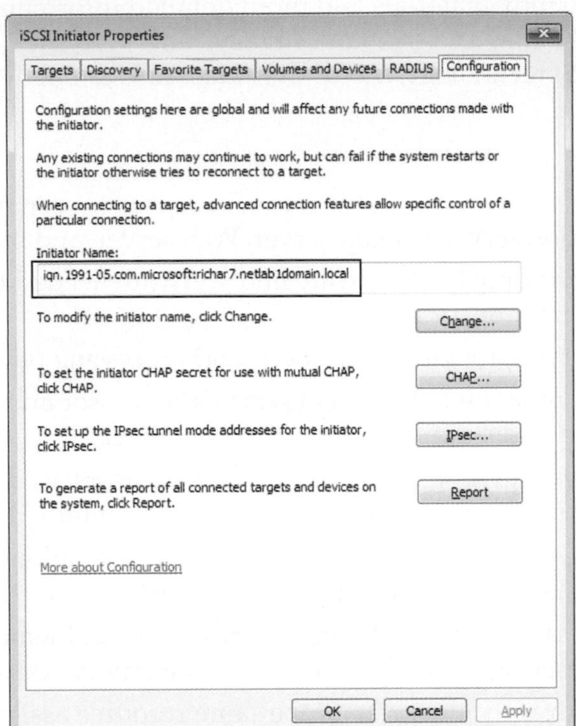

Figure 9-29. **Configuration** tab of the **iSCSI Initiator Properties** dialog box.

The string of characters consists of letters *A–Z*, numbers *0–9*, and special symbols dash (-), period (.), and colon (:). The string of characters typically provides a general description, but this is not a requirement. The string of characters can represent anything. Everything before the colon is a mandatory standard. Everything after the colon is entirely up to the naming authority.

The IQN address in the example is first identified by "iqn". Following this are the date of origination of the address "1991-05," the reverse domain name of the authority "com.microsoft," and the computer name and domain.

The IEEE has developed another naming format known as the *Extended Unique Identifier* or the *IEU-64* format. The IEU format consists of the prefix "ieu" followed by a period and then by a string of hexadecimal numbers. For example, ieu.0123D0123F0A. This type of address is issued by IEEE and is used by equipment manufacturers to identify its network storage devices.

Furthering Your Study

You may be interested in further study and possible certification as a server technician. The CompTIA organization has a certification called *Server+*, which is designed to verify your competence for installing, repairing, and maintaining servers. You can download a complete description of the exam objectives from the CompTIA Web site.

Many of the areas in the Server+ Certification exam overlap those on the A+ Certification exam. However, even if you have scored high on the A+ Certification exams, there are sufficient differences between the certifications that will prevent you from passing the Server+ Certification exam without specialized study.

For additional study materials and more detailed information about server hardware, access the IBM and the Sun Microsystems Web sites. For detailed information on SCSI technology, access the Adaptec Web site.

Summary

- Servers play many roles in a network, such as print server, file server, database server, application server, backup server, Web server, and mail server.
- A thin server has only the hardware and software needed to support and run a specific function, or role.
- A thin client server provides applications and processing power to a thin client.
- The thin client relies on a thin client server's processor and memory for processing data and running software applications.
- Typically, entry-level servers contain 1 to 8 processors; mid-range servers contain 9 to 30 processors; and high-end servers contain 31 to 106 processors.
- Servers typically incorporate hot-swap technology to allow components to be removed or installed while the system is running.
- System resources associated with hardware are Direct Memory Access (DMA), interrupt request (IRQ), I/O port address, and memory address assignment.
- When two hardware devices share the same resource assignment, a system conflict occurs.
- The most common RAID levels are RAID 0, RAID 1, and RAID 5.
- RAID 0 is known as striping. Striping increases data read/write speed but does not provide fault tolerance.
- RAID 1 is mirroring or duplexing two hard disk drives.
- RAID 5 is known as striping with parity, which combines data read/write speed with fault tolerance.
- Network Attached Storage (NAS) is a device or collection of devices used to provide storage for a local area network. The NAS shares the bandwidth of the local network.
- Storage Area Network (SAN) is a separate network dedicated to data storage. It does not affect the bandwidth of the other connected networks.
- The iSCSI standard is an IP-based storage technology that uses IPv4 and IPv6 network addresses to identify storage devices on a LAN, MAN, or WAN.

Review Questions

Answer the following questions on a separate sheet of paper. Please do not write in this book.

1. What are some typical services that servers provide?
2. What is a thin server and what applications can it be used for?
3. What is a thin client server and what applications can it be used for?
4. What does the term *hot-swap* mean?
5. What type of motherboard is commonly used for servers?
6. Which server component is responsible for the POST?
7. How many devices can be connected to a Fast/Wide SCSI-2 chain?
8. What is the bus width of Fast SCSI-2?
9. What is the bus width of Fast/Wide SCSI-2?

10. What must be done to the last device on a SCSI chain?
11. What does the acronym LUN represent?
12. What does the acronym ACPI represent?
13. What is the purpose of ACPI?
14. What does the acronym ACPICA represent?
15. What is the goal of ACPICA?
16. Name the four system resources that may be assigned to a hardware device?
17. How many IRQ settings are there in a typical computer?
18. What does the acronym RAID represent?
19. How is parity used to replace data lost on a damaged disk?
20. Which RAID level(s) provide no fault tolerance?
21. Which RAID levels provide disk mirroring?
22. What is the difference between disk mirroring and duplexing?
23. Which RAID level provides both striping and parity?
24. Your system storage is accessed many times throughout the day by many users. The data is not critical. Rather, it is a collection of application software. A tape backup system is used to restore data from a system failure. Which RAID level would *most likely* be appropriate and why?
25. Which RAID level is denoted by the use of two hard disk drives each containing identical data?
26. What does the acronym NAS represent?
27. What does the acronym SAN represent?
28. What is the difference between NAS and SAN?
29. What type of media is used for Fibre Channel?
30. What are the three common Fibre Channel topologies?
31. What does the acronym iSCSI represent?
32. What are the two main advantages to iSCSI storage?
33. What two protocols are used to send SCSI commands across the network?
34. What does the acronym NAA represent?
35. What two naming formats are used to identify iSCSI targets?
36. What naming format is used to identify Fibre Channel storage devices?
37. Identify the following address type: iqn.2008-06.com.rmroberts:myiSCSIstorage.

Sample Network+ Exam Questions

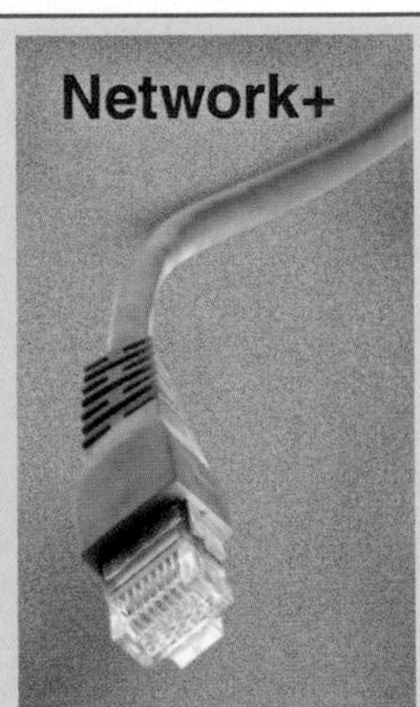

Answer the following questions on a separate sheet of paper. Please do not write in this book.

1. Which RAID level provides the fastest reading and writing data transfer time?
   A. RAID 0
   B. RAID 1
   C. RAID 5
   D. RAID 0 and RAID 1
2. Which network RAID level provides a duplicate copy of one hard disk drive on another hard disk drive?
   A. RAID 0
   B. RAID 1
   C. RAID 5
   D. RAID 4

3. How does SAN differ from NAS?
   A. SAN provides access to a SCSI disk exclusively, while NAS provides access to SCSI, ATA, and EIDE drives.
   B. SAN offers encryption; NAS does not.
   C. SAN does not increase local network traffic; NAS does.
   D. SAN is connected to the local network system, while NAS is accessed remotely via a WAN link.
4. What is the minimum number of drives required for implementing a RAID 5 installation?
   A. 1
   B. 2
   C. 3
   D. 4
5. What does the term *fault tolerance* mean?
   A. The ability to find faults in data before it is backed up.
   B. The ability of the network administrator to tolerate system policy breeches by users.
   C. The ability to recover from a system failure.
   D. The ability to continue normal operation despite a system failure.
6. Which of the following describes the ability to change a module such as hard disk drive or power supply on a server without the need to shut down the server?
   A. System substitution
   B. On the fly changes
   C. Hot-swap
   D. Infinite run ability
7. What is the function of disk striping?
   A. Reduces the total amount of time it takes to store large amounts of data.
   B. Stores duplicate data across two or more drives.
   C. Ensures data integrity.
   D. Aids in disaster recovery.
8. How does a client access files on a NAS device?
   A. Through NAS client software.
   B. Through a server that is attached to the NAS device.
   C. Directly through Category 5e cable.
   D. Directly through high-speed, fiber-optic cable.
9. An investment broker is installing a network system for his employees and to provide customer access. Money transactions will occur on a continuous basis. Which RAID level would you recommend for this business?
   A. RAID 0
   B. RAID 1
   C. RAID 1 (with duplexed drives)
   D. RAID 5
10. Multiple CPUs in a server can perform which of the following?
    A. Unilateral processing
    B. Multiplexed processing
    C. Synchronous processing
    D. Parallel processing

Suggested Laboratory Activities

Do not attempt any suggested laboratory activities without your instructor's permission. Certain activities can render the PC operating system inoperable.

1. Create several partitions on a hard disk drive and then format the partitions using FAT32.
2. Convert a basic FAT32 partition to an NTFS partition and then convert the NTFS partition to dynamic disk.
3. Use the **diskpart** command to view the contents of a hard disk drive. Familiarize yourself with the DiskPart command line options.
4. Install a RAID 0, RAID 1, and RAID 5 system. Remove a hard disk drive to simulate a disk failure and then replace the hard disk drive with a new hard disk drive and rebuild the missing data.
5. Explore the iSCSI Initiator administrative tool in Windows 7.

Interesting Web Sites for More Information

http://computer.howstuffworks.com/scsi.htm
http://msdn.microsoft.com/en-us/library/ee681827(VS.85).aspx
http://serverwatch.internet.com
www.acnc.com/raid.html
www.faqs.org/rfcs/rfc3720.html
www.molex.com
www.pcguide.com/topic.html
www.starwindsoftware.com/white-papers

An enterprise business typically depends on hundreds of servers to meet user demands.

Chapter 9
Laboratory Activity

Using the DiskPart Command Interpreter

After completing this laboratory activity, you will be able to:

- Use the DiskPart command interpreter.
- Use common DiskPart commands to retrieve information about the number of disks installed in a system and about disk partitions or volumes.
- Use DiskPart **help** command to reveal a list of DiskPart commands.

Introduction

Disk management is usually performed in the Disk Management utility. The DiskPart command interpreter is an alternative way to manage disks and partitions. At times, the DiskPart command interpreter may be the only alternative for inspecting and manipulating the master boot record (MBR) and partition table should the GUI fail. Also, certain tasks can be performed using the DiskPart command interpreter that cannot be performed using the Disk Management utility. For example, you must use the DiskPart command interpreter to convert a dynamic disk to a basic disk and to delete or replace the MBR in the active partition. The Disk Management utility does not allow the performance of these tasks because it is designed to protect the integrity of the disk structure from accidental deletion.

You can think of the DiskPart command interpreter as an updated version of the **fdisk** command. Windows XP no longer supports the **fdisk** command. The DiskPart utility is used in place of **fdisk** to inspect, create, and delete partitions or volumes on a disk drive.

The DiskPart command interpreter will not make changes to removable media such as a USB drive and an IEEE-1394 drive. These types of media are identified as a "super floppy" by the DiskPart utility rather than as a hard disk drive.

In this laboratory activity, you will perform some basic DiskPart operations to become familiar with this utility. While you most likely will never need to use the full capability of this utility, more information can be obtained at the Microsoft Tech Support Web site.

Look at the following screen capture. Notice that the **detail disk** command has been entered at the DiskPart command line. The **detail disk** command reveals details about the selected disk, such as the hard disk drive manufacturer and type. It also shows that the hard disk drive has two partitions or volumes. Volume 1 is assigned letter *C* and volume 2 is assigned letter *D*. Notice that both volumes are indicated as healthy.

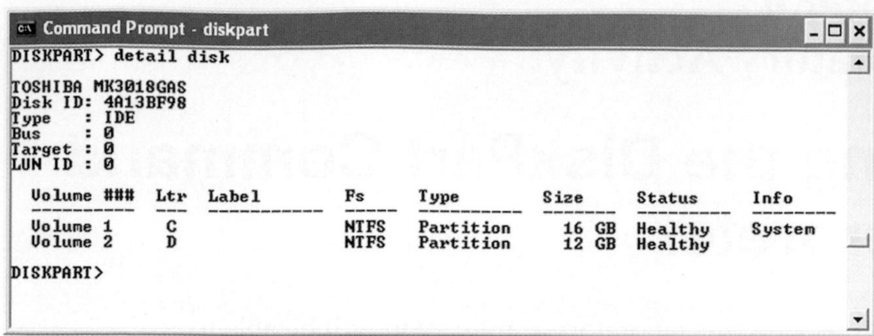

The **list** command can be used with the disk, volume, and partition object. When using the DiskPart command interpreter, disks, partitions, and volumes are referred to as *objects*. Look at the following screen capture. It shows the **list disk**, **list partition**, and **list volume** commands. The **list disk** command lists the disk(s) installed starting with disk 0. The **list volume** command lists the volumes contained in the system. The **list partition** command lists the partitions located on a selected disk. Notice how the DVD-ROM drive is identified after issuing the **list volume** command. Also, notice how the removable drive is identified even though it is no longer present.

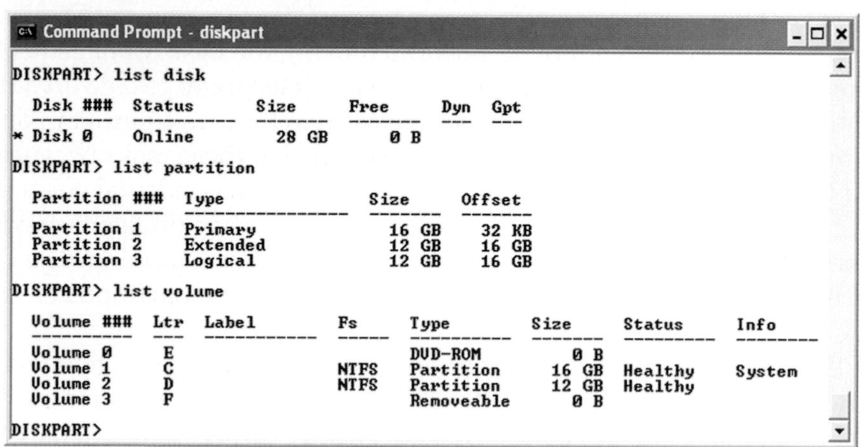

Before issuing the **list partition** command, you must select the disk you wish to view. For example, to view the partition information for a single hard disk drive, you would issue the **select disk** command. Then you would issue the **list partition** command. Otherwise, you will generate an error message stating, "There is no disk selected to list partitions."

Selecting the disk is also known as *setting focus*. When you set focus, you focus the **list partition** command on a selected disk. You must also set the focus on the partition you wish to list. If you do not, the default partition you are presently running the DiskPart command interpreter from is automatically selected.

For more information on the DiskPart command interpreter, read the following Microsoft Support article: 300415—A Description of the DiskPart Command Line Utility.

Equipment and Materials

- Computer with Windows XP, Windows Vista, or Windows 7 installed. (A server is not required for this laboratory activity.)

Procedure

1. ______ Report to your assigned workstation.
2. ______ Boot the computer and verify it is in working order.
3. ______ Open the command prompt (**Start | All Programs | Accessories | Command Prompt**, or **Start | Run** and enter **cmd** in the **Run** dialog box).
4. ______ At the command line, type and enter the **DiskPart** command. If successful, the prompt will display > DiskPart to let you know that you are now using the DiskPart command interpreter.
5. ______ Enter the **Help** or **/?** command to reveal a list of commands.
6. ______ Enter the **list** command to display the objects that can be specified with the **list** command. Disk, partition, and volume are listed.
7. ______ Try each of the following commands to reveal information about the disk drive(s): **list disk**, **list partition**, **list volume**. Remember, the **list partition** command requires focus. You must use the **select** command to select the disk drive you wish to list partition information about. For example, you would enter **select disk 0** to set the focus on the first disk in the system. The **select** command is only required for the **list partition** command. After running each command, record on a separate sheet of paper the information revealed.
8. ______ The **detail** command reveals similar content but with more detailed information about an object. Enter each of the following commands and then record on a separate sheet of paper the information revealed: **detail disk**, **detail volume**, **detail partition**.
9. ______ Practice using the commands covered thus far until you are very familiar with them. They are difficult to learn at first because some involve setting focus and using two words for a valid command.
10. ______ Use the **help** command to reveal what the following commands are used for. Do *not* attempt to use any of the following commands without explicit permission from the instructor.

Command	Purpose
add	
active	
assign	
break	
clean	
create	
delete	
detail	
exit	
extend	
help	
import	
inactive	
list	
online	
rem	
remove	
repair	
rescan	
retain	
select	

11. _____ Enter the **exit** command to return to the command prompt and then again to return to the Windows desktop. Leave your computer in the condition as specified by your instructor.

12. _____ Answer the review questions.

Review Questions

Answer the following questions on a separate sheet of paper. Please do not write in this book.

1. What are objects when using the DiskPart command interpreter?
2. What command is used to reveal information about a particular partition?
3. Which command is used to set focus on a particular drive?
4. What does the command prompt look like when you are running the DiskPart command interpreter?
5. How can you see a list of the various DiskPart commands?
6. A particular computer has only one hard disk drive. What command is used to set focus on that one hard disk drive?
7. What command will stop the DiskPart command interpreter and return you to the default prompt?

10 TCP/IP Fundamentals

After studying this chapter, you will be able to:

- ❑ Explain the operation of the Network Address Translation (NAT) protocol.
- ❑ Use the **ipconfig** command to determine the IP address and subnet mask on a workstation.
- ❑ Explain the operation of the Domain Name System (DNS).
- ❑ Map UDP, TCP, and IP to the OSI model.
- ❑ Explain the operation of the Windows Internet Naming Service (WINS).
- ❑ Explain the operation of the Dynamic Host Configuration Protocol (DHCP).
- ❑ Identify Automatic Private IP Addressing (APIPA) addresses.
- ❑ Differentiate between IPv4 and IPv6 addresses.
- ❑ Recall the three key IPv4 to IPv6 transition technologies and their function.
- ❑ Interpret the displays of TCP/IP troubleshooting utilities.

Network+ Exam—Key Points

The Network+ Certification exam requires extensive knowledge of how IP addresses function in a network. You need to have a solid grasp of the relationship of IP addresses and subnet masks as well as the common TCP/IP troubleshooting command line utilities: **ping**, **tracert**, **nbstat**, **ipconfig**, and **winipcfg**. Be able to explain how WINS, DNS, DHCP, and APIPA services operate in a network. You cannot study this chapter too much! Be sure to perform laboratory activities relating to the topics in this chapter.

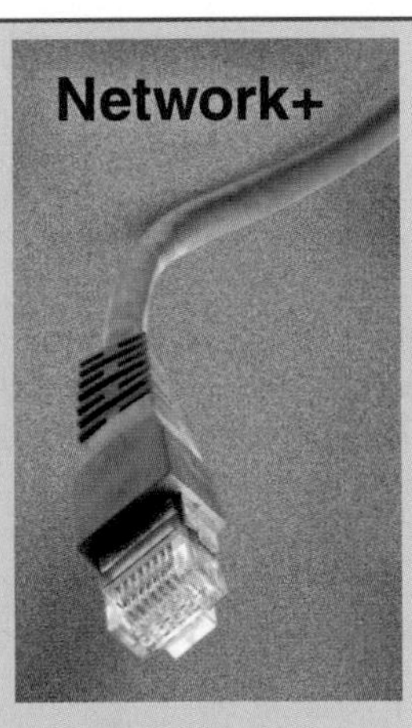

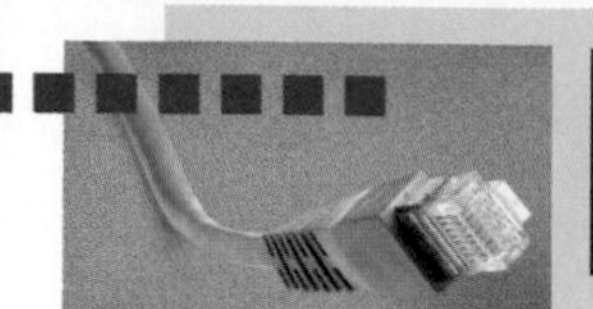

Key Words and Terms

The following words and terms will become important pieces of your networking vocabulary. Be sure you can define them.

6to4
Address Resolution Protocol (ARP)
anycast address
Automatic Private IP Addressing (APIPA)
Bootstrap Protocol (BOOTP)
Class A network
Class B network
Class C network
default gateway address
diskless station
Domain Name System (DNS)
dynamic addressing
Dynamic Host Configuration Protocol (DHCP)
dynamic IP assignment
EUI-64 identifier
Fully Qualified Domain Name (FQDN)
global address
host
Integrated Network Information Center (InterNIC)
Internet Corporation for Assigned Names and Numbers (ICANN)
Intra-Site Automatic Tunneling Address Protocol (ISATAP)
IPv6
link-local
loopback address
multicast address
Neighbor Discovery
Network Address Translation (NAT)
octet
port number
registrar
resolver
Reverse Address Resolution Protocol (RARP)
socket
static addressing
static IP assignment
subdomain
subnet mask
subnetwork
Teredo
unicast address
unique-local
Windows Internet Naming Service (WINS)

The TCP/IP protocol is used for network communications by all major network operating systems. It was especially designed for the Internet. Entire textbooks have been written on the subject of TCP/IP, and it accounts for a large portion of the Network+ Certification exam. Other certifications from Novell, Nortel, Microsoft, Linux, and IBM also rely heavily on TCP/IP principles for their certification exams.

As a network administrator, you need to be able to configure a host to use the TCP/IP protocol and to troubleshoot network connection problems in a TCP/IP environment. To be able to do this, you need to understand the Domain Name Service (DNS) structure, TCP/IP addressing, and how services such as Dynamic Internet Connection Protocol (DHCP) work. You also need to be able to use TCP/

IP troubleshooting utilities and interpret their output to solve communication problems.

This chapter introduces TCP/IP addressing and the Domain Name Service (DNS), which provide functionality and structure to the Internet. It takes a detailed look at how TCP/IP hosts are identified and relates TCP/IP communications to the OSI model. Lastly, a brief overview of some of the many TCP/IP troubleshooting utilities is presented.

IPv4 Addressing

The TCP/IP protocol was developed by the Department of Defense (DoD). It was specifically designed for communication over the Internet. As the Internet evolved, it became evident that a means of identifying network nodes was needed. The IP address was the solution and was approved in 1980.

There are two types of IP addressing schemes: IPv4 and IPv6. IPv6 addressing is covered later in this chapter. An IPv4 address consists of four octets, **Figure 10-1.** An ***octet*** is an eight-bit (or one-byte) value. Each octet in an IPv4 address is composed of eight digits of 0s and 1s. Periods separate each octet from neighboring octets.

octet
an eight-bit (or one-byte) value.

The term *IP address* could mean either IPv4 or IPv6.

Although IPv4 numbers are computed in the binary form, they are interpreted and used in the decimal form. When an octet is interpreted as a decimal number, the values range from 0 through 255. This range is based on the maximum possibilities of an eight-position binary number. **Figure 10-2** shows an IPv4 address specified in binary and decimal. As you can see, the decimal expression of an IPv4 address is much shorter than the binary expression of the same address. It is also much easier to read and interpret.

IPv4 addressing is a method of identifying every node or host on a network. The terms ***host*** and ***node*** are used interchangeably to identify individual PCs, printers, and network equipment that may require an address.

host
a name for a computer, printer, and network device associated with an IP address on a TCP/IP network. Also called a *node*.

A near perfect analogy of IPv4 addressing is the telephone system. The telephone system is hierarchical in that it uses area codes to identify areas outside a local area. The first three digits identify the area code, and the last seven digits identify the telephone inside the area code. See **Figure 10-3.**

IPv4 addresses work in much the same way. An IPv4 address has two parts: the network number and the host number. The network number identifies the network you are trying to connect to and the host number identifies the host or

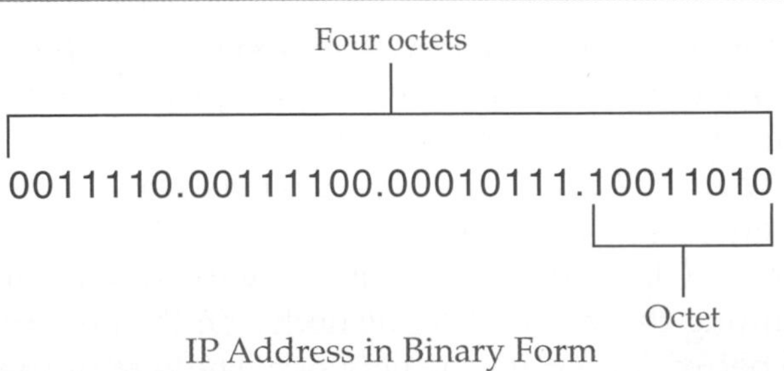

Figure 10-1.
An IPv4 address consists of four octets (eight-bit units).

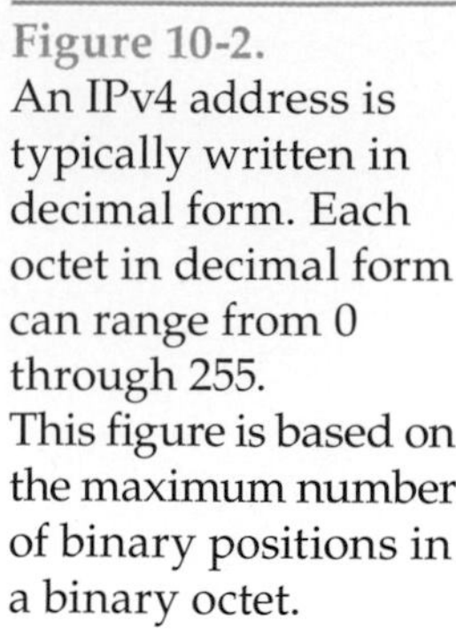

Figure 10-2. An IPv4 address is typically written in decimal form. Each octet in decimal form can range from 0 through 255. This figure is based on the maximum number of binary positions in a binary octet.

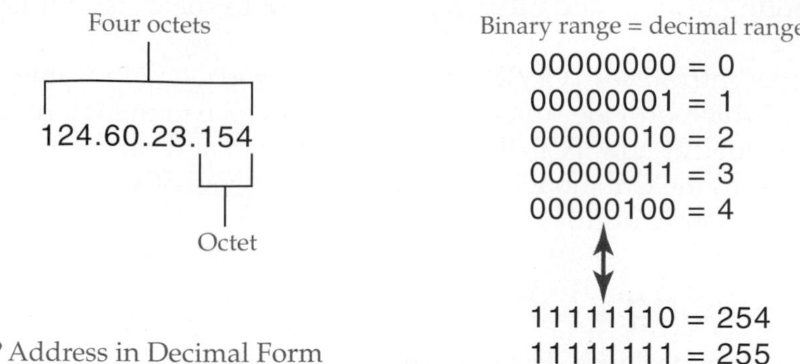

Figure 10-3. The IPv4 addressing scheme can be compared to the telephone system. In a telephone system, a three-digit number indicates the area the telephone is in, and the telephone number indicates the telephone. In an IPv4 address, part of the address indicates the network the host is in and the other part indicates the host.

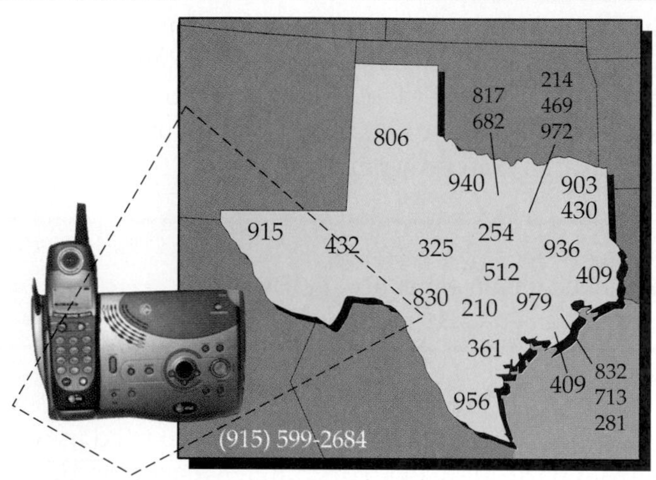

network node. The relationship of IPv4 addresses to the network system is the same as telephone numbers to the telephone system. Each telephone is identified with a unique telephone number, and each node on a network is identified by a unique IPv4 number.

Network Class

Class A network an IPv4 network classification that supports up to 16 million hosts on each of 127 networks.

Class B network an IPv4 network classification that supports up to 65,000 hosts on each of 16,000 networks.

Class C network an IPv4 network classification that supports 254 hosts on each of 2 million networks.

For the purpose of assigning IPv4 addresses, networks are divided into three major classifications: Class A, Class B, and Class C. Large networks are assigned a Class A classification. A ***Class A network*** can support up to 16 million hosts on each of 127 networks. Medium-sized networks are assigned a Class B classification. A ***Class B network*** supports up to 65,000 hosts on each of 16,000 networks. Small networks are assigned a Class C classification. A ***Class C network*** supports 254 hosts on each of 2 million networks.

Networks are assigned an IPv4 address based on their network classification. Look at **Figure 10-4.** In the table, you can see that the class of the network determines the numeric value of the first octet in its IPv4 address. The range for a Class A network is from 1 to 127, for a Class B network it is from 128 to 191, and for a Class C network it is from 192 to 223.

IPv4 addresses for Class A networks use only the first octet as the network address. The remaining three octets define nodes on the network. The first two octets of a Class B network identify the network. The remaining two octets

Class	Range	Number of Networks	Number of Hosts
Class A	1–127	127	16,000,000
Class B	128–191	16,000	65,000
Class C	192–223	2,000,000	254

Figure 10-4. IPv4 address classifications.

identify nodes on the network. A Class C network uses the first three octets to identify the network and the last octet to identify the nodes. For example, a typical Class C network might have an IPv4 address of 201.100.100.12. The network is identified by the 201.100.100, and the node is identified as 12.

Network+ Note

For the Network+ Certification exam, be sure you can identify IPv4 addresses by their class.

Subnet Mask

A company may divide their network into several, smaller networks. A network within a network is known as a ***subnetwork***. A ***subnet mask*** is a number similar to an IP address. It is used to determine in which subnetwork a particular IPv4 address belongs. The subnet mask can be used to identify the class of network, but it is really intended to allow the network address to be broken down into subnetworks.

subnetwork
a network within a network.

subnet mask
a number similar to an IP address used to determine to which subnetwork a particular IPv4 address belongs.

When the subnet mask is encountered, it is usually viewed in the decimal form—a series of four three-digit numbers. At first glance, a subnet mask may appear identical to an IPv4 address. However, a subnet mask is distinguishable from an IP address because it begins with one or more octets of 255. An IPv4 address cannot begin with 255.

The octets of a subnet mask correspond to octets in the IPv4 address. The numbers found in a subnet mask depend on the class of the network and the number of subnetworks into which the network is divided. The subnet mask is combined with the IPv4 address using the bitwise AND operation. The details of this operation are beyond the scope of this textbook. The resulting address is the subnet address. For now, just remember that the subnet mask is used to identify any subnetwork at a network address. Chapter 11—Subnetting covers the subnet mask in more depth.

Reserved IPv4 Addresses

A number of IPv4 addresses are reserved for private networks. They are often used for offices sharing an Internet address or for experimentation. They are not valid for use as a direct connection to the Internet. Look at the following chart of private IPv4 addresses.

Class	Range	Subnet Mask
A	10.0.0.0 – 10.255.255.255	255.0.0.0
B	172.016.0.0 – 172.31.255.255	255.255.0.0
C	192.168.0.0 – 192.168.255.255	255.255.255.0

Network+ Note

For the Network+ Certification exam, be sure you can identify a private IPv4 address.

Microsoft Windows uses the Class C IPv4 range for implementing a small-office/home-office network. Typically, one computer is connected to the Internet through an ISP and other computers share the connection by creating a small TCP/IP network. The host is assigned the 192.168.0.1 IPv4 address while the clients are assigned IP addresses 192.168.0.2 through 192.168.0.255. While the term *host* is used typically to describe any device on a network that has an IP address, the host in this scenario is the computer that hosts the Internet connection. Computers that connect to the Internet through the host are called *clients*.

Network Address Translation (NAT) a protocol used to translate private network addresses into an assigned Internet address, and vice versa.

Microsoft refers to this type of connection as Internet Connection Sharing (ICS). ICS uses the ***Network Address Translation (NAT)*** protocol to translate private network addresses into an assigned Internet address, and vice versa. NAT was especially designed for implementing private network configurations. It allows an unregistered private network address to communicate with a legally registered IP address. For example, a client that wishes to access the Internet sends a request to the host. The host, in turn, uses the IP address assigned by the ISP to connect to the Internet. See **Figure 10-5.** Three main advantages of using NAT are as follows:

- Provides a firewall type of service by hiding internal IP addresses.
- Allows computers on a network to share one common IP address to access the Internet without the need of multiple IP addresses to be assigned to the subnetwork.
- Allows multiple ISDN connections to be combined into one Internet connection.

Network+ Note

For the Network+ Certification exam, be sure to know the purpose of the Network Address Translation (NAT) protocol.

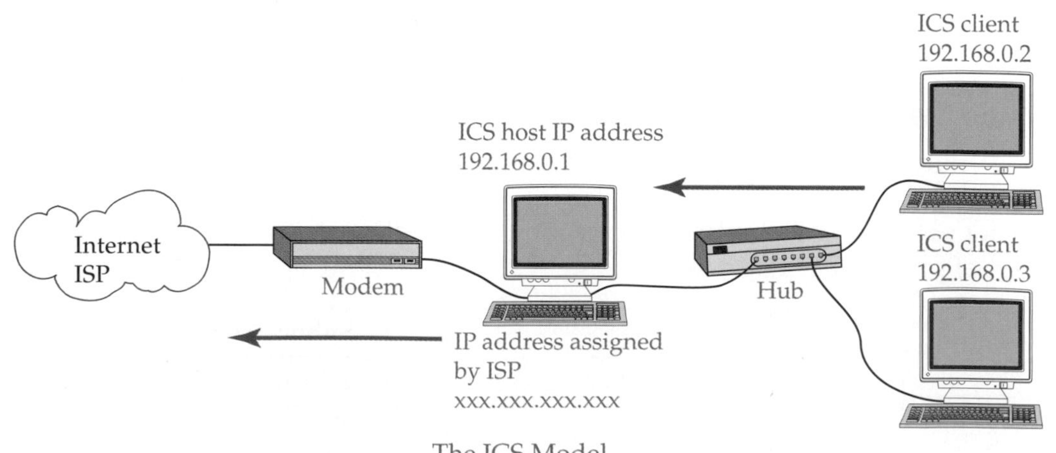

Figure 10-5. Internet Connection Sharing (ICS) uses the Network Address Translation (NAT) protocol to translate unregistered IP addresses to a registered IP address. In this example, an ICS client sends an Internet request to the IP address of the ICS host, 192.168.0.1. The ICS host uses the ISP assigned address to access the Internet.

It is important to note that a private network such as an Intranet may use any possible IP address as long as it does not connect to the Internet. Using a number that is assigned to a URL would not only confuse the network system, it is illegal. The reserved private addresses can be used even when the network connects to the Internet. The Internet does not recognize the private network addresses, so they do not affect the system. This is why private network addresses are ideal for creating a subnetwork.

The NAT protocol is commonly installed automatically in Microsoft Windows 2000 and later versions when the Network Setup Wizard is used. For example, when installing the Internet Connection Service (ICS) through the Network Setup Wizard, the user is asked a series of questions. Based on the responses that are entered by the user, the operating system automatically sets up a connection share for a single Internet connection.

Figure 10-6 shows the **Local Area Connection Properties** dialog box from Windows 7, which provides an option to allow other network computers to access the Internet through its Internet connection. This option will automatically create an ICS configuration.

Note

With the development of the NAT protocol, the numbers of IPv4 addresses are lasting longer than expected. By using the NAT protocol to translate private IPv4 addresses on a home or office network, thousands, if not millions, of IPv4 addresses are saved.

Viewing IP Configuration Settings

The IPv4 configuration is a group of settings made on a host that allows it to communicate in a TCP/IP environment. The IPv4 configuration consists of the host's IPv4 address, the subnet mask, and the default gateway. The ***default gateway address*** is the address of the computer that provides a connection to the Internet. The Internet service provider's software or the network DHCP server usually determines these settings automatically. Occasionally, you may have to adjust the settings manually or verify the information while working with an ISP

default gateway address
the address of the computer that provides a connection to the Internet.

Figure 10-6.
The **Local Area Connection Properties** dialog box for a Windows 7 computer provides an option to allow networked computers to access the Internet through the computer's Internet connection.

to troubleshoot a connection. On a Windows-based computer, you can use the IP Configuration utility to verify the settings.

Windows XP and later use the **ipconfig** command issued from the command prompt to run the IP Configuration utility. See **Figure 10-7.** The assigned IPv4 address, the subnet mask, and the default gateway address are displayed. To reveal more information about the connection, use the **ipconfig /all** command. See **Figure 10-8.** Notice that the MAC address (physical address), DHCP server address, and DNS server are revealed as well as other information. The additional information provided, such as the IPv4 address of the DHCP server and the DNS server, will become more relevant to you later in the chapter.

Note

UNIX/Linux systems use the **ifconfig** command to produce similar results as **ipconfig**.

Tech Tip

The terms *physical* and *logical* are often used to describe network systems and devices. It is important to be able to determine the difference between a physical and a logical component. For example, the IP address is a logical address assigned to a network host. It is logical because it is assigned and can be changed at any time. In contrast, the MAC address is a physical address electrically etched into the network interface card associated with each host.

Domain Name System (DNS)

Since IP addresses are difficult to remember, the Internet uses a ***Domain Name System (DNS)*** or ***Domain Name Service*** to make it easier for people to identify and find networks on the Internet. It does this by allowing a name, called

Figure 10-7.
IP Configuration display when the **ipconfig** command is issued.

```
C:\DOCUME~1\JKELTNER.GWP>ipconfig

Windows IP Configuration

Ethernet adapter Local Area Connection:

        Connection-specific DNS Suffix  . : gwp.com
        IP Address. . . . . . . . . . . . : 192.0.0.187
        Subnet Mask . . . . . . . . . . . : 255.255.255.0
        Default Gateway . . . . . . . . . : 192.0.0.110
```

Figure 10-8.
The **IP Configuration** display when the **ipconfig /all** command is issued.

```
C:\DOCUME~1\JKELTNER.GWP>ipconfig /all

Windows IP Configuration

        Host Name . . . . . . . . . . . . : EDIT84
        Primary Dns Suffix  . . . . . . . : gwp.com
        Node Type . . . . . . . . . . . . : Hybrid
        IP Routing Enabled. . . . . . . . : No
        WINS Proxy Enabled. . . . . . . . : No
        DNS Suffix Search List. . . . . . : gwp.com
                                            gwp.com

Ethernet adapter Local Area Connection:

        Connection-specific DNS Suffix  . : gwp.com
        Description . . . . . . . . . . . : Intel(R) PRO/100 VE Network Connecti
on
        Physical Address. . . . . . . . . : 00-0D-60-3F-B5-2B
        Dhcp Enabled. . . . . . . . . . . : Yes
        Autoconfiguration Enabled . . . . : Yes
        IP Address. . . . . . . . . . . . : 192.0.0.187
        Subnet Mask . . . . . . . . . . . : 255.255.255.0
        Default Gateway . . . . . . . . . : 192.0.0.110
        DHCP Server . . . . . . . . . . . : 192.0.0.10
        DNS Servers . . . . . . . . . . . : 192.0.0.10
        Primary WINS Server . . . . . . . : 192.0.0.10
        Secondary WINS Server . . . . . . : 192.0.0.105
        Lease Obtained. . . . . . . . . . : Wednesday, December 15, 2004 3:07:48
 PM
        Lease Expires . . . . . . . . . . : Sunday, December 19, 2004 3:07:48 PM
```

a *domain name*, to be associated with a network address. You can communicate on the Internet by using a domain name or an IP address. For example, when you use a Web browser you can enter the domain name for the URL or an IP address. The IP address connects faster to a distant location than a domain name. When a domain name is entered, it must be converted to an IP address before communication can begin. The amount of time it takes varies according to conditions. Many of these conditions are discussed throughout this chapter.

Domain Name System (DNS)
a system that associates a host or domain name with an IP address, making it easy to identify and find hosts and networks. Also referred to as *Domain Name Service.*

Internet Corporation for Assigned Names and Numbers (ICANN)

The ***Internet Corporation for Assigned Names and Numbers (ICANN)*** is a private, not-for-profit organization that coordinates the assignment of domain names and IP addresses. It does so by allocating domain name registration to select, private companies. Each of the select, private companies is called a ***registrar.*** To obtain a domain name and an IP address, a business or organization places an application through a registrar. Once the registrar processes the application, the business or organization receives an official second-level domain name and an IP address that is registered to the domain name they have been issued.

Internet Corporation for Assigned Names and Numbers (ICANN)
a company that manages domain name registration by allocating domain name registration to select, private companies.

registrar
a select, private company that is assigned a pool of IP addresses from ICANN and handles domain registration.

IP addresses were once regulated and assigned through the government organization known as the ***Integrated Network Information Center (InterNIC).*** InterNIC was a branch of the United States government under the direction of the Department of Commerce. It was responsible for regulating the Internet, overseeing the issue of domain names, and assigning IP addresses to them. InterNIC managed the domain root for .com, .net, .org, .edu, and .gov top-level domains.

Integrated Network Information Center (InterNIC)
a branch of the United States government under the direction of the Department of Commerce that was responsible for regulating the Internet, overseeing the issue of domain names, and assigning IP addresses to them.

The Internet Assigned Numbers Authority (IANA) was the original authority that the US contracted in the early 1990s. IANA established the Internet Network Information Center (InterNIC) funded by the National Science Foundation. Late in the 1990s the government felt that the assigned numbers and names should be somewhat privatized, so they subcontracted the responsibilities to ICANN, a not-for-profit organization. ICANN assumed many of the responsibilities of IANA, but the ultimate authority for assigned numbers and names rests with the US government.

Currently, InterNIC is a Web site that provides services and information about Internet assigned names and numbers and is a registered service mark of the US Department of Commerce. The Department of Commerce licensed InterNIC to ICANN, which operates the InterNIC Web site. The US Department of Commerce is responsible for the overall assignment of the assigned numbers and names in the United States. To find out more about ICANN, visit their Web site at www.icann.org.

Fully Qualified Domain Name (FQDN)

To locate a host on a large network, you need to use the complete name of the host, which includes a combination of the host name and domain name. The complete name of the host is referred to as the ***Fully Qualified Domain Name (FQDN).*** For example, a host called *Station12* in the domain xyzcorp.com would have an FDQN of station12.xyzcorp.com. *Station12* is the host name, and xyzcorp.com is the domain name.

Fully Qualified Domain Name (FQDN)
a combination of a host name and domain name.

As you have seen in previous chapters, network operating systems follow the domain name structure for naming servers, workstations, and other network devices. This was not always the case. Earlier systems using NetBIOS and NetBEUI had their own naming schemes. These naming schemes are not consistent with naming rules used for Fully Qualified Domain Names.

Network operating systems such as Linux and Windows 2000 and later follow the rules of Fully Qualified Domain Names when creating their network structure. However, these operating systems can still communicate with older networking technologies.

Realizing the difference between a host name and a NetBIOS name can help you understand how communication can occur between systems that use Fully Qualified Domain Names and those that use NetBIOS names. A NetBIOS name is a computer name limited to a maximum of 15 characters. A host name can be a Fully Qualified Domain Name or the first part of the Fully Qualified Domain Name. A host name is limited to 63 characters. Many of the symbols allowed in NetBIOS names cannot be used in Fully Qualified Domain Names. These symbols include the following:

; : " < > * + = \ / ? ,

To allow for communications between a system that uses NetBIOS names and one that uses host names, computer names are converted automatically for compatibility. For example, consider a network that contains computers with legacy operating systems. Many legacy operating systems use NetBIOS names to identify computers on a Microsoft network. Modern operating systems use the Fully Qualified Domain Name to communicate. However, to communicate with the legacy computers, the Fully Qualified Domain Name is shortened automatically to match the NetBIOS maximum length of 15 characters. Windows computers can use NetBIOS names to communicate with other Windows computers on the network. However, when communicating with Windows 2000 computers, any symbols in the NetBIOS name need to be replaced with hyphens.

Figure 10-9 shows a warning message that displays on a Windows 7 computer when you configure it with a computer name longer than 15 characters. Compare the NetBIOS name in the message with the name displayed in the system information shown in **Figure 10-10.** Notice that the Computer name is "Richard7asAlongNameTooLongForNetBIOS," which is shortened to RICHARD7ASALONG to be compliant with the 15-character NetBIOS name requirement.

DNS Structure and Operation

DNS is hierarchical, similar to a typical file system structure comprising directories and files, **Figure 10-11.** At the top of DNS is the root. Directly under the root are the top-level domains. The top-level domains start the process of

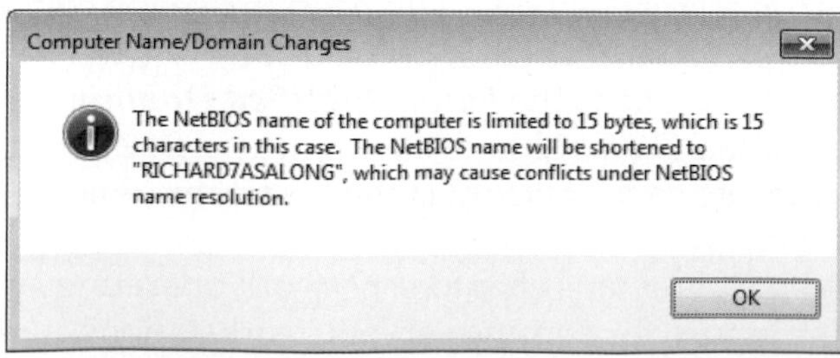

Figure 10-9.
Message box stating that the computer name will be shortened to 15 characters.

Figure 10-10.
Notice that the computer name "Richard7asAlongNameTooLongForNetBIOS" is shortened to "RICHARD7ASALONG" to be compliant with the 15-character NetBIOS name requirement as shown in Figure 10-9.

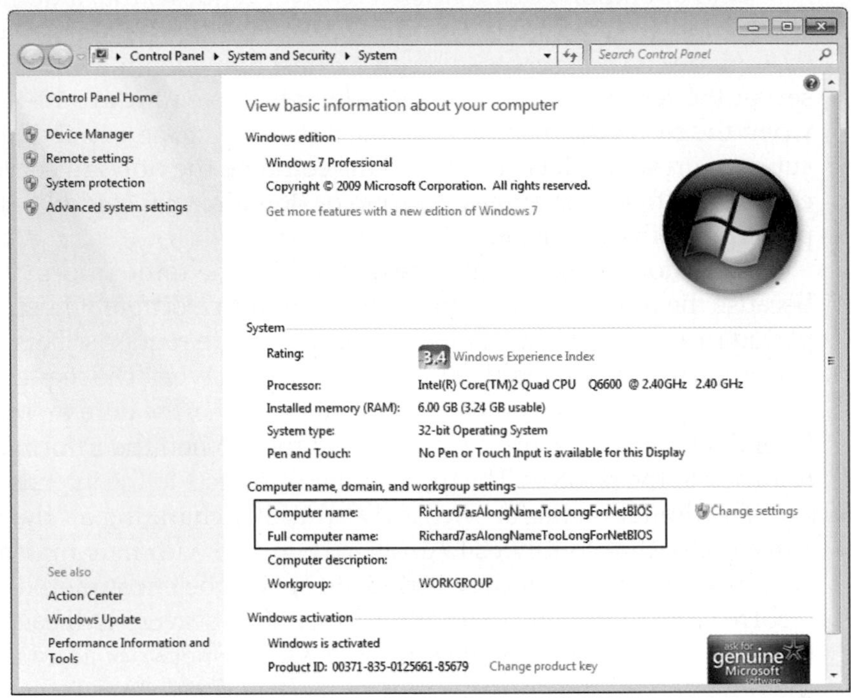

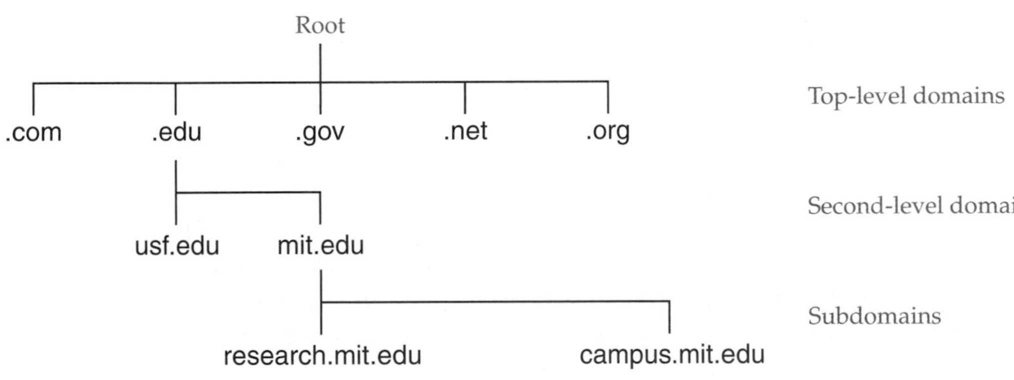

Figure 10-11.
The Domain Name System structure.

dividing the organizational structure into specialized areas. The most common top-level domains are .com, .edu, .gov, .int, .mil, .net, and .org.

The next level of the structure is composed of second-level domains. Second-level domains represent the domain names as assigned by ICANN. Second-level domains identify various companies and organizations. For example, the Massachusetts Institute of Technology domain name is known as mit.edu. The structure is further divided into subdomains controlled by the second-level domains. A ***subdomain*** is any level domain located beneath the secondary domain. For example, the mit.edu, second-level domain can be divided into subdomains such as faculty.mit.edu, research.mit.edu, and students.mit.edu. A subdomain can also be called a *lower-level domain*.

subdomain
any level domain located beneath the secondary domain. Also called a *lower-level domain*.

DNS root servers are located at the top of the domain name hierarchy structure. The root domain server stores the ultimate database for resolving an Internet domain name to a specific IP address. Currently, there are thirteen DNS root servers. A top-level domain server stores DNS information of all top-level domains. A second-level domain server stores DNS information of all second-level domains.

DNS operation begins when a resolver requests that a domain name be resolved to an IP address. The ***resolver*** is a software program located on a host that queries a DNS server to resolve a host name to an IP address. The first DNS server the resolver contacts is a subdomain server, **Figure 10-12.** For example, when the resolver attempts to connect to research.mit.edu, it queries the first subdomain server it encounters. This could be the domain server the host is connected to as part of a workgroup or domain, or it could be the Internet service provider (ISP) for a home PC.

resolver
a software program located on a host that queries a DNS server to resolve a host name to an IP address.

A subdomain server may be queried for the same information many times. Because the request is likely to occur again from a different host, domain names are placed in a cache on the domain server for future requests. This method speeds up the process of supplying IP address information when the request is repeated. If the IP address for the domain name is not in the cache, the domain server queries higher-level domain servers until reaching the root. When the information is found, it is returned to the resolver. The resolver then connects to the intended host.

The domain name service is dynamically changing all the time. It is like a live entity that continues to grow and update with new information and changes. During the update period, errors can be encountered while trying to resolve a domain name to an IP address. Most servers will cache domain name information for approximately three days. The network administrator controls the time period. If a domain changes its IP address during the three-day period, an error can be generated attempting to connect to the domain site. This is because the old information about the IP address is still in the server cache and has not been updated.

Let's take a closer look at how DNS is used to acquire information about a domain name and its associated IP address. The following are the possible steps that occur when a resolver requests the IP address of a domain name. Refer to **Figure 10-13.**

1. The user types in www.g-w.com in the browser.
2. The browser checks if the domain name g-w.com exists in its own browser cache.
3. If not, the browser sends a DNS query to the network's domain name server. The domain server checks its own cache for the requested domain IP address. If this information is in the cache, it connects the host to the destination IP address.
4. If the information is not stored in the domain server cache, it is then requested from a higher-level domain server. The highest level is the top-level domain server located beneath the root.

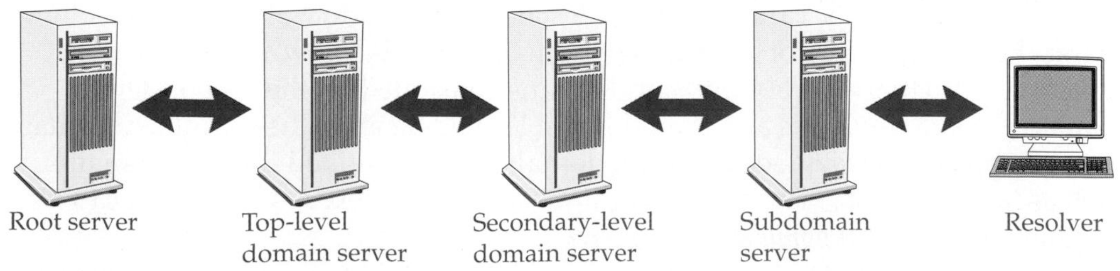

Figure 10-12.
The resolver queries the closest DNS server for IP information. If the DNS server does not have this information, the DNS server passes the request to a higher-level DNS server.

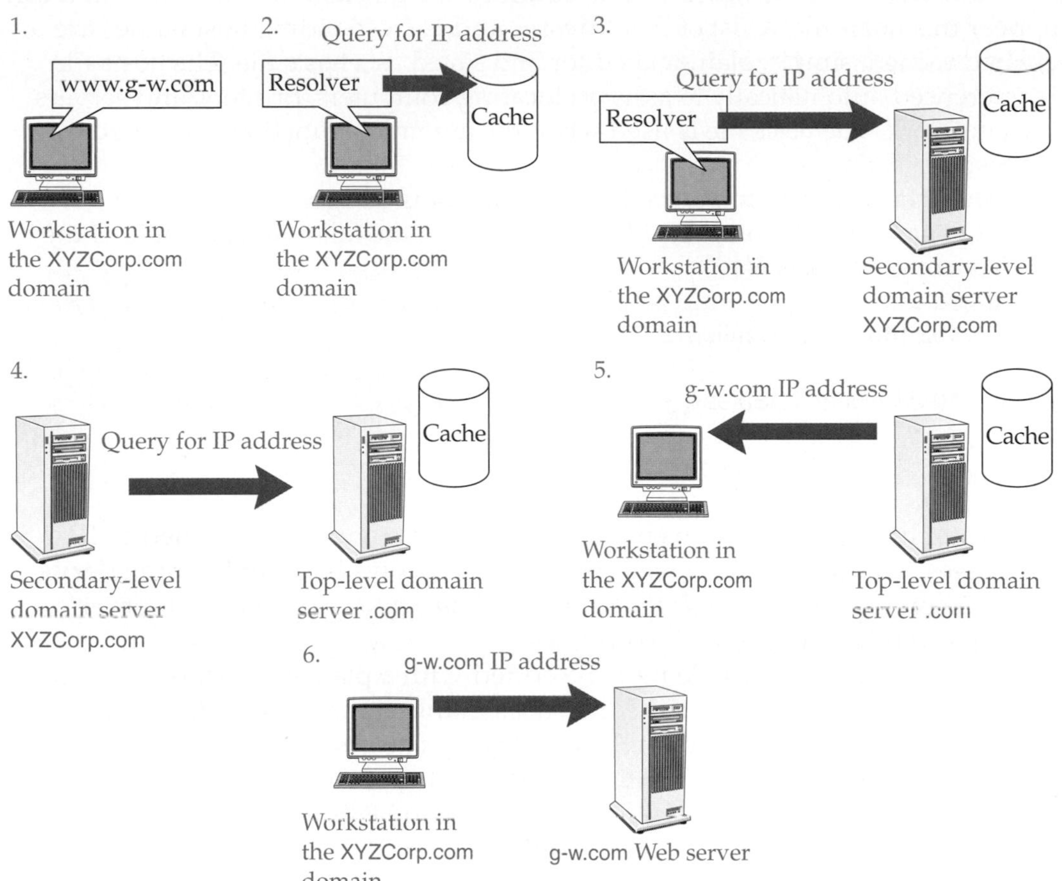

Figure 10-13. This example shows the possible steps that can occur while resolving a domain name to an IP address.

5. If the domain name is an authorized domain name, the top-level domain server returns the IP address information. This information is added to the domain server and workstation cache.
6. The computer that originally attempted to connect to www.g-w.com now uses the IP address to connect to the Web server located at www.g-w.com.

Hosts and Lmhosts Text Files

Originally, all computer names were resolved using a text database. The text database is simply a text file that contains IP addresses and related information. The two text files used to resolve host and NetBIOS names to IP addresses are hosts and lmhosts. These files can still be used as a backup in case other means of resolving computer names to IP addresses fail.

The text file hosts was the original method used by UNIX systems to match computer names to corresponding IP addresses. The following is an example of the contents of a hosts file.

```
127.0.0.1       Localhost
192.168.0.25    PcsAreUs.com
10.100.50.25    Station23.XYZcorp.com
172.63.10.24    USF.edu
```

Note that Fully Qualified Domain Names are considered host names and can appear in a hosts file. A list of IP addresses and corresponding host names are created using a simple, plain-text editor and saved as a hosts file. The hosts file is referenced automatically to assist in locating computers, printers, and servers on a network. The hosts file is used when the automatic functions provided by a DNS server fails.

The lmhosts file is similar to the hosts file but is designed for use with NetBIOS name resolution to IP addresses. Look at the following example of the contents of an lmhosts file.

```
192.168.23.104 Station12

10.23.105.21.1  Sales4

173.76.22.231  Computer25
```

Note that the file contains NetBIOS names of computers matched to IP addresses. The lmhosts file is read when the Windows Internet Naming Service (WINS) server fails. A ***Windows Internet Naming Service (WINS)*** server resolves NetBIOS names to IP addresses.

Windows Internet Naming Service (WINS)
a service that resolves NetBIOS names to IP addresses.

The hosts and lmhosts file must be edited with a plain-text editor such as Notepad. A more sophisticated editor uses many different fonts that make the file unreadable by the network client software. The hosts and lmhosts file must be in plain, ASCII text to be read. The key point to remember is that the hosts file resolves host names to IP addresses related to DNS, and the lmhosts file resolves NetBIOS names to IP addresses related to WINS.

IP, TCP, and UDP Protocols

TCP/IP is actually a suite of protocols. The three most commonly used protocols in the TCP/IP suite are Internet Protocol (IP), Transmission Control Protocol (TCP), and User Datagram Protocol (UDP). IP is designed to control data transmission between two nodes and to ensure that a link has been established between source and destination. IP does not care if the packet is delivered correctly. IP simply transmits the data. IP is a connectionless protocol. UDP functions similar to IP. It establishes a link but does not ensure that data is delivered correctly. It is also a connectionless protocol.

TCP ensures packets arrive intact and in correct order. TCP is a connection-oriented protocol. The main difference between TCP and UDP is that TCP can break large amounts of data into smaller packets and UDP cannot. UDP sends a single packet to transmit control information and data. This section looks at how the IP, TCP, and UDP move data from source to destination.

Relationship to the OSI Model

Figure 10-14 shows the relationship of some TCP/IP protocols to the OSI model and typical data formats. In the illustration, you can see that the three upper layers—application, presentation, and session—take raw data and send it down to the transport layer. At the transport layer, large blocks of raw data are broken into smaller units referred to as *segments*. The segments are placed into the data portion of the TCP or UDP frame. The selection of TCP or UDP frame depends on three factors:

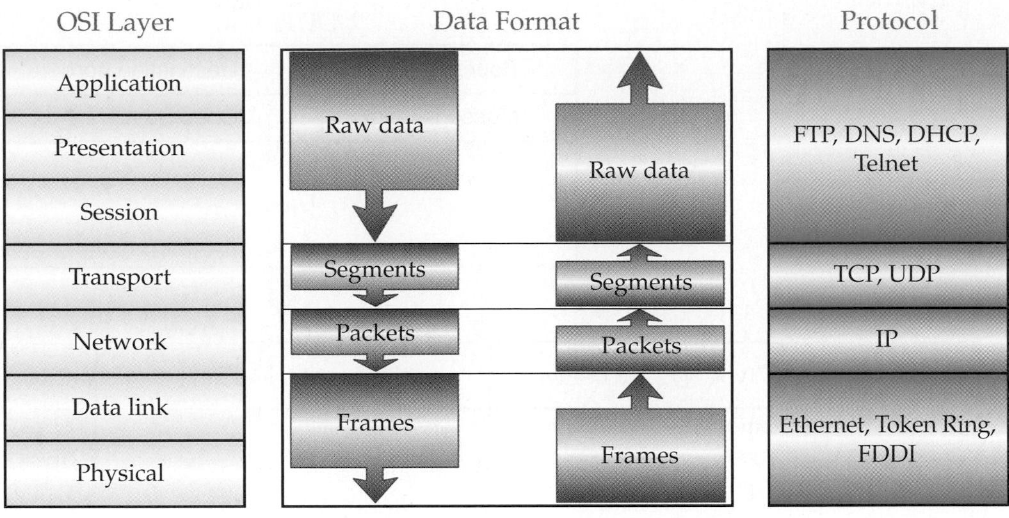

Figure 10-14. The relationship of TCP/IP protocols and data formats to the OSI model.

- The software used in the upper layers of the OSI model.
- The amount of data to be sent.
- If a connectionless or connection-oriented transport of data is desired.

Both the TCP and UDP frame formats provide the port number of the source and destination. For UDP, the port number is optional, but for TCP, the port number is required. There will be more about port numbers later in the chapter.

The content of the TCP or UDP protocol is then moved to the network layer. At the network layer, the TCP or UDP frame is enclosed in an IP protocol frame. The entire unit is referred to as a *packet*. The IP packet contains a source and destination IP address and is sent to the data link layer.

The data link layer performs the final encapsulation of the combined frame formats (TCP or UDP and IP). The data link layer supplies the physical address of the destination and source. The physical address is the MAC address associated with the network card of the source and destination computer. The collective unit of frame formats is referred to as a *frame*.

The frame is placed on the physical media as a series of digital pulses. If the network is Ethernet, the frame is broadcast to all nodes in the segment of the network. When the frame arrives at the destination, the process is reversed. As the data moves up the OSI model, each of the protocol frame formats is removed until the raw data is received at the highest level of the OSI model, the application layer.

Frame Formats

Now let's take a closer look at the frame formats of IP, TCP, UDP, and Ethernet to get a better understanding of the mechanics of the process. Look at **Figure 10-15.** In the illustration, a UDP frame is inserted into the data portion of an IP frame.

The UDP frame format is simple in construction. The header information contains only four significant items: source port, destination port, message length, and checksum. The frame's structure reveals that only port addresses are used to identify the source and destination. There is no way to identify the source or destination by IP address or MAC address. UDP and TCP rely on the IP frame format for the IP address of the destination and source. The IP frame relies on the Ethernet frame for the source and destination MAC address.

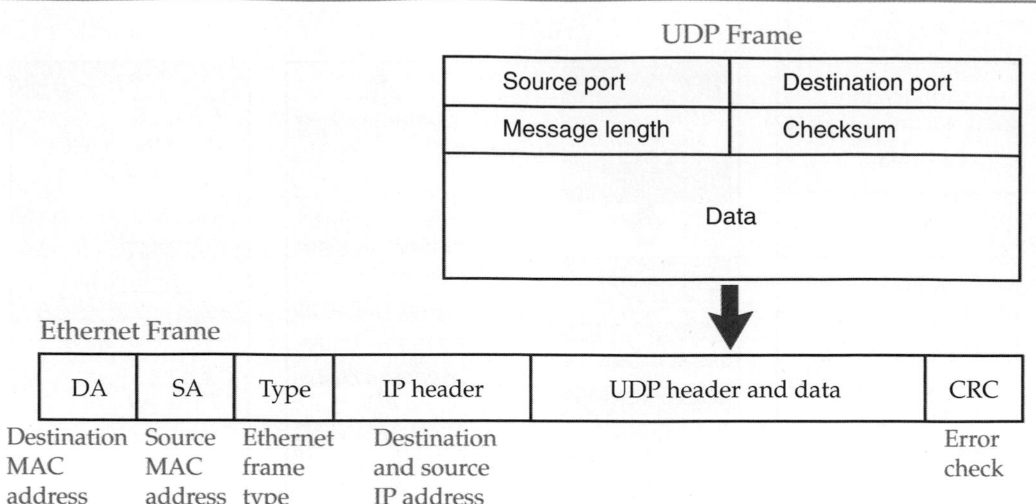

Figure 10-15. UDP is framed in an IP packet, and then the IP packet is framed in an Ethernet frame.

Now look at **Figure 10-16.** Notice that the TCP header contains more information than the UDP header. The TCP header contains additional information such as a sequence number, which is used to reassemble data in a correct order. UDP does not need a sequence number. It is used to transfer small blocks of data or commands.

As the protocol frames reach the data link layer of the OSI model, the final step is to encapsulate the entire set of protocol frames into a frame matching the network standard used, such as Ethernet, Token Ring, and FDDI. Look at **Figure 10-17.** In the example, Ethernet has been chosen. The Ethernet frame relies on the MAC addresses for transmitting between workstations. Remember that a unique MAC address is embedded into each network interface card. The Ethernet frame is broadcast to all the network interface cards on the LAN. When the destination network interface card receives the entire frame of protocol formats and data, it removes the Ethernet frame

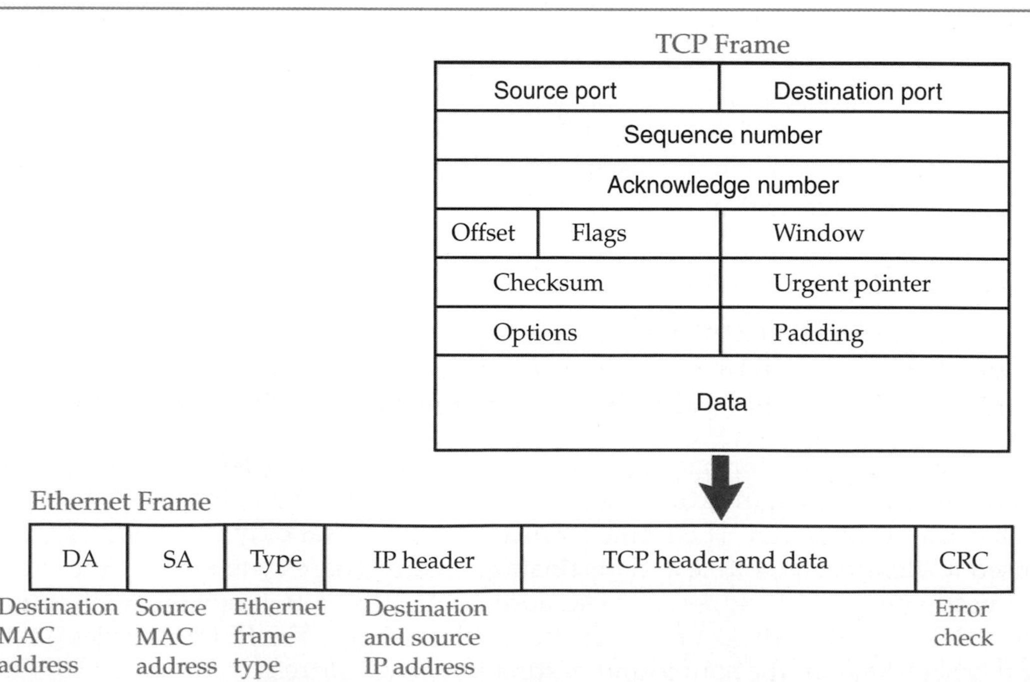

Figure 10-16. TCP is framed in an IP packet, and then the IP packet is framed in an Ethernet frame.

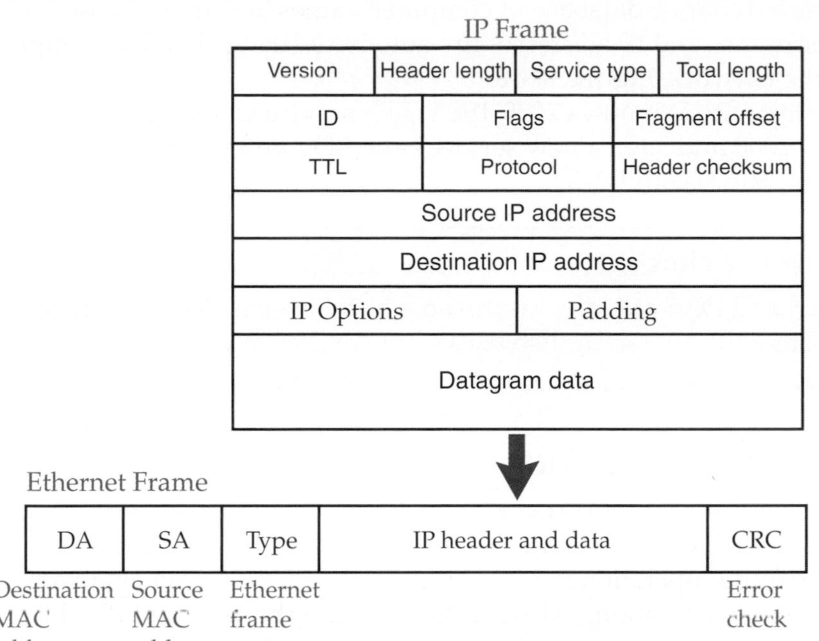

Figure 10-17. IP is framed in an Ethernet frame. The Ethernet frame is then placed on the network media.

and passes the remaining protocol frame formats to the OSI model at the destination. If the destination is on the same LAN as the source, then the remaining formats are removed until the data reaches the application layer.

If the destination is at a distant location that requires navigation across the Internet or a WAN link, a network device such as a router removes the Ethernet frame. The IP address is used to deliver the entire contents to the distant location. At the distant location, the remaining protocol formats are removed until the raw data is revealed.

This is a simplified explanation of the role of the various protocol frame formats. You will rely on these basic concepts to understand how bridges, switches, routers, and gateways operate. Other protocols classified as application protocols, such as FTP, TFTP, Telnet, and SNMP, fit inside a TCP or UDP frame.

To learn more about various protocol formats associated with TCP/IP visit www.protocols.com. This Web site has an extensive listing and a complete explanation of each field within the frame format. There are also hot links, acronyms, and technical papers available, which will assist you in furthering your network expertise.

Assigning IP Addresses

There are several methods for assigning IP addresses. The assignment of IP addresses falls into two broad categories: static and dynamic. A ***static IP assignment*** means that an IP address is entered manually for each host on the network. This is typically done when the network interface card is configured. A ***dynamic IP assignment*** means that the IP address is issued automatically, typically when the computer boots and joins the network.

static IP assignment an IP address that is entered manually for each host on the network.

dynamic IP assignment an IP address that is issued automatically, typically when the computer boots and joins the network.

Windows Internet Naming Service (WINS)

Windows Internet Naming Service (WINS) is used to resolve computer NetBIOS names to IP addresses. WINS is unique to Microsoft networks. WINS maintains a dynamic database of computer names and IP addresses. The computer names and IP addresses are automatically updated as computers log on and off the network, **Figure 10-18.**

Starting with Windows 2000, the WINS service is no longer required. In Windows 2000 and later, a new service called Dynamic DNS incorporates the features of WINS with DNS.

Network+ Note

WINS and DNS are often confused. For the Network+ Certification exam, be sure you can distinguish between DNS and WINS.

Dynamic Host Configuration Protocol (DHCP)

static addressing assigning an IP address manually.

Dynamic Host Configuration Protocol (DHCP) a service that assigns IP addresses automatically to the hosts on a network.

dynamic addressing automatically assigning IP addresses.

Originally, computers on a network had to have their IP addresses assigned manually. This method was called ***static addressing.*** Static addressing was a time-consuming operation if a large number of PCs were on a network. A log of computer names, locations, MAC addresses, and the assigned IP addresses had to be recorded manually. An administrator or network technician had to be careful not to use the same IP address on another computer. This is because each IP address has to be unique. Using the same IP address for two different computers causes communication conflicts, resulting in erratic behavior.

Dynamic Host Configuration Protocol (DHCP) is designed to replace the manual setup of IP addresses on a network. When a server runs DHCP, the IP addresses are assigned automatically. The act of automatically assigning IP addresses is known as ***dynamic addressing.***

The DHCP server has a pool, or list, of IP addresses to draw from, **Figure 10-19.** Each computer that logs on to the network is assigned an address from the pool. The IP address assignment is temporary. The address is released after a period of time and may be reissued to another computer.

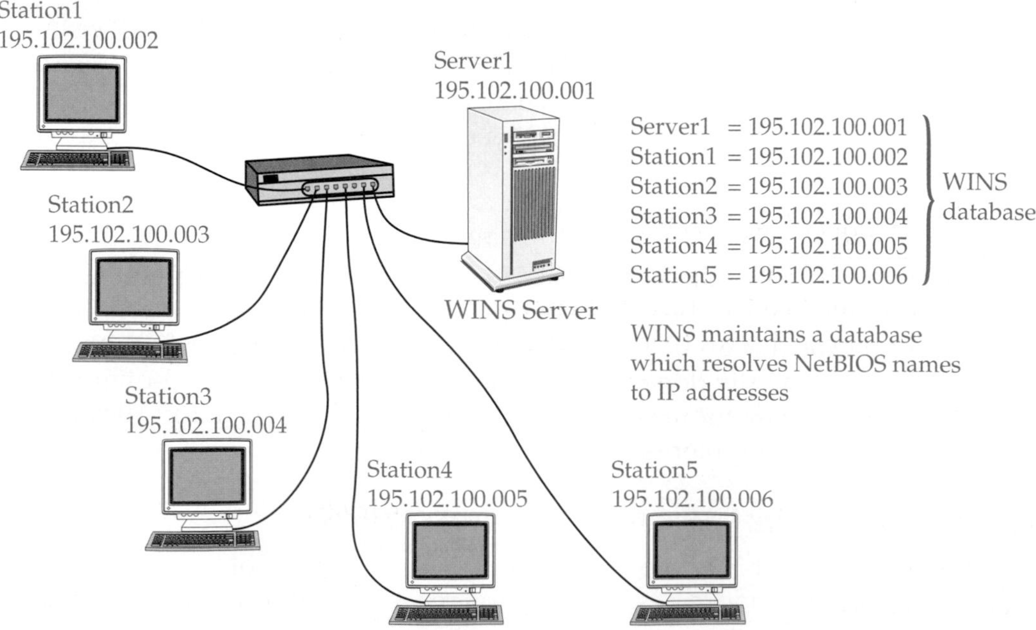

Figure 10-18. The Windows Internet Naming Service (WINS) resolves NetBIOS computer names to IP addresses.

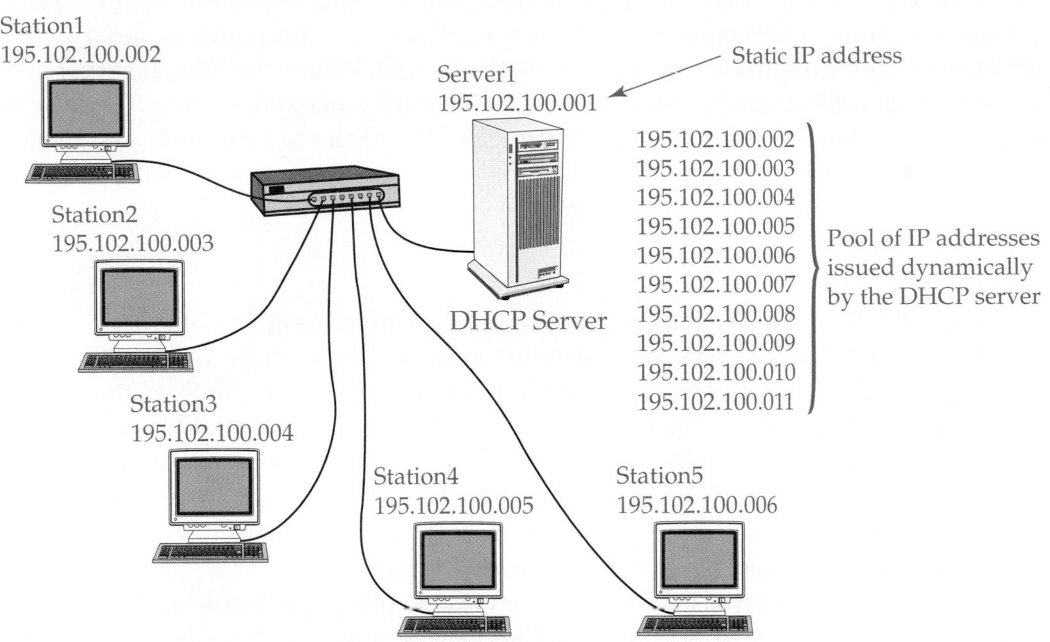

Figure 10-19. The Dynamic Host Configuration Protocol (DHCP) on a DHCP server automatically assigns a temporary IP address to a host. The IP address is randomly selected from a pool of addresses. The temporary IP address is returned to the pool when the lease expires. Certain types of equipment, such as servers, must maintain the same address all of the time. They are assigned an IP address manually. When an IP address is manually assigned, it is said to be a static IP address.

This is how a client is assigned an IP address from a DHCP server. First, when *Station3* is booted, it automatically requests an IP address assignment from the DHCP server. *Station3* does not know where the DHCP server is, so it sends out the request for an IP address as a broadcast to all nodes on the network segment. The protocol used for the request is UDP, which is especially designed for broadcast communication.

Second, the DHCP server receives the request and returns an unassigned IP address from its pool of IP addresses. This is also done in the form of a broadcast. The server returns the information as a UDP broadcast so that any other device connected to the same network as *Station3* will have the IP address information.

Third, *Station3* accepts the assigned IP address and acknowledges this with a UDP broadcast to all nodes on the network. This allows any other device, like a backup DHCP server, to update its database of IP address assignments.

Fourth, the DHCP server acknowledges that *Station3* has accepted the assigned IP address. This completes the four-step process.

The temporary assignment of the IP address to *Station3* requires four broadcast packets. This is not a lot of network traffic compared to several hundred or even thousands of computers logging on to the network at the beginning of the workday. Each computer generates four broadcasts to acquire an IP address from a DHCP server. In addition, each computer generates traffic when downloading e-mail. The traffic on a network in this scenario is heavy, and the number of collisions can greatly increase.

During the IP address negotiation between the DHCP server and *Station3*, other information is transmitted, such as the lease period for the assigned IP address, the subnet mask, and the location of the default gateway. The IP address assignment can be easily confirmed by using **ipconfig**.

It is important to note that when you are setting up a network using a DHCP server, you must assign static IP addresses to all servers and printers and any other equipment required to have a static IP address. When the DHCP server assigns an IP address to a host, it does not necessarily assign the same IP address to the same piece of equipment each time. The IP address is randomly assigned. For computers to be able to consistently find devices such as servers and printers, the devices must have static IP addresses assigned to them.

DHCP Lease

The DHCP server sets a lease period for IP address assignments. The default lease period is 8 days, but the network administrator can modify the lease period. The length of the lease period depends on factors such as the type of network, number of users, typical user profiles, and available number of IP addresses assigned to the network. A large corporate network would need a longer lease period. It is up to the professional judgment of the network administrator to determine the lease period. If the network belongs to an ISP, the ISP administrator would issue a shorter lease period.

If the lease period spans 30 days, for example, the client would not need to request an IP address from the DHCP server the next time they log on as long they log on during the 30-day time period. If the lease period expires, the computer must request a new temporary IP address from the DHCP server.

However, when a lease has expired, it is important that a user properly log off or shut down their computer when ending a session. The IP address is only released when a user logs off or properly shuts down the computer. If a person simply shuts down the computer using the power switch, the computer cannot properly release the IP address. The IP address will still be in use and will not be available to other clients.

Automatic Private IP Addressing (APIPA)

A special set of IP addresses have been set aside by IANA to use when a DHCP server cannot be reached. The range is 169.254.0.0 through 169.254.255.255. If a network interface card fails to connect to a DHCP server and if the card has not been set up with a static IP address, the workstation automatically generates an IP address in the range from 169.254.0.1 to 169.254.255.254. It uses this IP address to communicate with other workstations on the same segment. Once the DHCP server comes back on line and can resume issuing IP addresses from its pool of IP addresses, the workstation releases the 169.254.xxx.xxx IP address and takes one from the DHCP server.

Automatic Private IP Addressing (APIPA)
a feature that assigns an IP address from a special set of IP addresses that have been set aside by IANA when a DHCP server cannot be reached.

This type of addressing is called ***Automatic Private IP Addressing (APIPA)*** and is compatible with all Microsoft products starting with Windows 98. This process was not necessary in prior versions of Windows because the NetBEUI protocol was automatically configured when a network interface card was installed. If the TCP/IP protocol failed because the DHCP server did not issue an IP address to the workstation, the workstation used the NetBEUI protocol. The NetBEUI protocol uses the MAC address to communicate with workstations on the local segment. On Windows 98 and later workstations, NetBEUI is not installed by default. When the DHCP server fails, there is no way for the computers to communicate on the local segment.

APIPA is configured in the **Internet Protocol (TCP/IP) Properties** dialog box, **Figure 10-20.** At the top of the dialog box is the **Automatic private IP address**

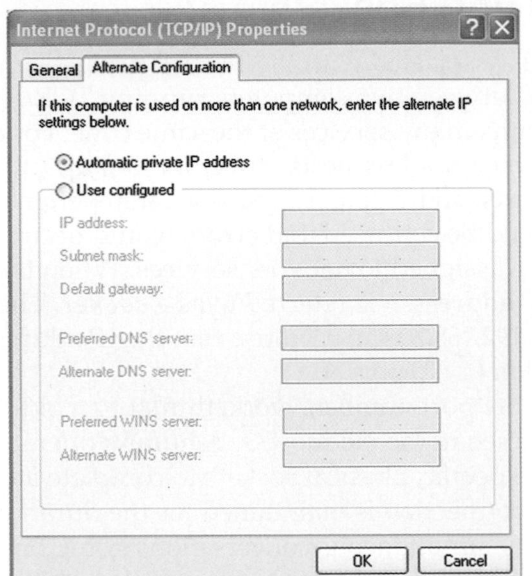

Figure 10-20.
The **Internet Protocol (TCP/IP) Properties** dialog box allows a workstation to be assigned alternate TCP/IP settings.

option. Notice that the other option, **User configured**, allows the workstation to be installed on more than one network by assigning an alternate set of IP settings and preferred DNS and WINS server settings. The **User configured** option is an excellent feature for laptop computers that may be moved to more than one location.

Bootstrap Protocol (BOOTP)

The ***Bootstrap Protocol (BOOTP)*** is a legacy protocol developed in the mid-1980s before DHCP protocol and service. BOOTP uses a centralized database of the MAC addresses and IP assignments of all devices on the network. The network administrator is required to enter every MAC address and IP address into the database. When a computer or other network device is booted, it automatically queries the BOOTP server and requests an IP assignment.

BOOTP is ideal for workstations or other network devices that do not have a hard disk drive. A workstation that does not have hard disk drives installed is referred to as a ***diskless station.*** The term *diskless station* is also used to refer to workstations that do not contain floppy disk drives. Both BOOTP and DHCP use the same port numbers, 67 and 68. IANA identifies port 67 as "bootps" for the server and port 68 as "bootpc" for the client.

Bootstrap Protocol (BOOTP)
a service that uses a centralized database of the MAC addresses and IP assignments of all devices on the network and assigns the appropriate IP address to a host when it boots.

diskless station
a workstation that does not have hard disk drives installed. It can also mean a workstation that does not contain a floppy disk drive.

Duplicate IPv4 Addresses

A static IP address is configured manually rather than using a DHCP server to automatically issue an IPv4 address to a workstation. You cannot manually configure a duplicate IPv4 address. Windows Vista and Windows XP will generate a warning message and will not allow you to complete the task of configuring a duplicate IPv4 address. Windows 7 will not generate a warning but will automatically assign an APIPA.

A duplicate IPv4 address is not a concern when IPv6 is configured by default because all exchanges of packets are performed in isolated local area network (link-local) by using IPv6 addresses.

TCP/IP Ports and Sockets

port number
a number associated with the TCP/IP protocol and used to create a virtual connection between two computers running TCP/IP.

socket
a port number combined with an IP address.

A ***port number*** is associated with the TCP/IP protocol and is used to create a virtual connection between two computers running TCP/IP. A computer, especially a server, runs many services at the same time. For example, a server could coordinate many e-mail requests, directory lookups, file transfers, Internet search requests, and Web page requests. If it were not for port numbers, communications would be confused and errors would occur.

Port numbers are assigned to network services. When the port number is combined with an IP address, it is referred to as a ***socket.*** The following is an example of a socket: 192.168.20.45:80. Notice that the IP address 192.168.20.45 is connected with a colon (:) to port 80.

To understand how port numbers work, think of an old-time telephone switchboard that you see in the old movies. A human operator plugs a connection cord into specific, physical sockets to complete a connection between two telephones. The connection is maintained for the duration of the call. The switchboard has many simultaneous conversations going on at the same time. Like the old-time telephone switchboard, socket technology allows multiple, simultaneous services to run between a server and a workstation.

Look at **Figure 10-21.** You can see how the server uses port numbers combined with an IP address to sort the various communications taking place. Note that two sockets are created between the workstation and the server for file transfer and another socket is created for Web page browsing. Port number assignments are not limited to client/server communications. They are used to communicate between any two devices on a network.

Figure 10-22 lists some typical port number assignments. Looking at the chart you can see some familiar port assignments such as port 80, which is associated with a Web server; port 20, which is assigned to data transfers using FTP; and port 21, which is used for FTP control commands. For a complete list of assigned ports, visit www.iana.org/assignments/port-numbers.

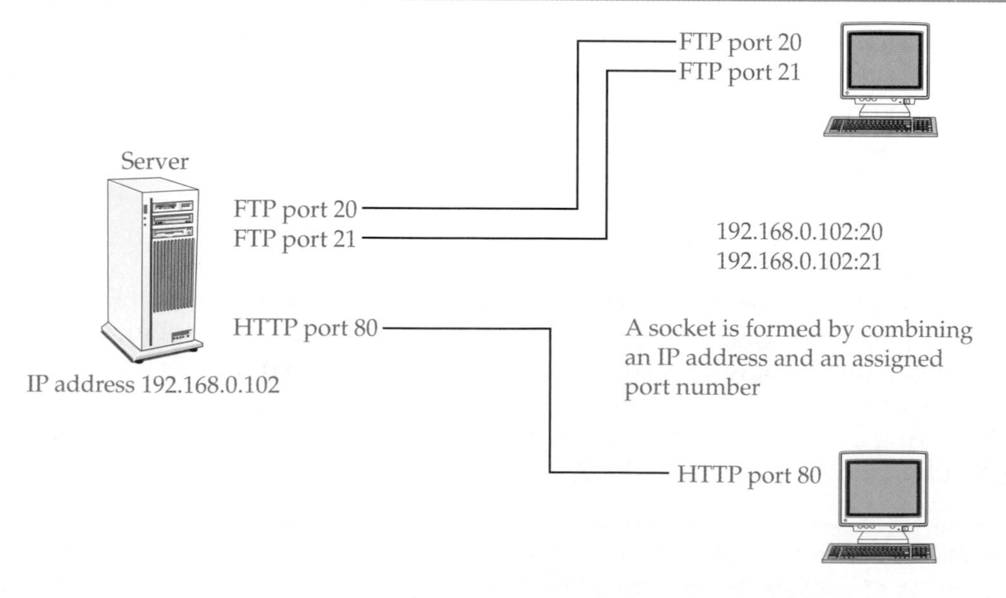

Figure 10-21. Communication can be sorted by the creation of a virtual circuit between a server and a workstation or between a workstation and a workstation. The virtual circuit is a combination of an IP address and a port number. This combination is called a *socket*. The socket creates and maintains a logical communications channel between two points on a network.

Port #	Service	Description
7	ECHO	Echo a reply
20	FTP	File Transfer Protocol data
21	FTP	File Transfer Protocol control commands
22	SSH	Secure Shell
23	TELNET	Terminal emulation connection
25	SMTP	Simple Mail Transfer Protocol
43	NICNAME	Who Is
49	LOGIN	Login Host Protocol
53	DNS	Domain Name Server
69	TFTP	Trivia File Transfer Protocol
80	HTTP	Hypertext Transfer Protocol
110	POP	Post Office Protocol
119	NNTP	Network News Transfer Protocol
123	NTP	Network Time Protocol
137	NETBIOS	NetBIOS name service
143	IMAP4	Internet Message Access Protocol version 4
161	SNMP	Simple Network Management Protocol
389	LDAP	Lightweight Directory Access Protocol
443	HTTPS	HTTP Security
500	IPSEC	IP Security
1723	PPTP	Point-to-Point Tunneling Protocol
5631	pcAnywhere data	pcAnywhere data
5632	pcAnywhere status	pcAnywhere status
3389	Windows Remote Desktop	Remote access to desktops

Figure 10-22. Typical port assignments.

The port number is derived from a sixteen-bit binary field, which means there are over 65,000 different possible port numbers available for use. Ports 0 through 1023 are assigned by IANA and are called *well-known port numbers* because they have typical assignments. The port numbers higher than 1023 are referred to as *upper-level port numbers*. They do not have typical assignments. Private companies commonly use the numbers from 1023 through 49151 to support their software utilities. The remaining numbers, 49152 through 65535, can be used by anyone.

Network+ Note

To be prepared for the Network+ Certification exam, memorize the common port numbers associated with TCP/IP and their function. The most common port numbers encountered on the exam are 20, 21, 23, 80, and 110.

Introducing the IPv6 Standard

The newest Internet addressing scheme is called ***IPv6***. It is referred to as a "classless IP addressing scheme" because there is no need for a subnet mask based on network class. Windows Vista, Windows 7, and Microsoft Server 2008 automatically configure an IPv6 address in addition to an IPv4 address. While

IPv6
an Internet addressing scheme that uses 128 bits to represent an IP address. The 128 bits are divided into 8 units of 16 bits. These units can be represented as a 4-digit hexadecimal number separated by colons.

IPv6 is still not fully implemented, it is now incorporated into all modern operating systems and is here to stay.

The original reason for developing a new IP address system was the rapid development of the Internet and the almost immediate shortage of available IP addresses. Today, almost all electronic communications equipment use the Internet and some form of an Internet address. The development of the IPv6 standard has lead to other network addressing improvements. We will now look at some of the advantages of using IPv6.

Advantages of IPv6

The IPv4 standard is still primarily the same as it was when it was finalized in 1980. IPv6 provides many advantages and improvements when compared with the limitations of IPv4 such as a larger pool of Internet and network addresses, reduced broadcast traffic, better security, and improved quality of service.

Note

The IPv6 standard is still evolving and not fully implemented at this time. While all information is accurate at the time of this writing, IPv6 standards may be modified in the future. You should check reliable references for the latest changes concerning IPv6.

Number of Possible IPv6 Addresses

The main reason IPv6 was developed was to increase the number of available Internet addresses. The IPv4 address is equal to 32-bits or approximately 4,000,000,000 billion possible addresses. IPv6 uses 128-bit addresses, which provides over 340,000,000,000,000,000,000,000,000,000,000,000,000 possible addresses. As you can see, the possible number of unique addresses seems inexhaustible.

Reduced Broadcast Traffic

IPv4 uses Address Resolution Protocol (ARP) to resolve IPv4 addresses to Media Access Control (MAC) addresses. IPv6 uses the Neighbor Discovery (ND) protocol, which is carried inside a series of Internet Control Message Protocol (ICMP) packets on the local area network. Basically, ND will eventually replace ARP broadcasts, which will significantly reduce network traffic on the local area network. At this time, the implementation of both IPv6 and IPv4 by default does not result in total reduced local area network traffic.

The ARP protocol produces bursts of three UDP packets every few minutes containing the ARP request. This is followed by UDP packets returning from the destinations. Each destination typically produces a series of three UDP packets. UDP packets do not guarantee delivery. They are connectionless, thus they can create more traffic than IPv6. The IPv6 address contains the MAC address identifier of the network device, so it does not require ARP to resolve the MAC to IPv4 assigned address.

Improved Security

IPv6 incorporates IPSec to provide better security than IPv4. IPSec is not a single protocol but rather a collection of protocols used to encrypt and authenticate each packet that uses an IP address over the Internet. The reason IPv6 has improved security is the use of IPSec is mandatory for IPv6 and optional for IPv4. There will be much more about IPSec in Chapter 15—Network Security.

Better Quality of Service

Quality of service refers to a protocol's ability to deliver certain packets in a timely fashion. For example, a long text document can have delays between packets that do not affect the content of the document. However, packets containing video or audio, such as a telephone conversation, must not have delays between the packets. A long delay between packets can cause a choppy conversation with parts of speech missing. IPv4 does have a quality of service feature, but when using security such as IPSec, packet delivery is slowed. The IPv6 standard significantly improves quality of service and does not let IPSec security cause long delays between packets.

IPv6 uses fewer packets to achieve the same results as IPv4. IPv4 uses Type of Services (TOS) field in the header in conjunction with UDP and TCP packet port numbers to deliver time-sensitive data. IPv6 contains header information that allows routers to immediately identify the packet priority and allow the router to act on the packet without the need for more information. The IPv6 packet allows the router to maintain direct flow of packets with an assigned priority. In short, the IPv6 format allows the router to process a priority packet faster than the IPv4 format, thus improving quality of service.

Support for Neighbor Discovery

Neighbor Discovery is an IPv6 data link layer mechanism used to identify network devices automatically, without the need of user intervention. IPv6 encapsulates ICMPv6 packets to exchange information with other devices connected in the same section (subnet) of a local area network. ICMPv6 supports two new message types that are not offered in ICMPv4. The two new message types that support discovery are Neighbor Solicitation and Neighbor Advertisement.

Neighbor Discovery an IPv6 data link layer mechanism used to identify network devices automatically, without the need of user intervention.

Proprietary discovery protocols are based on the Neighbor Discovery protocol standard. For example, Cisco Discovery Protocol (CDP) and Microsoft Link Layer Topology Discovery Mapper/Responder are both examples of the Neighbor Discovery mechanism.

Internet Control Message Protocol Version 6 (ICMPv6) is designed to exchange messages between neighboring nodes on the same link. This is the basis of the Network Discovery protocol, which allows a computer to identify other devices connected in the local link. Network Discovery also allows for automatic configuration of network devices and the discovery of router devices attached to the local area network.

IPv6 Address Format

Modern computer equipment and software readily accepts IPv6 addresses and uses them to communicate across a network. The IPv6 standard uses a total address length of 128 bits. The 128 bits are divided into 8 units of 16 bits. These units can be represented as a 4-digit hexadecimal number separated by colons. See **Figure 10-23.** The IPv6 address is assigned to network interface cards and equipment in a similar fashion as IPv4 addresses.

IPv6 EUI-64 Identifier

The original IEEE 802 MAC address consists of a 24-bit manufacturer's ID and a 24-bit unique ID associated with each network interface card. The IPv6 standard uses a 24-bit manufacturer's ID and a 40-bit unique ID to identify each network interface card. See **Figure 10-24.** Together they make up the last 64 bits of an IPv6 address known as the *EUI-64 identifier*. The ***EUI-64 identifier*** serves the same function as the IPv4 MAC address. Since the original MAC address is 48-bits and the EUI-64 identifier is 64-bits, the original MAC address is modified to fit inside the 64-bit frame. The hexadecimal values "FF" and "FE" are inserted in the middle

EUI-64 identifier an IPv6 address that serves the same function as the IPv4 MAC address.

Figure 10-23.
The IPv6 addressing scheme.

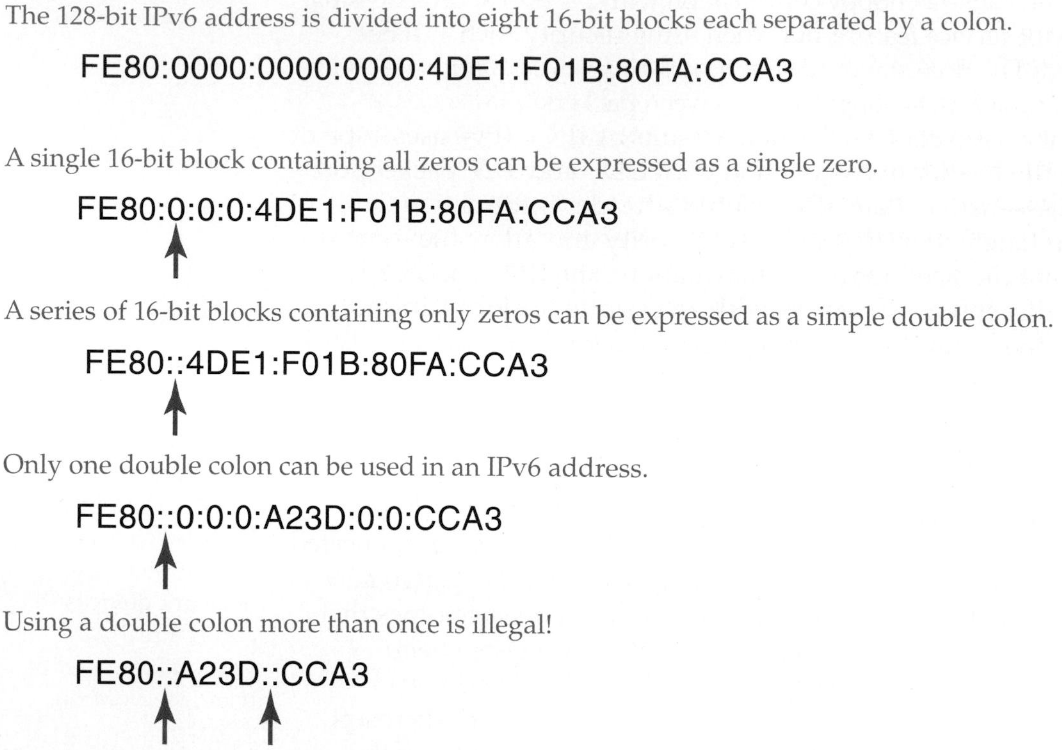

The 128-bit IPv6 address is divided into eight 16-bit blocks each separated by a colon.

FE80:0000:0000:0000:4DE1:F01B:80FA:CCA3

A single 16-bit block containing all zeros can be expressed as a single zero.

FE80:0:0:0:4DE1:F01B:80FA:CCA3

A series of 16-bit blocks containing only zeros can be expressed as a simple double colon.

FE80::4DE1:F01B:80FA:CCA3

Only one double colon can be used in an IPv6 address.

FE80::0:0:0:A23D:0:0:CCA3

Using a double colon more than once is illegal!

FE80::A23D::CCA3

Figure 10-24.
IPv4 MAC address compared with an IPv6 EUI-64 identifier.

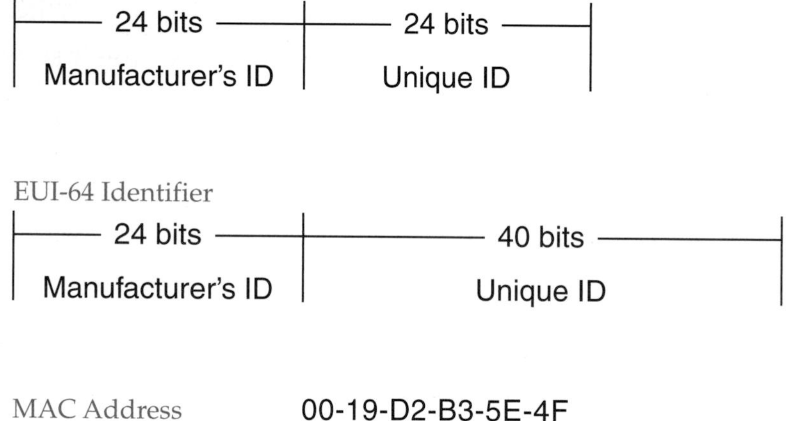

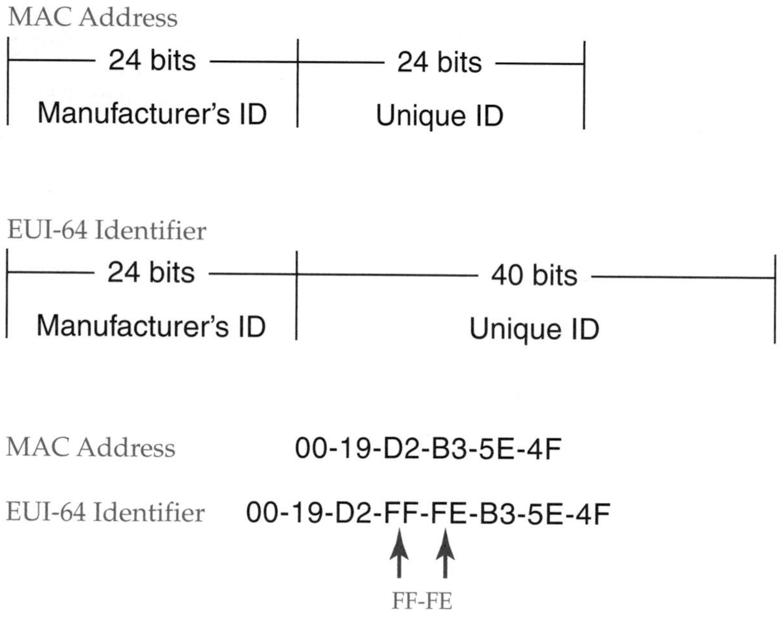

MAC Address 00-19-D2-B3-5E-4F

EUI-64 Identifier 00-19-D2-FF-FE-B3-5E-4F

FF-FE

of the original 48-bit MAC address which results in a 64-bit EUI-64 identifier. For example, an original MAC address of 00-19-D2-B3-5E-4F would be expressed as 00-19-D2-FF-FE-B3-5E-4F after being converted to a EUI-64 identifier.

EUI-64 identifiers are standard in Windows XP SP1 and Windows Server 2003. However, in Windows Vista, Windows 7, and Windows Server 2008, the EUI-64 no longer uses the original MAC address of the adapter. The EUI-64 is randomly generated. This change was made because incorporating the MAC address into the EUI-64 is a security risk. Transmitting an IPv6 address with a MAC address across the Internet could result in the computer or network device being identified. For example, a network sniffer that is used to probe packets exchanged over a network could record all IPv6 addresses along with the MAC addresses. Over time, the addresses could be associated with specific persons that use the specified computers and with the days these persons leave early from work or are absent. A hacker could then access the employee's computer when the employee has left work.

Look at **Figure 10-25,** which compares the results of the **ipconfig /all** command issued at a Windows 7 and Windows XP computer. Notice how the MAC address is incorporated into the IPv6 address in the Windows XP screen capture. However, in the Windows 7 screen capture notice that the EUI-64 identifier is different than the MAC address.

IPv6 Topography Terminology

IPv6 introduced new terminology to redefine the network topography. The new terms are used to classify portions of an organization's network. When using IPv4 addressing, an organization can subdivide the network into subsections using subnet masks or subnets. IPv6 does not use a subnet mask but rather incorporates a similar function into the complete IPv6 address. IPv6 classifies the scope or range of an IPv6 address by its prefix, such as FE80 and FEC0.

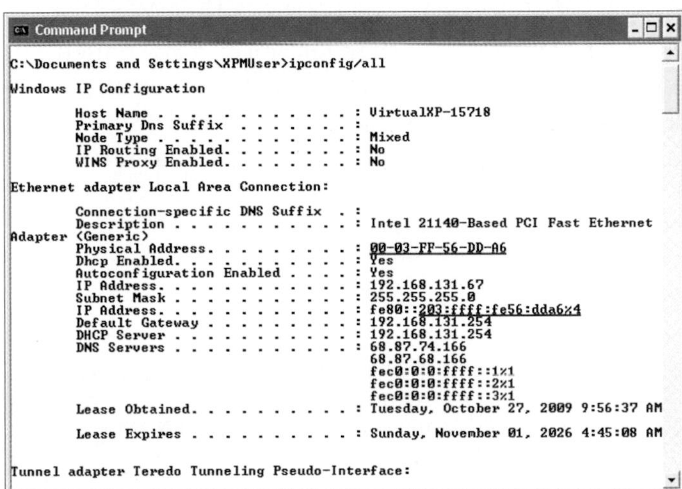

Windows XP

```
C:\Windows\system32\cmd.exe
C:\Users\Richard>ipconfig/all

Windows IP Configuration

   Host Name . . . . . . . . . . . . : Richar7
   Primary Dns Suffix  . . . . . . . :
   Node Type . . . . . . . . . . . . : Hybrid
   IP Routing Enabled. . . . . . . . : No
   WINS Proxy Enabled. . . . . . . . : No
   DNS Suffix Search List. . . . . . : hsd1.fl.comcast.net.

Ethernet adapter Local Area Connection:

   Connection-specific DNS Suffix  . : hsd1.fl.comcast.net.
   Description . . . . . . . . . . . : Intel(R) 82566DC-2 Gigabit Network Connec
tion
   Physical Address. . . . . . . . . : 00-1F-E2-57-DD-A6
   DHCP Enabled. . . . . . . . . . . : Yes
   Autoconfiguration Enabled . . . . : Yes
   Link-local IPv6 Address . . . . . : fe80::55c7:254c:4bf7:712b%11(Preferred)
   IPv4 Address. . . . . . . . . . . : 192.168.1.100(Preferred)
   Subnet Mask . . . . . . . . . . . : 255.255.255.0
   Lease Obtained. . . . . . . . . . : Wednesday, October 28, 2009 10:00:45 AM
   Lease Expires . . . . . . . . . . : Thursday, October 29, 2009 10:00:44 AM
   Default Gateway . . . . . . . . . : 192.168.1.1
   DHCP Server . . . . . . . . . . . : 192.168.1.1
   DHCPv6 IAID . . . . . . . . . . . : 234889186
```

Windows 7

Figure 10-25.
EUI-64 identifier in Windows XP and Windows Vista.

Three terms used to describe the scope of the network are *global*, *link-local*, and *unique-local*. See **Figure 10-26.** IPv6 addresses can divide the entire network of an organization into separate parts in much the same way as a separate subnet mask does for IPv4 addressing. This limits communication to portions of the entire network.

The term *site-local* was originally used in the series of RFCs that specified the IPv6 address standard. Later in October of 2005, the term *Unique Local IPv6 Unicast Address* was defined in RFC 4193 and used to clarify and replace the term *site-local*. In September 2004, RFC3879 "depreciated" the term *Site Local Address*. Also, the terms are not hyphenated in the RFCs.

global address the Internet address as assigned by the IANA organization used to uniquely identify a location on the IPv6 Internet.

link-local a portion of an organization's network.

unique-local the entire organization's network or a portion of it.

Global address is the public (Internet) address used to identify the local network, and it is administered by IANA. It is equivalent to the IPv4 public (Internet) address and can be routed.

Link-local is a portion of the organization's network. For example, the entire network might be the whole network within the XYZ Corporation. Within the XYZ Corporation are three smaller units such as payroll, sales, and management. Each of these three subunits is referred to as *link-local* or portions of the XYZ Corporation network. Routers will not forward packets that have a link-local address.

Unique-local is the entire organization's network or a portion of it. A router can forward packets to any portion of the organization's network but not outside the organization's network.

Network+ Note

The IEEE uses the term *interface* when describing the assignment of an IPv6 address to a device rather than the term *node*, which is commonly used to identify connections on a network. The main difference between these terms is a node can only have one IP address assigned to it. In contrast, an interface can have more than one IPv6 address assigned to it. This might seem like a trivial difference, but look for the term as it will most likely appear on the CompTIA Network+ exam.

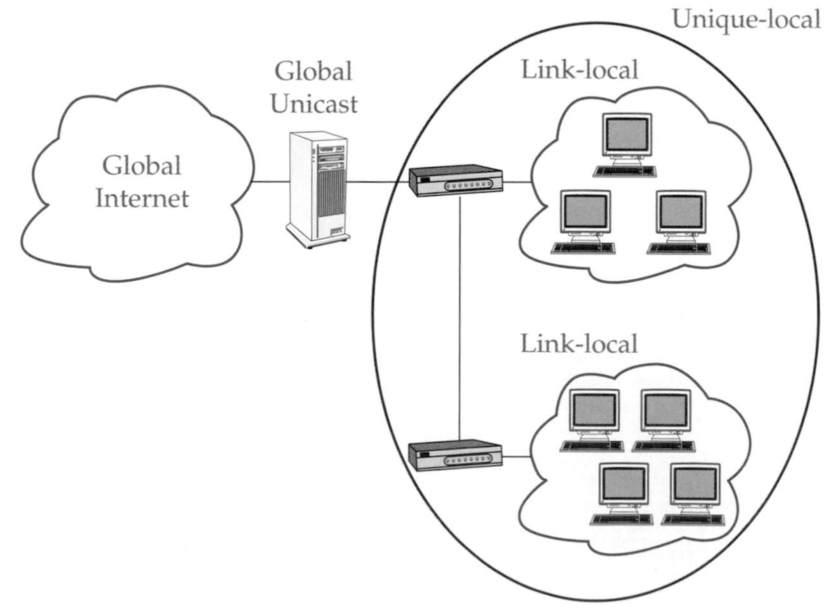

Figure 10-26. IPv6 network classifications. The global IPv6 address is routable and serves as the Internet address. It is used to communicate outside the confines of the corporation network. The link-local IPv6 address identifies a portion of the corporation's network and is not routable. The unique-local IPv6 address spans portions of a corporation's network or the entire network.

Types of IPv6 Addresses

There are three broad classifications of IPv6 addresses: unicast, multicast, and anycast. A ***unicast address*** delivers packets to a single network address. A ***multicast address*** delivers packets to multiple addresses and is also referred to as *many-to-one*. An ***anycast address*** delivers packets to the nearest interface and is used mainly for supporting router functions.

unicast address an IPv6 address that delivers packets to a single network address.

multicast address an IPv6 address that delivers packets to multiple addresses. It is also referred to as *many-to-one*.

anycast address an IPv6 address that delivers packets to the nearest interface and is used mainly for supporting router functions.

Unicast Addresses

A unicast address is organized by the scope of the address such as global unicast, link-local, site-local, unique-local, and special. Global is used for the IPv6 portion of the Internet and is similar in function as an IPv4 public (registered) address. Link-local is used on a local area network when there is no router or gateway available. Site-local serves the same function as local area network. The site-local can encompass part of the local area network or the entire local area network to include remote locations. Each of these unicast address types will now be discussed in detail. Other special unicast addresses covered in this section are loopback address, unspecified address, and zone IDs.

Global Unicast Address

A global unicast IPv6 address is similar to an IPv4 public (registered) address. The global unicast address is unique and used for Internet addresses. A global unicast address can broadcast to all IPv6 addresses in the IPv6 portion of the local area network as well as to other global IPv6 addresses across the IPv6 portion of the Internet. The scope of the IPv6 global unicast address is the entire Internet as well as the local area network. The global unicast address starts with 2000: or written as 2000:/3. The first three bits are set to 001, **Figure 10-27.** This is how a global address is identified and distinguished from other IPv6 addresses. The subnet ID is used to identify subnets or sections of an organization's network. The interface ID is used to identify a specific interface or device on the subnet.

Link-Local Unicast IPv6 Address

A link-local IPv6 address is used to communicate on the local area network and will not be forwarded by a router. The link-local address serves the same function as an IPv4 APIPA address (169.254.xxx.xxx). The IPv6 link-local address always starts with FE80 or FE80::/64. A link-local IPv6 is never forwarded beyond the local-link by an IPv6-capable router.

Link-local IPv6 addresses are automatically assigned by the operating system. Link-local IPv6 addresses are required for the Network Discovery feature. Without a link-local IPv6 address, Network Discovery will not function. This is why Microsoft operating systems configure a link-local address automatically for network devices.

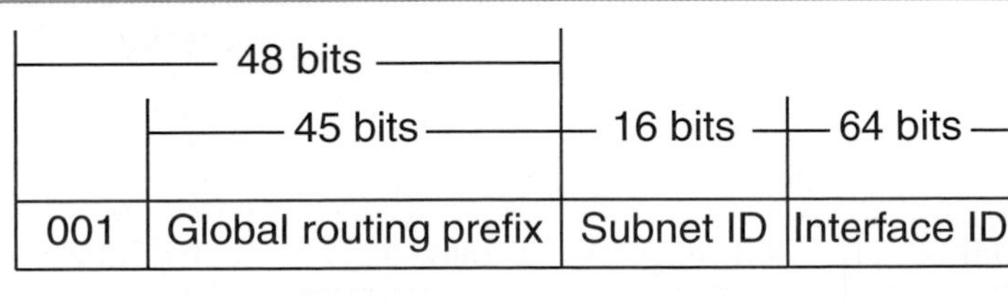

Figure 10-27.
Global unicast address format.

Look at **Figure 10-28** and compare the link-local, site-local, and unique-local address format. You will notice immediately that the link-local address does not have a subnet ID. This part of the IPv6 is usually filled with zeros or simply ::. The link-local address can be easily identified because it always starts with the prefix FE80.

The global, site-local, and unique-local addresses use a subnet ID, which makes it different from a link-local address. The subnet ID serves same function as a subnet mask.

Unique-Local Unicast IPv6 Address

The unique-local unicast IPv6 address is a replacement for site-local address. Site-local is still valid but is now considered "depreciated." The term *depreciated* means that it is no longer being developed and will be replaced by unique-local address.

The unique-local address serves the same function as the site-local address. The unique-local address can represent the entire local area network or just a portion. The unique-local address can also represent multiple locations such as New York and Chicago as long as the two locations are members of the same network. Look at Figure 10-28 and compare the site-local address to the unique-local address. Notice that a global ID and a subnet ID is assigned to the address. The unique-local address is easily identified by the prefix FC00.

Note

You will see the unique-local address expressed as FC00::/7 or FC00::/8. The correct version is FC00::/7. What has happened is there is a single bit that follows the first 7 bits of the unique-local address. This single bit is always set to binary 1, which results in the address being expressed as FC00::/8.

Figure 10-28. Global unicast, link-local, site-local, and unique-local IPv6 address comparison.

Global Unicast

48 bits	16 bits	64 bits
001 Global routing prefix	Subnet ID	Interface ID

Local-link FE80::/64

10 bits	54 bits	64 bits
1111 1110 10		Interface ID

Site-local FEC0::/10

10 bits	54 bits	64 bits
1111 1110 11	Subnet ID	Interface ID

Unique-local FC00::/7

7 bits		40 bits	16 bits	64 bits
1111		Global ID	Subnet ID	Interface ID

Site-Local Unicast IPv6 Address

The site-local unicast IPv6 address serves the same function as the IPv4 private addresses (10.0.0.0, 172.16.0.0, and 192.168.0.0). Site-local addresses always start with FEC0 or FEC0::/10. Site-local IPv6 addresses are designed to not be routable beyond the local area network but are routable among the local-link sections of the local area network. Site-local IPv6 addresses are used for an organization with a defined geographic area such as a business, school, campus, or local area network or a portion of that organization's local area network. In contrast to link-local addresses, site-local must be assigned manually.

IPv6 Loopback Address

The IPv6 ***loopback address*** is the reserved IP address of the network interface card. It is used to test if an IP address is configured for the network interface card and if the network interface card is functioning normally. The loopback address for IPv4 is 127.0.0.1. The loopback address for IPv6 is 0:0:0:0:0:0:0:1 or ::1. Note that the double colon eliminates fields containing only zeros.

loopback address the reserved IP address of a network interface card. It is used to test if an IP address is configured for the network interface card and if the network interface card is functioning normally.

IPv6 Unspecified Address

The IPv6 unspecified address is 0:0:0:0:0:0:0:0: or simply a double colon :: to represent a string of zeros. It is the equivalent of the IPv4 address 0.0.0.0. The unspecified address is used when an interface is checking for its own duplicate address during the initial connection to the network. Because the identifier is randomly generated, there is a possibility that two devices could have the same identifier. When a device first comes on the network, it identifies itself with an all zero address and checks if its random address has already been assigned to another device. If no other device is using an address that matches the random address, then the randomly generated address will be used.

Local-Use Address Zone IDs

Zone IDs are used for local-use addresses to indicate which zone on a local area network a site-local address is used. The geographical area of the network is a section of the network that spans one or more link-local sections or a lesser part of a site-local section. Local-use IPv6 addresses can be used more than once to identify computers connected on different zones within the same geographic local area network (LAN or WAN). A zone ID is represented at the end of an IPv6 address as a percent sign followed by a number. For example, in **Figure 10-29** the zone ID is %10.

Zone ID is also referred to as a *scope ID*. Numeric values used for the zone ID are selected by the sending network device, not the receiving network device. It is possible for a single computer to be identified by more than one zone ID.

IPv6 Prefixes

An IPv6 prefix is the portion of the address with a fixed value that informs network devices of what action to take. For example, FF00::/8 is a prefix indicating a multicast address.

Prefixes for IP addresses may be expressed using Classless Inter-Domain Routing (CIDR), which indicates what portion of the network IP address represents the subnet or network address. CIDR is covered in much more detail in Chapter 11—Subnetting.

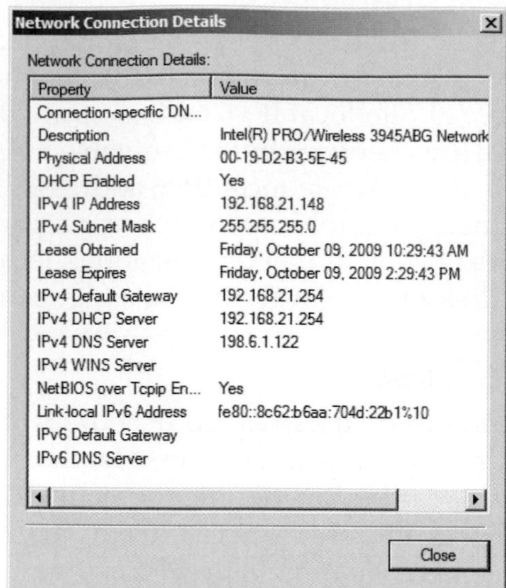

Figure 10-29. **Network Connection Details** dialog box displaying the link-local IPv6 address with the zone ID "%10."

IPv6 has been designed not to use a separate subnet mask, but it does use a prefix which serves the same purpose as the IPv4 subnet mask. The IPv6 prefix is expressed as address/prefix. For example, FE80::/64 means that the first 64 bits represent the network address. You will see IPv6 addresses expressed in both forms: the entire IPv6 address or the CIDR. See **Figure 10-30** for a list of common IPv6 address prefixes.

To see a more complete list of multicast IPv6 address prefixes, visit the IANA Web site: www.iana.org/assignments/ipv6-multicast-addresses. For more information on IANA IPv6 addresess, visit www.iana.org/assignments/ipv6-address-space.

IPv6 Transition Technologies

There are several technologies used to help in the transition from IPv4 to IPv6. Three of these technologies are Teredo, 6to4, and ISATAP. These technologies are intended to be used until IPv6 is fully implemented and IPv4 is fully depreciated.

Figure 10-30. Common IPv6 address prefixes.

Prefix	Address Type
2000::/3	Global unicast
FE80::/10	Link-local unicast
FC08::/10	Site-local unicast
FD08::/8	Unique-local unicast
FF00::/8	Multicast
FF01::1	Interface multicast local all nodes
FF02::1	Link-local multicast all nodes
FF01::2	Interface-local multicast all routers
FF02::2	Link-local multicast all routers
FF05::2	Site-local multicast all routers

6to4

6to4 is a mechanism that provides a means of communicating across the IPv4 Internet while preserving the original IPv6 assigned address of the network device. The **6to4** address technology supports network-to-network communications between routers. 6to4 solves compatibility issues between IPv6 and IPv4 addresses. For example, the IPv4 address 134.175.27.10 displayed as a 6to4 IPv6 address is 2002::86AF:1B0A. Each set of IPv4 decimal numbers are converted to IPv6 hexadecimal pairs, where

6to4 an IPv6 transition mechanism that provides a means of communicating across the IPv4 Internet while preserving the original IPv6 assigned address of the network device.

Decimal 134 = Hex 86

Decimal 175 = Hex AF

Decimal 27 = Hex 1B

Decimal 10 = Hex 0A

The IPv6 unicast 6to4 address always starts with 2002 or is represented by 2002::/16. A global unicast address is followed by a subnet ID and finally an interface ID. For example, Global site prefix:Subnet ID:Interface ID or 2002::WWXX:YYZZ, where WWXX:YYZZ corresponds to the original IPv4 address:

Octet 1 = WW

Octet 2 = XX

Octet 3 = YY

Octet 4 = ZZ

Thus,

2002::86AF:1B0A = 134.175.27.10

6to4 is designed for router-to-router communications. A router must be designed to support 6to4 to be able to forward 6to4 packets.

Intra-Site Automatic Tunneling Address Protocol (ISATAP) a node-to-node and node-to-router technology used for existing IPv4 network devices to eliminate the need to upgrade network devices. It works by tunneling IPv6 addresses inside existing IPv4 packets at the data link layer.

Teredo a network address translator similar to the NAT protocol. It creates a tunnel that allows incoming IPv6 traffic through a firewall designed for IPv4.

ISATAP

Intra-Site Automatic Tunneling Address Protocol (ISATAP) was developed jointly by Microsoft and Cisco Systems. ISATAP is designed to tunnel IPv6 addresses inside IPv4 packets at the data link layer. ISATAP is a node-to-node and node-to-router technology used for IPv4-based network devices to eliminate the need to upgrade these devices.

ISATAP supports Neighbor Discovery, which identifies computers and network devices such as local routers. The main advantage of ISATAP over 6to4 is ISATAP is used to discover routers using the ICMPv6 protocol. ISATAP has been implemented in all versions of Windows since Windows XP and Windows Server 2003.

Teredo

Teredo is configured by default in Windows Vista and Windows 7 and is considered a last-resort technology when ISATAP cannot be used. Teredo functions as a network address translator similar to the NAT protocol. NAT devices are used to convert an IPv4 public address to one or more private addresses. 6to4 requires a 6to4-enabled router at the edge of the network system that connects to the Internet. Teredo does not. Teredo creates a tunnel in similar fashion to 6to4 and allows incoming IPv6 traffic through a firewall designed for IPv4. This is especially important for small office systems and homes that use a router/gateway firewall system.

Teredo was first implemented by Microsoft Windows XP SP2 and later and has been continually refined. You will see a reference to "automatic tunneling pseudo interface" or to "tunneling" when you issue the **ipconfig /all** command on a Windows Vista or later computer.

Broadcast and Multicast Addresses

A broadcast address sends packets to all network addresses while a multicast address sends packets to a specific set of addresses. IPv4 uses broadcast and multicast addresses to distribute packets. IPv6 uses multicast addresses.

Multicast addressing is used for topology discovery, gateway discovery, and group discovery. A computer or network device can announce its presence to other computers and devices on the local-link using a multicast address. For example, an IPv6 address with the prefix of FF02 is used to distribute a packet to all computers on a link-local.

The Link-Layer Multicast Name Resolution (LLMNR) protocol uses both IPv4 and IPv6 for name resolution through multicast. The IPv4 multicast destination address is 224.0.0.252. The IPv6 multicast destination address is ff02::1:3. These two multicast addresses will not be forwarded by a router, thus limiting the broadcast to the local-link. These two multicast destination addresses are used by the LLMNR protocol. The LLMNR protocol is used by Windows Vista, Windows 7, and Windows Server 2008 for name resolution using the multicast addresses and the NetBIOS Name Service (NBNS) protocol.

IPv6 Lifetimes

IPv4 addresses are leased for a definite period of time. IPv6 addresses are configured with two lifetime values: valid lifetime and preferred lifetime. Valid lifetime is typically a week, and a preferred lifetime is a day. A valid lifetime value has been validated by a router. An IPv6 address with a valid lifetime value can send and receive unicast messages. A preferred lifetime value is the period of time that an interface can start new communication sessions.

Windows XP and IPv6

IPv6 is not configured by default in Windows XP. To install IPv6, enter **ipv6 install** at the command prompt. To remove IPv6, enter **ipv6 uninstall** at the command prompt. Windows XP uses the **ping6** and **tracert6** commands to ping and trace the route of an IPv6 address.

Originally, Windows XP incorporated the MAC address directly into the IPv6 address. Now, a randomly-generated number is used in place of the MAC address for the interface portion of the IPv6 address. Microsoft offers advanced support for Windows XP and IPv6. You can download the "Advanced Networking Pack for Windows XP" from the Microsoft Web site for free. It consists of a software package with complete Windows XP support for the latest IPv6 protocols and technologies.

Disabling IPv6

IPv6 is configured by default in Windows Vista, Windows 7, and Windows Server 2008. You can disable IPv6 through the **Network Connection Properties** dialog box. Some administrators may wish to disable IPv6 because they feel that the network will be overloaded by exchanging both IPv4 and IPv6 packets across the network. Most exchanges of packets in the link-local part of the network are duplicate functions of IPv4 and IPv6. However, most networks use network adapters that are rated at 100 MB and higher and can easily handle the increase in network traffic without adversely affecting the network.

Also, Microsoft has designed several features that take advantage of IPv6, and these features will be adversely affected by disabling IPv6. Some of the Windows 7 features that depend on IPv6 are HomeGroup and Direct Access as well as features found in other Windows operating systems such as Remote Assistance, Windows Mail, and Network Discovery. See **Figure 10-31** for a summary of the major differences between IPv4 and IPv6.

To learn more about IPv6, visit the Microsoft Web site http://technet.microsoft.com/en-us/network/bb530961.aspx or conduct a Web search using the key words "TechNet Microsoft IPv6."

TCP/IP Troubleshooting Utilities

There can be many types of problems associated with TCP/IP technology. Fortunately, there are a number of useful utilities that can identify the problem. These utilities are **netstat**, **nbtstat**, **ping**, **tracert**, **arp**, and **nslookup**. This section only introduces these tools. Further experience can be gained by using these tools in the lab and in the field.

Netstat

The **netstat** command displays current TCP/IP and port statistics. It can be used to determine network problems such as excessive broadcasts on the network. It also allows the user to monitor network connections.

IPv4	IPv6
32-bit/4-byte address.	128-bit/16-byte address.
ARP broadcast to discover nodes.	Network Discovery replaces ARP.
Uses regular broadcasts to all nodes on local area network.	Replaces broadcasts with multicast to specific nodes.
Addresses are configured manually or through DHCP.	DHCP or manual configuration is not required. IPv6 is configured automatically by computer.
IPSec optional.	IPSec mandatory.
Uses decimal numbers for address consisting of 0-255.	Uses hexadecimal numbers consisting of 00–FF.
Uses a subnet mask to identify the network and host portions of an IPv4 address.	Uses a prefix that provides a similar function as a subnet mask.
Assigns a single IPv4 address per single network adapter.	Can have more than one IPv6 address assigned to a single network adapter.

Figure 10-31.
Summary comparison of IPv4 and IPv6.

Figure 10-32 shows the results of the **netstat -a** command issued at the command prompt. Notice that the **netstat -a** command has returned a list of services, port addresses, and type of packet sent (TCP or UDP). The **-a** switch is just one of the many switches available to use with the **netstat** command.

Nbtstat

The **nbtstat** command is used to display NetBIOS over TCP statistics. In **Figure 10-33,** you can see a list of NetBIOS names of equipment connected to the local area network and workgroup names.

Remember, NetBIOS does not use IP addresses to identify computers on a network. Windows-based networks use the Server Message Block (SMB) protocol and NetBIOS names to identify computers on a network. For TCP/IP to resolve NetBIOS names, the WINS utility must be running or the lmhosts file must be manually configured.

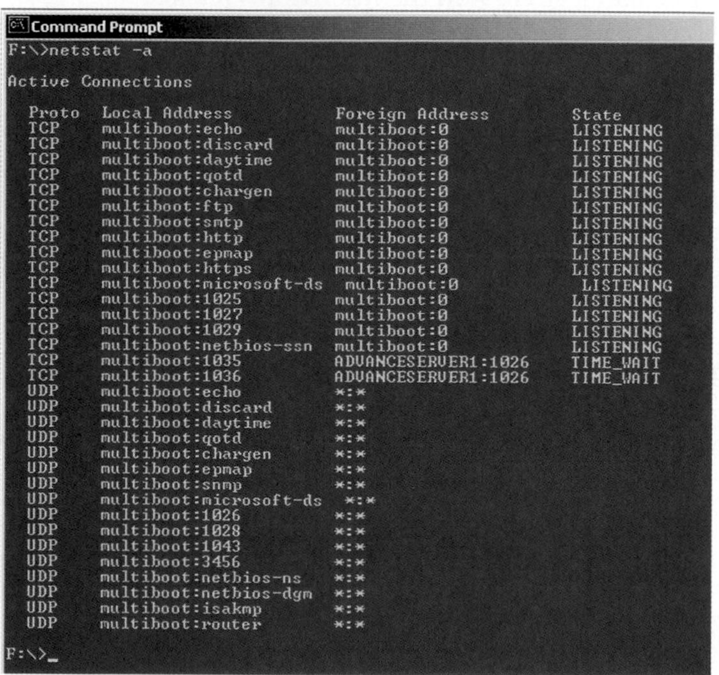

Figure 10-32.
The **netstat -a** command displays a list of services, port addresses, and type of packet sent (TCP or UDP).

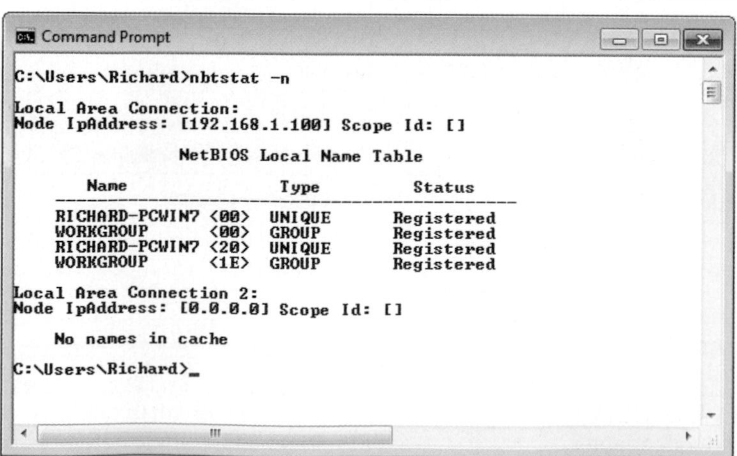

Figure 10-33.
The **nbstat -n** command displays NetBIOS over TCP statistics including computer and workgroup names.

SMB, CIFS, and SMB2 are the Microsoft network protocols designed to support print and file sharing on a Microsoft network.

The **nbtstat** command can be issued from the command prompt with various switches that affect the outcome of the command. Remember, switches for commands issued from the command prompt can be revealed by using the **/?** or **/help** switch after typing the command at the command prompt. Be sure to leave a space between the switch and the end of the command.

Ping

The **ping** command is used to send a packet from one host to another on a network and then echo a return reply. It is commonly used to quickly check the connection state of network media between two hosts on a network. The **ping** command can be used on LANs and WANs. To run the **ping** utility, you simply issue the **ping** command at the command prompt followed by the IP address or the host name with which you wish to test communication.

Figure 10-34 shows two ways to issue the **ping** command. In the top portion of the screen, the command is issued using the destination host name *multiboot* (**ping multiboot**). When a host name is used, the reply displays the destination IP address. In this example, it is 192.168.0.3. In the middle portion of the screen, the **ping** command has been issued using the destination IP address. The same results as in the previous command are displayed. Note that each reply from the destination indicates the number or bytes, lapse time in microseconds, and the Time to Live (TTL) of the packet sent.

The **ping** command uses the Internet Control Message Protocol (ICMP) to carry troubleshooting data across the network. The Internet Control Message Protocol (ICMP) is a part of the TCP/IP suite of protocols and provides the ability to remotely troubleshoot and monitor devices on network systems.

Microsoft designed Windows XP **ping6** as the equivalent of the IPv4 **ping** command. However, Windows Vista and Windows 7 do not recognize the **ping6** command. Instead, **ping -6** is used. The **-6** switch forces the command to use the IPv6 address. Look at **Figure 10-35** of **ping -6** results. When the **ping -6** command is entered followed by the name of a local network computer, the echo response

```
Command Prompt
Pinging multiboot [192.168.0.3] with 32 bytes of data:

Reply from 192.168.0.3: bytes=32 time<10ms TTL=128
Reply from 192.168.0.3: bytes=32 time<10ms TTL=128
Reply from 192.168.0.3: bytes=32 time<10ms TTL=128
Reply from 192.168.0.3: bytes=32 time<10ms TTL=128

Ping statistics for 192.168.0.3:
    Packets: Sent = 4, Received = 4, Lost = 0 (0% loss),
Approximate round trip times in milli-seconds:
    Minimum = 0ms, Maximum =  0ms, Average =  0ms

F:\>ping 192.168.0.3

Pinging 192.168.0.3 with 32 bytes of data:

Reply from 192.168.0.3: bytes=32 time<10ms TTL=128
Reply from 192.168.0.3: bytes=32 time<10ms TTL=128
Reply from 192.168.0.3: bytes=32 time<10ms TTL=128
Reply from 192.168.0.3: bytes=32 time<10ms TTL=128

Ping statistics for 192.168.0.3:
    Packets: Sent = 4, Received = 4, Lost = 0 (0% loss),
Approximate round trip times in milli-seconds:
    Minimum = 0ms, Maximum =  0ms, Average =  0ms

F:\>
```

Figure 10-34.
The **ping** command sends a packet from one host to another on a network and then echoes a return reply.

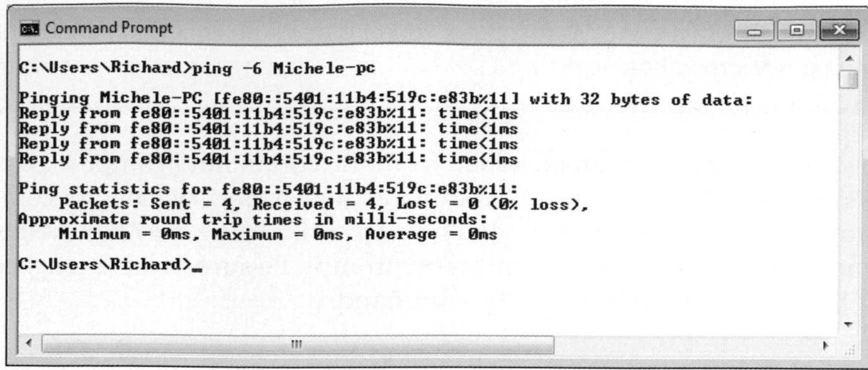

Figure 10-35.
Windows Vista and Windows 7 use the **-6** switch to force the **ping** command to use the IPv6 address.

will display the IPv6 address of the destination computer. Using the **-4** switch with the **ping** command forces the command to use the IPv4 address.

The **ping -6** command is carried inside the ICMPv6 packet.

Tracert or Traceroute

You can think of the trace route utility, **tracert** or **traceroute**, as an advanced **ping** utility. Unix/Linux systems use the **traceroute** command, while Microsoft systems use the **tracert** command. In this section, examples of the trace route utility use the **tracert** command.

The trace route utility sends a packet to a destination host, gathers statistics and information along the way, and displays the information on the monitor of the originator. The final destination point echoes information such as who owns the site's domain name, the IP address, and geographic location. Also displayed is each connection point along the route of the trace with information about its location. Most of the connection points displayed are routers.

The trace route utility also displays the approximate hop lapse times between points along the route. The amount of time delay can help analyze network failure or problems caused by excessive time delays.

Figure 10-36 shows the information revealed when a **tracert** command has been issued from the local host to the www.novell.com Web site. A series of hops, or router connections, are revealed along with the amount of time between each hop. Trace route is a good utility for troubleshooting a path to a distant destination.

Address Resolution Protocol (ARP) a service that resolves IP addresses to MAC addresses.

Reverse Address Resolution Protocol (RARP) a service that finds the MAC address of a host when the IP address is known.

ARP

Address Resolution Protocol (ARP) is used to map the host MAC address to the logical host IP address. For a computer to be able to run ARP, ARP must know the computer's IP address. ARP is a protocol in the TCP/IP suite of protocols. Since it is dependent on TCP/IP, it needs to have an IP address assigned before it can reveal any information. ARP also caches information about contacts on the network.

Reverse Address Resolution Protocol (RARP) is used to find the MAC address of the host when the IP address is known. It serves the opposite function

Figure 10-36.
The trace route utility is used to gather and display statistics and information about the route to a destination host.

```
Tracing route to novell.com [192.233.80.9]
over a maximum of 30 hops:

  1   247 ms   247 ms   261 ms  tc101.strato.net [209.26.168.249]
  2   248 ms   247 ms   261 ms  tc102-254.strato.net [64.45.197.254]
  3   357 ms   412 ms   247 ms  host193.strato.net [207.30.98.193]
  4   261 ms   261 ms   247 ms  host4.utelfla.com [207.30.208.4]
  5   288 ms   275 ms   275 ms  sl-gw25-atl-9-9.sprintlink.net [144.223.29.9]
  6   261 ms   275 ms   275 ms  sl-bb23-atl-6-0.sprintlink.net [144.232.22.9]
  7   275 ms   288 ms   288 ms  sl-bb25-fw-4-3.sprintlink.net [144.232.20.61]
  8   288 ms   289 ms   274 ms  144.232.11.37
  9   289 ms   288 ms   302 ms  sprint-gw.dlstx.ip.att.net [192.205.32.53]
 10   288 ms   288 ms   302 ms  gbr4-p50.dlstx.ip.att.net [12.123.16.246]
 11   316 ms   329 ms   330 ms  gbr4-p50.dvmco.ip.att.net [12.122.2.102]
 12   329 ms   330 ms   329 ms  gbr3-p60.dvmco.ip.att.net [12.122.5.33]
 13   329 ms   330 ms   329 ms  gar1-p360.slkut.ip.att.net [12.122.2.237]
 14   344 ms   329 ms   330 ms  12.127.106.34
 15   316 ms   330 ms   329 ms  192.94.118.221
 16   330 ms   329 ms   330 ms  192.94.118.2
 17   330 ms   329 ms   330 ms  prv1-mx.provo.novell.com [192.233.80.9]

Trace complete.

C:\WINDOWS>
```

of ARP. RARP was originally developed to support the BOOTP protocol. Remember that BOOTP is used to obtain an IP address automatically from the BOOTP server.

In **Figure 10-37**, the **arp -a** command lists IP addresses resolved to MAC addresses. The information displayed comes from the ARP cache on the 192.168.0.3 host. The ARP cache contains the IP and MAC addresses the 192.168.0.3 host has communicated with in the last two minutes. The information presented is displayed in a database format. The **arp** command can be used to verify IP address and MAC address assignments.

Nslookup

The **nslookup** command is a UNIX/Linux utility used to query domain servers when seeking information about domain names and IP addresses. The **nslookup** command maps, or resolves, domain names to IP addresses. This is a convenient tool when looking for information about a particular domain or IP addresses. **Nslookup** is very similar to the **whois** command found at many Web server providers.

```
Command Prompt
Microsoft Windows 2000 [Version 5.00.2195]
(C) Copyright 1985-1999 Microsoft Corp.

F:\>arp -a

Interface: 192.168.0.3 on Interface 0x1000003
  Internet Address      Physical Address      Type
  192.168.0.4           00-20-78-07-06-51     dynamic
  192.168.0.73          00-a0-cc-7c-70-38     dynamic

F:\>
```

Figure 10-37.
The **arp -a** command reveals information found in the ARP cache. The ARP cache stores the IP and MAC addresses the host has communicated with in the last two minutes.

Summary

- An IP address is used to identify a host on a TCP/IP network.
- There are two types of IP addressing schemes: IPv4 and IPv6.
- IPv4 uses four octets separated by periods to uniquely identify each host.
- The decimal number located in the first octet of an IP number can identify its class: Class A network is identified by the 0–127 range, a Class B network by the 128–191 range, and a Class C network by the 192–223 range.
- The IPv4 assignment uses a subnet mask that identifies which portion of the IP address is the network address and which portion is the host address.
- The three reserved, or private, IP addresses are: 10.0.0.0, 172.16.0.0, and 192.168.0.0.
- The Network Address Translation (NAT) protocol provides the technology to allow multiple workstations to share one common Internet connection.
- A Fully Qualified Domain Name (FQDN) consists of a host name and a domain name.
- The Domain Name System (DNS) matches host and domain names to IP addresses.
- DNS is a hierarchical system composed of top-level domains, second-level domains, and subdomains.
- Servers are typically assigned a static IP address.
- A hosts file is used to resolve computer names to IP addresses when a DNS server is unavailable.
- WINS matches IP addresses to NetBIOS names.
- The Dynamic Host Configuration Protocol (DHCP) is used to dynamically, or automatically, assign IP addresses to workstations.
- Automatic Private IP Addressing (APIPA) is a technique that temporarily issues an IP address in the range of 169.254.0.1 to 169.254.255.255 in case of a DHCP server failure.
- Four advantages of IPv6 are larger pool of Internet addresses, better security through mandatory IPSec, better quality of service, and reduced number of network broadcasts.
- IPv6 uses eight sets of 16-bit hexadecimal numbers to uniquely identify each host; it does not require a subnet mask.
- A EUI-64 identifier serves the same purpose as a MAC address.
- The three broad classifications of IPv6 addresses are unicast, multicast, and anycast.
- Link-local IPv6 addresses always start with FE80 and are not routable.
- Site-local IPv6 addresses always start with FEC0 and are routable.
- Unique-local IPv6 addresses begin with FD00 and are routable only within the private network.
- The loopback address for an IPv4 address is 127.0.0.1.
- The loopback address for an IPv6 address is ::1.
- A single network adapter can have more than one IPv6 addresses assigned.
- 6to4 addresses always starts with 2002:. and are used to support communication between IPv6 and IPv4 addresses on an IPv4 network system.

- ISATAP is designed as a node-to-node and node-to-router technology supporting IPv6 tunneling over an IPv4 network.
- Teredo creates a tunnel to allow incoming IPv6 traffic through a firewall designed for IPv4.
- Link-layer Multicast Name Resolution (LLMNR) protocol uses both IPv4 and IPv6 for name resolution through multicast.

Review Questions

Answer the following questions on a separate sheet of paper. Please do not write in this book.

1. What is the default protocol for communication across the Internet?
2. How many bytes are in an IPv4 address?
3. How many bits are in an IPv4 address?
4. How many octets are in an IPv4 address?
5. What is the range of numbers in an IPv4 octet?
6. List the IP addresses commonly assigned as private networks.
7. The _____ protocol allows an unregistered private network address to communicate with a legally registered IP address.
8. Briefly explain how the NAT protocol works.
9. A technician using Windows 7 wishes to inspect the subnet mask used for a workstation. How might the technician find the subnet mask information?
10. What two parts make up an FQDN?
11. What two methods are used to assign an IP address to a host?
12. Compare and contrast DNS and WINS.
13. What is contained in a typical lmhosts file?
14. What is contained in a typical hosts file?
15. Identify each of the following protocols as either connectionless or connection-oriented.
    A. TCP
    B. IP
    C. UDP
16. Briefly describe how TCP, UDP, and IP relate to the OSI model.
17. On what does the TCP frame rely to identify source and destination IP addresses?
18. On what does the UDP frame rely to identify source and destination IP addresses?
19. On what does the IP frame rely to identify the source and destination MAC addresses?
20. What is the function of DHCP?
21. Briefly describe how DHCP works.
22. What type of addressing automatically generates an IP address in the range of 169.254.0.1 to 169.254.255.255 if a network interface card fails to connect to a DHCP server?
23. What port is indicated by the following address: 192.168.23.45:80?
24. What are the three broad classifications of IPv6 addresses?
25. Which IPv6 address type is similar in function as the IPv4 public addresses?
26. Which IPv6 address type serves the same function as IPv4 APIPA?
27. How is a MAC address converted to a EUI-64 address in operating systems earlier than Windows Vista and Windows Server 2008?
28. How is the EUI-64 identifier generated in the Windows Vista, Windows 7, and Windows Server 2008 operating systems?

29. How many bytes are represented by an IPv6 address?
30. How many bits are represented by an IPv6 address?
31. What special character is used to separate the sections of an IPv6 address?
32. What are the three transition technologies used to implement IPv6?
33. What utility is *most likely* used to quickly verify a connection between two network points?
34. What TCP/IP utility can reveal the number of hops between the source and destination host?
35. What TCP/IP utility displays current network protocol statistics, such as the number of packets sent?
36. What TCP/IP utility displays a current listing of NetBIOS names and their associated IP addresses?

Sample Network+ Exam Questions

Answer the following questions on a separate sheet of paper. Please do not write in this book.

1. Which network operating system(s) use TCP/IP as a default protocol? (Select all that apply.)
   A. Windows 2000
   B. Linux
   C. Windows NT
   D. UNIX
2. Which technology supports the automatic assignment of IP addresses to network hosts?
   A. WINS
   B. DHCP
   C. ARP
   D. DNS
3. Which command reveals the assigned IP address and MAC address on a Windows 7 computer?
   A. **ipcfg**
   B. **ifconfig**
   C. **ipconfig**
   D. **winipcfg**
4. Which IP address is commonly assigned to private networks?
   A. 123.244.12.0
   B. 192.168.0.0
   C. 255.255.255.255
   D. 1.1.1.0
5. Identify the subnet mask of a Class B network.
   A. 255.0.0.0
   B. 255.255.0.0
   C. 0.0.255.255
   D. 255.255.255.0
6. What is the IPv4 loopback address?
   A. 127.0.0.1
   B. 255.255.255.255
   C. 0.0.0.0
   D. 255.0.0.0

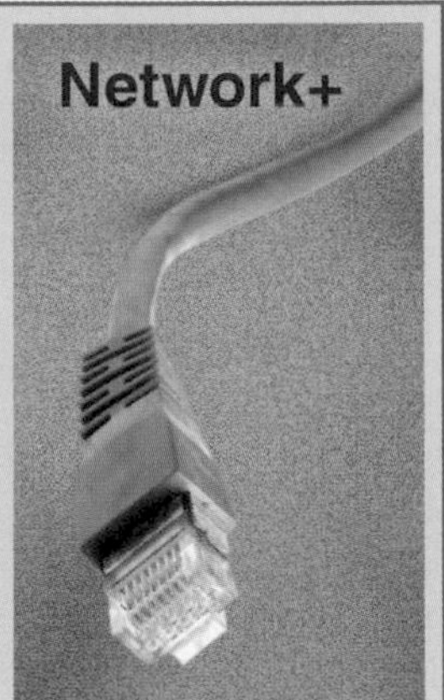

7. What function does a WINS server perform?
   A. Automatically assigns a Mac address to a network adapter.
   B. Resolves IP addresses to MAC addresses.
   C. Resolves NetBIOS names to IP addresses.
   D. Resolves domain names to IP addresses.
8. Which is an example of a Fully Qualified Domain Name?
   A. 3F 2B 12 CC D2 1F
   B. //workstation1/server
   C. //server1/client23
   D. workstation1.auditing.abc.com
9. A technician enters **ipconfig** at the command prompt of a Windows Vista workstation and sees the assigned IP address for the workstation is 169.254.1.12. What can the technician surmise from the assigned address?
   A. The workstation is using a static IP address.
   B. The DHCP server is down.
   C. The WINS server is not on line.
   D. The network is functioning normally.
10. What type of information is stored in the ARP cache?
   A. IP and MAC addresses
   B. IP addresses only
   C. IP addresses and domain names of workstations
   D. MAC addresses only

Interesting Web Sites for More Information

http://technet.microsoft.com/en-us/network/bb530961.aspx
www.3com.com/other/pdfs/infra/corpinfo/en_US/501302.pdf
www.iana.org/assignments/port-numbers
www.iana.org/numbers
www.icann.org
www.internic.org
www.neoworx.com

Suggested Laboratory Activities

1. Locate the sample lmhosts file called lmhosts.sam on a Windows computer by using the **Search** option located on the **Start** menu. Once you have located the lmhosts.sam file, open it in Notepad. A sample file should be displayed with information about how to create and modify the file.
2. Run **ipconfig** from the command prompt to reveal information about a computer such as its IP address assignment and MAC address. Run the utility when the computer is not connected to the Internet and then again after connected to the Internet to reveal changes in the IP address information.
3. Run **netstat** from the command prompt and use the **/?** option to reveal information about the command. Experiment with the command options while the computer is connected as part of a peer-to-peer network and when connected to the Internet.

4. Run **nbtstat** from the command prompt and use the **/?** option to reveal information about the command. Experiment with the command options while the computer is connected as part of a peer-to-peer network and when connected to the Internet.
5. Set up a DHCP server and then configure a workstation to connect to it.
6. Create identical hosts files on several computers to resolve PC names to IP addresses without a DNS server.
7. Use a protocol analyzer to capture some typical TCP/IP frames on a network. Identify the parts of the frame, such as the IP address of the source and destination, MAC address of the source and destination, and contents of the data section.
8. Using Windows XP Professional, install the IPv6 protocol. Use Windows Help and Support for assistance.
9. Try out the **ping ::1** command.

Chapter 10
Laboratory Activity

Configuring a Static IPv6 Address

After completing this laboratory activity, you will be able to:

- Use the **Internet Protocol Version 6 (TCP/IP) Properties** dialog box to configure a static IPv6 address.
- Use the **Network Connection Details** dialog box to view details about a network adapter card's settings.

Introduction

In this laboratory activity, you will configure a static IPv6 address and then view the change in the **Network Connection Details** dialog box. In general, you most likely will not need to configure a static IPv6 address for a workstation, but you may need to configure a static IPv6 address for a server or a router.

Two values you will need to enter are the IPv6 address and the subnet prefix length. The IPv6 address includes a subnet prefix. The *subnet prefix* determines how a router should handle the IPv6 packets. The *subnet prefix length* indicates which portion of the IPv6 address is the network portion. The following screen capture shows the static IPv6 address fe80::1234 with a subnet prefix length of 64 bits. The default subnet prefix length is 64 bits, but the length can be changed to any value within the range of the IPv6 address 128-bit length.

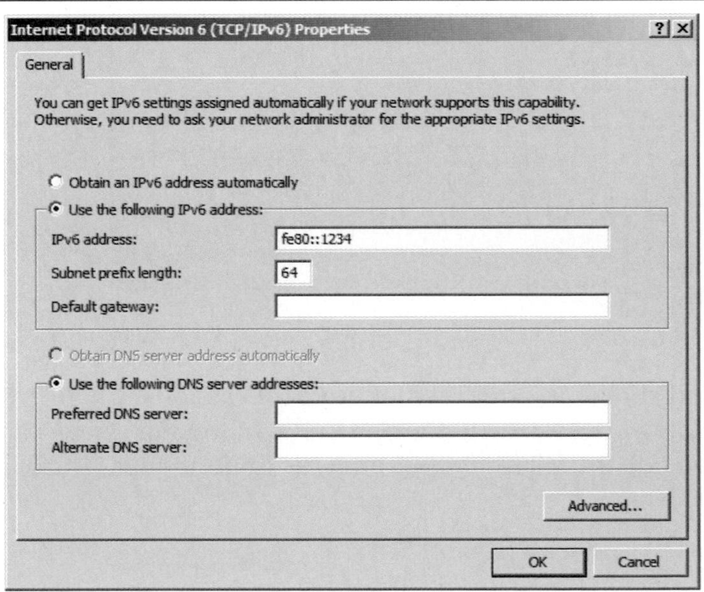

The DNS server address and the default gateway are optional. These device addresses are located automatically by Network Discovery and the exchange of protocols.

Equipment and Materials

- Computer with Windows Vista or Windows 7.

Note
Do not attempt this lab activity using Windows XP.

Procedure

1. ______ Report to your assigned workstation.
2. ______ Boot the computer and verify it is in working order.
3. ______ Access the **Local Area Connection Properties** dialog box either through Network and Sharing Center or through Control Panel. Select **Internet Protocol Version 6 (TCP/IPv6)** as shown in the following screen capture and then click the **Properties** button.

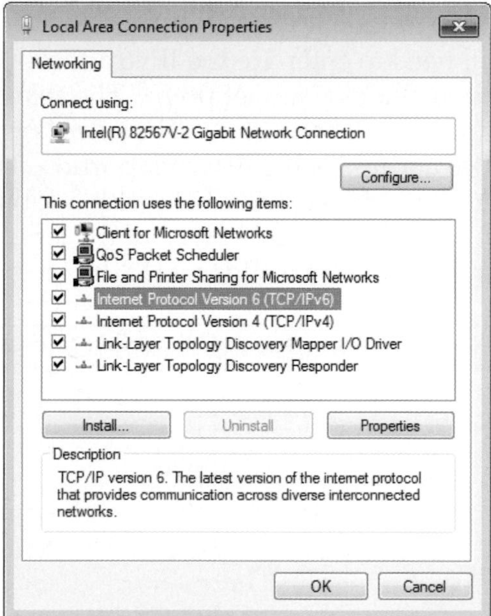

4. ______ You should see the **Internet Protocol Version 6 (TCP/IPv6) Properties** dialog box similar to the one in the following screen capture. Select the **Use the following IPv6 address** option. Then, enter the following information:

   IPv6 address: fe08::1234

   Subnet prefix length: 64

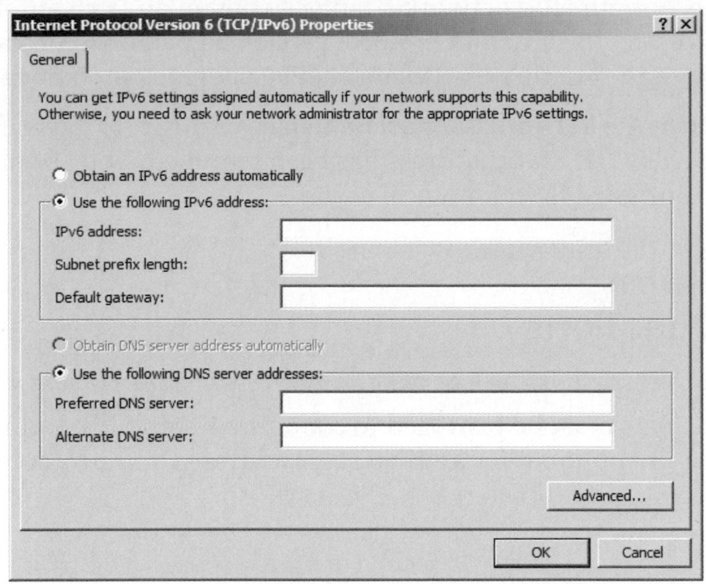

5. ______ Click **OK** to close the **Internet Protocol Version 6 (TCP/IPv6) Properties** dialog box. Then, close the **Local Area Connection Properties** dialog box by clicking **OK** again.

6. ______ Access the **Network Connection Details** dialog box (**Network and Sharing Center | Local Area Connection | Details** button) to view the status of the IPv6 address. You should see two IPv6 addresses assigned to the network adapter. The original link-local IPv6 address and the static IPv6 address you just configured.

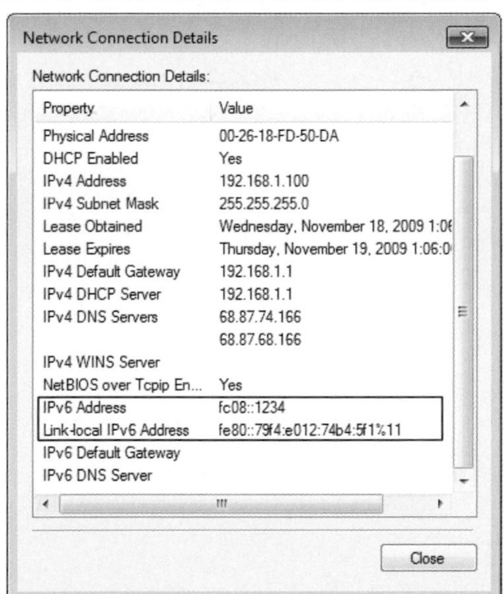

7. ______ Call your instructor to inspect your **Network Connection Details** dialog box.

8. ______ Reconfigure the network adapter to obtain an IPv6 automatically by accessing the **Internet Protocol Version 6 (TCP/IPv6) Properties** dialog box and selecting the **Obtain an IPv6 address automatically** option.
9. ______ Open the **Network Connection Details** dialog box to verify that the "fc08::1234" static address has been removed. You should only see the original IPv6 link-local address.
10. ______ Answer the review questions.

Review Questions

Answer the following questions on a separate sheet of paper. Please do not write in this book.

1. What two items must be provided to configure a static IPv6 address?
2. What items are optional for an IPv6 static address configuration?

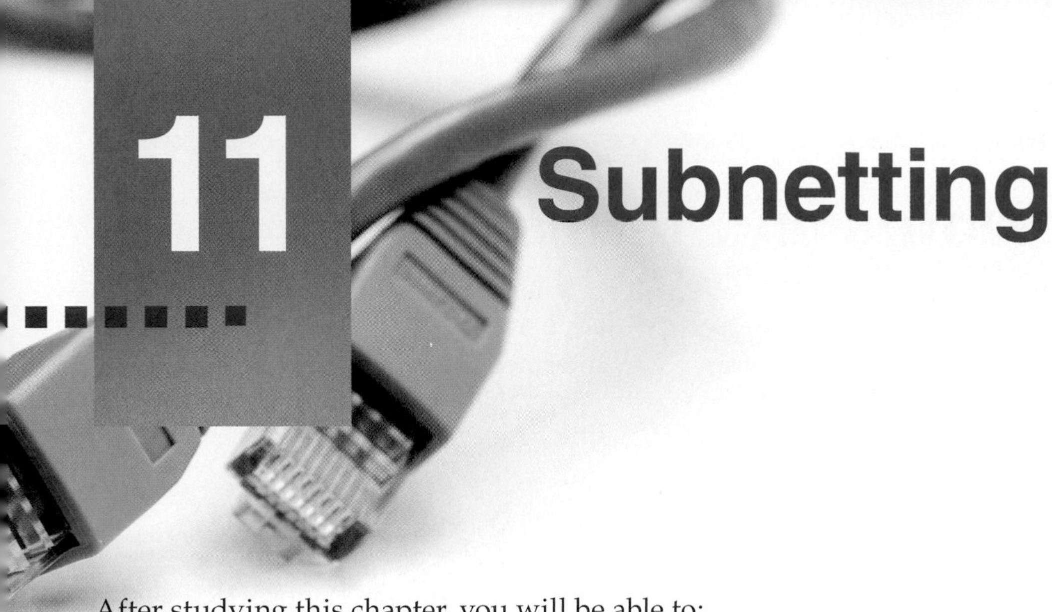

11 Subnetting

After studying this chapter, you will be able to:
- ❑ Interpret binary bit patterns.
- ❑ Summarize the purpose, advantages, and disadvantages of subnetting.
- ❑ Carry out subnet mask calculations.
- ❑ Identify subnet network characteristics by inspecting a subnet mask.
- ❑ Compare the bridge, switch, and router as applied to subnetting.
- ❑ Summarize the characteristics and purpose of a Virtual LAN.
- ❑ Compare common router protocols.
- ❑ Interpret CIDR notation.

Network+ Exam—Key Points

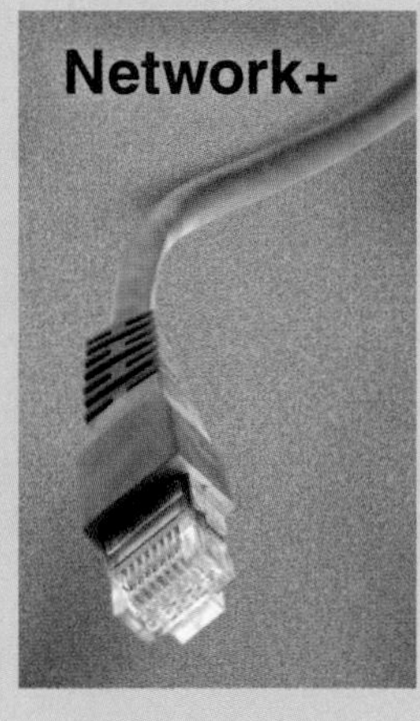

The Network+ Certification exam requires only a basic understanding of TCP/IP addressing and its relationship to the subnet mask. You should know how to identify a network class by looking at the first octet of an IPv4 address. The numeric value of the first octet will identify the network class. Questions concerning the network class can be quite difficult unless you memorize the decimal values associated with each class. You should be very familiar with switches and VLANs. Questions concerning subnetting, bridges, switches, routers, and VLANs will typically make up 10% to 15% of the test. Be prepared.

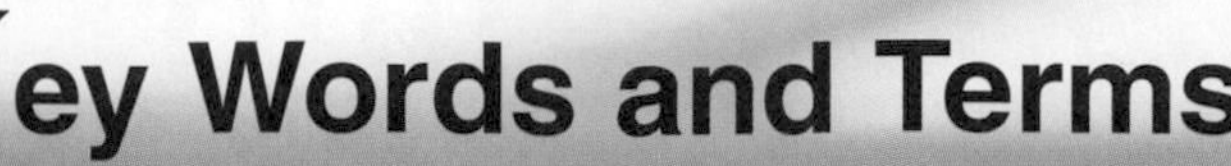

Key Words and Terms

The following words and terms will become important pieces of your networking vocabulary. Be sure you can define them.

adaptive cut-through
Border Gateway Protocol (BGP)
Classless Internet-Domain Routing (CIDR)
convergence
cut-through
distance vector protocol
dotted decimal notation
dynamic IP address table
dynamic VLAN
Enhanced Interior Gateway Routing Protocol (EIGRP)
Exterior Gateway Protocol (EGP)
filtering
Fixed Length Subnet Mask (FLSM)
fragment-free
hop
Interior Gateway Protocol (IGP)
Interior Gateway Routing Protocol (IGRP)
Intermediate System to Intermediate System (IS-IS)
link aggregation
link state protocol
Open Shortest Path First (OSPF)
RIP next generation (RIPng)
Router Information Protocol (RIP)
router metric
routing
Spanning Tree Protocol (STP)
static IP address table
static VLAN
store-and-forward
subnetting
trunking
Variable Length Subnet Mask (VLSM)
Virtual Local Area Network (VLAN)
Virtual Trunking Protocol (VTP)

This chapter covers the most difficult concept to master concerning networking fundamentals: subnetting. Subnetting means taking a single IP address issued from a registrar or an ISP and creating two or more subnetworks from it. For example, if a small business is issued only one IP address, it can increase security or subdivide the network by creating two different networks from the issued IP address. It can do this by using the subnet mask technique explained in this chapter.

To learn how to subnet, pay close attention to the information presented in this chapter, and practice the calculations. Before going any further in this unit, you must master binary-to-decimal conversion and decimal-to-binary conversion. The term *mastery* means a complete understanding and ability to use and apply a concept, not simply becoming familiar with it. A simple familiarity is not sufficient. Without fully understanding binary counting and conversion to decimal, the following information is difficult to understand and impossible to apply in the field.

For this unit, you may be able to use a calculator for making binary to decimal conversions. One such calculator is available in Microsoft Windows 98 or later under **Accessories**. However, some certification exams require subnet masks to be calculated manually. If you plan to take one of the other various certification exams, please check if calculating subnet masks by hand is required. If they are, make sure you get plenty of practice making binary to decimal conversions without a calculator or reference table.

The Binary Number System

The binary number system is a perfect match for digital electronic systems, such as computer systems. Digital electronics consists of circuits that have only two electrical states: on and off. The binary number system consists entirely of ones (1s) and zeros (0s). The ones typically represent electrical energy, and the zero represents the absence of electrical energy.

Digital circuit patterns can be represented by binary bit patterns. The major problem with the binary number system is reading and interpreting the numeric values of the binary bit patterns. We are used to the decimal number system and our minds are trained to interpret and do calculations based on decimal numbers. In addition, decimal numbers require much less space than binary numbers when written out.

The fact that large numeric expressions written in binary can be quite lengthy adds to the difficulty of using the binary number system and quickly interpreting their numeric value. For this unit, you will need to be able to convert binary numbers to their decimal equivalents. You may use the tables provided as you progress through this chapter, but you should be able to convert an eight-digit binary number to its decimal equivalent without a table to fully understand the technology. Think of the exercises in this chapter as learning an entirely new numbering system, such as Roman numerals.

Following this paragraph is a simple table that can help you convert binary numbers to their decimal equivalents. The table is limited to eight positions. This is equal to one byte, the most common unit you will encounter. It is also equal to one octet of an IPv4 IP address.

1	1	1	1	1	1	1	1
128	64	32	16	8	4	2	1

To convert a binary bit pattern to a decimal value, simply insert the decimal value for each individual bit position represented by a one, and then add the decimal values together. Study the following example.

1	0	0	1	0	1	0	1
128	0	0	16	0	4	0	1
128 + 16 + 4 + 1 = 149							

Dotted Decimal Notation

Typically, the IPv4 address numeric values encountered in computer technology are displayed in decimal form, not binary. This form is referred to as ***dotted decimal notation.*** Look at **Figure 11-1** to see an example of a Class B IPv4 address and subnet mask expressed as both binary and dotted decimal notation.

dotted decimal notation
an IPv4 address displayed in decimal form.

Figure 11-1.
A Class B IPv4 address and subnet mask in binary and decimal form. Notice that in the subnet mask, all ones indicate the network and all zeros indicate the host.

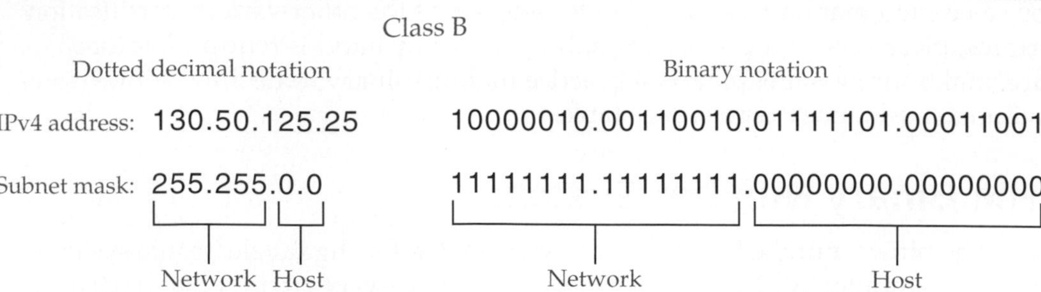

The figure shows a network IPv4 address of 130.50.125.25 with a subnet mask of 255.255.0.0. The subnet mask, like the IP address, is divided into two parts: the network address and the host address. In the example, the subnet mask network address is 255.255.0.0 and the host address is 0.0. All IPv4 addresses indicate a host address and a network address.

Subnetting

subnetting
dividing a network into subnetworks, or subnets.

You should recall from Chapter 10—TCP/IP Fundamentals that a subnet mask serves to identify the class of an IPv4 network and to allow the network address to be divided into subnetworks. Dividing a network into subnetworks, or subnets, is called ***subnetting.*** Router technology also relies on subnetting for creating large sections of network communication paths.

A subnet is a network created by borrowing bits from the host portion of an assigned network IP address. Look at **Figure 11-2.** In the example, a Class B network subnet mask has been extended into the first host octet. The first three bits borrowed from the host portion of the address are used to identify the subnets created from the original IP address. By borrowing the first three bits from the host portion, six subnets may be formed. Take particular notice of the new dotted decimal notation of the subnet mask. It is now 255.255.224.0. The original subnet mask was 255.255.0.0.

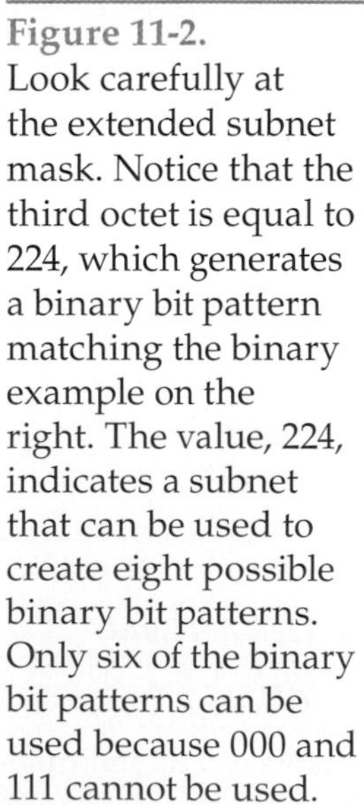
Figure 11-2.
Look carefully at the extended subnet mask. Notice that the third octet is equal to 224, which generates a binary bit pattern matching the binary example on the right. The value, 224, indicates a subnet that can be used to create eight possible binary bit patterns. Only six of the binary bit patterns can be used because 000 and 111 cannot be used.

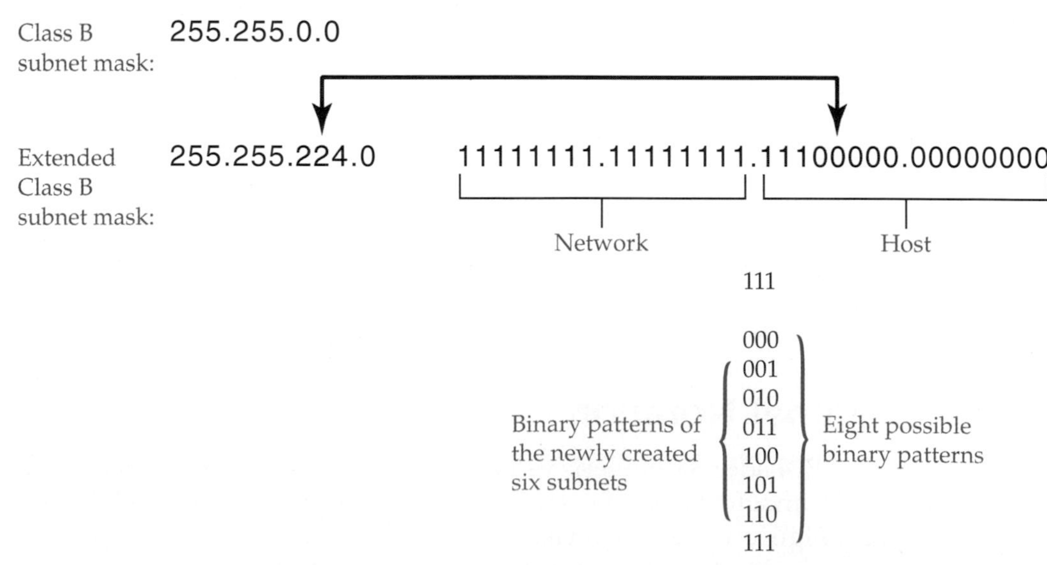

The three bits borrowed from the host can create a total of eight binary patterns. Refer to Figure 11-2. Notice that only six of the eight possible binary patterns can be used to identify the subnets. The binary pattern containing all zeros and the binary pattern of all ones are reserved values. The fact that they are reserved means they cannot be used to identify a particular network.

When messages are broadcast to all network nodes, a pattern of all ones is used in the destination address. This indicates that the message is intended for all network addresses. A bit pattern of all zeros is normally used for special functions such as a temporary address of a network card when it is set up for an automatic IP address assignment from a DHCP server. The all zero pattern indicates to the DHCP server that an IP address needs to be issued to the network card.

So when you are looking at binary bit patterns for subnet masks, be sure to subtract all zeros and all ones from the total possible number of patterns. When a binary bit pattern is converted directly to a decimal equivalent, subtract one from the total. For example, an extended portion of a subnet mask consisting of three binary ones equals 4 + 2 + 1 = 7. Subtract one from the total to derive the total number of subnets. See **Figure 11-3.**

A subnet reduces broadcasts and provides additional security. Broadcasts on Ethernet networks are typically limited to their immediate network, which is identified by the network portion of an IPv4 address. When traffic becomes too heavy, creating subnets reduces the number of broadcasts. Users with similar duties can be placed into the subnet areas to reduce the number of broadcasts affecting the immediate network. Subnets also increase security because they do not normally appear when viewed by intruders from outside the network area.

Now let's look at a Class C IP address and subnet mask, **Figure 11-4.** (Class B and Class C are the most common networks to be used to create subnets.) When

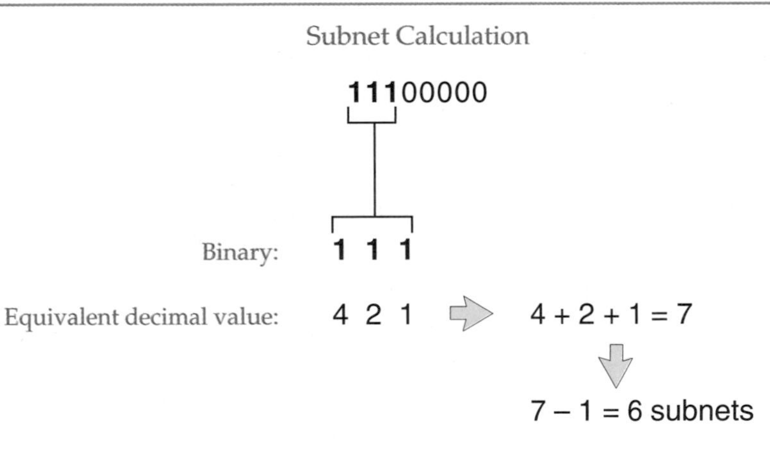

Figure 11-3.
To calculate the total number of subnets, simply add the value of the three bits together and then subtract one from the total.

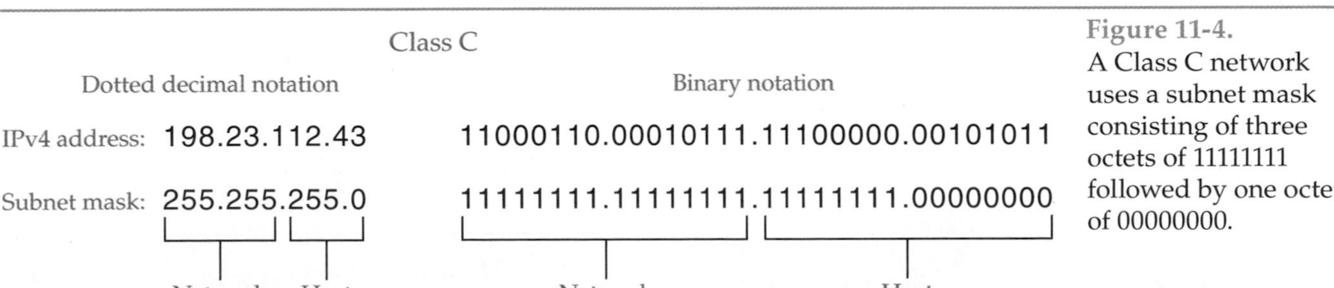

Figure 11-4.
A Class C network uses a subnet mask consisting of three octets of 11111111 followed by one octet of 00000000.

a Class C network is used to create subnets, bits are borrowed from the fourth octet, which is the host portion of the address.

In addition to determining the number of subnetworks that can be created, **Figure 11-5,** the number of actual hosts on each subnetwork are determined, **Figure 11-6.** The number of zeros in the address determines the number of hosts. To calculate the number of hosts available for each subnet, simply convert the bit pattern to decimal numbers and then add them together as shown in Figure 11-6. Subtract one from the total to find the number of hosts per subnet.

A point of normal confusion for students is the difference between total possible binary bit patterns and total decimal equivalent value. The total number of binary bit patterns always includes a bit pattern consisting of all zeros. When completing a conversion of binary to decimal, a pattern of all zeros is not considered. Just remember to subtract one from the total number of hosts when converting from binary to decimal. Also, you can use the tables in **Figure 11-7, Figure 11-8,** and **Figure 11-9** to assist you. The first table, Figure 11-7, is designed for determining the dotted decimal value based on the subnet mask bit pattern. In the last column of the table are the decimal values that correspond to the binary bit patterns displayed in the table. This is valuable for determining the subnet mask in dotted decimal format.

Figure 11-5.
In this example, three bits have been borrowed from the host of a Class C network.

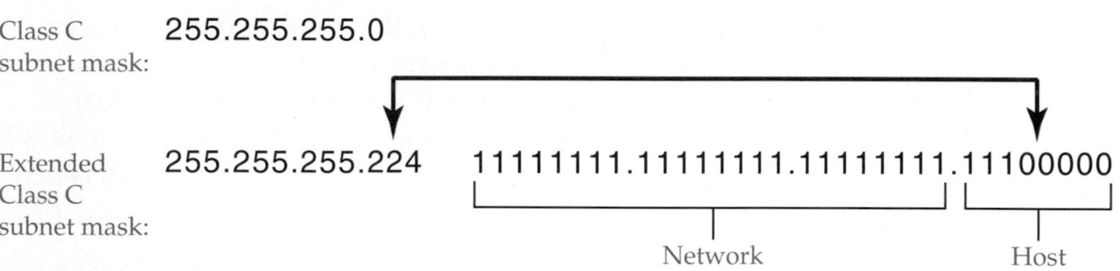

Figure 11-6.
To calculate the total number of hosts per subnetwork, convert the binary value to decimal and then subtract one from the total.

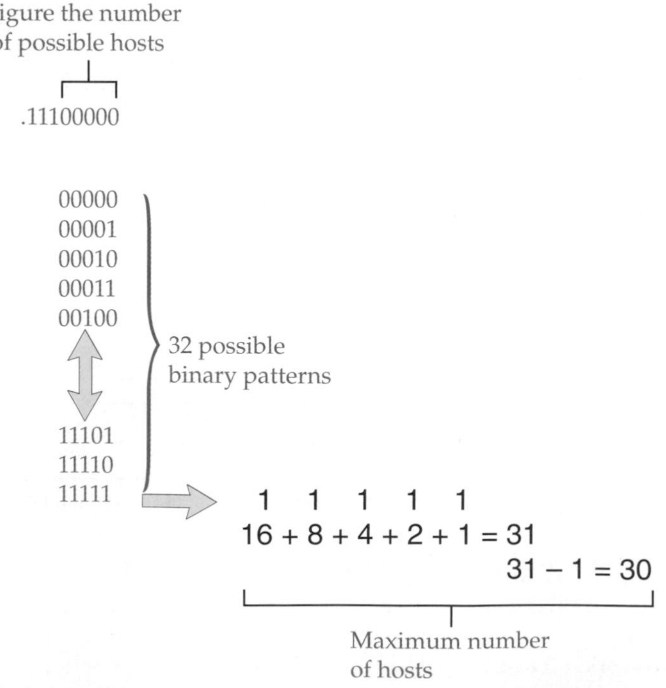

128	64	32	16	8	4	2	1	
1	0	0	0	0	0	0	0	**128**
1	1	0	0	0	0	0	0	**192**
1	1	1	0	0	0	0	0	**224**
1	1	1	1	0	0	0	0	**240**
1	1	1	1	1	0	0	0	**248**
1	1	1	1	1	1	0	0	**252**
1	1	1	1	1	1	1	0	**254**
1	1	1	1	1	1	1	1	**255**

Figure 11-7. Binary bit pattern to decimal conversion table. This table can be used to convert decimal values to subnet mask bit patterns.

Number of Bits	Subnet Mask	Number of Subnets	Number of Hosts
2	255.255.192.0	2	16,382
3	255.255.224.0	6	8,190
4	255.255.240.0	14	4,094
5	255.255.248.0	30	2,046
6	255.255.252.0	62	1,022
7	255.255.254.0	126	510
8	255.255.255.0	254	254
9	255.255.255.128	510	126
10	255.255.255.192	1,022	62
11	255.255.255.224	2,046	30
12	255.255.255.240	4,094	14
13	255.255.255.248	8,190	6
14	255.255.255.252	16,382	2

Note: Values for all binary patterns of all ones and all zeros in the network portion of the subnet mask have been eliminated from the table.

Figure 11-8. Common values used for Class B subnetting. Notice that a Class B subnet mask can span across two octets.

The second table, Figure 11-8, will help you determine the number of subnets and the number of hosts based on the subnet mask of a Class B network. The table has fourteen entries. This is because a Class B network has two host octets. When creating subnets, it is possible to borrow bits from both host octets to create the subnet mask.

Number of Bits	Subnet Mask	Number of Subnets	Number of Hosts
2	255.255.255.192	2	62
3	255.255.255.224	6	30
4	255.255.255.240	14	14
5	255.255.255.248	30	6
6	255.255.255.252	62	2

Note: Values for all binary patterns of all ones and all zeros in the network portion of the subnet mask have been eliminated from the table.

Figure 11-9. Common values used for Class C subnetting. Notice that the Class C subnet mask values match many of the Class B subnet mask values and host values. However, for the same network subnet masks, the quantities of subnets generated do not match.

The third table, Figure 11-9, is used to determine the number of subnets and hosts corresponding to a Class C network. Notice that there are only six possibilities for a Class C subnet mask. Also, pay attention to the fact that a Class C and a Class B network have several matching subnet masks in dotted decimal form, but the quantity of subnets differ.

A Closer Look at Subnets

In **Figure 11-10**, a subnet mask of 255.255.255.192 has been applied to a Class C IP address of 202.130.46.125. When applied, two subnets containing 62 hosts each are created. Note that the only two valid network addresses are 202.130.046.64 and 202.130.046.128. The other two calculated network addresses 202.130.046.0 and 202.130.046.192 cannot be used. The first address is based on a network binary bit pattern of all zeros, and the other is based on a binary pattern of all ones. Remember that you cannot use those two binary bit patterns while subnetting.

Some software/hardware combination equipment are able to use a network address using all zeros and all ones that increases the total possible number of subnets and hosts. You will encounter both systems until one becomes the dominant system. For now, consider the subnet mask system that does not allow the use of consecutive ones or zeros in the network portion of the subnet mask as the legacy system. The system that does allow the use of ones and zeros is the preferred system because it allows the use of more possible combinations of IP addresses. RFC 1874 allows the use of all ones and all zeros in the extended portion of the subnet mask.

Variable Length Subnet Mask (VLSM)
a subnet mask that is not expressed in standard eight-bit or one-byte values. It occurs when a subnet is further divided into smaller subnets, which are not equal to the original subnet in length or in the number of hosts.

A subnet mask that is not expressed in standard eight-bit or one-byte values is often referred to as a ***Variable Length Subnet Mask (VLSM)***. The term *Variable Length Subnet Mask* is derived from the fact that by subnetting, the total length of the binary one-bit pattern can vary in length rather than be held to the traditional series of eight-bit or one-byte patterns. Look at **Figure 11-11.** Notice how two additional subnets have been created out of two subnets. This makes a total of four subnets—two

Figure 11-10.
Subnetting two subnets.

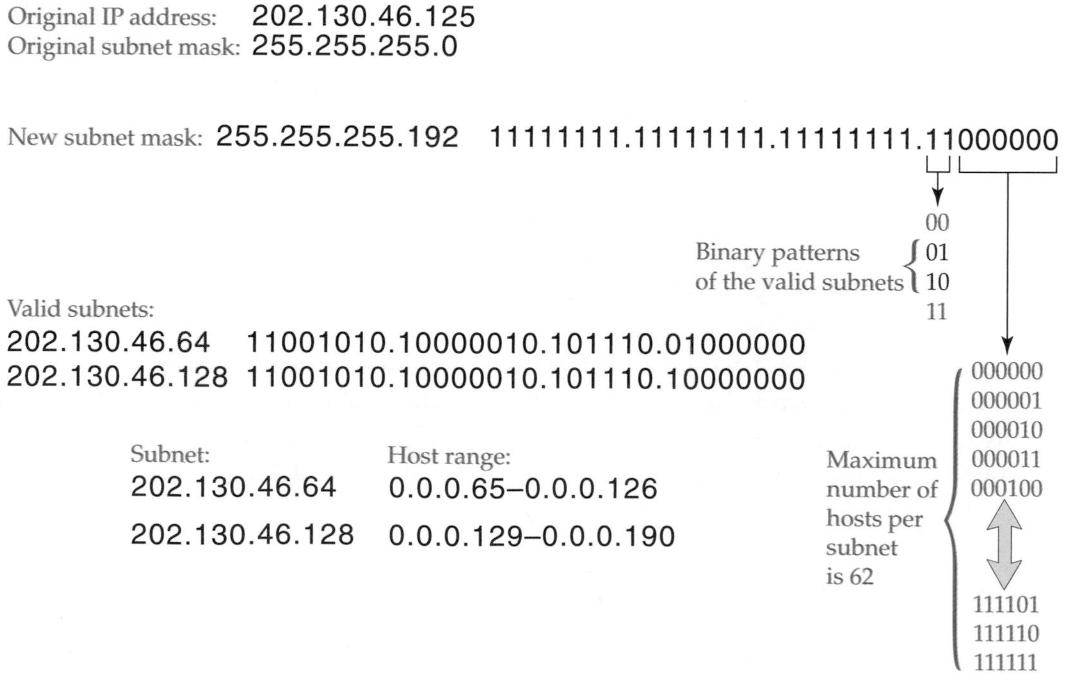

Original IP address: 202.130.46.125
Original subnet mask: 255.255.255.0

New subnet mask: 255.255.255.192 11111111.11111111.11111111.11000000

Binary patterns of the valid subnets: 00, 01, 10, 11

Valid subnets:
202.130.46.64 11001010.10000010.101110.01000000
202.130.46.128 11001010.10000010.101110.10000000

Subnet:	Host range:
202.130.46.64	0.0.0.65–0.0.0.126
202.130.46.128	0.0.0.129–0.0.0.190

Maximum number of hosts per subnet is 62
000000
000001
000010
000011
000100
111101
111110
111111

Figure 11-11.
A Variable Length Subnet Mask (VLSM) is formed when a subnet is used to create an additional subnet, which is not equal to the original subnet in length or in the number of hosts.

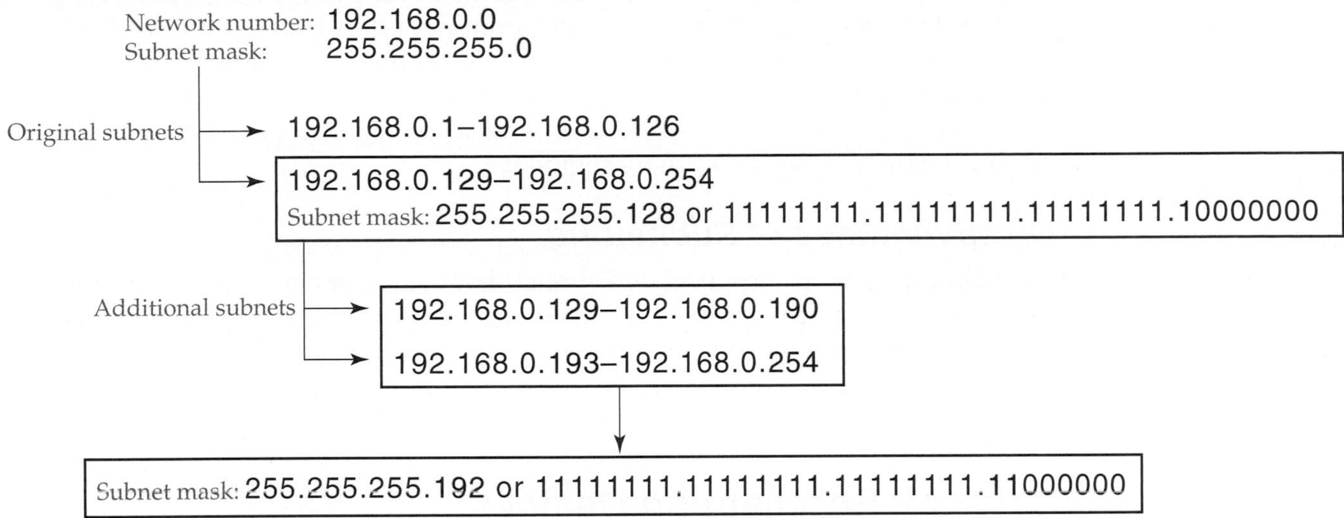

original subnets plus two smaller subnets created from the originals. The original subnets are referred to as *fixed length* because each subnet is of equal length.

A ***Fixed Length Subnet Mask (FLSM),*** therefore, has subnets that are equal in length and have an equal number of hosts. With the additional subnets, however, there is more than one length of subnet mask. The term *Variable Length Subnet Mask* applies because multiple subnets with more than one length of subnet mask have been created. The length refers to the binary ones used to identify the network and the host.

Fixed Length Subnet Mask (FLSM)
a subnet mask that is expressed in standard eight-bit or one-byte values. Its subnets are equal in range and have an equal number of hosts.

Subnetting can cause confusion, which has led to IP addresses being presented in a different written manner at times. For example, you may see an IP address that contains a Variable Length Subnet Mask written as 202.130.046.125/26. The /26 indicates that a mask with a total length of 26 bits is used for the mask. Do not confuse the slash (/) symbol with the colon (:) symbol, which follows an IP address to identify a port number. Variable Length Subnet Mask notation, also known as *Classless Internet-Domain Routing (CIDR),* is covered in detail later in this chapter.

There are many software programs available that can automatically calculate the number of subnets, hosts, subnet mask, and all addresses for a given IP address. A free network subnet calculator is available from www.wildpackets.com.

Unfortunately, you cannot use software or a calculator on any actual certification exams at the time of this writing. This procedure may change in the future. For now, you must learn to calculate these values manually to pass most certification exams that involve IP addressing and the TCP/IP protocol. Many certification authorities feel that when students can successfully perform the necessary calculations, they prove they have mastered the basic concept of subnetting networks.

Advantages of Subnetting

As stated earlier, subnetting creates a more secure network by placing hosts on separate networks. Network users cannot readily access resources on a host of a different subnet unless the system administrator creates the necessary user profile to allow it. Subnetting creates two or more segments out of the original network. When the original network is divided into two or more segments, broadcast packets from one network are not forwarded to the other network. If broadcast packets are not forwarded, the amount of data traffic is reduced. When the amount of data traffic is reduced, fewer collisions occur. As the number of collisions is reduced, the network appears faster to users. Subnetting, therefore, also reduces the amount of collisions on a network segment by dividing the original segment into two or more segments.

Disadvantages of Subnetting

Subnetting by using calculated subnet mask assignments could be difficult to manage because of the inherent confusion of the IP address assignments. There is also confusion because some equipment is designed to use subnets based on all one and all zero bit patterns to increase the total number of possible subnets and hosts.

Network Segmenting Devices

Another way to segment a network is to use a physical device such as a bridge, switch, or router. The bridge and switch segment a network at the data link layer or layer 2 level. The router segments a network at the network layer or layer 3 level. The bridge, switch, and router were covered earlier in the textbook. In this chapter, these devices are covered in more depth since you have a better understanding of networking principles involving physical and logical addresses.

Bridge

A bridge is a device that segments a network by filtering network traffic based on MAC addresses. Because the bridge filters MAC addresses, it is considered a layer 2 or data link layer device. Bridges are not associated with a particular protocol. As frames pass through the bridge, the bridge automatically creates a bridging table. The bridge refers to the table when determining whether to pass or block a frame based on its MAC address. The selective passing and blocking of frames is referred to as ***filtering***. Bridges only pass frames which reside on the other side of the bridge. Bridges also forward broadcast frames. All devices connected to the bridge must have the same subnet when using a bridge.

filtering the selective passing and blocking of frames.

Tech Tip

Technically, switches and bridges filter frames and operate at layer 2. Routers filter packets and operate at layer 3. Frames are associated with the data link layer while packets are associated with the network layer. However, you will often see the terms "packet" and "frame" used interchangeably from a variety of sources.

Bridges are seldom encountered because electronic network devices are becoming more reasonably priced. Network designers are, therefore, opting to use more sophisticated devices such as switches. They do not cost much more than a bridge.

The most commonly encountered bridges are wireless bridges or wireless access points, which incorporate the bridge function. The switch is often referred to as a *multiport bridge*.

The IEEE standard still uses the term *bridge* when describing devices that filter frames by MAC address. You will also see the term *bridge* used to describe individual ports of a switch.

Switch

Switches are the most commonly used device for segmenting a wired network. Subnetting is based on the principle of using an IP address subnet mask to isolate sections of a network, thus creating small broadcast zones. Subnetting by subnet mask requires no special hardware and is considered a logical, not a physical, way to create a subnet. Switches use MAC addresses to create isolated segments of a network, but they do not create a subnet. Switches do not prevent broadcasts because they do not filter frames by IP address. All network broadcasts are still forwarded through a switch.

Switches filter network activity by the physical address of the destination device without broadcasting each and every frame to all devices. For example, a network could be organized by corporate workgroups such as accounting, engineering, administration, or by physical locations such as building 1 and building 2. A switch could be used to create network segments for each corporate workgroup or location so that overall network traffic is reduced. Only broadcasts would be forwarded to all devices through the switch.

Switches can be programmed or can operate in automatic mode to learn about adjacent devices. In many ways, a switch is like a multiple port bridge. Each port on the switch can be programmed to act independently of the other ports.

Network+ Note

When taking the Network+ Certification exam, be careful not to confuse the term *port* used for the switch physical port with the term *port* used to describe the port address, such as port 80 for HTTP used with TCP and UDP packets.

Switches are a great way to segment a network or create a Virtual Local Area Network (VLAN). A VLAN creates a group of network devices that operate in a single broadcast domain even when the devices are located on physically-separated networks. VLANs are covered later in this chapter.

A switch is often used to correct network conditions such as reduced bandwidth caused by too many devices in the same broadcast domain. Since the devices share the same bandwidth, network performance is reduced as more and more devices are added to the network.

Switch vs. Hub

A hub is an inexpensive common connection point used for multiple Ethernet network connections. However, the hub passes all broadcasts. The hub can be replaced with a switch to correct this problem. Each port on a switch can support the same bandwidth as the network. For example, a 1-Gb switch can support 1 Gb through each of its ports. The bandwidth does not need to be shared with other devices connected to the switch. A 100-Mb hub shares the 100-Mb bandwidth with other devices connected to the hub, thus reducing the amount of bandwidth for each device. For example, if five devices are connected to a 100-Mb hub, each would use approximately 1/5 of the total bandwidth or approximately 20 Mb. If the same five devices are connected to a 100-Mb switch, each device would have 100 Mb of bandwidth. Therefore, there is no reduction of bandwidth when connecting with a switch.

Look at **Figure 11-12** and **Figure 11-13** to compare the actions of a hub and switch. Notice that the hub in Figure 11-12 forwards the frame sent from PC-1 to the server to all nodes, including the Internet gateway. In other words, the hub forwards all frames and does nothing to limit broadcasts or correct collisions. The hub shares the bandwidth with all devices connected to the hub. Each device can send an Ethernet frame onto the network. Frames from each device can collide with other frames causing frames to become corrupted. When an Ethernet frame is corrupted, it is sent again, thus reducing bandwidth.

In Figure 11-13, the hub is replaced with a switch. A switch reads the destination MAC address and then forwards the frame to only that address. The switch limits

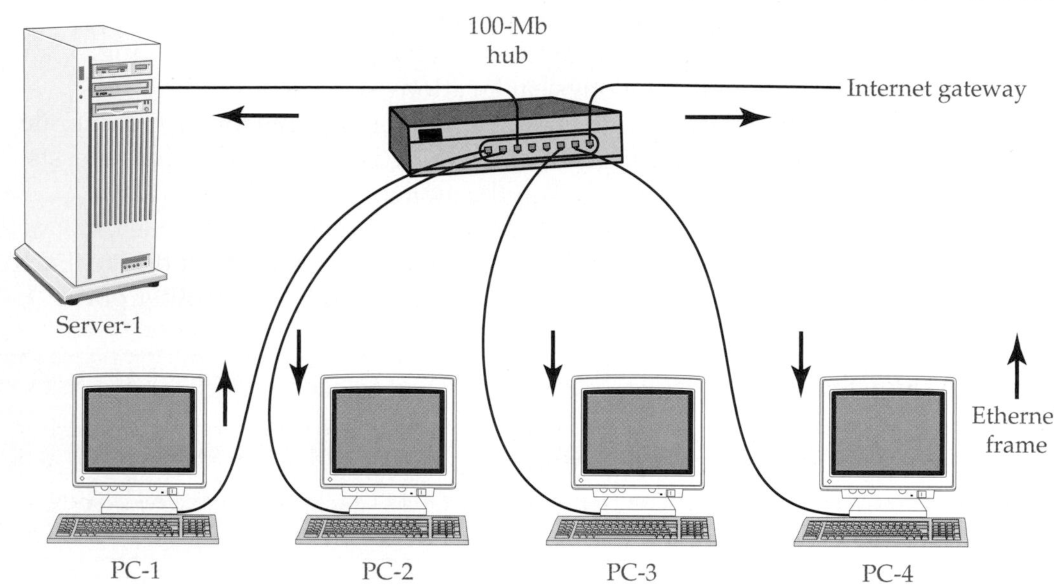

Figure 11-12. Each network device must share the 100-Mb bandwidth of the local network segment.

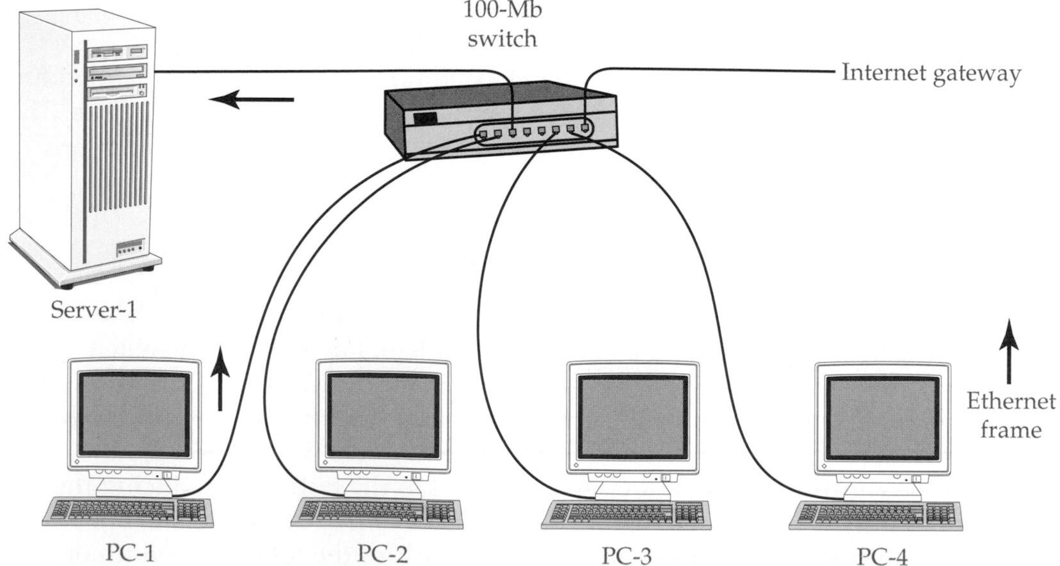

Figure 11-13. Each PC can use the full 100-Mb bandwidth between it and other devices connected to the switch.

the number of frame collisions and provides full bandwidth for each device. The exception is for a broadcast frame with an address such as 255.255.255.255. Broadcast frames are sent to all devices.

You must consider that we are talking about the local area network and connections between two devices. When connections are shared through another device such as an Internet gateway or a server with Internet Connection Sharing, then bandwidth will be reduced. Look at **Figure 11-14.**

The switch only provides the maximum bandwidth within the local segment of the network. If most of the workstations are constantly accessing resources on the Internet or on a centralized shared device such as a file server, then the switch will not provide significant benefit, except for reducing collisions. To increase network bandwidth to the gateway, install higher bandwidth cable, network cards, routers, gateways, or modems. For example, replace all the 100-Mb devices and cable with 1-Gb devices and cable.

Switch vs. Bridge

To better understand how a switch is superior to a bridge, you must first look at how a switch operates. A switch automatically learns the location of hardware devices by reading a frame's source MAC address as the frames are transmitted to the switch. This is similar to the way a bridge learns the location of a device. The switch then maps the MAC address to the switch port, thus creating a switch port table.

Note

Cisco refers to a switch port table as *content-address memory (CAM).*

A bridge simply passes or blocks a frame based on the MAC address. Switches are designed with forwarding modes. The forwarding mode determines how packets are passed through the switch. The common forwarding modes are cut-through, store-and-forward, fragment-free, and adaptive cut-through. All but cut-through mode are used to detect packet errors and then react according to design.

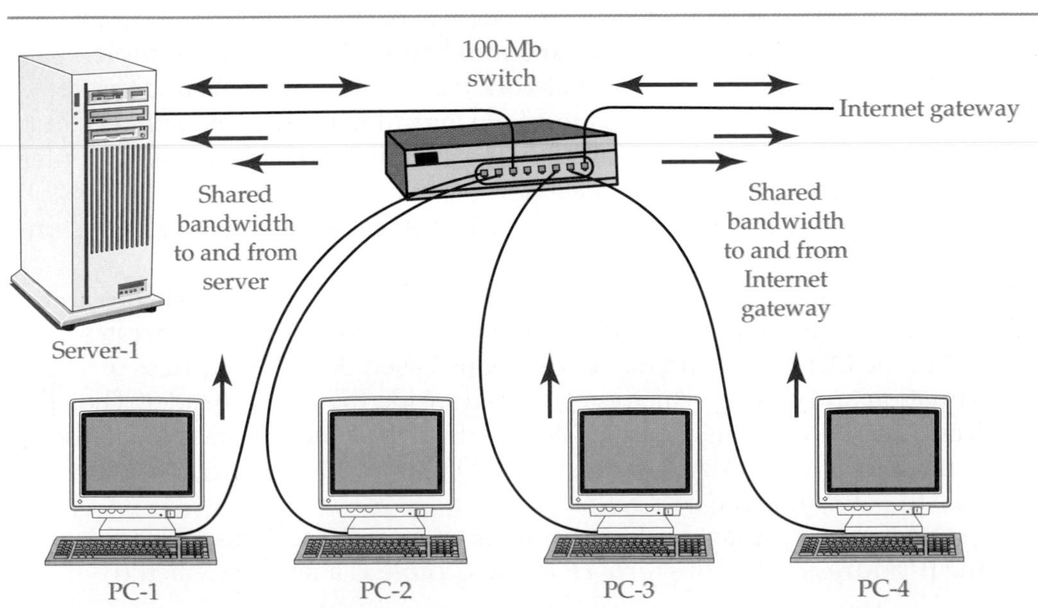

Figure 11-14. Devices on a switch share bandwidth when accessing server resources or the Internet gateway.

cut-through a method of switching that forwards the frame immediately after receiving it. Also referred to as *low latency*.

store-and-forward a method of switching that reads the entire contents of the frame before forwarding the frame to its destination.

fragment-free a method of switching that checks the first 64 bytes of an Ethernet frame before forwarding it.

adaptive cut-through a method of switching in which a switch operates in cut-through mode by forwarding the frame immediately after receiving it until it detects an unacceptable number of corrupt frames. Then, the switch operates in store-and-forward mode or fragment-free mode until the number of corrupt frames is reduced to an acceptable number.

routing the process of selecting the "best route" to send packets through a network.

static IP address table a table of IP addresses that have been entered manually.

The ***cut-through*** method forwards the frame immediately after receiving it. Cut-through, also known as a *low latency*, is the quickest method of switching. *Latency* refers to the delay created by networking devices receiving and transmitting frames.

Store-and-forward reads the entire contents of the frame before forwarding the frame to its destination. The store-and-forward method drops corrupt frames. The cut-through method does not drop corrupt frames. Store-and-forward has a much higher latency than cut-through because each frame is inspected.

Fragment-free is a mixture of the store-and-forward and cut-through methods. This method inspects the first 64 bytes of an Ethernet frame. Since most errors are detected in the first 64 bytes, there is no need to check the entire frame. This means that the latency is less than that with the store-and-forward method but not quite as good as that with the cut-through method.

The last method, ***adaptive cut-through,*** is unique in the way it operates as cut-through until an unacceptable number of corrupt frames are detected. After a certain number of corrupt frames are detected, the switch operates in a store-and-forward mode or fragment-free mode until the number of corrupt frames is reduced to an acceptable number. Then, the switch once more operates as a cut-through switch.

Router

The main function of a router is to route packets to their proper destination within an IP-based network or across the Internet. ***Routing*** is the process of selecting the "best route" through which to send packets. Networks, especially large networks covering great distances, can comprise a variety of media and network devices. There may be several different paths from the source to the destination using a variety of network media such as copper core, fiber, and wireless as well as network systems managed by different communication companies and ISPs. The router determines the best network and Internet path on which to forward packets. Routers interface with other routers and exchange routing table information. The routing tables contain information about the other routers and networks. This information is processed by the router and then used to determine the best route to send the packet to its final destination.

The router is the most diverse network device because it can be programmed to perform a much wider amount of functions than a switch. For example, routers can be programmed to filter network traffic and can be used to create more networks. Routers can be used to create logical networks and subnets, but it is more practical and less expensive to use a switch for these purposes. Routers can limit broadcast domains and create new broadcast domains. Unlike hubs, bridges, and switches, routers do not forward broadcasts. This reduces collision domains.

One major disadvantage of routers is they can be slower than switches and bridges because they analyze the data in the routing table. A router operates at layer 3 of the OSI model and makes decisions based on the IP address of the destination and source, which is contained inside the packet header. The IP address is also known as the *logical address*. Switches and bridges need only to examine the physical (MAC) address and do not need to analyze logical addresses to determine the best path.

Routers can be programmed to operate from static IP address tables or dynamic IP address tables. A ***static IP address table*** is a table in which IP addresses are entered manually. A ***dynamic IP address table*** is a table in which IP addresses are generated automatically by a software program that communicates with nearby routers. The software program allows a router to exchange IP address information with other routers and build a reference table based on this information.

Convergence is a routing table term that applies to dynamic routing. With static routing, all routing tables are always the same. With dynamic routing, tables are constantly changing. When all dynamic routing tables contain the same information, a state of convergence is said to exist. Convergence is also referred to as *steady state.*

Router Metric

A ***router metric*** is the mechanism used to determine or measure the best route. Some of the various elements of a router metric are throughput, reliability, packet loss, latency, and number of hops. ***Hop*** is a measure of how many network devices such as routers and gateways a packet must pass through until the packet reaches its destination. The hop is the oldest and most basic metric used for determining the best route. When you issue a **tracert** command, you will see the number of hops that the **tracert** packet has passed through to reach the final destination.

Routing protocol metrics vary according to the routing protocol design. For example, the Router Information Protocol (RIP) simply uses the number of hops to determine the best route. More sophisticated routing protocols take into account other factors such as throughput, reliability, and latency.

Routing Protocol Classifications

Two basic routing protocol classifications are Interior Gateway Protocol (IGP) and Exterior Gateway Protocol (EGP). ***Interior Gateway Protocol (IGP)*** is confined to an autonomous network. The term *autonomous* is used by the IEEE organization to describe the confines of the network system protocol. Autonomous means that the network is under one authority or is a single domain. For example, a campus network with a domain name of USF.edu would be under one authority. ***Exterior Gateway Protocol (EGP)*** is designed to exchange information between different autonomous networks. For example, exchanging information between a campus network and some other network location across the Internet. Examples of IGP are RIP, IGRP, OSPF, and IS-IS. Examples of Exterior Gateway Protocol are BGP and EGP. Exterior Gateway Protocol is both a type of protocol and a protocol. See the table in **Figure 11-15,** which lists various routing protocols and identifies them as IGP, EGP, link state, or distance vector.

Two additional classifications of routing protocols are link state and distance vector. A ***link state protocol*** performs its own calculations of the best route. It only transfers information about connections and does not pass its routing table to other devices. A ***distance vector protocol*** shares its routing table with other routers. Eventually, the routers will be in a state of convergence when all of the routers contain the same routing table information. Convergence rarely occurs with link state systems.

Examples of link state protocols are IS-IS and OSPF. Examples of distance vector are RIP, IGRP, EIGRP. The following sections will briefly introduce some of the most common router protocols.

dynamic IP address table
a table of IP addresses generated by a software program that communicates with nearby routers.

convergence
the state in which all dynamic routing tables contain the same information. Also referred to as *steady state.*

router metric
the mechanism used to determine or measure the best route. Some of the various elements of a router metric are throughput, reliability, packet loss, latency, and number of hops.

hop
a measure of how many network devices such as routers and gateways a packet must pass through until the packet reaches its destination.

Interior Gateway Protocol (IGP)
a basic routing protocol that is confined to an autonomous network. Examples of IGP are RIP, IGRP, OSPF, and IS-IS.

Exterior Gateway Protocol (EGP)
a basic routing protocol that exchanges information between different autonomous networks. Examples of Exterior Gateway Protocol are BGP and EGP.

Figure 11-15.
Routing protocols.

Routing Protocol	Internet Gateway Protocol (IGP)	Exterior Gateway Protocol (EGP)	Link State Protocol	Distance Vector Protocol	Comment
BGP		×			Exchanges routing information between different autonomous networks.
EGP		×			Exchanges routing information between different autonomous networks.
EIGRP	×		×	×	Guarantees loop-free operation. Cisco advertises EIGRP as a link state protocol and a distance vector protocol.
IGRP	×			×	Allows a maximum hop count of 255 and uses a metric based on bandwidth, latency, route traffic, and reliability.
IS-IS	×		×		Detects router types as level 1 or level 2 when determining shortest route.
OSPF	×		×		Can detect network link failures and then automatically determine next best path.
RIP	×			×	Supports a maximum of 15 hops.
RIPng	×			×	IPv6 version of RIP.

link state protocol a routing protocol that only transfers information about connections and does not pass its routing table to other devices.

distance vector protocol a routing protocol that shares its routing table with other routers.

RIP and RIP2

The ***Router Information Protocol (RIP)*** is one of the oldest protocols ever developed for routers. RIP periodically exchanges an entire table of routing information with nearby routers. Each router maintains a database containing information about the devices connected to the network. RIP sends the information to other routers so that they can update their own router table.

Each router location in the network structure is referred to as a *hop*. RIP supports a maximum of 15 hops, which means it will forward a message update for a total of 15 locations. The router hop is also referred to as the *metric*. Maximum metric or hop is the distance the packet can travel before being dropped.

Each frame sent contains a time stamp. The time stamp is used to determine the time-out or Time to Live (TTL) for each frame. RIP and RIP2 are examples of an interior gateway protocol. RIP and RIP2 can forward information to other devices located on the network domain but cannot forward information outside the domain, which makes it an example of IGP. RIP also uses distance vector algorithms which allow it only to exchange routing table information with its neighboring devices and not the entire domain. RIPv2 has a simple authentication feature not supported in RIP.

Router Information Protocol (RIP) one of the oldest router protocols, which determines the best path based on number of hops.

RIPng

RIP next generation (RIPng) is an IPv6 version of RIP. RIP was designed for IPv4 networks and has certain limitations associated with IPv4. RIPng is designed for IPv6 type devices and does not need the intervention of translation protocols as long as the routing devices used support RIPng. Also, RIP provides authentication as part of the protocol. RIPng does not provide authentication as part of the protocol because IPv6 provides authentication.

RIP next generation (RIPng) an IPv6 version of RIP.

Open Shortest Path First (OSPF) a link state, interior gateway routing protocol used in an autonomous network system.

OSPF

Open Shortest Path First (OSPF) is a routing protocol that only exchanges the most recently changed information in the table. OSPF saves bandwidth because it does not transfer the large amounts of data associated with RIP. It is a Cisco proprietary, IGP, and link state protocol. It is a dynamic protocol in that it uses link state to update its routing table. OSPF in contrast to RIP uses more than just hop count to determine the best path. OSPF can detect network link failures and then automatically determine the next best path if one exists. OSPF also contains an authentication mechanism to ensure that the exchange of data is only from trusted routers. Router data tables can be corrupted by unethical hackers, causing network security to be compromised.

Intermediate System to Intermediate System (IS-IS) an IGP link state protocol that determines a router type as level 1 or level 2 when detecting the best path for data.

All routing protocols are designed as dynamic. The classification of static refers to changes to a router table made manually which override dynamic entries.

IS-IS

Intermediate System to Intermediate System (IS-IS) is an IGP link state protocol. IS-IS is pronounced "eye–sys." IS-IS is used in similar applications as OSPF but has a different approach to router communication and the exchange of data. IS-IS determines router type as level 1 or level 2. Level 1 routers are typically inside the autonomous network. Level 2 routers are outside the autonomous network. Level 1 routers can communicate with level 1 or level 2 routers. Level 2 routers can only communicate with other level 2 routers.

Interior Gateway Routing Protocol (IGRP) a distance vector protocol that has a maximum hop count of 255 and a default value of 100 hops. It uses a complex metric calculation based on items such as bandwidth, latency, route traffic, and reliability to determine the best path for data.

IGRP

Interior Gateway Routing Protocol (IGRP) is a Cisco proprietary distance vector protocol. Cisco developed IGRP as an improved version of RIP. For example, RIP is limited to a 15-hop count, but IGRP has a maximum hop count of 255 and a default value of 100 hops. IGRP has a more complex metric calculation than RIP. RIP uses hops for the metric. IGRP metric is based on items such as bandwidth, latency, route traffic, and reliability. To learn more about the various routing protocols, visit the Cisco Web site.

EIGRP

Enhanced Interior Gateway Routing Protocol (EIGRP) a distance vector protocol that guarantees loop-free operation.

Enhanced Interior Gateway Routing Protocol (EIGRP) is another Cisco proprietary distance vector protocol and an improved version of IGRP. EIGRP is a sophisticated routing protocol that guarantees loop-free operation. Router loops can occur with older dynamic protocol versions and thus corrupt routing table data. The corrupt data can cause packets to circulate endlessly in the network. Cisco has advertised EIGRP as a hybrid routing protocol that combines both distance vector and link state characteristics.

BGP

Border Gateway Protocol (BGP) an Internet routing protocol that supports the exchange of routing information between autonomous networks.

Border Gateway Protocol (BGP) is an Internet routing protocol that supports the exchange of routing information between autonomous networks. BGP is a type of Exterior Gateway Protocol and has replaced the Exterior Gateway Protocol. BGP routers contain typically over 90,000 route entries. BGP routers are assigned a unique IP address and domain name by IANA, the same authority that assigns IP addresses to corresponding domain names for Web sites. IANA assigns each authorized BGP router an Autonomous System (AS) number in the range from 1 to 64511. One AS number can be assigned to more than one router. For example, a collection of routers under the same administrative authority can be represented by one AS number. The AS number is embedded into the BGP packet in much the same way the IP address is embedded into a packet.

Figure 11-16 shows the results of a **tracert** command issued as **tracert www.comcast.net**. The path to the Comcast network is traced starting with the client computer with IP address 192.168.1.1. Each hop or router is identified by a unique domain name and IP address. The AS number is not apparent because it is embedded into the packet when BGR exchanges information about the best route to use. To learn more about assigning Internet numbers, visit the IANA Web site at www.iana.org.

Router vs. Multilayer Switch

The main difference between a router and a multilayer layer switch is their physical construction and intended use. A router is constructed around a programmable microprocessor. The microprocessor is very similar to the microprocessor used in a computer referred to as the *CPU*. You can think of a router as a computer with multiple network adapters installed, one adapter for each port. The router can be programmed and reprogrammed numerous times and is designed to specifically route frames based on IP addresses. A basic switch cannot

Figure 11-16. The **tracert** command reveals the names of the routers along the Internet path.

```
Command Prompt

C:\Users\Richard>tracert www.comcast.net

Tracing route to a1526.g.akamai.net [96.17.75.25]
over a maximum of 30 hops:

  1     1 ms    <1 ms    <1 ms  192.168.1.1
  2     8 ms     8 ms     6 ms  73.17.116.1
  3     8 ms     7 ms     7 ms  ge-2-2-sr01.sebring.fl.westfl.comcast.net [68.86.199.77]
  4     7 ms     7 ms     7 ms  te-3-2-sr01.arcadia.fl.westfl.comcast.net [68.87.238.105]
  5     8 ms     9 ms     9 ms  te-9-4-ur01.portcharlott.fl.westfl.comcast.net [68.87.238.101]
  6     7 ms     9 ms     9 ms  te-8-2-ur01.northport.fl.westfl.comcast.net [68.87.238.65]
  7    10 ms    10 ms    10 ms  te-8-4-ar02.venice.fl.westfl.comcast.net [68.87.238.25]
  8    12 ms    15 ms    12 ms  te-7-1-ar01.bonitasprngs.fl.naples.comcast.net [68.85.229.249]
  9    11 ms    11 ms    18 ms  te-9-1-ar02.bonitasprngs.fl.naples.comcast.net [68.87.236.106]
 10    16 ms    19 ms    17 ms  te-0-2-0-5-ar03.northdade.fl.pompano.comcast.net [68.85.229.253]
 11    20 ms    36 ms    18 ms  pos-0-5-0-0-cr01.miami.fl.ibone.comcast.net [68.86.91.81]
 12    33 ms    32 ms    32 ms  pos-2-3-0-0-cr01.atlanta.ga.ibone.comcast.net [68.86.85.193]
 13    32 ms    33 ms    34 ms  pos-0-2-0-0-pe01.56marietta.ga.ibone.comcast.net [68.86.86.166]
 14    33 ms    36 ms    32 ms  a96-17-75-25.deploy.akamaitechnologies.com [96.17.75.25]

Trace complete.

C:\Users\Richard>_
```

communicate directly across the Internet. The basic switch needs to be assisted by a router to reach a distant Internet address.

A multilayer switch typically has much simpler electronic components than a router. An additional electronic chip known as *Application Specific Integrated Circuit (ASIC)* is incorporated into the switch. The addition of the ASIC gives the layer 2 switch additional capabilities typically found at upper levels of the OSI model. Hence the name *multilayer switch*. The multilayer switches are generally limited to a specific task and have limited programmable functions. For example, a layer 2 switch with an ASIC can perform specific layer 3 functions necessary to pass frames associated with IP phone addresses to their appropriate location and to block all others.

Multilayer switches are referred to by many different ways such as *layer 3 switch*, *4-7 switch*, *layer 7 switch*, *URL switch*, *Web content switch*, and *content switch*.

A layer 3 switch has a dedicated function and can use IP information in addition to MAC information to route frames/packets. Since it uses the layer 3 IP address, it is commonly referred to as a *layer 3 switch*.

A content switch routes frames based on the content of the packet. For example, a content switch can be used for load balancing a cluster of Web servers. Another application might be to provide support for Voice over IP (VoIP) applications, providing dedicated ports, and ensuring maximum bandwidth for the VoIP application.

Other names for content switches are *4-7 switch* and *layer 7 switch* because they route frames based on applications that align with the upper layers of the OSI model, such as mail services, printing services, HTTPS, and video streaming.

Note

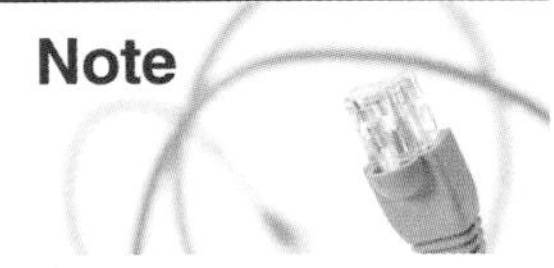

The CompTIA Network+ Certification uses the term *multilayer switch* in place of *content switch*. Read exam questions carefully and look for specific terms such as *basic switch*, *layer 3 switch*, and *content switch* as a clue to the correct answer. For example, a basic switch is limited to layer 2 functions while a content switch is related to higher level functions.

Router communications can be quite complex and require several semesters of study. This section was simply a short introduction of routers so that you might obtain a general understanding of their role in networking. Cisco Systems has a complete curriculum devoted to router studies and router programming. Visit the Cisco Networking Academy online to look at the contents of their complete certification program. The link to the Cisco Networking Academy is www.cisco.com/web/learning/netacad/index.html or conduct an Internet search using the key terms "Cisco Academy."

Virtual LAN

A ***Virtual Local Area Network (VLAN)*** is a broadcast domain created by one or more switches based on logical (MAC) addresses. VLANs are typically used to improve network performance by reducing the size of collision domains. VLANs can also be used to create secure subnets on shared network media.

Virtual Local Area Network (VLAN) a broadcast domain created by one or more switches based on logical (MAC) addresses.

Switches are the most common choice for the creation of a VLAN on a wired network. A VLAN is based on the layer 2 physical address (MAC). A switch automatically creates a VLAN for each physical port because each port isolates the transfer of frames. Each port sends frames to the attached devices by filtering the frame based on physical (MAC) address contained inside the frame. Broadcasts are sent to all devices based on the IP address. Look at **Figure 11-17.**

A broadcast domain is a segment of the network that forwards all broadcasts to all devices on that segment. In Figure 11-17, the switches forward broadcasts based on IP addresses. The typical broadcast IP address is 255.255.255.255. Notice how the router segments the network into two separate broadcast domains.

A switch can create virtual LANs based on the physical (MAC) address. Look at **Figure 11-18.** Notice how multiple VLANs have been created by the switches. Each port on a switch is assigned to a specific VLAN such as VLAN1 and VLAN2. You can connect to a programmable switch using the Telnet service. Once connected, you can assign ports to a specific VLAN. When a hub is connected to a specific port, the hub becomes part of that particular VLAN. All devices connected to the hub become part of the assigned VLAN.

Switches cannot connect to other switches in separate broadcast domains directly. A router is used to connect two or more switches that are in separate networks or separate domains. After connecting the switches together with a router, the switches can extend a VLAN connection to include devices in the other network. In **Figure 11-19**, you can see how a VLAN can be extended to a separate network switch.

This is a key difference between routers and switches. Routers can create networks and separate networks. Switches are confined to a single network. Remember that routers operate at layer 3 and communicate through IP addresses. Switches operate at layer 2 and communicate through MAC addresses. They are thus confined to a network and cannot route frames directly through the Internet.

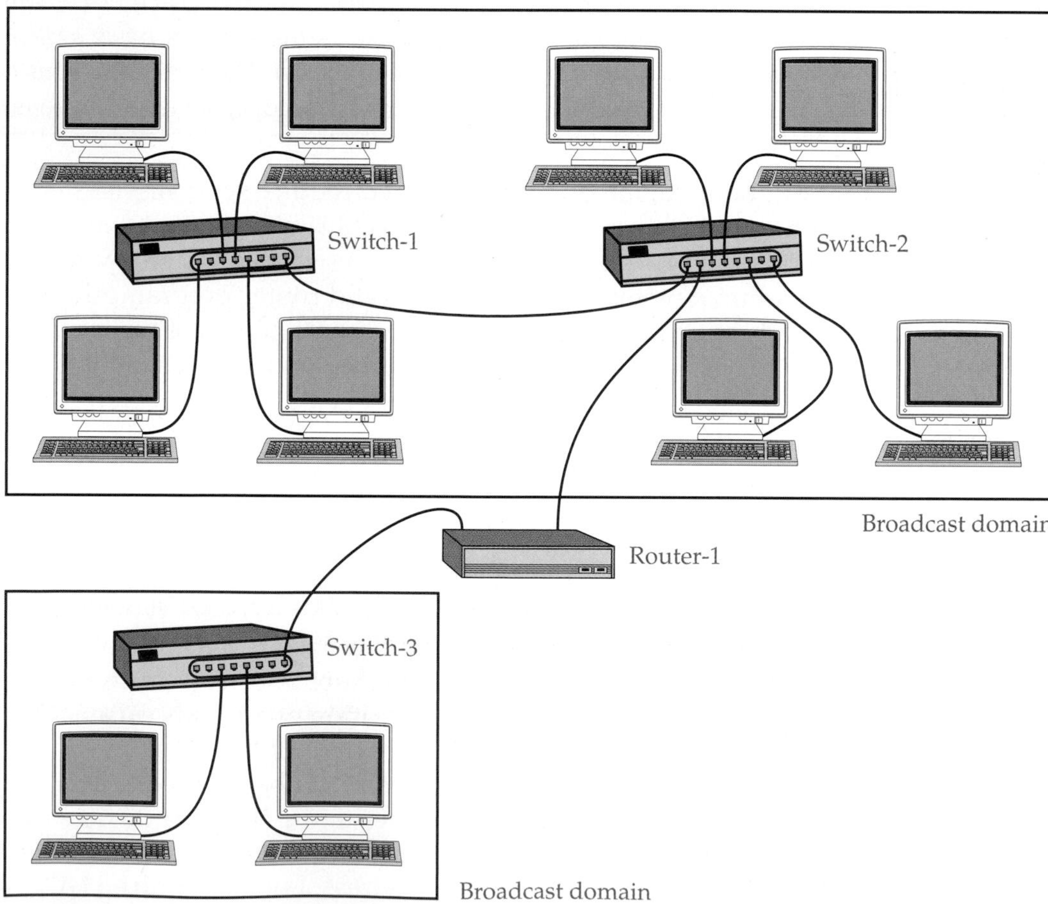

Figure 11-17.
A VLAN is created for each physical port on each switch shown. Each port sends frames to the attached device by filtering the frame based on the MAC address. Broadcasts are sent to all devices in a broadcast domain based on the IP addresses.

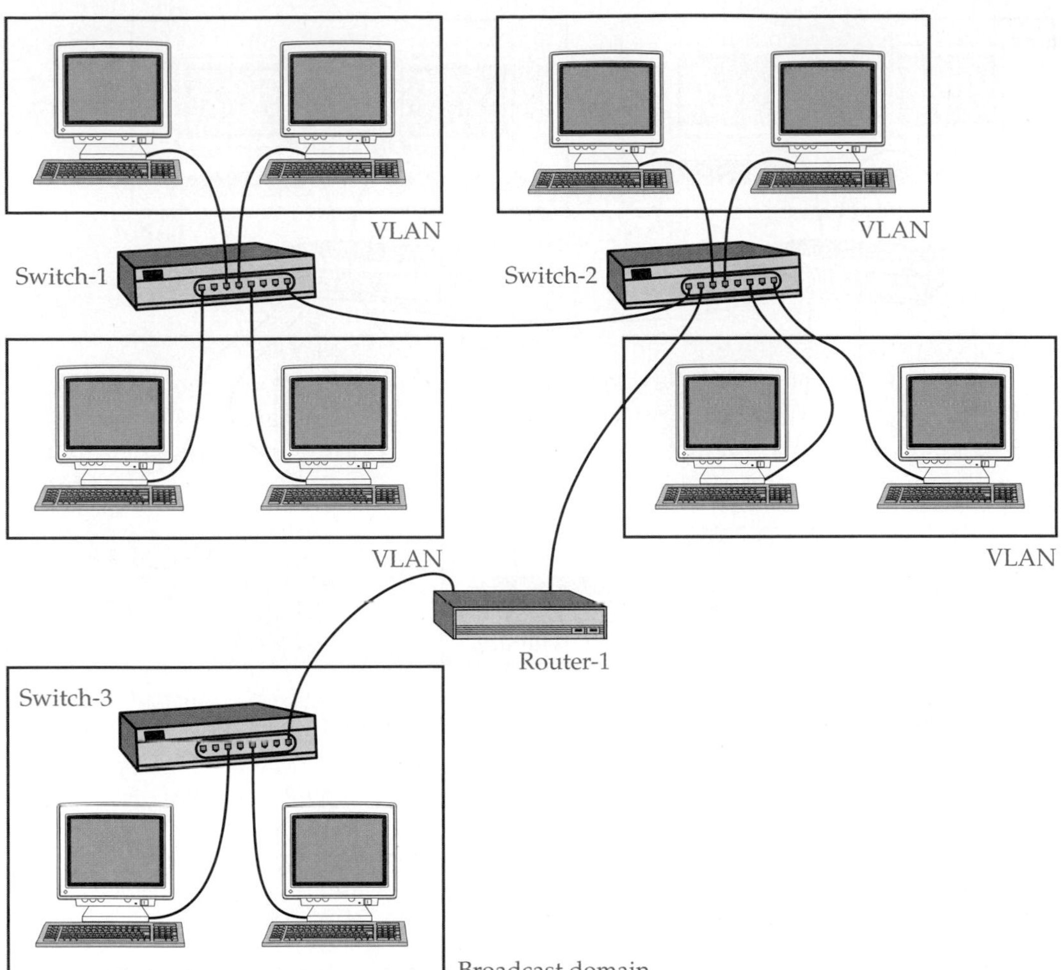

Figure 11-18. Multiple VLANs are created with switches based on MAC addresses. Each port on a switch is assigned to a specific VLAN such as VLAN1 or VLAN2.

Static vs. Dynamic VLAN

VLANs can be created statically or dynamically. A ***static VLAN*** is created when physical ports on a switch are assigned manually to a particular VLAN. A ***dynamic VLAN*** is created through software without the need of manual intervention. A dynamic VLAN will assign the device MAC address and the user name automatically to a VLAN. For example, when two devices are connected to two different ports on a switch and they exchange packets, the switch automatically assigns a default VLAN to these ports.

static VLAN created when physical ports on a switch are manually assigned to a particular VLAN.

dynamic VLAN created automatically using software by assigning the device MAC address and the user name to a VLAN.

VLAN Trunking

VLAN technology is described in the IEEE 802.1Q standard and is referred to as *VLAN Trunking*. The standard describes the use of VLAN tags to identify individual network sections or broadcast zones. ***Trunking*** is the technique of connecting different VLANs together using a single network link. Switches are connected to each other through a router or routers. The router then can be used to exchange information between switches using the Spanning Tree Protocol (STP), which is discussed in the following section. The cable that is used for trunking is referred to as the *trunk*. The ports used for trunking are referred to as the *trunk ports*.

trunking the technique of connecting different VLANs together using a single network link.

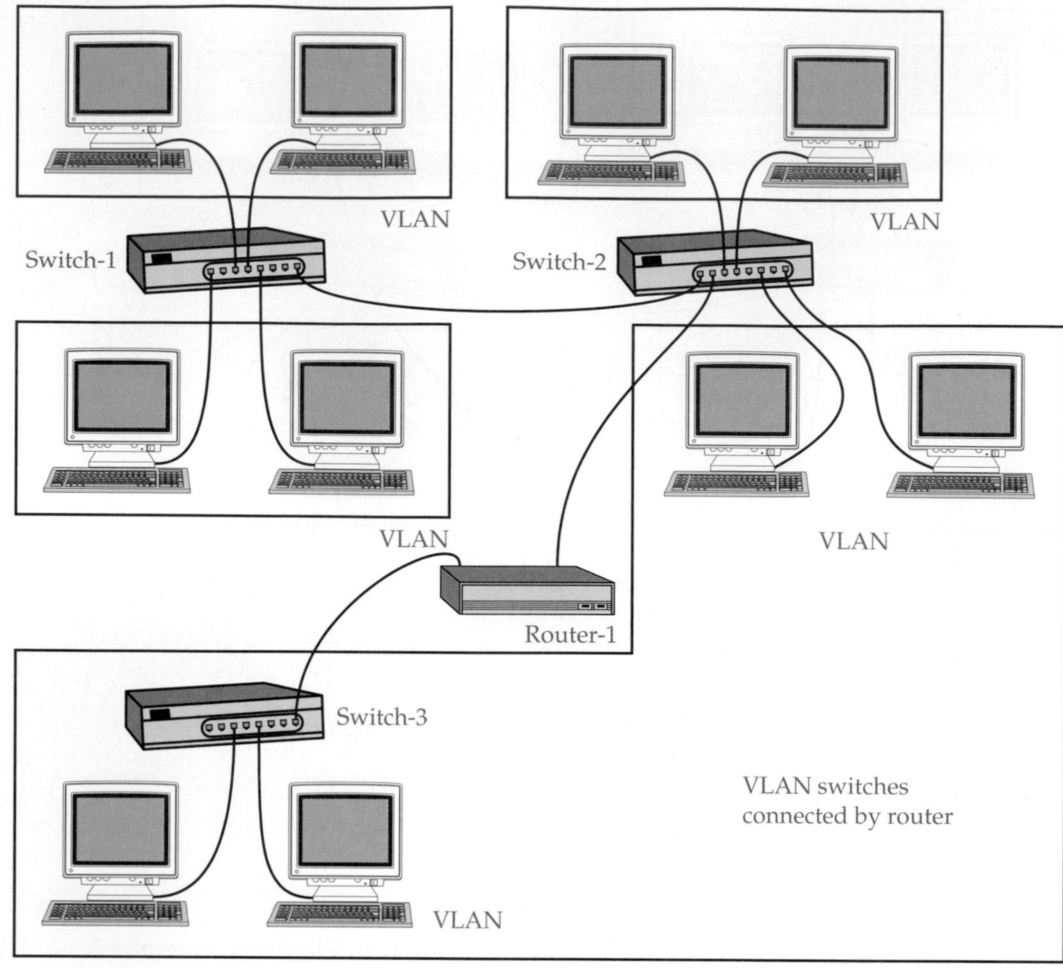

Figure 11-19. A router must be used to connect two or more switches that are in separate networks or separate domains. After connecting the switches together with a router, the switches can extend a VLAN connection to include devices in the other network.

Virtual Trunking Protocol (VTP) a proprietary protocol developed by Cisco Systems to provide automatic reconfiguration of multiple switches across an entire network.

Virtual Trunking Protocol (VTP) is a proprietary protocol developed by Cisco Systems that automatically reconfigures multiple switches across an entire network. This drastically reduces administration time when changes need to be made. A technician can make configuration changes to one switch. The switch will then automatically forward message packets to the other switches throughout the network to update its configurations.

Cisco VTP does not conform to the IEEE 802.1Q standard but rather exceeds it. Cisco switches typically can be configured to run in two different modes to ensure compatibility between legacy switches: IEEE 802.1Q mode and Cisco VTP mode. The 802.1Q mode restricts switches to communicating with MAC addresses and does not allow switches to communicate with other switches. Switches need to be connected together by routers to communicate. Cisco VTP controls the exchange of information such as switch tables between all switches without the need of a router to be directly connected to each switch. Cisco VTP mode allows for the direct connection of switches with or without the use of routers. Look at **Figure 11-20.** Notice that the router connects directly to the switch and then the switch connects directly to the next switch. This is referred to as *trunking*.

For very detailed information about the IEEE 802.1Q standard in PDF format, visit http://standards.ieee.org/getieee802/download/802.1Q-2005.pdf. You must log

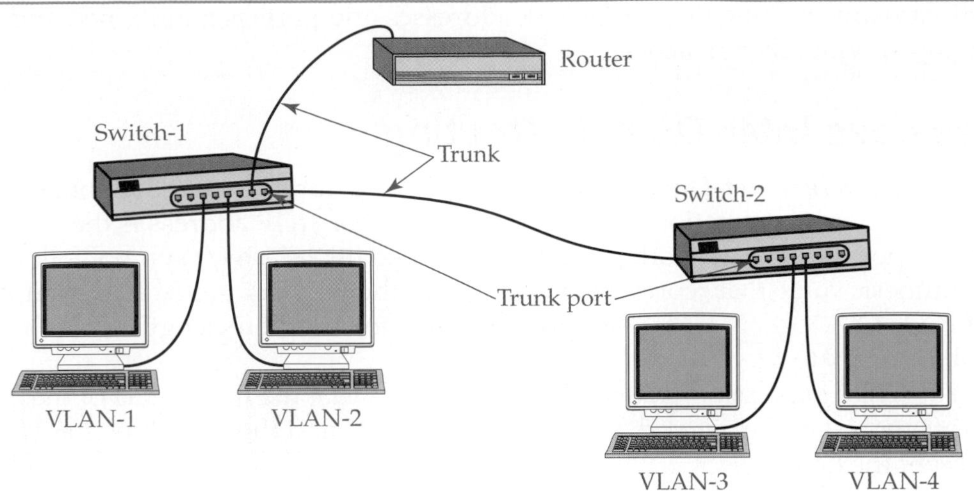

Figure 11-20. Cisco VTP mode allows for the direct connection of switches with or without the use of routers.

in first, but the Web site does not require any information other than identifying yourself as a student. Then you will be directed to the link.

Note

The IEEE 802.1Q standard treats switches as multiport bridges. You will see the term *bridge* used throughout the document. When you encounter the term *bridge* in the IEEE standard, you can think of a port on a switch.

Spanning Tree Protocol

The ***Spanning Tree Protocol (STP)*** is a layer 2 protocol designed to manage networks based on MAC addresses. STP was originally designed to prevent broadcast storms created from improperly-configured bridges and or switches. Bridges can be accidentally wired incorrectly, resulting in a physical network loop. When a network loop is created, frames are continually circulated in the loop causing a broadcast storm that renders the network inoperable.

Spanning Tree Protocol (STP) a layer 2 protocol designed to manage networks based on MAC addresses and to prevent bridge loops.

Switches that act as multiport bridges, are often intentionally configured with redundant connections or "loops" to provide a backup link in case one of the links fail. If the redundant links are misconfigured, the switch will send a continuous stream of packets, causing a bridge loop, also known as a *broadcast storm*. The Spanning Tree Protocol uses a special method to detect misconfigured backup links and prevent the creation of broadcast storms. Most misconfigurations occur when routers are added to a network with multiple switches. A misconfigured (incorrectly programmed) router will cause a broadcast storm.

The Spanning Tree Protocol prevents broadcast storms caused by network loops. The combination of the Spanning Tree Protocol and the Discovery Protocol(s) allows switches and routers to discover other network devices and to be self-programmed for the most appropriate configuration.

STP uses the Spanning Tree algorithm to determine and eliminate the presence of a physical or logical network loop. The algorithm calculates and compares MAC address locations to identify bridge and switch ports. The protocol then automatically assigns specific MAC address to specific ports and eliminates any existing loop. A table of addresses and ports is maintained and exchanged with other switches.

Classless Inter-Domain Routing

Classless Internet-Domain Routing (CIDR)
a special notation that identifies which part of an IP address is the network portion. The network portion is identified by a slash (/) symbol followed by a numeric value that represents the length of the network prefix. Also referred to as or *Variable Length Subnet Mask.*

Classless Internet-Domain Routing (CIDR) or Variable Length Subnet Mask uses a special notation to identify which part of an IP address is the network portion. The network portion is identified by a slash (/) symbol followed by a numeric value that represents the length of the network prefix. For example, XXX.XXX.XXX.XXX/N where *N* represents the network prefix length and is a number from *0* to *32*.

The CIDR expression 192.168.123.106/24 means that the first 24 bits of the address represent the network address or 192.168.123 and the last 8 bits, 106, represent the host.

The CIDR correlates to the IPv4 address by assuming each portion (octet) of the IPv4 address represents a maximum value of eight bits. To figure out the CIDR, simply think of each part of the IPv4 address of having a value of eight bits. For example, to figure out the CIDR for the network address 192.168.123 you would add together three values of eight:

$$8 + 8 + 8 = 24$$

Figure 11-21 shows examples of how the subnet mask is derived based on the CIDR. Notice that as each of the binary patterns are reduced by one, the final octet representing the subnet mask also changes. For example, look at the subnet mask and binary pattern for 255.255.254.0. The complete binary form of the network portion of 255.255.254.0 is 11111111.11111111.11111110. Adding the bits together octet by octet, we have the following:

$$8 + 8 + 7 = 23$$

Thus, the CIDR notation will be /23 for the IPv4 address represented by the subnet mask of 255.255.254.0. See **Figure 11-22** for a table of CIDR lengths and related subnet masks.

Figure 11-21.
Deriving the CIDR from a subnet mask

Subnet Mask	Binary Pattern	CIDR	
255.255.255.0	11111111.11111111.11111111.00000000	8+8+8	**/24**
255.255.254.0	11111111.11111111.11111110.00000000	8+8+7	**/23**
255.255.252.0	111111111.11111111.11111100.00000000	8+8+6	**/22**
255.255.248.0	111111111.11111111.11111000.00000000	8+8+5	**/21**
255.255.240.0	11111111.11111111.11110000.00000000	8+8+4	**/20**
255.255.224.0	11111111.11111111.11100000.00000000	8+8+3	**/19**
255.255.192.0	11111111.111111111.11000000.00000000	8+8+2	**/18**
255.255.128.0	11111111.11111111.10000000.00000000	8+8+1	**/17**

CIDR Length	Subnet Mask	# of Networks	Class	# of Hosts
/1	128.0.0.0	128	A	2,147,483,392
/2	192.0.0.0	64	A	1,073,741,696
/3	224.0.0.0	32	A	536,870,848
/4	240.0.0.0	16	A	268,435,424
/5	248.0.0.0	8	A	134,217,712
/6	252.0.0.0	4	A	67,108,856
/7	254.0.0.0	2	A	33,554,428
/8	255.0.0.0	1	A	16,777,214
/9	255.128.0.0	128	B	8,388,352
/10	255.192.0.0	64	B	4,194,176
/11	255.224.0.0	32	B	2,097,088
/12	255.240.0.0	16	B	1,048,544
/13	255.248.0.0	8	B	524,272
/14	255.252.0.0	4	B	262,136
/15	255.254.0.0	2	B	131,068
/16	255.255.0.0	1	B	65,024
/17	255.255.128.0	128	C	32,512
/18	255.255.192.0	64	C	16,256
/19	255.255.224.0	32	C	8,128
/20	255.255.240.0	16	C	4,064
/21	255.255.248.0	8	C	2,032
/22	255.255.252.0	4	C	1,016
/23	255.255.254.0	2	C	508
/24	255.255.255.0	1	C	254
/25	255.255.255.128	2	C subnets	124
/26	255.255.255.192	4	C subnets	62
/27	255.255.255.224	8	C subnets	30
/28	255.255.255.240	16	C subnets	14
/29	255.255.255.248	32	C subnets	6
/30	255.255.255.252	64	C subnets	2
/31	255.255.255.254*	NA	NA	NA
/32	255.255.255.255*	NA	NA	NA

*255.255.255.255 and 255.255.255.254 reserved for broadcast.

Figure 11-22. CDIR table for IPv4 networks.

Link Aggregation

link aggregation when two or more network cables are paralleled to increase bandwidth and provide redundancy.

Link aggregation is when two or more network cables are paralleled to increase bandwidth and provide redundancy. For example, a server can be configured with two network adapters and then the two cables can be run to two ports on a switch. This configuration results in twice as much bandwidth available to the devices connected through the switch.

Link aggregation is a great way to increase bandwidth for network backbones. The redundancy ensures availability when one of the cables or connections fails. A switch can be placed on each end of the backbone and multiple cables can be connected to each switch.

Tech Tip

You should always completely configure both ends of a link aggregation before physically connecting the switches together. If you physically connect the two switches first and then configure the link aggregation, a network loop could be created, causing a broadcast storm and packet loss.

Summary

- The subnet mask uses a series of ones to identify the network portion of an IP address and a series of zeros to identify the host portion.
- To create a subnet, bits are borrowed from the host portion of an IP address to expand the network portion of the IP address.
- An IP address with all zeros in the host portion cannot be assigned to any network device.
- An IP address with all ones in the host portion cannot be assigned to any network device.
- A Fixed Length Subnet Mask (FLSM) has two or more equal-sized subnets.
- A Variable Length Subnet Mask (VLSM) occurs when you create additional subnets from a subnet.
- Subnetting provides security because subnetworks cannot be seen from outside the subnetwork.
- Subnetting reduces network traffic by isolating broadcasts to each subnet.
- Bridges and switches are layer 2 devices that filter frames based on physical (MAC) addresses.
- Routers are layer 3 devices and filter frames based on logical addresses (IP addresses).
- A router is used to connect switches that are located in a separate network.
- Routers make decisions based on source and destination IP addresses.
- Routers do not forward broadcasts and, therefore, reduce collision domains.
- A router metric is the mechanism used to determine or measure the best route.
- A metric calculation may be based on but not limited to throughput, reliability, packet loss, latency, and number of hops.
- A hop is a device such as a router located in the network path between the destination and the source.

- Two basic routing protocol classifications are Interior Gateway Protocol (IGP) and Exterior Gateway Protocol (EGP).
- An autonomous network is a network under one authority.
- RIP is one of the oldest router protocols and determines the best path based on number of hops.
- EIGRP is a sophisticated routing protocol that guarantees loop-free operation.
- An Application Specific Integrated Circuit (ASIC) is incorporated into a switch to expand its function.
- A multilayer switch is a dedicated switch that uses IP information and packet contents to route frames or packets.
- A Virtual LAN (VLAN) is a communication path between workstations on separate or the same network segment.
- Switches can be used to create VLANs.
- Switch loops are generally caused by misconfigured routers and switches or corrupt data.
- Spanning Tree Protocol detects and corrects switch loops.
- Link aggregation is when two or more network cables are paralleled to increase bandwidth and provide redundancy.

Review Questions

Answer the following questions on a separate sheet of paper. Please do not write in this book.

1. Convert the following binary bit patterns to decimal number values. Do *not* use a calculator for this activity. You may use the following tables for support.

1	1	1	1	1	1	1	1
128	64	32	16	8	4	2	1

1	0	0	1	0	1	0	1
128	0	0	16	0	4	0	1

A.

0	0	0	0	1	1	0	0

B.

0	0	0	0	1	1	1	1

C.

1	1	0	0	0	0	0	0

D.

0	0	0	1	0	1	0	1

E.

1	1	0	1	1	1	1	1

2. A subnet mask can be divided into two descriptive sections. What are the two sections called?
3. Why would a network administrator create subnets?
4. What do the binary ones in a subnet mask indicate?
5. What do the binary zeros in a subnet mask indicate?
6. Using the information provided, identify which part of the IP address 190.134.124.112 with a subnet mask of 255.255.255.0 is the network address and which part is the host address?
7. How many bits are borrowed from a Class B host address to create 30 new subnets?
8. How many bits are borrowed from a Class C host address to create 6 new subnets?
9. How many subnets can be formed using a subnet mask of 255.255.255.224 for a Class C network and using hardware that allows the use of all zeros and all ones in the network portion of the subnet mask?
10. How many hosts are created from the following Class C subnet mask: 255.255.255.240?
11. A network administrator decides to partition an existing Class C network into six equal parts. Each part of the network must hold at least 22 computers. What subnet mask must be used to satisfy the requirement?
12. How many subnets can be created from the following Class C subnet mask: 255.255.255.224?
13. How many subnets can be created from the following Class C subnet mask: 255.255.255.248?
14. What is the difference between a router and a layer 3 switch?
15. What is an autonomous network?
16. A bridge filters frames based on which type of address?
17. A switch filters frames based on which type of address?
18. What IEEE term is used to represent individual ports on a switch?
19. A router filters frames based on which type of address?
20. What is a VLAN?
21. How many VLANs are created by default on a network switch?
22. At which layer of the OSI model do bridges and switches operate?
23. At which layer of the OSI model do routers operate?
24. What is a broadcast domain?
25. Name three devices that will forward a broadcast?
26. Name one device that will not forward a broadcast?
27. Which IGP router protocol uses only hop count to determine the best path?
28. What is the difference between an Interior Gateway Protocol and an Exterior Gateway Protocol?
29. Name four IGP protocols.
30. What network class is represented by the following CIDR: XXX.XXX.XXX.XXX/16?
31. What is the network portion of 179.124.244.2/16?
32. What is the host portion of 179.124.244.2/16?

Sample Network+ Exam Questions

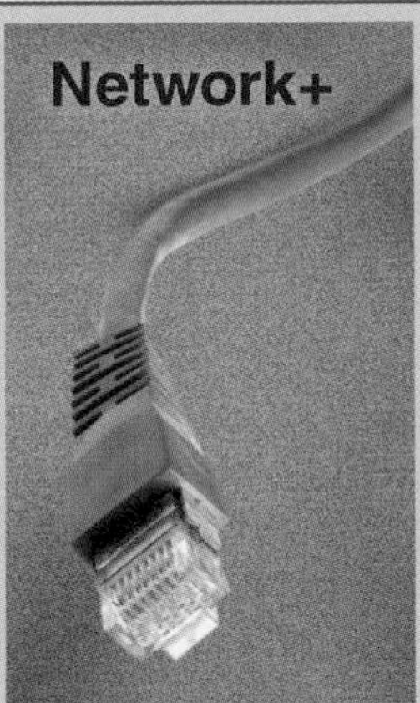

Answer the following questions on a separate sheet of paper. Please do not write in this book.

1. What subnet mask is used to identify a typical Class A network and host?
   A. 255.255.255.255
   B. 255.255.255.0
   C. 255.255.0.0
   D. 255.0.0.0
2. Which devices can filter network frames? (Select two.)
   A. Hub
   B. Repeater
   C. Bridge
   D. Switch
   E. Router
3. What is the network class *most likely* associated with the IP address 150.150.23.34? (Hint: The network class can be identified by the first octet.)
   A. Class A
   B. Class B
   C. Class C
   D. Class D
4. Which of the following IP addresses is a reserved address and cannot be used when connecting to the Internet?
   A. 123.001.001.21
   B. 192.168.0.23
   C. 154.23.168.32
   D. 200.200.200.200
5. What is the host address for an IP address of 199.200.12.45 with a subnet mask of 255.255.255.0?
   A. 199.200.12
   B. 45
   C. 255.255.255
   D. .0
6. What subnet mask is used to identify a typical Class B network and host?
   A. 255.255.255.255
   B. 255.255.255.0
   C. 255.255.0.0
   D. 255.0.0.0
7. What is the network class *most likely* associated with the IP address 198.150.25.10? (Hint: The network class can be identified by the first octet.)
   A. Class A
   B. Class B
   C. Class C
   D. Class D
8. Which protocol is designed to prevent switch loops?
   A. ICMP
   B. STP
   C. FTP
   D. SSL

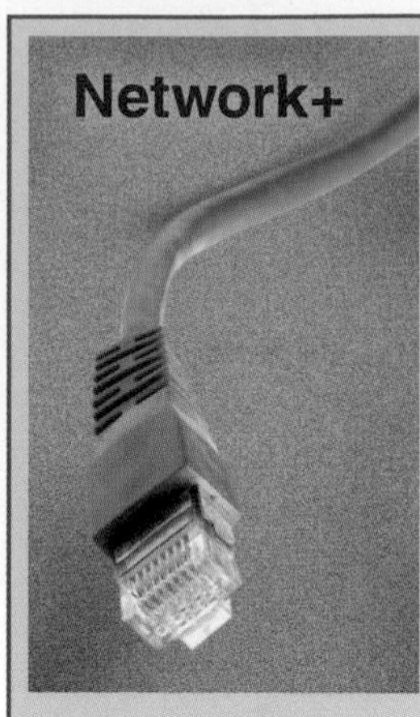

9. What does a router use to determine the best route?
   A. Metric
   B. Vector
   C. MAC address
   D. TTL
10. Which two are link state router protocols?
   A. RIP
   B. OSPF
   C. IS-IS
   D. RIPng

Interesting Web Sites for More Information

www.3com.com
www.boson.com/FreeUtilities.html
www.cisco.com
www.faqs.org/rfcs/rfc1878.html
www.solarwinds.net
www.subnet-calculator.com
www.subnetmask.info
www.wildpackets.com/products/ipsubnetcalculator

Suggested Laboratory Activities

1. Create two subnets using the reserved IP address 192.168.0.0. This should be a team project. You will need one PC acting as a server and two or more PCs to serve as workstations in different subnets.
2. Install Internet Connection Sharing (ICS). Use at least two computers: one for the host and the other for the client.

Chapter 11 Laboratory Activity

Subnet Mask Calculator

After completing this laboratory activity, you will be able to:

- Carry out installation procedures for the WildPackets IP Subnet Calculator.
- Use the WildPackets IP Subnet Calculator to determine the number of hosts and subnetworks associated with a given subnet mask.
- Interpret the binary pattern associated with a given subnet mask or IP address.

Introduction

In this laboratory activity, you will download the WildPackets IP Subnet Calculator from the WildPackets Web site and install it. The calculator is free. If the WildPackets IP Subnet Calculator is not available, you can conduct an Internet search to locate another subnet calculator. The WildPackets IP Subnet Calculator is a very handy utility.

> ***Note***
> *While the Network+ Certification exam does not require network subnet mask calculations at this time, some other network certifications do require subnet mask calculations by hand. You cannot use a calculator during these exams. Always check for the latest test specifications concerning this area.*

The calculations for subnets can be very difficult for students and also for many technicians. It is one of the most difficult aspects of networking fundamentals. However, the concept of creating a subnet out of an assigned IP address is very simple. The subnet mask is divided into two portions: the network portion and the host portion. For example, the subnet mask of a typical Class C network is 255.255.255.0. Each of the first three octets has the number *255* representing the network portion of the subnet mask and the number *0*, representing the host portion of the subnet mask. The value 255 is equal to eight binary ones (11111111), or an entire octet filled with ones. The series of ones represents the network portion of the subnet mask.

To create a subnet from a Class C network assignment, the host assignment of 0 is changed to some other value, such as 160, 192, or 224. The new value extends the network portion into the host portion of an assigned address. Remember, when subnetting, bits are borrowed from the host portion of an IP address. The borrowed bits are the extended portion of the network address. In a Class C subnet mask, this means that the fourth octet will begin (starting at the left of the octet) with a series of ones.

To calculate the decimal number that represents the series of binary ones is difficult for most people, especially if they do not have a background in digital electronics. This is where the WildPackets IP Subnet Calculator comes in handy. The calculator allows you to choose a class of network, such as Class A, Class B, or Class C, and select the number of subnets you desire. The WildPackets IP

Subnet Calculator instantly gives you all the information you need. Let's see how this is done.

When provided with an IP address, the calculator immediately displays the network class, the bit-map pattern of the host and network, and the hexadecimal equivalent of the address. The following screen capture shows the information given for the IP address 128.15.10.5.

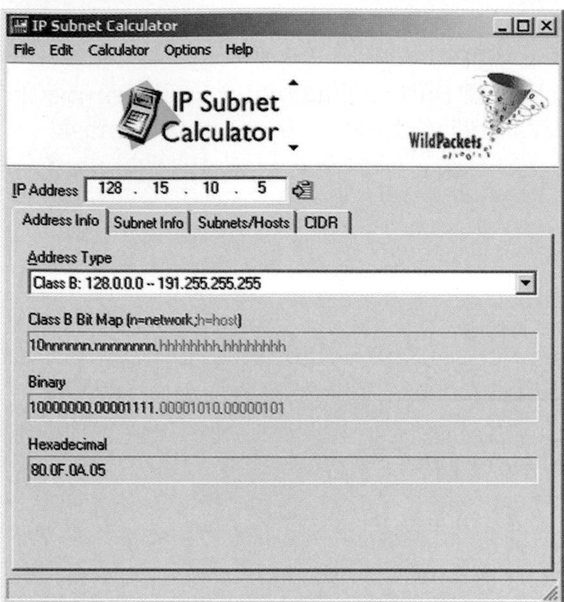

Now look at the next screen capture. Notice the tabs beneath the **IP Address** textbox. The **Subnet Info** tab allows you to enter values for the calculation such as the number of subnets required or the number of hosts required for each subnet. These two values are the main values you will typically work with.

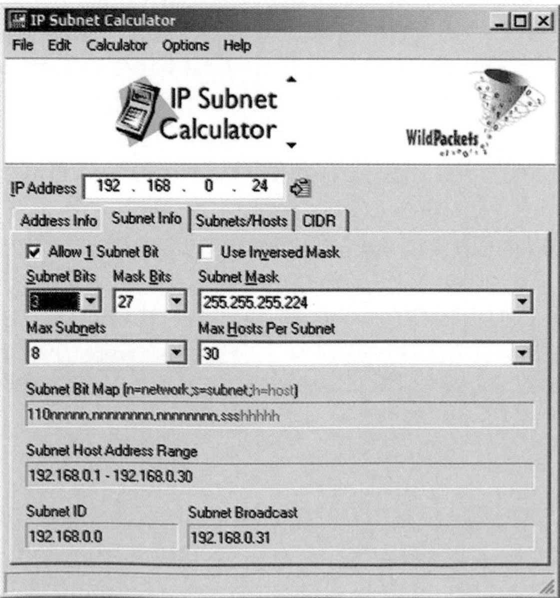

Network	Network	Network	Host	
NA	NA	NA	0000000000	**All zeros**
NA	NA	NA	0100000000	
NA	NA	NA	1000000000	
NA	NA	NA	1100000000	**All ones**

Note: NA = Not Applicable

Notice the **Allow 1 Subnet Bit** option. This option allows all zeros and all ones to be used in the extended portion of a network address. Look at the following table. Notice the first two binary positions of the host portion of the address.

Originally, all zeros and all ones were not allowed in the lead position of the host address used for subnetting. The binary pattern containing all zeros and all ones were reserved values. A bit pattern of all zeros is typically used for special functions, such as a temporary address of a network card when it is configured for an automatic IP address assignment from a DHCP server. Some routers recognize the use of the binary one in the first part network address as reserved for broadcasts. Today, the generally-accepted convention is to allow all zeros and ones. Notice in the previous table that four subnets can be created when all zeros and ones are allowed.

Note

While running the laboratory activity, select and deselect the **Allow 1 Subnet Bit** *option to see the effect on the number of hosts and subnetworks.*

Now look at the following screen capture. Notice that a complete list of all possible host IP addresses is automatically listed under the **Subnets/Hosts** tab. As you can see, the WildPackets IP Subnet Calculator is a handy tool. The best way to learn how to use this calculator is by downloading it and experimenting with different scenarios.

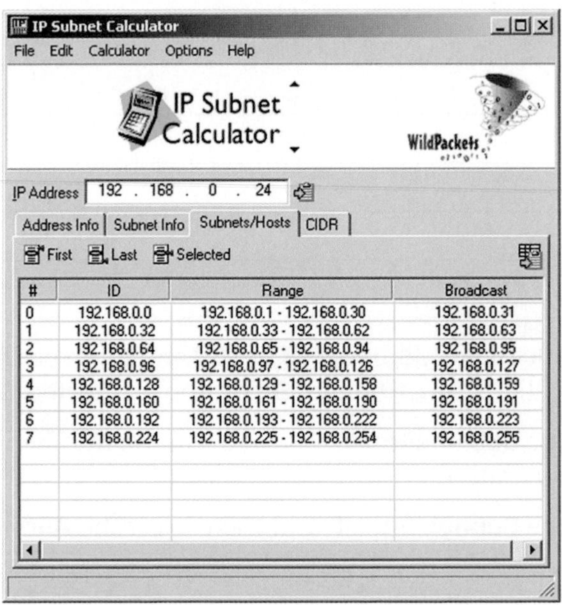

Equipment and Materials

- Computer with Internet access.
- E-mail address. (An e-mail address is typically required by WildPackets. The e-mail address is used to supply a user name and password for completing the download and the installation of the software package.)

Procedure

1. ______ Report to your assigned workstation.
2. ______ Boot the computer and verify it is in working order.
3. ______ Use the following URL to locate the WildPackets IP Subnet Calculator: www.wildpackets.com. The WildPackets IP Subnet Calculator is found under the Resources | Free Utilities link.
4. ______ Download and install the WildPackets IP Subnet Calculator.
5. ______ Open the WildPackets IP Subnet Calculator program.
6. ______ In the IP Address textbox, enter the following IP addresses and identify the class of network for each. Record your answers on a separate sheet of paper.

IP Address	Network Class
192.168.0.0	
202.111.0.0	
68.0.0.0	
234.0.0.0	
254.0.0.0	
127.1.1.1	
126.0.0.0	
128.0.0.0	
192.0.0.0	
191.0.0.0	

7. ______ Now, enter the IP address 192.168.0.0 and then select the **Subnet Info** tab. Check if the **Allow 1 Subnet Bit** option is selected. If it is, deselect it.
8. ______ Select the **Subnets/Hosts** tab to reveal the number of subnets and hosts generated.
9. ______ Select the **Subnet Info** tab and then select the **Allow 1 Subnet Bit** option.
10. ______ Return to the **Subnets/Hosts** tab and observe the effect on the total number of hosts and subnets.

11. ______ Experiment with the calculator.
12. ______ When you have finished experimenting with the calculator, answer the review questions.
13. ______ Return your workstation to its original condition.

Review Questions

Answer the following questions on a separate sheet of paper. Please do not write in this book.

1. What is the generally-accepted convention of having all zeros and ones in the extended portion of a network address?
2. What is the number of hosts for any Class C network?
3. What is the maximum number of hosts for one subnet on a Class C network that has been divided into two subnets?
4. What is the maximum number of hosts for one subnet on a Class C network that has been divided into six subnets?
5. What is the maximum number of hosts for a Class C network that has been divided into 14 subnets?
6. A Class C network is divided into six equal subnets. What is the range of IP addresses of host IP assignments for the first subnet when the **Allow 1 Subnet Bit** option is selected?
7. A Class C network is divided into six equal subnets. What is the range of IP addresses of host IP assignments for the first subnet when the **Allow 1 Subnet Bit** option is not selected?
8. What is the broadcast IP address of the first IP range for a Class C network that is divided into six equal subnets with the **Allow 1 Subnet Bit** option selected?
9. What decimal number is represented by 11110000?
10. What decimal number is represented by 01000000?

The InterNIC Web site (www.internic.net) hosts a Whois search engine. The Whois engine provides information about registered domains, registars, and name servers.

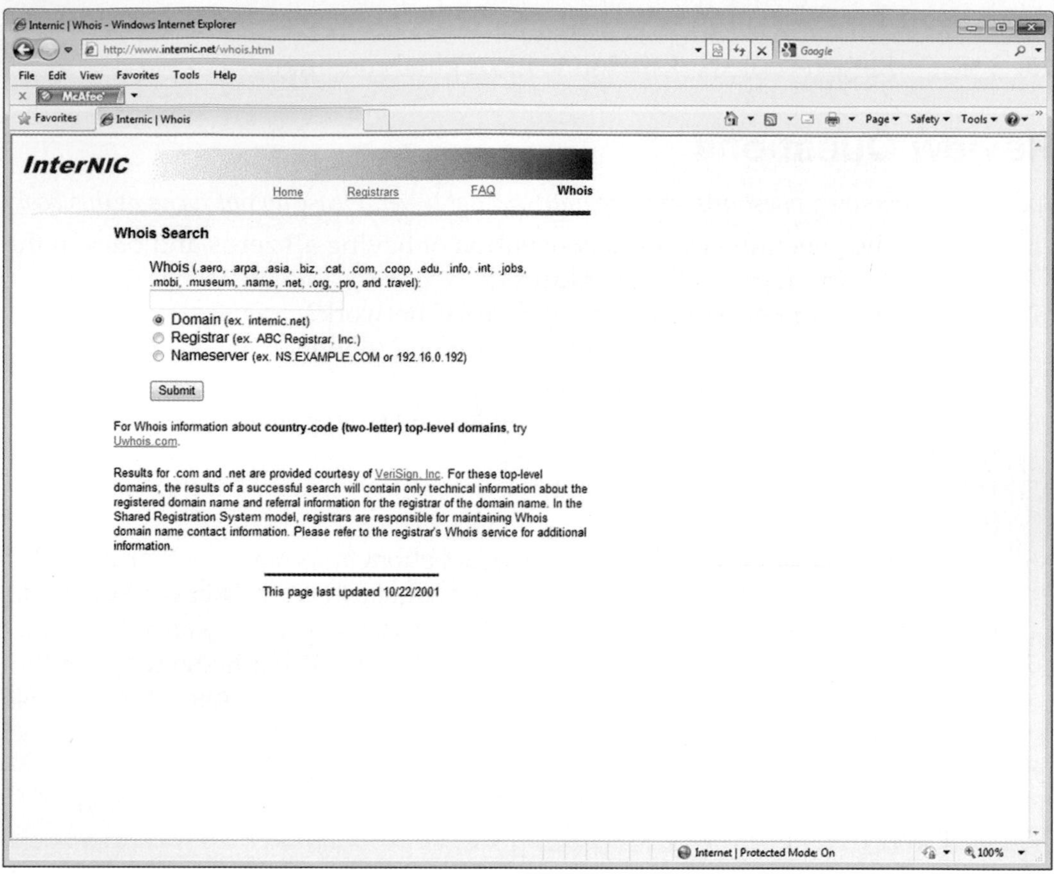

12 Multimedia Transmission

After studying this chapter, you will be able to:

- ❑ Explain how signals are converted between analog and digital.
- ❑ Explain how latency affects the transfer of audio and video signals.
- ❑ Explain how data is compressed and decompressed.
- ❑ Recall the purpose and characteristics of multimedia transmission protocols X.25, Frame Relay, ATM, VoIP, RTP, and SIP.
- ❑ Apply proper troubleshooting methods to identify and fix multimedia transmission problems.
- ❑ Recall the purpose and characteristics of a bandwidth shaper.

Network+ Exam—Key Points

There will most likely be at least one question concerning the transfer of multimedia across a network system. Since ATM is used extensively to transport multimedia, be prepared to answer questions about the ATM protocol and multiplexing.

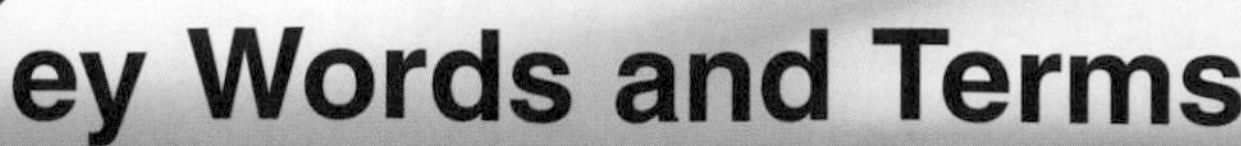

Key Words and Terms

The following words and terms will become important pieces of your networking vocabulary. Be sure you can define them.

acoustical echo
Analog-to-Digital Converter (ADC)
Asynchronous Transfer Mode (ATM)
Available Bit Rate (ABR)
bandwidth shaper
bit rate
codec (compressor/decompressor)
Committed Information Rate (CIR)
Constant Bit Rate (CBR)
Digital-to-Analog Converter (DAC)
Frame Relay
hard phone
H.323
impedance mismatch
jitter
latency
MPEG (Moving Picture Experts Group)
permanent virtual circuit (PVC)
Public Switched Telephone Network (PSTN)
Quality of Service (QoS)
Real-time Transport Protocol (RTP)
sampling frequency
sampling rate
Session Initiation Protocol (SIP)
soft phone
telephone gateway
Unspecified Bit Rate (UBR)
Variable Bit Rate (VBR)
Variable Bit Rate-Non Real Time (VBR-NRT)
Variable Bit Rate-Real Time (VBR-RT)
Voice over IP (VoIP)
X.25

This chapter introduces network technologies that support the transfer of audio, video, and multimedia (a mixture of audio, video, text, and images). When transferring these types of data, there are some concerns that are not found in typical file transfer situations consisting of text only documents. The beginning of the chapter introduces some basic concepts about audio and video that will help you better understand the technologies used to transport multimedia. Later in the chapter, protocols such as X.25, Frame Relay, ATM, and VoIP and the technologies that support them are introduced.

This area of networking can be quite complex and challenging. It is the fastest growing area of network technology. Soon, all industries, such as telephone, television, music, and movie, will use network technology to deliver their data all over the world. Individuals are already using personal Web cams to transmit video anywhere in the world. Telephone calls can be made to any location a computer can reach without necessarily using the standard telephone systems. Data can also be sent across existing telephone lines or a mixture of network, telephone, and wireless systems. As you will see, the transfer of audio, video, and multimedia requires special techniques.

Voice and Audio Signals

Anyone reading this sentence has most likely transmitted their voice over a section of network owned by a long-distance telephone company. Digitizing a voice and transporting it over existing telephone lines began in the early 1970s. It was brought on in part by the rapid development of digital electronics.

The human voice and other audio signals are analog signals. Remember from earlier chapters: an analog signal fluctuates in amplitude (voltage level). For an audio signal (analog signal) to be transported across a network system, it must be converted into a series of digital pulses that represent the analog waveform. After the digital pulses reach their destination, the digital pulses must be converted into an analog signal so that the human ear can detect and understand it.

Converting digital pulses to an analog waveform is called *digital-to-analog conversion*. Converting an analog waveform to digital pulses is called *analog-to-digital conversion*. The following section takes a closer look at both of these processes.

Signal Conversion

Audio signals must be converted into digital signals and placed in packets before transmitted across a network. When the packets of digital signals reach their destination, they are reassembled and converted into an analog signal. The quality of the analog signal depends on the detail of the digital coding.

The analog signal is converted into a digital code by taking samples of the analog signal's amplitude at specific times. The number of times the sample is taken during a specific period is referred to as the ***sampling rate.*** The number of bits used to represent the amplitude of the analog signal is referred to as ***bit rate, bit resolution,*** or ***bit depth.*** The quality of the sound conversion is directly related to the sampling rate and the bit resolution. In other words, the higher the sampling rate and the greater the bit resolution, the better the sound.

sampling rate
the number of times during a specific period that a sample of a signal's amplitude is taken.

bit rate
the number of bits used to represent the amplitude of an analog signal.

sampling frequency
the number of times per second that a sample of a signal's amplitude is taken.

How often amplitude is measured per second is called ***sampling frequency.*** Sampling frequency varies significantly. A typical voice sampling frequency is approximately 11 kHz, or 11,000 times per second. The sampling frequency of quality sound applications, such as music, is approximately 44 kHz. Look at **Figure 12-1.**

A typical human voice or any other audio signal fluctuates over a period of time. Figure 12-1A shows how an audio signal's amplitude is plotted against time. Amplitude is plotted vertically on the graph, and the time period is plotted horizontally on the graph. The quality of the analog-to-digital conversion depends on the sampling frequency, which is based on the number of bits available to store the sampling.

Compare the two sampling rates in Figure 12-1B and Figure 12-1C. Notice that the low sampling rate has fewer sampling points than the high sampling rate. The high sampling rate contains more sampling points to represent the original analog signal. As the sampling rate increases, a better representation of the original signal is made.

The maximum number of sampling points represented in digital form depends on the number of bits used to represent the analog signal at any given point of time. The maximum number of possible bits per sample represents the bit rate. The higher the number of bits used, the better the digital description of the analog signal. For example, if only 4 bits are used to represent the voltage level, a total of 16 distinct voltage levels are represented. Four bits can have a maximum of 16 binary patterns. Look at **Figure 12-2.** Notice that 16 voltage levels (0 volts

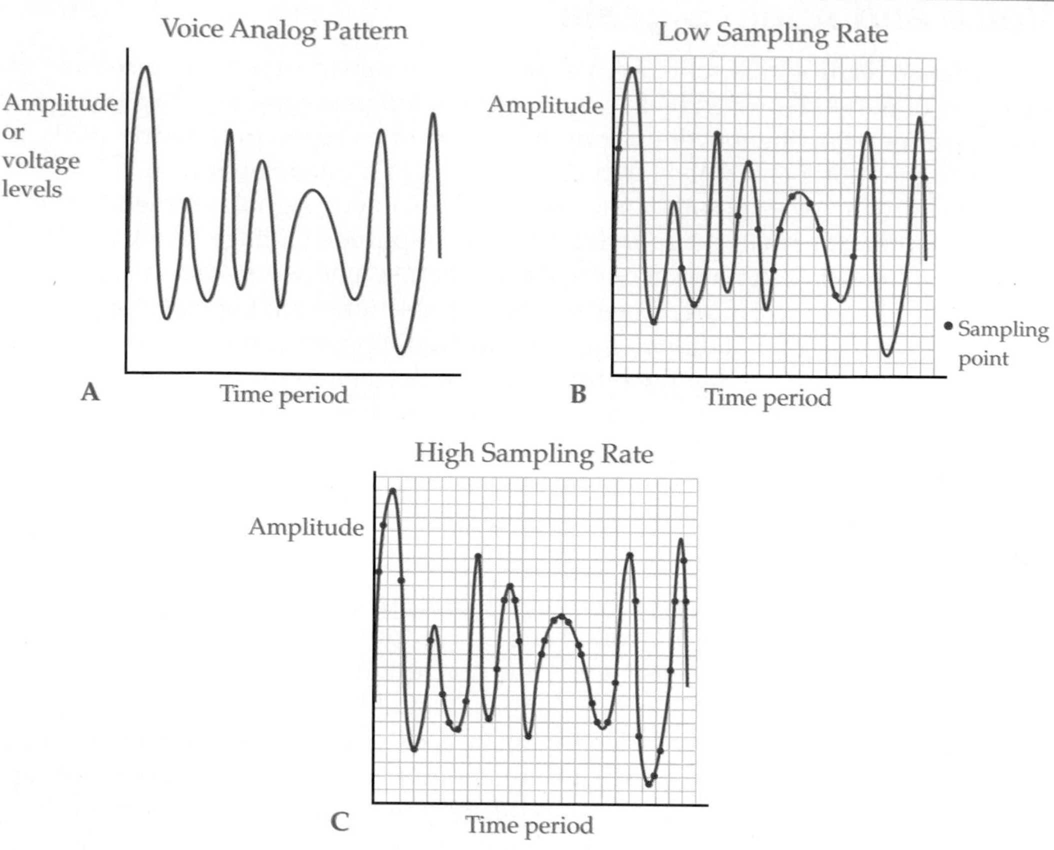

Figure 12-1. The sampling rate of the human voice. A—In this graph, the amplitude of the human voice is plotted on the vertical axis. The time period represents the frequency of the human voice and is plotted on the horizontal axis. B—This graph depicts a low sampling rate. Each point on the graph represents the point at which a sample is taken. C—This graph depicts a high sampling rate. In a high sampling rate, more data about the original signal is collected.

Figure 12-2. Voltage levels, 0 volts through 15 volts, represented by 4-bit binary patterns.

Voltage Level	Binary Code
0 volts	0000
1 volts	0001
2 volts	0010
3 volts	0011
4 volts	0100
5 volts	0101
6 volts	0110
7 volts	0111
8 volts	1000
9 volts	1001
10 volts	1010
11 volts	1011
12 volts	1100
13 volts	1101
14 volts	1110
15 volts	1111

through 15 volts) are represented by 16, 4-bit binary patterns. A distinct binary pattern represents each voltage level. Now look at **Figure 12-3.** In this example, 8 bits are used to represent the voltage levels 0 volts through 15 volts. A maximum of 256 distinct voltage levels are represented. Notice the intervals at which the voltage

Voltage Level	Binary Code
0 volts	0000 0000
0.05859 volts	0000 0001
0.11718 volts	0000 0010
0.17577 volts	0000 0011
0.23436 volts	0000 0100
0.29295 volts	0000 0101
0.35154 volts	0000 0110
0.41013 volts	0000 0111
0.46872 volts	0000 1000
0.52731 volts	0000 1001
0.58594 volts	0000 1010
0.64449 volts	0000 1011
0.70308 volts	0000 1100
0.05859 volts	0000 1101
0.82026 volts	0000 1110
0.87885 volts	0000 1111
0.93744 volts	0001 0000
0.99603 volts	0001 0001
1.05462 volts	0001 0010
↓	↓
14.94141 volts	1111 1110
15 volts	1111 1111

Figure 12-3.
Voltage levels, 0 volts through 15 volts, represented by 8-bit binary patterns.

increases. In the first example, the voltage increases by 1 volt with each increment. In this example, the voltage increases by 0.05859 volts with each increment. If 16 bits are used, a total of 65,536 levels can be used to represent voltage levels 0 volts through 15 volts. With each increment, the voltage level would increase by 0.000229 volts. Therefore, the greater the number of bits used, the more levels of voltage can be sampled, resulting in a better representation of the analog signal.

The human analog voice can be converted to a digital signal using a relatively low sampling rate. Originally, speech was recorded using an 8-bit, or 1-byte, voltage level at a low frequency such as 11 kHz. This resulted in a poor but acceptable quality of recorded voice.

Today, higher sampling rates are used to achieve higher sound quality. As you can see in **Figure 12-4,** quality sound equal to recording studio levels can be achieved through sampling rates and bit depth such as "2 channel, 24-bit, 48000 Hz."

When working with sounds that require a high degree of quality, such as music and singing voices, a high sampling rate is needed. Musical instruments have a much wider range of fluctuating sound patterns compared with human speech. Look at **Figure 12-5.** You can see high rates for speakers, which improve the quality of sound for the listener. A 24-bit, 48-kHz output is constructed from a sampling rate as high as 1.5 Mbps.

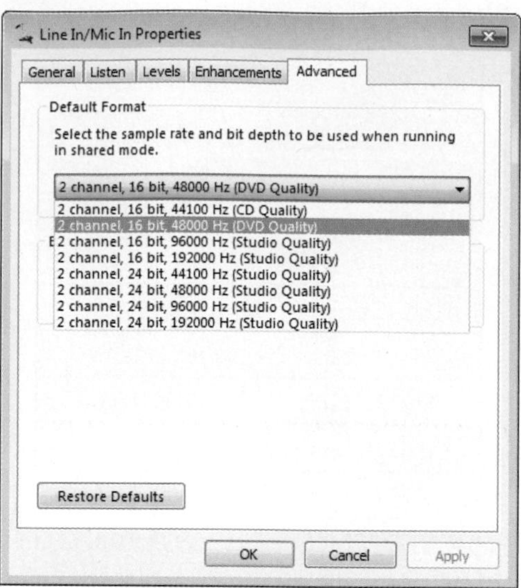

Figure 12-4. The sound level of a microphone can achieve studio quality.

Jitter

jitter the small staggers or hesitations in the delivery sequence of audio or video data caused by latency or missing packets.

A high sampling rate requires high bandwidth, or throughput. A practical compromise between the maximum obtainable bandwidth of the network media and the sampling rate of the audio signal must be reached. If the sampling rate is too high, there will be too much data to transmit across the network, and some of the packets will be dropped to accommodate the inefficient bandwidth. This results in jitter. ***Jitter*** is the small staggers or hesitations in the delivery sequence of audio or video data caused by latency or missing packets. A good example of jitter can be seen at times during a television news broadcast. A reporter located in some distant country is talking in real time to a news correspondent

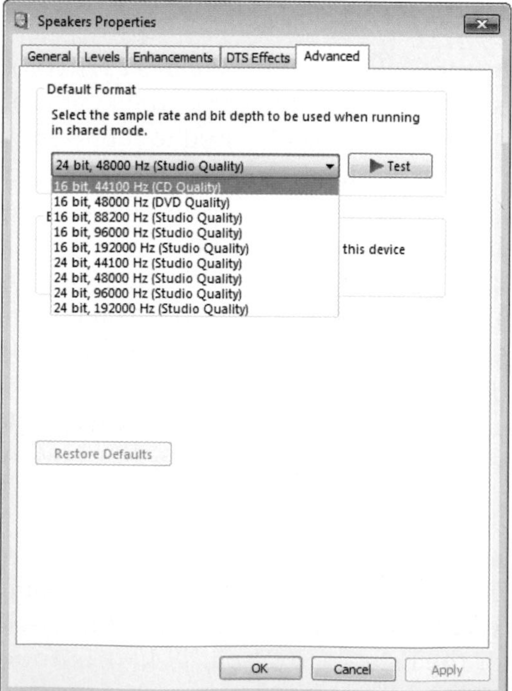

Figure 12-5. Speaker output can also achieve studio quality.

in the United States over a videophone or a similar device. You will often see a disrupted picture and time delay of responses to questions while the broadcast takes place. If the sampling rate is too low, the quality of the sound suffers, resulting in an artificial sound produced at the destination point.

Multimedia data transmitted across a large network requires network media such as T1 or fiber-optic. Low-quality data, such as voice, can be transmitted over traditional copper cabling, such as Cat 5. The distance traveled by the data and the type of data (voice, music, and video, multimedia) determine the cabling requirements.

Latency

latency
the amount of time it takes a signal to travel from its source to its destination.

The term ***latency*** means the delay of data as it travels to its destination. Latency may not be a problem for text file transfers or e-mail exchange. Even the common practice of downloading music has an acceptable latency period. Audio files contain a tremendous amount of data. When music is downloaded, it is buffered before it is played. *Buffering* means data is stored in memory until a sufficient amount of data is stored. When a sufficient amount is stored, the music begins to play. If buffering did not occur, there would be many momentary interruptions in the music.

A music file contains a large amount of data. This data must be processed at a very high data rate. If something acts as a bottleneck, the flow of data could slow. For example, if a music file required a data rate of 1 Mb per minute to produce a steady stream of music and there was a restriction between the origin and the destination, such as a modem, the music would start and stop every time the data-transfer rate fell lower than the required data rate to produce a steady sound. When buffering takes place, a large volume of data is stored in memory before the music begins to play. This reserve ensures a steady flow of music data is provided while the music is playing. This same technique is used for video.

When a real-time application such as a telephone conversation occurs, only a minimal latency period can be tolerated. The human ear can tolerate small breaks in the flow of audio data. If the breaks are small, they will go completely unnoticed. For example, a break in the data flow of less than 150 milliseconds (150/1000 or 0.15) can be tolerated. The human ear will not detect any break in the conversation. When a latency period of approximately 250 milliseconds is present, the listener will notice it, but tolerate it. A period of 500 milliseconds, however, is unacceptable to the listener.

Latency occurs because of several factors. One factor can be equipment such as gateways that change the data frame from one format to another while connecting two dissimilar network systems. Satellite transmission can generate delays from 50 milliseconds to 500 milliseconds. The time it takes a software compression program to compress data can increase latency. Lost or destroyed frames can add to the latency.

The total amount of latency between data packets produces jitter. Remember, jitter is the effect on the quality of sound or images when they arrive at their destination in other than regularly spaced, minimum intervals. See **Figure 12-6.** As the data packets enter the Internet system, latency periods between the packets may increase to an undesirable level. In the illustration, notice that each packet leaves the source in regularly spaced intervals, but after navigating long distances, irregular spacing develops. If the spaces are too large (250 milliseconds), jitter is produced at the destination.

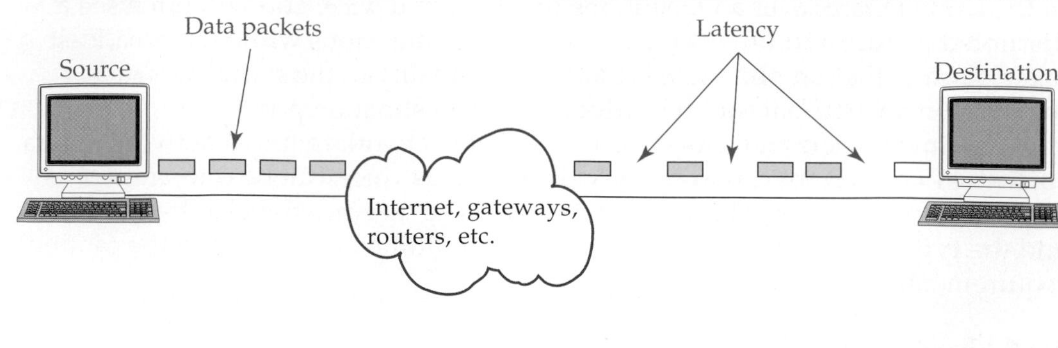

Figure 12-6. Packets leaving the source are evenly spaced with minimal delay. After they traverse the Internet, latency increases causing packets to arrive at their destination in other than regularly spaced, minimum intervals. The total amount of latency between data packets produces jitter.

Acoustical Echo

acoustical echo
a condition that takes place when a microphone and a speaker are in close proximity or the audio is improperly adjusted, causing feedback.

Acoustical echo is a condition that takes place when a microphone and a speaker are in close proximity or the audio is improperly adjusted, causing feedback. The sound coming from the speaker is so loud that it is received by the microphone, thus generating an echo effect. The electronic sound components convert the sound wave sent to the microphone to digital and then back to analog for output on the speaker(s). The echo effect occurs because the conversion of analog to digital to analog is not instantaneous. The echo effect can be prevented by decreasing the level of amplification.

Acoustical echo is commonly encountered in VoIP when using laptop computers and computer audio headsets equipped with microphones. Acoustical echo can be easily corrected by reconfiguring the sound level of the equipment.

Some audio devices are equipped with echo cancellation components. These components detect an echo condition and then automatically change circuit conditions to eliminate the echo. Echo cancellation components are just one of the reasons for the difference in prices between inexpensive audio devices and more costly devices.

Other conditions that contribute to echo conditions for VoIP are packet latency and packet loss. Latency problems are typically increased by long distances and mixing media such as telephone lines and satellite signals to carry audio packets. Latency is the main reason for packet loss. Since audio requires a constant stream of packets in a timely fashion, corrupt packets are dropped and not retransmitted. They are not retransmitted because it would not serve any useful purpose. By the time a missing or corrupt packet is discovered and retransmitted, it would no longer fit correctly into the sequence of packets without increasing the delay of the packet stream.

A whole field of electronics is referred to as *digital signal processing (DSP)*. DSP is, as the name infers, dedicated to processing digital signals through all types of electronic equipment and signal carrying media. At times, the DSP equipment and components can cause problems rather than correct them. For example, some systems insert a "best guess" of the missing packet contents to fill in audio gaps so the listener does not experience gaps in sound. At times, this technique can result in echo.

Also, be aware that there is a direct correlation in the number of participants in a conference call and the generation of echo. It only takes one participant to experience echo to produce echo affecting all participants in the conference call.

When experiencing echo, you must consider the following factors: impedance mismatch, acoustical echo, latency, and packet loss. For more detailed information about acoustical echo, visit www.adaptivedigital.com/product/echo_cancel/echo_explain.htm. To find this Web site, you can also conduct a search using the key terms "impedance mismatch echo." Some Web search results can be very technical and, therefore, require an understanding of basic electronics.

Video

Video is a result of flashing still images in front of a viewer at a rate faster than the human eye can detect. For example, a typical movie consists of a series of still images running through a projector at a rate of 24 frames per second. In other words, 24 images flash in front of the viewer every second. A frequency lower than this would cause the picture to be choppy, and a jitter effect would be detected.

Look at **Figure 12-7.** This figure shows a set of still images taken from a digital movie of a dog named Daisy who is returning a ball in a game of catch. Look closely at Daisy's front legs to see the gradual change in position. When the series of frames are displayed on a monitor at 24 frames per second, a smooth video motion is displayed. Full motion video for Internet and Intranet require the same number of frames per second. However, there are more variables than frame rate that need to be considered, such as picture resolution, color depth, the processing speed of the computer, the amount of video RAM available, and the type of network medium used to transfer the video.

Video Resolution

Video resolution is described in pixels and is measured horizontally and vertically across a display. For example, a typical VGA resolution is 640 × 480, or 640 pixels on each of the 480 lines of the display. See **Figure 12-8.**

Assuming that an image was at a VGA resolution in full color (32-bit), the amount of RAM required to contain the image would be approximately 1 MB (480 × 640 × 32) per second. If 24 frames (images) were required for full-motion video, approximately 24 MB of data would need to be delivered across the network every second. A three-minute video sequence would require approximately a 4320 MB (180 sec × 24 MB) data stream.

As you can see, video requires many computer resources and a lot of network media bandwidth. While most computers will support video as well as audio, many network systems will not. Full motion video with audio requires a network medium with high bandwidth, or the color resolution and frame rate will need to be significantly reduced. Think of the actual bandwidth of a telephone modem rated for 56 kbps. It would be impossible to produce a live videoconference using a 56 kbps modem.

Compression

All video systems use a form of compression and decompression to reduce the total number of bytes required for each image. The term ***codec (compressor/decompressor)*** is used to represent software, hardware, or combination of software and hardware that compress and decompress video and audio information. Some common codecs are MPEG, Indeo, and Cinepak.

Let's take a closer look at one of the most common codecs in use—MPEG. ***MPEG (Moving Picture Experts Group)*** is an industry standard that ensures compatibility between different cameras, displays, and other multimedia equipment.

codec (compressor/decompressor) software, hardware, or combination of software and hardware that compresses and decompresses video and audio information.

MPEG (Moving Picture Experts Group) an industry standard that ensures compatibility between different cameras, displays, and other multimedia equipment.

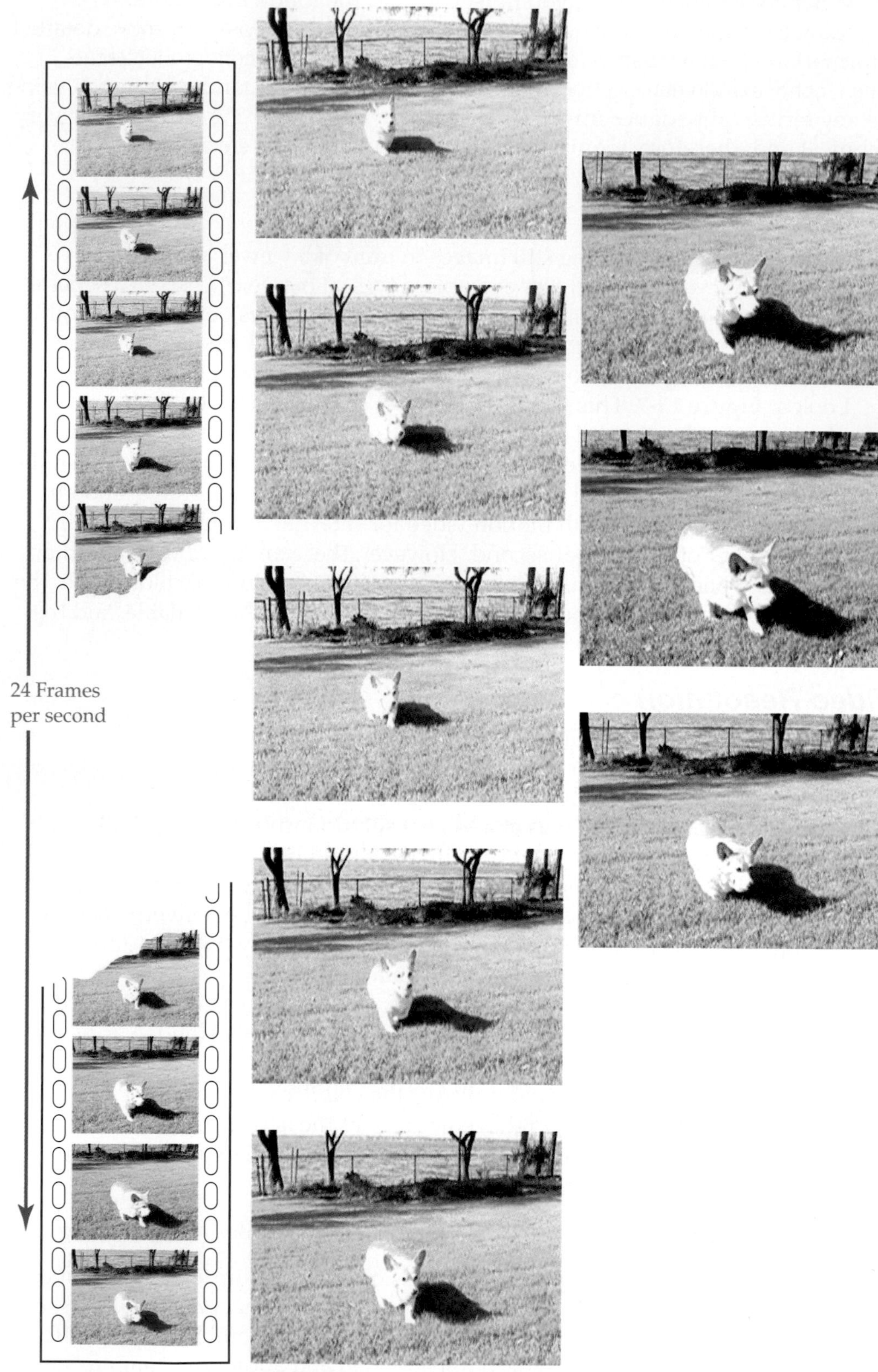

Figure 12-7.
A typical strip of movie film must change at a rate of 24 frames per second. The film consists of a string of still prints. Each frame contains a slight change in position of the object in motion.

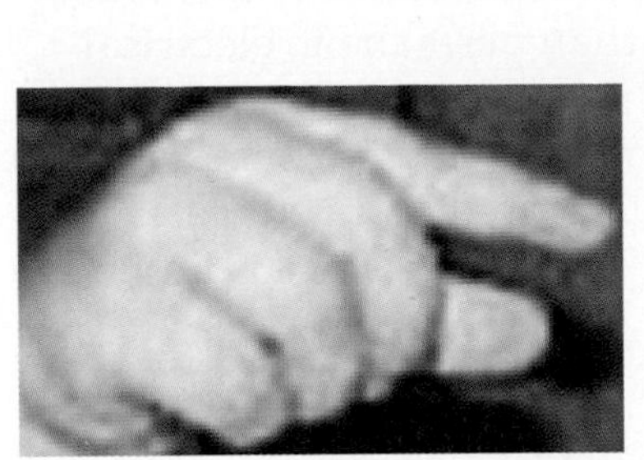

A closeup of the hand area reveals the pixel pattern

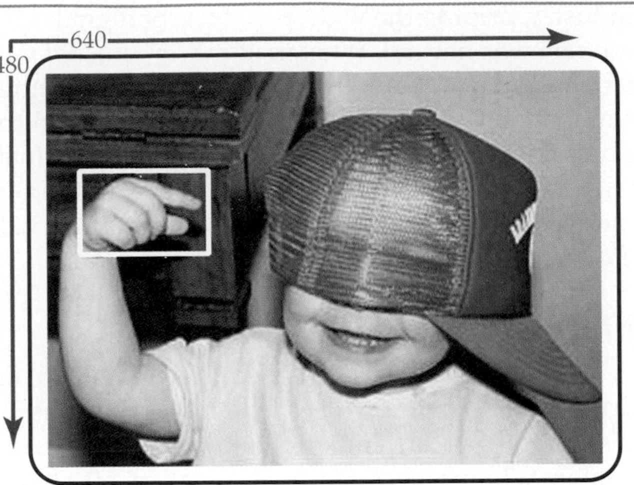

Figure 12-8.
The image in the display represents a VGA resolution of 640 × 480 pixels, or a total of 307,200 pixels. Each pixel location may require as many as 3 bytes to represent a color depth of 256 possible colors. This means that one frame of an image would require approximately 1 MB of memory or storage.

The compression technique that MPEG uses is simple to understand. Look again at Figure 12-7 of the dog playing ball. Notice how much of the image is redundant. Most of the background image does not change. MPEG capitalizes on this typical video feature. The MPEG compression software is written to predict which areas of the next frame will change and which areas will not. The prediction is based on the likelihood that if an area has not changed from one frame to the next, it is likely not to change in the next frame. The areas that do not change do not need to be transmitted or stored. The result is a reduction of the total amount of data that needs to be stored or broadcast.

There are various MPEG standards such as MPEG-1 and MPEG-2. MPEG-1 produces a relatively low-resolution image of approximately 320 × 240 pixels with a data rate of approximately 1.5 Megabits. This is an excellent standard for applications such as e-mail, where high resolution is not required. MPEG is also used to compress audio files. MPEG-2 produces a resolution of 720 × 480 pixels with a data rate of approximately 6 Mb and quality CD audio. The development of MPEG-3 was canceled and never fully developed. It was to support High Definition Television (HDTV). The MPEG-2 standard, however, is adequate to support HDTV.

MPEG-4 is a new standard used on multimedia applications for the Internet. It is designed to meet the requirements to support broadcast quality audio and video. For full motion video, MPEG-4 supports data rates higher than 1 Gb per second. This is a vast improvement over MPEG-2 data compression.

Multimedia Transmission Protocols

Early network systems were used for transferring text files and still images. Today, multimedia is incorporated into many different network systems. Network videoconferencing is becoming commonplace in the business world. This section looks at some of the protocols designed to support high data rate audio and video streaming.

X.25

X.25
a protocol that uses analog signals to transmit data across long distances.

The ***X.25*** protocol is unusual because it uses analog signals to transmit data across long distances. It was developed in the early years of the telecommunications industry, prior to the widespread use of digital signals. An analog transport design for data was natural. What makes X.25 unusual when compared with other analog technologies is that it uses packet switching rather than permanent, electrical connections. Analog signals are routed around the world in packets that many times follow different routes to reach their destination. X.25 laid the foundation for packet switching technology. X.25 is not commonly used in the United States, but many locations overseas are still committed to X.25. The X.25 protocol is limited to a maximum data rate of 56 kbps.

Frame Relay

Frame Relay was designed to replace X.25. Frame Relay is a packet switching protocol that typically uses leased lines such as T1 to carry data over long distances. You can think of Frame Relay as an upgraded digital version of the analog X.25 protocol. Frame Relay allows for a data rate as high as 1.544 Mbps. Whereas, X.25 is limited to 56 kbps.

Both X.25 and Frame Relay can be configured as a ***permanent virtual circuit (PVC).*** A PVC behaves like a hard-wired connection between the destination and source. It can follow many different paths while transmitting data between the destination and source. A PVC is not committed to following a single path such as a T1 line.

This may sound confusing because Frame Relay is generally transmitted over T1 lines to ensure a minimum data rate known as a Committed Information Rate (CIR). A ***Committed Information Rate (CIR)*** is a guaranteed bandwidth a commercial carrier will provide a subscriber. Many times, a T1 line is shared with other users. When the T1 line is shared, the data rate can fluctuate because of the variations in traffic, which includes the number of users and the type of data on the line. Frame Relay data transfer speeds are limited to the media used. A T1 line has a bandwidth of 1.544 bps. T-3 is limited to 45 Mbps.

Frame Relay
a packet switching protocol that typically uses leased lines such as T1 to carry data over long distances.

permanent virtual circuit (PVC)
a type of connection that behaves as if it were a hard-wired connection between the destination and source.

Committed Information Rate (CIR)
a guaranteed bandwidth a commercial carrier will provide a subscriber.

ATM

Asynchronous Transfer Mode (ATM) is a widely used protocol that is especially designed for carrying audio, video, and multimedia. It can support a bandwidth of 622 Mbps. ATM technology was designed in the 1970s at Bell Labs for use as a telephone technology. At that time, digital electronics was rapidly expanding and replacing electronic analog devices. Bell Labs was experimenting with a way to transmit analog voice signals as digital signals across telephone lines and networks. ATM technology was developed very early during the evolution of network communications and really did not come into common use for WAN applications until the 1990s.

ATM is designed specifically to transfer audio, video, and multimedia. ATM maintains a constant stream of voice or video from the source to the destination and avoids jitter. Traditionally, audio and video was transferred over analog media, such as telephone lines and radio and television frequencies. An analog signal can be converted into a digital signal through the use of specialized electronic chips referred to as ***Analog-to-Digital Converter (ADC)*** and ***Digital-to-Analog Converter (DAC)***. As the names imply, the chips are designed to change an analog signal into a digital signal and vice versa.

Figure 12-9 is a simplification of ATM technology. The sound of a person's voice is converted into electrical energy. The electrical energy is a series of voltage fluctuation patterns known as an *analog signal*. The voltage fluctuation patterns

Asynchronous Transfer Mode (ATM)
a protocol designed especially for transmitting data, voice, and video.

Analog-to-Digital Converter (ADC)
a computer chip designed to change an analog signal to a digital signal.

Digital-to-Analog Converter (DAC)
a computer chip designed to change a digital signal to an analog signal.

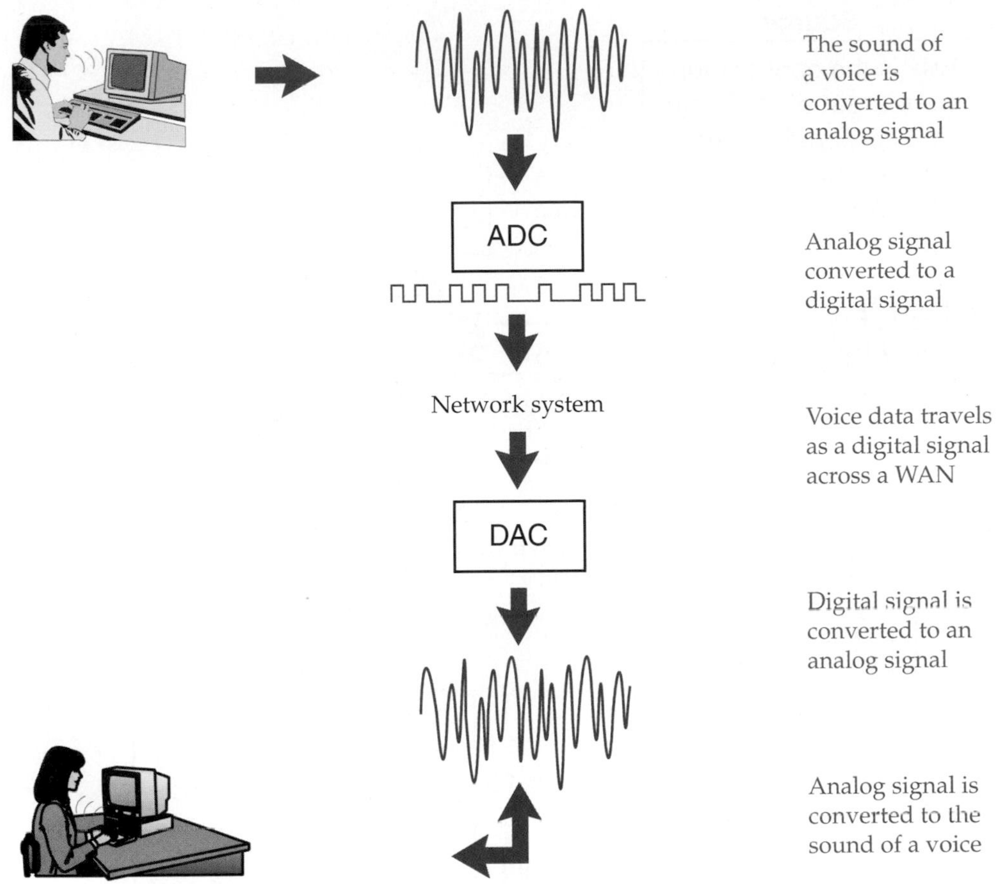

Figure 12-9. An example of analog-to-digital and digital-to-analog conversion.

are converted into a series of digital signals. At the destination, the digital signal is converted into an analog signal. The analog signal is amplified and applied to a speaker, which converts the analog signal into the sound of the voice.

ATM Data Transmission Model

ATM is designed to divide text and audio/video into cells of 53 bytes each. **Figure 12-10** illustrates how ATM technology works. Notice that the cells are placed in sequence giving higher priority to the audio/video cells. Remember that the audio/video packets cannot tolerate excessive latency. Any delay in transporting the cells disrupts the audio and video during a live transmission, resulting in jitter.

ATM can be transmitted at a Constant Bit Rate (CBR) or as a Variable Bit Rate (VBR). A ***Constant Bit Rate (CBR)***, as the name implies, is a steady stream of ATM cells moving at a predictable rate. CBR is best used for video conferencing, telephone conversations, television broadcasts, or anywhere real-time data transfer is required. When a CBR is desired, a dedicated circuit or a virtual circuit must be established between two points. By establishing a constant connection between the two points, the data rate can be guaranteed. A guaranteed data rate is required for a live or a real-time exchange of data.

A ***Variable Bit Rate (VBR)*** is an ATM cell rate that automatically adjusts to support time-sensitive data. It uses multiplexing techniques to provide a minimum CBR for time-sensitive audio and video transmissions while controlling the data rate of non-time-sensitive data, such as text or plain e-mail. A VBR may be used when cost prohibits a CBR system. For example, a high bandwidth system

Constant Bit Rate (CBR)
an ATM data transfer classification in which a steady stream of ATM cells move at a predictable rate.

Variable Bit Rate (VBR)
an ATM data transfer classification in which the ATM cell rate automatically adjusts to support time-sensitive data. It uses multiplexing techniques to provide a minimum Constant Bit Rate for time-sensitive audio and video transmissions while controlling the data rate of non-time-sensitive data, such as text or plain e-mail.

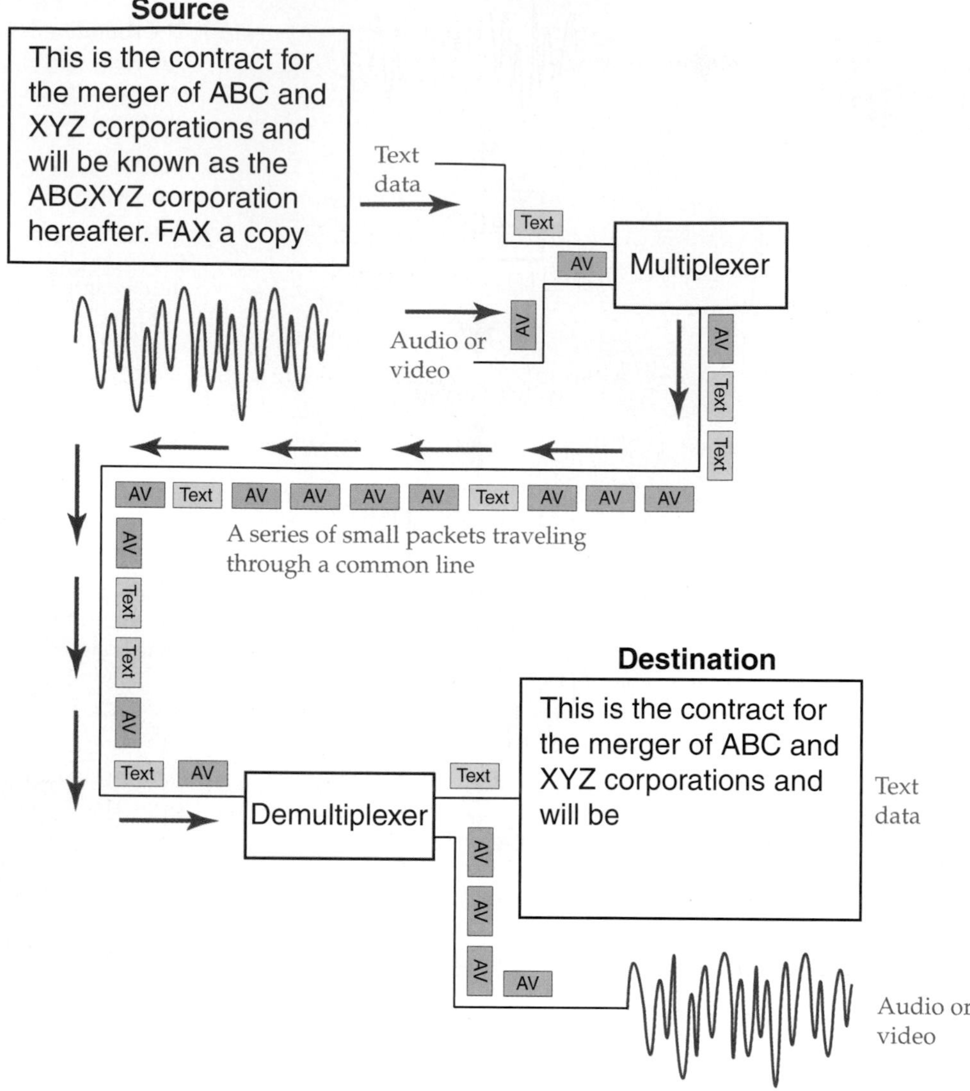

Figure 12-10. In this example, two forms of data, text and audio/video are separated into cells and multiplexed. All cells are placed on a single line as a series of packets. Priority is given to the time-sensitive audio/video cells. At the destination, a demultiplexer separates the two forms of data.

equipped with a multiplexer at one end and a demultiplexer at the other end can transfer telephone conversations, e-mail messages, and files across a single carrier. The trick is to maintain a minimum data transfer rate for the telephone conversation and video, both of which are time-sensitive, while allowing delay to occur in the e-mail and file transfer. The ATM cells carrying audio and video are given the highest priority so that a constant flow of the time-sensitive data can be maintained. The cells carrying e-mail and file transfers can be delayed.

Before ATM, separate systems were required to accommodate the various types of data. ATM allows text, voice, and video to be carried on the same network system. This can prove to be cost-effective in certain instances. For example, a corporation spanning the globe generates a large number of long-distance telephone calls. It is less expensive to use the corporate WAN for voice transmission than separate telephone lines. ATM communication may also prove to be an effective way of holding corporate meetings, which would otherwise require employees from various locations to converge and meet at a central location. Conferencing over a network is more economical than traveling, and, in many instances, it is a more effective use of employee time.

ATM Switch

The ATM switch provides virtual circuits between various points on the network system and is used with the ATM protocol. An ATM switch can provide a separate virtual circuit between several computers at the same time.

Look at **Figure 12-11.** In the illustration, the ATM switch provides virtual circuit connections between *Computer A*, *Computer B*, and *Computer C* and at the same time provides a connection between *Computer D* and *Computer E*. The computers are connected as virtual circuits, not permanent circuits. During the communication period between two or more computers, the ATM switch makes the connection appear to be a permanent connection. When the transfer of text, audio, or video is complete, the circuits disconnect. A computer can then connect to a different computer.

In the illustration, the ATM switch is used to provide a temporary connection between designated computers. The switch can also be set up to provide a permanent, virtual connection that provides a guaranteed bandwidth between two or more computers.

ATM Data Transfer Classifications

There are five ATM classifications: CBR, VBR-NRT, VBR-RT, ABR, and UBR. Each classification describes the degree to which the virtual circuit is dedicated to ATM cell transmission.

You have already learned that Constant Bit Rate (CBR) is a steady stream of ATM cells moving at a predictable rate. CBR is used for applications such as video conferencing and telephone communications. Variable Bit Rate (VBR) has the ability to change the rate of flow in contrast to CBR. VBR is divided into two major classes: VBR-Real Time (VBR-RT) and VBR-Non Real Time (VBR-NRT).

Variable Bit Rate-Non Real Time (VBR-NRT) allows ATM cells to move at a variable rate. The rate of movement depends on the type of data contained in each cell. For example, an e-mail that contains a text and multimedia attachment contains two types of data. Each type of data needs to be handled with a different

Variable Bit Rate-Non Real Time (VBR-NRT) an ATM data transfer classification that allows cells to move at a variable rate. The rate of movement depends on the type of data contained in each cell.

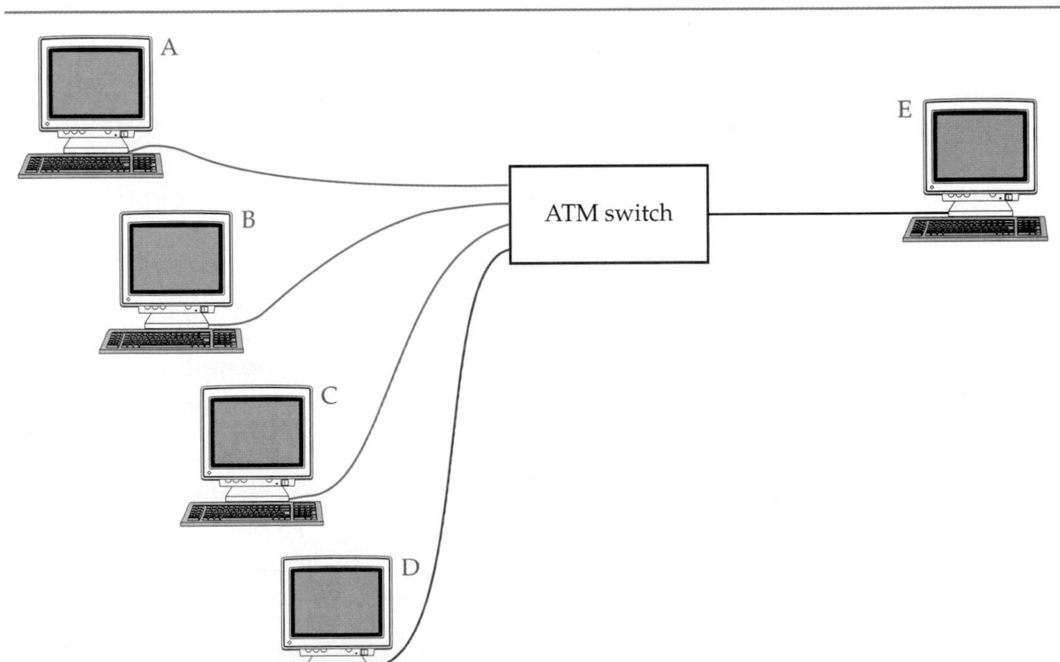

Figure 12-11. *Computer A* provides video to *Computer B* and *Computer C* while *Computer D* exchanges a file with *Computer E*. The ATM switch creates a separate virtual circuit between these computers, which behave as though they were wired directly to each other.

priority. The multimedia data would have the highest priority. However, there is no need for the cells that contain multimedia data to be transferred in real time because the communication is strictly in one direction, not two-way like in a telephone conversation.

Variable Bit Rate-Real Time (VBR-RT) an ATM data transfer classification that allows cells to move at a variable rate depending on the cell's contents to support real-time audio and video transfers.

Available Bit Rate (ABR) an ATM data transfer classification most appropriate for file transfer. It uses the available bit rate associated with the networking medium. The speed of a file transfer using the ABR classification is affected by the amount of traffic on the network system.

Variable Bit Rate-Real Time (VBR-RT) is similar to VBR-NRT in that it moves cells at a variable rate depending on the cell's contents. The main difference between the two bit rates is VBR-RT adjusts the bit rate to support real-time audio and video transfers. For example, when transferring text files and telephone conversation at the same time, the telephone conversation is transferred in real time while the text file is sent at a lower rate.

Available Bit Rate (ABR) is most appropriate for file transfer. It uses the available bit rate associated with the networking medium. The speed of a file transfer using the ABR classification is affected by the amount of traffic on the network.

Unspecified Bit Rate (UBR) is as implied. It does not guarantee any speed or meet requirements of any special application such as multimedia or telephony. This classification is typically applied inside TCP/IP frames. A good example is a Web cam that updates the image every thirty seconds or so, rather than providing full-motion video.

The ATM data transfer classifications reflect a matching cost factor. The highest quality is CBR, and it is the most expensive to use. The least expensive is UBR, which is minimal to no cost when used across the Internet as part of a TCP/IP frame. The minimal cost is the cost of the ISP.

ATM Cell Design

The ATM cell is simple in design. The maximum size of the cell is 53 bytes, consisting of a 5-byte header and a 48-byte payload. See **Figure 12-12.**

Tech Tip

The ATM cell is at times referred to as a *packet* or *frame*. This is incorrect according to the ATM forum organization.

Unspecified Bit Rate (UBR) an ATM data transfer classification that does not guarantee any speed or meet requirements of any special application such as multimedia or telephony. This classification is typically applied inside TCP/IP frames.

The most significant characteristic of the ATM cell is it carries only a 48-byte payload. While this may seem small, you must consider that the idea behind the design is to be able to mix many different cells on the same network medium. Remember, it is important not to cause too much latency or destroy a multimedia cell. Any cells that are destroyed or do not reach the destination are not retransmitted over the media. There is no time to retransmit a cell or to reorder cells if they become out of order when traveling across a network.

The 4 bits in the Generic Flow Control (GFC) field were originally designed to contain information about the function of the cell. It is not used at the time of this writing. The 8 bits in the Virtual Path Identifier (VPI) field and the 16 bits in the Virtual Channel Identifier (VCI) field identify the path from the source to the destination using a series of ATM switches. The 3 bits in the Payload Type

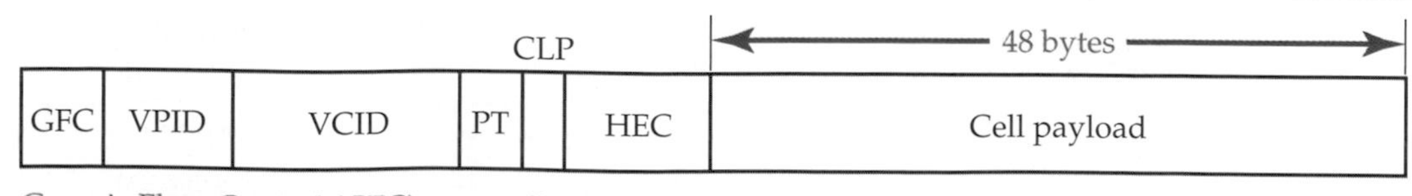

Figure 12-12. The ATM protocol is designed for efficiency. Compared with other protocols, such as IP, the ATM protocol is quite small.

(PT) field indicate the type of payload carried in the cell, such as data or control instructions. The 1 bit in the Cell Loss Priority (CLP) field indicates if the cell should be dropped if it encounters severe congestion on the network. The CLP field keeps time-sensitive transmissions, such as live video and audio, up-to-date and prevents latency issues. The 8-bit Header Error Control (HEC) field detects errors in the header portion of the cell, not in the payload.

ATM is a connection-oriented protocol. This means that it establishes a logical connection between the source and destination. Logical connections are also referred to as *virtual connections*. Remember that a virtual connection is not a permanent, physical connection but rather a connection that behaves as a physical connection. A virtual connection is set up and controlled by a software program. There are two types of virtual connections associated with ATM, and they are identified in the header of the ATM cell. The two types of connections are Virtual Path Connections (VPC) and Virtual Channel Connections (VCC). See **Figure 12-13.**

The illustration shows a backbone running between two ATM switches. The backbone is considered a virtual path. The virtual path contains the individual virtual circuits, or virtual channels, between specific computers or network equipment. In the illustration, there are two virtual channels, *A* and *B*. The virtual channels merge into the virtual path when traveling between the switches and then split into separate virtual channels when serving the computers identified as *A* and *B*.

To better understand virtual path connections and virtual channel connections, a complete highway system can be used as an analogy. A complete highway system includes state highways and an interstate highway. The state highways can be compared to virtual channels and an interstate highway can be compared to a virtual path. State highways connect at different points along the interstate highway. A car travels from its home (source) across a state highway, merges onto the interstate

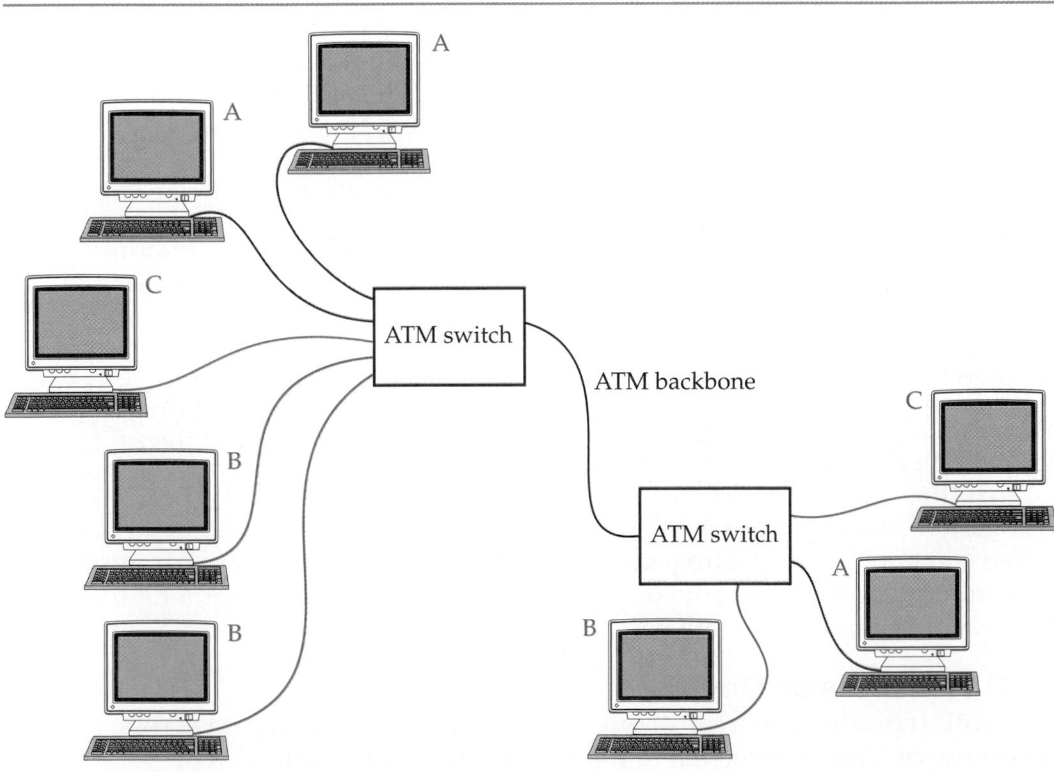

Figure 12-13.
The ATM backbone contains paths, which consist of two or more virtual channels. The backbone is referred to as the *virtual path*.

highway where it travels with other cars from various state highways, and then exits onto a state highway to reach its destination.

In reality, there can be many virtual path connections between ATM switches. The virtual path connections can be set up as Permanent Virtual Circuits (PVC) or Switched Virtual Circuits (SVC). For example, a corporation may have a PVC established between its Chicago and St. Louis offices to maintain a constant update of a critical database. Other connections can be set up as an SVC. The SVC would be used as needed. It would typically be used by individuals who only connect to resources at the other locations on a temporary basis. Remember that connections across long-distance lines are very expensive. Even virtual connections are expensive. A dedicated, physical connection between two locations is more expensive than a switched circuit that is only connected temporarily. The ATM and other cell switching technologies are designed with flexibility in mind. However, because of the flexibility, much confusion can arise.

ATM switches are designed to support ATM protocol functions. The ATM switch processes millions of cells per second and provides multiplexing, which is required to deliver each cell in a timely fashion while sharing a common media. Each ATM switch maintains routing tables based on information contained in the ATM cell header. A routing table for the ATM switch is similar in design and purpose to the routing table used for a router. Remember that the virtual path identifier and the virtual channel identifier are used to locate and maintain the connection between two devices. Based on the information contained in the header, the ATM switch sets up the virtual channels and paths between end users.

The ATM switch controls the bandwidth allocated to each virtual circuit and controls the cells by priorities set in the Cell Loss Priority (CLP) field in the ATM cell header. The switch also drops some of the cells if cell traffic exceeds the capacity of the switch, media attached to the switch, or both.

The typical ATM switch is designed with multiple ports. The switch is used to make a physical connection to various network media such as fiber-optic cable, twisted pair cable, and coaxial cable. Because of costs, ATM switches are mostly found on long-haul communication portions of a WAN rather than on a LAN.

VoIP

Voice over IP (VoIP) an Internet telephony protocol designed for high-performance data delivery and quality of service. It relies on existing TCP/IP technology and existing TCP/IP networking equipment.

Voice over IP (VoIP), also known as ***Internet telephony,*** is similar in concept to ATM in that it is designed for high-performance data delivery and quality of service. VoIP, however, relies on existing TCP/IP technology and existing TCP/IP networking equipment. ATM is a protocol separate from the TCP/IP stack and uses special equipment designed for the protocol, such as ATM switches and dedicated communication lines. ATM requires expensive equipment for support, while support for VoIP is inexpensive.

At the time of this writing, VoIP is still evolving and is considered an inexpensive alternative to ATM. VoIP is less expensive for long-distance calls when compared with existing telephone technologies. This is why it is appealing to so many people, especially to corporations communicating over long-distance lines with overseas corporations.

VoIP Transmission Model

VoIP typically uses a series of UDP packets to send voice data across the network. The construction of the UDP packet is similar to that of ATM.

Remember that ATM designed its packet for efficiency. The ATM packet is a short packet with little overhead like the UDP packet. UDP provides a best effort delivery of data with no mechanism to check if the data arrived in sequence or intact. The UDP packet does not generate high latency because it does not attempt to resend lost packets.

VoIP uses the TCP protocol for applications such as video or audio streaming. Streaming is the continuous downloading of multimedia files without interruption. The TCP protocol has a sequence number in the header, which ensures packets are arranged in proper sequence when they arrive at the final destination. Remember, TCP uses a sequence number as part of its header information so packets can be reassembled at the destination. UDP does not have a sequence number, so it cannot guarantee assembly of data packets in their proper sequence.

VoIP Infrastructure

For TCP/IP to be an excellent means of carrying multimedia, a media carrier from source to destination with high bandwidth is required, such as Gigabyte Ethernet or fiber-optic cable.

One of the major technical problems with Internet communications has been the location of the last few hundred feet of cabling to the home computer, known as the *local loop*. The local loop is typically designed for low-bandwidth analog voice communications. Since the bandwidth is low, it is the bottleneck for the entire system, even if the rest of the communications link uses the very latest technology. The last few hundred feet of the system can affect the overall latency of packet transmission, which negates the latest technology. Traditional telephone lines cannot adequately carry audio and video in real time. For VoIP to work successfully, there must be adequate bandwidth. Without adequate bandwidth, latency becomes a problem. DSL and Cable Internet access provide adequate bandwidth for VoIP to run without latency. DSL and Cable are not connected to the local loop.

There are several ways VoIP can be used. These include the following:

- Communicating from PC to PC using TCP/IP.
- Mixing TCP/IP telephone technology with existing and modern telephone technologies.
- Communicating from a PC to a cell phone via traditional LAN cabling network, a Public Switched Telephone Network (PSTN), and wireless technology.

VoIP can communicate from PC to PC using only the TCP/IP protocol. This is easy to set up and is similar to using Windows XP NetMeeting, Windows Vista Meeting Space, and Windows 7 People Near Me. All three programs are collaboration programs that support the exchange of text messages and documents and remote desktop access. NetMeeting supports audio and video and is therefore a VoIP application. This feature is not included in Meeting Space and People Near Me. Microsoft claimed that support for video and audio used too much bandwidth which caused latency problems in the peer-to-peer network. As an alternative, Microsoft offers a subscription collaboration software package called Microsoft Office Live Meeting. Also, Windows 7 can be incorporated with Skype to provide video and audio during a meeting session. Both the Windows Vista and Windows 7 collaboration require IPv6 for support.

VoIP can be used by mixing TCP/IP with modern telephone technologies. For example, a PC can connect to a standard telephone via a TCP/IP network,

Public Switched Telephone Network (PSTN), and the more modern ISDN or FDDI technologies. ***Public Switched Telephone Network (PSTN),*** or ***Plain Old Telephone Service (POTS),*** usually refers to the older telephone technology that uses twisted pair cable and analog signals.

Public Switched Telephone Network (PSTN)
the older telephone system that uses twisted pair cabling and analog signals rather than digital.

Mixing TCP/IP with telephone technologies is very complex. It requires translating TCP/IP into traditional telephone protocols and vice versa. There can be substantial delays or latency using a hybrid, or mixed, protocol system required for communications over the variety of media encountered.

VoIP can also be used to communicate from a PC to a cell phone via traditional LAN cabling, a Public Switched Telephone Network (PSTN), and then wireless technology. This type of communication is even more complicated than the last scenario and can create even longer delays. Look at **Figure 12-14.**

A PC can communicate with a wide variety of communication devices. There are many communication scenarios that mix PC communication with conventional telephone, wireless cell phones, and personal digital assistants. Each of these communication technologies requires special protocols and protocol conversions. Each set of protocols varies according to the communication path. The path can be over public analog telephone lines, public digital telephone lines, private company lines, fiber-optic cable, infrared, satellite, and wireless.

Bandwidth-Shaping Techniques

VoIP often relies on bandwidth-shaping techniques to ensure quality of service. A ***bandwidth shaper,*** or ***traffic shaper,*** is used to prioritize network packets to ensure quality of service for time-sensitive applications such as VoIP. A bandwidth shaper prioritizes network traffic by protocol or assigned switch port or port number.

bandwidth shaper
a technique implemented in a network by hardware or software to control the bandwidth through a particular device such as a gateway, shared Internet connection, network switch, or router.

The bandwidth shaper can delay the delivery of low-priority packets, thus allowing high-priority packets the maximum throughput. For example, to ensure the delivery of VoIP packets, Web pages requested for download to a workstation are throttled back, ensuring the highest quality of service to the VoIP packets. The term *throttled back* means that the number of packets to be downloaded during a given period of time is limited to reduce bandwidth consumption. Bandwidth shapers are commonly employed by Internet Service Providers and other large providers of Internet access such as corporations and educational institutions.

Bandwidth shaping can be accomplished with hardware or software and is used to control the bandwidth through a particular device such as a gateway,

Analog telephone lines
Digital telephone lines
Internet backbones
LANs
MANs
WANs
Wireless

Figure 12-14.
Computers can communicate with a wide variety of communication devices such as cell phones, pagers, palmtops, personal digital assistants, and landline telephones. The wide variety of equipment and devices require a wide variety of communication lines and equipment.

shared Internet connection, network switch, or router. When a switch is used, the bandwidth rate for a switch port can be manually set. For example, you could configure the switch port for 10 Mb, 100 Mb, or 1 Gb maximum throughput. When bandwidth- or traffic-shaping software is used, the bandwidth can be limited for a particular set of IP addresses, type of protocol such as HTTP, or a particular application. To learn more about bandwidth-shaper equipment and applications, visit the NetEqualizer Web site at www.netequalizer.com.

Telephone Gateway and H.323

A ***telephone gateway*** is a specialized piece of equipment that connects a packet-style network communications system to a telephone system using the H.323 protocol. The ***H.323*** standard is the telecommunications standard for audio, video, and data communications using IP or packet-type networks defined by the International Telecommunication Union (ITU). On one side of the telephone gateway is the telephone system and on the other side is the network system. The telephone system side is the H.323 side. You can think of the gateway as the H.323 server and the computers on the network side as the H.323 clients. Look at **Figure 12-15.**

H.323 is not one specific protocol but rather an entire suite of protocols similar to the TCP/IP suite of protocols. There are over 20 different protocols designed to work with H.323. The protocols are systems that control processes such as name to telephone number conversion, call forwarding, caller ID, call blocking, conversion from TCP/IP to wireless, and conversion to European telephone systems.

telephone gateway
a specialized piece of equipment that connects a packet-style network communications system to a telephone system using the H.323 protocol.

H.323
a telecommunications standard and protocol used for audio, video, and data communications using IP or packet-type networks defined by the International Telecommunication Union (ITU).

Quality of Service (QoS)

The biggest problem in using packet-based networking systems is latency. The ***Quality of Service (QoS)*** protocol was developed to minimize latency. The QoS protocol gives time-sensitive packets, such as those carrying telephone conversations, a higher priority than data packets. The QoS Packet Scheduler is available in Windows XP and later, **Figure 12-16.**

Windows operating systems later than Windows XP install QoS by default during installation if the computer supports a network connection. The QoS feature works for both wired and wireless networks.

Frame Relay and ATM are sometimes carried over typical Internet backbones packaged inside the IP protocol. These technologies are referred to as *ATM over*

Quality of Service (QoS)
a protocol that gives time-sensitive packets, such as those carrying telephone conversations, a higher priority than data packets.

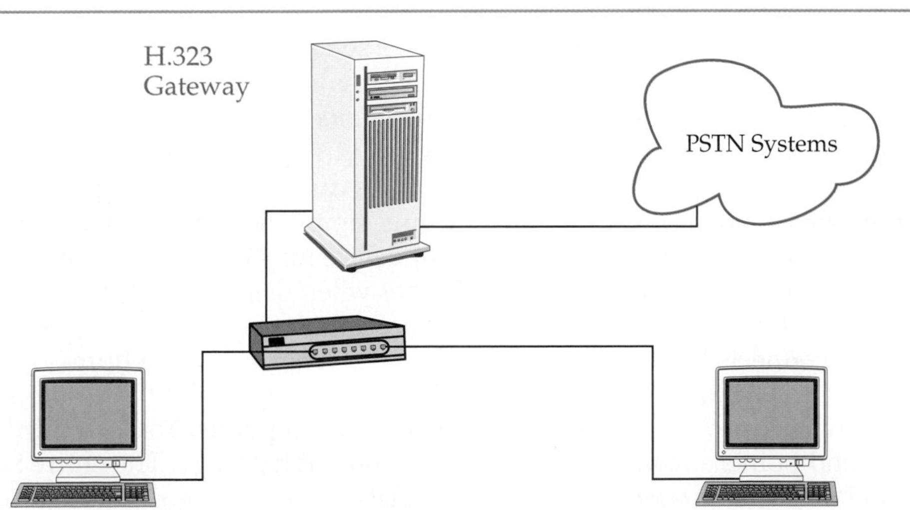

Figure 12-15.
The H.323 client is installed on the workstations, while the H.323 gateway service is part of the telephone system.

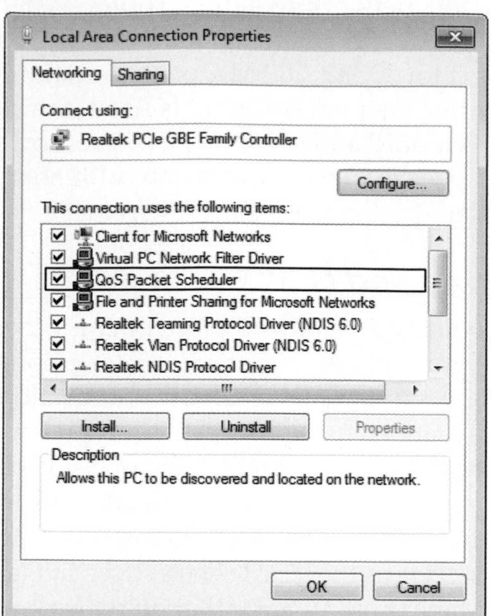

Figure 12-16. Quality of Service (QoS) is an optional protocol available in Windows XP and installed by default in later Windows operating systems. The QoS protocol gives time-sensitive packets a higher priority than data packets.

IP (ATMoIP) and *Frame Relay over IP (FRoIP)*. Chapter 14—Remote Access and Long-Distance Communications takes a closer look at how these systems work.

Tech Tip

Nortel Networks specializes in integrating telecommunications and networking. You may want to visit the Nortel Web site at www.nortelnetworks.com to learn more about the telecommunications industry as a possible source of employment. Nortel also offers a variety of certifications. Many of these certifications involve a detailed understanding of networking.

Session Initiation Protocol (SIP)

Session Initiation Protocol (SIP) a standard and a protocol for initiating, maintaining, and terminating the exchange of voice, multimedia, gaming, chat, and more.

hard phone a physical telephonic device.

soft phone a virtual telephonic device.

Session Initiation Protocol (SIP) is a standard and a protocol. The SIP standard was specified by the Internet Engineering Task Force (IETF). SIP is used for initiating, maintaining, and terminating the exchange of voice, multimedia, gaming, chat, and more. SIP does not carry the data but rather establishes and maintains the session until the session is terminated. The control of a VoIP session is referred to as *call signaling*.

An example of a SIP application is Skype, a software program which supports telephone communications across the Internet using soft or hard phones. A ***hard phone*** is a physical telephonic device. A ***soft phone*** is a virtual telephonic device. An example of a soft phone is shown in **Figure 12-17.** Notice the keypad for entering telephone numbers. The software takes care of establishing a connection with the entered phone number. A user would simply need a headset connected to the computer to serve as an input/output device for the conversation.

SIP usually does not generate any charges when using the Internet for conversations between two soft phones. Charges are typically incurred when a soft phone connects to a hard phone using the Internet as the medium.

The typical default port for SIP is 5060 for UDP and 5061 for TCP. SIP is an application layer protocol for connecting network end points. You can think of network end points as configured in a point-to-point topology. The entire SIP RFC can be viewed at www.ietf.org/rfc/rfc3261.txt.

Figure 12-17.
The Skype software application provides "soft phone" local and long-distance service for a PC and also incorporate video as an option.

Real-Time Transport Protocol (RTP)

Real-time Transport Protocol (RTP) is a standard as well as a protocol developed by IETF. The term *real time* means delivering the packets as fast as possible without any delay. To achieve this, RTP uses UDP; hence, it does not guarantee packet delivery.

Real-time Transport Protocol (RTP)
a standard and a protocol used to stream voice and video in real time.

RTP is used to stream voice and video as used in video conferencing and gaming. RTP is typically used in conjunction with Real-time Transport Control Protocol (RTCP). RTP is a packet design that carries the streaming data. RTCP is used to ensure quality of service and to monitor performance.

RTP may also use other protocols, such as SIP, H.225, and H.245, to accomplish its task. For example, a session may use SIP to establish a multimedia link, RTP to carry the multimedia, and SIP to terminate the session. RTP is an open standard that can be used by anyone when designing a communications system. It is up to the designer as to which protocols it uses with RTP to accomplish the task.

Check the following Web site for a list of open source RIP and SIP software applications: www.voip-info.org/wiki/view/Open+Source+VOIP+Software?navmenu. You can also conduct an Internet search using the terms "SIP open source software" and "RTP open source software."

Basic VoIP Troubleshooting

The exact procedure for troubleshooting VoIP applications depends on the type of system installed, the topology, and the symptoms of the problem. First, you must determine if the problem is performance related or a complete failure of the system. A performance issue is generally related to the quality of the VoIP service. In other words, how well a person can hear the conversation. Is the conversation clear, or is it garbled or broken up? Performance issues are typically caused by latency and jitter. A complete failure of the VoIP system generally relates to a connection failure between the destination and source. Both performance and complete failure can be verified in many cases by the use of a protocol analyzer. The protocol analyzer will prove to be of vital importance when troubleshooting VoIP systems.

Using a Protocol Analyzer to Verify Packet Exchange

A protocol analyzer can be used to verify the exchange of packets needed to support a VoIP service. Look at **Figure 12-18.** It shows a collection of packet exchanges between a VoIP destination and source captured with the Microsoft Network Monitor protocol analyzer. The packets were captured while a telephone call was made using a PC to a cell phone. As you can see, there are several IP addresses associated with the Skype VoIP call. The IP addresses are associated with the Skype Luxembourg office, the Comcast Internet Service Provider, and the IP address of the final destination.

In the capture, packet exchanges to and from the destination are verified. This is an indication that there is a complete network path and that the Skype VoIP system is in fact configured properly.

The use of a protocol analyzer can also be used to view the time it takes to exchange packets. In the capture, the time is listed in the **Time Offset** column. A latency of 250 microseconds will be very noticeable by the user.

The protocol analyzer can also be used to verify jitter by performing a TCP/IP trace. When a trace is performed, the protocol analyzer will automatically verify the stream of packets and indicate if any are missing from the stream. Missing packets results in jitter.

VoIP Jitter

Jitter as associated with VoIP will cause sound quality problems. It is caused by dropped or lost packets and results in a choppy voice transmission. If the jitter is severe enough, the conversation can be unintelligible. Many devices such as routers, switches, and gateways allow for the configuration of QoS, which improves VoIP quality and may completely eliminate jitter. For example in **Figure 12-19,** a

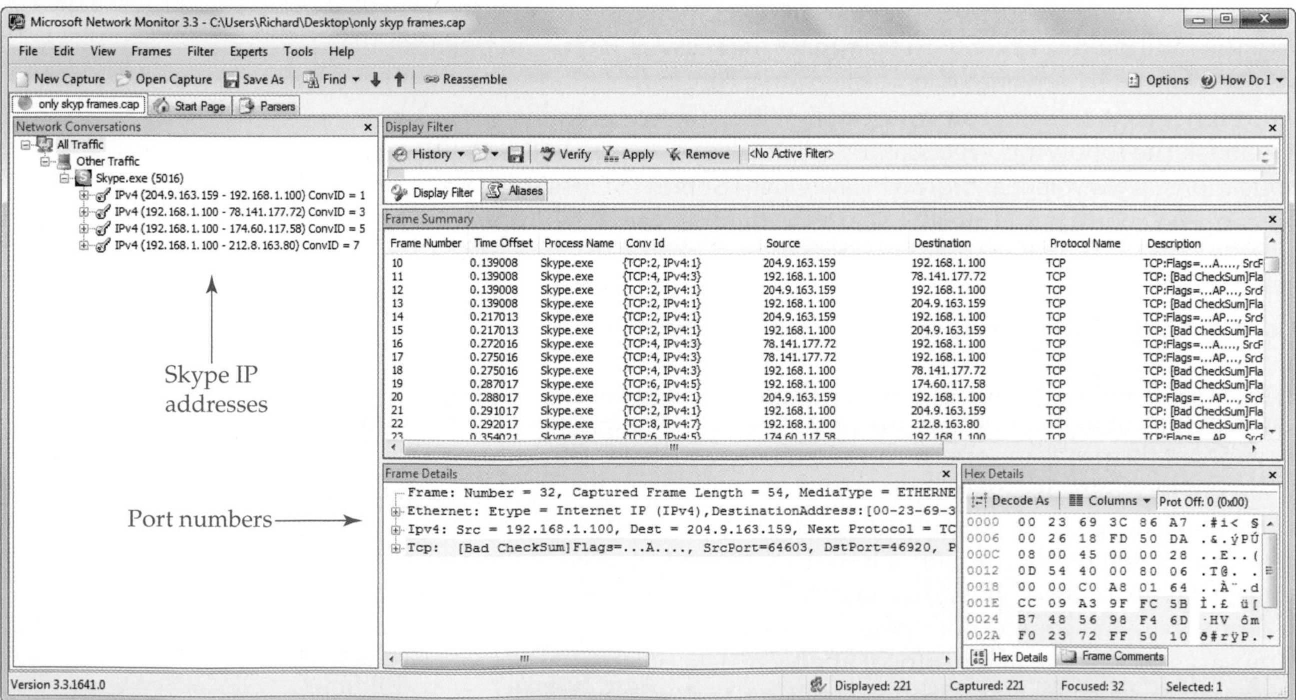

Figure 12-18.
The Microsoft Network Monitor protocol analyzer can be used to verify the packet exchange of a VoIP system such as Skype.

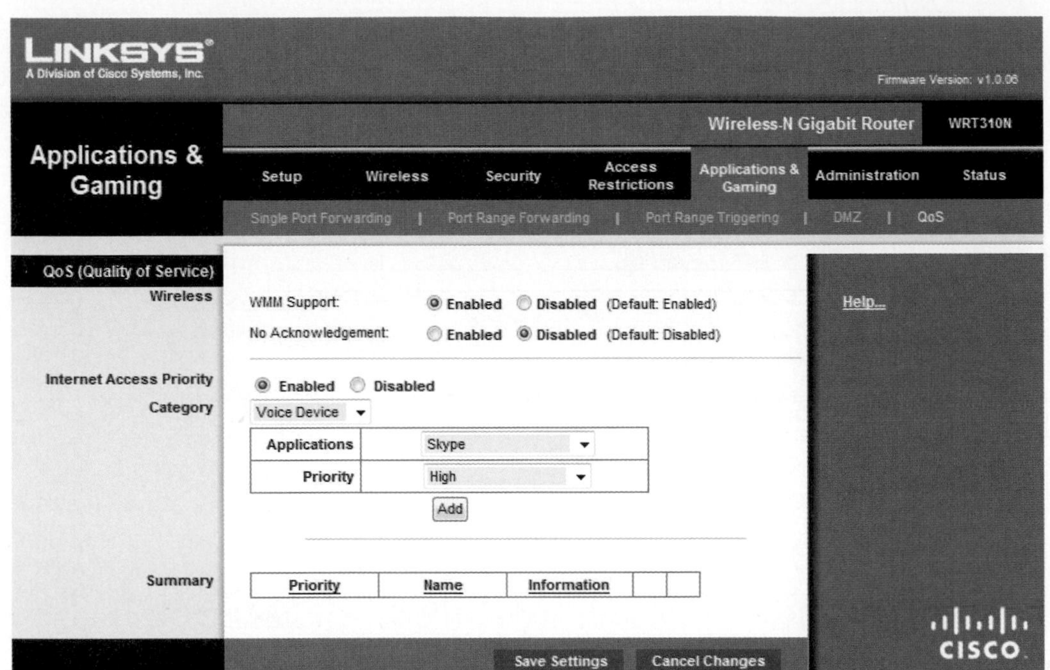

Figure 12-19. The Cisco Linksys router provides support for QoS. You can configure priority for specific applications, which means the packets associated with the application will be sent through the router before other packets.

Linksys router is configured to enable the voice device "Skype" to have a high priority. This will allow Skype-related packets to be passed through the router before other types of packets associated with other software application.

QoS can also be configured for other software applications, such as online gaming, MSN Messenger, and Yahoo! Messenger. When the specific software application is not an identified option in the selection box, you can simply assign a priority to the port numbers directly related to the application.

Firewall Blocking VoIP Packets

One of the most common sources of VoIP problems is the computer's firewall blocking the packets. The firewall should be configured automatically during the VoIP software installation process to allow the exchange of VoIP packets. If the VoIP software application is newer than the existing computer operating system, then the computer's firewall may need to be configured manually to allow the packets to pass. See **Figure 12-20.** The port numbers associated with the VoIP software application can be found in the VoIP manufacturer's Web site, typically listed under support or Frequently Asked Questions (FAQs). The PC may be connected to a switch or router before the modem in a small-office or home-office. When a router or switch is used to share the Internet connection, that device may need to be configured to allow the VoIP application to pass through. Again, the device should be configured to accommodate specific port assignments associated with the VoIP software application.

If the VoIP system has never worked, then you have most likely made an error in the system configuration. You will need to check the installation instructions carefully and follow each step closely.

Audio Device Configuration

Another reason for complete failure could be due to the microphone, speaker, or headset. Sometimes and more often than you think, a user cannot get their

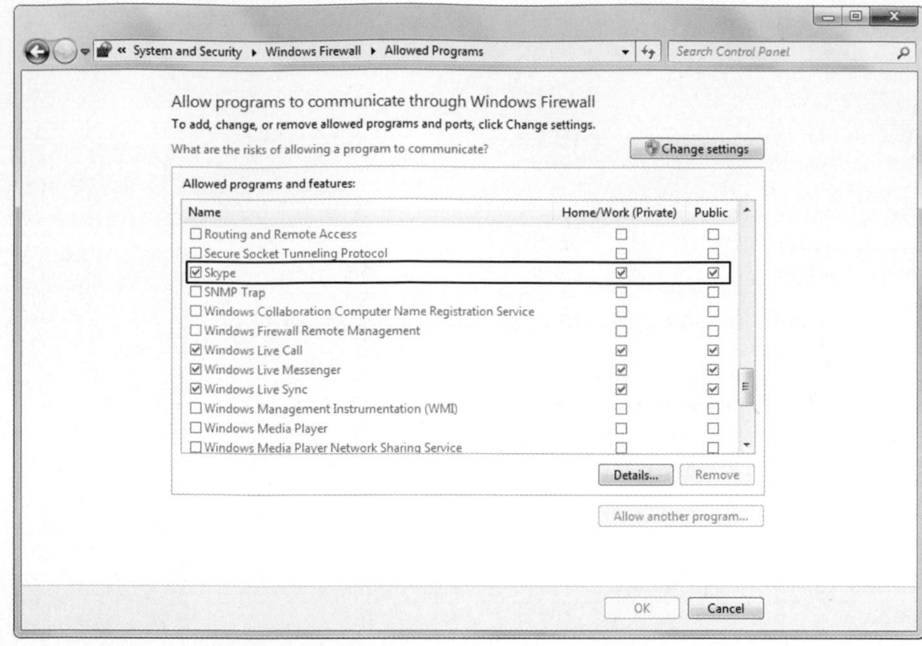

Figure 12-20. Windows Firewall configured to allow packets associated with Skype to pass when the computer is in the Private or Public setting.

VoIP system to work properly because they did not turn on the speaker switch on the headset or the microphone. Speaker and microphone configuration and testing can be completed through Windows Control Panel. Look at **Figure 12-21,** which shows the **Hardware and Sound** menu in Windows 7 Control Panel. This menu is very similar to that in Windows Vista Control Panel. By selecting the **Manage audio devices** option, you can verify the configuration of sound devices such as the microphone and speakers. You can also test these items to ensure they are working properly.

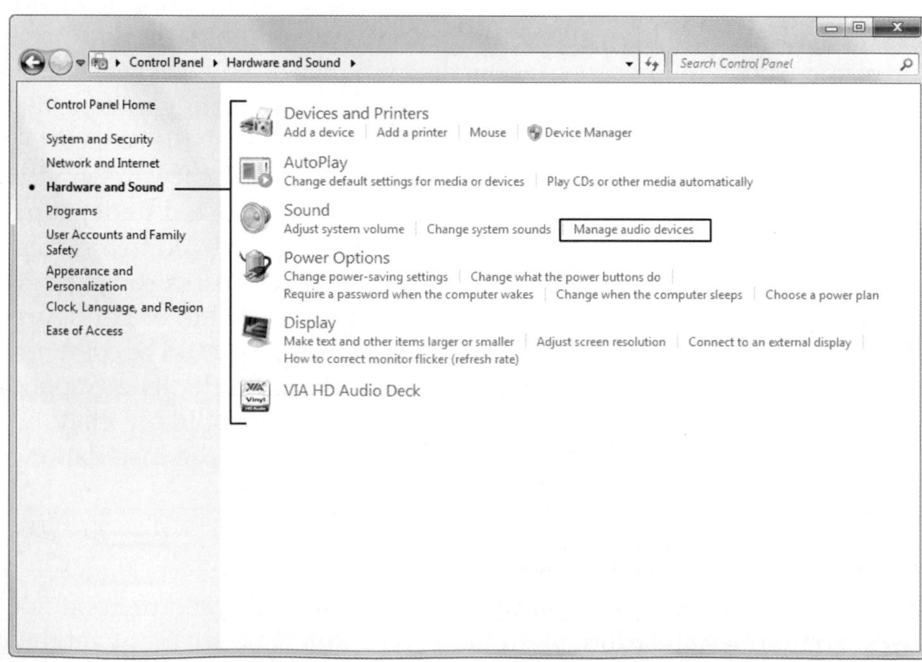

Figure 12-21. You can configure and verify an audio device, such as if the speakers and microphone are working correctly, by accessing the **Manage audio devices** option in the Windows 7 Control Panel **Hardware and Sound** menu.

As you can see, troubleshooting a simple VoIP system is not very difficult—most of the time. A much more complex system that involves traditional telephone equipment merged into an Ethernet network system is more difficult to troubleshoot. You must refer to the manufacturer's resource guides when troubleshooting the system. Manufacturers supply complete step-by-step guides to assist the network technician in correctly performing the troubleshooting task. The basic concepts presented in this section will most likely also be present in the manufacturer's materials.

Impedance Mismatch

Impedance mismatch is an electronics term which refers to the effect of connecting two different electronic audio systems that have different electronic characteristics. When the two systems have different electronic characteristics you will have an impedance mismatch. A common example of impedance mismatch is connecting a two-wire local loop telephone circuit to a four-wire telephone circuit. The two-wire circuit uses half-duplex communication because only one person can talk at a time. The same two wires carry the conversation to and from the source and destination. The four-wire circuit uses hybrid duplex communications, which means it can carry source and destination audio signals separately and simultaneously. This mismatch of two-wire and four-wire circuits is the most common cause of telephone audio echo. Impedance mismatch also occurs when VoIP technology uses telephone transmission cables for part of the circuit. Impedance mismatch is one of the most common causes of VoIP echo.

impedance mismatch
the effect of connecting two different electronic audio systems that have different electronic characteristics.

Summary

- An analog signal is converted into a digital code by taking samples of the analog signal's amplitude at specific times.
- Sampling rate is the number of times a signal is sampled during a specific period.
- Sampling frequency is the number of times a signal is sampled per second.
- Jitter is the small staggers or hesitations in the delivery sequence of audio or video data and is caused by latency or missing packets.
- Video images typically occur at a minimum rate of 24 frames per second.
- The term *latency* means the delay of data as it travels to its destination.
- While latency with a delay of approximately 250 milliseconds will be noticed by a user, it is acceptable.
- The term *codec* represents software, hardware, or combination of software and hardware that compresses and decompresses video and audio information.
- X.25 is one of the early protocols used to transfer data over telephone lines.
- Frame Relay is a packet switching protocol that typically uses leased lines such as T1 to carry data over long distances.
- The Asynchronous Transfer Mode (ATM) protocol is designed to carry audio, video, and multimedia.
- The five ATM classifications are CBR, VBR-NRT, VBR-RT, ABR, and UBR.
- The maximum size of an ATM cell is 53 bytes, consisting of a 5-byte header and a 48-byte payload.

- Voice over IP (VoIP) is a technique that relies on the TCP/IP protocol suite to carry audio and video data.
- VoIP uses the UDP protocol when sending time-sensitive data, such as a telephone conversation.
- VoIP uses the TCP protocol when sending audio and video streaming data.
- The H.323 protocol is used by telecommunications and telephone equipment.
- A gateway is used to convert the TCP/IP protocol to the H.323 protocol.
- The Session Initiation Protocol (SIP) is used for initiating, maintaining, and terminating the exchange of data.
- The Real-time Transport Protocol (RTP) is used to stream voice and video as used in video conferencing and gaming.
- A bandwidth shaper prioritizes network packets to ensure quality of service for time-sensitive applications.
- A protocol analyzer is an excellent tool for identifying VoIP-related problems.
- Impedance mismatch refers to the effect of connecting two different electronic audio systems that have different electronic characteristics.

Review Questions

Answer the following questions on a separate sheet of paper. Please do not write in this book.

1. Converting digital pulses to an analog waveform is called _____ conversion.
2. Converting an analog waveform to digital pulses is called _____ conversion.
3. What is jitter?
4. The delay of data from its origin to the final destination is called _____.
5. Name four factors that contribute to echo.
6. What is the principle use for MPEG compression?
7. What communications protocol is characterized by analog packets rather than digital packets for communication?
8. What is the maximum data rate of X.25?
9. What protocol could be called an upgrade of the X.25 protocol?
10. What is the maximum data rate of Frame Relay?
11. Which scenario requires the Constant Bit Rate (CBR) classification of ATM communications?
    A. Live telephone conversation
    B. FAX
    C. Real-time broadcast of a movie
    D. Business conference call
    E. Cell phone conversation
    F. Transfer of an image from an archive
12. Which ATM classification provides the best support for video conferencing?
13. What does the term *Variable Bit Rate* mean in reference to ATM classifications?
14. What is the total length of a typical ATM cell including the header?
15. What happens when one of the ATM cells is destroyed or does not reach the destination?
16. Why is the ATM cell payload so small (48 bytes)?
17. An ATM virtual path may contain two or more _____.
18. A Switched Virtual Circuit (SVC) is a (temporary, permanent) _____ connection between two devices on a network.

19. Based on what two factors will an ATM switch drop a cell?
20. Which VoIP protocol is used to establish and terminate a VoIP session?
21. Which VoIP protocol is used to stream multimedia in real-time between two network nodes?
22. What is another name for bandwidth shaper?
23. What is the purpose of a bandwidth shaper?
24. What is the purpose of the QoS protocol?
25. What is the most common source of VoIP echo?

Sample Network+ Exam Questions

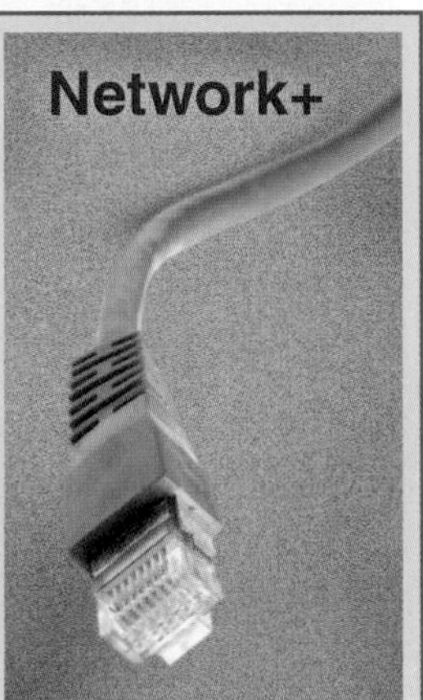

Answer the following questions on a separate sheet of paper. Please do not write in this book.

1. The delay of video/audio data packets is referred to as _____ in networking terminology.
   A. Packet Loss Ratio
   B. latency
   C. Variable Rate Overflow
   D. heading
2. Which ATM data transfer classification provides the highest quality of ATM service?
   A. VBR
   B. CBR
   C. UBR
   D. ABR
3. Which upper-layer protocol is typically used to package voice data that is to be transferred using Voice over IP (VoIP) technology?
   A. PPP
   B. SLIP
   C. UDP
   D. CHAP
4. Which definition best describes multiplexing as it applies to ATM?
   A. Combining multiple signals or sequencing different data packet streams over a single medium.
   B. Combining several different protocols to use as a single protocol.
   C. Combining several different types of networking media to form one cohesive media.
   D. Combining separate data packets into one large data packet before transmitting across a single network line.
5. Which of the following statements are true concerning ATM? (Select all that apply.)
   A. The ATM protocol allows voice, video, and text data to be carried on the same media.
   B. The maximum cell size for ATM is 1500 bytes.
   C. ATM is a connection-oriented protocol.
   D. ATM is a connectionless protocol.

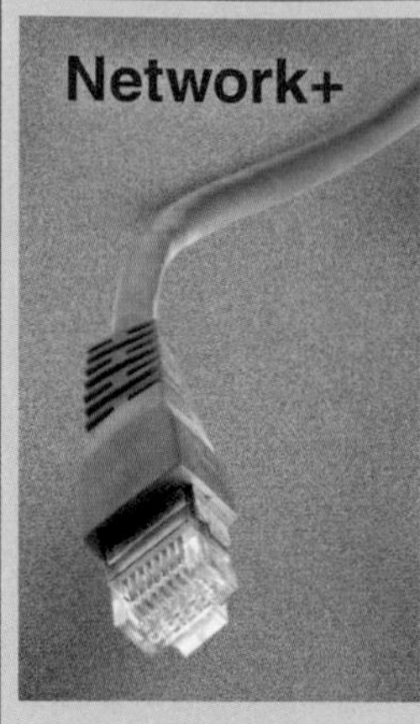

6. Which protocol transmits data in the form of an analog signal?
   A. IP
   B. IPX
   C. X.25
   D. ATM
7. Which compression method is used to achieve the highest data rates for multimedia over a network?
   A. MPEG-1
   B. X.25
   C. SLIP
   D. MPEG-4
8. Which protocol is used to support Internet telephony?
   A. CHAP
   B. VoIP
   C. SLIP
   D. AppleTalk
9. Which protocol is designed specifically to ensure the delivery of time-sensitive packets and reduce latency?
   A. QoS
   B. TCP
   C. X.25
   D. MPEG
10. Which telephone protocol suite is designed to support audio, video, and data communications?
    A. SLIP
    B. RADIUS
    C. RAS
    D. H.323

Interesting Web Sites for More Information

www.imtc.org
www.nortelnetworks.com
www.webtutorials.com

Suggested Laboratory Activities

1. Download and configure Skype on two PCs and then set up a video call between the two PCs. A protocol analyzer can be used to view the packet exchange and identify related video protocols.
2. Install two Web cams in the lab area and monitor the performance between the two cameras. You may wish to use a protocol analyzer to measure the amount of traffic generated between the two.
3. Access a Web cam on the Internet and use a protocol analyzer to examine the amount of network traffic required to support the download of images from the Web cam.

Chapter 12
Laboratory Activity

Windows Meeting Space

After completing this laboratory activity, you will be able to:

- Use the Windows Meeting Space set up dialog boxes to configure Meeting Space.
- Use Windows Meeting Space to set up an online collaboration activity.
- Use Windows Meeting Space to join an online collaboration activity.

In this laboratory activity, you will become familiar with Windows Vista Meeting Space. Microsoft has developed many different online collaboration tools, such as Windows XP NetMeeting, Windows Vista Meeting Space, and Windows 7 People Near Me.

Windows XP NetMeeting allowed for conferencing and collaboration and provided a white board feature and live video and audio support. Windows Vista Meeting Space does not include these features. Windows 7 People Near Me requires an e-mail account for configuration.

Windows Vista Meeting Space allows you to share your documents, programs, and your desktop with selected individuals or a group on the local area network or across the Internet. You can also connect to a network-enabled projector and make a presentation using Meeting Space. Invitations to join the meeting can be sent directly to individuals by Instant Messenger or by e-mail.

All data exchanged is encrypted, and all users can be authenticated by password to join the meeting. Data encryption for Microsoft collaboration is new starting in Windows Vista.

Earlier versions allowed microphone support for online sound exchange and video support for Web cams. These two options are not included in Meeting Space.

Equipment and Materials

- Two Windows Vista computers set up as part of a peer-to-peer network.
- The following information provided by your instructor:

  Display name: ______________________________

  Allow invitations from: ______________________________

Procedure

1. _____ Report to your assigned workstation.
2. _____ Boot the computers and verify they are in working order.
3. _____ On one of the computers, open Windows Meeting Space from the **Start** menu (**Start | All Programs | Windows Meeting Space**).

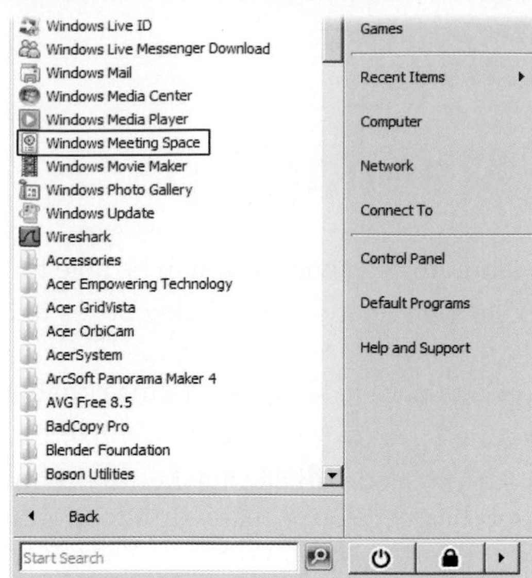

The first time Windows Meeting Space is opened, the program will automatically run in configuration mode. The next two screen captures show what you will see if Windows Meeting Space has not been configured.

4. ______ If Windows Meeting Space has not been previously configured, configure it now by filling in the display name and selecting from whom to allow invitations. Refer to the information that was provided by your instructor.
5. ______ After Windows Meeting Space is configured, open Meeting Space. A dialog box similar to the one in the following screen capture will appear.

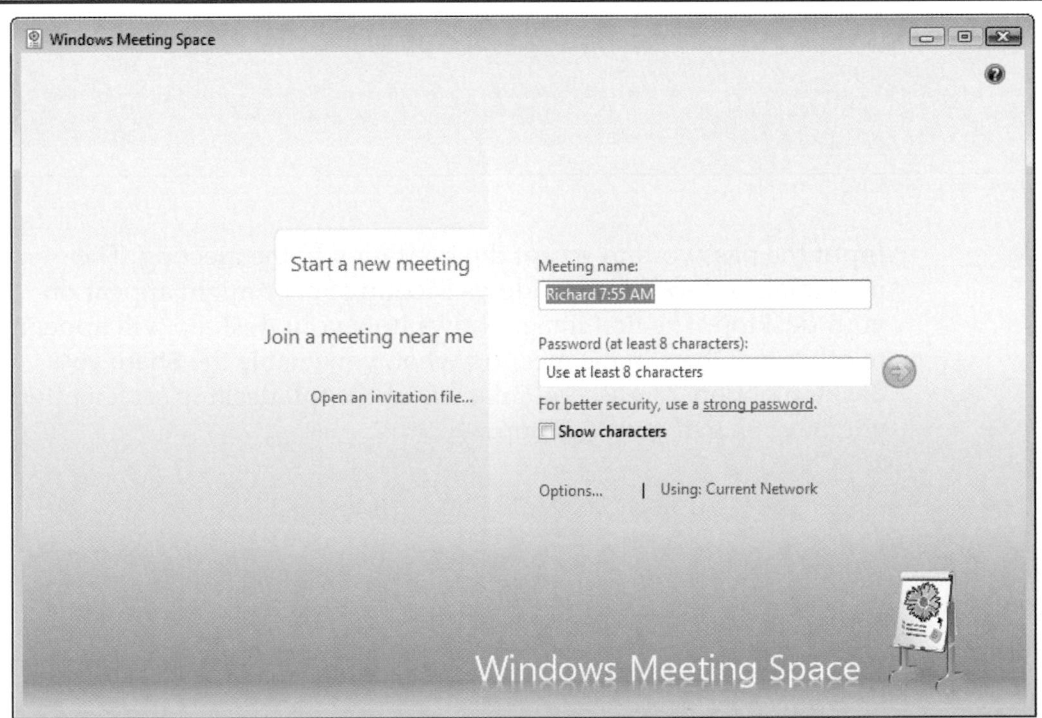

The meeting name has a default title of the account user name and time. You can change the meeting title if you want it to be more meaningful such as "Budget Meeting."

You are also presented with an option to create a password. Users joining the meeting must supply the matching password. You may use the default meeting title and then use "Pa$$word" for the meeting password.

6. ______ The invitations are automatically sent out to all Windows Vista computers in the peer-to-peer network. Invitees will see a dialog box similar to the one in the following screen capture.

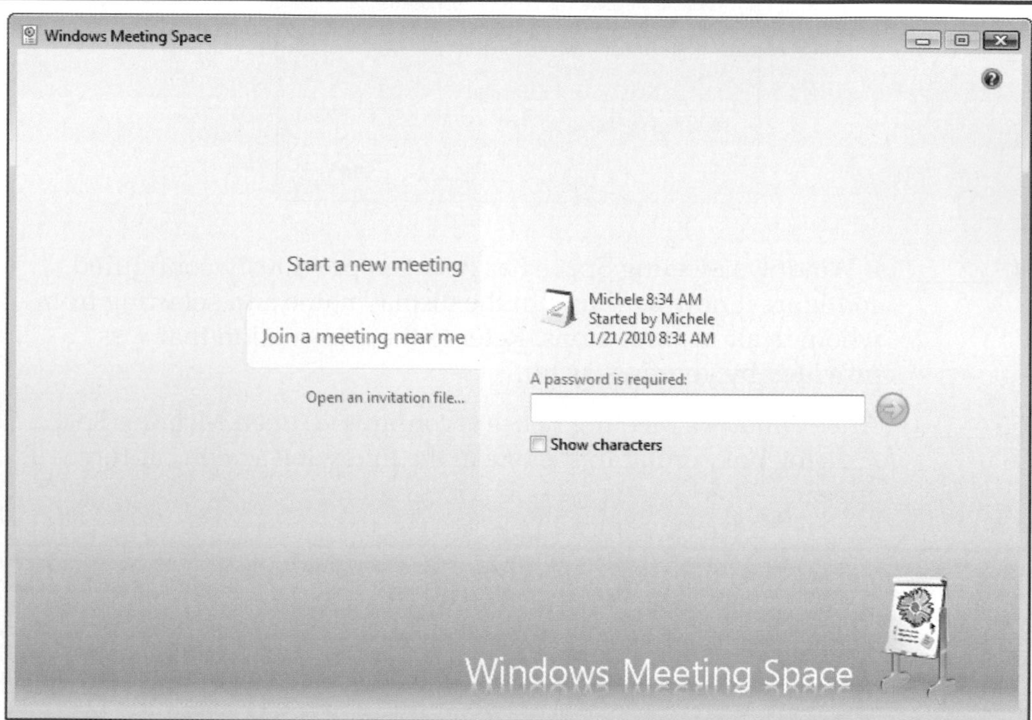

7. ______ Input the password to accept the invitation to the meeting. The next images show how Windows Meeting Space might appear on your desktop. The first image shows how your desktop will appear to other members in the meeting when you enable the **Share your desktop** option. The second image is of the full desktop screen after you have shared your desktop.

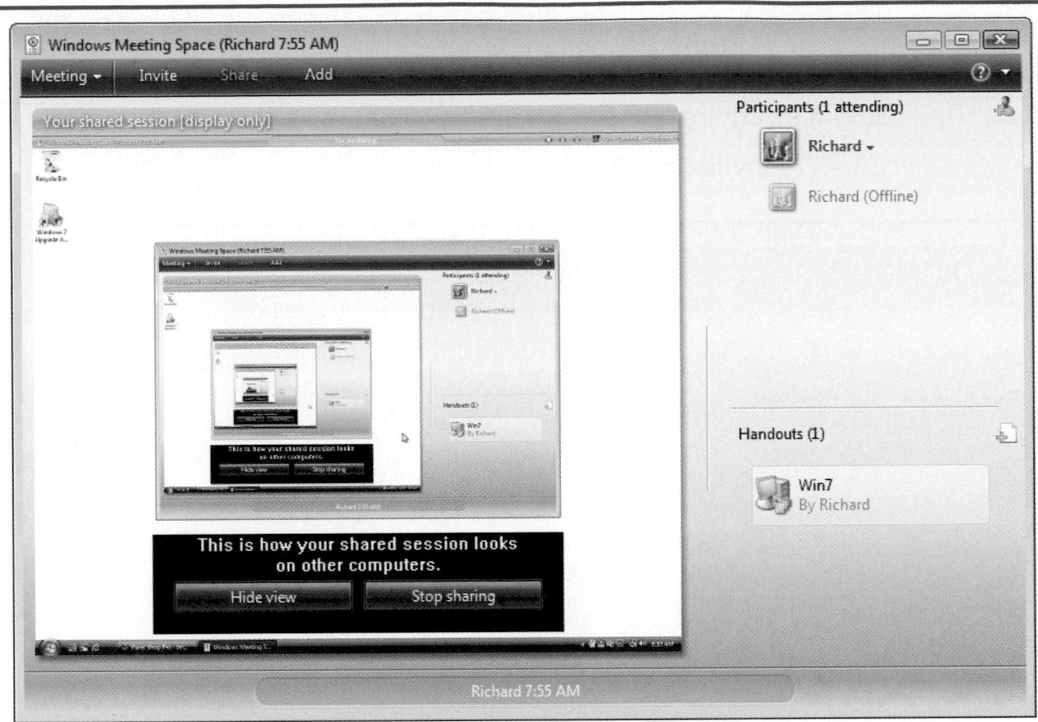
Windows Meeting Space (Richard 7:55 AM)
Meeting
Invite
Share
Add
Your shared session [display only]
Participants (1 attending)
Richard
Richard (Offline)
Handouts (1)
Win7
By Richard
This is how your shared session looks on other computers.
Hide view
Stop sharing
Richard 7:55 AM

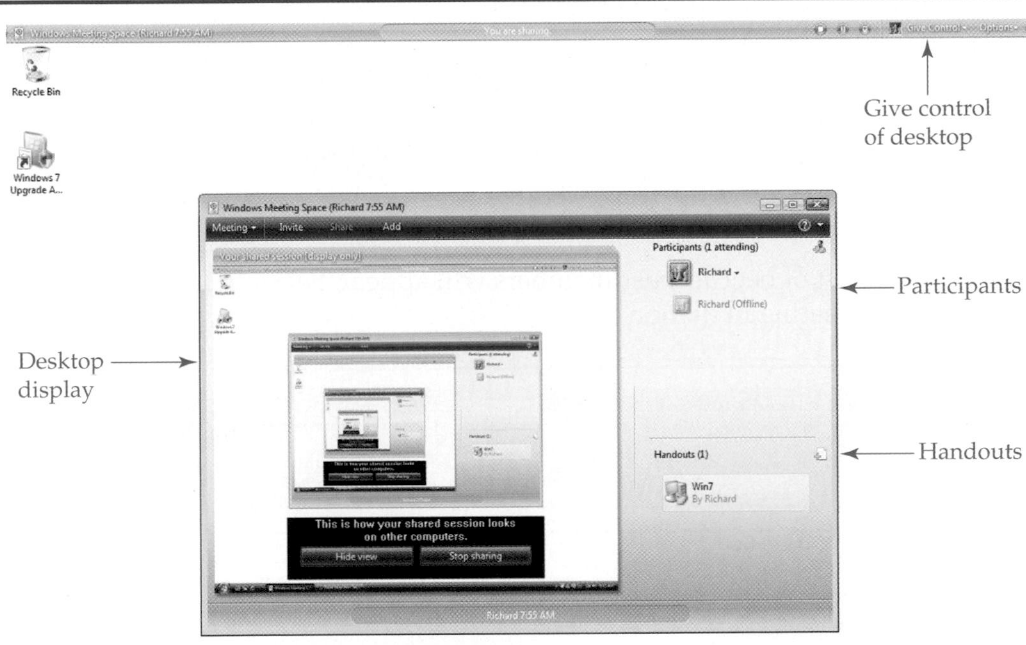
Recycle Bin
Windows 7 Upgrade A...
Give control of desktop
Participants
Desktop display
Handouts
Windows Meeting Space (Richard 7:55 AM)
Meeting
Invite
Share
Add
Participants (1 attending)
Richard
Richard (Offline)
Handouts (1)
Win7
By Richard
This is how your shared session looks on other computers.
Hide view
Stop sharing
Richard 7:55 AM

Windows Meeting S...
Paint Shop Pro - Im...
8:12 AM

The meeting participants will appear as a list on the right side. You have an option to share your desktop and another option to provide handouts for the meeting. The handout, such as a document, will be automatically sent to the other participants as a shared folder.

8. _____ Click the **Invite** option.

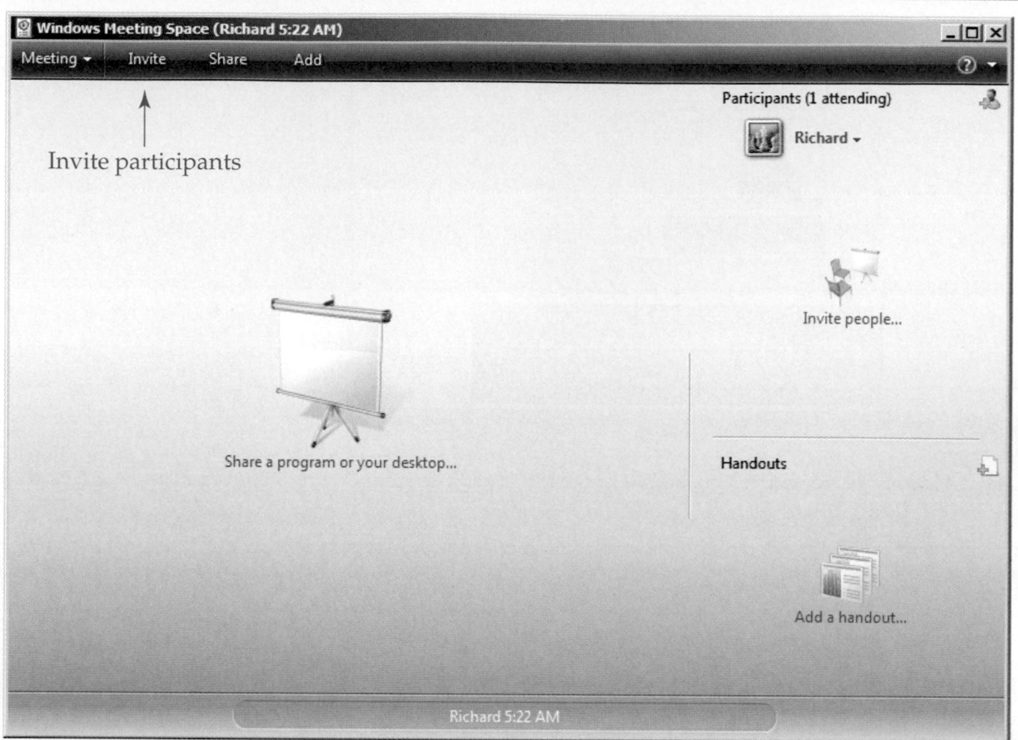

A list of peer-to-peer members will appear. Select individuals to send a meeting invitation to.

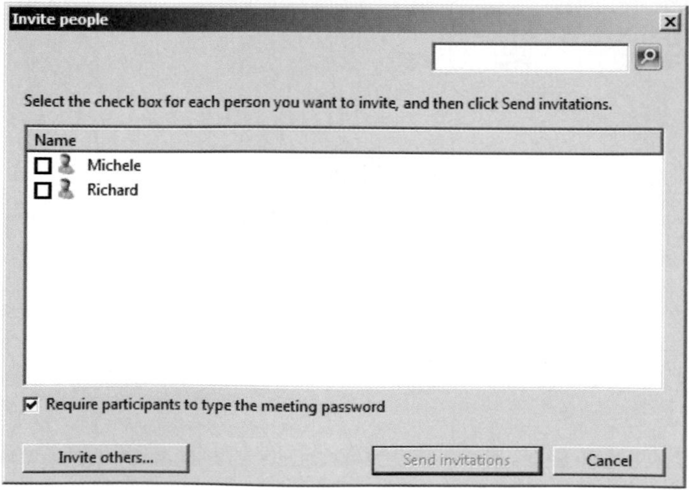

You also are presented with an **Invite others** button, which will allow you to send an e-mail to persons who do not appear in the list. After you have selected people to join the meeting, you can send them text messages. To text a member of the meeting, simply double-click the participants name.

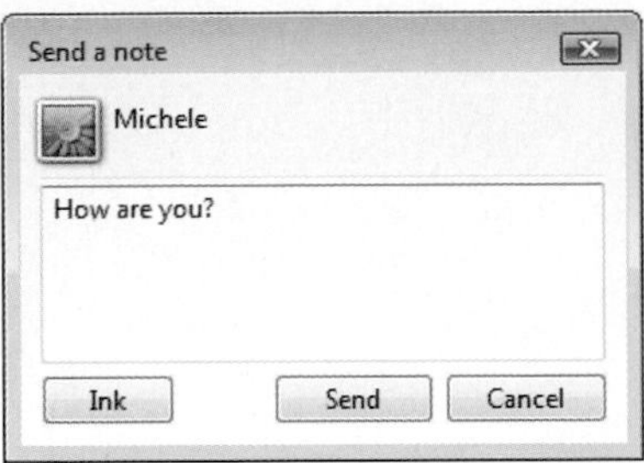

9. _____ Take a few minutes to explore the features of Windows Meeting Space by trying the following tasks:
   - Sharing a file as a handout
   - Sending a text message to the other participants
   - Sharing your desktop with the other participants
10. _____ Close Windows Meeting Space and then answer the review questions.

Review Questions

Answer the following questions on a separate sheet of paper. Please do not write in this book.

1. Which version of Microsoft Windows uses Meeting Space?
2. Can you share your desktop in Windows Meeting Space?
3. In which two ways can invitations be sent in Windows Meeting Space?
4. Which two featured options that were available in Windows NetMeeting are no longer available in Windows Meeting Space?

A computer, headset, and software application such as Skype can be used to make voice and video calls over the net.

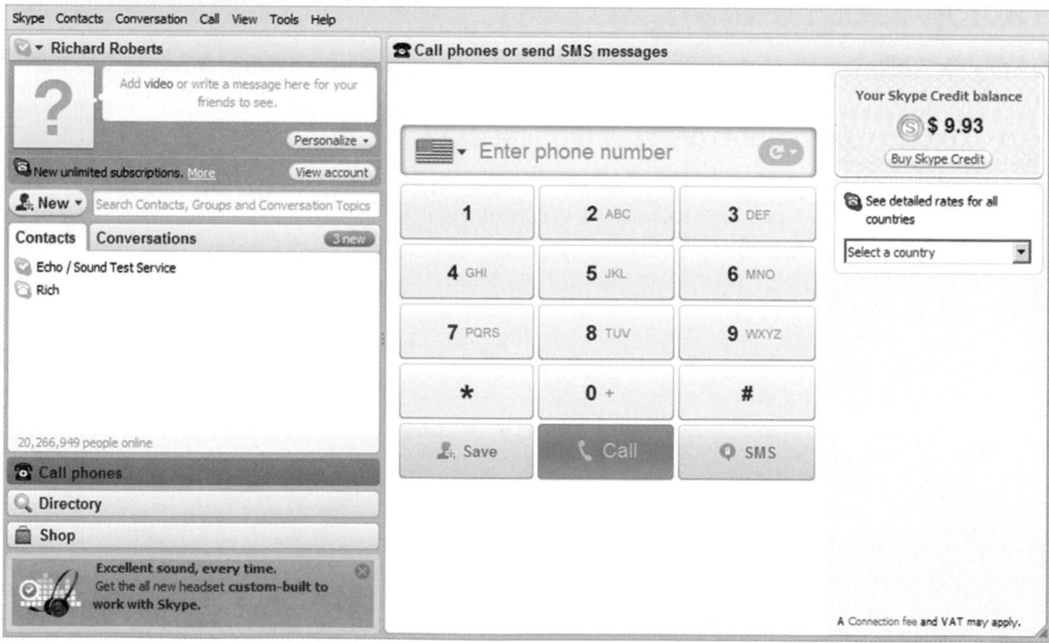

13 Web Servers and Services

After studying this chapter, you will be able to:

- ❑ Differentiate between Internet, intranet, and extranet.
- ❑ Identify the parts of a URL.
- ❑ Identify the features of a Web browser.
- ❑ Explain how markup languages work.
- ❑ Explain how e-mail messages are transported.
- ❑ Differentiate between common e-mail protocols.

Network+ Exam—Key Points

The Network+ Certification exam presents questions about Web server basics. It does not contain in-depth questions in this area. Rather, it tests your knowledge of protocols such as HTTP, HTML, POP3, IMAP4, SMTP, and FTP commonly used in conjunction with Web servers and e-mail servers. You need a basic understanding of how these protocols are used. Also, be sure you can configure a workstation for e-mail.

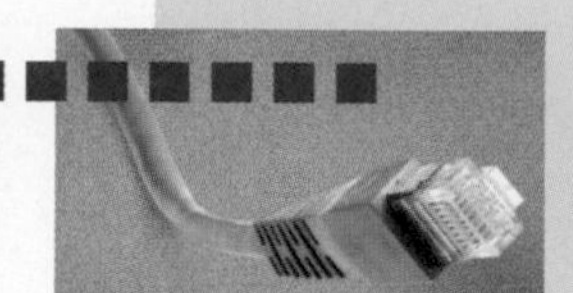

Key Words and Terms

The following words and terms will become important pieces of your networking vocabulary. Be sure you can define them.

anonymous FTP site
cascading style sheets (CSS)
Extensible Markup Language (XML)
extranet
File Transfer Protocol (FTP)
HTML tag
hyperlink
Hypertext Markup Language (HTML)
Hypertext Transfer Protocol (HTTP)
Internet
Internet Message Access Protocol (IMAP)
intranet
JavaScript
mail filter
mail gateway
Multipurpose Internet Mail Extensions (MIME)
Network News Transfer Protocol (NNTP)
newsgroup
Post Office Protocol (POP)
search engine
Secure File Transfer Protocol (SFTP)
Simple Mail Transfer Protocol (SMTP)
Simple Object Access Protocol (SOAP)
spam
spammer
spamming
Standard Generalized Markup Language (SGML)
Trivial File Transfer Protocol (TFTP)
Uniform Resource Locator (URL)
Web browser
Web server
Web site

The need for Web servers has greatly increased over the years. Web servers provide a means to display informational pages to viewers across the World Wide Web or a local area network. E-mail has rapidly grown to become one of the most common forms of communication.

In this chapter, you will learn the differences between the three types of networks that provide Web page distribution. You will also be introduced to two of the most popular Web server software packages and to the basic operation of an e-mail system.

Internet, Intranet, and Extranet

There are three types of networks that provide Web page distribution: Internet, intranet, and extranet. The type of access allowed to a network's Web pages (Web site) determines each classification.

Internet
a collection of interconnected networks from all around the world.

Internet

An ***Internet*** is a collection of interconnected networks from all around the world. Therefore, when you install a Web server for the Internet, you are setting up a computer to be accessed by anyone in the world. The Internet relies on the TCP/IP suite of protocols to transport Web pages. The Internet is also referred to as the *World Wide Web* because when the various network cable connections that make up the Internet are diagrammed, the diagram resembles a spider's web.

There are other types of networks that function similar to the Internet but on a limited or restricted basis. These networks are called *intranet* and *extranet* and are commonly found in business environments.

Intranet

A Web server need not be connected to the Internet to serve as a way for companies to communicate and to distribute information. A Web server can be connected to an intranet. An ***intranet*** is a private network that serves a specific group of users within a LAN. For example, a corporation or an educational institution may set up a private Web server to be accessed only by a designated group of users from within its local area network. In the corporation, an intranet is designed for only the employees. In the educational setting, it may be accessed only by school employees and students. Normally, an intranet cannot be freely accessed by anyone. If the intranet is accessible from the World Wide Web, the intranet uses a firewall to isolate it from the outside world. The main reason for access limitations is security.

intranet
a private network that serves a specific group of users within a LAN.

An intranet can be used to post forms, explanations and examples of forms, policy books, maps, address books, and such. The advantage of using an intranet is users already know how to surf the Internet and can start using the system immediately. In a traditional network, a new user often needs training in how to access network shares and navigate directory structures.

Extranet

An ***extranet*** allows internal access to Web pages and allows authorized personnel from outside the network to access the network's Web pages. An extranet is often designed to allow employees, business partners (other businesses), and customers access to the intranet from outside the network, through the Internet. Access to the extranet is available only if the user has a valid user name and password. The user name and password determines what areas of the extranet are accessible. For example, members of partner companies may have only limited access to the Web site while employees may have full access to the Web site.

extranet
a network that allows internal and external access to Web pages by authorized personnel.

Look at **Figure 13-1** for a comparison of an intranet and an extranet. Remember that an extranet does not let the general public access the Web site—only partner companies, employees, and authorized customers.

Domain Name and URL Resolution

Since the TCP/IP protocols use IP addresses to transfer data, the Internet must use the Domain Name Service (DNS) to translate domain names and Uniform Resource Locators (URLs) to an IP address. A ***Uniform Resource Locator (URL)*** is a user-friendly name such as http://support.microsoft.com. When a URL is typed into a Web browser, the Web browser uses a DNS server to translate or resolve the URL name to an IP address.

Uniform Resource Locator (URL)
a user-friendly name such as http://support.microsoft.com, which allows users to access Web-based resources.

A user can directly access a Web page by typing in the IP address of the Web server that hosts the Web page. This eliminates the need to use a DNS server

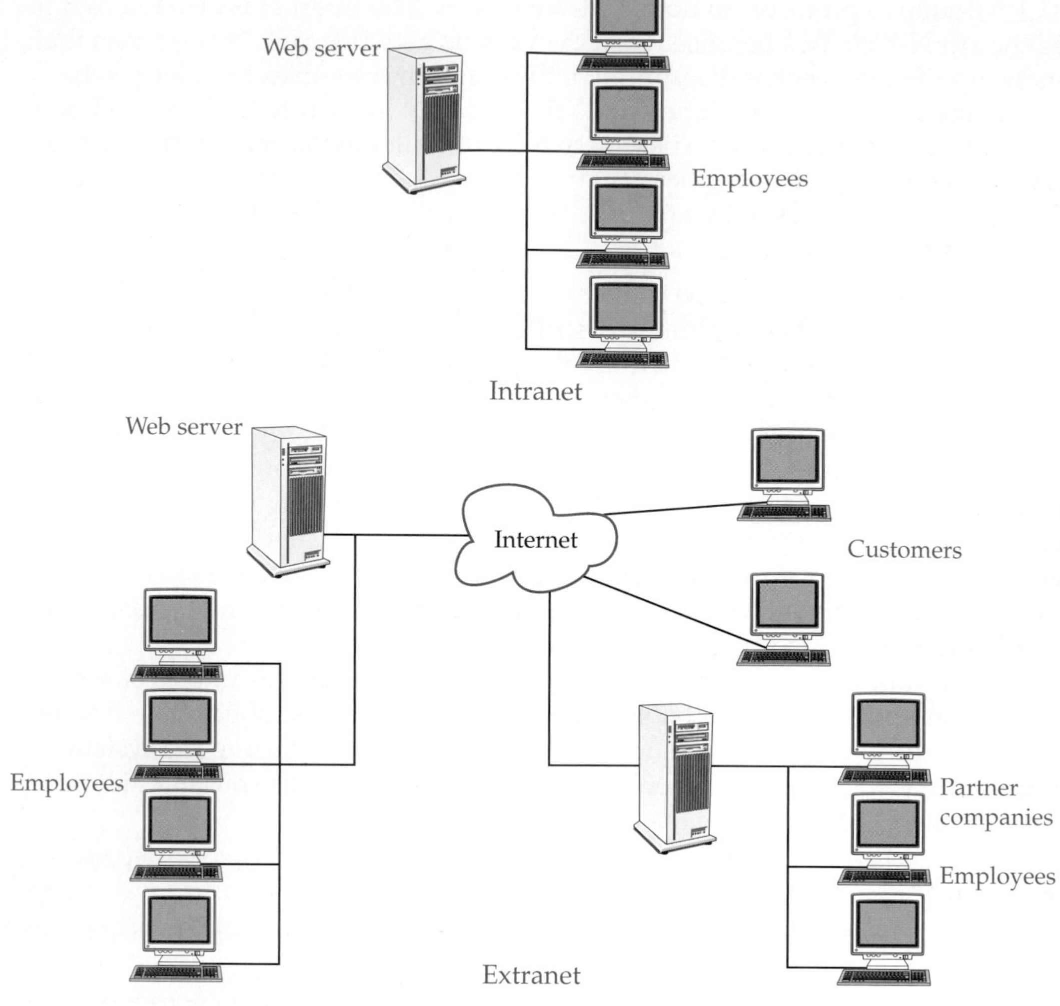

Figure 13-1.
An intranet allows employees limited access to a company Web server. The Web server is accessible only through the company LAN. It is not accessible through the Internet. An extranet provides limited access to the company Web server to both employees within the LAN and to customers, partner companies, and employees through the Internet.

to resolve the URL name to an IP address and may expedite access. However, people do not generally communicate by IP addresses. They use domain names.

Tech Tip

Network proxy servers store IP and URL addresses in their cache to expedite the connection process. A proxy server intercepts all requests for Web sites and then provides the requested Web page without the need to connect to the Web site. If the proxy server does not contain a copy of the requested page, it forwards the request to the Web site.

A complete URL can be seen in **Figure 13-2.** Note the way the URL is expressed. The first item in the URL is the protocol. Typical choices are HTTP and FTP. The next part of the URL is the domain name of the Web server hosting the site

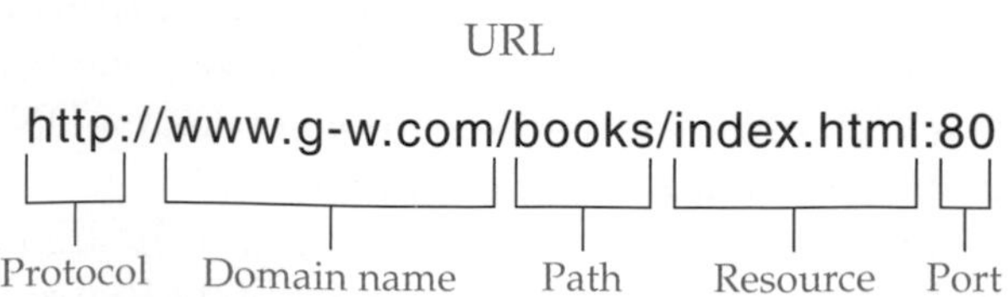

Figure 13-2.
Structure of a URL.

followed closely by the path to the resource or page desired. The path is actually a directory or directory and subdirectories on the Web server that lead to the Web page file. In the example, the index.html Web page is located in the /books directory. The port number at the end of the URL is optional and is not generally used. The default port number of a Web page TCP/IP connection is 80.

DNS is organized as a hierarchical structure with the root at the top. As you have seen in Chapter 7—Microsoft Network Operating Systems, Microsoft Active Directory (AD) has a similar structure as DNS. NetBIOS domain names of earlier systems have come to look like a URL. Lightweight Directory Access Protocol (LDAP) has made it possible for Microsoft AD and DNS to look and function similarly. In each structure, the entire directory appears as though it is one structure on one computer; when in reality, it can comprise many computers spread across the world. You may wish to review the DNS structure in Chapter 10—TCP/IP Fundamentals.

Web Servers

Web server
a server configured to provide Web services, such as Web pages, file transfer, and HTML-based e-mail.

Web site
a location on the World Wide Web that contains a collection of Web pages and files, which can be accessed through the Internet. A Web site is owned and managed by an individual, company, or organization.

A ***Web server*** is, as the name implies, a server configured to provide Web services, such as Web pages, file transfer, and HTML-based e-mail. To create a Web server, a software package, such as Apache HTTP Server or Microsoft Internet Information Services (IIS), is installed on a computer. The computer can be a server or a PC. Typically, Web server software is installed on a server that is running a network operating system, such as Windows Server 2008. You can also install a light version of IIS on a PC running a workstation version of the Microsoft operating system. The only requirement is the computer should provide sufficient resources such as memory, CPU speed, and hard disk drive space to accommodate the software package.

A ***Web site*** is traditionally defined as a location on the World Wide Web. The Web site contains a collection of Web pages and files, which can be accessed through the Internet. A Web site is owned and managed by an individual, company, or organization.

An intranet has almost all of the characteristics of a Web site, but it is not a true Web site by strict definition.

For a Web server to operate while connected to the Internet, it must be assigned a domain name and IP address. A domain name can be acquired through a domain name provider or a Web hosting service. A domain name must be registered before an IP address can be assigned to a Web server. To obtain an IP address and domain name combination, the user submits an application to a domain name provider or Web hosting service for a nominal fee. Once the information is processed, an IP address is assigned to the domain name.

A domain name must be unique. In other words, the domain name you choose cannot be in use by another person or company. You can check if the domain name you've selected is unique by using the **whois** utility on the InterNIC Web site (www.internic.net). If the domain name you enter is in use, the **whois** utility displays information such as the domain name's registrar, the names of the name servers on which the domain name is listed, the date the domain name was assigned, and the date the domain name expires.

Figure 13-3 shows the **whois** utility screen prior to a request for information. **Figure 13-4** shows the detailed results of a search for the g-w.com domain name.

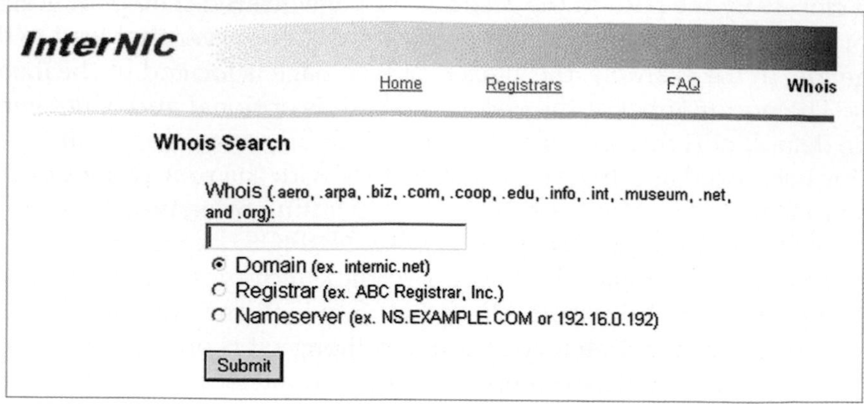

Figure 13-3.
The **whois** utility can be accessed through the InterNIC Web site.

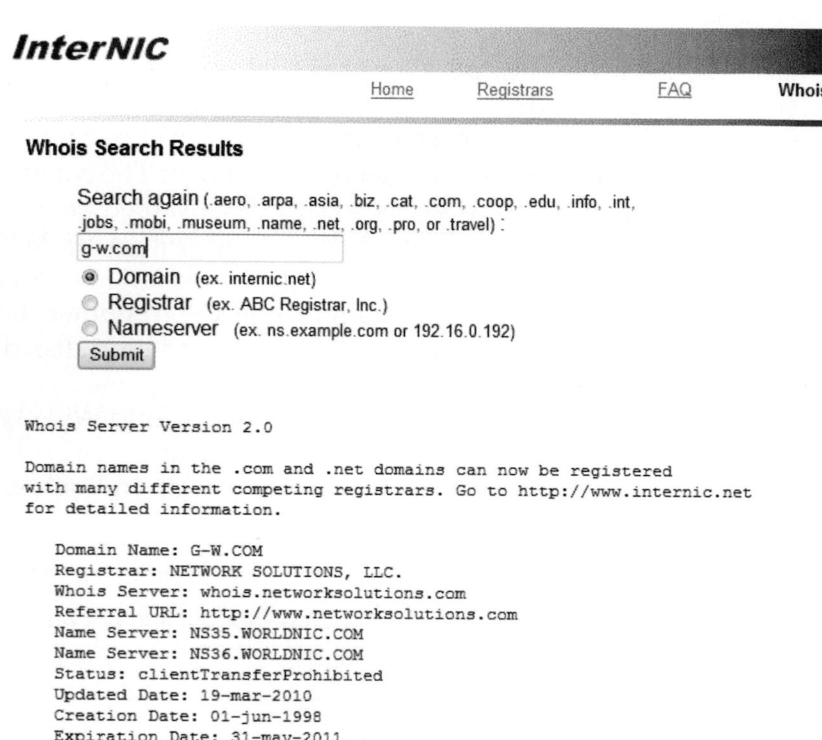

Figure 13-4.
The results of a **whois** search.

The **whois** utility can conduct searches by the domain name, registrar name, or nameserver. The nameserver can be listed as a domain name or an IP address.

There are several ways to set up a Web server. A Web server can be set up on the same server as the network server, a server dedicated to only Web services, and a Web hosting company's Web site.

A Web server can run on the same server as the network server, especially if the LAN has only one server. In fact, you can run Web server services from a workstation. For example, installing Internet Information Services (IIS) on a Windows workstation allows the workstation to run a single Web site that can be accessed by a maximum of ten simultaneous users.

A dedicated server can be used to host Web services. A dedicated server serves only one function. However, more than one Web site can be hosted from a single server.

A company or organization may choose to have a Web hosting company host its Web site. A Web hosting company sells space on its Web server, allowing a company or organization to set up a Web site without the need of owning and supporting a Web server.

Figure 13-5 and **Figure 13-6** illustrate the two most common scenarios of Web hosting. Each has advantages and disadvantages. For a large Web site consisting of many pages and a large volume of traffic, it is probably less expensive to install a Web server in-house. For a smaller Web site with a low volume of traffic, using a Web hosting company is more appropriate. Using a company that provides most of your Web hosting needs is called *outsourcing*. Look at the chart in **Figure 13-7** to see how some of the factors of Web site operation compare between hosting your own Web site and outsourcing your Web site.

Apache HTTP Server

The most widely used Web server software is Apache HTTP Server. The main reason for its popularity is its price. Programmers with a common interest developed the Apache HTTP Server software for free. The Apache HTTP Server software can be downloaded from the Apache Software Foundation Web site at www.apache.org, or it can be bought as a package with documentation and extra utilities for a modest price. Documentation and additional references are available at the Apache Software Foundation Web site. Once Apache is installed and started on a server, a manual can

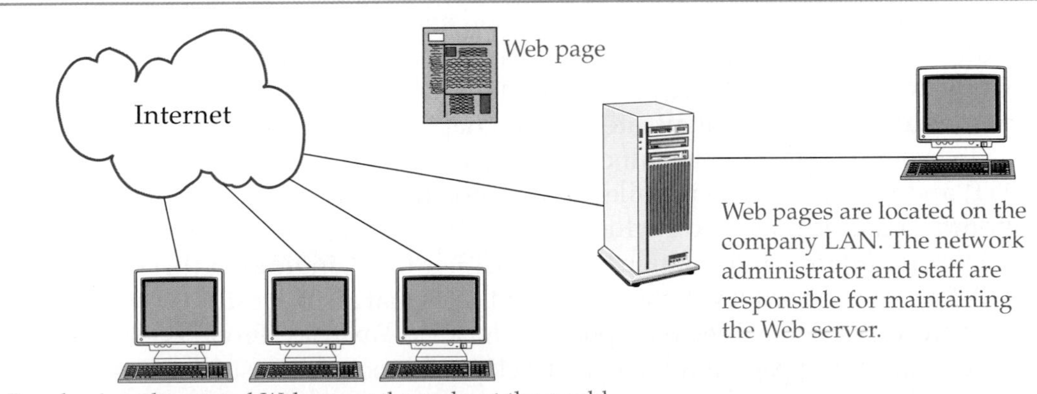

Figure 13-5.
When a Web server is part of a company's LAN, the network administrator and staff are responsible for maintaining the server.

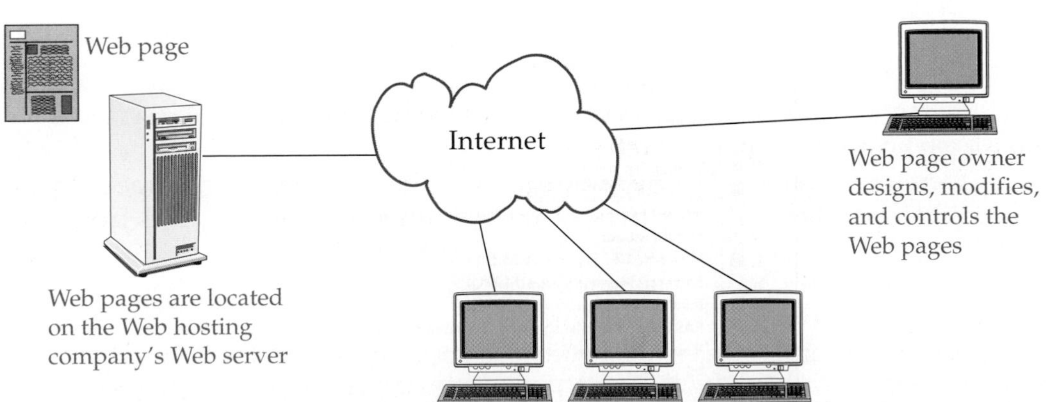

Figure 13-6.
Web hosting companies can provide Web services. In this scenario, the Web page owner is responsible for the content and design of Web pages. The Web hosting company is responsible for supporting and maintaining the server.

Figure 13-7.
Comparison of outsourcing a Web site and hosting your own Web site.

Outsourcing Your Web Site	Hosting Your Own Web Site
Server space used is prorated.	Owner must purchase and install server hardware and software.
Technical support is provided.	An expert technician is required.
Connectivity is provided. Fee varies according to traffic volume.	Owner must obtain and pay for connectivity such as DSL, Cable modem, T1 line, or other high-bandwidth connection.
Most services, such as administration and maintenance, are provided.	Frequent administration, maintenance, and security checks are needed.
Web site design is not provided. Some companies offer a one-time design service for free on a limited number of pages.	Need Web page design software and personnel competent to use it.

be accessed through http://localhost/manual/index.html. The manual is a complete user guide with information about all aspects of installing and using Apache HTTP Server.

Apache HTTP Server software is generally associated with Linux and UNIX systems. However, versions of Apache HTTP Server software are available for all the major network operating systems, such as Microsoft and Linux.

Internet Information Services (IIS)

The Internet Information Services (IIS) is the Microsoft Windows Web server default service. IIS supports Web site creation and management. Some service protocols that are supported by IIS are the Network News Transfer Protocol (NNTP), File Transfer Protocol (FTP), and Simple Mail Transfer Protocol (SMTP). These protocols are covered in detail later in this chapter.

IIS is not installed by default on a Microsoft server. Services such as IIS, FTP, SMTP, and NNTP must be installed as additional services. **Figure 13-8** shows the **Windows Features** dialog box, which lists additional services to turn off or on. The checkbox for Internet Information Services (IIS) is filled, indicating that only part of the IIS feature is turned on. A checkmark indicates that all of a feature is turned on.

Microsoft's original Web page program is called *FrontPage*. FrontPage is not as robust as other Web page and Web site development tools. Microsoft has a new Web

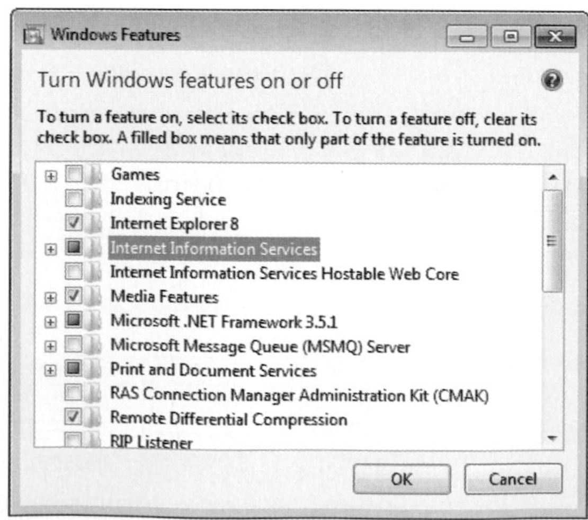

Figure 13-8.
Internet Information Services and other services can be installed through the **Windows Features** dialog box.

Figure 13-9. Default IIS Web page displayed on the Web server or from a Windows workstation.

page suite of tools called Microsoft Expression. Microsoft Expression does not require extensions (supportive software programs) to be installed on the host server as is required with FrontPage. Microsoft Expression is a complete suite of programs and utilities that are as powerful as any other Web page suite today. To learn more about the Microsoft Expression Web suite, visit www.microsoft.com/expression.

Figure 13-9 shows the results of using Microsoft Internet Explorer to access the default Web page after IIS7 has been installed. The page shown will display on the Windows Web server and from a workstation accessing the Web server.

Tech Tip

You can install IIS on a Windows workstation and support a maximum of ten simultaneous connections. This is a great way to experiment with Web page designs and Web server technologies.

Web Browsers

A ***Web browser*** is a software program that permits the user to navigate the World Wide Web and then interpret and display Web pages. The most common Web browsers incorporate other software programs such as e-mail clients and security features. Two of the most popular Web browsers are Microsoft Internet Explorer and Mozilla Firefox.

Web browser
a software program that permits the user to navigate the World Wide Web and then interpret and display Web pages.

Search Engines

A ***search engine*** is a software program that is designed to locate Web sites and pages by relevant terms entered into the search text box. Most Web browsers incorporate a search engine, but Web browsers and search engines are technically two different software applications. For example, Internet Explorer and Mozilla Firefox are Web browsers, but Google is a search engine. The term *search engine,*

search engine
a software program that is designed to locate Web sites and pages by relevant terms entered into the search text box.

however, has become synonymous with *Web browser* because the Web browser and search engine are configured as a single software application.

Two new Web software applications are Microsoft Bing and Google Chrome. Chrome is the new Web browser introduced by Google the search engine company. Bing is the new search engine developed by Microsoft to incorporate into Internet Explorer. As you can see, Microsoft and Google have become two competitive rivals each trying to dominate the Internet by providing free search engines and Web browsers.

Tech Tip

To determine if a software application is a Web browser or a search engine, enter "C:" into the address bar. A Web browser software application such as Internet Explorer or Mozilla Firefox will display the contents of the C partition. If you enter "C:" into a search engine text box, results will be displayed with Web page and Web site locations related to the term "C:".

Figure 13-10 shows Internet Explorer (the Web browser) with Google (the search engine) set as the default search engine. The Web browser has an address bar in which you can enter the Web site URL or IP address. The search engine has a search text box in which to enter relevant key terms. Notice in Figure 13-10 the term "fireplaces" is used to generate a list of corresponding Web pages and Web sites.

The reason Web browsers and search engines are free software applications is they display advertised links as part of an Internet search. Sponsored links or paid advertisements are used to generate money for the search engine company,

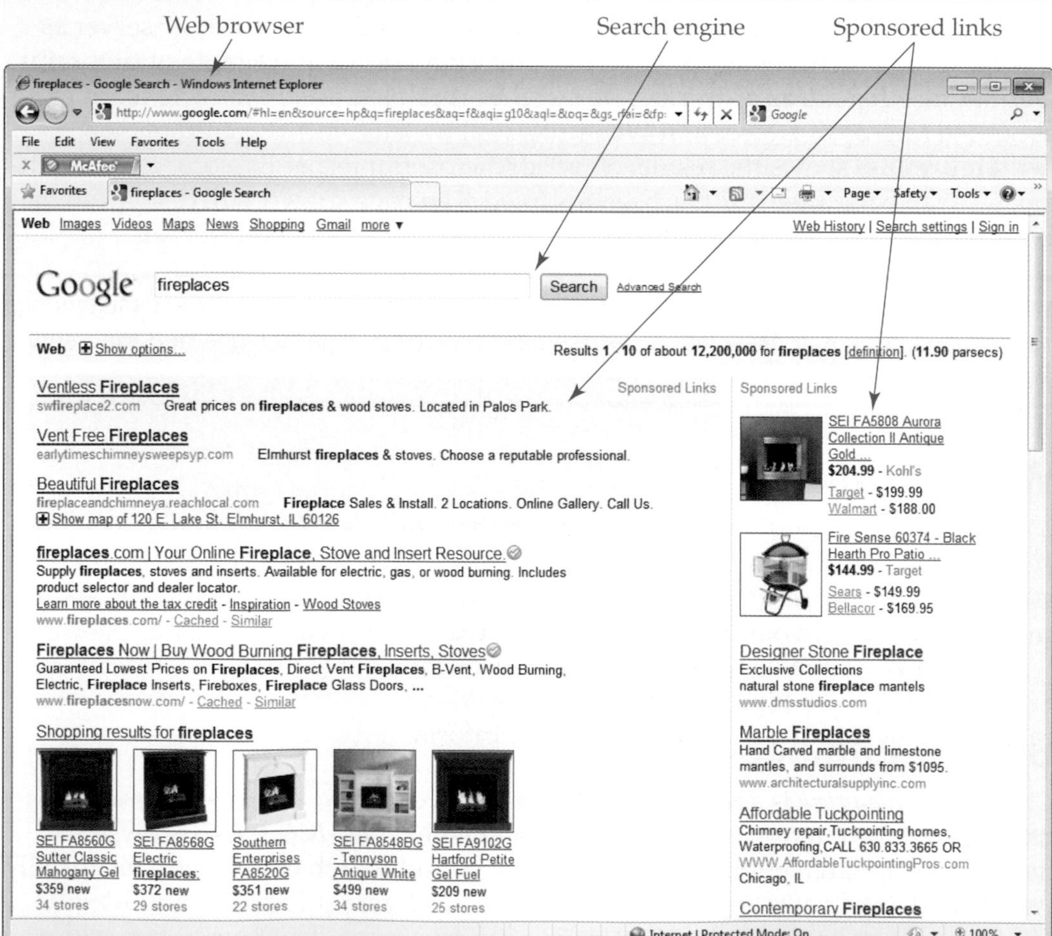

Figure 13-10. The Internet Explorer Web browser with Google set as the default search engine.

thus providing the search engine software application for free to users. The actual results relevant to the search term(s) begin just below the colored background area.

Search engine companies maintain millions of listings in a database correlated to search terms. The exact method used by search engine companies to rate Web pages and Web sites is a closely guarded secret. Even though the exact method is kept secret; there are some commonly known factors which influence search engine results.

One factor is that you can apply directly to the search engine company to have your Web site and Web pages listed. Some companies will list the site for free while others charge a fee.

Another factor is a search engine searches the entire World Wide Web using software programs known as *spiders* or *bots*. The spiders or bots collect information about Web page content such as terms found on the page and links to other Web pages and Web sites. The search engine company collects the data and stores it in large server farms. When you enter search terms or key words into a search engine text box, the terms are compared to terms in the database.

Finally, a Web site can have a high ranking. One key to having a high ranking in a search engine is to have a Web page that has many links to it from other Web sites. The more links to the page from other Web sites, the more popular the Web page, hence, a higher ranking by the search engine company.

Web Site Communications

Web site communications is based on the Hypertext Transfer Protocol (HTTP) and the Hypertext Markup Language (HTML). The ***Hypertext Transfer Protocol (HTTP)*** is a protocol designed for communication between a Web browser and a Web server. ***Hypertext Markup Language (HTML)*** is a programming language used to create Web pages. It can be interpreted by any type of computer with any type of Web browser.

Hypertext Transfer Protocol (HTTP)
a protocol designed for communications between a Web browser and a Web server.

Hypertext Markup Language (HTML)
a programming language used to create Web pages.

HTML

HTML also provides a means for linking to other Web pages or to an area on the same Web page. A link to another Web page or to an area on the same Web page is called a ***hyperlink***. A user simply clicks the hyperlink and the Web browser automatically replaces the current Web page with the Web page designated in the hyperlink or "jumps" to a specified area within the Web page.

hyperlink
a link to another Web page or to an area on the same Web page.

A Web page contains text and special symbols defined by HTML tags. HTML tags are also referred to as *markups*. An ***HTML tag*** is an instruction for how the text and graphics should appear when displayed in a Web browser. For example, HTML tags determine the size, style, and color of the text font and identify the placement of graphics. A Web browser interprets the HTML tags to make the text and graphics appear on the display as specified.

HTML tag
an instruction for how the text and graphics should appear when displayed in a Web browser.

Figure 13-11 shows the Goodheart-Willcox Publisher Web page as it appears in Internet Explorer. **Figure 13-12** shows a section of coding used to represent the page. You can see how the HTML tags and information combine to present the information in a Web browser.

The HTML standard was developed by the World Wide Web Consortium (W3C). As you have previously learned in Chapter 1—Introduction to Networking, W3C is a nonprofit organization dedicated to the development of voluntary standards for the Web. The consortium has spent many years developing the standards for SGML, HTML, and XML.

Figure 13-11. A Web browser interprets the HTML tags in the Web page coding to display the text and graphics.

SGML

Standard Generalized Markup Language (SGML) the original standard for both HTML and XML.

Standard Generalized Markup Language (SGML) is the original standard for both HTML and XML. HTML is a compact version of SGML. XML was developed to enhance HTML. Today, Extensible Hypertext Markup Language (XHTML) is a variation of XML and is the recommended replacement for HTML.

XML

Extensible Markup Language (XML) a markup language based on the same principles as HTML, with the added ability to create custom tags.

Extensible Markup Language (XML) is greatly enhanced compared with HTML. XML is designed especially for large enterprise business applications running on Web servers. While XML is based on the same principles as HTML, it has one very important difference: XML allows the creation of custom tags. XML also identifies the data contained inside the tags, while HTML only identifies how to display the data identified by the tag. For example, HTML uses tags to identify the size, font, or color of a block of text. XML can do the same, but it can also identify the contents, such as a numerical calculation for a database or spreadsheet. This allows the contents to be easily accessed and manipulated by a database or spreadsheet program. XML was designed with business applications in mind. XML can be easily converted to HTML and displayed through a browser. This ensures downward compatibility for systems.

CSS

cascading style sheets (CSS) an enhancement to HTML tags that can be embedded into a Web page or exist as a separate script to control all pages in a Web site.

The latest markup language is ***cascading style sheets (CSS).*** You can think of CSS as an enhancement to HTML tags rather than a separate new language. CSS

Figure 13-12.
Example of coding used to create the Goodheart-Willcox Publisher home page.

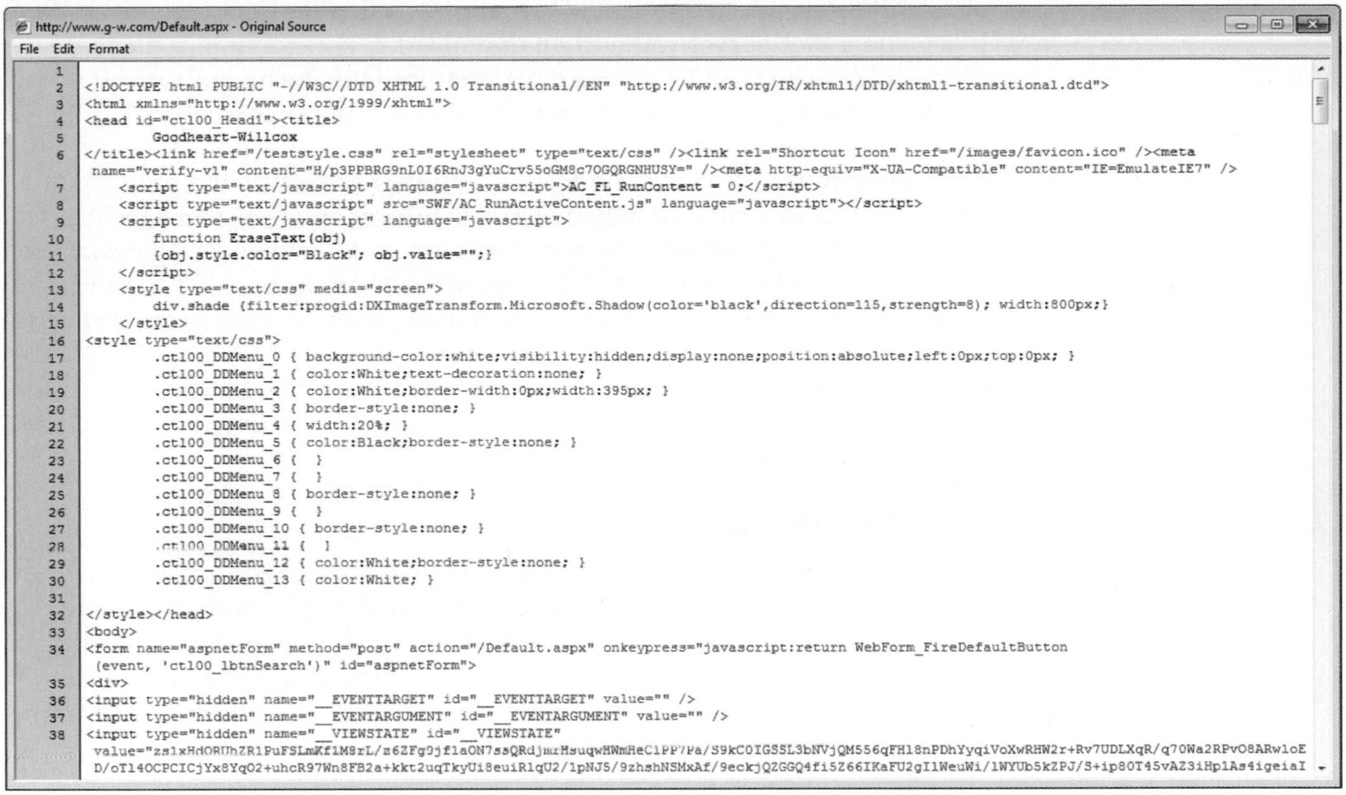

http://www.g-w.com/Default.aspx - Original Source

File Edit Format

```
<!DOCTYPE html PUBLIC "-//W3C//DTD XHTML 1.0 Transitional//EN" "http://www.w3.org/TR/xhtml1/DTD/xhtml1-transitional.dtd">
<html xmlns="http://www.w3.org/1999/xhtml">
<head id="ctl00_Head1"><title>
        Goodheart-Willcox
</title><link href="/teststyle.css" rel="stylesheet" type="text/css" /><link rel="Shortcut Icon" href="/images/favicon.ico" /><meta
 name="verify-v1" content="H/p3PPBRG9nL0I6RnJ3gYuCrv55oGM8c7OGQRGNHUSY=" /><meta http-equiv="X-UA-Compatible" content="IE=EmulateIE7" />
    <script type="text/javascript" language="javascript">AC_FL_RunContent = 0;</script>
    <script type="text/javascript" src="SWF/AC_RunActiveContent.js" language="javascript"></script>
    <script type="text/javascript" language="javascript">
        function EraseText(obj)
        {obj.style.color="Black"; obj.value="";}
    </script>
    <style type="text/css" media="screen">
        div.shade {filter:progid:DXImageTransform.Microsoft.Shadow(color='black',direction=115,strength=8); width:800px;}
    </style>
<style type="text/css">
        .ctl00_DDMenu_0 { background-color:white;visibility:hidden;display:none;position:absolute;left:0px;top:0px; }
        .ctl00_DDMenu_1 { color:White;text-decoration:none; }
        .ctl00_DDMenu_2 { color:White;border-width:0px;width:395px; }
        .ctl00_DDMenu_3 { border-style:none; }
        .ctl00_DDMenu_4 { width:20%; }
        .ctl00_DDMenu_5 { color:Black;border-style:none; }
        .ctl00_DDMenu_6 {  }
        .ctl00_DDMenu_7 {  }
        .ctl00_DDMenu_8 { border-style:none; }
        .ctl00_DDMenu_9 {  }
        .ctl00_DDMenu_10 { border-style:none; }
        .ctl00_DDMenu_11 {  }
        .ctl00_DDMenu_12 { color:White;border-style:none; }
        .ctl00_DDMenu_13 { color:White; }

</style></head>
<body>
<form name="aspnetForm" method="post" action="/Default.aspx" onkeypress="javascript:return WebForm_FireDefaultButton
 (event, 'ctl00_lbtnSearch')" id="aspnetForm">
<div>
<input type="hidden" name="__EVENTTARGET" id="__EVENTTARGET" value="" />
<input type="hidden" name="__EVENTARGUMENT" id="__EVENTARGUMENT" value="" />
<input type="hidden" name="__VIEWSTATE" id="__VIEWSTATE"
 value="zs1xHdORUhZR1PuFSLmKf1M8rL/z6ZFg9jf1aON7ssQRdjmrHsuqwHWmHeC1PP7Pa/S9kCOIGSSL3bNVjQM556qFH18nPDhYyqiVoXwRHW2r+Rv7UDLXqR/q70Wa2RPvO8ARwloE
 D/oTl4OCPCICjYx8YqO2+uhcR97Wn8FB2a+kkt2uqTkyUi8euiRlqU2/1pNJ5/9zhshNSMxAf/9eckjQZGGQ4fi5Z66IKaFU2gI1WeuWi/1WYUb5kZPJ/S+ip80T45vAZ3iHp1As4igeiaI
```

can be embedded into a Web page or exist as a separate script that is used to control all pages in a Web site. A CSS script is a set of program instructions written as plain text and saved as a file on the Web site. When CSS is used as a separate script file, it can be referenced by any and all Web pages in the entire Web site. The advantage of using CSS is a Web designer can make changes to all Web page content or "html tags" in every page in the Web site from a single location. For example, the CSS file can contain a description of the navigation bar that appears on every Web page in the site. By modifying the contents of the CSS file, you will automatically change the navigation bar on every Web page. Before CSS, a Web designer would need to make changes to the navigation bar on each Web site page. As you can see, CSS can save a Web designer many hours of work caused by Web site changes.

JavaScript

JavaScript is a programming language that is designed to be embedded into a HTML Web page and allows the user to interact with the Web page. For example, an online order form is most often written in JavaScript. The information filled into the text boxes of the form are typically sent to a server and inserted into a database. The database information can then be acted on.

JavaScript
a programming language that is designed to be embedded into an HTML Web page and allow the user to interact with the Web page.

To learn more about Web page programming languages, visit the W3Schools Web site at www.w3schools.com. W3Schools has an extensive collection of excellent tutorial programs. Try out the HTML tutorial. There is an interactive tutorial Web page that allows you modify Web page content and view the effect immediately. This is a great way to learn the basics of Web page programming and construction.

Simple Object Access Protocol (SOAP) a set of rules constructed from XML for Web-based messages. It is designed to allow a client to freely interact with a Web page on a Web server, rather than download it.

SOAP

Simple Object Access Protocol (SOAP) is a set of rules for Web-based messages and is constructed from XML. It allows a client to freely interact with a Web page on a Web server, rather than download it. For example, a database stored on a Web server can be accessed and manipulated by an authorized client without downloading any database records. Also, a program can be run on the Web server while viewed by the client.

SOAP combined with XML and HTML technologies solves the problem of exchanging data and information between two incompatible systems such as Windows and UNIX. Normally, the two operating systems require a gateway or the installation of additional protocols to support communication. By using HTML, XML, and SOAP technologies, the two incompatible systems are able to communicate without additional modifications.

The use of SOAP to access and run applications on a Web server has lead to a phrase coined by Microsoft—*Web Services*. The phrase *Web Services* means that services can be provided through Web pages.

FrontPage Extensions

FrontPage extensions are a set of programs that support the authoring, browsing, and administration of the Microsoft FrontPage program. If you are using Microsoft FrontPage to design your Web site, you must install IIS and the FrontPage extensions. This is true for a corporate intranet and Internet service. Extensions provide software tools for managing site security, checking site traffic, and organizing the hierarchy of Web page structures.

File Transfer Protocol (FTP)

File Transfer Protocol (FTP) a service that can be incorporated into a Web server to support file transfers between a client and server. It is often used to upload Web pages to Web hosting servers.

The ***File Transfer Protocol (FTP)*** can be incorporated into a Web server to support file transfers between a client and server. FTP uses TCP packets and establishes a connection between the client and server. FTP is accessed using an FTP client that is either text-based or GUI-based. When using a text-based FTP client, a series of commands are issued at an FTP prompt similar to the way commands are issued at a DOS prompt. The following is a list of some common FTP commands and their function.

bye	Exit the FTP program
cd/*directory*	Change the directory on the FTP site
get	Transfer a file from the FTP site to the client
help	Display FTP commands
lcd	Change the directory on the client
open	Open a connection to an FTP site
put	Transfer a file from the client to the FTP site
pwd	Display the current directory of the FTP site
quit	Close the FTP session

To start the FTP utility, go to the DOS prompt and enter the **ftp** command. Use the **help** command to display a list of FTP commands, **Figure 13-13.** To get

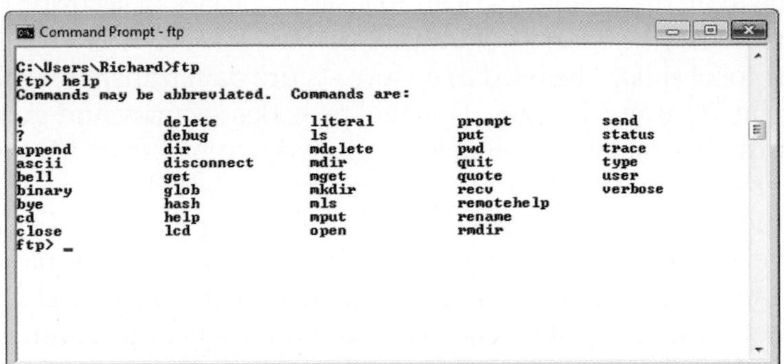
```
C:\Users\Richard>ftp
ftp> help
Commands may be abbreviated.  Commands are:

!               delete          literal         prompt          send
?               debug           ls              put             status
append          dir             mdelete         pwd             trace
ascii           disconnect      mdir            quit            type
bell            get             mget            quote           user
binary          glob            mkdir           recv            verbose
bye             hash            mls             remotehelp
cd              help            mput            rename
close           lcd             open            rmdir
ftp> _
```

Figure 13-13. A list of **FTP** commands can be displayed by entering **help** at the FTP command prompt.

help with a specific command, type **help** followed by the command. To exit the FTP program, enter the **bye** command.

Most Web page software has its own utility for uploading a file to the Web server FTP directory. There are also many third-party utilities available.

You can also use most Web browsers to access an FTP site by simply changing the protocol in Web browser's address bar from http: to ftp:. One important difference between most Web sites and an FTP site is you can upload files to an FTP site but not to a Web site. You can, however, download files from a Web site and an FTP site.

Figure 13-14 shows the Microsoft FTP site accessed through Internet Explorer using the ftp: protocol at the beginning of the URL. Look closely at how the FTP site is indicated in the DNS host name portion of the URL. Access to this FTP site was made as an anonymous user. An anonymous user does not require a password or user name. Anyone can access the FTP site to download files.

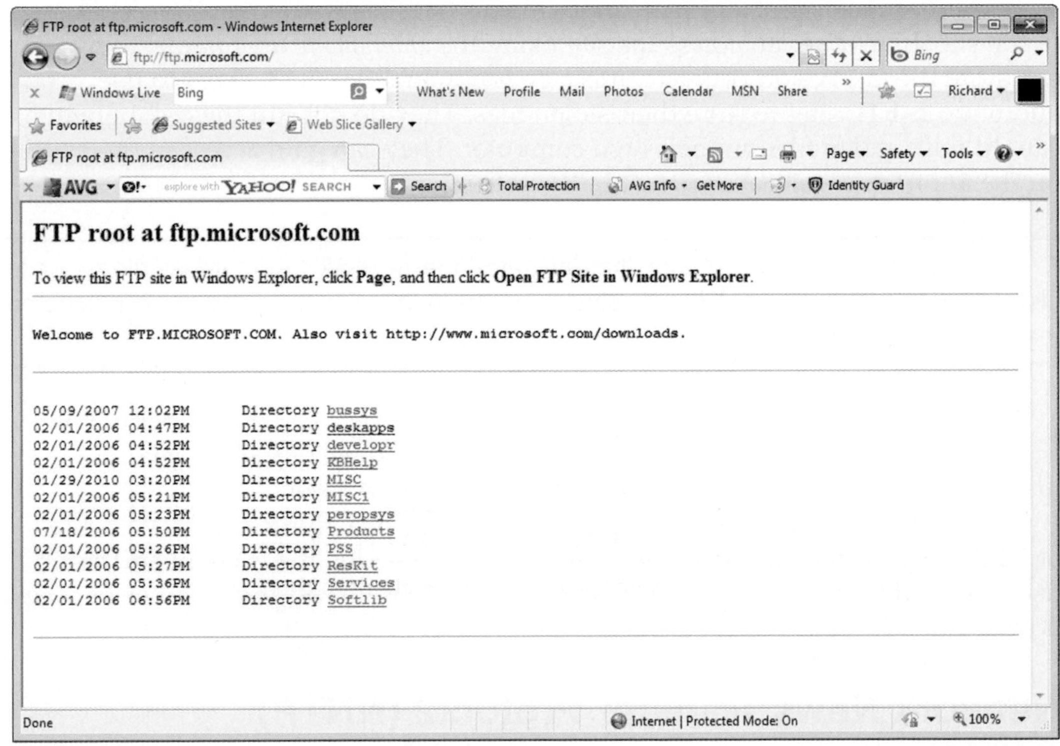

Figure 13-14. Example of an FTP site displayed through the Internet Explorer browser.

One of the main disadvantages of an FTP site is the lack of security. FTP does not encrypt passwords or the contents of transferred files. If security is a concern, another utility and protocol should be used to ensure secure data transfers. One such tool is Microsoft File Transfer Manager. This tool provides security and guaranteed file delivery over the Internet. It is available as a free download from Microsoft.

Trivial File Transfer Protocol (TFTP) a lightweight version of FTP that does not require the use of a user name and password because it uses UDP packets for transferring data. It allows a client to transfer files, but not to view the directory listing at the FTP site.

Secure File Transfer Protocol (SFTP) a secure version of FTP that encrypts the user name, password, and data to provide the highest level of security compared to FTP and TFTP.

anonymous FTP site an FTP site that allows anyone to access the site and download or upload files. No password or any other form of authentication is required.

Two other variations of the FTP protocol are Trivial File Transfer Protocol and Secure File Transfer Protocol. ***Trivial File Transfer Protocol (TFTP)*** is a lightweight version of FTP. TFTP never requires the use of a user name and password because it uses UDP packets for transferring data. Since UDP packets are used, a connection is never established between the client and server. The client is allowed to transfer files, but not to view the directory listing at the FTP site. TFTP uses fewer commands than FTP.

Secure File Transfer Protocol (SFTP) is a secure version of FTP. SFTP uses TCP packets and therefore establishes a connection using a user name and password. It encrypts the user name, password, and data to provide the highest level of security compared to FTP and TFTP. SFTP should be used when transferring sensitive data and when security is required.

Anonymous FTP Site

One of the easiest FTP sites to administer is an anonymous FTP site. An ***anonymous FTP site*** allows anyone to access the site and download or upload files. No password or any other form of authentication is required. Since no real form of authentication is required, the site is always at risk of being vandalized. It is better to require some form of authentication such as an e-mail address or to have a list of authorized user names and passwords. With proper authentication required, you can determine who accessed the site, when the site was accessed, and what files were downloaded or uploaded.

Another major problem with anonymous FTP sites is the unauthorized use of the site. If anyone can access the site using the *anonymous* user name, they can store illegal files on your site. It is a common practice of crackers to use anonymous FTP sites to store their stolen files. They do not run the risk of being caught with stolen files on their own computer. They can gain access to their files on the anonymous site at any time in the future.

Tech Tip

A *cracker* is an unauthorized user that infiltrates the network to create problems or to disrupt or steal information. A *hacker* simply breaks in to see if he or she can but does no real damage.

If you set up the FTP site as a secure FTP site, always test the security. Try accessing the FTP site from another computer using some of the commands mentioned earlier.

Network News Transfer Protocol (NNTP) a TCP/IP protocol designed to distribute news messages to NNTP clients and NNTP servers across the Internet.

Internet Information Services can activate a log of activities at the Web site or FTP site. Common information contained in the IIS log file is client address, user name, date and time of access, server name, IP address, and number of bytes downloaded or uploaded.

Network News Transfer Protocol (NNTP)

Network News Transfer Protocol (NNTP) is part of the TCP/IP suite of protocols. It is designed to distribute news messages to NNTP clients and NNTP servers across the Internet. News articles are stored in a central NNTP server and distributed automatically to other NNTP servers and clients.

News articles are arranged in groups or categories referred to as *newsgroups*. A ***newsgroup*** is also referred to as a ***discussion group.*** There are many different newsgroups available. **Figure 13-15** shows a list of available newsgroups run by Microsoft. Each newsgroup is dedicated to a particular Microsoft product and contains a collection of messages posted by individuals. The messages consist of questions and answers. You can join a discussion or post a question to a newsgroup. Members of the group will post responses to your question. A complete listing of all responses is available for reading.

newsgroup
news articles that are arranged in a group or category on an NNTP server. Newsgroups are also referred to as *discussion groups.*

A client is required in order to access, download, and read the contents of an NNTP server. There are various newsreader clients designed for accessing and reading the messages posted on an NNTP server. You can use Microsoft Outlook to access a network news server and read and post messages.

Figure 13-16 shows an example of a newsgroup message being posted on one of Microsoft's newsgroups. The message concerns three quick fixes for stubborn PC problems. The message and link are being displayed in Microsoft Outlook. Notice in

Figure 13-15.
A partial list of Microsoft newsgroups.

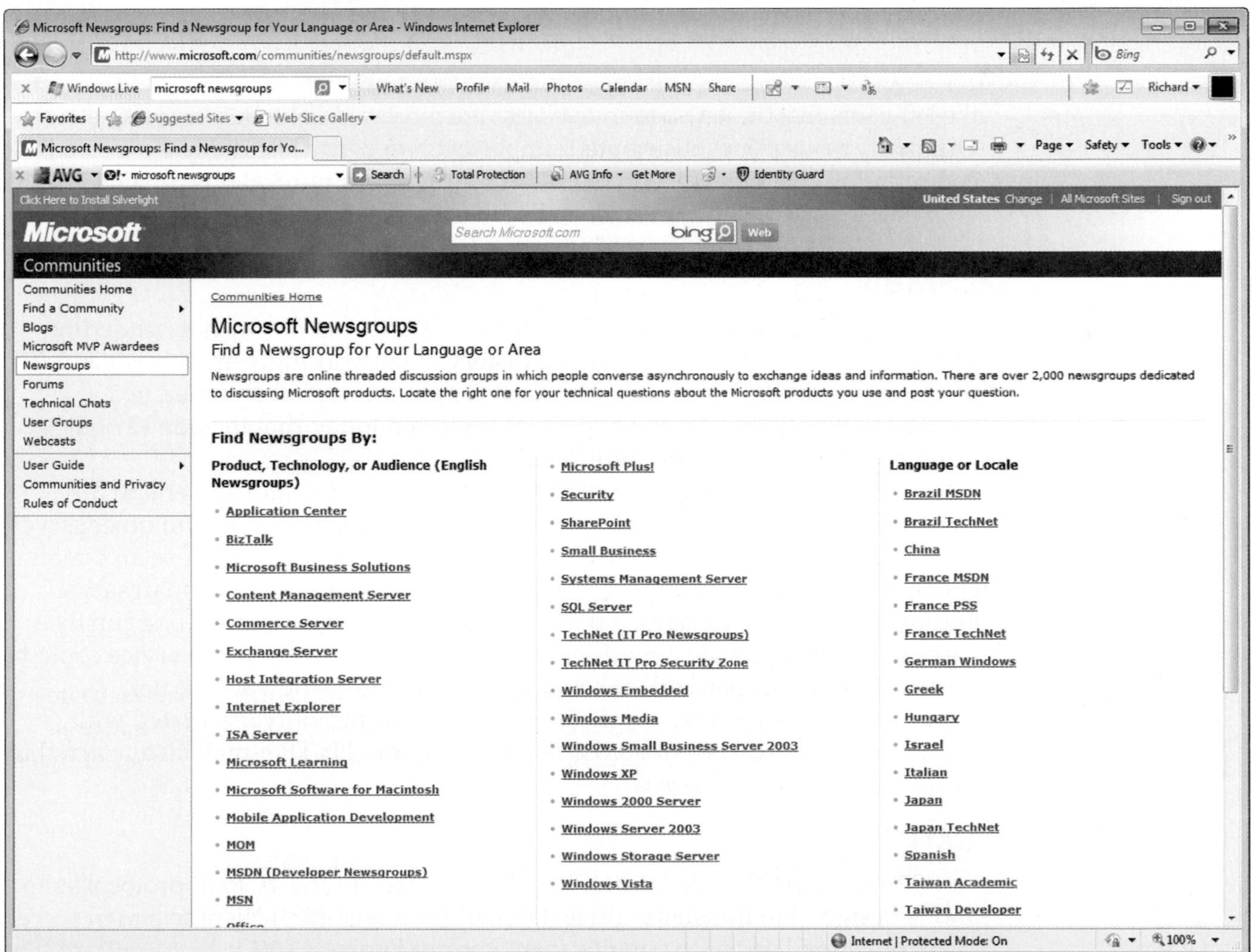

Figure 13-16.
Example of a newsgroup message displayed in Microsoft Outlook.

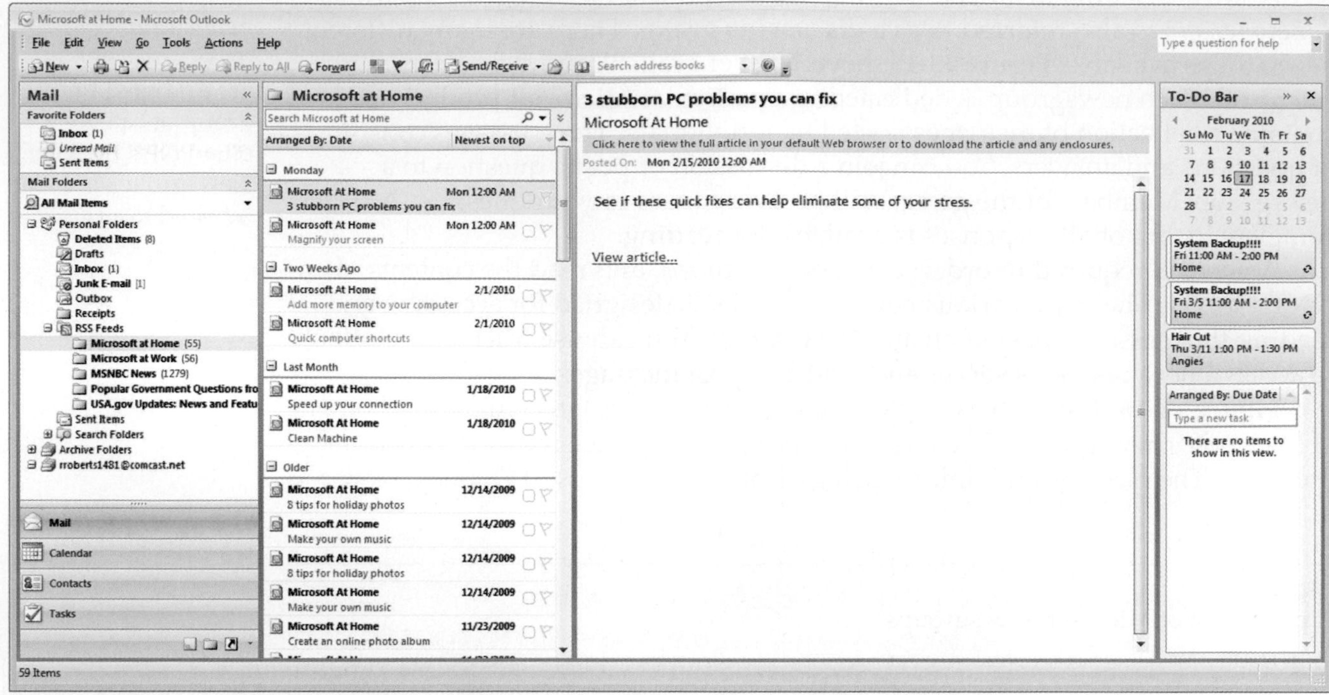

the left panel that the newsgroup messages are displayed separately from the e-mails. Originally newsgroups distributed simple text-based articles. Today, newsgroup communications is greatly enhanced. Newsgroup communications provide links to Web pages that contain the article rather than displaying simple text messages.

E-Mail

You are probably familiar with e-mail as a user, but not with its underling protocols and standards. Early in the history of networking, e-mail was viewed as a novelty rather than a necessity. Early e-mail messages contained text information only and not the rich formats viewed today that include various fonts, pictures, sounds, and multimedia.

In the simplest terms, an e-mail system consists of a mail server and an e-mail client. The mail server is responsible for forwarding e-mail to other servers and storing e-mail until a client can retrieve them. The user must use an e-mail client, also referred to as an *e-mail agent*, to communicate with the mail server and to retrieve the messages. An ISP or a private network, such as one run by a corporation, can provide a mail server. In other words, the e-mail service could be limited to a private network or could span the world using the Internet.

In the following sections, the protocols most commonly associated with e-mail are covered. They are SMTP, POP, IMAP, and HTTP e-mail also referred to as *HTML e-mail* or *Web e-mail*.

Simple Mail Transfer Protocol (SMTP) a TCP/IP protocol designed to transfer plain text e-mail from an e-mail client to a mail server and from a mail server to a mail server.

SMTP

Simple Mail Transfer Protocol (SMTP) is part of the TCP/IP protocol suite and is designed to transfer plain text e-mail from an e-mail client to a mail server and from a mail server to a mail server. Look at **Figure 13-17.**

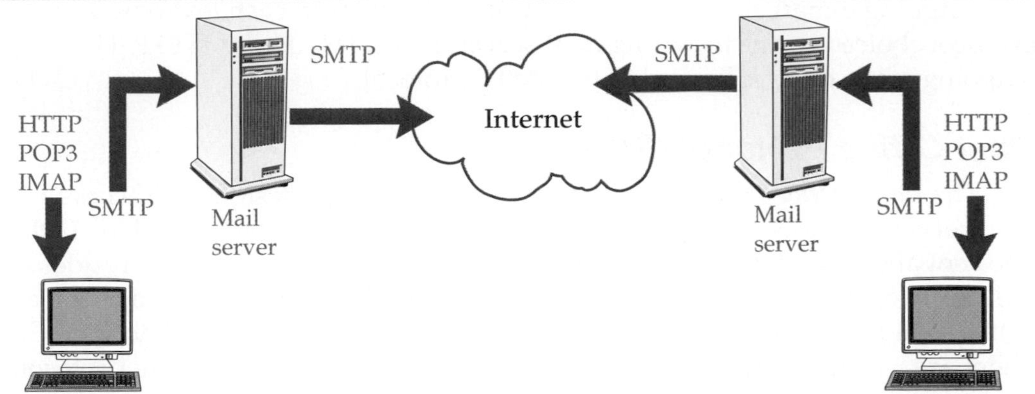

Figure 13-17.
The SMTP protocol is used to send mail from an e-mail client to a mail server and from a mail server to a mail server. The POP3, IMAP, and HTTP protocols are used to retrieve e-mail from mail servers.

In the illustration, you can see that a mail server is connected to the Internet where it forwards messages to other mail servers. The PC uses an e-mail client, with the POP or IMAP protocol, to access messages on a mail server. The mail server uses the POP or IMAP protocol to communicate with and to download e-mail to the client.

When setting up an e-mail account, the mail server is designated as an SMTP server for sending e-mail and as a POP3 or IMAP server for retrieving e-mail. Two separate mail servers may be used—one for sending e-mail and the other for receiving e-mail—or one server may be used for sending and receiving e-mail. In either case, two server names typically need to be supplied when setting up an e-mail account.

An e-mail server that hosts the POP or IMAP protocol can be called a *POP server* or an *IMAP server*. A server that hosts the SMTP protocol can be called an *SMTP server*.

Figure 13-18 shows a typical Windows **Internet Connection** dialog box associated with setting up an e-mail account. Notice the requirements, such as selecting the type of incoming mail server, the name of the incoming mail server, and the name of the outgoing mail server. If the same server is used for incoming

Add New E-mail Account
Internet E-mail Settings
Each of these settings are required to get your e-mail account working.
User Information
Your Name: Joe Smith
E-mail Address: JoeSmith@rmroberts.com
Server Information
Account Type: POP3
Incoming mail server:
Outgoing mail server (SMTP):
Logon Information
User Name:
Password:
Remember password
Require logon using Secure Password Authentication (SPA)
Test Account Settings
After filling out the information on this screen, we recommend you test your account by clicking the button below. (Requires network connection)
Test Account Settings ...
More Settings ...
< Back Next > Cancel

Figure 13-18.
Setting up an e-mail account with the Windows **Internet Connection**. Notice the choices for the type of incoming mail server. Also note that an incoming mail server and an outgoing mail server must be specified.

and outgoing e-mail, the same server name will appear in each text box. The protocol choices for the incoming mail server: POP3, IMAP, and HTTP. The outgoing mail server is limited to the SMTP protocol.

Post Office Protocol (POP)

Post Office Protocol (POP)
a simple protocol designed to access a mail server and download e-mail to the e-mail client.

The ***Post Office Protocol (POP)*** is a simple protocol designed to access a mail server and download e-mail to the e-mail client. In contrast to IMAP, POP does not allow you to store messages on the mail server. Stored e-mail resides on the user's local hard drive, not the mail server's hard drive. Typically, as soon as you open a POP mail account, the server begins downloading e-mail to the PC. There are various versions of POP: POP, POP2, and POP3. Today, these protocols are simply referred to as *POP* or *POP3*.

Internet Message Access Protocol (IMAP)

Internet Message Access Protocol (IMAP)
a sophisticated mail access protocol that can manipulate e-mail while it is on the server. It also allows a user to access his or her e-mail and then leave the e-mail on the server.

Internet Message Access Protocol (IMAP) is used to access messages stored on a mail server in similar fashion to POP. There are various releases of IMAP such as IMAP, IMAP2, IMAP3, and IMAP4. When compared with POP, IMAP is a more sophisticated protocol because it can manipulate the e-mail while it is on the server. You can view the e-mail headers and content before downloading the e-mail. IMAP allows you to select the e-mail that you want to download rather than automatically downloading all of the e-mail for you. You can also store the e-mail on the mail server rather than on the client. One advantage of storing e-mail on the server is the server may be automatically backed up each day. Important e-mail can be retained even if your PC's hard drive fails.

The IMAP protocol also allows the user to access his or her e-mail from more than one PC. A user can access e-mail and then leave the e-mail on the server. This means that a user can access e-mail from home, work, or while traveling. Copies of the e-mails can be stored on more than one computer such as a home computer or laptop. With the POP protocol, all e-mail is downloaded to a PC and is deleted from the e-mail server. If a user accesses the mail server from another PC, the previously downloaded e-mail is no longer available. Any new e-mail on the mail server is downloaded instead. E-mail is spread across the total number of computers you use to access your e-mail rather than stored in one central location.

The downside to the way IMAP handles e-mail storage is the mail server must provide sufficient space for all e-mail users. Storage space could be limited, which forces the e-mail user to remove some of his or her e-mail from the server to provide space for new e-mail. Also, a large e-mail, such as one with a graphic or sound attachment, might very well use all the storage space provided for the e-mail account, causing other e-mail delivery attempts to be rejected.

It may seem that all e-mail clients should use IMAP rather than POP. This is not always the case. For example, a corporate organization may choose to use POP rather than IMAP because POP is less resource intensive than IMAP. POP e-mail would not burden the network server the way IMAP would. Also, IMAP would create more network traffic than POP because IMAP allows a greater amount of port numbers.

HTTP E-Mail

The newest version of an Internet e-mail client is HTTP e-mail. It is also referred to as *Web-based e-mail*. To use the HTTP e-mail service, you need only a Web browser for the e-mail client. You do not need a specific e-mail client designed strictly for e-mail. There are numerous HTTP e-mail clients based on the HTML protocol.

HTTP e-mail is usually advertised as free e-mail. The HTTP e-mail client is designed similar to Web pages. You can transfer messages that contain animation, graphics, and sound. It also allows users to access e-mail from anywhere the Internet is accessed. All the user needs to do is access the Internet to connect to the mail server and then enter his or her user name and password.

There are a few disadvantages of using HTTP e-mail. One disadvantage associated with HTTP-based e-mail is security. HTTP e-mail uses HTML coding that can easily hide viruses and worms. A Trojan horse can easily be hidden in the contents of an HTTP e-mail. When the client opens the e-mail, the computer is immediately infected. The only way to use HTTP securely is with certificates and a secure Web site. This ensures a secure connection. When a secure connection is used, the protocol in the Web address is identified with https rather than http. The *s* at the end of http indicates a secure site.

Another disadvantage to HTTP e-mail is it is typically associated with free e-mail. With free e-mail, you have a small amount of designated storage space. Once that set amount is reached, the provider of the free e-mail service will charge you for additional space. The provider may also attempt to sell you many add-ons to enhance your e-mail, like fancy paper, animated characters, and sounds attached to your e-mail message. While these items are fun, they can cause you to use up valuable storage space.

For example, you send a cute e-mail to a friend that has an animated character and plays a familiar tune when he or she opens it. The free e-mail company will probably solicit your friend to download a free version of the e-mail client. After your friend does, he or she composes an e-mail and returns the message to you. Soon, everyone you know is using the free e-mail client and your inbox is exceeding the maximum allowed capacity. All those fancy additions to the e-mail, like music and animated characters, take up a lot of storage space because they are coded into the e-mail message. You eventually will be prompted to buy space at a nominal monthly fee or suffer the consequences of losing e-mail messages.

The main advantages of Web mail is it can be obtained free of charge, has many graphic display enhancements, and can typically be accessed from anywhere on the Internet, which makes it especially appealing to travelers. There are numerous free e-mail services available: some reputable and some not so reputable.

Multipurpose Internet Mail Extensions (MIME)

Multipurpose Internet Mail Extensions (MIME) is a protocol that encodes additional information known as mail attachments to e-mail protocols that normally could not transfer attachments such as graphics. SMTP is designed only to transfer text material between servers and from clients. MIME allows e-mail attachments to be transferred as separate files using SMTP as the transport protocol. Not all mail servers support MIME, but most do. Some do not support MIME by design to reduce the amount of traffic on a network. Remember that mail attachments such as music and animation require a lot of bandwidth and can congest a network. Simple text messages do not cause severe congestion.

Multipurpose Internet Mail Extensions (MIME) a protocol that encodes additional information known as mail attachments to e-mail protocols that normally could not transfer attachments such as graphics.

E-Mail Address Format

The e-mail address is based on the domain name system of addresses. The following are typical e-mail address formats:

someone@Somewhere.com

someone@NewAccounts.Somewhere.com

someone@Somewhere.com.uk

The user name or mailbox name in the example is *Someone*. The @ (at) symbol is called the *axon*. The host name follows the @ symbol. Then the type of domain is identified after the period. The type of domain in the example is .com for commercial. There are many domain types and names, such as .gov for government or .org for organization. For addresses outside the United States, there is an additional country code such as .uk for United Kingdom.

E-Mail Structure

Figure 13-19 shows an example of an e-mail structure. In the example, you can see how HTML commands, or tags, are used to form e-mail. The HTTP **<message>** tag is used with the attributes **to =**, **from =**, and **subject =**. These attributes form the e-mail header. The HTML **<text>** tag identifies the text portion of the e-mail.

Of course, e-mail clients are much more sophisticated than the previous example. The example is used to illustrate how HTTP commands are combined with HTML tags to form a basic e-mail structure. Typical e-mail incorporates icons and visual elements from other programming languages to hide HTML coding. The same message would appear in an e-mail client as in the screen capture shown in **Figure 13-20.**

mail filter
blocks, or filters, unwanted e-mail messages.

spam
an unwanted or unsolicited e-mail such as advertisement.

spamming
the distribution of unsolicited e-mail.

spammer
a person who engages in distributing unsolicited e-mail or sending e-mail with some sort of advertisement as a probe.

Mail Filter

A ***mail filter*** blocks, or filters, unwanted e-mail messages such as ***spam***. ***Spamming*** is the distribution of unsolicited e-mail. E-mails are sent as broadcasts to numerous mailboxes using a list of known mailboxes or programs that randomly generate mailbox addresses. A ***spammer*** often sends e-mail with some sort of advertisement as a probe. The spammer often includes a line that says something like, "If you received this e-mail by mistake or want to be removed from our mailing list, simply reply to this e-mail address." If the recipient responds to the e-mail, the spammer receives an e-mail reply with a legitimate e-mail address to add to his or her list of e-mail addresses. The spammer can use this e-mail address in the future or sell it. Many legitimate companies or organizations do offer a genuine removal from an e-mail list service. If you receive unsolicited e-mail from an unknown source, the best advice is do *not* reply!

Mail filters can be placed on servers or desktops. The filtering technique varies between the different mail filter systems available. Most e-mail clients contain some sort of filtering feature. For example, Microsoft Outlook allows you to identify undesirable sources of e-mail. Look at **Figure 13-21.**

Figure 13-19.
Example HTML commands, or tags, used to form an e-mail.

```
<message to="KeltnerJ@g-w.com" from="Richard@rmroberts.com"
        subject="Here is the latest chapter revision.">
        <text>
        Good morning JoAnne
        Attached is the latest chapter revision for Networking Fundamentals.
        </text>
/message>
```

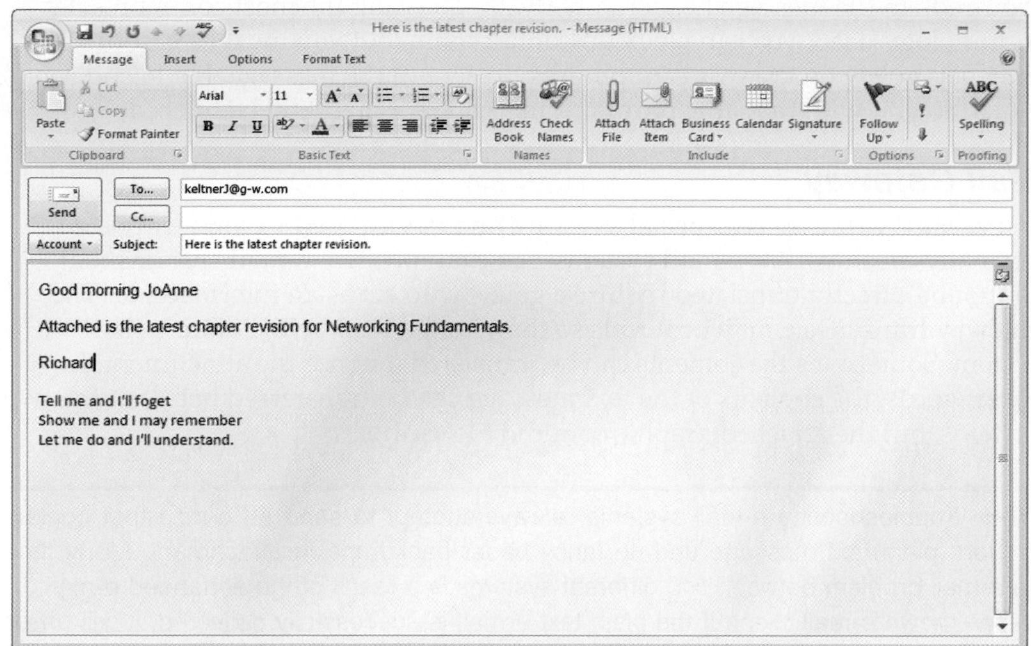

Figure 13-20.
E-mail client software hides the HTML coding from the user.

Microsoft Outlook has two features available called *block sender* and *message rule*. Block sender blocks messages based on the mailbox address of the sender. Message rule filters mail contents based on header or letter body contents, or both. The filter can be based on one or more words. For example, you can filter all incoming mail that contains the phrase "act now" or "immediate response

Figure 13-21.
Microsoft Office Outlook e-mail can apply filters to messages to block the source or to allow the source if the message has been sent to the junk folder.

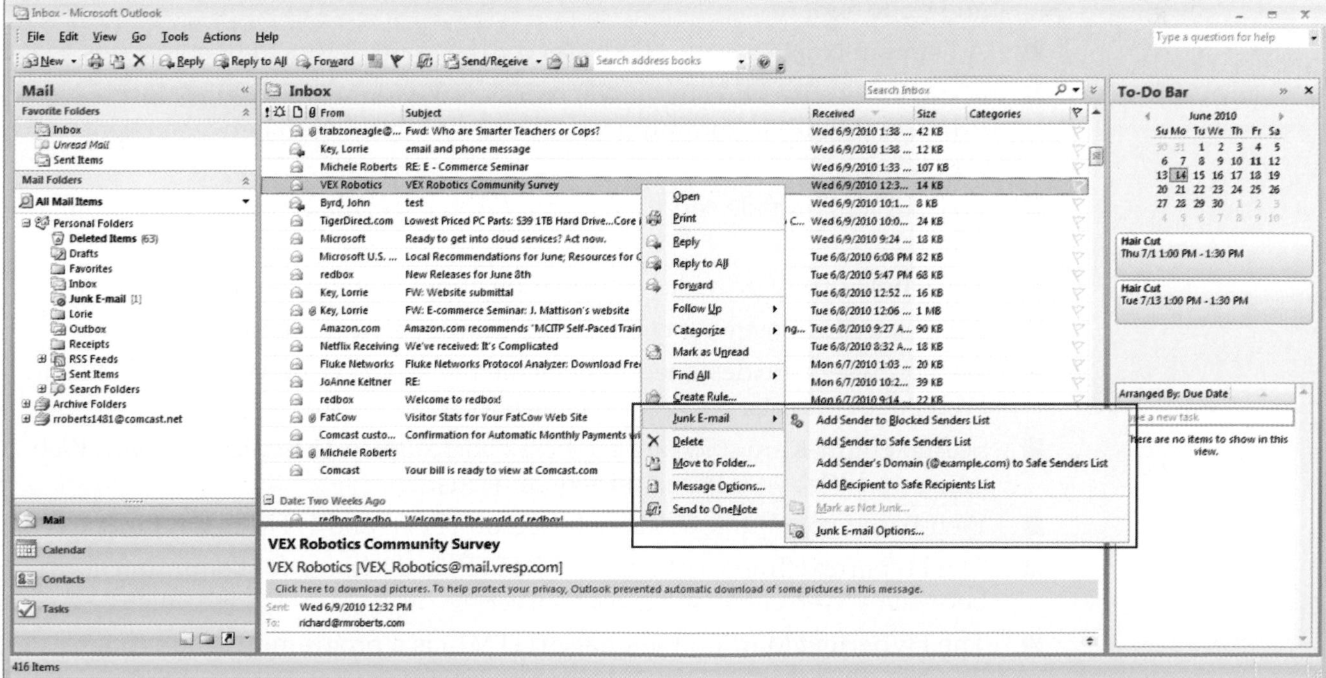

required" in the message header or body. By guessing the most common sales terminology used, you can block unwanted spam, but you must be careful. The filter acts solely on the words or phrases present in the message. If a friend sends e-mail to you with the same phrase, your friend's e-mail will be filtered.

Mail Gateway

mail gateway
a special software and device used to connect two normally incompatible e-mail systems.

A ***mail gateway*** is a special software and device used to connect two normally incompatible e-mail systems. For example, two e-mail systems that cannot be directly translated require a gateway to act as an intermediate. The gateway translates e-mail protocols so they can be read by the other e-mail system. Sometimes the contents can be translated, but not the attachment. In other words, the contents of the text message can be transferred between the two systems, but the attached graphic or audio file cannot.

Tech Tip

When troubleshooting e-mail systems, *always* attempt to send an e-mail that contains a short, plain text message and no fancy paper backdrops or attachment. Many times an e-mail problem between two different systems is a result of the enhanced e-mail or a lesser-known e-mail client. If the plain text e-mail is successfully delivered, it will ensure that the network infrastructure is intact and that the SMTP system is working correctly. You can then turn your attention to e-mail client compatibility.

Summary

- The Internet is a worldwide network that anyone can use for communication.
- An intranet is typically a private, Web-based network limited to a select set of clients.
- An extranet is a combination of a private and public Web-based network.
- A Uniform Resource Locator (URL) is a user-friendly name that resolves to an IP address.
- A Domain Name System (DNS) server translates URLs to IP addresses.
- Microsoft Active Directory (AD) relies on the Lightweight Directory Access Protocol (LDAP) to communicate directory information between clients and servers.
- Web servers provide services, such as Web page, file transfer, and e-mail, to clients.
- The **whois** utility provides information about domain name owners.
- Apache is the most widely used Web server software package.
- Web browsers are designed to navigate the World Wide Web and to display Web page contents.
- Search engines are software applications designed to located relevant Web pages and Web sites based on search terms.
- Web-based communication are based on HTTP and HTML standards.
- The Hypertext Transport Protocol (HTTP) is designed for communication between a Web client and a Web server.
- The Hypertext Markup Language (HTML) is a programming language.

- XML is an enhanced markup language that supports client interaction with server applications.
- SOAP is a protocol designed to support XML and run applications on a Web server.
- The File Transfer Protocol (FTP) supports file transfers between a client and an FTP server.
- TFTP is a simpler version of FTP that uses fewer commands.
- SFTP securely transfers of data by encrypting user names, passwords, and data.
- An anonymous FTP site permits file transfers without the need of a required password or user name.
- Incoming mail server choices are typically limited to POP3, IMAP, and HTTP.
- An outgoing mail server is typically an SMTP server.
- One server may function as both the incoming and outgoing mail server.

Review Questions

Answer the following questions on a separate sheet of paper. Please do not write in this book.

1. What are the three types of networks that provide Web page distribution?
2. A(n) _____ is a network in which employees can only access a company Web server from within the company.
3. A(n) _____ allows internal access to Web pages and allows authorized personnel from outside the network to access the network's Web pages.
4. What is the purpose of a DNS server?
5. What protocol is common to Microsoft Active Directory (AD)?
6. What is the purpose of a Web server?
7. What does the **whois** utility do?
8. What are some things to consider when choosing to set up your own Web server rather than choosing to use a Web hosting service?
9. Name three ways to conduct a **whois** search?
10. Name two software packages that are designed to turn a server into a Web server?
11. What does the acronym IIS represent?
12. What is the name of the default Web server software installed on a Microsoft server?
13. What are the two most common Web browsers?
14. What is the difference between HTML and HTTP?
15. What is a markup?
16. What is the purpose of HTML tags?
17. What does the acronym W3C represent?
18. What is the difference between HTML and XML?
19. SOAP is closely associated with which markup language?
20. What is an anonymous FTP site?
21. What protocol is used to send e-mail to a mail server or to transfer e-mail from one mail server to another mail server?
22. What protocols download e-mail from a server?
23. Which e-mail protocol is used to download e-mail automatically without the option to store it on the mail server?
24. How does MIME enhance e-mail?

Sample Network+ Exam Questions

Answer the following questions on a separate sheet of paper. Please do not write in this book.

1. What protocol is used to transport Web page information from a Web server to a client?
   A. HTML
   B. HTTP
   C. IPX/SPX
   D. SMTP
2. Which protocol is designed to download files from a Web site?
   A. ATM
   B. FTP
   C. SNMP
   D. ICMP
3. A(n) _____ is a network in which only employees from within a company can access the company Web server.
   A. Internet
   B. Intranet
   C. Extranet
   D. LAN Net
4. The typical port number used for making a Web server connection is _____.
   A. 33
   B. 80
   C. 125
   D. 440
5. Which protocol is specifically designed to store e-mail messages on a mail server?
   A. FTP
   B. POP
   C. IMAP
   D. HTML
6. Which type of server is designed to receive e-mail messages from an e-mail client?
   A. DNS
   B. DHCP
   C. SMTP
   D. POP
7. Your company is setting up an e-mail system for the sales department. The sales department wants to be able to access and read its current e-mail as well as stored e-mail while traveling outside the office. Which type of e-mail server will best meet its needs?
   A. POP3
   B. FTP
   C. TFTP
   D. IMAP

8. Which is the correct e-mail format for a salesman from the United Kingdom with a user name of Bjones?
   A. BJones@Sales.Homeoffice.com.uk
   B. BJones@uk.com/homeoffice.sales
   C. BJones@Sales/HomeOffice/com/uk
   D. BJones.HomeOffice.Sales.com@uk
9. What type of server translates URLs to IP addresses?
   A. DNS
   B. DHCP
   C. IMAP
   D. IIS
10. Which program or utility would you use to determine who owns and operates a specific Web site?
    A. **netstat**
    B. **tracert**
    C. **whois**
    D. **ping**

Interesting Web Sites for More Information

www.apache.org
www.arin.net
www.internic.net
www.linux.org
www.microsoft.com
www.novell.com
www.redhat.com

Suggested Laboratory Activities

1. Set up an intranet for your networking class. Install Microsoft IIS and then use a Web-authoring tool, such as FrontPage, to design and install a Web site. The Web site should permit students to access information. Each student can design a page for the Web site.
2. Download and explore anyone of several free HTML authoring tools available and design a simple Web page. Use the authoring utility to expose the hidden HTML code.
3. Set up an FTP site as part of the Web site you created in the first laboratory activity. Load a file on the FTP site that can be distributed to all the students using anonymous access.
4. Set up restrictions on the FTP Web site so that only users with a user name and password can access the site.
5. Explore the InterNIC Web site or conduct a Google search for the **whois** utility. Look up some familiar URL names and see what information is revealed.
6. Search for three different Web-hosting services and compare prices and services.
7. Configure a workstation for a connection to an e-mail server. Obtain step-by-step instructions from your ISP's Web site.

Apache HTTP Server is the most popular open-source Web server software package available. It is continuously developed and maintained by the Apache Software Foundation.

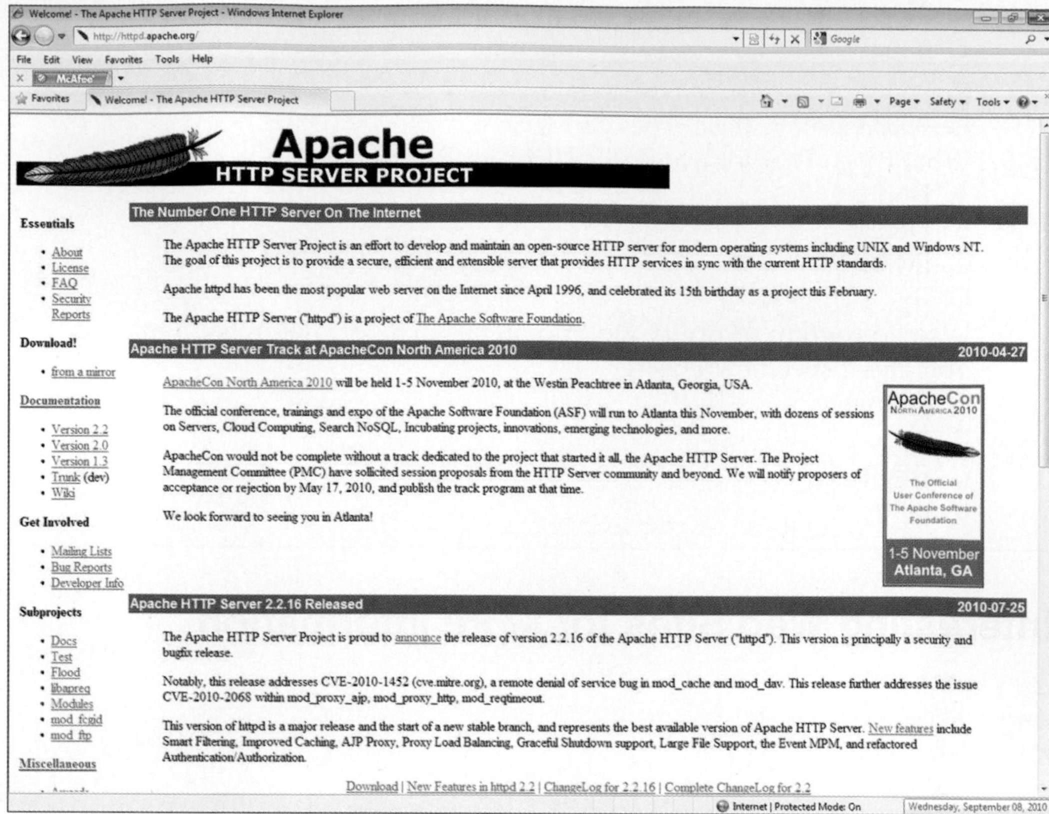

Chapter 13 Laboratory Activity

Installing Internet Information Services (IIS)

After completing this laboratory activity, you will be able to:

- Recall the limitations of Internet Information Services (IIS) on a Windows Vista and Windows 7 computer.
- Recall the purpose and characteristics of Internet Information Services (IIS).
- Carry out proper procedures to install Internet Information Services (IIS).
- Use an Internet browser to access and display the default Internet Information Services (IIS) Web page.
- Use Computer Management to explore the IIS directory structure.

Introduction

In this laboratory activity, you will install Internet Information Services (IIS) on a Windows Vista or Windows 7 computer to provide Web site and FTP services to a maximum of ten simultaneous computer connections. IIS can be installed on a workstation that is part of a peer-to-peer network to form an intranet. IIS can also be installed on a stand-alone computer to test Web page development before posting the Web pages to a company Web site.

IIS is not installed during a typical Windows installation. To install IIS, you must access **Start | Control Panel | Programs | Turn Windows features on or off**. The **Windows Features** dialog box will display. In the following screen capture, you can see Internet Information Services listed. Select this component by clicking the checkbox.

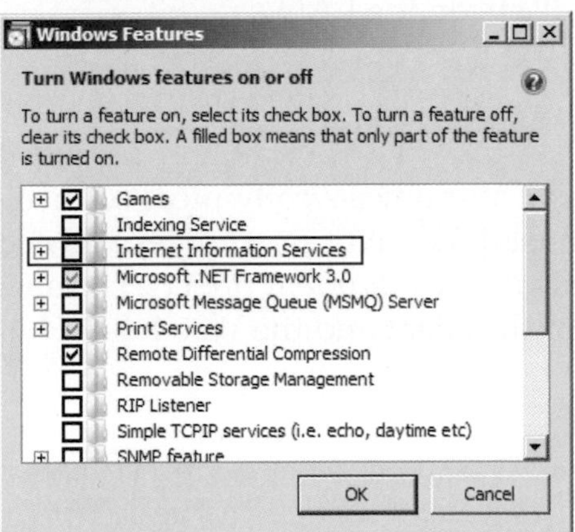

Setting up a computer as a Web server limited to LAN access is equal to an intranet. Compared with the Internet, an intranet is limited in scope. The Internet is a World Wide Web service while an intranet is limited to a single corporation, business, school, or such. The intranet is intended for a specific audience rather than for users on the World Wide Web. The intranet can be used as a means of accessing company information and providing a mechanism for downloading files. Many employees find it easier to navigate a Web site than a network environment. The Web site can be set up to provide to all employees a newsletter, a business calendar, company forms, a company policy book, employee benefits, and files for download. The use of the intranet is limited only to the designer's imagination.

After IIS has been installed, you can test the service by typing **http://localhost**, **http://127.0.0.1**, or the assigned IP address in the Internet Explorer address bar. The first part of the URL is the type of protocol used: typically, HTTP or FTP. The second part of the URL after the double slash (//) is the location of the Web server. The location will be the Web server's domain name or IP address. To resolve a domain name, a DNS server is required. A direct connection using the IP address does not require a DNS server.

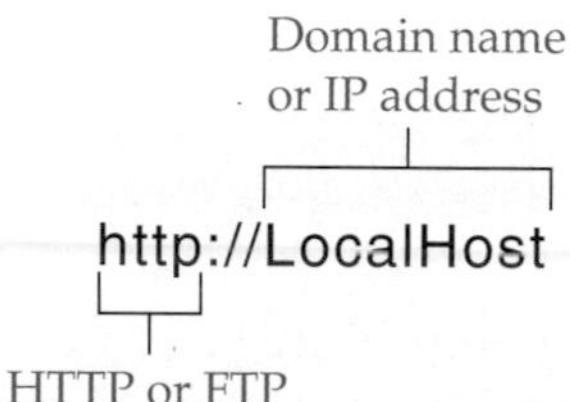

IIS can be used to provide Web services to users on the Internet; however, there are several requirements with which you need to be familiar. Your local Internet Service Provider (ISP) can provide you with the first three items on the following list.

- The Web server must have an assigned IP address.
- The Web server must have a legal domain name, such as MyCorporation.com.
- The Web server will need to stay connected to the Internet 24/7.
- A router is recommended so that the Web site and the Internet connection can be shared with users on the LAN.

Equipment and Materials

- Two Windows Vista or Windows 7 computers connected as peer-to-peer network. (You will install IIS on one computer and access the Web server from the other. If this is a two-student project, simply take turns, switching the responsibility for the client and the Web host.)

Warning
Do not install IIS on a workstation connected to a client/server network. The IIS installation can create unexpected results, such as system lockups.

Note
Windows Home Basic will not support this laboratory activity, but Home Premium or better editions will.

Procedure

1. ______ Report to your assigned workstation.
2. ______ Boot the computers and verify they are in working order.
3. ______ Create a Restore Point on the computer on which you will install IIS. This will allow you to uninstall IIS if a problem arises.
4. ______ Access **Start | Control Panel | Programs | Turn Windows features on or off**. The Turn **Windows features on or off** option is similar in Windows Vista and Windows 7.

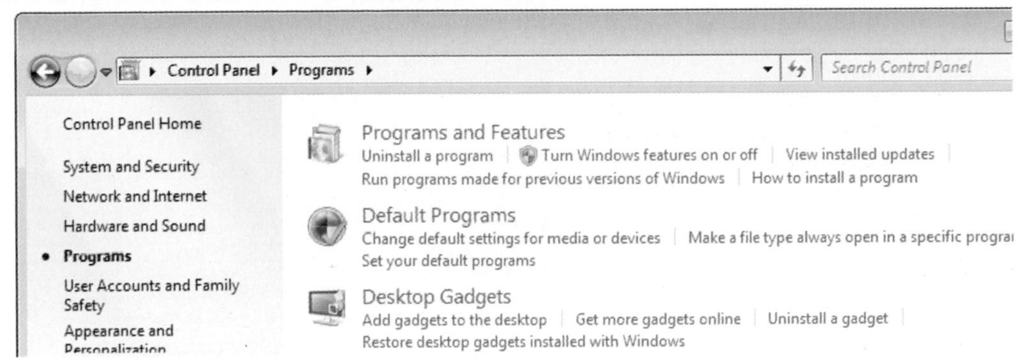

The **Windows Features** dialog box will open.

5. ______ From the **Windows Features** dialog box, select **Internet Information Services**.

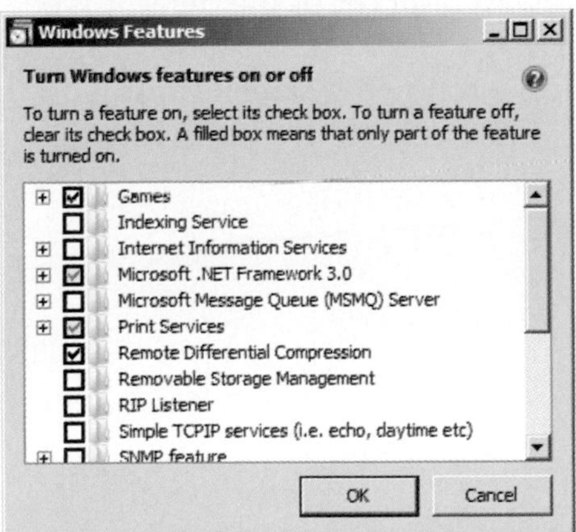

6. ______ Click **OK** to automatically install the most commonly required IIS components. After Internet Information Services (IIS) and its subcomponents have been installed, the wizard will display a window informing you the components have been successfully installed.

7. ______ Verify IIS has been installed by opening Computer Management (right-click **Computer** and select **Manage** from the shortcut menu). You should see the Internet Information Services (IIS) Manager folder listed under the Services and Applications folder. If you do not see this folder, call your instructor.

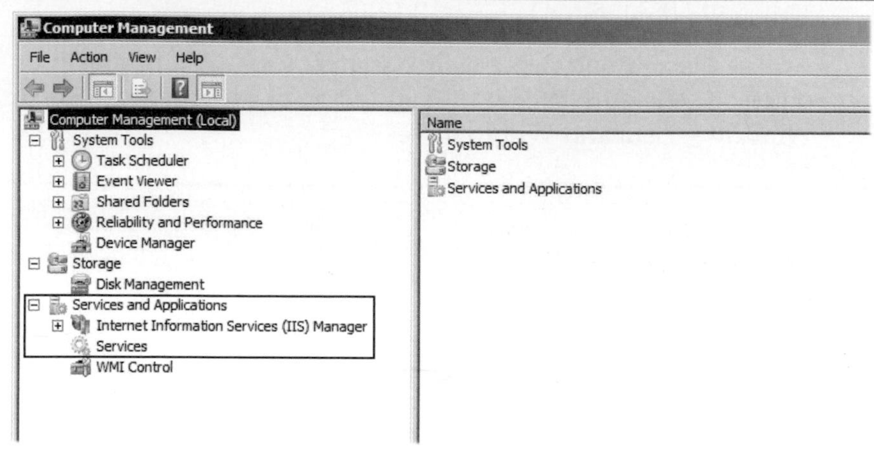

8. ______ Before you can access the default Web page, you may need to disable the firewall on the Web page hosting computer. After you turn off the firewall, you can access the default Web page from any computer on the local area network. To turn off the firewall, access the **Control Panel | System and Security | Windows Firewall**. Enabling and disabling the firewall is intuitive.

9. ______ From the other workstation (the one without IIS), enter the IP address of the Web server or the default Web site folder. For example, http://192.168.000.075. A Web page should appear similar to the one in the following screen capture. If the Web page does not appear, call your instructor.

If you have an Internet connection on your workstation, you can double-click the IIS7 image, which will automatically redirect you to the Microsoft IIS Web site. The Web site contains extensive information about IIS.

10. ______ Enter the following URLs and observe the results. First, test the URL address from the Web server and then from the workstation. Use the IP address of the Web server in place of 192.168.0.75 used in the examples.

Web Server:

- Use http://localhost at the Web server to display the default Web page.
- Use http://192.168.0.75 at the Web server to display the default Web page.
- Use http://*<hostname>* at the Web server and use the computer name of the Web server in place of *<hostname>*. For example, http://station1.

Second Workstation:

- Use http://192.168.0.75 at the workstation to display the default Web page.
- Use http://*<hostname>* at the workstation to display the default Web page.
- If you installed and configured the FTP Service, use ftp://*<hostname>* or ftp://192.168.0.75 from the workstation to expose any files available for file transfer from the Web hosting computer. (The

FTP Service is not installed by default in Windows Vista and Windows 7.)

Note
To view help and information, simply click the default Web page when it appears on the screen.

11. _____ If you have a Web page authoring utility, make a Web page to replace the default IIS Web page. Simply create a Web page and save it as default.htm in the C:\inetpub\wwwroot directory. You could use Microsoft Word to create a Web page. To create a Web page using Microsoft Word, simply open Word and create a document. When you save the document, save it in the HTML format by using the **Save As** command from the **File** menu. Locate the C:\inetpub\wwwroot directory in the **Save in** list box and then select **Web Page** from the **Save as type** list box. Enter the file name default in the **File name** text box and then click **Save**.

12. _____ Open Computer Management on the hosting computer (right-click **Computer** and select **Manage** from the shortcut menu). You should see Internet Information Services (IIS) Manager folder located under the Service and Applications folder in the left pane.

You can expand the Internet Information Services (IIS) Manager folder by selecting it with the mouse. After selecting it, you will see related Web site functions such as Authentication, Default Document, and Error Pages similar to that in the following screen capture.

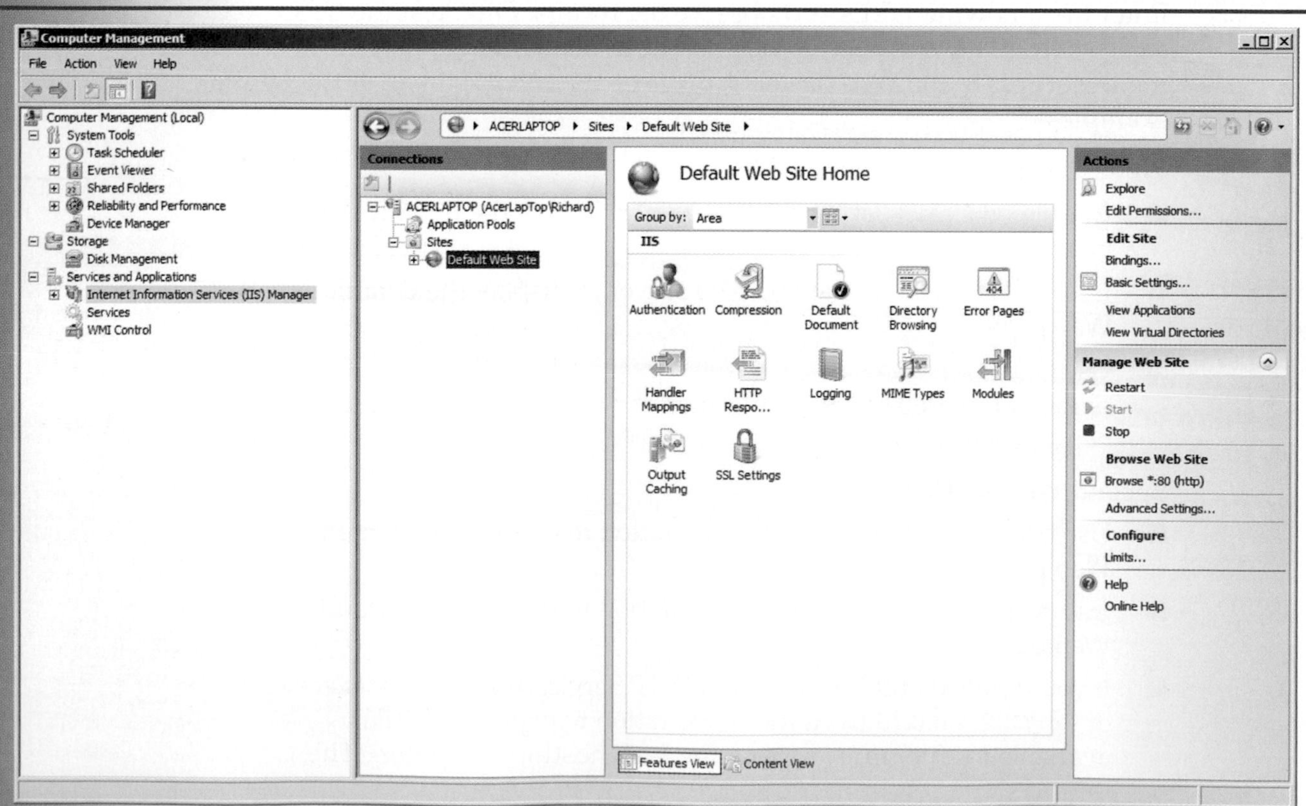

The **Default Web Site Home** pane contains an array of features that modify the default Web page. You may take a minute to view the options, but you will not understand most of the features presented. Web host configuration is an extensive topic, well beyond the scope of this lab activity. Do take note of the option in the right pane that allows you to stop and start the Web service.

13. _____ Close all open dialog boxes and then answer the review questions.
14. _____ Leave the workstation and IIS server in the condition specified by your instructor.

Review Questions

Answer the following questions on a separate sheet of paper. Please do not write in this book.

1. What does the acronym IIS represent?
2. On what version of Windows can IIS be installed?
3. What is the maximum number of simultaneous connections IIS allows when installed on Windows Vista or Windows 7?
4. True *or* False. IIS is installed by default when a typical installation of Windows is performed.
5. What is the difference between the URL of a Web page and the URL of an FTP site?
6. What common Windows program will prevent network users from viewing the default home page?

The World Wide Web Consortium (W3C) has many online tutorials and courses on Web-related topics such as HTML, CSS, and Web services.

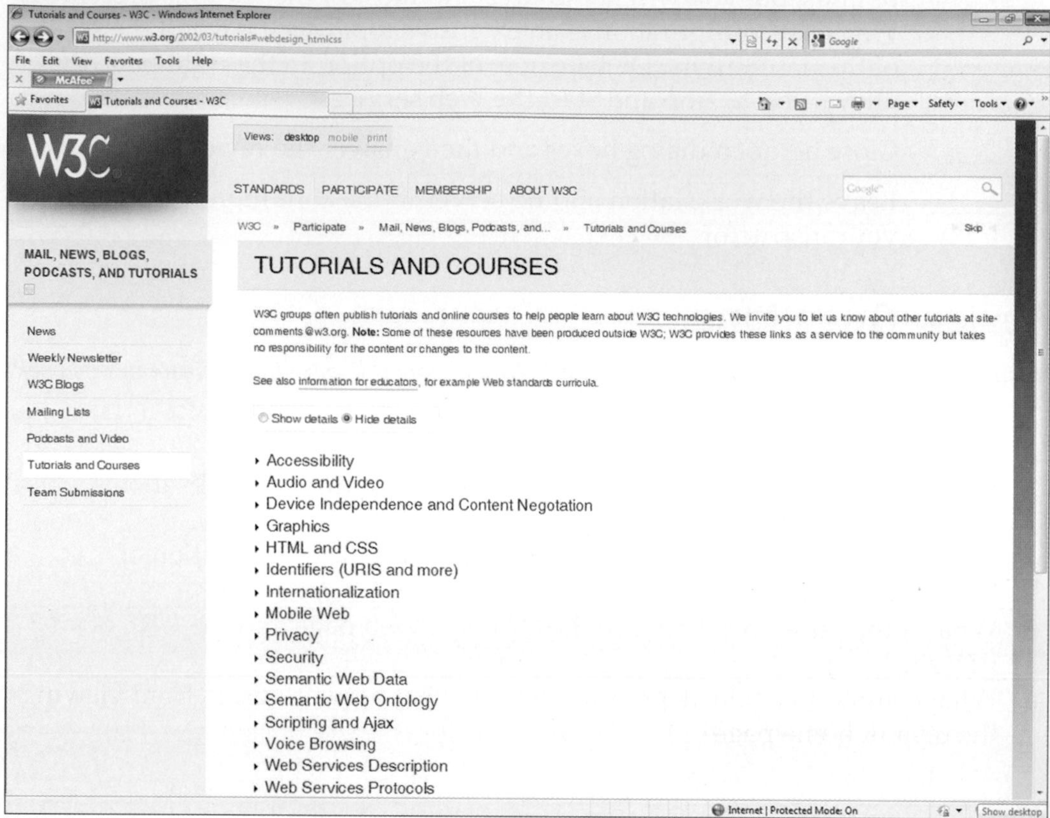

14 Remote Access and Long-Distance Communications

After studying this chapter, you will be able to:

- ❑ Recall the function of each major part of the public telephone system.
- ❑ Compare remote connection technologies.
- ❑ Explain how remote access to a network is achieved.
- ❑ Compare common remote access protocols.
- ❑ Recall the function and characteristics of a Virtual Private Network (VPN).

Network+ Exam—Key Points

The Network+ Certification exam covers the various types of media associated with the telecommunications industry. Typical questions are based on descriptions of the media and media performance limits. Be sure you are familiar with VPN and the associated protocols that support VPN.

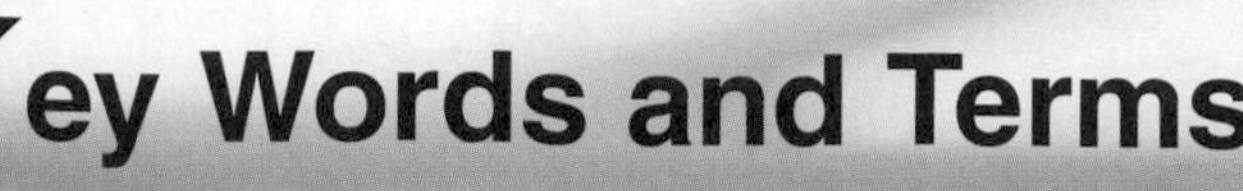

Key Words and Terms

The following words and terms will become important pieces of your networking vocabulary. Be sure you can define them.

Bandwidth Allocation Protocol (BAP)
Basic Rate ISDN (BRI-ISDN)
Broadband ISDN (B-ISDN)
Channel Service Unit/Data Service Unit (CSU/DSU)
dial-up networking
Digital Subscriber Line (DSL)
edge router
head-end
Integrated Services Digital Network (ISDN)
International Telecommunications Union (ITU)
Layer 2 Forwarding (L2F)
Layer 2 Tunneling Protocol (L2TP)
loading coil
Local Central Office
Local Exchange Carrier (LEC)
local loop
Multilink Point-to-Point Protocol (MLPPP)
Multi-Protocol Label Switching (MPLS)
Point of Presence (PoP)
Point-to-Point Protocol over Ethernet (PPPoE)
Point-to-Point Protocol (PPP)
Point-to-Point Tunneling Protocol (PPTP)
Primary Rate ISDN (PRI-ISDN)
remote access server
Remote Desktop Protocol (RDP)
Serial Line Internet Protocol (SLIP)
sunspots
Synchronous Optical Network (SONET)
T-carrier
trunk line
upconverter
Virtual Private Network (VPN)

This chapter explains the requirements for communicating remotely with a network and for communicating between LANs and to and from a MAN or a WAN. Remote communications rely on either public communications systems or private communications systems. The communications system we are most familiar with is the public telephone system.

Remote connection technology is at the very heart of a MAN and WAN. To understand a MAN and WAN, you must have an excellent understanding of remote connection technologies, such as T1, ISDN, and SONET. This chapter explores remote connection technologies and the different types of media used to transfer data across vast distances. We will begin the chapter with an introduction to the telecommunications system.

Introduction to Telecommunications Systems

The telecommunications industry has existed for almost a hundred years. During most of this period, it existed as an analog system and has been steadily converting to a complete digital system. The typical telephone system with which you are familiar consists mainly of two systems: local carriers and long-distance carriers.

Originally, local and long-distance carriers were the same entity. Rates were controlled to an extent by the government. The breakup, or deregulation, of telephone companies began as a series of legal disputes beginning in the late 1940s and ending in 1984 with the complete deregulation of the telephone industry. Large companies such as AT&T and Bell Telephone Company were separated into individual companies.

The two major service parts, local service and long-distance service, were also separated. This meant the customer would use one company for local telephone service, or local calls, and another for long-distance calls. Deregulation eliminated the monopolistic nature of the telecommunications industry. The concept was to make the market more competitive so that the consumer could benefit from the competition.

Deregulation created many local service and long-distance carriers. A local carrier is often referred to as a ***Local Exchange Carrier (LEC)*** and is made of one or more Local Central Offices. The ***Local Central Office*** is where the customer's telephone lines connect to the switchgear. The Local Central Office connects to long-distance carriers to provide long-distance access to individual residencies. Look at **Figure 14-1.** Notice that the ***local loop*** is the section of wiring between customer premises and the Local Central Office. The Local Central Office can be tied to other Local Central Offices via trunk lines. A ***trunk line*** consists of hundreds of pairs of twisted pair cable or fiber-optic cable.

The ***Point of Presence (PoP)*** is the point where the telephone company line connects to the subscriber line. The subscriber line begins at the customer's premises. Before deregulation, the telephone company was responsible for all wiring and

Local Exchange Carrier (LEC)
a local carrier, which is made of one or more Local Central Offices.

Local Central Office
the location where the customer's telephone lines connect to the switchgear. The Local Central Office connects to long-distance carriers to provide long-distance access to individual residencies.

local loop
the section of wiring between customer premises and the Local Central Office.

trunk line
consists of hundreds of pairs of twisted pair cable or fiber-optic cable.

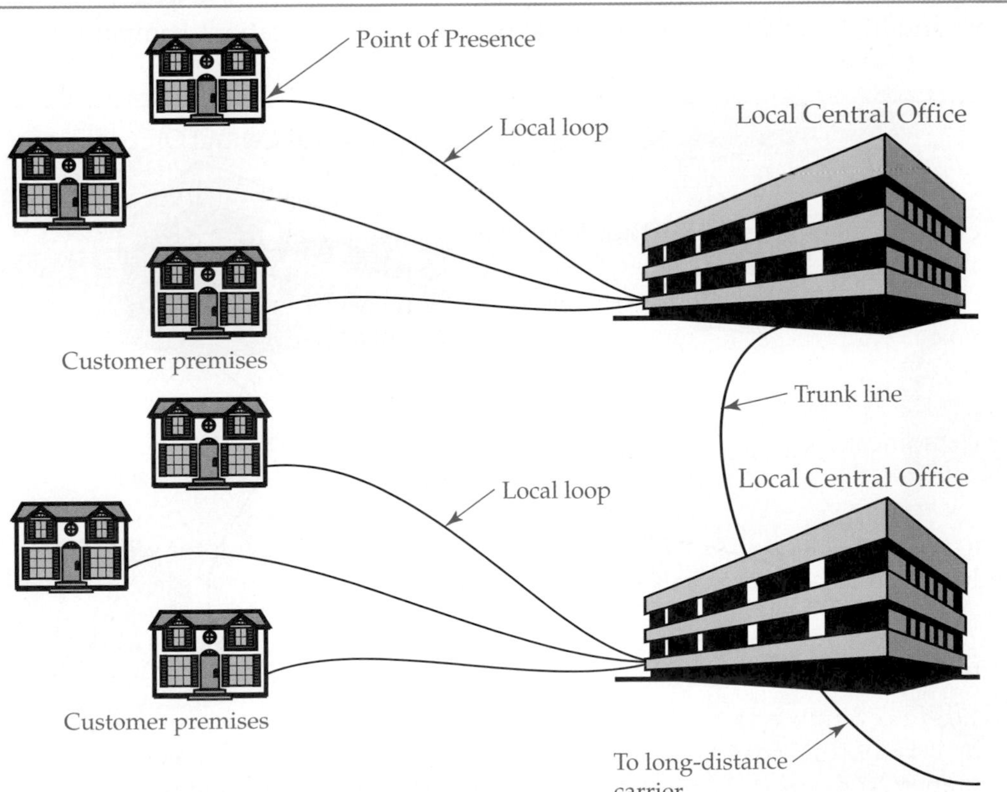

Figure 14-1.
A local loop is typically a low-bandwidth, twisted pair line between the telephone company's Local Central Office and the customer premises.

Point of Presence (PoP) the point where the telephone company line connects to the subscriber line.

equipment provided to the customer. The telephone company provided, installed, and repaired telephones and telephone lines inside the customer's home or business. Today, as you know, you must purchase a telephone and are responsible for repairing any telephone lines and equipment inside your home or business.

Remote Connection Technologies and Media

The worldwide communications system is quite complex, offering a variety of media to use and many different long-distance providers. While a LAN usually has a limited scope of communications media, a MAN and a WAN have a large variety of communications media and technologies from which to choose.

Both public and private communications companies often control the media. Communications companies are referred to as *carriers* or *providers*. These companies provide and maintain the media for data transmission.

Small businesses and private residencies typically connect to their ISP via the Local Central Office, **Figure 14-2.** Therefore, they usually use the low-bandwidth local loop between their site and the Local Central Office. Enterprises or large businesses require high bandwidth for telecommunications and Internet access. They typically avoid the low-bandwidth local loop by using high-speed leased lines, such as a T1 line, to access other business locations and their ISP.

The geographic area of a residence or business often affects the choice or availability of remote connection media. Connecting to a remote network from an office in a metropolitan area does not typically present the same bandwidth limitations as connecting to a remote network in a rural or suburban area. Access to the Local Exchange Carrier from a metropolitan area is usually accessible using media that provides a much higher bandwidth than is typically found in suburban residential or rural areas.

In a metropolitan area, there is the option of using leased lines, which provide private and high-bandwidth communications. Telecommunications companies

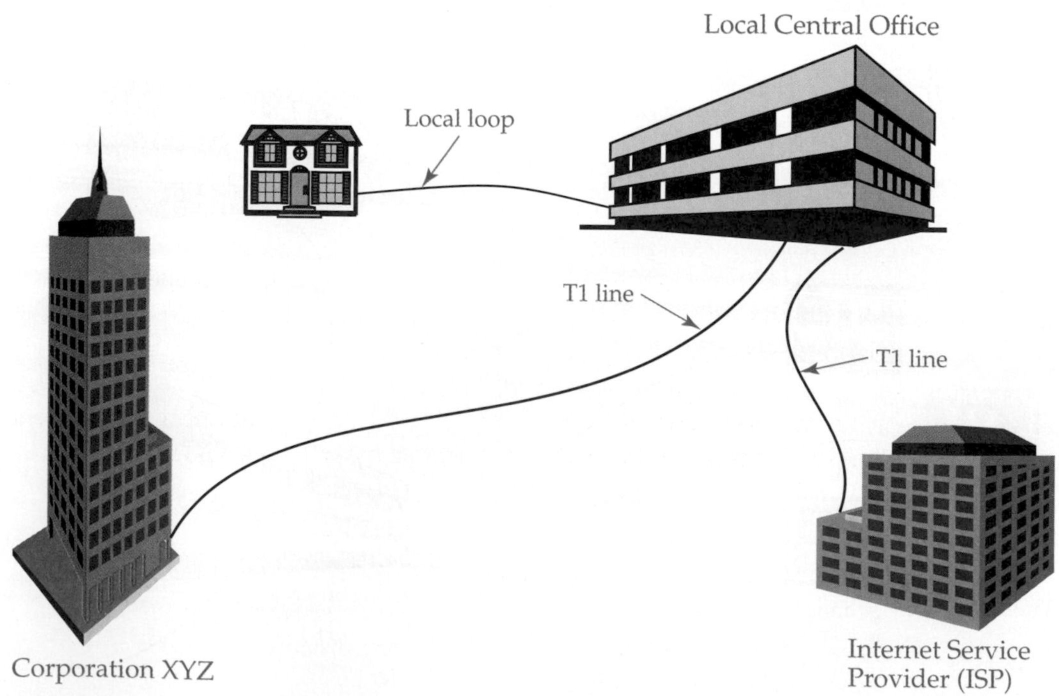

Figure 14-2. While typical residencies use a low-bandwidth, twisted pair line for telecommunications and Internet access, Internet Service Providers (ISPs) and enterprise businesses use a high-bandwidth line, such as T1.

make leased lines available between major metropolitan areas all over the world. In general, private communications systems are typically available in densely populated, metropolitan areas that contain numerous businesses with a need for high-speed communication. In contrast, public communications systems are typically located everywhere but do not always offer the same high bandwidth.

As you will see in the following sections, there are many different types of media, such as PSTN, ISDN, Cable, DSL, satellite, and T-carrier lines, available for communicating over long-distances. Each of the media covered is offered at various speeds and costs.

Public Switched Telephone Network (PSTN)

As you have previously learned in Chapter 12—Multimedia Transmission, a Public Switched Telephone Network (PSTN) is an older telephone technology that uses twisted pair cabling and analog signals rather than digital. Another name for a *Public Switched Telephone Network (PSTN)* is *Plain Old Telephone Service (POTS).*

The public telephone system was originally analog. After digital electronics emerged, the telephone industry began switching the public telephone system equipment and lines to that which supports digital technology. Today, the public telephone system is a mixture of digital and analog systems. While long-distance connections are usually digital, the short run between a residence or small business to the local loop is usually analog. Connections between the major telephone equipment are digital. It is possible, however, to have an entirely digital system that includes the local loop. Several options to achieve an entirely digital connection are discussed later in the chapter.

Typically, the PSTN is used when making a dial-up connection. A dial-up connection is a type of connection made using a traditional telephone line to reach a distant computer or network system. For example, a businessman using a laptop will typically connect the laptop modem to a telephone jack and dial a telephone number. This will connect the laptop modem to the modem at the distant network. Home users use a dial-up connection to reach their ISP when accessing their ISP through the telephone line.

It is important to note that a remote connection to a distant network or other computer has a total bandwidth equal to its weakest link. The weakest link is typically the local loop. This is especially true when attempting to connect to a remote computer from a residence. The existing residential telecommunications technology is largely influenced by the original telecommunications technology.

The original telephone system was an analog system requiring 48 volts to communicate across telephone lines. The telephone lines were designed to carry voice, not digital data. The original line did not require the twist in the conductor pairs, which is required for a high data rate. The telephone lines were designed to carry a maximum frequency of 4 kHz. This frequency is more than adequate for voice communications. Historically, the first network systems were designed to run at these slow transmission rates to take advantage of the millions of miles of existing telephone cables. Although this speed is usable, it is unacceptable by today's standards.

ISDN

Integrated Services Digital Network (ISDN) was developed in the 1980s. It provides the means for a fully digital transmission. ISDN lines are commonly found in small businesses, but there are some homes that are wired with ISDN. ISDN requires an ISDN modem. The ISDN modem can be installed either

Integrated Services Digital Network (ISDN) a long-distance-connection technology that provides a means for a fully digital transmission over channels that are capable of speeds of up to 64 kbps.

internally in the PC as an expansion card or externally, connecting through a serial port.

There are three categories of ISDN from which to choose: basic rate, primary rate, and broadband. ***Basic Rate ISDN (BRI-ISDN)*** consists of three conductors: two B channels, referred to as *bearer channels*, and one D channel, referred to as the *delta channel*. See **Figure 14-3.** The B channels carry data, voice, video, or a combination of voice and data. Each B channel carries a maximum of 64 kbps or a combined maximum data rate of 128 kbps. This data rate is approximately two to five times faster than the traditional telephone modem, which is 56 kbps. The D channel has a maximum bandwidth of 16 kbps. The D channel carries control signals. The control signals are used to set up, maintain, and terminate transmission on the B channels.

Basic Rate ISDN (BRI-ISDN)
a category of ISDN that consists of three conductors: two B channels, referred to as *bearer channels*, and one D channel, referred to as the *delta channel*.

Primary Rate ISDN (PRI-ISDN) consists of twenty-three B channels and one D channel. It has a total data rate of 1.544 Mbps. ***Broadband ISDN (B-ISDN)*** is designed to carry multiple frequencies. It has a total data rate of 1.5 Mbps. Remember that Broadband refers to media that can carry multiple frequencies. Baseband refers to media that can carry only one frequency. Basic Rate ISDN and Primary Rate ISDN are digital technologies and can carry only one frequency; hence, they are both Baseband.

Primary Rate ISDN (PRI-ISDN)
a category of ISDN that consists of twenty-three B channels and one D channel. It has a total data rate of 1.544 Mbps.

Broadband ISDN (B-ISDN)
a category of ISDN designed to carry multiple frequencies.

Cable Internet Service

Cable Internet service uses the Cable television distribution system to provide Internet access. Typically, Cable Internet service requires a Cable modem connection and a twisted pair or USB connection. The Cable modem connection connects to the F-type connector on the Cable service coaxial cable. The RJ-45 or USB connection on the Cable modem connects via twisted pair or USB cable to the network interface card on the computer. The RJ-45 or USB connection on the Cable modem may also connect to a hub, switch, gateway, or router to provide a shared Internet connection.

Tech Tip

A Cable modem is also called a *transceiver*. The word *transceiver* is a combination of the words *transmit* and *receive*.

Cable Internet service is an asymmetrical form of communication. The term *asymmetrical* is used to describe Cable Internet service communication because the uplink and downlink have two different transfer speeds. Upstream connections vary between 320 kbps and 10 Mbps, while downstream data rates vary between

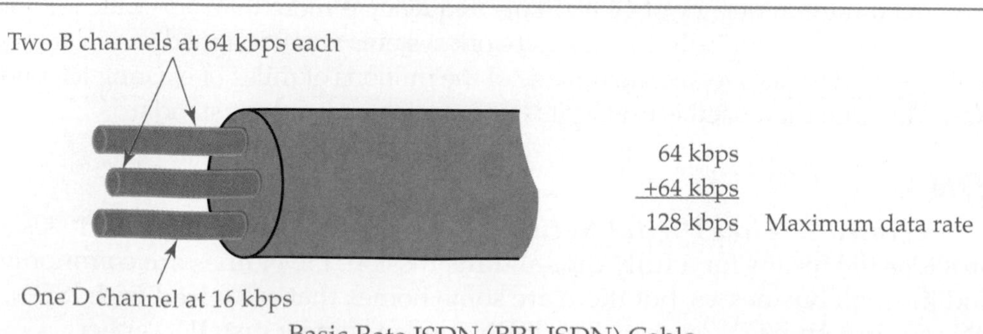

Figure 14-3.
A Basic Rate ISDN (BRI-ISDN) cable consists of two 64-kbps B channels and one 16-kbps D channel. The two B channels can be combined for a total bandwidth of 128 kbps.

27 Mbps and 37 Mbps. The term *downstream* is used to describe the data flow direction from the carrier or provider site to the customer. The term *upstream* is used for the data flow direction from the customer to the carrier. These speeds are advertised by the Data Over Cable System Interface Specification (DOCSIS), which is the industry standard.

The DOCSIS standard was developed by a group of Cable industry representatives before the IEEE 802.14 standard was developed. The IEEE 802.14 standard was an early attempt to standardize Cable modems and high-speed access. It failed because of a lack of support by the manufacturers who opted to follow the DOCSIS standard.

The speeds advertised by DOCSIS are theoretical speeds and are far from the actual speeds you can expect. In fact, it is difficult to obtain the actual speed because speed is affected by various factors, such as time of day, type of data downloaded, and overall distance from the Cable provider.

The amount of bandwidth available is mostly influenced by how many other subscribers are using the Cable service in the local area. The local area distribution point is referred to as the ***head-end.*** See **Figure 14-4.** There can be hundreds of subscribers connected to the cable before accessing the head-end. As the volume of subscribers increases, the bandwidth decreases.

head-end the local area distribution point of a Cable television service provider.

The actual bandwidth fluctuates according to the number of users on line at the same time and the type of data downloaded. For example, in the middle of the night, a typical user should have remarkable download speeds because there are very few users on line. In contrast, the late afternoon hours offer slower speeds due to the large number of users, typically just home from school. At that time, students are on the system doing homework and downloading music and games. All this traffic puts a stress on the bandwidth, thus decreasing it substantially.

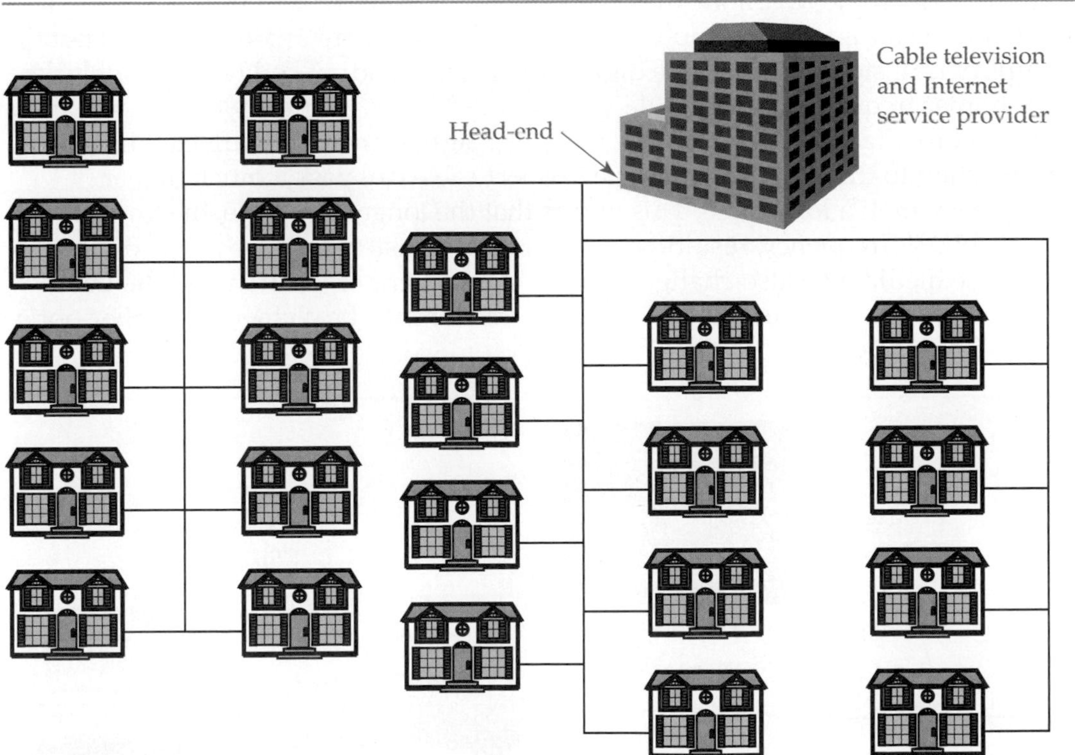

Figure 14-4. While Cable Internet access offers a high-bandwidth Internet connection to residencies, the total number of simultaneous Internet connections through the Cable system affects the amount of bandwidth used by each residence.

As stated earlier, Cable Internet service requires a special piece of equipment called a Cable modem. The Cable modem provides a connection to the Cable television service media and to the network interface card in the PC. **Figure 14-5** shows how a splitter can be used to share the Cable television coaxial cable with the Cable modem.

Not all Cable companies can provide Internet service because Internet access requires special equipment to distribute Internet access through the Cable company's distribution system. Original Cable distribution equipment was designed for the downstream distribution of video and music and not designed to accept upstream communication. The cabling and the equipment at the Cable company's distribution center usually have to be upgraded. The original coaxial cable is replaced with hybrid fiber-coax cable. The fiber-optic portion supports the high bandwidth while the coaxial portion supports the control.

Digital Subscriber Line (DSL)

Digital Subscriber Line (DSL)
a leased line dedicated to networking that uses multiple frequencies as separate channels on the existing telephone local loop. The multiple channels combine to carry more data than the original telephone modem design.

loading coil
a device used to amplify voice signals.

Digital Subscriber Line (DSL) is a high-speed Internet access technology that uses existing local loop telephone lines. It is much faster than ISDN and is designed to replace it. DSL comes in a variety of standards that vary in the techniques used to make data transmission faster.

DSL uses modulation techniques similar to those discussed in Chapter 4—Wireless Technology. Multiple frequencies are used as separate channels on the existing telephone local loop. The multiple channels combine to carry more data than the original telephone modem design. The original telephone modem design does not use multiple frequency signals. It uses only one.

Maximum distance for DSL is limited due to the high frequencies transmitted. The typical maximum distance for DSL is 1,000 feet to 18,000 feet and is measured from the DSL modem to the telephone company's Local Central Office. The exact limit depends on the variation of DSL used and any special equipment that might exist on the telephone line, such as loading coils, or a change in the media. A ***loading coil*** is used to amplify voice signals, which are analog, and will not amplify DSL signals, which are digital. In fact, the loading coil reduces or blocks the higher frequency DSL signal.

Another factor is the length of the cable. Signal strength is affected in direct proportion to the length of the cable. A short cable can pass a much higher frequency than a long cable. This means that the longer the cable, the lower the applied DSL frequency, resulting in lower data transfer rates.

The media may also change between the subscriber location and the Local Central Office. For example, the copper conductor may be changed to a fiber-optic

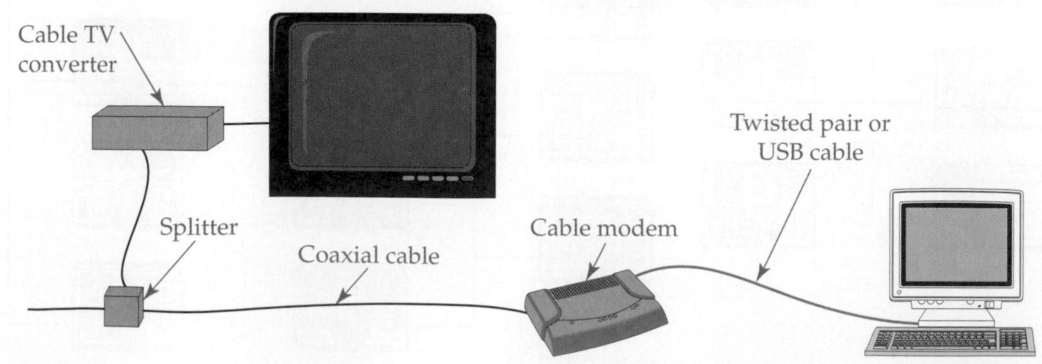

Figure 14-5. The television Cable service can provide Internet access. A Cable modem is needed to connect the PC to the Cable service.

DSL Type	Description	Upstream Data Rate	Downstream Data Rate	Maximum Distance between DSL Modem and Central Office
ADSL	Asymmetrical DSL	1.544 Mbps	1.5 Mbps–8 Mbps	12,000 ft.–18,000 ft.
SDSL	Symmetric DSL	1.544 Mbps	1.544 Mbps	10,000 ft.
HDSL	High bit-rate DSL	1.544 Mbps	1.544 Mbps	14,000 ft.
VDSL	Very high bit-rate DSL	1.5 Mbps–2.3 Mbps	13 Mbps–52 Mbps	1000 ft.–4500 ft.

Figure 14-6. DSL technologies.

cable at some point, which will prevent the application of DSL. The DSL technique is applied only to copper core cable, not fiber-optic cable.

DSL varies in upstream and downstream bandwidth based on the transmission technique used. Some varieties of DSL are listed in **Figure 14-6.** The main points to remember about DSL is it is a high-speed Internet access technology that uses existing local loop telephone lines, and the actual download rate is affected by the length of the cable.

Satellite

A satellite system can be used for Internet access and for data communication, **Figure 14-7.** A typical satellite system consists of a satellite dish at the satellite service provider location, a satellite, and a satellite dish at the consumer location. Satellite system installations are available in consumer-grade and business-grade. The typical consumer-grade installation consists of a small dish for downloading and a landline, such as a traditional telephone line, for uploading. Before you can connect to the Internet, you need to make an initial connection to the satellite Internet service provider through a modem. Thereafter, you must use the telephone line connection via the modem to communicate (upload) Web page requests and to send e-mail.

Typical download speeds for consumer satellite communications are 400 kbps to 500 kbps. Upload speeds are limited to the particular land-based technology

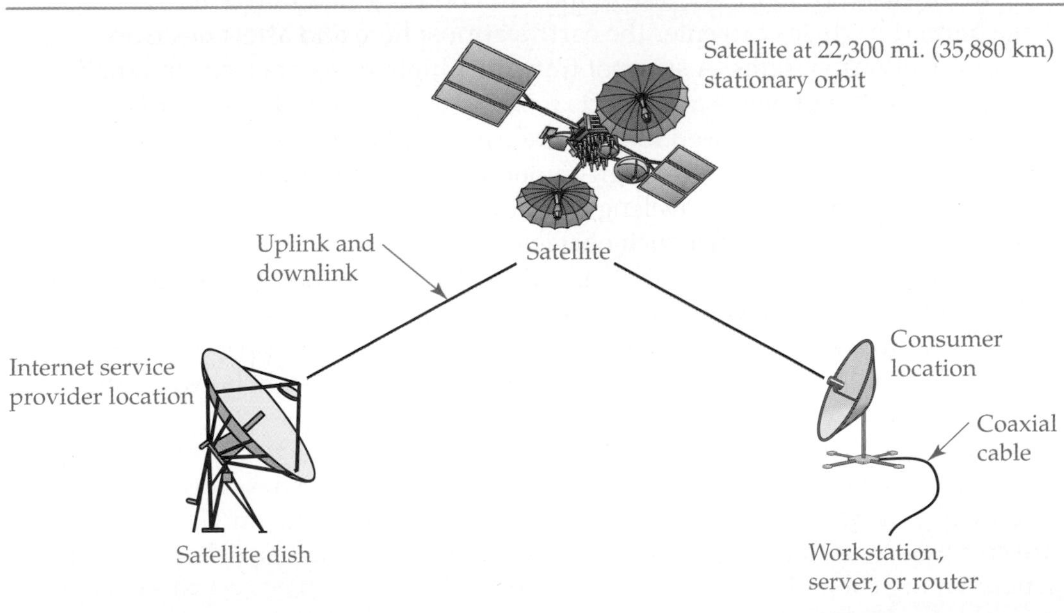

Figure 14-7. Typical satellite system components.

used for upload. For example, a telephone modem offers speeds of 56 kbps and an ISDN modem offers speeds of 1.54 Mbps and 128 kbps. Often, the only real advantage for consumer satellite technology is access from remote locations.

Business-grade satellite communications offer higher speeds, typically up to 1.5 Mbps in the US and up to 2 Mbps in Europe and other countries. The speed difference between the US and other countries is due to different wireless regulations. Business-grade satellite communications are designed with more expensive equipment while consumer-grade satellite communications are designed with less expensive equipment. Using less expensive equipment for consumer-grade satellite communications allows satellite communications to be competitively priced among other Internet access technologies. Business-grade satellite communications, however, offer uplink and downlink capabilities. Uplink requires a radio transmitter to be integrated into the satellite dish. The radio transmitter is referred to as an ***upconverter***.

upconverter a radio transmitter integrated into a satellite dish.

The main advantages of using satellite communications is it is ideal for temporary connections such as sporting events or remote locations where landlines are not readily available. The disadvantages of satellite communications are latency, security, and interference. As you have already learned in Chapter 4—Wireless Technology, the satellite is located 22,300 miles from the surface of the earth and is in a geosynchronous orbit (synchronized with the earth's rotational speed). The great distance the radio wave must travel causes the transmitted signal to experience propagation delay. The propagation delay for a signal transmitted from a satellite to a satellite dish is approximately 250 milliseconds. The propagation delay does not noticeably affect the downloading of Web pages with text-based contents, but it is unacceptable for telephone support or full-duplex video conferencing.

Security is also a problem because all transmissions are based on radio transmissions, which can be easily intercepted. An encryption program is needed to secure sensitive data. Radio wave transmissions to and from the satellite can be adversely affected by certain conditions.

Atmospheric conditions due to stormy weather (rain, lightning, etc.) affect satellite communications, causing data loss. Another phenomenon known as *sunspots* also affects communications. ***Sunspots*** are magnetic energy storms that occur at the surface of the sun. The magnetic fields produce charged particles that are released from the surface of the sun and projected into outer space. The charged particles can enter the earth's atmosphere and affect electronic communications systems. A sunspot transmits high levels of electromagnetic energy across the universe and affects to some degree all radio transmissions.

sunspots magnetic energy storms that occur at the surface of the sun.

The radio frequency used for satellite transmission is classified as microwave. Microwaves have a high-frequency pattern with short wavelengths. The high-frequency, short wavelength radio waves are easily disrupted by trees, buildings, bridges, and other such obstacles. A clear line of sight is required between the receiving satellite dish and the orbiting satellite. This is in contrast to low-frequency radio waves like the one used for wireless networks. Wireless network radio waves can penetrate some objects that are not very dense. In summary, satellite communications require a clear line of sight between the destination and source. See **Figure 14-8.**

The same principle used to transmit data between the satellite and satellite dish can be used between a series of microwave satellite dishes. You can see microwave dishes located on towers all over the country. The microwave dishes are commonly used by telephone communications systems, especially in areas where laying cables is difficult or impossible.

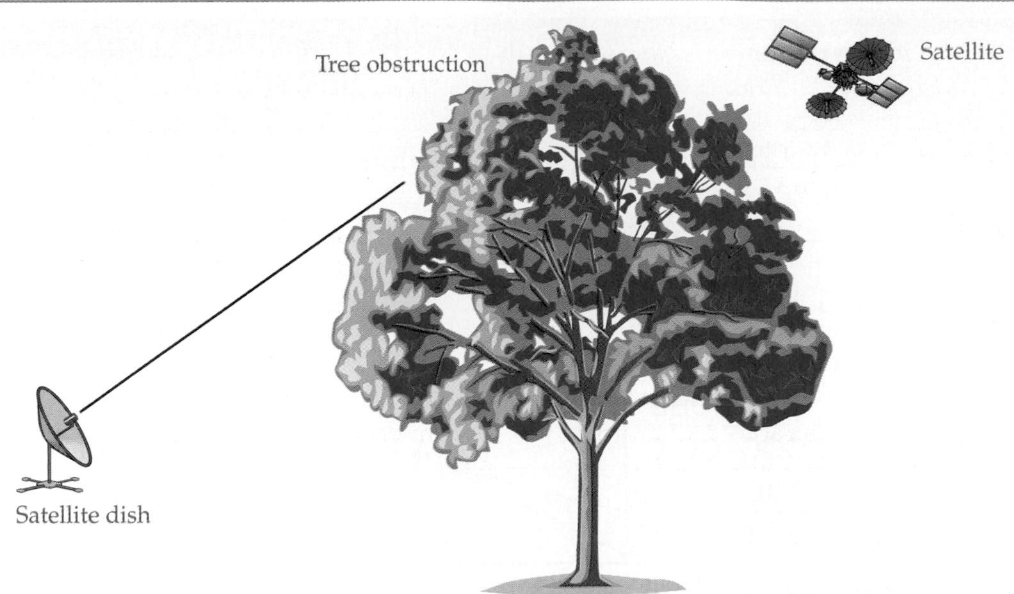

Figure 14-8.
There must be a clear line of sight between the satellite dish and the satellite. Trees, buildings, bridges, and such interfere with satellite radio transmissions.

Another location where microwave dish transmission is often used is across bodies of water, such as bays and wide rivers, or over large tracts of flat land. Again, the line of sight principle must be applied, and the series of dishes must be precisely aimed at one another.

T-Carrier

A ***T-carrier*** is a leased line that follows one of the standards known as T1, fractional T1, T2, or T3. The T-carrier is a dedicated, permanent connection that is capable of providing high bandwidth. A T1 line consists of 24 channels, each with a data rate of 64 kbps or a total bandwidth of 1.544 Mbps. A fractional T1 only uses part of a T1 line's full capability, usually in increments of 64 kbps. See **Figure 14-9** for a summary of T-carrier standards.

T-carrier
a leased line that follows one of the standards known as T1, fractional T1, T2, or T3. The T-carrier is a dedicated, permanent connection that is capable of providing a high bandwidth.

The European counterpart to a T1 leased line is E1, which has a maximum rate of 2.048 Mbps. The Japanese counterpart is J1. Notice in **Figure 14-10** that data rates for T1, E1, and J1 differ.

T-carriers were developed to carry data and voice signals. You will often see T1 lines as a mixture of voice and data lines. To accomplish the task of sharing T1 media with different signals, a pair of multiplexers is used. One multiplexer is placed on each end of the T-carrier line. The multiplexer combines the different signal types (voice and data) into an organized manner and places the different signal types onto a single T1 line for transmission. Look at **Figure 14-11.**

T-Carrier Standard	Number of T1 Lines	Number of Channels	Maximum Data Rate
T1	1	24	1.544 Mbps
T2	4	96	6.312 Mbps
T3	28	672	44.736 Mbps
T4	168	4032	274.176 Mbps

Figure 14-9.
T-carrier technologies.

Figure 14-10.
Comparison of T1, E1, and J1 lines.

USA		Europe		Japan	
T1	1.544 Mbps	E1	2.048 Mbps	J1	1.544 Mbps
T2	6.312 Mbps	E2	8.448 Mbps	J2	6.312 Mbps
T3	44.736 Mbps	E3	34.368 Mbps	J3	32.064 Mbps
T4	274.176 Mbps	E4	139.264 Mbps	J4	97.728 Mbps
NA	NA	E5	564.992 Mbps	J5	397.200 Mbps

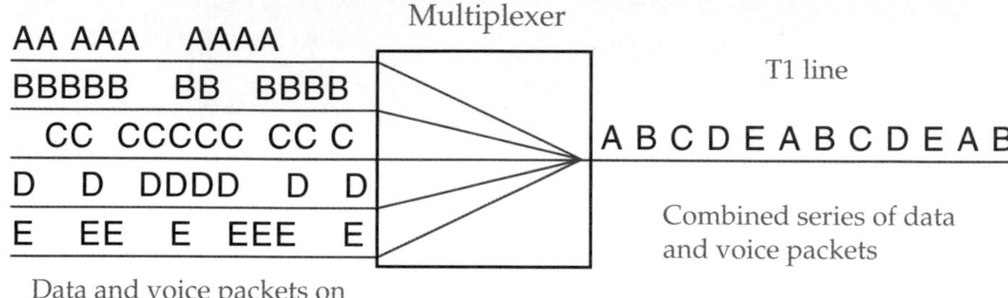

Figure 14-11.
A multiplexer typically combines multiple lines of incoming data into a single series of data packets on a T1 line. A demultiplexer at the destination reverses the process.

When mixing voice and data, voice packets must be placed onto the T-carrier line in close proximity to one another. If voice packets are spaced too far apart (interspersed between data), the received voice transmission will have undesirable pauses. It is the multiplexer's responsibility to place the voice packets on the T-carrier line often enough so that there will not be any detectable sound gaps or pauses when reassembled at the destination multiplexer. It is not as critical for data packets to be placed in close proximately to one another.

Often, the multiplexer and a Channel Service Unit/Data Service Unit (CSU/DSU) are incorporated into a single unit. A ***Channel Service Unit/Data Service Unit (CSU/DSU)*** converts signals from the LAN to signals that can be carried by the T1 line, and vice versa.

Channel Service Unit/Data Service Unit (CSU/DSU) electronic circuitry that converts signals from the LAN to signals that can be carried by a T1 line, and vice versa.

FDDI

The Fiber Distribution Data Interface (FDDI) is a dual ring, fiber-optic arrangement. FDDI was covered earlier in Chapter 3—Fiber-Optic Cable. FDDI is mentioned here because it is often used in a MAN distribution system because of its reliability and its high bandwidth. FDDI can be used for distances of up to 62 miles. This distance is more than adequate for MAN installations.

Synchronous Optical Network (SONET) similar in design to T-carrier technology except SONET bases its technology on fiber-optic cable.

SONET

Synchronous Optical Network (SONET) is similar in design to T-carrier technology except SONET bases its technology on fiber-optic cable. Because SONET is based on fiber-optic cable, it can provide a much higher bandwidth—as high as 9.9 Gbps. SONET is the standard choice for connecting global-sized networks spanning across the nation and oceans. See **Figure 14-12** for a summary of SONET levels.

SONET is similar to T-carrier in that special termination equipment, such as a multiplexer, is needed at the customer location. SONET often uses multiplexer technology to carry a mix of data, voice, and video on the same channel.

SONET is designed as a ring topology similar to the dual-ring structure of FDDI. One ring is the primary communication ring, and the other ring serves

SONET Level	Maximum Data Rate
OC-1	51.84 Mbps
OC-3	145.52 Mbps
OC-12	622 Mbps
OC-24	1244 Mbps
OC-48	2488 Mbps
OC-192	9953 Mbps

Figure 14-12. SONET levels.

as a backup. The backup ring ensures reliability. If the primary ring fails, data transmission is automatically switched to the backup ring.

Enterprise companies spanning long distances, such as across the nation or the globe, most often use SONET. Small or mid-size companies do not typically use SONET because it is quite expensive to lease when compared with other technologies. It has, however, the best design for reliability.

X.25

X.25 is a packet switching analog network technology developed in the 1970s. X.25 can support a maximum bandwidth of 56 kbps. For over twenty years, X.25 was used to transmit data over long distances. It was used almost exclusively for transmissions around the world because the ***International Telecommunications Union (ITU)*** recognized it as a standard. ITU is responsible for standardizing communications on an international level. The ITU regulates radio, television, and satellite frequencies and standards and telephony standards. Although X.25 dominated worldwide communications, Frame Relay has been the first choice since the early 1990s.

International Telecommunications Union (ITU) an organization responsible for standardizing communications on an international level. The ITU regulates radio, television, and satellite frequencies and standards and telephony standards.

X.25 is not usually available in the USA. However, knowledge about X.25 is required for working with WAN systems that connect all over the world. This protocol is often included in the list of protocols available in many different operating systems.

Frame Relay

Frame Relay uses digital media rather than analog like X.25. Frame Relay is a packet switching technology similar to X.25. Both X.25 and Frame Relay are Permanent Virtual Circuits. A Permanent Virtual Circuit (PVC) typically uses numerous paths between two points. A packet switching technology reduces data into smaller units (packets) and uses a number of different routes (switching) to transport the packets. Remember, a packet contains a destination and source address and a packet sequence number. The sequence number allows the packets to be arranged in their original order when they reach the destination.

One main advantage of Frame Relay technology is, because it is a shared, leased line, it can be leased at a reduced rate. This can mean a significant cost reduction when compared with T-carrier, especially for expensive overseas communication. The fact that Frame Relay is a shared leased line can also be viewed as a disadvantage. The available bandwidth could fluctuate from 56 kbps to 1.544 kbps. For example, the bandwidth available to a user in the morning can be significantly reduced because of the traffic generated by personnel checking for data transactions from the night before. At another time of day, the full 1.544 Mbps bandwidth could be available. See **Figure 14-13** for a summary of WAN connection technologies.

Figure 14-13. Summary of WAN connection technologies.

WAN Connection Technology	Access Method	Data Rate	Comments
ATM	Direct connection	25 Mbps–622 Mbps	Virtually private.
Cable Internet Service	Direct connection	Downstream: 27 Mbps–37 Mbps (theoretical). 300 kbps–500 kbps (actual) Upstream: 320 kbps–10 Mbps	TV Cable service. Requires a cable modem. Cable service uses MPEG-2 for data compression.
FDDI	Direct connection	100 Mbps	High reliability and bandwidth.
Fractional T1	Direct connection	64 kbps	T-carrier technology. Can use multiple channels to increase speed by increments of 64 kbps.
Frame Relay	Virtual connection	56 kbps–45 Mbps	Virtually private.
ISDN	Dial-up	64 kbps and 128 kbps	Requires a leased line and an ISDN modem. Can carry only one frequency.
PRI-ISDN	Direct connection	1.544 Mbps	Requires a leased line and an ISDN modem. Can carry only one frequency.
Public Switched Telephone Network (PSTN)	Dial-up	56 kbps	This is also known as Plain Old Telephone Service (POTS). Requires a telephone modem.
Satellite Internet Service	Direct connection	400 kbps–2 Mbps	May use a dial-up service to connect to the satellite Internet provider. Experiences propagation delay.
SONET	Direct connection	51 Mbps–9953 Mbps	Commonly used to span long distances such as across the nation and overseas.
T1	Direct connection	1.544 Mbps	T-carrier technology.
T3	Direct connection	44.736 Mbps	T-carrier technology.
X.25	Virtual connection	56 kbps	Packet switching, analog technology.
xDSL	Direct connection	1.544 Mbps–52 Mbps	Data rate depends on the version of DSL. Requires an xDSL modem. Limited distance from the DSL modem to the telephone company's Local Central Office is between 1,000 ft.–18,000 ft.

dial-up networking a network system in which a dial-up connection is used to access a remote access server.

Dial-Up Networking

Remote connections can be made to distant networks using existing telephone lines. The term ***dial-up networking*** describes a network system in which a dial-up connection is used to access a remote access server. A ***remote access server,*** therefore, is a server that is accessed through dial-up networking. To set up a dial-up network, a modem must be installed at the client location and on the remote access server. Remote access software must also be installed. The remote access software specific to Microsoft operating systems are Dial-Up Networking (DUN) and Remote Access Service (RAS). DUN is installed on the client side of the remote access network, and RAS is installed on the remote access server.

remote access server a server that is accessed through dial-up networking.

Windows 2000 Server, Windows Server 2003, and Windows Server 2008 use an enhanced version of RAS called *Routing and Remote Access Service (RRAS)*.

Look at **Figure 14-14.** A laptop at a distant location is connected to a telephone line. The laptop connects to the home-office network through the remote access server. Once a connection is established, the remote access user can check his or her office e-mail, print out customer orders, access files on his or her office desktop computer, and access the company database. There are three common ways to set up remote dial-in access on a server:

- Allow dial-in to the remote access server only.
- Allow dial-out from the remote access server only.
- Allow full-service dial-in and dial-out on the remote access server.

Dial-In Only

The dial-in only configuration allows remote access clients to connect to the network server, but does not allow hosts on the network to dial out. This prevents personnel from surfing the World Wide Web, but allows the hosts on the network to accept incoming calls. This is a good business scenario that prevents workers from wasting time when they should be providing service to customers.

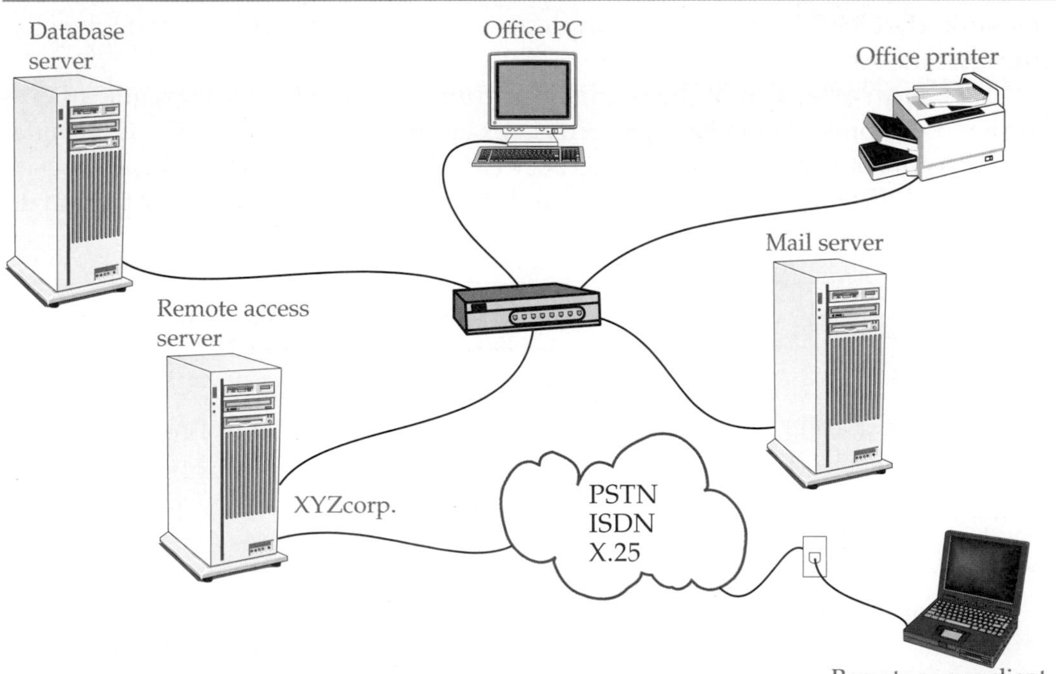

Figure 14-14. A laptop computer can connect to the corporate office by using dial-up networking software. A server must be set up with remote access server software. Once this is accomplished, the remote client can access items such as the office computer, printer, company database, and e-mail.

Dial-Out Only

Dial-out only access adds security to a network system by allowing calls to be placed from the network but not into the network. This prevents unauthorized persons from accessing the network through a telephone modem connection.

Full Service

Full service access allows the remote client to dial-in to the network and also allows network hosts to dial-out to remote locations. This type of access is perfect for a small-office environment or a limited number of users in an enterprise business environment. Security policies can control individual user access to telephone features in much the same way file-sharing access can be controlled. Specific users can be identified and granted various levels of modem use and specific hours or times of modem access.

Remote access can be configured to allow the business to bear the cost of a long-distance call. For example, a remote access client calls into the office server. The office server detects the incoming call but does not accept it. The call is terminated and the server immediately returns the call to the remote access client so that the server side bears the cost of the long-distance call rather than the remote access client.

A network may also be accessed remotely through an Internet connection if the network has a network server with a modem and the remote access service running. Not all offices have a network server. In this scenario, remote access must take place from telephone modem to telephone modem between a network PC and a remote access PC.

Remote Desktop Protocol (RDP)

Remote Desktop Protocol (RDP) a presentation protocol that allows Windows computers to communicate directly with Windows-based clients.

The ***Remote Desktop Protocol (RDP)*** is a presentation protocol that allows Windows computers to communicate directly with Windows-based clients. The Remote Desktop Protocol is transmitted across any TCP/IP connection. RDP provides security by encrypting the contents of packets sent across the TCP/IP network. Port 3389 is the default port used for RDP and must be opened when a firewall is used.

RDP is an extension of the original Terminal Services technology, an earlier version of the presentation type protocol. Look at **Figure 14-15.** The original Terminal Service technology allowed a Terminal Services Client to send keyboard and mouse control to the Terminal Services Server and the Terminal Services Server to send its

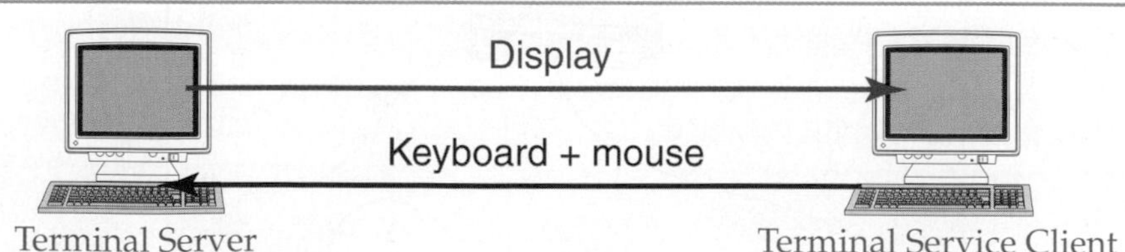

Figure 14-15. Terminal Services technology allows a Terminal Services Client to send keyboard and mouse control to the Terminal Services Server and the Terminal Services Server to send its display to the Terminal Services Client.

display to the Terminal Services Client. For example, after the client establishes a connection with the Terminal Services Server, it sends commands via the keyboard or mouse to manipulate the directory and file structure. The Terminal Services Server sends the screen image to the client as the files are manipulated. The client experiences the session as though he or she were sitting at the server.

When using RDP with a Windows Professional system, the roles of Terminal Service Client and Terminal Server are simply called the *client* and *host*, respectively. The client uses the Remote Desktop Connection software to connect to the host.

RDP is based on the International Telecommunications Union (ITU) T.120 protocol.

Remote Access Protocols

Dial-up access uses special protocols for negotiating a connection between a PC and a network, two networks, or two PCs. Some of the most common remote access protocols are briefly introduced in this section. You will see that many remote access protocols were developed to better address the issues of security. See **Figure 14-16** for a summary of remote access protocols.

Serial Line Internet Protocol (SLIP) a remote access protocol that enables a PC to connect to a remote network using a serial line connection, typically through a telephone line. SLIP is an asynchronous protocol that supports only IP.

PPP and SLIP

Serial Line Internet Protocol (SLIP) and Point-to-Point Protocol (PPP) enable a PC to connect to a remote network using a serial line connection, typically through a telephone line. The ***Serial Line Internet Protocol (SLIP)*** protocol was introduced

Remote Access Protocol	Full Name	Description
L2F	Layer 2 Forwarding	Enhances security and makes use of a VPN using the public Internet. L2F requires special equipment on the host side to support data transfers.
L2TP	Layer 2 Tunneling Protocol	Combines the features of L2F and PPTP.
MLPPP	Multilink Point-to-Point Protocol	Combines two or more physical links in such a way that they act as one, thus increasing the supported bandwidth. Works with ISDN lines, PSTN lines, and X.25 technology.
PPP	Point-to-Point Protocol	A synchronous protocol that supports multiple protocols such as IPX and AppleTalk. Enables a PC to connect to a remote network using a serial line connection, typically through a telephone line.
PPPoE	Point-to-Point Protocol over Ethernet	Supports multiple clients connected to an ISP over Ethernet.
PPTP	Point-to-Point Tunneling Protocol	Enhanced version of PPP that makes use of a VPN using the public Internet. It encapsulates the existing network protocol (IP, IPX, AppleTalk, and such) into the PPTP protocol.
SLIP	Serial Line Internet Protocol	An asynchronous protocol that supports only IP. Enables a PC to connect to a remote network using a serial line connection, typically through a telephone line.

Figure 14-16. Summary of remote access protocols.

with UNIX and supports only TCP/IP. ***Point-to-Point Protocol (PPP)*** is a vast improvement over SLIP and can support multiple protocols such as IPX, AppleTalk, and TCP/IP.

Point-to-Point Protocol (PPP) a remote access protocol that enables a PC to connect to a remote network using a serial line connection, typically through a telephone line. PPP is a synchronous protocol that supports multiple protocols such as IPX and AppleTalk.

SLIP is strictly an asynchronous protocol while PPP is both asynchronous and synchronous. Remember from earlier chapters that synchronous transmission relies on a separate timing signal so that both the transmitting and receiving equipment are in step during the exchange of data. Asynchronous means that the data is transferred without a timing signal. Data is transferred from one point to another without being in step.

PPP is much easier to set up than SLIP because most of the required settings can be automatically negotiated. SLIP requires information such as the IP address to be entered manually. You will seldom encounter SLIP because it doesn't support authentication, encryption, or VPN connections.

PPTP

Point-to-Point Tunneling Protocol (PPTP) a remote access protocol that is an enhanced version of PPP. It is designed to enhance security and to make use of a virtually private network using the public Internet.

Point-to-Point Tunneling Protocol (PPTP) is an enhanced version of PPP. It is designed to enhance security and to make use of a virtually private network using the public Internet. The Internet is used by millions of people. While it is an excellent system of communication, it has security issues. The term *virtually private* means that the network connection appears to be a private network, similar to a dedicated network media such as a T1 line. A T1 line offers a much higher level of security than an Internet connection because it is a privately leased line in contrast to a publicly accessed connection.

When using PPTP, you can gain access to a corporate network by using a dial-up connection through an ISP and then negotiating data transfers over the public Internet. The term *tunneling* refers to encapsulating the existing network protocol (IP, IPX, AppleTalk, and such) into the PPTP protocol.

PPTP incorporates methods to encrypt data. The PPTP protocol also supports the necessary remote access service and network access authentication.

PPPoE

Point-to-Point Protocol over Ethernet (PPPoE) a remote access protocol that allows one or more hosts on an Ethernet network to establish an individual PPP connection with an ISP. PPPoE frames the PPP protocol so that the PPP frame can travel over an Ethernet network.

Point-to-Point Protocol over Ethernet (PPPoE) provides one or more hosts on an Ethernet network the ability to establish an individual PPP connection with an ISP. PPPoE frames the PPP protocol so that the PPP frame can travel over an Ethernet network.

Look at the **Figure 14-17.** Notice that each computer using the PPPoE protocol has the ability to establish and maintain an individual connection with an ISP. With Internet Connection Sharing (ICS), one computer establishes a connection to the ISP and must remain on for the other computers to have the ability to connect to the Internet. With the PPPoE protocol, each PPPoE client has direct access to the ISP. The PPPoE clients are arranged as a typical Ethernet network and use a DSL or Cable modem to connect to the ISP. The DSL or Cable modem may be incorporated into a router or serve as an individual piece of equipment. A PPPoE access server is located at the ISP. The server provides individual connections as needed to each of the PPPoE clients.

The PPPoE connection has two stages: discovery and session. In the discovery stage, the PPPoE client attempts to discover the location of the PPPoE server. There may be more than one PPPoE server. The client must locate and establish a connection with only one PPPoE server. Typically, the PPPoE client and the PPPoE server exchange network identification consisting of an IP address and MAC address. After addressees are exchanged, a connection is established

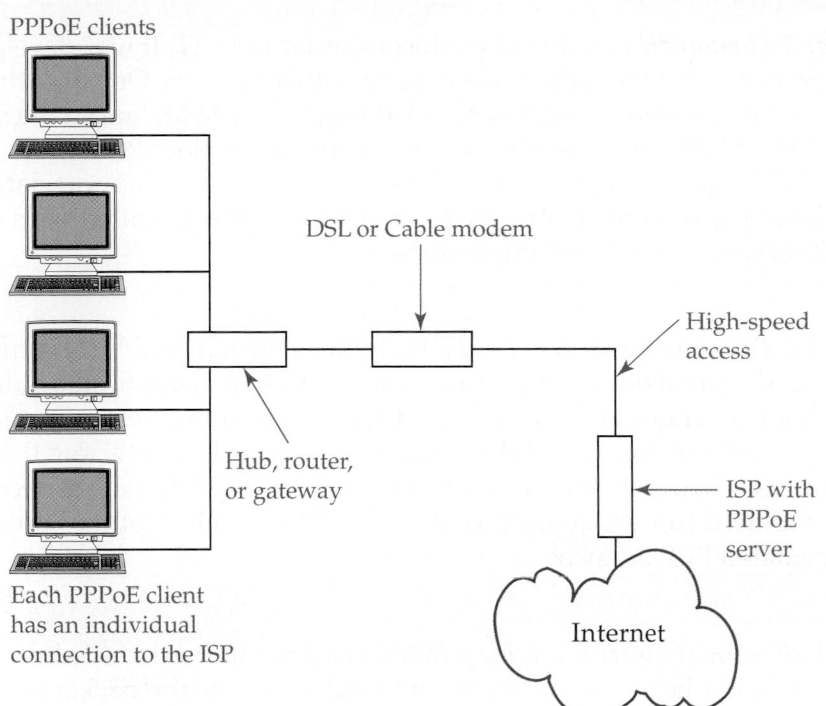

Figure 14-17. PPPoE is an effective means of creating individual high-speed connections for Internet access.

and maintained indefinitely. The established connection is referred to as a *session*. Each session is independent of other connections to the PPPoE.

In Figure 14-17, all computers are on the same network. In another scenario, the computers connecting to the ISP may reside in an office building consisting of many different businesses. Individual users may need to be billed rather than the entire site. The MAC address provides a way of billing the user and establishing a user account for authentication purposes. The ISP can then provide billing based on a per-user, rather than per-site basis.

PPPoE establishes a virtual serial connection to the ISP in the same way a single PPP connection creates a true serial connection. In other words, when using PPPoE, each computer establishes a virtually private PPP connection to the Internet.

MLPPP

Multilink Point-to-Point Protocol (MLPPP), also known as ***Multilink dialing,*** can combine two or more physical links in such a way that they act as one, thus increasing the supported bandwidth. For MLPPP to operate, the access server and the client must have MLPPP enabled. MLPPP works with ISDN lines, PSTN lines, and X.25 technology.

Multilink Point-to-Point Protocol (MLPPP) a remote access protocol that can combine two or more physical links so that they act as one, thus increasing the supported bandwidth. This protocol works with ISDN lines, PSTN lines, and X.25 technology. Also called *Multilink dialing.*

MLPPP can use the ***Bandwidth Allocation Protocol (BAP).*** BAP allows the number of lines used by MLPPP to change on demand. For example, if simple text is downloaded, a single line will suffice for the low-bandwidth data. If multimedia is downloaded to multiple workstations, such as for a videoconferencing, BAP will automatically increase the number of lines to support the increased bandwidth. Once the high-bandwidth data transmission has ended, the number of lines is reduced to minimum. Remember, there is a high cost associated with telephone and leased lines. Controlling the number of lines used based on demand is cost-effective.

Bandwidth Allocation Protocol (BAP) a communications protocol that can change the number of lines or channels according to current bandwidth.

L2F

Layer 2 Forwarding (L2F) a remote access protocol, similar to PPTP, designed to enhance security and to make use of a virtually private network using the public Internet. It was developed by Cisco Systems and then released for use by other vendors. L2F requires special equipment on the host side to support data transfer whereas PPTP does not.

Layer 2 Forwarding (L2F) is a protocol similar to PPTP. It was developed by Cisco Systems and then released for use by other venders. One big advantage of L2F is that it can work directly with ATM and Frame Relay, and it does not require TCP/IP. L2F also supports more than one connection. PPTP does not. However, L2F requires special equipment on the host side to support data transfer. The only requirement for PPTP is that the host is installed with a Microsoft server class of operating system.

L2TP

Layer 2 Tunneling Protocol (L2TP) a tunneling protocol that uses IPSec to encrypt the contents of the encapsulated PPP protocol.

Layer 2 Tunneling Protocol (L2TP) combines the L2F and PPTP protocols. Microsoft and several other companies developed PPTP. Cisco Systems developed L2F. The Internet Engineering Task Force (IETF) wanted to create a protocol that had the best features of both L2F and PPTP protocols. Jointly, the IETF, Cisco Systems, Microsoft, and many others designed L2TP. L2TP has become an industry standard tunneling protocol that uses IPSec to encrypt the contents of the encapsulated PPP protocol.

MPLS

Multi-Protocol Label Switching (MPLS) a routing protocol that allows a label to be attached to an IP packet in order to route the packet to a specific destination.

edge router the router at the entrance and exit of a WAN.

Multi-Protocol Label Switching (MPLS) allows the network administrator to attach a label or header to an IP packet in order to route the packet to a specific destination. This protocol is designed for high-speed packet routing networks. Traditional routing protocols require that every router in the route inspect the contents or at least a portion of the contents of the Ethernet packet and then calculate or refer to a table to determine the best route for the packet. MPLS-enabled routers simply inspect the attached label and then forward the packet based on the contents of the label.

The MPLS label and route are predetermined by the network administrator, thus eliminating the need for a router CPU to calculate the best route or search routing tables for the best route. The overall effect is reduced packet latency. The MPLS label contents also contain a priority code, which ensures quality of service. Thus, MPLS provides a faster means of distributing packets from edge router to edge router. The term ***edge router*** refers to the router at the entrance and exit of the WAN.

The Internet Engineering Task Force (IETF) developed the standard for MPLS because of the need to provide a quicker method of routing packets across the Internet and large enterprise networks. The IETF design specifies a very small MPLS label of approximately 3 bytes. The MPLS label can be attached to IPv4 or IPv6 packets, ensuring compatibility now and in the future.

MPLS is not intended by design for routing on a local area network but rather for moving packets from point to point across large network systems controlled by a single authority. For example, Sprint networks or an Internet provider such as Comcast. The MPLS label is removed on entering the local area network. Traditional routing protocols such as IS-IS and OSPF can be used to forward the packet across the local network after the label has been removed.

The two main network applications for MPLS are traffic shaping and support for VPN. MPLS traffic shaping is when the system administrator decides which route will be taken between distant nodes. A VPN can be created by the label attached to the packet.

The main advantage of MPLS when compared with ATM is MPLS is designed to work with existing IP network technology. ATM is not and requires special equipment and support. Also, ATM is designed to create small packets of a fixed size (48-byte). MPLS simply adds a small 4- to 8-byte header to the existing IP packet, which has no size limitation. The larger packets can be moved more efficiently across large IP networks.

The main advantage of MPLS when compared with Frame Relay is cost. Frame Relay generally requires leased lines, which can be very expensive. As stated earlier, MPLS can use existing Internet networks.

The concept of how MPLS works is simple. At each end of the MPLS portion of the WAN are routers referred to as *Label Edge Routers*. Between the Label Edge Routers are other MPLS routers called *Label Switch Routers*. The network administrator inserts information into the label portion of the MPLS, specifying the destination for all MPLS packets. The label information is distributed throughout the network to all MPLS devices by the Label Distribution Protocol (LDP). The LDP distributes the information in advance so that the label can be interpreted immediately on arrival and forwarded to the predetermined destination. The MPLS tag is added when the packet enters the WAN and is removed when the packet leaves the WAN and enters a local area network.

The administrator can control the packet flow through the WAN thus "shaping" network traffic. The administrator through the use of MPLS can guarantee a specific minimum bandwidth and quality of service to customers. In other words, an Internet service provider can guarantee quality of service to specific customers when using MPLSs over private network systems.

MPLS is referred to as a "layer 2.5" protocol because it does not align with either layer 2 or layer 3 of the OSI model. It does, however, perform similar functions as layer 2 and layer 3 devices. To learn more about MPLS, visit www.mplsrc.com/mplsfaq.shtml.

Virtual Private Networks (VPN)

A ***Virtual Private Network (VPN)*** is a simulated, independent network created by software over a public network. An example of a public network is the Internet. Since anyone can access and use a public network, there is a possibility of unauthorized access to any network connected to it. A VPN makes it possible to create a private connection over a public network with no additional cost. For example, a company may wish to use the Internet to connect to its many branch offices spread throughout the country. The main reason for using the Internet is it is inexpensive when compared with leased lines and other physical private connections. However, the company may wish to keep its data and transmissions secure while using the Internet for data transfers and communications. The answer to this dilemma would be to implement a VPN.

Virtual Private Network (VPN) a simulated, independent network created by software over a public network.

A VPN is created through a software package that provides security. Adding special equipment, such as a firewall, can further increase the security of the VPN. All operating systems support a form of VPN.

Not all firewalls are equipment-based technologies. Some firewalls are strictly software packages.

Most VPN software encapsulate transport protocol packets inside a secure protocol packet and encrypt the contents as well. In the early days of networking, security was not considered a real threat. The original TCP/IP protocol suite was not very secure. In fact, the early designs were made public to encourage the development of the Internet by the private sector. Today, security is a prime concern of all Internet users. Through the utilization of VPN technology, a secure link can be created through an unsecure public network like the Internet. VPN is not just limited to the Internet but is also used to create private links inside a private network system like a company network or a school network. Since most local area networks use the TCP/IP suite of protocols, security concerns still exist in the local network.

Four of the most common protocols used in a VPN are PPTP, L2F, L2TP, and IPSec. These protocols allow a VPN to provide four basic features common to all VPN connections: authentication, access control, confidentiality, and data integrity. *Authentication* (in relation to a VPN) is the process of assuring the person who is accessing the remote system is really the person who is authorized to use the system. *Access control* is the act of allowing only authorized users access to the VPN. *Confidentiality* is the act of preventing anyone else from reading the data that flows through the VPN. *Data integrity* is the process of ensuring the data that leaves the source and arrives at the destination has not been tampered with. These topics are covered in detail in Chapter 15—Network Security.

Summary

- The deregulation of the telecommunications industry allows for separate local telephone systems and long-distance telephone systems, which increases competition and reduces overall costs.
- The Point of Presence (PoP) is the point where the public telephone line ends and the customer premises telephone line and equipment begin.
- Since the deregulation of the telecommunications industry, residents and business owners are responsible for the telephone system on their side of the Point of Presence (PoP).
- There are many types of media available for communicating over long-distances, such as Cable, DSL, ISDN, PSTN, satellite, SONET, and T1. Each is offered at various speeds and costs.
- Basic Rate ISDN (BRI-ISDN) consists of two B channels and one D channel with a total bandwidth of 128 kbps.
- Primary Rate ISDN (PRI-ISDN) consists of twenty-three B channels and one D channel with a total data rate of 1.544 Mbps.
- Broadband ISDN (B-ISDN) is the newest category of ISDN and is designed to carry multiple frequencies; hence, the term *Broadband*.
- Cable Internet service offers data rates as high as 36 Mbps downstream and 10 Mbps upstream. However, 10 Mbps is a theoretical speed.
- Cable Internet service is defined by the Data Over Cable System Interface Specification (DOCSIS) standard developed independently of IEEE 802.14.
- DSL is offered in many varieties, such as ADSL, SDSL, HDSL, and VDSL.
- The maximum allowable distance between a DSL modem and the Local Central Office is typically 1,000 feet to 18,000 feet. This distance varies according to the type of DSL used and any special equipment that might exist on the telephone line, such as loading coils or a change in the media.
- DSL bandwidth varies from 1.5 Mbps to 52 Mbps depending on the DSL variation used and the distance from the Local Central Office.
- Satellite communications is ideal for remote locations and offers various speeds based on cost of equipment and service.
- Consumer satellite service bandwidth is typically 400 kbps to 500 kbps.

- Commercial satellite service bandwidth is a maximum 1.5 Mbps in the USA and 2 Mbps in Europe.
- Satellite communications use microwave technology and must have a clear line of site between the satellite and the satellite dish.
- T-carriers are leased lines and range from fractional T1 to T4. The most common T-carrier lines encountered in networking are fractional T1, T2, and T3.
- A T1 line consists of 24 channels with 64 kbps of bandwidth available per channel.
- T1 offers a maximum bandwidth of 1.544 Mbps, and T3 offers 44.736.
- Synchronous Optical Network (SONET) offers the highest bandwidth and the greatest distances.
- X.25 is an older telephone line technology that is rarely encountered in the USA but still exists in other parts of the world.
- Frame Relay is the replacement for X.25 and employs a Permanent Virtual Circuit (PVC).
- Frame Relay and X.25 are packet switching technologies.
- Dial-up networking allows a user to access a network remotely using telephone lines.
- Dial-up networking requires a modem and remote access software to be installed on the client side of a remote connection and on a remote access server.
- Serial Line Interface Protocol (SLIP) is an older protocol used to support remote connections over telephone lines. It has been replaced by PPP and PPTP.
- Point-to-Point Tunneling Protocol (PPTP) encapsulates other protocols inside the PPTP packet, resulting in a secure connection.
- Multi-Protocol Label Switching (MPLS) can be used with IPv4- or IPv6-based networks as well as, ATM, Frame Relay, or most any networking technology available today.
- MPLS provides a more efficient method of routing packets than traditional routing protocols.
- The main two applications of MPLS are network traffic shaping and support for VPN.
- A Virtual Private Network (VPN) is a secure connection over a public network system based on software, not hardware.

Review Questions

Answer the following questions on a separate sheet of paper. Please do not write in this book.

1. What is the name used for the telephone line running between customer premises and the Local Central Office?
2. Where is the Point of Presence (PoP) located?
3. What does the acronym ISDN represent?
4. How many channels are there in a BRI-ISDN cable assembly?
5. What is the maximum bandwidth of a BRI-ISDN service?
6. What is the maximum bandwidth for a telephone modem?
7. What is the purpose of the D channel in an ISDN cable assembly?
8. What is the maximum theoretical bandwidth for Cable Internet access?
9. What factors influence the speed of a Cable Internet service connection?
10. What is the difference between a T1 and a fractional T1 line?

11. How many T1 lines make up a T3 line?
12. Which has the highest bandwidth: a T1 connection or a telephone modem connection?
13. Which has the highest bandwidth: SONET or ISDN?
14. Which has the highest bandwidth: T1 or X.25?
15. What high-speed technology is used for long-distance communications especially overseas via underwater?
16. Which has a highest bandwidth: ISDN or consumer satellite service?
17. What does the acronym CSU/DSU represent?
18. What type of media is a CSU/DSU associated with?
19. Match the following:

1. ISDN	A. Fiber-optic system used for overseas connections.
2. DSL	B. Typically the slowest connection technology.
3. SONET	C. Two B channels and one D channel.
4. T3	D. Typically 45-Mbps bandwidth.
5. Telephone modem	E. Digital telephone line.

20. What is the main difference between SLIP and PPP?
21. In what situation is the PPPoE protocol used?
22. What is the main difference between PPTP and PPP?
23. What is the difference between a Virtual Private Network (VPN) and a network that uses a T1 line to connect two branch offices?
24. What does the MPLS represent?
25. What are the two main applications for MPLS?
26. To which layer of the OSI model does MPLS align?
27. Which protocol is used to distribute MPLS label information to all MPLS-enabled routers?

Sample Network+ Exam Questions

Answer the following questions on a separate sheet of paper. Please do not write in this book.

1. Which technology provides the most bandwidth when connecting two networks located approximately 18 miles apart?
   A. PSTN
   B. DSL
   C. ISDN
   D. T1
2. What is the typical bandwidth of one ISDN B channel?
   A. 56 kbps
   B. 64 kbps
   C. 128 kbps
   D. 1.5 Mbps
3. What is the typical data rate of a fractional T1 line?
   A. 56 kbps
   B. 64 kbps
   C. 128 kbps
   D. 1.544 Mbps

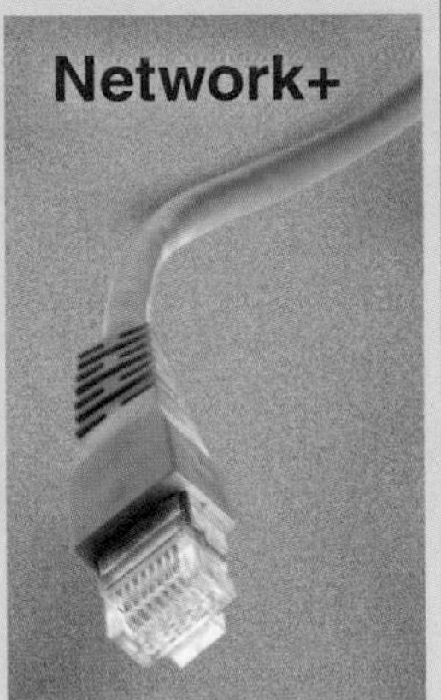

4. What would *most likely* affect the bandwidth of a DSL line?
   A. The number of subscribers sharing the DSL line.
   B. The distance from the DSL modem to the DSL provider.
   C. The distance to the ISP.
   D. The amplitude of the signal modulation.
5. What network media does DSL use?
   A. Shielded twisted pair
   B. Coaxial cable
   C. Fiber-optic cable
   D. Telephone line
6. Which of the following protocols is commonly used to create a VPN?
   A. FTP
   B. HTTP
   C. PPTP
   D. SLIP
7. Which of the following protocols would be most appropriate for creating multiple, individual dial-up connections from an Ethernet network through a common DSL or Cable modem to an ISP.
   A. PPP
   B. PPPoE
   C. SLIP
   D. TFTP
8. Which medium provides the best security when transmitting data between two points?
   A. Satellite
   B. Internet
   C. T1 line
   D. IEEE 802.11a
9. Which of the following statements is true concerning X.25 and Frame Relay technologies?
   A. Frame Relay uses analog technology and X.25 does not.
   B. X.25 uses analog technology and Frame Relay does not.
   C. Frame Relay and X.25 both use analog technology.
   D. Frame Relay and X.25 both use digital technology.
10. Which communications medium is used for SONET?
    A. Wireless 2.5 GHz
    B. UTP
    C. RG-58
    D. Fiber-optic

Suggested Laboratory Activities

1. Install and configure a variety of modems such as a Cable modem, DSL modem, and an ISDN modem.
2. Using the **tracert** command from the command prompt, trace the route taken by the packet to a remote location. Some test locations are www.novell.com and www.microsoft.com. Identify the amount of time it takes to reach each router along the route. (Each router along the route to the destination is called a *hop*.)
3. Go to the Microsoft support Web page and research Remote Desktop and VPN.

4. Using the knowledge gained from the previous suggested laboratory activity, set up a remote connection to a PC across the Internet.
5. Research the average cost for the following services if available to your school or geographic area. Do *not* write in this book. Use a separate sheet of paper to copy and fill in the chart. Access the information by using the Internet.

Technology	Availability Yes/No	Cost	Comments
Telephone line			
ISDN			
DSL			
Cable			
Fractional T-1			
T-1			
Satellite			

Interesting Web Sites for More Information

www.cable-modem.net
www.howstuffworks.com
www.iec.org
www.protocols.com

Chapter 14
Laboratory Activity

Routing and Remote Access Service (RRAS)

After completing this laboratory activity, you will be able to:

- Recall the purpose of each Routing and Remote Access Service (RRAS) option.
- Use the RRAS Setup Wizard to configure the Routing and Remote Access Service.
- Explain the Callback feature.

Introduction

In this laboratory activity, you will configure the Routing and Remote Access Service (RRAS), which is available in Windows Server 2008 and earlier Microsoft server systems. Microsoft provides an RRAS Setup Wizard, which automatically walks a technician through RRAS configuration. RRAS allows a server to pose as a remote access server or as a network router.

When configured as a router, the server is used to connect various network segments or subnets. You will not configure the server as a router during this laboratory activity. You will only configure the server as a remote access server accessible by telephone.

The following figure shows one way a client might access a company server. A salesperson that is traveling across the United States might use a dial-up connection from a laptop to the home office to place an order, check e-mail, or access files on the server. The server has a telephone modem installed and configured to receive incoming calls. This modem is dedicated to remote access and is not used for Internet access.

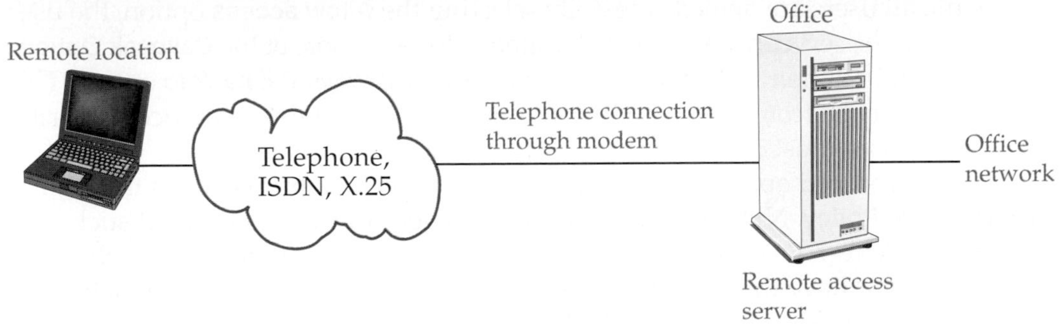

More than one telephone modem can be installed in a server to provide multiple access points to the server. Each modem is assigned a unique telephone number. Several manufacturers make a dial-up telephone modem bank. A dial-up telephone modem bank is a separate group of telephone modems that provide multiple access points to the server. Large, corporate network servers that have a high demand for remote access commonly use a modem bank.

A small-office server might have two modems installed in a single server: one for dialing out and the other for dialing in. The server may also be configured as a multiple connection location for Virtual Private Network (VPN) connections or may be configured as a Network Address Translation (NAT) server providing access to the Internet for multiple workstations through a modem or high-bandwidth connection.

After a server is configured for dial-in remote access, user profiles must be configured so that users can access the server using a dial-up connection. Look at the following screen capture of the dial-in properties for user Richard Roberts.

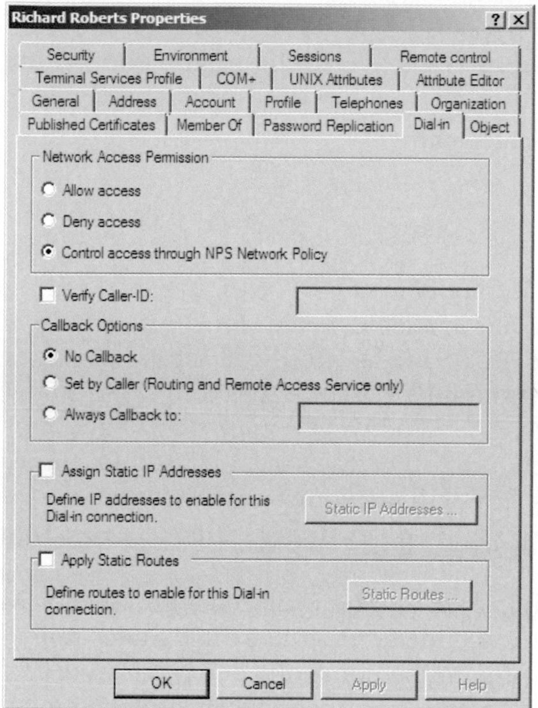

Take note of the **Allow access** option in the **Network Access Permission** section. By default, all users are denied access. By selecting the **Allow access** option, the user can dial in to the server from a remote location. Also, take note of the **Callback Options** section. A callback number can be entered next to the **Always Callback to** option. This enables a call back from a specified telephone number and thus enhances security because the user must call from the specified telephone number.

A new featured option for Windows Server 2008 is **Control access through NPS Network Policy**. NPS options allow security features to be enforced such as Network Access Protection (NAP). NAP is a new feature that requires the client computer have the latest updates installed before it can access the network. Another security feature is RADIUS. The RADIUS feature requires that the user who is connecting to the network from a remote location be Authenticated, Authorized, and Audited, and it is commonly referred to as *triple A* or simply *AAA*. To use the RADIUS service, the client computer's network adapter needs to be configured for the 802.11x. RADIUS and AAA are covered in Chapter 15—Network Security.

At the server, properties for the remote configuration can be set up to limit telephone calls to specific days and hours and for the maximum length of a connection. For example, all dial-in calls can be limited to a maximum of five minutes. This way, no one single user can monopolize the dial-in service.

The RRAS Setup Wizard provides a link to more information about RRAS. Also, extensive information is available through **Help and Support** accessed from the **Start** menu.

At the end of this laboratory activity, your instructor will most likely want you to uninstall the RRAS service. Be sure to check with your instructor before you begin the laboratory activity.

Equipment and Materials

- A Windows 2008 server with a modem installed.

Note
All features of the RRAS Setup Wizard may not be available for viewing without a modem installed, but you can still perform the lab activity.

Procedure

1. _____ Report to your assigned workstation.
2. _____ Boot the computer and ensure it is in working order.
3. _____ Add the Network Policy and Access Services role to the server by opening Server Manager and selecting the **Add Roles** option. Select **Network Policy and Access Services** and click **Next**.

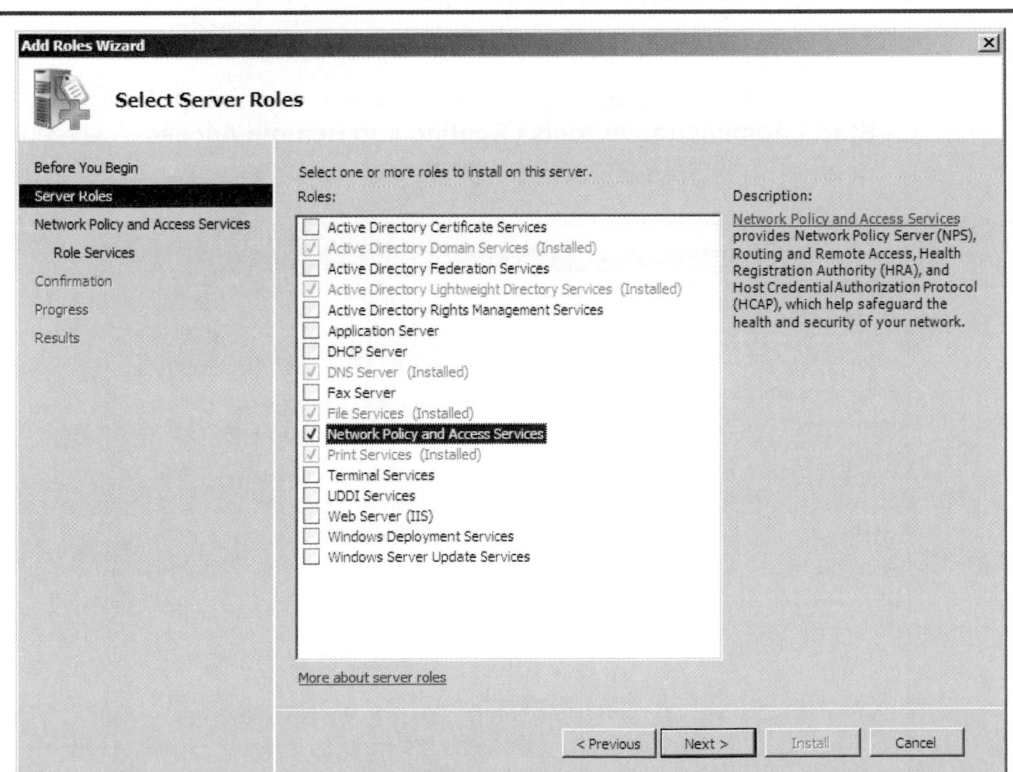

4. _____ In the **Select Role Services** screen of the Add Roles Wizard, select **Routing and Remote Access Services** and the services listed beneath this item as shown in the following screen capture. Click **Next** and then **Finish**.

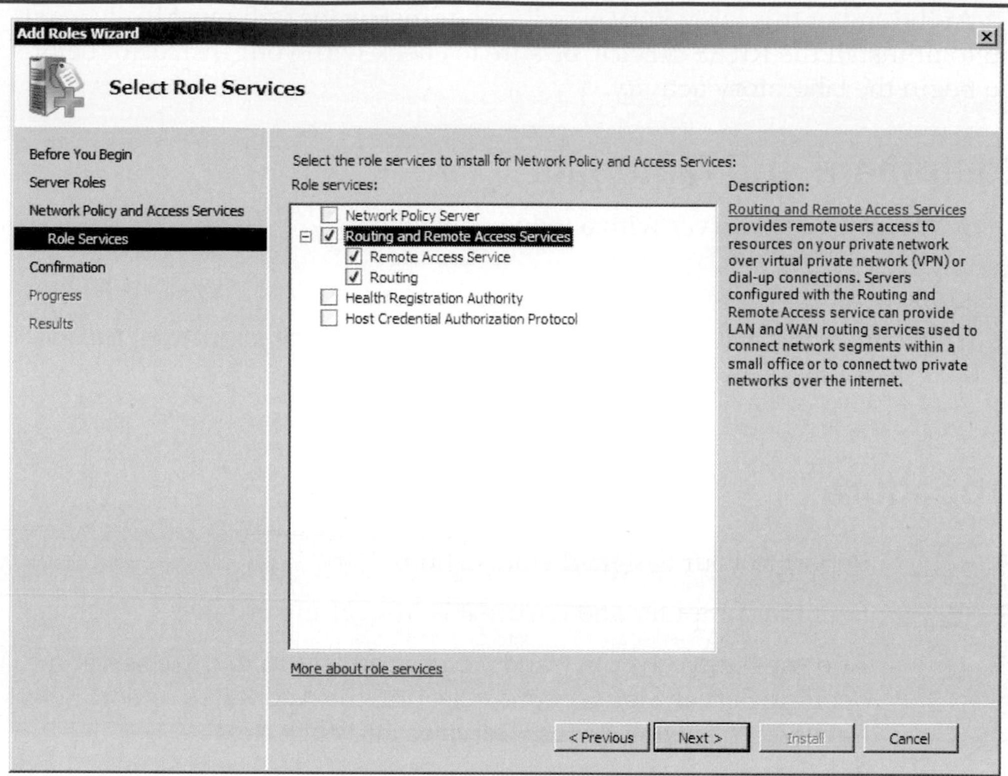

5. _____ To access the Routing and Remote Access Server Setup Wizard, open **Start | Administrative Tools | Routing and Remote Access**. A screen similar to the following will appear.

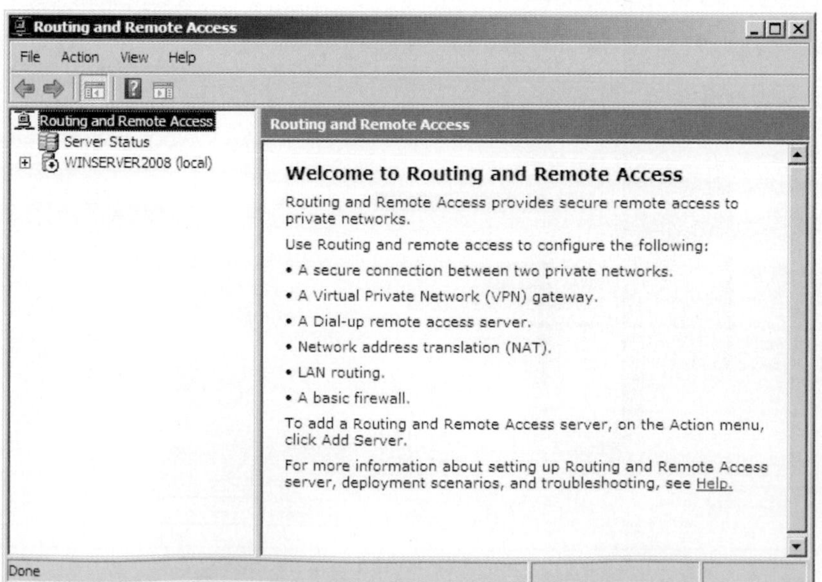

Read the **Welcome to Routing and Remote Access** screen to learn about the types of routing and remote access RRAS will allow you to configure.

6. ______ Right-click the server name located beneath **Routing and Remote Access** and then select **Configure and Enable Routing and Remote Access** from the shortcut menu.

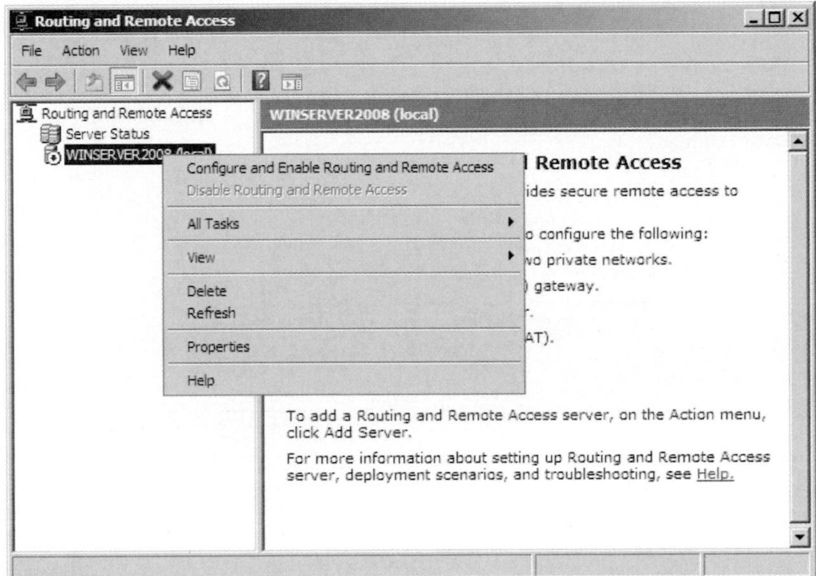

The RRAS Setup Wizard will display and look similar to that in the following figure. The RRAS Setup Wizard provides an easy to follow step-by-step process for setting up the server for remote access and routing.

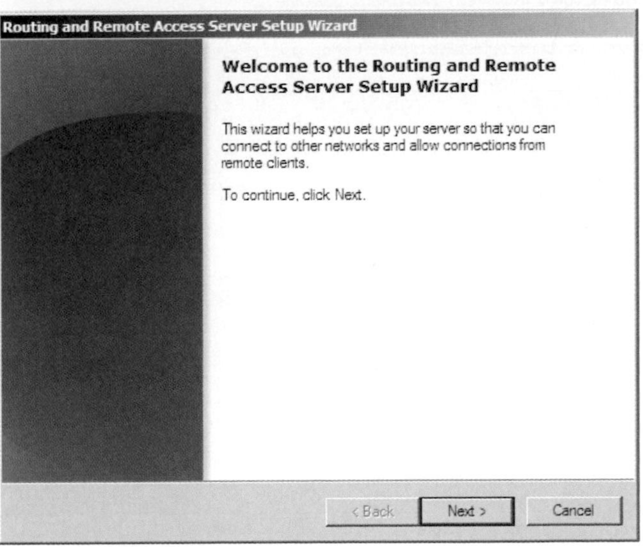

7. _____ Click **Next**. The RRAS Setup Wizard will display various configuration options, such as **Remote access (dial-up or VPN)** and **Network address translation (NAT)**. Record these five configuration options on a separate sheet of paper.

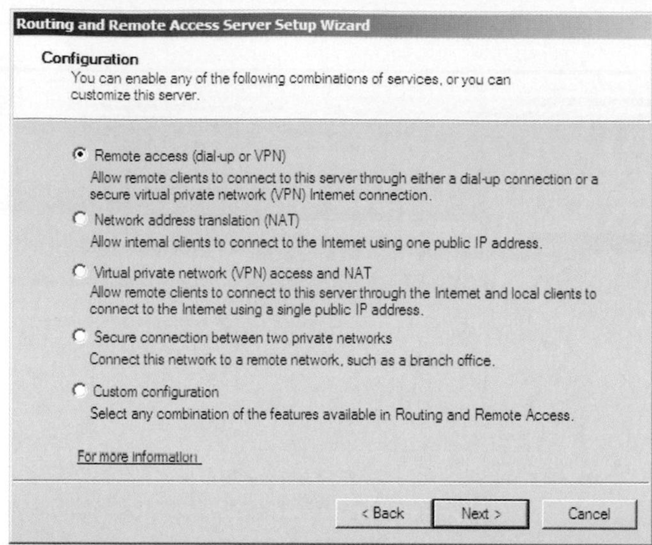

8. _____ Select **Remote access (dial-up or VPN)**. At the bottom of the screen is a **For more information** link that will provide more information about RRAS. Take a few minutes and explore this link, and then return to the current RRAS Setup Wizard screen.

9. _____ Click **Next**. You will be presented with two options: **VPN** and **Dial-up**. Select **Dial-up**.

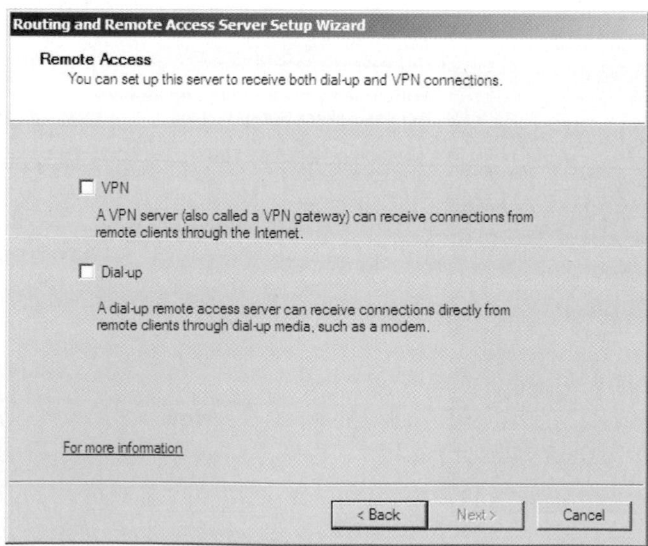

Notice the difference between the two remote access options. The VPN option allows the user to connect remotely to the server through the Internet and does not require a physical telephone line connection. Also notice that the other name used for *VPN server* is *VPN gateway*.

10. _____ Click **Next**. If you have more than one connection available from the server, the **Network Selection** screen will display and prompt you to select which connection to use. Choose the option that is associated with the telephone modem, not the network adapter.

If you have only one connection available from the server, the **IP Address Assignment** screen will display. The **IP Address Assignment** screen allows you to select the IP address assignments method. You can select either **Automatically** or **from a specified range of addresses**. To be able to use the **Automatically** option, you must have DHCP configured on this server or another server. If you are not using a DHCP server, you must manually assign IP addresses by selecting the **From a specified range of addresses** option. When using a specified range, you only need to reserve one or more IP addresses to be used by remote access clients.

11. _____ For this laboratory activity, select **From a specified range of addresses** option and then click **Next**. The **Address Range Assignment** screen will display.

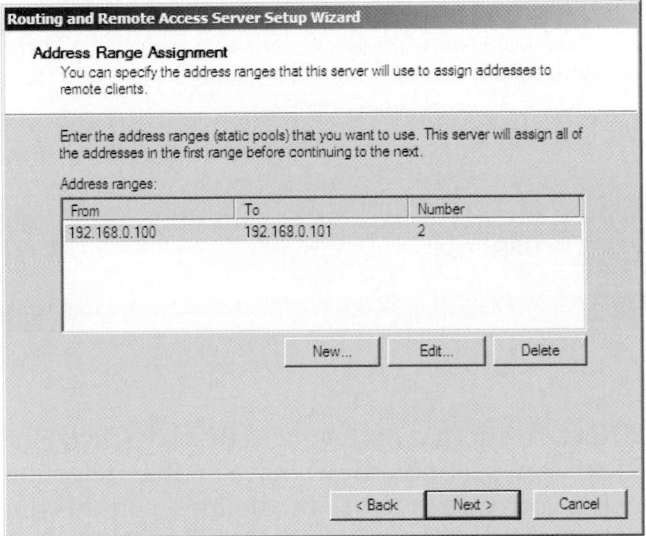

12. _____ To enter a range of IP addresses, click **New** and then enter the starting IP address and ending IP address. Alternatively, you can enter the starting IP address and then the number of IP addresses desired. In the following figure, notice that two IP addresses are reserved: 192.168.000.100 and 192.168.000.101.

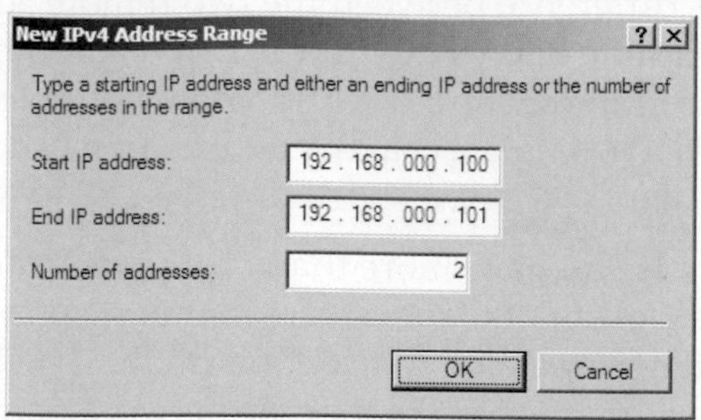

13. ______ Click **OK** and then click **Next**. The **Managing Multiple Remote Access Servers** screen will display. You will be asked if you want to set up this server to work with a RADIUS server. RADIUS is typically used on large networks that have more than one Wireless Access Point (WAP) for accessing the network system. For this laboratory activity, select **No, use Routing and Remote Access to authenticate connection requests**.

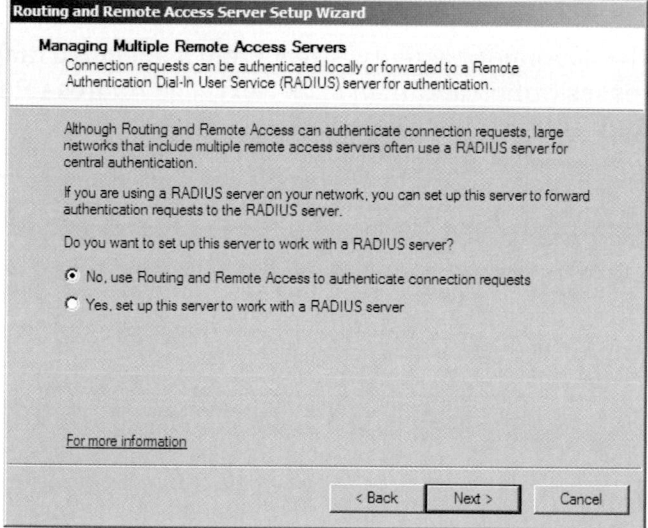

14. ______ Click **Next**. A summary screen will display. Click **Finish** to complete the RRAS configuration. If you have another telephone line available in the lab, you can test RRAS by dialing in on this line from a separate computer.

15. ______ In this step, you will delete the Routing and Remote Access Service from the server by deleting the server from the Routing and Remote Access utility. To remove RRAS from the server, open the Routing and Remote Access utility (**Start | Administrative Tools | Routing and Remote Access**). When the utility appears, right-click the server icon and then select **Delete** from the shortcut menu.

16. ______ After you have removed the Routing and Remote Access Service, answer the review questions.

Review Questions

Answer the following questions on a separate sheet of paper. Please do not write in this book.

1. How do you access the Routing and Remote Access utility?
2. A technician has just successfully configured remote dial-in access for a server, but no one can access the server. What might be the problem?
3. Where is the **Callback** option configured for a client?
4. What are the five configuration options available in the RRAS Setup Wizard?
5. What are the two options for assigning an IP address to the dial-in clients?

Back side of a Cable modem. Notice the F-type, USB, and RJ-45 connectors.

15 Network Security

After studying this chapter, you will be able to:

- ❑ Give examples of common network security breaches and vulnerabilities.
- ❑ Differentiate between symmetrical and asymmetrical encryption.
- ❑ Recall the role of a Certificate Authority (CA).
- ❑ Compare RADIUS and TACACS+.
- ❑ Compare authentication protocols.
- ❑ Summarize the characteristics of a secure password.
- ❑ Give examples of how a firewall can be used to secure network access.
- ❑ Recall the purpose of various computer and network security tools.

Network+ Exam—Key Points

The Network Security domain of the CompTIA Network+ exam objectives has been expanded in recent years to include many of the latest security technologies. While an in-depth knowledge of any particular security technology is not required, you should be familiar with all of the objectives in the Network Security domain.

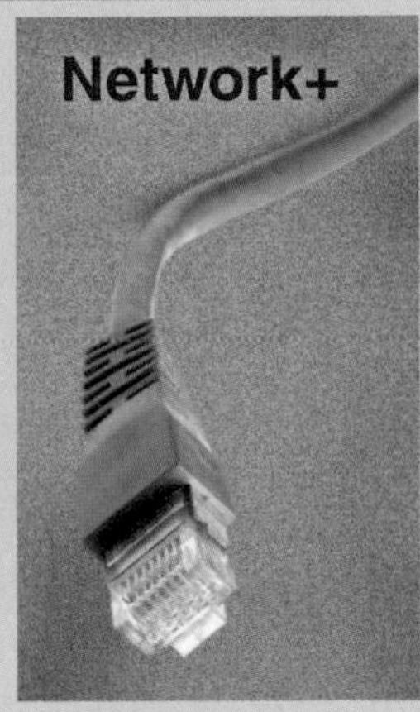

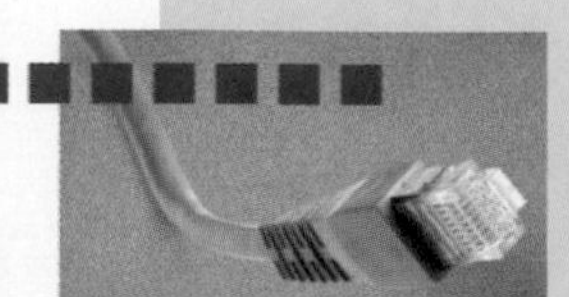

Key Words and Terms

The following words and terms will become important pieces of your networking vocabulary. Be sure you can define them.

AAA proxy
application gateway
asymmetric-key encryption
authentication
Authentication, Authorization, and Accounting (AAA)
backdoor
biometrics
California SB 1386
Certificate Authority (CA)
Challenge Handshake Authentication Protocol (CHAP)
ciphertext
circuit-level gateway
content filter
cracker
cryptology
demilitarized zone (DMZ)
Denial of Service (DoS)
Diameter
digital certificate
encryption
firewall
firewall signature identification
hashing
Health Insurance Portability and Accountability Act (HIPAA)
Independent Computer Architecture (ICA)
Internet Protocol Security (IPSec)
Intrusion Detection System (IDS)
Intrusion Prevention System (IPS)
Kerberos
key
Lightweight Extensible Authentication Protocol (LEAP)
macro virus
man in the middle (MITM)
Media Access Control (MAC) filter
Microsoft Challenge Handshake Authentication Protocol (MS-CHAP)
packet filter
packet sniffer
Password Authentication Protocol (PAP)
Payment Card Industry Data Security Standard (PCI DSS)
phishing
port monitoring
Protected Extensible Authentication Protocol (PEAP)
protocol analyzer
proxy server
Public Key Infrastructure (PKI)
Remote Authentication Dial-In User Service (RADIUS)
replay attack
rogue access point
Sarbanes-Oxley (SOX)
Secure Copy Protocol (SCP)
Secure HTTP (S-HTTP)
Secure Shell (SSH)
Security Sockets Layer (SSL)
service pack
smart card
Smurf attack
social engineering
spoofing
stateful packet inspection
stateless packet inspection
symmetric-key encryption
TACACS+
Transport Layer Security (TLS)
transport mode
Trojan horse
tunnel mode
virtual network connection (VNC)
Wi-Fi Protected Access 2 (WPA2)
worm
Zero Configuration (Zeroconf)

This chapter presents the basics of network security. Network security is transparent to the user in almost all applications. The term *transparent* means that the user is not aware of the underlying security system except for entering of the user name and password. Your responsibility as a technician is to select the most appropriate security system for a given situation, detect security breaches, and prevent security intrusion. You must have a general understanding of security terminology and specifications as it relates to configuring hardware and software systems.

Network security can be very confusing because of the many proprietary software systems. Private software and hardware companies are reluctant to reveal detailed information about their security technology. If they did reveal more details than absolutely necessary, they might compromise the security system and its purpose. Also, there are many variations of security technologies that at first appear similar or perform the same function. This is because network security technologies are steadily evolving and improving.

In this chapter, you will receive a general overview of security systems and principles. In its simplest form, network security comprises two main elements: authentication and encryption. ***Authentication*** is the process used to identify a user and ensure the user is who he or she claims to be. Typically, authentication is accomplished through a combination of user name and password. This method is probably the one you are most familiar with. However, it is not sufficient to authenticate a user. The user's presence on the network should be tracked and it should be determined what resources the user is permitted to view, use, and alter.

authentication
the process of identifying a user and ensuring the user is who he or she claims to be.

There are other forms of authentication such as digital certificates, smart cards, and biometrics. We will look at these and other methods of authentication as well as security protocols and security methods, such as encryption, authorization, and accounting.

The field of network security is vast and complex. This chapter covers the basics of network security. A complete presentation of network security would require an entire course with a textbook completely dedicated to network security and an intensive series of lab activities.

Hackers, Crackers, and Intruders

The term *hacker* originally described any computer enthusiast who lacked formal training. The term has now been redefined to identify anyone who gains unauthorized access to a computer system. A ***cracker*** is defined as anyone who gains access to a computer system without authorization and with the intent to do harm or play pranks. They are said to "crack" a password or security system. The terms are debatable. The exact meaning of the term *hacker* depends on the content in which it is used and by whom. A self-proclaimed hacker does not think of himself or herself as a cracker. For the sake of clarity, in this textbook, anyone who gains access to a computer system they are not authorized to access is called an *intruder*.

cracker
anyone who gains access to a computer system without authorization and with the intent to do harm or play pranks.

Common Network Security Breaches

The topic of network security is very complex and would easily fill thousands of pages. In this next section, the most commonly encountered security breaches are covered to provide you with a basic understanding of network vulnerability. As you will see, people, not equipment, generate most of the security breaches.

Unprotected Network Shares

Many times employees will set up a network share to allow other employees to access or copy their files. They do not realize that setting up a network share with minimal to no security sets up a possible entry point for an attack from the outside. Many hacker tools can probe and access available shares on a network. This is a common way networks are compromised. Employees also create network shares with minimal to no security so that they might be able to access their own files from home. Network shares with minimal to no security and remote access enabled combine for a security breach waiting to happen. See **Figure 15-1.**

Social Engineering

social engineering the manipulation of personnel by the use of deceit to gain security information.

Social engineering is a term used to describe the manipulation of personnel by the use of deceit to gain security information. One of the weakest security areas is the gullibility of typical users and their respect for assumed authority. For example, consider the following scenario. A telephone rings on a user's desk and the following conversation takes place:

Caller: Hello. This is Bob down at IMS operations conducting a security check. We believe we may have an intruder in our system.

Gene Gullible: Yes. What can I do to help?

Caller: Well Gene, I need to look at your PC files to see if there have been any possible intrusions. I need your user name and password to inspect your system. It will only take a minute and will save me a lot of time rather than coming down there.

Gene Gullible: Sure. My user name is ggullible and the password is toocool.

You see, that is all there is to it. Gene's system has been compromised by the social engineering technique.

Open Ports

Ports, such as HTTP port 80, are used to connect to computers during communication sessions. Legitimate users normally use them for browsing a Web page, network meetings, and performing file transfers and downloads. Open ports can also be a way for intruders to gain access to the network system. Open ports are

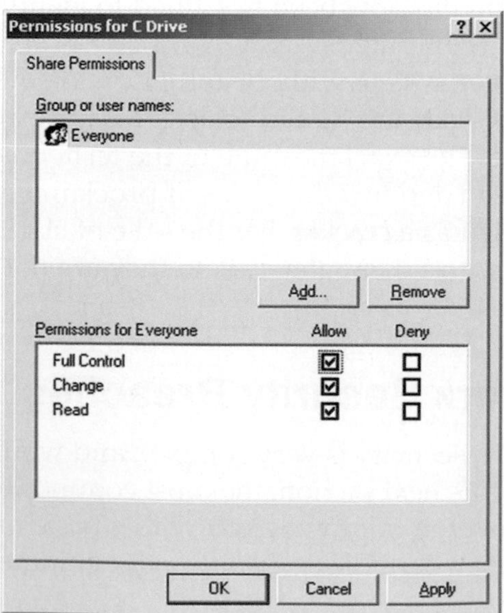

Figure 15-1.
In this example, an employee has given the group *Everyone* full access to the C drive.

one of the most common security problems for any site. All unused ports should be closed, and all ports should be monitored for activity. A third-party utility or the **netstat** utility can be used to check for open ports. The **netstat** utility is covered later in this chapter.

Zero Configuration (Zeroconf)

Zero Configuration (Zeroconf) is a standard developed by IEEE which recommends how to design a device that automatically detects other devices on the same network or on a nearby network segment without the need of intervention by an administrator or a DHCP or DNS server. Identification is based on MAC addresses, which are unique for each device. Network devices are any devices that can be identified by a MAC address and can include communication devices and electronic appliances.

Zeroconf devices must have a unique IP address, subnet mask, and gateway address issued automatically. The Zeroconf protocol must also be able to resolve duplicate IP addresses automatically and translate between IP addresses and host names.

The main reason for the development of Zeroconf protocol is to enable an easy method of networking devices without the intervention of an administrator. Microsoft operating systems as well as MAC OS 9 and later incorporate the Zeroconf standard. For example, the Microsoft wireless device protocol automatically configures a wireless network card when it is physically inserted into the computer.

The downside of Zeroconf is it makes a network less secure. A person could simply purchase a similar device and connect it to a network system and then gain access. An example is a wireless device, such as a WAP, that uses a default SSID and automatic IP addressing. If the device is installed with the default settings and it uses Zeroconf to configure the clients, anyone with a similar device installed can access the same network.

Zero Configuration (Zeroconf)
a standard developed by IEEE which recommends how to design a device that automatically detects other devices on the same network or on a nearby network segment without the need of intervention by an administrator or a DHCP or DNS server.

Denial of Service (DoS)

Denial of Service (DoS) is one of the most common attacks on servers. Denial of Service is, as the name implies, denying access to a server by overloading the server with bogus requests. The DoS attack overloads the server to the point that the server crashes or is not able to complete legitimate user requests.

Denial of Service (DoS)
denying access to a server by overloading the server with bogus requests.

Man in the Middle (MITM)

Man in the middle (MITM) is a method of intercepting a network transmission, reading it, and then placing it back on route to its intended destination, **Figure 15-2.** It is a serious security breach. The contents may or may not be modified. This method can also be used for a replay attack. A ***replay attack*** occurs when the data in the network transmission is copied and stored. Later, information such as an IP address and MAC address can be used to establish an unauthorized connection to the destination by impersonating the original source. Replay attacks are generally avoided by using a time stamp as part of the communication structure. The time stamp is used to verify the time of each transmission. If the time that is recorded in the time stamp exceeds a specific value, the entire packet is dropped because it is assumed to be bogus.

man in the middle (MITM)
a method of intercepting a network transmission, reading it, and then placing it back on route to its intended destination.

replay attack
a method of using information, such as an IP or MAC address, that had previously been copied and stored during a network transmission to establish an unauthorized connection with the destination.

Figure 15-2.
A man in the middle attack occurs when a third party intercepts a data transmission with the intent to use vital information it contains for a later attack. Once the third party reads and stores the data transmission, it is placed back on route to its destination.

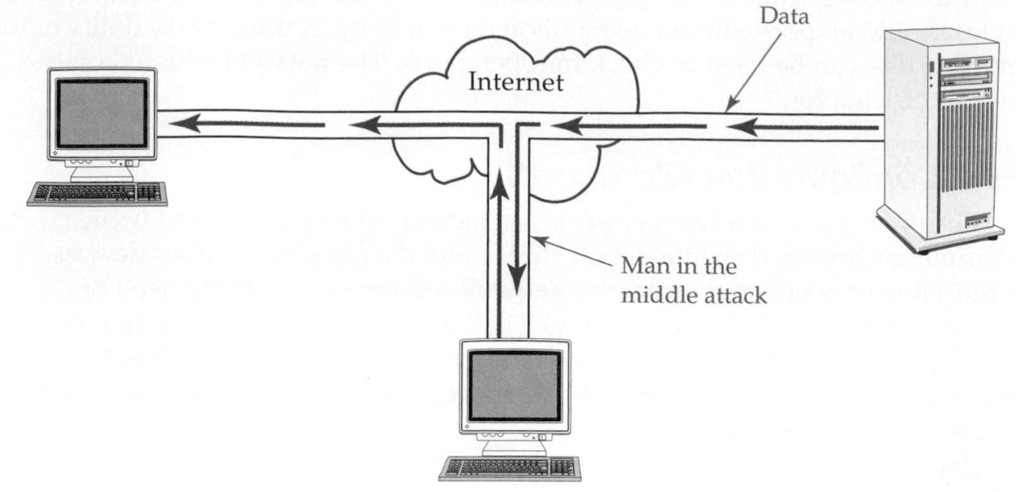

Spoofing

spoofing
fooling the destination by using an IP address other than the true IP address of a source to create a fake identity.

Spoofing is fooling the destination by using an IP address other than the true IP address of a source to create a fake identity, **Figure 15-3.** For example, to gain access to a network, an unauthorized person may try to use what they think is a valid IP address to fool a server. Another example is to use a bogus IP address and ID when sending an unsolicited e-mail to someone. The e-mail can be used to solicit information or release a worm.

It is a good policy never to respond to an unsolicited e-mail. A common ploy is to send unsolicited e-mails to millions of possible legitimate e-mail addresses using a software program that generates possible e-mail addresses. In the e-mail, a line is included that states: "If this e-mail was sent by mistake and you wish to be removed from our e-mail list, please click the link below." The link is intended to generate a list of everyone who replies. The list is valuable because it contains a list of real e-mail addresses that can be sold or distributed to interested parties, such as advertisers. By responding to the removal link, you verify the e-mail address used was a genuine e-mail address.

Smurf attack
a type of DoS that consists of spoofing the target address and then pinging the target broadcast address.

Smurf Attack

The ***Smurf attack*** is a type of DoS. It consists of spoofing the target address and then pinging the target broadcast address. This generates a large number of ping relays from the target. The most common way to deal with a DoS attack is to configure a computer firewall not to respond to ICMP ping requests. Another

Figure 15-3.
Spoofing is the act of using a fake IP address to gain access to a network.

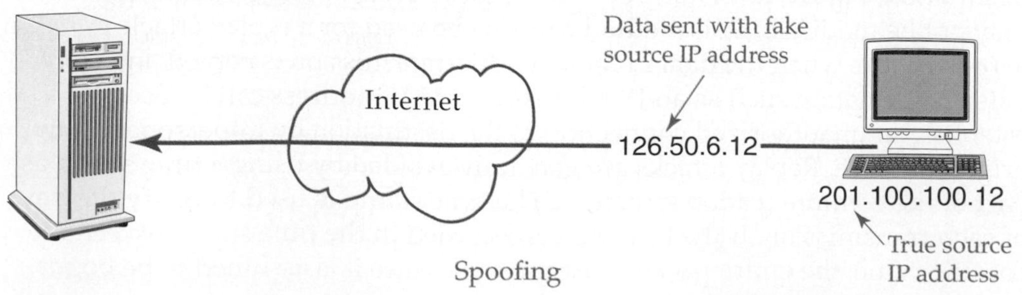

safeguard is to configure routers not to forward ICMP echo requests to broadcast addresses in the network.

Trojan Horse

The ***Trojan horse*** is a program designed to gain access to a computer while pretending to be something else. For example, a user downloads what they think is a free game. A real game may indeed be inside the download, and for a good Trojan horse design, it should be. However, in addition to the game program code is code of a malicious nature. The malicious code could contain a virus, worm, or what is known as a *backdoor.* A ***backdoor*** is a software access port to the computer the Trojan horse has infected. Another common purpose for a Trojan horse is to download a program that imitates the logon screen of a legitimate operating system. When the user logs on using the Trojan horse fake logon screen, the user's name and password is sent to an unauthorized user for later use in gaining access to the computer.

Trojan horse
a program designed to gain access to a computer while pretending to be something else.

backdoor
a software access port to the computer a Trojan horse has infected.

E-mail Attachments

The most commonly encountered viruses come as e-mail attachments. E-mail attachments can be written from a variety of software programs. A person could use Visual Basic, C, C++, Visual C++, Java, and other programming tools, such as a common word processing macro tool. Once the program is written, it is attached to an e-mail. When the recipient opens the e-mail attachment, the program is activated.

Macro Virus

One of the most common and most easily written virus programs is a ***macro virus***. Many legitimate software programs, such as word processing packages, contain a special tool called a *macro writer.* The macro writer records and saves certain keystroke sequences as a convenience for the user. For example, a user can make a macro that inserts their return address into a document when they press a specific key sequence. The macro program is handy for reducing the amount of work involved for repetitive tasks. The same principle can be used to create viruses. A series of commonly used keystrokes can be linked to a virus. The macro is sent as an e-mail attachment and is launched when the e-mail recipient opens the attachment. The macro virus may infect a template file like normal.dot and then execute when the user presses a certain combination of keys.

macro virus
a virus created by storing a series of keystrokes known as a "macro" produced by a word-processing software application.

Worm

A ***worm*** is a software program that can spread easily and rapidly to many different computers, **Figure 15-4.** A typical virus cannot spread automatically. There are many famous worm programs, and more are released each day. The most common worm programs use e-mail to replicate and spread. The most sophisticated worm programs use the list of e-mail contacts on the target computer to spread automatically.

The only way to keep ahead of a new worm is to check one of the many centers dedicated to worm and virus detection. Check with sans.org, cern.org, and commercial antivirus Web sites. A common practice of securing a network system against worms is to install a dedicated e-mail server to limit the infection. The e-mail server can be interrupted without disrupting service from the

worm
a software program that can spread easily and rapidly to many different computers.

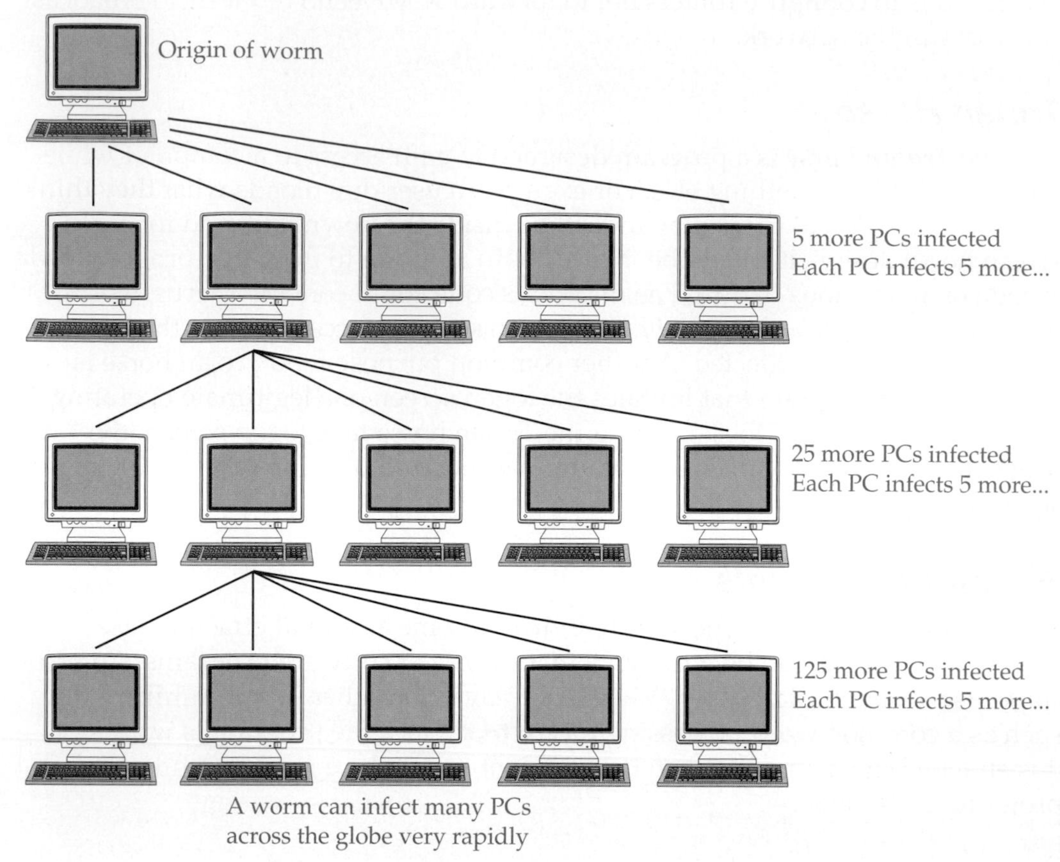

Figure 15-4. E-mail is the most common method of transmitting a worm. Using this method, the worm multiplies at an exponential rate.

database server, Web server, or any other server. Placing the e-mail service on a server that performs other services could cause the other services to fail.

Phishing

phishing
a method of Internet fraud that involves using e-mail to steal a person's identity and other sensitive information, such as financial.

Phishing (pronounced *fishing*) is the latest method of Internet fraud that involves using e-mail to steal a person's identity and other sensitive information, such as financial. In a phishing attack, e-mail is sent that appears to be from a legitimate enterprise in an attempt to solicit personal information. For example, a person may receive an e-mail that appears to be from the legitimate company eBay. The e-mail may even use the eBay artwork and logo. The contents of the e-mail requests the person's personal information, such as a bank account PIN number, credit card number, password, social security number, and anything else that can be used for identity theft.

Another example is an e-mail that poses as a known and often accessed company, such as a credit card company. The e-mail states that a virus has compromised all user accounts and that the company must reconstruct all user account information. The e-mail contains a Web site link. The e-mail recipient is told in the e-mail to go to the Web site and enter the requested information. When the e-mail recipient clicks the Web site link, he or she is directed to an illegal site created to look like the Web site of the legitimate company. However, the domain name of the illegal site is slightly different than the domain name of the legitimate company. The bogus domain name goes undetected by the e-mail recipient because of slight changes in the characters. Look at **Figure 15-5.** Notice how similarly shaped characters and numbers have been substituted.

Legitimate Site	Bogus Site	Look at the following in the bogus Web site:
www.paypal.com	www.paypa1.com	The number *1* used in place of the letter *l*.
www.firstfederal.com	www.firstfedera1.com	The letter *l* again.
www.payonline.com	www.pay0nline.com	The number *0* for the letter *O*.

Figure 15-5.
A domain name can be disguised by making slight changes in the characters. Notice how a lowercase *l* looks similar to the number *1* and an uppercase *O* looks similar to the number *0*.

You can see how easy it is to create a bogus Web site that could fool a trusting user. Also, be aware that rolling the mouse over a Web site link embedded in the text of an e-mail created with HTTP can automatically take you to a site that resembles the Web site indicated in the link. The Web site link can be easily programmed to direct you to a different Web site altogether. Never send personal information in response to e-mail, even if the e-mail looks legitimate. Call the company first to confirm the legitimacy of the e-mail.

Administrator Laziness

Administrator laziness, rather than a lack of knowledge, causes the most common security breaches. Common security breaches are a result of quick fixes, lack of user training, and naivety about being a target. Administrators and users often think, "Why would anyone want to hack into this site?" The truth is many intruders simply want to access any network. The network's contents are not the important issue. The challenge of a successful, unauthorized access is sufficient reward for many intruders. Never assume that any network or PC is safe from an intruder.

Intrusion Detection and Intrusion Prevention Systems

An Intrusion Detection System (IDS) and Intrusion Prevention System (IPS) are designed to monitor host and network systems for unauthorized activity. All security protection systems, both software and hardware, can be classified as either IDS or IPS.

An ***Intrusion Detection System (IDS)*** is a passive system which only detects unauthorized activity, **Figure 15-6.** For example, Microsoft Event Viewer is a type of IDS system. It monitors activities on a host computer but does not prevent unauthorized activity.

Intrusion Detection System (IDS)
a passive security protection system which only detects unauthorized activity.

An ***Intrusion Prevention System (IPS)*** is a reactive system which means it not only detects unauthorized activity, it also performs some function to stop the activity, **Figure 15-7.** For example, most antivirus software programs not only detect unauthorized activity such as an attempt to download and install malware, it can also remove malware.

Intrusion Prevention System (IPS)
a reactive security protection system that detects unauthorized activity and performs some function to stop the activity.

The detection system can be either host-based or network-based. A host-based system is installed on the individual computer and monitors and prevents unauthorized activity. Network-based systems monitor and protect the entire network.

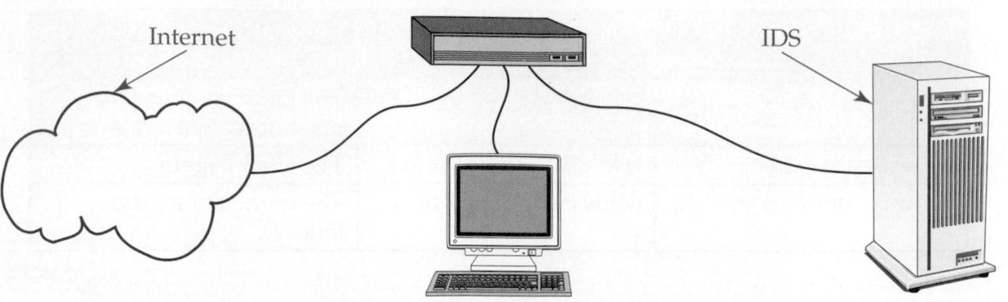

Figure 15-6.
An Intrusion Detection System (IDS) passively monitors all packets and detects unauthorized activity. It does not prevent unauthorized activity.

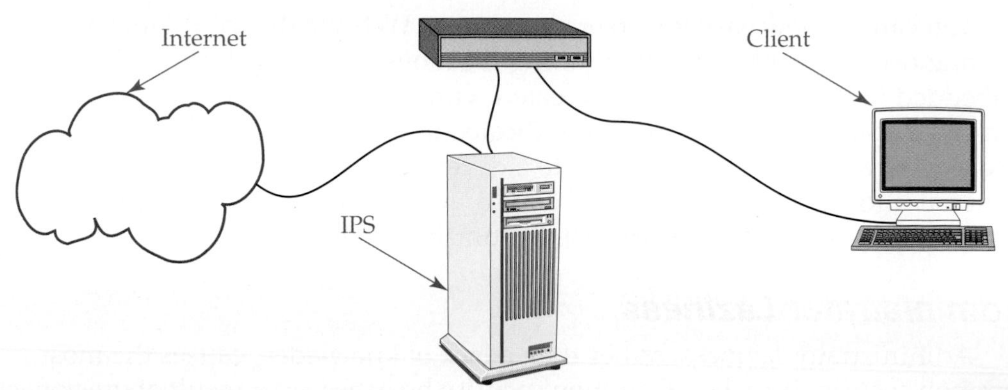

Figure 15-7.
An Intrusion Prevention System (IPS) actively monitors all packets by detecting unauthorized activity and performing some function to stop the activity.

Both IDS and IPS can generate false positives. A false positive is when a file is detected and perceived as harmful to the system. The file is then quarantined or deleted and a notice is sent to the system administrator. After reviewing the file, it is typically found to be a driver update that was downloaded with the intention of being installed automatically or some other equally harmless file. A perfect IDS/IPS solution does not exist and will most likely never be obtained.

port monitoring when a particular port on a switch is connected directly to the IDS or IPS and monitors all activity through another port on the same switch.

Network IDS and IPS typically require some form of port monitoring. ***Port monitoring*** is when a particular port on a switch is connected directly to the IDS or IPS and monitors all activity through another port on the same switch. In other words, two ports carry identical packet information. One port is used to carry packets to other parts of the network while the other port (the mirror) analyzes the packets.

Security Methods and Protocols

The two basic building blocks of secure network communications are authentication and encryption. These security methods are supported by security protocols. The concepts presented in this section are critical for a basic understanding of the sophisticated world of network security.

Public Key Infrastructure (PKI) the use of public keys (encryption keys) to create a secure environment for the exchange of data between network devices.

Public Key Infrastructure (PKI)

Public Key Infrastructure (PKI) is the use of public keys (encryption keys) to create a secure environment for the exchange of data between network devices. PKI is a form of encryption and authentication. A key is generated and used for encryption and a certificate is generated and used to verify authentication. To gain a better understanding of PKI, we will look at the encryption process.

Encryption is the method of using an algorithm to encode data. The algorithm converts the data into a form that cannot be easily decoded. The science of encoding data is called ***cryptology.*** Encrypted data is referred to as ***ciphertext.*** The number of bits used in the encryption code is often used to express the level of security provided. The maximum number of code variations depends on the maximum number of bits used to encode the message. For example, a 48-bit code can produce fewer combinations compared with a 128-bit encoding scheme.

encryption
the method of using an algorithm to encode data.

cryptology
the science of encoding data.

ciphertext
encrypted data.

key
an algorithm used to encode data.

This is how the system of encryption works. A sender writes a message and then encrypts the message using an algorithm. An algorithm used to encode data is called a ***key.*** The key is unique for each transmitted message. It is randomly generated and then applied to the message. The key can scramble the original message and add additional misleading characters to the text. The message is transmitted and then received by the destination. At the destination, the message is decrypted using a key. There are two main types of key encryption methods: symmetric-key encryption and asymmetric-key encryption.

Symmetric-Key Encryption

Symmetric-key encryption, or ***secret-key cryptography,*** uses a key that only the sender and the receiver know. Both parties use the same key to perform encryption and decryption, **Figure 15-8.** The term *symmetric* is used because the same key is used for both coding and decoding the message.

symmetric-key encryption
a key encryption method in which the sender and receiver use the same key.

Symmetric keys are typically used when large amounts of data are to be encrypted. The symmetric key encodes and decodes faster than more complex methods and can be just as secure.

Asymmetric-Key Encryption

Asymmetric-key encryption, or ***public-key cryptography,*** uses two keys: a private key and a public key, **Figure 15-9.** Typically, the originator of the encryption system owns the private key. For example, a teacher who wishes to communicate with his or her students across the Internet but ensure privacy would retain a private key. A public key is issued to all students. A message is encoded using the private key and can only be decoded using the public key. The owner of the public key can send a message in return that can only be decoded by the private key.

asymmetric-key encryption
a key encryption method in which the sender and receiver use two different keys: a private key and a public key.

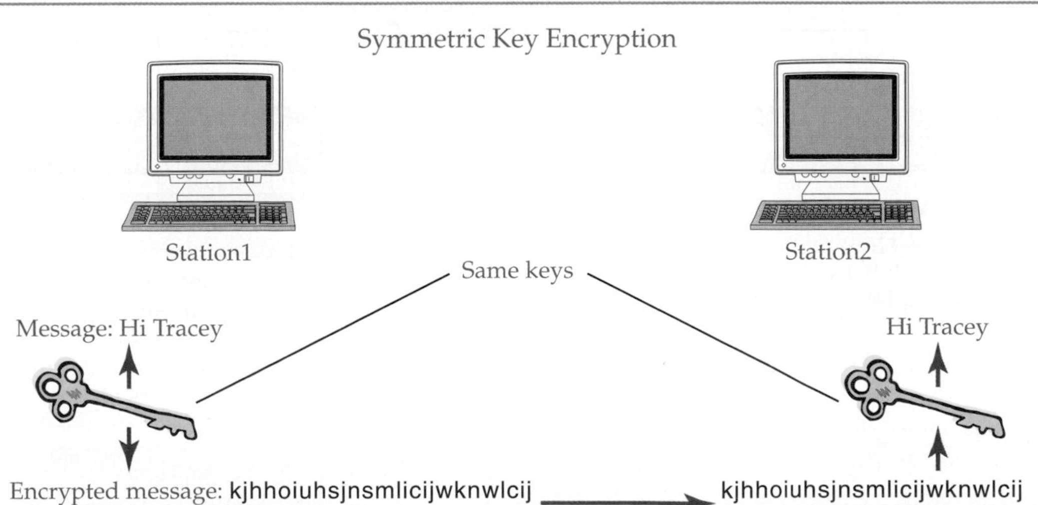

Figure 15-8. The symmetric key encryption system uses the same key to encrypt and decrypt data.

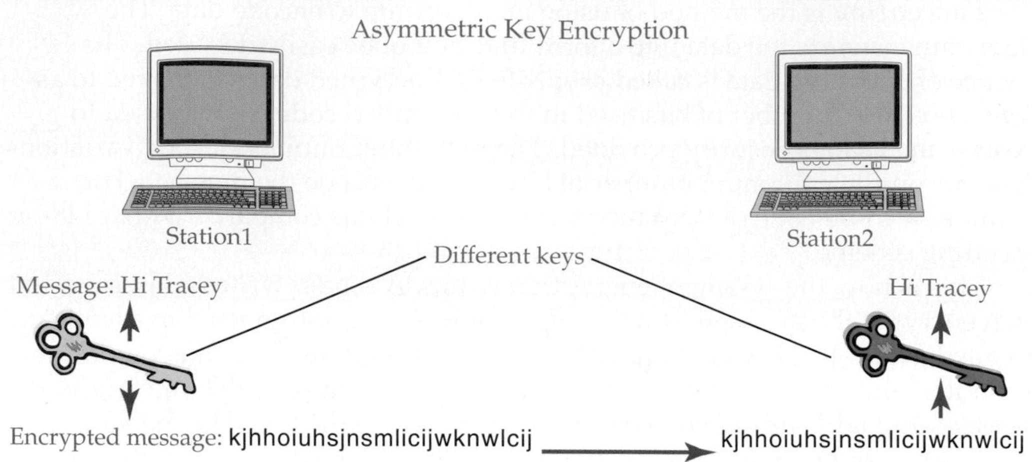

Figure 15-9. The asymmetric key encryption system uses two different keys—one key for encrypting the data and the other for decrypting the data.

Certificate Authority (CA) a service that contains the security list of users authorized to access the private key owner's messages, using a public key.

digital certificate a file that commonly contains data such as the user's name and e-mail address, the public key value assigned to the user, the validity period of the public key, and issuing authority identifier information.

In this method, a message created with a private key can only be decoded with a public key, and a message encrypted with a public key can only be decoded with a private key. A message created with a public key cannot be decoded with another public key. This means that all the encryption and decryption is centered on the owner of the private key. It takes both the public and private keys to code and decode an encrypted message.

Certificate Authority (CA)

Typically, a service referred to as the ***Certificate Authority (CA)*** contains the security list of users authorized to access the private key owner's messages, using a public key. See **Figure 15-10.** The private key owner consults the CA for this information before sending a message. The CA sends the requested information in the form of a digital certificate. A ***digital certificate*** is a file that commonly contains data such as the user's name and e-mail address, the public key value assigned to the user, the validity period of the public key, and issuing authority identifier information.

This is how the encryption/decryption process works, **Figure 15-11.** *Station1* wants to send an encrypted message to *Station2*. *Station1* applies for a digital certificate from a CA. The CA issues a digital certificate, which contains the user's

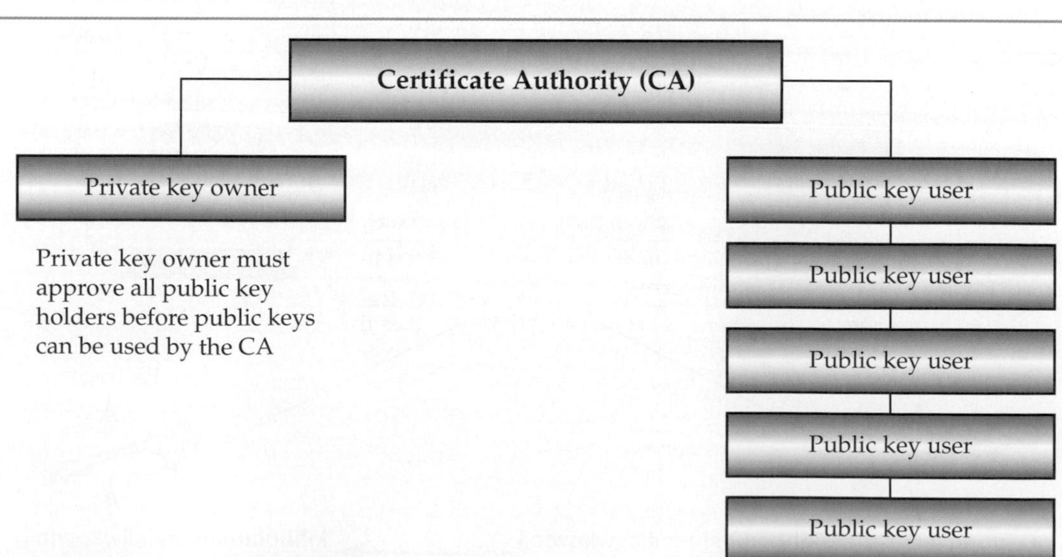

Figure 15-10. The CA issues a private key to the private key owner and then issues public keys to public key users approved by the private key owner.

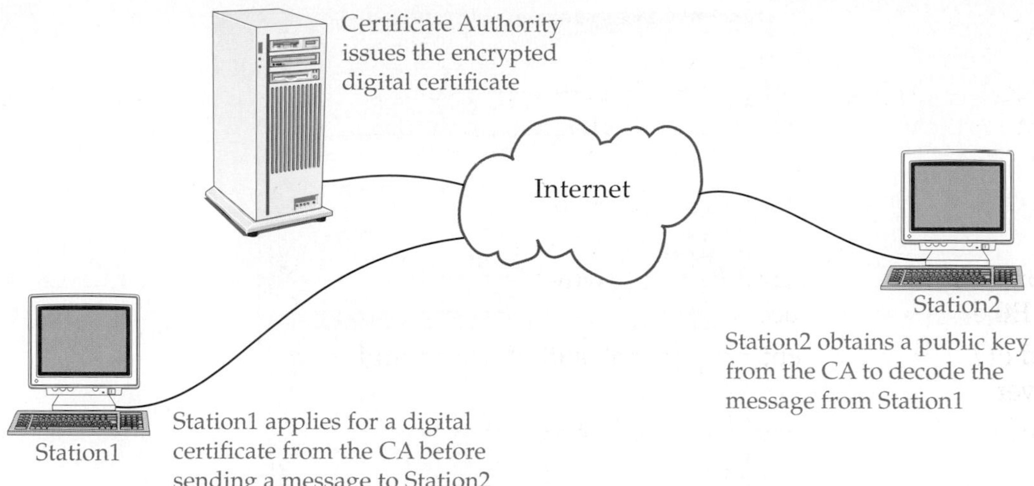

Figure 15-11.
Station1 applies for and receives a digital certificate from the CA. *Station2* uses the public key provided by the CA to decode the message and to verify the sender is really *Station1*. After verifying and receiving the message from *Station1*, *Station2* can send an encrypted reply to *Station1*.

public key/private key and security identification information known only to *Station1* and the CA. *Station1* uses the private key to encrypt the message. *Station1* can now send a message to *Station2*. When *Station2* receives the message, it uses the public key to decode the encrypted message. If *Station2* sends an encrypted reply to *Station1* using the public key, *Station1* will decode the reply using the private key.

VeriSign is one of the largest commercial digital certificate companies in the world. A certificate from VeriSign can be obtained by applying for one at their Web site. **Figure 15-12** shows a VeriSign security certificate. You can see the list of protection services offered by this particular certificate. In **Figure 15-13,** you can see some of the details about this certificate. Looking closely, you can see the validity period of the certificate, the particular algorithm used, and the length of the public key, which is 2048 bits.

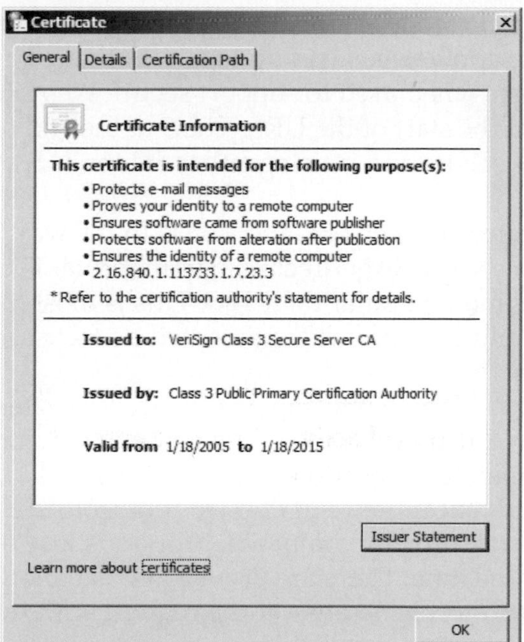

Figure 15-12.
A digital certificate issued from VeriSign.

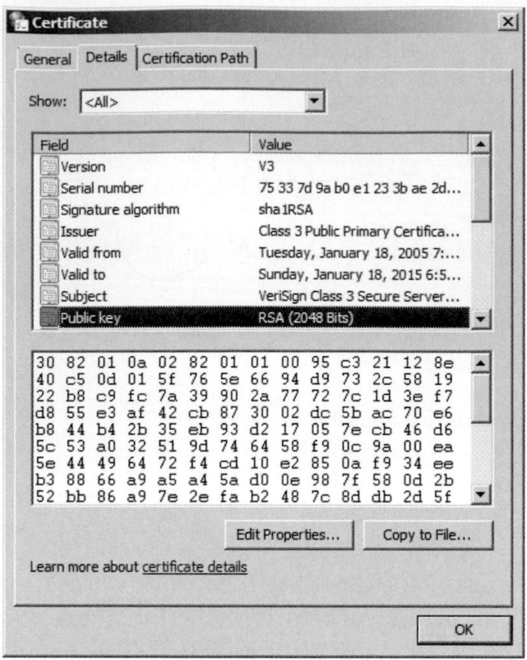

Figure 15-13. Details of a digital certificate from VeriSign.

Security Sockets Layer (SSL)

Security Sockets Layer (SSL) a security protocol developed by Netscape Communications Corporation to secure transactions between Web servers and individuals using the Internet for such purposes as credit card transactions.

Security Sockets Layer (SSL) is a security protocol used to authenticate clients and servers and to encrypt data. SSL was first introduced and developed by Netscape Communications Corporation. It was designed to secure transactions between Web servers and individuals using the Internet for such purposes as credit card transactions. SSL has been well accepted, and as a result, there have been several revisions of the SSL protocol. SSL 3.0 is the latest version.

Transport Layer Security (TLS)

Transport Layer Security (TLS) a security protocol developed by the Internet Engineering Task Force (IEFT) to secure transactions between Web servers and individuals using the Internet for such purposes as credit card transactions.

Transport Layer Security (TLS) is an Internet Engineering Task Force (IEFT) standard that was developed after SSL. It serves the same purpose as SSL. Both SSL and TLS are application layer protocols. Both are based on public key encryption technology. When used to support secure Web site connections, they both display https:// at the start of the URL. The *S* at the end of "https" means that the connection is secure and is using either SSL or TLS as the security mechanism.

The main difference between SSL and TLS is in the way they secure the connection. According to the SANS Technology Institute, TLS is more secure than SSL. Ironically, SSL is more popular than TLS. This is most likely because SSL was introduced first and has become the accepted de facto security protocol for Web site transactions.

Originally, SSL was designed to support secure Web site connections. Today, SSL and TLS security functions have been expanded to include applications such as VoIP, e-mail, and remote connections.

Although the differences between the two protocols SSL and TLS are minor, the two protocols are not directly compatible. You must use either SSL or TLS, but not both at the same time. There are provisions that allow you to attempt a connection with one protocol and answer the request with the other protocol. A negotiation takes place between the client and server, and an agreement is reached where both the client and server will use either TLS or SSL to complete the secure connection. SSL and TLS are similar in the following ways:

- They are application layer protocols.
- They are based on public key cryptology.
- They are supported by all major Internet browsers.
- Neither one requires that the client have a preconfigured user account on the server.

To learn more about TLS and SSL, visit http://technet.microsoft.com/en-us/library/cc784450(WS.10).aspx.

Secure HTTP

Another protocol used to securely send messages across the Internet is ***Secure HTTP (S-HTTP).*** S-HTTP and SSL are used for similar purposes. S-HTTP was developed by Enterprise Integration Technologies (EIT), which was acquired by VeriFone. Not all Web browsers support S-HTTP. S-HTTP uses symmetric keys, not public keys like SSL. SSL is the most widely used method of secure Web connectivity. The main difference between S-HTTP and SSL is SSL creates a secure connection between the client and server. S-HTTP secures individual messages between the client and server rather than the connection.

Secure HTTP (S-HTTP) an Internet security protocol that secures individual messages between the client and server rather than the connection.

Both S-HTTP and HTTPS are often referred to as *Secure Hypertext Transfer Protocol.* This is incorrect. S-HTTP and HTTPS are two different protocols.

Virtual Network Connection (VNC)

A ***virtual network connection (VNC)*** is a term used to describe the broad category of remote connection systems that allow a user to connect to a network device such as a server or a desktop computer from a remote device such as a laptop, palmtop, or cell phone. Typically, the user attaches to the remote network either wirelessly or through an Internet connection. Because the remote user is not actually a physical part of the network the user is accessing, the connection is considered "virtual."

virtual network connection (VNC) a point-to-point connection through a public or private network that acts like a separate network for security purposes.

Independent Computer Architecture (ICA)

Independent Computer Architecture (ICA) is a proprietary protocol designed by Citrix Systems to support the exchange of software applications between a server and client. Citrix ICA and Microsoft Remote Desktop Protocol (RDP) are the two main choices for this application.

Independent Computer Architecture (ICA) a proprietary protocol designed by Citrix Systems to support the exchange of software applications between a server and client.

Internet Protocol Security (IPSec)

Internet Protocol Security (IPSec) provides end-to-end security across the public Internet and private networks. IPSec was developed by the Internet Engineering Task Force (IETF) and has been incorporated into many different vender security systems. IPSec is an optional security feature for IPv4 but is not optional for IPv6.

IPSec consists of a wide collection of security protocols, hashes, and algorithms. The security protocols, hashes, and algorithms can be implemented in various

Internet Protocol Security (IPSec) an IETF standard for securing point-to-point connections in an IP-based network using encryption techniques.

combinations to make IPSec more unique for a given vender. Some of the more common software applications are firewalls, VPNs, and authentication software.

tunnel mode
an IPSec mode that encrypts the payload and the header.

transport mode
an IPSec mode that only encrypts the payload.

There are two standard modes of IPSec implementation: transport mode and tunnel mode. In ***tunnel mode,*** the payload and the header, which contains routing information, is encrypted. In ***transport mode,*** only the payload is encrypted. See **Figure 15-14.** Transport mode is typically used for a host-to-host connection that already provides another form of security so that only the payload needs protection. Tunnel mode provides a greater degree of security and is commonly used for VPN applications.

Some of the more common security technologies that can be implemented with IPSec are ESP, IKE, AH, MDS, SHA-1, 3DES, AES, and more. The two common protocols associated with IPSec are Encapsulated Security Payload (ESP) and Authentication Header (AH). Authentication can also be verified using Kerberos, a preshared key, or digital certificate. IPSec VPNs typically use public and private keys for encryption. IPSec works at the network layer and is transparent to the user. Microsoft first started incorporating IPSec into Windows Server 2003.

Secure Shell (SSH)

Secure Shell (SSH)
a protocol that provides secure network services over an insecure network medium such as the Internet.

Secure Shell (SSH) is a protocol that provides secure network services over an insecure network medium such as the Internet. SSH was originally designed for UNIX systems to replace Remote Login (**rlogin**), Remote Shell (**rsh**), and Remote Copy (**rcp**). These utilities are known as *r commands* by UNIX and Linux users. The r commands do not directly support encryption, which means files and commands are sent in plain text and can be intercepted and read by a protocol sniffer or analyzer. SSH is associated with TCP/IP port 22. It requires the use of a private and a public key as well as a password. The r commands do not require a password, but do require to be issued by the root user. While the r commands require root privileges, which provide a level of system security, many security experts do not consider this a sophisticated means of authentication.

Today, the open source SSH protocol can be used on any operating system that supports the TCP/IP suite. This means SSH can be used on Microsoft and MAC OS. Microsoft does not directly support SSH because it uses its own security mechanisms. However, a third-party software program that supports SSH can be installed.

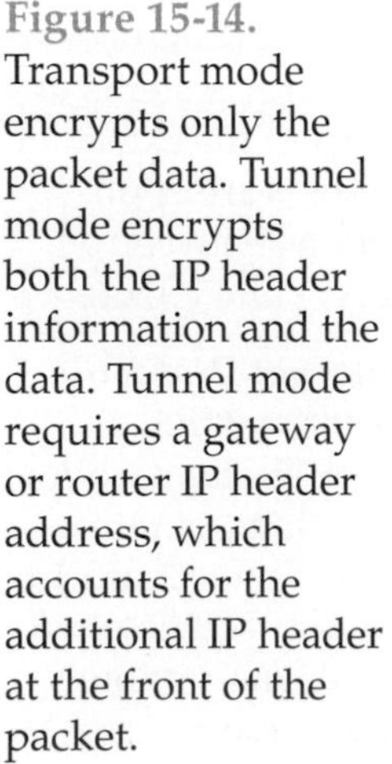
Figure 15-14. Transport mode encrypts only the packet data. Tunnel mode encrypts both the IP header information and the data. Tunnel mode requires a gateway or router IP header address, which accounts for the additional IP header at the front of the packet.

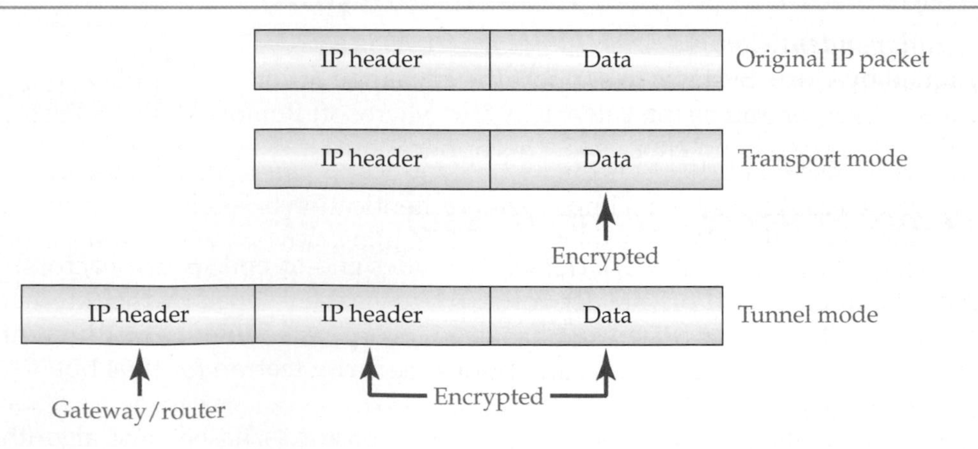

Secure Copy Protocol (SCP)

Secure Copy Protocol (SCP) provides a secure way of transferring files between computers. It is the replacement for **rcp**. Similar to anonyms FTP, the **rcp** command does not require a password.

Secure Copy Protocol (SCP) a protocol that provides a secure way of transferring files between computers. It is the replacement for **rcp**.

SSH, SCP, and SFTP are all issued as commands in the UNIX/Linux environment. Linux commands are case-sensitive, so they must be issued in lowercase form, such as **ssh, scp, sftp**. There are third-party GUI programs that incorporate the open source SSH, SCP, and SFTP protocols so that the user does not need to issue text commands at the command prompt.

Network+ Note

The letters *SFTP* can represent two different acronyms in networking: Secure File Transfer Protocol and Simple File Transfer Protocol. Secure File Transfer Protocol usually uses the acronym S/FTP, but not always. S/FTP is actually a software program rather than a true protocol. When asked a question about SFTP, look at the context of the question for clues.

Wireless Security

Wireless devices are inherently insecure because the wireless medium, the radio wave, is an unbound medium. Wired networks can be installed inside walls, ceilings, floors, and metal conduits, which provide a degree of physical security. Someone attempting to tap into a wired network would need to at least access the inside of the building. The wireless network, because of the nature of the radio wave, can extend beyond the physical limits of a building. This means that anyone can automatically have physical access to the network without entering the building if certain security measures are not set in place. For example, a small wireless network may have no security enabled or have only limited security provided by the Wireless Access Point (WAP).

The original solution to wireless network security involves three mechanisms: Service Set Identifier (SSID), Media Access Control (MAC) filtering, and Wired Equivalent Privacy (WEP). Wireless network security has evolved at a remarkable rate. In less than seven years, four major security implementations have been developed: WPA, WPA2, 802.1x, and 802.11i. This section covers the original solution to wireless network security, SSID, MAC filtering, and WEP, plus the most recent security implementations, WPA, WPA2, 802.1x, and 802.11i.

Wireless Access Point Authentication

Wireless device authentication can be achieved in more than one way. A Wireless Access Point (WAP) is the first authentication mechanism. However, not all Wireless Access Points implement authentication based on user name and password. Typically, a WAP is set by default to allow anyone with the same brand of wireless network device to connect automatically to the WAP, and thus to the wired network.

Tech Tip

If a WAP has more sophisticated options, such as a user name and password feature, it is referred to as a *wireless gateway* or *router*.

Wireless networks use a Service Set Identifier (SSID) to identify the wireless network. The SSID is similar to a workgroup name. Multiple wireless networks can coexist within range of each other and operate independently by using different SSIDs. All wireless devices have a default SSID. To increase security, the SSID should be changed when the WAP is installed.

Media Access Control (MAC) Filter

Media Access Control (MAC) filter a feature that allows or restricts WAP access based on the MAC address of a wireless network card.

A ***Media Access Control (MAC) filter*** is a feature that allows or restricts WAP access based on the MAC address of a wireless network card. To set up a MAC filter, an administrator creates an Access Control List (ACL). The ACL contains a list of MAC addresses belonging to authorized wireless network devices. The ACL is stored in the WAP. When a wireless network device attempts to access the network through the WAP, the WAP checks the ACL to see if the wireless network device is authorized to access the network.

Wired Equivalent Privacy (WEP)

Wired Equivalent Privacy (WEP) was the first attempt to secure with encryption the data transferred across a wireless network. It was part of the original IEEE 802.11 wireless standard. Not long after WEP was implemented, it was discovered that there were flaws in the encryption method. The WEP algorithm was not as complex as it was first thought to be. A determined hacker could crack the encryption in several hours. In fact, several tools are available on the Internet that can be used to crack WEP encryption keys.

While WEP might be adequate for a low-risk network, such as a home network that does not participate in financial transactions, it is inadequate for high-risk networks, such as a business where financial transactions are commonplace. Creating a VPN, however, can compensate for WEP vulnerability. A VPN can incorporate an authentication and an encryption method, adding to the security set in place by WEP.

Wi-Fi Protected Access (WPA)

Wi-Fi Protected Access (WPA) was developed by the Wi-Fi organization and is not an IEEE standard. When vulnerabilities were discovered in the algorithm used for WEP, a more restrictive encryption was needed to protect data transferred across a wireless network. The Wi-Fi organization sponsored the development of Wi-Fi Protected Access (WPA) as a solution to the vulnerabilities discovered in WEP. WPA uses a more complex encryption technique to protect data. It has become the replacement for WEP. WPA is designed to be compatible with 802.11 devices. WPA encryption is selected from the **Associations** page of the **WLAN Properties** dialog box, **Figure 15-15.**

Wi-Fi Protected Access 2 (WPA2)

Wi-Fi Protected Access 2 (WPA2) an improved version of the WPA standard that provides authentication like WPA, but uses an enhanced encryption method.

Wi-Fi Protected Access 2 (WPA2) was developed by the Wi-Fi organization as an enhanced version of WPA. It is designed to be compatible with the IEEE 802.11i standard.

802.11i

The IEEE ratified the IEEE 802.11i standard in June of 2004 to remedy the original security flaws in 802.11. The 802.11i standard specifies the use of a 128-bit

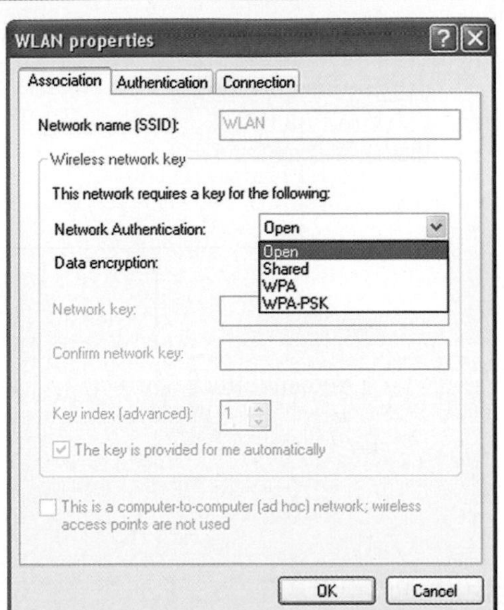

Figure 15-15. WPA encryption is set on the **Associations** page of the **WLAN Properties** dialog box.

Advanced Encryption Standard (AES) for data encryption. It also incorporates a mechanism for generating a fresh set of keys for each new connection. This means enhanced security because the keys are constantly changed rather than reused. 802.11i is downward compatible with existing 802.11 devices. However, this does not mean that the security standards of the 802.11 devices are improved. It simply means that an 802.11i device will use WEP for security when communicating with an 802.11 device.

802.1x Authentication

802.1x provides port-based, network access control. Port-based, network access control supports authentication for Ethernet network access. The term *port-based* refers to any location point represented as a point of access. Do not confuse the term *port-based* with the term *port*, which is used in conjunction with an IP address to identify a service, such as port 80 for HTTP. 802.1x is primarily used for client/server-based networks. It allows the network server to authenticate a wireless network device when the wireless network device attempts to connect to the wired network through a WAP. Older wireless network hardware does not support Advanced Encryption Standard (AES) and therefore cannot fully support the 802.1x enhancements.

802.1x requires three components: supplicant, authenticator, and authentication server, **Figure 15-16.** The *supplicant* is the wireless network device that is requesting network access. The WAP functions as the *authenticator* and does not allow any type of access to the network without proper authentication. A server running Remote Authentication Dial-In User Service (RADIUS) acts as the *authentication server*. ***Remote Authentication Dial-In User Service (RADIUS)*** is a service that allows remote access servers to authenticate to a central server.

Remote Authentication Dial-In User Service (RADIUS) a service that allows remote access servers to authenticate to a central server.

802.1x provides a much easier way to manage numerous Wireless Access Points. By using a server to provide centralized authentication, there is no need to maintain an ACL at each WAP. For example, a university campus might incorporate hundreds of Wireless Access Points, which permit students and faculty to access the system from anywhere on campus. Every semester, new

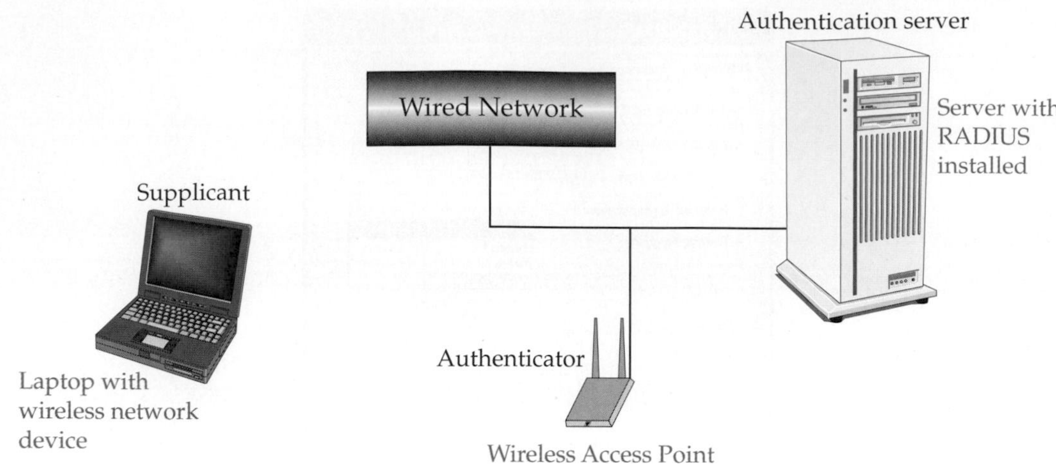

Figure 15-16. The 802.1x standard provides centralized authentication for wireless LANs. It incorporates three components: supplicant, authenticator, and authentication server.

students and faculty need to be added to the ACL. 802.1x allows for a much easier security model by allowing an administrator to manage security from a centralized location.

To set up IEEE 802.1x on a wireless network client, IEEE 802.1x must be enabled. Look at **Figure 15-17.** Notice that security type 802.1x and encryption type WEP have been selected. Also, there are numerous authentications methods available to choose from. Many of these methods are proprietary designs by such companies as Microsoft, Cisco, and Intel. The authentication method selected must match the method used by the RADIUS server.

IEEE 802.1x authentication is enabled in the **Wireless Network Properties** dialog box. The exact number of security, encryption, and authentication types will vary according to operating system version and network adapter manufacturer support. If no security type is selected, no encryption types or authentication options will be available, **Figure 15-18.**

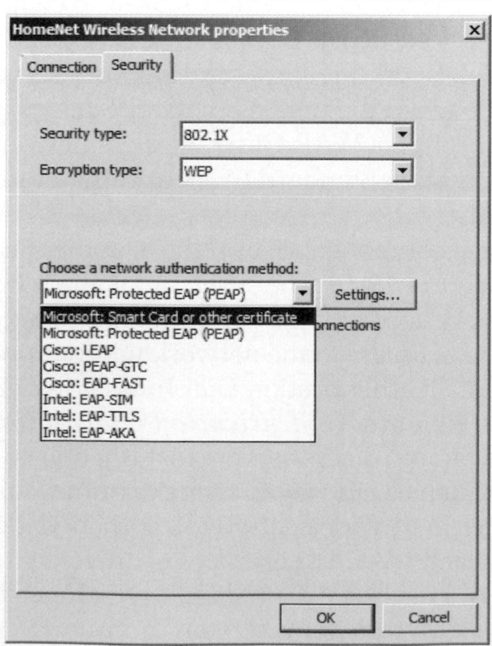

Figure 15-17. IEEE 802.1x authentication is enabled in the **Wireless Network Properties** dialog box. The exact number of security types, encryption types, and authentication methods available will vary according to the operating system version and network adapter manufacturer support.

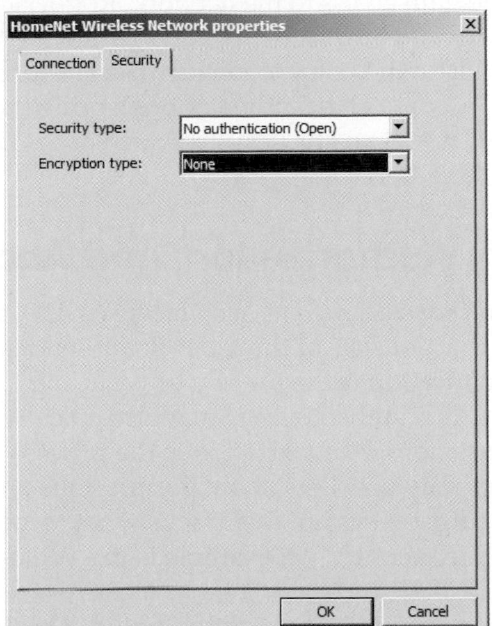

Figure 15-18.
No encryption options are available when the **Security type** option is set to **No authentication (Open)**.

If encryption is disabled for the wireless client or the wireless client is part of a peer-to-peer network, the message as shown in **Figure 15-19** will display. The message says that if encryption is disabled for the wireless client, IEEE 802.1x cannot be used for authentication—nor can 802.1x be used on a peer-to-peer network. Remember, a peer-to-peer network does not have a server to verify authentication, which is one of the requirements of 802.1x.

Rogue Wireless Access Points

A ***rogue access point*** is an unauthorized Wireless Access Point that is installed on a network system. Rogue access points provide a means to compromise the security of a network. Any network user could add a WAP to an existing network,

rogue access point an unauthorized WAP that is installed on a network system.

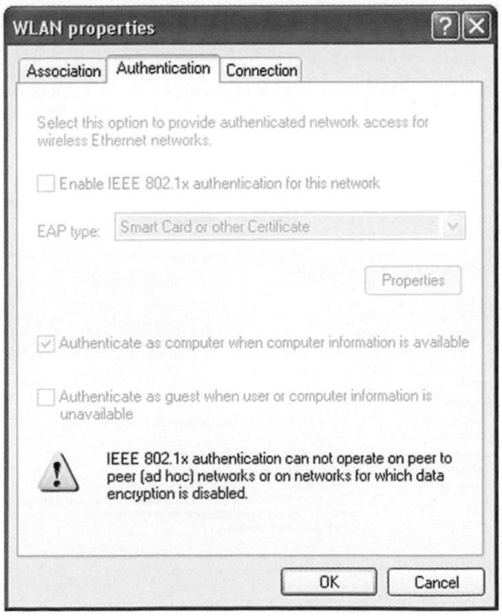

Figure 15-19.
IEEE 802.1x cannot be used for authentication if encryption is disabled for the wireless client. It also cannot be used on a peer-to-peer network because a peer-to-peer network does not have a server to perform authentication.

thus allowing anyone to gain access to the network. Rogue access points can be prevented by using a wireless intrusion prevention system (WIPS). The WIPS will automatically conduct radio scans to identify the existence and location of the rogue access point location. One method of preventing the successful use of a rogue access point is the use of an 802.1x system such as RADIUS, which requires authentication through a server.

Authentication, Authorization, and Accounting

Authentication, Authorization, and Accounting (AAA) a security standard that consists of three parts: authentication, authorization, and accounting.

Authentication, Authorization, and Accounting (AAA), also known as ***triple A,*** is a security standard that consists of three parts: authentication, authorization, and accounting. Authentication is the process of verifying the identity of the user. It incorporates various authentication models typically designed around a user name and user password. Authorization is the process of identifying which system resources a user may use. User share permissions are an example of authorization. Accounting is a system that tracks what resources a user accesses and keeps a record of user activity. An example is the Windows security log, **Figure 15-20.**

Another form of accounting is the activity log used by Internet service providers that host Web pages. The ISP uses logs to track total bandwidth and disk space used and to maintain a list of IP addresses that access each Web page.

Note

When using the Internet to research Authentication, Authorization, and Accounting (AAA), you will be directed to Cisco and its AAA security model and not to the intent of the AAA identified in the CompTIA Network+ objectives. Cisco provides a security system for router and server access referred to as *Cisco IOS AAA* and *Cisco NX-OS*. The IOS is an acronym representing *Internetwork Operating System* and the NX-OS is an acronym representing *NeXt-generation Operating System*.

Windows security log

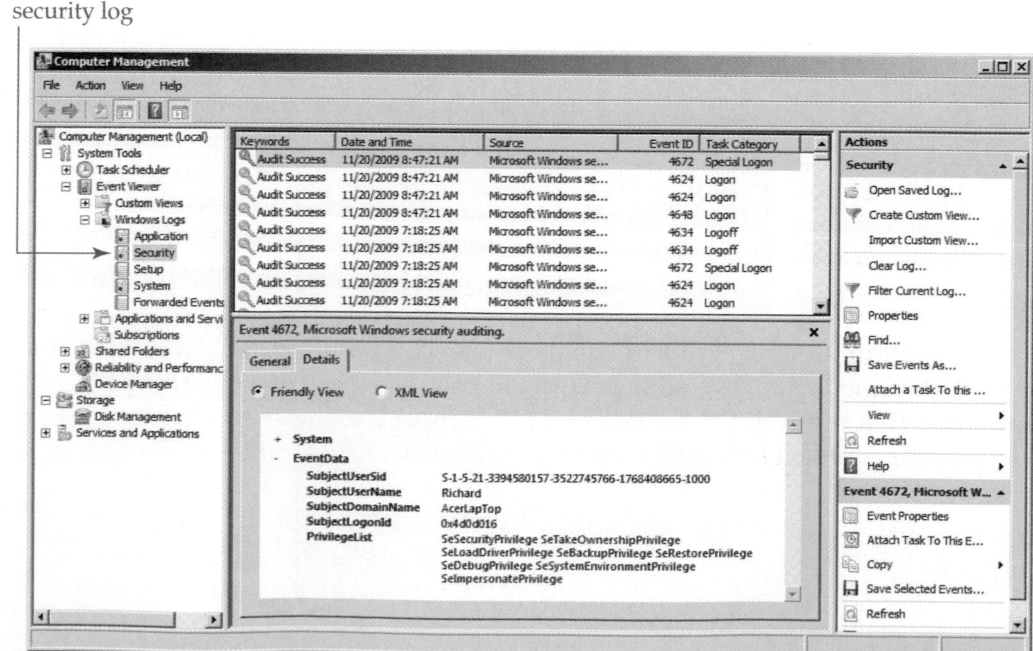

Figure 15-20. Windows 7 security log as accessed through Computer Management. The security log can be used to track user activity.

The triple *A* security standard is the most common model used for network access today. The dominate client/server security models that support the AAA concept are RADIUS, TACACS+, and Diameter. Each of these security systems provide authentication, authorization, and accounting but in different ways.

RADIUS

RADIUS is the acronym for Remote Authentication Dial-In User Service and is an IETF standard that describes how to access client/server network systems. RADIUS is the default method of network security used by Microsoft and is incorporated into many of the Microsoft security features such as Internet Authentication Service (IAS), Network Policy Server (NPS), and remote access service.

Note

Internet Authentication Service (IAS) is the Microsoft implementation of RADIUS for Windows Server 2003 and Network Policy Server (NPS) is the Microsoft implementation of RADIUS for Windows Server 2008.

RADIUS systems authenticate users on a client/server network. The server is referred to as the *Network Access Server (NAS)*. Today, RADIUS is used for more than just dial-in access to a network. It is also used for wireless access and Internet access to the NAS. RADIUS provides a centralized location, typically a server that is used to store user account credentials. Many Internet service providers use RADIUS to store user names and passwords and record user activity. A token is typically assigned to the user after authentication. The token is used to authorize the user account to various portions of the network which match the user permissions. The token is also used to track user activity.

RADIUS is referred to as a "port authentication" standard. Microsoft refers to it as an "802.1x security standard." Some switches have an advanced feature referred to as "port authentication." Port authentication is a method in which a switch restricts access through a specific switch port until access is authenticated by a RADIUS or TACACS+ server.

Diameter

Diameter is an IETF standard and a next-generation authentication protocol designed to secure a connection between two or more devices. The Diameter standard is especially applicable to roaming devices, such as cell phones. In contrast to RADIUS, Diameter does not require a client/server model and can be used in a peer-to-peer network for applications such as a cell phone peer-to-peer wireless network. Diameter allows for "attributes" to be added to the basic Diameter protocol structure. By adding attributes, Diameter is enhanced to meet AAA security requirements.

Diameter an Internet Engineering Task Force (IETF) standard and a next-generation authentication protocol designed to secure a connection between two or more devices.

Diameter in its simplest form is not directly compatible with RADUIS, but the IETF designed Diameter so that it can be compatible with a client/server application that uses a RADIUS server. For example, attributes can be added to the Diameter protocol that will allow a Diameter device to authenticate with a RADIUS server. Diameter can be compatible with a RADIUS server without the need to translate protocols or use a gateway.

When Diameter is extended to meet the AAA requirements, it can be used not only for authentication and authorization, but also accounting. Cell phone billing information can be included in the accounting portion of AAA.

For example, a user with a Diameter-enabled portable communication device can make a secure connection with the home-office network. The user will authenticate through the network RADIUS server and be tracked not only by the client/server network but also by the cell phone service provider. You can think of it as a shared AAA environment.

AAA proxy
an intermediate device used as a relay between an AAA authenticator and client.

The ***AAA proxy*** is any network device that acts as an intermediary to exchange security packets between the AAA server and the AAA client. For example, when a portable device such as a cell phone receives a request, it acts as the server by forwarding the authentication request to a RADIUS server for verification. The cell phone acting as a server will then act as a client to the RADIUS server when it receives verification. As you can see, the cell phone acts as an AAA proxy server.

Diameter uses TCP packets only and uses IPSec and TLS for security. To learn more about Diameter visit www.ibm.com/developerworks/library/wi-diameter/index.html.

Note

Diameter is a play on words with Radius—"diameter" and "radius." Who says geeks don't have a sense of humor!

RADIUS typically requires the clients and server be configured manually, whereas Diameter supports automatic dynamic discovery through DNS.

TACACS+

TACACS+
a Cisco proprietary client/server security method that directs client requests to the authentication server in similar fashion as Microsoft RADIUS.

TACACS+ represents the acronym Terminal Access Controller Access-Control System plus. It is an alternative to RADIUS for security. TACACS+ is often confused with TACACS and thought to be an improved version of TACACS. It is actually an entirely new system, not a derivative of TACACS, which is a much older security system originally implemented for UNIX servers. TACACS+ is a client/server proprietary AAA security system developed by Cisco systems. The following is a brief comparison of RADIUS and TACACS+:

RADIUS	TACACS+
Uses connectionless UDP.	Uses connection-oriented TCP.
Uses one database for authentication, authorization, and accounting.	Uses separate databases for authentication, authorization, and accounting.
Encrypts only the password.	Encrypts the entire exchange of logon packets.
Uses a token-based authentication method.	Uses a token-based authentication method.

To learn more about Microsoft RADIUS, visit the following Microsoft TechNet links.

- http://technet.microsoft.com/en-us/network/bb643123.aspx
- http://technet.microsoft.com/en-us/library/bb742381.aspx
- http://technet.microsoft.com/en-us/library/cc731320.aspx

Authentication Protocols

Chapter 14—Remote Access and Long-Distance Communications introduced SLIP, PPP, and many variations of PPP such as PPTP, PPPoE, and MLPPPP. While PPP and SLIP are primarily concerned with remote connection security over dial-up telephone lines and ISDN, there are many protocols designed to provide secure connections over Ethernet networks and the Internet, such as PAP, CHAP, and Kerberos. This section takes a look at these protocols.

Password Authentication Protocol (PAP)

Password Authentication Protocol (PAP) is the basic password authentication technique used for HTTP and remote dial-up access. PAP sends the user name and password in plain text format, also referred to as *clear text*. The user name and password are sent over the network and then compared to a database of user names and passwords to determine if they may access the server. PAP was developed when security on the Internet using TCP/IP was not a real problem. The clear text used inside the packet allows the password and user name to be easily intercepted.

Password Authentication Protocol (PAP) an authentication protocol that sends a user name and password in plain text format.

Note

PAP is basically obsolete because of the clear text characteristic.

Challenge Handshake Authentication Protocol (CHAP)

The ***Challenge Handshake Authentication Protocol (CHAP)*** is an authentication protocol that sends an encrypted string of characters representing the user name and password. It does not send the actual user name and password. CHAP was designed to be used with PPP when making a remote connection to a server. ***Microsoft Challenge Handshake Authentication Protocol (MS-CHAP)*** is an enhanced version of CHAP that encrypts not only the user name and password but also the data package. MS-CHAP must be used with Microsoft operating systems. It is not compatible with other operating systems.

Challenge Handshake Authentication Protocol (CHAP) an authentication protocol that sends an encrypted string of characters representing the user name and password. It does not send the actual user name and password.

Microsoft Challenge Handshake Authentication Protocol (MS-CHAP) an enhanced version of CHAP that encrypts not only the user name and password but also the data package. MS-CHAP must be used with Microsoft operating systems.

This is how CHAP works. Using the PPP protocol, a computer connects to a remote system. After a connection is established, the server, also known as the *authentication agent*, sends a challenge to the client, or peer. The authentication agent sends a key to the client so that it can encrypt its user name and password. The client responds with an encrypted key representing the password and user name. The server either accepts or rejects the client user name and password based on a matching encryption key. The actual user name and password are not sent. Only a key generated from the characters used in the user name and password is sent.

The authenticating agent randomly generates challenges to verify it is still connected to an authorized peer and not to an impostor that has intercepted packets. CHAP prevents the replay attack by repeating the challenge at random intervals to detect an unauthorized connection. The technical names *authentication agent* and *peer* are used because CHAP can be used for more than server access, such as to authenticate two routers when using a tunneling protocol or VPN connection.

MS-CHAP began being phased out with the introduction of Windows Vista. The latest version used for authentication is MS-CHAPv2. MS-CHAPv2 provides stronger encryption and supports two-way authentication. MS-CHAP only supports one-way authentication. One-way authentication only verifies with the authenticator who the client is. Two-way authentication takes it one step further and also verifies who the authenticator is to the client.

Kerberos

Kerberos
a security authentication system that provides both authentication and encryption services. It uses a two-way method of authentication.

The Massachusetts Institute of Technology (MIT) developed a security authentication system called ***Kerberos.*** The name Kerberos (also spelled *Cerberus*) comes from Greek mythology. It is the name of the mythical three-headed dog that guards the entrance to Hades. Kerberos allows two computers to communicate securely over a network that is not typically secure, such as the Internet. While Kerberos was developed and distributed as an open protocol, it has been incorporated into many proprietary software systems.

Kerberos provides both authentication and encryption services. It uses a two-way method of authentication. In this method, the client is authenticated to the server, and the server is authenticated to the client. When encrypting and decrypting data, Kerberos uses a key to ensure privacy. Two different keys are used similar to the public and private key concept—one key to encode the data (encryption key) and the other key to decode the data (decryption key). Possession of only one key is of no use to the intruder because the same key cannot be used to encode and decode the data.

As you can see in **Figure 15-21**, a key encodes the text message. The message is transmitted from the source to the destination. At the destination, another

Figure 15-21.
Kerberos uses two different key codes. The first key code is used to encrypt the data, and the second key code is used to decrypt the data.

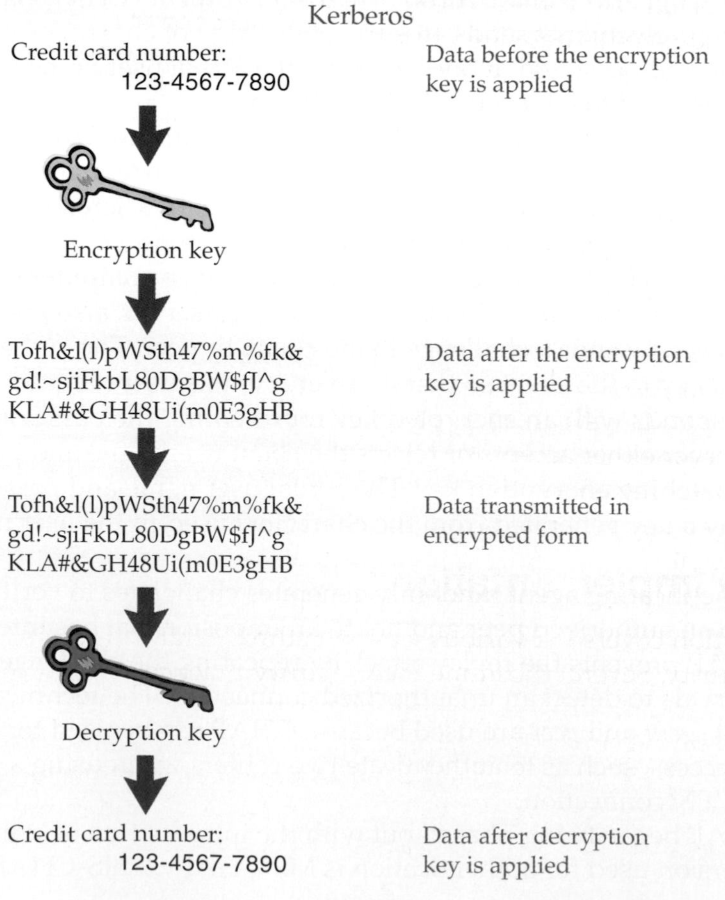

key is applied to the ciphered text to decode it into plain text. Remember, two different keys are used in the Kerberos security system. If the data is intercepted along the way, it is unreadable because it cannot be deciphered without the destination key.

Extensible Authentication Protocol (EAP)

Extensible Authentication Protocol (EAP) is an Internet Engineering Task Force (IETF) standard that is used for network access and authentication in a client/server environment when IP is not available. For example, a dial-up connection to an Internet service provider uses a telephone line to make the connection using the Point-to-Point Protocol (PPP). There is no existing network. EAP was originally developed for use with PPP. Later EAP was adopted for use with wireless connections. Microsoft used EAP for applications such as PPP and dial-up, VPN, and site-to-site and remote access connections. EAP is also used for 802.1x wireless connections and for access and authentication to network switches.

There are numerous variations of the original EAP standard such as EAP-MD5, EAP-TLS, EAP-IKEv2, EAP-AKA, EAP-FAST, and EAP-SIM. We will limit our coverage to only the most commonly encountered variations: PEAP and LEAP.

Protected Extensible Authentication Protocol (PEAP)

Protected Extensible Authentication Protocol (PEAP) is a proprietary protocol developed jointly by Cisco Systems and Microsoft. PEAP is an extension to the original EAP. EAP sends clear text messages which can be intercepted. PEAP is an enhanced version of EAP, which first establishes a secure connection using Transport Layer Security (TLS). TLS provides encryption for the EAP connection and ensures data integrity.

Protected Extensible Authentication Protocol (PEAP) a protocol developed jointly by Cisco and Microsoft that enhances EAP authentication by encapsulating the EAP protocol inside an encrypted PEAP packet over a wireless network.

Lightweight Extensible Authentication Protocol (LEAP)

Lightweight Extensible Authentication Protocol (LEAP) is a proprietary authentication system developed by Cisco Systems for its line of Wireless Access Points. Cisco released this improved EAP standard before the IETF completed the 802.11i standard for wireless network security. One of the major improvements of Cisco LEAP security is periodically the LEAP wireless connection is reauthenticated, thus ensuring that the client is still the original authenticated client and that the connection has not been hijacked by an unauthorized person.

Lightweight Extensible Authentication Protocol (LEAP) a proprietary authentication system developed by Cisco Systems.

Wi-Fi Protected Access (WPA)

Wi-Fi Protected Access (WPA) provides both authentication and encryption for wireless devices. WPA was covered earlier in this chapter.

Security Implementations

This section covers the various ways an administrator can implement network security. Several recommended security practices for new network installations are installing the latest software updates and patches, setting up an account for daily administrative tasks, and changing the default administrator's name. A network administrator needs to constantly educate system users in routine security practices. Yearly seminars, e-mail alerts, and reminders at department meetings are all good efforts.

An administrator should add software or hardware devices that block open ports or filter incoming and outgoing traffic to secure the network. Physically securing the server and other vulnerable points of the network, such as wiring closets, hubs, and router, should also be seriously considered.

Software Installation Patches

Security begins immediately after the initial installation of the network operating system and associated software programs. There are hundreds of known vulnerabilities to operating systems and software packages. For example, when a network operating system such as Windows Server 2008 is installed and configured, it has many known vulnerabilities. Before the installation can be considered complete, the latest patch must be installed. Software patches contain many software fixes that close security holes and fix software bugs. Microsoft releases collections of patches and fixes referred to as a ***service pack.***

service pack
a collection of software patches and fixes.

Administrator Account

Many network operating systems are installed with a default administrator account. During installation, you are given the opportunity to enter a password of your choice for this account. The default user name, such as *Administrator,* provides one half of authenticity to a potential intruder. To secure this potential breach, choose a new administrator name to use in place of the default administrator name, assign the account full administrative privileges, and then delete the default account.

Tech Tip

The ability to delete or rename the administrator account varies according to operating system and version.

For example, Windows Server has the default system administrator name of *Administrator.* A new account should be made with a new name such as *Operat0r1$.* It should be created with full administrative privileges. After the new account has been created, the original account, *Administrator,* should be deleted from the system.

It is also recommended an account be set up that the administrator can use to perform daily duties and that does not require a complete set of administrative powers. The idea behind using a limited administrator account is to protect the system in the event an intruder compromises the account. If an intruder were to gain access of the system using a Trojan horse, the intruder could use a password-stealing program to acquire the administrator's password when the administrator logs on to maintain the system. The intruder could use the administrator account to set up his or her own account that has administrative powers.

If an administrator uses an account with less than full administrative powers, the powers of an intruder are limited if the system is cracked. A user account cannot create another user account that is more powerful than itself. It can only create an account that has equal or lesser powers. By using a less powerful account for daily business, you leave the most powerful account in reserve for when it is really needed. Remember, if the intruder has power equal to the administrator, the intruder can delete everything the system administrator account has created!

Tech Tip

Some network administrators set up a fake administrator account and limit the fake administrator's abilities to control or modify the network resources. This is intended to mislead unauthorized intruders.

User Account Passwords

After installing the network operating system and patches, the next major item of concern is password protection. The network administrator can do much to ensure proper passwords and techniques are used. An administrator can educate system users on choosing a proper password and set up password policies. Educating users includes teaching them about poor and secure passwords. Setting up password policies includes setting defaults for password histories, age, and length.

Poor passwords contain common names, words, or sequential numbers or letters. The following are some examples of poor passwords:

Jamie
Reds
password
secret
TopSecret
love
12345
abcde
AbCdE
A1B2C3
1q2w3e4r

Poor passwords match words commonly found in the dictionary or contain names familiar to the password's owner. Poor passwords also include keyboard combinations that are easy for the password owner to remember. Look at the password *1q2w3e4r* in the previous list. The *1q2w3e4r* password may look like a secure password. However, by locating the letters and numbers on your keyboard to reveal the pattern, you will see that it is not. Keyboard patterns are not secure, but they are better than most typical poor passwords.

Another common password that should be avoided is a social security number. A social security number is easily identified by its nine-number sequence. When a social security password is cracked, the intruder can gain access to other personal information. Never use your social security number as a password under any circumstance.

Secure passwords do not match words commonly found in a dictionary. Instead, they incorporate numbers and special characters, which makes them much more difficult to crack. The following are some examples of secure passwords:

AceHat$_301
Bob_$ecure4PC
Open_Lock231!

No password is 100% secure. However, there are passwords that are difficult to guess or hash. ***Hashing*** is a technique that relies on an algorithm or encryption device based on mathematical algorithms for guessing a password. Passwords are so critical to authentication that network operating systems can control many of the important characteristics required of good passwords.

hashing
a technique that relies on an algorithm or encryption device based on mathematical algorithms for guessing a password.

An administrator can set policies or default settings that can aid in password security. **Figure 15-22** shows the Group Policy Management utility associated with Windows Server 2008. You can readily see the list of password policies available such as history, age, length, and complexity.

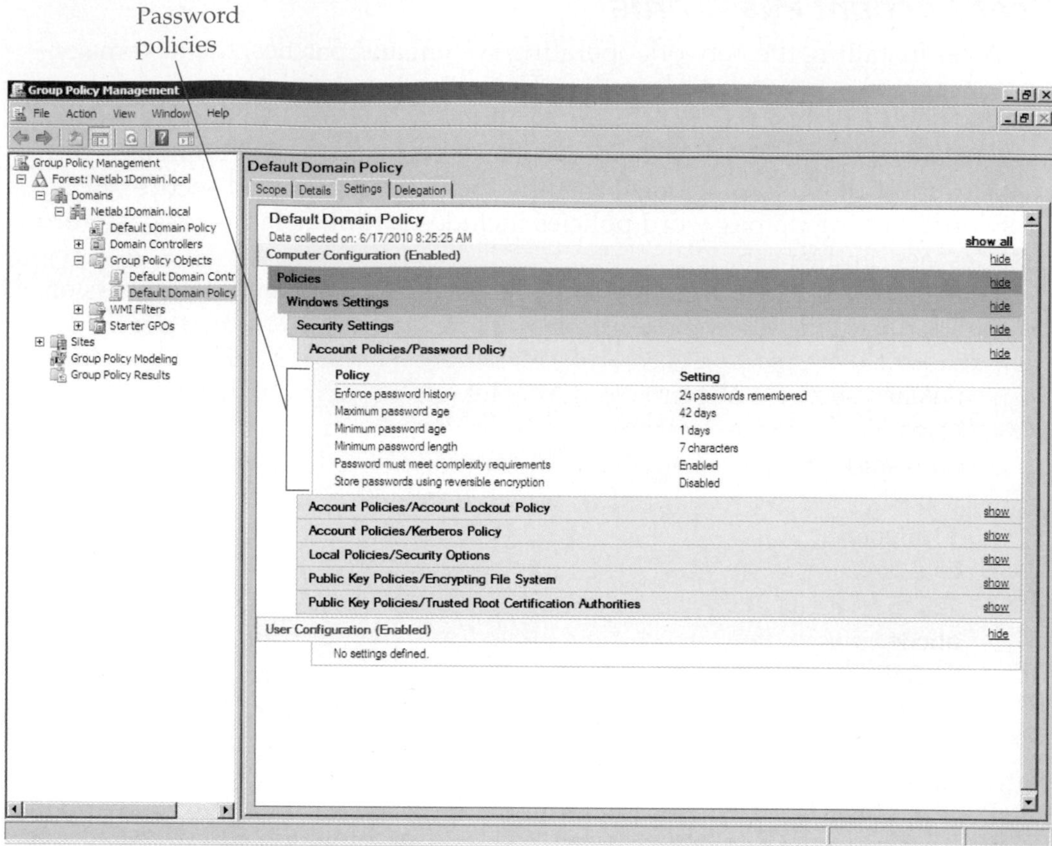

Figure 15-22. Windows Server 2008 password policies for the domain.

Password History

As passwords are changed, the old passwords can be stored and used for comparison against the most recent password. For example, a user may be required to change his or her password every 90 days. This practice is compromised if the user constantly switches between two passwords such as *MySecret* and *Secure*. Not only are these poor passwords, by constantly switching between the two, there is little protection offered by changing the password. Some network operating systems, therefore, allow the administrator to set a minimum password history, which forces the user to use a new password that does not match any of their old passwords. For example the history password policy can be set to store the last 24 passwords. By enforcing the password history, users are forced to continually use new passwords. This can also be easily compromised by ingenious techniques, such as adding a number to the end of a password and then simply incrementing the number by one each time a new password is required—for example, *MySecret1*, *MySecret2*, and *MySecret3*.

Password Age

Passwords should be changed frequently, but not so often that it becomes a real annoyance to the users. A good rule of thumb is to require passwords to be changed every 90 days.

Minimum Password Length

The exact password length depends on the company and network administrator's perception of the need for security. Passwords that are too long are not practical for most applications. A password should be of sufficient length to allow a variety of characters and symbols to be used but not so long that the support desk is constantly reassigning forgotten passwords.

A good rule of thumb is eight characters minimum. Administrators and special operators, such as department heads with administrative privileges to assign passwords to individual workgroups, should be required to use a password of at least 12 characters.

Other Password Security Measures

For further password security, it is a recommended practice to move the location of the password storage file. Depending on the network operating system, it is also a good practice to relocate other security files from the default location. When security files are left in the default location, intruders can easily locate them. Also, when a database with user name and password information is saved on a computer, the database should be encrypted and placed under an unassuming file name such as Tax Report Summaries rather than Personnel Security Passwords.

Any password can be hacked, but not all intruders can hack all password methods. For example, an intruder can hack a highly secure password, but it can be very difficult and take even a month or more. A nonsecure password can be compromised very easily and in a very short time.

You can audit the network security passwords by using special software packages designed for this purpose. Many operating system Web sites provide such tools at no cost.

Firewall

A ***firewall*** is designed to monitor and pass or block packets as they enter or leave a network system, **Figure 15-23.** A firewall may consist of either hardware or software or a combination of both. Servers, routers, and individual computers may be used as firewalls.

firewall
a hardware device or software that passes or blocks packets as they enter or leave a network system.

Firewalls are designed to filter inbound and outbound flow of network packets based on factors such as IP address, port numbers, software application, packet contents, and protocols. The exact selection of factors can vary according to the firewall design, purpose, and configuration.

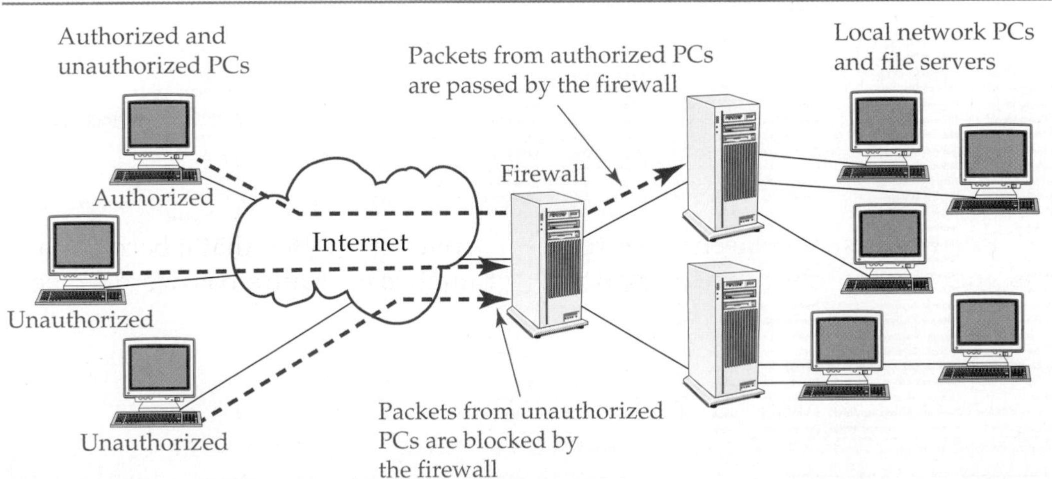

Figure 15-23.
A firewall inspects data packets and either allows the packet to pass, or it blocks the packet.

Windows Firewall is very sophisticated and can filter both inbound and outbound packets. The Windows 7 Firewall and Windows Server 2008 Firewall are almost identical in design. Look at **Figure 15-24,** which shows the Windows 7 Firewall. As you can see, there are many default firewall settings that are directly coordinated with the network location. Most users do not comprehend how a sophisticated firewall system works. Microsoft simply asks the user to pick the type of environment he or she is in such as Public, Private, or Domain. Then, Microsoft automatically configures Windows Firewall for the type of environment selected.

Users have the option to configure individual software program access and specific port access. Notice in Figure 15-24 that every software application and computer service is associated with a protocol such as TCP or UDP and a corresponding port number. The basic operation of all firewalls is based on filtering port numbers that are directly correlated to network services. For example, NetBIOS Name Resolution and UDP port 137 as shown in **Figure 15-25.**

Specific well-known port numbers (0–1023) are correlated to specific services assigned by the IANA organization. Well-known port numbers are typically assigned to system services. Registered ports (1024–49151) are also assigned by IANA and are typically assigned to specific software applications. Dynamic or private ports (49152–65535) are not assigned and can be used for any purpose by any software designer. You may wish to review the list of typical port number assignments in Chapter 10—TCP/IP Fundamentals. A complete list of port numbers can be found at: www.iana.org/assignments/port-numbers. You can also conduct an Internet search using the key terms "IANA.org port numbers."

There are several classifications of firewalls such as packet filter, application gateway, content filter, and circuit level gateway. A typical firewall consists of two

Figure 15-24.
Windows Firewall with Advanced Security has many default firewall settings that are directly coordinated with the network location or environment, such as Public, Private, or Domain.

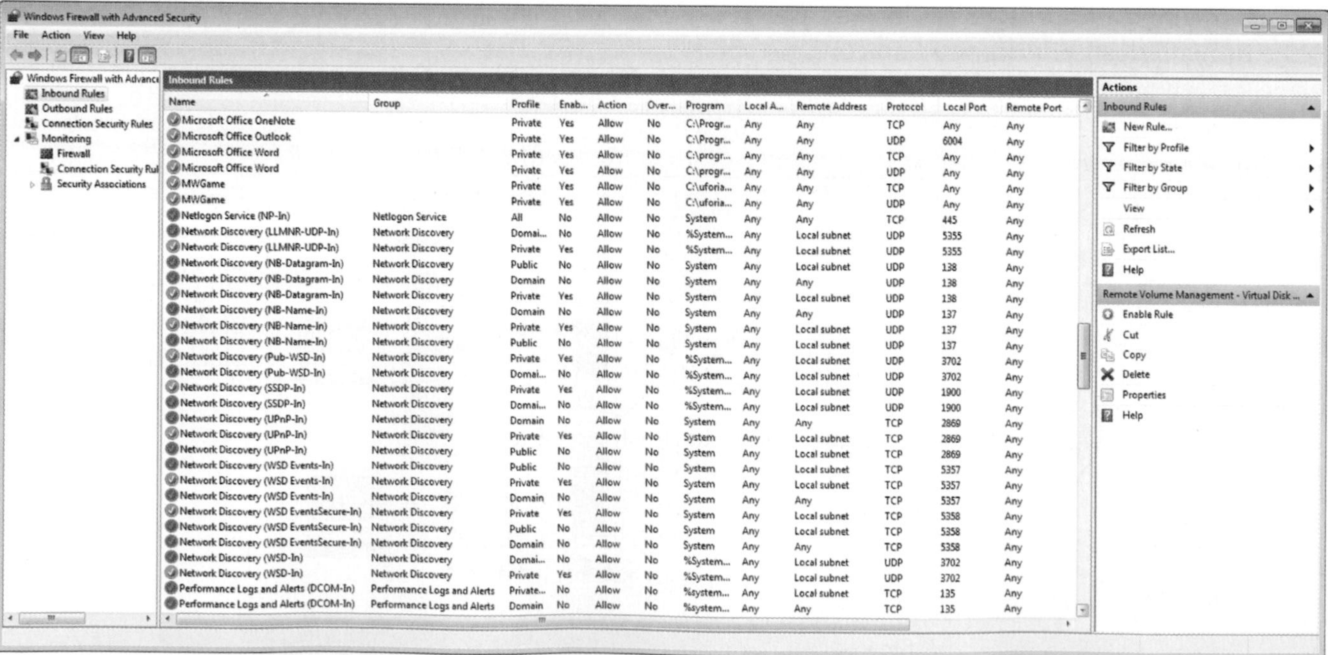

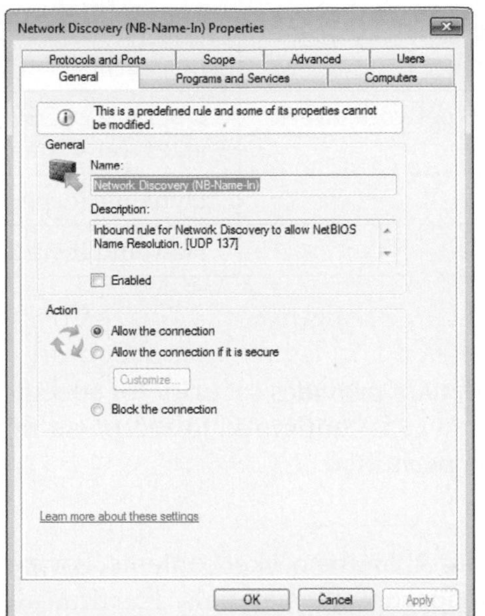

Figure 15-25. The firewall is configured to allow packets related to Network Discovery NetBIOS Name Resolution through assigned UDP port 137.

or more filtering techniques. Often network devices are identified as performing firewall functions in addition to their intended purpose. For example, a network gateway can also perform functions associated with a firewall by filtering packets based on IP address, port number, or MAC address.

Packet Filter

A ***packet filter*** inspects each packet as it passes through the firewall and then accepts or rejects the packet based on a set of rules. The terms *stateful* and *stateless* as applied to firewall technology is the way the packets are inspected. When configured for ***stateless packet inspection,*** a firewall inspects individual packet attributes such as IP address, port number, and protocols. It then applies a filter based on the individual packet attributes. The filter is based on static information. It does not take into account packet flow. For example, a malicious program can delete a section of packets or alter the sequence. A stateless packet inspection will not detect the missing packets. Stateful packet inspection aligns with layer 3 of the OSI model.

A firewall configured for ***stateful packet inspection*** applies a filter based on the sequence of packets. A stateful packet inspection can detect missing packets or an altered sequence of packets. For example, a firewall configured for stateful packet inspection could detect a man in the middle exploit, but a firewall configured for stateless packet inspection could not. Stateful packet inspection aligns with layer 3 and 4 of the OSI model because it not only inspects packet contents related to layer 3 (network layer), it also inspects the packet sequence as related to layer 4 (transport layer).

Stateful packet inspection requires packets to be stored and the firewall CPU to process information before applying a filter. As a result, stateful packet inspection is slower than stateless packet inspection and can cause network latency. Stateless packet inspection is quicker because it simply compares packet data against a set of firewall rules and then applies the filter. Stateless packet inspection causes less network latency compared with stateful packet inspection. The following table summarizes stateful and stateless packet inspection.

packet filter software that inspects each packet as it passes through the firewall and then accepts or rejects the packet based on a set of rules.

stateless packet inspection a firewall inspection method in which individual packet attributes such as IP address, port number, and protocols are inspected and filtered.

stateful packet inspection a firewall inspection method in which the sequence of packets is inspected in order to detect missing packets or an altered sequence of packets.

Stateless Inspection	Stateful Inspection
Inspects individual packets.	Inspects packet flow.
Operates at OSI layer 3 (network layer).	Operates at OSI layer 3 (network layer) and layer 4 (transport layer).
Static inspection.	Dynamic inspection.
Fast.	Slow and increased network latency.

application gateway a hardware device or software that provides security for specific applications by accepting traffic based on the exact match of the application permitted.

content filter a hardware device or software that provides security based on the packet contents.

circuit-level gateway a hardware device or software that monitors a connection until the connection is successfully established between the destination and source host.

firewall signature identification a hardware device or software that works in similar fashion as antivirus protection by intercepting a packet and comparing it to specific malware attributes. When the attributes match, it removes the packet.

demilitarized zone (DMZ) the area of a network that permits access from a host located outside the local area network. It is not protected by the firewall.

Application Gateway

An ***application gateway*** provides security for specific applications such as FTP and Telnet. The gateway is configured to accept traffic based on the exact match of the application permitted.

Content Filter

A ***content filter*** is based on the packet contents. For example, there are many Web sites that contain inappropriate materials. The firewall is configured to block specific Web sites or specific packet contents that contain specific terms. Most content filtering packages require a subscription to a service that updates the filtering components on a routine basis. Content filtering can also incorporate protection from malware. Typically, a content filter is based on a list of search terms such as *alcohol*, *cult*, and *drugs*. The exact list can be controlled by the system administrator. For example, the word *drug* may not be appropriate for a middle school, but would be appropriate for a medical college.

Circuit-Level Gateway

A ***circuit-level gateway*** monitors a connection until the connection is successfully established between the destination and source host. After the connection is established, packets can flow freely between the two hosts. Since the packet sequence is encoded, it is usually quite difficult for an intruder to access the stream of data moving between the hosts.

Firewall Signature Identification

Firewall signature identification works in similar fashion as antivirus protection and is often considered the same thing. Malware can often be classified by a collection of distinct attributes such as port number, payload size, and source address. When a packet is intercepted, it can be compared to specific attributes. When the attributes match, the packet is removed. The main weakness of signature identification is the same as it is for antivirus software. Both require constant updates of new signatures or definitions. New malware is created every day. There is no signature immediately available for new malware.

Demilitarized Zone (DMZ)

Demilitarized zone (DMZ) is the area of the network that permits access from a host located outside the local area network. Network administrators configure a firewall to allow Internet access to part of the network while restricting access to the private portion of the network. See **Figure 15-26.**

The DMZ is the portion of the network that permits access from the Internet. A DMZ can be created with a router or a server with three network adapters installed. One network adapter is connected directly to the Internet, another is connected to the DMZ, and the other is connected to the private section of the network.

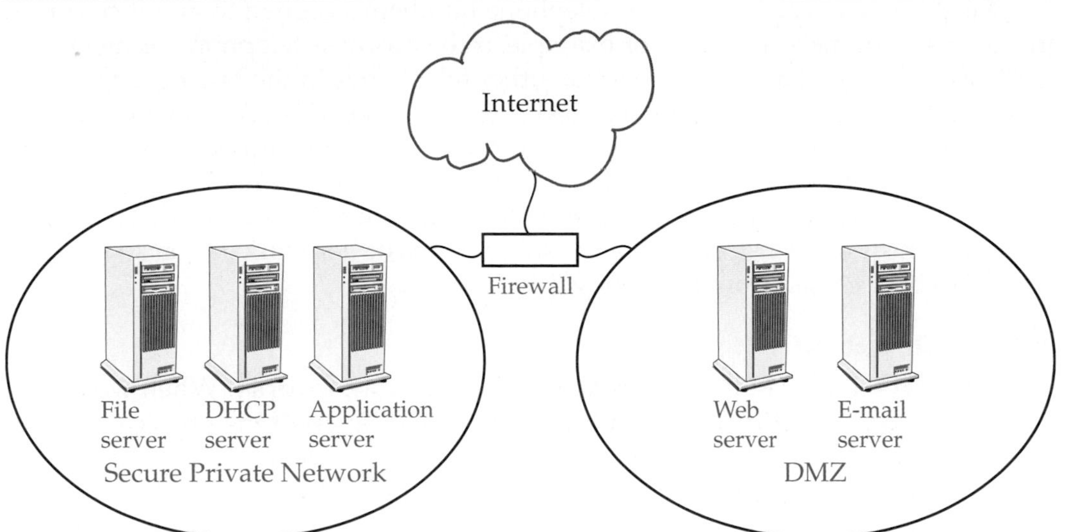

Figure 15-26.
The DMZ is the portion of the network that permits access from the Internet.

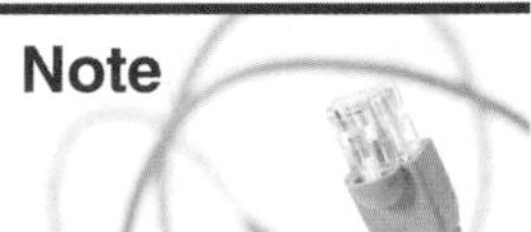

Cisco introduced the term *zone based policy* to distinguish its new method of firewall protection in which it divides the network into zones and applies firewall policies to each zone.

Proxy Server

A ***proxy server*** is a firewall component that is typically installed on a server and resides between the Internet server and the LAN hosts. It appears as a destination host while hiding the address of the true host inside the LAN. To anyone outside the network, only the proxy server is seen. Proxy servers replace the IP address of outgoing packets with the IP address assigned to the proxy server. For incoming packets that are allowed to flow into the network, the reverse is true.

proxy server
a firewall component that is typically installed on a server and resides between the Internet server and the LAN hosts. It appears as a destination host while hiding the address of the true host inside the LAN.

The proxy server can be configured to allow packets to flow into and out of the network if they meet certain conditions. The conditions configured can be items such as specific IP addresses, certain protocols, and server names or URLs.

Proxy servers may also cache information such as frequently visited Web sites. By caching the Web sites and their IP addresses, connections can be made faster than when searching for the Web site. Proxy servers are sometimes referred to as *gateways*.

Securing Remote Access

Remote access is sometimes a necessity, especially for sales personnel who travel. Sales personnel typically need to attach to the office file server to check their e-mail, place customer orders, and check an order's status. While remote access is necessary, it can also pose as a vulnerable access point.

It is interesting to note that remote access can occur without the direct knowledge of network administrators. An employee can secretly attach a modem to his or her workstation so that he or she may access office files from home. Software such as pcAnywhere and Windows Remote Desktop Connection are designed for such capabilities. A hacker can gain access the exact way the employee did.

Most intruders are aware that telephone numbers assigned to an office run in successive numerical order. For example, if the business telephone number is 333-1234, it is probably a safe bet that other telephones in the business are assigned telephone numbers such as 333-1235, 333-1236, 333-1237, and 333-1238. The pattern is easily revealed. This is also true for telephone number extensions.

When an employee attaches a telephone modem to his or her computer at work, he or she leaves a backdoor open to an intruder. As stated earlier, the employee most likely has created a file share on his or her workstation so the file share can be accessed from home or while traveling.

Physical Security

Physical security is an important aspect of network security. When we discuss physical security, we are talking about the location of the physical system. File servers should be placed in a secure room. A secure room means that it is physically locked and can only be accessed by authorized personnel. This policy should apply to the file server room, wiring closets, Point of Presence location, and anywhere along data lines where someone can gain access. Devices which connect the workstations to the network, such as hubs and routers, must also be secured but generally not at such a high level as the file server and wiring closets.

Workstations should also be physically secured. Many users leave their workstation connected to the network when they go home for the day. When they leave, the workstation is still logged on to the network with their user account. This is an open invitation to unauthorized personnel. This is especially true in a large, open office environment when 50 or more workers have open access to every computer in the office area. What if a sensitive document such as a salary schedule for the entire corporation was downloaded, reproduced, and posted on the company lounge bulletin board? Management would most likely be upset. The network administrator could trace the event to your workstation using a standard event-monitoring utility. You would then have to explain this incident and hope you can save your job in the process.

Biometrics

biometrics
the science of using the unique physical features of a person to confirm his or her identification for authentication purposes.

Biometrics is the science of using the unique physical features of a person to confirm a person's identification for authentication purposes. Some examples of unique physical features are fingerprints, speech, eye color patterns, and facial features. One or more of these physical traits can be scanned and encoded as data to be used for comparison when a person attempts to enter a secure area. See **Figure 15-27.** Biometrics can also be used in conjunction with traditional authentication methods, such as user name and password.

It is assumed that because biometrics is unique it cannot be compromised. It is a well-known fact that even foolproof security models can be compromised. A group of college students once cracked a biometrics fingerprint scanner by getting a sample of a network user's fingerprint from a glass. Next, they made a mold of the fingerprint and poured a plastic substance similar to rubber into the mold. They used the rubber form of the fingerprint to crack a biometrics fingerprint scanner. As this story exemplifies, any security model can be broken. However, certain models are much more difficult to crack than others.

smart card
a technology that incorporates a special card into the security system. It is used in conjunction with a personal identification number (PIN).

Smart Card

A ***smart card*** incorporates a special card into the security system. It is used in conjunction with a personal identification number (PIN), **Figure 15-28.** A card reader is attached to the computer system via any standard port such as a serial or

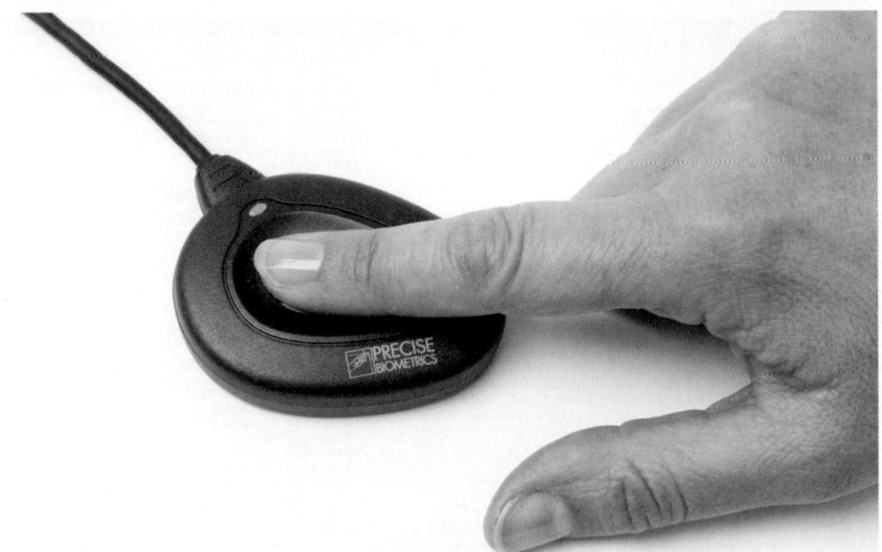

Figure 15-27.
A biometric device that uses the fingerprint for authentication. (Precise Biometrics)

Figure 15-28.
A smart card security system typically uses a smart card and a PIN for authentication. (Gemplus)

USB port. Once the smart card is inserted into the card reader, the user is prompted for a PIN. After the correct PIN is entered, access to the computer system is granted. Smart card technology is not only designed for a single PC, it can also be used to access a network workgroup or domain. Access to the network is limited to the permissions assigned to the user account by the system administrator.

Security Tools

There are numerous security tools available on the market that are designed to identify common network security weaknesses by probing the network and searching for vulnerabilities. The tools are similar to tools used by hackers and crackers to probe a network. Security tools can help you determine if a potential problem exists. One such tool is GFI LANguard.

In **Figure 15-29,** the GFI LANguard utility has revealed some potential problems that exist on a network. Since this information is taken from an actual site, the IP address has been blocked out for protection. As you can see, numerous

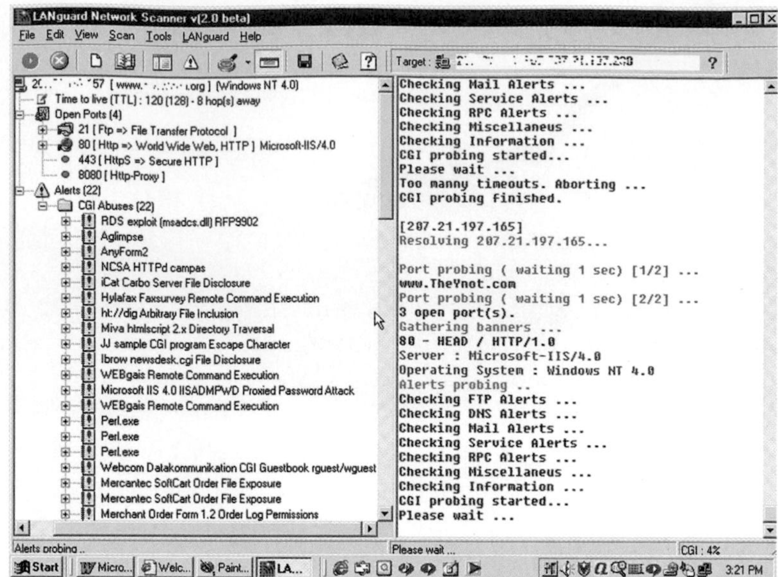

Figure 15-29.
The GFI LANguard utility can be used to check for security problems on a local area network.

possible security problems exist on this network. A person with some expertise could easily penetrate this site and cause a tremendous amount of damage. GFI LANguard is designed to check security problems on the local area network, but can be used by a hacker or cracker as well.

Netstat Utility

The **netstat** utility can help determine which ports are open on a computer. To check for open ports using the **netstat** utility, enter **netstat -a** at the command prompt. A display will appear similar to the one in **Figure 15-30,** which shows the TCP and UDP protocols, the port number of each port currently opened, and the name of the computer associated with the protocol. Any port listed that is not being used should be closed. A utility that periodically detects open ports and alerts you to unauthorized intrusions should also be used.

Audit Tools

User authentication and encryption may not be a sufficient measure of security. A system of auditing user activities should be set up. Not all network attacks or probes come from outside the network. Many network attacks come from inside the network by employees. The activities of users or intruders can be

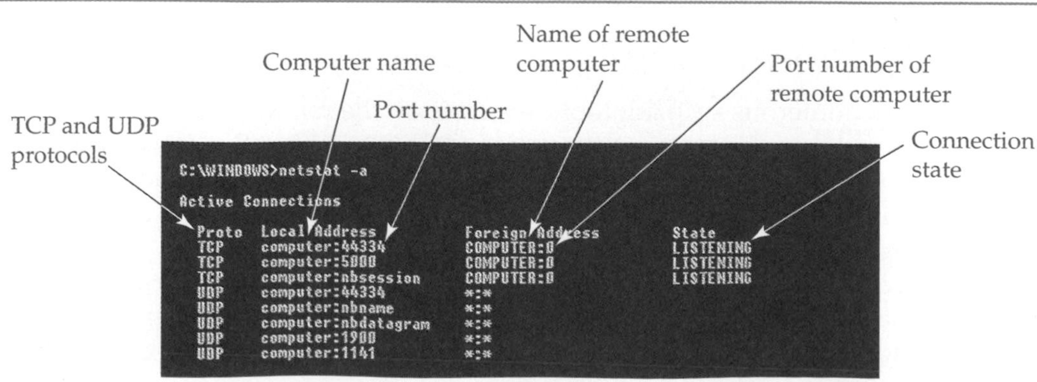

Figure 15-30.
An administrator can use the **netstat** utility to detect open ports on a computer.

recorded in a log, or the network can be set up to generate messages to alert the administrator of a possible attack. Activities such as repeated logon failures are a good sign of intruder activity.

The Event Viewer allows network activities to be monitored that may indicate an attempted or successful system intrusion. Look at the Event Viewer security log events of a Windows Server 2008 system in **Figure 15-31.** The security log lists logon events, successes and failures, dates, and times. By clicking a failed event in the security log, specifics about the event are revealed in more detail. Notice the Audit Failure event that is highlighted in middle pane in Figure 15-31. It refers to the failed logon event of a user named *richard* in the workgroup *WORKGROUP* who attempted to log on to the computer system and was denied access because of either a bad user name or bad password.

Self-Hack Tools

Several companies have self-hack tools available. These tools are typically built into a security package and offered as an additional feature. For example, GFI LANguard is not only designed to provide security measures for a network, it can also test network security using common methods such as password cracking. GFI LANguard probes the LAN for open communication ports and general security weaknesses. It also provides a password-cracking tool.

Protocol Analyzer

A ***protocol analyzer*** is a special software application used to monitor a network and inspect frame/packet contents. It can reveal information about protocols such

protocol analyzer
a tool used to inspect protocol activity and contents.

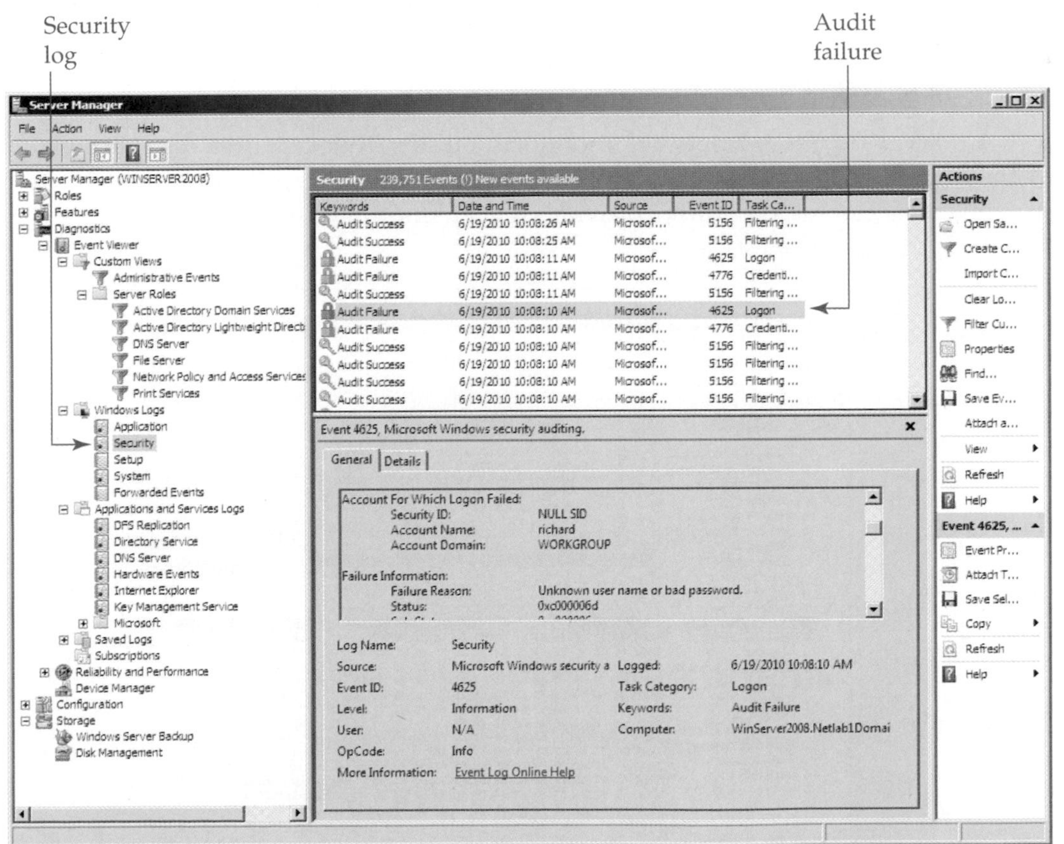

Figure 15-31.
The Event Viewer security log can be used to monitor the system for an attempted or successful system intrusion.

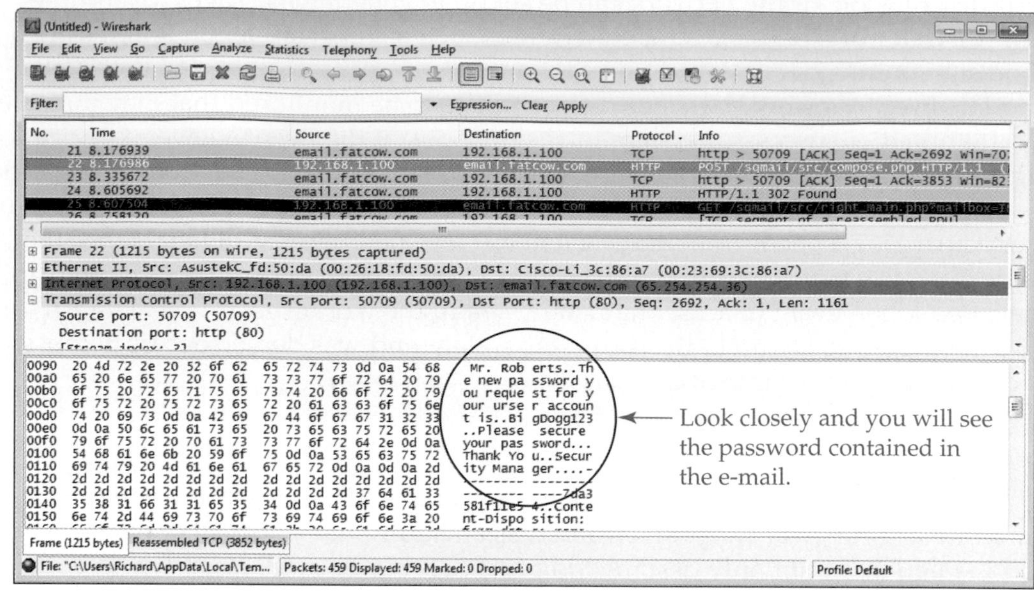

Figure 15-32. Notice how the contents of an unencrypted e-mail can be revealed to anyone using a protocol analyzer or protocol sniffer.

as the source and destination IP address, MAC address, port address, time of transmission, and the contents of unencrypted packets.

Figure 15-32 shows an e-mail transmission. Take a close look at the contents of the e-mail, which are translated on the right side of the screen. In the translation, you will see the password and the user name issued to the recipient because the e-mail was not encrypted. The contents of this e-mail are revealed to anyone using a protocol analyzer or protocol sniffer on this network.

Another excellent tool is the Fluke OptiView Protocol Analyzer. In fact, Fluke has an entire series of network analyzing tools to help you inspect a network system.

Packet Sniffer

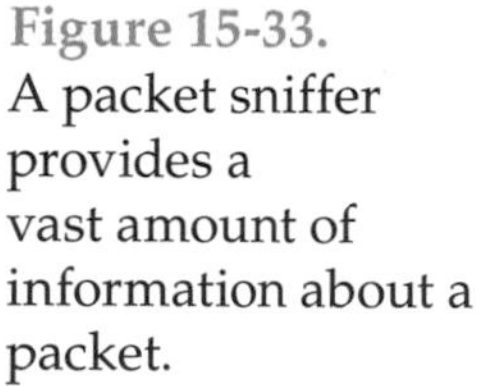

packet sniffer a network monitoring utility that captures data packets as they travel across a network.

A ***packet sniffer*** is a network monitoring utility that captures data packets as they travel across a network. Look at the packet sniffer utility in **Figure 15-33.** As you can see, a packet sniffer provides a vast amount of information such

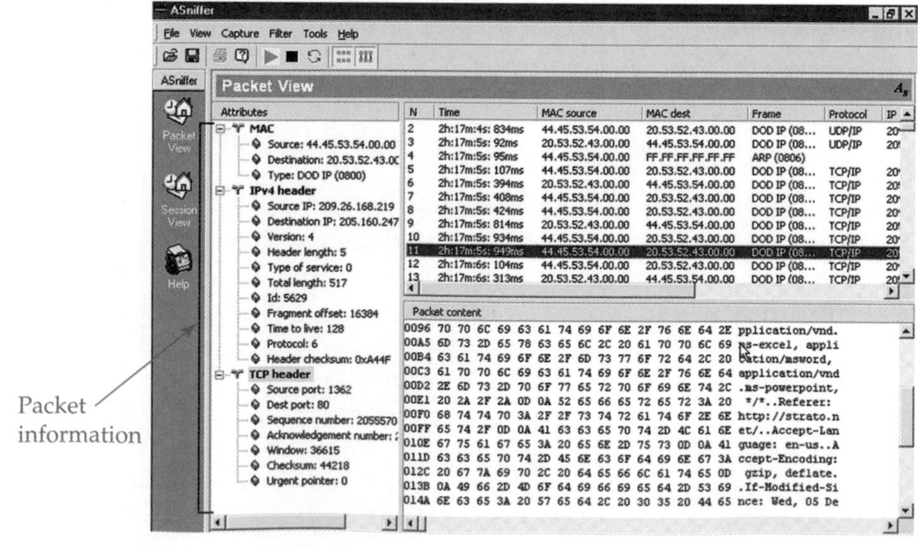

Figure 15-33. A packet sniffer provides a vast amount of information about a packet.

as packet size, protocol, and the source and destination address expressed as an IP address and a MAC address. On the right side of the screen, you can see some of the information contained inside the decoded packet. This particular packet sniffer can capture and perform a complete analysis of TCP, IP, ARP, and UDP protocols. This utility can be very useful in analyzing network problems. However, in the wrong hands, it can be a security threat.

The terms *packet sniffer* and *protocol analyzer* are commonly used interchangeably. A packet sniffer is mainly designed as a tool to capture packet contents and header information and to provide limited information. The protocol analyzer provides these same functions and much more, such as analyzing network traffic patterns, producing graphical representations of protocol characteristics and the network infrastructure, and analyzing network problems.

System Backups

System backups are necessary for recovering lost data. However, the common system backup will restore most data lost from an attack, but will not restore all the data. Any data saved during routine operation, which has not been backed up since the last incremental backup, will be lost.

For example, a system is backed up every night at 7:00 p.m. The next day, the office opens at 8:00 a.m. and begins business for the day. At 2:00 p.m., an intruder enters the system and formats the hard drive of the file server and then releases a virus on the workstations. All data stored since 8:00 a.m. is lost and cannot be recovered.

Network security is a rapidly growing field. It has its own special certification. The certification requires an intensive study of security far above the limited scope of this textbook. If you think you would like to become an expert in network security, visit the SANS organization Web site to find out more about the requirements. This certification is well respected and much in demand.

Data Security Compliance Requirements

There are several security standards and laws aimed at securing user personal data such as medical records, banking records, health records, and credit card information. The difference between a standard and a law is that a standard is voluntary and a law is legally binding.

Both standards and laws typically require the network to be tested for security vulnerabilities. Most require network access and activity to be tracked, monitored, and recorded. They also require that network security features be tested on a regular basis. A policy and procedure guide should also be created and maintained, and all network users be instructed in security-related procedures, such as password and e-mail security.

A standard contains rules such as no wireless devices can be used in the company for processing customer information and the network must be scanned periodically to identify any rogue access point. As you leaned earlier in this chapter, a rogue access point is one that has been installed without company authorization. For example, a credit manager installs a WAP so that she can use her own laptop from any location in the store to access user account information. The WAP installed by the credit manager would be considered a rogue access point.

Tech Tip 

A standard can be incorporated into a contract, making it legally binding. For example, when a network construction contract states that "all work shall conform to the latest IEEE standards," then the standard has become the legally binding part of the contract.

Another key requirement to data security compliance is the creation and enforcement of an incident response plan. An incident response plan contains step-by-step instructions to be followed immediately after a security incident has occurred. For example, on discovery of unauthorized access to the network, all network servers containing customer data will be shut down until the breach has been secured. The network will not be considered secure until notification has been distributed by the network security chief.

Health Insurance Portability and Accountability Act

Health Insurance Portability and Accountability Act (HIPAA)
a set of standards designed to protect health records.

The ***Health Insurance Portability and Accountability Act (HIPAA)*** is a set of standards designed to protect health records. All health care organizations are required to protect patient-related records. This applies to all health care organizations and insurance companies. HIPAA has three broad areas of compliance requirements: administrative safeguards, physical safeguards, and technical safeguards.

Administrative safeguards require that policies and procedures be designed, maintained, and implemented to ensure patient record confidentiality. The administrative safeguard must also include an employee training component.

Physical safeguards require that all patient information must be physically secured. For example, patient information must be kept in a safe, secure area and only authorized personnel can access the data and only on a need-to-know basis. The information must be secured from access when no one is present.

Technical safeguards include items such as all exchange of patient data must be encrypted when transferred over public networks. There is an exception at the time of this writing concerning encryption. E-mail to and from a patient is not required to be encrypted unless requested by the patient. All access to the network must be authenticated. This means that at a minimum, user names and passwords are required for all users on an individual basis. Also, access from other health entities such as insurance companies or other health professionals must have their identity verified. Another aspect of technical safeguards is the establishment of policy and procedures to ensure security of patient records.

Payment Card Industry Data Security Standard (PCI DSS)
a set of credit card security standards designed to protect credit card information.

California SB 1386
a legislative act that requires all organizations that own or have access to personal information of California residents to notify the person of any breach of security of his or her personal data.

Payment Card Industry Data Security Standard

Payment Card Industry Data Security Standard (PCI DSS) is a set of credit card security standards designed to protect credit card information. This is not a law but rather a voluntary set of security standards. PCI DSS typically requires all data to be encrypted when transferred, a firewall to be installed and maintained, and a written policy and procedure manual to be used as a guide for personnel dealing with customer data security.

California SB 1386

The ***California SB 1386*** act requires all organizations that own or have access to personal information of California residents are required to notify the person of any breach of security of his or her personal data. This act would require that all IT organizations that handle California residents' information be monitored by an intrusion detection system at the very minimum.

Sarbanes-Oxley

Sarbanes-Oxley (SOX) is a legislative act that imposes standards on financial institutions to secure personal financial records. As part of the legislative act, the IT portion of the organization is required to perform routine security checks of the network system and data storage.

You can learn more specific details of the data security requirements by conducting a search using combinations of the key terms "data security compliance requirements" and the name of the corresponding standard or law. Many states have their own laws related to personal data security. Conduct a search to view regulations for your state.

An excellent PDF file covering wireless standards for processing credit cards is www.pcisecuritystandards.org/pdfs/PCI_DSS_Wireless_Guidelines.pdf. To access this site, you can also conduct a search using the key terms "PCI DSS Security Standards Org".

Sarbanes-Oxley (SOX)
a legislative act that imposes standards on financial institutions to secure personal financial records. As part of the legislative act, the IT portion of the organization is required to perform routine security checks of the network system and data storage.

Summary

- Authentication is the procedure of verifying a user's identity.
- Social engineering is an activity that uses personal skills rather than technical knowledge to gain access to a network or secure area.
- Spoofing is fooling the destination by using an IP address other than the true IP address of a source to gain access to a system.
- A Trojan horse often contains a program that can reveal user names and passwords.
- The most common way worms and other undesirable content are spread is through e-mail attachments.
- A macro virus is written using readily available macro writers that come as part of a word processing program.
- Encryption is a method of using an algorithm to encode data.
- A key is a software code used to encode or decode data.
- Public Key Infrastructure (PKI) is a security method that uses encryption keys and certificates to encrypt and authenticate users.
- There are two main types of key encryption methods: symmetric-key encryption and asymmetric-key encryption.
- A symmetric key is a key classification that uses the same key to encrypt and decrypt data.
- An asymmetric key is a key classification that uses two different keys to encrypt and decrypt data.
- Digital certificates are issued by Certificate Authorities and are used to verify identities.
- Digital certificate keys are typically asymmetric.
- The Secure Socket Layer (SSL) protocol was developed by Netscape to secure transactions between Web servers and individuals using the Internet for such purposes as credit card transactions.
- Transport Layer Security (TLS) was developed after SSL by the Internet Engineering Task Force (IETF). It serves the same purpose as SSL but is more secure.

- IPSec is a protocol designed to secure IP packets on an unsecured network medium.
- The original solution to wireless device security includes a Service Set Identifier (SSID), Media Access Control (MAC) filtering, and Wired Equivalent Privacy (WEP).
- IEEE 802.11i is a standard that was developed to remedy the original security flaws in 802.11.
- 802.1x provides port-based, network access control, which supports authentication for Ethernet network access.
- 802.1x is composed of three components: supplicant, authenticator, and authentication server.
- AAA represents Authentication, Authorization, and Accounting.
- TACTACS+, RADIUS, and Diameter are all models of AAA.
- Password Authentication Protocol (PAP) was an early development of user name and password authentication that transmits the user name and password as clear text.
- The Challenge Handshake Authentication Protocol (CHAP) encrypts the user name and password.
- Microsoft Challenge Handshake Authentication Protocol (MS-CHAP) is a Microsoft version of CHAP that can only be used with Microsoft operating systems.
- Kerberos was designed at the Massachusetts Institute of Technology (MIT) and is used to authenticate the client and the server.
- The Kerberos system uses two different keys similar to a public and private key for security.
- After installing a network operating system, you should immediately apply any available software patches to the system.
- The system administrator default user name should be changed to lessen the chance of the system being cracked.
- A strong password is composed of letters, numbers, and special symbols.
- Network operating systems typically incorporate password policy features such as password history, minimum length, age, and complexity.
- A firewall monitors data packets as they enter or exit the network system and either blocks or passes them.
- A proxy server is a special firewall designed to hide clients inside the network from unauthorized personnel outside the network.
- Biometrics is the use of physical characteristics for the basis of user authentication.
- A smart card integrates electronics into a card for authentication.
- A protocol analyzer is a tool that inspects protocol activity and contents.
- A packet sniffer is a type of network monitoring utility that inspects data packets.

Review Questions

Answer the following questions on a separate sheet of paper. Please do not write in this book.

1. What is using a false IP address or identity called?
2. What method is used to counter a Smurf attack on a network?
3. What is the purpose behind using a Trojan horse?
4. Where are macro writers commonly found?
5. Through what method are worms typically spread?
6. What is the difference between symmetrical key encryption and asymmetrical key encryption?
7. Another name for symmetric key encryption is _____.
8. What does the acronym PKI represent?
9. What is the purpose of a Certificate Authority (CA)?
10. Who developed SSL?
11. What is the purpose of SSL?
12. Which two protocols are specifically designed to make Web site transactions safe?
13. What is IPSec?
14. What is the difference between IPSec tunnel mode and transport mode?
15. What two protocols are common to IPSec?
16. What are the three original wireless device security mechanisms?
17. What encryption mechanism was developed as a replacement for WEP?
18. What is 802.11i?
19. What is 802.1x?
20. What are the three components of an 802.1x configuration?
21. Identify three security technologies that meet the AAA requirements?
22. Which protocol could be considered as the next generation RADIUS?
23. Why is PAP considered an unsecured system of authorization?
24. What does the acronym CHAP represent?
25. Why is CHAP considered an improvement over PAP?
26. What operating system is MS-CHAP designed exclusively for?
27. Of the three different protocols, PAP, CHAP, and MS-CHAP, which encrypts the contents of the packet?
28. What is Kerberos?
29. The initial network operating system should not be considered complete until the latest software _____ is installed.
30. Describe the characteristics of a poor password.
31. Describe the characteristics of a good password.
32. How is a firewall used to secure network access?
33. What factors are used by firewalls to filter inbound and outbound network traffic?
34. What is the difference between stateful and stateless firewall inspection?
35. How is a proxy server used to secure network access?
36. What is biometrics?
37. What technology uses a plastic card with embedded electronics for identification?
38. What TCP utility displays open ports?
39. What is a protocol analyzer used for?
40. What is a packet sniffer?

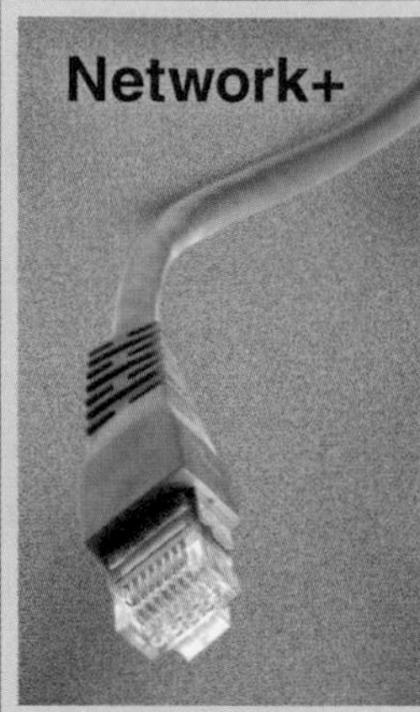

Sample Network+ Exam Questions

Answer the following questions on a separate sheet of paper. Please do not write in this book.

1. What common security measure should be performed immediately after the new network operating system has been installed?
   A. Change the default administrator user name and give it a difficult password to crack.
   B. Immediately write down the administrator user name and password, and then delete the administrator account to prevent it from being penetrated by unauthorized persons.
   C. Access the BIOS settings and change the network administrator's password.
   D. Install a protocol analyzer to see if a cracker detected the installation.
2. Which of the following software packages or utilities is used to analyze the contents of individual packets on an Ethernet network?
   A. **arp**
   B. Packet sniffer
   C. **tracert**
   D. **ping**
3. Which of the following is the *least* secure authentication method?
   A. CHAP
   B. PAP
   C. Kerberos
   D. 802.1x
4. Which utility can record security events as they take place on a Windows network?
   A. Event Viewer
   B. Network Monitor
   C. Directory Service
   D. Device Manager
5. Which is the best example of a secure password?
   A. BigDog
   B. Star$Read1345
   C. NtsysFive
   D. Pass123456789
6. Which security term is used to describe the act of obtaining a person's identity through fraudulent means?
   A. Trojan
   B. Phishing
   C. Man in the middle
   D. DoS
7. Which is a centralized security method that uses a server for wireless authentication?
   A. WEP
   B. WAP
   C. WPA
   D. 802.1x

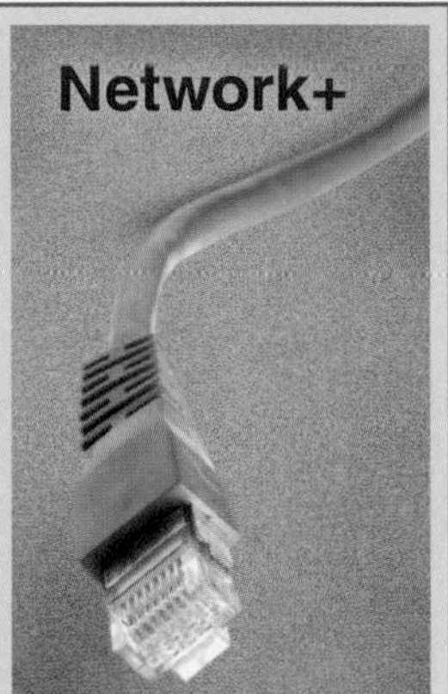

8. Which of the following is used to identify a wireless network?
   A. MAC filter
   B. SSID
   C. EAP
   D. Subnet mask
9. Which is the most common means of spreading a computer worm?
   A. Uploading data from a disc
   B. Newly installed hardware devices
   C. Opening e-mail attachments
   D. Newly installed software utilities
10. Which protocol was designed to provide secure communication between a Web server and a Web browser?
    A. SSL
    B. FTP
    C. PPP
    D. RADIUS

Suggested Laboratory Activities

1. Install and configure Windows Internet Connection Sharing (ICS).
2. Experiment with Windows password policy settings.
3. Search the Internet and then download and configure trial versions of security software.
4. Apply for a trial version of a digital certificate from a CA such as VeriSign. After obtaining the digital certificate, try it out with a classmate.
5. Access Windows Firewall and then open Help to learn more about the firewall configuration options.
6. Open Event Viewer and explore its options.
7. Visit the SANS organization Web site for the latest security information and information about security certification.
8. Visit the GFI Web site (www.gfi.com/lannetscan) and then download and install GFI LANguard.

Interesting Web Sites for More Information

http://technet.microsoft.com/en-us/library/cc725770(WS.10).aspx
http://technet.microsoft.com/en-us/library/cc732283(WS.10).aspx
http://technet.microsoft.com/en-us/library/cc784886(WS.10).aspx
http://technet.microsoft.com/en-us/security/cc297183.aspx
http://web.mit.edu/kerberos/dist/index.html
http://web.mit.edu/kerberos/www
www.cert.org
www.gfi.com/lannetscan
www.hackingexposed.com/tools/tools.html
www.ietf.org/old/2009/ids.by.wg/ipsec.html
www.incidents.org
www.insecure.org
www.sans.org
www.sans.org/security-resources/glossary.php

Chapter 15
Laboratory Activity

Security Event Monitoring

After completing this laboratory activity, you will be able to:

- Use Event Viewer or Computer Management to open the security log.
- Interpret a failed security event.
- Identify the type of events that are recorded in the security log.
- Use Event Viewer or Computer Management to modify the security log configuration.

Introduction

In this laboratory activity, you will access and modify the security log configuration. The security log can be accessed directly through Event Viewer or through Computer Management. To open Event Viewer, enter **eventvwr.exe** in the **Search** dialog box off the **Start** menu and select **Event Viewer** from the search results. The same executable command can be used for Windows XP and later operating systems. To open Computer Management, right-click **Computer** from the **Start** menu and then select **Manage** from the shortcut menu. When Computer Management opens, you will see Event Viewer listed as a folder in the left-hand pane.

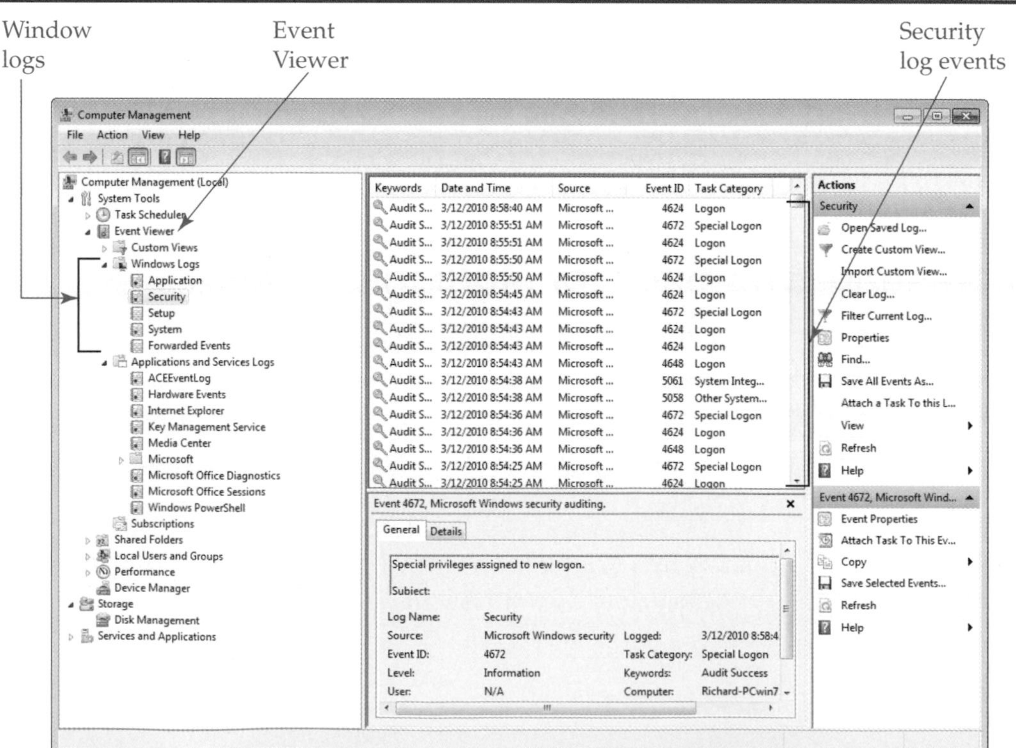

Event Viewer contains many different types of files. For example, the screen capture shows the list of events contained in the security log. A detailed set of information about the event can be viewed by simply double-clicking the selected event. An **Event Properties** dialog box will appear similar to the one in the following screen capture.

You can see the information gathered about an attempted logon using explicit credentials. The event took place on 3/12/2010 at 10:16:12 AM. The user account name entered for authentication was *BobbyG* and his credentials are located at account domain RICHARD-PCWIN7. BobbyG attempted to log on to the server WinServer2008.Netlab1Domain.local and failed. This record can be copied to the clipboard as a single event and then printed so the administrator has a hard copy to work from or to add to a security report. The event can also be e-mailed to an account for viewing as well. As you can see, Event Viewer is an important utility that can monitor user authentication. If a series of failed events occur using the same name, an administrator will know that either the user *BobbyG* is having a problem with his password or that someone is attempting to access the server using the *BobbyG* account name and guessing the password.

Certain security log properties can be modified, such as the size of the security log file. The entire file can be saved to a separate folder for storage or review. Look at the following screen capture and note the three overwrite options listed near the bottom of the **Log Properties–Security** dialog box: **Overwrite events as needed (oldest events first)**; **Archive the log when full, do not overwrite events**; and **Do not overwrite events (Clear logs manually)**.

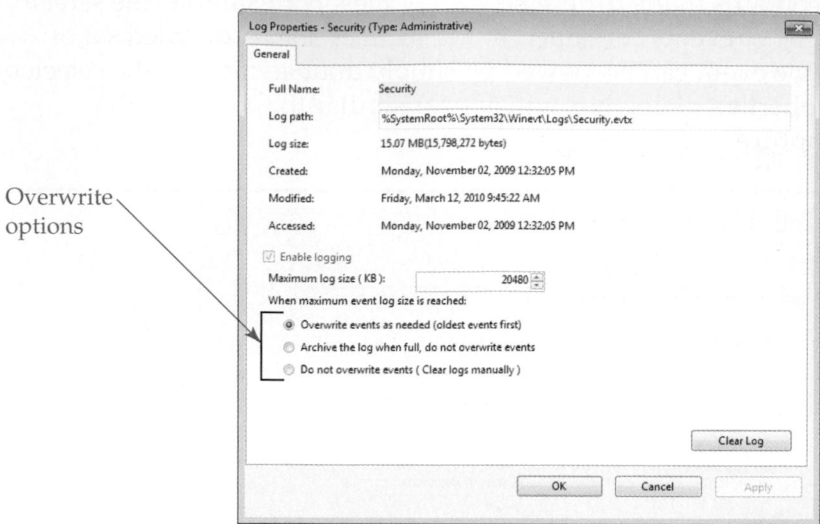

The default setting is **Overwrite events as needed (oldest events first)**. This means when the allotted amount of file space is used, the oldest event will be erased as new ones are generated. **Do not overwrite events (clear log manually)** is not often used because if the log reaches its limit, the computer will generate an error message or a blue screen and then lock the computer when a new event needs to be recorded. The server must then be restarted and the log manually cleared.

The entire log or events can contain an overwhelming number of events numbering into the tens of thousands. To overcome the extensive number of events collected in the log, the event can be filtered. Look at the following screen capture of the **Filter Current Log** dialog box.

Filter Current Log
Filter XML
Logged: Any time
Event level: Critical Warning Verbose
Error Information
By log Event logs: Security
By source Event sources:
Includes/Excludes Event IDs: Enter ID numbers and/or ID ranges separated by commas. To exclude criteria, type a minus sign first. For example 1,3,5-99,-76
<All Event IDs>
Task category:
Keywords:
User: <All Users>
Computer(s): <All Computers>
Clear
OK Cancel

You can filter events by time period such as days, weeks, or hours. You can also filter events by level such as critical, warning, verbose, error, or information. To learn more detailed information about the Event Viewer options and logs, conduct an Internet search using the key terms "Microsoft TechNet Event Viewer." You can also locate information on the local computer by entering "Event Viewer" in Help and Support located off the **Start** menu.

Equipment and Materials

- Computer with Windows 7 or Windows Server 2008 installed as part of a peer-to-peer network. You will need administrative privileges.

  Note
  The Windows 7 and Windows Server 2008 Event Monitor are very similar.

Procedure

1. ______ Report to your assigned workstation.
2. ______ Boot the computer and make sure it is in working order.
3. ______ Access Event Viewer by entering **eventvwr.exe** in the **Search** dialog box located off the **Start** menu. Event Viewer will appear in the search results before you finish typing the entire name.
4. ______ After Event Viewer opens, exit Event Viewer by selecting **File | Exit**.
5. ______ Now access Event Viewer by selecting **Start**, right-clicking **Computer**, and selecting **Manage** from the shortcut menu. The Computer Management console will open. The Event Viewer is listed as a folder in the left-hand pane.
6. ______ Expand the Event Viewer folder so that you can see the five Windows log types: **Application**, **Security**, **Setup**, **System**, and **Forward Events**.
7. ______ Select **Security**. Look at the security events listed in the center pane of the window. If your system is new, there may be few events listed. Take note of what the latest event is by double-clicking the event. The **Event Properties** dialog box will display. When you are finished viewing the event details, click **OK** to close the **Event Properties** dialog box.
8. ______ Sort the events by type, date, user, and computer by clicking on the top of each column.
9. ______ Log off the computer.
10. ______ Generate a failed logon event by attempting to log on to the computer from a different computer in the peer-to-peer using a bogus name and password.
11. ______ Now, log on to the original computer and open the security log to see if the failed event was recorded. If the failed logon attempt is not listed, call your instructor for assistance.
12. ______ View the details of the failed event by double-clicking the event or by right-clicking the event and selecting **Properties** from the shortcut menu. Answer the following questions on a separate sheet of paper.
    - Is the bogus name listed?
    - What other information is listed in the **Event Properties** window?

13. ______ Close the **Event Properties** window by clicking **OK**.

14. ______ Right-click the **Security** folder listed under the Event Viewer folder and then select **Properties**. Look at the options listed on the **General** page. Practice changing the log size and the overwrite options. When you are finished experimenting, click **Cancel** to exit the dialog box without saving any changes.

15. ______ Answer the review questions and then return the computer to the condition specified by your instructor.

Review Questions

Answer the following questions on a separate sheet of paper. Please do not write in this book.

1. What is the name of the executable file that will start the Event Viewer?
2. What are the three overwrite options for the security log?
3. What is the default overwrite option?
4. What does the **Filter current log** option allow you to do?
5. List the five Event Viewer logs.

16 A Closer Look at the OSI Model

After studying this chapter, you will be able to:

- ❑ Compare the OSI model with the DoD model.
- ❑ Explain the structure and operation of the logical link control (LLC) and the media access control (MAC) sublayers.
- ❑ Recall the function of each layer of the OSI model.
- ❑ Match common network hardware to the layers of the OSI model.
- ❑ Match common IEEE standards to the layers of the OSI model.
- ❑ Explain the encapsulation process.
- ❑ Match the TCP/IP protocol suite to the OSI model.

Network+ Exam—Key Points

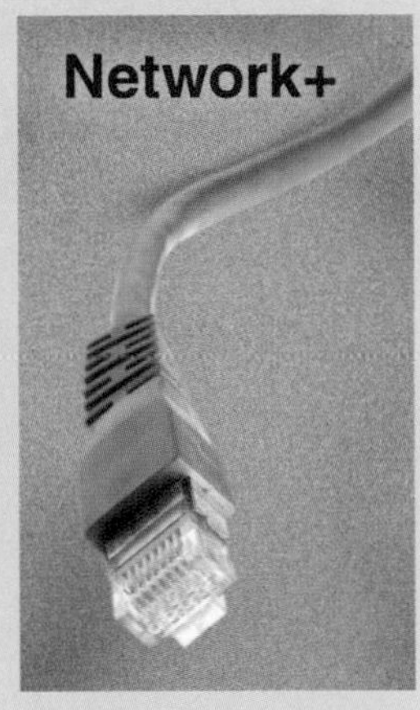

The Network+ Certification exam references the OSI model and the TCP/IP protocol suite. You should not encounter any questions related to legacy protocols such as IPX/SPX, AppleTalk, and NetBEUI. Although, you may still encounter these protocols in reference materials and see network device configuration options for these protocols, especially in protocol analyzers.

When studying for the Network+ Certification exam, concentrate on the TCP/IP protocol suite and the OSI model layer definitions. You should also be able to describe the protocol encapsulation process and the responsibility of each protocol.

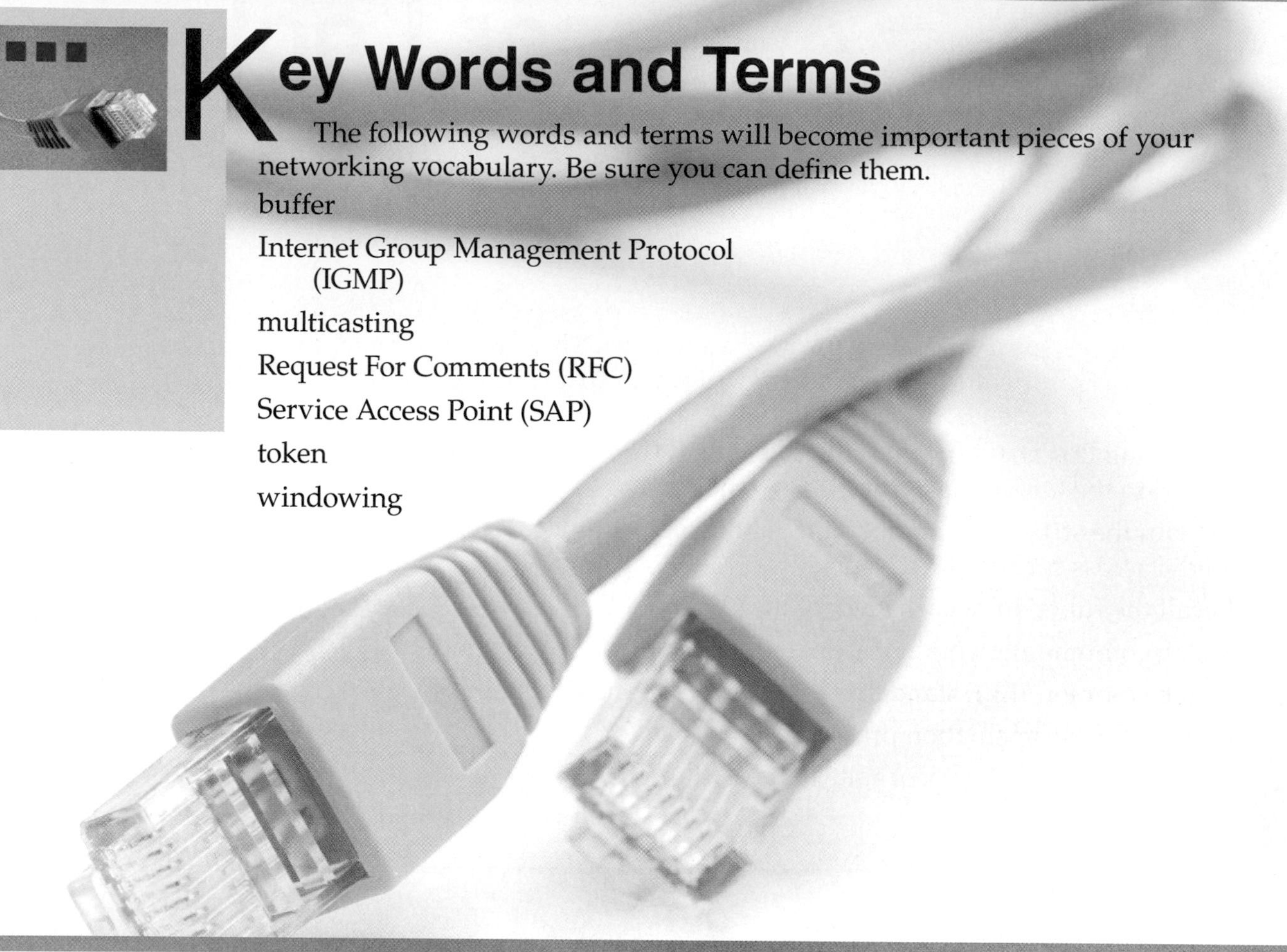

Key Words and Terms

The following words and terms will become important pieces of your networking vocabulary. Be sure you can define them.

buffer
Internet Group Management Protocol (IGMP)
multicasting
Request For Comments (RFC)
Service Access Point (SAP)
token
windowing

An in-depth understanding of the OSI model has been one of the most difficult concepts for students to master. Simply explaining the OSI model once in any textbook is insufficient. Only after the student masters the concepts of the various protocols, hardware, and software can they truly begin to grasp the concepts related to the OSI model. In this chapter, a more detailed study of the OSI model is presented with special emphasis on the physical, data, network, and transport layers.

This chapter presents the OSI model as it relates to the TCP/IP protocol stack, how it compares to network equipment, and how it relates to various network operating systems. It is the intent of this chapter to clear much of the fog surrounding the functions of the OSI model and its relationship to hardware and software. A detailed study and review of this chapter will help you prepare for the Network+ Certification exam and provide you with an excellent refresher before going on to the following chapters, which cover maintaining, troubleshooting, designing, and installing networks.

History and Purpose of the OSI Model

The original model, or design, of TCP/IP communications over the Internet was first developed by the Department of Defense (DoD) in the 1970s. The DoD model is simpler in design than the OSI model. See **Figure 16-1.** Notice that the DoD model has four layers and the OSI model has seven.

When the DoD model was designed, the Internet structure was new and concepts were much simpler. The communications protocol was TCP/IP. There were not an overwhelming number of applications used in the early days of the Internet. Security was not considered a real problem, and encryption was not used. There was only one dominant operating system—UNIX. As long as all hardware models adapted to the DoD model and used the TCP/IP protocol, compatibility was not an issue.

The original network media was existing telephone lines. Only plain ASCII text was exchanged, not graphics, sound, or animation. There was no exchange of e-mail, as we know it today. The DoD model was based on the simple concept of exchanging text materials using TCP/IP over the Internet. As networking systems became more robust with full multimedia features, many more types of networking media and security features evolved along with a more complex model.

The requirements of such advances led to the development of the OSI model, as we know it today. Software (protocol) developers and network equipment manufacturers use the OSI model as an outline when developing software and hardware devices.

The Institute of Electrical and Electronic Engineers (IEEE) is concerned with the electronic aspects of the OSI model. This organization is composed of engineers, students, scientists, and manufacturing representatives who form standards that promote interoperability of hardware devices. In other words, they set standards that ensure hardware, such as network adapter cards, cables, cable connectors, switches, and routers, will easily interconnect and support each other rather than be proprietary.

The IEEE organization is nonprofit and many members donate their time toward the development of the standards. Since the IEEE is concerned with the electrical aspects of network communications, they redesigned the OSI model to reflect their interests. The IEEE version of the OSI model splits the data link layer

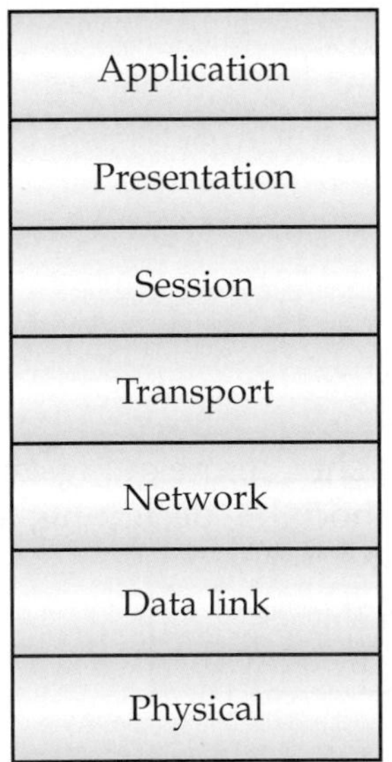

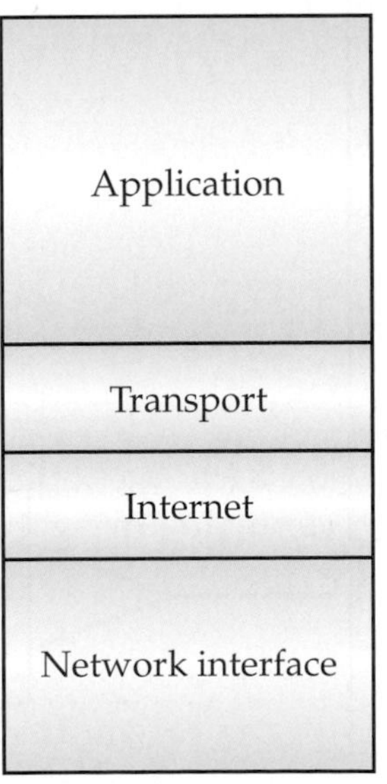

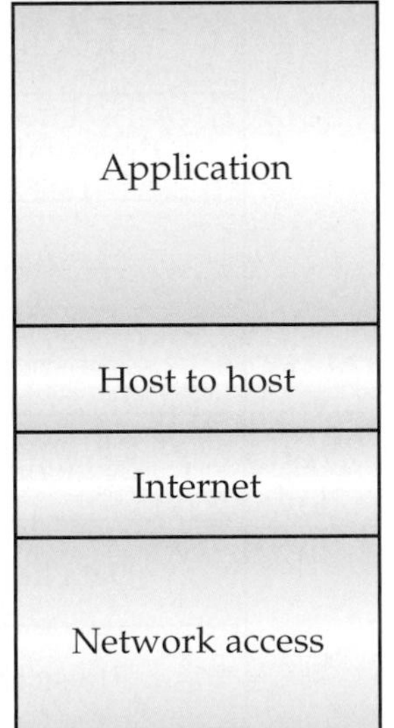

Figure 16-1.
The original DoD model was much simpler in design than the OSI model. Note that there are two versions of the DoD model.

into two sublayers: logical link control (LLC) and media access control (MAC). This version became known as the IEEE 802 model. See **Figure 16-2.**

Notice how the data link layer of the OSI model has been subdivided into the LLC sublayer and the MAC sublayer. The LLC sublayer communicates with the upper-level protocols and is software in nature. It is responsible for framing the contents of the upper levels and includes the node address of the source as identified by the network interface card's MAC address.

The MAC sublayer is concerned with accessing the network medium and converting the contents of the frame into a serial stream of bits that will be carried by copper core cable, fiber-optic cable, or by wireless means. There will be more about the data link layer later in the chapter.

The OSI Layers

This section takes a closer look at the layers of the OSI model. Compare the characteristics of the various OSI layers in **Figure 16-3.** The top four layers are primarily descriptions of software functions and are hardware independent. The software in these upper layers are Web browsers like Internet Explorer, Firefox, and Mozilla; e-mail clients; instant messaging; FTP; and such. The lower three levels are directly related to specific hardware types.

The physical and data link layers are dominated by hardware, especially the physical layer. Hardware consists of such devices as routers, switches, hubs, network interface cards, and cabling. Notice that the gateway is assigned to the upper layers of the OSI model. This is because the gateway acts as a translator when two different operating systems attempt to communicate. Remember that an operating system is software. The term *gateway* is often confused to mean a specific piece of equipment when in reality it is a software service typically installed on a router or server. The gateway translates the different file formats used to form packets. The gateway interprets the packets and then translates the contents.

The data link layer is where data in the packets are transformed into electrical digital pulses and then placed on the network medium such as copper cable,

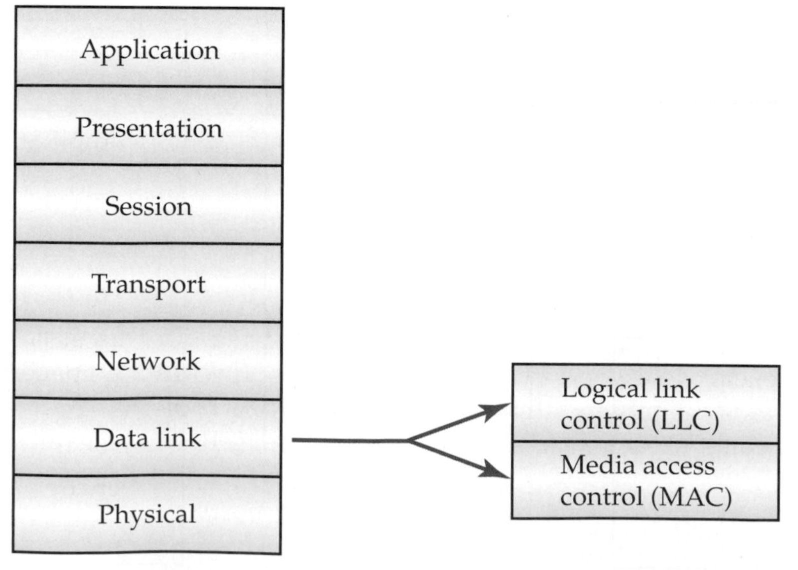

Figure 16-2. The revised OSI model, referred to as the *IEEE 802 model*, divides the data link layer into two sublayers: logical link control (LLC) and media access control (MAC).

OSI Layer	Function	Hardware	Protocols	Keywords
Application	User interface	Gateways	HTTP, FTP, WWW, SNAP, SMB, SMTP, Telnet, POP, IMAP	Browser, e-mail, network applications
Presentation	Convert to common format such as ASCII, data encryption, and compression	Gateways	MPEG, WAV, MIDI, QuickTime	ASCII, Unicode, EBCDIC, CODEC, and bit order
Session	Establish and close communication between two nodes Coordinates communication	Gateways	NFS, DNS, SQL, RPC, NetBIOS, X.25, SMB	Establish and terminate a communication session, log on, user name, password, authentication, assign services through port numbers
Transport	Sequence packets Ensure error free delivery Takes over after the session has been established	Gateways (layer 4 switches)	TCP, UDP, SPX	Segments, windowing, flow control, transport packets, error checking (if required), port numbers
Network	Navigates outside of the LAN	Routers (layer 3 switches)	IP, IPX, AppleTalk, ICMP, RIP, RIPv2, ARP, OSPF, IGRP, RARP, BGP, NLSP, IS-IS, EIRGP	IP address, routing, packets, datagrams, network address, packet switching, logical address, best and shortest route
Data Link	Prepares data for media access Defines frame format	Bridges, switches, Wireless Access Points, network interface cards	CSMA/CD, CSMA/CA, LLDP	MAC address, hardware address, LLC, CRC, frame types, frames, topologies, contention
Physical	The physical aspect of the network	Copper core cable, fiber-optic cable, wireless, hubs, repeaters, transceivers, amplifiers, transducers	NA	Bit, byte, cable, media, topology, transmission, voltage, digital signals

Figure 16-3. OSI layer comparison table.

fiber-optic cable, or wireless radio signals. The network layer is where hardware and software combine to allow packets to traverse great distances using the IP addressing scheme. It is also where the router is located. The router is responsible for routing packets based on the IP address contained within the packets. The network layer is designed with the WAN in mind. It is typically concerned with using IP for routing packets to and from distant hosts. IP can be used for a LAN as well.

There are many exceptions to the OSI model. No one networking system follows the model perfectly. Always remember that the OSI model is a suggested, voluntary model for network communications. It is not mandatory. It is an attempt to help unify network communications by serving as a design guideline. The following sections cover each OSI layer in more detail. Refer to Figure 16-3 as you read through them.

Application Layer

The application layer is where the networking application interfaces to the OSI model. The term *application* should not be confused with software applications such as spreadsheet, word processing, and database programs. You can think of the application layer as the location of the networking specific application. For example, FTP, HTTP, SMTP, SMB and Telnet reside at the top of the OSI model. Each of these high-level protocols typically represents a network application. The protocols at the application layer perform services such as Web browsing, exchanging e-mail messages, and file transfer, **Figure 16-4.**

For example, when an e-mail client (application) receives e-mail, it uses one of the various protocols designed for e-mail retrieval, such as POP3 or IMAP. POP3 and IMAP are application layer protocols. The e-mail client interface is a GUI. The user is completely unaware of the complexities behind the scenes, such as the data flowing up and down the OSI layers to receive the e-mail.

Presentation Layer

The presentation layer is concerned with negotiating a common set of symbols that the source and destination hosts can interpret. For example, the content of a message can be in ASCII format or coded as EBCDIC. You should recall that EBCDIC is the coding format IBM mainframes use to represent data, and ASCII is the format PCs use to represent data. The two coding schemes do not directly convert but rather must be interpreted to exchange data, **Figure 16-5.**

Both the destination and source must agree on the format used for coding information and compression. Compression techniques are generally referred to as *CODECs*. When security is an issue, the contents should be encrypted. The encryption method used will be one that can be interpreted by both ends of the communications link.

The exact sequence of bits is also of major concern of the presentation layer. The bit order of data can be read from left to right or from right to left. For example, the Motorola 68000 processor and the IBM 8086 processor read the stream of bits in the opposite order. In other words, the binary stream 11110000 from one computer

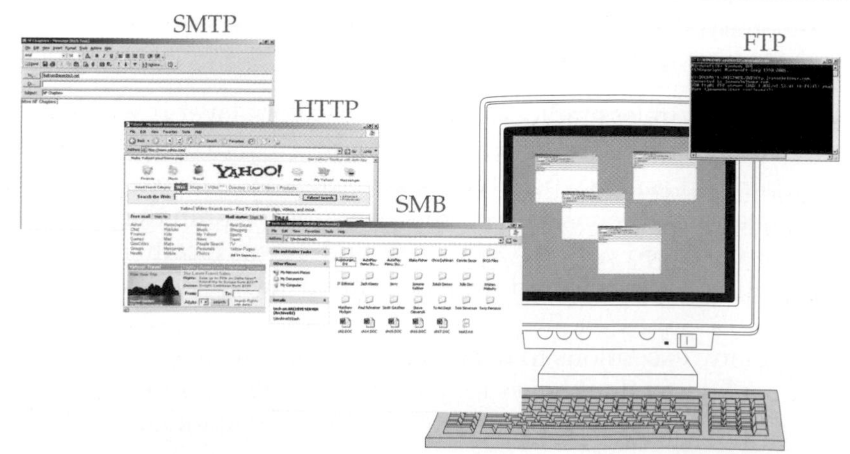

Figure 16-4.
The application layer is the OSI layer in which networking specific applications, such as SMTP, HTTP, SMB, and FTP, operate.

Figure 16-5.
The presentation layer negotiates a common set of symbols that the source and destination hosts can interpret. In this example, an ASCII text file is interpreted as EBCDIC.

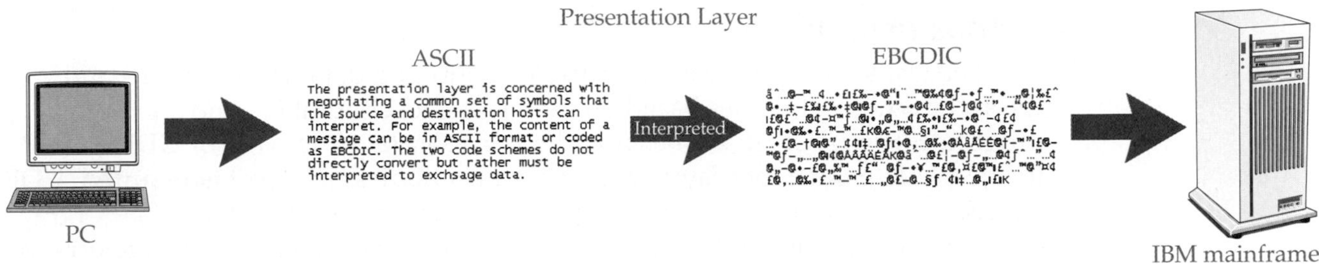

is represented as 00001111 on the other computer. The data binary pattern is reversed. This must be corrected before transmitting data. It is the responsibility of the presentation layer and associated protocols to correct the problem of bit order. In short, the presentation layer is concerned with packaging the raw data into a form that both the source and the destination can interpret.

Session Layer

The session layer establishes, maintains, and terminates the connection with the destination. It determines what the correct virtual connection is by matching the port number to the service required to support the layers above it. For example, when connecting to a distant location, not only does the IP address need to be encapsulated into the packet, the port number that corresponds with the provided service must also be encapsulated. If the requested port number is busy, the session layer determines if the connection can wait or if another port number can be assigned. System logon activities and passwords can take place during the session layer.

Communication between the two hosts must be synchronized. Synchronized means that each host must recognize the other is ready to communicate or end the session. Properly ending a session between two hosts is important. The connection must be released at both ends so the port addresses are freed for future communication. Therefore, there must be a way of letting both computers know when the session is over. To do this, the session layer resynchronizes the connection by regularly checking if both hosts desire to continue communicating.

The session layer is where differences in the programming mechanics or code are worked out for communicating between two nodes in the same network or distant networks. The session layer solves problems, such as how to establish a connection between nodes on the same system architecture and diverse architecture. For example, the session layer solves communication problems between a Windows client on an Ethernet network and an IBM Linux server on a Token Ring network.

Negotiations between the destination and source are accomplished using a token. A ***token*** is the name given to the packet that exchanges session information between the source and destination. Do not confuse the term *token* as used here with the term *token* used in Token Ring network technology.

token
the name given to the packet that exchanges session information between the source and destination.

The decisions determined at the session layer concerning the connection are carried out at the next layer, the data layer. For example, in the data layer, the port number is inserted into each segment that reflects the service requested or provided.

Some of the protocols closely associated with the session layer are DNS, X.25, NetBIOS, RPC, SMB, and NFS. When you think of the session layer, think of establishing, maintaining, and terminating a connection. See **Figure 16-6.**

Transport Layer

The transport layer provides reliable end-to-end data transmissions and error-checking techniques based on sequence packet numbers and software programs. For a TCP/IP connection, the transport layer uses either UDP or TCP to encapsulate the upper-layer data. If a connectionless protocol is required, UDP is used. If a connection-oriented protocol is required, TCP is used.

The integrity of the data is checked at the transport layer. The transport layer checks the contents of a frame and for the proper sequence of frames to ensure the data will be reassembled in the correct order at the destination. The transport layer is also where port numbers are inserted into the segments. Remember that the port number is assigned in the session layer, and the IP address is assigned in the network layer. Together, the port number and IP address form what is known as a *socket*.

The transport layer divides large blocks of data into smaller blocks of data. Dividing large blocks of data into smaller blocks of data is called *segmenting* and results in a segment. The segment is associated with the transport layer. The size of a typical segment is negotiated with the destination host. Together, the destination host and the source host decide the maximum size of each segment and the amount of segments that will be sent before requiring an acknowledgment, **Figure 16-7.** The process is often referred to as ***windowing,*** or ***flow control.***

windowing
the process of negotiating the maximum size of each segment and the amount of segments that will be sent before requiring an acknowledgment.

Windowing, or controlling the amount of data between two hosts is essential. A window size must be established between the destination and the source

Figure 16-6.
The session layer is concerned with deciding on a communications port and synchronization, establishing a common form of communication, and terminating the session.

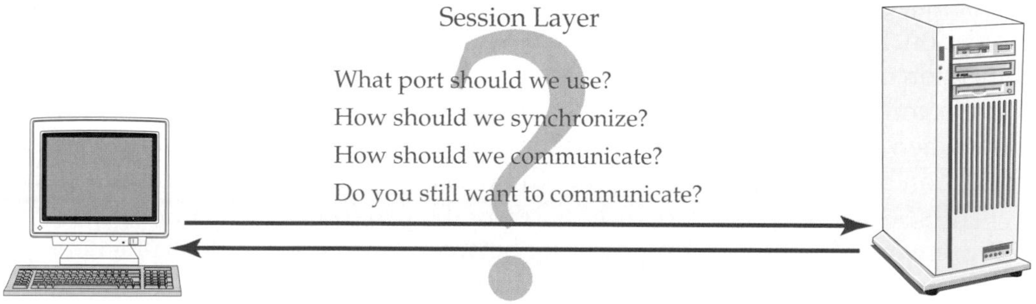

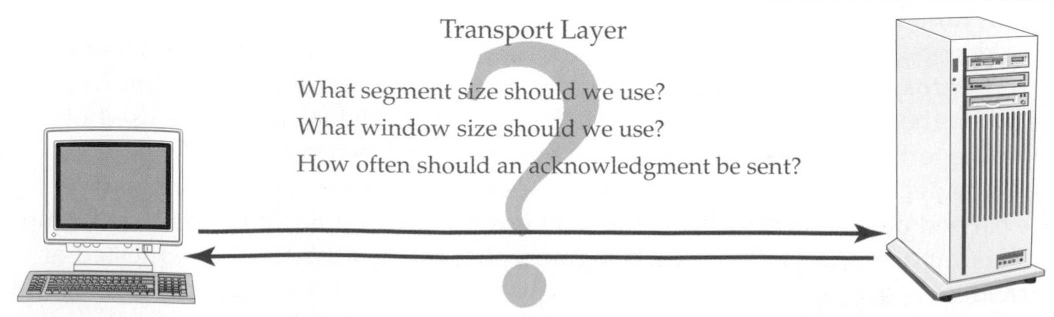

Figure 16-7.
The transport layer is concerned with determining the segment size and how often an acknowledgement should be sent.

before large volumes of data can be exchanged in the most efficient manner. The large blocks of data can be moved between two nodes using several different techniques. For example, a live telephone conversation needs to be moved as rapidly as possible without any form of acknowledgment between the two nodes. A data transmission consisting of a large, detailed graphic may require that each block of data delivered be confirmed to ensure integrity.

In the last scenario, the size of the packet must be determined. Both the source and destination must agree on the maximum size that can be transmitted between the two nodes. The size is based on physical factors such as the buffer size at each location. A ***buffer*** is a small amount of memory used to temporarily store data. If the packets sent exceed the buffer size at the destination, only the packets that fill the buffer are left intact. The rest are discarded.

buffer
a small amount of memory used to temporarily store data.

The next major issue of the windowing technique concerns the efficiency of delivering a large quantity of data packets. For instance, is it necessary to send a confirmation or acknowledgment after each packet has reached its destination? It may be more efficient to send an acknowledgment after several packets are received.

Part of the process of windowing is determining the error rate associated with data packet delivery. If the number of errors in delivery is low or nonexistent, then a large number of packets can be delivered before returning an acknowledgment to the sender. If the error rate is high, then an acknowledgment after every packet may be required. The size of the packets and how many are delivered before an acknowledgment from the destination is how windowing affects the efficiency of data exchange.

Network Layer

As the name of this layer implies, the network layer is concerned with navigating the network by using IP addresses, **Figure 16-8.** The network layer is where the IP address is added to the segment. The segment is turned into a packet by including the IP address of the destination and source with the port numbers that were inserted in the transport layer.

Packets are also referred to as *datagrams* by some reference materials.

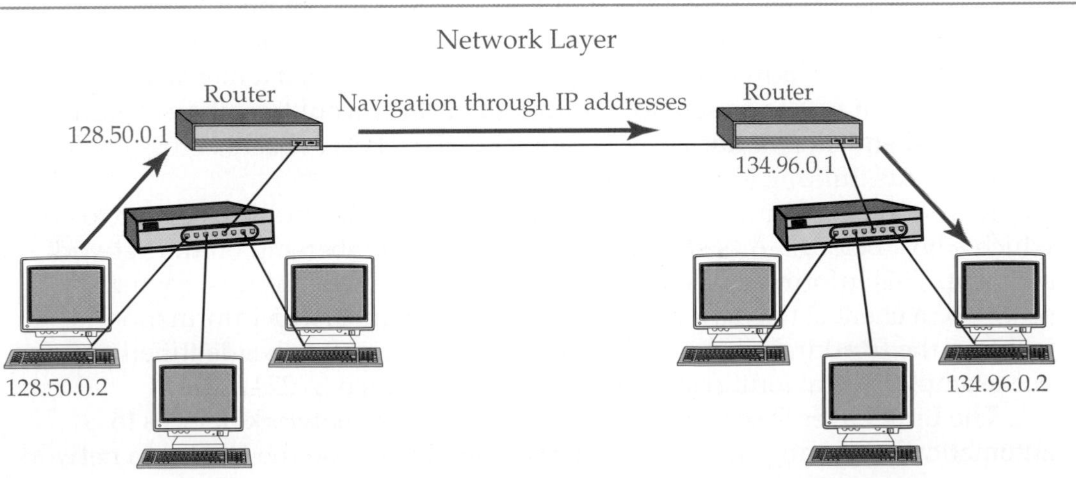

Figure 16-8. The network layer is concerned with navigating the network using IP addresses.

The network layer is associated with routers. You should recall from Chapter 1—Introduction to Networking that routers are devices that route packets to various networks based on the IP address inside the packet. This is the way packets are able to traverse the complexity of the World Wide Web.

The entire World Wide Web structure is composed of thousands of routers that are capable of directing the flow of packets to and from destination and source hosts based on IP addresses. The way each packet is forwarded depends on the routing protocol used. The most common router protocols are BGP, IGP, IGRP/EIGRP, IS-IS, NLSP, OSPF, RIP, RIPng, and RIP2. For detailed information on these protocols, see Chapter 11—Subnetting.

You should recall from Chapter 11—Subnetting that routers can be programmed to operate from static IP address tables or dynamic IP address tables. A static IP address table is a table of IP addresses entered manually. A dynamic IP address table is a table of IP addresses generated by routing protocols that communicate with nearby routers. The routing protocols allow routers to exchange IP address information automatically and build reference tables based on information that is exchanged with other routers.

The information contained in the router tables determines which network path is used to deliver the packet. The routing protocols are designed with specific variables in mind for forwarding packets. The variables include things to be considered such as the shortest path based on physical distance, time, and the cost of the connection. The cost is very important because there are numerous private, leased lines that can be used to transmit a packet. The cost may vary considerably between different vendors.

Some other protocols closely associated with the network layer are Address Resolution Protocol (ARP), Reverse Address Resolution Protocol (RARP), Internet Control Message Protocol (ICMP), Internet Group Management Protocol (IGMP), and Link Layer Discovery Protocol (LLDP). You should recall that ICMP is used to generate messages and carry commands inside an IP packet. Some of the more common messages deal with attempts to reach a destination. ICMP carries error messages regarding unreachable hosts and message timeouts based on the TTL value.

Internet Group Management Protocol (IGMP) is a TCP/IP protocol designed to support multicasting. ***Multicasting*** is sending the same data packet to a group of hosts identified by one IP address. Multicasting conserves bandwidth on a network because packets are identified for delivery to hosts that belong to a particular multicast group. When a message is sent to a multicast group, the single set of packets for that group reach a router and are then forwarded only to members of the multicast group. Without multicasting and the IGMP protocol, the same message would need to be sent to each member of the multicast group as individual sets of packets. For example, if a message contained 5 packets and it was to be sent to 20 different hosts, it would result in sending 100 packets. When using multicast, only one set of 5 packets are sent across the local network, thus limiting local area network traffic.

Internet Group Management Protocol (IGMP)
a TCP/IP protocol designed to support multicasting. It informs a multicast router of the names of the multicast group to which a host belongs.

multicasting
sending the same data packet to a group of hosts identified by one IP address.

IGMP informs a multicast router of the names of the multicast group to which a host belongs. A host broadcasts its group membership on the network segment. This information is recorded in a database on a multicast router, a server, or a client acting as a database container. Membership information includes the IP address of each client and the IP address of the identified group. For example, a local multicast group might be identified as 224.0.3.1.

The Link Layer Discovery Protocol (LLDP) allows network devices to automatically exchange information with other devices on the local area network that have LLDP configured. Microsoft incorporates LLDP in Windows Vista and later operating systems. Cisco Systems has a version of LLDP called Cisco Discovery Protocol (CDP).

A detailed study of routers and router protocols is beyond the scope of this textbook. To learn more about routers and routing protocols, visit the Cisco Systems Web site. Cisco Systems sponsors training academies throughout the United States dedicated to training Cisco router specialists. You may want to do a search to find the nearest Cisco academy to pursue additional training.

Data Link Layer

As mentioned in the beginning of this chapter, the data link layer was first defined by the ISO when it developed the OSI model. Later, the IEEE redefined the data link layer by dividing it into two sublayers called the LLC and the MAC. See **Figure 16-9** for a summary of LLC and MAC sublayer functions.

The IEEE published extensive details concerning the LLC, known as the IEEE 802.2 standard. The LLC sublayer is concerned with framing the contents of the upper levels, including the MAC addresses of the source and destination. The LLC sublayer deals with physical addresses rather than logical addresses. Remember that the MAC address that is programmed into every network interface card is used to uniquely identify network nodes along the network media.

The LLC sublayer also ensures the reliability of the physical connection rather than of the data contained within the frame. The error check performed at the LLC sublayer is much simpler in design than that performed at the transport layer. It consists of a Cyclic Redundancy Check (CRC). The CRC is incorporated into the Frame Check Sequence (FCS) field of the frame and represents the overall size of the frame, which includes the size of the header and the data. The CRC check uses a simple mathematical formula that checks the size of the entire frame when it is delivered at the destination data link layer or while in route to the destination.

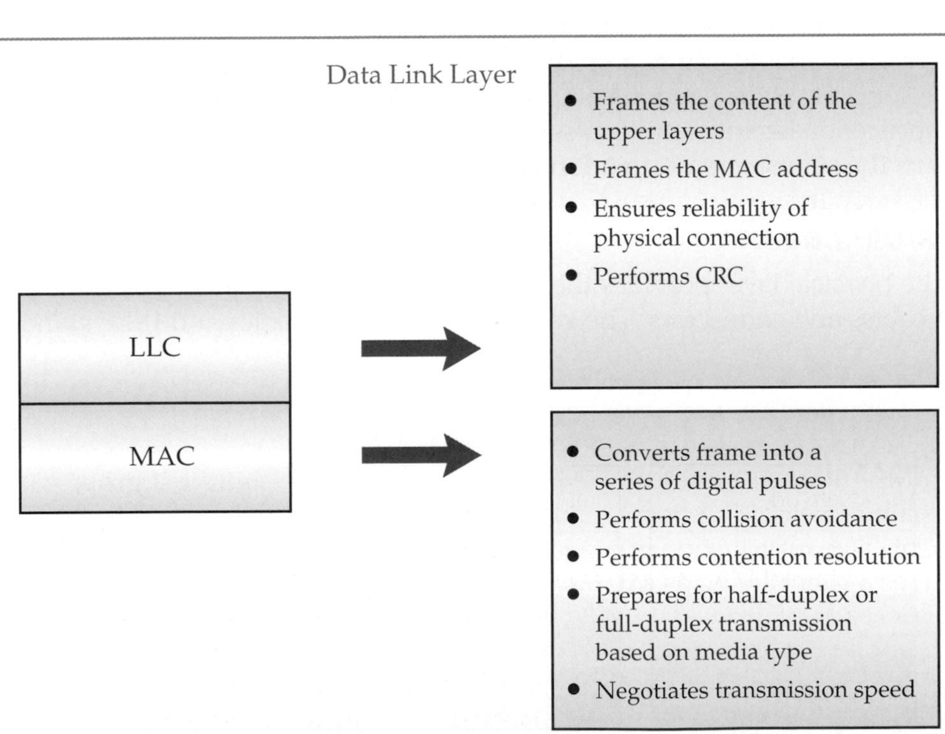

Figure 16-9. LLC and MAC sublayer functions.

Network+ Note

It is very easy to confuse the transport layer and the data link layer when asked a question about error checking in the OSI model. You must carefully read any questions concerning the OSI model and error checking and concentrate on what type of error is being checked. The transport layer is concerned about the content of the protocol data unit (PDU) while the data link layer is concerned about the overall content of the frame, which includes the data content. Think of the transport layer as ensuring error-free data or contents of the PDU. The data link layer looks at the entire frame based on the CRC and then decides to either pass the frame along or drop it entirely. The corruption may be in the header rather than the data content.

The MAC sublayer converts the frame and its contents into a series of digital pulses to be carried on the media (physical layer). For example, the binary electrical pulse sequence for Token Ring is different than wireless or Ethernet framing. Novell has used four different Ethernet framing techniques for communication in their NetWare network. Each of the four is slightly different. If two different frame types were used on two different computers in a NetWare network, the computers would not be able to communicate properly.

The IEEE standards such as Ethernet 802.3, Token Bus 802.4, and Token Ring 802.5 define the data link layer and the physical layer. **Figure 16-10** shows the relationship of many different standards that define various network media architecture and physical attributes. The standards are very detailed so that programmers and hardware designers can use it as a model for designing software and hardware devices. In other words, the standards address the type of materials to be used.

Service Access Point (SAP)
a combination of MAC address and a number that identifies a protocol and its service. SAP addresses exist for the source and destination computer. It provides a means of direct communication between protocols at different layers of the OSI model and between the source and destination computers.

The data link layer uses Service Access Points (SAPs) to communicate with protocols at various layers of the OSI model. The MAC and LLC also each have a SAP and use it to communicate with one another. The SAP is used in similar fashion as a port address, which is used to exchange information between computers. The ***Service Access Point (SAP)*** consists of a MAC address and a number that identifies a protocol and its service. SAP addresses exist for the source and destination computer. The SAP provides a means of direct communication between protocols at different layers of the OSI model and between the source and destination computers.

Physical Layer

The physical layer provides the path for the raw digital pulses that are moved along cables and connectors. The various network topologies and IEEE standards

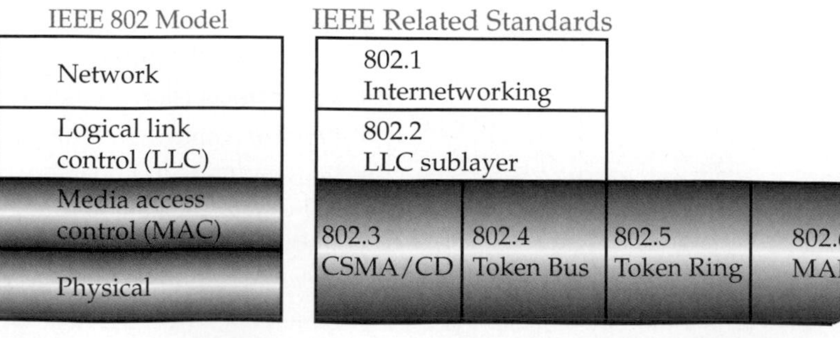

Figure 16-10. The majority of IEEE standards deal with the physical layer and the MAC sublayer.

for equipment are identified at this layer. For example, the type of connectors used for various mediums such as BNC, RJ-45, D-shell, RS-232, ST, and SC connectors. Exact dimensions of connectors, materials, voltage level, frequency, data rates, Baseband and Broadband signaling techniques, and any other concerns about the physical communications circuit between the destination and source is described at this layer.

The Encapsulation Process

Encapsulation is the process of adding information to the segment that identifies such things as the source address, the destination address, the end of the segment, and the size of the segment. The size of a segment is determined by the protocol selected to communicate between two points. Segments have additional information added, which is necessary in order to complete the transmission from one point to another. For example, if the data is transferred across a vast distance using the Internet, information such as the destination IP address and the source IP address must be added. Also, a sequence number must be added to ensure the segments are rearranged in the proper order and that no segments are missing. The following is a summary of the encapsulation process:

- User data is converted into standard data format such as ASCII and EBCDIC.
- Data is broken into segments.
- Segments are placed into packets and header information is added.
- Packets are placed into frames and more header information is added.
- Frames are converted into a serial stream of data.
- The serial stream of data is converted to digital pulses.

Refer to **Figure 16-11** as the process of encapsulating raw data into a frame at the source and then disassembling the frame at the destination is reviewed. To transfer data between two locations, the source and destination must first establish a connection with each other. We will assume that the connection between the two points has been established and the data format, communication rules, encryption (if necessary), security, and any other communication details

Application	Connection between the two points has been established and the data format, communication rules, encryption, security, and any other communication details have been agreed on
Presentation	
Session	
Transport	Segment
Network	Packet
Data link	Frame/bit stream
Physical	Digital signals

Figure 16-11. Data flow and packaging in relation to the OSI model.

have been agreed on. All these concerns are accomplished mainly at the top three layers: application, presentation, and session.

Next, the data is divided into small units. This process is referred to as *data segmentation* or simply *segmenting*. A segment of data is simply a portion of the total amount of raw data broken into sizes that can be handled. The size is decided when the source and destination negotiate their connection and set up their rules for communication.

Each segment is placed into a packet. First, the segment is typically enclosed in either a UDP or TCP envelope. If a large amount of data is to be transferred, TCP is used for constructing the envelope. Since TCP is used to carry the data segment, a port number must be assigned. The port number is necessary to set up a constant connection with the other workstation and to acknowledge the data has arrived intact or not. If only a small amount of data such as a command were sent between the source and destination, UDP could be used. UDP does not require a port number because it does not require verification that the data was delivered.

After a segment has been enclosed in a TCP envelope, it is enclosed in a packet. The packet adds the IP address to the envelope carrying the data. An IP address for the destination and source are included in every packet.

Next, each packet is enclosed in a frame. A frame adds the MAC address for the destination and source to the packet. The frame is converted into a serial stream of data and then converted to digital pulses and placed on the network media. The type of media, such as Ethernet, Token Ring, or wireless is identified in the frame. The MAC address is used to move the frame through the LAN. The MAC address identifies the workstation and equipment along the LAN path until the frame reaches the outer edge of the LAN. When the frame encounters the first piece of Internet equipment, typically a router, the MAC address is stripped away, leaving the IP address of the source and destination. Remember that the Internet uses IP addresses to locate nodes, not MAC addresses. The frame can travel over thousands of miles using only an IP address to find the destination network.

When the frame reaches the destination LAN, the network operating system uses ARP to resolve the IP address to a MAC address. Inside the destination LAN, the MAC address identifies the final destination node or workstation. At the destination, the envelopes around the data are stripped away until the raw data is revealed. The segments of raw data are put back together in proper sequence to display the data at the destination. The data could be plain text or multimedia. Any missing segments invoke a request for retransmission.

This is the classic explanation of how data is transported across the Internet. At this point, it might seem that each level of the OSI model only takes one or two frames for communication to take place, but that is far from reality. Even a simple request takes many steps to perform. The OSI model is at best an abstract model of how network communications should work. In reality, an actual network communication sequence is more complex.

Figure 16-12 shows a screen capture of the Microsoft Network Monitor utility. A series of frames are captured as related to the network devices identified in the left pane. The frame details (bottom pane) reveal the encapsulated protocols for each frame. In this particular set of frame captures you can see the Microsoft SMB2 protocol, which is being used to negotiate a sharing transaction between two network devices. The frame capture sequence involves both IPv4 and IPv6.

A great reference for information about protocol encapsulation can be found at the WildPackets Web site: www.wildpackets.com. You may wish to view its collection of white papers as well as its seminar series.

Figure 16-12.
The Microsoft Network Monitor utility can be used to capture and analyze frames.

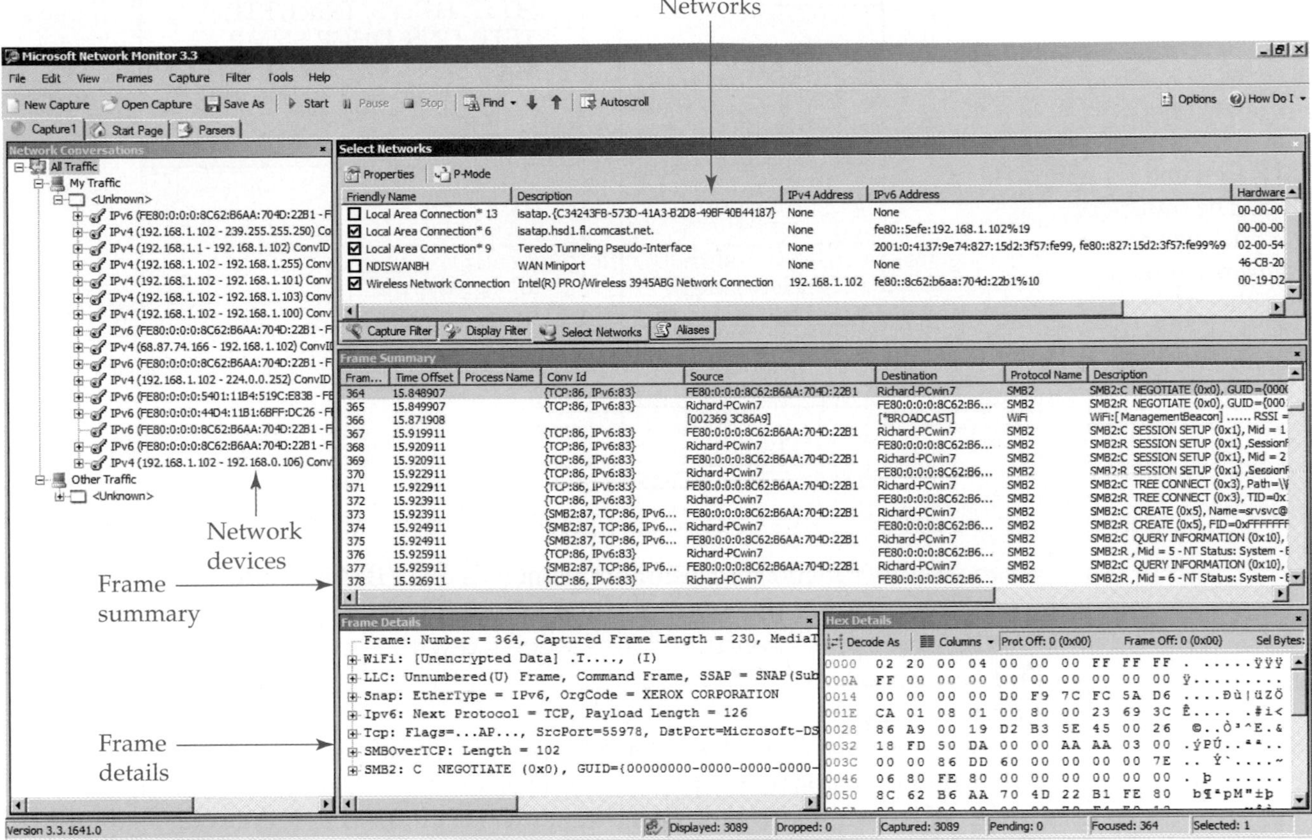

The OSI Model and the Major Protocol Suites

The OSI model was developed after the majority of network protocols were already in use. As a result, not all network protocols match neatly to the OSI model design. For example, many protocols must span more than one layer to be properly represented when compared to the OSI model. Typically, higher-level protocols can perform multiple functions that span several layers of the OSI model. This section takes a closer look at how the dominate protocols of the major network operating systems compare to the OSI model.

TCP/IP Protocols

Look at **Figure 16-13.** The TCP/IP protocol suite is collected into three main areas: the top layers, which consist of the application, presentation, and session layer; the transport layer; and the network layer. The top layers are concerned with application protocols, such as HTTP, FTP, and Telnet. The transport layer packages the upper-level protocols into either TCP or UDP segments. The network layer encapsulates the TCP or UDP segments into packets. The protocols used at the network layer are IP, ICMP, and ARP.

Novell IPX/SPX Protocols

Novell developed a proprietary set of protocols referred to as the *Internetwork Packet Exchange/Sequenced Packet Exchange (IPX/SPX)* protocol suite. The IPX/SPX

Figure 16-13.
The TCP/IP protocol suite is collected into three main areas. The top layers are concerned with application protocols, such as HTTP, FTP, and Telnet. The transport layer packages the upper-level protocols into either TCP or UDP segments. The network layer encapsulates the TCP or UDP into IP packets.

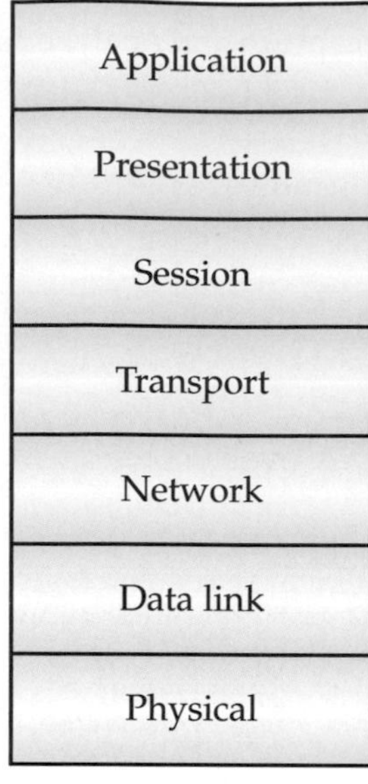

Application, Presentation, Session	HTTP, HTTPS, Telnet, FTP, TFTP, DNS, DHCP, SNMP, SMTP, POP, IMAP, NTP
Transport	TCP, UDP
Network	IP, ICMP, ARP

protocol suite functions in a similar fashion as TCP/IP. **Figure 16-14** shows how the NetWare protocols align with the OSI model. The NetWare Core Protocol (NCP) handles the upper-layer functions associated with application, presentation, and session layers. NCP provides services between the server and clients and provides support for file services, Novell Directory Services (NDS), printing, messages, security, network synchronization, auditing, and more. The Service Advertising Protocol (SAP) is used to locate servers and services on the network. Tables of information, such as the server hosting the service and its location, are typically located on routers to assist in locating the desired service and server.

Internetwork Packet Exchange (IPX) is the original network layer protocol used to route packets in the Novell NetWare network. When routed outside the NetWare network and across the Internet, IPX is encapsulated inside the IP packet. IPX is a connectionless protocol responsible for identifying destination

Figure 16-14.
The IPX/SPX protocol suite.

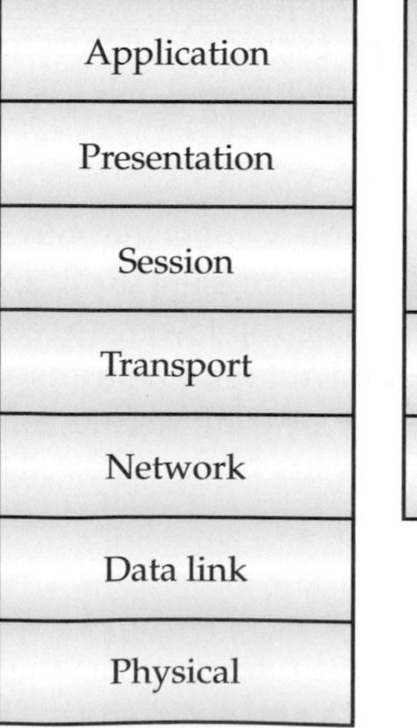

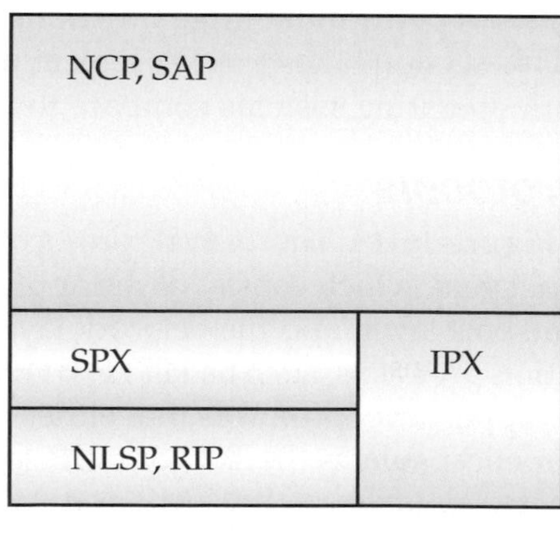

and source network, node, and socket. Sequenced Packet Exchange (SPX) is a connection-oriented protocol designed to enhance IPX by guaranteeing packet delivery. SPX is similar in function to TCP, while IPX can be compared to IP.

RIP and NLSP, as mentioned earlier in this chapter, are routing protocols. NetWare Link Services Protocol (NLSP) was developed by Novell to overcome some of the limitations of RIP and SAP. Both RIP and SAP work on small networks, but for large networks a better protocol such as NLSP is needed. For example, RIP is limited to 15 hops and NLSP is limited to 127 hops. NLSP uses smaller packet sizes than RIP and SAP. It also supports multicasting.

The lower layers are designed to be physical and data link independent, which means that Novell NetWare can communicate over various vendor equipment.

As TCP/IP has become the de facto standard for Internet communications, Novell has offered native support for TCP/IP since NetWare 5. IPX/SPX is still offered in NetWare 5 systems a choice of protocols, mainly to ensure downward compatibility within older existing NetWare systems.

AppleTalk Protocols

The AppleTalk Filing Protocol (AFP) handles functions associated with the application and presentation layers. As the name implies, AFP provides services for file sharing, printing, messages, and other upper-layer services. The session layer aligns with the Zone Information Protocol (ZIP), AppleTalk Session Protocol (ASP), and AppleTalk Data Stream Protocol (ADSP). ADSP provides functions for full-duplex communication. Note that ADSP spans both the session layer and the transport layer. Not all protocols align perfectly with the OSI model. See **Figure 16-15.**

ASP provides general support for communications between the server and clients. ZIP provides support for zone information and name resolution. AppleTalk divides the network into zones, which is the equivalent to groups or workgroups.

OSI layer	AppleTalk protocols	
Application	AFP	
Presentation		
Session	ASP, ZIP	ADSP
Transport	AEP, ATP, NBP, RTMP	
Network	DDP	
Data link	LocalTalk	
Physical		

Figure 16-15.
The AppleTalk protocol suite is similar in function to TCP/IP and IPX/SPX protocol suites. Both IPX/SPX and AppleTalk are designed to be data link independent, which allows both protocol suites to be used with a variety of technologies.

The transport layer aligns with AppleTalk Transaction Protocol (ATP), AppleTalk Echo Protocol (AEP), Name Binding Protocol (NBP), and Routing Table Maintenance Protocol (RTMP). These various protocol functions combine collectively to ensure reliable data communication.

At the network layer is the Datagram Delivery Protocol (DDP). It is a best effort, connectionless protocol similar in design to IP and IPX. There is no one matching protocol to ensure data delivery at this level. DDP relies on upper-level protocols to ensure accurate delivery of data.

The lower level of the AppleTalk protocol suite is denoted by the LocalTalk protocol. LocalTalk supports communication on an Apple LAN by providing support for Apple networking devices. Apple can also communicate with other standard interfaces such as Ethernet, Token Ring, and FDDI.

Tech Tip

Both Apple and Novell protocols can be placed inside IP and be transported across the Internet.

AppleShare IP Protocols

AppleShare is a networking suite developed by and for Macintosh computers based on the AppleTalk protocol. AppleShare IP is an improvement over AppleShare and is a protocol suite based on AppleShare and TCP/IP. AppleShare IP provides services over the Internet or LAN using IP addresses instead of node identification as in AppleTalk. By using the IP address as a means of location identification, AppleShare IP can provide remote printing and file sharing using the TCP/IP protocol suite of protocols. AppleShare IP provides three types of file sharing technology: Apple File Sharing (AFP) over TCP/IP, SMB/CIFS over TCP/IP, and File Transfer Protocol (FTP). In addition, it provides common network services such as Web hosting, e-mail, and DNS.

With the introduction of the Mac OS X server operating system in 2001, AppleShare IP became obsolete. The latest version of Mac OS X provides support for sharing resources with older Macintosh computers through AFP. Mac OS X supports SMB/CIFS, FTP, and NFS for sharing resources with modern day computers.

Today, all modern network and desktop operating systems are based on the TCP/IP suite of protocols and have basically abandoned or have very limited support for their earlier native protocols. Also, all modern operating systems support IPv6 and are ready for the complete transition from IPv4 to IPv6 on the Internet.

Request For Comments (RFC)

Request For Comments (RFC) a series of technical reports and proposals concerning protocols and network standards.

The ***Request For Comments (RFC)*** is a series of technical reports and proposals concerning protocols and network standards. The Internet Engineering Task Force and other closely related organizations publish RFCs. RFCs continuously evolve as new technologies are implemented. Each RFC is assigned a unique identification number and name such as RFC 2131 Dynamic Host Configuration Protocol. There are several classifications of RFC documents such as the approved Internet standard, proposed Internet standard, and Internet best practices.

When a proposal is first submitted, it is viewed as a proposed Internet standard and is circulated in draft form. The draft form tells all concerned that the proposal is open for discussion and comment but has not yet been formally adopted.

Approved Internet standards have been examined by a special committee and formally adopted as a standard. Standards are provided to help manufacturers, computer programmers, scientists, and such to develop resources conforming to standard lines of communication. You have already seen how protocols have a set sequence of fields that provide certain types of information. Once the protocol standard has been accepted, the standard can be used as a basis for designing other software and hardware to interface with the protocol.

Anyone can write a proposal for an RFC. It is an open forum, but there are some guidelines that an RFC must follow before it can be accepted as a proposal. The guidelines spell out the written format of the proposal. For example, it may only be written in standard ASCII text with a maximum of 72 characters per line; a maximum height of 58 lines followed by an end of page character, such as a form feed (FF); a suggested table of contents; and rules about the size of the page and margins. There can be no special additional features added to the ASCII characters, such as underlining or double strike. The text must be kept as plain as possible because it will be converted into other forms for storage and transmission, such as FTP. You can visit www.rfc-editor.org to see the typical layout of an RFC.

Summary

- The OSI model is an abstract representation of data communications developed by the ISO.
- Network systems do not necessarily exactly match all layers of the OSI model.
- The application layer is where the user interfaces with the network system using network programs such as a Web browser, FTP, Telnet, and an e-mail client.
- The presentation layer is concerned with bit sequence and with using an acceptable data format such as ASCII, EBCDIC, and CODEC.
- The session layer is concerned with establishing, maintaining, and terminating a connection between two nodes.
- The transport layer is concerned with providing reliable, accurate data in the most efficient manner.
- The network layer is where IP addressing is inserted into a packet and where decisions based on IP addresses are made.
- The data link layer is where frames are converted into a serial stream of data and decisions based on MAC addresses are made.
- The physical layer provides the path for digital signals and represents the media, connectors, and passive components.
- While the OSI model tends to make encapsulation appear simple and direct, actual communication is complex and generates hundreds or even thousands of frames while carrying out the simplest of networking tasks.
- Novell NetWare IPX is a connectionless protocol, and SPX is a connection-oriented protocol.

- AppleTalk Datagram Delivery Protocol (DDP) is a connectionless protocol used to route packets across a network.
- AppleTalk Datagram Delivery Protocol (DDP) relies on upper-level protocols to form connection-oriented communication.
- The Apple LocalTalk protocol is used to access network media in an Apple network environment.
- AppleShare IP is a protocol suite based on AppleShare and TCP/IP.

Review Questions

Answer the following questions on a separate sheet of paper. Please do not write in this book.

1. How does the ISO OSI model compare with the DoD model?
2. Why is the DoD model so simple when compared to the OSI model?
3. What is the major difference between the ISO version of the OSI model and the IEEE 802 version of the OSI model?
4. The IEEE divided the data link layer into two sublayers. What are the two sublayers called?
5. Briefly describe the function of each IEEE data link sublayer.
6. At which layer of the OSI model does a network interface card operate?
7. At which layer of the OSI model does a hub operate?
8. At which layers of the OSI model does a gateway operate?
9. At which later of the OSI model does a router operate?
10. Match the following terms to their definitions.

1. Application	A. Cabling and connectors.
2. Presentation	B. Converts frames codes to a serial stream of data.
3. Session	C. Responsible for connecting across WAN systems.
4. Transport	D. Repackages long messages into smaller units.
5. Network	E. Establishes rules for communication between two computers.
6. Data link	F. Translates data into a common compatible format.
7. Physical	G. File transfer service, e-mail, and Web browser programs.

11. At which layer does windowing take place?
12. At which layer is the MAC address inserted into the frame?
13. To which two layers of the OSI model do the IEEE 802.3 standards relate?
14. To which two layers of the OSI model do the Token Ring standards relate?
15. Briefly describe the encapsulation process.
16. Which Novell protocols align with the upper layers of the OSI model?
17. Which Novell protocol is similar in function to IP?
18. Which Novell protocol is similar in function to TCP?
19. Which Apple protocol is similar in function to IP?
20. What Apple protocol is used to access the network media?
21. Which Apple protocol aligns with the upper two layers of the OSI model?
22. How does the Apple protocol suite ensure delivery of data if the Datagram Delivery Protocol (DDP) is a connectionless protocol?
23. What does the acronym RFC mean?
24. Who may write an RFC proposal?

Sample Network+ Exam Questions

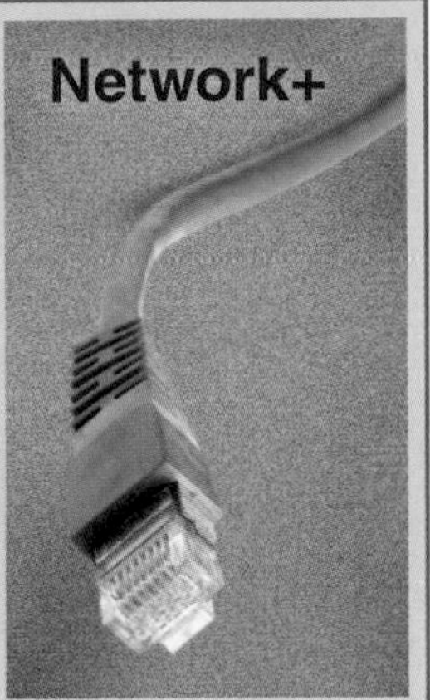

Answer the following questions on a separate sheet of paper. Please do not write in this book.

1. What is the name of the two sublayers of the data link layer as defined by the IEEE 802 standard?
   A. Network layer, session access control
   B. Logical link control, media access control
   C. Protocol control, data control
   D. Physical layer, network layer
2. Which is the correct order of encapsulation moving from the application layer to the data link layer?
   A. Packet, segment, frame, raw data
   B. Raw data, segment, frame, packet
   C. Frame, packet, segment, raw data
   D. Raw data, segment, packet, frame
3. Which of the following protocols are closely or directly related to the network layer? (Select all that apply.)
   A. HTTP
   B. ARP
   C. RIP
   D. TCP
   E. UDP
   F. IP
   G. FTP
4. Which of the following protocols are connectionless? (Select all that apply.)
   A. UDP
   B. TCP
   C. IP
   D. SPX
5. Which of the following statements best describe the transport layer?
   A. Provides an end-to-end connection with reliable and efficient data transfer.
   B. Provides routing information using IP addresses when sending packets across a WAN.
   C. Converts the data into an acceptable form such as ASCII.
   D. Provides services to the client such as Web browsing.
6. Which IEEE standard is responsible for detailed information concerning the LLC?
   A. 802.2
   B. 802.4
   C. 802.6
   D. 802.16
7. Which two items are used to create a socket? (Select all that apply.)
   A. IP address
   B. MAC address
   C. Port number
   D. NetBIOS name

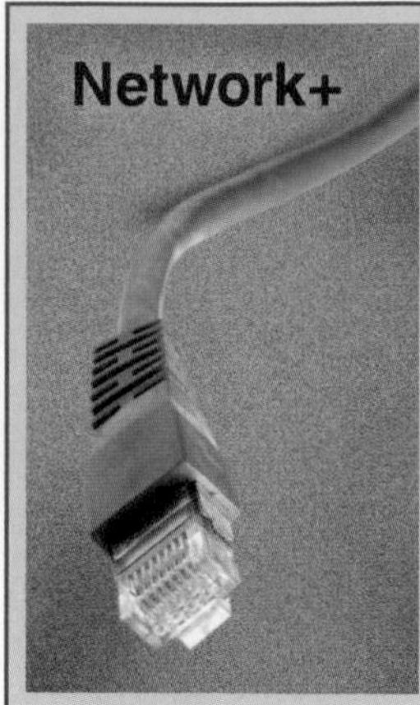

8. At which layer of the OSI model do routers operate?
   A. Application
   B. Session
   C. Network
   D. Data link
9. Which OSI layer is responsible for checking frame errors based on Cyclic Redundancy Checks (CRC)?
   A. Application
   B. Session
   C. Network
   D. Data link
10. With which layer of the OSI model would an RJ-45 connector be associated?
    A. Application
    B. Transport
    C. Physical
    D. Network

Suggested Laboratory Activities

1. Install Microsoft Network Monitor. Generate frames by using common functions such as **ping**, **tracert**, and opening a share. Capture a series of frames. An excellent experiment is to start a capture while there is no activity on the network. Then, turn on another PC. Observe the activity created when a workstation boots and joins the network.
2. Go to the CompTIA Web site and look at the Network+ Certification exam objectives. List all of the protocols that are listed in the objectives. Write out the complete name for each acronym. Write a brief description of each.
3. Visit the www.iso.org Web site and see what standards they are responsible for.

Interesting Web Sites for More Information

www.certyourself.com
www.ietf.org
www.lex-con.com/osimodel.htm
www.protocols.com
www.split.org/storage/osireference.pdf
www.wildpackets.com/support/

Chapter 16 Laboratory Activity

Wireshark OSI Model Exploration

After completing this laboratory activity, you will be able to:

- Use the Wireshark Network Protocol Analyzer to match protocols to the OSI model.
- Identify the protocols responsible for MAC address, IP address, and port numbers.
- Explain how protocols encapsulate data and other protocols.

Introduction

In this laboratory activity, you will use the Wireshark Network Protocol Analyzer to compare the relationship of specific protocols to the layers of the OSI model. You can typically determine the OSI layer a protocol aligns with by looking at its relative position in the hierarchy of protocols in the Wireshark program. Look at the following screen capture. Notice that the hierarchy of protocols is displayed in the middle pane of the Wireshark screen. Each frame that is selected displays its own hierarchy. The typical hierarchy lists at the top of the pane the protocol related to the bottom-most OSI layer.

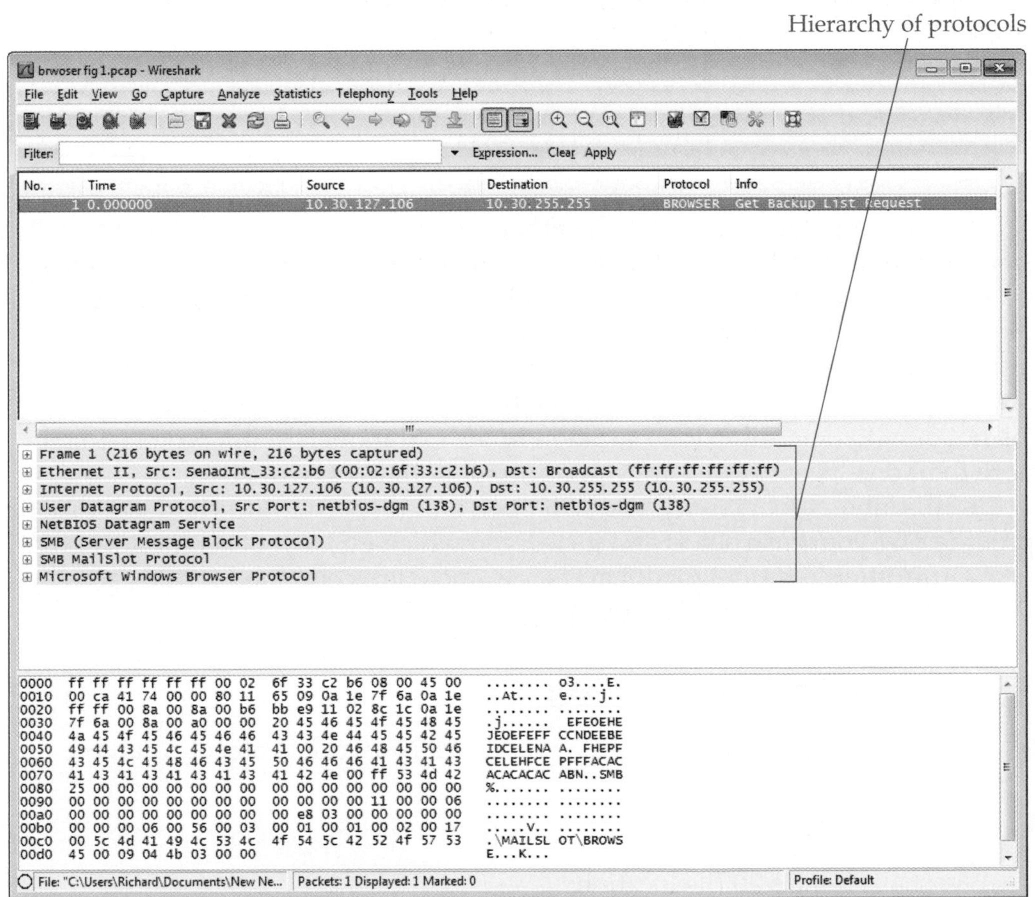

Clicking the box with a plus sign in it can reveal more information about each protocol listed in the hierarchy. This information may reveal items such as source, destination, MAC, and port addresses.

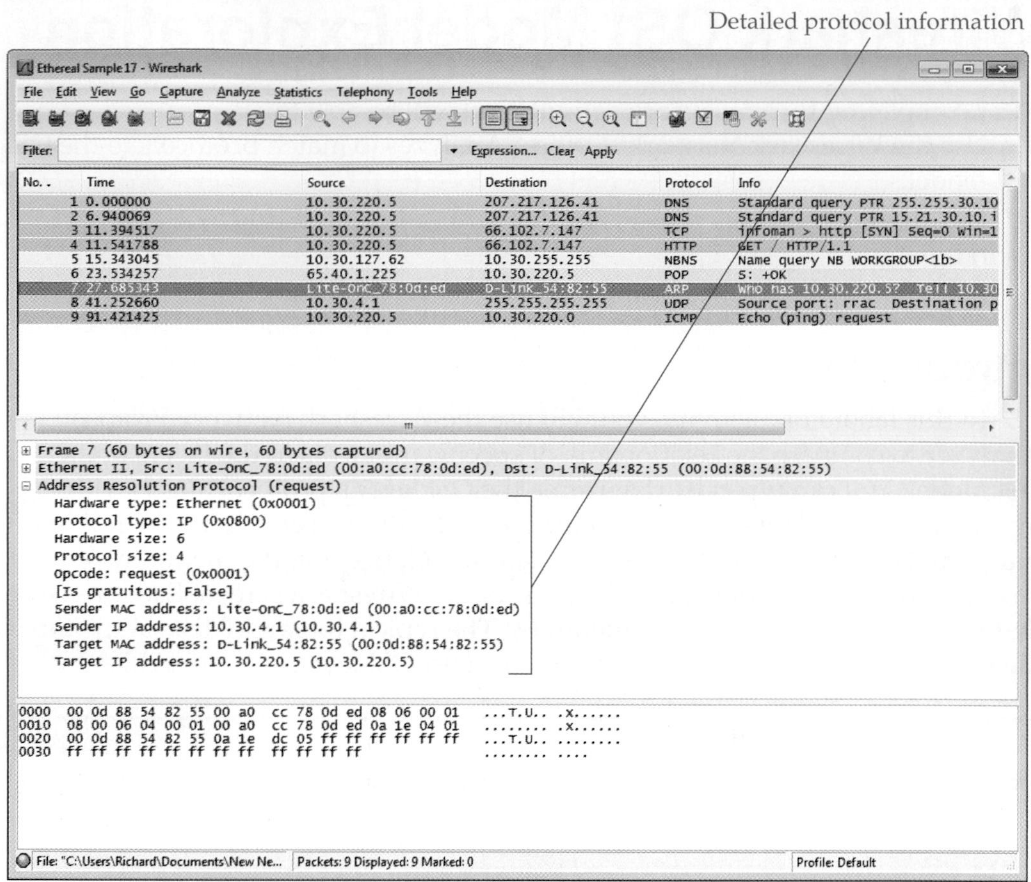

According to the OSI model, the Ethernet II protocol is a layer 2 protocol. It contains the MAC address of the destination and source. The Internet Protocol is a layer 3 protocol. It contains the IP address of the destination and source. The User Datagram Protocol is a layer 4 protocol. It contains the source and destination port numbers. The remaining protocols are upper-level protocols (layers 5, 6, and 7). Unless you know the function of these upper-level protocols, it is not easy to determine their location in the OSI model. Many protocols span more than one layer because they perform more than one function.

In this laboratory activity, you will open and inspect a Wireshark capture file (provided by your instructor) and identify to which OSI layer each protocol in the capture should be assigned. Layers 5, 6, and 7 are combined for this activity. Layer 1 does not exist for this activity.

Equipment and Materials

- Windows 7 workstation with the Wireshark Network Protocol Analyzer installed.
- Wireshark Sample 20 file.

  Wireshark Sample 20 file location: ______________________________

Procedure

1. ______ Report to your assigned workstation.
2. ______ Boot the computer and verify it is in working order.
3. ______ Start the Wireshark Network Protocol Analyzer utility.
4. ______ Open the Wireshark Sample 20 file.
5. ______ Copy the following chart onto a separate sheet of paper. For each protocol displayed in the capture, place an *X* in the corresponding OSI model layer in the chart and write out the protocol name.

Protocol	Layer 2	Layer 3	Layer 4	Layers 5,6,7	Protocol Name
Ethernet II					
ARP					
IP					
TCP					
UDP					
SMTP					
POP					
NBNS					
HTTP					
SMB2					
DNS					
LLMNR					
ICMP					
RIPv2					

6. ______ After completing the chart, go on to answer the review questions.
7. ______ Return the workstation to its original condition.

Review Questions

Answer the following questions on a separate sheet of paper. Please do not write in this book.

1. Which protocol was found at layer 2 throughout this lab activity?
2. Which protocols were found at layer 3 throughout this lab activity?
3. Which protocols were found at layer 4 throughout this lab activity?
4. Which protocols were not specifically identified, but are typically found at layers 5, 6, and 7?
5. What protocols are used to encapsulate the upper-level (5, 6, and 7) protocols?

6. Which protocol uses the MAC address to identify the location of the destination and source?
7. Which protocol uses the IPv4 address to locate the source and destination?
8. Which protocols use the port number to identify the source and destination?
9. Explain how protocol encapsulation provides all the required information for data packet delivery.

17 Maintaining the Network

After studying this chapter, you will be able to:

- ❑ Use a baseline to determine the performance of a network or server.
- ❑ Carry out general procedures for installing patches, upgrades, and service packs.
- ❑ Give examples of commonly accepted practices for protecting data.
- ❑ Identify types of fault tolerance.
- ❑ Distinguish between fault tolerance and disaster recovery.
- ❑ Compare server data backup strategies.
- ❑ Differentiate between a continuous UPS system and a standby UPS system.
- ❑ Give examples of commonly accepted antivirus procedures and policies.

Network+ Exam—Key Points

Questions concerning maintaining the network are drawn from such topics as patches, upgrades, and fixes; data backup strategies; antivirus procedures; disaster recovery; and fault tolerance. Maintaining the network requires knowledge about all aspects of networking and of some basic concepts associated with PC support.

Even if you do not have access to your own Windows server, you can still become very familiar with network maintenance because many of the tools discussed here are almost identical in Windows desktop operating systems.

Key Words and Terms

The following words and terms will become important pieces of your networking vocabulary. Be sure you can define them.

antivirus suite
archive bit
average utilization
backdoor virus
baseline
blackout
brownout
bug
cluster
cold spare
continuous UPS
differential backup
disaster recovery
electrical spike
electrical surge
frame size average
frame size peak
full backup
generator
hoax
hot spare
incremental backup
isolation transformer
joke program
lightning arrestor
logic bomb
macro
macro virus
malware
MBR virus
password virus
peak utilization
polymorphic virus
power conditioning
scan engine
service pack
Simple Network Management Protocol (SNMP)
standby UPS
stealth virus
swap file
system migration
Trojan horse
Uninterruptible Power Supply (UPS)
virus
virus pattern file
worm

Network+ Note

Be aware that you may see A+ type questions on the Network+ Certification exam.

A network only comes to a user's attention after it fails or is slow to respond to a user's requests. In reality, after a network is installed, it requires constant maintenance to be in near perfect condition and to ensure data integrity. Only with constant maintenance will the network be in good condition to ensure user satisfaction and smooth company operation.

This chapter introduces some new concepts and reintroduces some concepts that have been taught much earlier. Earlier concepts are applied directly to network maintenance. Most of the maintenance of a network system is the result of constant monitoring by the network administrator. While the network technician may perform routine daily maintenance under the direction of the network administrator, the administrator is ultimately responsible for the type, extent, and frequency of the maintenance to be performed.

Monitoring the Server and Network

The network system needs to be constantly monitored to determine when failures occur and to predict possible or imminent failure. Activity can be monitored, recorded, and expressed statistically to predict failure. For example, as a company grows, so will the amount of network traffic generated by the number of employees and customers. Statistical data based on network media bandwidth, total CPU activity, data storage space, and memory utilization can be monitored, and a predicted failure rate can be forecasted through data analysis.

The predictions are based on system history. For example, if a company consumes storage space at a rate of 6% per month, network storage will be compromised in less than 18 months. A server's CPU activity can be monitored, such as when and how often CPU utilization reaches 100%. Another example is memory (RAM) activity. When exceeded, it typically causes more storage space activity. For example, operating systems use hard disk drive space to assist RAM. A block of hard disk drive space is used to augment RAM. When RAM is full, the operating system uses the block of hard disk drive space to supplement the RAM.

Hard drive disk space that supplements the RAM is referred to as a ***swap file***, or ***page file***. The swap file on the hard disk drive serves the same purpose as RAM. When the swap file is used, data processing slows because the hard disk drive cannot perform at the same high speed as the RAM. The slower swap file causes data processing to slow and affects the time it takes to retrieve data across the network. While the network is not the cause for the slow down, the network appears to be responding slowly to the user.

swap file
hard drive disk space that supplements the RAM.

Establishing a Baseline

The only way to objectively determine the performance of a network or a server is to establish a baseline immediately after the network or server is installed. A ***baseline*** is a measurement of performance characteristics that can be used at a later date to objectively determine if the network or server is performing satisfactorily. Typically, a baseline can be established by software utilities especially designed for such tasks. Many network operating systems have their own set of utilities that can perform routine baseline assessments.

baseline
a measurement of performance characteristics that can be used at a later date to objectively determine if the network or server is performing satisfactorily.

One of the most important aspects of establishing a baseline is testing the network or server under normal and stressed conditions. Some software packages are designed to simulate network traffic so that the network can be stress-tested.

One of the best times to monitor a network or server is early in the morning. Start the monitoring process before the first shift of personnel arrives. At this time, activity should be at a minimum. As personnel report to their offices and start the workday, network traffic increases dramatically. For example, the mail server will experience the most activity when the greatest number of personnel check their e-mail and send return e-mails. The times that typically generate the most e-mail traffic are first thing in the morning, after the lunch break, and at the end of the workday.

It is important to understand that a baseline is not a collection of data at a particular point in time, but rather a collection of data over a period of time. A baseline of the system should be established as soon as a new network or server is installed and is operational. After that, the baseline information should be routinely collected and reviewed to predict events that could affect network or server performance. By predicting events, such as reaching an unacceptable level of collisions or running out of data storage space, preventive maintenance can be scheduled.

Network Baseline

Look at a sample form in **Figure 17-1** for collecting and recording baseline information for a network. Baselines can be very detailed, but the one in the example is brief. It is meant only to present you with an idea of what type of data is gathered and why.

peak utilization
the highest level of utilization experienced by the network.

Peak utilization is the highest level of utilization experienced by the network. Peak utilization occurs when there is the most traffic on the network segment. This can happen several times during a day—for example, first thing in the morning, lunchtime, and at the end of the day. This is normal and is mainly generated by users logging on to the network, opening files (especially large ones), and reading and sending e-mail. Peak utilization should not exceed 80% for long periods of time.

average utilization
the average amount of utilization or traffic on the network in the time period monitored.

Average utilization is as the name implies—the average amount of utilization or traffic on the network in the time period monitored. The average utilization for the network segment should not exceed 40%. Most new network segments will operate at 10% to 25%. The average and peak utilization is of major concern. When high rates occur, the network should be evaluated as to the cause. After the cause is determined, a plan for corrective action should be proposed.

Figure 17-1.
A simple form like the one in this example or a more detailed form can be created to record baseline information.

Network Segment ID ____________________

Date and Time Period ______________________________

Segment	**Value**	**Comments**
Peak Utilization		
Average Utilization		
Frame Size Peak		
Frame Size Average		
Number of Protocols		
Number of Nodes		
Most Active 10 Nodes		
Collisions		
Packets Dropped		

Frame size peak is a record of the largest frame size recorded during the time period monitored. ***Frame size average*** is the average of all frame sizes during the period monitored. Frame size varies, but the factors that affect frame size are the type of protocol and equipment used, the amount of traffic on the segment, and the type of data transmitted. An average TCP frame will be approximately 500 bytes. Very small TCP frames can indicate a problem.

frame size peak a record of the largest frame size recorded during the time period monitored.

frame size average the average of all frame sizes during the period monitored.

Number of protocols is the number of different protocols transmitted in the network segment. A large number of different protocols can reflect an improperly configured network device such as a network adapter, router, switch, or wireless access point. There can also be existence of legacy devices on the network that are still configured for old Ethernet frame types or older protocols. Legacy devices typically broadcast more than one frame type until they receive a response from the other device or the service they are requesting. For example, many devices automatically configure the network device for older network protocols to ensure backward compatibility. You may see protocols related to NetBEUI, IPX/SPX, or AppleTalk. A large number of duplicate protocol frames and packets are generated across network segments caused by the network devices being configured for IPv4 and IPv6 by default. The number of protocols can be reduced by manually configuring devices and selecting only the appropriate protocols and services.

Number of nodes is the number of nodes communicating on the network segment. The number of nodes normally increases as time goes by. This is because economically healthy organizations grow. When comparing segment statistics over long periods of time (years), the number of nodes generating network traffic needs to be taken into account.

The *Most active 10 nodes* entry is an indicator of possible network problem locations. For example, a workstation with a bad cable connection may be dropping an unusually large number of frames, which in turn causes new frames to be generated and transmitted. A node that must retransmit many frames will most likely be in the top ten of this list.

The *Collisions* entry represents frame or packet collisions on the network segment. Collisions are the primary indicator of a problem. There should be very few collisions on a healthy Ethernet segment. Less than 1% is not unusual. *Packets dropped* also indicate a problem. Packets dropped are a good indication that there is a cable or connection problem.

Excessive collisions and excessive network traffic can be reduced through traffic-shaping techniques. When a network link is experiencing too many collisions or excessive traffic, routers or layer 3 switches can be installed to provide additional segment links. Another advantage to multiple segment paths is increased network reliability provided by link redundancy.

While a form was used in the example, many systems can typically collect data and export the data to spreadsheet format. The spreadsheet format can be incorporated into a word processor application or simply printed out as a direct report with graphs. Most protocol analyzers can also record system baseline information.

Be aware that a server, not just network devices, can cause network bottlenecks. The three main causes of server bottlenecks are insufficient resources, unbalanced client loads, and incorrectly configured service(s). Insufficient server resources include too many users for the amount of server resources available. This is especially true of server memory and hard disk drive activity. To alleviate this type of problem, add more memory or configure more hard disk drives and map users to the additional drives.

When resource sharing is unbalanced, too many users are logging on to the same server when other servers are available. In this case, the default server logon for a portion of the users should be changed to balance the load.

A service may be incorrectly configured to handle the given client load. For example, a DHCP server may be configured with a limited IP address pool or with a long lease period duration. In this case, the administrator may need to increase the number of available IP addresses or shorten the lease period.

Server Baseline

Some of the most commonly monitored categories for establishing a server baseline are memory utilization, hard disk activity, CPU utilization, and server access activity. Memory utilization will determine if more memory needs to be installed in the server. Baselines include determining the amount of RAM available and paging file (swap file) activity. Legacy server systems depended on a paging file to augment the installed limited amount of RAM. The page file is a section of hard disk drive used to act as memory to supplement the available RAM. In general, a maximum page file of 1.5 times the actual amount of RAM installed was created.

Beginning with Windows Server 2003 and Windows XP, the 64-bit operating system was introduced. Today, all modern servers are typically 64-bit systems.

Note

The original release of Windows Server 2008 could be installed as 32-bit or 64-bit. Starting with the second release of Windows Server 2008, only the 64-bit system is available.

The 32-bit operating systems recognize 4 GB maximum of RAM. Any more RAM in a 32-bit system is wasted. The 64-bit operating systems can recognize up to 16 TB (terabytes) of RAM. Page file size is not as critical for 64-bit systems because these systems can handle more physical memory than 32-bit systems, thus reducing the need for page files. In fact, Microsoft has no recommended size of page file for a 64-bit system. Microsoft even states that there may be no need at all for a page file if there is sufficient physical RAM installed on a 64-bit system.

Hard disk drive activity, or disk I/O activity, is monitored to determine when additional hard drives need to be installed. When a hard drive reaches approximately 80% capacity, additional storage should be installed.

CPU utilization determines if the CPU is overloaded with requests. CPU utilization should not exceed 85%. When 85% threshold is reached, a faster CPU or additional CPUs should be installed. Additional servers can also be installed to share the processing load. When additional servers are configured for load balancing, they are often referred to as *server clusters* or *server farms*. It is very common to have two or more servers providing Web services for a high demand Web site location. For example, Google uses a server farm, which is a collection of over 50,000, 64-bit servers. The exact number of servers is constantly changing because the capability of individual servers is constantly changing. In 2007, it was estimated that the Google server farm contained over 450,000 servers. Most likely, 32-bit core type of servers with limited storage space was the reason for such a high number.

Note

Do *not* confuse the term *load balancing* with *traffic shaping*. Load balancing is balancing the demand of network clients to utilize system resources such as files or CPU processing. Traffic shaping is used to provide more bandwidth across the network system by providing alternate pathways.

It is important to note that running performance monitoring software applications adversely affects server performance. Server performance monitoring tools use system resources such as RAM and CPU. A healthy server can handle performance monitoring applications with no problem. However, if the server is already overburdened, the use of a performance monitoring tool can cause a server to increase response time to network clients.

Monitoring Tools

Network events need to be monitored to detect and predict problems. The exact problems can vary a great deal, from simple user problems to detecting an intruder's attempts to break into the system. All major operating systems have monitoring utilities. There are also many good third-party tools available. Monitoring tools not only monitor events but also record the events into a log, which is then saved as a file. Event logs can be used to assist in analyzing system problems involving hardware, software, and security issues.

Performance Monitors

Most major operating systems come with some type of performance monitoring utility. Microsoft Server provides Performance Monitor, which monitors network activity and system resources, **Figure 17-2.**

A utility such as Performance Monitor provides the network administrator with the information needed for making objective decisions about the system. Performance Monitor can be configured to send alerts to the system administrator when resources are critical.

Performance Monitor can be used to predict system failure or to isolate the cause of poor performance. When used properly, the administrator can schedule routine hardware replacements, additions, and upgrades that will minimally affect user access. For example, if the CPU is at maximum performance for extended periods of time, a better CPU can be installed or more CPUs can be added during a period of low usage like a weekend or evening. Scheduling routine repairs and upgrades prevents unexpected and predictable network system failures. Many failures can be avoided by routine monitoring of system activities.

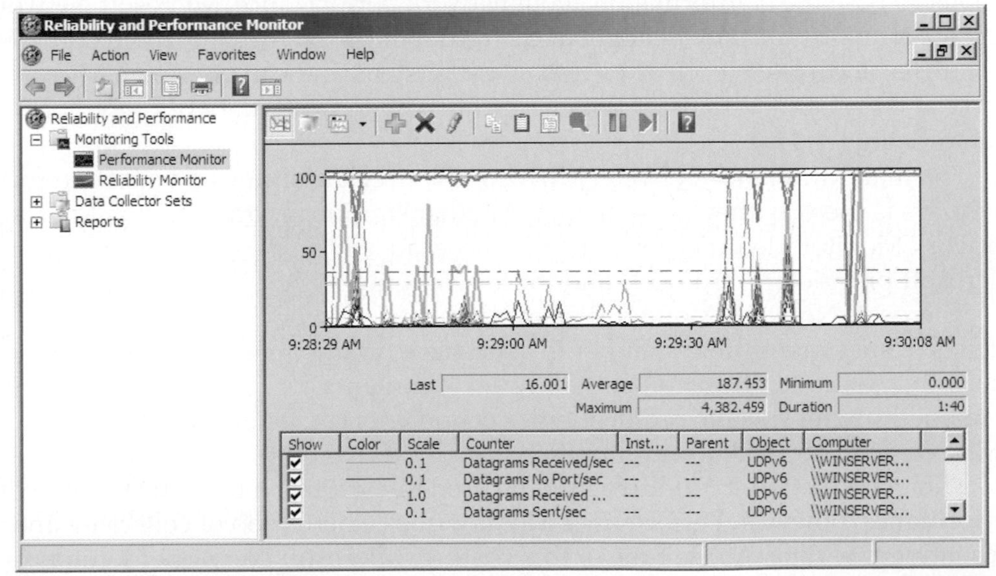

Figure 17-2.
The Performance Monitor is part of the diagnostic tools available in Microsoft Server.

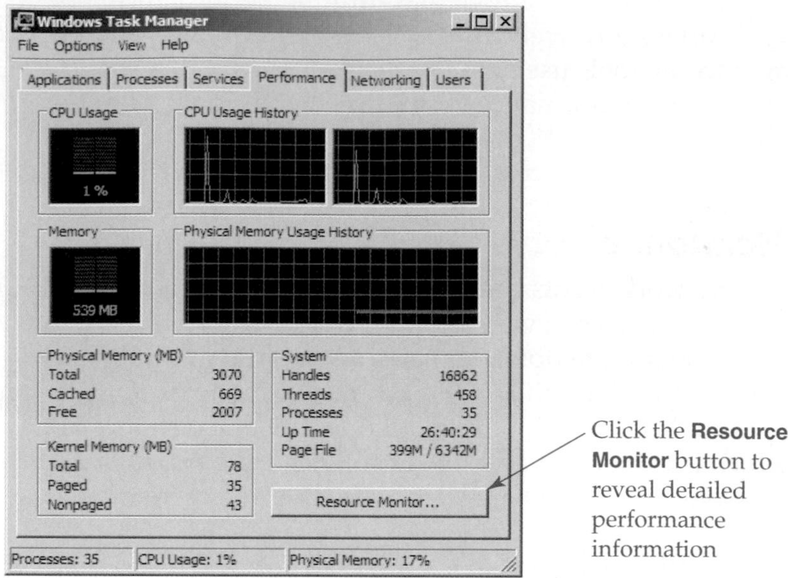

Figure 17-3.
Windows Task Manager can be used to display a quick view of system performance.

Windows Server operating systems have many of the same tools that are available in the Windows desktop operating systems. **Figure 17-3,** shows the screen capture of Windows Task Manager taken from a Windows Server 2008 computer. It has the same appearance as the Task Manager in a Microsoft desktop system.

Windows Task Manager provides a quick view of system performance and can also show what software applications, processes, and services are running. For a more detailed view of performance factors, click the **Resource Monitor** button. Notice in **Figure 17-4** a more detailed view of system resources and network performance is presented. The graphs at the top of the **Resource Overview** dialog box provide a picture of the CPU, disk, network, and memory performance.

Microsoft Network Monitor has evolved over the years from a simple introductory protocol analyzer into a full protocol analyzer with many features found only in very expensive third-party protocol analyzers. It can be used to establish a baseline of information about network performance. Microsoft Network Monitor is not installed by default but can be downloaded from the Microsoft Web site for free. It comes in both 32-bit and 64-bit versions and can be run on Microsoft server and desktop systems. A screen capture of Microsoft Network Monitor is shown in **Figure 17-5.**

The main difference between Microsoft Network Monitor and other protocol analyzers is the way they present data. Another significant difference is Microsoft Network Monitor identifies fewer protocols because it is designed to identify only Microsoft proprietary protocols and those belonging to the TCP/IP protocol suite.

Microsoft Network Monitor displays all active network connections and collects frames in a similar manner to Wireshark or any other protocol analyzer. The encapsulation of the protocols and packet contents are displayed. Filters can be applied so that specific protocol types or contents can be isolated from the total collection of packets and frames.

Microsoft Network Monitor could be used to establish a baseline for network performance; however, Performance Monitor does a better job of collecting and presenting raw data. At the time of this writing, Microsoft Network Monitor

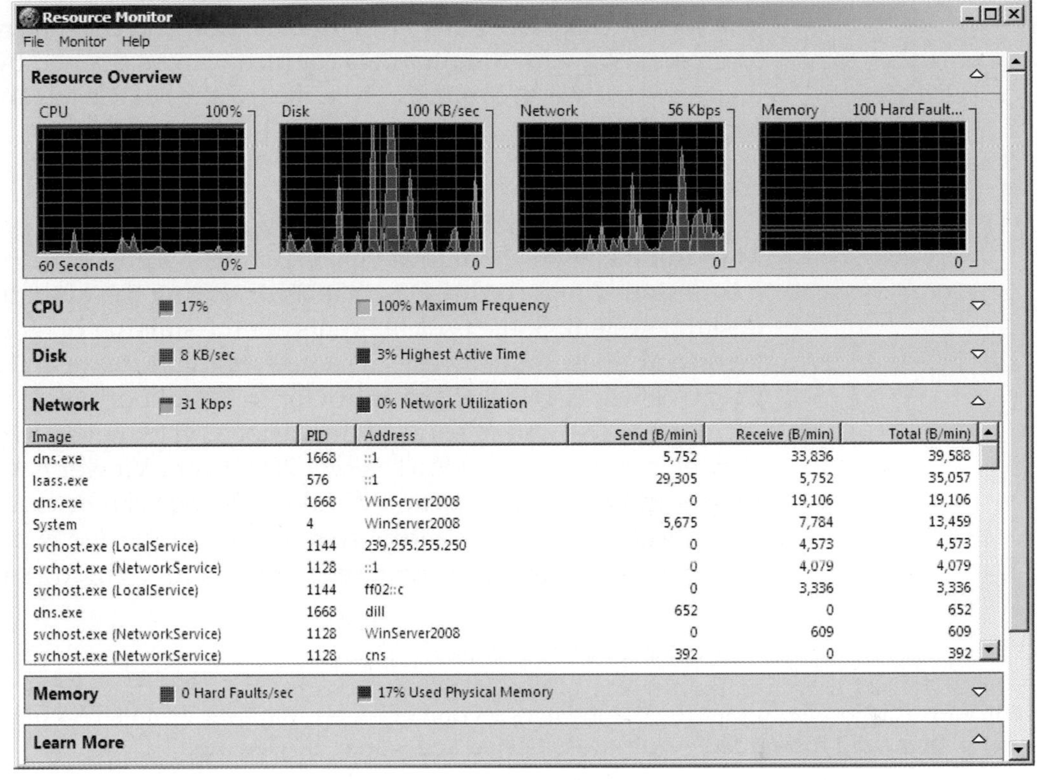

Figure 17-4.
By clicking the **Resource Monitor** button in Windows Task Manager, detailed performance information can be displayed.

Figure 17-5.
Microsoft Network Monitor is a protocol analyzer that can be used to monitor network performance.

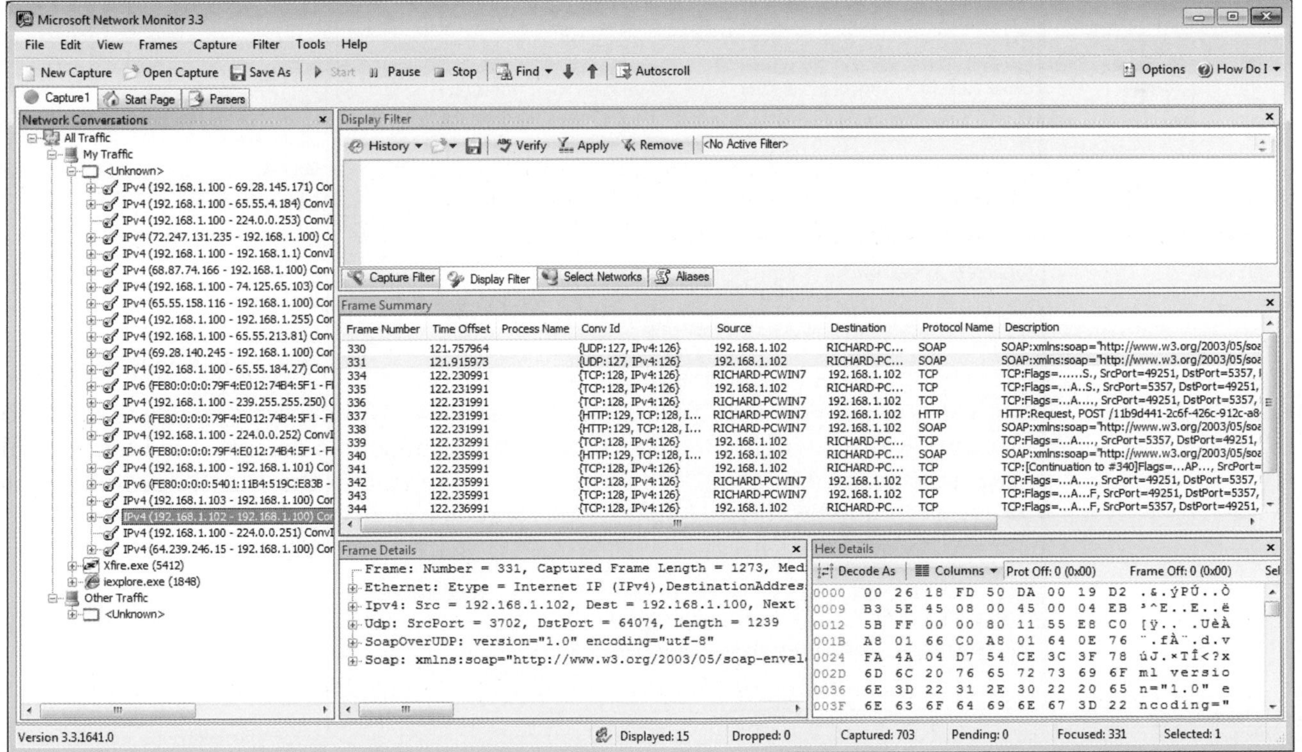

lacks many of the advanced features found in other protocol analyzers such as graphically displaying statistical information and presenting written reports. Microsoft Network Monitor data captures can be opened by other protocol analyzers such as Wireshark. Then, the features of the advanced protocol analyzer can be used to study the data.

Event Viewers

All major operating systems include some form of an event monitoring utility. Microsoft provides in many of its operating systems a utility called *Event Viewer.* It is designed to record events that occur during the operation of the server or desktop system. Some typical events are the starting or stopping of a service, user logon activities, share access, file access, and hardware and software information. Event Viewer is an excellent utility for troubleshooting system failures.

Figure 17-6 shows some of the various system events recorded in the Event Viewer system log. Windows Server 2008 Event Viewer is very similar to Event Viewer in Windows Vista and Windows 7. Logs can be created for events related to applications, security, setup, system, and forwarded events. In **Figure 17-7,** information is displayed about the failure of the Windows Update service.

Figure 17-6.
Event Viewer is located under the **Diagnostics** section of Server Manager. Events relating to applications, security, setup, system, and forwarded events are collected and stored for viewing.

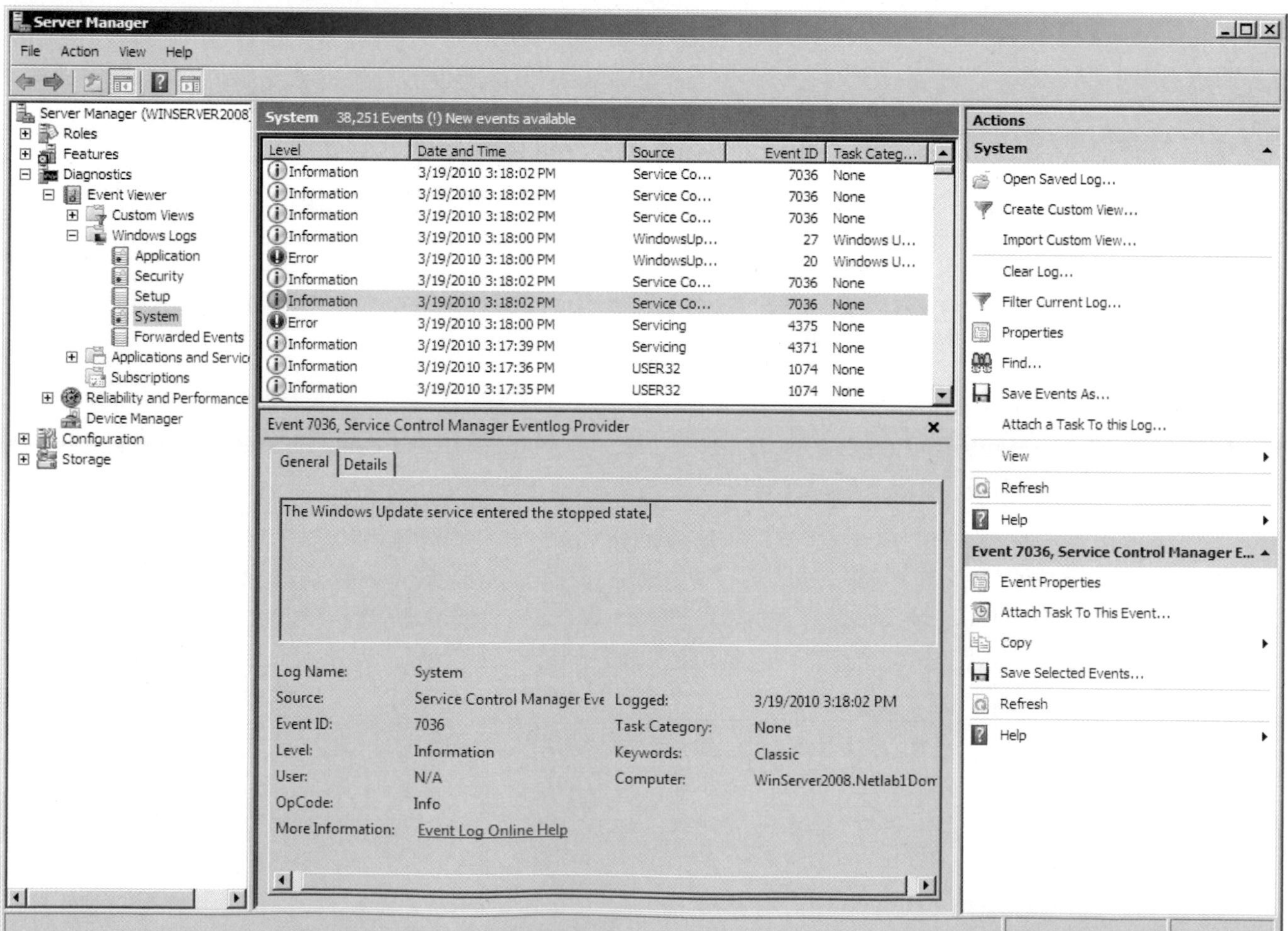

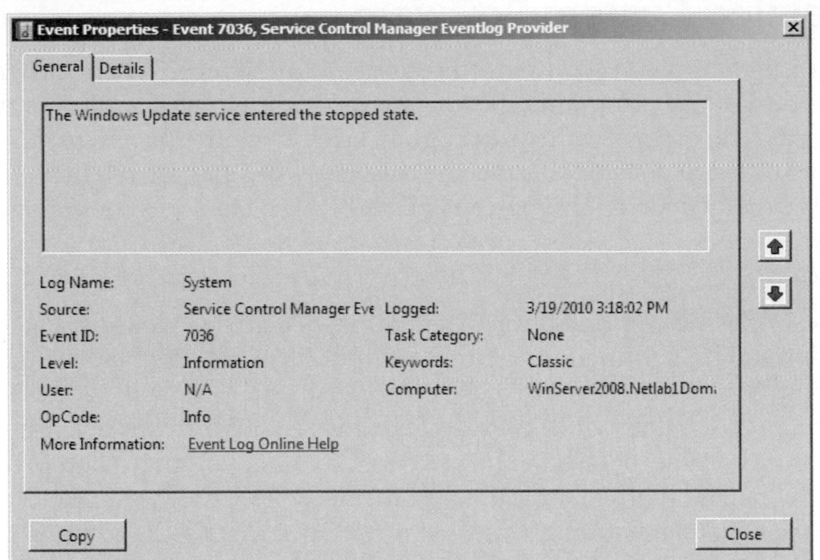

Figure 17-7. The individual event can be opened as a separate window by double-clicking the event item in Event Viewer.

Simple Network Management Protocol (SNMP)

The ***Simple Network Management Protocol (SNMP)*** was designed by the ITEF to support network management, allowing an administrator to manage and monitor network devices and services from a single location. SNMP is an application layer protocol that uses UDP packets for delivery.

Simple Network Management Protocol (SNMP) a protocol designed by the ITEF that allows an administrator to manage and monitor network devices and services from a single location.

The ITEF SNMP protocol is not a complete finished protocol but rather a framework that is used by third-party software companies. The third-party software designers finish the framework to perform a function, such as network monitoring of devices or remote configuration of network devices. SNMP applications are designed to monitor and configure items on a network from a centralized location. Some items that can be configured and monitored are servers, routers, switches, IP video cameras, IP phones, and just about any device that uses the TCP/IP suite of protocols.

The SNMP agent is installed on the devices that are to be monitored by the Network Management System (NMS). The NMS collects the data and stores the data in a Management Information Base (MIB).

Microsoft server and desktop operating systems do *not* enable SNMP by default. **Figure 17-8** shows the Windows Server 2008 **Windows Features** dialog box. Notice that SNMP must be selected manually. This is because Microsoft has developed its own protocols used for network management.

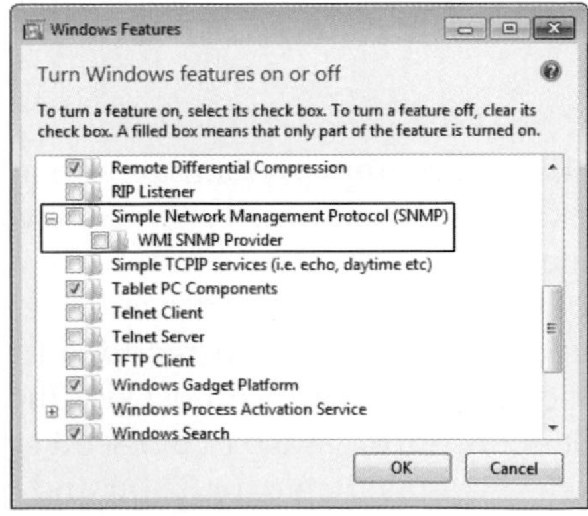

Figure 17-8. SNMP can be enabled through **Control Panel | Programs | Programs and Features | Turn Windows features on or off**.

Maintaining System Software

bug
a software program error.

service pack
a collection of software patches, or fixes.

Software packages typically need routine maintenance. When software developers design their programs, they do the very best job they can, but problems, or program errors, do occur. A software program error is referred to as a ***bug.*** Software patches, or fixes, are developed after the discovery of a bug or security problem. Software is usually updated through patches, service packs, and system upgrades.

Patches

Software patches for operating systems are released frequently. Patches should be tested on a limited number of computers or servers before installing them across the entire network. Patches can cause problems with your existing system because of unknown or untested hardware software applications. After carefully and thoroughly testing the effects of a patch, you may then proceed to install the patch on other computers in the network. Another reason for the caution is most patches cannot be uninstalled. Once installed and an unforeseen critical problem develops, you may be forced to do a backup of important data, wipe the system clean, and then do a new operating system installation. When talking about hundreds or thousands of computers, this could be very time-consuming.

Service Packs

Microsoft uses the term ***service pack*** to describe a collection of software patches, or fixes. After every release of a major operating system, a series of service packs is provided free of charge to users to update the system. A typical service pack consists of program modifications that provide security fixes and updated drivers for new hardware technologies. For example, Windows NT 4.0 went through a series of six major service packs. The first service pack released for Windows XP was a collection of 324 fixes that dealt with network, hardware, security, and basic operating system issues. You can download a detailed list of each fix included in the service pack. Details about the nature of each problem are also provided.

Windows Vista and Windows Server 2008 Service Pack 2 (SP2) contained 838 changes. Microsoft provided a downloadable Excel spreadsheet that the technician could use to link to information about the fixes and changes, **Figure 17-9.** The technician simply clicked on the link to access detailed information about the fix.

Keeping the operating system up-to-date with service packs and individual patches as they are released is good insurance against program security flaws and other problems as they are discovered. Service packs should be tested before installing them on a network system.

Upgrades

A software upgrade is a major improvement or enhancement to existing software programs. For example, Windows Server 2008 was released in February 2008 and then released again in July 2009 as Windows Server 2008 R2. The "R2" represents "release number two" or "second release." There were many changes to the operating system and many more features added that it justified a new release rather than a service pack. One of the most significant changes was that Windows Server 2008 R2 is only available for 64-bit systems. The original Windows Server 2008 release was available for 32-bit and 64-bit systems.

Figure 17-9.
Microsoft provided a spreadsheet containing a list of 838 changes for Windows Vista and Windows Server 2008 in the release of Service Pack 2 (SP2). Links to details about each change were embedded into the spreadsheet.

Hotfixes and Security Updates included in Windows Server 08 Service Pack 2 and Windows Vista Service Pack 2

Windows Server 2008 Service Pack 2 (SP2) and Windows Vista Service Pack 2 (SP2) includes all previously released updates for Windows Server 2008 and all released updates since Windows Vista Service Pack 1. Many of these updates are available to the public on the Microsoft Download Center and Windows Update, while others are only available to specific customers or partners. It is standard practice to include all of these updates in a Service Pack and as such they are included in Windows Server2008 SP2 and Windows Vista SP2.

This document contains a list of these updates with links to their descriptive webpages on http://support.microsoft.com. There are other updates in Service Pack 2 which have not been released as updates and therefore are not presented in this list.

KBArticle	Title	IssueTy	Component	Link
941693	MS08-025: Vulnerability in Windows Kernel could allow elevation of privilege	Security	Base Technologies	http://support.microsoft.com/kb/941693
950974	MS08-049: Vulnerability in Event System could allow remote code execution	Security	Base Technologies	http://support.microsoft.com/kb/950974
954211	MS08-061: Vulnerabilities in Windows kernel could allow elevation of privilege	Security	Base Technologies	http://support.microsoft.com/kb/954211
971284	A hotfix is available to enable crash on CTRL-SCROLL support on Vista SP1 and Windows Server 2008 on a USB keyboard	Hotfix	Drivers	http://support.microsoft.com/kb/971284
952004	MS09-012: Description of the security update for MSDTC Transaction Facility: April 2009	Security	Security	http://support.microsoft.com/kb/952004
956841	MS08-064: Vulnerability in Virtual Address Descriptor manipulation could allow elevation of privilege	Security	Base Technologies	http://support.microsoft.com/kb/956841
957095	MS08-063: Vulnerability in SMB could allow remote code execution	Security	Base Technologies	http://support.microsoft.com/kb/957095
957097	MS08-068: Vulnerability in SMB could allow remote code execution	Security	Base Technologies	http://support.microsoft.com/kb/957097
958687	MS09-001: Vulnerabilities in SMB could allow remote code execution	Security	Base Technologies	http://support.microsoft.com/kb/958687
958690	MS09-006: Vulnerabilities in Windows Kernel could allow remote code execution	Security	Base Technologies	http://support.microsoft.com/kb/958690
954459	MS08-069: Description of the security update for XML Core Services 6.0: November 11, 2008	Security	Data Services	http://support.microsoft.com/kb/954459
955069	MS08-069: Description of the security update for XML Core Services 3.0: November 11, 2008	Security	Data Services	http://support.microsoft.com/kb/955069
958623	MS08-075: Description of the security update for Windows Search: December 9, 2008	Security	Desktop Shell	http://support.microsoft.com/kb/958623

The term *upgrade* generally refers to changing from one operating system to another that uses the same basic core operating system features. A system upgrade occurs when the basic core of the operating system is still the same without significant changes. When there is a great difference between the old operating system and the new operating system, you cannot perform a system upgrade.

For diverse operating systems, you must perform a system migration. The term *migration* means combining two diverse operating systems or network systems into one system. For example, you cannot upgrade Windows Server 2008 32-bit to Windows Server 2008 R2, which is a 64-bit operating system. You must migrate it because of the significant changes to the basic structure, such as the 64-bit feature. There will be more about migration later in this chapter as applied to different network operating systems being merged into one network system.

Software Installations

New software programs should be tested before they are installed on a network server or distributed to network clients. Software developers do a good job of testing their software on numerous types of computers with various types of hardware and software configurations. Often, a beta version of the software package is released so the developer can gain more knowledge about the software compatibility of the software package.

Microsoft and other software developers routinely allow users to have access to beta versions of an upcoming release of a software package. For example,

Microsoft Windows Server 2008 was released as a beta version months before it was distributed through retail outlets. By releasing beta versions, thousands of copies of the software can be tested by many different users running various software packages and using many different types of hardware. Numerous flaws can be detected and remedied before releasing the software package.

Hardware manufacturers work hand in hand with software developers to write driver programs to support their hardware. If the hardware drivers are developed in time, they are included in the beta version of the operating system so they can also be tested. After the release of new operating system hardware, developers must provide drivers for the system by packaging a disk or disc with the hardware device or offering free downloadable drivers from their Web site. As you can see, the development of a new operating system can be quite involved.

Before you install a new software package on a server or client, it should be fully tested. A test network consisting of a few workstations and a server can be set up using the same software and hardware that exists in the real network. The test network is separate from the real network and is used to test software package compatibility with hardware and software applications. A corporation or institution should have a lab or training room set aside that can be used for testing purposes.

Installing a new software system on a network can cause unpredictable problems. Some problems are not reversible. Any administrator or technician would want to avoid having to reformat the server hard drive, reinstall the operating system and software applications, and restore the data that was last backed up. During this time period, all personnel who use the network for work purposes would be idle. Production loss can be very expensive. Think about the hundreds or even thousands of employees that are being paid while waiting for the network to be functional. Think about how many customers a business could lose.

Before installing any new hardware or software on a network system, you should also check the hardware or software compatibility list at both the hardware manufacturer's Web site and the operating system Web site, **Figure 17-10.**

Often, information on one Web site will conflict with another. For example, the operating system Web site might indicate that the hardware device is not compatible with the operating system. By going to the hardware manufacturer's Web site, you may find that a driver has been released that will allow the hardware to work on that operating system. Conflicting information about hardware compatibility is a common occurrence.

Operating systems often offer patches or fixes for security problems as they are discovered. Security is an ongoing issue. Breaches in network security happen constantly. E-mail newsletters are offered free of charge at all leading operating system Web sites. You should subscribe to these newsletters and read them often to become aware of the latest developments. You must stay ahead of intruders. Leading antivirus developers also provide newsletters. Not only do antivirus developers provide you with timely information, they typically release fixes in 24 hours or less of initial virus detection.

Maintaining System Hardware

The proper maintenance of system hardware is cost-effective. A system failure during business hours can be very costly to the company. Whenever possible, all system hardware maintenance should be performed when business and clients will be least affected.

Figure 17-10.
A—Microsoft maintains a complete list of hardware- and software-compatible products at its Web site for all of its currently-supported operating systems. B—A lengthy list of hardware that is certified to be compatible with Microsoft Server 2008.

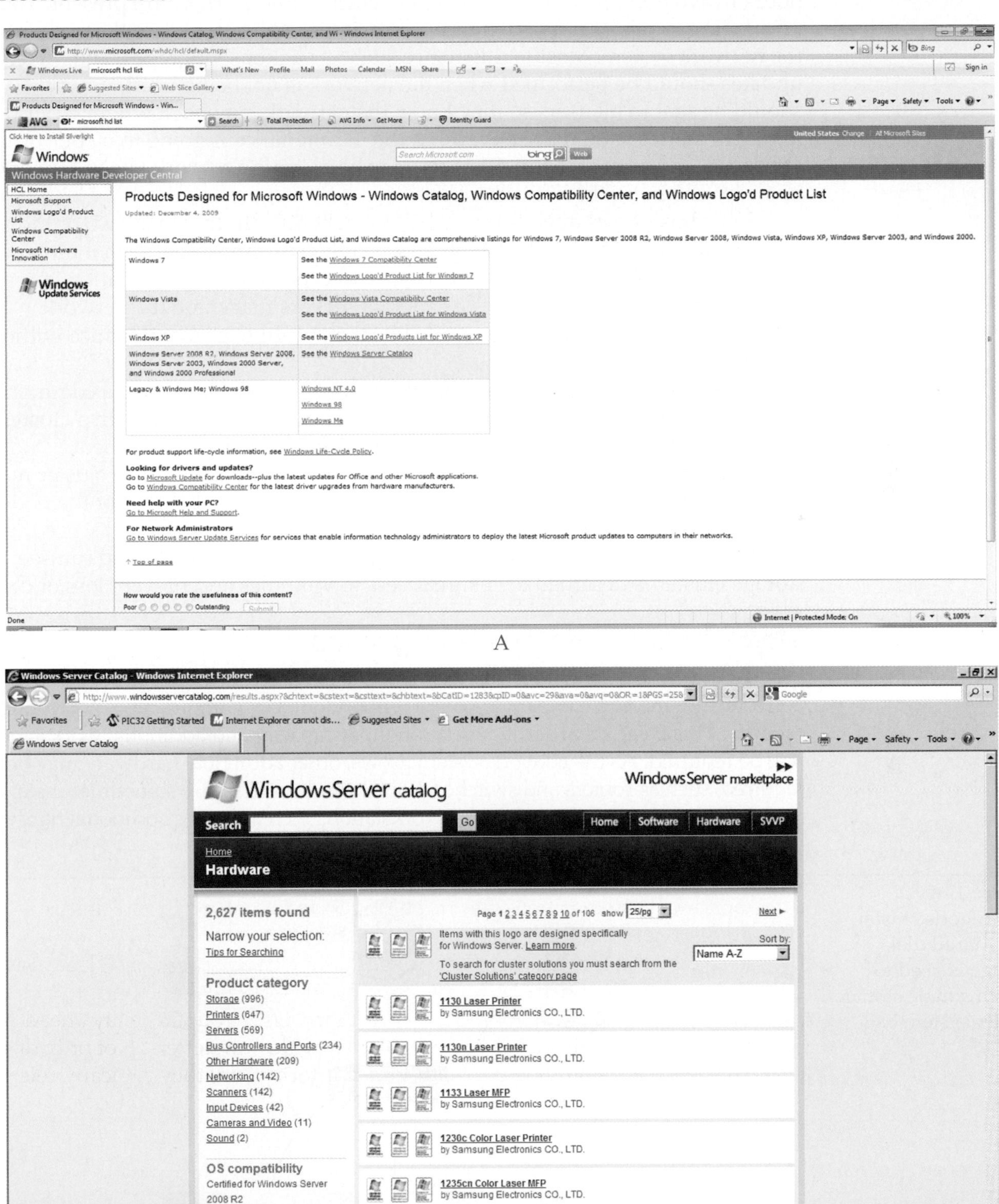

Scheduling Downtime

Scheduling downtime is an important aspect of maintenance. A small network with a single server should have maintenance performed after business hours to avoid the possibility of a system crash while workers are present. You never want to perform maintenance that may possibly jeopardize the use of the network system. Most maintenance such as backups, upgrades, and virus updates should be performed when the network is not being used. A notice should be sent to all users so they know the network may be down for a period of time. The notice should be sent even if the maintenance is going to be performed after regular business hours. Workers may be planning to work late or to work at home by accessing the network remotely.

Some businesses operate on a 24/7/365 schedule. In this case, two or more servers are routinely installed. One may be taken off-line to perform maintenance while the other carries the network. A special type of server installation is referred to as *cluster.* A ***cluster*** is a group of servers that share the network demand. One of the servers can easily be taken off-line for maintenance without disrupting network activities.

cluster
a group of servers that share the network demand.

Look at **Figure 17-11.** Notice that there are two servers sharing a common storage unit. The two servers share the same IP address and name. In a cluster configuration, the servers are referred to as *node 1, node 2,* etc. The client computers connect to the network through a switch or a router. The cluster may also have two or more switches or routers for redundancy. If either of the nodes goes down or are taken off-line for maintenance, the other node will serve the clients. The shared storage is usually a RAID 5 configuration. As you can see, a storage cluster is designed to ensure access to vital files and prevent loss of data.

Major Network Hardware Upgrades

Backbones, additional servers, routers, switches, and such may be added to the network system. As a company grows, it will undoubtedly require more networking capacity. This means that additional throughput capacity and additional workstations will be required. As the network system grows, other additional hardware may be required, such as routers and switches. Routers and switches are sometimes installed on existing systems as the number of workstations increases. The additional hardware

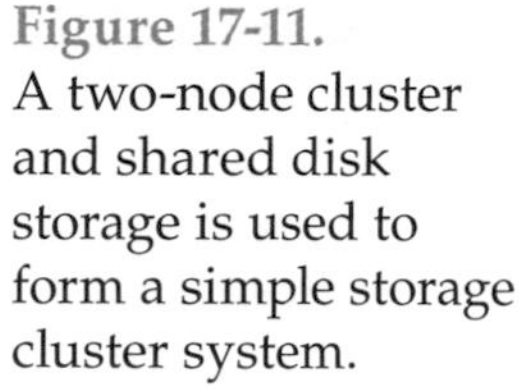
Figure 17-11.
A two-node cluster and shared disk storage is used to form a simple storage cluster system.

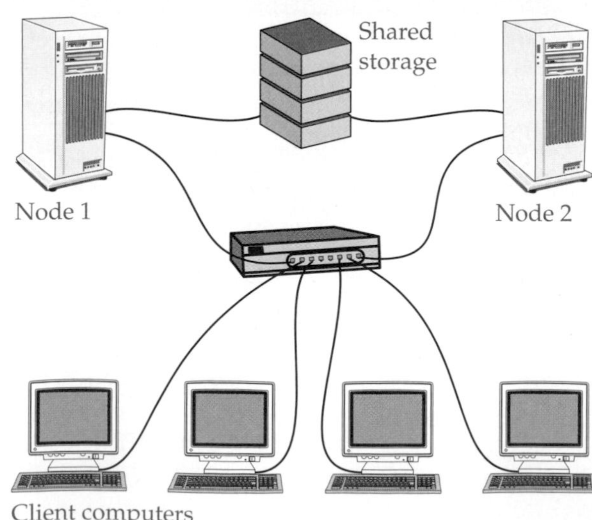

is used to create Virtual LANs (VLANs). A VLAN increases the available bandwidth. The bandwidth is increased because each VLAN acts as its own separate network, thus reducing the amount of collision zones.

Each VLAN has the same throughput as the original LAN. For example, it is possible to divide an existing 1000BaseT network consisting of 100 workstations into two separate VLANs by using switch technology. The network is divided according to workgroups. Workgroups often communicate within their own workgroup but seldom outside of the same workgroup. By dividing the network into two separate LANs, the bandwidth is technically doubled by creating two networks, each with 1000 Mbps bandwidth. However, this is not always practical. Bandwidth is based on the actual working conditions of two or more workgroups within the network.

Maintaining System Integrity

The completeness and accuracy of data is referred to as *system integrity* or *data integrity*. Maintaining system integrity requires protecting the data while the server is running. To protect data, fault tolerance and disaster recovery must be designed into the network. You should recall from Chapter 9—Introduction to the Server that fault tolerance is a system's ability to continue operation during a system hardware or software error. Fault tolerance strategies include some RAID systems and electrical power systems. Electrical power systems are covered in detail later in this chapter. ***Disaster recovery*** is the restoration of a system to normal operation after a disaster has occurred. It includes data backups; hot and cold spares; and hot, warm, and cold sites.

disaster recovery the restoration of a system to normal operation after a disaster has occurred.

Network+ Note

For the Network+ Certification exam, be sure you know the difference between fault tolerance and disaster recovery and can identify devices, systems, and strategies related to each. Remember, fault tolerance includes RAID systems, server clustering, and UPS units. Disaster recovery includes data backups and data backup media storage. RAID 0, however, does not provide fault tolerance.

Fault Tolerant RAID Systems

RAID will only be quickly reviewed in this chapter. For a detailed explanation of each RAID system, review Chapter 9—Introduction to the Server. While there are many different RAID styles, the predominant RAID systems that provide fault tolerance are RAID 1 and RAID 5.

RAID 0 does *not* offer fault tolerance. It is designed strictly for data storage speed.

RAID 1 consists of two disk drives with matching data on each drive. If one drive fails, the other has a complete copy of data. RAID 1 is also known as *disk mirroring*. RAID 5 combines parity and striping to provide an economical way to protect data should a hard disk drive fail. At least three hard disk drives are required for a RAID 5 configuration. Data blocks are striped across two hard disk drives, and parity for those two blocks is stored on a third hard disk drive. Parity and data blocks alternate across the drive system so that each hard disk drive consists of approximately two part data blocks and one part parity. This method ensures equal restoration time if any of the three hard disk drives fail.

Backup Data Methods

Even with fault tolerant RAID systems, data can still be corrupted or damaged beyond repair. For example, a virus could infect each disk drive in the RAID system. A natural disaster, storm, hurricane, tornado, flood, or a fire could destroy the computer system. A backup data method must be employed to restore valuable data in case any of these events occur. Backing up data is part of a disaster recovery system. Backups should be made at regular intervals. This way the data can be restored up to the last, good backup.

The term *backup* refers to making copies of the data on a storage system. Backups can be made manually or automatically through the use of software applications designed for such purposes. Copies of data can be made to most any type of data storage medium such as DVD drives, tapes, and network attached storage devices. The most common storage device is a tape backup drive, but DVD-RW drives are becoming more appropriate for small storage systems. Three types of backups can be performed: full, incremental, and differential.

Full Backup

full backup
a backup method that backs up all designated data.

As the name implies, a ***full backup*** is a complete backup of all designated data. You do not need to back up everything on a server during a full backup. You need only copy the data. If the hard disk drive is replaced because it failed, the operating system and applications can be reinstalled from discs. The data is the real concern. A full backup operation copies all identified data during a single backup period.

Incremental Backup

incremental backup
a backup method which copies only data that has changed since the previous backup.

An ***incremental backup*** copies only data that has changed since the previous backup. Compared to full backups, incremental backups are time savers.

A typical scenario of using the incremental backup method is to perform a full backup once a week and then incremental backups daily. In a week's time, this would equal seven backup sessions: one full backup and six incremental backups. This process saves time when compared with making daily full backups. The only disadvantage is that when data is restored, the last full backup must be restored first and then each incremental backup in sequential order. If one incremental backup is restored out of sequence, the data restoration is flawed. See **Figure 17-12.** Keep in mind that large data systems may require more than one tape each day for differential as well as incremental backups. One tape was used in the example to keep the concept simple.

Figure 17-12.
An incremental backup requires separate media for each incremental backup.

Differential Backup

A ***differential backup*** backs up all data that has been changed since the last full backup. There is no need to use a series of tapes. One tape for the differential backup will do because all data changes since the last full backup are recorded. See **Figure 17-13.**

differential backup
a backup method that backs up all data that has been changed since the last full backup.

Tech Tip

Tape drive media is vulnerable to damage through wear and electromagnetism. It is a good idea to alternate between two or more tapes when performing backups. For example, if performing a weekly full backup, you should overwrite a tape every other backup. This will increase the life of the tape and serve as a backup in case one of the tapes becomes damaged.

A typical scenario of using the differential backup method is to perform a full backup once a week and a differential daily on the other days of the week. To restore data, the full backup is restored and then the last differential backup.

You may wonder how the technology knows if a full backup has been performed or an incremental or a differential change has occurred. A file attribute, called *archive*, provides this information. Remember that files have file attributes such as read only and system. The archive attribute is actually a bit that is set when changes are made in the file's contents. The ***archive bit*** identifies if a file has changed since the last full or incremental backup. By indicating which files have changed since the last full backup, the backup system can copy only the changed files. The archive bit is reset every time a full backup or an incremental backup is performed. The archive bit is not reset when a differential backup is performed or when a file is copied using commands such as **copy** and **xcopy**.

archive bit
a file attribute that identifies if a file has changed since the last full or incremental backup.

Remember, an incremental backup copies only files that have changed since the last full backup or last incremental backup. Both incremental and full backups reset the archive bit. When the contents of a particular file changes by being opened and then closed during a business transaction, the archive bit is set, indicating that it should be backed up during the next backup operation.

A differential backup does not reset the archive bit. It simply copies all files that have changed since the last full backup. Note that differential and incremental backups are never mixed. Only one type of backup, incremental or differential, can be performed after a full backup.

Data Backup and Restoration Methods

Backup data consists of a collection of many different files. Not all files are accessed on any given day. For example, if a bank maintains one file per customer, then that single file's content remains unchanged until the customer performs

Figure 17-13.
A differential backup can use the same media for each backup.

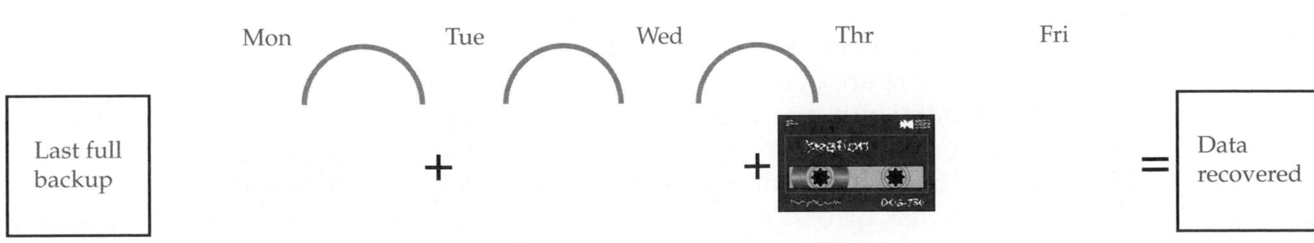

a bank transaction. A bank may have thousands or even millions of customers, which equates to millions of files. There is no need to back up every file every day, especially if the vast majority of files have not changed. In this scenario, performing a full backup once a week with incremental backups during the week is sufficient and will speed the backup process. Small data systems, on the other hand, can perform a full backup every day or a full backup once a week followed by a daily differential backup.

Remember, when restoring data from an incremental backup, each incremental tape is needed as well as the last full backup. The incremental backups must be restored in the exact order they were created since the last full backup. When restoring data from a differential backup, only the last full backup and the last differential backup created are needed.

Storing Backup Data

Backups of critical information are a must, but what if the facility experiences a disaster such as a fire, flood, severe storms, or vandalism? The tape backups must be stored in a secure, climate-controlled, off-site environment. You may have additional copies of the same backups on-site for easy access if needed, but critical data must be stored away from the site. Key points concerning data backup storage include the following:

- Store backups off-site.
- Store backups in a secure area with limited access.
- Store backups in a climate-controlled storage area.
- Avoid storing backups in direct sunlight.
- Avoid storing backups near electrical panels or in equipment rooms.
- Avoid exposing backups to magnetic fields generated by electrical equipment, such as motors and speakers.

Never store magnetic tape, disc media, or any computer equipment in direct sunlight. Direct sunlight can damage sensitive magnetic media. The magnetic tracks on backup media can lose part or all of their magnetic qualities due to exposure to direct sunlight and the heat generated by the exposure. Backup media should never be stored in equipment rooms of buildings that contain electrical equipment, HVAC (Heat Ventilation and Air Conditioning), or other forms of electrical equipment and electrical motors. Storage areas need to be climate-controlled. Backup media, especially tapes, are easily damaged by excessive heat and humidity. Always store backup media in a secure area that has limited access by personnel. Someone can easily throw away a collection of backup media while on a routine cleanup assignment of a dusty storage area. Also, remember that backup media will prove to be of little value if the disaster that destroys the original data such as fire also destroys the backup copies.

Hot and Cold Spares

hot spare
a backup component that can automatically replace a failed system component without the intervention of a technician.

A ***hot spare*** is a backup component that can automatically replace a failed system component without the intervention of a technician. A hot spare is typically a spare disk drive that is part of a RAID system but not in regular use. It is a standby unit that activates when one of the disk drives in the RAID unit fail. On failure of any disk drive, the hot spare automatically replaces the failed disk drive. The disk controller will automatically begin rebuilding the lost data on the new disk drive. The process of rebuilding the data onto the new drive is only possible with a fault tolerant RAID system, such as RAID 1 or RAID 5. The hot spare provides excellent fault tolerance and zero down time for the server.

A failed hard disk drive can also be replaced by a cold spare. A ***cold spare*** is any compatible disk drive that is in storage and is used to replace a failed disk drive. If the server supports hot swap drives, the cold disk drive can be hot swapped with the failed disk drive. As soon as the failed drive is hot swapped with the cold spare, the disk controller will automatically begin to rebuild the data onto the new disk drive. The advantage of a hot spare over the cold spare is obvious. There is a minimum amount of server down time when hot spares are used. See **Figure 17-14.**

cold spare
any compatible disk drive that is in storage and is used to replace a failed disk drive.

Hot, Cold, and Warm Sites

The terms *hot*, *cold*, and *warm* are used to describe the readiness of an off-site data storage facility to recover from a failure at the primary site, **Figure 17-15.** A cold site refers to a data storage facility where backup data is stored. A warm site consists of hardware and data, but the data has not yet been loaded onto the hardware. A hot site is a data storage facility where a backup of data is stored as well as a running system containing the most up-to-date data. The system is ready to serve users in case of a complete system failure at the original site. The only thing missing from the system is the last incremental or full backup.

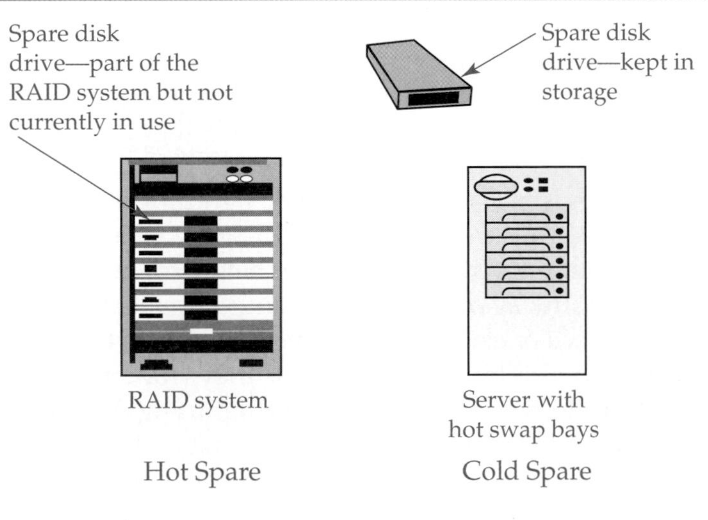

Figure 17-14.
Hot and cold spares. A—A hot spare requires no technician intervention. B—A cold spare requires a technician to install it into the system after removing the failed component.

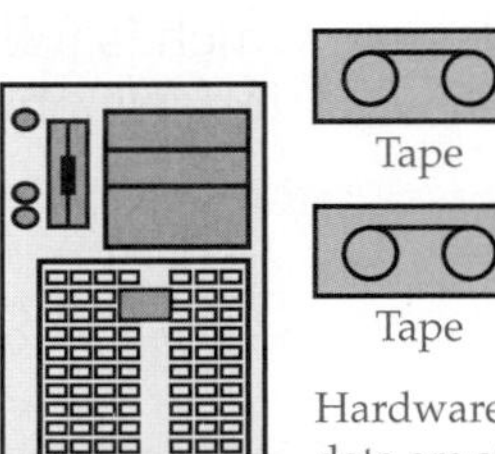
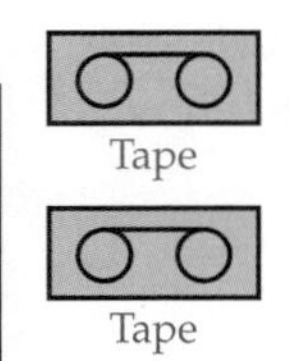

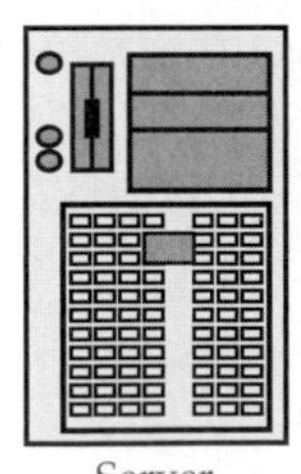

Figure 17-15.
Differences between a cold site, warm site, and hot site.

As you can obviously see, the choice of off-site storage is directly related to cost and the value placed on the time it takes to recover from a data loss scenario. The cold site is the least expensive but takes the longest to set up and recover. The hot site offers the quickest recovery but is the most expensive to maintain.

Maintaining Stable Electrical Power

A good supply of electrical power is essential for keeping the server running. Most people assume the electrical power coming from the 120-volt outlet is a steady stream of 120-volt electricity. The fact is, the electrical power coming from the outlet is not a steady stream and, most times, is not exactly 120 volts. Commercial electrical power suffers from conditions such as spikes, surges, brownouts, and blackouts. This section contains a detailed discussion of electrical power conditions and the electrical power devices used to overcome the ill effects of these conditions.

Electrical Surges and Spikes

electrical surge
a higher-than-normal voltage level, typically caused by lightning.

electrical spike
a very short burst of abnormally high voltage, typically caused by electrical equipment.

lightning arrestor
a special piece of electrical equipment designed to dampen the effects of the electrical surge caused by lightning.

Electrical surges and spikes are a very common occurrence in commercial electrical power. An ***electrical surge*** is a higher-than-normal voltage level, typically caused by lightning. An ***electrical spike*** is a very short burst of abnormally high voltage, typically caused by electrical equipment. See **Figure 17-16.** Electrical surges and spikes happen many times throughout the day and typically go unnoticed. The magnitude of the voltage level varies. Normally, electrical spikes are not of sufficient magnitude to harm most electrical systems, even delicate electronic equipment. Over the years, electronic designers have incorporated techniques that limit the effect of most electrical surges and spikes. Occasionally though, they are of sufficient strength to damage equipment.

The most severe electrical surge is caused by lightning strikes. A thunderstorm need not be in close proximity to equipment to damage it. After the lightning strikes a power line, the surge can travel over twenty miles before reaching its final destination. Equipment along the pathway of the electrical surge can be damaged. A ***lightning arrestor*** is a special piece of electrical equipment designed to dampen the effects of the electrical surge caused by lightning. While they work most times, they do not always prevent the destruction caused by the lightning. Most network systems are adequately protected from lightning damage by a good quality Uninterruptible Power Supply (UPS). UPS devices are discussed in detail later in this section.

Another cause of electrical surges through electrical systems is automobile accidents. Many times an automobile will strike a utility pole. When the automobile strikes the pole, the power lines swing together causing the two lines to touch. This causes a momentary electrical explosion, which is followed by an electrical surge and occasionally a brownout or blackout condition.

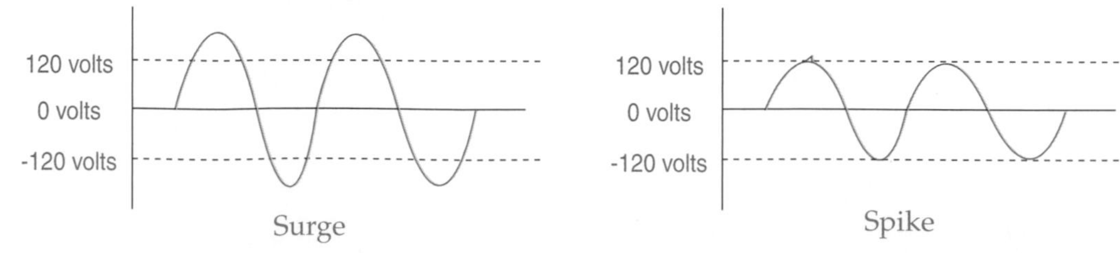

Figure 17-16.
An electrical surge is a higher-than-normal voltage level. An electrical spike is a very short burst of abnormally high voltage.

Electrical equipment, such as motors, welders, and even electrical switches, cause electrical spikes. The spike is the result of an electrical phenomena referred to as *inductive reactance*. Inductive reactance is very common and is associated with the windings (coiled wire) inside motors, transformers, appliances, tools, and various other pieces of electrical equipment. When an electrical circuit that uses alternating current (AC) is opened or closed and the circuit has inductive properties (windings), an electrical spike is produced. The exact voltage level of the spike depends on the electrical characteristics of the circuit. In short, there are many electrical spikes during a normal 24-hour period. Most electrical spikes go unnoticed because of the way electrical systems are designed. The amount of information required to adequately understand inductive reactance is far beyond the scope of this book. In fact, it is one of the most difficult principles to master in the study of electronics. For now, just remember that electrical equipment, such as the items mentioned, can generate electrical spikes during normal usage.

Standards and best practices are used to reduce the effects of electrical spikes. For example, computer system electrical circuits are typically isolated from electrical circuits that provide power to lighting and electrical equipment. By isolating the electrical circuits serving computer equipment, the possibility of electrical spikes produced by equipment in the building is reduced. For example, commercial buildings, hospitals, and schools use a bright orange color to identify electrical outlets to be used strictly for computer or sensitive electronic equipment, such as hospital monitoring or life support equipment. These outlets should never be used for equipment that can produce electrical noise or spikes, such as vacuum cleaners, drills, microwaves, and other common equipment found in the workplace. Many electrical appliances and power tools produce unwanted distortions in the AC signal, which may damage sensitive electronic equipment or corrupt data. A worker using a drill plugged into one of the designated orange outlets will produce thousands of small spikes that will affect equipment on the entire dedicated circuit.

Brownouts and Blackouts

Brownouts and blackouts are a classification of electrical energy loss dependent on the amount of voltage lost. A ***brownout*** is a partial loss of electrical energy while a ***blackout*** is a total loss of electrical energy, **Figure 17-17.** For example, during a blackout, there is no voltage available. During a brownout, there is a measurable, lower-than-normal voltage level. A brownout sometimes appears to the naked eye as a dimming effect.

brownout
a partial loss of electrical energy.

blackout
a total loss of electrical energy.

Blackouts are routinely caused by equipment failure, automobiles striking utility poles, fires, and natural disasters such as earthquakes, storms, tornadoes, and hurricanes. While a blackout can cause a loss of data, a brownout can actually damage electrical equipment. When a brownout occurs, the voltage level

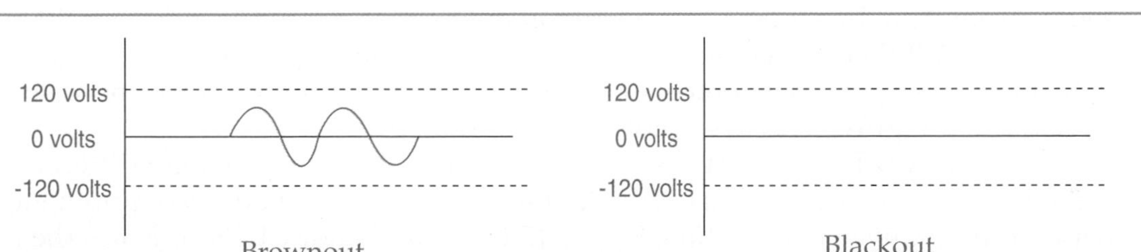

Figure 17-17. A brownout is a partial loss of electrical energy. A blackout is a total loss of electrical energy.

at the electrical equipment is lower than the equipment normally expects. Most electrical equipment will attempt to compensate for the lower voltage level by allowing the amperage to increase. The increased amperage will be in excess of what the system can safely handle. Normally, a fuse will blow or a breaker will trip, thus protecting the equipment. If not, the high electrical current (amperage) will damage components in the electrical system. The effects of blackouts and brownouts on the network server and other related equipment could be prevented by the use of an Uninterruptible Power Supply (UPS).

Brownouts may occur on any power system. The main cause of brownouts is excessive consumption of electricity. Excessive consumption happens most often when there are severe weather conditions, such as extremely high or low temperature. Electrical heating and cooling equipment requires large amounts of electrical energy during extreme temperature conditions. Most electrical devices specify that the ideal voltage for equipment should be within 10% of the indicated voltage level of the appliance or machine. For example, an electrical device rated for 120 volts AC requires a safe operating voltage level plus or minus 10% of 120 volts. That would be a range of 108 volts to 132 volts. Any voltage level outside this range could have serious side effects.

Uninterruptible Power Supply (UPS)

Uninterruptible Power Supply (UPS) a device that ensures constant and consistent network performance by supplying electrical energy in case of a power failure or blackout.

power conditioning the process of eliminating spikes and any type of variation in the desired AC signal pattern.

standby UPS a type of UPS that waits until there is a disruption in commercial electricity before it takes over the responsibility of supplying electrical energy.

continuous UPS provides a steady supply of electrical energy at all times, even when there is no electrical problem.

An ***Uninterruptible Power Supply (UPS)*** is a device that ensures constant and consistent network performance by supplying electrical energy in case of a power failure or blackout. UPS systems are also designed to provide protection from electrical surges, spikes, and brownouts. A UPS provides a steady voltage level to equipment even when the input voltage level is higher or lower than needed. The exact length of time the UPS supplies power during a blackout depends on the amount of electrical load it must support and the size or amp-hour capacity of the batteries in the UPS unit. A UPS also provides power conditioning. ***Power conditioning*** is the process of eliminating spikes as well as any type of variation in the desired AC signal pattern.

There are two major categories of UPS units: standby and continuous. Many other names are used to describe UPS units, such as *off-line*, *on-line*, and *line-interactive*. Off-line and line-interactive are standby UPS units. On-line is a continuous UPS unit. Manufacturers often coin these names. What you need to understand is the characteristics of each. This will help you know which one is the correct style for your computer system's protection. For this chapter, we will use the terms *standby* and *continuous* for the two major categories.

A ***standby UPS*** waits until there is a disruption in commercial electricity before it takes over the responsibility of supplying electrical energy. A ***continuous UPS*** provides a steady supply of electrical energy at all times, even when there is no electrical problem. The reason for using a continuous UPS is to eliminate the possibility of data corruption. A standby UPS quickly takes over to supply electrical energy when commercial power is lost. The standby UPS can switch from standby mode to full operation in less than 5 milliseconds, or 5/1000 of a second. While that may seem fast, it is not fast enough to ensure error-free data during computer data processing. The best solution is to use a continuous UPS. Look at **Figure 17-18** to see how the two compare.

Both types of UPS systems use an inverter and a battery. The main difference is the continuous UPS provides a constant flow of electrical energy to equipment without the slightest interruption, Figure 17-18A. The standby UPS activates the switching mechanism when low or no voltage is detected. In the Figure 17-18B, a pair of relay contacts indicates the switching mechanism. Some units use solid-state electronic switches, but even the electronic switches cause a slight interruption in power. Even though this may only take a few milliseconds and go unnoticed in conventional lighting, television, and other pieces of equipment, it is serious enough to lose valuable data during data transactions such as saving, loading, or transferring.

A UPS should be sized at approximately 130% of the average load, but not less than 110% of the expected maximum load.

Microsoft operating systems earlier than Windows Server 2000 and Windows XP provided options for managing UPS systems as part of the **Power Options** dialog box. For Windows Server 2000 and Windows XP and later Windows operating systems, UPS manufacturers supply their own software applications for configuration, monitoring, and notification. The typical UPS system connects to the computer through a USB port.

Look at **Figure 17-19,** which shows a screen capture of the PowerChute software utility that is used to monitor and configure an APC UPS system. The monitoring option provides information such as the battery charge state and the amount of electrical energy consumed by the computer expressed in watts. Configuration options such as voltage levels can be adjusted. In **Figure 17-20,** the default values for the maximum and minimum voltage levels are displayed. These levels can be adjusted up or down as desired.

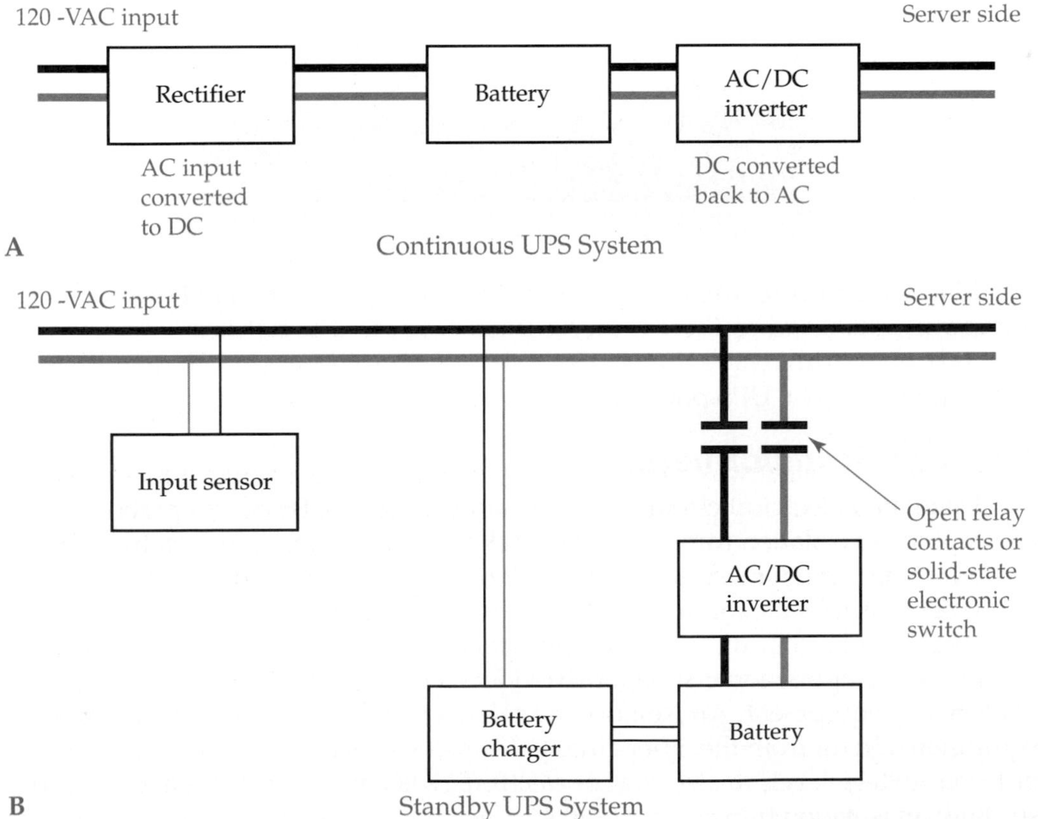

Figure 17-18. The two major categories of UPS unit are continuous and standby. A—Continuous UPS supplies a constant flow of electrical power to the server. When the commercial power goes off, there is no momentary interruption of electrical power to the server because power is continuously supplied. B—Standby UPS does not provide a steady continuous supply of electrical power. There is always a momentary power interruption while switching to backup power.

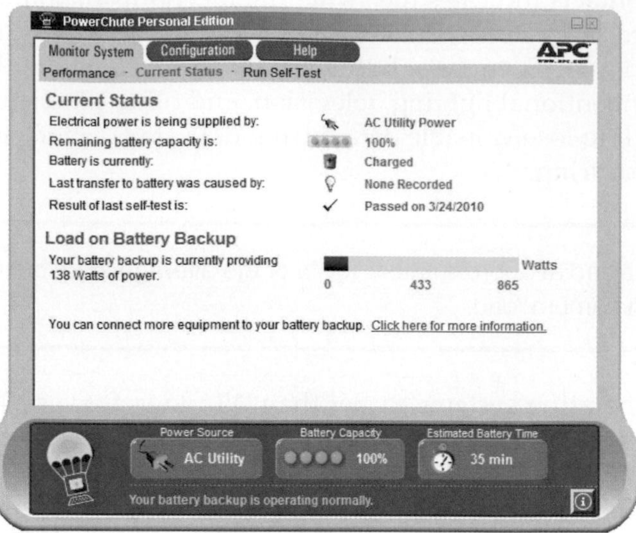

Figure 17-19. The PowerChute software utility provides options to monitor and configure the UPS.

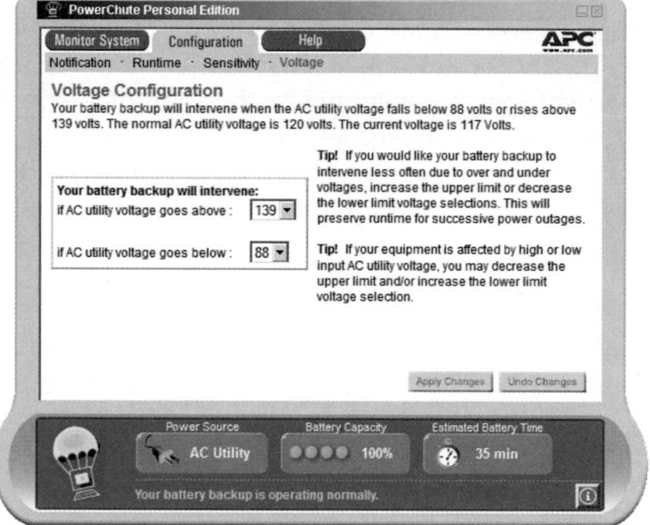

Figure 17-20. PowerChute can be used to configure the maximum and minimum voltage levels for the APC UPS system.

Many other configuration options are available such as automated notification to network clients when there is an AC power failure. The notification provides network users with ample time to close any open programs and shut down the computer before the UPS power supply is completely drained.

Isolation Transformers

Dedicated electrical circuits used for supplying computer equipment typically have isolation transformers installed near the source or electrical panel. An ***isolation transformer*** is a device that uses a transformer to isolate a circuit from other circuits emanating from the same electrical source. For example, electrical circuits coming from the electrical panel feed regular purpose outlets used for coffee pots, copiers, paper shredders, pencil sharpeners, and other types of electrical equipment. An isolation transformer isolates the special computer equipment circuit from the other circuits. Transformers are normally used to raise or lower voltage levels in electrical or electronic systems. Look at **Figure 17-21** to see how an isolation transformer works.

isolation transformer
a device that uses a transformer to isolate a circuit from other circuits emanating from the same electrical source.

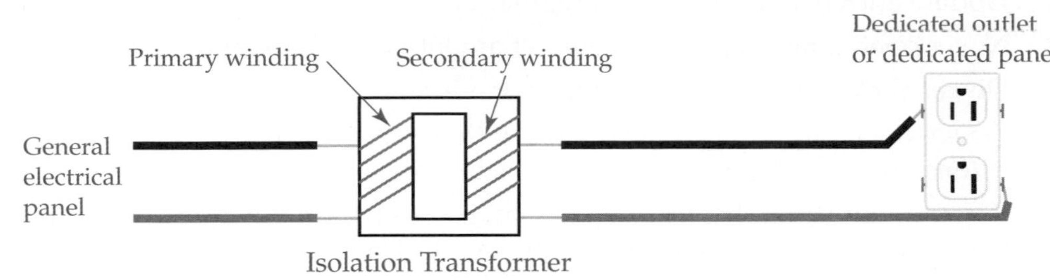

Figure 17-21.
An isolation transformer is used to isolate, or separate, dedicated power outlets from the other power outlets in an electrical distribution system. Isolation transformers suppress electrical voltage spikes.

The transformer consists of a primary, or input, winding and a secondary, or output, winding. The two windings are not electrically connected. They connect through a magnetic field produced in the primary winding. The magnetic field passes through the secondary winding, which in turn produces voltage in the output that mirrors the input voltage. One of the by-products of using an isolation transformer is its natural ability to suppress voltage spikes. The isolation transformer isolates the circuit on the output side of the transformer from the effects of spikes generated on the input side of the transformer. The isolation transformer will not eliminate very large spikes, but it will suppress the voltage level, which can damage computer equipment.

Generators

A ***generator*** is a device that creates and provides electricity. It is used for computer systems that require 24/7/365 uptime. A generator can maintain power for a few minutes to several hours depending on the size of the unit. Critical systems require one or more generators—for example, a system of computers used in an airfield control tower. If severe weather took the commercial power out, the control tower could still monitor airplanes and provide information to pilots. Other systems that rely on computer technology and require generators are hospitals, police, fire, rescue, security, military, banking, high-rise buildings, and large enterprise businesses.

generator
a device that creates and provides electricity.

Protecting Networks from Malware

In Chapter 15—Network Security, you learned that some of the ways a network could be compromised is through malicious code such as Trojan and Macro. However, malicious code cannot only compromise security, it can damage data and cause system failure. An administrator must be on constant guard against computer malicious code, or malware. A network administrator's best protection for the network is a combination of user policies and antivirus software.

Establishing Network System User Policies

All network users need user and system policies that are set in place and enforced. Policies outline how users are to use and not use their workstation and the network. Basically, policies and procedure are a list of dos and don'ts for the user. Typically, these are called an *Acceptable Use Policy*. An Acceptable Use Policy that helps protect a system against malware may include the following:

- Do *not* open any e-mail file attachments from unknown sources.
- Do *not* download any files from unknown sources.

- Update antivirus software on a regular basis.
- Never open e-mail advertisements, chain letters, or junk mail.
- Do *not* click icons embedded in files or e-mails.
- Do *not* open any e-mail attachments with an exe, com, bat, vbs, shs, pif, ovl extension or double extensions such as in GreatPicture.jpg.exe.
- If you doubt the authenticity of an e-mail, check with the indicated source before opening the e-mail, especially an attachment.

Antivirus Software

Antivirus software is typically used to scan files and e-mail for viruses. It can be configured to run in the background and scan files and e-mail as they are accessed. When an antivirus program detects a virus in this mode, it will display a message that says that a virus has been detected. Depending on how the antivirus software is configured, it will either prompt the user for an action to take or alert the user that it has cleaned, deleted, or quarantined the infected file or e-mail. A file is typically quarantined (moved to a quarantine directory) when the antivirus software program is unable to remove the virus. The user can then use the antivirus software program to view the file and delete it.

A user can also scan files and e-mail at anytime by opening the antivirus program and selecting the storage locations or directories to scan. When an antivirus program detects a virus in this mode, it will display a report after it has scanned all of the selected files. Depending on how the antivirus software is configured, it will either display the action taken or allow the user to clean, delete, or quarantine the infected file or files. **Figure 17-22** shows a report of infected e-mail. Notice that the antivirus software lists the name of the malware with which the file is infected.

virus pattern file
a database of virus signatures, or codes, unique to each known virus.

scan engine
a software program that performs the function of reading each file indicated in the scan configuration and checking it against the virus signatures in the virus pattern file.

Antivirus software should be installed on the server and on each workstation in the network. Antivirus software comes in enterprise versions that allow an administrator to easily install and update antivirus software on all workstations from a single location.

Antivirus software consists of a scan engine and a virus pattern file. The ***virus pattern file*** is a database of virus signatures, or codes, unique to each known virus. The ***scan engine*** is a software program that performs the function of reading each file indicated in the scan configuration and checking it against the virus signatures in the virus pattern file. Since antivirus companies continuously update the virus

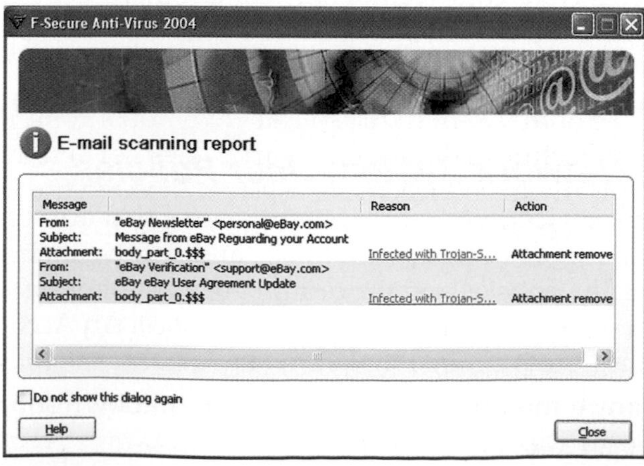

Figure 17-22.
An antivirus scan report typically lists the names of all infected files, the name of the malware with which each file is infected, and the action taken.

pattern files as new malware is discovered, the virus pattern file should be updated on a regular basis.

An antivirus software program can only remove known viruses. Every day, there are new viruses or variations of old viruses. Virus pattern files are constantly updated to include virus signatures for all known viruses. Sometimes a virus is so new, the latest virus pattern file does not include a virus signature for the new virus. In this case, the administrator must remove the virus manually. Most antivirus sites provide a detailed, step-by-step virus removal process. The process usually involves accessing the system registry and changing values or removing a specific registry key. Normally, you are cautioned never to modify system registry contents because doing so could be disastrous. You could change the wrong area of the registry or make a typographical error, which can cause the system to not be able to load the Windows operating system. You should always back up the registry before making any changes to its contents.

Most antivirus software packages include additional features such as a firewall, protection against spam, and a popup ad blocker. An antivirus software package that includes additional features is typically referred to as an ***antivirus suite.***

antivirus suite
an antivirus software package that includes additional features.

Malware

Malicious software is referred to by the term *malware*, which is a contraction of the two-word descriptor *malicious software.* ***Malware*** is a software program designed to perform some type of unauthorized activity on a computer system. The unauthorized activity can be harmless, such as that provided by a joke program, or destructive, such as a program designed to erase all data stored on the system.

malware
a software program designed to perform some type of unauthorized activity on a computer system.

The term *malware*, *virus*, and *worm* are often used interchangeably even though this is not technically correct.

There are many terms used to classify malware, such as *virus, worm, logic bomb, Trojan horse, backdoor, joke program, hoax, stealth, polymorphic*, and *boot sector.* The exact classification can be confusing when a particular program has a combination of several characteristics. For example, a malware program could be used as an e-mail attachment disguised as a Trojan horse, which is designed to spread throughout the Internet as a worm and infect the boot sector of the hard disk drive in each host. Therefore, we now have a Trojan horse, worm, boot sector virus. This section looks at some of the common classifications of malware based on basic characteristics.

Virus

A ***virus*** is a type of malware that replicates itself on a computer after infecting it. By strict, technical definition, a virus does not automatically spread itself. A virus is typically introduced into a system through the use of a disk or disc. It can then be spread by an e-mail attachment. Confusion arises because of the common use of the term *virus* to represent any form of malicious software. The news media is especially fond of the term *virus.*

virus
a type of malware that replicates itself on a computer after infecting it.

A virus usually has three phases: infection, replication, and execution. The infection comes from a source such as a floppy disk, CD, e-mail, or network connection such as the Internet. Replication is when the virus duplicates itself to other programs, files, drives, or other computers on a network. If a virus continually replicates itself, it can easily consume all available hard disk drive space. Execution can take many forms, such as harmless, annoying, and destructive.

Worm

worm
a type of malware that infects files on a computer and automatically spreads to other computers.

A ***worm*** penetrates a computer and may reproduce itself. It does, however, infect other computer systems. Technically speaking, a worm is not a true virus, but rather its own destructive program. A virus replicates itself on one computer and infects files on that particular computer. A worm infects files on the infected computer and automatically spreads to other computers. The fact that the worm automatically spreads its own infection is what makes it different from a virus. A classic example of distributing a worm is through the use of e-mail. When a worm is sent as a file attachment, it replicates itself by using the list of contacts in the e-mail database. The people on the contacts list receive an e-mail, which may or may not need to be opened to infect the people on their contacts list. Worms are also referred to as *bacterium virus* by some authorities.

Trojan Horse

Trojan horse
a type of malware that appears as a gift, utility, game, or an e-mail attachment.

A ***Trojan horse*** appears as a gift, utility, game, or an e-mail attachment. When the file is opened, the malware is activated. It can cause immediate damage or wait until a later preset date. It can have an outward appearance of a harmless JPEG file or a utility to assist you with some sort of computer operation. You may not even realize that it is a virus. After all, that is the objective of the intruder. After a while, things happen. The hard disk drive is erased or filled with duplicates of the original program, leaving no space for any other files to be saved. A Trojan horse can cause most anything imaginable.

Joke Program

joke program
a type of malware designed with some sort of joke as the payload.

A ***joke program*** is designed with some sort of joke as the payload. For example, when the user invokes a certain action, the joke program is triggered. The joke might be designed to display a dialog box on the screen similar to the one in **Figure 17-23.** This joke program was written in Visual Basic. It looks like a real dialog box because it is! Visual Basic uses the same dialog boxes and other features found in the Microsoft operating system family of products.

While this joke appears harmless, there are some that are not. For example, there are joke programs that can render the user's computer unusable. The screen spins before the user's eyes and cannot be stopped until a secret key combination is used. The prank is harmless, unless the person who receives the joke program never receives the key combination to stop the program. Then the joke program is as destructive as any other malicious software program. Much production time is lost while attempts are made to remove the program. Joke programs are really no joke at all, especially in the world of business.

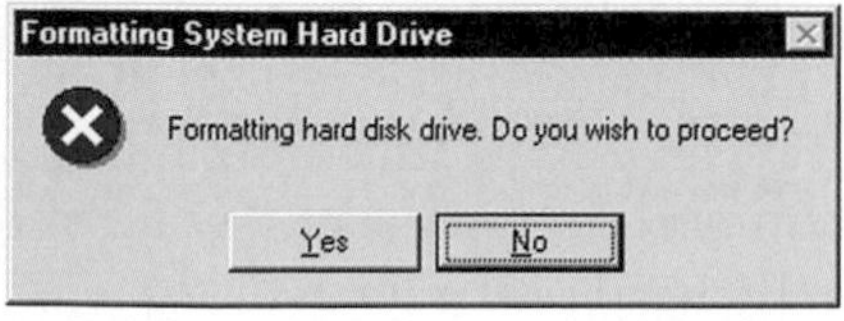

Figure 17-23.
Example of a joke program written in Visual Basic. A message box like this could panic a user because it looks like a dialog box produced by the Microsoft operating system.

MBR Virus

An ***MBR virus*** is a type of malware that attacks the master boot record (MBR) of a hard disk drive. It is considered extremely destructive. When activated, the virus plants hexadecimal codes in the MBR, rendering the MBR useless. This results in a system boot failure. Damage is usually limited to only the master boot record, which can be rebuilt if backups of system files have been made. Note that this includes the system files, and not just the data files. Many antivirus programs perform MBR backups as part of their installation and require a floppy to save necessary records for rebuilding the system.

MBR virus
a type of malware that attacks the master boot record (MBR) of a hard disk drive.

One point of particular interest is the **fdisk/mbr** command used to repair the MBR. Certain known virus programs such as the Monkey virus move the location of the MBR. Applying the **fdisk/mbr** command will not remedy the problem and most likely will do more damage.

Logic Bomb

A ***logic bomb*** remains dormant until a certain event takes place. The event could be a date, time, a certain number, word, file name, or even the number of times the virus program is loaded. The idea behind the design of a logic bomb is to wait for a period of time, which allows the virus to spread to other computers before releasing its destructive payload.

logic bomb
a type of malware that remains dormant until a certain event takes place.

Backdoor Virus

A ***backdoor virus*** is designed to go undetected and create a backdoor on your system. It is not designed to be directly destructive, but rather to breach security systems. Once the backdoor is created, the computer's file system can be accessed despite standard password and standard security systems. Backdoors are usually associated with network systems, but can also be used on stand-alone PCs.

backdoor virus
a type of malware designed to go undetected and create a backdoor on a computer.

Password Virus

A ***password virus*** is not a virus in the sense that it is designed to destroy a system or replicate itself, but rather, like the backdoor, it is designed to breach security by stealing passwords. The password is stolen and then redirected to another location, possibly on some other network on the Internet to be accessed later. The administrator of the network that houses the stolen password will probably not be aware that the network is being used to store a stolen password. A password virus is closely associated with backdoor viruses and may be used in combination. Both the password and backdoor virus are designed mainly for illegal access to networks. Either can be used to access a private PC when connected to the Internet.

password virus
a type of malware designed to breach security by stealing passwords.

Stealth Virus

A ***stealth virus*** hides from normal detection by incorporating itself into part of a known and usually required program. The signature of a stealth virus is difficult to detect unless the computer had an antivirus program installed when new. When the antivirus program is installed on a clean PC, it monitors changes in all files, especially those susceptible to a stealth virus. For example, if the program changes in length, it is a sign that a stealth virus has infected it.

stealth virus
a type of malware that hides from normal detection by incorporating itself into part of a known and usually required program.

Polymorphic Virus

A ***polymorphic virus*** is any malware that changes its characteristics or profile as it spreads to resist detection. It can change its program length randomly and also change the location of the files it chooses to infect. By constantly changing

polymorphic virus
a type of malware that changes its characteristics or profile as it spreads to resist detection.

its virus profile, it can go undetected by antivirus programs that compare files or programs to the signature or profile of a known virus. The most dangerous viruses use both the polymorphic and stealth characteristics to protect themselves.

Hoax

hoax
a message that is spread about a real or unreal virus.

A ***hoax*** is as the name implies. It is not a real virus, but a message that is spread about a real or unreal virus. It could be classified as a prank. Hoaxes are not harmless because they can cost money through the loss of production. The hoax may warn of a virus, such as a logic bomb, that will start infecting systems at noon on June 5. People who believe the hoax may shut down their computer at that time. Afterwards, they may wait for an antivirus program to clean their computer before resuming work. It may take time before they realize that this is just a hoax and that no virus exists. Much time could be lost, especially if the scenario takes place in the corporate environment involving thousands of computers. As you see, while not incurring harm to the PC and its data or system files, the hoax consumes valuable production time, which costs a company money in the form of labor costs.

Macro Virus

macro
a symbol, word, or key that represents a command or list of keystrokes.

macro virus
a virus created by the macro feature of a software application program.

A ***macro*** is a symbol, word, or key that represents a command or list of keystrokes. Most word processing applications, such as Microsoft Word, include a macro utility. A ***macro virus*** is named after the macro utility. A non-virus macro is designed to assist a computer user by converting repetitive tasks into one simple key code or name. Macros can record a set of user keystrokes and then save the set of keystrokes under a file name. When needed, the user can press the keystrokes to invoke the task or set of tasks the keystrokes relate to. For example, a set of keystrokes for creating a company heading to be used repeatedly can easily be created in the Microsoft Word program. A typical heading with the company's name, address, phone number, contact person, and greeting can all be created and saved as a macro. When loaded, the macro automatically recreates the keystrokes producing the desired company name, address, and such. This same method is used to create virus programs. The virus macro is usually distributed as an e-mail attachment.

One way malicious file attachments are hidden from users is by taking advantage of the fact that a filename can be 255 characters long, use periods in the name, and use blank spaces. For example, saving a file with a long string of blank spaces can hide an exe file extension. Look at the following example:

```
The Report.txt                              .exe
```

The filename in the example is over fifty characters long. If an e-mail was sent to someone with this filename, only the The Report.txt portion of the file name would show in the attachment field at the top of the e-mail. The exe file extension would be hidden from view. The person receiving the e-mail with the attachment would activate the malware when they opened the attachment, unaware that the attachment is an executable program.

Merging Networks

Mergers and acquisitions of different corporations are common in corporate environments. Two competing companies often merge as a way to increase profitability. When two companies merge, many costs can be eliminated. It results in reduced overhead or operational costs, while maintaining the same productivity and customer base. For example, if two competing widget manufacturers merge, they will still have the same total number of widget customers and have the same combined gross income. However, after the merger, some personnel positions can be reduced or eliminated. The number of high-level management positions can be reduced and departments, such as finance, can be eliminated from one company and absorbed by the other, or one could be greatly reduced. As the departments of the two companies are merged and personnel is reduced, equipment costs and business square footage required can also be reduced or merged. This reduces the total cost of production and thus increases the profits for stockholders and investors.

When the two companies merge, they may also combine two entirely different networking systems, such as Microsoft Windows and Novell NetWare or Unix/Linux. The networking technicians and administrators are charged with the task of making two different operating systems and networks compatible in the most efficient manner. This is not always an easy challenge. Combining the two systems may also involve turning the entire network into one network operating system. Combining two diverse network systems into one is often referred to as ***system migration.***

system migration combining two diverse network systems into one.

The term *system migration* is also used to describe converting from one operating system to a newer version of the operating system that uses different technologies. For example, Windows Server 2008 and Windows Server 2008 R2. One of the new technologies introduced in Windows Server 2008 R2 is Live Migration. In earlier operating systems, a server would need to be rebooted to complete the migration process. This meant that clients would be disconnected. With Live Migration, you can perform a migration without disconnecting the network clients. The server must be running Hyper-V, which is a virtualization software application. The clients are transferred transparently from one server to the other without interrupting services.

All major network operating systems can be based on TCP/IP communications. This means that all equipment on the network can be identified with IP addresses. When modifying or adding equipment such as printers to a network, the equipment's IP address must be static, not dynamic. It is important that all static addresses be unique.

Also, when using Dynamic Host Configuration Protocol (DHCP) services from the servers of the two different network systems, the technician must be careful not to duplicate IP address assignments. The two IP address pools should be merged to form one large pool.

There are many aspects to be concerned about when maintaining an existing network. At the technician level, you typically are not responsible for these decisions. The network administrator or administrative team must carry the burden of responsibility for decisions that affect the entire network. The decisions must be made carefully based on an existing body of knowledge. There are many case studies provided at vendor Web sites. Case studies are documented studies of how certain companies proceeded to achieve goals, such as system migration, upgrading, expansion, and new installations. The case studies should be used to serve as a model or as a possible guide to accomplishing a similar task. There is little or no need to plan your own merger from scratch.

Summary

- A baseline of the system should be established and then routinely collected to predict events that may occur.
- Monitor the network performance and do periodic comparisons between the current indicators and the original baseline to spot trends.
- Software programming flaws are referred to as *bugs*.
- Patches or fixes are used to correct bugs and security problems as they are discovered.
- Microsoft periodically releases collections of fixes and patches called *service packs*.
- Software patches, fixes, and service packs should be tested before applying them to the entire network.
- Adding a switch to create two or more virtual LANs (VLANs) can increase an existing network's bandwidth.
- The two types of UPS units are standby and continuous.
- Data integrity is the completeness and accuracy of data stored on the network system.
- Ensuring system integrity requires regular data backups and protecting the data while the server is running.
- The three backup types are full, incremental, and differential.
- A full backup makes a complete copy of the original data and resets the archive bit.
- A differential backup copies changed files since the last full backup. It does not reset the archive bit.
- An incremental backup copies changed files since the last incremental backup and then resets the archive bit.
- A good antivirus software suite and human resource training regarding computer policies and procedures are the best defenses against malicious software programs.
- A virus is a self-replicating program that wastes hard disk drive space.
- A worm is a malicious software program that automatically distributes itself across a network system.
- A Trojan horse is a malware program that has a deceptive or harmless appearance as a gift.
- There is no way to completely protect a system from malicious software programs.
- Caution should be used when making changes to the system registry as part of the steps to remove a virus problem. Always back up the system registry before making any changes.
- System migration can be defined as combining two diverse network systems into one or converting from one operating system to a newer version that uses different technologies.
- When adding equipment such as printers, use a static IP address, not a dynamic IP address.

Review Questions

Answer the following questions on a separate sheet of paper. Please do not write in this book.

1. Why are networks monitored?
2. Why is a baseline established?
3. What are some types of information gathered for a network baseline?
4. What are some typical events that can be monitored on a server?
5. Problems in software programs are referred to as _____.
6. Software programs installed periodically to solve problems with security or hardware are called _____ or _____.
7. Microsoft periodically releases a major collection of software patches and fixes and refers to them as _____.
8. Why should patches be tested before installing them on a network system?
9. What should you do before installing a new software package on a network system?
10. What should you do before installing a new hardware device on a network server or client?
11. Explain how bandwidth is increased by installing a switch and creating two or more virtual LANs?
12. Which RAID system does *not* ensure data integrity?
13. What are the three types of system data backups?
14. Which backup system takes the least amount of time to perform for a daily backup?
15. Which backup system takes the most amount of time when restoring data?
16. Which backup system is performed using a series of individual tapes that must be reinstalled in the exact order they were created?
17. When is the archive bit for a file reset?
18. What device is used to protect a server from power blackouts and brownouts?
19. Will a UPS protect against voltage spikes and surges?
20. What are the two major classifications of UPS systems?
21. What is an isolation transformer?
22. All viruses and worms can be referred to as _____.
23. What is the name for a malicious software program that infects files on an infected computer and automatically spreads to other computers?
24. What term is used to describe a malicious software program that appears as a gift, utility, game, or an e-mail attachment?
25. What type of virus is commonly created using a simple word processing program?
26. List seven things that a user can do and not do to help protect a system against malware.
27. What does the term *system migration* mean in reference to networking systems?
28. What precaution must be taken when combining two network systems that are both using DHCP?

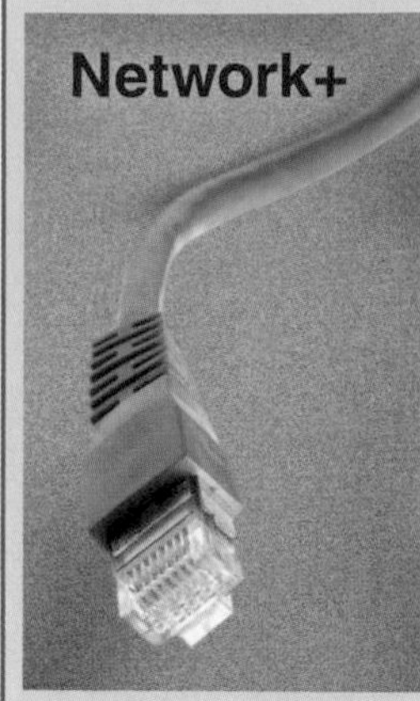

Sample Network+ Exam Questions

Answer the following questions on a separate sheet of paper. Please do not write in this book.

1. Which device is required to provide a steady stream of continuous electrical power to a server?
   A. A power strip with surge protection.
   B. A generator rated for at least 12 kW.
   C. A standby UPS system rated for at least 2000 W.
   D. An online UPS system rated for at least 2000 W.
2. You need to design a fault tolerant system for backing up critical data stored on a single network server. The system is in operation five days per week, Monday through Friday. You want to be able to restore the data as fast as possible after a hard disk drive failure. Which fault tolerance system will best meet the requirement of restoring the lost data as quickly as possible?
   A. Perform a full backup Fridays and an incremental backup each day of the week.
   B. Perform a full backup each day of the week.
   C. Perform a full backup Friday and a differential backup each day of the week.
   D. Install a RAID 1 system in the server.
3. You notice that the network has slowed over the last several weeks. While in the server room, you notice that the hard disk drive activity light seems to be constantly blinking. What might be the *most likely* cause of both symptoms, the network speed appearing slower and an increase in hard disk drive activity?
   A. The CPU does not have sufficient processing speed to accommodate network requests and activity.
   B. The existing RAM is not of sufficient size to support the amount of network requests and activity.
   C. The power supply is heating up, causing a slowdown in processing speed.
   D. A loose or faulty cable is causing too many packets to be dropped thus resulting in increased hard disk drive activity on the server.
4. What should be done before installing an operating system upgrade?
   A. Run **chkdsk** before you install the upgrade to provide more available disk space.
   B. Back up all critical files.
   C. Remove all existing applications before the system upgrade to ensure there will be no software conflicts during the initial boot. Then reinstall the applications.
   D. Stop all support services on the server so that they are not corrupted during the system upgrade.
5. Many more user workstations have been added to your existing Ethernet network since it was first installed. Over a period of time, demand has increased beyond for what the network was originally designed. Which recommendation would best remedy the problem in the shortest amount of time with the least amount of cost?
   A. Install a new server with more RAM, at least two CPUs, and more hard disk space.
   B. Evaluate the system and install a switch that will separate the traffic flow by departments.

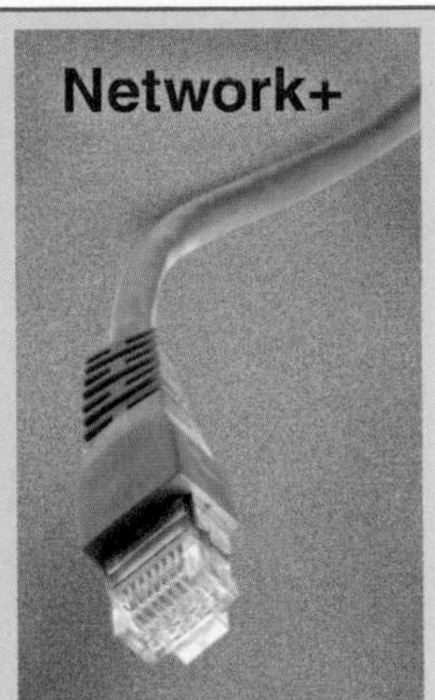

C. Remove the logon and authentication requirement for network users to release more hard disk drive space, decrease CPU demand, and decrease most of the network traffic.
D. Subdivide the network by department using hubs to block broadcasts from department to department and reduce the overall amount of broadcast across the entire network.

6. What does a file archive bit indicate?
   A. How many times the data has been copied.
   B. The file is not an original.
   C. A backup of the data has been made.
   D. A file accessible to legacy software programs.
7. Which of the following would be required for a cold backup site for the corporate accounting department?
   A. Copies of daily backup tapes.
   B. Equipment matching the corporate headquarters and backup copies of data.
   C. Operating software loaded on backup site computers and copies of data.
   D. Accounting software, operating system software, and backup copies of data loaded on the backup site computers.
8. Which backup technology only copies files that have changed since the last full backup and does not reset the file archive attribute?
   A. Incremental
   B. Differential
   C. Sequential
   D. Sparse
9. Which UPS system provides the best protection for a network server?
   A. Off-line
   B. Standby
   C. Continuous
   D. Generator
10. Which RAID system provides no fault tolerance protection?
    A. RAID 0
    B. RAID 1
    C. RAID 5
    D. RAID 1 and 5

Suggested Laboratory Activities

1. At a vendor Web site, locate and download several case studies concerning system migrations. Study the details of how it was accomplished and make a report to the class.
2. Locate a manufacturer that makes switches. Download information on how a switch can affect bandwidth.
3. Do an Internet search to find a Hardware Compatibility List (HCL) that could help you upgrade an existing network operating system to a newer network operating system.
4. Visit a major antivirus Web site, and then download and install a trial-basis antivirus suite on a server.
5. Look up the steps required to remove some of the more commonly known or latest viruses.

Interesting Web Sites for More Information

www.adaptec.com
www.antivirus.cai.com
www.apcc.com
www.ca.com/virusinfo
www.f-secure.com
www.grisoft.com
www.mcafee.com
www.sans.org
www.symantec.com
www.trendmicro.com
www.vcatch.com

Chapter 17
Laboratory Activity

LANguard Network Security Scanner

After completing this laboratory activity, you will be able to:

- Carry out proper procedures to download and install GFI LANguard.
- Use GFI LANguard to determine if the latest patches and service packs are installed on a system.
- Use GFI LANguard to identify network client and server potential security problems.
- Use GFI LANguard to inventory workstations, servers, and other network devices.

Introduction

In this laboratory activity, you will download and install a third-part utility called GFI LANguard Network Security Scanner. GFI LANguard is a software utility designed to check for potential security problems and scan for needed maintenance items, such as software patches and service packs. Identifying missing network operating system patches and updates are critical in keeping the network system secure and in working order.

GFI LANguard checks and identifies many security vulnerabilities and recommends corrective actions. The security items include open ports, open shares, passwords that do not meet minimum security requirements, and programs that run automatically, such as Trojans. GFI LANguard also checks for USB devices that might be connected to the network and considered a violation of company security policy, such as wireless adapters, wireless access points, hard drives, cameras, and other devices that use a USB port. As you can see, GFI LANguard is a versatile utility that conducts an in-depth check of the network.

GFI LANguard not only identifies missing patches and service packs, it can be configured to install them from one location. It can also install third-party software patches and updates. GFI LANguard also identifies and inventories most of the devices connected to the network, including the type of operating systems installed, MAC and IP addresses, domain names, and user names.

The highlights of GFI LANguard are presented in this laboratory activity. To achieve a more detailed and comprehensive understanding of GFI LANguard, you need to read the user manual, which is in PDF form. It can be downloaded for free from the GFI Web site. Using the GFI LANguard is very simple. You simply select the type of scan you wish to perform, such as **Quick Scan** or **Full Scan**.

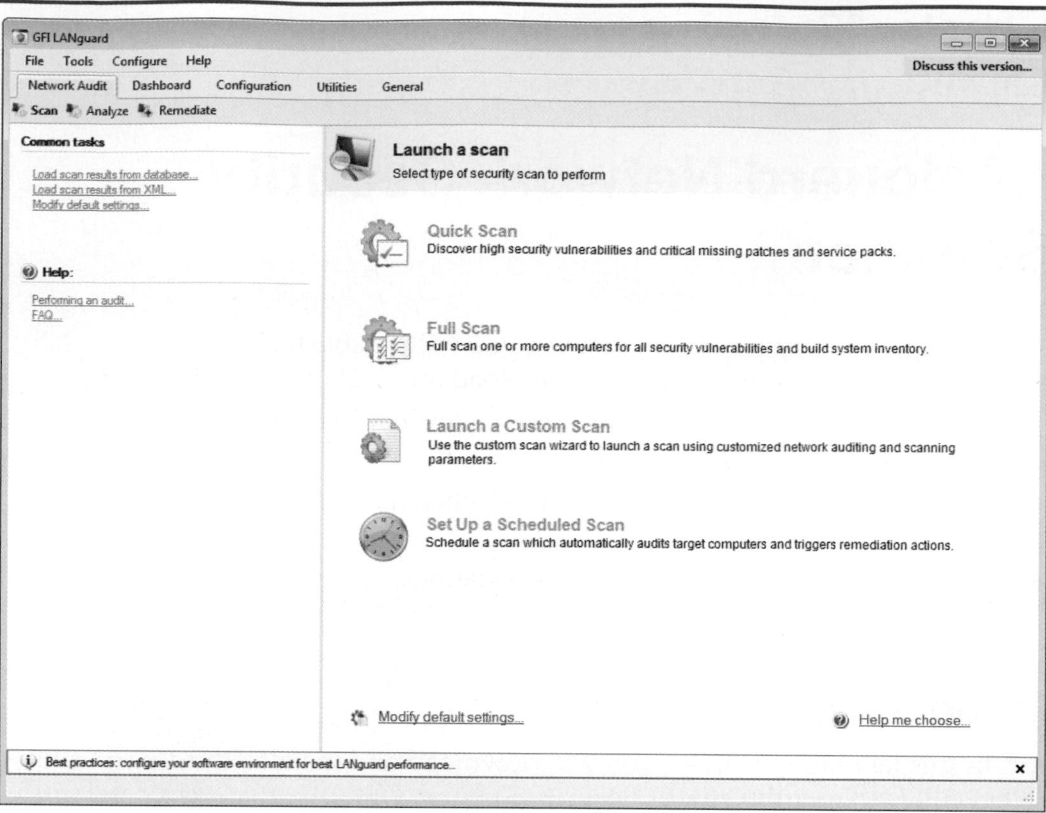

The next dialog box to appear prompts you to select the target to scan. The options are **Scan this computer**, **Scan another computer**, or **Scan the entire domain/workplace**. You can also configure a custom scan and even schedule an automatic scan.

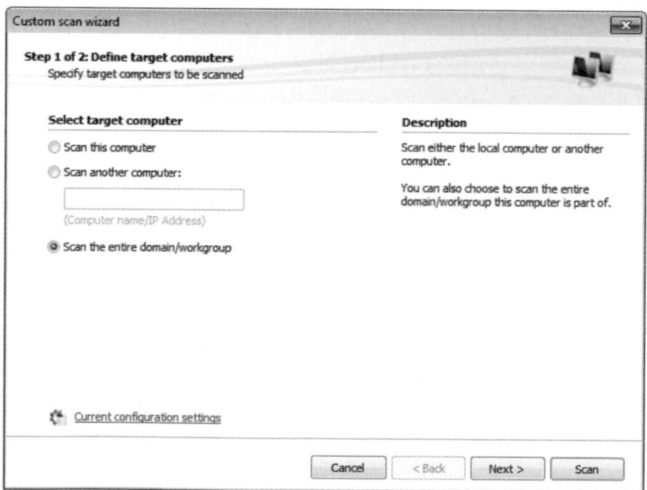

After selecting the target, you will be prompted to select credentials for the scan. This is shown in the following screen capture.

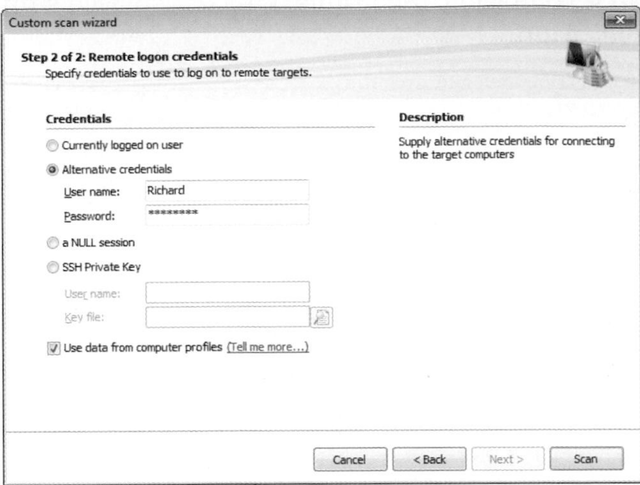

The credential options are **Currently logged on user**, **Alternative credentials**, **a NULL session**, and **SSH Private Key**. Using the **Alternative credentials** or **Currently logged on user** option allows the system administrator to detect missing patches and see vulnerabilities.

The **a NULL session** option allows you to see the network or selected target the same way a hacker would view the network. It is used to test network vulnerability to unauthorized personnel. The **SSH Private Key** option is required for connections to UNIX and Linux systems.

After selecting a credential option, you will need to press the **Scan** button to start the scan. The approximate amount of time to complete the scan will be presented along with a progress bar.

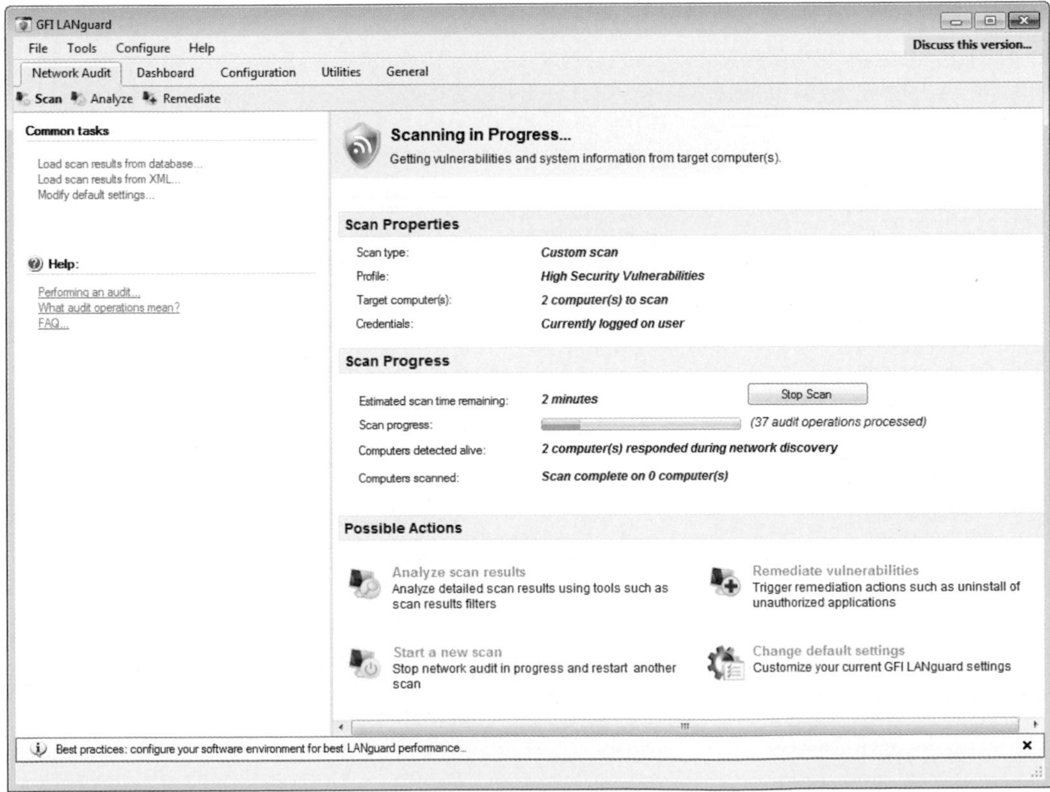

After the scan is completed, the results will be displayed similar to that in the following screen capture.

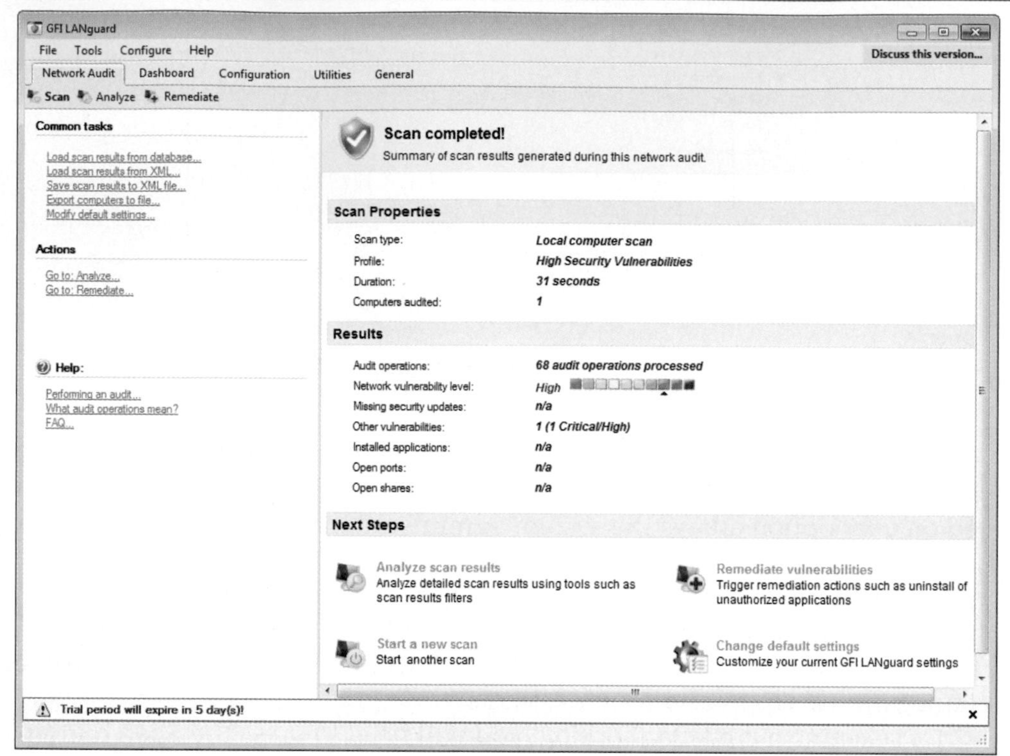

A more detailed view of scan results will be displayed when the **Analyze** option is selected under the **Network Audit** tab.

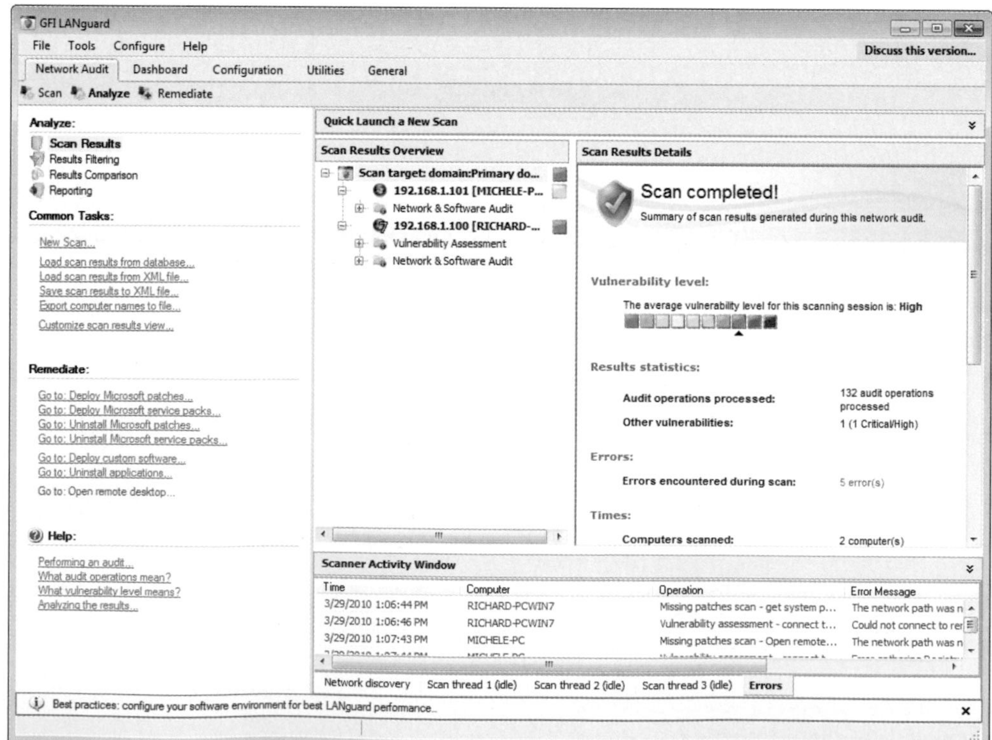

The scan results are displayed by IP address, and an overall vulnerability level is displayed as well.

Equipment and Materials

- Computer with Windows XP or later. Must be part of a peer-to-peer or client/server network.
- The following information provided by your instructor:

  Administrator user name: ______________________________

  Password: ______________________________

  Note
  Your instructor may supply you with a copy of GFI LANguard. This lab activity is based on GFI LanGuard version 9.

Procedure

1. _____ Gather all required materials and report to your assigned workstation.
2. _____ Boot the computer and verify it is in working order.
3. _____ If you already have a copy of GFI LANguard, skip to step 6. If not, create a LANguard folder on your computer. This is where you will download the GFI LANguard program and documentation.
4. _____ Locate GFI LANguard on the Internet by either conducting an Internet search using the keywords "GFI LANguard" or going to www.GFI.com and accessing the GFI LANguard download page.
5. _____ After locating GFI LANguard, download the trial copy, the accompanying manuals, and the quick start or installation guide. You will need to refer to the installation guide when installing GFI LANguard on your computer. Make sure it is GFI LANguard that you download. GFI has many different software utilities that allow you to scan the network and check for vulnerabilities and maintenance items.
6. _____ Read the instructions carefully before installing GFI LANguard.
7. _____ After reading the instructions, install GFI LANguard.
8. _____ After installing GFI LANguard, scan the network using your own credentials (user name and password). Review the results.
9. _____ Run the scanner a second time with the NULL session credentials. Again, review the results.
10. _____ Take a few minutes to look over the tools available under the **Tools** menu.
11. _____ Remove the GFI LANguard utility if requested by your instructor.
12. _____ Answer the review questions. You may use the GFI LANguard manual to assist you with the review questions.

Review Questions

Answer the following questions on a separate sheet of paper. Please do not write in this book.

1. What four types of scan options are available in GFI LANguard?
2. What kind of information does **a NULL Session** option reveal?
3. What does the **Alternative credentials** option allow you to do?
4. What type of information can be revealed by GFI LANguard?
5. How would you determine which devices needed patches and had security vulnerabilities if you did not use a program like GFI LANgurard?

18 Fundamentals of Troubleshooting the Network

After studying this chapter, you will be able to:

- ❑ Apply the CompTIA network troubleshooting strategy when diagnosing network problems.
- ❑ Plan the best course of action to remedy a network problem.
- ❑ Recall in detail the boot sequence for Windows NT–based computers.
- ❑ Evaluate if a problem is user-, hardware-, or software-generated.
- ❑ Give examples of the most common network problems encountered.
- ❑ Use common TCP/IP utilities for troubleshooting the network.

Network+ Exam—Key Points

Questions concerning troubleshooting consume a major portion of the Network+ Certification exam. You must be familiar with common TCP/IP troubleshooting commands and proper troubleshooting procedures. The most common command-line utilities used in test items are **tracert**, **ping**, **nslookup**, **netstat**, **nbtstat**, **ipconfig**, **arp**, **dig**, **mtr**, and **route**.

You will also be asked about common network troubleshooting devices such as multimeter, OTD, OTDR, and tone probe. Most troubleshooting questions are scenario-type questions. These types of questions require more thought than standard fact-recollection questions. Generally, you will be provided with a situation and then asked what is the best approach or the most appropriate utility for solving the problem.

A portion of the troubleshooting questions will require knowledge of wireless systems. You will have a difficult time answering troubleshooting questions without some practical experience.

Key Words and Terms

The following words and terms will become important pieces of your networking vocabulary. Be sure you can define them.

active partition
boot partition
dead drop
hardware abstract layer (HAL)
master boot record (MBR)
power-on self-test (POST)
signal bounce
system image
system partition

This chapter presents commonly accepted troubleshooting utilities and techniques, and in many ways, serves as a review of all of the areas covered thus far. Troubleshooting requires not only knowledge about the various utilities and tools available, but also their application. Practice using the utilities is essential to becoming proficient and skilled in troubleshooting.

Troubleshooting a network involves not only knowledge and skills for diagnosing a network problem but also knowledge and skills for diagnosing a PC. If you have not already completed a course in PC support and repair, it is highly recommended you do so. The need will become apparent while studying this chapter.

Much of this chapter is simply a brief review of already mastered knowledge but is presented in the context of troubleshooting. It is important that you bring together these concepts so that you can apply them in a work setting.

CompTIA Network+ Troubleshooting Methodology

This chapter introduces troubleshooting based on CompTIA's recommended troubleshooting procedures. **Figure 18-1** lists the CompTIA procedures for troubleshooting a network problem. These steps are critical. Use them regularly.

Given a scenario, implement the following network troubleshooting methodology:

1. Information gathering—identify symptoms and problems.
2. Identify the affected areas of the network.
3. Determine if anything has changed.
4. Establish the most probable cause.
5. Determine if escalation is necessary.
6. Create an action plan and solution identifying potential effects.
7. Implement and test the solution.
8. Identify the results and effects of the solution.
9. Document the solution and the entire process.

Figure 18-1. CompTIA's network troubleshooting procedures.

The following sections discuss each procedure in detail and relate them to real-world, network-troubleshooting situations.

1. Information Gathering—Identify Symptoms and Problems

Troubleshooting a network typically begins with answering a call to the help desk from a system user. The first thing you need to do to begin the troubleshooting process is gather information and identify symptoms and problems. This description is important so that you can clearly establish the symptoms. An accurate description is not always easy to obtain from a user because he or she does not understand root causes. Users will typically describe problems in vague terms and will not be able to establish any patterned behavior of the problem. Descriptions such as the following are common:

- The computer will not start.
- The computer keeps crashing.
- I can't get to my files.
- The computer is making a funny sound.
- My Adobe Dreamweaver program won't work.
- The printer won't work.

As you can see, most users cannot give you a true, technical description of a problem. Rather, they make general statements about the problem that is readily visible to them. You must be able to communicate with the user without frustration and work with the user through a dialog that will better help you understand the problem, while maintaining a good working relationship with the user. Now is not the time to laugh at the user's description or joke about the terminology he or she uses. They are not technical experts.

As a skilled technician, you can ask the user a series of simple questions to find out more about the nature of the problem. A series of simple questions will typically lead you in the direction of the problem. Some of these questions might include:

- Is this the first time the problem has occurred?
- When did the problem first occur?
- Is anyone else in the department having the same problem?
- Has anyone added new hardware or software to the system?
- What was the last change in the system?

When a problem is first reported by a user or noticed by the IT staff, a series of questions needs to be asked and answered to better understand and isolate the problem. Correctly approaching the problem by analyzing the situation before attempting repairs can save valuable time and frustration. The troubleshooting process *always* begins with questions. Be sure to ask good questions that will lead to a clear understanding of the problem.

Typically in a large networking environment, an incident report is completed by the person at the help desk or when the call is transferred to a technician who will work with the problem. See **Figure 18-2** for a sample of a help desk request form.

2. Identify the Affected Areas of the Network

When diagnosing a network problem, you must first determine the affected area or scope of the problem. The affected area can range from a single PC to the entire network. Remember, a network provides connectivity to local and remote hosts and provides services, file sharing, Internet access, e-mail, and more. There are many areas in a network that can be affected; however, these areas can be

Figure 18-2. An example of an incident report form.

Help Desk Ticket Number ______________

Caller: ________________ Date: _____________ Time: __________

Location: ________________ Phone Number/Ext: ___________

Department: _______________ Tech. Assigned: _______________

Complete Description ____

____

____

____

____

____

____

Help Desk Action Taken ______________________________________

____

____

____

____

Follow-up Date: ______________ Time: ______________

____

____

____

divided into major areas. A simple LAN can be divided into three major areas: workstation, network infrastructure, and server. A large network can be divided into five major areas:

- Isolated workstation (host).
- Workgroup.
- Network infrastructure.
- Server(s).
- Outside the LAN (Internet or remote access).

To correct an existing problem, you must first isolate the problem area and then proceed to diagnose and correct the problem. The problem can be thought of in separate areas, such as the workstation, department the network segment belongs to (workgroup), cabling and equipment (infrastructure), server, and remote access (outside the LAN). See **Figure 18-3.** When you determine the scope of the problem, you are determining how much of the network system is affected. Is the problem limited to a single workstation, several workstations, the entire department, a large section of the network, or the entire network? By determining the scope of the problem, you can start a list of probable equipment or software items to inspect. The amount of network area affected will help you determine the device(s) responsible for the problem.

When first establishing the symptoms, you may be isolating the affected areas by applying user information. The user may say, "I can't get to www.toysrfun.com. There's something wrong." You must follow up and ask, "Can you connect to any other sites? Can anyone else near you connect to the site? When did this problem first occur?"

The user's response to the first question starts the troubleshooting process. You do not ask them for the scope of the problem. You ask them a few simple questions.

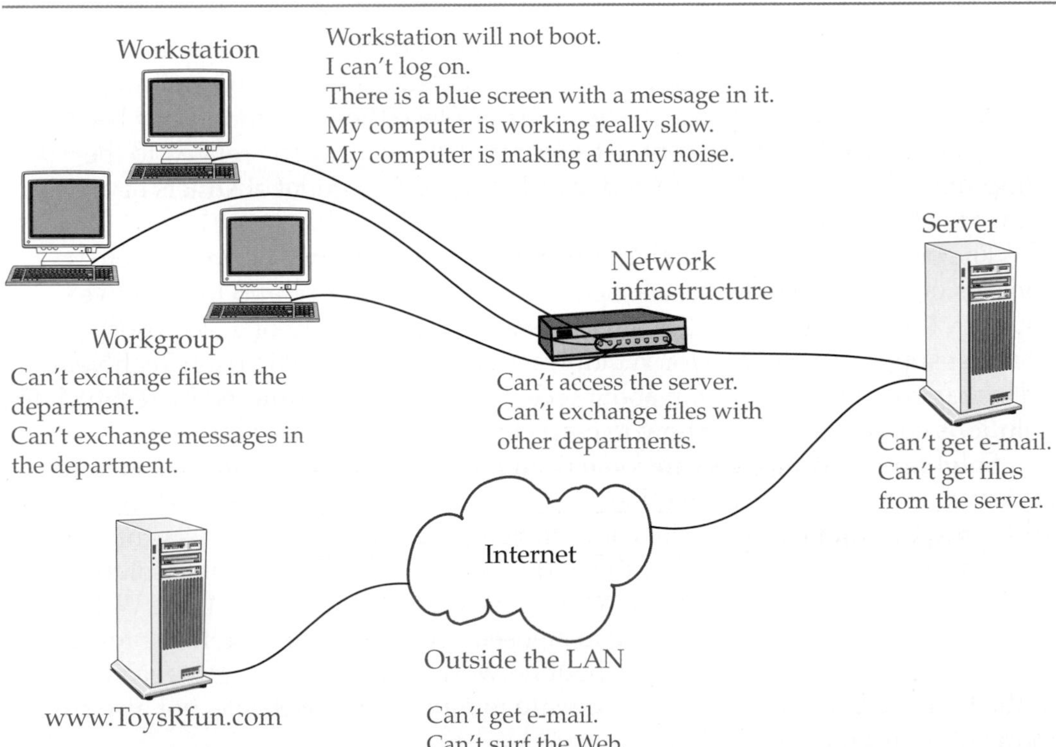

Figure 18-3. Network problems can be divided into five major areas: workstation, workgroup, server, network infrastructure, and outside the LAN.

From these questions, you will be able to determine the scope and will have gained valuable information about the problem. The user who is experiencing the problem may or may not have the expertise to help you. For example, they may not know if anyone else is having a problem. By using some of the various TCP/IP utilities available, you should be able to determine the scope of the problem quickly. TCP/IP tools are covered in more detail later in this chapter.

One of the most important items to assist you when troubleshooting a large network system is a detailed site plan that has all of the major networking devices identified. Many times the symptoms will provide you with short lists of devices to check. The map will help you identify the location of these devices.

3. Determine If Anything Has Changed

One of the most important things you must ask yourself and others is, "What has changed?" This question can be asked in many different ways. For example, you may ask one or more of the following questions:

- What has happened recently that could have caused a problem?
- Was there a new software package installed recently?
- Was a new service started on the server?
- Was a new hardware device recently installed?

Any of the answers to these questions could help determine the cause of a network problem. Perhaps, nothing has changed. The system failure may have occurred because of other reasons such as hard disk drive failure, IC failure, or a corrupted system or device file. A device failure and an unrelated event can easily confuse the troubleshooting process. Be aware that coincidences do occur.

4. Establish the Most Probable Cause

Troubleshooting requires a series of best guesses. Sometimes the solution to the problem is obvious, and other times the problem can be much more difficult to diagnose. Usually, someone else has encountered the same problem at some other location. There are thousands of documented problems and solutions available for review at no cost on the Internet. Once the symptoms have been clearly established, you can conduct a search using key words related to the symptoms. The search should produce a listing of document abstracts or articles from which to choose.

The operating system vender typically provides online support which consists of free knowledgebase articles, free e-mail support, and limited live support. Look at **Figure 18-4,** which shows a screen capture of a Microsoft TechNet support Web page for Windows Server 2008. The Microsoft TechNet Web site provides information about recent problems encountered by technicians. Solutions contain steps to follow to correct the problem.

Solutions for problems can come from numerous sources, such as operating system manufacturer Web sites, hardware manufacturer Web sites, and commercial Web sites. Commercial Web sites offer mixed product support, focus groups, organizations, and more. One of the best ways for locating a possible solution to a networking problem is the Google search engine. The World Wide Web has an extensive resource base waiting to be used. Google is highly reliable for hits concerning technical information about networks. You will not only receive hits at the hardware manufacturer or software manufacturer Web site, but also from many other reputable sources.

Figure 18-4.
Windows Server 2008 Troubleshooting and Support Web site contains information to assist the technician when troubleshooting server problems. The Web site contains expert information about problems encountered and reported to Microsoft and solutions.

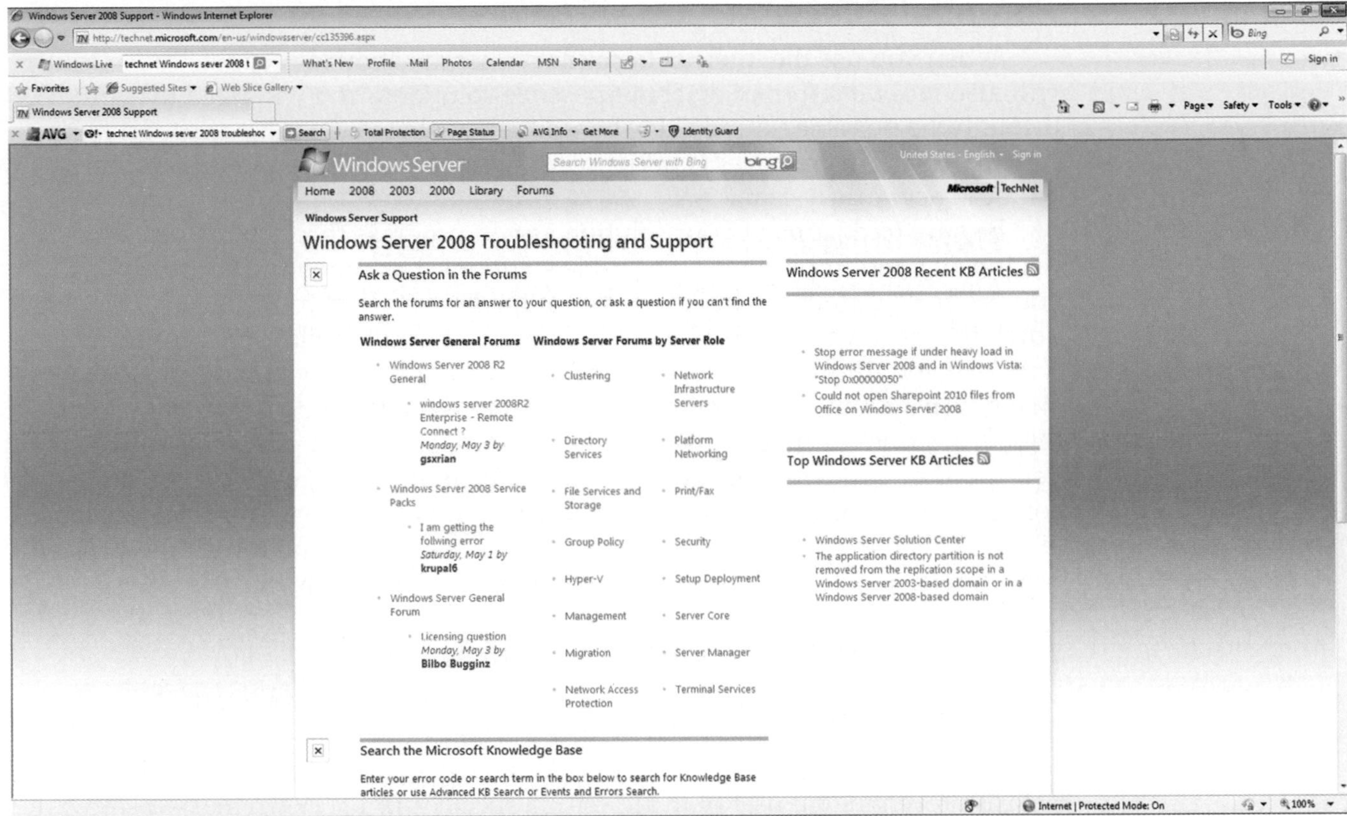

Technical support is also available by your specific operating system. The support can be provided by Web site and telephone. Support may be free or fee-based. Vendor diagnostic software CDs, especially for hardware tests, are also available.

5. Determine If Escalation Is Necessary

You will not be able to solve all problems. At times it will be necessary to escalate the problem to a supervisor or someone with more expertise. This is especially true for a network technician with limited experience. For example, if you determine that the problem involves permission shares on a particular server and you do not have the skills or authority to make changes to the server shares, you will need to escalate the problem to your immediate supervisor. Never attempt to troubleshoot a network device or software package that you are not thoroughly familiar with. Never make configuration changes to any network device that you are not familiar with or when you do not have authority to make changes.

Network infrastructure problems that generally require escalation by an inexperienced network technician include switching loops, routing loops, route problems, proxy ARP, and broadcast storms. When these conditions are detected, they should be immediately escalated to your immediate supervisor.

Again, identifying the specific problem requires an experienced technician. The important thing is to remember not to be afraid to request the help of a more experienced person or supervisor. More damage can be done by attempting to correct a problem that you are not thoroughly familiar with.

6. Create an Action Plan and Solution Identifying Potential Effects

When you use the Internet to conduct a search about a probable cause, you will also receive information about possible solutions. You will need to think through the possible solutions to choose the one that is the most appropriate to the situation. This requires experience and broad knowledge of and familiarity with the network system.

Be sure to document your solution as you progress through the process of diagnosing and implementing possible solutions. Documenting your work as you progress cannot be emphasized enough. Do *not* trust your memory. Writing down the steps you take is like leaving a trail for you to follow next time and will save you time and effort in the future. For example, if you have made any changes in system configurations, you need to write them down. A technician often loses track of time as they attempt to solve a network problem. As time goes by, they suddenly realize they have made many changes to the system configuration, and may have created additional problems or symptoms caused by those changes made. *Always* record the changes made and return the system configuration to its original settings before trying other changes.

7. Implement and Test the Solution

This may sound simplistic, but you need to test the fix you made. Not all problems need to be replicated or tested, but some do. For example, you suspect a new software package recently installed on a workstation has caused a problem, such as preventing the user from accessing a specific printer. When the new software package was removed, the workstation user could access the printer once again. If the new software package really was the culprit, you should be able to duplicate the problem. Try installing the software package on a different workstation and see if the same problem develops. If the problem of connecting to the printer occurs on the new workstation, then the software did actually cause the problem.

If the second workstation did not experience a problem connecting to the printer, then you may have a different problem. For example, a loose network cable connection could cause an intermittent problem with the connection to the printer. You uninstall the suspected software package and the problem clears. While uninstalling the software package, the bad or loose connection reconnects and the printer is accessible once again. If you truly solved a problem, you should be able to duplicate it.

Not all problems need to be replicated or tested. For example, obvious solutions such as a problem identified by a Windows message box may provide you with the problem solution, such as a recent patch. Once the patch is installed, the error no longer occurs. The solution was obvious because it was identified for you, and the recommendation worked.

8. Identify the Results and Effects of the Solution

You must realize the full ramification of the corrective action you are taking. Before you apply a possible solution, you need to know the extent of how it will affect the existing system. For example, when all else fails to repair the workstation or server, you can always reinstall the operating system. However, reinstalling the operating system could produce adverse effects on the network or workstation.

You typically have two choices for reinstalling an operating system: perform a clean installation or perform a system upgrade. When you perform a clean installation, all data on the existing partition and possibly on the entire hard disk drive is lost! You must have backups of all data files available, as well as all application software and any required device drivers.

When performing a system upgrade, the original operating system files are replaced. Typically, data files, application software, and original drivers are not required. A bit of caution is necessary when performing an upgrade. You may see messages asking if you want to install the original version of a file or driver or leave the existing file intact. This message occurs when an original system has had patches or service packs installed since the original installation. When performing an upgrade, the existing files are compared to the files about to be installed.

When two file names match but their creation dates differ, the installation process will typically ask, "Do you want to leave the existing file or replace it with the original or older file?" You should answer, "No," and leave the latest copy of the file. The only exception to this rule is if you suspect the latest version is the cause of the system abnormality. In that case, you would install the original operating system as an upgrade and later add each service pack or patch one at a time until you reach the latest, which is the suspected cause of the abnormality. In most cases, a patch or service pack will not have adverse effects on a system. Always check the support documentation at the software vendor's Web site for the latest information when repairing a system.

9. Document the Solution and the Entire Process

Most network troubleshooting scenarios start with an incident report filed with the help desk. The incident report typically includes an area for the technician to write down the implemented fix for the problem. This documentation will serve as a future reference.

Documentation is an important part of network administration and should be completed thoroughly and in a timely fashion. Documentation will save the company and personnel valuable time and money and should be considered by all technicians as a professional courtesy, as well as a necessity. Documentation can be shared with other workers especially in a large organization where workers do not get the opportunity to converse on a regular basis. The sharing of documentation can give other workers an insight to problems they may encounter in the future. Documentation also acts as a history of the system. For example, if a network interface card is replaced by another brand or version, you have a record available. The record can be used to update equipment inventories and equipment descriptions.

Knowing what type of equipment is installed on the network is very important, especially when performing a migration to a new operating system. For example, when upgrading from Windows Server 2003 to Windows Server 2008, an accurate list of system hardware is invaluable. The list can be checked against the Hardware Compatibility List (HCL) to ensure that all hardware used on the existing system is compatible with the new operating system. Without a way to check, a new operating system can be installed and problems may develop. These problems may expend a long period of time troubleshooting only to find out later that a hardware compatibility problem was the issue. Always keep an up-to-date and complete set of documentation for the existing network and associated equipment.

Software programs, such as HelpSTAR, are available to help an administrator keep track of service requests, computer inventory, and history, **Figure 18-5.** HelpSTAR is especially designed for the help desk. It is the only practical way to keep track of help desk calls when working with a large network consisting of many users or when supporting several companies. HelpSTAR can be used to initiate purchase orders and can keep an inventory of all new material and equipment as it is ordered for the network. By controlling the ordering process, the help desk also knows when the equipment needed to repair or replace a device is delivered and can match it to the correct job order. A service request can be initiated by e-mail or telephone request. The request is entered into the HelpSTAR database and assigned a reference number. The technician assigned to the problem can follow up by entering details about the progress and outcome of the incident.

Stages of Computer Operation

Troubleshooting the workstation and server involves a strong knowledge of PC operation, operating system software, and operating system boot sequences. If you are not knowledgeable about PC repair, it is strongly recommended that you take a computer repair course. A computer repair course will not only provide you with a background in PC hardware and repair, it will provide you with basic knowledge about the various desktop operating systems. This section assumes that you have a background in PC hardware and repair and are familiar with the various Microsoft desktop operating systems.

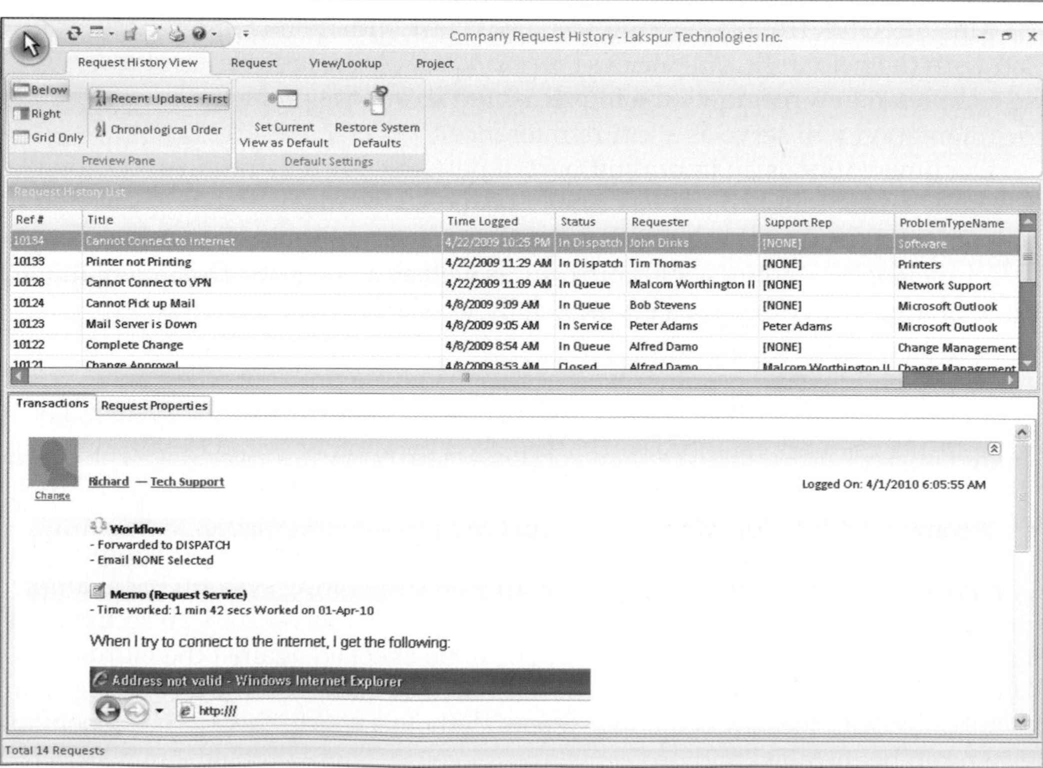

Figure 18-5.
The HelpSTAR program is a valuable tool in managing help desk requests.

When troubleshooting a computer or server, you need to determine at which stage of computer operation the system failure occurs. You do this by observing computer operation beginning with the POST and continuing until after a successful system logon. There are three general areas of server/computer operation to consider: POST, operating system loading and initiation, and the time period after a successful logon.

Note

The information presented here are general guidelines based on the most likely causes, and are not all-inclusive.

During the POST

The ***power-on self-test (POST)*** is the first stage of computer operation. Failure during the POST is generally an indication that there is a hardware failure. Some physical component is preventing the system from completing the startup operation. Failures during the POST are typically caused by such items as hard disk drives, RAM, CPU, motherboard, modem, and a failing power supply. Any essential computer hardware component can cause failure during the POST. If you suspect a POST failure caused by hardware, you should remove all nonessential components and attempt the boot process once more.

power-on self-test (POST)
a BIOS routine that performs a series of hardware checks to determine if the computer is in minimal working order.

Loading and Initializing the Operating System

This phase of operation occurs immediately after completing the POST and continues to a successful user logon. During this period, the operating system loads and initiates system configuration files. A failure during this time usually indicates a corrupt operating system or driver file.

If the startup process fails here, you will see the Microsoft infamous blue screen error. The blue screen error provides some idea of the cause of the failure, typically with an alphanumeric error code. The error code can be used as an Internet search term to locate information concerning the failure. You can also conduct a search at Microsoft's Web site using the blue screen error code.

This type of failure can typically be resolved by using the Windows installation disc. You simply place the disc into the CD/DVD drive and then reboot the system. The disc will be detected automatically, and you will be presented with recovery options based on the Windows operating system version. For example, Windows XP and Windows Server 2003 will present the Windows Recovery Console. The Windows Recovery Console is a command prompt that allows you to enter commands in an attempt to recover from the failure. In Windows Vista, Windows 7, and Windows Server 2008, the **System Recovery Options** menu is a much more sophisticated method of recovery with several options in addition to the command prompt. More will be covered later in this chapter concerning recovery using the installation disc.

After a Successful Logon

After a successful user logon, the most likely cause of a system failure is an installed software application or service. Software applications and services are started after a successful logon. A corrupt essential file could cause a system to hang or even crash after logon. Any problems such as the computer freezing

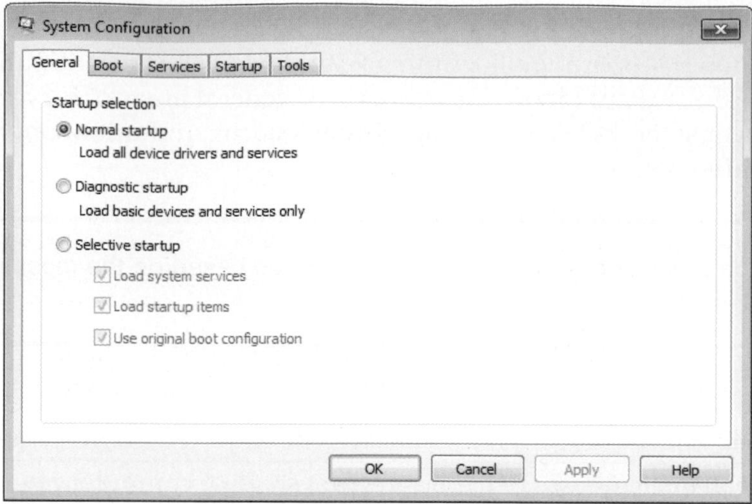

Figure 18-6. System Configuration is an excellent tool for determining if a system failure is caused by application software or a service.

or a long delay before the user desktop appears are associated with the startup files and services. One of the best utilities to identify the offending software application is System Configuration (msconfig.exe), **Figure 18-6.** Using the System Configuration tool to troubleshoot a computer is covered later in this chapter.

The System Configuration tool provides many different options for correcting system problems caused by software applications during and after the system startup. The System Configuration tool also provides access to the most common troubleshooting tools and provides a means of identifying suspected services.

Tech Tip

Malware can cause a system failure at any point of operation after the POST and, in some rare cases, during the POST. In general, malware affects the system after the POST.

Detailed Computer Startup Process

A good understanding of the computer startup process is an essential part of troubleshooting. Knowledge of the computer boot process will better enable you to determine in which general area of server/computer operation the problem failure is occurring. **Figure 18-7** compares the boot process phases of Windows 2000 and later operating systems. Notice that boot process phases three and four differ between Windows 2000/XP/Server 2003 and Windows Vista/7/Server 2008. Whereas boot process phases one, two, five, and six are similar. The following sections discuss each boot process phase. **Figure 18-8** and **Figure 18-9** summarize the boot sequences for Windows 2000/XP/Server 2003 and Windows Vista/7/Server 2008.

1. Power-On Self-Test (POST)

When a computer has power first applied to the motherboard by pressing the power switch, the system firmware (BIOS or EFI) starts the boot process by performing a quick check of hardware components and verifying that all hardware devices listed in the configuration database are present and appear to

Phase	Windows 2000	Windows XP and Server 2003	Windows Vista, Windows 7, and Windows Server 2008
1	POST	POST	POST
2	Initial Startup	Initial Startup	Initial Startup
3	Bootstrap Loader	Boot Loader	Windows Boot Manager
4	Detect and Configure Hardware	Detect and Configure Hardware	Windows Boot Loader
5	Kernel Loading	Kernel Loading	Kernel Loading
6	Logon Phase	Logon Phase	Logon Phase

Figure 18-7.
Boot process phase comparison of Windows 2000 and later operating systems.

Windows 2000/XP/Server 2003 Boot Sequence

1. The BIOS performs the power-on self-test (POST).
2. The BIOS reads the master boot record and loads its code into memory.
3. The MBR loads the NT boot loader (ntldr) into memory.
4. The NT boot loader (ntldr) loads the kernel (ntoskrnl.exe) and the hardware abstract layer (hal.dll) into RAM.
5. The kernel (ntoskrnl.exe) calls the ntdetect.com program.
6. The ntdetect.com program detects system hardware information and passes it to the NT boot loader (ntldr).
7. The NT boot loader (ntldr) passes hardware information to the NT kernel (ntoskrnl.exe).
8. The NT kernel (ntoskrnl.exe) loads the device drivers, initializes the HAL, and initializes the computer settings using the values stored in the system registry.
9. The NT kernel (ntoskrnl.exe) loads the session manager (smss.exe).
10. The session manager (smss.exe) runs an abbreviated version of Chkdsk and determines if the system volumes and partitions are in working order.
11. The windows logon file (winlogon.exe) is executed and the logon dialog box appears.
12. After a successful logon, the Local Security Authority (LSA) process (lsass.exe) and service subsystem (services.exe) load and run.

Figure 18-8.
Windows 2000/XP/Server 2003 boot sequence summary.

be in working order. The hard disk drive and standard hardware devices such as memory are automatically detected and configured. All configuration data is then stored in CMOS.

Note

Extensible Firmware Interface (EFI) is a new approach to the BIOS system. EFI is required on computers in order to use a new file system directory structure referred to as *GUID*. In the future, EFI is expected to replace BIOS as it exists today. Many computers run a hybrid combination of BIOS and EFI.

When POST completes, some adapters such as video cards or hard disk drives may carry out their own firmware diagnostics routine that is built into the device. This is independent from BIOS diagnostics.

Figure 18-9.
Windows Vista/7/Server 2008 boot sequence summary.

Windows Vista/7/Server 2008 Boot Sequence

1. The BIOS performs the power-on self-test (POST).
2. The BIOS reads the master boot record and loads its code into memory.
3. The BIOS loads the Windows Boot Manager (bootmgr).
4. The Windows Boot Manager (bootmgr) displays a boot menu if more than one operating system is installed, and it starts the Windows Boot Loader (winload.exe).
5. The Windows Boot Manager (bootmgr) passes control to the Windows Boot Loader (winload.exe).
6. The Windows Boot Loader (winload.exe) loads the NT kernel (ntoskrnl.exe) and hardware abstract layer (HAL) into RAM memory and then executes the kernel.
7. The NT kernel (ntoskrnl.exe) loads the session manager (smss.exe).
8. The session manager (smss.exe) runs an abbreviated version of Chkdsk and determines if the system volumes and partitions are in working order.
9. The windows logon file (winlogon.exe) is executed and the logon dialog box appears.
10. After a successful logon, the Local Security Authority (LSA) process (lsass.exe) and service subsystem (services.exe) load and run.

2. Initial Startup

master boot record (MBR)
an area located on the first sector of the hard drive that contains information about the hard drive partitions (partition table) and the location of the bootable partition (active partition).

active partition
the partition that contains the operating system files the computer should use to boot.

system partition
the partition that contains the core files that are used to start the operating system.

boot partition
the partition that contains the files needed to operate the computer. These files include device drivers, library files, services, commands, and utilities and are stored in a separate directory.

The initial startup phase is when the POST completes and then starts the operating system boot or bootstrap program. The POST routine looks for the boot device where the ***master boot record (MBR)*** is stored. The location of the boot device is stored by BIOS in CMOS memory. For example, the next boot device after POST may be a floppy disk, hard disk drive, CD or DVD drive, or a USB flash drive. The exact order can be changed in the BIOS setup program and then stored in the CMOS memory.

After identifying the location of the MBR, BIOS loads the MBR into RAM and then turns the boot routine over to the boot code located in the MBR. The MBR contains the boot code of the operating system and the partition table used to locate the additional startup files. The MBR is located on the first sector of the active partition on the hard disk drive. Additional duties of the MBR are to identify the system file type (FAT16, FAT32, NTFS etc.) and locate ntldr (NT boot loader file). The ntldr file is designed to load Windows XP Windows and earlier Windows NT-based operating systems. It is located on the active partition. On a Windows Vista and later system, the MBR loads the Windows Boot Manager (bootmgr). The ntldr is incorporated into the kernel, but is only used to boot NT-based operating systems prior to Windows Vista.

Often the terms *active partition*, *boot partition*, and *system partition* are used interchangeably, but actually they have different technical meanings. The ***active partition*** describes the partition that contains the operating system files the computer should use to boot. The ***system partition*** contains the core files, such as ntldr and ntdetect.com, which are used to start the operating system. The ***boot partition*** contains the files needed to operate the computer. These files include device drivers, library files, services, commands, and utilities and are stored in a separate directory, such as \windows and \winnt.

3. Boot Loader Phase (Windows 2000/XP/Server 2003)

On a Windows 2000/XP/Server 2003 computer after the initial startup, the boot loader phase first loads the kernel (ntoskrnl.exe) into RAM but does not execute it yet. Next, the hardware abstract layer (hal.dll) is loaded into RAM as well as the system registry hive. The ***hardware abstract layer (HAL)*** is designed to prevent third-party software applications and programs from directly accessing hardware. Only the Microsoft operating system can directly communicate with system hardware such as the memory. Certain key services are started to support various device drivers that are required during the boot process.

hardware abstract layer (HAL) a software layer located between the hardware devices and third-party vendor driver software.

4. Detect and Configure Hardware (Windows 2000/XP/ Server 2003)

Next on a Windows 2000/XP/Server 2003 computer, ntldr calls the ntdetect.com program. The ntdetect.com program detects the system hardware information, such as the computer ID, adapters, video information, keyboard, ports, and hard disk drives. The ntdetect.com file passes this information back to the ntldr, which in turn passes the information to the NT kernel (ntoskrnl.exe).

5. Windows Boot Manager (Windows Vista/7/Server 2008)

On a Windows Vista, 7, and Server 2008 computer after the initial startup, the BIOS loads the Windows Boot Manager (bootmgr). The Windows Boot Manager displays the boot menu, **Figure 18-10,** when more than one operating system is present on a computer and starts the Windows Boot Loader (winload.exe).

6. Windows Boot Loader (Windows Vista/7/Server 2008)

The Windows Boot Manager (bootmgr) then passes control to the Windows Boot Loader (winload.exe), which loads the NT kernel (ntoskrnl.exe) and hardware abstract layer (HAL) into RAM memory. It then executes the kernel.

7. Kernel Loading Phase

For all NT-based operating systems, the NT kernel (ntoskrnl.exe) is executed and takes over operation of the computer system. The NT kernel loads the device drivers, initializes the HAL, and initializes the computer settings using the values stored in the system registry.

The Windows kernel and HAL work together to communicate with software applications, drivers, and hardware. Driver files that do not require user security clearance are typically loaded. For example, the driver and services required to minimally run the printer is loaded at this time.

The kernel and HAL work together to process information stored in the registry, which is required to complete the boot process. The kernel also creates a

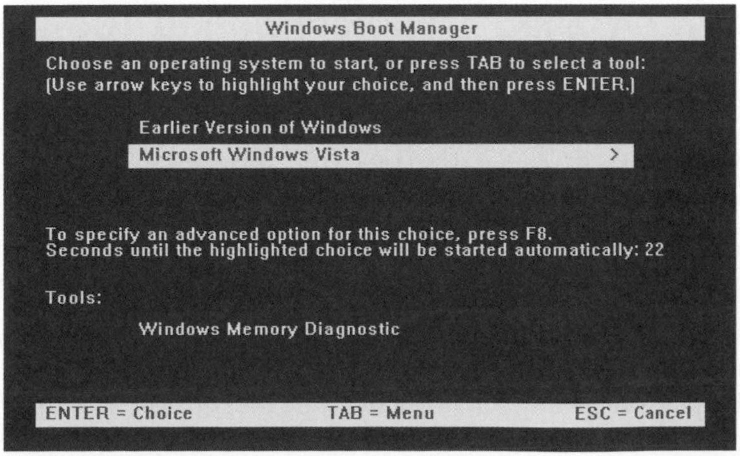

Windows Boot Manager
Choose an operating system to start, or press TAB to select a tool:
(Use arrow keys to highlight your choice, and then press ENTER.)
Earlier Version of Windows
Microsoft Windows Vista >
To specify an advanced option for this choice, press F8.
Seconds until the highlighted choice will be started automatically: 22
Tools:
Windows Memory Diagnostic
ENTER = Choice TAB = Menu ESC = Cancel

Figure 18-10. The Windows Boot Manger will display a menu if more than one operating system is installed on the computer, allowing the user to select an operating system to which to boot.

new registry key that contains information about the drivers and devices loaded thus far and those loaded through the rest of the boot operation. This information is used for the **Last Known Good Configuration** boot option when troubleshooting the system or attempting to recover from a system failure.

The session manager (smss.exe) is loaded and started by the kernel. This is when the boot process switches from text mode to graphics mode. In Windows XP, you will see a splash screen. In Windows Vista, you will see the progress bar appear at the bottom of the screen. The session manager will continue to run in the background until the computer is shut down.

The session manager starts and runs an abbreviated version of Chkdsk and determines if the system volumes and partitions are in working order. The session manager is also responsible for loading the page file or virtual memory. The page file supplements the amount of RAM installed on the computer.

Microsoft does not allow third-party software applications to directly access hardware and certain operating system files. But when access is needed by the third-party software applications, the session manager manages the activities.

8. Logon Phase

The windows logon file (winlogon.exe) is executed and the logon dialog box appears. A user typically enters his or her logon name and password to proceed to the computer desktop.

After a successful logon, the Local Security Authority (LSA) process (lsass.exe) loads and runs, and then the service subsystem (services.exe) loads and runs. The exact services loaded and started are determined by the computer configuration and the user credentials. Only the service the user is allowed access to or through will start. If there is only one default user and the computer is not connected to a network with a server, the user will be able to access and run all services for the computer. If a user has a limited account, he or she will only be able to run services allocated by the system administrator.

Startup programs are loaded and run at this point. If a computer user installs many programs over a period of time, it will take longer for the desktop to appear after completing the logon.

The boot process is not considered successful until an error-free logon has been completed. After a successful logon, the registry is updated and will become the registry reference for the **Last Known Good Configuration** boot option selected during the next startup process. Most problems encountered after a successful logon can be solved using System Restore or System Configuration tools.

Windows NT–Based Troubleshooting Tools

There are many tools and generally-accepted procedures for recovering a failed NT–based operating system. Some of these utilities are briefly covered in this section. To master these troubleshooting concepts, you need to practice using them. See **Figure 18-11** for a complete list of diagnostic utilities and the Microsoft operating systems in which they are included. This section covers Safe Mode, System Restore, Last Known Good Configuration, Recovery Console, Roll Back Driver, and System Configuration. It also covers using an emergency repair disk.

Safe Mode

Safe mode is accessed through the **Advanced Boot Options** menu. This menu is activated by pressing the special function key [F8] during the system startup. Safe mode can then be selected from the list of menu items, **Figure 18-12.**

Diagnostic Utility	Windows XP	Windows Vista	Windows 7	Windows Server 2003	Windows Server 2008
System Restore	×	×	×	×	×
Roll Back Driver	×	×	×	×	×
Recovery Console	×			×	
System Recovery Options Menu		×	×		×
Safe Mode	×	×	×	×	×
System Configuration (msconfig)	×	×	×	×	×
System Information (msinfo32)	×	×	×	×	×
DirectX Diagnostic Tool	×	×	×	×	×
Registry Editor (regedit)	×	×	×	×	×
Registry Editor (regedit32)	×	See note	See note	×	See note
Net	×	×	×	×	×
Dr. Watson	×	×	×	×	×
File Signature Verification	×	×	×	×	×
Network Diagnostics (netdiag) See note	×			×	
Network and Sharing Center		×	×		×
Performance Monitor	×	×	×	×	×
Reliability Monitor		×	×		×

Note: Windows operating systems later than Windows XP and Server 2003 have only one registry editor. It is called *regedit* and performs registry edits for 16-, 32-, and 64-bit registries.

Note: Network Diagnostics is now incorporated into Network and Sharing Center.

Figure 18-11. Common diagnostic utilities listed by various Microsoft NT–based operating systems.

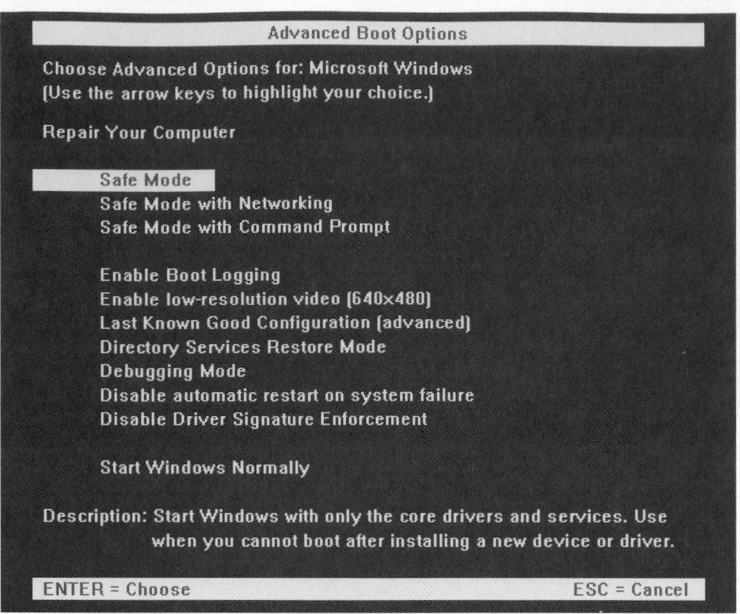

Figure 18-12.
Safe Mode is the first option (after **Repair Your Computer**) in the **Advanced Boot Options** menu. When booting a computer in safe mode, Windows loads only standard video drivers and essential drivers that are needed for the keyboard, mouse, and storage devices.

During a safe mode boot, only standard video drivers are loaded and essential drivers that are needed for the keyboard, mouse, and storage devices. No network connection is made. Starting the computer in safe mode can help determine if there is a problem with the PC or with the network. If the system appears to be working correctly with the minimum set of drivers, you may be able to correct the suspected source of the problem. For example, if a recently loaded software or hardware device is suspected of causing the system boot failure, you can delete it from the system and then attempt to boot the computer system normally.

System Restore

The System Restore utility does as the name implies. It restores the operating system to a condition established at a previous time. The System Restore utility can be accessed through **Start | All Programs | Accessories | System Tools** even when the computer is running in safe mode. You may use the System Restore utility to roll the operating system back to a previous time when the system was working perfectly. For example, you may have installed a new pointing device and loaded the required drivers only to find the computer will not boot properly or freezes during the boot process. You can start the computer in safe mode, start the System Restore utility, and select an earlier time. The System Restore utility rolls back the registry but does not change the existing data files, e-mail, and other common file types that you would not want to be removed or changed. The System Restore utility does remove executable files, which means that programs that were installed after the rollback date may be inoperable.

For example, a user experienced no problem with his computer yesterday. Today, he starts his computer and he cannot access any of his software applications. A system restore may correct the problem. You would simply start the System Restore tool and then select an earlier date to restore the computer system to. See **Figure 18-13.**

If you can only start the computer in safe mode, you can access System Restore through Control Panel or from the **Start** menu. You can also use the command prompt to start System Restore by entering **rstrui.exe**.

System Restore can also be used to solve problems such as when a computer suddenly starts to run slowly or develops problems associated with

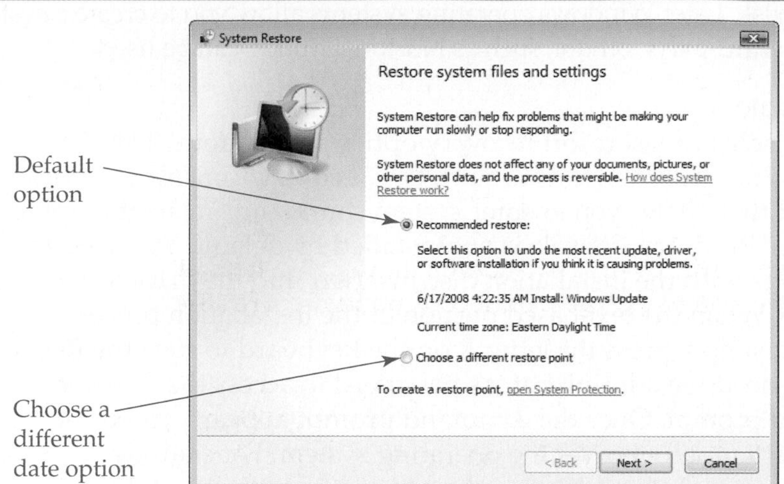

Figure 18-13. The System Restore tool can automatically reconfigure your computer with the registry settings from an earlier time.

a recent download, a new driver, a new patch, or any recent change to the system configuration. System Restore does not change the contents of any user application files such as e-mails, pictures, documents or other personal data. Any executable programs installed after the selected rollback date will not run properly because their registry settings will be changed.

Last Known Good Configuration

The **Last Known Good Configuration** option in the **Advanced Boot Options** menu is essential for correcting most boot problems on an NT–based system. Every time an NT–based computer has a successful logon after a completed boot, a backup of the system registry is made. The backup is available for use when a computer fails to boot properly because of some change in the system. The change in the system could be the installation of a new or updated software driver or a change in some hardware configuration. If an error during the boot operation is detected, a message will display such as, "Restore the system to the last known good configuration." When the **Last Known Good Configuration** option is selected, the last copy of the registry made during a successful boot replaces the existing registry.

Emergency Repair Disk

All modern operating systems have what is called an *emergency repair disk* or *system repair disc*. An emergency repair disk is used to repair or replace items such as the master boot record, file allocation tables, system registry files, or system configuration files. There is one very important aspect to using an emergency repair disk. It can only restore the system to the way it was configured when the disk was made. If the emergency repair disk was made right after the original installation of the operating system, the system will be set up in its original state. Any modifications to the system since the emergency repair disk was made will be lost if you use the emergency repair disk to repair the system. You may lose the use of any new software systems that were installed, hardware drivers, and system updates or patches. An emergency repair disk should be made whenever changes to the system occur. This will ensure an updated system will be restored rather than the original system.

Windows NT (Workstation and Server), Windows 2000 (Professional and Server), Windows Server 2003, and Windows XP Professional allow you to create an emergency repair disk. Later Windows operating systems allow you to create a system repair disc. Also, a third-party vendor, such as Norton Utilities, can be used.

Recovery Console

Recovery Console is a last resort recovery option in Windows 2000, XP, and Server 2003. When a system fails to start, the Recovery Console provides a command prompt that allows you to enter system commands in an attempt to recover the system. Recovery Console is not installed by default. You need to reboot the computer with the installation disc inserted into the drive to access Recovery Console. When the text-based portion of the installation process begins, you would simply press the letter *R* on the keyboard to start the Recovery Console. You will need the administrator's password to access the Recovery Console command prompt. Once the command prompt appears, you could issue commands in an attempt to recover the operating system. For example, you could run the **chkdsk** command to resolve sector problems from the hard disk drive or run **fixboot** to repair the boot sector. Look at **Figure 18-14** to view some of the most common Recovery Console commands. To read a detailed explanation of Recovery Console, see the Microsoft link at http://support.microsoft.com/kb/314058. To locate this site, you can also conduct an Internet search using the key terms "Recovery Console TechNet."

Roll Back Driver

The **Roll Back Driver** option has been part of Windows operating systems since Windows XP. The Roll Back Driver feature is available through the **Properties** dialog box of any hardware device installed on the computer. **Figure 18-15** shows the **Properties** dialog box of a Realtek PCI GBE Family Controller. The dialog box contains buttons that allow you to view driver details, update the driver, roll back the driver, or uninstall the driver.

The Roll Back Driver feature is a better alternative than using System Restore. System Restore rolls back all driver and configuration settings to the selected date. This can result in losing the configuration settings of devices you did not intend to change. The Roll Back Driver feature only reverts to the last driver configured for a specific device. For example, if you suspect a newly installed driver or driver update is causing a problem with a hardware device, you can use the Roll Back Driver feature to return to the previous version of the driver.

System Configuration

Another handy tool for solving computer problems such as software application or services is the System Configuration tool. See **Figure 18-16.** It can be accessed by entering **msconfig.exe** at the command prompt. The System Configuration tool has three broad options under the default **General** tab. The three options are **Normal startup**, **Diagnostic startup**, and **Selective startup**. When the **Diagnostic startup** option is selected, only basic devices and services are loaded. When the **Selective startup**

Figure 18-14.
Common Recovery Console commands.

Recovery Console Command	Description
chkdsk	Checks the hard disk drive platters for bad sectors.
diskpart	Displays and manages the partitions on a hard disk.
bootcfg	Modifies the boot.ini file.
fixboot	Writes a new boot sector on the system partition.
fixmbr	Repairs the master boot record.

Figure 18-15. The Rollback Driver feature is available through the **Properties** dialog box of any hardware device.

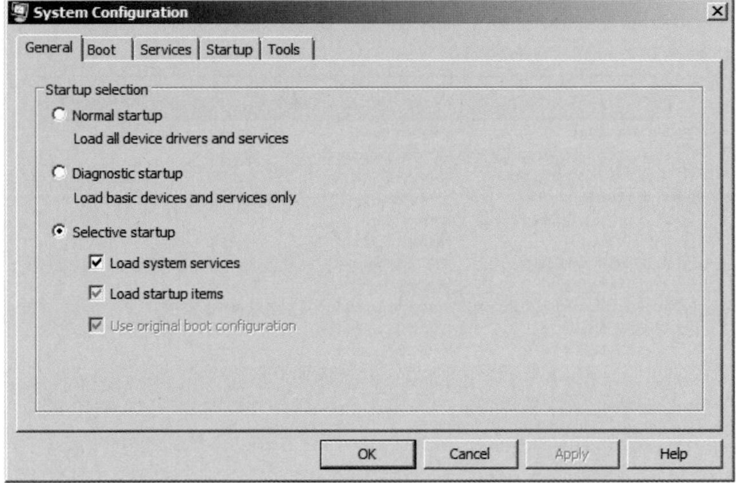

Figure 18-16. The System Configuration tool can be used to perform a diagnostic startup or a selective startup. You can use the tool to eliminate any or all services and software programs during computer startup.

option is selected, you can choose to load or not load system services and or startup items. These options are broad and are selected to quickly isolate the area of the problem. For example, you could have a startup item causing the computer to have a very long boot. Many printer programs automatically install software applications that inspect your printer and check ink supply levels. They also perform routine diagnostics and even automatically check for newer drivers through your Internet connection. You could have several programs installed on your computer that automatically start during the boot process and perform routine checks. The more programs that automatically start up during the boot period, the longer the boot process will take. Problems such as this can be pinpointed by selecting which programs run during startup.

The **Startup** tab allows you to view which items are run automatically during and after startup, **Figure 18-17.** You can enable or disable all items or simply select items by the corresponding check box. It is recommended to first disable all items. If the problem is corrected, reintroduce items one by one until the offending item is identified.

The **Services** tab allows you to choose which services can run during and after startup, **Figure 18-18.** You would use the same process as with startup items to

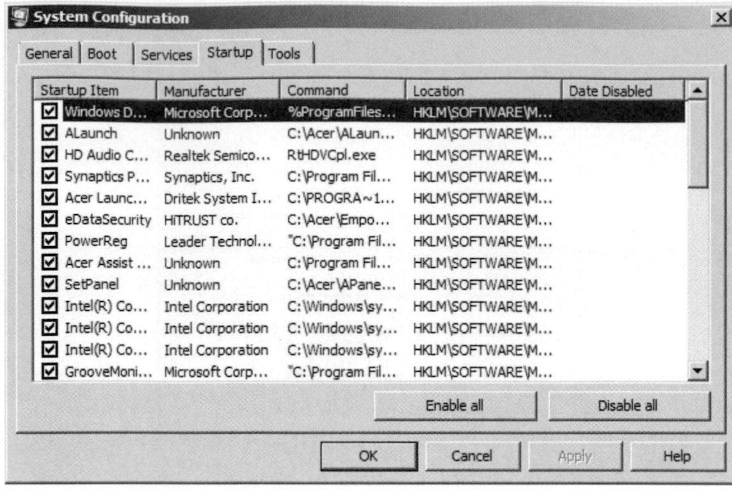

Figure 18-17. The System Configuration **Startup** tab allows you to choose suspect startup items.

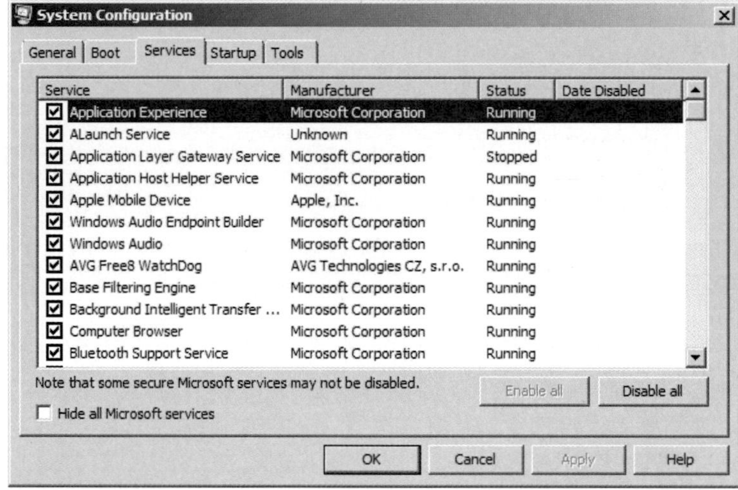

Figure 18-18. The System Configuration **Services** tab allows you to view and then select suspect services.

locate the problem. First, disable all services and see how computer performance is affected. Then, reintroduce services until the problem service is identified. See **Figure 18-19** for a description of all of the System Configuration tabs.

System Recovery Strategies and Methods

System recovery involves two major steps: recovering data and recovering the operating system. The best protection from a virus, worm, or unforeseen disaster is regular system and data backups. When other methods such as System Restore or System Configuration fail to repair the system, you can perform a new installation and then follow up with restoring lost data files from the most recent backup. This is why performing regular backups is emphasized.

All Windows operating systems provide some form of backup program. Windows XP has the Backup Wizard, which will allow you to back up files. Windows Vista has Backup and Restore, which allows you to back up system files or create a complete PC backup, or disk image. Windows 7 has Backup and Restore, which allows you to create a system repair disc as well as create a system image. The following are some tips to keep in mind to aid in the recovery process.

System Configuration Tab	Description
General	Perform broad diagnostics such as eliminating all nonessential items from startup.
Boot	Provides access to boot configuration options associated with dual-boot or multiboot operating systems.
Services	Select which services to enable or disable during and after startup.
Startup	Select startup items to enable or disable during and after startup.
Tools	Provides access to many common troubleshooting and configuration tools.

Figure 18-19. Description of System Configuration tabs.

- Always make a system image while the computer is running correctly.
- Perform system backups often or configure for automatic backups.
- Back up your system to a separate or external drive or to a network storage device.

Windows Installation Disc

The Windows Setup or installation disc can be used to recover from a system failure. You simply begin the installation by placing the installation disc into the appropriate CD/DVD drive and rebooting the computer. Under normal circumstances, the existing operating system is detected during the installation process, and you are presented with an option to perform a system repair. On rare occasions, the system can be so badly damaged that an existing operating system cannot be detected and a recovery option may not be presented.

Caution

Using the Windows setup or installation disc to restore or recover the computer system can sometimes destroy all data stored on the computer. For this reason, this method should be used as a last resort.

After selecting the option to perform a system repair, you will see the following menu items. The menu items will vary, depending on the Windows operating system you are using. As you can see in the following menu lists for Windows 7 and Windows Vista, the items are very similar but not an exact match.

Windows Vista

- Startup Repair
- System Restore
- Windows Complete PC Restore
- Windows Memory Diagnostic
- Command Prompt

Windows 7

- Startup Repair
- System Restore

- System Image Recovery
- Windows Memory Diagnostic
- Command Prompt

The main difference is **System Image Recovery** is available in Windows 7, but not in Windows Vista. This option or feature allows you to perform a complete system image backup. A complete ***system image*** is a snapshot of the entire storage structure to include files not normally backed up such as the MBR or GUID. Typical backup programs only back up system files and data files. For example, when performing a complete backup, the MBR or the GUID is not copied. When you create a system image, all sectors are copied, including the MBR or GUID and hidden disk sectors.

system image a snapshot of the entire storage structure, including files not normally backed up such as the MBR or GUID.

The option **Repair Your Computer** is available at the top of the **Advanced Boot Options** menu for operating systems that have the System Recovery program installed on a hard disk partition, **Figure 18-20.** Some computer systems do not have this option available. This option provides a list of recovery tools that can be used to repair startup problems, run diagnostics, or restore your system, **Figure 18-21.**

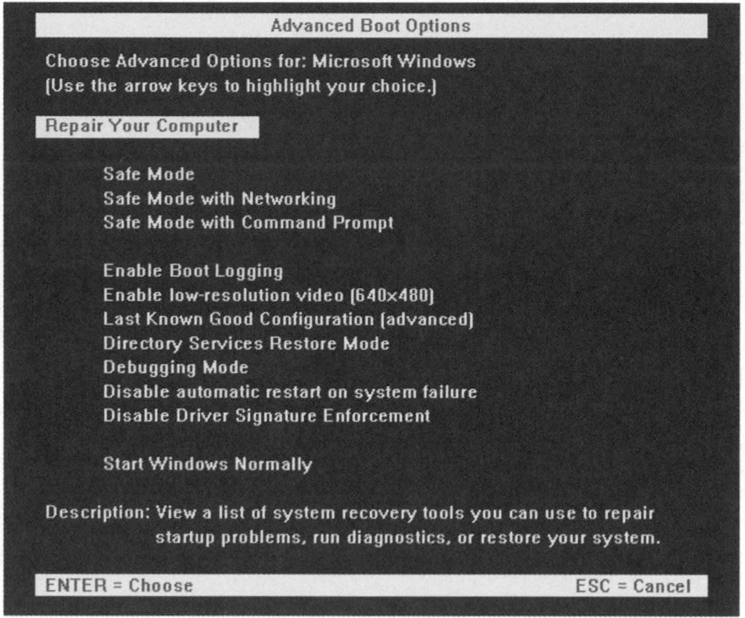

Figure 18-20. Selecting the **Repair Your Computer** option from the **Advanced Boot Options** menu in Windows 7 will allow you to access the **System Recovery Options** menu and recover the system.

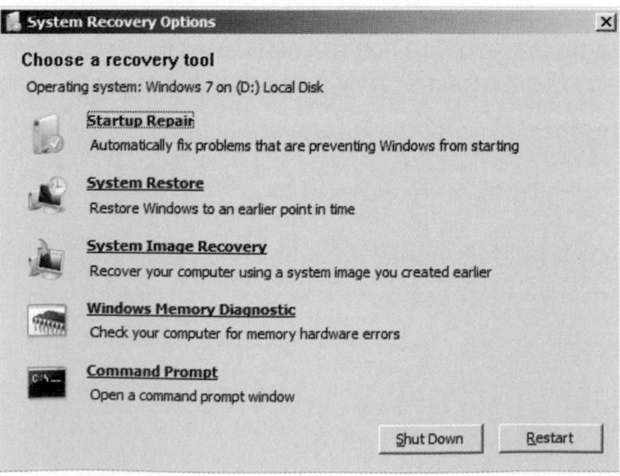

Figure 18-21. Windows 7 **System Recovery Options** menu.

These are the same options that appear when using an installation disc for recovery.

To access the **Advanced Boot Options** menu, press [F8] within two seconds after the POST completes.

Windows Backup and Restore

Windows Server 2008 has a similar option as Windows 7 for system image recovery located in its Backup and Restore tool. **Figure 18-22** shows a screen capture of the Windows 7 Backup and Restore tool. Notice that there are options to create a system image, create a system repair disc, and to restore from a backup. In this particular screen capture you will note that a backup has never been performed, so the option to restore files from a backup is not available.

When using the **System Image Recovery** or **Windows Complete PC Restore** option from the **Advanced Boot Options** menu, the system restoration will match a previously made backup of the system. Therefore, you must keep system backups and images current. You should make a new backup or image after every computer configuration change.

Windows XP Automated System Recovery (ASR)

Both Windows Server 2003 and Windows XP use the Automated System Recovery (ASR) feature to restore the computer operating system and important files. ASR is similar to the Windows 7 **System Image Recovery** and the Windows Vista **Windows Complete PC Restore** options. ASR is a backup option for Windows XP and Windows Server 2003. When you run a system backup in Windows XP or Windows Server 2003, you are presented with an option to create an ASR disk. System files and selected data files are backed up on a disk and can be used to restore the system at a later date after a system failure or loss of data. You can also opt to back up to a storage device such as a USB-connected drive or a location on a network. The main problem with ASR is every time you make a change to the system configuration you need to make a new ASR disk. Otherwise, the system will only be restored to the condition associated with the date the ASR disk was created. To learn more about Windows XP ASR, see http://support.microsoft.com/kb/818903.

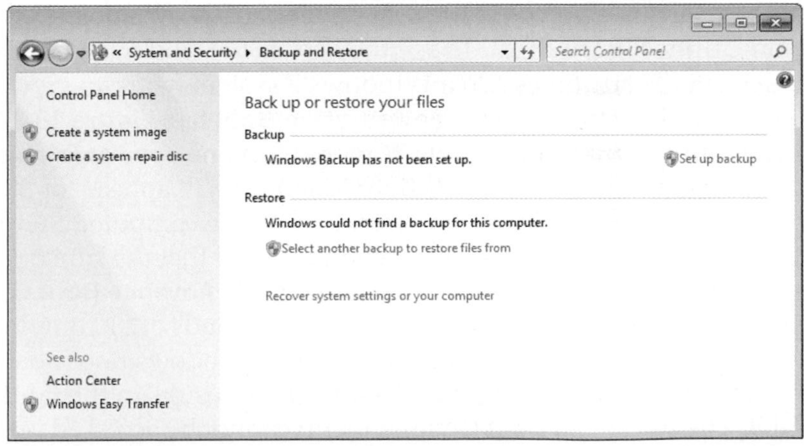

Figure 18-22.
The Windows 7 Backup and Restore tool has options to create a system image, create a system repair disc, and to restore data from a backup.

OEM and Repair Shop Disc Image

You can always restore your computer to new or factory condition by using the original installation disc or an image of the original system. There is one main problem with this method. You will lose all your saved files and software applications. You will need to create user accounts and reconfigure the computer system such as e-mail and Internet access. You will have a new system but no data unless you made a current backup. Ironically, when restoring the computer using a recent image, you may also be recreating the problem you were attempting to solve. For example, if the computer problem was caused by a virus such as a logic time bomb, the virus might very well be on the image. Using the infected disc image will infect the computer once more.

A disk image is often used by the Original Equipment Manufacturer (OEM) and computer repair shops when they configure their computers for resale. First, they make two separate partitions. They install the operating system and all software applications and drivers on the first partition. Then, an image of the first partition is made and stored on the second partition. The second partition is used to reimage the first partition to recover it from a disaster. Some manufacturers hide the second partition so that the user does not inadvertently damage the backup image.

Troubleshooting Dual-Boot Systems

Dual-boot and multiboot systems are becoming more common as users switch or upgrade from one operating system to a newer one. When users are comfortable with an operating system, they are typically hesitant to change, even if the newer operating system is better. For some users, it is a severe struggle to relearn some common tasks. For example, new operating systems often change the location of features. It is frustrating for the user to locate these features in the new operating system. A common practice is to install the new version as an optional system until the user has been trained on the new version.

Two operating systems on one computer, however, can generate their own unique problems. A common problem is the corruption of the boot.ini file or the Boot Configuration Data (BCD). The boot.ini file is used for Windows XP systems and the BCD is used for Windows Vista and Windows 7 systems.

The boot.ini and BCD file provide the user with a choice or selection of operating systems after the POST. An accidental modification or corruption of the boot.ini or BCD may prevent any of the operating systems to completely boot or cause only one of the operating systems to boot and not the others.

Look at the contents of a boot.ini file as it appears in the Windows XP System Configuration Utility, **Figure 18-23.** To see the boot.ini file, you must remove the hidden and system file attributes. On a Windows 7 system, you can view and modify the BCD settings the System Configuration **Boot** tab, **Figure 18-24.** Notice the default **Timeout** setting of 30 seconds. If more than one operating system is installed on the computer, the Windows Boot Manager will appear for 30 seconds. When there is only one operating system installed on the computer, there will be a two-second delay. It is during this two-second interval that the function key [F8] can be pressed to interrupt the boot process causing the **Advance Boot Options** menu to appear. If you do not press [F8] within two seconds after completion of the POST, the operating system will quickly load the Windows Boot Loader and the kernel. Then, the session manager will load, which results in the familiar Windows GUI. The **Advanced Boot Options** menu cannot be accessed once the

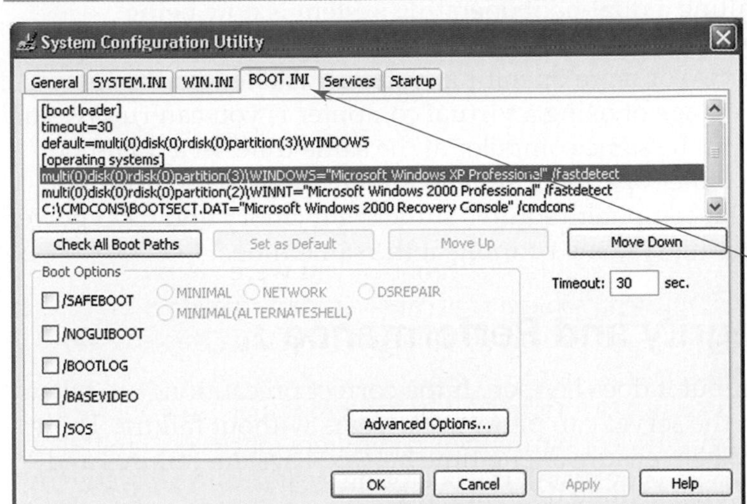

Figure 18-23. The boot.ini file in a multiboot system contains the locations of system files for each operating system on the computer. Its contents can be viewed from the System Configuration Utility.

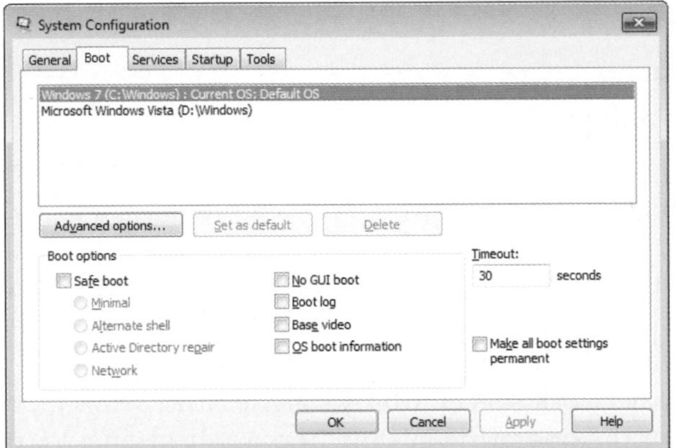

Figure 18-24. In Windows 7, the contents of the BCD can be viewed and modified from System Configuration.

computer reaches this point. You must restart the computer and press the [F8] key before POST is finished to access the **Advanced Boot Options** menu.

When the **Advanced Boot Options** menu appears, you can select the **Command Prompt** option and then enter the **bootrec** command, which is used to repair the MBR and the BCD. You can issue any one of several commands that will help you repair a corrupt system on a Windows Vista or Windows 7 computer. This tool is not available for Windows XP, Windows Server 2003, or Windows Server 2008. The following table lists the **bootrec** command with commonly-used switches.

Bootrec Command	Description
bootrec /RebuildBCD	Resolves a corrupt BCD.
bootrec /FixMBR	Resolves a corrupt MBR.
bootrec /FixBoot	Writes a new boot sector on the system partition.
bootrec /ScanOS	Scans for Windows 7 and Windows Vista compatible operating systems installed on the computer.
bootrec /RebuildBCD	Scans for operating systems installed on the computer and adds them to the BCD.

The practice of installing a dual-boot operating system is now being replaced by virtual PC and virtual server programs. A virtual PC and virtual server allow you to have two or more operating systems installed on the same computer. The main advantage of using a virtual computer is you can run two or more operating systems on the same computer at the same time. In a dual-boot installation, you can run either operating system, but not at the same time. The disadvantage of the virtual computer requires sufficient memory and CPU power to support multiple operating systems running at the same time.

Server Data Integrity and Performance

Server failure is rare, but it does happen. If the correct precautions are taken when installing a server, the server can perform for years without failure. There are several items that can help ensure a long time between system failures and data loss. Some of these items include the following:

- UPS unit.
- RAID system.
- Backup system.
- Virus program.
- Service packs and patches.

When setting up a server, it is important to install an uninterruptible power supply (UPS). You should also select a fault tolerance type of RAID system that is appropriate for the company budget and for the type of data stored. Because failure is unavoidable, be sure to perform regular data backups or use an off-site storage facility service. Be sure to install patches and service packs as they become available. Remember to test the service pack or patch before installing it on the network server. Many patches and service packs can cause severe problems for the operating system and application programs. Install a virus protection software package designed especially for servers. In addition to a virus package for the server, it is also desirable to install a virus protection package on each workstation in the network. Do not overlook laptops used by the organization. Company laptop computers are also frequently attached to the network and can infect the network system.

Detailed troubleshooting information covering each of the major network operating systems for servers is beyond the scope of this textbook. For troubleshooting information about a particular server network operating system, you can review the information available at Novell, Microsoft, Sun Micro Systems, IBM, Dell, Red Hat, and Hewlett Packard. Expertise in one or more of these individual server network operating systems may be a certification you wish to obtain after completing this course of study.

Troubleshooting the Network Infrastructure

The network infrastructure consists of cabling and cabling devices such as hubs, switches, and routers. One of the most commonly encountered infrastructure problems is a loose cable connection. The second most encountered network problem is forgotten user passwords. Many of the tools described in this section were previously explained earlier in the textbook. You may wish to review them at this time.

Windows XP Network Diagnostic Utility

Windows XP and Windows Me include a powerful network diagnostic tool known as Network Diagnostics. The Network Diagnostics utility can be accessed by running **msinfo32** (System Information) from the **Run** dialog box off the **Start** menu. When the **System Information** window displays, select **Net Diagnostics** from the **Tools** menu, **Figure 18-25.** Selecting the **Scan your system** option in the Network Diagnostics utility automatically runs a series of network diagnostics on the local computer.

The Network Diagnostic utility combines many traditional network utilities into one. It can check network connections, hardware, and services related to networking at one time. Some of the items it automatically checks are the network interface card, telephone modem (if one exists), e-mail, WINS, DNS, and DHCP. Network Diagnostics is a versatile and powerful tool. Look at **Figure 18-26** to see the results of a typical Network Diagnostics scan performed from a Windows XP workstation.

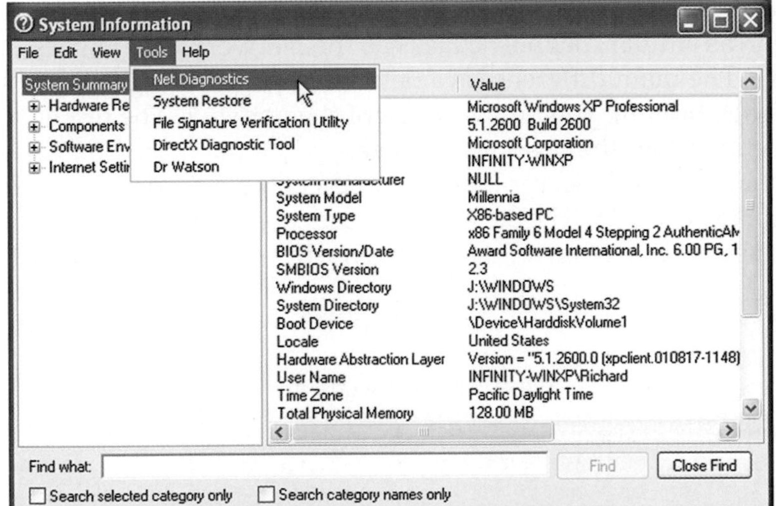

Figure 18-25. The Network Diagnostics utility can be accessed through the System Information (**msinfo32**) **Tools** menu.

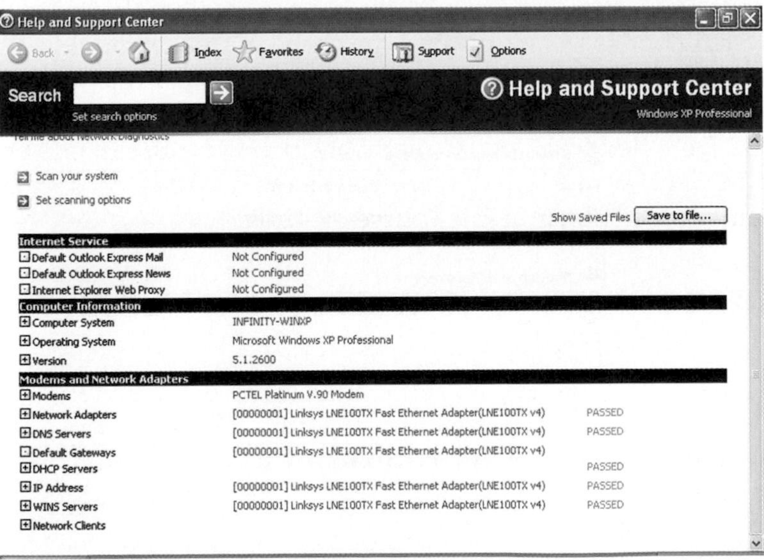

Figure 18-26. The results of a system scan in Network Diagnostics.

As you can see, when a particular device passes the test, the word *Pass* in bright green lettering appears to the right side of the device name. If it fails to pass a test, then the word *Failed* is presented in bright red lettering. The Network Diagnostic utility also identifies any items that were scanned but not configured in the workstation by displaying the words *Not Configured* in bright blue.

Network Diagnostics allows the user to customize the objects to scan and to save the results to a file for viewing at a later date. Saving the results to a file allows a technician or any users to see what the original settings are and compare them to a scan at a later date. A technician could also run a scan of the workstation, save the results to a file, and then transfer the file across the network to a central location. At the central location, it can be added to a network documentation folder containing information about every workstation on the network. This makes network documentation much easier for the technician and the system administrator.

Network and Sharing Center

Windows Vista introduced the Network and Sharing Center. The Network and Sharing Center provides a centralized location to diagnose a network problem. Look at **Figure 18-27** and notice the **Diagnose and repair** option. This option performs similar diagnostic tasks as the Network Diagnostics utility in Windows XP. The main difference is a detailed report is not generated but rather a short message briefing you on the status of the network. The test either passes or a message identifies the possible problem.

You can also consult Server Manager and generate a LAN Diagnostics report as shown in **Figure 18-28.** The Server Manager can automatically generate a LAN Diagnostics report as well as a System Diagnostics report. The LAN Diagnostics

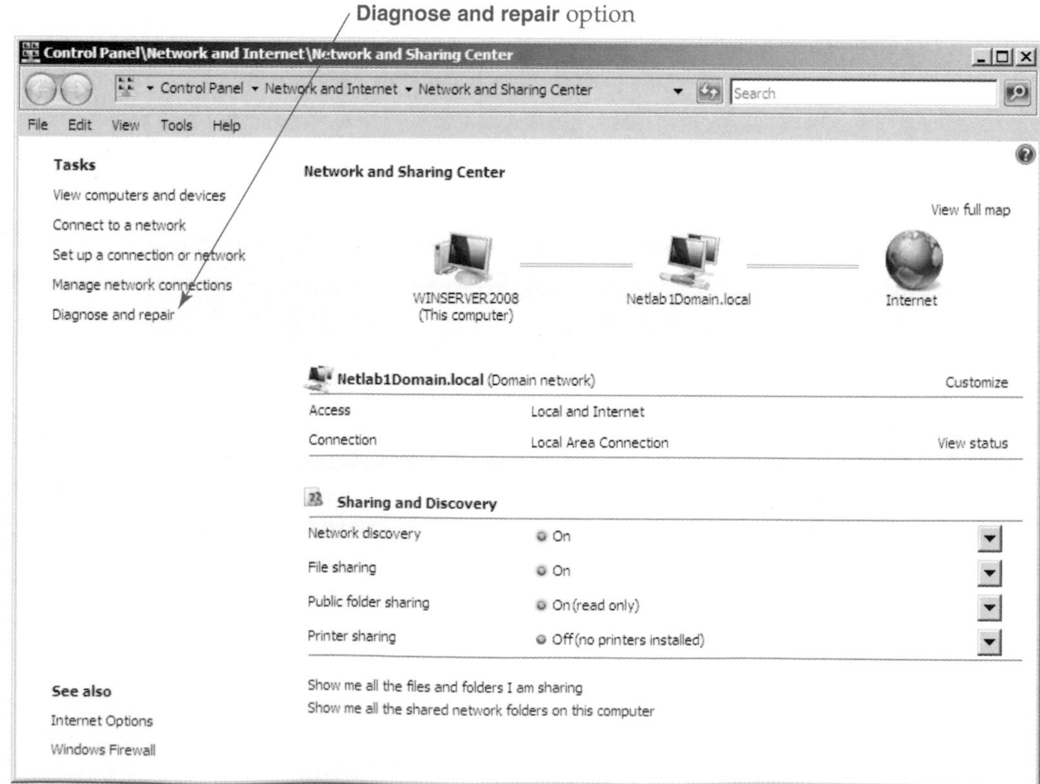

Figure 18-27. The Network and Sharing Center was first introduced in Windows Vista and Windows Server 2008. It contains an option to diagnose and repair the LAN connection.

Figure 18-28.
Server Manager has an option to automatically generate a LAN Diagnostics report.

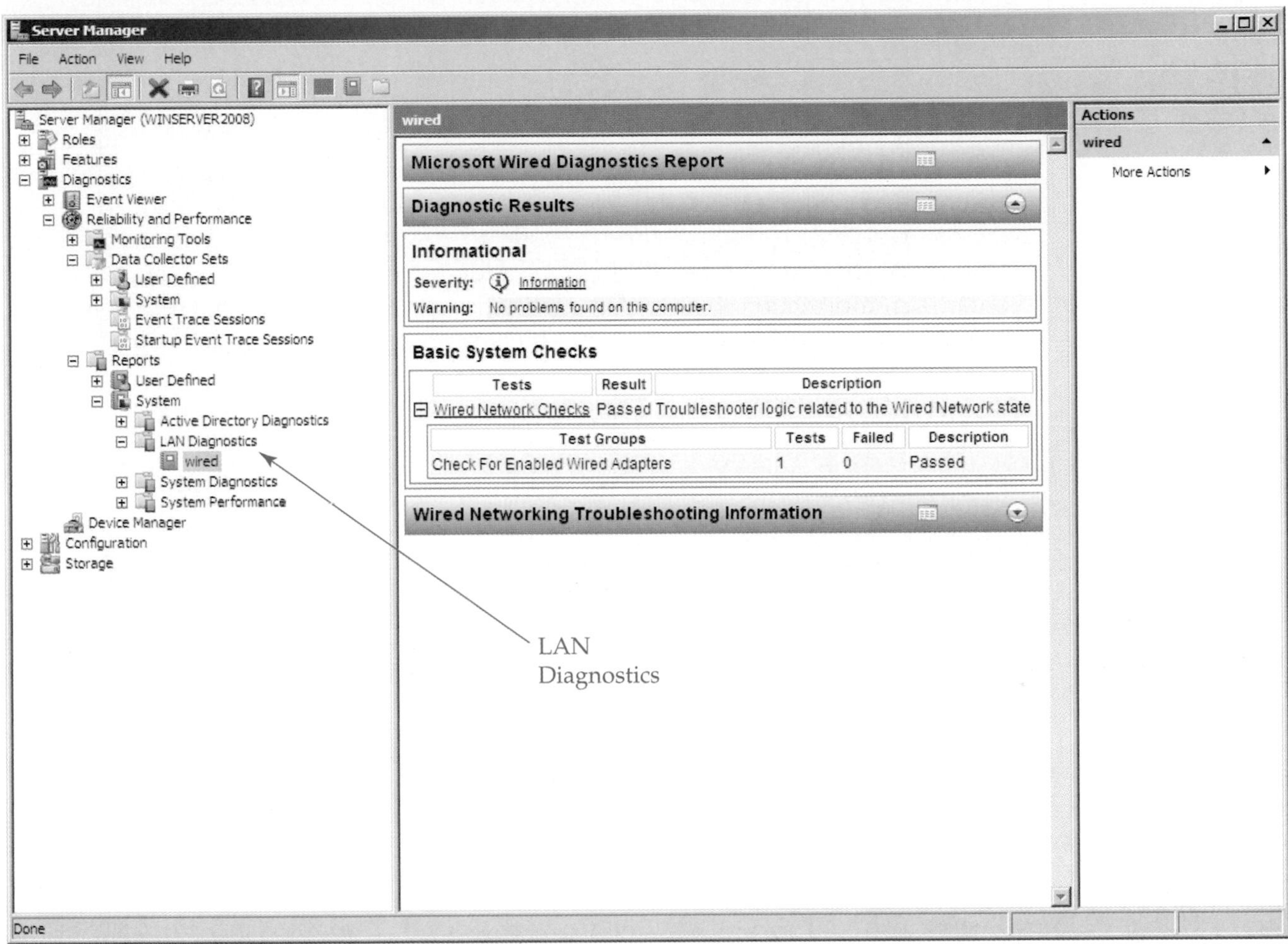

feature is disabled by default so that it will not use valuable network bandwidth. You must enable the related service for it to record LAN Diagnostics events.

Windows 7 also has the Network and Sharing Center, but it is not an exact match to the Network and Sharing Center in Windows Server 2008 and Windows Vista. Look at **Figure 18-29.** Notice that the options in Windows 7 are rearranged as compared with those in Windows Vista and Windows Server 2008, Figure 18-27.

In both versions of the Network and Sharing Center, a problem with the computer connection to the network is indicated by a yellow triangle containing an exclamation mark (!). A problem with a connection to the Internet is indicated by a red *X* drawn across the network wire icon. See **Figure 18-30.**

When a problem is identified with the yellow triangle containing an exclamation mark (!) or red *X*, you can obtain more detailed information by double-clicking the icon. After the problem is corrected and after a short delay usually of no more than one or two minutes, the trouble-indicating icons will disappear. The network browser scans the local area network periodically to detect changes in the condition or to automatically discover problems.

Another great feature of the Network and Sharing Center is the ability to create a map of all devices connected in the local network. You can identify how the network devices in the LAN relate to each other logically. Legacy devices

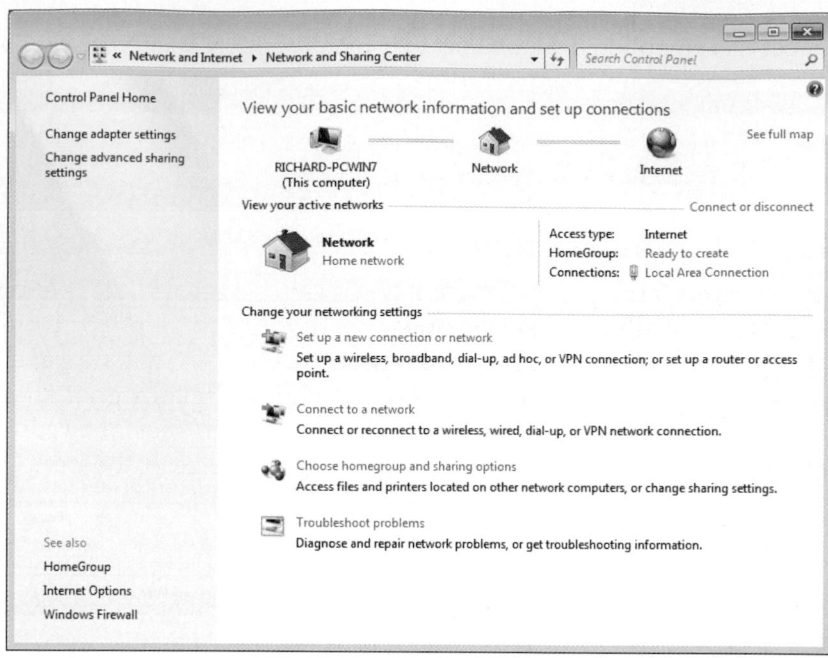

Figure 18-29. Windows 7 modified the look of the original Network and Sharing Center.

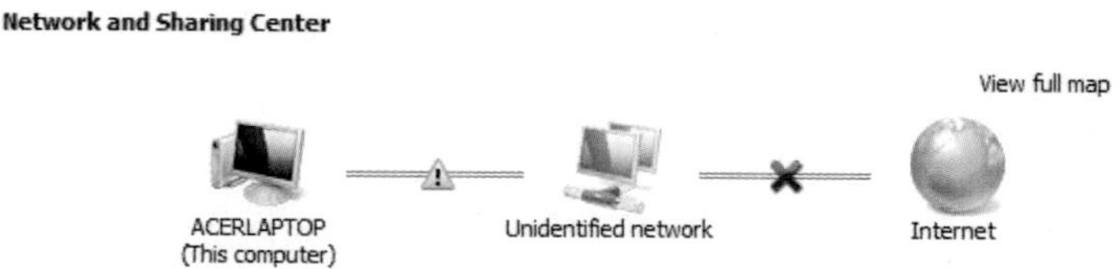

Figure 18-30. The Network and Sharing Center immediately diagnoses problems with computer LAN connections and will indicate the problem using a red *X* or yellow triangle with an exclamation mark.

such as Windows XP and older switches, routers, and gateways may not appear correctly in the map. The map relies on IPv6 and the Network Discovery protocols to create the map. Any device that does not support the Network Discovery feature or is only configured for IPv4 may not show up correctly in the map. There are downloadable patches or updates available for Windows XP and for some legacy network devices so that they will appear.

The Network Discovery feature is disabled by default for Windows Server 2008. To view the Windows Server 2008 correctly in a network map, it must be enabled. Microsoft considers enabling the Network Discovery feature for a server a security risk.

To learn more about the Network and Sharing Center, see the guide at http://technet.microsoft.com/en-us/library/cc770751(WS.10).aspx. To locate this site, you can also conduct an Internet search using the key terms "Microsoft TechNet Network and Sharing Center."

Network Cable Tester

Cables can be analyzed quickly using hardware tools such as a network cable tester. Cable testers go by many different names, such as digital cable analyzer and cable analyzer. A network cable tester performs a series of checks of cable integrity. Cable faults such as opens, shorts, and grounds can be quickly determined and located. Many cable testers can also check for crosstalk, radio interference, EMI, and excessive cable lengths and can determine the exact location of a cable fault. Some of the more expensive models can record troubleshooting data and download it to a computer. The computer can store or print the information.

Tone Generator and Tracer

A tone generator and tracer allow a technician to trace the exact location of cable runs inside walls, ceilings, or under the floor or to identify unmarked cables. The tone generator and tracer are separate devices. The tone generator attaches to one end of a cable. It produces an analog or digital signal and transmits it through the cable. The tracer is designed with special circuitry that receives the signal and produces a tone if it is in close range of the cable. When a cable fault is encountered, the signal ends or changes pitch.

The fact that the tone generator and tracer are designed to trace the path of a conductor is an advantage over a cable analyzer, which does not have this feature incorporated. An old term still used by technicians to describe the tone generator and detector is *fox and hound*. The tone generator represents the fox and the tracer represents the hound. In essence, the hound (tracer) follows the fox (signal) until reaching the end of the cable.

Fiber-Optic Cables

Fiber-optic cable requires specialized tools for troubleshooting. Typically, an Optical Time Domain Reflectometer (OTDR), sometimes abbreviated as OTD, is used to locate faults in the fiber-optic cable core. The OTDR uses a light source to detect faults. The light source sends a pulse of light energy through the fiber-optic core. As the light pulse encounters defects in the core and connectors, the light reflects to the source, which also acts as a receiver. The amount of reflected light and the time it took to travel to the fault and back is instantly calculated. The intensity of the reflected light and the calculated time indicate the type of flaw and the location in meters where it occurred. A more in-depth explanation of the OTDR can be found in Chapter 3—Fiber-Optic Cable.

Tech Tip

A Time Domain Reflectometer (TDR) is used to test copper core network cable and should not be confused with OTDR or OTD. The TDR works by sending an electronic pulse down the copper core cable and then reads signal bounce to locate cable faults.

NIC Loopback Test

The network interface card loopback test typically employs the use of the **ping** command as part of its diagnostics. A loopback test checks a hardware device's ability to transmit and receive signals. It consists of diagnostic software and an adapter (connector) called a *loopback*. The loopback is plugged into the back of the network interface card. When the diagnostic software is run, the loopback completes the electrical circuit between the transmit and receive pins. Without a connection between the transmit and receive pins, a complete series of diagnostic tests cannot be run.

Indicator Lights

All network adapters and network devices such as hubs and switches are equipped with indicator lights known as LEDs. There is no standard interpretation of what the light patterns represent. To interpret the exact meaning of the light patterns, such as a flashing or steady light, you must consult the manufacturer's resources. However, there are some general assumptions that can be made. If none of the indicator lights are lit, a cable problem may exist. A cable problem may include a disconnected cable at the hub or switch or a bad connection at either end of the cable. There is also a possibility that the network card is bad, but this is rare. Generally, it is safe to assume network activity when the indicator lights are blinking. The more rapid the lights blink, the higher the rate of activity. A steady light can also indicate high activity.

Network Analyzer

Typically, the entire network infrastructure can be tested using a network analyzer. A network analyzer can be software or a combination of software and hardware. Network analyzers are typically the most expensive of all network testing devices and exceed the budget of IT departments with small LANs. The best network analyzers combine features found in all network testing software and hardware and have elaborate display capabilities.

Protocol Analyzer

Protocol analyzers are used to capture and monitor data frames traveling across the network media. While most protocol analyzers monitor only TCP/IP, more sophisticated protocol analyzers can monitor hundreds of different protocols. Protocol analyzers vary greatly in their features. Protocol analyzers can filter the data they gather by limiting the capture of data to one or more nodes, thus reducing the total amount of data that needs to be analyzed. Many of the more sophisticated protocol analyzers can chart their results in graph form. Protocol analyzers are commonly incorporated into network analyzers.

While protocol analyzers vary somewhat, all have similar functions and characteristics. Look at **Figure 18-31** to view some of these features. Displayed are three viewing panes. The top pane displays the series of frames captured during the brief period the protocol analyzer was running. The frame that is highlighted contains the Simple Mail Transport Protocol (SMTP).

The middle pane displays detailed information about the highlighted frame, such as the IP address of the source and the destination, the time of the capture, and the type of protocol. The bottom pane displays the contents of the packet. The characters on the left side of the bottom pane display the contents as hexadecimal pairs. The ASCII equivalents of the hexadecimal pairs are on the right. Characters outside the range of the basic standard 128 characters are not displayed or are displayed as meaningless symbols. This particular SMTP captured packet contains a plain-text e-mail message. If you look closely at the contents, you will see who sent the message. By scrolling through the pane, the entire contents of the message and the e-mail addresses of the sender and destination are displayed.

A technician in the workplace can use a protocol analyzer to analyze network conditions, observe network traffic patterns, and identify bottlenecks. Most protocol analyzers provide features to allow the user to filter packets by source, destination, protocol type, or by most any characteristic of a frame or packet.

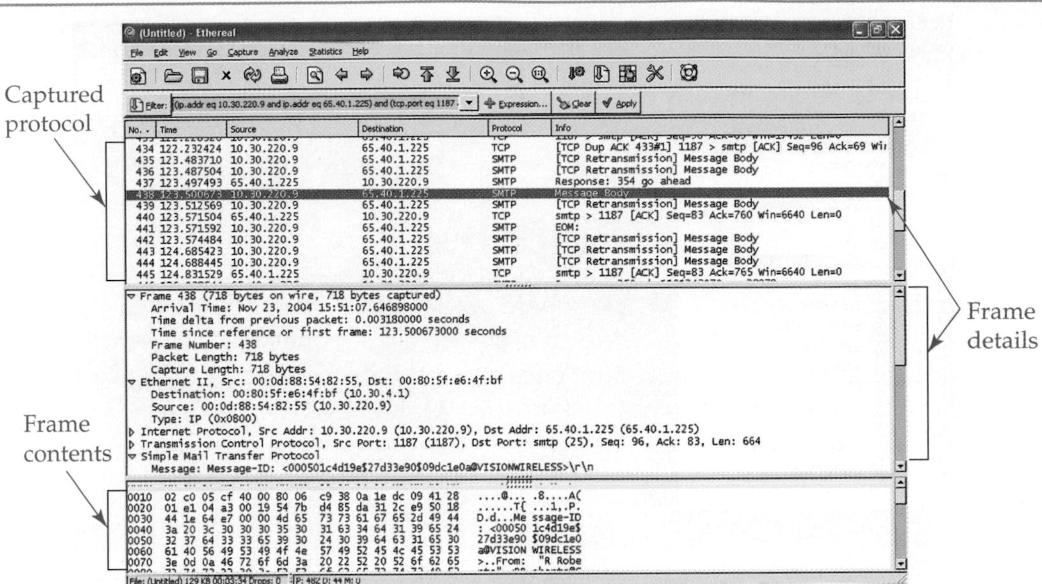

Figure 18-31. A protocol analyzer is used to capture frames and monitor frames of data traveling across the network media.

Conditions such as switching loops, routing loops, route problems, proxy ARP, and broadcast storms generally can only be detected by a protocol analyzer. You must be familiar with a protocol analyzer to be able to recognize a looping condition. If you configure a protocol analyzer to a network and you see the same protocol repeated excessively between two or more devices, then you most likely have a looping problem. For example, if the predominate protocol is ARP, you most likely have one of these above mentioned problems. If you see a large number of corrupt packets, you most likely are seeing a broadcast storm.

Wireless Network Tester/Analyzer

While not all protocol analyzers capture wireless protocols, many do. Wireless network analyzers often require hardware to perform a more in-depth analysis of the wireless infrastructure. Wireless analyzers are often designed to check signal strength and to measure radio and electromagnetic interference.

You may want to visit the Fluke Web site at www.fluke.com to see the many different types of network test equipment available. It is an excellent way to become more familiar with the various test instruments available for network troubleshooting. Limited trial protocol analyzers are available for download.

A freeware tool for checking a wireless network adapter and wireless access point is Network Stumbler, **Figure 18-32.** Network Stumbler displays the signal-to-noise ratio picked up by the wireless device. This can be a very valuable aid if you suspect there might be radio signals (noise) interfering with the wireless network.

Troubleshooting the Most Common Network Problems

After all of the training and certification you receive, you may be disappointed to find that the most common networking problems consume about 90% of a technician's time. In fact, most of the problems will be quite easy to solve with patience. This section presents some of the most common problems encountered.

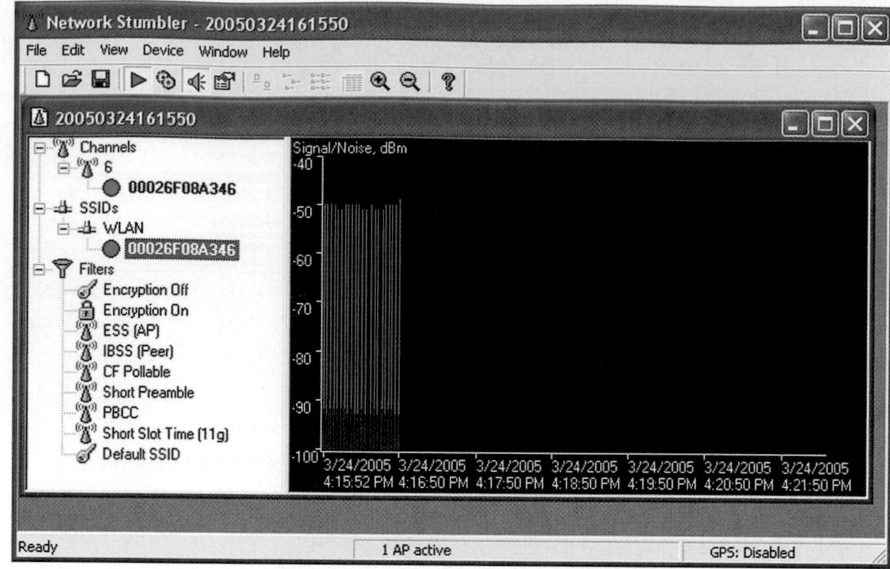

Figure 18-32. The Network Stumbler utility can aid in detecting interference in a wireless network.

A technician that has a sound knowledge of PC repair and support can easily solve many of these problems.

Cannot Log On to the Network/Computer

The most common help desk request is assistance for logging on to the network. Some of the most common user logon problems are listed in **Figure 18-33.** A logon problem is without a doubt the most common problem encountered. Users generate the largest number of network failures, not the hardware or software. Do not

Figure 18-33. Common logon problems and an explanation of how they happen.

Logon Problem	Explanation
Wrong password	Users forgot their latest password, which is a very common occurrence, especially if regular changing of passwords is required.
Typographical errors and spelling	Users often misspell their password or perform typographical errors while attempting to log on to the network.
[Caps Lock] key	The [Caps Lock] key is struck accidentally and remains on during the logon procedure. The password is case-sensitive, which results in the user being denied access.
[Num Lock] key	The user accidentally hits the [Num Lock] key, which causes the number pad function to change. If the user has a password that includes numbers and uses the number pad to enter the numbers, password errors will be generated when attempting to log on to the network. This is common with users that do accounting and use the number keypad frequently in their work.
Wrong domain or server	Users may inadvertently attempt to log on to the wrong server or domain when prompted by the logon dialog box. Depending on the network system, some users are capable of logging on to more than one domain controller or server and may have different user names or passwords for each domain controller or server. While not a good practice, this is a real possibility.

blame the user. The fact that users produce so many problems is caused by the lack of user expertise. Users need training, and it is the responsibility of the network administrator to provide that training. The better you train the users, the less you will encounter common problems.

Loose or No Connection

After logon problems, the most commonly encountered network problem is loose cable connections. I cannot count the times when simply removing and reinserting a cable from a hub, network interface card, or network device has cleared a connection problem. Connections of this type are mechanical connections, not soldered connections. Consequently, they can become loose or slightly oxidized.

Oxidation normally occurs at mechanical connection points where electrical energy flows through the connection. All metal oxidizes at various rates. The oxidation rate is accelerated when electrical energy flows through the connection. The amount of oxidation required for a connection failure need not be detectable by the human eye. There is no need for a heavy layer of electrical corrosion to exist. A microscopic, translucent layer of oxidation can render any electrical connection as an open circuit and produce a system failure.

For example, have you ever had a battery-operated electronic device, such as a television remote control, that quit working? You simply removed and reinserted the batteries, and it began to work. Or, you might have given the remote control a whack or two by hitting it against an object, and it began working. The effect was the same in both cases. The sliding motion of the battery terminals across the remote control contacts removed the microscopic layer of oxidation.

The memory module in **Figure 18-34** illustrates the excessive buildup of oxidation on metallic parts. Oxidation is particularly bothersome on low-voltage applications such as computers. A common pencil eraser has been used to remove a small section of oxidation from the memory module contacts that run along the edge. Pay particular attention to how shiny the copper contacts are now that the oxidation has been removed.

Oxidation can occur on any metal connection point in a computer, such as the contact edge of network interface cards and the pins of a CPU or hard disk drive. It can also occur on network cable connections.

No connection is also referred to as a ***dead drop.*** The network cable running through the building structure ceiling and wall is referred to as a "drop" so

dead drop
a network cable running through the building structure ceiling and wall that is not connected to the network.

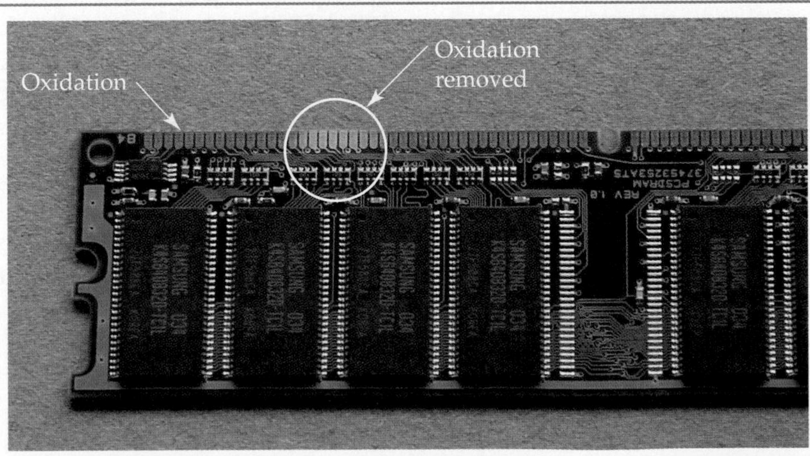

Figure 18-34.
The metal contacts of computer and network hardware are susceptible to oxidation. Note the oxidation on the contacts of this memory module.

consequently the term "dead drop" means the cable drop is dead or does not provide a complete path back to the patch panel.

The two main reasons for dead drops are security and new construction oversight. Many network administrators do not allow unassigned network outlets to be patched into the patch panel in the main utility room as a matter of system security. They feel that anyone could plug in a laptop computer to an existing network wall outlet and access the network system. While it is true that the unauthorized user does not have a server account, he or she still have made physical access to the network system and is on his or her way to compromising network security.

The second most common reason for a dead drop is during construction of the new system, the network cable was never patched through at the patch panel, thus creating an open network circuit. This is easily remedied by simply making the appropriate patch at the patch panel.

Cannot Access a Share

There are several reasons a user may not be able to access a network share. You can determine why by first making sure the user can connect to the share location by using the **ping** command with the IP address of the share location. The inability to access the share location through the **ping** command may indicate a network media problem or network device program. If connectivity with the share location is intact as indicated by the **ping** command, check if the user has rights or permissions to the share. This situation usually happens when the user or the share is new.

Cannot Print to Network Printer

Most printer problems are easy to resolve if the printer has worked correctly prior to the problem. Many users do not understand the basics of printer operation, especially if they have never used a networked printer. If a user is experiencing a printer problem, check if electrical power is applied to the printer. This means that the printer is plugged in, the outlet has power, and the printer is turned on. Next, see if the printer will perform a self-test. All printers have a preprogrammed self-test that is activated through the printer menu selections or activated by a button combination or sequence. You may need to check the printer manual for instructions.

If the printer is connected to or managed by the server, check if there is sufficient disk space for the print job(s) that are waiting to print. Check if a print job has stopped because of some other problem, thus preventing any job sent to the printer to be processed. Make sure the person attempting to print has permissions or user rights to print. The user may be trying to use a printer he or she doe not have permissions to use, especially if he or she is new. Check if the print server is down. Many of the reasons that a user cannot connect to a network printer would be the same as for connecting to a network share. Check if the DNS or WINS service/server is running.

Printer Is Printing Gibberish

Another common printing problem is a printer that has been working suddenly starts printing gibberish. The following is a list of common printer items to check:

- Does the cache or print spooler need to be cleared?
- Is the printer misidentified?
- Did the user attempt to connect to the wrong printer?

The print job in the cache or print spooler may have become corrupted, or the user may have used the wrong printer driver to print to the selected printer. Many times, it is quicker to simply dump all the files waiting to be printed, remove the printer drivers, reinstall the drivers, and reconfigure the printer share. You do not know what has taken place before you arrived at the problem printer. Someone may have already attempted to fix the printer. That person would not typically be a technician, just someone who may have fixed a printer problem before and believes that he or she can most likely fix this one. They may have tried to change many of the settings and even attempted to connect to a different printer share, thus sending the waiting files to a printer in a different location. Remember your people skills and be patient.

Computer Has a Virus or Worm

Worms are the real danger for computer networks. Worms are typically distributed by e-mail systems and use the list of e-mail contacts to spread the worm program. A good virus suite of programs that contain e-mail scanning services is essential to protect against worm attacks. There is no way to stop all virus or worm attacks. New viruses and worms are created daily. You can protect the system against known viruses and worms, but you must constantly update the protection package. E-mail alerts from virus protection vendors are sent to users as soon as a new virus or worm is identified.

Most user-reported and inexperienced technician-reported viruses are not really viruses at all. Many suspected viruses are actually the results of users and technicians misconfiguring software or hardware.

Cannot Obtain a Proper IPv4 Address

A network administrator may continue to add users and workstations to a large network system but inadvertently forget to expand the IP address pool at the DHCP server. The address pool is a range of IP addresses used by the DHCP server to assign to workstations. The total number of IP address assignments in a pool is referred to as the *scope*. If there are 250 addresses in the DHCP scope and more than 250 users, it is impossible for all workstations to be assigned an IP address. The DHCP scope must be expanded to allow for more users.

Also, the DHCP server may be off-line or the network path to the DHCP server may not be complete because of an open cable or device failure such as a switch or hub. When the computer cannot obtain an IP address from DHCP server, the computer will automatically assign itself an IP address known as Automatic Private IP Address (APIPA) in the range from 169.254.0.1 to 169.254.255.254. When you run the **ipconfig** command and see a corresponding APIPA in this range, you know the computer has not been able to obtain a DHCP IPv4 address. IPv6 automatically assigns a random IPv6 address at this time and does not rely on DHCP for an assignment.

Cannot Connect to an Application Server

A very common help desk request is that the user cannot access an application server such as a mail server. After ruling out a user logon error and issuing the **ping** command to ensure a complete path to the application server exists, you must look for other causes of the problem. Are there any switches or routers between the user's workstation and the application server? Is the problem isolated to a single user, or is the problem shared by other users as well? Is the shared problem spread across the entire network or limited to a specific segment or department?

Many times all physical network equipment is working properly and there simply is too much demand for the application server. For example, a mail server would experience the most workload the first thing in the morning. The combination of the morning workload, a group of e-mails with several large attachments, and the workstation downloading updates would make it appear that the network is not performing or is performing very slowly. This type of condition can be verified with a protocol analyzer to see the traffic load. An overloaded network system could be remedied by adding additional network switches.

Cannot Access VoIP Services

The most common reason users cannot access VoIP services is VLAN switch failure or an incorrectly-configured VLAN assignment. The most common reason for incorrect VLAN assignments is technician error when configuring the switch. Each port on the VLAN switch must be checked and verified to ensure it is assigned to the correct VLAN tag. If you are not familiar with the VLAN switch configuration, you must escalate the problem to a more qualified technician.

Duplex Mismatch

Network devices operate in either half-duplex or full-duplex mode. When operating in full-duplex mode, the device can send and receive packets simultaneously. When configured as half-duplex mode, the device can send or receive but not send and receive packets simultaneously. Almost all network devices have the ability to auto-configure their mode of operation as either half-duplex or full-duplex. Typically, the two communicating devices are matched correctly, but, there will be times when the proper match fails and one device will be in full-duplex mode and the other device in half-duplex mode. The failure to automatically configure the duplex mode correctly can be caused by packet corruption for wired devices and radio interference for wireless devices.

When two devices are exchanging packets and one is in full-duplex mode and the other is in half-duplex mode, the network segment appears to lose bandwidth or appears to have degraded performance. The full-duplex device is freely transmitting packets and not waiting on the half-duplex device. This condition causes packet collisions, and thus corrupt packets.

You can reset network devices suspected of duplex mismatch, such as switches or computers. You can also manually configure both devices for either half- or full-duplex to correct this problem.

Cannot Access the Internet

Internet connection failure on a network can be caused by circumstances inside the local network or outside the local network. The type of physical Internet access used by the network determines the exact method of troubleshooting. For example, if a telephone modem is used to access the Internet through an ISP, then a simple test such as dialing a cell phone number using the Internet connection modem will verify if the modem is working. If a T1 line is used, you may need to call the provider to test the connection from its support office. In general, check if the problem is isolated to the Internet connection equipment, Internet service provider equipment, or a service on the LAN, such as the Internet Connection Sharing (ICS) service.

There are several common issues related to Internet access problems. The problem is usually directly related to Domain Name Service (DNS). Either the

DNS server or service is down or the network adapter has been configured for the wrong DNS server or gateway. The DNS service protocol uses UDP packets to transmit DNS information to the requesting client. UDP is not reliable and does not verify the delivery of the DNS packet. As a result, corrupt DNS packet or failure to deliver the DNS packet can result in a failed Internet connection. Also, be aware that some locations do change their assigned Web service provider. If the Internet connection information was stored in a local area network proxy server, router, or server cache, then the wrong address could be used when attempting to connect to a site on the Internet. Two possible remedies are the following:

- Purge the Internet DNS cache on all related network equipment.
- Use a protocol analyzer to determine if there is an excessive amount of corrupt packets caused by collisions on the network.

If there is excessive packet corruption, you will need to alleviate the problem by using traffic management techniques such as increasing bandwidth or the addition of switches in the network.

Another important factor to consider is the network firewall configuration. If the problem is not with the DNS server, it might very well be caused by the system firewall. A user might be able to connect to an Internet location but may not be able to establish a connection with a service at that location. When the user cannot establish a service, he or she will generally report to the service desk that they are experiencing an Internet connection failure. However, the firewall most likely is configured to block the port related to the desired service. For example, a user might report that he or she cannot establish a connection to the Internet for his or her BlackBerry®. Normally the BlackBerry uses port 110, the same port as POP3, which is used for the mail client. If the user is attempting to make a secure connection such as with SSL, then port 995 is used. If port 995 is blocked, the user will not be able to establish a secure connection through the BlackBerry.

Remember, port numbers are directly correlated to specific services. If a required port number is blocked (filtered), the user cannot use the service, and it will appear as an Internet connection problem to the user.

Another reason for failure to connect to the Internet is when the network adapter is manually configured for the wrong or nonexistent gateway. It is not unusual for a network technician to make a typo or transpose the correct numbers of the default gateway address. This results in Internet access failure. Technicians often fail to catch their own mistake when the numbers are transposed. You can completely remove the default gateway IP address and let the system find the gateway automatically if the network adapter is installed on a computer with an operating system that supports this capability. Windows 7 and Windows Vista will usually automatically find the correct default gateway. On larger networks containing two or more subnets, it is very easy to assign the wrong default gateway to a computer. You can usually ping the default gateway to verify it is online and reachable from your location. After verifying the gateway, check your network adapter configuration carefully.

Troubleshooting Common Wireless Problems

Three common problems associated with wireless networks are wrong ESSID, signal bounce, and mismatched encryption configurations.

ESSID Mismatch

When two or more Wireless Access Points (WAPs) are used to support roaming and are connected to a common wired network, they must have matching SSIDs. The configuration of matching SSIDs to support device roaming is referred to as *Extended SSID (ESSID)*. An inexperienced technician might replace an existing WAP or add a new WAP and not change the default SSID to match the SSID of the other WAPs. When this happens, an ESSID mismatch has occurred and the roaming wireless device will not always be able to connect to the network.

At times, it is desirable to have a mismatch condition. You may want to create two different wireless network systems in the same wired network. For example, you could create two wireless networks, one for students and one for faculty. You could assign two different SSIDs for each of the wireless networks. In addition, you would also want to set up a passphrase or wireless key to prevent unauthorized persons from connecting to the wireless network. The SSID is not sufficient to prevent an unauthorized connection.

Signal Bounce

signal bounce
a condition where the wireless signal is reflected or "bounced" off a metal object such as a metal building, file cabinets, some types of glass, and certain building materials.

Signal bounce refers to a condition where the wireless signal reflects off or "bounces" off a metal object such as a metal building, file cabinets, some types of glass, and certain building materials. Signal bounce can corrupt the wireless signal. You can usually eliminate signal corruption caused by signal bounce by simply repositioning the wireless devices. Even moving a WAP a few feet can eliminate the problem. Ironically, signal bounce will actually improve a signal if its reflection is in close approximation to the original signal.

Encryption Enabled

When encryption is enabled on a wireless device such as a WAP, all devices expected to communicate with the WAP must have a matching encryption passphrase or security key. Even if the wireless device is detected by the computer system and the SSID or ESSID matches, you will still not be able to connect with the device if it is configured for encryption without a matching encryption passphrase or security key.

Other items to consider when troubleshooting wireless devices are wireless channels, frequency, maximum distance, and IEEE standard mismatch. You may want to review Chapter 4—Wireless Technology.

Troubleshooting with TCP/IP Utilities

TCP/IP is the predominant network communications protocol in use. All major operating systems use TCP/IP for communicating across the Internet and LAN. Microsoft NetBEUI and IPX/SPX are obsolete. An excellent understanding of TCP/IP utilities is mandatory for a network technician. There are several common TCP/IP utilities designed to diagnose problems with the TCP/IP protocol suite. Most of the commands are the same in all operating systems with only a few exceptions. Exceptions are pointed out in this section when appropriate.

Ping

The **ping** command is designed to send an echo request message to another node using the Internet Control Message Protocol (ICMP). The **ping** command is used to verify that a connection exists between the destination and the source. It is also used to verify that the TCP/IP protocol is configured properly. For example, you can issue the **ping localhost** command to verify that the TCP/IP protocol is configured for the host's network interface card. Let's look at how you might use the **ping** command to troubleshoot a LAN and beyond. The following sequence will help you troubleshoot a connection on a TCP/IP-based network:

1. Ping the workstation. Use the **ping 127.0.0.1** or **ping localhost** command. This is used to verify that TCP/IP has been configured for the network interface card. Failure indicates a problem with the network interface card.
2. Ping the assigned IP address. If a static address has been assigned to the desktop, ping that assigned IP address. If DHCP has been selected for an automatic IP address assignment, skip this step.
3. Ping another workstation on the LAN. Ping it by name and then by the assigned IP address. If the **ping** command returns successfully when the IP address is used but fails when the name of the distant workstation is used, it is a good sign of a DNS server or WINS server failure. WINS is used on older Windows systems to resolve NetBIOS computer names to IP addresses.
4. Ping the default network server, gateway, or router. This will verify a complete cable connection from the workstation to the server, gateway, or router. The device you choose will vary according to each network design. Basically, you are verifying a connection to the outer edge of the LAN.
5. Ping the DNS server used for the network. This will verify that the server responsible for resolving domain names to IP addresses is accessible. Ping the DNS server when you are experiencing problems with Internet connections. This may not be necessary for a small network.
6. Ping a distant location, such as Google, AOL, Microsoft, and Novell to verify that connections can be made outside the network. This is especially important when resolving Internet connection problems. You may experience a timeout for the **ping** command. This is because many sites block the ping request for security reasons. The **ping** command appears as a probe of the network and may not be successful. You may need to try several well-known sites before one replies to your ping request. If either of the last two recommended ping steps fail, it may indicate that a DNS server problem exists.

In **Figure 18-35,** you can see a list of inbound firewall rules available in Windows Server 2008. The red circle with a diagonal line indicates that the inbound connection for ICMP has been blocked, thus preventing the ping echo request.

There are some **ping** switches available that can modify its use. The **-n** switch is used to change the number of echo requests to be sent. The **-l** switch may be used to increase the timeout value for special applications. For example, if you are pinging a site that requires a satellite connection, the time interval may need to be increased because of the inherently slow transmission times associated with satellite communications.

The switches available for the **ping** command can vary according to the operating system used.

Pathping

The **pathping** command is a combination of the **ping** and **tracert** commands. It sends an ICMP echo request message to all routers and gateways along the path to the destination address. See **Figure 18-36.** The destination address can be

Figure 18-35.
List of inbound firewall rules in Windows Server 2008.

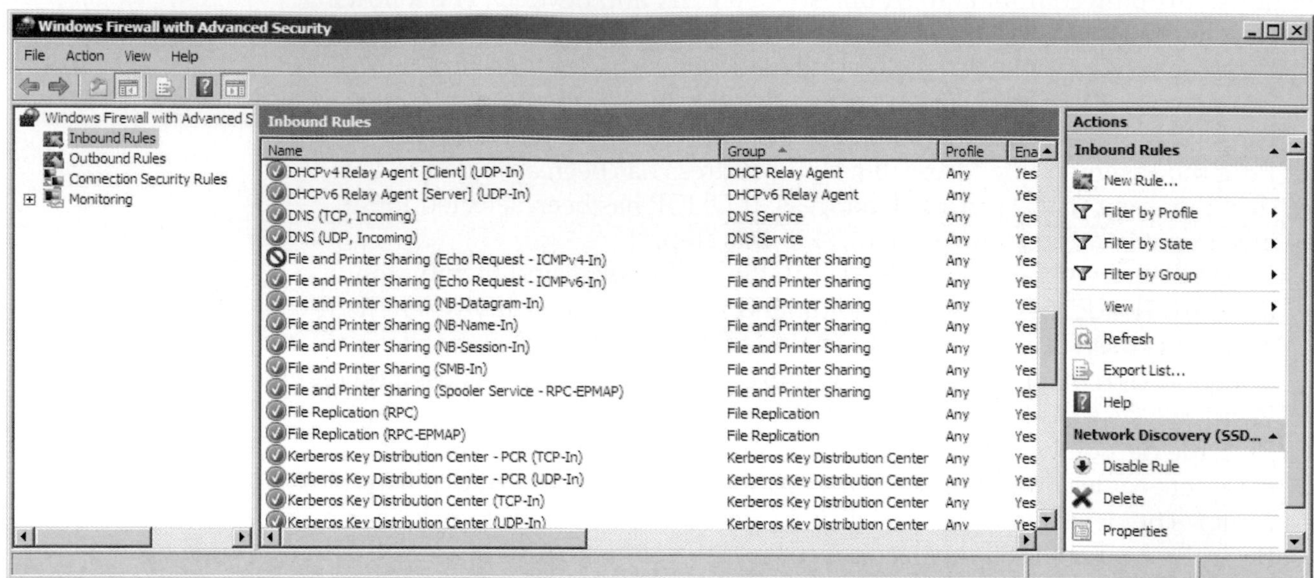

expressed as an IP address, a URL or domain name, or FQDN. The disadvantage of the **pathping** command is it can take 5 to 10 minutes to obtain the final results. The advantage is the results are quite detailed when compared with **ping** or **tracert** and help to identify the exact device causing the bottleneck. The **pathping** command not only traces the router to the destination, it also continues to send out a series of pings over a period of time and after the initial route has been displayed. The additional series of pings are used to provide a statistical analysis of the route to each router or gateway along the path. The statistical information can be used to identify sources of network latency. Notice that in Figure 18-36 **pathping** generated a report after 500 seconds or approximately 8 minutes. The extended time period can better identify intermittent network bottlenecks that may be missed by **tracert**, **route**, or **ping**.

UNIX/Linux systems use a similar command as **pathping** called **mtr**.

The **ping**, **tracert**, and **pathping** commands rely on ICMP echo requests to obtain their results. If a router or gateway is configured to filter echo requests, the command will not produce any result.

Tracert

The **tracert** command traces the route from the workstation to a remote location and displays information about the path taken by the **tracert** packets. Look at **Figure 18-37** to see a typical **tracert** display. The utility displays a series of hops taken along the route from the workstation to the requested destination.

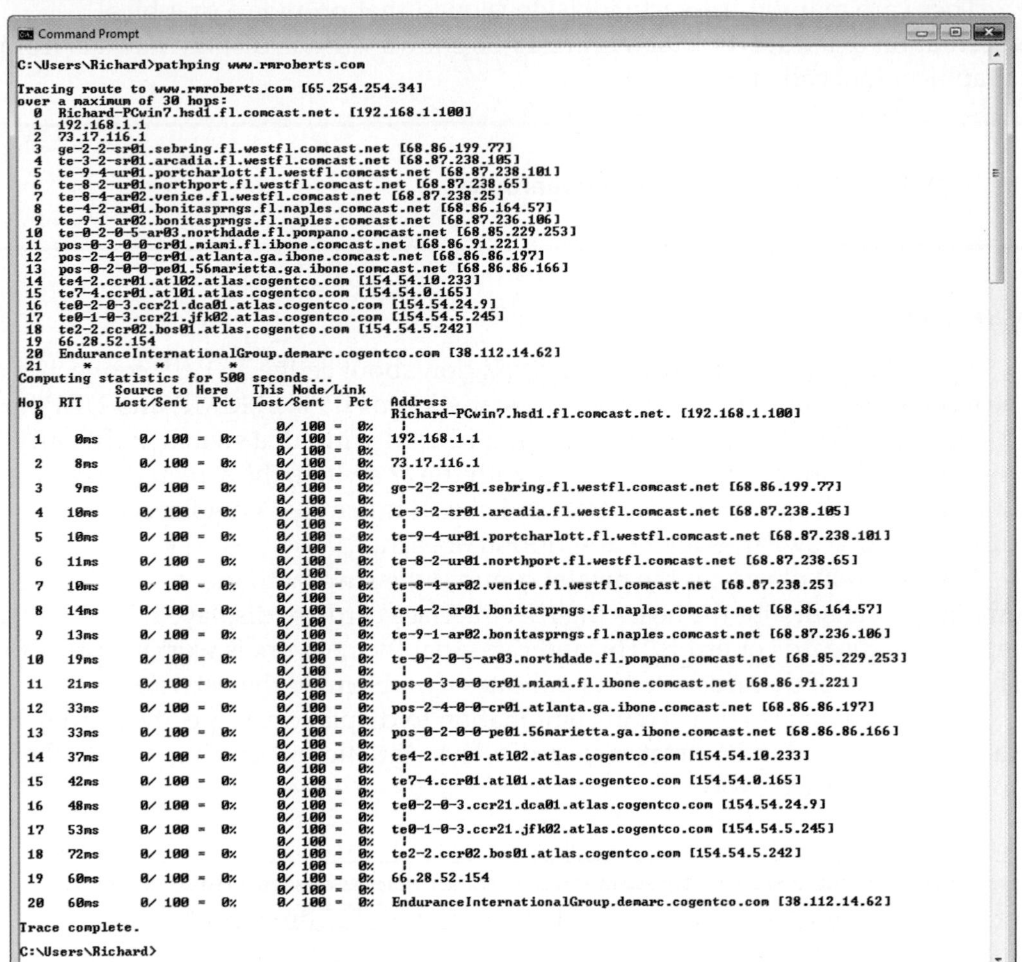

Figure 18-36.
The **pathping** is a combination of the commands **ping** and **tracert** and produces detailed information about the network route to the final destination.

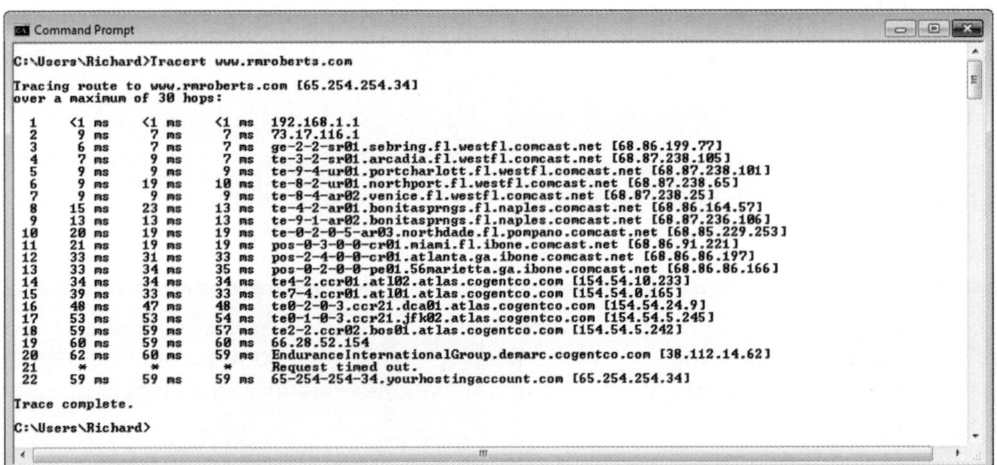

Figure 18-37.
Typical display of the **tracert** command used with a DNS name. Notice that each router along the path to the destination is listed along with the time in milliseconds it took to reach the router.

The amount of time taken to reach each router along the route is displayed in milliseconds. The **tracert** command sends a series of **ping** packets from the source to the destination. At each router or gateway encountered along the path, an echo is sent back to the source. Each additional **ping** packet increases the time-to-live to enable the packet to reach the final destination.

There are many third-party tools developed that provide a graphical presentation of a **tracert** result. **Figure 18-38** shows various display formats from a graphical tool called NeoTrace.

Tech Tip

The UNIX/Linux **tracert** command is **traceroute**.

Netstat

The **netstat** command displays information about active TCP/IP connections. The **netstat** command displays Ethernet statistics for IP, TCP, ICMP, and UDP for IPv4 and IPv6. When the **netstat** command is used without a switch, it lists all active TCP/IP connections. When used with the **/?** switch, the screen displays a summary of all the common **netstat** switches. **Figure 18-39** displays a list of common **netstat** switches and a description of each.

Figure 18-40 illustrates the **netstat** command issued with the **-e** switch. The cumulative statistics for the host's Internet interface card are displayed. Notice that there are no discards or errors. This indicates that the network is working properly. A high number of discards or errors indicates a problem on the network.

Switches may also be used in combination to display very specific results. For example, the command **netstat -s -p ip** displays statistics pertaining only to the IP protocol. See **Figure 18-41.**

Figure 18-38. The NeoTrace utility can display traced routes in various formats.

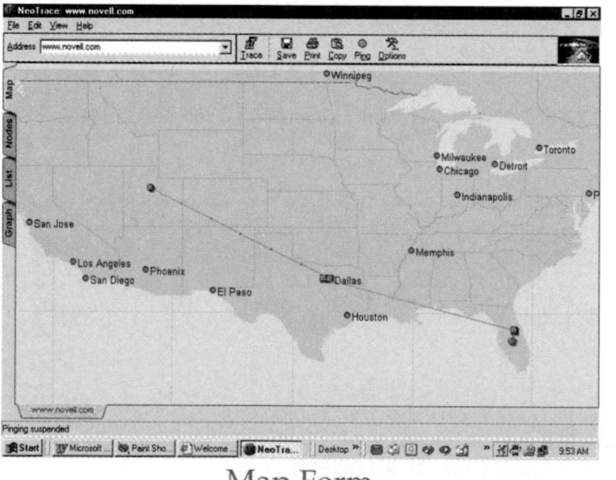

Map Form

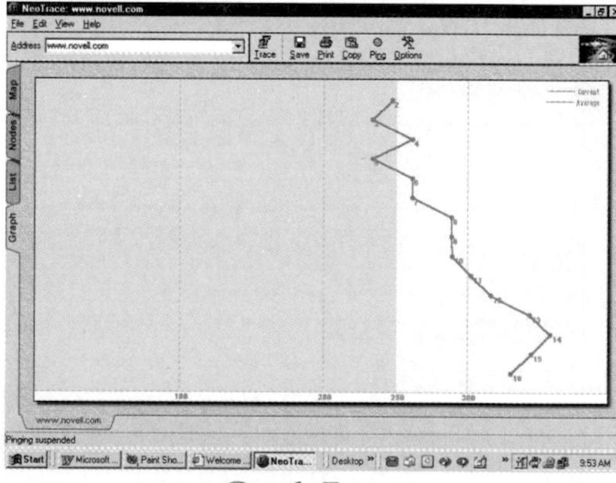

Graph Form

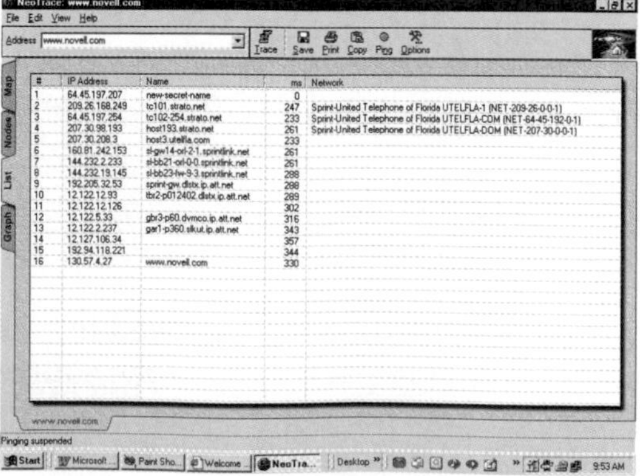

List Form

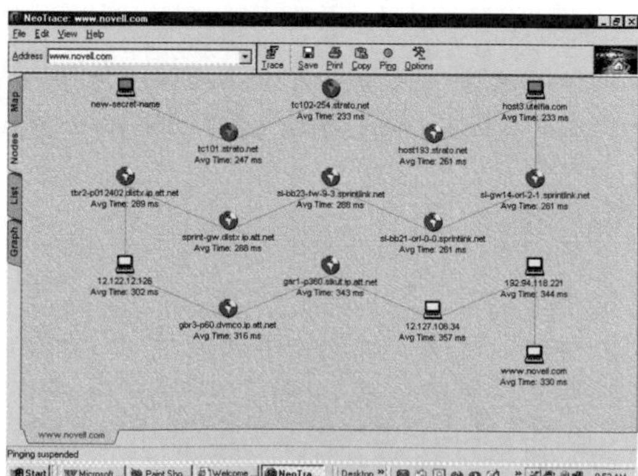

Node Form

netstat switch	Description
-a	Displays all active TCP and UDP connections.
-e	Displays Ethernet statistics.
-f	Displays the Fully Qualified Domain Name (FQDN).
-n	Displays active TCP connections expressed numerically.
-p	Displays active connections for a specific protocol.
-s	Displays statistics by protocol.
-r	Displays contents of routing table.
/?	Displays help.

Figure 18-39. Summary of **netstat** switches.

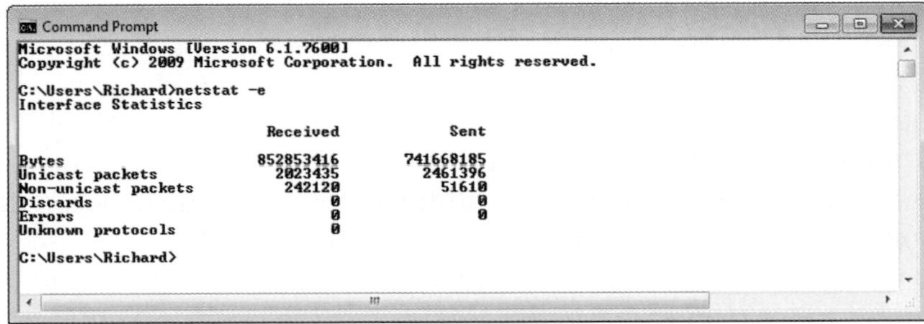

Figure 18-40. The **netstat -e** command can be used to check if the network is working properly. A high number of discards or errors indicates a problem.

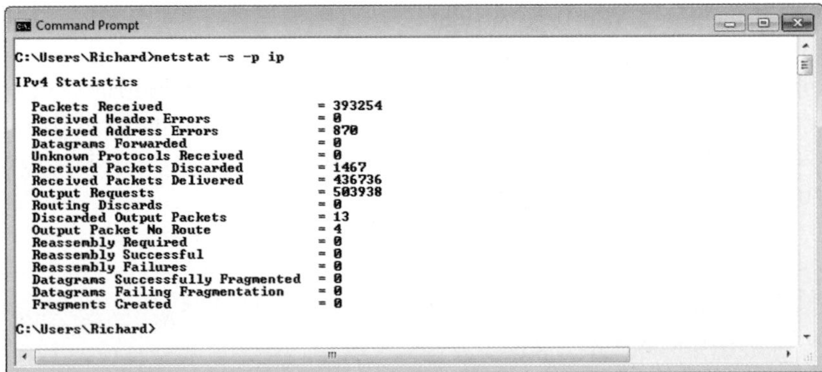

Figure 18-41. The **netstat -s -p ip** command displays statistics relating to the IP protocol.

As you can see, the **netstat** command can be very handy as a troubleshooting tool. It is a way to collect statistics about TCP, IP, UDP, and ICMP. Of course, commercial analyzers display all this same data and more. Commercial network protocol analyzers can display statistics not only as raw data but also in bar, pie, or line chart form in a wide array of colors. These charts can be easily imported into a word processing package to make formal presentations or written reports.

Nbtstat

The **nbtstat** command displays NetBIOS over TCP/IP statistics and information gathered from broadcasts, NetBIOS cache, and WINS services. It can be a very handy tool for verifying that the WINS server is functioning properly or that NetBIOS over TCP has been configured correctly for the network interface card. Look at the list of the common switches in **Figure 18-42** that can be added to the **nbtstat** command to achieve the indicated results.

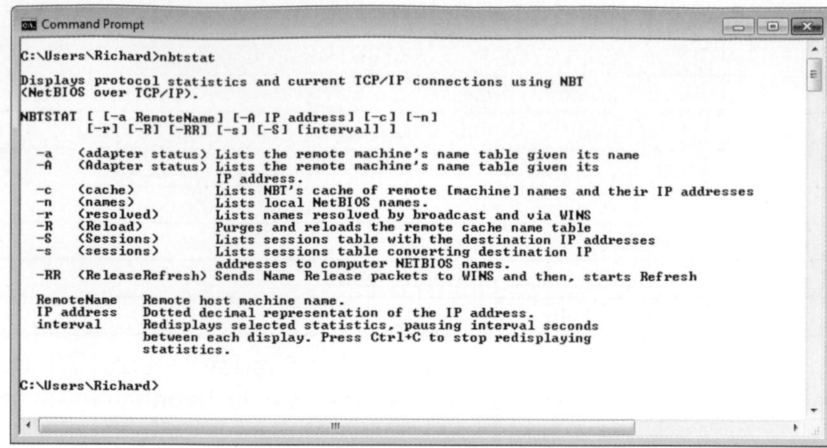

Figure 18-42. Issuing the **nbtstat** command at the command line displays a list of switches and their descriptions.

By applying a switch, you can achieve specific results. For example, by using the **nbtstat -c** command, you will display the contents of the cache of NetBIOS names, their host IP address, and the amount of time in seconds that the information will remain in the name cache. See **Figure 18-43.**

Notice the hexadecimal numbers located inside the greater than and lesser than symbols (< >) following the NetBIOS names in the list. The NetBIOS name actually contains 16 characters. The sixteenth character is a hexadecimal number used to provide additional programming information about the NetBIOS-named device. The hexadecimal number indicates if the device is a server or a workstation or if the name contains blank characters and other program writing concerns. While a user can only enter 15 alphanumeric characters for a NetBIOS name, 16 characters are actually stored for each device. The user is unaware of the sixteenth character. To better illustrate the power of **nbtstat**, see the command examples listed in **Figure 18-44.**

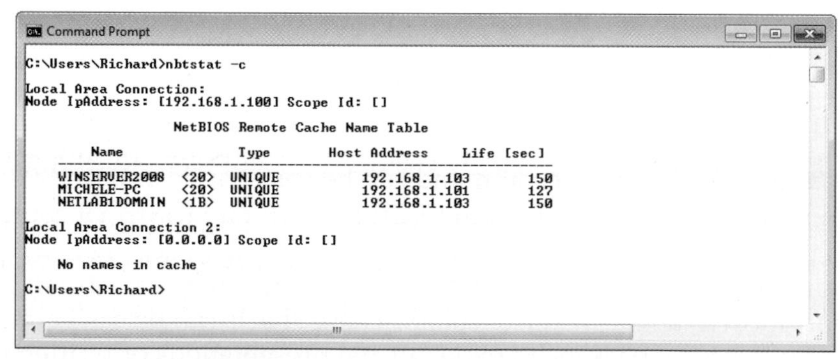

Figure 18-43. The **nbtstat -c** command displays a list of NetBIOS names that are stored in a cache on the localhost.

Figure 18-44. Some **nbtstat** command examples.

Command	Description
nbtstat -n	This command displays the contents of the local computer NetBIOS name table.
nbtstat -a station24	This command displays the NetBIOS name table of the computer with the NetBIOS name of *Station24*.
nbtstat -A 192.168.0.23	This command displays the NetBIOS name table of the computer with the IP address 192.168.0.23.

ARP

The **arp** command is used to inspect the contents of the ARP table. The ARP table maps MAC addresses to IP addresses. The **arp** command can be useful when attempting to verify the physical address of another client or device on the local network. Simply ping the IP address or name of the other workstation or device and then check the ARP cache using the **arp -a** command.

IPconfig

Ipconfig is used on the Windows NT family of operating systems to identify the IP configuration of a computer. It reveals the assigned IP address, subnet mask, and default gateway. The equivalent command for Windows 98 and Windows 95 is **winipcfg**. On a UNIX/Linux system, you would use the **ifconfig** command.

Network+ Note

For the Network+ exam, be sure you can identify which IP configuration tool command is used on each of the following operating systems: Windows NT-based, Windows 95 and 98, and UNIX/Linux.

Nslookup

The **nslookup** command is used to display information about DNS servers. For example, by issuing the **nslookup** command from the command prompt, a reply would identify the name and IP address of the first available DNS server. The **nslookup** command can be used to verify that the DNS server is available and that there is a complete network media path to the DNS server.

When **nslookup** is used alone, it returns the network's default DNS server name and location. When used with a domain name, **nslookup** returns information about that domain. See **Figure 18-45.** Notice that **nslookup** was used to gather information about the default Comcast server. It returned the complete default server name as well as the assigned IP address. To find out more about the **nslookup** command, issue the **/?** or **help** at the **nslookup** prompt.

Two UNIX/Linux tools that perform a similar function as **nslookup** are **dig** (Domain Information Digger) and **host**. Both commands are run from the UNIX/Linux command line. The **dig** and **host** commands are not supported by Windows operating systems.

Be aware that there are many third-party tools that use the same name as the command. Instead of the third-party tool using a command line, they typically

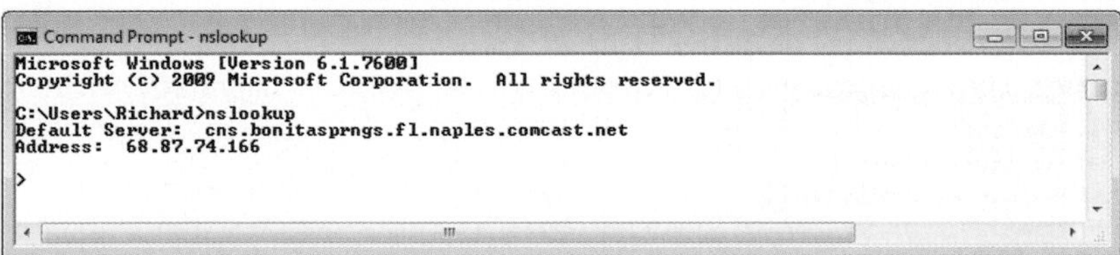

Figure 18-45.
When the **nslookup** command is used alone, information about the network's default DNS server is given. When used with a domain name, information about that domain is given.

provide a graphical user interface and display the retrieved information in a graphical form rather than a text-based form.

Route

The **route** command is used to view information contained in the local routing table. **Figure 18-46** shows the results of issuing the **route print** command. The route command displays both IPv4 and IPv6 addresses, subnet masks, the default gateway, and the assigned IP address of the default gateway. The **netstat -r** command displays similar information to the **route print** command, **Figure 18-47.**

Net

A very handy command line tool is the **net** command. It is the Microsoft command-line tool that can be used to investigate the local network. It is activated by typing **net** at the command prompt followed by a specific command. The commands can be used to obtain information about the local network such as a list of all the computers or shares on the LAN or statistics as related to the LAN. It can also be used to start or stop a service. Entering **net** at the command line will display the commands and syntax to be used with this command, **Figure 18-48.**

One of the most handy net commands is **net view**. This command will reveal all workstations and servers currently online in the LAN. You can also display information about the current user by typing and entering the command **whoami** at the command prompt. The command **hostname** will display the assigned host name of the computer. The **net stats workstation** command will display a list of network statistics for the workstation at which the command is issued, **Figure 18-49.**

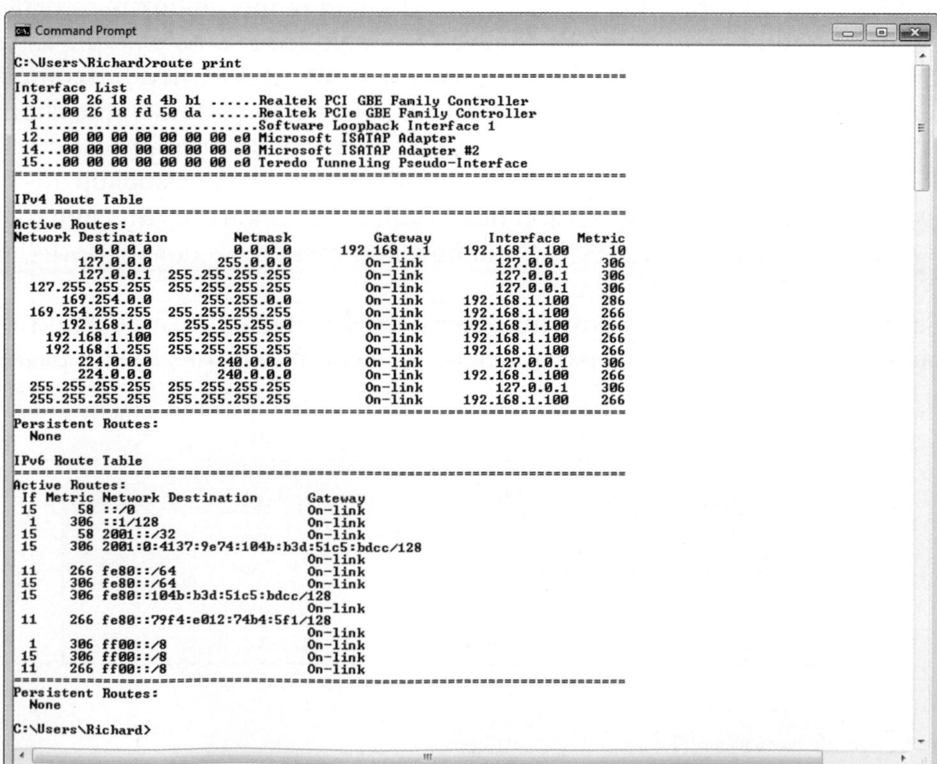

```
Command Prompt
C:\Users\Richard>route print
===========================================================================
Interface List
 13...00 26 18 fd 4b b1 ......Realtek PCI GBE Family Controller
 11...00 26 18 fd 50 da ......Realtek PCIe GBE Family Controller
  1...........................Software Loopback Interface 1
 12...00 00 00 00 00 00 00 e0 Microsoft ISATAP Adapter
 14...00 00 00 00 00 00 00 e0 Microsoft ISATAP Adapter #2
 15...00 00 00 00 00 00 00 e0 Teredo Tunneling Pseudo-Interface
===========================================================================

IPv4 Route Table
===========================================================================
Active Routes:
Network Destination        Netmask          Gateway       Interface  Metric
          0.0.0.0          0.0.0.0      192.168.1.1    192.168.1.100     10
        127.0.0.0        255.0.0.0         On-link         127.0.0.1    306
        127.0.0.1  255.255.255.255         On-link         127.0.0.1    306
  127.255.255.255  255.255.255.255         On-link         127.0.0.1    306
      169.254.0.0      255.255.0.0         On-link     192.168.1.100    286
  169.254.255.255  255.255.255.255         On-link     192.168.1.100    266
      192.168.1.0    255.255.255.0         On-link     192.168.1.100    266
    192.168.1.100  255.255.255.255         On-link     192.168.1.100    266
    192.168.1.255  255.255.255.255         On-link     192.168.1.100    266
        224.0.0.0        240.0.0.0         On-link         127.0.0.1    306
        224.0.0.0        240.0.0.0         On-link     192.168.1.100    266
  255.255.255.255  255.255.255.255         On-link         127.0.0.1    306
  255.255.255.255  255.255.255.255         On-link     192.168.1.100    266
===========================================================================
Persistent Routes:
  None

IPv6 Route Table
===========================================================================
Active Routes:
 If Metric Network Destination      Gateway
 15     58 ::/0                     On-link
  1    306 ::1/128                  On-link
 15     58 2001::/32                On-link
 15    306 2001:0:4137:9e74:104b:b3d:51c5:bdcc/128
                                    On-link
 11    266 fe80::/64                On-link
 15    306 fe80::/64                On-link
 15    306 fe80::104b:b3d:51c5:bdcc/128
                                    On-link
 11    266 fe80::79f4:e012:74b4:5f1/128
                                    On-link
  1    306 ff00::/8                 On-link
 15    306 ff00::/8                 On-link
 11    266 ff00::/8                 On-link
===========================================================================
Persistent Routes:
  None

C:\Users\Richard>
```

Figure 18-46.
The **route print** command displays the contents of the local routing table.

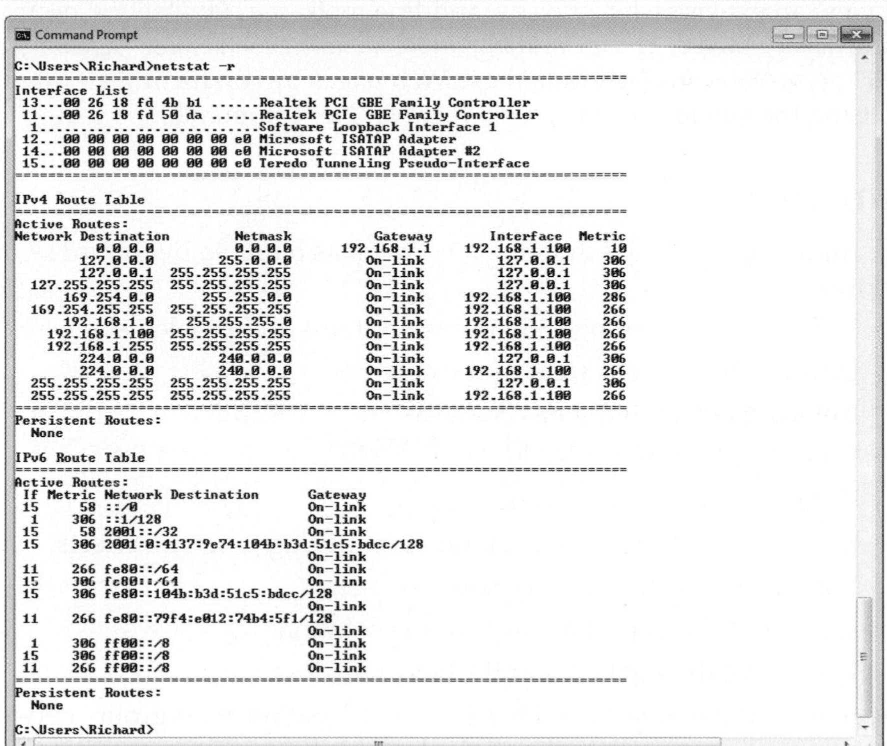

```
Command Prompt

C:\Users\Richard>netstat -r
===========================================================================
Interface List
 13...00 26 18 fd 4b b1 ......Realtek PCI GBE Family Controller
 11...00 26 18 fd 50 da ......Realtek PCIe GBE Family Controller
  1...........................Software Loopback Interface 1
 12...00 00 00 00 00 00 00 e0 Microsoft ISATAP Adapter
 14...00 00 00 00 00 00 00 e0 Microsoft ISATAP Adapter #2
 15...00 00 00 00 00 00 00 e0 Teredo Tunneling Pseudo-Interface
===========================================================================

IPv4 Route Table
===========================================================================
Active Routes:
Network Destination        Netmask          Gateway       Interface  Metric
          0.0.0.0          0.0.0.0      192.168.1.1   192.168.1.100     10
        127.0.0.0        255.0.0.0         On-link        127.0.0.1    306
        127.0.0.1  255.255.255.255         On-link        127.0.0.1    306
  127.255.255.255  255.255.255.255         On-link        127.0.0.1    306
      169.254.0.0      255.255.0.0         On-link    192.168.1.100    286
  169.254.255.255  255.255.255.255         On-link    192.168.1.100    266
      192.168.1.0    255.255.255.0         On-link    192.168.1.100    266
    192.168.1.100  255.255.255.255         On-link    192.168.1.100    266
    192.168.1.255  255.255.255.255         On-link    192.168.1.100    266
        224.0.0.0        240.0.0.0         On-link        127.0.0.1    306
        224.0.0.0        240.0.0.0         On-link    192.168.1.100    266
  255.255.255.255  255.255.255.255         On-link        127.0.0.1    306
  255.255.255.255  255.255.255.255         On-link    192.168.1.100    266
===========================================================================
Persistent Routes:
  None

IPv6 Route Table
===========================================================================
Active Routes:
 If Metric Network Destination      Gateway
 15     58 ::/0                     On-link
  1    306 ::1/128                  On-link
 15     58 2001::/32                On-link
 15    306 2001:0:4137:9e74:104b:b3d:51c5:bdcc/128
                                    On-link
 11    266 fe80::/64                On-link
 15    306 fe80::/64                On-link
 15    306 fe80::104b:b3d:51c5:bdcc/128
                                    On-link
 11    266 fe80::79f4:e012:74b4:5f1/128
                                    On-link
  1    306 ff00::/8                 On-link
 15    306 ff00::/8                 On-link
 11    266 ff00::/8                 On-link
===========================================================================
Persistent Routes:
  None

C:\Users\Richard>
```

Figure 18-47.
The **netstat -r** command displays similar information as the **route print** command.

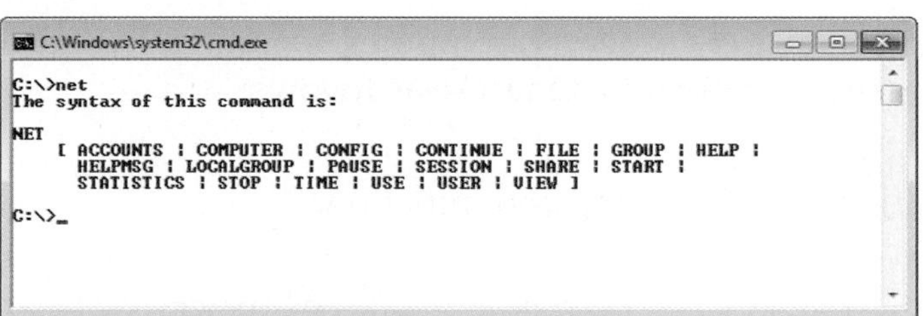

```
C:\Windows\system32\cmd.exe

C:\>net
The syntax of this command is:

NET
    [ ACCOUNTS | COMPUTER | CONFIG | CONTINUE | FILE | GROUP | HELP |
      HELPMSG | LOCALGROUP | PAUSE | SESSION | SHARE | START |
      STATISTICS | STOP | TIME | USE | USER | VIEW ]

C:\>_
```

Figure 18-48.
The **net** command can be used to view LAN information such as the assigned computer name, user name, and what shares are available.

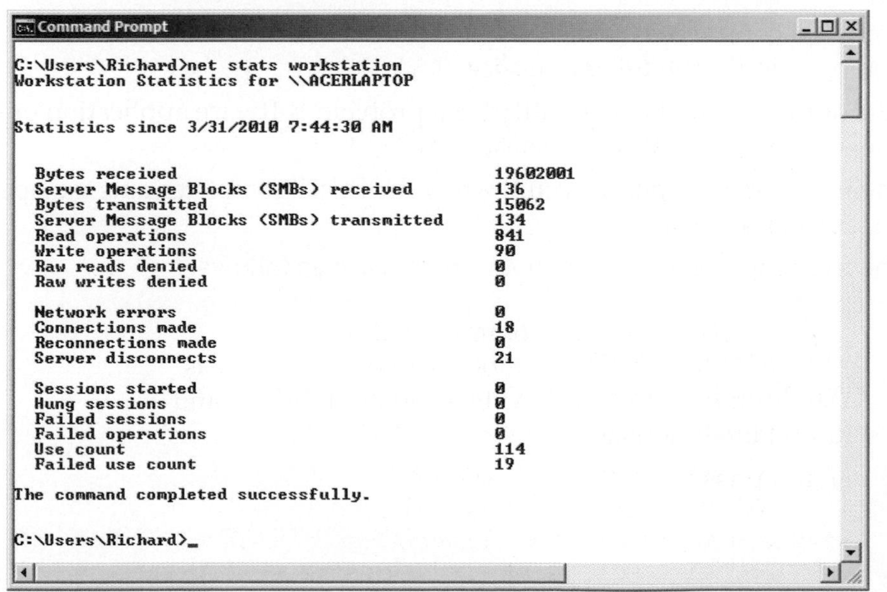

```
Command Prompt

C:\Users\Richard>net stats workstation
Workstation Statistics for \\ACERLAPTOP


Statistics since 3/31/2010 7:44:30 AM


  Bytes received                               19602001
  Server Message Blocks (SMBs) received        136
  Bytes transmitted                            15062
  Server Message Blocks (SMBs) transmitted     134
  Read operations                              841
  Write operations                             90
  Raw reads denied                             0
  Raw writes denied                            0

  Network errors                               0
  Connections made                             18
  Reconnections made                           0
  Server disconnects                           21

  Sessions started                             0
  Hung sessions                                0
  Failed sessions                              0
  Failed operations                            0
  Use count                                    114
  Failed use count                             19

The command completed successfully.


C:\Users\Richard>_
```

Figure 18-49.
The **net stats workstation** command produces a list of workstation network statistics.

To view an extensive list of command-line tools, see http://technet.microsoft.com/en-us/library/bb490719.aspx and http://technet.microsoft.com/en-us/library/bb490890.aspx. You can also locate these Web pages by conducting an Internet search using the key terms "Microsoft TechNet Net commands."

Summary

- The nine steps to troubleshooting a network as outlined by CompTIA are as follows:
  - Information gathering—identify symptoms and problems.
  - Identify the affected areas of the network.
  - Determine if anything has changed.
  - Establish the most probable cause.
  - Determine if escalation is necessary.
  - Create an action plan and solution identifying potential effects.
  - Implement and test the solution.
  - Identify the results and effects of the solution.
  - Document the solution and the entire process.
- The five areas of network problems are: workstation, workgroup, network infrastructure, server(s), and outside the LAN.
- Always ask, "What has changed recently?" that could have caused the problem.
- The three general areas of server/computer operation to consider when troubleshooting computer systems are as follows:
  - During the POST.
  - Operating system loading and initiation.
  - After a successful logon.
- The most common reason for failure during the POST is a hardware failure.
- The most common reason for failure after the POST and before a successful logon is corruption of an essential operating system file or a driver failure.
- The most common reason for a system failure after a successful system logon is application software or a service.
- One of the best tools for identifying a problem software application or service is System Configuration (msconfig.exe).
- The initial startup phase occurs when the POST completes and the operating system starts to load.
- The five major phases of the boot process are as follows:
  - POST.
  - Initial startup phase.
  - Windows Boot Loader or Boot Manager phase.
  - Kernel loading phase.
  - Logon phase.

- Extensible Firmware Interface (EFI) is a new approach to the BIOS system.
- EFI is required on computers to use a new file system directory structure called *GUID*.
- The Windows Boot Manager used in Windows Vista/7/Server 2008 allows you to select which operating system to load when more than one operating system is installed.
- Press [F8] after the POST and before the operating system loads to access the **Advance Boot Options** menu.
- The Windows Boot Manager and Boot Loader were introduced in Windows Vista and Windows Server 2008.
- The **Safe Mode** option allows the computer to boot with a limited number of system drivers and memory space.
- System Restore replaces the current registry settings with an earlier set of registry settings.
- The **Last Known Good Configuration** option will attempt to load the operating system using the last set of registry data.
- A disk image is an exact copy of the operating system and all files sector by sector.
- The Windows 7 System Recovery Options items are **Startup Repair**, **System Restore**, **System Image Recovery**, **Windows Memory Diagnostic**, and **Command Prompt**.
- The **Repair Your Computer** option in the **Advance Boot Options** menu is new in Windows 7.
- The System Configuration tool (msconfig.exe) can be used to select which startup programs and services run during the startup process.
- The Windows XP boot.ini file has been replaced with the Boot Configuration Data (BCD) starting with Windows Vista.
- Ways to ensure network server data integrity and performance involve UPS units, RAID systems, frequent data backups, malware protection, and applying service packs and patches.
- The Network Diagnostics utility is designed for Windows XP to diagnose common network problems and identify possible causes.
- Network and Sharing Center was first introduced in Windows Vista and Windows Server 2008 and provides a centralized location for network configuration and troubleshooting.
- In Network and Sharing Center, a red X indicates no connection and a yellow triangle containing an exclamation mark indicates a problem.
- The most common network errors are caused by human interaction with the network system.
- The command-line tools used to verify the network path are **ping** and **tracert**.
- The command-line tools used to verify the network path and identify possible bottlenecks by sending a series of ICMP echo request over a period of time is **pathping**.

Review Questions

Answer the following questions on a separate sheet of paper. Please do not write in this book.

1. List the nine steps recommended for network troubleshooting as outlined by CompTIA.
2. What are the five major areas, or locations, of computer/network problems?
3. What is the start of any computer boot process?
4. What controls the sequence of boot device hardware, such as the hard disk drive, floppy disk, and CD-ROM?
5. When troubleshooting a computer or server, what three major stages of computer operation should you observe to determine at which stage the system failure occurred?
6. Which program in Windows Vista, Windows 7, and Windows Server 2008 replaced the boot loader (ntldr)?
7. How can you tell when the startup text mode is complete?
8. What are the two types of system firmware?
9. What is the final stage of the boot process?
10. When is the network workstation boot process considered complete?
11. What is the name of the Windows logon executable file?
12. Which two tools will solve most problems that occur after the system logon?
13. What executable file is loaded and run immediately after a successful logon?
14. Which special function key is used to access the **Advanced Boot Options** menu?
15. What are the typical **Advanced Boot Options** menu selections for Windows 7?
16. What provides the best protection from viruses, worms, and unforeseen disasters?
17. Which **Advanced Boot Options** menu option will use the registry settings from the last successful boot?
18. Explain the term *loopback test*.
19. What is the most common network problem?
20. What are the most common reasons users cannot log on to a network? (List at least three.)
21. What is a dead drop?
22. What would an assigned IP address of 169.254.0.12 indicate?
23. What is the most common problem that prevents a user from accessing VoIP services?
24. What condition occurs when one network device is configured for half-duplex and the other is configured for full-duplex?
25. What service is typically directly related to Internet access?
26. What network device could be responsible for preventing an ICMP echo request?
27. What wireless connection problem can usually be cleared by repositioning the wireless device?
28. What two wireless configuration options can prevent a user from establishing a connection?
29. What TCP/IP utility is designed to quickly verify a connection between the source and destination?
30. Which TCP/IP utility performs the same functions as **tracert** and also performs a statistical analysis of the path over a period of time?
31. What is the UNIX/Linux command equivalent of the Windows NT **tracert** command?

32. Which TCP/IP utility is designed to list all routers along a path to a distant destination?
33. Which TCP/IP utility will display statistics for IP, TCP, ICMP, and UDP?
34. What command is used to view information contained in the local routing table?

Sample Network+ Exam Questions

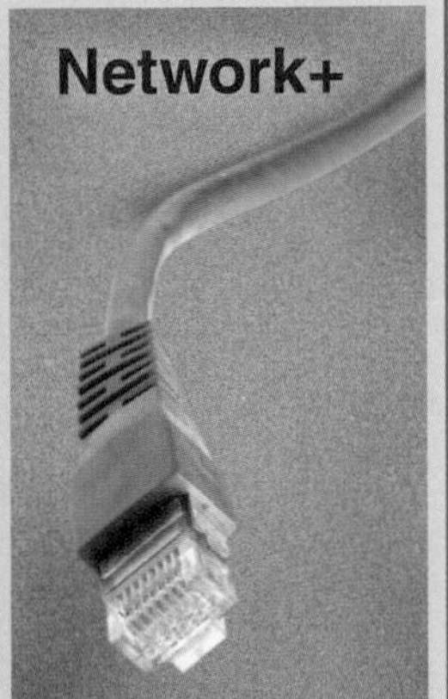

Answer the following questions on a separate sheet of paper. Please do not write in this book.

1. Which command would you *most likely* use to verify a cable connection to the server on the LAN?
   A. **netstat**
   B. **ping**
   C. **ifconfig**
   D. **tracert**
2. Where is the **Last Known Good Configuration** option located?
   A. It is located in the System Configuration collection of tools.
   B. It appears after inserting the operating system installation DVD immediately after the computer is rebooted.
   C. It is an option located in the **Advanced Boot Options** menu list.
   D. It is an option located off the **Start** menu under the **Administrative Tools.**
3. Which tool can be used to select or limit startup programs in Windows Server 2008?
   A. File Server Resource Manager
   B. Sysconfig
   C. Msconfig
   D. Network Policy Server
4. A workstation is connected to an Ethernet 100BaseT network. All workstations are configured for DHCP. You run **ipconfig** and see that the following IPv4 address is being used: 169.254.0.123. What would be the next most appropriate action?
   A. Replace the network adapter.
   B. Replace the network cable.
   C. Ping the DHCP server.
   D. Check the network adapter properties to see if a static IPv4 address has been assigned.
5. Which network tool would you use to view all the active TCP and UDP ports?
   A. ARP
   B. Netstat
   C. Nslookup
   D. Ipconfig
6. Which type of meter would be most appropriate for checking a 100BaseFX cable?
   A. Ohmmeter
   B. Ammeter
   C. Multimeter
   D. OTDR meter

7. You have just successfully booted a Linux server. Which command would be the most appropriate to check the server network adapter IP address assignment?
   A. **dig**
   B. **nslookup**
   C. **ifconfig**
   D. **pingpath**
8. Which protocol would you block using a firewall to prevent probes by the **ping** command?
   A. TFTP
   B. ICMP
   C. HTTP
   D. SSL
9. Which command would you issue from the command prompt to view the total number of packets sent and received from a workstation?
   A. **ping -w**
   B. **arp -a**
   C. **tracert -d**
   D. **netstat -e**
10. What is the first thing you should do when troubleshooting a network problem?
    A. Establish what has changed.
    B. Identify the symptoms and problems.
    C. Select the most probable cause.
    D. Implement an action plan.

Suggested Laboratory Activities

1. Inspect the boot.ini file using the System Configuration (msconfig.exe) utility in Windows XP.
2. Install Windows XP in Windows 7 using Windows Virtual PC. Details are at the Microsoft Web site. Conduct a search using the terms "Windows 7 Virtual PC" to locate the Web page instructions and download information.
3. Practice using the Windows Recovery Environment, which is accessed through the Windows Vista, Windows 7, or Windows Server 2008 installation disc. Explore the various options available.
4. Back up a portion of the files on a computer using storage media such as DVD-RW.
5. Inspect the contents of each tab in System Configuration (msconfig.exe).
6. Inspect the System Information (msinfo32.exe) utility closely, especially the available tools and system hardware/software information. Note: Tools are only available in Windows XP.
7. Run System Restore and create a restore point in Windows XP, Windows Vista, or Windows 7.
8. Start a computer in safe mode by pressing [F8] during the startup and observe the menu selections closely. Also, try various menu options.
9. Use Help and Support on a Windows Server 2008 computer to research common printer problems.

Interesting Web Sites for More Information

http://support.microsoft.com/default.aspx
http://support.microsoft.com/kb/325375
http://technet.microsoft.com/en-us/library/bb727023.aspx
http://technet.microsoft.com/en-us/library/cc766215(WS.10).aspx
http://technet.microsoft.com/en-us/library/cc770751(WS.10).aspx

Chapter 18 Laboratory Activity

Using the Netstat Command

After completing this laboratory activity, you will be able to:

- Recall the function of **netstat**.
- Identify the screen display results for each **netstat** command switch.
- Use the **netstat** command as a diagnostic tool.

Introduction

This laboratory activity is designed to familiarize you with the **netstat** command. The **netstat** command displays the active TCP and UDP protocols and port connections. In this laboratory activity, you will use the **netstat** command and several common switches to view active port connections. The following is a screen capture of the **netstat** command results issued while the computer is connected to the Internet and conducting a search.

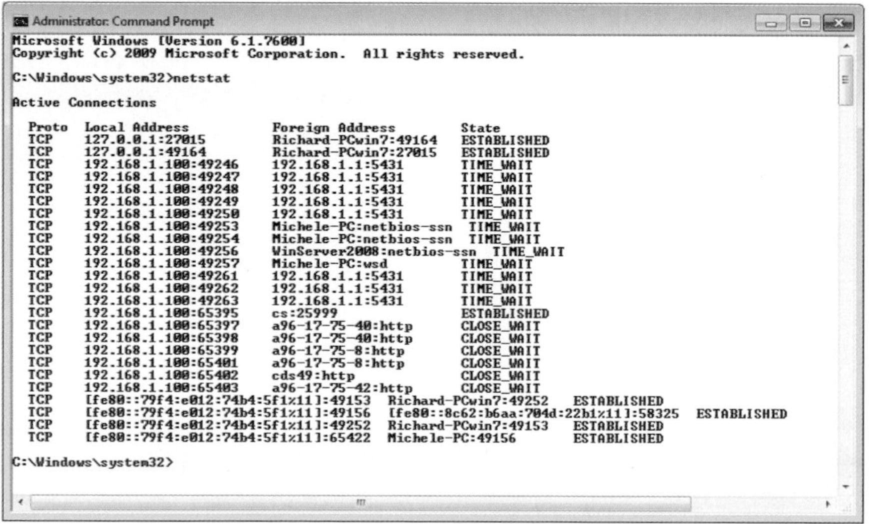

The **netstat** command was issued without any command switches. As you can see, the protocol (**Proto** column), local machine name and port number (**Local Address** column), address the port is connected to (**Foreign Address** column), and the connection status (**State** column) is displayed.

Common **netstat** command switches and their function are listed in the following table.

Switch	Results
/?	Displays help.
-a	Displays all active TCP and UDP connections and ports.
-e	Displays Ethernet statistics.
-f	Display a Fully Qualified Domain Name (FQDM) for foreign addresses.
-n	Displays addresses and port numbers in numerical form but does not resolve names.
-p proto	Displays results by specific protocol. For example **netstat –p icmp** will display results for the ICMP protocol.
-s	Displays statistics for protocols and can be used with the **–p** switch to display statistics for a specific protocol.
-r	Displays the contents of the routing table.
-o	Displays the Process ID (PID) in addition to the protocol. The process ID identifies the program running in similar fashion to the way Task Manager displays processes running currently on the computer.

Many software utilities such as packet analyzers display the same information in a GUI form as **netstat**. You need to be familiar with the **netstat** command to perform a quick spot check when more sophisticated utilities are not available. Also, be aware that the **netstat** command can be part of a CompTIA Network+ exam question. You should be familiar with the command if you plan to take the certification exam.

Equipment and Materials

- Windows Vista or Windows 7 computer with an Internet connection.

Note
The lab activity can be run without an Internet connection, but the results of the **netstat** *command will be limited.*

Procedure

1. ______ Report to your assigned workstation.
2. ______ Boot the computer and verify it is in working order.
3. ______ Access the command prompt and enter **netstat /?** and view the results.
4. ______ Type the **netstat** command using a variety of uppercase and lowercase letters to determine if the command is case-sensitive. Write your conclusion on a separate sheet of paper.
5. ______ Issue the **netstat** command using the **-a** switch and view the results.

6. _____ Issue the **netstat** command using the following switches and observe the results of each: **-e**, **-r**, **-f**, and **-s**.
7. _____ Issue the **netstat** command again using each of the switches **-a**, **-e**, **-r**, **-f**, **-s** after establishing an Internet connection to a Web site.
8. _____ Carefully study each of the **netstat** command switches and be sure you can identify the screen display results for each.
9. _____ Go on to answer the review questions before shutting down the computer.

Review Questions

Answer the following questions on a separate sheet of paper. Please do not write in this book.

1. Is the **netstat** command case-sensitive?
2. What is the purpose of the **netstat** command?
3. What effect does the **-e** switch have on the **netstat** command output?
4. What effect does the **-r** switch have on the **netstat** command?
5. What effect does the **-f** switch have on the **netstat** command?
6. Which **netstat** command switch was used to produce the following displayed results?

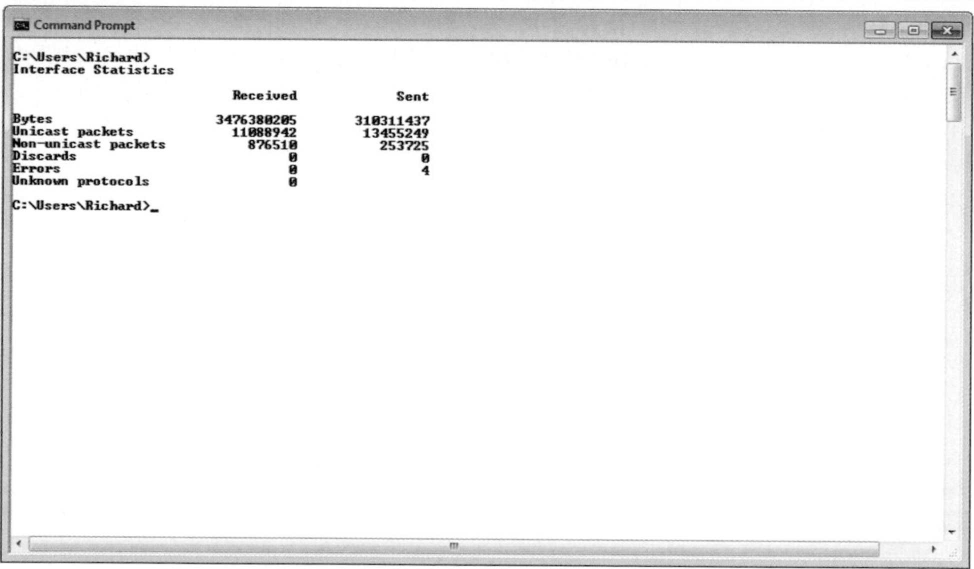

7. Which **netstat** command switch produced the following displayed results?

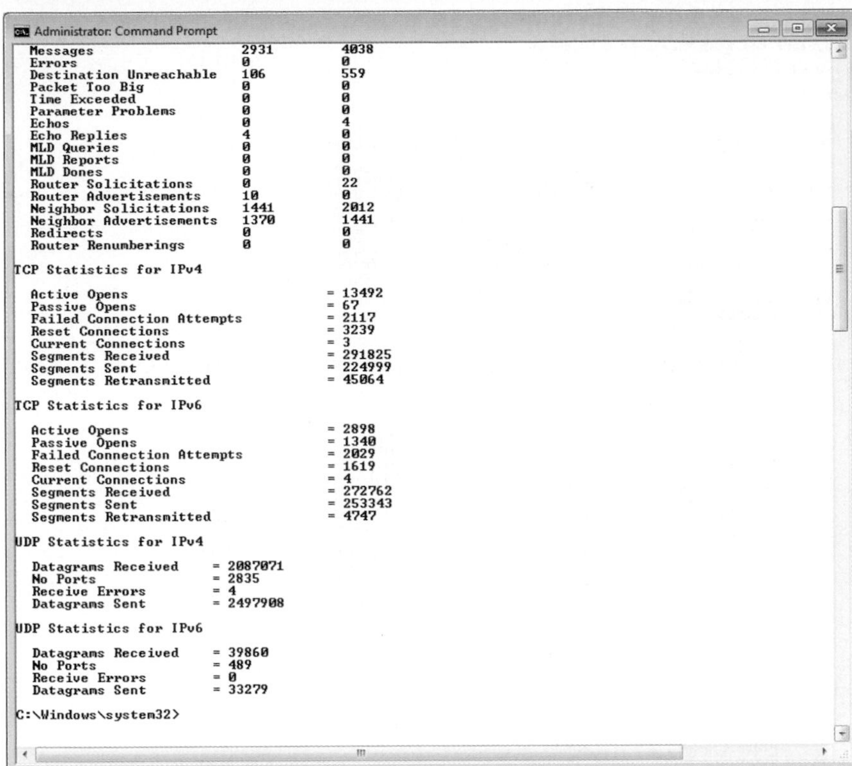

8. Which **netstat** command switch produced the following displayed results?

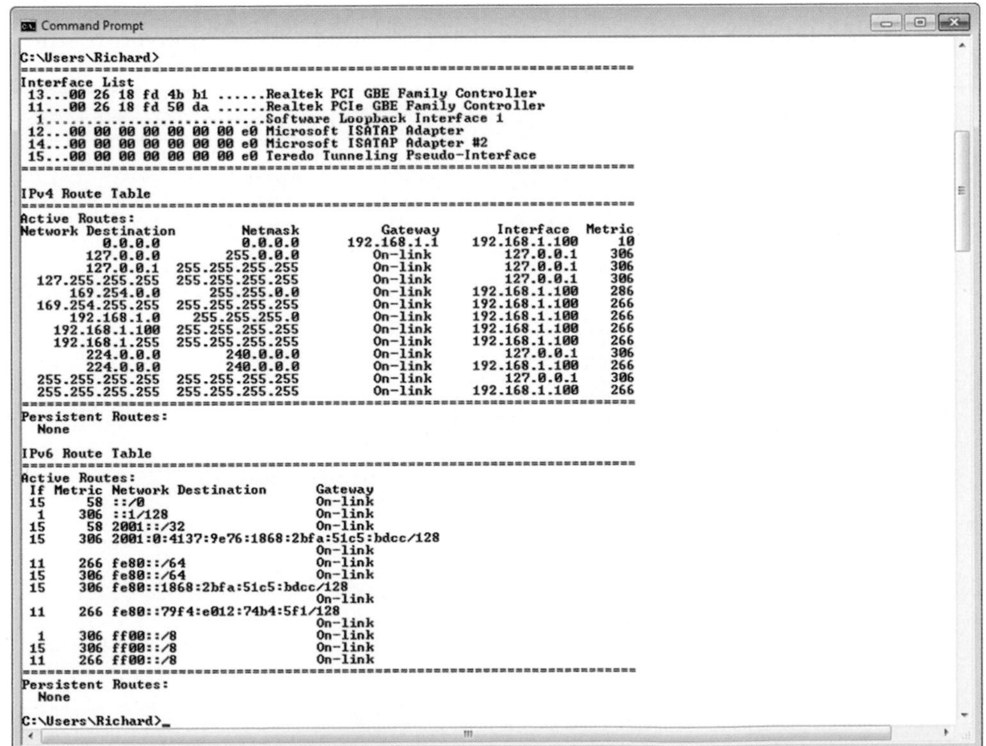

9. Which **netstat** command switch produced the following displayed results?

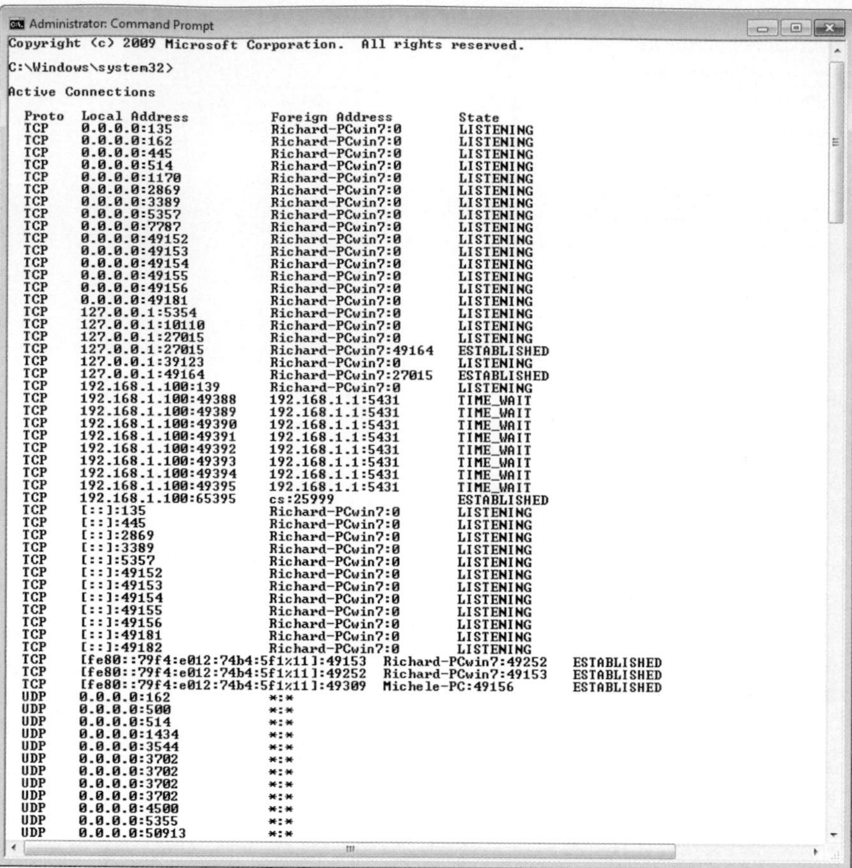

```
Administrator: Command Prompt
Copyright (c) 2009 Microsoft Corporation.  All rights reserved.

C:\Windows\system32>

Active Connections

  Proto  Local Address          Foreign Address        State
  TCP    0.0.0.0:135            Richard-PCwin7:0       LISTENING
  TCP    0.0.0.0:162            Richard-PCwin7:0       LISTENING
  TCP    0.0.0.0:445            Richard-PCwin7:0       LISTENING
  TCP    0.0.0.0:514            Richard-PCwin7:0       LISTENING
  TCP    0.0.0.0:1170           Richard-PCwin7:0       LISTENING
  TCP    0.0.0.0:2869           Richard-PCwin7:0       LISTENING
  TCP    0.0.0.0:3389           Richard-PCwin7:0       LISTENING
  TCP    0.0.0.0:5357           Richard-PCwin7:0       LISTENING
  TCP    0.0.0.0:7787           Richard-PCwin7:0       LISTENING
  TCP    0.0.0.0:49152          Richard-PCwin7:0       LISTENING
  TCP    0.0.0.0:49153          Richard-PCwin7:0       LISTENING
  TCP    0.0.0.0:49154          Richard-PCwin7:0       LISTENING
  TCP    0.0.0.0:49155          Richard-PCwin7:0       LISTENING
  TCP    0.0.0.0:49156          Richard-PCwin7:0       LISTENING
  TCP    0.0.0.0:49181          Richard-PCwin7:0       LISTENING
  TCP    127.0.0.1:5354         Richard-PCwin7:0       LISTENING
  TCP    127.0.0.1:10110        Richard-PCwin7:0       LISTENING
  TCP    127.0.0.1:27015        Richard-PCwin7:0       LISTENING
  TCP    127.0.0.1:27015        Richard-PCwin7:49164   ESTABLISHED
  TCP    127.0.0.1:39123        Richard-PCwin7:0       LISTENING
  TCP    127.0.0.1:49164        Richard-PCwin7:27015   ESTABLISHED
  TCP    192.168.1.100:139      Richard-PCwin7:0       LISTENING
  TCP    192.168.1.100:49388    192.168.1.1:5431       TIME_WAIT
  TCP    192.168.1.100:49389    192.168.1.1:5431       TIME_WAIT
  TCP    192.168.1.100:49390    192.168.1.1:5431       TIME_WAIT
  TCP    192.168.1.100:49391    192.168.1.1:5431       TIME_WAIT
  TCP    192.168.1.100:49392    192.168.1.1:5431       TIME_WAIT
  TCP    192.168.1.100:49393    192.168.1.1:5431       TIME_WAIT
  TCP    192.168.1.100:49394    192.168.1.1:5431       TIME_WAIT
  TCP    192.168.1.100:49395    192.168.1.1:5431       TIME_WAIT
  TCP    192.168.1.100:65395    cs:25999               ESTABLISHED
  TCP    [::]:135               Richard-PCwin7:0       LISTENING
  TCP    [::]:445               Richard-PCwin7:0       LISTENING
  TCP    [::]:2869              Richard-PCwin7:0       LISTENING
  TCP    [::]:3389              Richard-PCwin7:0       LISTENING
  TCP    [::]:5357              Richard-PCwin7:0       LISTENING
  TCP    [::]:49152             Richard-PCwin7:0       LISTENING
  TCP    [::]:49153             Richard-PCwin7:0       LISTENING
  TCP    [::]:49154             Richard-PCwin7:0       LISTENING
  TCP    [::]:49155             Richard-PCwin7:0       LISTENING
  TCP    [::]:49156             Richard-PCwin7:0       LISTENING
  TCP    [::]:49181             Richard-PCwin7:0       LISTENING
  TCP    [::]:49182             Richard-PCwin7:0       LISTENING
  TCP    [fe80::79f4:e012:74b4:5f1%11]:49153  Richard-PCwin7:49252   ESTABLISHED
  TCP    [fe80::79f4:e012:74b4:5f1%11]:49252  Richard-PCwin7:49153   ESTABLISHED
  TCP    [fe80::79f4:e012:74b4:5f1%11]:49309  Michele-PC:49156       ESTABLISHED
  UDP    0.0.0.0:162            *:*
  UDP    0.0.0.0:500            *:*
  UDP    0.0.0.0:514            *:*
  UDP    0.0.0.0:1434           *:*
  UDP    0.0.0.0:3544           *:*
  UDP    0.0.0.0:3702           *:*
  UDP    0.0.0.0:3702           *:*
  UDP    0.0.0.0:3702           *:*
  UDP    0.0.0.0:3702           *:*
  UDP    0.0.0.0:4500           *:*
  UDP    0.0.0.0:5355           *:*
  UDP    0.0.0.0:50913          *:*
```

10. Which **netstat** command switch produced the following displayed results?

```
Command Prompt

C:\Users\Richard>

Active Connections

  Proto  Local Address          Foreign Address        State
  TCP    127.0.0.1:27015        Richard-PCwin7:49164   ESTABLISHED
  TCP    127.0.0.1:49164        Richard-PCwin7:27015   ESTABLISHED
  TCP    192.168.1.100:49162    192.168.1.1:5431       TIME_WAIT
  TCP    192.168.1.100:49163    192.168.1.1:5431       TIME_WAIT
  TCP    192.168.1.100:49165    192.168.1.1:5431       TIME_WAIT
  TCP    192.168.1.100:65395    cs.xfire.com:25999     ESTABLISHED
  TCP    192.168.1.100:65397    a96-17-75-40.deploy.akamaitechnologies.com:http  CLOSE_WAIT
  TCP    192.168.1.100:65398    a96-17-75-40.deploy.akamaitechnologies.com:http  CLOSE_WAIT
  TCP    192.168.1.100:65399    a96-17-75-8.deploy.akamaitechnologies.com:http  CLOSE_WAIT
  TCP    192.168.1.100:65401    a96-17-75-8.deploy.akamaitechnologies.com:http  CLOSE_WAIT
  TCP    192.168.1.100:65402    cds49.mia9.msecn.net:http  CLOSE_WAIT
  TCP    192.168.1.100:65403    a96-17-75-42.deploy.akamaitechnologies.com:http  CLOSE_WAIT
  TCP    192.168.1.100:65517    192.168.1.1:5431       TIME_WAIT
  TCP    192.168.1.100:65520    192.168.1.1:5431       TIME_WAIT
  TCP    192.168.1.100:65521    192.168.1.1:5431       TIME_WAIT
  TCP    192.168.1.100:65523    192.168.1.1:5431       TIME_WAIT
  TCP    192.168.1.100:65524    192.168.1.1:5431       TIME_WAIT
  TCP    192.168.1.100:65525    192.168.1.1:5431       TIME_WAIT
  TCP    192.168.1.100:65528    a72-246-45-82.deploy.akamaitechnologies.com:http  ESTABLISHED
  TCP    192.168.1.100:65531    wwwco1vip.microsoft.com:http  ESTABLISHED
  TCP    [fe80::79f4:e012:74b4:5f1%11]:49153  Richard-PCwin7.hsd1.fl.comcast.net.:49252  ESTABLISHED
  TCP    [fe80::79f4:e012:74b4:5f1%11]:49156  [fe80::8c62:b6aa:704d:22b1%11]:58325  ESTABLISHED
  TCP    [fe80::79f4:e012:74b4:5f1%11]:49252  Richard-PCwin7.hsd1.fl.comcast.net.:49153  ESTABLISHED
  TCP    [fe80::79f4:e012:74b4:5f1%11]:65422  Michele-PC:49156       ESTABLISHED

C:\Users\Richard>_
```

19 Designing and Installing a New Network

After studying this chapter, you will be able to:

- Apply the various stages of network design to designing a network.
- Design or modify a network based on specifications for network design.
- Create a naming convention for network objects.
- Identify network cable connection locations using standards terminology.
- Identify the various facilities used in a telecommunications infrastructure.
- Summarize the use of a Multi-User Telecommunication Outlet Assembly (MUTOA) and Consolidation Points (CPs).

Network+ Exam—Key Points

The Network+ Certification exam does not cover in-depth specifications and standards or installing network systems. CompTIA typically limits its questions to the general installation topics provided in this chapter, such as TIA/EIA standards and architectural design elements. Be sure to know the common horizontal wiring cable standards for distances.

Key Words and Terms

The following words and terms will become important pieces of your networking vocabulary. Be sure you can define them.

backbone
Consolidation Point (CP)
demarcation point
entrance facility
equipment room
horizontal cross connect
horizontal wiring
insulation-displacement connector (IDC)
Main Distribution Frame (MDF)
main entrance room
Multi-User Telecommunication Outlet Assembly (MUTOA)
naming convention
Network Interface Device (NID)
Optical Network Terminal (ONT)
patch panel
punch down block
punch down tool
smart jack
telecommunications closet
telecommunications room
work area

This chapter introduces the concepts and related knowledge needed to design network systems. At this point in your networking course, you should be capable of designing a small-office/home-office (SOHO) network without assistance. Larger networks can be a challenge. System designers for large networks require years of training in all aspects of networking. The Microsoft Learning Web site (www.microsoft.com/learning/en/us/default.aspx) has a complete listing of Microsoft certifications as they relate to network installation, maintenance, and design.

This chapter is not intended to prepare you for a network infrastructure design examination, but rather to provide you with an introduction to network design concepts. This chapter also reinforces concepts learned earlier in the textbook.

Tech Tip

Now that you have mastered the basics, you may wish to further your education after finishing this course by taking a course on network design. You can go online and download the requirements from Microsoft and Novell to see what is expected to pass their certification exams.

Needs Assessment and Design

The first step of any design project is conducting a needs assessment. A needs assessment may be a formal or an informal process, depending on the size of the project. For example, a needs assessment for a change in a small-office network can be as simple as interviewing the owner of the company on a one-on-one basis. A complex change involving hundreds or thousands of workstations and thousands of employees may involve a series of formal meetings with numerous personnel. It may also involve several surveys conducted over a long period of time. The scope of the needs assessment is dictated by the complexity of the project.

There are many factors to consider when designing a new network or modifying an existing network. **Figure 19-1** lists questions to consider when designing a network. The questions are organized by physical network structure, security, application, organizational structure, and fault tolerance and data integrity. The following sections take a closer look at some of these questions.

Questions to Consider When Designing a Network
Physical Network Structure
❑ What type of business is performed at the site?
❑ What network requirements are necessary for business operations?
❑ How large is the geographic area to be networked?
❑ How many users will there be on the network?
❑ What types of resources are needed (Internet access, printers, and such)?
❑ Is remote access by sales personnel or other staff required?
❑ What services will be provided (e-mail, Internet, videoconferencing, and such)?
❑ How will the Internet be accessed (modem, DSL, ISDN, T1, fractional T1, Satellite)?
❑ What type of electrical concerns should be considered?
❑ Where will equipment be placed?
❑ What is the total IT budget?
Security
❑ What level of security is required?
❑ What is the physical security level available and required?
❑ Will there be a firewall?
❑ Will there be a VPN?
❑ Will security procedures include passwords, shares, and encryption?
Application
❑ How much storage will each user require?
❑ What types of software application packages will be needed on the network (word processing, accounting, spreadsheet, database, and such)?
Organizational Structure
❑ How do different people, departments, or groups within the organization share data?
❑ How can services be divided and resources allocated to reduce network traffic?
❑ Should the security database be divided or replicated to reduce network traffic?
Fault Tolerance and Data Integrity
❑ How important is data integrity?
❑ How important is availability?
❑ What are the data recovery requirements?
❑ What are the data integrity requirements?
❑ What are the data redundancy requirements?
❑ What type of RAID level should be implemented?
❑ Should server clustering be implemented?
❑ What data backup method will be implemented?

Figure 19-1. Questions to consider when designing a network. The questions are organized by physical network structure, security, application, organizational structure, and fault tolerance and data integrity.

Physical Network Structure

The physical structure of the network is typically the first concern of the network designer. The physical structure consists of network devices and media. The number of users and geographic layout determine the type of network equipment and media needed. A company with ten employees working in a small office may only require a single hub to link workstations to the network. Cable length and network traffic will most likely not be an issue. A large company that spans several floors of a building and has many departments will typically need to divide the physical structure of the network into several LANs or virtual LANs to overcome cable length and network traffic issues. This type of network may require a fiber-optic backbone and many switches. A company that spans several geographic locations will need to use leased lines or implement a Virtual Private Network (VPN).

Note

The term *network infrastructure* is often used to describe the physical aspects of the network such as cabling and network devices.

Other factors that determine the type of network equipment and media needed are remote access to and from the network. A company sales force often requires remote access to the network while they are on the road or working from various locations within the state or country. For mobile employees, wireless access may be suitable or a VPN connection over the Internet. A router, firewall, and high-bandwidth Internet access device will be needed for employees working within the company who need to access the Internet.

Many businesses require a Web site for providing an online catalog of products and supporting online sales. The Web site can be set up as part of the network system or be outsourced to a Web hosting service. When outsourced, the business leases space from the Web hosting service. The Web hosting service provides hardware and software support on 24/7/365 basis. It also provides security.

Setting up a company Web site using a server inside the company network requires expertise and can be quite an expensive proposition. In general, small Web sites should be outsourced to be cost-effective. When a large Web site is required for a business, it may be less expensive for the business to host its own Web site by installing the necessary hardware and software and hiring additional personnel.

Security

Security is vital for a business of any size that provides online sales or remote access. A firewall is typically required to control traffic to and from the network and to block access to sensitive data. The type of firewall to be installed, such as firewall software or a firewall device, must be decided. Cost is typically a main factor when selecting a firewall.

A set of written security procedures needs to be established and enforced. This includes passwords, network access, and the physical security of file server rooms and individual workstations. All personnel using the network need to be trained in security procedures.

Application

The network designer must note the types of applications the network users will need. A company using only a word processing and spreadsheet program will typically not require a large amount of hard drive space on the server for data files. A company using a database program with a large database of customers will require a large amount of hard drive space. A network designer must determine the current size of the database and determine the future size due to growth.

Organizational Structure

Organizational structure questions determine the number of servers, directory structure, location of resources, and partition and volume configuration. It is important to note how the company is organized and how data is shared among departments or workgroups. The organizational structure of a company is typically reflected in the organizational structure of the security database, or directory. In a large company, services and resources must be allocated to reduce network traffic. A directory structure must be partitioned to do the same. Server hard drive partitions and volumes should also reflect how the company is organized and how data is shared. This will aid in security and system recovery. A network designer must also establish a naming convention for network objects such as users, printers, servers, and workstations and must establish the types of attributes that will be filled in for each user. The implementation of TCP/IP and domain names should be planned at this time.

TCP/IP

Typically, all new networks use TCP/IP as their default protocol or they incorporate TCP/IP into their list of protocols bound to the network interface card. How TCP/IP will be implemented for the network requires planning. A network designer must decide if the IP addresses will be statically or dynamically assigned. If dynamically assigned, the designer should determine which server will act as a DHCP server and document the IP address ranges of the IP address pools.

Online purchasing and catalogs are a part of most businesses. An assigned IP address will most likely be required. Also, most companies require a domain name to be used as their URL. To see if a domain name is in use by another company, a simple search can be conducted on the Internet. Most Web hosting sites provide a domain name search for free such as that shown in **Figure 19-2.** After a unique name is

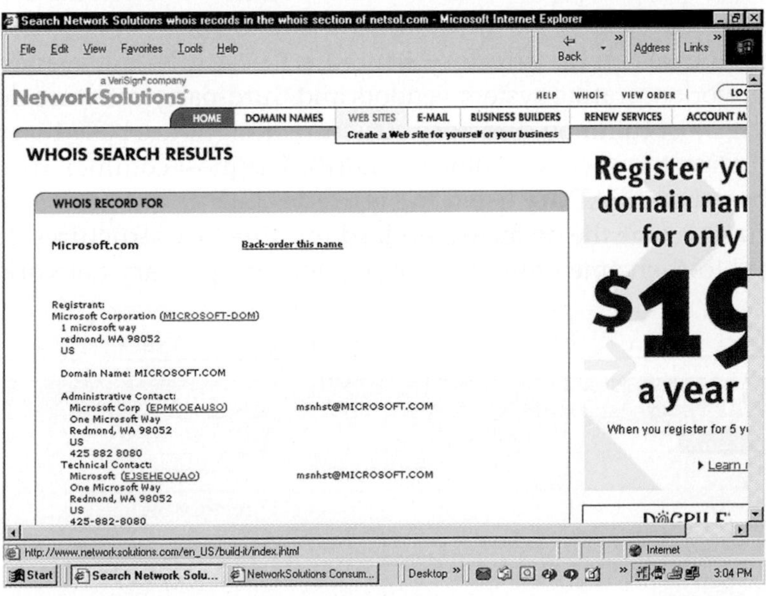

Figure 19-2. A domain name search engine provided by a domain name registration company

found for the company, it can be purchased through a Web host provider. There is a recurring cost each year for the ownership of the name. You can also purchase domain names from commercial vendors. Originally, URL names were purchased from the U.S. government. As the demand increased, the U.S. government allowed commercial vendors to distribute the names for a reasonable cost—under government supervision, of course.

Number of Servers

A single server may be sufficient for the entire network, or several servers may be required. The overall requirements of the network structure determine the number of servers needed. Look at the following list of possible server roles:

- File server.
- Application server.
- SQL server.
- Mail server.
- DNS server.
- DHCP server.
- RAS server.
- RADIUS server.
- Web server.
- Gateway.
- Firewall.
- Thin client terminal service server.

As you can see, there are many roles and services that may be required by the network server based on the requirements of the business. A server may serve a single role or several. This is typically determined by a server's resources and physical location in the network.

Designing the Directory Structure

After all the information has been gathered concerning the structure of the organization (people, groups, services, software, workflow through the departments, and business requirements), the directory structure can be designed. There are tools that can help you design the directory structure. These tools are available from all the major network operating system vendors and third-party software developers.

All of the most common directory structure designs are based on the Lightweight Directory Access Protocol (LDAP). The most common directory structures based on LDAP are listed in **Figure 19-3.**

LDAP has become the de facto standard for directory structures. LDAP was designed to overcome limitations of previous proprietary network designs.

Figure 19-3.
Common directory structures based on LDAP.

Operating System	Directory
Microsoft	Active Directory
Novell	eDirectory
IBM	Directory Server
Sun Microsystems	ONE Integrated Server
Open Source UNIX/Linux	OpenLDAP

Many of the network designs were very complex and often required third-party software solutions for integrating different systems into a single unit. With the adoption of TCP/IP as the default internet protocol of all major network systems and LDAP serving as the core for directory structures, networking systems from different companies (Microsoft, Red Hat, Novell, Sun Micro, HP) are becoming easier to integrate.

LDAP is organized into major areas including the root, country, organization, organizational units, objects, and individuals. The exact name used for the components vary somewhat by each network operating system vendor. The name may be different, but the concept and function of the features are the same. See **Figure 19-4.**

The top of the directory structure is the root. Next, is the country container, which is optional in most operating systems. The structure is then divided into organizations followed by organizational units. The last elements are objects. As you can see, the structure closely resembles the Internet hierarchical structure.

This is a very brief summary of the LDAP directory structure. The amount of knowledge required to design an LDAP directory structure requires a complete course. You may wish to take a course on directory design later in your studies.

Microsoft Visio includes templates to assist you in designing an LDAP directory structure.

Directory Structure Schema

The directory structure is composed of many different objects. Each object has a set of attributes associated with it. Some attributes are mandatory, such as logon name and full name, and some are optional, such as the user's home address and fax number. The network designer should determine and document which attributes are standard for all users.

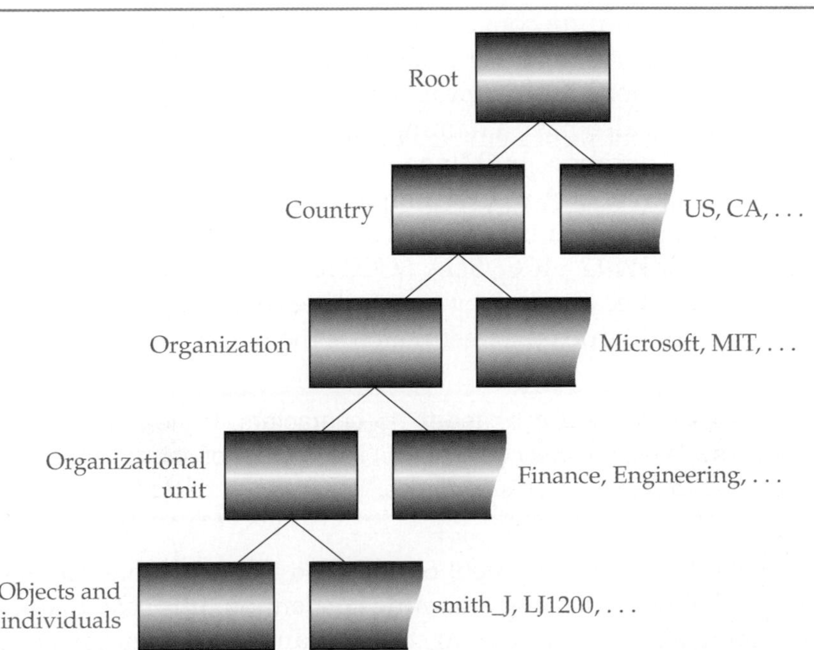

Figure 19-4. LDAP organization.

Naming Conventions

naming convention a standard naming format used when providing names for network objects.

A ***naming convention*** is a standard naming format that is used when providing names for network objects. A naming convention should be established and a written policy developed, especially for a large network installation that involves many technicians. Establishing a naming convention for objects, such as users, printers, and servers, provides for consistency throughout the system. The consistency makes the system much easier to troubleshoot and to locate objects.

A user name may be established in several different ways. Look at the various possible logon names for James Smith:

- Jsmith
- SmithJ
- Smith_J
- J_Smith

The most commonly accepted form is last name, underline, and the initial of the first name. While this is a common form, a more security conscious company may want a different naming convention that would be much harder for an outsider to guess, such as *Smith_J123*. When a user name is easy to guess, the administrator has jeopardized one half of the authentication process. Only the password needs to be guessed to access the network. This is why a more difficult to guess naming convention should be considered. In fact, the user name does not have to resemble the user's name.

A naming convention should be established that describes and identifies all equipment classified as an object. For example, thought should be given to how workstations, servers, printers, and other hardware are named. A workstation may reveal its location as part of the name, such as *WS-23-Bld4Rm110*. The location and the purpose of the server can be incorporated into the server name. This helps a technician to readily identify a server in a large corporate environment or in a network that is spread across the country or world. Some examples of abbreviations that can be incorporated into object names include those in **Figure 19-5.**

A server name may look like the following: *HQServer1*. The server may also follow the LDAP naming convention to match an Internet URL such as HQServer1.ABCcorp.com. This server is located at the headquarters of ABC Corporation and functions as a gateway to the Internet.

Workstations will also have a naming convention based on similar abbreviations. Room numbers, building letters, or departments can be incorporated into the name. A workstation name for the 12th workstation in the accounting department in room 302 of building H might look like *WS12ACCBldH302* or *WS12_ACC_BLD_H302*. It is best to avoid user names to identify workstations because employees often leave the job or are promoted, which means the user name no longer matches the workstation name.

Tech Tip

Remember, NetBIOS names are limited to 15 characters. If the network has Windows legacy operating systems, you may want to limit the number of characters in a name to 15; otherwise, name-resolving problems can arise.

It is important that all equipment or nodes on a network have a unique name. Be careful when designing a naming convention. It is easy to duplicate a workstation name while attempting to create a naming convention. For example,

Classification	Name	Abbreviation
Business locations	California	CA
	Chicago	CHI
	Florida	FL
	Headquarters	HQ
	New York City	NYC
	Operations	OPS
Server role identification	Applications	APPS
	Backup server	BKUP
	Domain Name Server	DNS
	File server	FS
	Gateway (router, proxy server, firewall, etc.)	GW
	Web server	WEB
Workstation and printer identification	Building	BLD
	Color laser printer	CLP
	Department	DPT
	Inkjet	IJ
	LaserJet	LJ
	Room location number	RM
	Workstation	WS

Figure 19-5. Examples of abbreviations that can be incorporated into object names.

if you simply use a workstation number and room number and not a building number, you could easily create duplicate names if more than one building exists. A name such as *WS12RM11*, which uses only a workstation number and room number, can exist in more than one building. This results in duplicate names.

A network designer should consider any naming restrictions. Is there a maximum number of letters that can be used? Are there any illegal symbols that cannot be used? Remember that the network may be remotely connected to another network with a different naming requirement. When creating names for users, workstations, servers, printers, and other network objects, remember to be consistent. Create a maximum length, and keep the name compatible with other operating systems.

Figure 19-6 lists typical symbols that should be avoided when creating object names. These symbols are the most universally recognized as reserved symbols and cannot be used by most operating systems for file or object names. You will see these symbols typically listed by Microsoft as well as Unix/Linux. These special symbols should also be avoided for LDAP directory structures. The symbols have special programming functions and should be avoided; otherwise, unexpected results could occur.

Some systems have a more extensive set of rules for naming conventions. This can cause some system interoperability problems. For example, some UNIX/Linux systems typically require only lowercase letters be used for object names because object names are case-sensitive.

Figure 19-6.
Typical symbols that should be avoided when creating names in any of the major operating systems.

Symbol	Description
/	Forward slash
\	Backslash
:	Colon
;	Semicolon
,	Comma
*	Asterisk
[]	Brackets
<>	Greater and lesser than
		Pipe
+	Plus sign
=	Equal sign
?	Question mark

Partition and Volume Structure

The partitioning of storage devices is an important aspect to consider. You should not simply create one partition and place all files in it. The design should reflect the work activities of the company and reinforce security. For example, from the security aspect, a separate partition should be used to house the operating system and operating system boot files. The partition can be set up to allow access to administrators. This will add an additional layer of security, in addition to typical user permissions. Work-related partitions can be used to isolate functions such as public shares, artwork, Internet downloads, workgroups, departments, or other features unique to the workplace. The partitioning design should be a reflection of the overall directory design.

The hard disk drive system structure must be designed before installing the network operating system. The two main concerns of partition design are security and data recovery. You need to design the partition to limit access and to accommodate system recovery after failure. You can design the system to allow users to access only specific parts of the hard disk drive system. Limiting access strengthens the security of the network from unauthorized users inside and outside of the organization.

The hard disk drive system should be organized to allow efficient system backups. For example, all data storage can be confined to a particular partition or volume. This will allow for easy back up of important system information. The drive that contains the data could easily be mirrored to provide a simple recovery system. The exact design of the partition or volume structure varies and depends mainly on the project administrator.

Fault Tolerance and Data Integrity

The importance a company places on fault tolerance determines the type of RAID system needed or if server mirroring or clustering should be used. Do not forget that fault tolerance also includes the directory structure. A designer should determine how the directory structure is partitioned and replicated, not only to reduce network traffic, but also to provide for redundancy should one of the servers that hosts the directory database fail.

The importance a company places on data integrity determines the type of electrical system that should be employed. Remember, a dedicated electrical system used for computers and networks helps ensure data integrity by eliminating surges produced by office equipment. Many electrical devices produce voltage spikes during normal usage, such as motor-driven devices that use a brush-type motor (kitchen appliances, office machines, vacuum cleaners, drills, saws, and such). The voltage spikes travel along the entire length of the circuit until they encounter suppression devices, such as transformers or voltage suppressers. If sensitive computer equipment share the same circuit as equipment that produce voltage spikes, computer equipment can be damaged.

The isolation of the electrical system starts in the electrical equipment room. Typically, a separate electrical panel is installed to serve only network equipment. The network equipment includes the computers throughout the facility. The electrical feed from the regular electrical supply to the dedicated network system panel typically uses isolation transformers to separate the two systems. The outlets used for computers are identified by a special color, such as orange.

Network Design Tools

There are many utilities and case studies available to help with network design. You may wish to visit the support Web site of the operating system you will be using and see what utilities and case studies are available. Case studies typically explain how an actual network was designed and implemented. They can provide a valuable insight into how you might approach your design.

Note

The guides and tools in this section are current at the time of this writing. When visiting the Microsoft support site for planning guides and tools, you may expect changes and updates as well as beta tools.

Microsoft Planning Tools

Planning a network system is not an easy task. To help with the planning Microsoft as well as other companies offer tools to assist you when planning or designing a network system. One such item you may be interested in is Microsoft's *Infrastructure Planning and Design Guide Series*.

The *Infrastructure Planning and Design Guide Series* is part of the Solution Accelerators technical library on the TechNet Web site. Other guides available cover topics such as security, virtualization, sever configuration, SQL server, and more. See **Figure 19-7.**

Microsoft Assessment and Planning (MAP) Toolkit

The Microsoft Assessment and Planning (MAP) toolkit is a free, downloadable tool to help you update or migrate an existing network system. Included in the MAP toolkit are manuals and guides to help you use the kit. See **Figure 19-8.**

The MAP toolkit will automatically survey the existing network and inventory all virtual and non-virtual computers and servers. The toolkit needs to be configured before conducting the assessment. You must supply information such as the administrator name and password and what type of assessment you wish to conduct.

The toolkit will automatically discover network computers and servers after you provide some information, such as a range of IP addresses and the Active Directory domain name.

The Microsoft Assessment and Planning Toolkit provides a summary of the inventory and assessment when completed. See **Figure 19-9.** Some of the items that are determined by the toolkit are how many computers in the network are ready for upgrade to Window Vista, Windows 7, Windows Server 2008, or

Figure 19-7.
Microsoft's *Infrastructure Planning and Design Guide Series* can help you to plan or design a network system. This series is part of the Solution Accelerators technical library on the Microsoft TechNet Web site

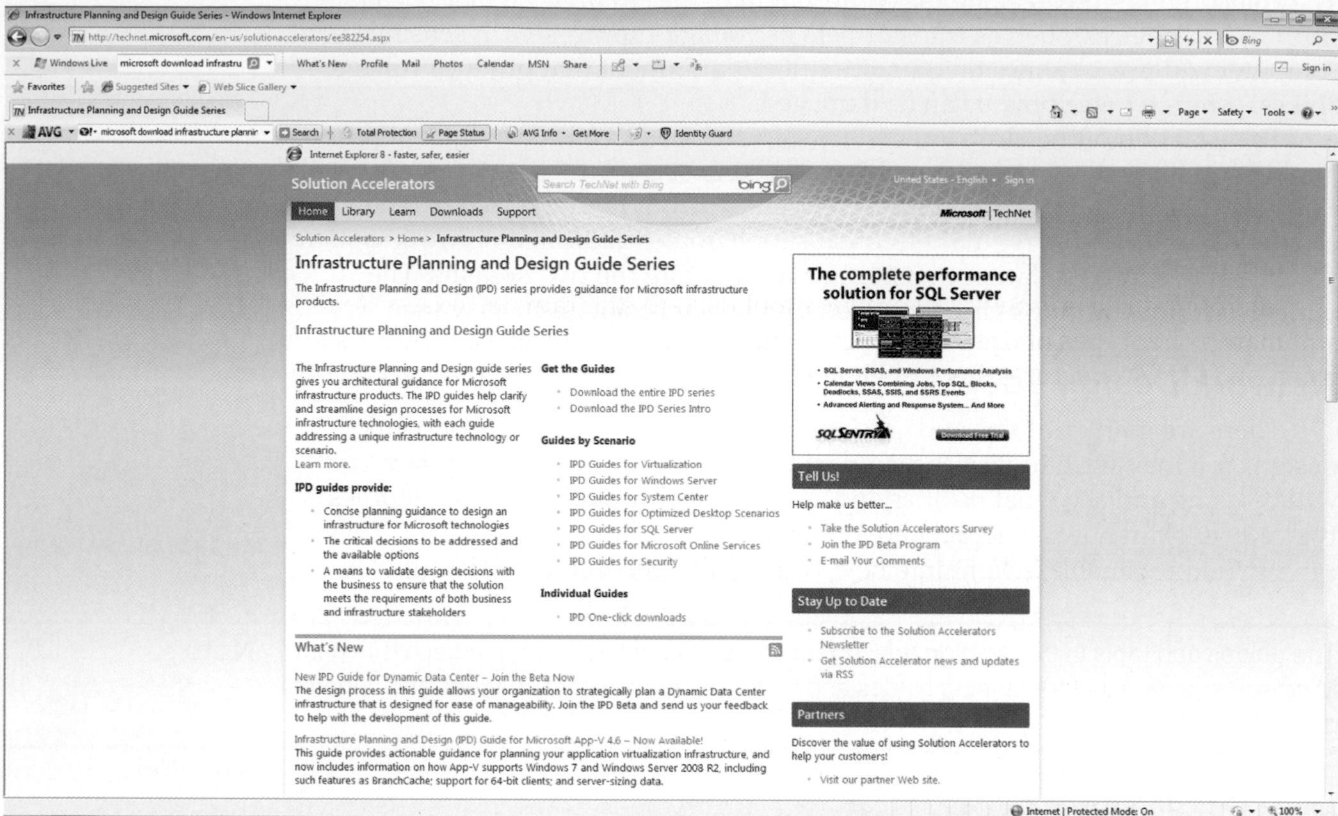

Figure 19-8.
The Microsoft Assessment and Planning Toolkit can help you plan a successful network upgrade or migration.

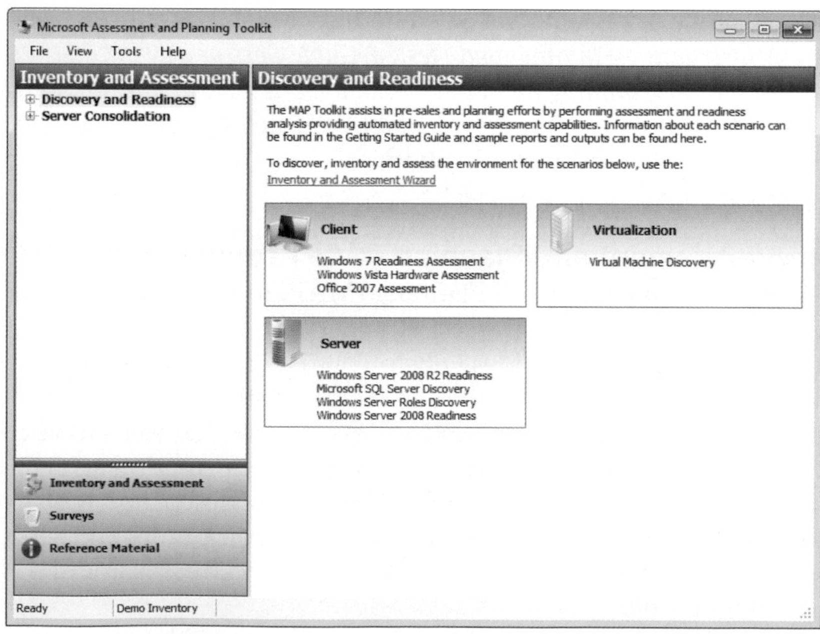

Windows Server 2008 R2. A detailed report of the results can also be exported to one of Microsoft's Office software applications such as Excel or Word. Then, the results can easily be incorporated into a formal report.

To learn more about Microsoft planning tools and guides, visit http://technet.microsoft.com/en-us/solutionaccelerators/ee382254.aspx. This Microsoft Web site provides an entire series of free, downloadable guides for planning Active Directory domain services, file services, print services, Windows Server virtualization, and more. To access this Web site, you can also use the key terms "Microsoft Active Directory Domain Services" or "Microsoft Infrastructure Planning and Design."

Microsoft Visio

Microsoft Visio is a powerful drawing tool used to diagram network systems and many other types of drawings, such as electrical, mechanical, floor plans, site plans, and LDAP structures. Look at **Figure 19-10.** Microsoft Visio displays a sample drawing of a network. As you can see, various symbols or icons are available to

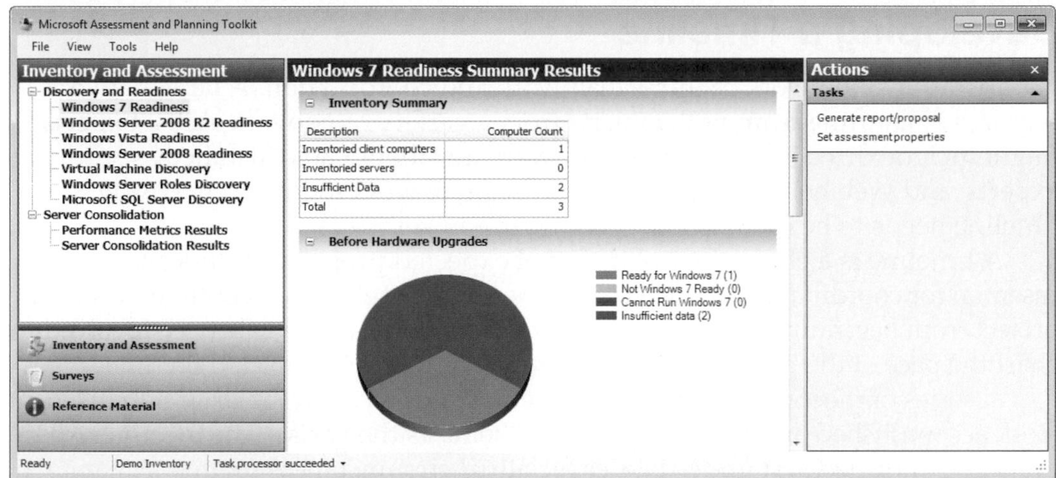

Figure 19-9.
The Microsoft Assessment and Planning Toolkit provides a summary expressed as a pie chart when the inventory is completed.

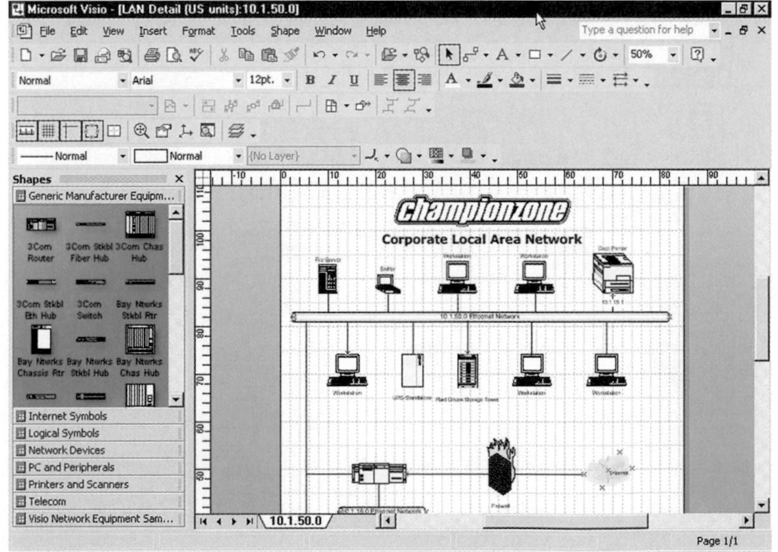

Figure 19-10.
A network designer can use the Microsoft Visio program to design the physical structure and directory structure of a network.

incorporate into the drawing. This drawing is only two dimensional, but Microsoft Visio is capable of three-dimensional drawings as well. This is an extremely important tool for planning and documenting network systems. Network analyzer and troubleshooting software from Fluke can export information into a Microsoft Visio graphical format. Equipment manufacturers provide stencils and templates of their hardware devices so they can be incorporated easily into a Microsoft Visio drawing. The stencils are available for download.

NetworkView

NetworkView can examine existing networks and document hardware located in the network system. It does this by sending out protocol probes to identify hardware IP addresses, names, operating systems, and more. See **Figure 19-11.**

The NetworkView software program identifies all TCP/IP nodes in a network, using DNS, SNMP, TCP ports, and MAC addresses. It draws a high-quality color map of any size that can be printed or saved for future use. This is an extremely valuable tool for identifying existing equipment in a network system that has incomplete or nonexistent drawings.

Developing a Timeline

Installing a network requires teamwork and coordination. A large network requires a planning team with experts from a variety of network skills. Experts might include directory designers, hardware installers, cable installers, security experts, and Web hosting experts. For the team to work together effectively, a timeline needs to be established.

A timeline is a chronological listing of expected project progress and is essential for coordinating all project activities. The timeline must outline the entire project from beginning to end. It is a planning tool that allows everyone involved to chart the pace of the project and to determine if it will be completed on time.

A series of meetings is set up with everyone involved in the project to discuss work accomplished and to identify any problems as they arise. The meetings keep everyone informed and up-to-date, especially if circumstances require a change in

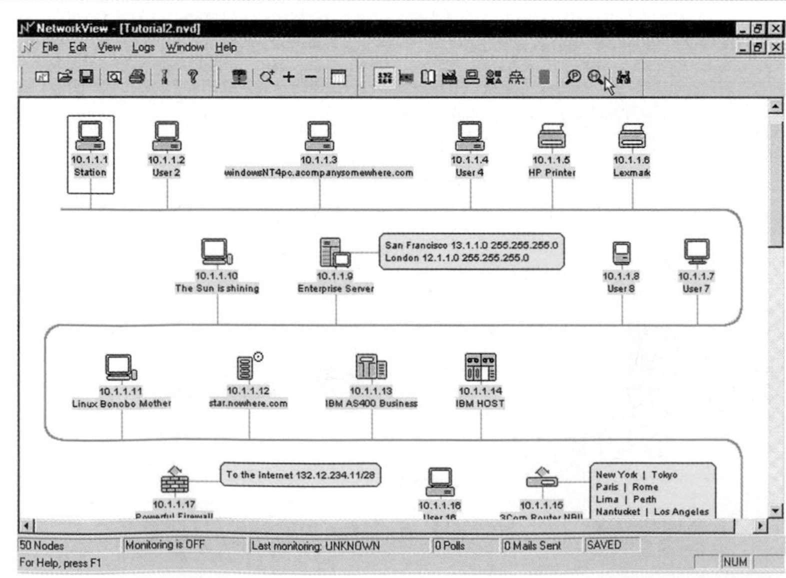

Figure 19-11. Some software programs, such as NetworkView, can examine an existing network and document hardware located in the network system.

the timeline. For example, a delay in delivery of a hardware item, such as a particular router or server, may require a change in the sequence of work activities. If it is expected that the server will be delivered late, the people responsible for installing the operating system and setting up the directory structure need to be notified.

Figure 19-12 shows an example of a timeline. There are several different styles of timelines. The timeline in the example is a Gantt chart. Notice that major tasks are listed. The duration of time they will take to perform is shown in a graphical form in the last column. Bars represent the time period allocated for the particular task. Notice that the time periods of some tasks run concurrently with the time period of other tasks. For example, task 1 and tasks 8, 9, 10 share some of the same time period. This means that while the conduit is installed at the job site, the server can be prepared away from the site.

Installation

Microsoft provides tools for automatic installation of multiple copies of software and operating systems. For example, original equipment manufacturers (OEMs) use an imaging toolkit to automatically install operating systems. One of the original kits used during the Windows XP era was called the *System Preparation tool (sysprep.exe)*. Today, Microsoft provides the Windows Automated Installation Kit (AIK), which is a set of tools that automates the installation process. In short, a disc image is created containing the operating system, needed hardware drivers, and software applications. In essence, a clone is created of an "ideal" computer. Each computer must have identical hardware components. The disc image is then automatically copied and installed on all computers. This method saves thousands of technician hours when creating or updating a large enterprise network. To learn more about Windows AIK, visit http://technet.microsoft.com/en-us/library/dd367840.aspx or conduct a search using the key terms "Microsoft Windows Automated Installation Kit."

Implementation

The next step after installing the network is implementation. Implementing and testing the network is a necessity that takes time. Most new, large networks will have problems, even those installed after many hours of planning. There are always oversights. All sections of the network need to be tested to ensure there are no bottlenecks and the hardware and software are in working order. This is typically a combined effort involving the installation crew and business personnel.

Business personnel need to test the system by simulating or actually performing their job duties. Such duties may involve using printers, accessing the Internet, saving

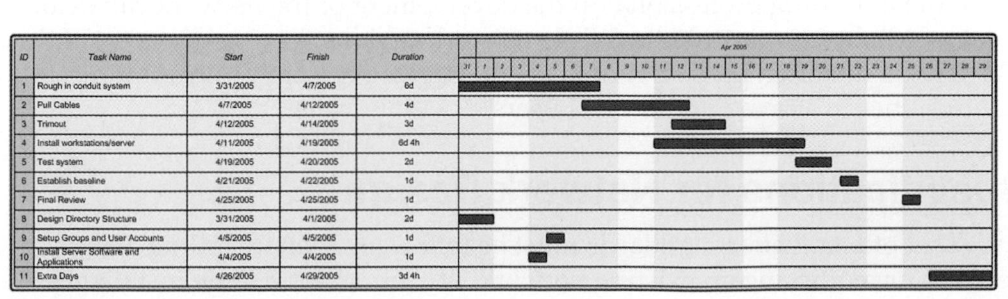
Waltmark Project

ID	Task Name	Start	Finish	Duration
1	Rough in conduit system	3/31/2005	4/7/2005	6d
2	Pull Cables	4/7/2005	4/12/2005	4d
3	Trimout	4/12/2005	4/14/2005	3d
4	Install workstations/server	4/11/2005	4/19/2005	6d 4h
5	Test system	4/19/2005	4/20/2005	2d
6	Establish baseline	4/21/2005	4/22/2005	1d
7	Final Review	4/25/2005	4/25/2005	1d
8	Design Directory Structure	3/31/2005	4/1/2005	2d
9	Setup Groups and User Accounts	4/5/2005	4/5/2005	1d
10	Install Server Software and Applications	4/4/2005	4/4/2005	1d
11	Extra Days	4/26/2005	4/29/2005	3d 4h

Figure 19-12. An example of a timeline for a network installation project.

data to the backup location, engaging in a network videoconference, exchanging e-mail, and remotely accessing the network. Only after exhaustive testing, can business personnel be sure the network hardware and software has been installed to expectation.

Documentation

Network documentation is vital to an organized approach of network installation and continued service. A set of network documents with specific procedures for security and other areas of network usage must be developed. Rules need to be established to ensure proper use of equipment and software and to prevent the company from being liable for actions taken by its employees.

For example, a set of policies needs to be established that clarify unauthorized use of the network and equipment. Some examples of unauthorized use of the network are gambling, distribution of materials that are not part of the company or part of the user's job, harassment, and unauthorized downloading of graphic material, music, and software. In general, any illegal activity is prohibited. Personal uses of equipment such as printing out your child's homework assignment, club activities, and personal correspondence are typically unauthorized in many companies and are viewed as fraud against the company by the misuse of company time and resources.

Drawings of the finished network system are also needed. Note the word finished. Changes occur as the system is built. Thus, the finished product can be somewhat different from the original proposal. Too often, a network system is installed, but no drawings of the finished system exist. Only the original proposed plan exists. Changes do occur, especially in complex systems. Documentation of changes that occur after an installation is also important because the network administrator may be the only person who knows how the system was changed.

Training

An essential part of installing a network system is to design a training program for the network users. The user must be trained in password and general security policies and procedures, remote access, e-mail fundamentals, and more.

The amount and depth of the training varies according to the size of the project. For example, a small modification to an existing network may require only a briefing. A large enterprise project may require training for hundreds of employees over a period of days, weeks, or months.

Company procedures and policies need to be developed before conducting training. Policies and procedures need to be disseminated as part of the training. Involving a training professional in the development of the network can be of great assistance in this process. While network designers are really good at their job, they do not often possess the skills and talents necessary to communicate technicalities to a broad audience of users.

Specifications for Network Design

A set of installation standards must be followed when installing a new network or modifying an existing network. A contract for a large installation typically includes a set of specifications or "specs," as they are often referred to in trade jargon. Specifications are used to specify details or expectations about materials and craftsmanship that are acceptable for the installation of the system. The specifications ensure that the owner and the contractor both know exactly what is expected. Without a set of specifications, there can be a wide variation of interpretation between what the owner expects and the finished product. Documentation that includes specifications reduces communication problems.

The overall size of a set of specifications can be quite lengthy. Most specifications make reference to other, previously-established standards to reduce the size of the document. There is no need to call out details about wall outlets and electrical circuits installed for the network. The specifications simply make reference to established specifications. For example, a specification in a document might read, "All electrical work shall conform to the minimum standards established by the National Electrical Code (NEC)."

The National Electrical Code (NEC) comprises hundreds of pages of specifications for wire sizes, conduit sizes, supports, and other materials that have been selected by an organization of electrical engineers, contractors, and fire and safety experts. Many years have been dedicated to researching the best, minimal standards that are adequate to ensure the safety of personnel.

This section discusses standard organizations and some standards related to networking. It also defines some architectural design element terms, such as *main entrance room* and *horizontal cross connect*. It is important that you be familiar with these terms because they are often used in the standards related to networking.

You will see different terms used to describe the same concept. This is because the terminology is often originated from conflicting industry standards and terminology developed by individual private companies. For example, you may see the following terms and acronyms used to describe the connection point where the customer and the commercial provider cable meets: Point of Presence (POP), Point of Entry (POE), Customer Connection Point (CCP), Service Delivery Point (SDP), demarc, and demarcation point. In the electronics industry, different terminology for the same concept is common. Consider the source of the term before dismissing it as incorrect.

Architectural Design Elements

The architectural design elements recognized by ANSI/TIA/EIA are demarcation point, Network Interface Device, main entrance room, Main Distribution Frame, entrance facility, equipment room, work area, horizontal cross connect, horizontal wiring, backbone, patch panel, punch down block, telecommunications room, and telecommunications closet. **Figure 19-13** illustrates the general locations of some of these architectural design elements.

Demarcation Point

Demarcation point or ***demarc*** is the spot where the customer equipment or cable meets the telecommunications provider cable or equipment. The demarcation point is where the customer and private/public telecommunications companies become responsible for the cable and equipment. If the private/public telecommunications company is directed to troubleshoot or make repairs on the customer side of the demarcation point, the customer is billed for the services.

demarcation point the point where the customer equipment or cable meets the telecommunications provider cable or equipment.

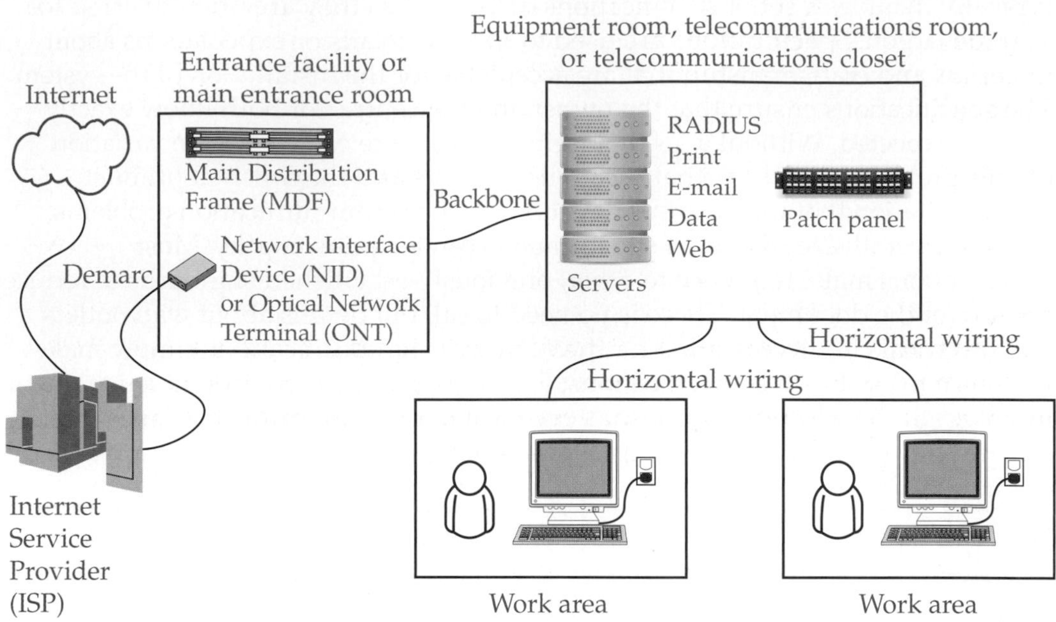

Figure 19-13. General locations of some of the architectural design elements recognized by ANSI/TIA/EIA.

The customer is not responsible for any work performed on the private/public telecommunications side of the demarcation point.

Network Interface Device

Network Interface Device (NID) any device that connects the commercial carrier local loop to the private customer's premises wiring.

smart jack an intelligent connection point, which incorporates additional electronics that allow it to perform specific functions.

Optical Network Terminal (ONT) a fiber-optic cable termination point between the customer and the service provider. It can provide multiple services such as telephone, television, and Internet access.

A ***Network Interface Device (NID)*** is a term used to describe a device that connects the commercial carrier local loop to the private customer's premises wiring. The NID can be considered the point of demarcation or demarc point for the communications system. Two common NID devices are smart jack and optical network terminal.

The term *jack* was used to describe the connection point between the communications provider (telephone company) and the customer. A jack provides a simple and quick connection point. A ***smart jack*** is considered an intelligent connection point because it incorporates additional electronics that allow it to perform specific functions. For example, a smart jack can perform a loopback test remotely from the service provider without the need to send a technician to the smart jack location. The smart jack can also automatically perform diagnostics and generate a report of the probable cause of the problem. The self-diagnostics by the smart jack helps the provider determine if the problem exists on the customer premises or on the service provider's side of the connection. Smart jacks typically obtain electrical power from the telephone line connection, which means the jack does not need a separate power supply in most cases. Smart jacks are commonly used for T1 and DSL terminations.

An ***Optical Network Terminal (ONT)*** is a fiber-optic cable termination point between the customer and the service provider. The ONT is more than just a simple fiber-optic cable connection point. Fiber-optic service can provide multiple services such as telephone, television, and Internet access. When the fiber-optic cable provides multiple services, the ONT acts as a multiplexer and de-multiplexer unit. Combining signals on a fiber-optic cable is called *multiplexing*. The separation of the signals at the destination is referred to as *de-multiplexing*.

The ONT typically obtains power from the customer site. There may also be a battery backup system to provide access even when the electrical power is out of service at the site. If the customer has a UPS system for the computer, then the customer can shut down the computer system safely, even if he or she is in the process of downloading or uploading data.

Both the smart jack and the Optical Network Terminal (ONT) can be identified as the demarcation point.

Main Entrance Room

The ***main entrance room*** is the room in which public or private telecommunications enter the building. In the past, the main entrance room not only housed the telecommunications equipment, but also the air conditioning, heating, electrical, and other equipment. As the building industry evolved, the telecommunications room was eventually established in a separate room in the building. This is preferred due to a multitude of reasons including access, security, and performance issues.

main entrance room the room in which public or private telecommunications enter the building.

Main Distribution Frame (MDF)

The ***Main Distribution Frame (MDF)*** is the cable connection point where the private telecommunications cables come into a building and then connect or distribute to other areas in the building. The MDF typically consists of a cable rack and physical cable connections for the individual cable conductors. The MDF can function as a test point when troubleshooting. The MDF is usually located in the main entrance room.

Main Distribution Frame (MDF) and *Intermediate Distribution Frame (IDF)* are relative terms. For example, when a multistory building requires telecommunications, there will be a combination of MDF and IDFs throughout the facility. Each floor would have an IDF that acts as the connection point from the MDF and distributes cable runs to all areas on that specific floor. The same terminology is often applied to network cable distribution.

Main Distribution Frame (MDF) the cable connection point where the private telecommunications cables come into a building and then connect or distribute to other areas in the building. It typically consists of a cable rack and physical cable connections for the individual cable conductors.

Entrance Facility

The ***entrance facility*** is the room that is used as the entrance location for public or private communications cables. The entrance facility may also serve as a telecommunications room or equipment room. Many times, the location depends on the availability of rooms and spaces in an existing building or the design or the complexity of the equipment required.

entrance facility the room that is used as the entrance location for public or private communications cables.

Equipment Room

An ***equipment room*** contains the telecommunications equipment for the building such as the Private Branch Exchange (PBX), servers, and telecommunications wiring system terminations. Most large companies have their own telephone system referred to as a *Private Branch Exchange (PBX)*. An equipment room may also serve the purpose of an entrance facility or a telecommunications room.

equipment room a room that contains the telecommunications equipment for the building such as the Private Branch Exchange (PBX), servers, and telecommunications wiring system terminations.

Work Area

The ***work area*** is where employees perform their normal office duties. The work area is given this designation because the standards are different than those for hallways, lounges, reception areas, storage areas, and various other areas in the building. When you consider the various rooms that might be found

work area the area in which employees perform their normal office duties.

in a building, designating a work area as a special room is not so unusual. The requirements for a work area are not the same as the requirements for a storage area or a reception area. However, if a reception area were also a work area, there would be different requirements than normal.

Tech Tip

The terminology for network facilities is based on telecommunications standards. The telecommunications industry existed long before computer network technology, and many of the terms used to describe network rooms are actually derived from that industry.

Horizontal Cross Connect

horizontal cross connect
a mechanical means of connecting horizontal cabling systems to other cables or equipment.

A ***horizontal cross connect*** provides a mechanical means of connecting horizontal cabling systems to other cables or equipment. For example, a horizontal cross connect is used to connect horizontal cabling to a backbone or to system equipment such as a router, switch, bridge, or server.

Horizontal Wiring

horizontal wiring
the section of cable that runs from individual work areas to the telecommunications closet.

Horizontal wiring refers to the section of cable that runs from individual work areas to the telecommunications closet. The telecommunications closet contains connection equipment for the workstations in the immediate area.

All work areas connect to the telecommunications closet horizontal cross connects. Horizontal cable distance is limited to 90 meters for the horizontal run from the telecommunications outlet to the telecommunications closet. The maximum total distance is 100 meters.

Tech Tip

Some specifications state that the total combined length of patch cables at each end of the horizontal run should be no more than 10 meters. However, as a general rule, a total combined length of patch cables over 10 meters is allowed as long as the maximum total distance for horizontal cabling does not exceed 100 meters.

At least two outlets should be installed in each work area. One outlet is used for voice communications and the other for data communications. Typically, more than two outlets are installed as a combination of network and telephone outlets. Category 3 is the minimum recommendation for telephone wiring, but a higher category of wiring is permitted. The media for data communications can be any one of the following:

- Four-pair UTP Category 5/5e/6/6e (Category 5e or higher is recommended).
- Two-pair STP.
- Two-strand, 62.5/125 μm fiber-optic cable.

Backbone

backbone
a cable that is located between the telecommunications closets, equipment rooms, and main entrance facility. It can run horizontally and vertically through a building. Also, a common cable path that often employs high-speed network cable such as fiber-optic.

A network ***backbone*** is located between the telecommunications closets, equipment rooms, and main entrance facility. The backbone connects these areas and does not serve individual workstations. A backbone can run horizontally and vertically through a building. When the backbone is run vertically, it is sometimes referred to as a *riser* and typically passes through 4-inch conduit sleeves in the floor or ceiling. The backbone cannot be run in elevator shafts. See **Figure 19-14** for a list of the approved cable and distances for backbones. Note that when UTP and STP are used for telephone communications (voice), the maximum distance is 800

Cable Type	Distance
UTP Category 3 or higher (Category 5, 5e, 6, or 6e recommended)	800 meters (voice)
	90 meters (data)
STP Category 3 or higher (Category 5, 5e, 6, or 6e recommended)	800 meters (voice)
	90 meters (data)
Multimode or 62.5/125 fiber-optic cable	2000 meters
Single-mode fiber-optic cable	3000 meters

Figure 19-14.
List of approved cable and distances for backbones.

meters. When UTP and STP are used for networks (data), the backbone is limited to 90 meters.

The most widely accepted material used for network backbones is fiber-optic cable. UTP can be used for small networks, but fiber-optic cable is the preferred media if it can be used within budget restraints. Coaxial cable is not recommended for new installations as either backbone or horizontal wiring. While coaxial cable has not been prohibited, it is not recommended for new installations.

patch panel
a rack-mounted device that has RJ-45 jacks on the front and a matching series of connections on the back.

punch down tool
a tool used for pushing individual twisted pair wires into an insulation-displacement connector (IDC) and automatically trimming conductor excess.

Patch Panel

A typical ***patch panel*** is a rack-mounted wiring device for network systems. The device has RJ-45 jacks on the front and a matching series of connections on the back, **Figure 19-15.** Patch panel cables are used for making connections between the front of the patch panel and equipment. The back of the panel is where the horizontal run cable is terminated.

The individual wires of each cable are pushed into the connections on the back of the patch panel using a punch down tool. A ***punch down tool*** is specifically made for this type of cable wiring termination, **Figure 19-16.** It is used to push

A

B

Figure 19-15.
A patch panel serves as a connection point between cable runs and network equipment. A—Front view. B—Back view.

Figure 19-16.
A punch down tool is used to connect twisted pair wire to the connections on the back of patch panels, RJ-45 outlets, and punch down blocks.

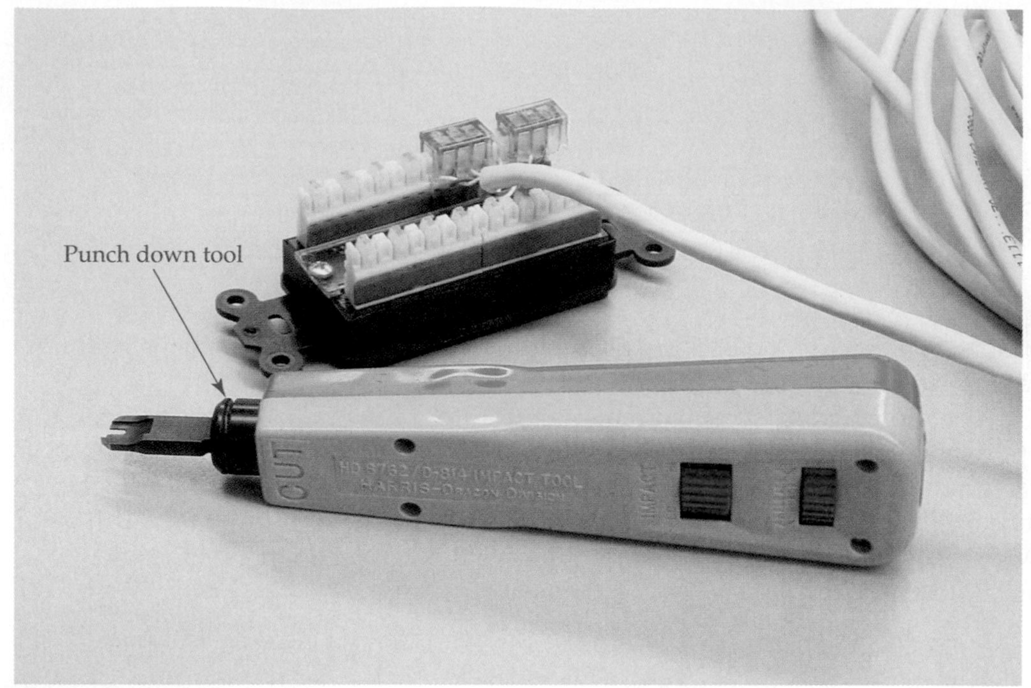

individual twisted pair wires into the connection and automatically trim conductor excess. The connections found on the back of patch panels are also found in outlets and punch down blocks. Punch down blocks are covered in the following section.

Patch panels are a convenient way to make connections and provide a means for easily modifying the cable connection system. The punch down tool uses a blade that corresponds to the termination style. For example, a 110 blade is used for a 110 block, and a 66 blade is used for a 66 block.

Punch Down Block

punch down block
a block of connections designed for terminating solid copper wire and typically consisting of a series of insulation-displacement connectors (IDCs).

insulation-displacement connector (IDC)
a type of network and telecommunications cable termination connector designed to remove the insulation of individual conductors while being inserted with a punch down tool.

A ***punch down block*** is a network system wiring device used to terminate communications cable for telephone systems. It is also used as an intermediate cable connection point for joining two cables. Punch down blocks are not normal network wiring devices; however, you may encounter them used to terminate DSL and Cable modems.

There are two main types of punch down blocks: 66 and 110. The 66 block is older than the 110 block. See **Figure 19-17.** The 110 block was designed to support higher cable frequencies and is less prone to crosstalk. It is the preferred style for network cable such as Cat 5, Cat 5e, and Cat 6. The 66 block was originally designed for telephone communications and is limited to Cat 3 or earlier types of twisted pair cable. It does not support high frequencies.

The cable termination for a 66 or 100 block is referred to as ***insulation-displacement connector (IDC).*** During the installation process, the outer cable sheath is removed, and the insulation (plastic cover) is left on the individual conductors for the installation process. A punch down tool is used to push the conductor into the IDC. There is no need to remove the insulation from the conductor because the IDC pierces the insulation. The punch down tool not only pushes the conductor into place, it also cuts off excess conductor. See **Figure 19-18.**

The number of punch down block terminals corresponds to the standard telecommunications cable design and is designated as pairs. For example, standard

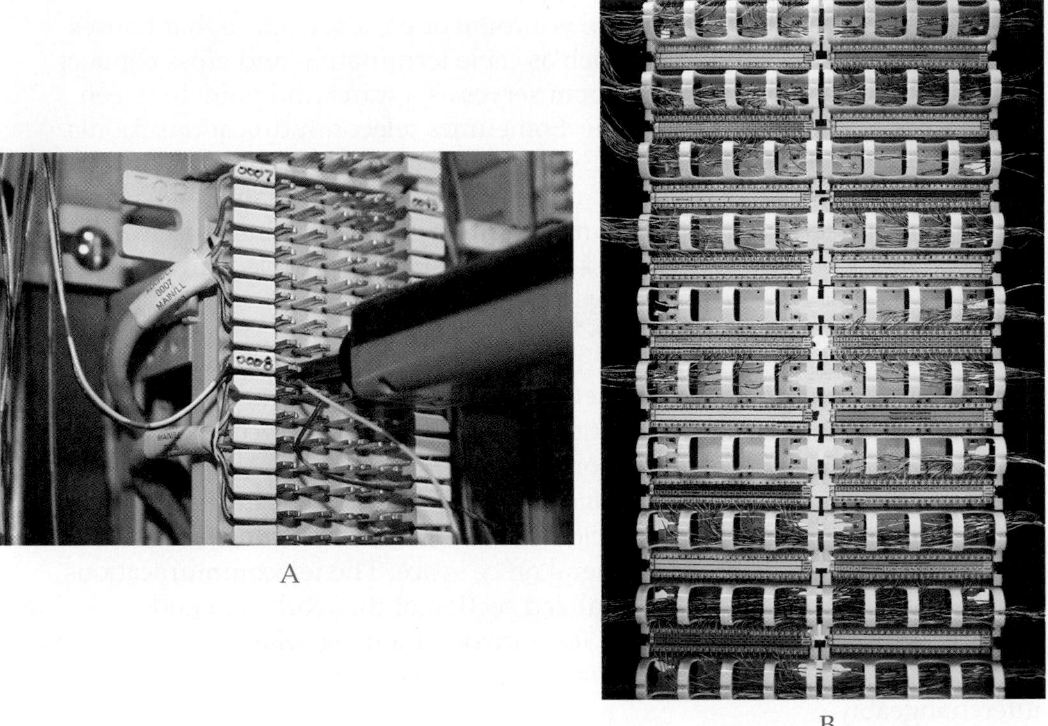

Figure 19-17. Punch down blocks. A—66 block. B—110 block.

telecommunications cable designs are 25, 50, 100, and 300 pair. Note that the cables are designated as "pairs," which means the conductor count is by pair. Thus, a 25-pair cable has 50 conductors.

When two cables are terminated to a punch down block, the individual cable conductors can be connected by individual jumpers or by a bridge clip. A bridge clip is the preferred method of joining conductors at a punch down block location.

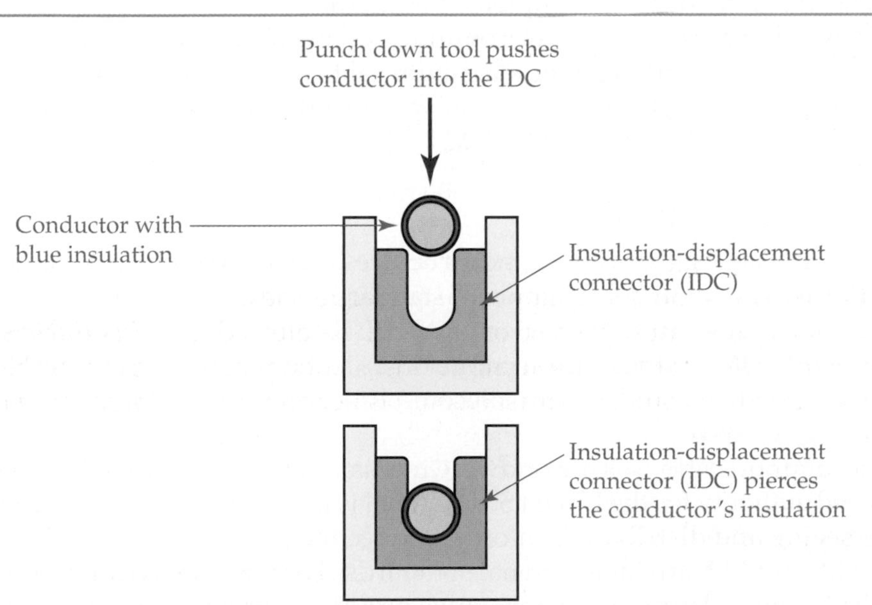

Figure 19-18. When the punch down tool pushes the conductor into the IDC, the IDC pierces the conductor's insulation and the punch down tool cuts off the excess conductor. The punch down tool blade must match the type of punch down block being used.

Telecommunications Room

telecommunications room a room or enclosed space that houses telecommunications equipment, such as cable termination and cross connect wiring. It serves as a transition point between the backbone and horizontal wiring.

The ***telecommunications room*** is a room or enclosed space that houses telecommunications equipment, such as cable termination and cross connect wiring. The telecommunications room serves as a transition point between the backbone and horizontal wiring. Sometimes telecommunications rooms are referred to as *equipment rooms*. Exact terminology depends on the source of the technology reference. For example, a network technician may use the term *equipment room* while a telecommunications technician may use the term *telecommunications room*. There must be a minimum of one telecommunications room per floor of a multistory building.

Telecommunications Closet

telecommunications closet an enclosed space used to house telecommunications cable termination equipment. It is the recognized transition point between the backbone and horizontal wiring.

The ***telecommunications closet*** is an enclosed space used to house telecommunications cable termination equipment. It is the recognized transition point between the backbone and horizontal wiring. The telecommunications closet is also referred to as *telecommunications room*. The closet can be a small room about the size of a standard clothes closet, or it can be an enclosed cabinet that is placed securely inside a general office space. The telecommunications closet is typically placed in a centralized section of the work area and is used to house the horizontal cross connect for horizontal wiring. Many companies and organizations use the terms *telecommunication room* and *telecommunication closet* interchangeably.

Standards Organizations

There are many organizations that write standards for communications and network systems. The standards of these organizations are often incorporated into the contract specifications for the new network. Many of the standards appear redundant. However, you must remember that the standards are not just for networks. Many of the standards are written for communications systems such as the telephone system. These communications systems overlap with network communications.

Many manufacturers publish their own set of standards, often exceeding the standards from the American National Standards Institute (ANSI), Electronic Industries Alliance (EIA), and Telecommunications Industry Association (TIA). This causes a lot of confusion for maximum cable ratings. For example, different manufacturers advertised Category 6 at various rates before it was ever a formal standard published by ANSI/TIA/EIA.

ANSI/TIA/EIA Standards

Network cabling, hardware, and structures are specified by a combination of standards. The set or combination of standards and recommendations used in the United States is a combination of ANSI, TIA, and EIA and is referred to as *ANSI/TIA/EIA*. While these are separate organizations, they come together for generally agreed on standards for telecommunications and networking, such as those in **Figure 19-19.**

Telecommunications is a worldwide media. The ANSI/TIA/EIA is the recognized authority for the United States. ANSI is the main organization responsible for overseeing and distributing information technology standards in the United States. TIA and EIA are international standards. To eliminate redundancy, the ANSI, TIA, and EIA formed a cooperative group to combine standards that cover

Standard	Description
TIA/EIA 569-A	Commercial Building Standard for Telecommunications Pathways and Spaces
TIA/EIA 568-B.1-2000	Commercial Building Telecommunications Cabling Standard
TIA/EIA 606-A	Administration Standard for Commercial Telecommunications Infrastructure
TIA/EIA 607-A	Commercial Building Grounding and Bonding Requirements for Telecommunications
TSB-75	Additional Horizontal Cabling Practices for Open Offices

Figure 19-19. ANSI/TIA/EIA standards for telecommunications and networking.

common areas. The International Standards Organization (ISO) is the European standards organization with similar responsibilities to the ANSI/TIA/EIA. The OSI model was developed by the ISO. The Canadian Standards Association (CSA) is a Canadian standards organization. As you can see, standards may change from country to country. Also, these are minimum standards. They may be superseded by higher standards written by individual organizations such as bodies of government, the airline industry, and universities.

TIA/EIA 569-A

The 569-A Standard for Telecommunications Pathways and Spaces recommends how communication cables are to be installed. The term *telecommunications* is not limited to data networks, but rather to the broad range of communications, such as telephone and video. It is important to remember when reading standards that many pertain to communications systems and may not meet the requirements of a network standard such as 100BaseT or higher. Keep this in mind when references are made to Category 3 cable systems.

TIA/EIA 568-B

The 568-B standards describe the wiring standards for commercial buildings. They generally define the construction practices and design for the media, connection points, termination, and topology. Note that standards are not solely concerned with network systems, but rather with all types of general telecommunications systems like telephone wiring. You must be careful when reading recommendations because Category 3 is still a recognized UTP for telephone wiring. An example of a 568-B standard is 568-B.1-2000 (Commercial Building Telecommunications Cabling Standard), which was introduced in 2000 when the use of Category 5e cable for network use was approved.

TIA/EIA 606-A

The 606-A Administration Standard for Commercial Telecommunications Infrastructure standard describes the telecommunications infrastructure design guidelines. This includes blueprint drawings, PBX records, equipment inventories, identification formats, color coding, and labeling.

TIA/EIA 607-A

The 607-A standard describes the grounding and bonding requirements for telecommunications in commercial buildings. To better understand the concepts relating to grounding and bonding, you must first understand some basic electrical concepts as they relate to personnel safety. Electrical systems carry electrical energy, which can be hazardous to personnel. When electrical equipment fails, electrical current attempts to find the best electrical path to the earth. The path can be provided intentionally for safety reasons or unintentionally, such as through people coming in contact with the equipment. When people provide the path to earth, they can be severely shocked—sometimes fatally.

Electrical cables are insulated to prevent electrical energy from energizing the boxes, conduits, and devices that contain electrical wiring and equipment. To prevent electrical shock, the metal parts of the equipment are grounded and bonded. When equipment is grounded, a better path to earth can be made than through people coming in contact with the equipment.

The term *ground* or *grounding* means the intentional or accidental electrical path between an electronic device and the earth. The TIA/EIA 607-A standard specifies that equipment, such as boxes, conduits, and other metal devices associated with electrical and telecommunications equipment provide protection from electrical shock by grounding. When parts of the system are connected to the grounding system, they are described as bonded. *Bonding* is a term, which means that a short copper jumper joins a noncurrent carrying device to the electrical system ground. Proper grounding and bonding is a standard safety practice and a requirement by the NEC and the ANSI/TIA/EIA organizations.

The National Electrical Code (NEC) states that there can only be one main system ground for a facility. The main system ground serves as the main ground for all electrical-related equipment, such as the electrical system, telecommunications equipment, and network equipment. A grounding electrode rod is driven into the earth at the main electrical entrance of the building, **Figure 19-20.** A typical

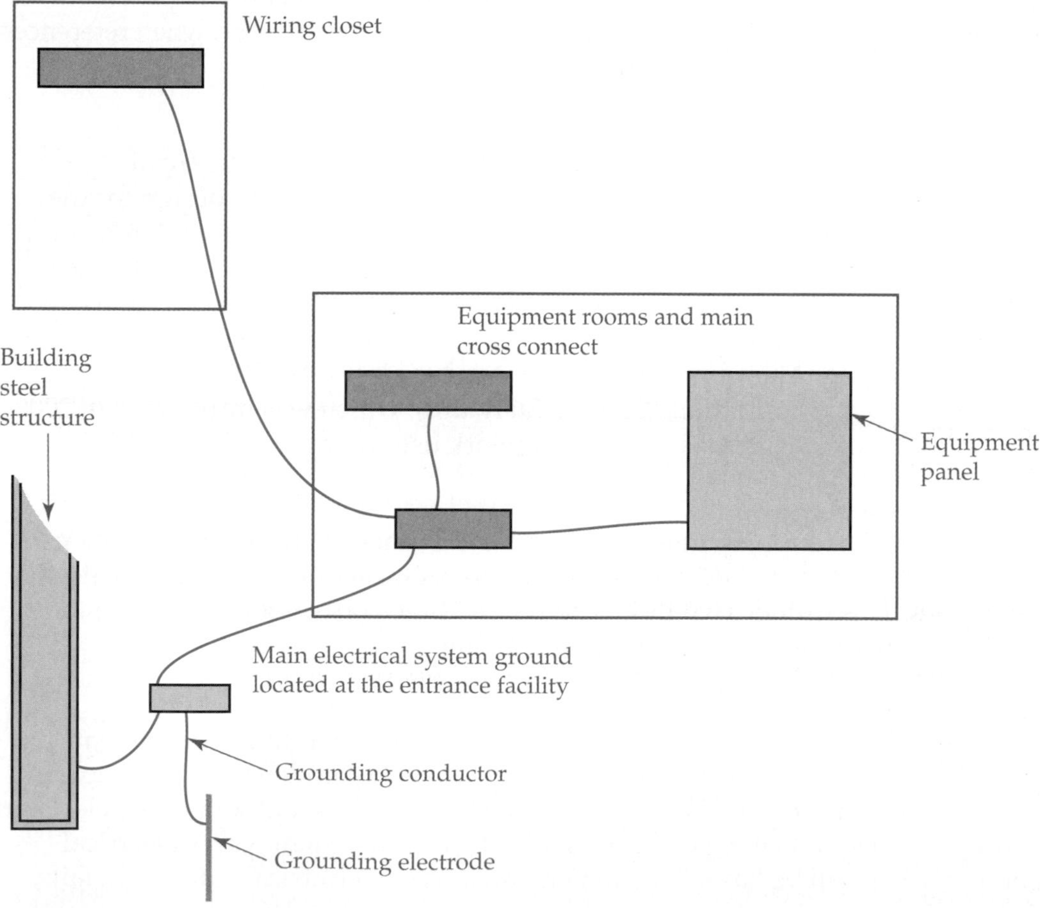

Figure 19-20.
A ground conductor is run throughout the entire facility, connecting all metal equipment and devices to the main electrical system ground located at the entrance facility.

grounding electrode is made of copper or copper-clad steel approximately 1/2″ in diameter and at least 8′ long. A grounding conductor made of either bare copper wire or green insulated wire is used to connect all required metallic devices in the system together. The building's steel structural support is also tied to the grounding system. The grounding conductor runs through each section of the facility, including the wiring closets.

TSB-75

The ANSI/TIA/EIA organization released TSB-75 to support the open office space design. TSB-75 is a supplement to the 568-A standard. ANSI/TIA/EIA often releases updated bulletins to support changes and exceptions to its standards rather than release an entirely new standard.

An open office space design requires a flexible wiring method that can easily support rewiring. Open office areas do not have permanent walls and typically consist of many office cubicles. The cubicle design is easily changed and rearranged. Many building owners who lease space to businesses prefer this style of construction. By using the open office design, the office area can be easily and quickly reorganized for many different types of businesses that require unique office floor arrangements. This type of design can also be used for convention centers and large assembly rooms, which often require the quick rearrangement of the floor plan.

TSB-75 states that a Consolidation Point (CP) and a Multi-User Telecommunications Outlet Assembly (MUTOA) can be used in open office spaces. See **Figure 19-21.** A ***Multi-User Telecommunication Outlet Assembly (MUTOA)*** is a grouping of outlets that serves up to 12 work areas. This is not a cross connect, but rather a prefabricated set of connection points. The MUTOA is mounted on the permanent building structure or on furniture that is permanently secured to the floor. Patch cables run from the MUTOA to the equipment in the work area.

The ***Consolidation Point (CP)*** is a connection to the horizontal wiring system, which in turn feeds to a wall outlet or an MUTOA. A patch cable can be plugged into the MUTOA and run directly to the equipment in the work area. Often the patch cable is run through channels in the furniture to conceal the presence of the cabling and ensure office safety. A Consolidation Point uses twisted pair cable with solid wire rather than stranded wire to connect to the outlets in the work area. See **Figure 19-22** for Consolidation Point and MUTOA systems.

Multi-User Telecommunication Outlet Assembly (MUTOA) a grouping of outlets that serves up to 12 work areas.

Consolidation Point (CP) a connection to the horizontal wiring system, which in turn feeds to a wall outlet or an MUTOA.

Figure 19-23 lists the maximum recommended distances of cable lengths for horizontal wiring and patch cables. It is important to note that the overall length of the horizontal wiring is limited to 100 meters. The same distances are used for Consolidation Points. Certain equipment manufacturers provide their own distance charts that include modified distances based on conductor characteristics such as diameter. Also note that the maximum length of a patch panel cable that can be used in a telecommunications room is 7 meters.

Network and Computer Electrical Requirements

The National Electrical Code (NEC) defines the electrical requirements and standards for networks. NEC specifies standards that ensure safety of personnel and serve as a guide to minimal equipment requirements. The NEC is used as a guide for electricians rather than for a certified network cable installer. Network system construction often requires the expertise of individuals from various backgrounds. All electrical work requires a licensed journeyman electrician

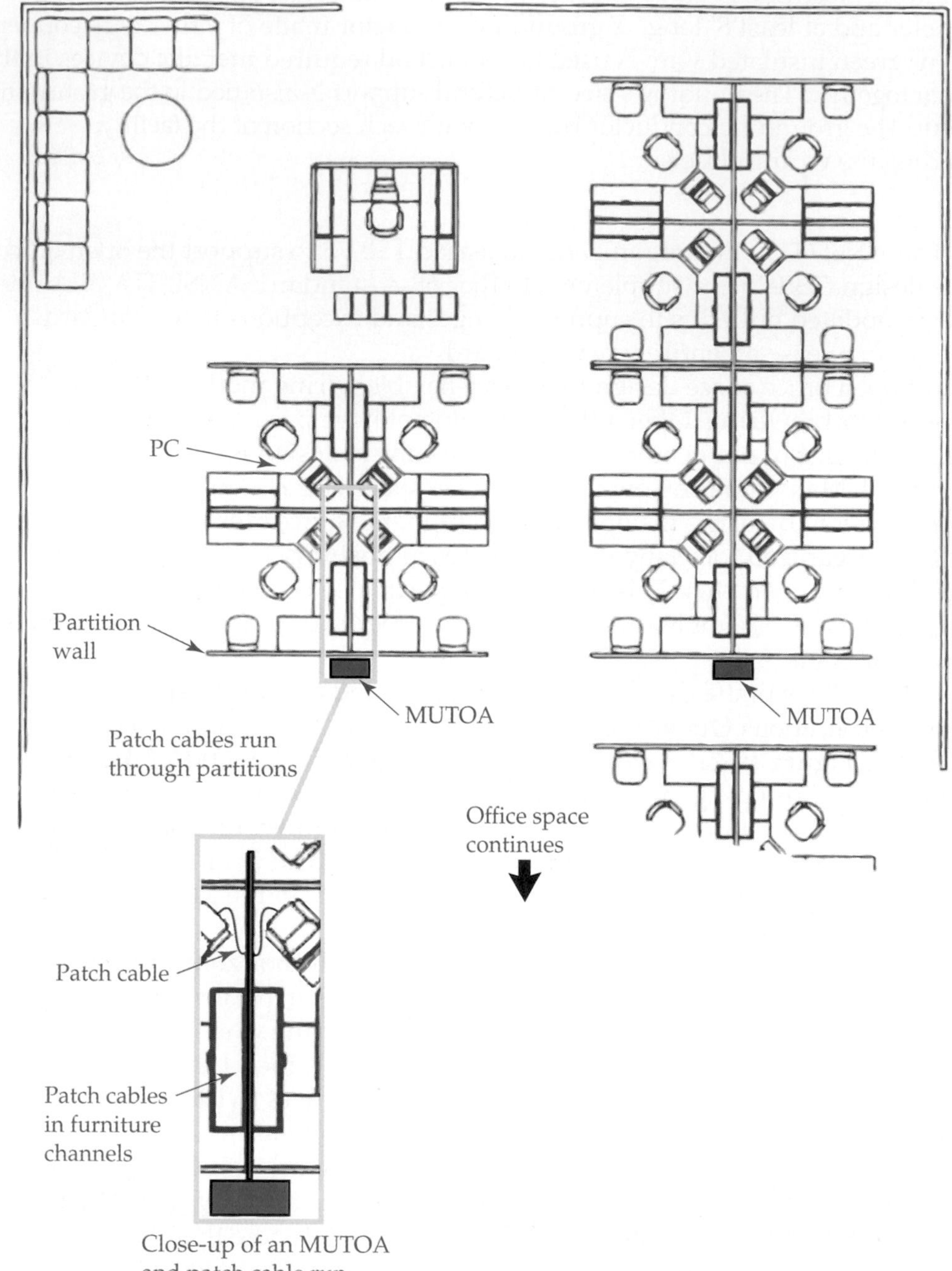

Figure 19-21. An open office area has no permanent wall structures. It is designed to be a flexible office area. Several MUTOAs can be placed in the open office area to serve work areas. If the design changes, the MUTOA can be easily rearranged to accommodate the new office layout.

and an electrical contractor. Network technicians should never engage in the installation or modifications of electrical systems. Electrical systems are classified in three general groups according to the voltage levels encountered in the system. See **Figure 19-24.**

Telecommunications, video, and signaling systems fall into the less than 50-volt category. Telecommunications wiring must never be in the same conduit or box as any system wiring of a higher voltage rating. The telecommunications must be isolated from the higher voltage systems not only to prevent data corruption and interference, but also to ensure the safety of personnel using network equipment.

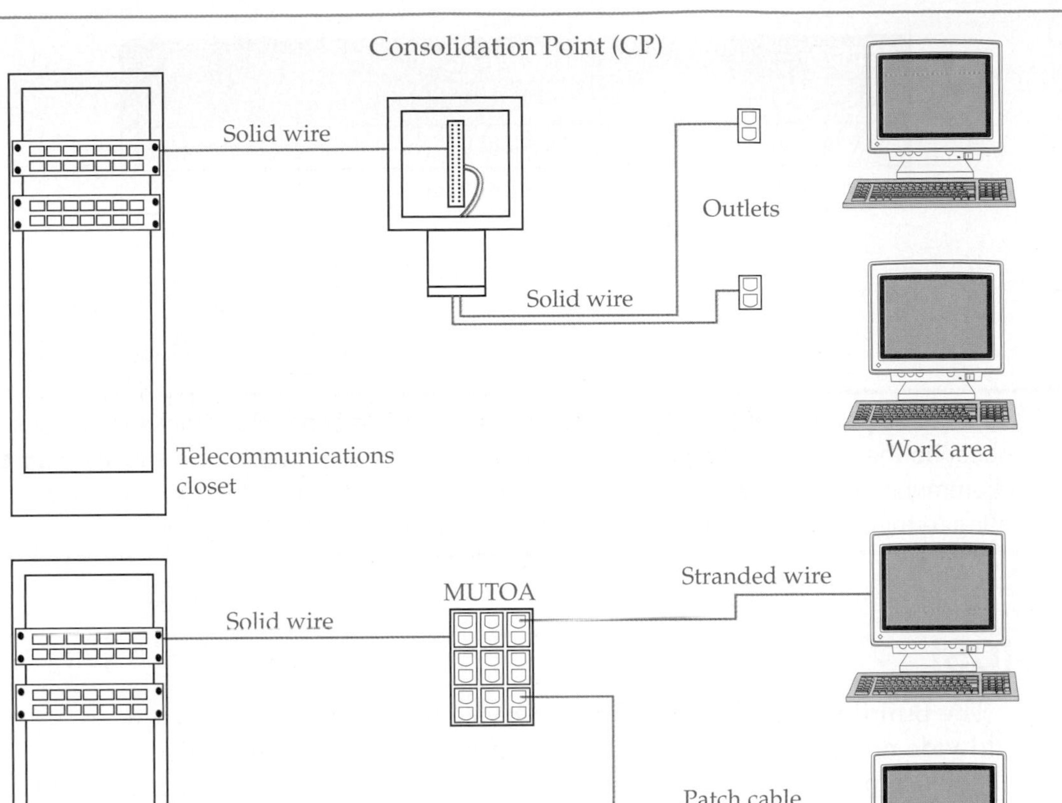

Figure 19-22. A Consolidation Point (CP) is a central point that provides connections for outlets in the work areas. An MUTOA is an assembly of outlets in a work area that equipment attaches to using patch cables.

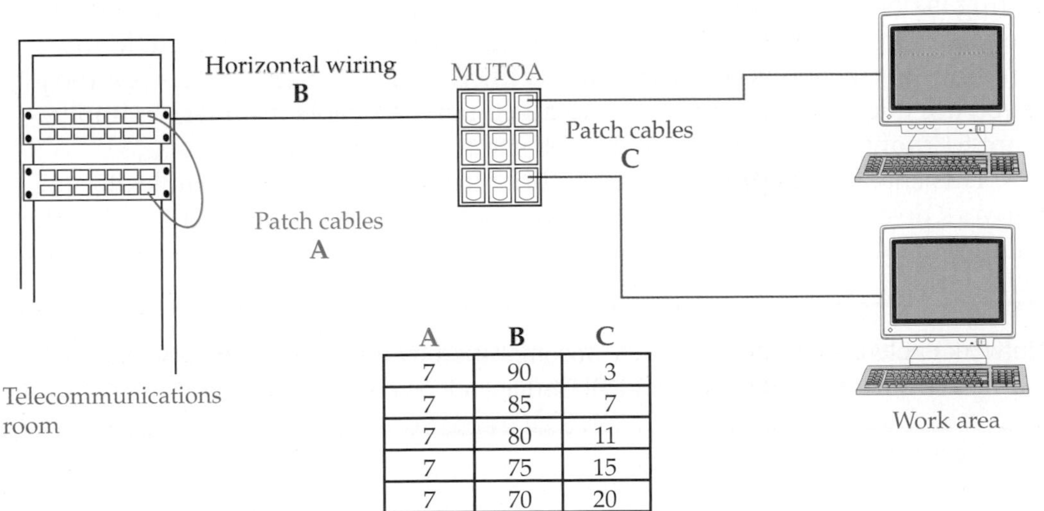

A	B	C
7	90	3
7	85	7
7	80	11
7	75	15
7	70	20

All distances are in meters

Figure 19-23. Maximum recommended distances of cable lengths for horizontal wiring and patch cables. Note that the total distance will never exceed 100 meters for the horizontal wiring length. Also note that the longest patch cable on the patch panel is 7 meters.

Voltage	Application
< 50 volts	Signaling and communications
50 volts–600 volts	Residential and commercial wiring
> 600 volts	High-voltage wiring

Figure 19-24. The three general groups in which electrical systems are classified. Note that they are classified according to the voltage levels encountered in the system.

Tech Tip

The main components of the network wiring system use telecommunications terminology to describe the various sections of the network. Network standards are a subcategory of telecommunications that existed long before networking systems. It is only natural that the existing terminology be used when describing the newer network wiring system.

BICSI

The Building Industry Consulting Service International (BICSI) is a worldwide non-profit association dedicated to the education of skilled workers in the telecommunications infrastructure and related fields. The organization is referred to by its acronym, which rhymes with *Dixie*. In recent years, BICSI has expanded its educational offerings in network cabling, and it is a recognized network cable infrastructure installation authority. The organization offers training programs, publications, and testing for certification.

One such certification is in network cabling, which consists of a written examination and a performance examination. In the performance examination, candidates are required to make connections or splices using several different media, such as Category 5e, fiber-optic cable, and coaxial cable. The performance testing is performed under the direction of a BICSI certified examiner, and the cables are sent to the BICSI organization where they are evaluated. Many building specifications state that only certified cable installers be used on the job. If you are interested in becoming a certified network cable installer or simply want to know more, visit the BICSI Web site at www.bicsi.org.

This chapter has presented only a brief introduction to the complexities of network design. Please visit the many recommended Web sites at the end of the chapter to find out more about this interesting aspect of networking technology.

Tech Tip

Network cable installation is typically accomplished by BICSI certified individuals. These individuals have passed the rigid BICSI Certification exam.

Summary

- The first part of the design process is to conduct a needs assessment.
- A timeline is a chronological listing of the expected sequence of work from the beginning of the project until the end.
- LDAP is the de facto directory standard used by network operating systems.
- A naming convention must be developed for all objects in the network environment to provide for easy identification.
- An isolated electrical system should always be used for network equipment.
- The demarc or demarcation identifies the point where the public/private telecommunications company cable terminates and the customer cabling begins.
- Smart jacks and Optical Network Terminals (ONTs) are common demarc locations.
- The Main Distribution Frame (MDF) is the cable connection point where the private telecommunication cables come into a building and then connect or distribute to other areas inside the building.
- Main Distribution Frame (MDF) and Intermediate Distribution Frame (IDF) are relative locations as related to the distribution of telecommunications cables.
- Horizontal cable distance is limited to 90 meters for the horizontal run from the telecommunications outlet to the telecommunications room.
- The maximum distance for backbone wiring using UTP as a network medium is 90 meters.
- The maximum distance for a multimode fiber-optic cable backbone is 2000 meters.
- The maximum distance for a single-mode fiber-optic cable backbone is 3000 meters.
- Punch down blocks are used to distribute, terminate, and connect telecommunications cables.
- Specifications are a set of guidelines that explicitly describe the workmanship and materials that will be used in the project.
- The main standard used for network design in the U.S. was developed jointly by several organizations and is referred to as ANSI/TIA/EIA.
- International Standards Organization (ISO) is the European standards organization similar to the ANSI/TIA/EIA.
- The Canadian Standards Association (CSA) is similar to ANSI/TIA/EIA.
- A Consolidation Point (CP) is a location in the horizontal wiring that provides an interconnection, which extends into the work areas.
- A Multi-User Telecommunication Outlet Assembly (MUTOA) is a grouping of outlets that serves up to 12 work areas.
- The maximum length of a patch panel cable that can be used in a telecommunications room is 7 meters.
- All electrical work for a networking system must follow the recommendations of the National Electrical Code (NEC) standards.
- Network technicians should not engage in the installation of electrical devices.
- BICSI is a nonprofit organization dedicated to telecommunications installation, training, and education.

Review Questions

Answer the following questions on a separate sheet of paper. Please do not write in this book.

1. What is the first step in the network design process?
2. What are some of the roles and services provided by a network server? (Name at least 10.)
3. On what protocol standard are all major directory structures based?
4. Why is a naming convention important?
5. List 10 keyboard symbols that should *not* be used in LDAP computer or other object names.
6. What is the purpose of specifications?
7. Name two Network Interface Devices.
8. What is a smart jack?
9. What name is used to represent a fiber-optic building termination point located at the demarc?
10. How many individual conductors are in a 50-pair cable?
11. Name three services that are typically provided by an ONT device?
12. What is the name of the room where the telephone system enters the building?
13. Name two other uses or room designations that an equipment room may serve.
14. What do the acronyms MDF and IDF represent?
15. What is the purpose of the MDF?
16. Where is backbone cable located in a building?
17. What is a work area?
18. Describe a patch panel.
19. What tool is used to connect cable to the back of a patch panel?
20. How many telecommunications rooms must there be in a building?
21. What do the three acronyms ANSI, TIA, EIA represent?
22. What is the difference between a Consolidation Point (CP) and a Multi-User Telecommunication Outlet Assembly (MUTOA)?
23. What is the maximum number of work areas a single MUTAO or Consolidation Point (CP) can serve?
24. Can an MUTOA be mounted behind a drop ceiling?
25. What characteristic does furniture need to allow a MUTOA or Consolidation Point (CP) to be attached to it?

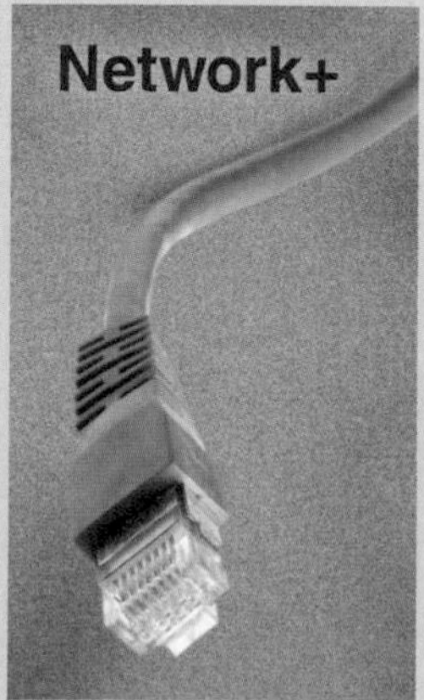

Sample Network+ Exam Questions

Answer the following questions on a separate sheet of paper. Please do not write in this book.

1. A metal fabrication manufacturer is setting up a production plant that will incorporate network computer-controlled machinery. Welding is commonly used in the metal fabrication process and is automated. Which type of network cable would you recommend be used to counter the effects of EMI generated by the welding equipment on the plant floor.
   A. 24 AWG UTP
   B. 22 AWG UTP
   C. Multimode fiber-optic
   D. 1000BaseT

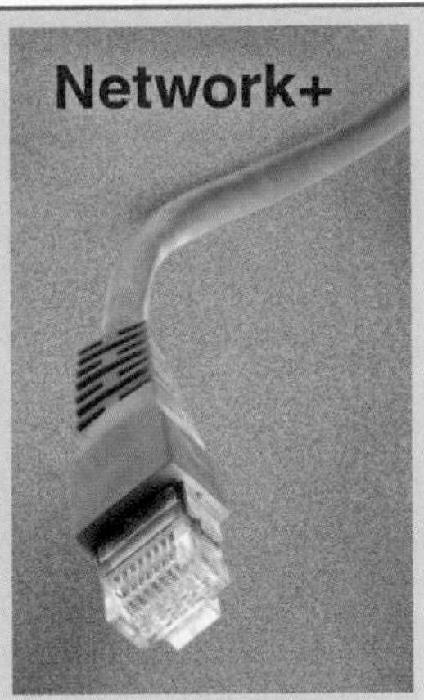

2. What type of tool is used to make 100BaseT connections at telecommunications outlets in a work area?
   A. RG-58 crimper
   B. Punch down tool
   C. Electric soldering iron
   D. 24 AWG cable stripper
3. What is the maximum length for a horizontal run of UTP cable from a telecommunications closet to the work area outlet?
   A. 800 meters
   B. 200 meters
   C. 100 meters
   D. 90 meters
4. What is the maximum length of a patch panel cable that can be used in a telecommunications room?
   A. 3 meters
   B. 5 meters
   C. 7 meters
   D. 9 meters
5. What is the maximum distance of a single-mode, fiber-optic backbone?
   A. 100 meters
   B. 800 meters
   C. 2000 meters
   D. 3000 meters
6. Which standard describes how to install communications cables in telecommunication pathways and spaces?
   A. NEC
   B. TIA/EIA 569-A
   C. TIA/EIA 606-A
   D. TIA/EIA 607-A
7. What is the name of the Ethernet network passive device that is used in an equipment room to serve as a connection between horizontal cable runs and the equipment in the server room?
   A. Gateway
   B. Router
   C. Patch panel
   D. MUTOA
8. Which type of cable would *most likely* be used to provide connections between the workstation and the RJ-45 wall jack?
   A. Stranded core coaxial cable with a copper shield
   B. UTP with stranded copper wires
   C. STP with solid copper wires
   D. UTP with solid copper wires
9. Which method provides the best protection from office equipment interference?
   A. Double insulate all electrical cables.
   B. Use only 120-VAC equipment in the office area.
   C. Use insulated RJ-45 connectors on all cable assemblies.
   D. Use isolated dedicated electrical circuits for all network equipment.

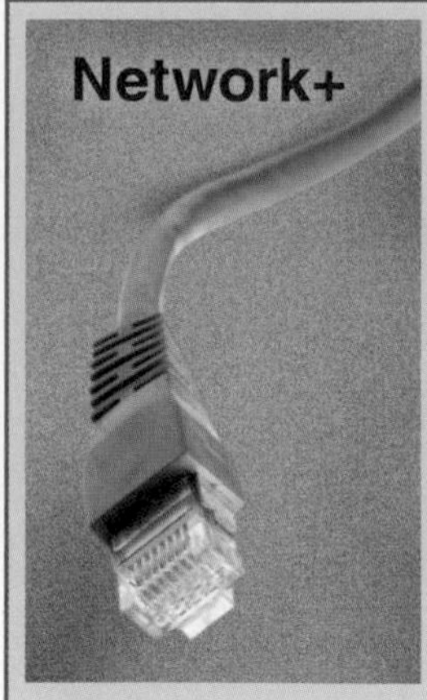

10. Which network device typically serves as the network system demarc?
    A. Router
    B. Gateway
    C. Smart jack
    D. Punch down block

Suggested Laboratory Activities

1. Download a free trial version of a network drawing tool such as Microsoft Visio. Use the tool to diagram a peer-to-peer network and a client/server network.
2. Design a complete system for your school. The system will include servers, backbones, workstations, and a directory structure.
3. Design a system for an insurance office with five, full-time agents, three secretaries, and one receptionist. The office requires a connection to the corporate headquarters in a neighboring state. Approximately 18 MB of data must be exchanged with the corporate office each 8-hour day. Make a materials list and a bid price for the entire project. You must decide on your own to install a client/server or peer-to-peer network. You will also decide on the software packages to include in the system. Come up with a written proposal and present it to the class.
4. Write an acceptable use policy for the proposed office in activity 3.
5. Write a comparison of features and pricing for three different network operating systems.
6. Visit several Web sites to obtain the latest network installation standards available.
7. Download the latest server and networking design guides from the Microsoft Web site.

Interesting Web Sites for More Information

http://technet.microsoft.com/en-us/default.aspx
www.bicsi.org
www.blackbox.com
www.cisco.com
www.hp.com
www.kroneamericas.com
www.siemon.com/us
www22.verizon.com/wholesale/solutionsbridge/solutionsbridge.html

Chapter 19
Laboratory Activity

Designing a Small Network

After completing this laboratory activity, you will be able to:
- Construct a simple materials list.
- Design a simple project timeline.
- Produce a price bid for the installation of a small office network.

Introduction

In this laboratory activity, you will design a small network system for a business office. You will decide on the workstations, network equipment, network media, and software. Your assignment is to carefully review the requirements as specified in the scenario and then construct a materials list, which includes prices for materials and labor. You will also calculate a profit figure. You will use the Internet for locating project items and obtaining prices.

Equipment and Materials

- Workstation and printer. (The workstation must have Internet access to conduct the research for the project. The printer is necessary to provide equipment specifications and pricing.)

Scenario

RMRoberts Inc. is setting up a brand new office for its Web design business. The office will consist of 16 workstations with the capability of supporting Web design functions. The office will require high-speed Internet access. Each person in the office will require a laser black and white printer. One full-color printer, centrally located, will be shared by all workstations. Each workstation must have installed a Microsoft operating system, Microsoft Office Professional software, and Adobe Studio Professional software. Also needed are office cubical dividers that will accommodate network and electrical wiring. The following figure illustrates what the final office design should look like as well as the office dimensions. Notice that the office has a drop ceiling.

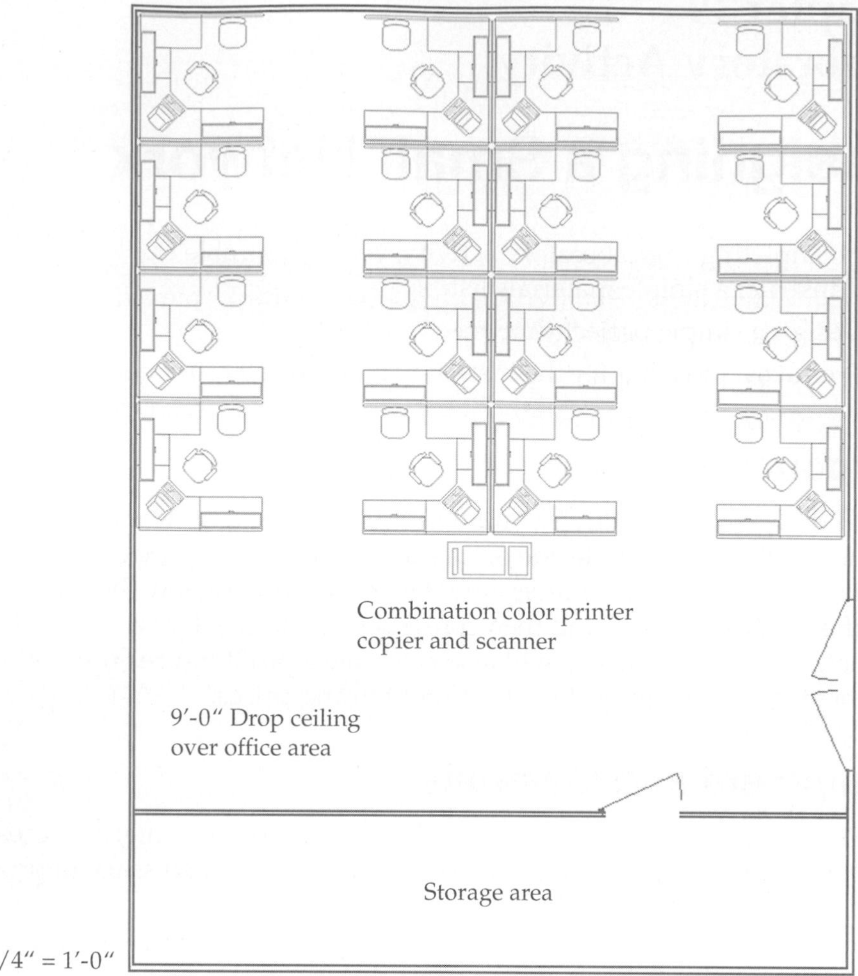

In summary, the materials should include the following:

- 16 workstations with a Microsoft operating system and Microsoft Office Professional.
- Microsoft Expression Web Suite for 16 workstations.
- Server(s).
- Network devices, such as hubs, switches, or routers.
- Network media.
- 16 laser black and white printers.
- 1 full-color printer.
- Office cubicle dividers.

Procedure

1. ______ Select appropriate computer workstations; any needed servers, hubs, switches, or routers; and network medium, such as copper wire, wireless, or fiber-optic for the network system. Be prepared to defend your selection of materials.
2. ______ Configure a detailed list of materials, material costs, a timeline for installing all hardware and software and providing at least one day of training for all office personnel on the system. A materials list must provide the following items:
   - Item name.
   - Manufacturer.
   - Part number.
   - Individual price.
   - Total cost.
   - Shipping cost.
   - Approximate delivery time.
3. ______ Submit the following items to your instructor:
   - Materials list.
   - Materials costs.
   - Labor cost.
   - Profit.
   - Timeline.
   - Hard copy of all prices and equipment specifications found in your Internet search.
4. ______ For extra credit, download a free demo version of Microsoft Visio or an equal drawing software program and make a drawing of the network system matching the proposal.

Project Tips

- Keep the system simple. Do *not* try to create an elaborate system.
- Sketch the network system before attempting to start a materials list.
- Less expensive materials may not necessarily be the best way to go.
- Feel free to be creative.

The BICSI organization (www.bicsi.org) provides resources, training, and certification for those in the telecommunications industry.

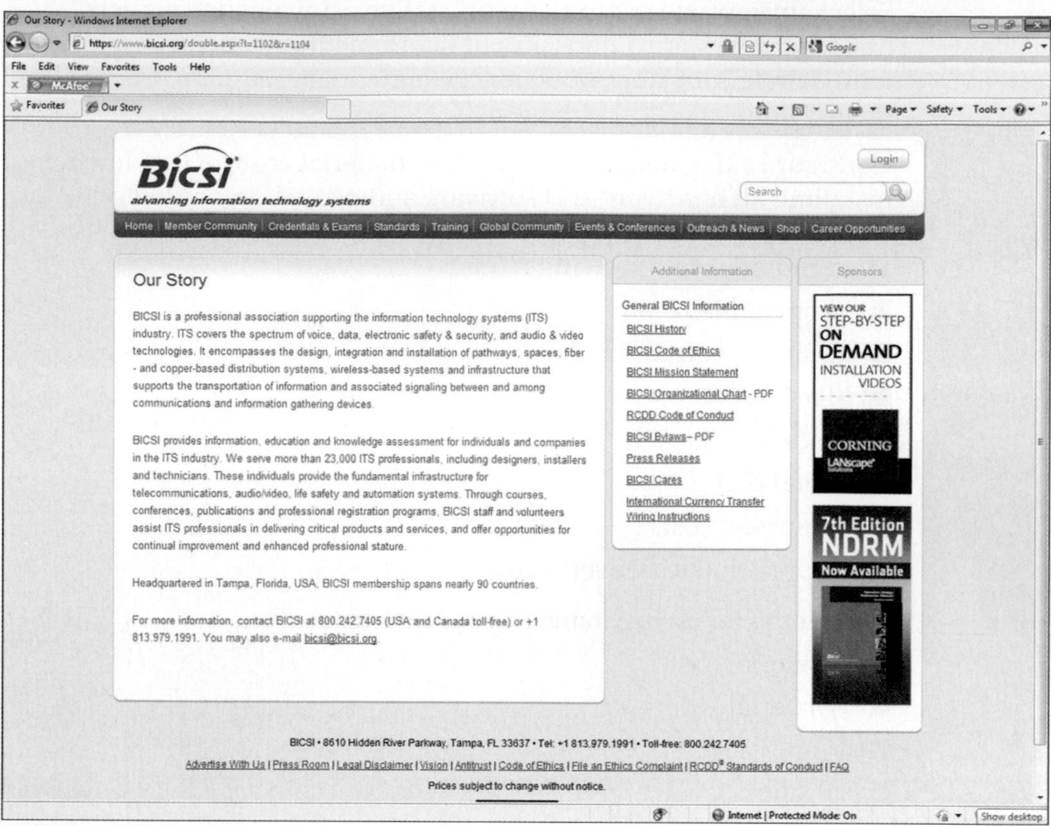

Network+ Certification Exam Preparation

After studying this chapter, you will be able to:

- ❑ Evaluate your level of preparedness for the Network+ Certification exam.
- ❑ Detect areas that require additional study.
- ❑ Plan a strategy for additional study in areas that show a need for improvement.

Network+ Exam—Key Points

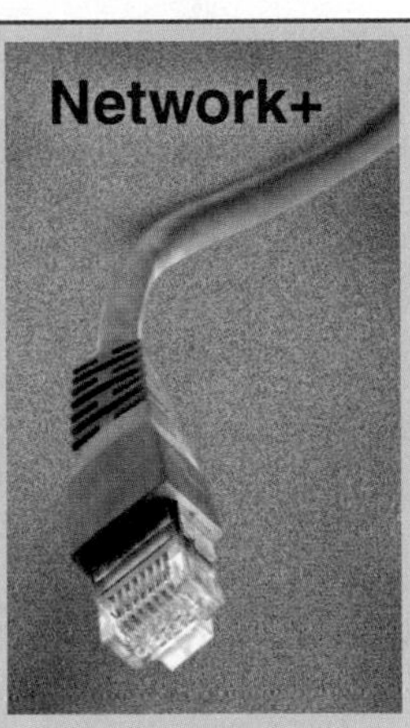

You should be able to install, configure, and troubleshoot basic network devices. You should also know the layers of the OSI model and be very familiar with all the common network protocols, especially those associated with the TCP/IP suite.

Be aware that some questions on the Network+ Certification exam will be based on A+ Certification exam knowledge. The CompTIA Web site states that all candidates for the Network+ exam should have the A+ Certification or equivalent knowledge.

Key Words and Terms

The following words and terms will become important pieces of your networking vocabulary. Be sure you can define them.

bridge exam

domain

Network+ Examination Objectives

weight

This chapter is designed to help you prepare for the CompTIA Network+ Certification exam. Test preparation strategies and a practice exam are included in this chapter. The practice exam simulates what you may encounter when taking the Network+ Certification exam. Every attempt has been made to closely simulate the Network+ Certification exam by covering the exact areas to be tested at the approximate knowledge level required. However, there is no guarantee successfully passing the practice exam will ensure your success on the Network+ Certification exam.

Note

At the time of this writing, CompTIA has changed its policy concerning the length of A+, Network+, and Security+ Certification from lifetime to 3 years. This will take effect starting January 1, 2011. Any certification obtained before January 1, 2011 will be good for a lifetime and, thus, will not need to be renewed.

The Network+ Certification Exam

Over 2500 industry representatives were surveyed to determine the critical job areas that would be tested by the Network+ Certification exam. The most common jobs performed by technicians form the basis of the exam. The exact areas to be tested are listed in the ***Network+ Certification Examination Objectives*** located on CompTIA's Web site. The Network+ Certification Examination Objectives are organized according to domains. A ***domain*** in relation to CompTIA objectives is an area of knowledge. The Network+ (2009 Edition) Certification exam covers six domains. Look at **Figure 20-1.** Notice that a certain percentage of exam questions are covered for each domain.

Network+ Certification Examination Objectives
a document that lists the exact areas tested on the Network+ Certification exam.

Network+ Note

The percentages listed in the Network+ (2009 Edition) Certification Examination Objectives are approximate and are subject to change.

The Network+ (2009 Edition) Certification exam consists of 100 questions to be completed in 90 minutes. The exam is graded on a scale of 100 to 900. The minimum passing score is 720. Test questions are not equally weighted. This means that each question is worth a different amount of points, or ***weight***. This makes it difficult to make a perfect pre-assessment tool, like the practice exam in this chapter. CompTIA keeps the weights of each question private. However, research has shown that there is a strong correlation between traditional test scores based on percentage and weighted question test scores.

domain
an area of knowledge on a CompTIA Certification exam.

weight
the amount of points assigned to a test question.

The Network+ (2009 Edition) Certification Examination Objectives present a disclaimer that is very important to anyone preparing to take the exam. It is a warning that the list is not all inclusive and there can be topics on the exam that are not specifically listed in the objectives. The objectives serves as a general outline of what areas are covered on the exam. The following is the exact wording taken from the CompTIA Network+ (2009 Edition) Certification Examination Objectives that is used as a disclaimer:

> **Note: The bulleted lists below each objective are not exhaustive lists. Even though they are not included in this document, other examples of technologies, processes or tasks pertaining to each objective may also be included on the exam.

In the introduction of the Network+ (2009 Edition) Certification Examination Objectives, CompTIA recommends the candidate have a CompTIA A+ Certification

Domain	Percentage	Approximate Number of Questions
1.0 Network Technologies	20 %	20
2.0 Network Media and Topologies	20 %	20
3.0 Network Devices	17 %	17
4.0 Network Management	20 %	20
5.0 Network Tools	12 %	12
6.0 Network Security	11 %	11
Total	100 %	100

Figure 20-1. Network+ (2009 Edition) domains and the percentage of questions asked in each domain.

before attempting the Network+ exam. The A+ Certification is not required, only recommended. Many of the test items require knowledge that directly correlates to the A+ Certification exam, especially test items relating to troubleshooting and computer hardware. CompTIA assumes that if you are taking the Network+ Certification exam, you have the skills commonly associated with PC support. If you do not have these skills, you will be at a disadvantage when taking the exam.

CompTIA also recommends the candidate have at least nine months work experience in network support or administration before taking the Network+ Certification exam. While there is no substitute for actual job experience, laboratory activities can provide you with much of the same experiences. Be sure to complete all laboratory activities included in this textbook and in the *Networking Fundamentals Laboratory Manual* before attempting the exam. Also, study the questions at the end of the laboratory activities. Many of these questions are designed to help you prepare for the Network+ Certification exam.

Use the *Networking Fundamentals Study Guide* to help reinforce concepts. Many of the concepts presented in the Network+ Certification Examination Objectives you will not have an opportunity to work with in the lab. For example, you may not have an opportunity to design and implement an FDDI or a 10GbaseSR network, yet you will need to know the specifications of these standards, such as the types of cable and connectors used and maximum and minimum cable distances. The *Networking Fundamentals Study Guide* will help you organize this information as well as help you review the material required for the Network+ Certification exam.

When working in the *Fundamentals Study Guide*, feel free to record your own notes and diagrams in the margins or available white space. This will personalize your learning experience. Organizing or presenting the material in your own way will help you gain a better understanding of the material.

Any person obtaining Network+ Certification before January 1, 2011 will be certified for life. However, a person certified after January 1, 2011 will need to renew his or her certification every 3 years by taking a bridge exam. A ***bridge exam*** only covers the newest objectives added since the previous edition of the exam. It consists of 50 questions at the time of this writing.

bridge exam a CompTIA Certification exam that only covers the newest objectives added since the previous edition of the exam.

Preparation Strategy

The secret to passing the Network+ Certification exam is having an organized strategy for preparation. The most common mistake made by students is to simply sit down and study their notes and available materials. A student needs to approach exam preparation in the most effective and objective manner. The following is a list of key steps to exam success:

1. Review and analyze the exam objectives.
2. Match exam objective details to resource materials.
3. Identify and practice laboratory activities that match the exam objectives.
4. Take practice exams.
5. Review problem areas.
6. Retake practice exams.
7. Schedule and take the Network+ Certification exam.

Network+ Note

When preparing for the Network+ Certification exam, be sure to check the CompTIA Web site for the very latest Network+ Certification Examination Objectives. The objectives are constantly revised.

1. Review and Analyze the Exam Objectives

The first step in the exam preparation strategy is to review and analyze the exam objectives outlined by the CompTIA organization. You need to know exactly what areas are required for certification. Networking is an extremely in-depth field that can easily fill volumes of books. The technical vocabulary alone spans over 10,000 words, not including all of the acronyms. Concentrate your studies on what is required for the Network+ Certification exam. For example, if subnet calculations are not required, do not spend hours on this area of networking.

Network+ Note

Subnet calculations are not required for the Network+ Certification exam, but it is required for other certification exams at the time of this writing. Also, note that changes in the exam composition change on a fairly frequent basis. It is always a good idea to check the CompTIA Web site for the latest content changes.

Too many people spend hours of study on areas that are not on the test. To avoid doing this, make an outline of the current exam objectives and fill in related facts for each objective. A sample of such an outline is presented in **Figure 20-2.**

On your outline, write several facts about each item mentioned in the objective. Use several references for each item in addition to the textbook. A variety of reference materials will greatly enhance your understanding of the topics in the outline.

There are many sites that will provide you with a detailed outline for free or for a small charge. While this would be the most convenient way to make a complete exam outline, it is not a sound learning strategy. To better retain the information, you need to construct your own outline and research the facts and details yourself! This method will better prepare you for the exam. Also, there are many ready-made study guides with inaccurate information and information which is outside the scope of the Network+ Certification exam. Also, much of the material is out of date. You will do a better job by constructing your own outline. This will ensure your study material is up-to-date. Also, by using multiple sources for information, you will be able to avoid inaccurate information.

Network+ Note

Since CompTIA recommends a Network+ candidate possess CompTIA A+ equivalent knowledge, you may want to download and review the exam objectives for the A+ Certification exams and use it as an outline for review in addition to the Network+ outline.

2. Match Exam Objective Details to Resource Material

You should gather the content needed to fill in your outline from a variety of reputable sources. Use your textbook, laboratory manual, and the Internet. There are many fine resources available, especially at operating system vendor Web

Figure 20-2.
Sample study guide.

My Study Guide

1.1 Explain the function of common networking protocols.

TCP ____________________

FTP ____________________

UDP ____________________

TCP/IP Suite ____________________

DHCP ____________________

TFTP ____________________

DNS ____________________

HTTP(S) ____________________

ARP ____________________

SIP (VoIP) ____________________

RTP (VoIP) ____________________

sites. For example, Microsoft has a lot of material on WINS because it was vital to its earlier network operating systems.

When looking up facts for network interoperability, do not simply check the Microsoft Web site to see how to set up communications between a Microsoft system and a Novell system. Check the Novell site as well for its recommendations.

Be careful of some sources, such as chat rooms. Chat rooms that discuss particular exams often have a lot of inaccurate information. It is always better to use only reputable and authoritative Web sites.

3. Identify and Practice Laboratory Activities That Match the Exam Objectives

Many of the objectives, especially those relating to troubleshooting, require the student have knowledge acquired through experience. The laboratory activities presented in this textbook and in the *Network Fundamentals Laboratory Manual* are designed to provide you with needed experiences. You may want to review and repeat these laboratory activities. You should be able to perform all past laboratory activities with minimal assistance. Laboratory activity experiences are much easier to remember than textbook materials. For example, setting up a DHCP service and troubleshooting one will give you an in-depth knowledge of the subject. This is better than simply memorizing facts.

Remember, becoming a network professional is not just about passing an exam. You need to know the subject area and be able to perform hands-on activities to obtain and keep a job in the industry. The industry does not pay you to answer questions, but rather to perform duties related to networking.

4. Take Practice Exams

Taking practice exams will help you to identify your areas for needed improvement in both subject matter and test-taking skills. All students have at least one area of weakness that could prevent them from passing the Network+ Certification exam. Take the practice exam included in this chapter and have your instructor score it. After all of the questions are scored, you can do an analysis of what areas you may need more study or laboratory experiences. Be careful of the many online exams offered for free on the Internet. Only use Web sites that your instructor recommends. Many of the Web sites have questions that do not exactly match the test objectives. Also, some of the provided answers are incorrect.

In general, most of the free practice exams are far more difficult than the actual Network+ Certification exam. Many of the free Internet exam sites are marketing tools to sell you other exams from their Web site. The sample exams may actually be harder than the CompTIA exam. The reason is it enhances their sales if you do poorly on the sample exam. Use caution before purchasing any set of test questions.

5. Review Problem Areas

After taking a practice exam, review your problem areas. Do not simply take a practice exam and study a set of questions. You need to learn the material covered. Review the test items missed. Go back and study these areas. Use the outline you developed from the Network+ Certification Examination Objectives to help you prepare.

6. Retake Practice Exams

Retake practice exams by taking a different practice exam to see if you have improved in the needed areas. Repeat steps four through six until you have gained sufficient confidence that you can pass the CompTIA Network+ Certification exam.

7. Schedule and Take the Network+ Certification Exam

One of the secrets of preparing for the Network+ Certification exam is to schedule an exact date and time to take the exam. Give yourself a real and practical deadline. Vague deadlines do *not* work and will actually work against you. By procrastinating, you will lose the knowledge learned for the current exam. For example, do not simply say, "I plan to take the exam in the fall." Chances are when fall comes you will still not be prepared and will procrastinate by saying, "I plan to take the exam this winter." Remember, procrastination is not a luxury; in this case, it is your enemy.

Set an exact date. This way you have committed both your financial and mental resources. Use your calendar to pick a date that gives you plenty of time to prepare by taking practice exams and reviewing. Don't wait until you think you are prepared to schedule the exam. In fact, scheduling the exam date should be one of the first things you do if you are serious about certification. Schedule the test, and then set up a specific schedule (timeline) for study.

Network+ Certification Practice Exam

This practice exam is structured according to the domains specified in the Network+ (2009 Edition) Certification Examination Objectives. Before each set of questions for the domain, the objectives for that domain are listed. The practice exam is 100 questions and should be taken within 90 minutes. After taking the exam, your instructor will score it.

Note

The CompTIA Network+ (2009 Edition) Certification Examination Objectives are subject to change without notice.

Domain 1.0—Network Technologies

- **1.1 Explain the function of common networking protocols:**
  TCP, FTP, UDP, TCP/IP suite, DHCP, TFTP, DNS, HTTP(S), ARP, SIP (VoIP), RTP (VoIP), SSH, POP3, NTP, IMAP4, Telnet, SMTP, SNMP2/3, ICMP, IGMP, and TLS.
- **1.2 Identify commonly used TCP and UDP default ports:**
  TCP ports (FTP–20, 21; SSH–22; Telnet–23; SMTP–25; DNS–53; HTTP–80; POP3–110; NTP–123; MAP4–143; HTTPS–443) and UDP ports (TFTP–69; DNS–53; BOOTPS/DHCP–67; SNMP–161).
- **1.3 Identify the following address formats:**
  IPv6, IPv4, and MAC addressing.

- **1.4 Given a scenario, evaluate the proper use of the following addressing technologies and addressing schemes:**
  Addressing technologies (subnetting, classful vs. classless, NAT, PAT, SNAT, public vs. private, DHCP) and addressing schemes (unicast, multicast, broadcast).
- **1.5 Identify common IPv4 and IPv6 routing protocols:**
  Link state (OSPF, IS-IS), distance vector (RIP, RIPv2, BGP), and hybrid (EIGRP).
- **1.6 Explain the purpose and properties of routing:**
  IGP vs. EGP, static vs. dynamic, next hop, understanding routing tables and how they pertain to path selection, and explain convergence (steady state).
- **1.7 Compare the characteristics of wireless communication standards:**
  802.11 a/b/g/n (speeds, distance, channels, frequency) and authentication and encryption (WPA, WEP, RADIUS, TKIP).

Domain 1.0—Practice Exam Questions 1–20

Answer the following questions on a separate sheet of paper. Please do not write in this book.

1. Which two ports are associated with FTP?
   A. 20, 21
   B. 21, 22
   C. 22, 23
   D. 23, 24
2. Which port number is associated with DNS?
   A. 25
   B. 53
   C. 80
   D. 112
3. Which protocol is used to download e-mail from a mail server?
   A. FTP
   B. SMTP
   C. POP3
   D. Telnet
4. Which port is the *most* secure when exchanging information with a Web site host?
   A. 21
   B. 80
   C. 110
   D. 443
5. Which network transmission is an example of transmitting packets to a select group of network nodes?
   A. Unicast
   B. Multicast
   C. Broadcast
   D. Selectivecast
6. Which wireless communication specification provides the *least* amount of bandwidth?
   A. 802.11a
   B. 802.11b
   C. 802.11g
   D. 802.11n

7. Which two are examples of a link state routing protocol? (Select two.)
   A. IS-IS
   B. OSPF
   C. RIP2
   C. IGRP
8. Which protocol is used to establish and then terminate a VoIP session?
   A. FTP
   B. RTP
   C. RIP
   D. SIP
9. Which is an example of an IPv6 address?
   A. 12:AD:2B:DF:23:C4
   B. 323.244.454.100
   C. fe80::1c7d:22de:51cc:efcd
   D. 10.23.24.12.66.46
10. Which is an example of router convergence?
   A. All routers connect to the same gateway.
   B. All routers share the same routing table information.
   C. All routers are connected to the same domain.
   D. A specified router designated as the "master router" is used to control all other router paths.
11. Which address can be forwarded from a local area network through a network router connected to the Internet?
   A. 192.168.0.5
   B. 169.254.0.12
   C. 10.0.12.23
   D. 56.123.45.134
12. Which is the correct network address for 192.168.12.35/24?
   A. 192.0.0.0
   B. 192.168.0.0
   C. 192.168.12.0
   D. 0.0.0.24
13. Which IPv4 address is an example of APIPA?
   A. 10.10.1.12
   B. 192.168.0.1
   C. 169.254.10.24
   D. 172.154.23.157
14. What is the assigned frequency for 802.11g devices?
   A. 5 GHz
   B. 5 MHz
   C. 2.4 MHz
   D. 2.4 GHz
15. What is the maximum speed specified by the 802.11g standard?
   A. 5 Mbps
   B. 11 Mbps
   C. 54 Mbps
   D. 300 Mbps

16. Which network node addresses are resolved by an IPv4 ARP request?
    A. Logical name and physical name.
    B. IP address and physical address.
    C. Assigned WINS name and MAC address.
    D. Physical address and MAC address.
17. Which is an example of a private IP address?
    A. 172.16.10.10
    B. 202.14.10.10
    C. 54.12.10.10
    D. 100.100.10.10
18. What is another name for a Wireless Access Point PSK?
    A. Passphrase
    B. SSID
    C. ESSID
    D. WEP
19. Which of the following will provide the *best* method of preventing WLAN access by an unauthorized person?
    A. Configure the WAP with WEP.
    B. Change the default SSID.
    C. Configure the WAP for MAC filtering.
    D. Change the default assigned channel of the WAP.
20. Which type of IP address should be assigned to a network printer?
    A. Classless
    B. Dynamic
    C. Static
    D. Public

Domain 2.0—Network Media and Topologies

- **2.1 Categorize standard cable types and their properties:**
  Type (Cat 3, Cat 5, Cat 5e, Cat 6, STP, UTP; multimode fiber, single-mode fiber, coaxial, RG-59, RG-6, serial, plenum vs. non-plenum) and properties (transmission speeds, distance, duplex, noise immunity, frequency).
- **2.2 Identify common connector types:**
  RJ-11, RJ-45, BNC, SC, ST, LC, and RS-232.
- **2.3 Identify common physical network topologies:**
  Star, mesh, bus, ring, point-to-point, point-to-multipoint, and hybrid.
- **2.4 Given a scenario, differentiate and implement appropriate wiring standards:**
  568A, 568B, straight vs. crossover, rollover, and loopback.
- **2.5 Categorize WAN technology types and properties:**
  Type (Frame Relay, E1/T1, ADSL, SDSL, VDSL, Cable modem, satellite , E3/T3, OC-x, wireless, ATM, SONET, MPLS, BRI-ISDN, PRI-ISDN, POTS, PSTN), and properties (circuit switch, packet switch, speed, transmission media, distance).
- **2.6 Categorize LAN technology types and properties:**
  Types (Ethernet, 10BaseT, 100BaseTX, 100BaseFX, 1000BaseT, 1000BaseX, 10GBaseSR, 10GBaseLR, 10GBaseER, 10GBaseSW, 10GBaseLW, 10GBaseEW, 10GBaseT) and properties (CSMA/CD, broadcast, collision, bonding, speed, distance).

- **2.7 Explain common logical network topologies and their characteristics:**
  Peer-to-peer, client/server, VPN, and VLAN.
- **2.8 Install components of wiring distribution:**
  Vertical and horizontal cross connects, patch panels, 66 block, MDFs, IDFs, 25 pair, 100 pair, 110 block, demarc, demarc extension, smart jack, verify wiring installation, and verify wiring termination.

Domain 2.0—Practice Exam Questions 21–40

Answer the following questions on a separate sheet of paper. Please do not write in this book.

21. Which topology will continue to provide client support when a single cable segment fails?
    A. Ring
    B. Star
    C. Mesh
    D. Point-to-point
22. Which cable or standard would provide the best protection from EMI?
    A. Cat 5e UTP
    B. 1000BaseT
    C. 10GbaseSW
    D. Cat 6 UTP
23. What is the expected maximum data rate for Cat 6 UTP cable?
    A. 100 Mbps
    B. 1 Gbps
    C. 10 Gbps
    D. 100 Gbps
24. Which cable type or standard is commonly used to provide high-frequency video signals associated with Cable television and satellite installations?
    A. Cat 5 UTP
    B. Cat 6a STP
    C. RG-6
    D. 1000BaseSW
25. Which connector is commonly used with coaxial cable?
    A. RJ-45
    B. RJ-11
    C. ST
    D. BNC
26. What is the *most* common unique characteristic of Cat 5e STP cable?
    A. Protection in wet and high humidity applications
    B. Protection from direct sunlight
    C. Protection from extreme temperature changes
    D. Protection from EMI
27. Which electrical measurement is used to express cable signal losses?
    A. Ohm
    B. Volt
    C. Resistance
    D. Decibel

28. Which technology eliminates the need for a network crossover cable?
    A. Auto-MDIX
    B. PoE
    C. PPP
    D. APIPA
29. Which is the location point where the commercial carrier cable meets the private customer network system?
    A. Plenum
    B. Demarc
    C. Gateway
    D. Point of no return
30. Which two statements are true concerning a 110 punch down block? (Select two.)
    A. 110 block terminates solid core wire.
    B. 110 block terminates stranded core wire.
    C. A 110 block can be used to terminate Cat 5 network cable or telephone communications cable.
    D. A 110 block can only be used to terminate Cat 5 cable.
31. Which cable type or standard supports the longest distances?
    A. 1000BaseT
    B. 10GBase ER
    C. 10GBaseSW
    D. 10GBaseLW
32. What is the speed of a T1 line?
    A. 1.544 Mbps
    B. 54 Mbps
    C. 11 Mbps
    D. 2.4 Mbps
33. Which media type supports the highest data transfer rate?
    A. T1
    B. ISDN
    C. 802.11n
    D. ADSL
34. Which two are examples of circuit-switched technologies? (Select two.)
    A. Ethernet
    B. POTS
    C. 802.11n
    D. ISDN
35. How do you change a 568A termination to a 568B termination?
    A. Switch termination pair 1-2 with pair 7-8.
    B. Switch termination pair 1-2 with pair 3-6.
    C. Switch termination pair 3-4 with pair 5-6.
    D. Switch termination pair 3–4 with pair 7–8.
36. Which device would *most likely* represent the demarcation point?
    A. 100 block
    B. Gateway router
    C. IDF
    D. Smart jack

37. Which is the correct example of BRI-ISDN?
    A. One B channel and one D channel.
    B. Two B channels and one D channel.
    C. One B channel and two D channels.
    D. Two B channels and two D channels.
38. Which device is commonly used to create a VLAN?
    A. Hub
    B. Bridge
    C. Switch
    D. Gateway
39. Which two protocols are used to support VPN connections?
    A. L2TP
    B. PPTP
    C. SMTP
    D. IMAP
40. What is the maximum distance a horizontal cross connect should be placed from the office computer cubical area outlet to comply with TIA-568B standard when using Cat 5e cable?
    A. 25 meters
    B. 50 meters
    C. 90 meters
    D. 300 meters

Domain 3.0—Network Devices

- **3.1 Install, configure, and differentiate between common network devices:**

  Hub, repeater, modem, NIC, media converters, basic switch, bridge, wireless access point, basic router, basic firewall, and basic DHCP server.
- **3.2 Identify the functions of specialized network devices:**

  Multilayer switch, content switch, IDS/IPS, load balancer, multifunction network devices, DNS server, bandwidth shaper, proxy server, and CSU/DSU.
- **3.3 Explain the advanced features of a switch:**

  PoE, spanning tree, VLAN, trunking, port mirroring, and port authentication.
- **3.4 Implement a basic wireless network:**

  Install client, access point placement, install access point (configure appropriate encryption, configure channels and frequencies, set ESSID and beacon), and verify installation.

Domain 3.0—Practice Exam Questions 41–57

Answer the following questions on a separate sheet of paper. Please do not write in this book.

41. Which protocol is used by default to automatically issue IPv4 addresses to client/server network workstations?
    A. FTP
    B. IMAP
    C. DHCP
    D. DNS

42. Which device is used to resolve IP addresses to host names?
    A. WINS server
    B. DNS server
    C. SMTP server
    D. DHCP server
43. Which device would be used to connect two different network media such as fiber-optic cable twisted pair?
    A. Hub
    B. Basic switch
    C. Basic router
    D. Media converter
44. Which device would you use to prevent a single user on a local area network from slowing the network response because they are constantly downloading large volumes of data from the Internet?
    A. Proxy server
    B. CSU/DSU
    C. Bandwidth shaper
    D. Bridge
45. Which device would you use to increase the data-carrying capacity between two network segments?
    A. Two switches with port trunking capabilities, one at each location.
    B. Two DHCP servers, one in each segment.
    C. Install a proxy server in each segment.
    D. Install a spanning tree switch that has a port connected to each segment of the network.
46. Which switch option would you implement to provide the best service for a VoIP device?
    A. Load balancing
    B. IDP
    C. Port mirroring
    D. Bandwidth shaper
47. Which technology would you implement on a network to prevent the occurrence of switch loops?
    A. Port mirroring
    B. IDP
    C. Spanning tree protocol
    D. ICMP protocol
48. You want to increase the range of a wireless network and have laptop users only connect once to the wireless network. Which configuration would satisfy the conditions stated?
    A. Assign the same IP address to all Wireless Access Points.
    B. Assign the same MAC address to all Wireless Access Points.
    C. Assign the same SSID to all Wireless Access Points.
    D. Disable beaconing at all Wireless Access Points.
49. Which wireless security requires an authentication server?
    A. WEP
    B. WAP
    C. 802.11x
    D. PAP

50. Which wireless encryption type provides the *least* security?
    A. WEP
    B. WPA
    C. WPA Personal
    D. 802.11x
51. Which device would be the *most* appropriate for speeding up network downloads by caching from a common Internet location?
    A. Load balancer
    B. VLAN
    C. Proxy server
    D. Repeater
52. A network bridge passes frames based on which type of address?
    A. IPv4
    B. IPv6
    C. physical
    D. logical
53. A basic switch forwards frames based on which type of address?
    A. IPv4
    B. IPv6
    C. physical
    D. logical
54. Which protocol does not use ARP requests to identify local area network computers?
    A. IPv4
    B. IPv6
    C. Ethernet
    D. IPv4 and IPv6
55. Which device is used to create a separate network?
    A. Hub
    B. Bridge
    C. Switch
    D. Router
56. Which device is the *most* commonly used to configure a VLAN on a small network?
    A. Bridge
    B. Repeater
    C. Switch
    D. Gateway
57. What is the main purpose of an IDS/IPS device?
    A. Perform load balancing on a local area network to ensure equal network access by all nodes.
    B. Set Internet access priorities according to software application types.
    C. Detect and protect against unauthorized network access.
    D. Provide equal access to clients connected to an ISP via a modem.

Domain 4.0—Network Management

Answer the following questions on a separate sheet of paper. Please do not write in this book.

■ **4.1 Explain the function of each layer of the OSI model:**

Layer 1—physical, Layer 2—data link, Layer 3—network, Layer 4—transport, Layer 5—session, Layer 6—presentation, and Layer 7—application.

- **4.2 Identify types of configuration management documentation:**
  Wiring schematics; physical and logical network diagrams; baselines; policies, procedures, and configurations; and regulations.
- **4.3 Given a scenario, evaluate the network based on configuration management documentation:**
  Compare wiring schematics, physical and logical network diagrams, baselines, policies and procedures, and configurations to network devices and infrastructure. Update wiring schematics, physical and logical network diagrams, configurations, and job logs as needed.
- **4.4 Conduct network monitoring to identify performance and connectivity issues using the following:**
  Network monitoring utilities (packet sniffers, connectivity software, load testing, throughput testers) and system logs, history logs, and event logs.
- **4.5 Explain different methods and rationales for network performance optimization:**
  Methods (QoS, traffic shaping, load balancing, high availability, caching engines, fault tolerance) and reasons (latency sensitivity, high bandwidth applications, VoIP, video applications, and uptime).
- **4.6 Given a scenario, implement the following network troubleshooting methodology:**
  Information gathering—identify symptoms and problems, identify the affected areas of the network, determine if anything has changed, establish the most probable cause, determine if escalation is necessary, create an action plan and solution identifying potential effects, implement and test the solution, identify the results and effects of the solution, and document the solution and the entire process.
- **4.7 Given a scenario, troubleshoot common connectivity issues and select an appropriate solution:**
  Physical issues (crosstalk, Near-End crosstalk, attenuation, collisions, shorts, open impedance mismatch, interference), logical issues (port speed, port duplex mismatch, incorrect VLAN, incorrect IP address, wrong gateway, wrong DNS, wrong subnet mask), issues that should be identified but escalated (switching loop, routing loop, route problems, proxy ARP, broadcast storms), and wireless issues (interference, incorrect encryption, incorrect channel, incorrect frequency, ESSID mismatch, standard mismatch, distance, bounce, incorrect antenna placement).

Domain 4.0—Practice Exam Questions 58–78

Answer the following questions on a separate sheet of paper. Please do not write in this book.

58. Which layer of the OSI model relates to establishing, maintaining, and terminating a connection between two network devices?
    A. Session
    B. Transport
    C. Network
    D. Application

59. Which layer of the OSI model is responsible for providing accurate and reliable data transfer?
    A. Session
    B. Transport
    C. Network
    D. Application
60. Which OSI layer would align with the FTP protocol?
    A. Session
    B. Transport
    C. Network
    D. Application
61. Which method would be *most* appropriate to reduce network collisions?
    A. Add additional Ethernet hubs, one for each major network department.
    B. Add an additional DNS server and then split the DNS assignments for all network adapters.
    C. Replace all existing Cat 5 cable with Cat 6.
    D. Replace network hubs with switches.
62. Which protocol is designed to prevent switching loops?
    A. FTP
    B. Spanning tree
    C. VLAN
    D. MS-CHAP
63. What would indicate that a workstation has been configured with an incorrect DNS address?
    A. The workstation will not complete a system boot.
    B. The workstation is causing a network broadcast storm.
    C. The workstation cannot successfully connect to other workstation shares on the network.
    D. The workstation cannot successfully ping the network server using the server IP address.
64. Which network condition can cause a broadcast storm?
    A. Defective NIC
    B. Attenuation
    C. Wrong subnet mask
    D. Incorrect static IP address assignment to workstation
65. A new additional 802.11n WAP has just been added to a LAN to expand the wireless service area. The WAP has been installed using the default configuration. What would prevent a laptop from connecting to the LAN through the new 802.11n-enabled WAP? Choose the *most likely* reason for failure to connect.
    A. Incorrect DHCP.
    B. The WAP does not support 802.11b connections.
    C. ESSID mismatch.
    D. Incorrect wireless channel.
66. Out of the items listed below, what would you do first when troubleshooting a network problem?
    A. Identify the affected areas of the network.
    B. Determine if anything has changed.
    C. Establish the most probable cause.
    D. Identify the symptoms.

67. What problem would be *most likely* encountered if a network backbone is extended too far beyond its design specification?
    A. NEXT
    B. FEXT
    C. Attenuation
    D. Excessive collisions
68. Which method will improve overall network performance for high-bandwidth applications?
    A. Load balancing
    B. Port mirroring
    C. Fault tolerance
    D. Traffic shaping
69. Which method would you implement to improve network system uptime?
    A. Load balancing
    B. Cache engine
    C. Fault tolerance
    D. Traffic shaping
70. Which method would you implement to improve VoIP performance?
    A. Caching engine
    B. Load balancing
    C. Traffic shaping
    D. Fault tolerance
71. Where would you look to compare the recent network scan to determine if there has been a significant change in network activity?
    A. Original construction specifications
    B. Proxy server cache
    C. ARP cache
    D. Baseline scan results
72. What is the technical term used to describe a port that can transmit and receive simultaneously?
    A. Full port
    B. Port mirror
    C. Duplex port
    D. Complex port
73. A small office area consists of two 802.11b wireless equipped workstations and an 802.11g gateway/router connected to a 2-Gb Cable modem. The 802.11g gateway/router is replaced by a new 802.11n gateway/router. What will be the maximum connection speed to the Internet from either of the workstations?
    A. 11 Mbps
    B. 54 Mbps
    C. 300 Mbps
    D. 2 Gbps
74. You are configuring a laptop wireless connection to a WAP on a client/server network. Which wireless security method will *most* closely match AAA security requirements?
    A. Reconfigure the laptop and WAP with a new matching SSID.
    B. Use 802.11x to configure the WAP, laptop, and network access server.
    C. Configure both the laptop and WAP using WEP.
    D. Configure the laptop and WAP with matching security keys and matching SSID.

75. A wireless laptop is configured with WEP encryption and to connect to a WAP that uses WPA2 encryption. What will be the *most likely* results when making a connection?
    A. The laptop will connect to the WAP forcing the WAP to automatically reconfigure as WEP to ensure backward compatibility.
    B. The laptop will detect the WPA2 encryption and automatically reconfigure the laptop to connect to the WAP using WPA2.
    C. The laptop will identify the WAP but will not be able to successfully connect.
    D. There is no problem because WPA2 encryption is backward compatible with WEP.
76. Which item is a common cause of VoIP echo?
    A. Cat 5e Near-End Crosstalk
    B. Line amplifier loss
    C. Impedance mismatch
    D. Attenuation
77. Where would you check if a change has taken place in the server's configuration that could be the source of a problem?
    A. System registry
    B. Event viewer
    C. Sysconfig
    D. System restore
78. Which item would cause the *most* limitation to a direct line of sight wireless network connection?
    A. Wooden door
    B. Drywall
    C. Metal file cabinets
    D. Concrete block wall

Domain 5.0—Network Tools

- **5.1 Given a scenario, select the appropriate command line interface tool and interpret the output to verify functionality:**
  Traceroute, ipconfig, ifconfig, ping, arp ping, arp, nslookup, hostname, dig, mtr, route, nbtstat, and netstat.
- **5.2 Explain the purpose of network scanners:**
  Packet sniffers, intrusion detection software, intrusion prevention software, and port scanners.
- **5.3 Given a scenario, utilize the appropriate hardware tools:**
  Cable testers, protocol analyzer, certifiers, TDR, OTDR, multimeter, toner probe, butt set, punch down tool, cable stripper, snips, voltage event recorder, and temperature monitor.

Domain 5.0—Practice Exam Questions 79–89

Answer the following questions on a separate sheet of paper. Please do not write in this book.

79. Which command would you use to view IP address and port number statistics?
    A. **tracert**
    B. **netstat**
    C. **dig**
    D. **ping**

80. A technician wishes to trace a UTP cable to check for a suspected break and to verify its physical path through the building. Which tool would be *most* appropriate?
    A. Tone generator and tracer
    B. ODT
    C. Protocol analyzer
    D. Multimeter
81. What information is revealed when issuing an **ipconfig** command with no switches, at the command prompt of a Windows Vista workstation on a TCP/IP Ethernet network? (Select all that apply.)
    A. Physical address
    B. IPv4 address
    C. Workgroup name
    D. Subnet mask
82. You are checking a network conductor pair using a VOM. What setting is *most* appropriate to verify there is no short between the two conductors?
    A. Amperes
    B. Volts
    C. Ohms
    D. Frequency
83. The time required to transfer a file has greatly increased recently. You suspect that there is an excessive amount of data transfers on the network. Which tool would you use to confirm your suspicions?
    A. Protocol analyzer
    B. OTD
    C. Network Neighborhood
    D. 1-GHz oscilloscope
84. You successfully ping the localhost but cannot ping anyone else in your workgroup. What is the *most likely* cause of the problem?
    A. The TCP/IP protocol is not installed on the workstation.
    B. The DNS server is down.
    C. There is a loose connection at the network interface card or hub.
    D. There is insufficient RAM installed in the workstation.
85. Users are complaining of very slow downloads in a particular workgroup. What would be the *most* appropriate course of action to take first?
    A. Ping each of the workstations in the workgroup to ensure each has a good connection.
    B. Run a protocol analyzer and compare the data to the network's baseline data.
    C. Use **netstat** to locate duplicate IP address assignments.
    D. Use a packet sniffer to see if users are using the appropriate user names and passwords.
86. Which of the following tools would be the *most* appropriate to check a fiber-optic backbone suspected as causing a network cabling problem?
    A. Digital multimeter
    B. OTDM
    C. Oscilloscope
    D. Tone generator

87. Which command is used to identify the default server and the assigned IP address of the server?
    A. **nslookup**
    B. **host**
    C. **dig**
    D. **whoami**
88. Which command would you use to view network latency between a series of existing routers?
    A. **ping**
    B. **tracert**
    C. **nslook**
    D. **dig**
89. Which command would be the most appropriate to view the assigned IPv6 address for a workstation?
    A. **arp/all**
    B. **dig**
    C. **arp/6**
    D. **ipconfig**

Domain 6.0—Network Security

- **6.1 Explain the function of hardware and software security devices:**
  Network-based firewall, host-based firewall, IDS, IPS, and VPN concentrator.
- **6.2 Explain common features of a firewall:**
  Application layer vs. network layer, stateful vs. stateless, scanning services, content filtering, signature identification, and zones.
- **6.3 Explain the methods of network access security:**
  Filtering (ACL, MAC filtering, IP filtering), tunneling and encryption (SSL VPN, VPN, L2TP, PPTP, IPSec), and remote access (RAS, RDP, PPPoE, PPP, VNC, ICA).
- **6.4 Explain methods of user authentication:**
  PKI, Kerberos, AAA (RADIUS, TACACS+), network access control (802.1x), CHAP, MS-CHAP, and EAP.
- **6.5 Explain issues that affect device security:**
  Physical security, restricting local and remote access, and secure methods vs. unsecure methods (SSH, HTTPS, SNMPv3, SFTP, SCP, Telnet, HTTP, FTP, RSH, RCP, SNMPv1/2).
- **6.6 Identify common security threats and mitigation techniques:**
  Security threats (DoS, viruses, worms, attackers, man in the middle, Smurf, rogue access points, social engineering) and mitigation techniques (policies and procedures, user training, patches and updates).

Domain 6.0—Practice Exam Questions 90–100

Answer the following questions on a separate sheet of paper. Please do not write in this book.

90. Which method provides the *best* network protection for preventing unauthorized access through a WAP?
    A. Change the default SSID.
    B. Change the access point frequency.
    C. Implement MAC filtering.
    D. Change the default channel.

91. What problem is caused by a DoS attack?
    A. The server and network is overwhelmed by requests.
    B. The operating system of each client in the network is corrupted.
    C. The assigned IP address for each device is switched, resulting in lost connections with the server.
    D. The antivirus suite is corrupted, resulting in a compromised network.
92. Which tool is the *most* appropriate to automatically detect unauthorized network access?
    A. Firewall
    B. Proxy server
    C. IDS
    D. Antivirus software
93. Which is the *best* method to prevent a Smurf attack?
    A. Change the subnet mask of all Wireless Access Points.
    B. Configure devices not to forward ICMP echo requests.
    C. Install IDS.
    D. Use static IP assignments.
94. Which is the *best* method of protection from malware embedded as an e-mail attachment?
    A. Install and configure an IDS.
    B. Install the latest software patches and updates.
    C. Configure all hosts as VPN clients.
    D. Conduct user training.
95. Which two security methods *most* closely match AAA requirements? (Select two.)
    A. IPSec
    B. RADIUS
    C. SSL VPN
    D. TACACS+
96. Which technology would be the *best* choice to detect and prevent the spread of a worm?
    A. Port scanner
    B. IDS
    C. IPS
    D. Protocol analyzer
97. Which is an example of social engineering?
    A. Smurf attack
    B. Man in the middle
    C. Rouge AP
    D. Phishing
98. Which two modes are associated with IPSec? (Select two.)
    A. Transport mode
    B. Tunnel mode
    C. Synchronous mode
    D. Secure mode
99. Which security method uses a trusted third party to verify identity?
    A. PKI
    B. CHAP
    C. IPSec
    D. PAP

100. Which protocol would be inspected by an application firewall?
   A. ARP
   B. PPTP
   C. HTTP
   D. IP

Scoring the Exam

Copy the following chart onto a separate sheet of paper and fill in your scores. Please do not write in this book.

Domain	Your Score (Number of correctly answered questions.)
1.0 Network Technologies	
2.0 Network Media and Topologies	
3.0 Network Devices	
4.0 Network Management	
5.0 Network Tools	
6.0 Network Security	
Total	

As a quick indication of how you performed on the practice exam, refer to the chart in **Figure 20-3.** The chart shows the total number of questions in each domain and the number of correctly answered questions you need to have to score an 80% in that domain.

Figure 20-3.
Use this chart to determine if you have achieved an 80% on the practice exam or in any of the domains.

Domain	Total Number of Questions by Domain	Approximate Number of Correct Answers Needed to Score 80%
1.0 Network Technologies	20	16
2.0 Network Media and Topologies	20	16
3.0 Network Devices	17	13–14
4.0 Network Management	20	16
5.0 Network Tools	12	9–10
6.0 Network Security	11	8–9
Total	100	80

Summary

- The Network+ Certification exam contains 100 questions.
- The maximum time allotted to answer the questions on the Network+ Certification exam is 90 minutes.
- Questions on the Network+ Certification exam are not equally weighted.
- Review and analyze all of the Network+ Certification exam objectives to become familiar with the knowledge areas for which the exam tests.
- Match the Network+ Certification exam objective details to quality resource material.
- Identify and practice laboratory activities that match the Network+ Certification exam objectives.
- Take practice exams, and then identify and review problem areas.

Review Questions

Answer the following questions on a separate sheet of paper. Please do not write in this book.

1. How many questions are on the Network+ Certification exam?
2. What is the minimum passing score for the Network+ Certification exam?
3. Outline the key points for an exam preparation strategy.
4. Why do you *not* want to depend on a commercial study guide to prepare for the exam?
5. What other CompTIA exam objectives may you want to use to help you prepare for the Network+ Certification exam?

Suggested Laboratory Activities

1. Download the latest Network+ Certification Examination Objectives.
2. Make a test objective outline and fill it in with facts and details about each objective.
3. Locate several Web sites that contain free test materials and evaluate the contents by comparing them to the current test objectives.

Interesting Web Sites for More Information

www.CompTIA.org
http://support.microsoft.com

Network+ Note

Visit the Microsoft's support Web site and look at articles that will reinforce knowledge required for the Network+ Certification exam. Examples are installing Windows Vista and Windows Server 2008. Pay particular attention to problems associated with the installation process. Also, look at the articles on troubleshooting tools provided by the operating systems. I have no doubt that many of these articles are a source of information for the Network+ Certification exam.

Visit the CompTIA Network+ Web page to download the Network+ Certification Examination Objectives and to learn more about the exam.

21 Employment in the Field of Networking Technology

After studying this chapter, you will be able to:

- ❑ Compare networking technology careers.
- ❑ Implement career information sources to plan a career in networking.
- ❑ Recall networking technology educational and certification requirements.
- ❑ Compare advanced training options.
- ❑ Carry out a successful job search.
- ❑ Construct a résumé.
- ❑ Apply appropriate interview skills.

Key Words and Terms

The following words and terms will become important pieces of your networking vocabulary. Be sure you can define them.

A+ Certification
business plan
Certified Linux Desktop Administrator (CLDA) Certification
Certified Novell Engineer (CNE) Certification
consultant
engineer
entrepreneur
Linux+ Certification
LPIC-1 Certification
LPIC-2 Certification
LPIC-3 Certification
Microsoft Certified Application Specialist (MCAS) Certification
Microsoft Certified Information Technology Professional (MCITP) Certification
Microsoft Certified Technical Specialist (MCTS) Certification
Microsoft Office Specialist (MOS) Certification
network administrator
network support specialist
Network+ Certification
Novell Certified Linux Administrator (CLA) Certification
Novell Certified Linux Engineer (CLE) Certification
Novell Certified Linux Professional (CLP) Certification
PDI+ Certification
practicum
programmer
programmer analyst
Security+ Certification
Server+ Certification
systems analyst
Web administrator
Web master

By successfully reaching this point in the textbook, you have probably decided whether or not to pursue a career in networking technology. Networking is one of the fastest growing fields within the scope of computer technology. If you have the interest, desire, and ability, you can find a rewarding career in this field.

Networking technology and related computer careers require a basic education in computers and networking as well as an advanced education in the field. Technology is constantly and rapidly advancing. New ideas become a reality every day. As a professional in the computer and networking field, this condition requires that you continually update your skills through education and training. Commercial certification in one or more technology fields is often required.

To keep up with the rapid changes in networking technology, you must form some type of action plan. Your personal plan must include strategies for gaining initial training and certifications and keeping up-to-date with the changes and ways to expand your opportunities for advancement in the IT field. This chapter discusses ways to gain employment and ways to advance your career. While you may already be employed in a networking, computer repair, or related job, this chapter may help you better define your career goals. First, let's look at some of the many different job titles in the IT industry.

Information Technology Industry Careers

There are a wide variety of careers in the Information Technology (IT) industry. Networking is the key to communications and information systems that play a major role in business and daily life. Think of all the things that depend on computer networks. For example, in the communications industry, the telephone, television, and radio are linked to computer networks. The manufacturing industry uses computers and networks to design, build, inventory, and sell most everything it makes. Computer networks control robots and automate assembly lines. In the business world, computer networks make communication and business nearly instantaneous. Sharing information within and among companies and the Internet is commonplace. Tasks that, in the past, required days and months to complete are now completed automatically or within minutes. The entire banking industry relies on networked computers to calculate and track money exchanges and post records of interest, earnings, and mortgage statistics.

Network technology has also saturated the field of medicine. Surgeons can perform laser and other surgery through long-distance communication over networks. Patient medical records are computerized, **Figure 21-1.** MRI scans can be transmitted instantly across a network to any distant city where other doctors can evaluate them. Architects and engineers rely on computers to design structures around the world. Not only can they design the structure, they can take a virtual tour of the design from another country. Law enforcement, the military, and other governmental units are completely reliant on networking technology.

Figure 21-1. Network technology plays a vital role in the field of medicine. It can provide access to patient records from remote locations, allow surgeons to perform laser and other surgery through long-distance communication, and transport MRI scans to any distant city where other doctors can evaluate them.

The need for people with networking and other computer skills has rapidly grown and will continue to grow. There are many careers in the IT industry from which to choose. Some of the many careers include the following:

- Network support specialist.
- Network administrator.
- Systems analyst.
- Consultant.
- Technical salesperson.
- Web administrator.
- Programmer.
- Software engineer.
- Entrepreneur.

Network Support Specialist

network support specialist
a person who assists users and customers whenever they encounter a network problem.

As a ***network support specialist***, you will be required to assist users and customers whenever they encounter a network problem. Often a network support specialist is assigned to a help desk. They answer phone calls, interpret user problems, and recommend solutions or dispatch a technician to the user's workstation. Most of the support they provide is through the Remote Assistance utility found in Windows operating systems, **Figure 21-2.** As a part of the role of support, network support specialists are often required to conduct training sessions for employees and write training manuals.

The network support specialist works under the direct supervision of a network administrator. The network administrator usually directs the network support specialist's activities for the day. Many network administrators started their careers as a network support specialist.

A network support specialist must continuously learn about new software packages, operating systems, hardware, security, data storage, and other key elements of networking. New hardware systems, software packages, service packs, and security

Figure 21-2.
A network support specialist is often assigned to a help desk. The network support specialist interprets user problems and can often provide support over the phone or remotely through a program like Remote Assistance.

software are continuously developed. You will need to expand your knowledge in these areas to make yourself even more valuable as a network support specialist and to advance to network administrator.

Network Administrator

Most of the maintenance of a network system is the result of constant monitoring by the network administrator. While the network support specialist may perform routine maintenance under the direction of the network administrator, the ***network administrator*** is ultimately responsible for the type, extent, and frequency of maintenance to be performed. The network administrator is also responsible for the installation, configuration, and maintenance of the LAN, MAN, or WAN. The network administrator may perform many routine administrative functions, such as work with hardware and software vendors, make written and oral presentations about the state of the network, interview prospective employees, evaluate employee performance, coordinate work schedules, order supplies and equipment, and prepare budget reports. It is not unusual for this type of position to require a four-year degree in addition to one to two years of technical training.

network administrator
a person responsible for the installation, configuration, and maintenance of the LAN, MAN, or WAN; making written and oral presentations about the state of the network; interviewing prospective employees; evaluating employee performance; coordinating work schedules; ordering supplies and equipment; and preparing budget reports.

Systems Analyst

A ***systems analyst*** is responsible for analyzing, evaluating, and recommending business software systems. Typically, a systems analyst is involved in designing systems and making recommendations rather than involved in day-to-day network operations. Many systems analysts work for hardware and software companies. The systems analyst works with clients by analyzing the client's business and making recommendations. He or she also designs network systems to match the needs of the client's business.

Some systems analysts work as independent contractors or consultants. As a consultant, they sell their expertise as a service to organizations that are about to install, upgrade, or modify a network system. A systems analyst must be able to communicate effectively with programmers, technicians, and engineers and with clients who have limited computer system knowledge. A systems analyst position usually requires a four-year degree.

systems analyst
a person responsible for analyzing, evaluating, and recommending business software systems.

Consultant

Consulting is another growing business in the IT industry. A ***consultant*** works with clients on projects and makes recommendations based on his or her expertise, **Figure 21-3.** The specific job the consultant does often depends on what work is needed. The client pays the consultant for his or her expertise. When the job is completed, the consultant is free to move on to a new job and client.

In the case of networking technology, it is recommended that a person become a consultant after extensive experience in the field. Consultants are expected to have answers to many challenges or be able to quickly research them. Consultants usually have vast expertise in one or more particular aspects of the IT industry, such as security, systems analysis, network design, and electronic marketing.

consultant
a person who works with clients on projects and makes recommendations based on his or her expertise.

Technical Salesperson

Technical salespersons are always needed in the industry to represent manufacturers of hardware and software. Many technical salespersons originally started out as a technician and then moved into sales. They are typically required to obtain a certification directly related to their field of expertise. For example,

Figure 21-3. Companies often rely on consultants for their expertise in certain areas.

if they are representing a virus software manufacturer, they will be required to obtain certification on the product they are selling. A person seeking a career in technical sales needs an outgoing personality, must be well groomed, and must like working with the people. This is not a job for the shy or timid.

Web administrator a person responsible for converting written documents into HTML or other Web page programming languages. This job requires training in Web page programming language and some expertise in networking technology.

Web Administrator

Web administration requires the design and implementation of Web pages for external and internal Web sites. The ***Web administrator*** is responsible for converting written documents into HTML or other Web page programming languages. The Web administrator usually has to interpret the needs of his or her employer and convert those needs into Web page presentations. This job requires not only training in Web page programming language, but also some expertise in networking technology. The Web administrator also requires some expertise in art and graphics. The ability to use a digital camera and video equipment and having video editing skills is beneficial.

Tech Tip

The Web page is often referred to as the *front end* while the support of the Web server is referred to as the *back end.*

Web master a person who has the expertise in Web programming languages, such as HTML, XML, JAVA, JavaScript, ActiveX, and familiarity with server management of IIS, Apache, UNIX, Linux, and Microsoft systems.

There are many self-taught Web page designers, but to land a job as a Web master, administrator, or technician requires additional training in networking and server technology. A ***Web master*** requires expertise in Web programming languages, such as HTML, XML, CSS, JAVA, JavaScript, ActiveX, and familiarity with server management of IIS, Apache, UNIX, Linux, and Microsoft systems. Certification is typically a minimal job requirement.

Programmer

A ***programmer*** writes, tests, and modifies software programs. There are many programming languages to choose from. Many programmers master more than one programming language. Some programming languages you may wish to learn are C, C++, Prolog, or JAVA. C and C++ are excellent programming languages to learn and a recommended starting point. Prolog is a programming language used in artificial intelligence and machines. One of the hottest programming languages today is JAVA. Other languages to consider are Visual Basic and XML.

programmer
a person who writes, tests, and modifies software programs.

Programmers vary from self-taught to college-educated. When college-educated, programmers are generally referred to as *software engineers*. Many programmers work as independent contractors who program or modify custom software packages to meet the needs of their employer. Some programmers are known as programmer analysts. A ***programmer analyst*** analyzes the needs of a client and performs the actual programming.

programmer analyst
a person who analyzes the needs of a client and performs the actual programming to meet those needs.

Engineer

An ***engineer*** is a degreed professional who possesses high-level skills necessary to solve problems related to his or her field of expertise. To become an engineer requires a four- to six-year college degree. Engineers require a strong background in mathematics, sciences, programming languages, and hardware. They typically advance to management and project leadership positions. If an engineer exhibits leadership skills, he or she often becomes the chief technology officer. Engineers command the highest salaries in the IT job market. Those that earn a doctoral degree often become university engineering and computer science faculty. They also are employed in the area of research where they are responsible for developing new technologies.

engineer
a degreed professional who possesses high-level skills necessary to solve problems related to his or her field of expertise.

Entrepreneur

An ***entrepreneur*** owns and operates a business. This person usually starts with an idea for filling a gap in the marketplace or identifying where a new product or service is needed. An entrepreneur then develops a business plan. A business plan is required if the entrepreneur is seeking financial support to open a business. The ***business plan*** outlines the goals for the business and includes action plans and a timetable for meeting those goals. A good business plan is vital if the business is to succeed.

entrepreneur
a person who owns and operates a business.

business plan
a document that outlines the goals for a business and includes an action plan and a timetable for meeting those goals.

In addition to a sound business plan, a successful entrepreneur possesses certain skills. The successful entrepreneur has knowledge of the product or service he or she plans to provide. This knowledge allows the entrepreneur to make smart business decisions. The successful entrepreneur also has sound management skills. These skills allow the entrepreneur to manage resources such as money, time, and employees. Resource management is critical to success. A serious lack of skill in any of these areas can lead to certain failure. The ability to think creatively and wisely are also important skills for the successful entrepreneur. These skills allow the entrepreneur to control the business and move it in the right direction.

Entrepreneurial opportunities are vast in the IT industry. Along with the growth of networking technologies and products, growth has occurred in servicing these technologies and products. Installing, maintaining, and servicing networks is and will continue to be a sound business in the industry.

Career Information Sources

The major source of job information, especially information regarding computer and networking, is the Internet. There are many Internet sources that contain job listings and job matching services. Nearly every college and school is connected to such a service. Another reference is the *Occupational Outlook Handbook*. It is published by the United States Department of Labor and Bureau of Statistics. Most school, community college, university, and public libraries have copies of this book. The book can be ordered from the Bureau of Labor Statistics Web site, www.bls.gov.

School guidance counselors and local labor market offices are other outstanding sources of career information. They can help you find information on particular careers and colleges, training programs, and military service opportunities. School guidance counselors and those who work in local labor market offices are typically well informed and ready to help you in your search for a job or training. Colleges typically have job information and placement services available.

A great amount of career and training information can be found on the Internet. Many company Web sites list employment opportunities, a brief job description, and the required skills and educational level for the job. The following are some careers you may find listed when searching these sources:

- Entry-level network technician.
- Network support professional.
- Network installer.
- Technical sales and marketing professional.
- Technical writer.
- Technical forensics technician.
- Customer service representative.
- Network security specialist.
- Internet Web site developer.
- Internet systems administrator.
- Database specialist.
- Network hardware specialist.
- Network engineer.
- Systems engineer.
- Software engineer.
- Programmer.
- Analyst.
- Chief information officer.
- Telecommunications data specialist.
- Voice over IP (VoIP) engineer.
- Data communications engineer.
- ATM engineer.
- Web master.
- Web developer.
- Industrial control engineer.
- IT consultant.
- Service/help desk technician.
- Network training specialist.

Each person must ask his or herself several questions before going further into the computer arena. Have you enjoyed this *Networking Fundamentals* textbook and the laboratory activities? The fact that you are studying networking shows that you already have a good background in computers and an interest in this area. Have you taken other classes in computer technology? Did you like them? Did you do well? Give serious thought to your responses to the above questions and guidelines. Your responses may be the start you need to achieve success in your chosen area.

General and College Education

The educational requirements for jobs in the IT industry vary. A minimum of a high school education is a solid foundation on which to build. Very few high school graduates enter the networking industry directly, but are required to receive specialized education in the training programs maintained by large companies. Specialized training may also come from formal training in colleges, technical schools, or the military. To gain promotions, however, advanced certifications and degrees are required.

College is an excellent option for advancement in the IT industry. A college education in one of the IT industry-related fields is an excellent choice because of the demand for people with a college degree. A college education not only provides a technical background, it provides preparation for the business world through other classes, such as technical writing, business writing, and speech. These classes teach basic communication skills, which are in as much demand as IT skills.

If you plan to advance in the IT business world, you must master the skills of communication, both written and spoken. You may need to give presentations not only inside your company but also to prospective clients for your company. You need to have the skills to prepare written materials and make a presentation that represents your company. For example, your company may be bidding to contract a networking project for a firm. During the process of meeting with the firm, a single person or a team representing your company will need to make a presentation to attempt to gain the firm's business. If you plan to be a part of the team, you will need the very best communication skills. A technician who knows the technology and who can communicate well is always in demand, **Figure 21-4.**

There is a direct correlation between salary and education level. Research proves that as your education level increases, so does your salary level. While the direct correlation indicates college as a major factor, additional certifications are also a direct influence. An ideal situation for a person planning a future in the IT industry is to combine technology education with another field of study such as business administration, finance, mathematics, science, electronics, medical, law enforcement, or any other field of interest. A combination of degrees greatly increases a person's employability.

Many community colleges offer courses and programs in the network technology field. You can take specific courses to learn more about a particular subject without going for a degree. Alternative pathways, such as military training, are also available to gain a particular skill. The military offers many specialized areas of study in the networking and computer technology fields. The opportunities for education and for gaining valuable work experiences are excellent in the military.

As an IT professional, you will be learning the rest of your life. The total knowledgebase related to the computer industry is never ending. Part of what you know now may be obsolete in just a few months. If you did not learn another thing from this point forward, many of your skills would be obsolete within a year or two.

Figure 21-4. Strong communication skills are a plus. In the networking field you may be required to present a product or a system plan to a group of clients. The ability to communicate technical information to those without your expertise is crucial.

Certification

Certification is a way to advance your knowledge and career in the IT industry. Many companies require certifications prior to hiring. Certification combined with work experience can prove your abilities to an employer. It can also advance your career inside a company and provide you with job security.

Obtaining your CompTIA Network+ and A+ Certification should just be the beginning for you. Once you have obtained these certifications, you should immediately start advancing toward other CompTIA certifications, such as Security+. You may also wish to start in an area of specialization, such as network administration, and obtain the Microsoft Certified Technical Specialist (MCTS).

Novell, Microsoft, Cisco Systems, and many other companies offer certification exams in many advanced fields of study. One of the most demanding certifications offered by Microsoft is the Microsoft Certified Information Technology Professional (MCITP). Training preparation for this certification can be delivered in many ways such as private schools, public schools, special seminars, online educational programs, and self-study. The main point is you must pass a series of exams to prove your knowledge and competency before you receive the certification. Let's look at some of these certifications.

CompTIA Certifications

The CompTIA organization offers certification in many areas. Receiving a CompTIA A+ and Network+ Certification is just the beginning. Some advanced CompTIA certifications that you may elect to pursue are Linux+, Server+, and PDI+.

A+ Certification a CompTIA certification that proves a person's knowledge related to PC support and repair.

A+

The ***A+ Certification*** is designed to test a person's knowledge related to PC support and repair. This certification requires passing two separate exams. The exams cover a broad range of topics as related to computers.

Over the years, the format of the test has changed. For example, for the original CompTIA A+ Certification, one exam covered hardware and another exam covered software. Later, the format was changed so that the first exam covered general knowledge as related to the PC, and the second exam matched an area of expertise, such as PC support technician, network support technician, or hardware support and repair. Currently, the 2009 A+ Certification consists of two similar exams. The main differences between these two exams are that one exam covers basic networking skills and knowledge related to specific operating systems, and the other requires more advanced skills such as using the command prompt for troubleshooting.

CompTIA revises the A+ Certification Examination Objectives approximately every three years or sooner to keep pace with the rapidly changing field of PC repair. Minor changes in the test objectives can occur at any time between major revisions. Always check the CompTIA Web site for the very latest information about the A+ Certification Examination Objectives.

Network+ Certification a CompTIA certification that measures the skills necessary for an entry-level network support technician.

Security+ Certification a CompTIA certification that measures a person's knowledge related to generally accepted security practices.

Server+ Certification a CompTIA certification that measures a person's knowledge of network server hardware and software, such as installing, configuring, diagnosing, and troubleshooting network server hardware and network operating systems.

Network+

The ***Network+ Certification*** measures the skills necessary for an entry-level network support technician. The typical Network+ candidate should have the A+ Certification or equivalent knowledge. It is also recommended that the candidate have at least nine months of network experience before attempting the exam. The exam is vender-neutral and is recognized by leading network organizations such as Novell, Cisco, and HP as part of their certification process. It is an excellent starting point for students interested in further certification in the networking technology areas.

Security+

The ***Security+ Certification*** requires knowledge related to generally accepted security practices. Some of the areas covered are network infrastructure, cryptography, access control, malware, and wireless security. As with all the other CompTIA certifications, the exam is vendor-neutral. The Security+ Certification is an excellent choice for the next certificate after achieving the Network+ Certification. CompTIA recommends, but does not require, that the Security+ candidate have two years of experience and Network+ Certification.

Note

CompTIA A+, Network+, and Security+ Certifications obtained before January 1, 2011 are valid for a lifetime. Certifications obtained in these areas starting January 1, 2011 are valid for three years from the date the candidate was certified.

Linux+ Certification a CompTIA certification that measures a person's knowledge of the Linux operating system, such as installing, configuring, administering, and troubleshooting the Linux operating system for a single PC and a network server.

Server+

The ***Server+ Certification*** tests a person's knowledge of network server hardware and software. The candidate is tested on installing, configuring, diagnosing, and troubleshooting network server hardware and network operating systems. The exam requires an in-depth knowledge of protocols, backup system standards, and system security.

Linux+

The ***Linux+ Certification*** tests a person's knowledge of the Linux operating system. It covers installing, configuring, administering, and troubleshooting the Linux operating system for a single PC and a network server.

PDI+

PDI+ Certification a CompTIA certification that measures a person's ability to configure and repair document imaging devices such as printers, copiers, scanners, fax machines, and multifunctional machines.

The ***PDI+ Certification*** measures the ability to configure and repair document imaging devices such as printers, copiers, scanners, fax machines, and multifunctional machines. The test covers the theory of imaging as related to printing and scanning devices and also knowledge of basic electronics. The electronics required is not in-depth but rather limited to general information about relays, power supplies, diodes, transistors, common ICs, using the multimeter, and electrical safety. Also tested for on the exam is basic knowledge of networking fundamentals limited to simple network configuration and simple sharing. There are no prerequisites for this exam, but CompTIA does recommend that the candidate have some work experience.

Microsoft Certifications

There are many different Microsoft certifications and levels of certifications, which are constantly evolving as new Microsoft products are developed and released. The entire scope of certifications can appear quite complex and confusing at first, but on further examination, you will see that there are only a few exams to actually start with based on which field of expertise you determine to master. The first Microsoft certification you might consider after achieving the CompTIA Network+ Certification is the Microsoft Certified Technical Specialist (MCTS).

Microsoft Certified Technical Specialist (MCTS) Certification a Microsoft certification awarded to an individual who masters a specific Microsoft technology.

MCTS

Microsoft Certified Technical Specialist (MCTS) Certification is awarded to an individual who masters a specific Microsoft technology. A few of the many different MCTS Certification exams are listed in **Figure 21-5.** This is just a partial

Figure 21-5. Some of the MCTS Certification exams offered from Microsoft.

MCTS	Exam	Description
Connected Home Integrator	70-625	This exam was developed by Microsoft for retail support industry employees who are responsible for implementing and configuring Windows Vista computer systems with home automation systems, entertainment systems, and home network systems.
Server 2008 Active Directory Configuration	70-640	This exam is designed for technicians who support medium to large network systems. The test covers technical skills required to support Active Directory such as server configuration, infrastructure, configuring forest and domains, DNS, server roles, and much more.
Server Visualization Configuration	70-652	This exam covers installing, configuring, and optimizing Hyper-V, which is Microsoft's virtualization software application.
Windows 7 Configuration	70-680	This exam covers installing, upgrading, and migrating Windows 7. The candidate is also tested on his or her knowledge of security, networking, hardware and software configuration, and mobile systems.
SQL Server 2008 Implementation and Maintenance	70-432	This exam covers installing, configuring, maintaining, and troubleshooting Microsoft SQL server.

listing of the more than 50 exam areas. Each of the Microsoft Office products, Web development software, and programming software has corresponding certification exams as well.

Two of the original Microsoft network certifications were the Microsoft Certified Systems Engineer (MCSE) and the Microsoft Certified System Administrator (MCSA). Both are still honored, but they will most likely be phased out over time. The certifications are based on Window 2000 Server and Windows Server 2003 operating systems. The MCSE and MCSA can no longer be earned. At the time of this writing, you can still renew these certifications by taking a combination of other related exams. The original certifications were good for three years and then required an update test. Microsoft now states that individual certifications will remain valid until the related technology is phased out.

MCITP

The next advanced certification is the ***Microsoft Certified Information Technology Professional (MCITP) Certification***, which typically requires passing two or more individual exams in a specific Microsoft technology. For example, you can earn an MCITP for the Windows 7 client called the *Enterprise Desktop Support Technician 7*. This area of certification consists of passing two separate exams: Windows 7, Configuring (70-680) and the Windows 7, Enterprise Desktop Support Technician (70-685). Earning the MCTS Certification is a prerequisite for earning the MCITP Certification.

Microsoft Certified Information Technology Professional (MCITP) Certification
a Microsoft certification that requires passing two or more Microsoft exams in a specific Microsoft technology.

MOS and MCAS

The ***Microsoft Office Specialist (MOS) Certification*** is based on Microsoft Office 2000, 2002, and 2003 products. Today, this certification area is based on Microsoft Office 2007 and is referred to as ***Microsoft Certified Application Specialist (MCAS) Certification.*** Some of the areas offered for certification are Microsoft Word, Excel, PowerPoint, Outlook, and Access. The contents of the certification exams are based on a particular release version of the Microsoft Office product. For example, there are several versions of Microsoft Word Certification exams, each based on the release date of the particular Microsoft Office product such as 2003 and 2007.

To learn more about the various Microsoft certifications, visit the Microsoft Learning Web site located at www.microsoft.com/learning/en/us/default.aspx. You can also locate this Web site by conducting an Internet search using the key terms "Microsoft certification learning."

Microsoft Office Specialist (MOS) Certification
a Microsoft certification based on Microsoft Office 2000, 2002, and 2003 products.

Microsoft Certified Application Specialist (MCAS) Certification
a Microsoft certification based on Microsoft Office 2007 and the Windows Vista operating system.

Novell Certifications

The original Novell certifications were based on the Novell NetWare operating system. The Novell NetWare operating system has been replaced by Open Enterprise Server 2, which allows NetWare to run on open source virtualization software called Xen Hypervisor. As a result, the original certifications have been either replaced by Linux versions of certifications, or they are in a state of transition from Novell NetWare certifications to Novell Linux certifications. In some cases, the original certification holders were allowed to upgrade their original NetWare certificates to Novell SUSE Linux versions by taking an upgrade certification test.

Novell now provides a variety of certifications based on Novell SUSE Linux. Some of the certifications only require a written test, but many require a practicum. A ***practicum*** or ***practical exam*** is a hands-on performance test that must be taken at an authorized testing center. The candidate is required to perform many different

practicum
a hands-on performance test. Also called a *practical exam*.

tasks based on a set of test objectives to prove his or her competency. Some of the most common Novell certifications at the present time are CLP, CLE, CLA, and CLDA.

CNE

The original ***Certified Novell Engineer (CNE) Certification*** still exists at the time of this writing, but it is being phased out and replaced by the Novell Certified Engineer Enterprise Services (NCE ES) certification. The original certification was based on the Novell NetWare operating system. The new certification is based on Novell Open Enterprise Server 2.

Certified Novell Engineer (CNE) Certification a Novell certification based on the Novell NetWare operating system.

Novell CLP

The ***Novell Certified Linux Professional (CLP) Certification*** is designed to prove a person has mastered the basic skills required to manage and maintain a Novell SUSE Linux Enterprise server. The skills measured are installing a Novell SUSE Linux Enterprise server, managing users and groups, troubleshooting the Novell SUSE Linux file system, and managing and compiling the Linux kernel. The CLP covers three training areas: SUSE Linux Enterprise Server fundamentals, SUSE Linux Enterprise Server administration, and SUSE Linux Enterprise Server advanced administration. The certification is based on passing a practicum that measures the skills reflected in these three training areas.

Novell Certified Linux Professional (CLP) Certification a Novell certification that proves a person has mastered the basic skills required to manage and maintain a Novell SUSE Linux server.

Novell CLE

The ***Novell Certified Linux Engineer (CLE) Certification*** is the next logical certification to pursue after achieving the Novell CLP. The Novell CLE Certification verifies expertise in Linux and Novell services that run on a SUSE Linux Enterprise Server system. A broad background in Linux administration is recommended before attempting the examination. This certification also requires a practicum rather than a written exam to prove competency. To see a complete listing of available courses and test objectives, visit the Novell Web site (www.novell.com).

Novell Certified Linux Engineer (CLE) Certification a Novell certification that verifies expertise in both Linux and Novell services that run on a Linux system. It is the next logical certification to pursue after achieving the CLP.

Novell CLA

The ***Novell Certified Linux Administrator (CLA) Certification*** is based on administrating a SUSE Linux Enterprise Server network. The candidate is tested on installation, configuration, and troubleshooting.

Note

Novell SUSE Linux certifications are classified by Linux version. For example, CLA11 means that the certification is based on SUSE Linux Enterprise Server version 11.

Novell Certified Linux Administrator (CLA) Certification a Novell certification based on administrating a Novell SUSE Linux Enterprise Server network system. The candidate is tested on installation, configuration, and troubleshooting.

CLDA

Certified Linux Desktop Administrator (CLDA) Certification is designed to prove expertise in SUSE Linux Enterprise Desktop installation, configuration, and management. This certification requires a single, written exam rather than a practicum. This certification is an excellent starting place before mastering higher Novell certification areas. To learn more about Novell certifications, visit www.novell.com/training/certinfo.

Cisco Certifications and Training

Cisco Corporation provides training opportunities at high schools and colleges all over the world. Cisco training sites are referred to as *academies*. The major emphasis at Cisco academies is network design, implementation, and troubleshooting as related to Cisco products.

The academy courses are designed as a combination of lecture, textbook, online learning, and hands-on laboratory activities. Some of the various certifications that can be earned at the Cisco academies are Cisco Certified Network Associate (CCNA), Cisco Certified Network Professional (CCNP), and Cisco Certified Entry Networking Technician (CCENT). There are also certifications available related to security, wireless devices, VoIP, VPN, and other specializations. The CCENT is one of the latest Cisco certifications and is designed for an entry-level job in networking, similar to the Network+ Certification. The biggest difference is that the Cisco CCENT requires basic knowledge and skills for programming switches and routers. You can locate the Cisco academy nearest you by visiting the Cisco Web site (www.cisco.com).

Certified Linux Desktop Administrator (CLDA) Certification a Novell certification that proves expertise in SUSE Linux Enterprise Desktop installation, configuration, and management. It is a single, written certification exam rather than a practicum.

LPIC

The Linux Professional Institute (LPI) offers certification for Linux through a vendor-neutral exam. Other organizations, such as CompTIA, Red Hat Linux, IBM, HP, Ubuntu, and Novell have started to award Linux Professional Institute Certification (LPIC) credit toward their own certifications. There are three levels of LPI certification exams: LPIC-1, LPIC-2, and LPIC-3. There are two exams each for LPIC-1 and LPIC-2 and one exam for LPIC-3. In the future, the LPIC-3 level is expected to require two exams.

LPIC-1 Certification a Linux Professional Institute certification that measures the basic skills associated with installing, configuring, and managing a Linux operating system. It emphasizes using the command line to configure the operating system.

LPIC-1

LPIC-1 Certification is the introductory level certification. It is designed to measure basic skills associated with installing, configuring, and managing a Linux operating system. Heavy emphasis is on using the command line to configure the operating system rather than the GUI. The LPIC-1 is a prerequisite to LPIC-2. It is also the certification level that is recognized for credit toward most other vendor-specific versions of Linux certification.

LPIC-2 Certification a Linux Professional Institute certification that requires more in-depth knowledge than that for the LPIC-1 exams. It covers basic skills associated with installing and configuring Linux server mail services, proxy server, news server, firewall, and Web server.

LPIC-2

LPIC-2 Certification is the second level of Linux certification and requires a more in-depth knowledge than LPIC-1. Areas of emphasis are small, mixed networks and configuring a Linux Internet gateway and Internet server. The test also covers basic skills associated with installing and configuring Linux server mail services, proxy server, news server, firewall, and Web server. It is a prerequisite to LPIC-3.

LPIC-3

LPIC-3 Certification measures the Linux skill set for supporting a large, enterprise Linux network. Areas of emphasis are mixed environment interoperability, virtualization, mail and messaging, and in-depth security configuration. To learn more about the LPI organization, visit www.lpi.org.

LPIC-3 Certification a Linux Professional Institute certification that measures the Linux skill set for supporting a large enterprise Linux network. Areas of emphasis are mixed environment interoperability, virtualization, mail and messaging, and in-depth security configuration.

Other Certifications

Many other companies have certification programs besides the ones outlined in the previous sections. Some of the companies are 3Com, Nortel Networks, HP, Red Hat, Sun Microsystems, and Oracle. More in-depth information about these certifications, such as exam outlines, study materials, available training, and prerequisites, can be found at the related Web sites. There are over 120 different companies and organizations that offer certifications and over 300 different types of certifications you may earn.

As you see, many different certifications are available for network technicians and IT professionals. You can customize your credentials by selecting different areas of certification similar to the way a university student selects classes for credit toward a degree. In fact, a collection of certifications is similar to a university degree.

After finishing this course, it is suggested that you select a field of specialization. This is the time to begin training for a specialized certification. Some of the most common areas are Microsoft, Novell, and Cisco. These three areas have shown the most interest of students at the entry level of training. You may wish to seek employment before beginning your next level of training or train concurrently while employed. Going to school while employed is an excellent method to reinforce what you are learning in the classroom. Remember, there is a direct correlation between knowledge and earnings. The more you know, the more you will earn.

The IT industry demands continuing education of its workforce. If you choose to join the IT workforce, be prepared for a lifetime of study, **Figure 21-6.** New systems, protocols, software, and hardware are constantly introduced. Often, these new systems demand new expertise to install, service, and repair. You can continue your education in a number of ways, such as attending college classes, seminars, online courses, and self-study.

You may choose to not pursue other certifications. This decision is acceptable, as long as you keep your skills up-to-date. You should subscribe to and read professional journals and newsletters in your area of work. Take as many courses as you possibly can, such as digital electronics, to enhance your networking and computer skills. If you are not willing to continuously hone your skills, then you should choose another, less demanding field of employment.

Employment

The three most important factors that will determine your ability to secure a position with an employer are your job history, technical expertise, and the job interview. A job history tells the employer a lot about your future as an employee, even if your job experiences are unrelated to the job for which you are applying. You may be just entering the IT profession. A solid recommendation from a past employer can make the difference. For example, if an applicant that has worked part-time while going to school for the last two years and a recommendation

Figure 21-6. To keep up with the continuously changing field of computer and networking technology requires constant study. Some of the ways you can continue your education include attending college classes and seminars, taking online courses, and self-study.

from the applicant's past employer shows a proven record of dependability, this applicant will have a great advantage. A person with no work experience leaves this aspect unknown.

Your training and work experiences show your technical expertise. If you have prior technical experiences, this can prove to be a real asset. Another applicant may have no technical employment history or any technical training. They may have simple, informal experience with a computer at home or have helped friends, and now they believe they can handle the job. This is where your training, experience, and especially your certification will put you ahead of the others.

Job Search Ideas

Finding a job can be a time-consuming and difficult task. The Internet has the most up-to-date information regarding job searches, **Figure 21-7.** Almost every computer-related site has a section devoted to career opportunities. You can often complete an application online. There are also many Web sites that will allow you to post a résumé.

The *Occupational Outlook Handbook* also has tips for conducting a job search. Start by talking to your parents, neighbors, teachers, or guidance counselors. These people may know of job openings that have not been advertised. Read the classified advertisements in the newspaper, especially in the Sunday editions. Look through the *Yellow Pages* to generate a list of local companies and their addresses and phone numbers. Companies are grouped according to industry in the Yellow Pages. City, county, or state employment services may provide useful job leads. Private employment agencies might also provide leads, but they often charge a fee for a job placement.

Preparing a Résumé

On your résumé, list all education and training you have had, in sequence. List all past employment in sequence, and do not leave gaps in your employment history. If you stopped your employment to go to school, note that in your employment history. This makes sure your potential employer does not think you are leaving out an employer who may not give you a good reference. List any reason there may be a

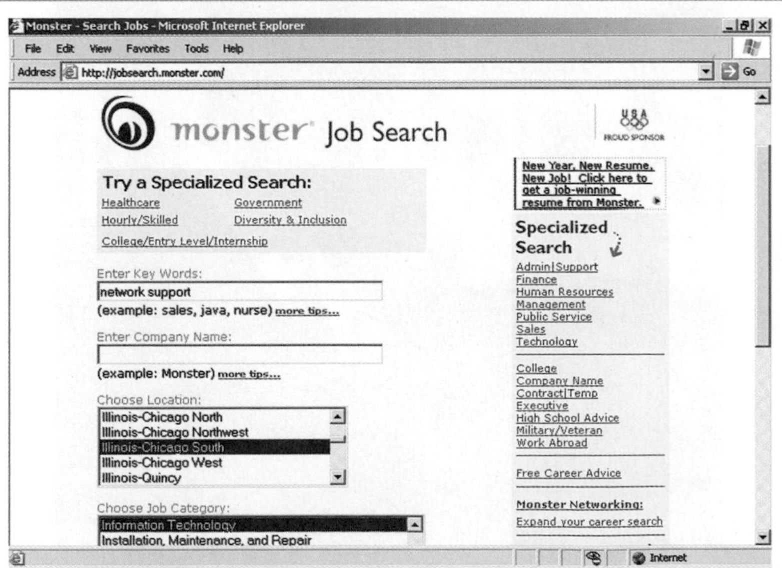

Figure 21-7.
The Internet is a great place to conduct a job search. Many sites have search engines that allow you to enter a key word, job category, and location.

break in employment. Additional material that is optional as a part of your résumé can include copies of certifications, transcripts, or letters of reference. Typically, these will be verified if listed on your résumé. However, you should not include more than a few. Employers do not appreciate lengthy résumés.

A quality résumé can make a great impression on an employer. Use a good-quality paper and a cover sheet. Make sure you have produced a good-quality copy that they may keep. Never give a potential employer a poor-quality copy.

Preparing for the Interview

Always learn about the company or prospective employer before your interview. Many times, this information is available on the company's Web site. This preparation lets the employer know you are truly interested in the company and that you possess the personal initiative to research and learn.

Have a specific job or jobs in mind, generally at an entry level. Most companies do not begin a new employee in a high-level job until the new employee has proven his or herself to the company. Remember, in the networking field, you will have access to the highest level of company security. A trustworthy employee is critical.

Review your qualifications for the job. Make sure your qualifications match those desired by the employer. Do not waste the employer's time or yours by interviewing for a job that is far beyond your level. If you are an entry-level technician, do not apply for a job as a network administrator.

Prepare to answer broad questions about yourself. It is wise to practice interviewing with someone who has knowledge about job interviews. A family member or friend who regularly does hiring for a company can be a great help, even if the hiring they do is not related to the field you are seeking. Practicing the interview will help you learn to control your natural nervousness.

Arrive at least 15 minutes prior to the scheduled time of your interview, **Figure 21-8.** Showing up late for your interview does not enhance your prospects for the job. It displays a lack of care for the job, the company, and the interviewer. Locate the building in advance. Make a practice run so that you will know exactly

Figure 21-8.
Always arrive fifteen minutes early for your interview. To predict how long it will take you to arrive at the interview site, make a practice run a day or two before. Be sure to take into consideration traffic conditions for the time of day in which your interview is scheduled.

how to get to the interview and how long it will take to get there. Consider the traffic conditions for that time of day. If you really want that job interview, have a backup plan in case you have difficulty with your transportation.

Personal Appearance at the Interview

Additionally, you should pay close attention to your physical appearance during a job interview. While some IT jobs allow a casual appearance, most employers require a more professional appearance. This is because technicians and administrators often interact with professionals within the company. Neat, clean, and professional appearance shows that you take pride in yourself and in your work. Even if the job is a backroom position, always dress appropriately for the interview. Blue jeans and a T-shirt are never appropriate.

Regardless of the job conditions, men and women should always dress up rather than down for an interview. This does not mean that you should dress for a party. Rather, you should dress for a formal business setting. Men should always wear a tie and a long-sleeved shirt at minimum. If you wear a suit or jacket, make sure it matches and fits properly. Women should always wear a suit or business dress.

Smile and use a firm handshake when you introduce yourself, **Figure 21-9.** This shows your confidence. Do not chew gum, eat candy, or smoke at any time when you are on the company premises. This is not a social visit. You may encounter your prospective supervisor on the premises prior to your interview.

Information to Bring to an Interview

The common information required at an interview is social security number, driver's license number, and a copy of your résumé. It is customary to provide references for a job. The quality of your references can mean a great deal to the employer. Some good references are teachers, past employers, supervisors, and fellow employees. Your immediate past employer will be required as a reference. Friends, family, and clergy are not considered good references. Get permission from people before using them as a reference. For each reference, provide a name, address, telephone number, and occupation. Also, note if the person was a past supervisor. You will need this information to complete a job application, which is typically required by the company's personnel office.

Job applications vary in appearance but are designed to gather the same basic information. Besides routine information, such as your name, address, telephone number, and social security number, the application typically requires

Figure 21-9. A neat appearance, good posture, and a firm handshake demonstrate self-confidence.

information about your references and work experiences. It will also ask about police records or any crimes for which you may have been convicted. The application may ask you to write a short summary of why you want the position.

Whenever you fill out the job application, do your best to make it legible to the reader, **Figure 21-10.** If the job application is not legible, it will often not be reviewed very thoroughly. In fact, some personnel offices will not even consider an application that is barely legible.

The Job Interview

The major factor that determines your employment is the job interview. The job interview gives the employer a chance to assess the applicant both physically and mentally with a series of questions. The way a question is answered is at times more important than the answer itself. For example, if an employer asks: "What would you do if you could not fix a networking problem?" The way you answer that question may tell the employer about your character, your confidence, and your ability to work with others. The employer is looking for certain traits in the individual the company is about to hire. Some common traits are honesty, confidence, dependability, and the ability to work well as a team member.

Employers many not ask the same questions for all applicants and will usually not be direct about the qualities they are seeking. The employer will ask questions to probe for the character and job-related qualities the company wants. For example, an employer may ask you to describe a time you had a problem with a fellow employee and how it was resolved. The answer to this question can tell an experienced interviewer a lot about the character of the applicant.

Once you have secured an interview, it is important to be prepared for it. Read the following tips for a successful interview:

- *Answer all questions to the best of your ability.* If you do not know the answer, simply say so. Do *not* try to devise an answer. Express your willingness to learn any new topics with which you may not be familiar. The person conducting the interview is an expert. You will not fool them by trying to invent an answer, and you will find they will most likely respect your honesty.
- *Use proper English and avoid slang.*
- *Speak slowly and concisely.*

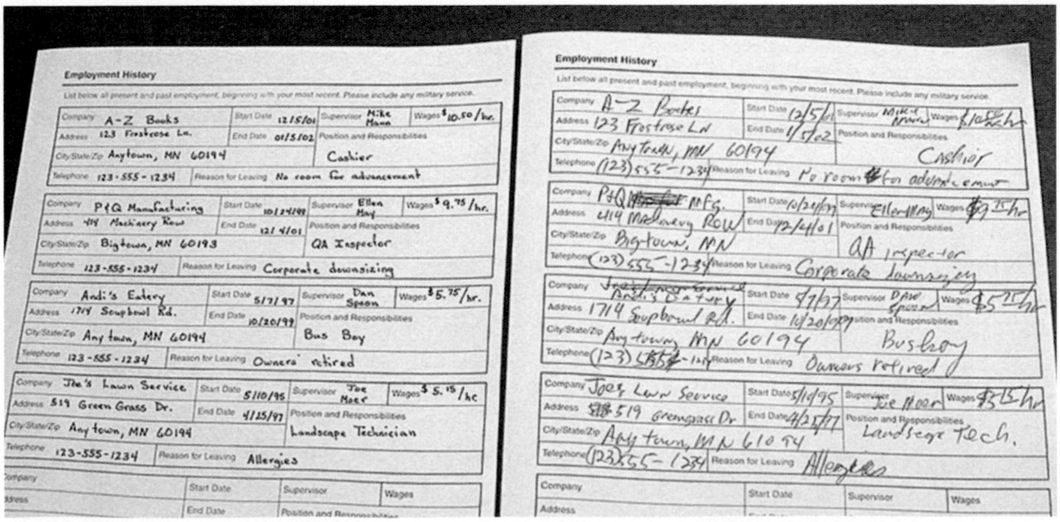

Figure 21-10. Write neatly (application on the left) when filling out employment applications or taking tests. Poor penmanship (application on the right) can make a bad impression on a prospective employer.

- *Use good manners.* Always address the persons who are conducting the interview as "Sir" and "Ma'am." Even if you are personally acquainted with your prospective employer, treat the employer as if he or she is a total stranger. Do *not* become complacent or presume you have the job, and never use foul language, even in a joking manner.
- *Convey a sense of cooperation and enthusiasm.* Your body language will convey a lot about your personality. Keep smiling.
- *Remember that the interview has not ended when you start asking questions.* As a matter of fact, your questions can reveal even more to the employer. Asking about how many breaks you will get during a day will send an undesirable message to the employer. It is not necessary to ask questions, especially if the interview has been thorough. However, do not hesitate if you believe there is pertinent information you must know. You may ask questions about the position and the organization, but limit your questions to operation conditions, which you do not understand. Many issues regarding a job can be obtained prior to the interview, especially if the information was posted.
- *Do not ask questions regarding salary unless it has not been covered in a job posting, uncovered through your research, or discussed by your prospective employer during the interview.* Remember, if you are offered the job, there will be additional time at that point to make any clarifications or salary negotiations that you believe are necessary.

Testing at the Interview

Employer testing is a common part of the job interview process. An employer can tell a lot about your technical knowledge and communication skills through a test, especially if written responses are required. Written responses reveal a lot about an interviewee. When taking a test, be sure you understand all test directions. Verbally confirm them if you have questions before you begin. The following guidelines will improve your testing success:

- Read each question carefully.
- Write legibly and clearly. If your handwriting is poor, print instead.
- Budget your time wisely. Don't dwell on one question.

Summary

- An entrepreneur owns and operates a business.
- There is a direct correlation between the amount of education for a specific field and salary.
- An information technology (IT) position requires continuous education.
- Recognized commercial certifications are a way of proving your expertise in most computer technology specialties, including networking.
- After gaining A+ Certification, Network+ Certification is a good, next step in your career advancement.
- CompTIA offers A+, Network+, Server+, Linux+, PDI+, and many more certifications.
- The Linux Professional Institute (LPI) offers vendor-neutral Linux certifications.
- Microsoft, Novell, Cisco, and many other companies offer certifications based on exams regarding their respective operating systems and hardware.

- You must continually update your knowledge and skills to remain vital to the IT industry.
- When you are interviewing for a new job, be sure to take your social security card, driver's license, and a good-quality copy of your résumé.
- Be able to produce a list of at least three references, including addresses and phone numbers. Make sure you obtain permission to use associates as references.
- Be on time or 15 minutes early for your interview.
- Smile and show a sense of cooperation and enthusiasm when interviewed.
- If tested by the prospective employer, be sure you understand the instructions for the test.

Review Questions

Answer the following questions on a separate sheet of paper. Please do not write in this book.

1. What is an entrepreneur?
2. Where can objective data be accessed for labor statistical information in the USA?
3. What is the correlation between education and salaries?
4. What certification would you like to achieve next?
5. Why is continuing education required for an employee in the IT industry?
6. What items should you bring to a job interview?
7. What is needed concerning your references?

Suggested Laboratory Activities

1. Research a possible certification you wish to obtain. List the approximate amount of time required to prepare for the certification. Find out the cost of the exam(s). Download a list of the knowledge areas, or objectives, required for the certification. Identify the type of job associated with the certification.
2. Research college degree IT programs. List the classes required for the degree. Identify and describe the type of job associated with the degree. What is the total cost of earning the degree, credit hour cost, and approximate textbook costs? What will the approximate cost be to support yourself during the period of time you are in school? This cost includes rent, utilities, food, clothing, transportation, and miscellaneous expenses.
3. Prepare a résumé.
4. Use the Internet to locate three different job descriptions for each of the following jobs. Make a composite of job skills required for each.
   - Web master.
   - Network administrator.
   - Network support specialist.
   - Help desk technician.

Interesting Web Sites for More Information

www.giac.org/certifications/roadmap.php
www.isc2.org
www.lpi.org
www.mcmcse.com/othercerts.shtml
www.novell.com/training/certinfo

Appendix A

List of Networking Acronyms

A

AAA	Authentication, Authorization, and Accounting
ABR	Available Bit Rate
ACL	access control list
ACPI	Automatic Configuration and Power Interface
ACPICA	ACPI Component Architecture
AD	Active Directory
ADC	Analog-to-Digital Converter
ADF	Automatic Document Feeder
ADSL	Asymmetric Digital Subscriber Line
AEP	American Electric Power
AES	Advanced Encryption Standard
AFP	AppleTalk Filing Protocol
AH	Authentication Header
AM	Amplitude Modulation
AMI	Alternate Mark Inversion
ANSI	American National Standards Institute
APIPA	Automatic Private IP Addressing
ARIN	American Registry for Internet Numbers
ARP	Address Resolution Protocol
ASCII	American Standard Code for Information Interchange
ASP	Application Service Provider
ATM	Asynchronous Transfer Mode
ATX	Alien Crosstalk
Auto-MDIX	Automatic Medium-Dependent Interface Crossover
AWG	American Wire Gauge

B

BAP	Bandwidth Allocation Protocol
BCD	Binary Coded Decimal
BDF	Building Distribution Frame
BERT	Bit-Error Rate Test
BGP	Border Gateway Protocol
B-ISDN	Broadband ISDN
BNC	British Naval Connector or Bayonet Neill-Concelman
BOOTP	Bootstrap Protocol
BPDU	Bridge Protocol Data Unit
BRI-ISDN	Basic Rate ISDN
BSS	Basic Service Set

C

CA	Certificate Authority
CBR	Constant Bit Rate
CDP	Cisco Discovery Protocol
CERN	*Centre European pour la Recherche Nucléaire*

CHAP	Challenge Handshake Authentication Protocol
CIDR	Classless Internet-Domain Routing
CIR	Committed Information Rate
CLA	Certified Linux Administrator
CLDA	Certified Linux Desktop Administrator
CLE	Certified Linux Engineer
CLP	Certified Linux Professional
CNAME	Canonical Name
CNE	Certified Novell Engineer
CP	Consolidation Point
CRAM-MDS	Challenge-Response Authentication Mechanism-Message Digest 5
CRC	Cyclic Redundancy Check
CSMA/CA	Carrier Sense Multiple Access with Collision Avoidance
CSMA/CD	Carrier Sense Multiple Access with Collision Detection
CSS	cascading style sheets
CSU	Channel Service Unit
CSU/DSU	Channel Service Unit/Data Service Unit
CUPS	Common UNIX Printing System

D

DAC	Digital-to-Analog Converter
dB	decibel
DDos	Distributed Denial of Service
DHCP	Dynamic Host Configuration Protocol
DLC	Data Link Control
DMA	Direct Memory Access
DMZ	demilitarized zone
DNS	Domain Name System *or* Domain Name Service
DOCSIS	Data-Over-Cable Service Interface Specification
DoS	Denial of Service
DSL	Digital Subscriber Line
DSU	Data Service Unit
DWDM	Dense Wavelength Division Multiplexing

E

E1	E-Carrier Level 1
EAP	Extensible Authentication Protocol
EBCDIC	Extended Binary Coded Decimal Interchange Code
EGP	Exterior Gateway Protocol
EIA	Electronic Industry Association
EIGRP	Enhanced Interior Gateway Routing Protocol
ELFEXT	Equal Level Far-End Crosstalk
EMI	Electromagnetic Interference
ESD	Electrostatic Discharge
ESP	Encapsulated Security Packets
ESSID	Extended Service Set Identifier

F

FDDI	Fiber Distributed Data Interface
FDM	Frequency Division Multiplexing
FEXT	Far-End Crosstalk
FHSS	Frequency Hopping Spread Spectrum
FIR	Fast Infrared
FLSM	Fixed Length Subnet Mask
FM	Frequency Modulation
FQDN	Fully Qualified Domain Name
FTP	File Transfer Protocol

G

GBIC	Gigabit Interface Converter
Gbps	gigabits per second
GUI	graphical user interface
GUID	globally unique identifier

H

HAL	hardware abstract layer
HDLC	High-Level Data Link Control
HIPAA	Health Insurance Portability and Accountability Act
HSRP	Hot Standby Router Protocol
HTML	Hypertext Markup Language
HTTP	Hypertext Transfer Protocol
HTTPS	Hypertext Transfer Protocol Secure
Hz	hertz

I

IANA	Internet Assigned Numbers Authority
IBSS	Independent Basic Service Set
ICA	Independent Computer Architecture
ICANN	Internet Corporation for Assigned Names and Numbers
ICMP	Internet Control Message Protocol
ICS	Internet Connection Sharing
IDC	insulation-displacement connector
IDF	Intermediate Distribution Frame
IDS	Intrusion Detection System
IEEE	Institute of Electrical and Electronic Engineers
IGMP	Internet Group Management Protocol
IGP	Interior Gateway Protocol
IGRP	Interior Gateway Routing Protocol
IIS	Internet Information Services
IKE	Internet Key Exchange
IMAP	Internet Message Access Protocol
InterNIC	Integrated Network Information Center
IP	Internet Protocol
IPP	Internet Printing Protocol
IPS	Intrusion Prevention System
IPSec	Internet Protocol Security
IT	Information Technology
IPv4	Internet Protocol version 4
IPv6	Internet Protocol version 6
IPX	Internetwork Packet Exchange
IRQ	interrupt request
ISATAP	Intra-Site Automatic Tunneling Address Protocol
iSCSI	Internet Small Computer System Interface
ISDN	Integrated Services Digital Network
IS-IS	Intermediate System to Intermediate System
ISO	International Organization for Standardization
ISP	Internet Service Provider
ITU	International Telecommunications Union

K

Kbps	kilobits per second

L

L2F	Layer 2 Forwarding
L2TP	Layer 2 Tunneling Protocol
LACP	Link Aggregation Control Protocol
LAN	local area network
LC	Local Connector
LDAP	Lightweight Directory Access Protocol
LDM	Logical Disk Manager
LEAP	Lightweight Extensible Authentication Protocol
LEC	Local Exchange Carrier
LED	Light Emitting Diode
LLC	Logical Link Control

LLDP	Link-Layer Discovery Protocol
LLDP-MED	Link-Layer Discovery Protocol–Media Endpoint Discovery
LLMNR	Link-Local Multicast Name Resolution
LLTD	Link-Layer Topology Discovery
LPR	Line Printer Request
LUN	logical unit number

M

MAC	Media Access Control
MAN	metropolitan area network
MAU	multistation access unit
Mbps	megabits per second
MBR	master boot record
MCAS	Microsoft Certified Application Specialist
MCITP	Microsoft Certified Information Technology Professional
MCTS	Microsoft Certified Technical Specialist
MDF	Main Distribution Frame
MDI	Media Dependent Interface
MDIX	Media Dependent Interface Crossover
MIB	Management Information Base
MIME	Multipurpose Internet Mail Extensions
MIMO	Multiple Input Multiple Output
MITM	man in the middle
MLPPP	Multilink Point-to-Point Protocol
MMF	multimode fiber
MOS	Microsoft Office Specialist
MPEG	Moving Picture Experts Group
MPLS	Multi-Protocol Label Switching
MS-CHAP	Microsoft Challenge Handshake Authentication Protocol
MSR	Microsoft Reserved
MT-RJ	Mechanical Transfer-Registered Jack
MUTOA	Multi-User Telecommunication Outlet Assembly
MX	Mail Exchanger

N

NAA	Network Address Authority
NAC	Network Access Control
NAS	network attached storage
NAT	Network Address Translation
NBNS	NetBIOS Name Server
NCP	Network Control Protocol
NetBEUI	Network Basic Input/Output Extended User Interface
NetBIOS	Network Basic Input/Output System
NEXT	Near-End Crosstalk
NFS	Network File System
NIC	network interface card
NID	Network Interface Device
nm	nanometer
NNTP	Network News Transfer Protocol
NOS	network operating system
NRZ	Non-Return to Zero
NTFS	New Technology File System
NTP	Network Time Protocol
NWLINK	Microsoft IPX/SPX Protocol

O

OCx	Optical Carrier
OFDM	orthogonal frequency-division multiplexing
ONT	Optical Network Terminal
OS	operating system
OSI	Open Systems Interconnection
OSPF	Open Shortest Path First

OTDR	Optical Time Domain Reflectometer

P

PAN	Personal Area Network
PAP	Password Authentication Protocol
PAT	Port Address Translation
PC	Personal Computer
PCI DSS	Payment Card Industry Data Security Standard
PEAP	Protected Extensible Authentication Protocol
PKI	Public Key Infrastructure
PoE	Power over Ethernet
PoP	Point of Presence
POP	Post Office Protocol
POST	power-on self-test
POTS	Plain Old Telephone System
PPP	Point-to-Point Protocol
PPPoE	Point-to-Point Protocol over Ethernet
PPTP	Point-to-Point Tunneling Protocol
PRI-ISDN	Primary Rate ISDN
PSTN	Public Switched Telephone Network
PVC	permanent virtual circuit

Q

QoS	Quality of Service

R

RADIUS	Remote Authentication Dial-In User Service
RAID	Redundant Array of Independent Disks
RARP	Reverse Address Resolution Protocol
RDP	Remote Desktop Protocol
RFC	Request For Comments
RFI	Radio Frequency Interface
RG	Radio Guide
RIP	Router Information Protocol
RIPng	RIP next generation
RJ	Registered Jack
RSA	Rivest, Shamir, Adelman
RSH	Remote Shell
RTP	Real-time Transport Protocol

S

SAN	storage area network
SAP	Service Access Point
SAS	serial attached SCSI
SC	Standard Connector/Subscriber Connector
SCP	Secure Copy Protocol
SCSI	Small Computer Systems Interface
SDSL	Symmetrical Digital Subscriber Line
SFTP	Secure File Transfer Protocol
SGML	Standard Generalized Markup Language
S-HTTP	Secure HTTP
SIP	Session Initiation Protocol
SLIP	Serial Line Internet Protocol
SMB	Server Message Block
SMF	Single Mode Fiber
SMTP	Simple Mail Transfer Protocol
SNAT	Static Network Address Translation
SNMP	Simple Network Management Protocol
SOA	Start of Authority
SOAP	Simple Object Access Protocol
SOHO	small-office/home-office
SONET	Synchronous Optical Network

SOX	Sarbanes-Oxley
SPS	Standby Power Supply
SPX	Sequenced Packet Exchange
SSH	Secure Shell
SSID	Service Set Identifier
SSL	Security Sockets Layer
ST	Straight Tip
STP	Spanning Tree Protocol

T

TA	Terminal Adaptor
TACACS	Terminal Access Controller Access-Control System
TACACS+	Terminal Access Controller Access-Control System plus
TCP	Transmission Control Protocol
TCP/IP	Transmission Control Protocol/ Internet Protocol
tcsh	Turbo C shell
TDM	Time Division Muliplexing
TDR	Time Domain Reflectometer
Telco	telephone company
TFTP	Trivial File Transfer Protocol
TIA	Telecommunications Industry Association
TKIP	Temporal Key Integrity Protocol
TLS	Transport Layer Security
TTL	Time to Live

U

UBR	Unspecified Bit Rate
UDP	User Datagram Protocol
UL	Underwriters Laboratories
UNC	Universal Naming Convention
UPS	Uninterruptible Power Supply
URL	Uniform Resource Locator
USB	Universal Serial Bus
UTP	Unshielded Twisted Pair

V

VBR	Variable Bit Rate
VBR-NRT	Variable Bit Rate-Non Real Time
VBR-RT	Variable Bit Rate-Real Time
VDSL	Variable Digital Subscriber Line
VLAN	Virtual Local Area Network
VLSM	Variable Length Subnet Mask
VNC	virtual network connection
VoIP	Voice over IP
VPN	Virtual Private Network
VTP	Virtual Trunking Protocol

W

W3C	World Wide Web Consortium
WAN	wide area network
WAP	Wireless Access Point
WAP	Wireless Application Protocol
WEP	Wired Equivalent Privacy
WINS	Windows Internet Naming Service
WPA	Wi-Fi Protected Access
WPA2	Wi-Fi Protected Access 2
WPAN	Wireless Personal Area Networks
WWW	World Wide Web

X

X.25	CCITT Packet Switching Protocol
XDSL	Extended Digital Subscriber Line
XML	Extensible Markup Language

Z

Zeroconf	Zero Configuration

Appendix B

Binary Math

Binary math accurately represents digital circuitry. In digital electronics, a circuit is either on or off or a voltage condition is high or low. For example, a digital circuit may have two distinct conditions: 5 volts present or 0 volts present.

Binary math uses only two numbers, 1 and 0, to represent an infinite range of numbers. The binary number system accomplishes this in basically the same way the decimal number system does, by placing numbers into discrete, digit positions. The decimal number system fills these digits with values 0 through 9. The first digit position is commonly referred to as the 1s. The maximum value that can be entered here is 9. The second digit position must therefore be the 10s. If the maximum value of 9 is entered in both the 10s position and the ls position, the resulting number is 99. The third position must therefore be the 100s position, and so on. Notice in **Figure B-1** that each of the positions can be expressed as an exponent of the base 10.

Figure B-1.

Digit Positions	1s	10s	100s	1,000s	10,000s	100,000s
Exponent	10^0	10^1	10^2	10^3	10^4	10^5
Range	0–9	10–90	100–900	1,000–9,000	10,000–90,000	100,000–900,000

Note
The Range row indicates the allowed values for each digit position.

Look at the number 2,753. This number includes the following:

2-1000s	2,000
7-100s	700
5-10s	50
3-ls	3
Total	2,753

Add the values together for a total of 2,753.

Binary numbers are expressed in similar fashion. However, instead of each digit position being 10 times greater than the position before it, the value of each position is double that of the position before it. See **Figure B-2.**

Figure B-2.

Digit Positions	1s	2s	4s	8s	16s	32s	64s	128s
Exponent	2^0	2^1	2^2	2^3	2^4	2^5	2^6	2^7
Value	0	2	4	8	16	32	64	128

Look at the binary number 101011000001 and compare it to **Figure B-3.** This number includes the following:

1-2048s	2,048
0-1024s	0
1-512s	512
0-256s	0
1-128s	128
1-64s	64
0-32s	0
0-16s	0
0-8s	0
0-4s	0
0-2s	0
1-1s	1
Total	2,753

Figure B-3.

2048s	1024s	512s	256s	128s	64s	32s	16s	8s	4s	2s	1s
1	0	1	0	1	1	0	0	0	0	0	1

As you can see, 101011000001 is the binary equivalent of 2,753.

To convert a binary number to a decimal number, simply record the decimal value assigned to the position for each position that contains a binary number 1 and then add the decimal numbers together. See **Figure B-4.**

Figure B-4.

32s	16s	8s	4s	2s	1s
1	0	1	1	0	1
32	+	8 +	4	+	1 = 45

When converting a decimal number to a binary number, you simply reverse the previous operation. For example, to convert the decimal number 178 to a binary number, you must divide it by a series of "powers of 2." The "powers of 2" are 1, 2, 4, 8, 16, 32, 64, 128, 256, 512, 1,024, 2,048, and so on.

To convert the decimal number 178 to binary, start by finding the largest "power of 2" that does not exceed 178. The largest "power of 2" value that does not exceed 178 is 128 (2^7). Place a 1 in the binary number position that represents 128. See **Figure B-5.**

Figure B-5.

Powers of 2	128	64	32	16	8	4	2	1
Binary Digit	1							

Subtracting 128 from 178 leaves 50. The number 50 is less than 64 (2^6), the next smaller "power of 2." Therefore, you must insert a 0 in the 64s position, as seen in **Figure B-6.**

Figure B-6.

Powers of 2	128	64	32	16	8	4	2	1
Binary Digit	1	0						

Next, 50 is larger than 32 (2^5), so place a 1 in the 32s position. See **Figure B-7.**

Figure B-7.

Powers of 2	128	64	32	16	8	4	2	1
Binary Digit	1	0	1					

Now, subtract 32 from 50. The difference is 18. The number 18 is larger than 16 (2^4), so place a 1 in the 16s position. See **Figure B-8.**

Figure B-8.

Powers of 2	128	64	32	16	8	4	2	1
Binary Digit	1	0	1	1				

Subtracting 16 from 18 leaves 2. The number 2 is smaller than the next two "powers of 2," 8 (23) and 4 (22). That means the next two positions in the binary number are both 0s. See **Figure B-9.**

Figure B-9.

Powers of 2	128	64	32	16	8	4	2	1
Binary Digit	1	0	1	1	0	0		

The next "power of 2" is 2 (2^1), and the number remaining from the last step is also 2. Therefore, a 1 goes into the 2s position. See **Figure B-10.**

Figure B-10.

Powers of 2	128	64	32	16	8	4	2	1
Binary Digit	1	0	1	1	0	0	1	

There are no decimal numbers remaining, so the 1s position should be filled with 0. The binary equivalent of the decimal number 178 is 10110010, **Figure B-11.**

Figure B-11.

Powers of 2	128	64	32	16	8	4	2	1
Binary Digit	1	0	1	1	0	0	1	0

Appendix C

Number Conversion Table			
Decimal	Binary	Octal	Hexadecimal
0	000000	0	0
1	000001	1	1
2	000010	2	2
3	000011	3	3
4	000100	4	4
5	000101	5	5
6	000110	6	6
7	000111	7	7
8	001000	10	8
9	001001	11	9
10	001010	12	A
11	001011	13	B
12	001100	14	C
13	001101	15	D
14	001110	16	E
15	001111	17	F
16	010000	20	10
17	010001	21	11
18	010010	22	12
19	010011	23	13
20	010100	24	14
21	010101	25	15
22	010110	26	16
23	010111	27	17
24	011000	30	18
25	011001	31	19
26	011010	32	1A
27	011011	33	1B
28	011100	34	1C
29	011101	35	1D
30	011110	36	1E

Number Conversion Table (continued)			
Decimal	Binary	Octal	Hexadecimal
31	011111	37	1F
32	100000	40	20
33	100001	41	21
34	100010	42	22
35	100011	43	23
36	100100	44	24
37	100101	45	25
38	100110	46	26
39	100111	47	27
40	101000	50	28
41	101001	51	29
42	101010	52	2A
43	101011	53	2B
44	101100	54	2C
45	101101	55	2D
46	101110	56	2E
47	101111	57	2F
48	110000	60	30
49	110001	61	31
50	110010	62	32
51	110011	63	33
52	110100	64	34
53	110101	65	35
54	110110	66	36
55	110111	67	37
56	111000	70	38
57	111001	71	39
58	111010	72	3A
59	111011	73	3B
60	111100	74	3C
61	111101	75	3D
62	111110	76	3E
63	111111	77	3F

Appendix D

Table of Standard ASCII Characters			(Continued)		(Continued)	
0	NUL	Null	43	+	86	V
1	SOH	Start of header	44	,	87	W
2	STX	Start of text	45	-	88	X
3	ETX	End of text	46	.	89	Y
4	EOT	End of transmission	47	/	90	Z
5	ENQ	Enquiry	48	0	91	[
6	ACK	Acknowledgment	49	1	92	\
7	BEL	Bell	50	2	93	]
8	BS	Backspace	51	3	94	^
9	HT	Horizontal tab	52	4	95	_
10	LF	Line feed	53	5	96	`
11	VT	Vertical tab	54	6	97	a
12	FF	Form feed	55	7	98	b
13	CR	Carriage return	56	8	99	c
14	SO	Shift out	57	9	100	d
15	SI	Shift in	58	:	101	e
16	DLE	Data link escape	59	;	102	f
17	DC1	Device control 1	60	<	103	g
18	DC2	Device control 2	61	=	104	h
19	DC3	Device control 3	62	>	105	i
20	DC4	Device control 4	63	?	106	j
21	NAK	Negative acknowledgment	64	@	107	k
22	SYN	Synchronous idle	65	A	108	l
23	ETB	End of transmit block	66	B	109	m
24	CAN	Cancel	67	C	110	n
25	EM	End of medium	68	D	111	o
26	SUB	Substitute	69	E	112	p
27	ESC	Escape	70	F	113	q
28	FS	File separator	71	G	114	r
29	GS	Group separator	72	H	115	s
30	RS	Record separator	73	I	116	t
31	US	Unit separator	74	J	117	u
32	SP	Space	75	K	118	v
33	!		76	L	119	w
34	"		77	M	120	x
35	#		78	N	121	y
36	$		79	O	122	z
37	%		80	P	123	{
38	&		81	Q	124	|
39	'		82	R	125	}
40	(		83	S	126	~
41	)		84	T	127	DEL
42	*		85	U		

E

Appendix E

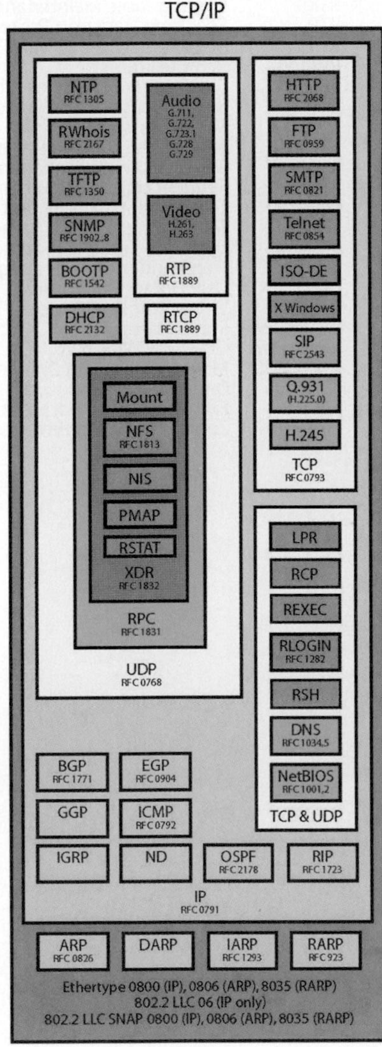

Protocol Family Encapsulations
TCP/IP
ISO
AppleTalk
Novell Netware
Layer 7 Application
Provides standard services to applications and end-user interfaces.
Layer 6 Presentation
Performs data format conversion. Provides compression, encoding, and encryption of data.
Layer 5 Session
Establishes sessions between services. Synchronizes and performs translations for naming services
Layer 4 Transport
Manages connections and provides reliable packet delivery. Operates in units of messages.
Layer 3 Network
Addresses and routes datagrams. Performs fragmentation and reassembly (IP). Operates in units of packets.
Layer 2 Logical Link
Provides hardware addressing and error detection/correction. Operates in units of frames.
Layer 1 Physical
Defines connection, electrical, and wiring specifications. Operates in units of bits.
NTP RFC 1305
RWhois RFC 2167
TFTP RFC 1350
SNMP RFC 1902..8
BOOTP RFC 1542
DHCP RFC 2132
Audio G.711, G.722, G.723.1 G.728 G.729
Video H.261, H.263
RTP RFC 1889
RTCP RFC 1889
Mount
NFS RFC 1813
NIS
PMAP
RSTAT
XDR RFC 1832
RPC RFC 1831
UDP RFC 0768
HTTP RFC 2068
FTP RFC 0959
SMTP RFC 0821
Telnet RFC 0854
ISO-DE
X Windows
SIP RFC 2543
Q.931 (H.225.0)
H.245
TCP RFC 0793
LPR
RCP
REXEC
RLOGIN RFC 1282
RSH
DNS RFC 1034,5
NetBIOS RFC 1001,2
TCP & UDP
BGP RFC 1771
EGP RFC 0904
GGP
ICMP RFC 0792
IGRP
ND
OSPF RFC 2178
RIP RFC 1723
IP RFC 0791
ARP RFC 0826
DARP
IARP RFC 1293
RARP RFC 923
Ethertype 0800 (IP), 0806 (ARP), 8035 (RARP)
802.2 LLC 06 (IP only)
802.2 LLC SNAP 0800 (IP), 0806 (ARP), 8035 (RARP)
FTAM
MMS
ODA
VTP
ASCE
CMIP
X.500 DS
ASCE/ROSE
X.400 MHS
ASCE/ROSE/RTSE
ISO PP
ISO SP
NetBIOS
ISO TP
CLNP/CONS
IS-IS
IDRP
802.2 LLC 14, 20, 34, 54, EC, FE
AARP
ADSP
AURP
TOPS
SoftTalk
ZIP
AEP
AFP
ASP
ZIP
ATP
Postscript
PAP
ATP & NBP
RTMP
DDP
802.2 LLC SNAP
809B (DDP), 80F3 (AARP)
LSP
NDS
NCP
NLP
NWBCAST
NWDIAG
NWSER
WatchDog
SAP
NetBIOS
SPX
SPX II
NLSP
PING
RIP
IPX
Ethertype 8137
Novell "Raw"
802.2 LLC EO
802.2 LLC SNAP 8137
NetBEUI
SMB
NetBEUI
802.2 LLC F0
WildPackets' Products:
Omni
EtherPeek VX
EtherPeek NX
PacketGrabber
AiroPeek NX
RFGrabber
GigaPeek NX
RMONGrabber
WANPeek NX
www.wildpackets.com

AARP	AppleTalk Address Resolution Protocol
ADSP	AppleTalk Data Stream Protocol
AEP	AppleTalk Echo Protocol
AFP	AppleTalk Filing Protocol
ARP	Address Resolution Protocol
ASCE	Association Control Service Element
ASP	AppleTalk Session Protocol
ATP	AppleTalk Transaction Protocol
AURP	AppleTalk Update Routing Protocol
BGP	Border Gateway Protocol
BOOTP	Boot Protocol
CLNP	Connectionless Network Protocol
CMIP	Common Management Information Protocol
CONS	Connection Oriented Network Protocol
DARP	Dynamic Address Resolution Protocol
DDP	Datagram Delivery Protocol
DHCP	Dynamic Host Configuration Protocol
EGP	Exterior Gateway Protocol
FTAM	File Transfer Access and Management
FTP	File Transfer Protocol
GGP	Gateway to Gateway Protocol
HTTP	HyperText Transfer Protocol
IARP	Inverse Address Resolution Protocol
ICMP	Internet Control Message Protocol
IDRP	Interdomain Routing Protocol
IGRP	Interior Gateway Routing Protocol
IP	Internet Protocol
IPX	Internet Packet Exchange
IS-IS	Intermediate System to Intermediate System Routing
ISO PP	Presentation Protocol
ISO SP	Session Protocol
ISO TP	Transport Protocol
ISO-DE	Development Environment
LPR	Remote Print
LSP	NetWare Lite Sideband Protocol
MMS	Manufacturing Message Service
Mount	Mount Server
NBP	Name Binding Protocol
NCP	NetWare Core Protocol
ND	Network Disk
NDS	NetWare Directory Service
NetBEUI	NetBIOS Enhanced User Interface
NetBIOS	Network Basic Input/Output System
NFS	Network File System
NIS	Network Information Services
NLP	NetWare Lite Protocol
NLSP	NetWare Link State Protocol
NTP	Network Time Protocol
NWBCAST	NetWare Broadcast Message Notification
NWDIAG	NetWare Diagnostic Support Protocol
NWSER	NetWare Serialization Protocol
ODA	Office Document Architecture
OSPF	Open Shortest Path First
PAP	Printer Access Protocol
PING	Packet Internet Groper
PMAP	Port Mapper
RARP	Reverse Address Resolution Protocol
RCP	Remote Copy
REXEC	Remote Execution
RIP	Routing Information Protocol
RLOGIN	Remote Login
ROSE	Remote Operations Service Element
RPC	Remote Procedure Call
RSH	Remote Shell
RSTAT	Remote Statistics
RTCP	RTP Control Protocol
RTMP	Routing Table Maintenance Protocol
RTP	Real-time Transport Protocol
RTSE	Reliable Transfer Service Element
RWhois	Remote Whois
SAP	Service Advertisement Protocol
SIP	Session Initialization Protocol
SMB	Server Message Block
SMTP	Simple Mail Transfer Protocol
SNMP	Simple Network Management Protocol
SPX	Sequenced Packet Exchange
TCP	Transmission Control Protocol
Telnet	Telecommunications Network Protocol
TFTP	Trivial File Transfer Protocol
TOPS	Transcendental Operating System
UDP	User Datagram Protocol
VTP	Virtual Terminal Protocol
WatchDog	Station Keep Alive
X Windows	Graphical Windows
X.400 MHS	Message Handling System
X.500 DS	Directory Services
XDR	Exchange Data Representative Protocol
ZIP	Zone Information Protocol

Glossary

1000BaseCX: an IEEE 802.3 classification that specifies a data rate of 1 Gbps, the use of Category 5 cable, a maximum segment length of 25 meters, and a minimum segment length of 0.6 meters.

1000BaseT: an IEEE 802.3 classification that specifies a 1-Gbps data rate using all four pairs of Category 5e cable, a maximum segment length of 100 meters, and a minimum segment length of 0.6 meters. Also known as *Gigabit Ethernet.*

100BaseT4: an IEEE 802.3 classification that specifies the use of all four pairs of Category 3, 4, or 5 cable and a data rate of 100 Mbps.

100BaseTX: an IEEE 802.3 classification that specifies the use of Category 5e cable on pairs 1 and 2 only. It is configured in a star topology and has a data rate of 100 Mbps.

10Base2: an IEEE 802.3 classification that specifies the use of RG-58 (thinnet) cable and a data rate of 10 Mbps.

10Base5: an IEEE 802.3 classification that specifies the use of RG-8 (thicknet) and a data rate of 10 Mbps.

10BaseT: an IEEE 802.3 classification that specifies the use of Category 3, 4, and 5 UTP cable. It is arranged in a star topology, follows the 100-meter rule, and has a data rate of 10 Mbps.

10GBaseT: an IEEE 802.3 classification that specifies a data rate of 10 Gbps at a distance of 100 meters using unshielded Category 6a cable or a distance of 55 meters using Category 6 cable. Also known as *10 Gigabit Ethernet* or *10BbT.*

6to4: an IPv6 transition mechanism that provides a means of communicating across the IPv4 Internet while preserving the original IPv6 assigned address of the network device.

A

A+ Certification: a CompTIA certification that proves a person's knowledge related to PC support and repair.

AAA proxy: an intermediate device used as a relay between an AAA authenticator and client.

access method: a method of gaining access to the network media.

access port: a connection on a hub to which cables attach.

acoustical echo: a condition that takes place when a microphone and a speaker are in close proximity or the audio is improperly adjusted, causing feedback.

ACPI Component Architecture (ACPICA): an extension to the original ACPI standard that provides a non-proprietary software package for hardware configuration.

Active Directory (AD): the Windows Server standard used to manage large and small network systems. It uses a hierarchical directory structure that is designed as a database containing information about objects belonging to the entire network.

active hub: a hub that can determine whether a packet should remain in an isolated section of the network or pass through to another section of the network. Also called an *intelligent hub* or *switch.*

active monitor: a computer that is responsible for monitoring the necessary administrative functions associated with Token Ring technology.

active partition: the partition that contains the operating system files the computer should use to boot.

ad hoc mode: a wireless network that does not contain a Wireless Access Point.

adaptive cut-through: a method of switching in which a switch operates in cut-through mode by forwarding the frame immediately after receiving it until it detects an unacceptable number of corrupt frames. Then, the switch operates in store-and-forward mode or fragment-free mode until the number of corrupt frames is reduced to an acceptable number.

Address Resolution Protocol (ARP): a service that resolves IP addresses to MAC addresses.

administrative server: a server that administers network security and activities.

Alien Crosstalk (AXT): a measurement of the noise introduced outside the cable jacket, typically caused by other network cables in close proximity.

American National Standards Institute (ANSI): a private, nonprofit organization that does not develop standards, but rather prompts voluntary conformity and standardization.

American Standard Code for Information Interchange (ASCII): a character code that uses eight bits to represent alphanumeric characters.

amplifier: an electronic device designed to raise a signal's amplitude.

amplitude: the maximum voltage, or height, of an electronic signal.

analog signal: an electronic signal that varies in values.

Analog-to-Digital Converter (ADC): a computer chip designed to change an analog signal to a digital signal.

anonymous FTP site: an FTP site that allows anyone to access the site and download or upload files. No password or any other form of authentication is required.

antivirus suite: an antivirus software package that includes additional features.

anycast address: an IPv6 address that delivers packets to the nearest interface and is used mainly for supporting router functions.

AppleTalk: a suite of protocols developed to support the Macintosh computers when configured as a network. Uses CSMA/CA as its access method.

application gateway: a hardware device or software that provides security for specific applications by accepting traffic based on the exact match of the application permitted.

application layer: a layer of the OSI model that works with specific networking applications such as Web browser programs, file transfer programs, and e-mail.

archive bit: a file attribute that identifies if a file has changed since the last full or incremental backup.

asymmetric-key encryption: a key encryption method in which the sender and receiver use two different keys: a private key and a public key.

Asynchronous Transfer Mode (ATM): a protocol designed especially for transmitting data, voice, and video.

asynchronous transmission: a type of transmission in which a digital signal is not synchronized with a reference signal.

ATM (Asynchronous Transfer Mode): a protocol designed especially for transmitting data, voice, and video.

attenuation: the loss of signal strength.

auditing: a service that tracks the events, use, and access of network resources and writes these actions to a log.

authentication: the process of identifying a user and ensuring the user is who he or she claims to be.

Authentication, Authorization, and Accounting (AAA): a security standard that consists of three parts: authentication, authorization, and accounting.

Automatic Configuration and Power Interface (ACPI): a standard for controlling the power options for computer hardware devices.

Automatic Medium-Dependent Interface Crossover (Auto-MDIX): an electronic chip technology incorporated into Gigabit Ethernet devices to automatically reassign pin functions and eliminate the need for a crossover cable.

Automatic Private IP Addressing (APIPA): a feature that assigns an IP address from a special set of IP addresses that have been set aside by IANA when a DHCP server cannot be reached.

Available Bit Rate (ABR): an ATM data transfer classification most appropriate for file transfer. It uses the available bit rate associated with the networking medium. The speed of a file transfer using the ABR classification is affected by the amount of traffic on the network system.

average utilization: the average amount of utilization or traffic on the network in the time period monitored.

AWG rating: a rating that describes the size of a conductor's diameter.

B

backbone: a cable that is located between the telecommunications closets, equipment rooms, and main entrance facility. It can run horizontally and vertically through a building. Also, a common cable path that often employs high-speed network cable such as fiber-optic.

backdoor: a software access port to the computer a Trojan horse has infected.

backdoor virus: a type of malware designed to go undetected and create a backdoor on a computer.

backplane: a simple motherboard designed with minimal components. It typically serves as the interface of all the major components.

bandwidth: a measurement of the network media's ability to carry data.

Bandwidth Allocation Protocol (BAP): a communications protocol that can change the number of lines or channels according to current bandwidth.

bandwidth shaper: a technique implemented in a network by hardware or software to control the bandwidth through a particular device such as a gateway, shared Internet connection, network switch, or router.

Baseband: a method of transmitting data in the form of a digital signal, using the entire bandwidth of a cable.

baseline: a measurement of performance characteristics that can be used at a later date to objectively determine if the network or server is performing satisfactorily.

basic disk: the term applied to the old system of hard disk drive configuration, which includes creating primary and extended partitions.

Basic Rate ISDN (BRI-ISDN): a category of ISDN that consists of three conductors: two B channels, referred to as *bearer channels*, and one D channel, referred to as the *delta channel*.

Basic Service Set (BSS): an IEEE term used to describe a group of wireless devices connected as an infrastructure network or an SSID.

beaconing: a recovery process used when a hardware failure occurs on the ring.

Binary Coded Decimal (BCD): a binary number format in which each number is represented as a four-digit binary code.

biometrics: the science of using the unique physical features of a person to confirm his or her identification for authentication purposes.

bipolar digital signal: a digital signal that fluctuates between a positive five-volt level and a negative five-volt level.

bit rate: the number of bits used to represent the amplitude of an analog signal.

blackout: a total loss of electrical energy.

blade server: a powerful server that is extremely thin. It is designed to be mounted in a small space with other blade servers.

boot loader: a program that starts the operating system load process.

boot partition: the partition that contains the files needed to operate the computer. These files include device drivers, library files, services, commands, and utilities and are stored in a separate directory.

Bootstrap Protocol (BOOTP): a service that uses a centralized database of the MAC addresses and IP assignments of all devices on the network and assigns the appropriate IP address to a host when it boots.

Border Gateway Protocol (BGP): an Internet routing protocol that supports the exchange of routing information between autonomous networks.

bridge: a network device that can be used to divide the network into smaller segments, reducing the chance of collisions.

bridge exam: a CompTIA Certification exam that only covers the newest objectives added since the previous edition of the exam.

Broadband: a method of transmitting data in the form of several analog signals at the same time.

Broadband ISDN (B-ISDN): a category of ISDN designed to carry multiple frequencies.

broadcast frame: a frame intended for every computer on the network.

broadcast storm: a condition in which a network is flooded with a continuous number of collisions and rebroadcasts.

brouter: a network device that combines router and bridge functions.

brownout: a partial loss of electrical energy.

buffer: a small amount of memory used to temporarily store data.

bug: a software program error.

bus topology: a network topology that uses a single cable or conductor to connect all nodes on the network.

business plan: a document that outlines the goals for a business and includes an action plan and a timetable for meeting those goals.

C

California SB 1386: a legislative act that requires all organizations that own or have access to personal information of California residents to notify the person of any breach of security of his or her personal data.

carrier wave: an electromagnetic wave of a set frequency that is used to carry data.

cascading style sheets (CSS): an enhancement to HTML tags that can be embedded into a Web page or exist as a separate script to control all pages in a Web site.

cell: an area or zone that is served by a radio access tower.

cellular technology: a technology based on radio waves connecting to designated areas referred to as *cells*.

centralized administration: the methodology used to administer a client/server network.

CERN: an organization responsible for the original development of the World Wide Web.

Certificate Authority (CA): a service that contains the security list of users authorized to access the private key owner's messages, using a public key.

Certified Linux Desktop Administrator (CLDA) Certification: a Novell certification that proves expertise in SUSE Linux Enterprise Desktop installation, configuration, and management. It is a single, written certification exam rather than a practicum.

Certified Novell Engineer (CNE) Certification: a Novell certification based on the Novell NetWare operating system.

Challenge Handshake Authentication Protocol (CHAP): an authentication protocol that sends an encrypted string of characters representing the user name and password. It does not send the actual user name and password.

Channel Service Unit/Data Service Unit (CSU/DSU): electronic circuitry that converts signals from the LAN to signals that can be carried by a T1 line, and vice versa.

channel: the bandwidth of a carrier wave.

ciphertext: encrypted data.

circuit switching: a type of transmission which establishes a permanent connection between two points for the duration of the data transfer period.

circuit-level gateway: a hardware device or software that monitors a connection until the connection is successfully established between the destination and source host.

Cisco Discovery Protocol (CDP): a variation of the Link-Layer Discovery Protocol (LLDP) designed to support equipment such as Cisco routers, switches, and telephones.

Class A network: an IPv4 network classification that supports up to 16 million hosts on each of 127 networks.

Class B network: an IPv4 network classification that supports up to 65,000 hosts on each of 16,000 networks.

Class C network: an IPv4 network classification that supports 254 hosts on each of 2 million networks.

Classless Internet-Domain Routing (CIDR): a special notation that identifies which part of an IP address is the network portion. The network portion is identified by a slash (/) symbol followed by a numeric value that represents the length of the network prefix. Also referred to as *Variable Length Subnet Mask.*

client/server network: a network that consists of computers connected to one or more servers.

cluster: a group of servers that share the network demand.

coaxial cable: a type of cable that consists of a copper core conductor surrounded by an insulator referred to as a *dielectric*. Also called *coax*.

codec (compressor/decompressor): software, hardware, or combination of software and hardware that compress and decompress video and audio information.

cold spare: any compatible disk drive that is in storage and is used to replace a failed disk drive.

collision domain: a section of a network where collisions occur.

command prompt: a text-based interface where commands are typed and entered.

command syntax: the correct manner and arrangement in which a command is to be typed.

Committed Information Rate (CIR): a guaranteed bandwidth a commercial carrier will provide a subscriber with.

Common UNIX Printing System (CUPS): a printer daemon designed to support network printing using the Internet Printing Protocol (IPP).

complex trust relationship: a trust relationship in which more than two domains have a full-trust relationship.

concentrator: a central connection point where all network cables are concentrated. It is classified as either active or passive. Also called a *hub.*

connectionless communication: a type of communication in which data is transmitted to the destination without first establishing a connection.

connectionless-oriented: a type of network connection that does not use a direct connection between the destination and the source.

connection-oriented communication: a type of communication in which a connection is first established between the source and destination computers before data is transmitted.

connection-oriented: a type of network connection that requires a direct connection between the source and the destination.

Consolidation Point (CP): a connection to the horizontal wiring system, which in turn feeds to a wall outlet or an MUTOA.

Constant Bit Rate (CBR): an ATM data transfer classification in which a steady stream of ATM cells move at a predictable rate.

consultant: a person who works with clients on projects and makes recommendations based on his or her expertise.

content filter: a hardware device or software that provides security based on the packet contents.

contiguous namespace: a namespace in which the location must use the root domain name as part of its URL or as its complete name.

continuous UPS: provides a steady supply of electrical energy at all times, even when there is no electrical problem.

convergence: the state in which all dynamic routing tables contain the same information. Also referred to as *steady state.*

copper core cable: a type of cable that consists of a copper wire surrounded by plastic or synthetic insulation.

cracker: anyone who gains access to a computer system without authorization and with the intent to do harm or play pranks.

crossed pair: a wiring fault that occurs when one of each of two cable pairs has become part of the other pair's connection.

crosstalk: interference that comes from neighboring conductors inside a wire's insulating jacket.

cryptology: the science of encoding data.

CSMA/CD (Carrier Sense Multiple Access with Collision Detection): a media access method used in Ethernet networks.

cut-through: a method of switching that forwards the frame immediately after receiving it. Also referred to as *low latency*.

Cyclic Redundancy Check (CRC): a sophisticated data integrity check that uses complicated mathematical algorithms to determine if one or more bits are corrupt.

D

daemon: a program that runs in the background and waits for a client to request its services.

data encryption: the encoding of data based on a mathematical formula, which converts the original data symbol into another symbol.

data link layer: a layer of the OSI model that describes how raw data is packaged for transfer from one network interface card to another.

database server: a server that contains data files and software programs to query the data.

datagram: a short message block that can be sent to a particular computer, sent to a group of computers, or broadcast to all computers connected to the media.

de facto standard: a standard developed because of its widely accepted use by industry.

dead drop: a network cable running through the building structure ceiling and wall that is not connected to the network.

decentralized administration: the methodology used to administer a peer-to-peer network.

decibel (dB): a unit of measurement that expresses the relationship of power between two electrical forces.

dedicated server: a server that provides a single function.

default gateway address: the address of the computer that provides a connection to the Internet.

demarcation point: the point where the customer equipment or cable meets the telecommunications provider cable or equipment. Also called *demarc*.

demilitarized zone (DMZ): the area of a network that permits access from a host located outside the local area network. It is not protected by the firewall.

demodulation: the process of separating a data signal from a carrier wave.

Denial of Service (DoS): denying access to a server by overloading the server with bogus requests.

device file: serves as a means of communication between the driver and the device.

dial-up networking: a network system in which a dial-up connection is used to access a remote access server.

Diameter: an Internet Engineering Task Force (IEFT) standard and a next-generation authentication protocol designed to secure a connection between two or more devices.

differential backup: a backup method that backs up all data that has been changed since the last full backup.

digital certificate: a file that commonly contains data such as the user's name and e-mail address, the public key value assigned to the user, the validity period of the public key, and issuing authority identifier information.

digital encoding: the conversion of data into a digital pattern acceptable to the network media.

digital signal: an electronic signal that has discrete values.

Digital Subscriber Line (DSL): a leased line dedicated to networking that uses multiple frequencies as separate channels on the existing telephone local loop. The multiple channels combine to carry more data than the original telephone modem design.

Digital-to-Analog Converter (DAC): a computer chip designed to change a digital signal to an analog signal.

Direct Memory Access (DMA) channel: a circuit that allows devices to communicate and transfer data to and from RAM without the need of CPU intervention.

direct sequencing: a spread spectrum technique that transmits data on multiple channels sequentially.

directional: the ability of an antenna to transmit electromagnetic signals in a focused or aimed direction.

disaster recovery: the restoration of a system to normal operation after a disaster has occurred.

disjointed namespace: a domain name that is a part of the Active Directory, but does not follow the contiguous namespace requirement.

disk mirroring: the act of writing the same information to two hard disk drives at the same time.

disk quota: the amount of disk space assigned to specific users.

disk striping: a storage technique that divides the data into sections and writes the data across several hard disk drives at the same time.

diskless station: a workstation that does not have hard disk drives installed. It can also mean a workstation that does not contain a floppy disk drive.

dispersion: the distortion of the light wave pattern as it reflects off the core cladding.

distance vector protocol: a routing protocol that shares its routing table with other routers.

distinguished name: a naming system that uniquely identifies the location of the object in the Active Directory structure.

domain: a logical grouping of users and equipment as defined by the network administrator. Also, an area of knowledge on a CompTIA Certification exam.

Domain Name System (DNS): a system that associates a host or domain name with an IP address, making it easy to identify and find hosts and networks. Also referred to as *Domain Name Service.*

dotted decimal notation: an IP address displayed in decimal form.

driver: a software program that allows a PC to communicate with and to transfer data to and from computer hardware, such as the network interface card.

dumb terminal: a type of computer that consists of only a display and keyboard. The keyboard contains the electronic components needed to support communication between the mainframe and the terminal. A dumb terminal does not contain a CPU.

duplexing: the technique of placing each mirrored hard drive on a separate hard disk drive controller.

dynamic addressing: automatically assigning IP addresses.

dynamic disk: a new system of disk configuration and management introduced with NTFS5.0. Dynamic disks are managed by the system as a group and allow for the creation of five different volume types: simple, spanned, mirrored, RAID-5, and striped.

Dynamic Host Configuration Protocol (DHCP): a service that assigns IP addresses automatically to the hosts on a network.

dynamic IP address table: a table of IP addresses generated by a software program that communicates with nearby routers.

dynamic IP assignment: an IP address that is issued automatically, typically when the computer boots and joins the network.

dynamic VLAN: created automatically using software by assigning the device MAC address and the user name to a VLAN.

E

edge router: the router at the entrance and exit of a WAN.

EFI partition: a partition on a GPT disk that contains all programs required to boot the computer in the same way the BIOS boots the computer.

electrical spike: a very short burst of abnormally high voltage, typically caused by electrical equipment.

electrical surge: a higher-than-normal voltage level, typically caused by lightning.

electromagnetic wave: a form of energy that behaves like a wave and can travel through a vacuum.

Electronic Industry Association (EIA): a trade association that is concerned with radio communications.

encapsulation: the process of adding information to the segment that identifies such things as the source address, the destination address, the end of the segment, and the size of the segment.

encryption: the method of using an algorithm to encode data.

engineer: a degreed professional who possesses high-level skills necessary to solve problems related to his or her field of expertise.

Enhanced Interior Gateway Routing Protocol (EIGRP): a distance vector protocol that guarantees loop-free operation.

entrance facility: the room that is used as the entrance location for public or private communications cables.

entrepreneur: a person who owns and operates a business.

Equal Level Far-End Crosstalk (ELFEXT): a measurement calculated by subtracting the effects of attenuation from the Far-End Crosstalk (FEXT) measurement.

equipment room: a room that contains the telecommunications equipment for the building such as the Private Branch Exchange (PBX), servers, and telecommunications wiring system terminations.

error correction: a RAID technique that uses traditional error-checking code (ECC) or parity.

EUI-64 identifier: an IPv6 address that serves the same function as the IPv4 MAC address.

Extended Binary Coded Decimal Interchange Code (EBCDIC): an IBM character code similar to ASCII.

extended partition: a partition that can contain one or more logical drives. Only one extended partition can exist on a hard disk drive.

Extended Service Set Identifier (ESSID): two or more Wireless Access Points or wireless devices using the same SSID.

Extensible Authentication Protocol (EAP): a protocol that ensures authorized access to the network system and network resources. It is used on both wired and wireless network systems.

Extensible Markup Language (XML): a markup language based on the same principles as HTML, with the added ability to create custom tags.

Exterior Gateway Protocol (EGP): a basic routing protocol that exchanges information between different autonomous networks. Examples of Exterior Gateway Protocol are BGP and EGP.

external trust: a trust relationship between Windows Server 2008 and an older server operating system or with another Windows Server 2008 computer or when the other domain is located in an entirely separate forest. The two forests are not joined in a trust relationship.

extranet: a network that allows internal and external access to Web pages by authorized personnel.

extrinsic losses: signal losses caused by physical factors outside the normal core, such as splices, connectors, and bends in the fiber core.

F

fabric switch: a switch designed especially for Fibre Channel networking and that provides a direct or switched connection between two points.

Far-End Crosstalk (FEXT): a measurement of reflective loss at the far end, or output end, of a cable. Far-end losses are expressed in decibels.

fault tolerance: as applied to RAID systems, it is the ability to recover from a hard disk or hard disk controller failure without the loss of stored data. As applied to a network infrastructure, it is the ability to continue operation during a system hardware or software error.

Fiber Distributed Data Interface (FDDI): a standard developed by ANSI that employs fiber-optic cable that can reach distances as far as 40 kilometers in length and support data speeds of 100 Mbps or higher. It is used mainly as a backbone for large network systems such as a MAN or a WAN.

fiber-optic cable: a type of cable that has a glass or clear plastic core.

Fibre Channel: a high-speed access method that typically uses fiber-optic cable as network media.

file server: a server that stores data files that can be accessed by a client.

File Transfer Protocol (FTP): a service that can be incorporated into a Web server to support file transfers between a client and server. It is often used to upload Web pages to Web hosting servers.

filtering: the selective passing and blocking of frames.

FIR (Fast Infrared): a protocol used for transmitting data from laptop computers to desktop computers without the use of cables.

firewall: a hardware device or software that passes or blocks packets as they enter or leave a network system.

firewall signature identification: a hardware device or software that works in similar fashion as antivirus protection by intercepting a packet and comparing it to specific malware attributes. When the attributes match, it removes the packet.

firmware: the combination of BIOS chip and the software program within the chip.

Fixed Length Subnet Mask (FLSM): a subnet mask that is expressed in standard eight-bit or one-byte values. Its subnets are equal in range and have an equal number of hosts.

forest: a collection of domain trees that share a common Active Directory database.

forest trust: a two-way trust that is designed to share resources between the two forests. In a forest trust, users can be authenticated in either forest.

fragment-free: a method of switching that checks the first 64 bytes of an Ethernet frame before forwarding it.

frame: a packet that is encapsulated with information needed to travel the Internet.

Frame Relay: a packet switching protocol that typically uses leased lines such as T1 to carry data over long distances.

frame size average: the average of all frame sizes during the period monitored.

frame size peak: a record of the largest frame size recorded during the time period monitored.

free space: the space on a hard disk drive that has not been partitioned.

frequency: the number of cycles of an electronic signal that occur in 1 second. It is measured in Hertz (Hz).

frequency hopping: a spread spectrum technique that transmits data on multiple channels simultaneously.

Fresnel reflection loss: a type of signal loss that commonly occurs at connection points in fiber-optic cabling and is due to refraction property differences in the core material, the connector materials used for sealing the connector, and air.

full backup: a backup method that backs up all designated data.

full-duplex: communication that occurs bi-directionally and simultaneously between two devices. An example of full-duplex communication is communication via telephone.

Fully Qualified Domain Name (FQDN): a combination of a host name and domain name.

fusion splice: joining two fiber-optic cores using heat to fuse the materials together.

G

gateway: a network device that connects the local area network to the Internet.

generator: a device that creates and provides electricity.

geosynchronous orbit: an orbit in which a satellite's rotational speed is synchronized with the earth's rotational speed, making the satellite appear to be in a stationary position.

global address: the Internet address as assigned by the IANA organization used to uniquely identify a location on the IPv6 Internet.

global security policy: a security policy that affects domain users.

globally unique identifier (GUID): a new partitioning style that uses a partition table called *GUID partition table (GPT).*

graded-index multimode fiber-optic cable: a type of multimode fiber-optic cable that has a varying grade of core material. It is designed for maximum light conduction at the center of the core and gradually diminished light conduction toward the cladding.

graphical user interface (GUI): a pictorial representation of commands and computer hardware that allows a user to access resources and programs with a click of a mouse button.

ground: a wiring fault that occurs when a conductor connects to the earth through a continuous path.

group account: a collection of users that typically share a common job-oriented goal or similar function.

H

H.323: a telecommunications standard and protocol used for audio, video, and data communications using IP or packet-type networks defined by the International Telecommunication Union (ITU).

half-duplex: communication that is bi-directional but can only occur in one direction at a time.

hard phone: a physical telephonic device.

hardware abstract layer (HAL): a software layer located between the hardware devices and third-party vendor driver software.

hashing: a technique that relies on an algorithm or encryption device based on mathematical algorithms for guessing a password.

head-end: the local area distribution point of a Cable television service provider.

Health Insurance Portability and Accountability Act (HIPAA): a set of standards designed to protect health records.

hierarchical star: a network topology created when two or more star topologies are merged using network devices such as hubs, switches, or routers.

hoax: a message that is spread about a real or unreal virus.

hop: a measure of how many network devices such as routers and gateways a packet must pass through until the packet reaches its destination.

horizontal cross connect: a mechanical means of connecting horizontal cabling systems to other cables or equipment.

horizontal wiring: the section of cable that runs from individual work areas to the telecommunications closet.

host: a name for a computer, printer, and network device associated with an IP address on a TCP/IP network. Also called a *node.*

hot spare: a backup component that can automatically replace a failed system component without the intervention of a technician.

hot swapping: the process of removing components without shutting down the system.

hot-swap technology: a technology that allows a component to be removed or installed while the system is running.

HTML tag: an instruction for how the text and graphics should appear when displayed in a Web browser.

hub: a network device that provides a common electrical connection to all nodes in a star topology, or a central connection point where all network cables are concentrated. It is classified as either active or passive. Also called a *concentrator.*

hybrid topology: a network topology that consists of a mixture of topology types connected together.

hyperlink: a link to another Web page or to an area on the same Web page.

Hypertext Markup Language (HTML): a programming language used to create Web pages.

Hypertext Transfer Protocol (HTTP): a protocol designed for communications between a Web browser and a Web Server.

I

impedance: the opposition to alternating current.

impedance mismatch: the effect of connecting two different electronic audio systems that have different electronic characteristics.

incremental backup: a backup method which copies only data that has changed since the previous backup.

Independent Basic Service Set (IBSS): a network that does not use an access point and usually is a direct connection between two wireless devices.

Independent Computer Architecture (ICA): a proprietary protocol designed by Citrix Systems to support the exchange of software applications between a server and client.

infrastructure mode: a wireless network that contains one or more Wireless Access Points.

inode: a table entry that contains information such as permissions; file size; name of the owner; the time stamps of the file's creation, modification, and last access; and a pointer to where the file is stored.

Input/Output (I/O) port: a small amount of memory assigned to a device that temporarily holds small amounts of data. It is used to transfer data between two locations.

Institute of Electrical and Electronic Engineers (IEEE): an organization that continually develops standards for the networking and communications industry.

insulation-displacement connector (IDC): a type of network and telecommunications cable termination connector designed to remove the insulation of individual conductors while being inserted with a punch down tool.

Integrated Network Information Center (InterNIC): a branch of the United States government under the direction of the Department of Commerce that was responsible for regulating the Internet, overseeing the issue of domain names, and assigning IP addresses to them.

Integrated Services Digital Network (ISDN): a long-distance-connection technology that provides a means for a fully digital transmission over channels that are capable of speeds of up to 64 kbps.

interactive logon: an authentication process in which the user is verified and given access to the Active Directory.

interference: an undesired electromagnetic signal imposed on a desired signal that distorts or corrupts the desired signal.

Interior Gateway Protocol (IGP): a basic routing protocol that is confined to an autonomous network. Examples of IGP are RIP, IGRP, OSPF, and IS-IS.

Interior Gateway Routing Protocol (IGRP): a distance vector protocol that has a maximum hop count of 255 and a default value of 100 hops. It uses a complex metric calculation based on items such as bandwidth, latency, route traffic, and reliability to determine the best path for data.

Intermediate System to Intermediate System (IS-IS): an IGP link state protocol that determines a router type as level 1 or level 2 when detecting the best path for data.

International Organization for Standardization (ISO): an organization interested in the standardization of computer equipment.

International Telecommunications Union (ITU): an organization responsible for standardizing communications on an international level. The ITU regulates radio, television, and satellite frequencies and standards and telephony standards.

Internet Corporation for Assigned Names and Numbers (ICANN): a company that manages domain name registration by allocating domain name registration to select, private companies.

Internet Group Management Protocol (IGMP): a TCP/IP protocol designed to support multicasting. It informs a multicast router of the names of the multicast group to which a host belongs.

Internet Message Access Protocol (IMAP): a sophisticated mail access protocol that can manipulate e-mail while it is on the server. It also allows a user to access his or her e-mail and then leave the e-mail on the server.

Internet Protocol Security (IPSec): an IETF standard for securing point-to-point connections in an IP-based network using encryption techniques.

Internet Small Computer System Interface (iSCSI): an IP-based storage technology that uses IPv4 and IPv6 network addresses to identify storage devices on a LAN, MAN, or WAN.

Internet: a collection of interconnected networks from all around the world.

interrupt request (IRQ): a circuit that communicates with the CPU.

intranet: a private network that serves a specific group of users within a LAN.

Intra-Site Automatic Tunneling Address Protocol (ISATAP): a node-to-node and node-to-router technology used for existing IPv4 network devices to eliminate the need to upgrade network devices. It works by tunneling IPv6 addresses inside existing IPv4 packets at the data link layer.

Intrusion Detection System (IDS): a passive security protection system which only detects unauthorized activity.

Intrusion Prevention System (IPS): a reactive security protection system that detects unauthorized activity and performs some function to stop the activity.

IPv6: an Internet addressing scheme that uses 128 bits to represent an IP address. The 128 bits are divided into 8 units of 16 bits. These units can be represented as a 4-digit hexadecimal number separated by colons.

ISM band: the band of radio frequencies associated with industrial, scientific, and medical devices.

isolation transformer: a device that uses a transformer to isolate a circuit from other circuits emanating from the same electrical source.

J

JavaScript: a programming language that is designed to be embedded into an HTML Web page and allow the user to interact with the Web page.

jitter: the small staggers or hesitations in the delivery sequence of audio or video data caused by latency or missing packets.

joke program: a type of malware designed with some sort of joke as the payload.

journal file: a log of file activity.

journaling file system: a type of file system that ensures file integrity whenever an unexpected system shutdown occurs, such as a power outage. The journaling file system maintains a log of all file activity.

K

Kerberos: a security authentication system that provides both authentication and encryption services. It uses a two-way method of authentication.

kernel: the core of an operating system.

key: an algorithm used to encode data.

L

latency: the amount of time it takes a signal to travel from its source to its destination.

layer 1 device: a network device that makes no decision about where a packet is sent.

layer 2 device: a network device that makes decisions about where a packet is sent based on a MAC address or a logical name.

Layer 2 Forwarding (L2F): a remote access protocol, similar to PPTP, designed to enhance security and to make use of a virtually private network using the public Internet. It was developed by Cisco Systems and then released for use by other vendors. L2F requires special equipment on the host side to support data transfer whereas PPPTP does not.

Layer 2 Tunneling Protocol (L2TP): a tunneling protocol that uses IPSec to encrypt the contents of the encapsulated PPP protocol.

layer 3 device: a network device that makes decisions about where a packet is sent based on the Internet protocol.

lightning arrestor: a special piece of electrical equipment designed to dampen the effects of the electrical surge caused by lightning.

Lightweight Extensible Authentication Protocol (LEAP): a proprietary authentication system developed by Cisco Systems.

link aggregation: when two or more network cables are paralleled to increase bandwidth and provide redundancy.

link state protocol: a routing protocol that only transfers information about connections and does not pass its routing table to other devices.

Link-Layer Discovery Protocol (LLDP): a protocol that identifies devices connected on the local area network and allows them to automatically exchange information.

Link-Layer Discovery Protocol-Media Endpoint Discovery (LLDP-MED): an enhanced version of the Link-Layer Discovery Protocol (LLDP) used for routers, switches, Voice over Internet Protocol (VoIP) devices, and Power over Ethernet (PoE) devices.

Link-Layer Topology Discovery (LLTD): Microsoft's version of the Link-Layer Discovery Protocol (LLDP).

Link-Local Multicast Name Resolution (LLMNR): a protocol that serves the same function as a DNS server when a DNS server cannot be reached. It resolves names of devices connected collectively on a local network.

link-local: a portion of an organization's network.

Linux+ Certification: a CompTIA certification that measures a person's knowledge of the Linux operating system, such as installing, configuring, administering, and troubleshooting the Linux operating system for a single PC and a network server.

loading coil: a device used to amplify voice signals.

local area network (LAN): a network that is usually confined to a single building and is managed by a single entity such as a company.

Local Central Office: the location where the customer's telephone lines connect to the switchgear. The Local Central Office connects to long-distance carriers to provide long-distance access to individual residencies.

Local Exchange Carrier (LEC): a local carrier, which is made of one or more Local Central Offices.

local loop: the section of wiring between customer premises and the Local Central Office.

local security policy: a security policy that affects local users.

LocalTalk: the network media in an AppleTalk network.

logic bomb: a type of malware that remains dormant until a certain event takes place.

Logical Disk Manager (LDM) partition: a partition on a GPT disk that contains information about dynamic volumes and is created during the conversion from NTFS4.0 to NTFS.0. There can be more than one LDM partition in a system.

logical drive: a partition on a hard disk drive that is assigned a drive letter.

logical identification: a name provided by the technician at the time of installation that uniquely identifies the computer on the network.

logical unit number (LUN): a numbering scheme to identify SCSI devices attached to an extender card.

logon right: the ability to log on to the network.

loopback address: the reserved IP address of a network interface card. It is used to test if an IP address is configured for the network interface card and if the network interface card is functioning normally.

loopback test: a signal that tests the network interface card to ensure it is functioning properly.

LPIC-1 Certification: a Linux Professional Institute certification that measures the basic skills associated with installing, configuring, and managing a Linux operating system. It emphasizes using the command line to configure the operating system.

LPIC-2 Certification: a Linux Professional Institute certification that requires more in-depth knowledge than that for the LPIC-1 exams. It covers basic skills associated with installing and configuring Linux server mail services, proxy server, news server, firewall, and Web server.

LPIC-3 Certification: a Linux Professional Institute certification that measures the Linux skill set for supporting a large enterprise Linux network. Areas of emphasis are mixed environment interoperability, virtualization, mail and messaging, and in-depth security configuration.

M

MAC (media access control) address: the physical ID of a network card, which is a six-byte, hexadecimal number such as 00 C0 12 2B 14 C5.

macro: a symbol, word, or key that represents a command or list of keystrokes.

macro virus: a virus created by storing a series of keystrokes known as a "macro" produced by a word-processing software application.

magnetic induction: an electrical phenomenon in which the magnetic field encircling a current-carrying conductor induces current in a conductor of close proximity. Also called *mutual induction*.

mail filter: blocks, or filters, unwanted e-mail messages.

mail gateway: a special software and device used to connect two normally incompatible e-mail systems.

Main Distribution Frame (MDF): the cable connection point where the private telecommunications cables come into a building and then connect or distribute to other areas in the building. It typically consists of a cable rack and physical cable connections for the individual cable conductors.

main entrance room: the room in which public or private telecommunications enter the building.

malware: a software program designed to perform some type of unauthorized activity on a computer system.

man in the middle (MITM): a method of intercepting a network transmission, reading it, and then placing it back on route to its intended destination.

Manchester encoding: an encoding scheme characterized by a digital pulse transitioning during the midpoint of the time period.

master boot record (MBR): an area located on the first sector of the hard drive that contains information about the hard drive partitions (partition table) and the location of the bootable partition (active partition).

MBR virus: a type of malware that attacks the master boot record (MBR) of a hard disk drive.

Media Access Control (MAC) filter: a feature that allows or restricts WAP access based on the MAC address of a wireless network card.

media converter: a device that changes one type of electrical signal into another or interfaces one cable type to another.

media: the general term that identifies the material used to transport packets and data streams between nodes.

memory address assignment: a large block of memory assigned to a device. It is used to transfer data between two locations.

mesh topology: a network topology in which each node on the network connects to every other node on the network.

metropolitan area network (MAN): a network that consists of two or more LANs connected with private or public communications lines within the same geographic area, such as a city or a university campus. It is managed by a single entity.

Microsoft Certified Application Specialist (MCAS) Certification: a Microsoft certification based on Microsoft Office 2007 and the Windows Vista operating system.

Microsoft Certified Information Technology Professional (MCITP) Certification: a Microsoft certification that requires passing two or more Microsoft exams in a specific Microsoft technology.

Microsoft Certified Technical Specialist (MCTS) Certification: a Microsoft certification awarded to an individual who masters a specific Microsoft technology.

Microsoft Challenge Handshake Authentication Protocol (MS-CHAP): an enhanced version of CHAP that encrypts not only the user name and password but also the data package. MS-CHAP must be used with Microsoft operating systems.

Microsoft Office Specialist (MOS) Certification: a Microsoft certification based on Microsoft Office 2000, 2002, and 2003 products.

Microsoft Reserved (MSR) partition: a partition on a disk that reserves disk space for use by system components.

modulation: the process of mixing a data signal with a carrier wave.

module: a small program, such as a hardware driver or a kernel enhancement, used to expand the kernel and to allow for flexibility.

monitor contention: the process of selecting an active monitor. Also called *monitor election*.

mount point: the location in the directory structure where a device is mounted or inserted.

MPEG (Moving Picture Experts Group): an industry standard that ensures compatibility between different cameras, displays, and other multimedia equipment.

multicast address: an IPv6 address that delivers packets to multiple addresses. It is also referred to as *many-to-one*.

multicast frame: a frame intended for a preselected number of computers, such as a specific workgroup.

multicasting: sending the same data packet to a group of hosts identified by one IP address.

multilayer switch: a switch that can make decisions about routing a packet based on packet content.

Multilink Point-to-Point Protocol (MLPPP): a remote access protocol that can combine two or more physical links so that they act as one, thus increasing the supported bandwidth. This protocol works with ISDN lines, PSTN lines, and X.25 technology. Also called *Multilink dialing*.

multimaster replication: a type of security database replication in which all domain controllers store a copy of the Active Directory database. Changes to the database can be made at any DC in the domain. When changes to the database are made, the changes are replicated to the other domain controllers.

multimode fiber-optic cable: a type of fiber-optic cable that has a large core diameter and is susceptible to attenuation due to dispersion.

Multiple Input Multiple Output (MIMO): a wireless networking technology that transmits two or more streams of data to increase data throughput and the range of the wireless network.

Multi-Protocol Label Switching (MPLS): a routing protocol that allows a label to be attached to an IP packet in order to route the packet to a specific destination.

Multipurpose Internet Mail Extensions (MIME): a protocol that encodes additional information known as mail attachments to e-mail protocols that normally could not transfer attachments such as graphics.

multistation access unit (MAU): a network device that allows for the quick connection and disconnection of Token Ring cables while maintaining the logic of the ring topology.

Multi-User Telecommunication Outlet Assembly (MUTOA): a grouping of outlets that serves up to 12 work areas.

N

namespace: the label that identifies a unique location in a structure such as the Internet.

naming convention: a standard naming format used when providing names for network objects.

Near-End Crosstalk (NEXT): a measurement of the reflected loss at the near end, or input end, of a cable. Losses are typically expressed in decibels.

Neighbor Discovery: an IPv6 data link layer mechanism used to identify network devices automatically, without the need of user intervention.

NetBIOS Name Server (NBNS): resolves NetBIOS computer names to IPv4 addresses.

network: an interconnected collection of computers, computer-related equipment, and communications devices.

Network Address Authority (NAA): a naming standard that consists of the "naa." prefix followed by a string of hexadecimal characters. It was developed by the International Committee for Information Technology Standards (ICITS).

Network Address Translation (NAT): a protocol used to translate private network addresses into an assigned Internet address, and vice versa.

network administrator: an overall administrator who controls access to the network and to its shares. Also, a person responsible for the installation, configuration, and maintenance of the LAN, MAN, or WAN; making written and oral presentations about the state of the network; interviewing prospective employees; evaluating employee performance; coordinating work schedules; ordering supplies and equipment; and preparing budget reports.

network attached storage (NAS): a device or collection of devices that provide storage for network data.

network authentication: an authentication process that occurs when a user accesses a resource.

Network File System (NFS): a protocol that supports file sharing from a UNIX and Linux operating system.

network interface card (NIC): a network device that contains the electronic components needed to send and receive a digital signal.

Network Interface Device (NID): any device that connects the commercial carrier local loop to the private customer's premises wiring.

network layer: a layer of the OSI model that is responsible for routing packets from one network to another using the IP addressing format.

network media: a general term for all forms of pathways that support network communication.

Network News Transfer Protocol (NNTP): a TCP/IP protocol designed to distribute news messages to NNTP clients and NNTP servers across the Internet.

network operating system (NOS): an operating system that provides communications between the computers, printers, and other intelligent hardware that exist on the network.

network share: a resource on the network that is shared among assigned users.

network support specialist: a person who assists users and customers whenever they encounter a network problem.

network topology: the physical arrangement of computers, computer-related devices, communications devices, and cabling in a network.

Network+ Certification Examination Objectives: a document that lists the exact areas tested on the Network+ Certification exam.

Network+ Certification: a CompTIA certification that measures the skills necessary for an entry-level network support technician.

New Technology File System (NTFS): the native file format for Windows NT and Windows Server operating systems.

newsgroup: news articles that are arranged in a group or category on an NNTP server. Newsgroups are also referred to as *discussion groups.*

node: any device attached to the network that is capable of processing and forwarding data.

noise: electromagnetic interference.

Non-Return to Zero (NRZ): a digital signal that fluctuates between a high (positive) voltage level and a low (negative) voltage level and never returns to zero for any measurable period of time.

Novell Certified Linux Administrator (CLA) Certification: a Novell certification based on administrating a Novell SUSE Linux Enterprise Server network system. The candidate is tested on installation, configuration, and troubleshooting.

Novell Certified Linux Engineer (CLE) Certification: a Novell certification that verifies expertise in both Linux and Novell services that run on a Linux system. It is the next logical certification to pursue after achieving the CLP.

Novell Certified Linux Professional (CLP) Certification: a Novell certification that proves a person has mastered the basic skills required to manage and maintain a Novell SUSE Linux server.

NTFS permissions: permissions assigned to directories and files. These permissions are effective locally and over the network.

O

object: any physical or logical unit that is defined as part of the network.

octet: an eight-bit (or one byte) value.

omni-directional: the ability of an antenna to transmit electromagnetic signals in all directions.

one's compliment: a digital-based mathematical calculation used to check for errors or corruption.

one-way trust relationship: a trust relationship in which one domain is the trusted domain and the other is the trusting domain. The trusting domain allows the trusted domain to access its resources, but the trusted domain does not allow the trusting domain to access it resources.

Open Shortest Path First (OSPF): a link state, interior gateway routing protocol used in an autonomous network system.

Open Systems Interconnection (OSI) model: a model that describes how hardware and software should work together to form a network communications system.

open: a wiring fault that occurs when the length of a conductor has an open spot.

Optical Network Terminal (ONT): a fiber-optic cable termination point between the customer and the service provider. It can provide multiple services such as telephone, television, and Internet access.

Optical Time Domain Reflectometer (OTDR): a meter for testing and troubleshooting long runs of fiber-optic cable. The OTDR conducts measurements based on the principle of attenuation.

organizational unit: a container that holds objects or other organizational units and is used to organize a network into manageable units.

orthogonal frequency-division multiplexing (OFDM): a transmission technique that transmits data over different channels within an assigned frequency range. Each channel is broadcast separately and is referred to as *multiplexed*. It can achieve data rates as high as 54 Mbps.

P

packet filter: software that inspects each packet as it passes through the firewall and then accepts or rejects the packet based on a set of rules.

packet sniffer: a network monitoring utility that captures data packets as they travel across a network.

packet switching: a type of transmission which does not use a permanent connection between two points for the duration of the data transfer period. Packets may travel different routes to the same destination.

parallel processing: processing a program through more than one CPU simultaneously.

parity check: a method of verifying the integrity of transmitted data.

partition: an area of the hard disk drive that is to be allocated to an operating system.

passive hub: a hub that acts only as a central connection point for network cables.

Password Authentication Protocol (PAP): an authentication protocol that sends a user name and password in plain text format.

password virus: a type of malware designed to breach security by stealing passwords.

patch panel: a rack-mounted device that has RJ-45 jacks on the front and a matching series of connections on the back.

Payment Card Industry Data Security Standard (PCI DSS): a set of credit card security standards designed to protect credit card information.

PDI+ Certification: a CompTIA certification that measures a person's ability to configure and repair document imaging devices such as printers, copiers, scanners, fax machines, and multi-functional machines.

peak utilization: the highest level of utilization experienced by the network.

peer-to-peer network: a network in which all computers are considered peers or equals.

permanent virtual circuit (PVC): a type of connection that behaves as if it were a hard-wired connection between the destination and source.

permission: the ability to access a network share.

phishing: a method of Internet fraud that involves using e-mail to steal a person's identity and other sensitive information, such as financial.

physical drive: the hard disk drive that is inside the computer.

physical layer: a layer of the OSI model that is concerned with how digital signals, the binary 1s and 0s, are carried electrically from one networked device to another.

piconet: a Bluetooth network. Also called a *Personal Area Network (PAN).*

plenum-rated: a rating that means a cable has a special type of insulation that will not give off toxic gases should the cable be consumed by fire.

Point of Presence (PoP): the point where the telephone company line connects to the subscriber line.

Point-to-Point Protocol (PPP): a remote access protocol that enables a PC to connect to a remote network using a serial line connection, typically through a telephone line. PPP is a synchronous protocol that supports multiple protocols such as IPX and AppleTalk.

Point-to-Point Protocol over Ethernet (PPPoE): a remote access protocol that allows one or more host on an Ethernet network to establish an individual PPP connection with an ISP. PPPoE frames the PPP protocol so that the PPP frame can travel over an Ethernet network.

Point-to-Point Tunneling Protocol (PPTP): a remote access protocol that is an enhanced version of PPP. It is designed to enhance security and to make use of a virtually private network using the public Internet.

polymorphic virus: a type of malware that changes its characteristics or profile as it spreads to resist detection.

port: a logical connection that matches a service with a computer.

port monitoring: when a particular port on a switch is connected directly to the IDS or IPS and monitors all activity through another port on the same switch.

port number: a number associated with the TCP/IP protocol and used to create a virtual connection between two computers running TCP/IP.

Post Office Protocol (POP): a simple protocol designed to access a mail server and download e-mail to the e-mail client.

power conditioning: the process of eliminating spikes and any type of variation in the desired AC signal pattern.

Power over Ethernet (PoE): an IEEE standard that specifies the supply of small amounts of electrical power to network devices such as cameras, IP phones, Wireless Access Points, speakers, and phone or PDA chargers.

power-on self-test (POST): a BIOS routine that performs a series of hardware checks to determine if the computer is in minimal working order.

practicum: a hands-on performance test. Also called a *practical exam.*

presentation layer: a layer of the OSI model that is responsible for converting character codes into a code that is recognizable by a computer that uses a different character code.

primary partition: a partition that stores a bootable copy of an operating system. Four primary partitions, or bootable partitions, may exist on a single hard disk drive, but only one primary partition can be active at a time.

Primary Rate ISDN (PRI-ISDN): a category of ISDN that consists of twenty-three B channels and one D channel. It has a total data rate of 1.544 Mbps.

print server: a server that coordinates printing activities between clients and printers.

programmer: a person who writes, tests, and modifies software programs.

programmer analyst: a person who analyzes the needs of a client and performs the actual programming to meet those needs.

propagation delay: the time it takes for data to be transmitted from the earth and satellite.

Protected Extensible Authentication Protocol (PEAP): a protocol developed jointly by Cisco and Microsoft that enhances EAP authentication by encapsulating the EAP protocol inside an encrypted PEAP packet over a wireless network.

protocol: a group of computer programs that handle packet formatting and control data transmission.

protocol analyzer: a tool used to inspect protocol activity and contents.

proxy server: a firewall component that is typically installed on a server and resides between the Internet server and the LAN hosts. It appears as a destination host while hiding the address of the true host inside the LAN.

Public Key Infrastructure (PKI): the use of public keys (encryption keys) to create a secure environment for the exchange of data between network devices.

Public Switched Telephone Network (PSTN): the older telephone system that uses twisted pair cabling and analog signals rather than digital.

punch down block: a block of connections designed for terminating solid copper wire and typically consisting of a series of insulation-displacement connectors (IDCs).

punch down tool: a tool used for pushing individual twisted pair wires into an insulation-displacement connector (IDC) and automatically trimming conductor excess.

Q

Quality of Service (QoS): a protocol that gives time-sensitive packets, such as those carrying telephone conversations, a higher priority than data packets.

R

radio interference: interference that matches the frequency of a carrier wave.

radio waves: electromagnetic waves with a frequency range of 10 kHz to 3,000,000 MHz.

realm trust: a trust relationship between a Windows Server 2008 domain and a non-Windows domain.

Real-time Transport Protocol (RTP): a standard and a protocol used to stream voice and video in real time.

receiver: an electronic device that receives a modulated signal and demodulates it.

Redundant Array of Independent Disks (RAID): a system of disks arranged for speed or fault tolerance, or both.

reflected loss: the amount of signal reflected from the end of a cable.

registrar: a select, private company that is assigned a pool of IP addresses from ICANN and handles domain registration.

remote access server: a server that is accessed through dial-up networking.

Remote Authentication Dial-In User Service (RADIUS): a service that allows remote access servers to authenticate to a central server.

Remote Desktop Protocol (RDP): a presentation protocol that allows Windows computers to communicate directly with Windows-based clients.

repeater: an electrical device that amplifies or reshapes a weak signal into its original strength and form.

replay attack: a method of using information, such as an IP or MAC address, that had previously been copied and stored during a network transmission to establish an unauthorized connection with the destination.

Request For Comments (RFC): a series of technical reports and proposals concerning protocols and network standards.

resistance: the opposition to direct current (DC) in a conductor.

resolver: a software program located on a host that queries a DNS server to resolve a host name to an IP address.

Reverse Address Resolution Protocol (RARP): a service that finds the MAC address of a host when the IP address is known.

reversed pair: a wiring fault that occurs when two pairs of a cable assembly have reversed two connections.

RG-58: a thin, flexible coaxial cable used in a 10Base2 network. Also called *thinnet.*

RG-6: a type of coaxial cable that has become the standard for Cable television (CATV) systems and satellite systems

RG-8: a thick, rigid coaxial cable used in a 10Base5 network. Also called *thicknet.*

ring polling: a process conducted by an active monitor to identify if a computer has logged on or off of the ring. Also called *polling the ring.*

ring purge: the process of removing a defective token and replacing it with a new token.

ring topology: a network topology that consists of a single cable that runs continuously from node to node.

RIP next generation (RIPng): an IPv6 version of RIP.

rogue access point: an unauthorized WAP that is installed on a network system.

rollover cable: a special cable where the pin order is completely reversed on one end of the cable. Pin 1 connects to pin 8, pin 2 connects to pin 7, and so on.

router: a network device that navigates packets across large networks, such as the Internet, using the most efficient route.

Router Information Protocol (RIP): one of the oldest router protocols, which determines the best path based on number of hops.

router metric: the mechanism used to determine or measure the best route. Some of the various elements of a router metric are throughput, reliability, packet loss, latency, and number of hops.

routing: the process of selecting the "best route" to send packets through a network.

S

sampling frequency: the number of times per second that a sample of a signal's amplitude is taken.

sampling rate: the number of times during a specific period that a sample of a signal's amplitude is taken.

Sarbanes-Oxley (SOX): a legislative act that imposes standards on financial institutions to secure personal financial records. As part of the legislative act, the IT portion of the organization is required to perform routine security checks of the network system and data storage.

scan engine: a software program that performs the function of reading each file indicated in the scan configuration and checking it against the virus signatures in the virus pattern file.

scattering: the loss of signal strength due to impurities in the core material.

search engine: a software program that is designed to locate Web sites and pages by relevant terms entered into the search text box.

Secure Copy Protocol (SCP): a protocol that provides a secure way of transferring files between computers. It is the replacement for **rcp**.

Secure File Transfer Protocol (SFTP): a secure version of FTP that encrypts the user name, password, and data to provide the highest level of security compared to FTP and TFTP.

Secure HTTP (S-HTTP): an Internet security protocol that secures individual messages between the client and server rather than the connection.

Secure Shell (SSH): a protocol that provides secure network services over an insecure network medium such as the Internet.

security policy: a blanket policy that secures resources on the network.

Security Sockets Layer (SSL): a security protocol developed by Netscape Communications Corporation to secure transactions between Web servers and individuals using the Internet for such purposes as credit card transactions.

Security+ Certification: a CompTIA certification that measures a person's knowledge related to generally accepted security practices.

segment: raw data that is divided into smaller units.

segmenting: the act of dividing a network into smaller sections to avoid collisions.

Serial attached SCSI (SAS): SCSI technology that transfers data in serial fashion.

Serial Line Internet Protocol (SLIP): a remote access protocol that enables a PC to connect to a remote network using a serial line connection, typically through a telephone line. SLIP is an asynchronous protocol that supports only IP.

server: a computer that provides services to networked computers, or clients.

server cluster: a group of servers connected both physically and logically to ensure constant service to clients.

Server Message Block (SMB): a protocol that supports file sharing from a Windows operating system.

Server+ Certification: a CompTIA certification that measures a person's knowledge of network server hardware and software, such as installing, configuring, diagnosing, and troubleshooting network server hardware and network operating systems.

Service Access Point (SAP): a combination of MAC address and a number that identifies a protocol and its service. SAP addresses exist for the source and destination computer. It provides a means of direct communication between protocols at different layers of the OSI model and between the source and destination computers.

service pack: a collection of software patches, or fixes.

session: a logical connection with the Linux computer. Also, communication that is limited between two particular computers.

Session Initiation Protocol (SIP): a standard and a protocol for initiating, maintaining, and terminating the exchange of voice, multimedia, gaming, chat, and more.

session layer: a layer of the OSI model that establishes a connection between two different computers and provides security based on computer and user name recognition.

share permissions: permissions assigned to a network share. Common share permissions are Full Control, Modify, Read, and Write.

share-level security: a type of security that provides password protection and minimal share permissions to network shares. Share-level security applies only to shares that are accessed over the network.

shell: a user interface that interprets and carries out commands from the user.

short: a wiring fault that occurs in cabling when two conductors are improperly connected, resulting in a shorter circuit path.

signal bounce: a condition where the wireless signal is reflected or "bounced" off a metal object such as a metal building, file cabinets, some types of glass, and certain building materials.

Simple Mail Transfer Protocol (SMTP): a TCP/IP protocol designed to transfer plain text e-mail from an e-mail client to a mail server and from a mail server to a mail server.

Simple Network Management Protocol (SNMP): a protocol designed by the ITEF that allows an administrator to manage and monitor network devices and services from a single location.

Simple Object Access Protocol (SOAP): a set of rules constructed from XML for Web-based messages. It is designed to allow a client to freely interact with a Web page on a Web server, rather than download it.

simple volume: a dynamic disk volume that exists on a single drive.

simplex: communication that occurs in one direction only. An example of simplex communication is the transmission that occurs between a television station and a television.

single-mode fiber-optic cable: a type of fiber-optic cable that has a small core diameter and limited dispersion. It can carry light farther than multimode fiber-optic cable.

Small Computer Systems Interface (SCSI): a computer bus technology that allows you to connect multiple devices to a single controller.

smart card: a technology that incorporates a special card into the security system. It is used in conjunction with a personal identification number (PIN).

smart jack: an intelligent connection point, which incorporates additional electronics that allow it to perform specific functions.

Smurf attack: a type of DoS that consists of spoofing the target address and then pinging the target broadcast address.

snap-in: a tool or utility that is added to the Microsoft Management Console (MMC).

social engineering: the manipulation of personnel by the use of deceit to gain security information.

socket: a port number combined with an IP address.

soft phone: a virtual telephonic device.

spam: an unwanted or unsolicited e-mail such as advertisement.

spammer: a person who engages in distributing unsolicited e-mail or sending e-mail with some sort of advertisement as a probe.

spamming: the distribution of unsolicited e-mail.

spanned volume: a single dynamic disk volume that spans many drives.

Spanning Tree Protocol (STP): a layer 2 protocol designed to manage networks based on MAC addresses and to prevent bridge loops.

spatial multiplexing: a wireless networking technology that transmits two or more streams of data in the same frequency channel.

split pair: a wiring fault that occurs when two pairs of conductors are reversed in connection with another pair.

spoofing: fooling the destination by using an IP address other than the true IP address of a source to create a fake identity.

spread spectrum: a transmission technique that uses multiple channels to transmit data either simultaneously or sequentially.

standard: a set of recommendations or practices presented by an organization that defines specific aspects about a technology.

Standard Generalized Markup Language (SGML): the original standard for both HTML and XML.

standby monitor: a computer on a Token Ring network that can become an active monitor if the current active monitor fails or logs off the network.

standby UPS: a type of UPS that waits until there is a disruption in commercial electricity before it takes over the responsibility of supplying electrical energy.

star topology: a network topology in which cables running from each node connect to a single point, such as a hub.

stateful packet inspection: a firewall inspection method in which the sequence of packets is inspected in order to detect missing packets or an altered sequence of packets.

stateless packet inspection: a firewall inspection method in which individual packet attributes such as IP address, port number, and protocols are inspected and filtered.

static addressing: assigning an IP address manually.

static IP address table: a table of IP addresses that have been entered manually.

static IP assignment: an IP address that is entered manually for each host on the network.

static VLAN: created when physical ports on a switch are manually assigned to a particular VLAN.

station address: an IPX/SPX-based address that consists of only a network number and node address.

stealth virus: a type of malware that hides from normal detection by incorporating itself into part of a known and usually required program.

step-index multimode fiber-optic cable: a general multimode fiber-optic cable that does not counter dispersion.

storage area network (SAN): a separate, high-speed network that provides a storage facility for one or more networks.

store-and-forward: a method of switching that reads the entire contents of the frame before forwarding the frame to its destination.

striped volume: a dynamic disk volume that increases the read/write access speed by spreading data across multiple hard disk drives.

subdomain: any level domain located beneath the secondary domain. Also called a *lower-level domain.*

subnet mask: a number similar to an IP address used to determine to which subnetwork a particular IPv4 address belongs.

subnetting: dividing a network into subnetworks, or subnets.

subnetwork: a network within a network.

sunspots: magnetic energy storms that occur at the surface of the sun.

swap file: hard drive disk space that supplements the RAM.

switch: a network device that filters network traffic or creates subnetworks from a larger network.

symmetric-key encryption: a key encryption method in which the sender and receiver use the same key.

Synchronous Optical Network (SONET): similar in design to T-carrier technology except SONET bases its technology on fiber-optic cable.

synchronous transmission: a type of transmission in which a digital signal is synchronized with a reference signal to ensure proper timing.

system image: a snapshot of the entire storage structure, including files not normally backed up such as the MBR or GUID.

system migration: combining two diverse network systems into one.

system partition: the partition that contains the core files that are used to start the operating system.

systems analyst: a person responsible for analyzing, evaluating, and recommending business software systems.

T

TACACS+: a Cisco proprietary client/server security method that directs client requests to the authentication server in similar fashion as Microsoft RADIUS.

tar ball: a compressed file containing one or more software programs.

T-carrier: a leased line that follows one of the standards known as T1, fractional T1, T2, or T3. The T-carrier is a dedicated, permanent connection that is capable of providing a high bandwidth.

TCP/IP (Transmission Control Protocol/ Internet Protocol): a protocol that was developed by the Defense Advanced Research Project Agency (DARPA) in the early 1970s and was designed to support communications over the Internet.

telecommunications closet: an enclosed space used to house telecommunications cable termination equipment. It is the recognized transition point between the backbone and horizontal wiring.

Telecommunications Industry Association (TIA): a standards maintenance organization mainly concerned with fiber optics, user equipment, network equipment, wireless communications, and satellite communications.

telecommunications room: a room or enclosed space that houses telecommunications equipment, such as cable termination and cross connect wiring. It serves as a transition point between the backbone and horizontal wiring.

telephone gateway: a specialized piece of equipment that connects a packet-style network communications system to a telephone system using the H.323 protocol.

Teredo: a network address translator similar to the NAT protocol. It creates a tunnel that allows incoming IPv6 traffic through a firewall designed for IPv4.

terminating resistor: an electrical device that absorbs transmitted signals, preventing the signals from deflecting and distorting.

thin client: a computer that relies on the thin client server's processing power and memory.

thin client server: a server that provides applications and processing power to a thin client.

thin server: a server that has only the hardware and software needed to support and run a specific function, such as Web services, print services, and file services.

time period: the rate of recurrence of an expected signal level change.

Time to Live (TTL): the maximum amount of time a packet is allowed to circulate through a network before it is destroyed.

token: a short binary code that is passed around to the computers on a ring topology and, in some cases, a bus topology. Also, the name given to the packet that exchanges session information between the source and destination.

transmitter: an electronic device that generates a carrier wave and modulates the data signal into the carrier wave.

transport layer: a layer of the OSI model that ensures reliable data by sequencing packets and reassembling them into their correct order.

Transport Layer Security (TLS): a security protocol developed by the Internet Engineering Task Force (IEFT) to secure transactions between Web servers and individuals using the Internet for such purposes as credit card transactions.

transport mode: an IPSec mode that only encrypts the payload.

tree: a collection of domains that share a common root domain name and Active Directory database. Also, a network topology created from two or more star topologies connected together by a common backbone.

Trivial File Transfer Protocol (TFTP): a lightweight version of FTP that does not require the use of a user name and password because it uses UDP packets for transferring data. It allows a client to transfer files, but not to view the directory listing at the FTP site.

Trojan horse: a program designed to gain access to a computer while pretending to be something else.

trunk line: consists of hundreds of pairs of twisted pair cable or fiber-optic cable.

trunking: the technique of connecting different VLANs together using a single network link.

trust relationship: a relationship between domains, which allows users from one domain to access resources on another domain in which they do not have a user account. The user can then access resources on another domain without having to log on to that domain. The user, however, must have permissions to access the resources.

tunnel mode: an IPSec mode that encrypts the payload and the header.

twisted pair: a type of cable that consists of four pairs of twisted conductors.

two-way trust relationship: a trust relationship in which both domains are designated as a trusted domain and a trusting domain. A two-way trust relationship allows both domains in the trust relationship to share its resources with the other.

U

unbounded media: an unrestricted path for network transmissions.

Underwriters Laboratories (UL): a nonprofit organization that tests products and materials for safety standards.

unicast address: an IPv6 address that delivers packets to a single network address.

Unicode: a character code that uses 16 bits to represent individual characters.

Uniform Resource Locator (URL): a user-friendly name such as http://support.microsoft.com, which allows users to access Web-based resources.

Uninterruptible Power Supply (UPS): a device that ensures constant and consistent network performance by supplying electrical energy in case of a power failure or blackout.

unipolar digital signal: a digital signal that fluctuates between a positive five-volt and zero-volt level.

unique-local: the entire organization's network or a portion of it.

Universal Naming Convention (UNC): a standard naming convention used by NetBIOS.

Unspecified Bit Rate (UBR): an ATM data transfer classification that does not guarantee any speed or meet requirements of any special application such as multimedia or telephony. This classification is typically applied inside TCP/IP frames.

upconverter: a radio transmitter integrated into a satellite dish.

user-level security: a type of security that requires a user to authenticate through a security database to access a share.

V

Variable Bit Rate (VBR): an ATM data transfer classification in which the ATM cell rate automatically adjusts to support time-sensitive data. It uses multiplexing techniques to provide a minimum Constant Bit Rate for time-sensitive audio and video transmissions while controlling the data rate of not time-sensitive data, such as text or plain e-mail.

Variable Bit Rate-Non Real Time (VBR-NRT): an ATM data transfer classification that allows cells to move at a variable rate. The rate of movement depends on the type of data contained in each cell.

Variable Bit Rate-Real Time (VBR-RT): an ATM data transfer classification that allows cells to move at a variable rate depending on the cell's contents to support real-time audio and video transfers.

Variable Length Subnet Mask (VLSM): a subnet mask that is not expressed in standard eight-bit or one-byte values. It occurs when a subnet is further divided into smaller subnets, which are not equal to the original subnet in length or in the number of hosts.

virtual circuit: a connection-oriented communication.

Virtual Local Area Network (VLAN): a broadcast domain created by one or more switches based on logical (MAC) addresses.

virtual network: a logical network within a LAN.

virtual network connection (VNC): a point-to-point connection through a public or private network that acts like a separate network for security purposes.

Virtual Private Network (VPN): a simulated, independent network created by software over a public network.

Virtual Trunking Protocol (VTP): a proprietary protocol developed by Cisco Systems to provide automatic reconfiguration of multiple switches across an entire network.

virus: a type of malware that replicates itself on a computer after infecting it.

virus pattern file: a database of virus signatures, or codes, unique to each known virus.

Voice over IP (VoIP): an Internet telephony protocol designed for high-performance data delivery and quality of service. It relies on existing TCP/IP technology and existing TCP/IP networking equipment.

volume: an accessible unit of hard disk drive space as seen through the Windows interface, such as in Windows Explorer. A volume may be assigned a single drive letter yet contain multiple partitions.

volume set: a volume that consists of partitions from two or more hard disk drives.

W

wavelength: the total distance an electromagnetic or light wave travels during one full cycle.

Web administrator: a person responsible for converting written documents into HTML or other Web page programming languages. This job requires training in Web page programming language and some expertise in networking technology.

Web browser: a software program that permits the user to navigate the World Wide Web and then interpret and display Web pages.

Web master: a person who has the expertise in Web programming languages, such as HTML, XML, JAVA, JavaScript, ActiveX, and familiarity with server management of IIS, Apache, UNIX, Linux, and Microsoft systems.

Web server: a server configured to provide Web services, such as Web pages, file transfer, and HTML-based e-mail.

Web site: a location on the World Wide Web that contains a collection of Web pages and files, which can be accessed through the Internet. A Web site is owned and managed by an individual, company, or organization.

weight: the amount of points assigned to a test question.

wide area network (WAN): a network that consists of a large number of networks and PCs connected with private and public communications lines throughout many geographic areas.

Wi-Fi: a term coined by the Wi-Fi Alliance that refers to 802.11 wireless network products.

Wi-Fi Protected Access (WPA): a protocol that combines the authentication method with encryption.

Wi-Fi Protected Access 2 (WPA2): an improved version of the WPA standard that provides authentication like WPA, but uses an enhanced encryption method.

windowing: the process of negotiating the maximum size of each segment and the amount of segments that will be sent before requiring an acknowledgment.

Windows Internet Naming Service (WINS): a service that resolves NetBIOS names to IP addresses.

windows manager: an application that controls the display such as by providing GUI icons, boxes, and buttons.

Wired Equivalent Privacy (WEP): a data encryption protocol that makes a wireless network as secure as a wired network.

Wireless Access Point (WAP): a wireless network device that provides a connection between a wireless network and a cable-based network and controls the flow of all packets on the wireless network.

Wireless Application Protocol (WAP): a protocol that ensures the safe exchange of data between a wireless network and a portable Wi-Fi device, such as a cell phone. It uses a set of keys to identify a device and to encrypt the data exchanged.

Wireless Personal Area Networks (WPAN): a small Ethernet network consisting of personal wireless devices such as a cell phone, laptop, palmtop, wireless printer, Wireless Access Point, iPod, Xbox 360, and similar items.

wireless topology: a network topology that does not use cabling.

work area: the area in which employees perform their normal office duties.

workgroup: a group of computers that share resources such as files and hardware.

working group: a standard not fully developed and adopted as an official standard recognized by IEEE.

World Wide Web Consortium (W3C): an organization that provides recommendations for Web page language standards.

worm: a software program that can spread easily and rapidly to many different computers.

X

X client: an application, such as a word processing program. The X client can also be a windows manager.

X server: a program that communicates with the computer hardware, such as the keyboard, mouse, and monitor.

X Windows: provides a GUI for UNIX and Linux systems.

X.25: a protocol that uses analog signals to transmit data across long distances.

Z

Zero Configuration (Zeroconf): a standard developed by IEEE which recommends how to design a device that automatically detects other devices on the same network or on a nearby network segment without the need of intervention by an administrator or a DHCP or DNS server.

Index

B

C

D

E

F

G

H

I

J

K

L

M

N

O

P

Q

R

S

T

U

V

W

X

Y

Z